Tax Planning 20

Tax Planning 2018/19

Edited by

Mark McLaughlin CTA (Fellow), ATT (Fellow), TEP, Consultant, Mark McLaughlin Associates and The TACS Partnership

With contributions by

Jackie Anderson LLB, ACA, CTA, LHA Consulting Ltd

Kye Burchmore LLB, RIFT Legal Services

Rebecca Cave CTA, FCA, MBA, FAIA (Hon), Taxwriter Ltd

George Duncan Solicitor, CTA, TEP, Partner, Charles Russell Speechlys LLP

Chris Erwood CTA, ATT, TEP, Director, Erwood & Associates Ltd

Anne Fairpo Barrister, CTA (Fellow), ATT

Adam Garrad BSc ATT MRICS, The Capital Allowances Partnership Ltd

Robert Maas FCA, FTII, FIIT, TEP, Consultant, CBW Tax Ltd

Pete Miller CTA (Fellow), Partner, The Miller Partnership

Donald Pearce-Crump BA (Hons), LLB, CTA (Fellow), ATT

Partha Ray Cameron & Associates Ltd

Peter Rayney FCA, CTA (Fellow), TEP, Peter Rayney Tax Consulting Ltd

David Whiscombe Barrister (Non-practising), CTA (Fellow), Consultant to BKL Tax

Chris Williams LLB, Senior Manager, Mazars LLP

Martin Wilson MA FCA, The Capital Allowances Partnership Ltd

Ken Wright BA, CA, CTA, Group Tax Manager, John Menzies plc

Bloomsbury Professional

LONDON · DUBLIN · EDINBURGH · NEW YORK · NEW DELHI · SYDNEY

BLOOMSBURY PROFESSIONAL
Bloomsbury Publishing Plc
41–43 Boltro Road, Haywards Heath, RH16 1BJ, UK

BLOOMSBURY and the Diana logo are trademarks of Bloomsbury Publishing Plc

First published in Great Britain 2018

British Library Cataloguing-in-Publication Data

A catalogue record for this book is available from the British Library.

ISBN: PB: 978 1 52650 761 7
      ePDF: 978 1 52650 763 1
      ePub: 978 1 52650 762 4

Typeset by Compuscript Ltd, Shannon
Printed and bound by CPI Group (UK) Ltd, Croydon, CR0 4YY

To find out more about our authors and books, visit www.bloomsburyprofessional.com. Here you will find extracts, author information, details of forthcoming events and the option to sign up for our newsletters.

Preface

Welcome to Bloomsbury Professional's *Tax Planning 2018/19*. This book is now in its twelfth year of publication.

The calendar year 2018 has seen a different cycle of Budget announcements and Finance Bills. There was no Budget in March unlike in previous years, but Royal Assent to *Finance Act 2018* was given in March 2018, whereas in previous years *Finance Acts* have normally become law during the summer. The next Budget is scheduled for the autumn and will be followed shortly thereafter by a Finance Bill, which will eventually become *Finance Act 2019*.

These changes to the tax legislation cycle have resulted in *Finance Act 2017*, *Finance (No 2) Act 2017* and *Finance Act 2018* being introduced in relatively quick succession. In addition, tax practitioners, accountants, solicitors, independent financial advisers, etc have had to contend with secondary legislation, tax cases and other new developments. This has happened against the backdrop of the government's continued drive to clamp down on tax avoidance and what it regards as unacceptable tax planning.

However, there is still much that can legitimately be done to save or reduce tax. *Tax Planning 2018/19* is therefore aimed at pointing out some of the areas where such planning opportunities still exist. Tax planning has an important role to play in managing one's financial affairs. Indeed, many clients of professional firms expect prompt, appropriate and up-to-date advice from their advisers on minimising tax liabilities. *Tax Planning 2018/19* is aimed at assisting professional advisers, among others, in delivering such advice.

Tax Planning 2018/19 takes into account new developments since the previous edition, including legislation introduced in *Finance (No 2) Act 2017* (which became law after the previous edition of this book was published) and *Finance Act 2018*, and a number of noteworthy tax case decisions. The aim of this book is to cover topical subjects, which are potentially relevant to the work of professional advisers etc. This edition therefore includes a new chapter on stamp taxes (including Land Transaction Tax in Wales) by Ken Wright. There is also a new chapter on capital allowances on property transactions by Martin Wilson.

The emphasis in *Tax Planning 2018/19* continues to be on providing topical content of practical use to the majority of small to medium-sized professional practices dealing with popular tax planning issues. However, the practical importance of tax subjects can vary in accordance with changes to the law and other developments. The publishers would therefore warmly welcome constructive suggestions from readers on subjects they would like to see covered in 2019/20 and subsequent editions.

As always, I wish to express my sincere gratitude to all the authors who have contributed material to this book with such skill, professionalism and commitment. Their extensive tax knowledge and experience will hopefully make this book a useful and practical reference work for the reader.

Finally, my thanks to everyone at Bloomsbury Professional. In particular, many thanks to Claire McDermott for her considerable efforts and help during the preparation and editing of the book.

The commentary is generally based on the law in England and Wales. That applying in Scotland and Northern Ireland may occasionally be different.

Whilst every care has been taken to ensure that the contents of this work are complete and accurate, no responsibility for loss occasioned by any person acting or refraining from action as a result of any statement in it can be accepted by the authors or the publishers.

Mark McLaughlin
General Editor
Manchester, 8 June 2018

Contents

Contents

Contents

Contents

Contents

Contents

Contents

Contents

Contents

Table of statutes

Table of statutes

1

Table of statutory instruments and other guidance

[All references are to paragraph number]

Table of cases

C

Table of cases

O

P

Q

R

X

Y

Z

List of examples

List of examples

Chapter 13

Chapter 14

Chapter 15

List of abbreviations

A&M	accumulation and maintenance
AA	annual allowance
ABA	agricultural building allowance
AC	amount crystallised
ACT	advance corporation tax
AFT	accounting for tax return
AIA	annual investment allowance
AIM	alternative investment market
APR	agricultural property relief
ASP	alternatively secured pension
ATED	annual tax on enveloped dwellings
AUST	apprentice upper secondary threshold
BCE	benefit crystallisation event
BEIS	Department for Business, Energy and Industrial Strategy
BEPS	Base Erosion and Profit Shifting
BES	Business Expansion Scheme
BMT	bereaved minor's trust
BPR	business property relief
CA	Companies Act
CAA 2001	Capital Allowances Act 2001
CBI	Confederation of British Industry
CEST	check employment status tool
CGT	capital gains tax
CIC	community interest company
CIHC	close investment holding company
CIOT	Chartered Institute of Taxation
CPI	consumer price index
CTA	Corporation Tax Act
CTAP	corporation tax accounting period

CTO	Capital Taxes Office
CTSA	corporation tax self-assessment
CVS	Corporate Venturing Scheme
CYB	current year basis
DOTAS	Disclosure of Tax Avoidance Schemes
DWP	Department for Work and Pensions
EBT	employee benefit trust
EEA	European Economic Area
EEIG	European economic interest grouping
EIS	Enterprise Investment Scheme
EMI	Enterprise Management Incentives
EP	enhanced protection
ER	entrepreneurs' relief
ERA 1996	Employment Rights Act 1996
ESC	Extra-Statutory Concession
FA	Finance Act
FAS	Financial Assistance Scheme
FCA	Financial Conduct Authority
FHL	furnished holiday letting
FIFO	first in, first out
FPS	Full Payment Submission
FSA	Financial Services Authority
FTT	First-tier Tribunal
FYA	first year allowance
GAAP	generally accepted accounting practice
GAAR	general anti-avoidance rule
GAD	Government's Actuary Department
GIA 2013	Growth and Infrastructure Act 2013
GPA	group payment arrangement
GWR	gifts with reservation
HMRC	Her Majesty's Revenue and Customs
IAS	International Accounting Standard
IBA	industrial building allowance

ICTA 1988	Income and Corporation Tax Act 1988
IHT	inheritance tax
IHTA 1984	Inheritance Tax Act 1984
IIP	interest in possession
IORP	institutions for occupational retirement provision
IOV	instrument of variation
IP	intellectual property
IPDI	immediate post-death interest
ISA	Individual Savings Account
IT	income tax
ITA 2007	Income Tax Act 2007
ITTOIA 2005	Income Tax (Trading and Other Income) Act 2005
LA	lifetime allowance
LBTT	Land and Buildings Transaction Tax
LBTT(S)A	Land and Buildings Transaction Tax (Scotland) Act
LEL	lower earnings limit
LIFO	last in, first out
LISA	lifetime Individual Savings Account
LLP	limited liability partnership
LP	limited partnership
LS	lump sum
LSDB	lump sum death benefits
LTT	Land Transaction Tax
LTTADT(W)A 2017	Land Transaction Tax and Anti-avoidance of Devolved Taxes (Wales) Act 2017
M&A	mergers and acquisitions
MSC	managed service company
MTD	making tax digital
NAO	National Audit Office
NEST	National Employment Savings Trust
NIC	National Insurance Contributions
NICA	National Insurance Contributions Act
NISA	New ISA
NMW	national minimum wage

NNP	non-natural person
NPV	net present value
NRB	nil rate band
OECD	Organisation for Economic Co-operation and Development
ONS	Office for National Statistics
OTS	Office of Tax Simplification
PA 1890	Partnership Act 1890
PAYE	Pay as You Earn
PEP	Personal Equity Plan
PENP	post-employment notice pay
PET	potentially exempt transfer
PILON	payment in lieu of notice
PIP	property-investment partnership
PLC	public limited company
PMA	plant and machinery allowance
POAT	pre-owned assets tax
PP	primary protection
PPR	principal private residence
PSC	personal service company
PT	primary threshold
QCB	qualifying corporate bond
QRP	qualifying residual profit
R&D	research and development
RAS	relief at source
REIT	real estate investment trust
RICS	Royal Institution of Chartered Surveyors
RIPP	relevant intellectual property profits
RPI	Retail Price Index
RTI	real time information
SAAC	special annual allowance charge
SAYE	Save as You Earn
SDLT	stamp duty land tax
SDRT	stamp duty reserve tax

SEIS	Seed Enterprise Investment Scheme
SIP	share incentive plan
SLA	standard lifetime allowance
SP	Statement of Practice
SRN	scheme reference number
SSCBA 1992	Social Security Contributions and Benefits Act 1992
SSE	substantial shareholdings exemption
STSP	single-tier state pension
TAAR	Targeted Anti-Avoidance Rules
TCGA 1992	Taxation of Chargeable Gains Act 1992
TEE	taxed-exempt-exempt
TIOPA 2010	Taxation (International and Other Provisions) Act 2010
TiS	Transactions in Securities
TMA 1970	Taxes Management Act 1970
TOGC	transfer of a going concern
TOPA 2014	Taxation of Pensions Act 2014
TNRB	transferable nil rate band
TUPE	Transfer of Undertakings (Protection of Employment) Regulations
UAP	upper accrual point
UEL	upper earnings limit
UITF	Urgent Issues Task Force
UT	Upper Tribunal
UTR	unique taxpayer reference
UURBS	unfunded unapproved retirement benefit scheme
VAT	value added tax
VATA 1994	Value Added Tax Act 1994
VCT	venture capital trust
VOA	Valuation Office Agency
VUR	value of uncrystallised rights
WDA	writing down allowance

Chapter 1

Starting a business – choosing an appropriate trading vehicle

Rebecca Cave CTA, FCA, MBA, FAIA (Hon)

SIGNPOSTS

- **Issues underlying the choice** – This will be guided by the number of people involved in the business and the flexibility needed for expansion or division of the business. Consider the administration and tax costs, as well as potential interest restrictions for property businesses (see **1.3–1.30**).

- **Why be a sole trader?** – Structure, regulation, business records, accounting date, cash-basis, fixed rate deductions and timing of tax payments (see **1.31–1.37**).

- **Why use a partnership?** – Distinguish between ordinary partnerships, limited partnerships, and LLPs. Also understand the tax benefits of all partnerships (see **1.38–1.70**).

- **Why use a company?** – Discussion of the tax benefits and the tax charges when loans are made to shareholders or directors (see **1.71–1.120**).

- **Company versus other vehicles** – Start as unincorporated, timing of tax payments, NIC burden, profit-extraction strategies, disadvantages of dividends, retention of profits (see **1.121–1.140**).

- **Long-term intentions** – Continuing or dissolving the business, double taxation charges (**1.141–1.145**).

PLAN AHEAD

1.1   When an individual wants to start a business, he must decide on the most appropriate medium through which to conduct that business. The choice of the business vehicle can contribute to the ultimate success of the business,

1

as it will affect the level and timing of tax payments, the availability of tax reliefs and the legal obligations of the business owners.

The basic choice for a new UK-based business is between a sole trader, ordinary partnership, limited partnership, limited liability partnership (LLP), or private limited company. Other alternatives for trading structures are: a trading trust, unlimited company, public limited company (PLC), co-operative, or a joint venture arrangement. Those alternative structures are not discussed in this chapter.

ISSUES UNDERLYING THE CHOICE

1.2   A business may be expected to trade in a certain form by its customers or for traditional reasons (see **1.19**). In the absence of such external pressures the initial choice of business vehicle will turn on these issues:

- the number of people involved;
- current or future flexibility required;
- administrative costs;
- need to protect personal assets; and
- tax costs.

There are also a number of commercial considerations that should be raised with the client when discussing the trading vehicle to be used to start the business. One form of trading vehicle is rarely suitable for the entire lifetime of the business, and the type of business operated (eg property investment or trading) may influence the structure to use.

Number of people involved

1.3   The choice of business structure is partly determined by the number of people who will be involved in running and owning the business. A sole trader is restricted to single-person ownership and management. An ordinary partnership is effectively a group of individuals who have come together to run a business. The partners are taxed like individual sole traders on their share of the profits made by the partnership. The partners may appoint managers to run the business on their behalf, but they remain fully jointly and severally liable for the debts of the business.

An LLP or a limited partnership can offer the partners some protection from the debts of the business (see **1.59**). It is possible to form a partnership between a one-man company (see **1.5**) and the individual who controls that company. See **Chapter 3** for discussion of partnerships that include a company as a member.

A company may have any number of shareholders, and some or all of those shareholders may also be the company directors who have responsibility for day-to-day management of the business. However, the company directors and managers can be a completely separate group of people from the owners (shareholders) of the business.

Flexibility

1.4   An ability to move smoothly from one form of business vehicle to another is important. Different levels of profits attract varying tax rates depending on the business structure, so a change from a sole trader or partnership to a limited company may be made to reduce the overall tax liability. The tax and other implications of incorporating a business are discussed in detail in **Chapter 2**.

A dynamic business will benefit from a regular review of its structure, particularly where new products or risks are taken on. Where the business involves several separate projects or products that have different chances of succeeding or failing, a separate business vehicle may be set up to contain each project. This will isolate these different commercial risks and ensure that a successful project is not brought down by one that fails. This approach may lead to forming a joint venture company, creating a number of associated companies or a combination of partnerships and companies.

A group of related businesses will also allow one project or product line to be extracted and sold on without disturbing the rest of the business. Where a series of similar ventures (eg property development) are carried on in successive companies or businesses, the taxation of the distributions on liquidation of the company may be subject to income tax rather than CGT under the new Targeted Anti-Avoidance Rules (TAAR) in *ITTOIA 2005, ss 396B* and *404A*, for further discussion of this point, see **Chapter 8**.

1.5   A private limited company is a particularly flexible vehicle as it may be owned and run by just one individual, who will normally be the sole director. The only limitation laid down by the *Companies Act 2006* is that a private company is obliged to have at least one director, who must be a natural person, not a company.

A private limited company is not required to appoint or retain a company secretary unless the company's articles specify that it should. The role of a company secretary would include taking responsibility for filing returns with Companies House, maintaining records of director's meetings and share registers, and distributing accounts to all the shareholders. In the absence of a company secretary the directors need to undertake these tasks. A public company must appoint a qualified company secretary. The company secretary need not hold any shares in the company, and thus need not be a part owner of the business, and need not be involved in the day-to-day running of the business.

Focus

Where an individual holds the position of company secretary or director, that person may qualify for entrepreneurs' relief on disposal of some or all of his shareholding in the company, if he holds at least 5% of the ordinary share capital and 5% of the associated voting rights (see **Chapter 8**).

Administrative costs

1.6 The administrative costs will tend to be higher where the business vehicle has greater reporting requirements, or it is required to run a PAYE scheme and thus make electronic returns under real time information (RTI). The costs of running a limited company tend to be greater than those for an ordinary partnership or sole-trader business, although the scale of the organisation and the complexity of the business will have a bearing on the total costs. The more reports a business is required to file with government bodies, the greater the risk of lateness or inaccuracy of a submission, which may well generate penalties.

1.7 A company can be registered at Companies House for as little as £10 if the process is undertaken online, but an ordinary partnership or sole-trader business has no such registration costs. An LLP must also be registered at Companies House for a basic fee of £12. Limited partnerships are required to be registered with Companies House, which costs £20, and online registration is not offered.

1.8 Companies and LLPs must both file confirmation statements at Companies House at a cost of £40, or £13 for electronic submission. The filing fee must be paid whether or not the business has traded during the year. Partnerships that are not LLPs, and sole-trader businesses, are not required to file a confirmation statement or annual return, submit to an audit, or file annual accounts at Companies House. This provides a high level of privacy for the business owners, and a cost saving.

Companies and partnerships, including LLPs, must submit an annual tax return to HMRC, in addition to the personal tax returns required for the business owners. Sole-traders submit details of their business profits or losses on their personal tax return, there is no separate tax return for the business. These annual returns are due to be replaced by quarterly filing under the making tax digital (MTD) regime, which is expected to be implemented from 2020 onwards; although the MTD regime to make VAT reports is due to commence for most VAT-registered businesses from April 2019.

1.9   The statutory accounts of companies and LLPs must be filed annually at Companies House and certain of those accounts must be subject to an audit before they are filed. Most LLPs and companies qualify as 'small', so they may take advantage of the audit exemption, under the *Accounts of Small and Medium-Sized Enterprises and Audit Exemption (Amendment) Regulations (SI 2004/16)*. However, some accounts will require an audit for other regulatory reasons, such as for businesses operating in the regulated financial services sector.

To qualify as 'small' the company or LLP must meet two of the three conditions set out in **Table 1.1** in its first financial year, or for later periods, in that year and the preceding year. Different limits apply to trading charities.

Table 1.1: Company size thresholds

For periods from 1 January 2016	*Micro-entity*	*Small Company*	*Medium Company*
Annual turnover not more than	£632,000	£10.2m	£36m
Balance sheet total not exceeding	£316,000	£5.1m	£18m
Average number of employees in financial year not exceeding	10	50	250

1.10   Companies and LLPs that qualify as 'small' or 'medium' (see **Table 1.1**) are also permitted to submit abbreviated accounts to Companies House, which only include a balance sheet and no profit and loss account. This prevents competitors from discovering the business turnover, profit, or whether a dividend has been paid. Medium-sized companies are required to include details of the business turnover within the abbreviated accounts.

Micro-entities, which can include LLPs, may prepare simplified financial statements which consist of an abridged profit and loss account, balance sheet with no notes and no director's report. The micro-entity is only required to file its balance sheet at Companies House. Charities and investment undertakings cannot qualify as micro-entities.

1.11   A full set of financial statements for a company including a profit and loss account and director's report must be submitted to HMRC to support the corporation tax return. Every figure in those documents must be 'tagged' using the extensible business reporting language (iXBRL) before it can be submitted with the corporate tax return.

Sole traders, partnerships and LLPs can still submit tax returns and accounts to HMRC in paper form, if the filing is completed by midnight on 31 October following the end of the tax year. A later filing of a partnership tax or individual tax return must be made electronically. Penalties for late filing of the partnership tax return apply per partner in addition to the penalty for late filing of the partnership return itself.

Tax costs

1.12   The tax burden borne by the business is influenced by the differing tax rates applicable to profits made within the structure (see **1.13**), but also by how those profits are calculated. A number of tax reliefs for costs or losses are only available to businesses who operate as a company, or conversely as a sole-trader or partnership (see **Table 1.5** at **1.144**).

From 6 April 2017 a residential property letting business which is run as a sole trade or partnership suffers a restriction on the amount of finance and interest charges that can be deducted for tax purposes. This gives the corporate structure a distinct advantage for property letting businesses (see **1.15**).

Where the business makes a loss, the ability to relieve that loss quickly can make an unincorporated structure more attractive, particularly in the early years of trading (see **1.14**).

If the business is expected to be consistently profitable, the choice of business vehicle may well be weighted towards a company. However, the expected profit level and the need to extract funds for personal use must be considered (see **1.89** onwards).

1.13   The income tax rates and bands, which apply to non-savings and non-dividend income, are now quite different for Scottish taxpayers as opposed to taxpayers who are resident in other parts of the UK. The tax rates and tax bands for dividends, savings and capital gains are the same across the UK.

National insurance contributions (NICs) are charged at the same rates and in the same bands across the UK. Class 2 NIC is payable by self-employed individuals at a flat rate of £153.40 for 2018/19 if the profits for the year exceed £6,205, Class 4 NIC is payable at 2% or 9% on various bands of self-employed profits. Class 2 and Class 4 NIC will be merged from 6 April 2019, and the revised rates should be announced in the 2018 Autumn Budget.

A comparison of the tax rates and bands for various profit levels is shown in **Table 1.2**. Different rates of corporation tax apply for companies in the oil and gas industry.

Table 1.2: Comparison of tax rates for 2018/19

Profits in band £	Rest of UK taxpayers %	Scottish taxpayers %	Class 4 NIC %	Corporation tax %
0–8,424	0	0	0	19
8,425–11,850	0	0	9	19
11,851–13,850	20	19	9	19
13,851–24,000	20	20	9	19
24,001–43,430	20	21	9	19
43,431–46,350	20	41	9	19
46,351–100,000	40	41	2	19
100,001–123,700	60*	61.5*	2	19
123,701–150,000	40	41	2	19
Over 150,000	45	46	2	19

*effective rate due to tapering away of personal allowance.

The comparison of net income after tax for different business structures will vary across the UK. For more detail on the tax due on profits of Scottish taxpayers trading as sole traders or as companies, please refer to *Incorporating and Disincorporating a business* (Bloomsbury Professional).

Timing of tax payments

1.14   The combined tax and national insurance liability for an unincorporated business is generally payable in two equal instalments by 31 January and 31 July, irrespective of the date the business has chosen to draw up accounts to each year.

The corporation tax is payable nine months and one day after the end of the accounting year, although large companies and corporate groups must generally pay their corporation tax liabilities by quarterly instalments.

A company may pay less tax on its profits than an unincorporated business of a similar size, but its liability to national insurance may be greater, depending on the level of salaries and benefits paid out. A straight comparison of tax costs between different business vehicles is complicated by the fact that some tax reliefs apply only to companies or only to unincorporated businesses (see **Table 1.5** at **1.144**). Certain benefits can be provided to employees and directors tax free through the medium of a company, but are taxable if provided to the owners of an unincorporated business.

An extra cost of using a company is the requirement to operate PAYE on the salaried remuneration of the owner. As such the company must also pay national insurance at 13.8% on salary, bonuses and benefits paid to employees or directors, which exceed £8,424 per year.

Focus

The choice of trading vehicle has a big effect on the quantum and timing of the tax liabilities generated by the business venture, but the choice should also be influenced by non-tax factors such as the need to protect the assets of the owner should the business fail.

Use of losses

1.15   Many new businesses expect to make losses in the first few periods of trading before moving into profit. If those trading losses are generated within a corporate structure before 1 April 2017, the losses are essentially trapped within that company with only three possible avenues of relief:

- set against the other income of the company (*CTA 2010, s 37*);

- carried back against the profits of the company for up to 12 months (*CTA 2010, s 37(3)*); or

- carried forward to set against future profits of the same trade (*CTA 2010, s 45*).

Corporate losses generated after 1 April 2017 are not automatically set against the company's taxable profits from the same trade in the same or future periods, but can be disclaimed in favour of later losses, or may be surrendered in the form of group relief to other group members. Where the company or group has profits of more than £5m, the relief for all brought-forward losses (generated at any time) is restricted to 50% of total profits in excess of £5m, but profits of up to £5m can be set-off in full against losses.

The losses made by an unincorporated business are not trapped within that business but can be relieved as follows:

(a)   Losses made within the first four years of the life of the business can be carried back up to three years and set against the trader's other income of that tax year (*ITA 2007, s 72*).

(b)   Trading losses made in any year can be set against the proprietor's other income of that year or the previous tax year (*ITA 2007, ss 64, 65*). This form of loss relief is known as sideways loss relief.

(c)   If the claims to set the loss against net income have not exhausted all of the loss, the taxpayer can opt to relieve the remaining trading losses against any capital gains of the same year and the preceding year (*ITA 2007, s 71*).

(d) Where the trading loss remains unrelieved the loss is automatically carried forward to be relieved against profits of the same trade, profession or vocation arising in future years (*ITA 2007, s 83*). The loss is set against the next available profit without restriction.

(e) On incorporation of the business any unused losses from the unincorporated trade can be set against income received from that company by the former owner, including dividends, salary, interest or rents, if certain conditions are met (*ITA 2007, s 86*).

There is an HMRC toolkit available to help taxpayers assess whether income tax losses have been correctly claimed, but it does not deal with the loss relief restrictions explained in **1.16** (http://tinyurl.com/psmxprv).

No loss relief can be claimed if the trade is not carried on commercially with a view to the realisation of profits (*ITA 2007, s 66*). Where losses arise from the trades of market gardening or farming, sideways loss relief is restricted if the losses have been made in each of the previous five years.

Loss restrictions

1.16   The use of sideways, opening years or capital loss relief may be limited by five separate restrictions summarised in **Table 1.3**. Any loss not relieved sideways, or carried back, is carried forward to be set against the future profits of the same trade without restriction.

Table 1.3: Loss restrictions

Type of restriction:	*LLP partner (active)*	*Limited partner*	*Non-active partner or sole-trader*	*Active partner or sole-trader*
1. Capital contribution cap (*ITA 2007, ss 104–114*)	Yes	Yes	Yes	No
2. £25,000 cap (*ITA 2007, ss 74A & 103C*)	No	Yes	Yes	No
3. Greater of £50,000 or 25% of income cap (*ITA 2007, s 24A*)	Yes	Yes	Yes	Yes
4. Denied entirely due to tax avoidance scheme (*ITA 2007, s 74ZA*)	Yes	Yes	Yes	Yes
5. Cash basis used (see **1.34**)	N/A	Yes	Yes	Yes

Non-active partners or sole traders can be any individuals, limited partners, or sleeping partners (see **1.44**) who are personally engaged with the trade for, on average, less than ten hours per week.

Where the business is a partnership, HMRC are clear that they will apply the first two loss restrictions in **Table 1.3** in the order shown in that table, ie capital contribution first. Those restrictions only apply to trades, not to professions or vocations (HMRC Business income manual BIM82640).

From 6 April 2013 the relief for losses, interest and a number of other tax reliefs is restricted where the total relief given in the tax year exceeds:

● £50,000; or

● 25% of the taxpayer's adjusted total income for the tax year.

The use of sideways, opening years or capital loss relief is completely denied where tax avoidance arrangements have been entered into (*ITA 2007, s 74ZA*). Although HMRC say this anti-avoidance rule is targeted at persons who enter into tax-avoidance arrangements, the legislation is not restricted to such circumstances (BIM85762).

There are special rules for losses derived from qualifying film expenditure and film partnerships (*ITA 2007, ss 74D and 103D*), which exclude the above loss restrictions, but impose their own restrictions to counter tax avoidance schemes.

Interest restrictions

1.17   Where a residential property letting business is carried on by individuals alone or in partnership, by trustees, or by personal representatives of deceased estates, the ability to deduct finance and interest charges from rental income is restricted as follows:

Tax year	Finance costs deductible:
2017/18	75%
2018/19	50%
2019/20	25%
2020/21	nil

The landlord receives a tax credit equivalent to 20% of the lower of:

● finance costs not deducted from rental income in the tax year;

- property business profits before deducting interest after deducting losses brought forward; and

- adjusted total income that exceeds personal allowances.

This tax credit is set at 20% irrespective of the marginal rate of income tax paid by the landlord. It is set against the taxpayer's income tax liability for the year (see **Example 1.1**). Any unused tax credit is carried forward to be relieved against the tax payable on the property income in a later tax year. This restriction on finance charges does not apply to corporate landlords.

Example 1.1 – Property letting run by sole trader or company

Peter is resident in England and lets residential property held in his own name, receiving net rents of £140,000 per year after agents' fees and repairs. He pays interest and finance charges of £112,000 per year. He does not pay national insurance on his letting income as it is not regarded as a trade.

Paul holds his let property in a company he controls, which also receives net rental income of £140,000 per year and pays £112,000 in interest. Paul extracts the net income from his company as a dividend.

The tax payable by the two property businesses is calculated as follows:

2018/19 tax year	Company	Individual	
	£	Paul £	Peter £
Letting income	140,000		140,000
Interest deductible (50% deductible for individual)	(112,000)		(56,000)
Net income	28,000		84,000
Less personal allowance	–		(11,850)
Net taxable profits	28,000		72,150
Income tax due at 20% on first £34,500			6,900
Income tax due at 40% over £34,500			15,060
Tax credit: 20% × 50% × 112,000			(11,200)
Corporation tax at 19%	(5,320)		–
Income after CT – paid as dividend to Paul	22,680	22,680	

Less personal allowance	(11,850)	
Less dividend allowance	(2,000)	
Subject to dividend tax at 7.5%	8,830	
Income tax paid	(662.25)	(10,760)
Cash in hand for individual:	22,017.75	17,240
Effective tax rate on net income of £28,000:	21.36%	38.42%

Other tax-related decisions

1.18   There are a number of tax-sensitive decisions for a new business (listed below), which need to be addressed, irrespective of the structure adopted:

●   choice of accounting date;

●   ownership of real property;

●   ownership of vehicles;

●   ownership of intellectual property;

●   how to attract investors;

●   how and when to extract profits;

●   how to provide for the proprietor's pension;

●   how to pass the business on;

●   how to extract capital.

Different business vehicles will produce different tax results for these issues. For example, the choice of accounting date for an unincorporated business can have a big influence on the timing and quantum of tax payable in the early years of the business (see **1.36**), but it is not so relevant for a corporate structure.

Commercial considerations

Credibility

1.19   A corporate structure can appear more credible to suppliers and customers, who may perceive unincorporated businesses as being small and risky. There may be considerable pressure from customers who receive a personal service from the proprietor of the business for that supplier business to be incorporated, to shift the risk of tax compliance on to the personal service company (PSC).

1.20 A corporate structure is thought to protect the customer from having to treat an individual contractor as an employee, subject to PAYE and NICs. Where an intermediary, such as a company or partnership, or even another individual such as an agent, is placed between the customer and the contractor who provides the personal service, the burdens of PAYE and employment rights for the individual should fall on the intermediary.

For contracts performed in the private sector, the intermediary is responsible for complying with the anti-avoidance rules known as IR35 (see **1.81**). From 6 April 2017, for contracts performed in the public sector, the public body that engages the PSC is responsible for deciding whether the IR35 rules apply. If IR35 does apply to the contract, the fee-payer who pays the PSC must deduct tax and Class 1 NIC under PAYE from the invoiced amount, as if it was gross pay, although VAT is paid on the gross amount of the invoice. This puts the contractor in a worse position than if he were an employee of his customer, so the advantages gained by working through a company are undermined.

The intermediary may also be subject to the additional constraints imposed by the Managed Service Companies (MSC) legislation (see **1.87**). There are particular rules for agency and temporary workers under which the worker may be treated as being an employee of the agency for tax and NIC purposes (see **Chapter 10**).

1.21 An LLP can also offer customers and suppliers a sense of security, as the reporting requirements mean the LLP's accounts are published for public view at Companies House. The LLP must also draw up accounts that comply with the same accounting standards as a company, and is not permitted to use the cash basis of accounting (see **1.34**).

Privacy

1.22 Those who prefer to keep the financial affairs of their business as a private matter between themselves and HMRC will see the disclosure requirements of a limited company or LLP as a disadvantage. However, micro-entities are permitted to file only a balance sheet at Companies House (see **1.10**).

Retention of control

1.23 The majority shareholders in a company, who hold more than 50% or 75% of the shares, can take the major decisions for the business, as those thresholds of share ownership provide rights under company law. The unanimous agreement of partners in a partnership is usually required for all major decisions, unless the partnership agreement states otherwise.

1.24   Shares in a private company can be created with diverse rights as to voting, dividends, entitlement to capital on winding-up, and so on. This offers not only great flexibility, but also the opportunity for the original proprietor to retain voting control in the company although he may not, at that stage, be entitled to the largest equity interest in the company. On the death of a shareholder, the legal continuity of the business is guaranteed. There is no automatic continuity of a partnership business on the death of a partner, but this may be provided for in the partnership agreement. The business of a sole trader will cease with the individual's death.

Raising finance

1.25   Companies may be able to raise additional finance from other shareholders, and minority and non-voting shareholders can provide finance that does not impinge on the majority's control over the running of the company. However, a private company cannot raise funds directly from the general public; only a public company can do this.

1.26   Companies may find it easier than unincorporated businesses to raise finance from other sources due to their equity structure. Although companies may become partners in most partnerships, a venture capitalist is unlikely to wish to become involved as a partner in an ordinary partnership, even as a limited partner. For further discussion of corporate partners see **Chapter 3**.

An LLP can offer a very flexible structure for companies and individuals to work together in a joint venture arrangement. However, the rules for taxing loans to participators (*CTA 2010, s 455*) can restrict the flow of funds within a group that consists of a close company and an LLP whose members are participators in the company (see **1.107**).

Focus

Anti-avoidance rules to prevent the manipulation of profits and losses, or the disposal of income streams or assets within mixed partnerships (ie partnerships with both individuals and non-individuals as members) apply from 6 April 2014. For further details see **Chapter 3**.

1.27   The personal liability of the business owners is often thought to influence the choice of business structure. However, in practice the limited liability achieved by the business owner by operating as a private limited company or an LLP is frequently undermined by the requirement to give personal guarantees to providers of business finance, or to provide a charge over their own personal assets in return for a business loan.

Unincorporated businesses are not able to offer a floating charge over their assets as security for borrowings, whereas companies and LLPs can do this.

National minimum wage

1.28   The national minimum wage (NMW) or national living wage (NLW) must be paid to all 'workers' (as defined for the NMW regulations). A director who does not have an explicit contract of employment with his company is unlikely to be a 'worker' for these purposes, so does not have to be paid the NMW (HMRC National Minimum Wage Manual NMWM05140). Family members who work in unincorporated businesses and live at home are also exempt from the NMW.

Sole traders and partners in ordinary partnerships, LLPs or limited partnerships are under no obligation to pay themselves any prescribed level of wages, as they are not treated as 'workers' for the purposes of the NMW. Although salaried partners in LLPs may be taxed as employees if they meet certain conditions, they are not actually employees and hence not treated as workers for the NMW legislation.

Share options

1.29   A company can incentivise employees by offering tax-advantaged share options or employee share schemes, which are not available to employees of a sole trader, partnership or LLP. For further details of the range of share-related incentives which can be provided, see *Employee Share Schemes* (7th edn, 2018, Bloomsbury Professional).

Exit strategy

1.30   A shareholder in a company can transfer small quantities of the company's shares to the next generation or to the management group, in order to gradually pass on control in the business. However, if shares are given to the company's employees, or to individuals who become employees when they acquire the shares, an income tax charge may arise under the employment-related securities legislation, on the basis that the shares are acquired due to the donee's employment (see **1.130**).

To transfer the interest of a sole trader or partner, the proprietor has to accept another person as a partner in the business, as an active or sleeping partner.

This transaction will normally require a partnership agreement to be drawn up or amended.

It is easier to sell shares in a private company than to sell a partnership share in a similar-sized business. If the intention is to develop the business to the point where it can be sold as a trading unit, a corporate structure will normally be more appropriate.

Having said that, the assets and trade of a business can be sold out of any form of trading vehicle. An asset sale is often favoured by the purchaser of a business, as any liabilities attached to the business can be excluded from the transaction. For further discussion of the tax issues concerning owner-managed company sales, see **Chapter 8**.

SOLE TRADER

Structure

1.31   A business operated by one person as a sole trader is the simplest possible business structure. The owner is personally liable for all the debts of the business and is taxed on all of the profits. Essentially there is no legal distinction between the individual and the business.

Regulation

1.32   The regulation of a sole-trader business is minimal, although HMRC require the individual to register for national insurance and tax purposes as soon as possible after the business commences. A failure to notify penalty may be imposed if the individual has not registered with HMRC by 31 January following the end of the tax year in which he commenced his business. However, if the individual is not already within the self-assessment system, he must notify HMRC by 5 October after the end of the tax year in which the new source of income arose, as a failure to notify penalty can arise after that earlier date.

Business records

1.33   All taxpayers have an obligation to keep sufficient records to support entries made on their tax returns (*TMA 1970, s 12B*), but the form and extent of those 'statutory records' is not specified in law, except for VAT purposes. HMRC have a right to inspect all statutory records, and the taxpayer cannot appeal against a notice to produce his statutory records (*FA 2008, Sch 36, para 29*).

> **Focus**
>
> A private bank account that is used to pay off a credit card debt comprising partly of business expenses, was found to form part of the business's statutory records (*J Beckwith v HMRC* [2012] UKFTT 181 (TC)). An appointment diary for a private doctor was found not to form part of her statutory records (*Dr K Long v HMRC* [2014] UKFTT 199 (TC)).

Cash basis of accounting

1.34   Unincorporated trading businesses can elect to calculate profits/ losses for tax purposes on the basis of the cash received and expenses paid out, known as the cash basis, as opposed to the accruals basis of accounting required by GAAP. The cash basis is supposed to make accounting easier for small businesses, who can start to used that method of accounting where their annual turnover is no more than £150,000.

Once a trading business has started to use the cash basis, it can carry on doing so until its annual turnover is twice the entry threshold (£300,000 from 6 April 2017). Alternatively, the business may leave the cash basis when its commercial circumstances change such that the cash basis is no longer appropriate.

Unincorporated landlords are expected to use a form of the cash basis from 6 April 2017, where their annual gross property income does not exceed £150,000, unless they explicitly opt out of the cash basis and use GAAP accounting instead.

The following businesses cannot use the cash basis:

- companies;
- LLPs;
- farmers using the herd basis;
- persons using profit averaging under *ITTOIA 2005, s 221*;
- persons carrying on a mineral extraction trade;
- persons who have claimed business premises renovation allowance or R&D allowance; and
- Lloyd's underwriters.

When using the cash basis for a trade, the individual cannot claim a deduction for loan interest of more than £500 per year, although a full deduction for hire purchase (HP) costs is permitted.

Landlords are subject to different restrictions for interest and finance charges when they use the property cash basis for periods from 6 April 2017. These interest restrictions for property businesses will apply in addition to the restrictions for residential property businesses described in **1.17**.

When using either form of cash basis, losses cannot be offset against other income (sideways relief), or carried back as set out in **1.15**, but those losses may be carried forward.

Fixed-rate deductions

1.35 Any unincorporated trading business or profession, which does not have a corporate partner, can use fixed-rate expenses to replace the calculation of actual costs incurred in three areas:

- car and motorcycle expenses;

- use of home for business purposes; and

- private use of a business premises which is also used as the proprietor's home.

For details of the relevant fixed rates see Bloomsbury's *Tax Rates and Tables 2018/19*. These fixed rate deductions can be used whether or not the business opts to use the cash basis described in **1.34**, and are not restricted by the turnover of the business.

Accounting date

1.36 The date to which the sole trader's accounts are made up each year can have a significant effect on the timing of tax payments, particularly in the early years of the business. This is because an unincorporated business reports the profits or losses, for the accounting period which ends within the tax year, on the tax return for that year.

For example, profits from the accounting period ending on 30 April 2018 will be reported on the tax return for 2018/19, but equally the results for the accounting period ending on 31 March 2019 will be reported on 2018/19 tax return. Although those accounting periods have only one month in common, the tax will be payable on the same dates:

- 31 January 2019: on-account payment equivalent to half of the 2017/18 liability;

- 31 July 2019: on-account payment equivalent to half of the 2017/18 liability; and

- 31 January 2020: any balancing payment due for 2018/19.

In the first tax year of a new business, the profits arising in that tax year are assessed to tax from the date of commencement of the business to the end of the tax year. This can lead to double taxation of profits made in the first 24 months of the new business – see **Example 1.2**. The accounting date chosen (early or late in the tax year) will affect the degree to which the early profits are doubly taxed.

Example 1.2 – Doubly taxed profits

Alistair started trading on 1 July 2017 and drew up his accounts for the ten months to 30 April 2018. He then draws up accounts to 30 April each year. The profits to be taxed in the first three tax years are calculated as follows:

Tax year	Profits taxed	Calculated from profits of:
2017/18	Actual profits from 1 July 2017 to 5 April 2018	9/10 × accounting period to 30 April 2018
2018/19	First 12 months	10/10 × accounting period to 30 April 2018 plus
		2/10 × accounting period to 30 April 2019
2019/20	Year ending 30 April 2019	12/12 × accounting period to 30 April 2019

The proportions of the accounting periods have been calculated in months, when strictly a proportion of days in each period should be used. However, it can be seen that the 9/10ths of the profits for the period to 30 April 2018 and 2/10ths of the profits for the period to 30 April 2019 have been taxed twice, and will make up the amount of overlap relief to be used when Alistair ceases to trade.

Overlap relief

1.37   Any doubly taxed profits are relieved as overlap relief, which reduces the final amount of profits taxed when the business ceases, or when the business changes the date to which its accounts are made up. Either of these events may occur many years after the original double taxation arose, but the amount of overlap relief deducted at that time is not adjusted for the effect of inflation. The overlap relief thus loses its value over time.

PARTNERSHIPS

Why use a partnership?

1.38   The decision to trade as either a sole trader or an ordinary partnership is likely to be influenced largely by family, professional, or other commercial considerations. For example, in a sector where there is a strong tradition of family continuity, such as farming, there may be powerful domestic reasons that induce the proprietor into taking his children into partnership.

The liability of a sole trader is unlimited in respect of his business debts. A partner will have joint, or joint and several liability for partnership debts. This means that any one partner could be called upon to satisfy the whole of the debts of the business, albeit with the right to claim a contribution from his fellow partners. However, each partner can only be required to pay the tax due on his individual profit share from the partnership. In spite of this, many large partnerships retain funds within the business to pay the income tax and NIC due on behalf of the partners.

Type of partnership

1.39   A partnership may be referred to as an ordinary or general partnership to distinguish it from the forms of limited partnership (see **1.52**) and limited liability partnership: LLP (see **1.56**).

Is there a partnership?

1.40   It is sometimes difficult to prove whether two or more people are operating a business as a partnership, or if only one person is in business, or there are a number of connected sole-trader businesses. This point will be important as reporting under Making Tax Digital comes into effect, as the reporting rules for partnerships will be different from those which will apply for sole traders.

Where there is no written partnership agreement in existence, the *Partnership Act 1890* governs the operation of ordinary partnerships, and defines a partnership as the relationship which subsists between persons carrying on business in common with a view to a profit. The *Partnership Act 1890, s 2* sets out certain transactions, which do not by themselves create a partnership, such as the co-ownership of property, or an employee receiving part of his salary by way of a share in the profits of the business.

A partnership is not required by law to have a partnership agreement, but the existence of such an agreement is very good, but not conclusive, evidence that a partnership exists. Sharing profits raises a presumption that a partnership exists, but, again, is not conclusive evidence of a partnership. A thorough analysis of whether a partnership existed is contained in the report of *Phillips (Raymond John) v HMRC* [2009] UKFTT 335 (TC), see also HMRC Business Income Manual para BIM82005.

Focus

HMRC will try to assert that a partnership existed, to collect tax and penalties owing from a person connected with the business, even if that person has not been named as a partner (see *Valantine (Pauline) v HMRC* [2011] UKFTT 808 (TC)).

Types of partners

1.41   Normally, a partner in an ordinary partnership will take an active role in the partnership business, and take a proportion of the trading profits in recognition of their contribution to the business. However, some partners take no active role, and are referred to as 'sleeping partners'. A partnership may contain 'salaried partners', who may be employees described as partners for prestige reasons only, or they may be full equity partners who take a fixed profit share of the partnership profits.

Both sleeping and active partners will normally contribute capital to the partnership when they join the partnership. The trading profits of the partnership need not be distributed in proportion to the amount of capital each partner has contributed to the business, and equally capital profits and losses may be shared in different ratios to income profits and losses.

Tax treatment

Income tax

1.42   The taxation of partnerships is relatively simple where there are only a few partners. For tax and national insurance purposes each partner is treated as an individual sole trader. The amount of profit or loss taxed on each partner is determined by the profit-sharing ratio the partnership operates.

Guidance on the taxation of partnerships is found in HMRC's Partnership Manual. Further detail on how partners and partnerships are taxed is found in **Chapter 3**, together with discussion of issues and opportunities which arise when using partnership.

1.43   When a partner joins a partnership, or the partnership starts trading there can be some double taxation of profits made from the date of commencement or from the date the new partner joins the partnership to the end of the tax year. This also applies when a sole trader starts to trade (see **1.36**). Overlap relief for the doubly taxed profits is given when the individual partner leaves the partnership, the partnership ceases to trade, or there is a change in the accounting date for the partnership.

Losses

1.44   A partner has the same choices as to how to relieve their portion of any trading loss as apply to a sole trader (see **1.15**). Each partner can make an independent choice as to how to obtain tax relief for their share of a trading loss, but see the restrictions for loss relief discussed in **1.16**.

1.45   The calculation of the tax charge for each individual partner can become complex if there are a large number of partners in the partnership and frequent changes in the profit-sharing ratios in any one tax year. A partner cannot have a taxable loss if another partner has a taxable profit in the same tax year. If a loss arises after allocating amounts paid out of the partnership profits as 'salaries', the loss must be reallocated to the partners with profits.

National insurance

1.46   Partners are generally self-employed earners for national insurance purposes (but see **1.60** for LLPs), so they must register as self-employed with HMRC and for self-assessment (on form SA401). Class 2 and Class 4 NIC are assessed and collected with the income tax self-assessment, and will be merged into one charge with effect from 6 April 2019.

Focus

HMRC and the DWP take the view that sleeping and inactive partners are subject to Class 2 national insurance on their rewards from the partnership, as they are 'gainfully employed' as self-employed earners for the purposes of *SSCBA 1992, s 2(1)(b)*.

Inheritance tax

1.47   An interest in a trading business, whether operated as a partnership or sole trader, potentially qualifies for 100% business property relief (BPR). However, BPR is denied if a binding contract for sale of the business or partnership interest exists at the date of death. To avoid this trap, the partnership agreement should contain an option for the existing partners to acquire the business interest following the death of a partner, but not a requirement that the business interest should be acquired. Alternatively, a tax liability may be avoided by claiming that the arrangements are part of a bona fide commercial bargain and were made without gratuitous intent.

Property held by a partner outside of the partnership and used by the partnership for its trade will qualify for 50% BPR, see further discussion in **Chapter 12**.

VAT

1.48   Although an ordinary partnership is not a separate taxable person in its own right in England and Wales, it is for VAT purposes. The partnership (not the individual partners) must register for VAT if its turnover exceeds the VAT registration threshold (frozen at £85,000 since 1 April 2017). However, the partners will be jointly and severally liable for the VAT debts of the partnership unless they have limited liability.

Partnerships formed in Scotland are treated as a separate legal person (*Partnership Act 1890, s 4(2)*).

1.49   No change in VAT registration is needed if there are changes in the composition of the partnership (ie partners leaving or joining). However, such changes should be notified to HMRC on form VAT2 as the departing partner will be regarded as a continuing partner and liable for the VAT debts of the business until the change is notified (see *Customs and Excise Comrs v Jamieson* [2002] STC 1418).

1.50   Where a sole proprietor takes another person into the business to form a partnership, or where a business carried on by two or more people in partnership is dissolved and continued by one person alone, HMRC must be informed. The change from sole proprietor to partnership or vice versa is a change of legal entity and will require registration of the new business for VAT purposes, although an election can be made to transfer the VAT registration number to the new entity (*VATA 1994, s 49(2)*).

1.51   If a sole trader carries on two or more distinct trades or businesses, the turnover of all those trades must be aggregated to determine if the individual is liable to be VAT registered. If he is VAT registered, all his trades must be subject to VAT. However, if the trades are conducted through separate legal entities such as a partnership, a limited company or sole trader, the trades will not be combined for VAT purposes, unless HMRC issue a direction for the businesses to be aggregated under *VATA 1994, Sch 1, para 2*.

Limited partnership

1.52 Limited partnerships are registered under the *Limited Partnerships Act 1907*. These are rarely used and should not be confused with LLPs incorporated under the *Limited Liability Partnerships Act 2000* (see **1.56**).

A limited partnership must include at least one general partner, whose liability is unlimited but it can be a limited company. Only the general partners can be involved in the management of the limited partnership. The liability of the limited partners for the debts and obligations of the partnership is limited to the amounts of their respective capital contributions. Limited partners lose their limited liability status if they become involved in the day-to-day running of the partnership.

Like an ordinary partnership, a limited partnership is not a separate legal entity when formed in England or Wales. Scottish partnerships do have a separate legal entity *(PA 1890, s 4(2))*.

Why use a limited partnership?

1.53 Limited partnerships are often used to undertake property developments or investments that are too big for a single person or organisation to take on. An investment manager will set up a subsidiary company to act as a general partner and invite third-party investors to become limited partners. Often the investment manager will then provide the general partner with the services of managing the limited partnership investment business.

Tax treatment

1.54 The tax treatment of a limited partnership is much the same as an ordinary partnership, as the partners are subject to tax on their share of the profits or losses as individuals. However, the partners' freedom to utilise trading losses from a limited partnership has been restricted by the various provisions described in **1.16**.

VAT

1.55 The VAT regulations relating to partnerships detailed at **1.48** do not apply to limited partnerships. A limited partnership does not have to have one VAT registration. The limited partners can be separately registered for VAT as decided in *H Saunders and TG Sorrell v Customs & Excise Commissioners* (1980) VATTR 51.

Limited liability partnership

1.56 A limited liability partnership (LLP) is a corporate body with its own legal personality, and is formed by incorporating under the *Limited Liability Partnerships Act 2000*. The LLP must be registered at Companies House, and must submit annual accounts and a confirmation statement, which are open to public view. The LLP must have a minimum of two members, but there is no maximum. Limited companies or other LLPs can also be members, but ordinary partnerships and limited partnerships cannot.

1.57 An advantage of an LLP is that it is a legal body separate from its members. An ordinary partnership only has a separate legal personality from the partners if it is formed under Scottish law. The members of an LLP have their liability limited to the amount of capital the member has contributed to the LLP.

1.58 An existing ordinary partnership can convert into an LLP without tax charges arising on the conversion. For income tax or corporation tax each partner's notional trade is treated as continuing. However, a new self-assessment reference number (UTR) will be set up by HMRC for the new LLP, and the nominated partner should tell HMRC whether it wishes to continue to use the old UTR or the new one.

The PAYE scheme can be transferred from the old partnership to the new LLP, but the partners must ask HMRC to do this. The VAT number of the old partnership can be reallocated to the LLP using the election under *VATA 1994, s 49(2)*.

Why use an LLP?

1.59 An LLP offers protection for all of the partners from the acts of the other partners as the members do not have joint and several liability for the debts of the LLP, as is the case with an ordinary partnership. Limited partnerships, as opposed to LLPs, only offer limited liability to partners who do not participate in the management of the business.

Tax treatment

1.60 The individual members of the LLP are not regarded as employed by the LLP for any purpose, unless the conditions in **1.61** apply. Thus the members of the LLP pay income tax and national insurance on a self-employed basis on their share of the profits. A corporate member pays corporation tax on its share of the profits.

1.61   A salaried member of an LLP (not of an ordinary partnership) is treated as an employee of the LLP for income tax and NIC purposes, if the individual meets all of the following conditions (*ITTOIA 2005, ss 863A–863C*):

A.   it is reasonable to expect that the member's remuneration for the work he performs for the LLP is substantially fixed, and does not vary in line with the overall profits or losses of the entire LLP (known as 'disguised salary');

B.   the member has no significant influence over the affairs of the entire LLP; and

C.   the member has contributed less than 25% of his disguised salary for the tax year as capital to the LLP.

Conditions A and B are considered only at the point when the individual becomes member of the LLP (or at 6 April 2014 if later); condition C must be examined annually.

Focus

Even if all the conditions A to C above are met, the individual continues to be treated as self-employed for employment law purposes until and unless his contract with the LLP is changed to an employment contract.

VAT treatment

1.62   As an LLP is a corporate body it is a recognised legal entity for VAT purposes and is separately liable for VAT registration, subject to the normal registration rules. As with ordinary partnerships this does not mean that the members will be seen as supplying their services to the LLP and therefore they will not normally have to register for VAT as individual partners.

1.63   As a corporate body the LLP can join a VAT group that has a company or other corporate bodies, such as universities, as members, as long as the conditions in *VATA 1994, ss 43* and *43A* are met. However, there are restrictions as to when an LLP can join a VAT group when it functions as the vehicle for a joint venture arrangement. For more information on VAT grouping see *HMRC VAT Notice 700/2: Group and divisional registration*. There are also anti-avoidance rules to consider in *VATA 1994, ss 43AA–44D* and *Sch 9A*.

Tax benefits of all partnerships

Income spreading

1.64   Tax issues may influence the decision to form a partnership. It is relatively common for a proprietor to take his spouse into partnership with a view to achieving an income tax saving. By spreading the profits of the business over two sets of basic rate income tax bands, and against two personal allowances, considerable tax savings may be achieved – see **Example 1.3**.

Example 1.3 – Comparing tax paid by sole trader or partnership

Frankie runs a sole trader business in England and makes taxable profits of £130,000 in the year to 31 March 2019, on which she pays £50,339 in tax and NIC, leaving £79,661 net income. If Frankie traded in partnership with Johnny, sharing the profits equally, the total tax and NIC payable would be £36,124, leaving a total net income of £93,876, thus increasing their net income by £14,215. Figures are rounded to nearest £.

2018/19 tax year	As sole trader	As partnership	
	Frankie	Frankie	Johnny
	£	£	£
Profits	130,000	65,000	65,000
Personal allowance*	Nil	11,850	11,850
Net taxable profits	130,000	53,150	53,150
Tax due at 20% on first £34,500	6,900	6,900	6,900
Tax due at 40% over £34,500	38,200	7,460	7,460
Class 2 NIC: £2.95 per week	153	153	153
Class 4 NIC: 9% between £8,424 and £46,350	3,413	3,413	3,413
Class 4 NIC: 2% above £46,350	1,673	136	136
Total tax and NICs payable	50,339	18,062	18,062
Net income after tax	79,661	46,938	46,938
Total effective tax and NI rate on gross profits:	38.72%	27.79%	27.79%

* Reduced to Nil where income is £123,700 or more.

1.65   HMRC should not challenge the apportionment of profits within a partnership but they may question the payment of a salary to a family member (see **1.95**). There is no legal requirement for the partners to contribute capital, participate in the management of the business, take an active part in running the business, or even be capable of performing the full range of activities of the business partnership (see HMRC Business Income Manual at BIM82020). Where there is a genuine partnership, the profits of that partnership may be split in any way which the partners desire, and that profit split may be changed at will.

1.66   Where the total business profits are split between two or more taxpayers, this can save considerable amounts of tax, as illustrated in **Example 1.3**. These tax savings are most effective where the income of an individual partner is reduced below a key tax threshold, such as £100,000 for loss of personal allowance, or £150,000 for the 45% tax rate (46% for Scottish taxpayers). Tax at the higher and additional rates may also be saved by making pension contributions, or gift aid donations on behalf of both partners to expand their basic and higher rate bands.

Focus

Families who claim child benefit also need to observe two further thresholds for the imposition of the high income child benefit charge (HICBC) that claws back child benefit received by the family. This tax charge applies where the highest earner in the family has net adjusted income of over £50,000. The full amount of child benefit is clawed back where the income of the highest earner is £60,000 or more.

Limits to tax saving

Settlements legislation

1.67   The main weapon HMRC can use to attack tax savings achieved through profit-sharing arrangements is the settlements legislation primarily contained in *ITTOIA 2005, Pt 5, Ch 5*. Following the House of Lords decision in *Jones v Garnett* [2007] STC 1536, it is unlikely that HMRC would use this legislation to attack husband and wife businesses as any profits diverted to a spouse or civil partner would be covered by the spouse exemption, see **1.116–1.119**.

Where the partners in the business are not married it is unlikely that the settlements legislation could be used to challenge the split of profits. However, where the partnership was not effective for some other purpose, for example where professional or trade rules barred the involvement in the business of certain individuals held out as partners, HMRC may be able to prove a partnership did not exist.

1.68   To provide a robust argument against the settlements legislation being invoked it is important that all the partners have the attributes and trappings of full equity partners. Good evidence of a genuine partnership should be available, such as a partnership agreement that provides for the sharing of income and capital losses as well as profits or gains. The trade should be conducted through a partnership bank account, for which all partners are signatories.

IR35 provisions

1.69   If the partnership provides the personal services of the partners or employees in circumstances where the worker would be an employee of the customer if the partnership did not exist, the IR35 rules for personal services provided through intermediaries may apply (see **1.81–1.86**).

Estate spreading

1.70   The prospect of saving inheritance tax can influence a business proprietor to form a partnership. In the case of a partnership between husband and wife, the tax saving can come from the equalisation of their estates. Where the partnership is between a parent and child or grandchild, the partnership arrangement can form the basis for a long-term transfer of the business down the generations.

COMPANIES

Type of company

1.71   The following types of company may be used by a new business:

- private company limited by shares;
- private company limited by guarantee and not having share capital;
- private unlimited company, with or without share capital; and
- community interest company (CIC).

There are also various forms of co-operative and common share-ownership arrangements, which are not dealt with in this chapter.

Private limited company

1.72   This is the most commonly used corporate form. Its defining criterion is that the liability of its members is limited to the amount, if any, unpaid on the shares held by each of them. A private company may convert to a public limited company (Plc), but discussion of that topic is outside the scope of this chapter.

Company limited by guarantee

1.73   A company limited by guarantee is commonly used by not-for-profit organisations that do not have a requirement for working capital, such as trade associations, clubs, charities and trade protection societies. Membership of a company limited by guarantee is not transferable and ceases on death or earlier retirement.

It is also possible to form a charitable incorporated organisation, under the *Charities Act 2006,* which is not considered further in this chapter.

Unlimited company

1.74   An unlimited company cannot have 'Limited' in its title, as it does not confer limited liability on its members. This means the members' liability is similar to that of partners in a general partnership. However, the unlimited company does have a separate legal existence and its members, unlike partners, have no direct obligation to contribute to the assets of the company while it is a going concern, save to be called upon to contribute to the company any capital unpaid on their shares.

Community interest company (CIC)

1.75   The CIC is designed to be used for community-based social businesses that are run as not-for-profit. A CIC may be a private or public limited company, limited by shares or guarantee. However, its articles of association must restrict the use of its assets for the benefit of the community. The CIC can attract investment under the social investment tax relief scheme.

Limited liability

1.76   Limited liability is perceived as being an important commercial advantage of carrying on a business through the medium of a limited company. The liability of the shareholders of a limited company is limited to the amount (if any) unpaid on their shares. Thus, if the company fails, they are not normally liable to make good any deficit. In the case of an unlimited company (see **1.74**), the shareholders' liability is not limited and they will be responsible for meeting all of the company's debts.

1.77   The actual degree of protection given by limited liability to the shareholders of private companies may be negated insofar as they have given any personal guarantees for the company's borrowings. A bank lending to a small company will almost invariably require personal guarantees from the directors or shareholders, and security over the personal assets of the major shareholders to support the loan provided. Shareholders will normally still be protected against claims by any creditors who have not taken such a security for their debts. The incorporation of a business will not absolve the proprietors from liability for pre-incorporation debts.

1.78   Individuals considering setting up a new business within a company, or incorporating an existing business, with a view to leaving creditors high and dry in the event of its being unsuccessful, should beware the provisions of the *Insolvency Act 1986, s 214* and the *Company Directors (Disqualification) Act 1986*. Under this legislation, directors can incur personal liability, notably in circumstances of wrongful trading or fraudulent trading, or when acting as a director when disqualified. For further discussion of the tax issues related to incorporation and disincorporation see **Chapter 2**.

Tax treatment

Corporate taxes

1.79   Corporation tax is levied at one rate for all sizes of company: 19% (from 1 April 2017), although different rates apply to companies in the oil and gas industry. This main rate of corporation tax is due to be cut to 17% from April 2020.

The tax savings to be made by operating through a limited company rather than as an unincorporated business have been diminished by the introduction of dividend tax from 6 April 2016, and by the reduction in the dividend allowance from £5,000 to £2,000 from 6 April 2018. However, tax savings can be realised by extracting profits from the company in a tax-efficient manner (see **1.89–1.110**).

1.80   In **Table 1.4** it is assumed the company owner is resident in England, takes a salary equal to the primary threshold for national insurance (£8,424) and extracts the balance of the profits as a dividend, of which the first £2,000 is taxed at 0%. This salary attracts no employees' or employer's NIC but the individual receives a full NI credit for the year. Note, these calculations would be different for an individual resident in Scotland, where the non-dividend and non-savings income is taxed at different rates and over different tax bands than for taxpayers in the rest of the UK.

Table 1.4: Comparison of net income in 2018/19

Gross profits by sole trader	Net taxable profits	IT @ 20%	IT @ 40%	Classes 2 and 4 NIC	Total tax and NI	Owner's net income
£	£	£	£	£	£	£
20,000	8,150	1,630	–	1,195.24	2,825.24	17,174.76
50,000	38,150	6,900	1,460	3,639.74	11,999.74	38,000.26
100,000	88,150	6,900	21,460	4,639.74	32,999.74	67,000.26
150,000	150,000*	6,900	46,200	5,639.74	58,739.74	91,260.26

Gross profits in company	Net profits after salary	CT @ 19%	Dividend tax @ 7.5% & @ 32.5%	IT @ 20% on salary	Total tax	Owner's net income
£	£	£	£	£	£	£
20,000	11,576	2,199.44	296.29	–	2,495.73	17,504.27
50,000	41,576	7,899.44	2,118.79	–	10,018.23	39,981.77
100,000	91,576	17,399.44	14,573.18	–	31,972.62	68,027.38
150,000*	141,576	26,899.44	27,735.68	1,684.80	56,319.92	93,680.08

* No tax-free personal allowance given when income exceeds £123,700.

The cash savings for incorporation range from £330 at the £20,000 profit level to £2,420 at the £150,000 profit level. However, that is not a linear progression as the savings from incorporation dip at various thresholds.

Personal service companies

1.81 Where an individual personally performs a contract through a third party, such as his own personal service company (PSC), that contract can fall foul of the wide-ranging anti-avoidance legislation for provision of personal services through intermediaries, known as IR35 (*ITEPA 2003, Pt 2, Ch 8*). These provisions do not prohibit the payment of dividends, but can mean that any dividends or payments to other employees must be paid out of income that has been subject to tax under PAYE and NICs.

1.82 The IR35 rules can apply where the intermediary is a company, partnership, or even an individual, but different qualifying conditions exist in each case:

- Intermediary is a PSC: the worker who performs the services must either hold a material interest in the company, broadly defined as 5% or more of the ordinary share capital, or receive payments from the company that can be taken to represent remuneration for the services performed for the final client.

- Intermediary is a partnership: the individuals who perform the personal services must share 60% or more of the profits of the partnership.

Sole traders who do not themselves act as intermediaries cannot fall under the IR35 legislation.

1.83   The IR35 legislation is designed to increase the tax burden of businesses that fall within it, and thus reduce the tax advantage from working through a PSC rather than as a direct employee for the final client. The tax advantages are principally the ability to receive income free of NICs, paid as dividends, and to achieve tax relief for business expenses on the wholly and exclusively basis (*ITTOIA 2005, s 34*) rather than the wholly, exclusively and necessarily basis required for tax relief of expenses incurred by an employee (*ITEPA 2003, s 336*).

The IR35 rules seek to apply PAYE and NIC to the proceeds of contracts that would be treated as employment contracts if they had been performed by the individual working directly for the client and not through the intermediary. Where the contract is performed in the private sector, the PSC must decide whether a particular contract is within IR35. From 6 April 2017, where the contract is performed for a public sector body, that body must decide whether the contract falls within IR35,rather than the PSC. In the private sector it is the PSC which bears the cost of the employer's NIC rather than the engager/client.

For contracts in the public sector, the amount invoiced by the PSC should be subject to PAYE and have income tax and employee's Class 1 NIC deducted, but the employer's Class 1 NIC should be paid by the fee-payer in the chain, which may not be the public body.

1.84   Whether income received by a personal service company falls within the IR35 rules will depend on the performance of the hypothetical contract represented by the actions of the worker, the final client, and any agency in between. Contractors and engagers are encouraged to use the HMRC: check employment status for tax (CEST) tool to determine if a contract is caught by IR35. However, CEST will only provide a definite answer in around 85% of cases, and many of those results may be incorrect as CEST has been programmed to assume that a mutuality of obligation between the parties always applies, when that is certainly not the case.

1.85   Although the IR35 rules may remove many of the benefits of operating through a personal service company, some are retained:

- If the company has some intrinsic value this may attract CGT relief through the application of entrepreneurs' relief and the capital gains exemption when the company is sold or formally liquidated (see **Chapter 8**).

- The company may make contributions into a registered pension scheme set up for the director and other employees, saving both corporation tax and NIC.

1.86 All business proprietors who are potentially affected by IR35 need to make the following judgments:

- What proportion of income is caught by the IR35 rules?

- What additional costs will the business incur by keeping records to comply with the rules?

- Do the benefits of operating through a company outweigh the immediate costs?

- Will the business make losses under the IR35 rules that cannot be relieved?

- What is the risk of the proprietor's view of which income falls under IR35 being successfully challenged by HMRC?

The Government is consulting on changes to the IR35 rules for private sector contracts, which are likely to take effect from 6 April 2019.

Managed service companies

1.87 A company whose business consists wholly or mainly of providing the personal services of a worker to others can be defined as a managed service company (MSC) under *ITEPA 2003, Pt 2, Ch 9*, if the following conditions also exist:

- more than half of the income of the MSC is paid on to the worker in some form;

- the manner of payment of this income to the worker increases the worker's net receipt above the amount he would have received if all those payments were treated as employment income; and

- a person who carries on a business of promoting or facilitating the use of companies to provide the services of individuals (an MSC provider) is involved with the company.

1.88 The consequences of being an MSC are serious for the MSC provider and the company. All non-employment income extracted from the MSC (such as dividends) is deemed to be earnings of the worker for both PAYE and national insurance purposes. The tax and NICs are payable when the payment to the worker is made, not at the end of the tax year as under the

IR35 provisions. The MSC provider, as well as the office holders of the MSC, and their associates, may also become liable to pay any PAYE and NICs debts which have been accrued by the MSC under the transfer of debt regulations (*SI 2007/1077* and *SI 2007/2068*), see *Christianuyi Ltd v HMRC* [2018] UKUT 10 (TCC). Where the MSC provisions apply to a company the IR35 provisions cannot also apply.

Profit extraction

Extract as dividends

1.89   Although tax is charged at only 19% on corporate profits, as compared to 19%, to 46% (for Scottish taxpayers) on profits made within unincorporated businesses (see **1.2**), the net income cannot easily be placed in the hands of shareholders without suffering a further charge to tax. The obvious way of distributing such profits is by the payment of dividends, which don't create a liability to NIC.

A company can only pay a dividend if it has sufficient realised distributable profits at the time that the dividend is paid. It may be necessary to prepare interim accounts to demonstrate the profits are available for distribution. If there are insufficient profits available, the dividend payment may be challenged by HMRC as a loan to the shareholder, or as remuneration of the director/ shareholder.

1.90   Individuals who receive company dividends in excess of £2,000 per year must pay dividend tax on the excess at 7.5% within the basic rate band (£34,500 for 2018/19), at 32.5% within the higher rate band, and at 38.1% on dividends in the additional rate band. Dividends form the highest slice of a taxpayer's income.

Disadvantages of dividends

1.91   Taking profits out of the company as dividends rather than as a salary or bonus can have a detrimental effect on the shareholder's financial affairs, as explained in **1.92–1.94**. Also paying dividends can increase the values of shareholdings for the purposes of IHT and CGT. However, the impact of IHT is usually limited because 100% business property relief is given on transfers of shares in qualifying unlisted companies that do not hold significant non-business investments.

1.92   Dividends do not count as pensionable earnings. Thus taking a large proportion of income in the form of dividends could restrict the individual's ability to make tax-relieved personal contributions to a pension. However, employer's pension contributions could be paid instead, see **1.107**.

Extract as bonus or salary

1.93 Profits extracted in the form of remuneration give rise to NIC charges for both the employee and the employer, which makes this method of profit extraction relatively expensive, once the NIC threshold of £8,424 is exceeded (for 2018/19). However, where the business is eligible to claim the employment allowance, that can be set against up to £3,000 of the employer's NICs.

In **Example 1.4** we have assumed the employment allowance is not available to set against NICs on the bonus, which will attract employer's NICs at 13.8%. The bonus is fully deductible for tax purposes, so there is no corporation tax charge where all the surplus profits are paid as a bonus. The dividend must be paid out of post-tax profits, so corporation tax must first be deducted from the gross profits. The employee is assumed to have already received a salary of exactly £11,850 which is covered by his personal allowance for the year. Figures are rounded to nearest £.

Example 1.4 – Choice between bonus or dividend		
2018/19 tax year	*Bonus*	*Dividend*
	£	£
Gross profits before tax (after salary of £11,850)	100,000	100,000
Less bonus	87,874	Nil
Less employer's NIC at 13.8%	12,126	Nil
Corporation tax charged at 19%	Nil	(19,000)
Payable to employee/shareholder before deductions	87,874	81,000
Employees NIC at 12% on first £34,500 (£46,350 – salary: £11,850)	(4,140)	Nil
Employees NIC at 2% above £34,500 of bonus	(1,067)	–
Gross receipt for employee before income tax	87,874	81,000
Income tax at 7.5% on dividends in band to £34,500 – £2,000	–	(2,438)
Income tax at 20% on first £34,500	(6,900)	–
Income/dividend tax at 40%/32.5% above £34,500	(21,350)	(15,113)
Net receipts	54,417	63,449
Effective total tax rate on gross profits of company	45.58%	36.55%

1.94 **Example 1.4** demonstrates that paying a dividend is still more tax efficient than a bonus or salary payment, taking into account the NIC payable. When considering whether to incorporate the business, the total effective tax and NIC payable on the gross profits should be compared to the total effective tax and NIC payable by the sole trader or partner on the same profits; see **Example 1.3** above.

1.95 If remuneration is paid to a director or employee in circumstances where little is done in return, or little responsibility for the business is taken on, HMRC will seek to disallow the deduction of excessive remuneration (see **1.111**).

Extract value by rent

1.96 Where a property is held by the proprietor or their family personally, but used for the company for its trade, the company may pay rent for the use of that property. The rent received must be declared on the individual's personal tax return, and be subject to income tax on the net amount after deduction of expenses such as loan interest, repairs and insurance.

1.97 The payment of rent to an individual can be a useful way to extract funds from the company, and it has the following advantages:

- rent payments do not carry national insurance charges;

- the rent can be paid whether or not the company has made a profit in the period, unlike a dividend;

- the rent payments are tax deductible for the company;

- the property can be placed in the hands of a member of the family who does not work directly for the business, and hence direct some income from the company to that individual where it may be taxed at a lower rate;

- the rent paid does not affect the business property relief (BPR) available on the value of the property, which will be 50% whether or not a market rent is paid.

A lease should be drawn up between the company and the property owner, and if the property owner is a director of the company the rents should be set at a reasonable market value. The grant of a lease may incur SDLT (LBTT in Scotland, or LTT in Wales) charges.

1.98 The proprietor of the business needs to balance the potential advantage of holding the property outside the company, in terms of profit extracted from the company, 50% BPR available on death compared to the 100% BPR available on the value of the property if it is held within the company. For further discussion of planning techniques available with BPR see **Chapter 12**.

A potential disadvantage of charging rent to the company for a building held privately is the loss of entrepreneurs' relief when the building is disposed of in association with the disposal of shares in the company and a withdrawal from the business. Where rent is received for the use of the building for periods after 5 April 2008, the entrepreneurs' relief will be restricted. Where the rent paid is less than the commercial market rent for the property the entrepreneurs' relief is restricted on a just and reasonable basis (*TCGA 1992, s 169P(2)*). For further discussion of entrepreneurs' relief on the disposal of a business see **Chapter 8**.

Extract value by interest

1.99 Where a shareholder or director has loaned money to the company, perhaps by not withdrawing amounts voted as dividends or remuneration, the company can pay interest on the outstanding balance. Where the interest is paid on a short-term loan from the individual to the company, the company can pay the interest due without deduction of tax.

If the period of the loan can exceed one year, the company should deduct income tax at 20% at the time the interest is paid, and report that tax deduction on a quarterly form CT61. Where the interest paid falls within the individual recipient's annual savings allowance (£1,000: basic rate taxpayer, £500: higher rate taxpayer), it is taxable at 0%, and the tax deducted at 20% can be reclaimed.

1.100 The interest paid by the company should be set at a commercial rate, which could be several points above the bank base rate. However, where HMRC perceive that the interest charge materially exceeds a commercial rate, they may seek to treat the excess interest as remuneration or a dividend distribution. There are also accounting issues to consider under FRS 102 or FRS 105 if the loan is not repayable on demand.

1.101 The payment of interest has the following advantages as a profit-extraction method:

● the interest can be paid whether or not the company has distributable profits, unlike a dividend;

● the interest payments do not carry national insurance;

● the interest payments are tax deductible for the company (but see **1.102**);

● payments are only made to those individuals who have outstanding credit balances with the company, rather than all of the shareholders, as with a dividend.

1.102 Where the company is a close company and the individual is a shareholder of that company, the company can only get a tax deduction for the interest due when it is actually paid, if the interest is paid more than 12 months after the end of the accounting period in which it was due (*CTA 2009, ss 373, 375*).

Extract value by benefits in kind

1.103   Value may be extracted from the company in the form of benefits in kind made available to directors, employees, and to shareholders who do not actually work for the company. Where the benefit is provided to a non-working shareholder, or an associate of that shareholder, the value of the benefit is not taxed as employment income, but is treated as a distribution under *CTA 2010, s 1064*.

1.104   Certain benefits in kind are tax free when provided to the company's employees or directors, but the private use of the asset or service would be taxable if paid for by the business and provided to a sole-trader or partner. Examples of tax-free benefits include:

- childcare vouchers – within limits;
- mobile phone;
- loan of up to £10,000 (see **1.106**);
- employer-provided training;
- relocation costs up to £8,000.

On the other hand, a car paid for by a partnership or unincorporated business may incur far lower tax charges than one provided for business and private use by the company.

Focus

A definite view on the potential tax savings which can be achieved by incorporating a business cannot be made without considering the levels of pension contributions, drawings or remuneration required by the individual, and the benefits in kind to be provided through the business, such as a company car.

Extract value by way of a pension

1.105   Pension contributions can be a tax-efficient way of extracting value from a company. An employer's pension contribution paid by the company into a scheme for a director or employee will be tax deductible if the individual's total remuneration package, including the pension contribution, is reasonable for the work done for the company.

Where the total pension contributions paid by or on behalf of the individual exceed the individual's annual allowance for the year, that individual will be subject to an annual allowance charge at their marginal tax rate.

Extract as a loan

1.106 Funds held within a private company may be loaned to directors, shareholders or employees, although tax charges may apply (see **1.107**). The following restrictions should also be noted:

- The *Companies Act 2006* prohibits loans to directors of more than £10,000 (*CA 2006, s 207*).

- A loan made available to an employee or associate of that employee through a third party may fall under the disguised remuneration provisions and thus be subject to PAYE (*ITEPA 2003, Pt 7A*).

- A loan to any director or to an employee which exceeds £10,000 at any point in the tax year, will generate a benefit in kind charge under *ITEPA 2003, s 175* equivalent to the interest due on the loan calculated at the official rate (2.5% since 6 April 2017), less any interest actually paid. The company will also be due to pay Class 1A NIC at 13.8% on the value of the benefit declared on the form P11D.

Loan to participators

1.107 Loans of any amount to participators in close companies can give rise to a charge under *CTA 2010, s 455* or *s 464A*, set at 32.5% of the loan advanced. This charge does not generally apply if the loan is repaid, written off or forgiven, within nine months of the end of the company's accounting period. However, the *CTA 2010, s 455* charge is extended in respect of loans or repayments where:

- A loan of £5,000 or more is repaid to the company, but within 30 days amounts totalling £5,000 or more are advanced to the same borrower or to one of his associates. The first loan is treated as not having been repaid, and continues for the purposes of calculating the corporation tax charge. However, if the repayment is made by a dividend declared by the company and chargeable to income tax on the participator, it is not brought within this rule (*CTA 2010, s 464C*).

- The loan is £15,000 or more, the 30-day rule is ignored if at the time of the repayment of the first loan, if the borrower intends to borrow at least £5,000 from the company or has arrangements in place to do so. If the later loan is made it is treated as a continuation of the first loan. As above if the repayment is made by a dividend declared by the company it is not brought within this rule (*CTA 2010, s 464C*).

- Loans channelled from the company through LLPs or partnerships in which the participator is a member are treated as if the loan was made directly to the participator. This also applies if the loan is advanced to a trust of which a participator in the company is a beneficiary, or potential beneficiary.

- An arrangement, perhaps a partnership structure between the company and a participator, is used to transfer value from the company to the participator (*CTA 2010, s 464A*).

- The charge under *CTA 2010, s 455(2)* does not apply if:

  - the amount of the loan does not exceed £15,000; and

  - the borrower works full-time for the close company or any of its associated companies; and

  - the borrower *does not* have a material interest in the company (being 5% or more of the ordinary shares); or

  - the debt is incurred for the supply of goods or services in the ordinary course of the trade or business of the company.

Where the loan from a close company to a participator is written off or forgiven, the borrower is liable to income tax on the amount written off, as if that sum was a net dividend (*ITTOIA 2005, s 415*). This tax charge takes precedence over a charge as employment income under *ITEPA 2003, s 118*. Where a loan which has given rise to a *CTA 2010, s 455* charge is written off, the company cannot claim a tax deduction for the loan write-off under the loan relationship rules.

When the loan is repaid the company must make a claim for repayment of the *s 455* charge within six years from the end of the financial year in which repayment is made.

HMRC will demand NICs on amounts paid to directors that cause their loan accounts to become overdrawn. HMRC claim the payment to the director is an advanced remuneration and thus generates a Class 1 NI liability at the date it is paid or the director becomes entitled to those funds (*SSCBA 1992, s 2(1)*). If it was always the intention to clear the loan with a dividend payment or some other private funds introduced to the company, the overdrawn amount cannot be an advance of remuneration. For further details, see para 30 of HMRC leaflet CA44: *National Insurance for Company Directors*.

Extract by way of purchase of own shares

1.108 Limited companies may issue redeemable shares and purchase their own shares under certain conditions. The amount by which the purchase price for the shares exceeds the amount paid on subscription must normally be treated as a distribution (*CTA 2010, s 1000*). The shareholder who receives value for the shares will have to pay income tax on the net proceeds as if they were a dividend.

The proceeds of a share buy-back are treated as a capital payment subject to capital gains tax, if the conditions of *CTA 2010, s 1033* can be met for the transaction. For a full discussion of the tax implications of the company purchasing its own shares see **Chapter 4**.

Extract value on death

1.109   Gifts of shares in an unquoted trading business or company qualify for 100% BPR for inheritance tax (*IHTA 1984, s 105(1)*). If the gift is made during the lifetime of the donor, the share must also qualify for BPR at the later date of death of the donor, or the tax relief will not apply. So the company must still be unquoted and trading within the definitions of those terms as they apply under the *Inheritance Tax Act 1984*.

1.110   Where an asset, such as land, buildings, plant or machinery, is held by an individual and used for the purpose of a business, the value of that asset will qualify for 50% BPR if:

● the business is the individual's own sole-trading business; or

● the business is a partnership in which the individual is a partner; or

● the business is an unquoted trading company in which the individual is a controlling shareholder.

Control for IHT purposes is measured by the voting power on all questions affecting the company as a whole, which if exercised would yield a majority of the votes capable of being exercised on them. For further discussion of BPR on gifts or transfers of business assets see **Chapter 12**.

Tax benefits of a company

Income spreading using salaries

1.111   To obtain a tax deduction for business expenses those expenses must be incurred wholly and exclusively for the purposes of the trade or profession (*CTA 2009, s 54* for corporation tax; *ITTOIA 2005, s 34* for income tax). This applies to salaries, bonuses, wages, pension contributions and other employee benefits just as it does to any other business expenses.

A wage paid to a spouse or child is often seen by business owners as a legitimate way to redistribute some of the profits of the business into hands of those who will pay tax at a lower rate on that income. A spouse who otherwise has no other income can be paid up to the earnings threshold for NIC (£162 per week for 2018/19), and pay no tax or NIC on that income. If the wages exceed the lower earnings limit (£116 per week for 2018/19), the individual will also receive a national insurance credit that counts as Class 1 NIC for qualification for state benefits.

1.112 Wages paid to relatives of the principal owner of the business are particularly vulnerable to attack by HMRC as being a disguised distribution of profits, and not a business expense wholly and exclusively incurred for the business. HMRC will want to know not only that the wage was actually paid to the individual (*Abbott v IRC* (1995) Sp C 58), but also that it fairly represents the value of the work done by that individual (*Copeman v William Flood & Sons Ltd* (1940) 24 TC 53).

1.113 Employees who are close relatives of the main proprietor should have service contracts in place that set out their duties and remuneration in commercial terms to deflect challenges from HMRC. Any family members employed by the family company should also be paid at least the national minimum wage, unless that individual acts purely as a director or company secretary and has no employment contract with the company (see **1.28**).

In **Example 1.3**, Frankie could have reduced the total tax paid by the business by employing Johnny rather than taking him into partnership. If his salary was set at £58,139, this would amount to a gross liability for the business of £65,000 including employer's NICs of £6,861. The total employers' and employees' NICs paid by the business on Johnny's salary would be £11,785 which would significantly reduce the tax saving of £14,215, achieved by forming a partnership.

An alternative position is shown in **Example 1.5** where Johnny's wage is set at the level such that the employer's NICs due would just be covered by the employment allowance of £3,000. Although Johnny is the only employee, the employment allowance can be claimed as the business is not incorporated.

Example 1.5 – Tax saved by sole trader employing one person

Frankie makes annual taxable profits of £130,000 in the year to 31 March 2019, on which she pays £50,339 in tax and NIC, leaving £79,661 net income. If Frankie employs Johnny, on a wage of £30,163, the total tax and NIC payable by them both would be £39,194, leaving a total net income of £90,806, thus increasing their net income by £11,145. Figures are rounded to nearest £.

2018/19 tax year	Sole trader	Sole trader	Employee
	Frankie	Frankie	Johnny
	£	£	£
Profits/ pay	130,000	99,387	30,163
Personal allowance*	Nil	11,850	11,850
Employers' NIC covered by employment allowance			(3,000)
Net taxable profits/pay	130,000	87,987	18,313
Tax due at 20% on up to £34,500	6,900	6,900	3,663
Tax due at 40% over £34,500	38,200	21,395	–
Class 2 NIC at £2.95 per week	153	153	–
Class 4 NIC at 9% on profits between £8,424 and £46,350	3,413	3,413	–
Class 4 NIC at 2% above £46,350	1,673	1,061	–
Employee's Class 1 NIC @ 12% above £8,424	–	–	2,609
Total tax and NICs payable	50,339	32,922	6,272
Net income after tax	79,661	66,465	23,891
Total effective tax and NI rate on gross profits/pay:	38.72%	33.13%	20.79%

* Reduced by £1 for every £2 of income over £100,000.

Income spreading using dividends

1.114   Any problem over obtaining a tax deduction for the relative's wages may be circumvented by paying a dividend instead of a salary, if the family member holds shares in the company. However, HMRC may challenge the use of the following structures to divert income from the main shareholders/ workers to other less active shareholders:

- dividend waivers;
- paying separate dividends on different classes of shares;
- the gift of shares with restricted rights; or
- dividends paid to the minor children of the main shareholder.

Settlements legislation

1.115   In any of these cases HMRC may argue that a settlement has been created by the main worker in favour of the person who received the dividends, on the basis that the main worker has made a gift of income to another individual. The anti-avoidance rules in the settlements legislation (*ITTOIA 2005, ss 619–648*) would then apply so the diverted income is taxed as if it was that of the donor.

1.116   The gift of ordinary shares between spouses, and the receipt of dividend income that arose from those shares was examined in: *Jones v Garnett (Inspector of Taxes)* [2007] STC 1536. The House of Lords decided in favour of the taxpayer, agreeing with HMRC that there was gift of income between the spouses, but that income was not caught by the settlement rules in *ITTOIA 2005, Ch 5,* as the spousal exemption applied. Mr Jones could not be taxed on the dividend income correctly received by Mrs Jones.

1.117   The decision in *Jones v Garnett* does not mean the settlement provisions can be ignored as the provisions could be applied where the shareholders are not married, or some of the shareholders are children, as the spousal exemption would not apply.

The guidance in the HMRC Trusts, Settlements and Estates Manual suggests a settlement is created where shares in the company are gifted to the child by someone other than the parents who are responsible for generating the profits of the company (see Example 16 at TSEM4300). This was shown in the case of *PA & FJ Bird v HMRC* [2008] SpC 720.

Mr and Mrs Bird initially owned all the shares in their company, but suggested that their daughters, then aged 15 and 10, should subscribe for some shares. The Special Commissioner accepted that the issuing of shares to the daughters comprised a settlement, and the income from that settlement should be taxed on the parents in equal parts. Although it was not clear in this case whether the funds used to subscribe for the shares came from the parents or an inheritance the girls received from their grandfather, the parents were deemed to be the settlors as they were the directors of the company and they arranged for new shares to be issued to the children.

1.118   Another example of the use of the settlements legislation to challenge the use of dividend waivers was the case *SP Buck v Revenue & Customs* [2008] SpC 716.

Mr Buck owned 9,999 of the shares in his company and his wife owned one share. Mr Buck waived his entitlement to his company's dividend, so the whole of the dividend was paid to his wife. The Special Commissioner found that

Mr Buck had formed a settlement in favour of his wife by waiving his dividend entitlement, and this settlement consisted purely of a right to income. As a result the income from that settlement should be taxed on Mr Buck.

1.119 When setting up a company in which family members are to hold shares, the following actions may reduce the risk of attack under the settlements legislation:

- The shares issued should be ordinary shares with full voting rights and rights to capital on a winding-up.

- Where the shareholders are a married couple or registered civil partners the ordinary shares should be gifted from one spouse/civil partner to the other.

- Both spouses/civil partners should be made directors of the company so they are equally responsible for the decisions the board of directors takes for the business, including suggesting the level of dividends to be paid.

- The duties undertaken by each family member for the company should be recorded to show that each shareholder plays a key role in the operation of the business.

IR35 rules

1.120 If the company is subject to the IR35 rules (see **1.81**), the payment of dividends may not be effective in reducing the effective total tax paid by the shareholder and the company on the income received. However, operating through a company has other commercial advantages and disadvantages, as discussed in **1.19–1.28**.

Company versus another medium

Starting as unincorporated

1.121 If the business is starting from scratch and expects to make losses for the first few years, trading within the medium of a partnership or sole-trader business for the first year or so will allow those losses to be relieved against the trader's other income (see **1.15**). An incorporation of the business when it is profitable may mean a capital gain arises on the transfer of assets including goodwill to the company (if the goodwill is transferrable). The gain arising on the transfer of the goodwill is unlikely to qualify for entrepreneurs' relief, but incorporation relief or hold-over relief may be used to hold-over the gain. For a further discussion of the tax reliefs and problems encountered on the incorporation of a business, see **Chapter 2**.

Timing of tax payments

1.122 Any comparison of the tax savings available by operating through a company, rather than as a sole trader or partnership needs to take into account the timing of tax payments. The timing of tax payments for a sole trader or partner starting in business is discussed in **1.36**.

Salary payments have the shortest time-lag for collection of the tax due, as they must be subject to PAYE and NIC deductions at the point of payment. Benefits in kind may also be taxed immediately through inclusion in the PAYE code, and the employer will have to pay Class 1A NICs on most benefits within three months of the end of the tax year.

Focus

The RTI system for reporting PAYE deductions provides HMRC with details of the PAYE due within three days of the payment date for salaries and wages, the HMRC banking and debt management section will issue demands for any apparent underpayment of PAYE without delay.

Companies

1.123 Most companies must pay their corporation tax nine months and one day after the end of the accounting period in which that tax liability arises. Large companies which have taxable profits in excess of £1.5 million a year, or which are part of a group, generally pay their corporate tax liability in four instalments commencing six months and 14 days from the start of the accounting period which gives rise to the tax liability.

National insurance

1.124 The national insurance burden can be a significant influence on the decision whether or not to take income in the form of earnings from a company, and if it is not possible to take NIC-free income, whether to incorporate at all. National insurance is payable on remuneration at levels over £8,424 per year (for 2018/19), and there is no upper limit on the remuneration that bears Class 1 NIC, although the rate payable by the employee drops to 2% once the upper earnings threshold is reached (£46,350 for 2018/19). Class 4 NIC payable by the self-employed are also unlimited in a similar fashion, but the Class 2 flat rate is set at the relatively low rate of £2.95 per week to reflect the minimum entitlement to social security benefits it carries.

1.125 The difference in the burden of NICs between the employed and self-employed is difficult to justify, as the only difference in terms of social security benefits is the entitlement to Jobseeker's Allowance, which is not available to those who have been self-employed. Nevertheless, NICs represent a very considerable fiscal impost in their own right, and their impact needs to be carefully considered by any individuals thinking of incorporating their business. The employer must also pay Class 1A NICs on almost all benefits in kind provided for employees where those benefits are also taxable.

Combination of personal and corporate taxes

1.126 The sole trader or partner is taxed on all the profits he makes whether or not he extracts those profits from the business, but the proprietor of a corporate business has the flexibility to control the level of personal tax he pays by extracting just enough income to keep his net adjusted income below the significant thresholds of £46,350 (£43,430 for Scottish taxpayers), £50,000, £100,000 or £150,000. This factor alone can influence the choice of business structure, particularly for businesses that expect to have widely fluctuating profits year on year.

Any profits extracted from the company, whether by way of remuneration, benefits in kind, dividends or other methods, will generally be chargeable to income tax, and in most cases, national insurance.

Profit-extraction strategy

1.127 The level of tax savings which can be made by operating a business through a company will depend on the method by which the proprietor extracts profits from the business. Where profits are extracted from the company as remuneration, which is subject to NIC, the impact of the combined employers' and employees' NIC are capable of resulting in the overall fiscal cost being in excess of that which would be suffered without incorporation.

1.128 The payment of dividends does not carry national insurance, and the first £2,000 received by the taxpayer in 2018/19 is taxed at 0%, so that can be a tax-efficient method of profit extraction for a basic-rate taxpayer.

Focus

Where the IR35 or the MSC provisions apply, dividend income may be reclassified as earnings and taxed as such (see **1.82** and **1.87**). This may tip the balance back in favour of an unincorporated business.

Small salary, high dividends

1.129   Where a director takes a small salary and extracts the balance of his income requirements from his company in a form that does not attract NIC, such as dividends, interest or rent – see **1.89–1.101**), significant savings may be made. However, this strategy is only tax efficient for certain companies, as the dividend is not tax deductible and so does not reduce the corporation tax payable, as a salary payment does. The tax savings also depend on the marginal tax rate of the shareholder.

Example 1.6 compares the standard profit-extraction strategy for a small company of paying a low salary with the balance of profits taken out of the company as a dividend, with the taxation of the same business as a partnership. It assumes both partners have a basic rate band of £34,500 available, which has not been extended by Gift Aid donations or by paying pension contributions. Figures are rounded to nearest £.

Example 1.6 – Tax paid by partnership compared to company

2018/19 tax year	As a company	As a partnership	
	F&J Ltd	Frankie	Johnny
	£	£	£
Profits	130,000	65,000	65,000
Wages from company up to personal allowance *	23,700	11,850	11,850
Net taxable profits	106,300	53,150	53,150
Corporation tax at 19%	20,197		
Net income extracted as dividend	86,103		
Tax due on 2 × divs: £32,500 @ 7.5% £2,000 @ 0%	4,875	–	–
Income tax due at 20% on next £34,500 profits	–	6,900	6,900
Tax due at 32.5% or 40% over £34,500 of dividend/profits/ person	5,558	7,460	7,460
Class 2 NIC at £2.95 per week	–	153	153
Class 4 NIC at 9% on profits of £37,926 + 2% on £18,650	–	3,786	3,786
Class 1 NIC @ 12% on wages	822	–	–

Net wages received (£11,439 each)	22,878	–	–
Total tax, including CT and NICs payable	31,452	18,299	18,299
Net income, including wages, after tax	97,726	46,701	46,701
* employers' NIC covered by employment allowance			

When operating as a partnership, Frankie and Johnnie have a net income after tax of £93,402. If they run their business through a company and take a salary equal to their personal allowances, they will have a net dividend income of £74,848 plus a net earned income of £22,878, giving a total net income of £97,726. Using the structure of a company could thus increase their net income by £4,324, but the exact savings will depend on the method used to extract profits from the company.

Employment-related securities

1.130   To take profits out of the company as dividends the individual must first hold an appropriate proportion of the company's shares. Where the individual already works for the company, holds a directorship, is related to someone who is employed by the company, or is about to be employed by the company, any shares acquired in that company will almost certainly be 'employment-related securities' as defined in *ITEPA 2003, Pt 7*. Where this is the case, tax charges can arise at the point when those shares are acquired, or when benefits connected with those shares, such as dividends, are received.

1.131   Where employees are awarded shares, it is clear that those shares are employment-related, but shares acquired in many other situations are also caught by deeming provisions in *ITEPA 2003, Pt 7*. Even gifts of shares between family members or others are caught unless the gift is made in the course of the normal domestic, family or personal relationships of the donor. Where such a gift of shares is made there should be some contemporaneous recording of the motive for the gift, and preferably a suitably worded deed of gift.

1.132   The tax charges on acquisition of employment-related securities normally only apply where:

- the shares have unusual terms (restricted securities, conditional securities or convertible securities); or

- the value of the shares is abnormal (high or low) as against a market value.

1.133   An income tax charge on dividends paid on shares classified as employment-related securities arises under *ITEPA 2003, s 447*, as the dividends paid on those shares are a benefit received in connection with those shares. However, the provisions in *ITEPA 2003, s 447* only apply where something has been done that affects the shares as part of a scheme or arrangement, the main purpose of which (or one of the main purposes) is the avoidance of tax or national insurance (*ITEPA 2003, s 447(4)*). If this is proven, the market value of the benefit from the share (the net dividend received) becomes chargeable as employment income instead of as dividend income (see *PA Holdings Ltd v HMRC* [2008] SSCD 1185).

As employment income, the amount of the 'dividend' must be subject to NIC and taxed under PAYE at the individual's marginal rate rather than at the rate that applies to dividends: 7.5%, 32.5% or 38.1% (for 2018/19).

1.134   The burden of proof would be on the taxpayer to demonstrate that whatever was done to the share (such as issuing the share or an alteration of terms), these actions were not intended to avoid tax and NICs. It is thought that paying a dividend on a share is not something that is '… done which affects the employment-related securities as part of a scheme or arrangement the main purpose (or one of the main purposes) of which is the avoidance of tax or national insurance contributions' (*ITEPA 2003, s 447(4)*). The ability of the provisions in *ITEPA 2003, s 447* to apply to dividends issued by owner-managed companies has not yet been tested in the courts. However, it is possible that a decision to pay dividends in the place of salary in a small company could be caught as a scheme or arrangement to avoid tax or NIC.

Disadvantages of dividends

Pension contributions

1.135   Dividends do not count as earnings for pension contribution purposes. The maximum pension contribution an individual may make per tax year and receive tax relief for is £3,600 (gross) or 100% of their UK earnings, if higher, although the employer may make higher contributions.

1.136   A tax-efficient strategy for most owner-managed companies is to have the company pay the pension contribution as the employer. The employer's and employee's contributions into the pension scheme should not exceed the employee's annual allowance for the year (nominally £40,000 for 2018/19), or an annual allowance charge at the taxpayer's marginal rate will be due. The employer's pension contributions do not have to be linked to the employee's salary, and should qualify in full for a corporation tax deduction if the company can show the total remuneration package was made wholly and exclusively for the business.

Flexibility

1.137 Where the directors and shareholders are different individuals it is difficult to use dividends to replace salaries to reward the directors separately from the non-working shareholders. Dividend waivers are commonly used to remedy this problem, although great care should be taken where these involve the shareholder's spouse, civil partner or minor children to avoid the possibility of the settlements legislation applying to the arrangement (see **1.118**). It is essential that any dividend waiver is made before the dividend is paid.

Different classes of shares (known as alphabet shares) may be issued to working and non-working shareholders, although this strategy can create problems, as the shares issued to the employees are likely to be employment-related securities (see **1.130**).

Focus

The use of alphabet shares to pay differential dividends to selected directors or employees or the blatant use of dividend waivers by controlling shareholders to divert what could effectively be seen as bonuses to colleagues working in the business, could be attacked by HMRC using the ruling in *PA Holdings Ltd v HMRC* [2008] SSCD 1185. In each case, the payments made as dividends would be charged to income tax and NIC as remuneration.

Administration

1.138 When paying a dividend certain administrative formalities have to be observed; dividend certificates, directors' minutes and resolutions should be prepared. If dividends have not been properly declared in accordance with company law formalities, HMRC may challenge the payment and seek to treat the dividend as remuneration subject to Class 1 NICs, and require PAYE to be applied.

Retention of profits

1.139 Normally some profits will be retained within the business for future investment or to use as working capital. A company will generally have paid less tax on such retained profits (at 19%) than a sole trader or partnership where the marginal tax rates will be 29% (including NI) on profits per person up to £46,350, and 42%, 47% or 62% (including NI) beyond that threshold. These marginal rates are different for Scottish taxpayers.

1.140 The proprietor needs to predict how long the business may remain in his hands and weigh up the difficulties of extracting capital value from the business in the long term. There is a potential double capital gains tax charge where appreciating assets are held within the company, and a potential double charge on retained earnings, both of which will crystallise when the company is liquidated (see **1.143**). If the company is sold rather than liquidated, this will not actually crystallise the double capital gains tax charge. However, the share price may reflect the gains held in the company and a charge on retained earnings will in effect arise at that time.

Long-term intentions

Continuing the business

1.141 The relative importance of the long-term disadvantage of the double charge on capital gains will depend upon the timescale that the proprietor has in mind for retaining the business. If he plans to run the company for many years, the cash-flow advantage from the lower tax rates on profits may outweigh the capital tax disadvantage at the time of liquidation or sale. Alternatively, there may in fact be no liquidation or sale because the business will be passed down to the next generation and continued within the family.

The decision in each case will depend very much on the precise circumstances of the business and the objectives of the proprietor. He will need to take a long view of the trends for both corporation tax and income tax rates, and weigh up the pros and cons of each course of action with considerable care.

Dissolving the company

1.142 Having once incorporated a business, it is not so easy to dissolve the company without incurring tax charges. Incorporation reliefs can apply to shelter gains when assets are transferred into a corporate body in return for shares, and disincorporation relief can protect the company from gains realised on the transfer of goodwill or property from a small company to the shareholders on its dissolution (see **Chapter 2**). However, the shareholders are not protected from the income tax or CGT charges that arise on the distribution of the company's assets.

Double tax charge

1.143 The received wisdom for capital gains tax planning has been to keep valuable assets used for the business outside the company if possible, to avoid the double tax charge when the company sells the asset and the shareholder extracts the proceeds. The potential double charge springs from:

- the charge to corporation tax in respect of a capital gain realised on disposal of the asset by the company; and

- the further charge to capital gains tax arising in the event of the shareholder wishing to liquidate the company and extract the net proceeds of the disposal of the asset; or

- a further charge to income tax when the shareholder extracts the proceeds of the sale from the company as a dividend.

The individual only obtains the benefit of the gain on the disposal of the asset by the company by suffering, at least to some extent, a duplicate tax charge.

Where the company pays corporation tax at 19% and the individual takes the net proceeds of the sale as a dividend, the total tax paid will be greater than the CGT rates of 10% and 20% that the individual would pay on the disposal of the asset (which is not a residential property) held outside the company, as shown in **Example 1.7**.

Example 1.7 – Gains made by company then distributed to shareholders

Assume the individuals have already received dividends of £2,000 each in that tax year which uses up the dividend allowance. The gain is calculated per person.

Company	£
Chargeable gain	10,000
Less corporation tax at 19%	(1,900)
Available for distribution	8,100

Distributed to taxpayers paying tax at:	*Basic rate*	*Higher rate*	*Additional rate*
	£	£	£
Gross dividend	8,100.00	8,100.00	8,100.00
Tax due at 7.5% / 32.5% / 38.1%	607.50	2,632.50	3,086.10
Corporation tax paid on the gain	1,900.00	1,900.00	1,900.00
Total tax paid on gain	2,507.50	4,532.50	4986.10
Effective tax rate on gain	25.075%	45.325%	49.861%

Reliefs available for different structures

1.144 Comparing the corporate and personal tax rates as in **Example 1.7** does not tell the full story, as in practice the maximum tax rate is likely to be reduced by the various tax reliefs available to both the individual and the company, as summarised in **Table 1.5** below.

Table 1.5

Tax relief	Unincorporated businesses	Companies
Indexation allowance	Not available	Reduces effect of inflation on asset values held since the later of acquisition or 31 March 1982, to 31 December 2017
Annual exemption	£11,700 for 2018/19	Not available
Entrepreneurs' relief on disposals (see **Chapter 8**)	CGT at 10% for gains on certain assets subject to a lifetime cap of £10m.	Not available
Substantial shareholding exemption (see **Chapter 6**)	Not available	Exempts gain or loss on shares if at least 10% stake is held for one year within six years of sale
Roll-over of gains on replacement of business assets in the following categories:	Land and buildings	Land and buildings
	Fixed plant and machinery	Fixed plant and machinery
	Ships, aircraft and hovercraft	Ships, aircraft and hovercraft
	Satellites and space stations	Satellites and space stations
	Goodwill	Lloyd's syndicate rights
	Basic payment rights for farmers	
	Fish quota	
	Lloyd's syndicate rights	

Roll-over relief on replacement intangible business assets	Included in the above categories of assets	For intangible assets acquired on and after 1 April 2002
Hold-over relief	Gifts of business assets and gifts of assets on which IHT is chargeable	Not available
EIS and SEIS to raise capital	Not available to raise business capital	Restricted to SMEs where investor is not connected to company
Transactions within a marriage/group (see **Chapters 16 and 6**)	Transfers between a married couple or civil partners who are living together are treated as no gain/no loss	Transfers within a group of companies where there is a 75% relationship are generally treated as no gain/no loss
R&D tax credits (see **Chapter 17**)	Not available	Enhanced deduction for revenue costs incurred in R&D projects. Losses made by small companies may be converted into tax credits
First-year tax credits	Not available	Surrender loss for payable tax credit where enhanced capital allowances claimed for the same period
Land remediation relief	Not available	Enhanced deduction for the cost of removing pollution from land or buildings
Patent Box regime (see **Chapter 18**)	Not available	Reduced rate of tax on profits derived from patented inventions or patent rights
Tax relief for production of British films, high end TV, video games, orchestra performances or museum exhibitions	Not available	Cash rebates of 20% or 25% of film production expenditure

| Cash basis accounting | Optional for most businesses where turnover is less than the VAT-registration threshold for the year | Not available |
| Interest relief for residential property lettings | Restricted from 2017/18, removed from 2020/21 | No restriction |

1.145   Where real capital gains are likely to arise, the potential double tax charge must be considered when incorporating a business that holds appreciating assets which are used for the trade. In such cases it may be sensible to leave the asset in the private hands of the proprietor and rent or lease the asset to the company. On the subsequent sale of the asset the individual will pay CGT on the gain at 10% or 20%, or at 18% or 28% if the asset is a residential property.

For further discussion of the current tax issues concerned with the sale of an owner-managed company, see **Chapter 8**.

Chapter 2

Incorporation and disincorporation

Mark McLaughlin CTA (Fellow), ATT (Fellow), TEP, Tax Consultant,
Mark McLaughlin Associates Ltd and The TACS Partnership
Jackie Anderson LLB, ACA, CTA, LHA Consulting Ltd

SIGNPOSTS

- **Scope** – The choice of trading medium is an important commercial decision, which should not generally be tax driven. However, a company can be a tax-efficient vehicle in which to shelter retained business profits at lower rates than personal tax rates for sole traders and individual partners in appropriate circumstances. Unfortunately, a number of tax measures have been devised to reduce the tax-efficiency of what has been termed 'tax motivated incorporations', but which potentially affect incorporations irrespective of their motive. A number of non-tax issues must be addressed when incorporating a business. Consideration should also be given to the implications if it is later decided to disincorporate the business (see **2.1–2.4**).

- **Income tax and NIC** – Incorporation gives rise to a number of income tax and national insurance contributions (NICs) issues, including cessation and overlap relief, the timing of tax payments, the treatment of stock and work in progress, capital allowances, income tax and NIC rates and planning, etc (see **2.5–2.32**).

- **Capital gains tax** – Incorporation often involves the disposal of chargeable assets to the company, such as business premises and goodwill. The sale of a business as a going concern may be subject to a claim for entrepreneurs' relief if the relevant conditions are satisfied. The scope for claiming entrepreneurs' relief on goodwill upon incorporation was restricted following changes introduced in *Finance Act 2015*, subject to certain exceptions (following changes introduced in *Finance Act 2016*). Other forms of capital gains tax relief may be available on a disposal of assets to the company (see **2.33–2.57**).

- **Goodwill** – Care should be taken in identifying and valuing goodwill. For example, personal goodwill cannot be transferred, and valuation difficulties can arise for certain businesses in respect of 'trade related property'. Overvaluations of goodwill can result in inadvertent tax charges (see **2.58–2.70**).

- **Other tax issues** – Various tax considerations resulting from incorporation can include whether the company may claim a deduction in respect of intangible fixed assets (although the ability to do so was adversely affected following changes introduced in *Finance Act 2015* and subsequently), stamp taxes (see **2.75–2.79**), inheritance tax, VAT and employment-related securities (see **2.71–2.102**).

- **Disincorporation** – While a company may have been chosen as the optimum operating vehicle for a business, there will be circumstances in which some businesses might benefit from 'disincorporating' and operating through a sole trader or partnership structure instead. Disincorporation can be implemented through a distribution or sale of the business to the shareholders (see **2.103–2.106**).

- **Key tax consequences of disincorporation** – These can include:

  (a) For the shareholder – the legislation (which replaced ESC C16) only permits distributions made under an informal winding-up to be treated as capital as long as these do not exceed £25,000 (see **2.107** and **2.118**).

  (b) For the company – the potential tax charges and events which arise on a disincorporation are similar to those which would occur on any sale of a company's business and assets to a 'third party' (see **2.108–2.117**).

- **Disincorporation relief** – A limited form of relief (introduced by *Finance Act 2013*) was available between 1 April 2013 and 31 March 2018, so that small business owners were potentially able to avoid a double charge to tax upon disincorporation (see **2.121**). However, as there could still be a tax charge on the shareholder, the relief was not always attractive to business owners.

INCORPORATION

Introduction

2.1   The choice of the most tax-efficient trading medium (ie sole trader, partnership or limited company) is a complicated subject, involving many different factors. With a top rate of income tax of 45% (for 2018/19), the incorporation of sole trader and partnership businesses is an important tax planning consideration. Incorporation might seem attractive to some business owners, particularly in view of a single corporation tax rate of 19% (for the financial year to 31 March 2019) for companies that do not have ring fence profits. Furthermore, the corporation tax rate was set at 19% for financial year beginning 1 April 2019 in *Finance (No 2) Act 2015*. The corporation tax rate for the financial year beginning 1 April 2020 was reduced to 17% in *Finance Act 2016*.

A company may therefore be seen as a useful vehicle in terms of sheltering retained profits at lower tax rates than the personal tax rates applicable to many sole traders and business partners. However, the future extraction of profits as dividends was adversely affected in many cases by the reform of the dividend tax system in *Finance Act 2016* (see **2.32**).

A separate chapter of this book has been dedicated to choosing an appropriate trading vehicle when a new business commences (see **Chapter 1**).

2.2   This chapter covers tax issues in connection with the process of incorporation. The subject has been a popular one for many years. Historically, the 'heyday' for business incorporations probably followed *Finance Act 2002*, with the introduction of a 0% starting rate of corporation tax. Much has changed since then, including the withdrawal of the starting rate and fluctuating corporation tax rates generally. In some cases, it may be attractive for owner-managers to disincorporate an existing company's business, and to operate as a sole trader or partnership instead.

However, disincorporation has its own set of tax problems associated with it. Prior to legislation introduced in *Finance Act 2013*, there was no statutory relief when a business disincorporated and reverted back to the medium of a sole trader or partnership. A measure of relief was temporarily available by allowing qualifying business assets to be transferred from the company to one or more of its shareholders with no immediate tax charge. However, disincorporation relief ceased to be available for business transfers following the expiry of its fixed five-year term on 31 March 2018 (see **2.121**).

The tax issues surrounding disincorporation are later considered in a separate section of this chapter.

2.3

Focus

Whilst this chapter does not deal with non-tax issues arising from incorporation, it should be borne in mind that there are a number of legal and commercial issues. Those issues broadly include:

- company formation (eg appointment of directors, allotment of shares etc);

- shareholders' agreement (if there is one);

- company law obligations, such as statutory forms and accounts filing at Companies House;

- formalities of transferring the unincorporated business (eg documenting the transfer, accounting for the incorporation, notifications to HMRC, the transfer of employees between businesses, etc);

- professional fees (ie in connection with the incorporation process, and the costs of preparing company accounts, which are often higher than for unincorporated businesses);

- other practicalities (eg company accounts and their filing in XBRL format to HMRC, financing, notifying customers, suppliers, insurance companies, employees, amending trade and telephone directories, etc).

2.4   In some cases, it will also be necessary to address any potential implications of incorporation in terms of the business owner's entitlement to state benefits. For example, the impact of being a company director and shareholder may need to be considered in the context of tax credits and universal credit, including the level of remuneration from the company and (for universal credit purposes) the level of company profits.

A subject as wide as incorporation (and disincorporation) cannot be covered in detail in a single chapter. Readers are directed to the latest edition of *Incorporating and Disincorporating a Business* (Bloomsbury Professional) for more comprehensive coverage.

Income tax

2.5   There are specific provisions aimed at simplifying the calculation of income tax for small unincorporated business.

First, eligible small businesses can elect for a 'cash basis' to apply for the purposes of accounting for trading profits, instead of using generally accepted accounting practice. *Finance (No 2) Act 2017* also introduced a mandatory cash basis with effect from the tax year 2017/18 in respect of property businesses with receipts for the tax year not exceeding £150,000, subject to an optional election facility for the cash basis not to apply.

Secondly, unincorporated businesses (ie self-employed individuals, or partnerships of individuals) can deduct certain expenses (ie motor expenses, use of home for business, and premises used for both home and business purposes) on a flat rate basis, if they choose (*ITTOIA 2005, ss 94B–94I*).

However, companies are excluded from applying these 'simplification' measures. This presents a potential disadvantage in terms of incorporating a business, or at least an additional consideration.

The incorporation of a business involves the cessation of a former sole trade or partnership. It must be remembered that the company is a totally separate entity, chargeable to corporation tax and not income tax. It is therefore necessary to apply appropriate cessation adjustments to the unincorporated business. The cessation will, of itself, cause certain adjustments to the tax computation, especially as regards stock and capital allowances (see **2.13, 2.17**).

Cessation computation

2.6   The general position under the current year basis (CYB) is that the income tax assessment for a given year is based on the profits of the accounting period ended in that year. Adjustments may be needed in the opening years to get to this position. Compensating adjustments may also be necessary when a business ceases.

There is no gap between the basis periods at cessation. The profits forming the basis of the assessment for the final tax year will be those earned in the period beginning immediately after the end of the basis period for the preceding year and ending on the date of cessation (*ITTOIA 2005, s 202*).

Depending on the accounting date and date of cessation, this could be a period of more or less than 12 months.

2.7   Unless the incorporation takes place on the usual accounting date, the accounts to cessation of the sole trade (or partnership) will be for a period other than 12 months. Use of a different date for the final accounting period will not normally trigger the change of basis period rules.

The cessation rules of *ITTOIA 2005, s 202* automatically take priority over the rules governing a change of accounting date (*ITTOIA 2005, ss 214–220*) for the year of cessation.

Overlap relief

2.8   Where 5 April has been used as the annual accounting date of a business, the total profits assessed will automatically equal the total profits earned. There will be no overlap between any income tax basis periods.

Accounts drawn up to 31 March (or 1, 2, 3 or 4 April) may be treated as coterminous with the tax year end (*ITTOIA 2005, s 209*).

Drawing up accounts to 5 April (or 31 March) has the advantage of simplicity. The profit earned during a tax year suffers income tax in that same year. No basis period adjustments are necessary. For that reason alone, many small sole traders and partnerships will choose this accounting date.

2.9   In using an accounting date other than one coterminous with the tax year end, there will be one or more years in which the basis periods for two adjacent tax years overlap. The logic to creation and use of overlap relief is that the profits earned throughout the life of a business are all subject to tax once, and once only. An adjustment may be made on a change of accounting date during the life of the business. Any remaining overlap relief can be useful in the tax year in which the business ceases.

Overlap relief is given as if it were an additional trading deduction incurred in that period (*ITTOIA 2005, s 205(1)*). In most instances, the use of overlap relief simply reduces the assessable profit in the final year. However, depending on the relative size of the profit and the overlap relief, a loss may be created. Equally, if a loss already arose in the period of cessation, the overlap relief will augment that loss.

A loss created or enhanced by overlap relief is generally treated in the same manner as any other trading loss; the usual loss relief claims may be made. The ability of sole traders and partners to obtain 'sideways loss relief' for trading losses against general income is subject to a limit (in *ITA 2007, s 24A*) on the amount of tax relief that can be deducted in their income tax calculation for the tax year (ie the greater of £50,000 and 25% of the individual's adjusted total income for the tax year). However, trading losses attributable to overlap relief may be deducted without restriction (*ITA 2007, s 24A(7)(c)*).

2.10

Focus

In any case other than a 31 March accounting date, there is no substitute for looking at the realised profits, projected future profits, amount of overlap relief and dates in each case. A wrong decision can result in a substantial income tax liability on cessation or, at least, a cash-flow disadvantage. The proprietor is not going to welcome that as a penalty for incorporation.

There is also the issue of adjustments which vary the profits. Particular issues here include stock valuation and capital allowances (see below).

Payment of tax

2.11   Very few sole traders (and partnerships) seem to make any provision for tax in their business accounts. For the most part, tax liabilities falling due now are paid out of profits earned now.

Example 2.1 – Timing of tax payments

Chris drew up accounts to 30 June each year. Ignoring incorporation, the tax due for 2018/19 (ie based on the accounts for the year ended 30 June 2018) would be payable by two payments on account on 31 January 2019 and 31 July 2019, with a balancing payment on 31 January 2020.

He will quite probably meet the 31 January 2020 bill out of incoming funds at the end of 2019, despite the fact that he began earning the relevant profits as long ago as 1 July 2017.

2.12   The proprietor needs to be warned in advance of the change in timing of tax payments which is occasioned by incorporation:

- Chris's sole-trader self-assessment for 2018/19 was based on profits earned in the period 1 July 2017 to 30 June 2018. Tax is payable in instalments falling due between 31 January 2019 and 31 January 2020. Payment of the tax therefore falls much later than the inflow of the corresponding funds.

- If the incorporated business draws up accounts to 30 June 2019, tax is payable on 1 April 2020, a delay of only nine months.

- If Chris draws a taxable salary from the company, income tax and NIC is normally payable only 17 days after the tax month of payment if paid electronically (or 14 days in any other case (*SI 2003/2682, reg 69(1)*).

The cash-flow considerations of funding the income tax (and NIC) liabilities of the unincorporated business up to the date of cessation should not be overlooked or underestimated. Forward planning (eg projecting tax liabilities and payment dates) based on the anticipated date of incorporation should be implemented as far as possible in advance.

However, it is proposed that 'making tax digital', when introduced, will provide unincorporated business owners with the opportunity to make regular payments towards their tax liabilities (HMRC consultation document 'Making Tax Digital: Voluntary pay as you go', 15 August 2016). This should help to mitigate cashflow difficulties resulting from incorporation in many cases.

Treatment of stock and work in progress

Trading stock

2.13 The basic position regarding the transfer of trading stock upon incorporation is that it is deemed to pass between connected persons at an arm's-length price (*ITTOIA 2005, s 177*).

The meaning of 'connected persons' is defined in *ITTOIA 2005, s 179*, and is rather wider than the usual definitions (in *CTA 2010, ss 1122–1123* or *ITA 2007, ss 993–994*). In particular, two persons are connected if one is a company and the other has control over it.

In most cases, the effect of the deeming provision in *ITTOIA 2005, s 177* is that the incorporation will result in additional taxable profits (ie if the arm's length value of stock exceeds its original cost) and a corresponding increase in the sole trader's or partner's income tax and Class 4 NIC liability.

2.14 However, the transferor and transferee (ie sole trader or partners and new company) may jointly elect that the stock is instead to be treated as transferred at the higher of cost or the amount actually paid (see *ITTOIA 2005, s 178*).

As the sale price or market value should be taken into account to determine the final profit of the unincorporated business, but is also deductible in arriving at the profits of the company, there is scope for planning. If the unincorporated business owner pays tax at (say) 40% but the company at only 19%, the stock should be transferred at a low value to reduce the income tax profits at the expense of corporate tax profits increasing but taxed at a lower rate. The choice of transfer value for these purposes is not infinitely variable though, as it must be lower than an arm's-length value (*ITTOIA 2005, s 178(2)*).

A flowchart illustrating the valuation of stock on cessation is included in HMRC's Business Income Manual at BIM33475. In addition, the practical application of the election is illustrated at BIM33480.

Where an election is appropriate, it must be made by the first anniversary of the normal self-assessment return filing date for the tax year of cessation (*ITTOIA 2005, s 178(4)*). However, it will often be practical to submit the election with the tax return covering the cessation period of the unincorporated business.

Note that such an election is only permissible where stock is sold or transferred for valuable consideration. It appears that if the stock is gifted to the company (which is not an impossible position in certain types of incorporation) then market value must prevail with no option available.

If a person who has made an election for the cash basis ceases carrying on a trade in that tax year, the value of any trading stock at the time of cessation is brought into account as a receipt on a basis that is just and reasonable in all the circumstances, for example, cost or net realisable value (*ITTOIA 2005, s 97A*). In the case of a person carrying on a profession or vocation, the value of any work in progress at the time of cessation is brought into account in the same way as trading stock for a trader (*ITTOIA 2005, s 97B*).

Work in progress

2.15   For the vast majority of businesses, everything so far mentioned about stock applies equally to work in progress. There are, though, distinct rules concerning the valuation of work in progress on discontinuance of a profession or vocation. These are to be found in *ITTOIA 2005, ss 182–185*.

The basic position is that where there is valuable consideration (eg on a business transfer in exchange for shares) the work in progress is taken to have that value (*ITTOIA 2005, s 184(1)*). On a gift, an arm's length value must prevail (*ITTOIA 2005, s 184(2)*).

HMRC are normally prepared to accept whatever value is attributed to work in progress, unless it is blatantly unreasonable. They will not seek to make any adjustment so long as the value attributed to work in progress follows the basis consistently used for accounting purposes.

HMRC guidance in their Business Income Manual on valuing professional work in progress states that the proper valuation depends on the correct application of generally accepted accounting practice to the facts. The guidance points out that uncompleted contracts for services should be valued in accordance with section 23 of FRS 102, and adds (at BIM33020):

> 'In most cases revenue for service contracts should be accounted for under what is known as the "percentage of completion" method. In very simple terms, this means that if a contract is in progress at the year end, then the supplier of services would include the proportion undertaken to that date in its accounts. So if the contract is 50% complete, 50% of the contract value will be recorded in the accounts as revenue.'

In the case of construction contracts, HMRC guidance (at BIM33025) states that where the outcome of the contract can be estimated reliably, contract revenue and contract costs should be recognised as income and expenses by reference to the stage of completion of the contract at the end of the reporting period.

2.16   There is a further provision relating to the cessation of a profession or vocation in that the taxpayer may elect for the closing work in progress on cessation to be taken as having its cost value (*ITTOIA 2005, s 185*).

Any amounts received on the transfer of work in progress which exceed the actual cost of the work is then treated as a post-cessation receipt (under *ITTOIA 2005, s 243*). As a general rule, on the cessation of trading a sum received for the transfer of work-in-progress (or trading stock) is not a post-cessation receipt if a valuation has been brought into account under *ITTOIA 2005, Pt 2, Ch 12* (valuation of stock and work in progress). However, this does not prevent a post-cessation receipt arising as the result of the above election under *ITTOIA 2005, s 185* (see *ITTOIA 2005, s 252(2)*).

The deadline for making the election is the first anniversary of the filing date for the self-assessment return in respect of the tax year of cessation (*ITTOIA 2005, 185(2)*).

Capital allowances

Plant and machinery

2.17   Writing down allowances (WDA), annual investment allowances (AIA) and first-year allowances (FYA) are not available in the final chargeable period (NB: since the introduction of the AIA (from 6 April 2008) the types of expenditure attracting FYA have been limited; see **2.22**).

Thus if a business incurs qualifying expenditure and incorporates very shortly afterwards, the opportunity to claim AIA and FYA may be lost (see, for example, *Keyl v Revenue & Customs* [2015] UKUT 383 (TCC)). The timing of incorporation may therefore be an important consideration.

The final chargeable period is (for the main pool or a 'special rate' pool) the chargeable period in which the qualifying activity is permanently discontinued (*CAA 2001, s 65(1)*). WDA in the final chargeable period is prohibited by *CAA 2001, s 55(4)*, AIA is prohibited by *CAA 2001, s 38B*, General Exclusion 1, and FYA is prohibited by *CAA 2001, s 46(2)*, General Exclusion 1.

2.18   In virtually every case, the new company will be connected with the proprietors of the unincorporated business. In most cases, the company's shareholders and directors will be identical to the sole trader or business partners. Connection follows under *CAA 2001, s 575*.

The disposal value of plant and machinery is to be interpreted in accordance with the table in *CAA 2001, s 61* ('Disposal events and disposal values'). Incorporation will involve either a sale of the plant and machinery, or a transfer for nil proceeds.

If the plant and machinery is sold, the disposal value for capital allowances purposes will generally be the net proceeds of sale (*CAA 2001, s 61(2),*

Table item 1). If there are no proceeds at all, so there is a pure gift, then market value prevails (*CAA 2001, s 61(2), Table Item 7*).

This bears careful consideration because there may be important planning advantages. The result of a disposal is generally a balancing allowance or balancing charge. A balancing allowance occurs when the disposal value is less than the written-down value of the pool (*CAA 2001, s 55(2)*) and is given as a deduction in the income tax computation in a similar fashion to a WDA, AIA or FYA. A balancing charge occurs when the disposal value is more than the written-down value of the pool (*CAA 2001, s 55(3)*) and is treated as an addition to profit.

There are anti-avoidance provisions for capital allowances purposes (*CAA 2001, Pt 2, Ch 17*), which apply to 'relevant transactions' such as the sale of plant and machinery (*CAA 2001, s 213*), including transactions between connected persons (*CAA 2001, s 214*). The effect is that no AIA or FYA is generally available for the buyer's expenditure (*CAA 2001, s 217*), and the buyer's qualifying expenditure is potentially restricted (*CAA 2001, s 218*).

In addition, the buyer's capital allowances are subject to adjustment (or other tax advantages such as in the timing of allowances may be cancelled out) where the transaction has an 'avoidance purpose' (as defined in *CAA 2001, s 215*), or relates to a scheme or arrangement with such a purpose. However, particularly in the latter case it is difficult to envisage an ordinary incorporation having a main purpose of obtaining a tax advantage in respect of plant and machinery, as capital allowances are not normally a primary consideration.

There is also a specific anti-avoidance rule to prevent the sale of a car allocated to a 'single asset pool' (ie within *CAA 2001, s 206*) at undervalue in order to generate a balancing allowance (*CAA 2001, s 208A*).

2.19   Connected parties do not necessarily have to suffer the balancing allowance or charge. Instead the transferor and transferee (eg the previous sole trader and the company) may make a joint election under *CAA 2001, s 266* that the plant and machinery be transferred at a price which gives rise to neither a balancing allowance nor a balancing charge. But what does that really mean?

There is nothing in *CAA 2001, s 267* to override the rules in *CAA 2001, ss 46, 38B* and *55* that prohibit a WDA, AIA or FYA in the final chargeable period. The trade of the former sole trader *is* discontinued at the point of incorporation. So, the plant and machinery is actually transferred at the tax written-down value at the *start* of the final period of account of the sole trade.

The above election generally fixes the value of plant and machinery at its tax written-down value, notwithstanding that the plant and machinery may be sold to the company, and for a different value (eg original cost). HMRC guidance confirms: 'When an election is made any sale or transfer price is ignored' (CA29040). An election may be made within two years from the date of incorporation (*CAA 2001, s 266(4)*). However, there is a special provision preventing the election in successions involving businesses of leasing plant or machinery (see *CAA 2001, s 267A*).

If an election is made under *CAA 2001, s 266* and any of the assets are fixtures (eg on a sale of the business premises), a joint election is also required under *CAA 2001, s 198* ('Election to apportion sale price on sale of qualifying interest') in order that the company is able to claim capital allowances on the fixtures. This is due to the 'fixed value requirement' (see *CAA 2001, ss 187A–187B*), which was introduced (in *Finance Act 2012*) from April 2012.

An election under *CAA 2001, s 266* prevents a balancing adjustment in respect of the unincorporated business, whereas a *CAA 2001, s 198* election allows the company to claim capital allowances on any fixtures that are transferred. In many cases, an election under *CAA 2001, s 266* will include both fixtures and other plant and machinery; hence the amount specified in the *CAA 2001, s 198* election should not exceed the amount in the *CAA 2001, s 266* election.

In some cases, consideration should be given to not making a *CAA 2001, s 266* election, and entering into a joint election under *CAA 2001, s 198* for a low value, as this may generate a balancing allowance.

A 'pooling' requirement also applies in relation to fixtures (from April 2014), whereby the availability of capital allowances to a purchaser of fixtures is generally conditional on the pooling of relevant expenditure prior to transfer.

For certain other assets, an election for an 'alternative amount' (as opposed to market value) may be possible to prevent a balancing charge arising on incorporation (see *CAA 2001, s 569*).

For guidance in this potentially difficult area, readers are referred to the latest edition of *Capital Allowances: Transactions and Planning* by Martin Wilson and Steven Bone (Bloomsbury Professional).

An election for transfers between connected persons is also available in respect of 'short life assets' (SLAs), if made within two years following the chargeable period of disposal (*CAA 2001, s 89*). The transfer of SLAs between connected persons otherwise takes place at market value (unless there is a tax charge under *ITEPA 2003*) (*CAA 2001, s 88*). The effect of a connected person election is broadly to treat the disposal as taking place at the capital allowances pool value, so that the original SLA election continues with the purchaser. If no such connected person election is made, the purchaser is still treated as having made the original SLA election with its original terminal date (see *CAA 2001, s 89(4)*), but a balancing allowance or charge will normally arise on the disposal.

2.20

Focus

The absence of any capital allowances at all in the final period of account means that great care should be taken in selecting the date on which to incorporate.

A tidy-minded adviser may favour incorporation at the traditional accounting date and make a *CAA 2001, s 266* election 'because it's easier'. This may result in the trader getting no capital allowances in the last period when, perhaps, there are substantial profits taxed at 40%, or possibly 45% (for 2018/19). The pay-off, of course, is that the company gets a higher writing down allowance in its first period of trade, but as companies generally pay corporation tax at 19% (for financial year 2018, commencing 1 April 2018) is this good planning, especially if the client bought a large piece of equipment just before incorporation in anticipation of capital allowances to mitigate tax on profits?

Pre-incorporation planning must encompass the effect on capital allowances.

Remember that capital allowances are given for a period of account (not a year of assessment). Where accounts have traditionally been drawn up to 31 March, incorporation on that date will mean the loss of AIA, FYA or WDA for a full accounting period. What about incorporating at 30 April instead? The final period of account in which no capital allowances can be given is therefore only one month – a far more acceptable proposition.

How short might the final period actually be? In theory, perhaps as little as a day (though this might be unduly provocative to HMRC); a month is probably realistic.

2.21   The above analysis (subject to the point about a sale and election in respect of plant and machinery at **2.19** above) applies to incorporation by the *TCGA 1992, s 162* route.

There is an alternative. This is to ignore the incorporation relief in that section and go for the alternative afforded by *TCGA 1992, s 165*. This relates to a gift of business assets, though payment of some proceeds is possible. The company could actually pay the sole trader for the plant and machinery. Where there are actual proceeds, they are taken as the disposal value under *CAA 2001, s 61(2)*, Table Item 1. Market value is not substituted even where the vendor and purchaser are connected.

The sale proceeds could be left outstanding on loan account with the company. The proprietor can then draw down on the loan account at a later date without further tax charge.

Capital allowances rates

2.22 Historically, the regime for plant and machinery allowances changed significantly from April 2008 (ie 1 April for businesses within the charge to corporation tax, or 6 April for businesses liable to income tax). Those changes resulted in a reduction in the main rate of WDA to 20% (from 25%). In addition, most FYAs disappeared (although 100% allowances continue to be available for qualifying 'green' expenditure).

Further significant capital allowances changes were introduced in *Finance Act 2011*, reducing the WDA rate to 18% (from 20%) for expenditure allocated to the main rate pool, and to 8% (from 10%) for expenditure allocated to the special rate pool. These reductions apply to chargeable periods from 1 April 2012 (corporation tax) and from 6 April 2012 (income tax).

Furthermore, the maximum amount of the AIA has fluctuated widely since its introduction. It was originally set at £50,000 from April 2008, but increased to £100,000 from April 2010. The maximum subsequently reduced from £100,000 to £25,000 from April 2012 (subject to transitional rules in respect of expenditure incurred during an accounting period that spans 1 April or 6 April 2012).

The maximum amount of AIA was later increased (in *Finance Act 2013*) from £25,000 to £250,000 for a temporary period of two years from 1 January 2013, for both incorporated and unincorporated businesses. The maximum amount of AIA was further increased (in *Finance Act 2014*) to £500,000 in relation to expenditure incurred from 1 or 6 April 2014 to 31 December 2015. Thereafter, the limit was set to fall back to £25,000. However, the maximum amount of AIA was subsequently set at £200,000 (following a change introduced in *Finance (No 2) Act 2015*) in relation to qualifying expenditure incurred from 1 January 2016 (*CAA 2001, s 51A(5)*).

The AIA of 100% applies to qualifying expenditure for businesses of any size, with WDAs being available on any excess expenditure over that limit.

The rate of allowances on fixtures integral to a building is only 8% and is expenditure subject to separate 'special rate' pooling, and the rate of WDA for long-life assets is also 8% (*CAA 2001, ss 104A, 104D*). If expenditure is eligible for allowances at differing rates, the AIA should be allocated to expenditure otherwise attracting the lowest rate of allowances where possible.

Perhaps unsurprisingly, AIA restrictions (in *CAA 2001, ss 51A–51N*) include 'anti-fragmentation' provisions to restrict the availability of AIA for one or more companies or businesses under common control if 'related' by reason of a 'shared premises' and/or a 'similar activities' condition being met. The effect is that a single AIA is shared between them. However, if business owners control a combination of an unincorporated business and a company, entitlement to AIA for each business remains unaffected, as AIA is considered separately for different business entities. This may be helpful if only a particular element of an unincorporated business is being incorporated (eg the audit or payroll functions of an accountancy practice).

The AIA is not available for expenditure incurred in the period in which the business is permanently discontinued (*CAA 2001, s 38B*, General Exclusion 1), or where an asset is acquired from a connected person (see **2.18**). 'Connected persons' is defined (in *CAA 2001, ss 575–575A*) in terms of control over the company. This may prevent AIA being available in many cases, such as immediately following the incorporation of a family business.

The AIA is also unavailable for certain transactions if a main purpose is to enable a person to obtain AIA to which they would not otherwise be entitled (*CAA 2001, s 38B*, General Exclusion 4). However, in practice capital allowances are unlikely to be a major consideration in the decision to incorporate in most cases.

Industrial and agricultural buildings

2.23 Following changes introduced in *Finance Act 2008*, industrial buildings allowances (IBAs) were gradually phased out, and ceased to be available altogether from April 2011 onwards (ie from 1 April for corporation tax purposes, or 6 April for income tax purposes) (*Finance Act 2008, ss 84, 85*).

2.24 In addition, *Finance Act 2007* withdrew balancing adjustments and the recalculation of WDAs on the sale of an industrial building with effect from 21 March 2007, subject to certain transitional and anti-avoidance rules.

2.25 Enterprise Zone Allowances were also withdrawn from April 2011, but are not subject to the phasing out rules for IBAs (*Finance Act 2007, s 36(1)*), and balancing charges therefore remain possible for a limited period of time thereafter (ie under *CAA 2001, ss 314, 328*); see CA35050.

However, first-year allowances of 100% were introduced in *Finance Act 2012* in respect of enterprise zones, which apply to companies investing in plant or machinery primarily for use in designated assisted areas within them, where qualifying expenditure is incurred in a specified eight-year period (*CAA 2001, s 45K*).

2.26 The phasing out provisions mentioned above also apply in the context of agricultural buildings allowances.

National insurance contributions

2.27 The impact on national insurance contributions (NICs) must be taken into account in any consideration of incorporation. In some ways, it may seem paradoxical that one should want to move from self-employment where the 'mainstream' rate (of Class 4 NICs) is 9% to employment where the mainstream rate (Class 1 primary and secondary) is 25.8% (for 2018/19), with employees paying 12% and employers paying 13.8%; this combined rate falls to 15.8% on earnings in excess of the upper earnings limit (£892 per week for 2018/19), with employees paying 2% and employers continuing to pay 13.8%.

Of course, self-employed earners over the age of 16 and under pensionable age are also liable to pay Class 2 contributions at a flat rate (*SSCBA 1992, s 11*), which (for 2018/19) is £2.95 per week. Class 2 NICs was to be abolished from April 2018 and Class 4 contributions reformed to provide the mechanism by which the self-employed build up entitlement to the state pension and contributory benefits. However, the government announced in Autumn Budget 2017 that the abolition of Class 2 NICs was being postponed until April 2019.

In an owner-managed company, where earnings fall between the Class 1 NIC 'Primary Threshold' and the 'Upper Earnings Limit' (UEL), as mentioned the total NIC payable by employers and employees is at a rate of 25.8%, a not inconsiderable sum. This is well in excess of the 9% NIC payable by a self-employed person.

The rate at which Class 4 contributions will be charged under the reforms to be introduced from 6 April 2019 had yet to be announced at the time of writing. Nevertheless, it is possible that the self-employed will face increases in the future.

NIC rates in respect of both employees and the self-employed for 2018/19 are as follows:

- the main rate of Class 1 NICs for employees and employers is 12% and 13.8% respectively;

- the additional rate of Class 1 NICs for employees is 2%;

- the main rate of Class 4 NICs for the self-employed is 9%, and the additional Class 4 NIC rate is 2%.

As mentioned above, self-employed earners also pay Class 2 contributions at the rate of £2.95 per week (for 2018/19).

However, the rate of employers' NIC is 0% (for 2018/19) for those under the age of 21 on earnings up to the level of the upper secondary threshold for under 21-year-olds (which is aligned with the UEL). On any earnings in excess of the upper secondary threshold, employer contributions are payable as normal at 13.8% (*SSCBA 1992, s 9A*). Furthermore, employers' NIC is also payable at 0% on the earnings of apprentices under the age of 25 up to the level of the apprentice upper secondary threshold (AUST), with employer contributions payable as normal at 13.8% on any earnings in excess of the AUST (*SSCBA 1992, s 9B*). The upper secondary threshold for under 21-year-olds and the AUST are aligned with the upper earnings limit for primary Class 1 purposes of £892 per week (for 2018/19).

To avoid paying Class 1 NIC rates, one must be prepared to withdraw funds from the incorporated business other than by way of salary. The payment of dividends is often the preferred method of profit extraction where possible, although difficulties can arise in certain circumstances if dividend payments take the place of a commercial salary (see **2.103** below). Further, the reform of the dividend tax regime from 6 April 2016 (and the reduction in the dividend allowance from 6 April 2018) generally reduced the tax advantage of extracting profits in the form of dividends, although dividends remain NIC-free.

Employment allowance

2.28   The employment allowance was introduced (in the *National Insurance Contributions Act 2014* (*NICA 2014*) from April 2014. Businesses and charities (including community amateur sports clubs) are generally entitled to an allowance of up to £3,000 (for 2018/19) against their employers' NIC liability. It broadly applies to most businesses, regardless of size, and irrespective of whether the business is incorporated or unincorporated (other than companies where the sole employee is also a director).

Regulations (introduced from 6 April 2016) prohibit certain companies from claiming the allowance (*Employment Allowance (Excluded Companies) Regulations 2016 (SI 2016/344)*). The legislation prevents companies where the sole employee is at the time that the earnings were paid also a director. HMRC's subsequent guidance states that affected companies are those where the director is the only employee paid earnings above the secondary threshold for Class 1 NIC purposes. HMRC's guidance can be found at: tinyurl.com/HMRC-EA-SDC. However, the legislation does not require a second employee to earn above the secondary threshold to preserve entitlement to the employment allowance. A company which has only one employee is also entitled to claim the allowance if at the time of the payment that employee is not a director. Personal companies where the sole employee is also the director may wish to consider resigning as a director and appointing another family member as the director.

Not all businesses can claim the employment allowance (*NICA 2014, s 2*). Excluded employers include those carrying functions wholly or mainly of a public nature (eg NHS or general practitioner services). In addition, personal and managed service companies can only claim the allowance in respect of actual (not deemed) payments of employment income. If companies or charities are connected, only one nominated PAYE scheme with employers' NIC liabilities can claim the allowance.

There is also a restriction from claiming the allowance on 'transfers of businesses', which would appear to affect the transfer of employees upon incorporation. In broad terms, if one business takes over another business during the tax year there will be no entitlement to any remaining balance of the employment allowance in respect of the employees who worked for the business taken over, or for employees who are carrying on the work of the business taken over.

An anti-avoidance rule also prevents an employer from qualifying for the allowance by reason of 'avoidance arrangements' (ie arrangements with a main purpose of which is to secure that a person benefits (or benefits further) from the application of the employment allowance provisions.

Detailed guidance on the employment allowance is available on the GOV.UK website (tinyurl.com/HMRC-EA-Guidance).

Maximum contributions

2.29   Unless the incorporation of the business takes place on 6 April, there will be a tax year in which the proprietor is both self-employed (as a sole trader or partner of the existing business) and an employed earner (as director/ employee of the new company). There may be a liability for Class 1, Class 2 and Class 4 contributions. Fortunately, there are rules to limit the amount of contributions payable where an individual has more than one employment or both employment and self-employment.

Where both Class 1 and Class 2 contributions are payable, the liability for primary Class 1 contributions and Class 2 contributions is not to exceed an amount equal to 53 primary Class 1 contributions payable on earnings at the UEL for the year (*Social Security (Contributions) Regulations 2001, SI 2001/1004, reg 21*). An annual maximum also applies for Class 4 contribution purposes (*SI 2001/1004, reg 100*).

However, the position is complicated because there is required to be made a further adjustment in respect of the additional rate of 2% (for 2018/19), which has no upper earnings limit.

2.30 The possibility of total contributions exceeding the relevant maxima may not be identified during the course of the tax year. Thus, contributions actually paid may be excessive. Overpaid contributions may be recovered from HMRC (see www.gov.uk/claim-national-insurance-refund).

Where the situation of overpayment is foreseen, it is possible to make application to defer payment of Class 1 contributions (although Class 4 contributions can no longer be deferred). In theory, such applications should be made before the beginning of the tax year to which they relate. This may make it an impractical option in the case of incorporation unless this occurs early in the tax year. If an application is successfully made and the contributions actually paid prove insufficient, the shortfall must be satisfied by direct payment to HMRC. For applications to defer Class 1 NICs, see tinyurl.com/ HMRC-NIC-CA72A.

None of the foregoing has any effect on the new company as secondary contributor. There are no provisions to limit the secondary contributions in respect of an employed earner. This is also true for Class 1A (and Class 1B) contributions which are payable only by employers.

State pension

2.31 A working individual (whether self-employed or an employee) pays NIC during his working life and generates a contribution record which determines the state pension which is paid after retirement age.

Focus

Employee Class 1 contributions start at the primary threshold (PT). However, contributions are treated as paid for state pension purposes where earnings are equal to or exceed the LEL, albeit that no contributions are actually paid (*SSCBA 1992, s 6A(2)*). On earnings between the LEL and PT notional contributions are paid at a zero rate in order to establish a contribution record for state pension purposes, even though no contributions are actually due.

> This has traditionally been a very useful planning tool in remunerating small company directors. Note that the company must still submit a full payment submission under the real time information (RTI) regime in order to record the earnings for this purpose, even if no income tax or NIC is actually payable.

The state pension regime changed following the introduction of legislation in the *Pensions Act 2014* (and secondary legislation in the *State Pension Regulations 2015 (SI 2015/173)*), for those individuals reaching state pension age from 6 April 2016 (NB: those who reached state pension age before that date remain subject to the previous pension rules).

Individuals reaching state pension age on or after 6 April 2016 receive a flat rate (or 'single-tier') state pension. Consequently, it is no longer possible to build up entitlement to the second state pension (S2P) in addition to the basic state pension. However, S2P will continue to be paid to those who reached state pension age before 6 April 2016 and who have built up entitlement to it. Consequently, the ability for members of a defined benefit occupational pension scheme to contract out of S2P ended on 5 April 2016.

Entitlement to the single-tier state pension is subject to the individual's NIC payment record, and requires at least 35 qualifying years of NICs in order to receive a full single-tier state pension. Those with fewer than 35 qualifying years, but with at least ten qualifying years will receive a proportionately smaller state pension (by contrast, a person needed 30 qualifying years for a full basic state pension if they reached state pension age before 6 April 2016). As indicated above, directors and employees can qualify for the state pension without actually paying any Class 1 contributions. Qualifying years under the new state pension are generated in the same way as qualifying years for the basic state pension. A qualifying year is broadly a tax year during an individual's working life in which they paid (or were treated as having paid, or were credited with) NICs on earnings of 52 times the LEL.

The scope and calculation of state pension entitlement is beyond the scope of this chapter. General guidance is available from the GOV.UK website (www.gov.uk/new-state-pension). Specialist advice from a pension expert should be sought if required.

Income tax rates

2.32   The basic personal allowance for income tax purposes gradually reduces (by £1 for every £2 of income) for individuals with adjusted net incomes over £100,000 a year (*ITA 2007, s 35(2)–(4)*). Based on current personal allowances levels (£11,850 for 2018/19) this means that the allowances would be extinguished for those with incomes of £123,700 a year or more.

Furthermore, an additional, higher rate of income tax of 45% (for 2018/19) applies to taxable incomes above £150,000.

The above restriction in personal allowances and a higher income tax rate of 45% could make incorporation seem a more attractive proposition for self-employed individuals who are potentially subject to higher income tax liabilities, in terms of sheltering profits at a lower rate of corporation tax. This assumes that the business owner would not need to extract all the profits, and may be prepared to restrict personal income levels to £100,000 (or £150,000) per annum or less.

Following the reform of dividend taxation (in *Finance Act 2016*) from April 2016, the 10% dividend tax credit was removed (ie such that dividends are received gross) and replaced with a dividend nil rate. This was originally up to £5,000 per tax year, but it was subsequently reduced (in *Finance (No 2) Act 2017*) to £2,000 for 2018/19 and subsequent tax years.

Furthermore, dividend tax rates (for 2018/19) are 7.5% for basic rate taxpayers, 32.5% for higher rate taxpayers and 38.1% for additional rate taxpayers.

It should be noted that dividends within the £2,000 'nil rate' still count towards an individual shareholder's basic or higher rate bands, and therefore affect the rate of tax paid on dividends received in excess of the allowance.

Those individuals who receive dividend income of £2,000 or less following incorporation, and/or who extract income from the company at relatively low levels (eg preferring to retain profits within the company, perhaps with a view to a company purchase of own shares on retirement (see **Chapter 4**) or a later sale or winding up of the company) will perhaps not be unduly concerned about the dividend tax regime.

Conversely, business owners who receive all or most of their income from dividends at substantial levels will need to consider their remuneration strategy carefully, particularly in relation to the traditional 'salary v dividend' comparison.

Planning in this area may therefore include considering the transfer of shares to a spouse (or civil partner) to make use of an extra £2,000 dividend nil rate, and to take advantage of the spouse's personal allowances and basic rate tax band, if appropriate. However, care must be taken in view of the settlements anti-avoidance provisions (in *ITTOIA 2005, Pt 5, Ch 5*).

For detailed commentary on extracting funds from the company and remuneration strategies, see *Tax Planning for Family and Owner-Managed Companies 2018/19* (Bloomsbury Professional).

In terms of the decision whether to incorporate, despite the government's desire to remove the tax advantages arising from incorporating the business, tax savings are still achievable in some cases, although, as mentioned, any such savings will in general be significantly lower than before the reform of the dividend tax regime. In some instances, the tax saving may be extinguished by the additional cost of operating through a company. In all cases, it is recommended to 'do the sums' before making the decision whether or not to incorporate in the context of tax.

Of course, incorporation has commercial implications for the business, which should (and generally does) take precedence over any tax considerations in practice.

Capital gains tax

2.33   Historically, fundamental changes to the CGT regime were introduced from 6 April 2008, including a standard CGT rate of 18%. However, an additional CGT rate of 28% was introduced from 23 June 2010 to the extent that the individual is chargeable to income tax at higher rates (and also for trustees and personal representatives).

Subsequently, the above 18% and 28% rates of CGT for individuals were reduced (in *Finance Act 2016*) to 10% and 20% (from 2016/17). However, gains on the disposal of residential property interests that do not qualify for private residence relief, and gains arising in respect of carried interest, remain subject to the 18% and 28% rates.

The most important changes to business owners who were considering incorporation at the time of the above CGT reforms from 6 April 2008 were the withdrawal of taper relief and indexation allowance. The government responded to protests by the private equity sector about the withdrawal of business asset taper relief (giving an effective CGT rate of around 10% for higher rate taxpayers) by announcing the introduction of entrepreneurs' relief from 6 April 2008.

For entrepreneurs' relief purposes, a CGT rate of 10% applies to qualifying gains of up to £10m, in relation to business disposals from 6 April 2011. This upper limit was increased from £5m, which applied in relation to business disposals between 23 June 2010 and 5 April 2011. For business disposals between 6 April 2010 and 22 June 2010, entrepreneurs' relief applied to the first £2m of qualifying gains. The relief limit was increased from an original ceiling of £1m, which applied to qualifying disposals in 2008/09 and 2009/10.

The entrepreneurs' relief maximum is a cumulative lifetime limit. However, disposals before 6 April 2008 do not affect this lifetime limit, subject to transitional rules regarding company reorganisations and qualifying enterprise investment scheme and venture capital trust investments.

Many sole traders and partnerships sought to incorporate their businesses prior to 6 April 2008 in order to 'bank' business asset taper relief (and possibly indexation allowance, in the case of established businesses), typically by selling their business to a newly formed company at an effective CGT rate of 10% (or possibly lower), with a view to extracting the proceeds in due course without further tax implications. Incorporating the business before 6 April 2008 would generally preserve entrepreneurs' relief entitlement on a later disposal of shares in the company, subject to the relevant relief conditions being satisfied.

2.34

Focus

The sale of the business to a newly formed company as a going concern in the manner described above may be seen as a potentially tax-efficient way to dispose of the business (or its chargeable assets, to be more precise) at the 10% CGT rate, if entrepreneurs' relief is available.

However, the scope for claiming entrepreneurs' relief on a disposal of goodwill upon incorporation was restricted by changes first introduced in *FA 2015* for business disposals from 3 December 2014, subject to exceptions from this general rule in certain circumstances (see **2.36**).

This strategy of selling the business requires careful thought. For example:

- A business sale will potentially trigger CGT liabilities. Whilst the tax charge could be financed via the company in part repayment of the debt owed following the sale, this assumes that the company is sufficiently in funds to do so.

- A sale of land and buildings (eg business premises) has stamp duty land tax (or land and buildings transaction tax in Scotland, or land transaction tax in Wales) implications (see **2.76**). In addition, an increase in value could result in a double layer of taxation (ie corporation tax on chargeable gains for the company,

---

and potential tax and NIC liabilities when the net proceeds are extracted by the company owners) on a subsequent disposal of the property.

● A sale of intangible assets such as goodwill can give rise to valuation difficulties, resulting in disposal proceeds being overstated (see **2.66**).

It should also be noted that entrepreneurs' relief applies to a 'material disposal of business assets' such as the whole or part of a business (*TCGA 1992, s 169I(2)(a)*). The disposal of an identifiable part of the taxpayer's business as a going concern was held to be eligible for entrepreneurs' relief in *Gilbert (t/a United Foods) v Revenue & Customs* [2011] UKFTT 705 (TC). By contrast, the disposal of business assets does not necessarily satisfy this requirement (*Russell v HMRC* [2012] UKFTT 623 (TC)). HMRC's views on the distinction can be found in the Capital Gains Manual (at CG64015 and following).

In some cases, it may be difficult to determine whether there has been a cessation of the unincorporated business (eg if the business owner carries on another, similar business thereafter), and if so, when that cessation took place for entrepreneurs' relief purposes (see *Rice v Revenue & Customs* [2014] UKFTT 133 (TC)). The importance of clear evidence regarding cessation in such cases cannot be overstated.

Of course, businesses will continue to incorporate for commercial reasons, if not for tax savings.

2.35   What assets might the business own? There could be stock, tools and equipment, land and buildings, goodwill and investments. In all but the smallest businesses, there will be CGT considerations on the transfer of a business to a company. Many items of plant, tools and equipment, motor vehicles, fixtures and fittings in buildings, etc will have attracted capital allowances as plant and machinery. Income tax adjustments will be necessary. That does not stop assets of this type being chargeable to CGT (though chattels having a value of £6,000 or less and motor cars are exempt (*TCGA 1992, ss 262, 263*)).

However, *TCGA 1992, s 37* excludes from the CGT computation any consideration taken into account as a receipt in computing income. An actual gain in respect of this type of asset will therefore only arise where it is transferred for a value greater than original cost (which will be rare). There is also an exclusion (see *TCGA 1992, s 37(1A)-(1C)*) in respect of capital receipts under, or after leaving, the cash basis.

There are provisions to restrict allowable CGT losses by the amount of capital allowances on an asset (*TCGA 1992, s 41*). The rationale is to prevent the person making the disposal receiving a 'double allowance', ie relief for capital allowances and an allowable capital loss. However, see 'Harvesting capital losses' by Arthur Conway (*Taxation*, 6 June 2013) for possible limitations on the ability of *TCGA 1992, s 41* to restrict capital losses on sales of plant and machinery.

Prior to the abolition of industrial and agricultural buildings allowances, income tax consequences often needed to be considered in respect of buildings used in the business. However, following the withdrawal of those allowances, it is now generally necessary to concentrate on the CGT aspects on a transfer of land and buildings.

2.36   Goodwill, and whether it can be transferred, is a subject in itself. In many instances, goodwill will not appear on the balance sheet of an unincorporated business. Business owners should ensure that it is of a type which is transferable.

As indicated at **2.34**, a sale of the business to a newly formed company as a going concern upon incorporation may be seen as a tax-efficient disposal, particularly if it qualifies for entrepreneurs' relief. However, the availability of entrepreneurs' relief on disposals of goodwill upon incorporation was restricted by changes introduced in *Finance Act 2015*, in response to concerns by the government that some business incorporations were motivated by the potential tax advantages of doing so, and that business proprietors had been gaining an 'unfair advantage' in selling the business to a related close company in order to effectively extract funds from the business at the entrepreneurs' CGT rate of 10%, rather than the normal rates of income tax and NICs.

The restriction (in *TCGA 1992, s 169LA*) as originally introduced in *FA 2015* applied broadly if the business owner transferred goodwill (directly or indirectly) to a 'related party' from 3 December 2014 as part of a qualifying business disposal for entrepreneurs' relief purposes, where the person was not a 'retiring partner'. However, the related party and retiring partner conditions were replaced (in *Finance Act 2016*) by different conditions in respect of close companies, ie broadly that immediately after the disposal the person (and any relevant connected person) together hold 5% or more of either the ordinary share capital or the voting rights in the company (or a group member). A 'relevant connected person' means a connected company or connected trustees, but not individuals in general. This restriction is subject to an exception in certain circumstances (see **2.37**). The changes in the entrepreneurs' relief restriction for transfers of goodwill were backdated, so that they apply to disposals from 3 December 2014.

The effect of the restriction, if it applies, is to exclude goodwill from the definition of 'relevant business assets' comprised in a 'qualifying business disposal' for entrepreneurs' relief purposes (in *TCGA 1992, s 169L*), so that a gain on an affected disposal of goodwill to a close company (or a company that would be close if it were resident in the UK) is charged at normal CGT rates (subject to other reliefs being claimed).

The entrepreneurs' relief restriction also applies where the goodwill disposal would otherwise be eligible for relief, but the business owner is party to 'relevant avoidance arrangements', ie broadly arrangements with a main purpose of ensuring that the above restriction does not apply.

2.37   If the entrepreneurs' relief restriction in **2.36** would otherwise apply by virtue of ownership of the company's share capital (ie by the disposer or any relevant connected person), it is nevertheless disapplied (by *TCGA 1992, s 169LA(1A)*) if certain conditions are satisfied. Firstly, there must be a disposal of all those shares to another company ('A') before the end of the 'relevant period' (ie 28 days beginning with the qualifying business disposal, or possibly longer if HMRC allow). Secondly, if company A is a close company, the disposer (and any relevant connected person) must hold less than 5% of the ordinary share capital and voting rights (of company A or any group member) immediately before the end of the relevant period (*TCGA 1992, s 169LA(1B)*).

Notwithstanding the entrepreneurs' relief restriction for transfers of goodwill in *TCGA 1992, s 169LA* (as amended by *Finance Act 2016*), an entrepreneurs' relief claim remains possible where, for example, the unincorporated business proprietor (and any relevant connected person) holds less than 5% of both the share capital and voting rights of the acquiring company; or where the business is incorporated prior to its disposal (within 28 days) to an unconnected company; or (say) on a disposal of the unincorporated business to a company wholly-owned by a family member. However, such exceptions from the restriction will probably not be relevant to most business incorporations.

2.38   It should be noted that the above entrepreneurs' relief restriction in respect of goodwill does not prevent the relief being claimed on other chargeable assets (eg business premises) that are relevant business assets comprised in the qualifying business disposal.

Other forms of CGT relief are considered in later sections of this chapter.

2.39   Capital gains are generally realised on the disposal of assets. There are various instances in *TCGA 1992* where tax on realised gains may be deferred until the happening of some later event. One such instance is where rollover relief is in point (*TCGA 1992, ss 152–160*). However, what if the gain does not relate to the (current) disposal of an asset? There is a potential trap for the unwary, as explained below.

A gain realised on the disposal of one asset, which has been used in a trade, may be deferred (or 'held over') against the acquisition of a second asset where the new asset is a wasting (or 'depreciating') asset, also used in the trade (*TCGA 1992, s 154*).

In that case, no adjustment is made to the base cost of the second asset. The gain on the first asset is calculated according to normal rules and simply deferred until the earliest of:

- the disposal of asset number two;

- the cessation of use of asset number two in a trade; or

- the expiry of ten years from the acquisition of asset number two.

If an asset carrying a deferred gain is transferred to a company on incorporation, there is a disposal. The original deferred gain comes back into charge; there is nothing you can do about it. None of the reliefs examined below cope with this. The deferred gain now chargeable arose on an earlier disposal and cannot be expunged by the incorporation reliefs. The tax will be due and payable.

Focus

In preparing to incorporate a business, always check whether there have been previous claims to rollover chargeable gains on business assets. Furthermore, note whether any such gains were merely deferred and not 'properly' rolled over.

2.40   The transfer of assets from an unincorporated business to a company is a disposal for CGT purposes. Further, it is invariably a disposal between connected persons. For this purpose, a company is connected with another person, if that person has control of it or if that person and persons connected with him together have control of it (*TCGA 1992, s 286(6)*).

Where the transactions are between connected persons, the rules of *TCGA 1992, s 18* prevail; in particular, the transaction is to be treated as a bargain not made at arm's length. This in turn brings *TCGA 1992, s 17* into play, to the extent that the consideration for the business proprietor(s) disposal of the assets is to be treated as their market value, and the company's corresponding acquisition value is also to be treated as market value. So, for the purposes of the CGT computation, the chargeable assets of a business are treated as passing at market value.

However, the actual consideration may be:

- shares in the company (which may be of more than one class);

- loan stock in the form of a debenture or similar (although this is rare in the case of small private companies);

- cash (often left outstanding on a director's loan account);

- nothing (it being quite common to gift the assets of a business to the company).

2.41 If there were to be a large chargeable gain, with tax payable, this would amount to a significant disincentive to incorporation. Certain reliefs exist to alleviate this problem and the rest of this chapter explores them:

- *TCGA 1992, s 162* ('Rollover relief on transfer of business');

- *TCGA 1992, s 165* ('Relief for gifts of business assets').

The latter is the more flexible of the two reliefs.

However, in addition EIS CGT deferral relief (*TCGA 1992, Sch 5B*) has sometimes been referred to as 'the third way'.

As indicated earlier, the sale of a business upon incorporation, whilst triggering a CGT charge, may nevertheless be an attractive alternative to the above reliefs, if a claim for entrepreneurs' relief is available at the reduced rate of 10% (although note the potential restriction in the relief at **2.36**).

TCGA 1992, s 162 **relief**

2.42 The relief under *TCGA 1992, s 162* (commonly referred to as 'incorporation relief') is mandatory if specified conditions are met, and therefore does not require a claim. The cost of the new assets (ie the company shares) is deducted from the chargeable gain. Correspondingly, the base cost of the new assets is reduced by the amount left out of the CGT computation on incorporation. There are provisions for apportionment where the consideration is not wholly in shares.

The relief applies where three conditions are satisfied (*TCGA 1992, s 162(1)*):

- a person who is not a company (ie sole trader or individual partner) transfers to a company a business as a going concern;

- together with the whole assets of the business, possibly excluding cash; and

- the business is so transferred wholly or partly in exchange for shares issued by the company to the person transferring the business.

With regard to the first bullet point above, it is important to ensure that what is transferred amounts to a 'business' as a going concern. There is no definition of 'business' for these purposes, although some assistance on its meaning may be derived from *Ramsay v HMRC* [2013] UKUT 226 (TCC). In that case, the Upper Tribunal allowed Mrs Ramsay's appeal against the decision of the First-tier Tribunal that she was not entitled to incorporation relief under *TCGA 1992, s 162*. Mrs Ramsay had inherited a one-third share of a large single building, which was divided into ten flats (five of which were occupied at the relevant time). She subsequently made a gift to her husband of one-half of her own one-third share, and later purchased the remaining two-thirds share of the property from her brothers. Mr and Mrs Ramsay transferred the property to a company, in exchange for shares in it.

Taking the activities of Mrs Ramsay as a whole, the Upper Tribunal concluded that Mrs Ramsay's activities fell within the business tests outlined in *Customs and Excise Commissioners v Lord Fisher* [1981] 2 All ER 147. The tribunal was also satisfied that the degree of activity undertaken in respect of the property overall was sufficient in nature and extent to amount to a business for the purpose of *TCGA 1992, s 162*.

It is also important to be able to demonstrate that the business is capable of being transferred, and that it was transferred as a going concern.

In *Roelich v Revenue & Customs* [2014] UKFTT 579 (TC), the taxpayer originally held 49 shares in a company (G). The other 51 of the 100 issued shares in G was held by another individual (B). In May 2006, the taxpayer made a transfer to G (valued at £523,363) in exchange for a further 49 shares (and at the same time B transferred a business into G in exchange for a further 51 shares). HMRC subsequently sought to charge CGT on the taxpayer's transfer to G. The taxpayer appealed, contending that incorporation relief under *TCGA 1992, s 162* was available in respect of the transfer.

HMRC considered that there was no business transferred to G that qualified for incorporation relief. The taxpayer had operated a property development consultancy business since 2003. In 2005, he reached an agreement with a contractor (PV), that if PV was successful in obtaining a landfill contract and if planning consent was obtained, PV would pay him a fee of £5 per load of infill. The infill contract was later awarded to PV. The taxpayer transferred the PV contract (which was valued on the basis of likely loads) to G in exchange for the 49 shares. The transfer was undertaken informally; there was no evidence of a disposal (or acquisition) of goodwill.

The First-tier Tribunal found that there was a business, and concluded that the business was a going concern from the outset. The tribunal did not accept HMRC's contention that the business was not capable of being transferred, as the taxpayer's knowledge was not incapable of being passed on to others. The tribunal also held that the business was transferred as a going concern, and was not merely the transfer of an income stream, as HMRC contended. Finally, the tribunal accepted that the issue of shares was primarily for the PV contract but was also in return for the transfer of the entire business. Incorporation relief was therefore available, and the taxpayer's appeal was allowed.

The taxpayer in *Roelich* was perhaps fortunate in the sense that the incorporation of his business was conducted informally, and there was very little documentary evidence of the transfer, whereas incorporation under *TCGA 1992, s 162* commonly involves some form of business transfer agreement.

Incorporation relief under *TCGA 1992, s 162* is very specific. All of the assets of the business (apart from cash which is, of course, not a chargeable asset) must be transferred to the company and this must be done wholly or partly in exchange for shares.

In fact, cash is not the only item which may be left out. HMRC Concession D32 states that relief under *TCGA 1992, s 162* is not precluded by the fact that some or all of the liabilities of the business are not taken over by the company. However, care is needed to ensure that liabilities remain within the terms of Concession D32. For example, if the company raises finance and uses the funds to pay the proprietors for the business to enable existing borrowings to be repaid, this will constitute (non-share) consideration for the business, resulting in any *TCGA 1992, s 162* relief being restricted.

'Cash' in the above context is considered by HMRC to include amounts left owing to the transferor as sums credited to a loan or current account with the company (see CG65720 and CG65760).

> **Example 2.2 – *TCGA 1992, s 162* relief in action**
>
> Janine decides to incorporate her business of producing personalised greetings cards from 1 June 2018. A very simplified closing balance sheet shows the assets to be stock £30,000, business premises £100,000 (cost £80,000) and goodwill £20,000 (cost nil). The entire business is transferred

to a newly formed company, Super Cards Ltd, and 1,000 ordinary £1 shares are issued to her.

(a) The market value of the 1,000 shares is £150,000 being the total value of the assets transferred in (market value applies as this is a connected persons transaction).

(b) The consideration (shares issued) is apportioned in a just and reasonable manner, thus:

	£
Stock	30,000
Shop premises	100,000
Goodwill	20,000

(c) The chargeable gains are:

	£	£
Shop – consideration	100,000	
Less: Cost	(80,000)	20,000
Goodwill, consideration	20,000	
Less: Cost	nil	20,000
Total gain		40,000

The whole of this gain will be rolled over under *TCGA 1992, s 162*.

(d) The CGT base cost of the shares, for a future computation on disposal is:

	£
Market value	150,000
Less: Gain rolled over *TCGA 1992, s 162*	(40,000)
Base cost	110,000

2.43 However, in some cases the gain may not be fully relieved. The business must be transferred as a going concern and must therefore reflect liabilities to be satisfied by the company. An undertaking to satisfy these liabilities amounts to further consideration. As indicated at **2.42**, Concession D32 prevents the assumption of liabilities from being treated as consideration for the purposes of the *TCGA 1992, s 162* computation. However, this does not mean that the liabilities can be ignored in determining the market value of the assets transferred.

Focus

Where the liabilities are relatively high, the net asset value of the business (which equals the value of the shares issued) may be low. If the chargeable assets have large inherent capital gains (watch out for goodwill off the balance sheet), it may be impossible to roll over all of the gain – the base cost of the shares cannot go below zero.

Example 2.3 – *TCGA 1992, s 162* relief limitation

Colin is a sole trader manufacturer of widgets. The balance sheet is as follows:

	£
Freehold property	300,000
Fixtures and fittings	25,000
Stock	25,000
	350,000
Less: Bank loan	(225,000)
Creditors	(50,000)
	£75,000
Represented by:	
Capital account	£75,000

The property originally cost £200,000, and there is goodwill off balance sheet of £75,000 for which Colin paid nothing.

He formed ABC Widgets Ltd on 1 May 2018 and 1,000 ordinary £1 shares were issued to him.

(a)   The market value of the shares issued is £150,000, being the total net value of the assets transferred in (ie £75,000 balance sheet net assets, plus £75,000 goodwill).

(b)   The chargeable gains are:

		£	£
Property:	Consideration (market value)	300,000	
	Less: Cost	(200,000)	100,000
Goodwill:	Consideration (market value)	75,000	

	£	£
Less: Cost	nil	75,000
		175,000
Less: Rolled over under *TCGA 1992, s 162*		(150,000)
Chargeable gain		25,000

Subject to the annual CGT exemption, this gain is immediately taxable. However, on the disposal of an unincorporated business a claim for entrepreneurs' relief is potentially available, if the relevant conditions are satisfied and subject to the amount of relief claimed in respect of any earlier qualifying disposals.

However, the restriction on claims for entrepreneurs' relief in respect of the disposal of goodwill upon incorporation should be noted (see **2.36**). In the above example, gains were made on the disposal of property and goodwill, but only part of the total gains could be rolled over. How is the chargeable gain to be allocated between those assets, for the purpose of determining any entitlement to entrepreneurs' relief on the residual aggregate gain in respect of the property? There has been no formal HMRC guidance or any precedent at the time of writing, but it is understood that HMRC would accept a 'just and reasonable' apportionment of the residual aggregate gain, by reference to the component chargeable gains (but not any losses) which were taken into consideration for *TCGA 1992, s 162* purposes.

HMRC's view on the general interaction between incorporation relief and entrepreneurs' relief is understood to be that incorporation relief takes precedence over a claim to entrepreneurs' relief. At the time of writing, HMRC's approach on the interaction of the reliefs is not explicitly stated in the Capital Gains manual. However, the guidance indicates that a claim made under a provision which rolls over that gain against the acquisition cost of a replacement asset (of which incorporation relief would presumably be one) takes precedence over a claim for entrepreneurs' relief (CG64136).

It should also be borne in mind that entrepreneurs' relief requires a claim, and that an election is available for *TCGA 1992, s 162* not to apply (*TCGA 1992, s 162A*). It would therefore seem possible for taxpayers effectively to choose between the reliefs (or perhaps to take advantage of a combination of the two in some cases).

Care should be exercised when considering goodwill valuations in property-related businesses, such as pubs or nursing homes (see **2.62** and following below).

(c)   The CGT base cost of the shares is:

Market value	150,000
Less: Gain rolled over *TCGA 1992, s 162*	(150,000)
	£nil

2.44   In the above situation where all the assets are transferred, only shares are issued and yet a chargeable gain still arises. Occasionally, though, other consideration might be taken. This could be in the form of loan stock issued by the company, or more simply the creation of a director's loan account with a credit balance.

In these circumstances, the gain which may be rolled over is limited to the fraction A/B of the amount of the gain on the old assets, where:

- A is the cost of the new assets (shares); and

- B is the value of the whole consideration received by the transferor in exchange for the business (*TCGA 1992, s 162(4)*).

Example 2.4 – Shares and other consideration (I)

Linda, a higher rate taxpayer, runs a fruit and vegetable wholesale business as a sole trader and decides to incorporate, with effect from 1 July 2018. The net asset value of her business is as follows:

Freehold property	200,000	(cost £100,000)
Fixtures and fittings	4,000	(cost £10,000)
Stock	6,000	(cost £6,000)
Goodwill	30,000	(cost nil)
Debtors	5,000	
	245,000	
Less: Trade creditors	(20,000)	
	£225,000	

Linda transfers the business to Fruit and Veg Ltd, which issues 1,000 ordinary £1 shares to her, and a director's loan account of £40,000 is created.

(a)   The market value of the shares issued is £185,000 being the net asset value of the business transferred in (£225,000), less the loan account (£40,000).

(b)   The chargeable gains are:

Property: Consideration	200,000	
Less: Cost	(100,000)	100,000
Goodwill: Consideration	30,000	
Less: Cost	nil	30,000
		130,000

Amount rolled over under *TCGA 1992, s 162*:

A/B × 130,000 =

$$\frac{185,000}{225,000} \times 130,000 = \qquad (106,889)$$

	23,111
Annual exemption (2018/19)	(11,700)
Amount chargeable to CGT	£11,411
CGT liability (see Note):	
Property: £11,411 (× £100,000/£130,000) × 10%	877
Goodwill: £11,411 (× £30,000/£130,000) × 20%	526
	£1,403

The CGT base cost of the shares is:

Market value	185,000
Less: Gain rolled over *TCGA 1992, s 162*	(106,889)
	£78,111

Note: As indicated at **2.43**, for the purpose of determining any entitlement to entrepreneurs' relief on the residual aggregate gain in respect of the property, it is assumed that HMRC would accept the above calculation of CGT based on a 'just and reasonable' apportionment, although there has been no formal HMRC guidance or any precedent at the time of writing.

2.45   The application of *TCGA 1992, s 162* is relatively inflexible, for two main reasons. First, it requires the transfer of all the business assets (with very limited exceptions) to the company. Secondly, most of the inherent value of the business is locked into the share capital of the company and cannot readily be extracted.

Some commentators recommend that if there is a substantial capital account in the unincorporated business then the proprietors should be advised to draw down on it before incorporation. Presumably such a capital account exists in the first place in order to fund continuing trading operations. If this is the case, then there is every likelihood that the funds withdrawn will be reintroduced into the company shortly afterwards by means of a credit to a director's loan account.

Perceived challenges to this process have sometimes been said to stem from *Furniss (Inspector of Taxes) v Dawson* HL 1984, 55 TC 324, in that the transactions are preordained and the intermediate one has no real purpose. The net effect is to re-characterise the transaction as if the business had been transferred for a consideration partly in the issue of shares and partly in cash. A counter-argument might be demonstrated by the incorporation agreement (assuming that there is one) showing the intention to transfer the entire assets of the business in return for shares. Could a similar challenge stem from the principle in *Ramsay (WT) Ltd v IRC* HL 1981, 54 TC 101, notably that there is a circular series of transactions leaving the business in the same position as before it started? The significance of *Ramsay* was effectively relegated to a rule of statutory construction following *Barclays Mercantile Business Finance Ltd v Mawson* [2004] UKHL 51.

However, a general anti-abuse rule (GAAR) was subsequently introduced in *Finance Act 2013*, and the government can also introduce targeted anti-avoidance rules where it is considered necessary to do so. Nevertheless, it is difficult (for the authors at least) to envisage business incorporations being affected by such measures.

It may be necessary to remove and retain part of the pre-incorporation capital account, for example to meet the tax liabilities of the unincorporated business. Provided that the final accounts of the unincorporated business have made full provision for outstanding tax liabilities, this should not be a problem.

2.46   It may be worthwhile thinking carefully about the consideration to be given by the company. If it is entirely the issue of shares, then the whole gain on the transfer of the business assets is (usually) deferred but then their full value is locked into the company. If some other consideration is given, there will be a chargeable gain, but does it need to be a taxable gain?

Example 2.5 – Shares and other consideration (II)

The facts are as in the previous example. The net asset value of Linda's business upon incorporation on 1 July 2018 is £225,000. The gross chargeable gains are £130,000.

Would Linda be better advised to create a loan account of (say) £20,000 as well as taking 1,000 ordinary shares?

(a)	The market value of the shares is £205,000, being the net asset value of the business transferred in, less the loan account (£225,000 – £20,000).	
(b)	Chargeable gains (gross), as before	130,000

Amount rolled over under *TCGA 1992, s 162*:

$$A/B \times 130,000 =$$

$$\frac{205,000}{225,000} \times 130,000 = \qquad (118,444)$$

$$11,556$$

Annual exemption (to cover)	(11,556)
Taxable gain	£nil

Linda has therefore created a director's loan account of £20,000 on which she is later free to draw with no additional tax liability, compared with a director's loan account of £40,000 in the previous example at a CGT cost of only £1,403.

(c)	The CGT base cost of the shares is:	
	Market value	205,000
	Less: Gain rolled over *TCGA 1992, s 162*	(118,444)
		£86,556

This is £8,445 higher than the previous example, in which Linda incurred a CGT liability of £1,403 but also had an additional credit of £20,000 to her loan account.

The availability of entrepreneurs' relief (in whole or part) may make a transfer in return for shares and a loan account with the company at a relatively low CGT cost seem like an attractive proposition, with the loan being repaid by the company as funds allow. The reduction in the base cost of the shares on a future disposal in those circumstances may be considered to be a price worth paying. However, the potential implications of a future increase in CGT rates should be borne in mind.

2.47 As mentioned, the CGT incorporation relief in *TCGA 1992, s 162* is mandatory. No claim is required. If the individual making the disposal of chargeable assets to the company meets the conditions laid down, then the relief is given.

However, *TCGA 1992, s 162A* permits a specific claim to disapply *TCGA 1992, s 162*. When this provision was introduced (in *Finance Act 2002*), it helped to overcome a potential problem involving the interaction of incorporation relief and taper relief, namely that the shares in the company issued on incorporation are a new asset and the qualifying holding period for taper relief must begin again. If the shares were sold shortly after incorporation, any previously earned entitlement to business asset taper relief on the assets transferred would be lost. This particular problem obviously disappeared with the withdrawal of taper relief from 6 April 2008.

However, the availability of entrepreneurs' relief for share disposals from that date is generally subject to a minimum ownership period of one year, and therefore the claim is still of some potential relevance.

2.48   If *TCGA 1992, s 162* relief is to be overridden, the business proprietor making the disposal to the company must make a claim, usually by the second anniversary of 31 January following the year of assessment in which the disposal took place (*TCGA 1992, s 162A(3)*). This is shortened to the first anniversary if the shares are sold before the end of the year following incorporation (*TCGA 1992, s 162A(4)*). Special rules apply where there has been a transfer between spouses (see *TCGA 1992, s 162A(5)*).

If the business was transferred from a partnership to a company, each individual partner may separately choose whether or not to make a *TCGA 1992, s 162A* claim (*TCGA 1992, s 162A(7)*).

The effect of the election is that the gain on disposal of business assets to the company is calculated in the usual way, taking the benefit of entrepreneurs' relief, if it is available and claimed. There is no deferral and tax is payable on the net gain. The base cost of the shares issued on incorporation is therefore market value.

TCGA 1992, s 165 relief

2.49   Many incorporations use the relief in *TCGA 1992, s 165* instead. Although the relief is headed 'Relief for gifts of business assets' it does not simply apply to gifts. It would be better termed a relief for transfers of business assets at undervalue.

A business asset for this purpose is defined as including an asset, or interest in an asset, used for the purposes of a trade, profession or vocation carried on by the transferor (*TCGA 1992, s 165(2)(a)(i)*). Any chargeable asset used in a sole trade or partnership by the asset owner is therefore encompassed.

2.50   The relief applies where the asset owner disposes of the asset by way of a bargain not at arm's length (*TCGA 1992, s 165(1)(a)*). As mentioned, the transfer of assets from an unincorporated business proprietor to the company will normally be such because it is a connected party transaction.

The effect of the relief is that a chargeable gain otherwise arising is reduced by the 'held over gain' and the amount of the company's CGT base cost is also reduced by the held over gain (*TCGA 1992, s 165(4)*).

2.51   Unlike *TCGA 1992, s 162* (application of which is mandatory in the relevant circumstances), a specific claim is required for gift relief to apply (*TCGA 1992, s 165(1)(b)*).

The claim must be made jointly by both the individual making the transfer and the company. HMRC require the claim to be made on the form contained in HMRC Helpsheet HS295 ('Relief for gifts and similar transactions') (tinyurl. com/HMRC-HS295).

No shorter time limit is specified, so the general time limit of four years from the end of the tax year in which the transfer takes place normally applies (*TMA 1970, s 43(1)*).

In practice, claims will nearly always be made long before the end of this time limit (normally in the business owner's tax return for the year of incorporation), because otherwise CGT on the gain would become payable.

Note that *TCGA 1992, s 165* contains no requirement that the transfer shall be the whole of the business or even all of the assets used in the business. It must simply be 'an asset' used in a trade, profession or vocation. Thus there is a flexibility which is absent from the *TCGA 1992, s 162* process.

Relief under *TCGA 1992, s 165* is available broadly if the asset is used for the purposes of the trade. The asset must be in 'trade' use immediately before it is gifted. Note that previous periods of non-trade use will generally restrict the relief (*TCGA 1992, Sch 7, para 5*).

Furthermore, if part of a property was used for the purposes of the trade and part of it was not, gift relief is generally subject to a restriction on a 'just and reasonable' basis (*TCGA 1992, Sch 7, para 6*).

2.52   The amount of the gain which can be held over is as follows:

- in the case of a pure gift (ie no proceeds at all), the gain which would otherwise arise in deeming the proceeds to be market value (*TCGA 1992, s 165(6)*), or

- in the case of a transfer at undervalue, the amount by which the deemed gain exceeds the excess of the actual consideration over the costs deductible in the CGT computation (*TCGA 1992, s 165(7)*).

The costs deductible are those given by *TCGA 1992, s 38* ('Acquisition and disposal costs etc').

Example 2.6 – *TCGA 1992, s 165* relief: gift or sale at undervalue

Grant runs a musical supplies business. He decides to incorporate it, and transfers to the company the business premises now valued at £180,000. The CGT base cost is £75,000.

£

(a) Capital gain arising:

Consideration (market value)	180,000
Less: Cost	(75,000)
	£105,000

(b) If Grant gifts the property to the company the whole of the gain is held over. The base cost of the property for the company is:

Market value	180,000
Less: Held over gain	(105,000)
Base cost for future disposal	£75,000

(c) If Grant sells the property to the company for £50,000:

Actual proceeds	50,000
Less: Allowable cost	(75,000)
Excess	£nil

The result is as in (b) above. This is probably not a realistic scenario as Grant is missing the opportunity to take a further £25,000 tax free; the proceeds might as well be £75,000 – the result is similar.

(d) If Grant sells the property to the company for £125,000:

Actual proceeds	125,000
Less: Allowable cost	(75,000)
Excess	£50,000
Gross gain	105,000
Less: Excess	(50,000)
Gain held over	£55,000

The excess is also the chargeable gain subject to the annual exemption, if available. Entrepreneurs' relief may also be available for qualifying business disposals. *TCGA 1992, s 165* relief and entrepreneurs' relief both require claims, and some scope for planning may therefore exist in terms of choosing which relief to claim.

With regard to the interaction of gifts hold over relief and entrepreneurs' relief, HMRC's view is that *TCGA 1992, s 165* relief takes priority over entrepreneurs' relief (CG64137).

In the case of a disposal at undervalue, a claim to entrepreneurs' relief may be possible in respect of the amount of any gain remaining chargeable.

However, the restriction on entrepreneurs' relief claims in relation to disposals of goodwill to close companies (*TCGA 1992, s 169LA*) should be taken into account, if appropriate.

The base cost of the property for the company is:

Market value	180,000
Less: Held over gain	(55,000)
Base cost for future disposal	£125,000

2.53

Focus

Unlike *TCGA 1992, s 162*, there is no fixed process to follow. An incorporation using *TCGA 1992, s 165* relief may therefore typically proceed on the following basis:

- Form the company (or acquire an 'off the shelf' company) and issue shares by cash subscription. Typically, the number of shares will be small.

- Some time later, on incorporation, transfer the required assets to the company either by pure gift or by sale for proceeds of a personally determined amount. Note that the company's undertaking to satisfy any liabilities of the unincorporated business will amount to proceeds for this purpose.

- At the outset, the company is unlikely to have substantial cash, so the proceeds are often left outstanding on the loan account.

- Sometime later, when the company is trading profitably, the proprietor may draw down from the loan account effectively taking the proceeds without further tax cost.

Prior to the entrepreneurs' relief restriction in respect of goodwill disposals (see **2.36**), it was relatively common for goodwill to be sold at market value, as opposed to being gifted. However, following the entrepreneurs' relief restriction, some business owners may prefer to gift the goodwill (or sell it at an undervalue) and claim relief under *TCGA 1992, s 165* instead.

There is perhaps less need in these circumstances for a formal incorporation agreement (which is essential for the *TCGA 1992, s 162* process). Any property transfer will be evidenced by a conveyance. However, because of its intangible nature, there ought to be a document evidencing any transfer of goodwill. Do not forget also that other items, such as stock and plant and machinery attracting capital allowances, may need to be sold to the company at particular prices. All in all, some sort of document is still a sensible step.

Summary – *TCGA 1992, ss 162* and *165* compared

2.54

		TCGA 1992, s 162	*TCGA 1992, s 165*
1	How the relief is given	Mandatory. If certain conditions are satisfied, the relief is given automatically.	Optional. Claim required.
2	Method of incorporation	Fixed method:	Method more flexible:
		– form company, issue a few shares;	– form company, issue required number of shares;
		– transfer entire business and assets to company;	– transfer only assets required to company;
		– company issues more shares (and loan/ cash) to the transferor of the business as consideration.	– company may pay for assets; price flexible.
3	CGT base cost of shares	Market value less gain rolled over.	Subscription price, minimal.
4	Base cost of assets in company	Market value. Incorporation was a connected party transaction; *s 162* depresses the share base cost, not that of the assets.	Market value less gain held over.

5	Flexibility	Can be overridden by a claim under *TCGA 1992, s 162A*. Partners in a partnership can separately choose to make this claim or not.	Claim may cover all assets or selected ones. Partners in partnership may make different claims to suit personal circumstances.
6	Funds potentially available	Value of assets locked into share capital of company unless cash/loan note issued. Amount which can be withdrawn relatively low.	Shareholder/director free to draw on loan account created as consideration for asset transfer, funds permitting. The amount may be quite high.
7	Debtors/other assets	Other assets, such as debtors, must go into the company.	Debtors may be left out of company. Care needed though if creditors exceed debtors and both are excluded from the transfer. The company's satisfaction of the creditors amounts to consideration for other assets transferred.
8	Losses	Permits the carry forward of losses under *ITA 2007, s 86*.	Cannot carry forward losses under *ITA 2007, s 86*.

For the most part, there is a straight choice between incorporation by the *TCGA 1992, s 162* route or the *TCGA 1992, s 165* route. There is no right or wrong answer. All the circumstances of the business, its asset values etc must be considered along with the future intentions of the proprietors. An appropriate decision must be made.

What you cannot do is to pick the best bits of *TCGA 1992, ss 162* and *165* and use them both. We have seen that there may be circumstances in which *TCGA 1992, s 162* can leave a residual chargeable gain. This is not eligible for a claim under *TCGA 1992, s 165* because there are actual market value proceeds (ie the shares).

Enterprise Investment Scheme (EIS)

2.55   A further opportunity in the CGT legislation to defer realised gains is afforded by EIS reinvestment relief under *TCGA 1992, Sch 5B*. This relief is related to investments in EIS companies and is perhaps better referred to as deferral relief. As mentioned at **2.41**, some refer to it as 'the third way'.

Following changes to the interaction of EIS deferral relief and entrepreneurs' relief from 23 June 2010, this potential route to incorporation may have been unattractive in many cases where entrepreneurs' relief would otherwise be available. However, the disincentive to claiming EIS deferral relief in respect of qualifying business disposals was relieved by further changes from 3 December 2014, as mentioned at **2.56**.

It has to be said that the EIS legislation (both for the income tax relief in *ITA 2007, Pt 5* and the CGT reliefs in *TCGA 1992, ss 150A–150C* and *Sch 5B*) is extraordinarily complicated. There are pitfalls aplenty and anyone seeking to use these reliefs should exercise great care. Even if a qualifying investment is successfully made, there is plenty of scope for things to go wrong after the event, due to a plethora of anti-avoidance rules. A detailed analysis of the EIS reliefs is beyond the scope of this chapter.

2.56 In broad terms, CGT deferral relief is potentially available where, *inter alia*, a 'qualifying investor' subscribes in cash for new ordinary shares which are fully paid up; in a 'qualifying company' which carries on a 'qualifying trade'; and the company uses the money received in a trade within specified time limits (*TCGA 1992, Sch 5B, para 1(2)*). If those and other relief conditions are satisfied, then a capital gain realised by the investor may be reduced by the amount of the investment (or a smaller amount specified in a claim) (*TCGA 1992, Sch 5B, para 2(1)*).

In theory, the route to EIS deferral relief upon incorporation appears to be as follows:

- Form the company and issue a small number of shares for cash. It is preferable that the initial shareholder is not (one of) the proprietor(s) of the business to be incorporated. This is for complex technical reasons which might lead the share issue to be regarded as a bonus or rights issue and not a new subscription (see *Dunstan v Young, Austen and Young Ltd* CA 1988, 61 TC 448.

- The business proprietor then enters into an agreement to sell the assets of the business to the company for cash. The deal must be at market value, realising a chargeable gain. It is preferable that the company borrows money to do this, rather than have the proceeds left outstanding on loan account.

- The business proprietor then uses all or part of the cash consideration to subscribe for new ordinary shares in the company and claims deferral relief under the provisions of *TCGA 1992, Sch 5B*. It is important that cash must change hands to avoid falling foul of the anti-avoidance provisions in *Sch 5B, para 13* ('Value received by investor'). Further, the second and third steps above must not be combined. The shares must be subscribed for in cash – linking the steps would mean an asset/share exchange and the relief would not be due.

●   The amount subscribed must be sufficient to cover the gain on disposal of the original business assets.

However, this approach must come with a huge health warning! The above is not necessarily a tried and tested route and HMRC could argue that the rather circular series of transactions is part of a scheme for the avoidance of tax.

There is an advance clearance procedure for establishing the qualifying nature of the shares to be issued and the company (form EIS(AA) 'Advance assurance application: Enterprise Investment Scheme/Seed Enterprise Investment Scheme'; see tinyurl.com/HMRC-EIS-SEIS-AA). Full explanation of the advance clearance procedure is included in HMRC's Venture Capital Schemes manual (at VCM14030-VCM14070), although individuals considering investing could contact the Small Company Enterprise Centre for comment on whether or not they would be eligible for EIS relief on their subscriptions.

Entrepreneurs' relief potentially applies to material disposals of business assets. If a gain on the disposal of the business qualifies for entrepreneurs' relief, a claim for relief can be made in respect of the gains arising. In terms of the interaction between entrepreneurs' relief and EIS deferral relief, it is possible (following changes introduced in *FA 2015*) for entrepreneurs' relief to be claimed on deferred gains when they are charged to tax, subject to the relief conditions that applied when they were first deferred, where the disposal resulting in the 'first eventual gain' (ie the first gain arising under the EIS legislation) is made on or after 3 December 2014 (see *TCGA 1992, ss 169U–169V*). Thus the individual can potentially benefit from both the deferral of gains and entrepreneurs' relief on the same gains. The entrepreneurs' relief claim in respect of the first eventual gain must be made on or before the first anniversary of 31 January following the tax year in which that gain accrues.

For gains accrued before 3 December 2014, the individual may effectively choose between claiming entrepreneurs' relief (for qualifying business disposals from 23 June 2010, following changes introduced in *Finance (No 2) Act 2010*) and paying CGT on the gain at 10%, or claiming EIS deferral relief and paying CGT at the prevailing rate when the gain later comes into charge (*TCGA 1992, Sch 5B, para 1(5A)*). However, in (perhaps rare) cases where a gain has exceeded the £10m lifetime limit for entrepreneurs' relief purposes, entrepreneurs' relief can be claimed up to the lifetime limit, and EIS deferral relief claimed on gains above that limit.

For business disposals before 23 June 2010, the gain is first reduced by entrepreneurs' relief (of 4/9ths), before EIS deferral relief is applied. The deferred gain (net of entrepreneurs' relief) comes back into charge when a 'chargeable event' occurs in respect of the EIS shares (eg upon a disposal of the shares).

Entrepreneurs' relief can be claimed even if the business disposal was before 6 April 2008 (ie when the relief was introduced) and the chargeable event in respect of the qualifying EIS investment occurs on or after that date, provided that the original business disposal would have qualified for entrepreneurs' relief had it been available at that time (*Finance Act 2008, Sch 3, para 8*). Where all or part of a pre-6 April 2008 gain comes into charge following a chargeable event on or after 23 June 2010, entrepreneurs' relief (at the 10% rate) can be claimed under the *Finance Act 2008* transitional rules, if the relief conditions were satisfied when the gain arose. This revised form of relief applies if the first chargeable event since 6 April 2008 takes place from 23 June 2010.

For pre-6 April 2008 deferred gains coming into charge before 23 June 2010, chargeable gains on the subsequent disposal of the EIS shares (or other chargeable event) is net of entrepreneurs' relief (of 4/9ths). Any gain still remaining can be further reduced by losses and the CGT annual exemption, if available.

Various changes to the EIS legislation were introduced in *Finance (No 2) Act 2015*. One such change concerned how money raised by a share issue must be used. For shares issued from Royal Assent (18 November 2015), money used to acquire (directly or indirectly) a trade, goodwill or other intangible assets used for trade purposes does not amount to using that money for the purposes of a qualifying business activity (*ITA 2007, s 175(1ZA)*). This would appear to prevent existing trades being acquired upon incorporation, in the manner outlined above. It is understood that, whilst this restriction applies to EIS income tax relief, it was not intended to apply for CGT deferral relief purposes. However, this is not expressly stated in the legislation.

Seed EIS

2.57   The seed enterprise investment scheme (SEIS) was introduced (in *Finance Act 2012*) to encourage support in small, early stage companies (*ITA 2007, Pt 5A; TCGA 1992, s 150E, Sch 5BB*). The relief is available for shares issued on or after 6 April 2012 (*ITA 2007, s 257A*).

The SEIS offers qualifying investors the opportunity to claim income tax relief (worth 50% of the amount invested up to an annual maximum of £100,000) on subscriptions for shares in a qualifying company where certain conditions are satisfied.

Incorporation and disincorporation

For CGT purposes, there is an exemption for gains on shares within the scope of the SEIS. Reinvestment relief at 50% is also available on gains realised from disposals of assets (in 2013/14 and subsequent tax years) which are reinvested in the SEIS (*TCGA 1992, s 150G, Sch 5BB, para 1*). Reinvestment relief at 100% was available on gains realised in 2012/13 only (where the gains were reinvested through the SEIS in that or the following tax year).

However, it should be noted that SEIS involves a 'new qualifying trade' of an issuing company, which broadly means a genuine new venture, which has not been carried on within a defined two-year pre-investment period (*ITA 2007, s 257HF*).

In addition, HMRC can withdraw SEIS relief broadly if (*inter alia*) the company or a qualifying subsidiary carries on all or part of a trade previously carried on by another person during a specified period, or takes over assets during that period which were previously used by the investor (either alone or with other persons) in their trade where the person(s) had or has more than a half share in the trade (*ITA 2007, s 257FP(1)*).

Thus it seems that SEIS is aimed at encouraging genuinely new investment in companies by outside investors, and to ensuring that relief is not available to anyone who directly or indirectly owned the trade before it came to be owned by the company (VCM36100). The relief was not intended to apply for the purposes of incorporations.

Goodwill

2.58 Prior to changes restricting the availability of entrepreneurs' relief on the disposal of goodwill to a close company from 3 December 2014 (see **2.36**), the planning opportunity afforded by the business owner selling goodwill upon incorporation was relatively popular. The basic process of incorporation under *TCGA 1992, s 165* would be as follows:

- Sell some or all of the assets of the business, including goodwill, to the company either for full value or undervalue, leaving the proceeds outstanding on loan account.

- The first step is perceived to have created a capital gain, which may be reduced by entrepreneurs' relief and the annual exemption, if available. A sale at less than full market value could be considered in conjunction with a claim for holdover relief under *TCGA 1992, s 165*.

- Once the company starts to make profits, the proprietor can draw down on the loan account (representing the proceeds of sale of goodwill) without incurring further tax liabilities.

However, as indicated at **2.36**, claims for entrepreneurs' relief on disposals of goodwill to a close company (within *TCGA 1992, s 169LA*) are no longer possible, except in certain limited circumstances. The relevant restriction was aimed at countering perceived 'unfair' tax disadvantages on incorporation.

It should be noted that goodwill may still be the subject of a holdover claim under *TCGA 1992, s 165*, and that entrepreneurs' relief remains available on other relevant business assets comprised in the qualifying business disposal, such as trading premises. Goodwill may alternatively be sold upon incorporation at market value, albeit that any chargeable gain will be subject to normal CGT rates (10% and/or 20% for 2018/19).

2.59

Focus

Best practice for advisers who use the business sale route would be to follow the CG34 procedure and, shortly after the transaction takes place, seek agreement from HMRC on the valuations of the capital assets transferred to ensure that the CGT computations submitted are accurate so that the correct tax (if any) may be paid on the due date.

Form CG34 ('Post-transaction valuation checks for capital gains') can be downloaded from HMRC's website: tinyurl.com/HMRC-CG34.

2.60 Some advisers may have experienced an unpleasant surprise following a goodwill sale, in the form of a letter from HMRC Shares and Assets Valuation. Typically, this will say that HMRC have sought guidance on the valuation of the goodwill transferred to the company, and in their view, this is little or nothing. What has been missed?

Nature of goodwill

2.61 What is goodwill? HMRC's Capital Gains Manual devotes a section to goodwill and intellectual property rights (see CG68000 and following). Readers who wish to steer clear (or at least be more aware) of potential conflicts with HMRC are advised to refer to that commentary.

The courts have tried to define goodwill, with varying success. Perhaps the leading commentary is that of Lord MacNaghten (in *IRC v Muller & Co's Margarine Ltd* [1901] AC 217, HL):

'What is goodwill? It is a thing very easy to describe, very difficult to define. It is the benefit and advantage of the good name, reputation and connection of a business. It is the attractive force which brings in custom. It is the one thing which distinguishes an old established business from a new business at its first start.'

HMRC's guidance on goodwill changed in September 2008. Previously, HMRC favoured a kind of zoological classification of goodwill, likening the behaviour of business customers to certain types of animal. Developing the theme there existed, in HMRC's view, three components to goodwill (ie personal, inherent and free) though they were not separable and, where the different types were present in one business, they became parts of an inseparable whole.

However, a Practice Note was issued by HMRC in January 2009 ('Apportioning the Price Paid for a Business Transferred as a Going Concern'), explaining that HMRC and the Valuation Office Agency (VOA) consider that the price paid for a business as a going concern should be apportioned between goodwill and other assets included in the sale, and describing how this should be done. Referring to the various goodwill components (ie 'personal', 'inherent' and 'free' goodwill), HMRC state: 'These subdivisions are no longer considered helpful as they tend to cause confusion'.

In the context of business incorporations, HMRC state the following (CG68050):

> 'If you are dealing with a transfer of goodwill between connected persons it is essential that you should establish by reference to the facts whether the transferee has, in fact, succeeded to the business as a going concern (as opposed to having acquired one or more of the business assets) before sending a request to SAV for a valuation of goodwill. You should not accept that there has been a disposal of goodwill unless there is factual evidence of a transfer of the business as a going concern.'

HMRC consider that, because goodwill is inseparable from the business from which it is derived, the disposal of a business as a going concern must involve the transfer of goodwill.

An unregistered trademark is considered by HMRC to be an intrinsic part of the goodwill of a business, which does not exist as a separate asset within the meaning of *TCGA 1992, s 21(1)*. HMRC's position is therefore that the unregistered trademark is not capable of assignment separate from the goodwill of the business in which it is used (CG68020). By contrast, a registered trademark is considered by HMRC to be a separate asset from the goodwill of the business (CG68220).

Goodwill and trade related property

2.62   In the case of businesses carried on from 'trade related property' (eg public houses, hotels, petrol stations, cinemas, restaurants, care homes etc), in their Practice Note (see **2.61**) HMRC appear to accept that there will be an element of goodwill in such businesses when sold as a going concern.

However, HMRC consider that the sale price will reflect the value of tangible assets and other assets such as goodwill, and that it is necessary to consider the contribution that each asset makes to the combined value. HMRC's approach appears to be to treat the difference between the purchase price of the business and values of the property, fixtures and fittings etc as being the value of the goodwill (and any other intangible business assets). Any goodwill etc will reflect the capitalised value of the excess of the estimated recurring profits of the actual business owner over those of what HMRC refer to as a hypothetical 'reasonably efficient operator'.

The broad implication of the Practice Note seems to be that goodwill valuations of businesses carried on from trade-related premises will generally be lower than for other types of businesses.

The Practice Note was expanded upon in September 2013, and includes a number of worked examples showing the approach of HMRC and the VOA in apportioning the proceeds on the sale of a business as a going concern, where the business was carried on from trade-related property (ie pubs and care homes). In each example, the HMRC/VOA approach results in a much lower goodwill valuation than had been claimed. The examples also outline the approach in calculating goodwill for the purposes of relief under the intangible fixed asset provisions. The current version of the Practice Note is available from the GOV.UK website (tinyurl.com/HMRC-PN-Price-TOGC).

Of course, the Practice Note is only a statement of HMRC's views regarding goodwill, and does not carry the force of law. The Royal Institution of Chartered Surveyors (RICS) rejected the approach described in the Practice Note. Discussions between HMRC, VOA and the Chartered Institute of Taxation (CIOT) subsequently took place with input from RICS and other professional bodies, but, at the time of writing, a consensus has still not been reached on a common approach.

In the meantime, the valuation of goodwill in trade-related properties should be treated with caution, and specialist valuation advice should be considered.

Personal goodwill

2.63

Focus

If any goodwill is attributable to the personal skills of the proprietor (eg a chef or hairdresser), in HMRC's view such personal goodwill is

---

not transferable on a sale of the business (CG68010). This view has not changed, but unfortunately it presents a trap for the unwary.

Some commentators have indicated that HMRC have previously challenged the valuation of goodwill in professional practices in some cases, including whether there is any 'free' goodwill that is capable of being transferred.

However, in *Wildin v Revenue & Customs* [2014] UKFTT 459 (TC), the tribunal commented: 'the success of the firm was dependent on [the taxpayer's] own local contacts and work ethic.' There was no suggestion that this gave rise to personal goodwill (which cannot be transferred).

Advisers who have had goodwill valuations challenged by HMRC Shares and Assets Valuation possibly valued the goodwill by reference to the 'super profit' of the business.

Example 2.7 – Personal goodwill 'trap'

Mike is the chef and proprietor of a successful restaurant business, which incorporated on 1 May 2018. Last year, the gross profit was £200,000. The super profit might be established thus:

Gross profit	200,000
Less: Drawings (say)	(50,000)
Less: Interest on capital (say)	(20,000)
Super profit	£130,000

Goodwill valued at 1–2 times super profit (say £125,000–£250,000).

The problem? Most of the goodwill is personal (attaching to Mike and his reputed skills as a chef), or attaches to the location of his premises. Mike's adviser forgot this and merely included £200,000 (on a multiplier of 1½) as the goodwill proceeds upon the incorporation of the business.

The adviser is faced with explaining to Mike why HMRC will not agree the valuation.

Following the introduction of the restriction in the availability of entrepreneurs' relief on the disposal of goodwill to a close company (within *TCGA 1992, s 169LA*) from 3 December 2014 (see **2.58**), the above scenario involving a goodwill sale will probably be much less prevalent than before the restriction was introduced. However, it will still be a relevant issue in some cases, including for many business incorporations that took place before 3 December 2014 and which are subject to HMRC enquiry.

2.64   In the above example, could Mike's adviser have done anything better? As regards the personal goodwill, the answer is probably not. Mike does not want a service contract with the company. The advantage of taking dividends as opposed to salary has been explained to him and he wants to exploit this. In any case, it is questionable whether a service contract would make any difference. It merely gives the company an opportunity to exploit Mike's goodwill: it does not effect a transfer. HMRC guidance states (at CG68010):

> 'Any goodwill attributable to the personal skills of the proprietor, for example the personal skills of a chef or a hairdresser, will not be transferred to the new proprietor. Advice should be obtained from the CG Technical Group if it is claimed that the goodwill attributable to the personal skills of the proprietor have been transferred with the business because his/her services have been retained for the foreseeable future by means of an employment contract.'

As regards the goodwill attributable to the restaurant premises, the answer is 'perhaps'. Mike had various personal reasons for not placing this in the company. In the Practice Note to the 'Goodwill in Trade Related Properties Background Note' (tinyurl.com/HMRC-Goodwill-TRP-Note; see **2.62** above), HMRC express the view that, if a business such as a restaurant was transferred without 'some form of property interest', its value would be 'substantially diminished or removed'. It therefore seems likely that some measure of goodwill would be attributable to a lease, so Mike could have leased the premises to the company. This does not, however, transfer all of it.

2.65   HMRC seem to take the view that much of the goodwill attaching to any small business derives from the skills, abilities and other personal attributes of the proprietor. In other words, the transfer of goodwill might be a nice idea, but in many instances the scope to do it may be severely limited. You may have to face the fact that the personal goodwill must be left outside the company.

There is anecdotal evidence of HMRC challenging goodwill valuations for professional practices, particularly medical practitioners, on the basis that the goodwill of a professional is personal and therefore non-transferable. Care is therefore needed, and specialist advice in this area should be sought, if necessary.

2.66 In the above example, Mike's new company is paying him £200,000 and HMRC Shares and Assets Valuation maintain that the value of the free goodwill truly transferable is well below this. The majority of the goodwill remains outside the company. What then is the nature of the payment?

The capital gain will be calculated by reference to the market value of the goodwill as the parties are connected. How should the excess be handled? At this stage the company has not traded and, in the absence of any borrowings, has no funds. Its payment is therefore, to all intents and purposes, an IOU represented by a credit balance on a loan account.

HMRC's view, as stated in *Tax Bulletin,* Issue 76 (April 2005), is that the excess could fall to be treated in alternative ways, as follows:

- **Employment earnings** – HMRC have indicated that if goodwill was '… deliberately overvalued when it was sold to the company' the excess payment made by the company will be taxable as employment income (ie as earnings or, exceptionally, a benefit). The same applies to payments by the company for future services to be provided by the former business owner. Earnings will be subject to PAYE, and any benefit is reportable on form P11D. In either case, HMRC consider that the excess payment is liable to Class 1 NICs.

- **Distribution** – It will normally be the case that goodwill is transferred before the company has commenced trading. HMRC consider that, in the majority of cases in which goodwill is transferred, any excess value will be received in the capacity of a shareholder, rather than an employee or director. A payment of excess value would therefore be treated by HMRC as a distribution (by reason of *CTA 2010, ss 1000(1)* or *1020(1)–(3)*).

HMRC's analysis of the tax treatment of payments for goodwill in *Tax Bulletin,* Issue 76 is based on the premise that the goodwill has been deliberately overvalued. HMRC appear to accept in the *Tax Bulletin* that goodwill valuations are not an exact science, and consider that distributions (within *CTA 2010, s 1020(1)–(3)*) can be 'inadvertent'. HMRC may therefore allow the transaction to be 'unwound' in those circumstances.

Focus

However, there are caveats to this let-out:

(1) 'Reasonable efforts' must be made to carry out the transaction at market value using a professional valuation (ie an 'independent and suitably qualified valuer on an appropriate basis').

---

(2)   There can be no unwinding of intentional overvaluations.

(3)   There must be no tax avoidance motive.

If a distribution is unwound, the shareholder must repay the excess value to the company. If the individual has already drawn down on the loan account then this repayment may give rise to an overdrawn loan account and a 'loan to a participator' under *CTA 2010, s 455*, leading to a tax charge on the company. There might also be an income tax charge on the individual as a beneficial loan under *ITEPA 2003, s 175*.

2.67   One could endeavour to ensure that the document of transfer includes an 'adjuster clause', which expresses the proceeds as being £x 'or such lesser amount as may be agreed with HMRC'. However, on enquiry this would seem likely to provoke a challenge, particularly if no serious attempt has been made to value the goodwill properly in the first instance.

Valuation of goodwill

2.68   The valuation of goodwill in businesses without trade-related property is presently less controversial than for those businesses with such property (see **2.62**). However, in both cases goodwill valuation is a specialist area. HMRC deal with such valuation issues through their Shares and Assets Valuation specialist office.

As mentioned, on incorporation it will be necessary to identify the value of non-personal goodwill which is readily transferable to the company. The usual method of valuation is by reference to the maintainable profits of the business. Allowance should be made for proprietor's remuneration, measured as the likely salary which an arm's length manager of the business might expect to be paid. Differential weighting might be applied over a period of time giving more significance to recent profits than the older ones.

In *Spring Capital Ltd v Revenue & Customs and Others* [2015] UKFTT 66 (TC), the First-tier Tribunal commented (albeit *obiter*) on whether, in valuing goodwill on its purported transfer by the proprietors of an unincorporated business to a company, a prudent purchaser would heavily discount the value of the business because there were no service contracts or non-competition clauses binding those individuals to the business, or whether it should be assumed (in the absence of such contracts or covenants) that the proprietors would remain with the company. The tribunal considered it reasonable to assume that the business should be valued on the latter basis. Whilst not creating any binding precedent, the tribunal's comments may be persuasive in appropriate cases, or at least act as a useful reminder of the complexities that can arise when valuing goodwill.

2.69 There is also the vexed question of an appropriate multiplier to use. Comparisons of quoted companies in similar fields of business are generally of little relevance. The business being transferred is non-corporate and probably relatively small. The well-advised purchaser will assess the risk and, on an arm's-length basis, may make an offer well below what the business proprietor considers reasonable. However, this is the principle to be adopted and in many small trades a multiplier of only 1 or 2 is probably realistic.

In the context of businesses carried on from trade-related properties, as mentioned at **2.62** above, the Practice Note originally issued by HMRC in January 2009, and an expanded version of the Practice Note published in September 2013, set out how HMRC and the VOA consider the price paid for such a business as a going concern should be apportioned between goodwill and other assets. A particularly careful and prudent approach is required when valuing goodwill in those businesses.

2.70 Where the amounts involved are material, an independent expert valuation will be worth considering, particularly in view of HMRC's comments in *Tax Bulletin,* Issue 76. At a minimum, a record of the considerations taken in establishing the figure adopted should be maintained as a defence should there be an enquiry, which is likely to involve HMRC Shares and Assets Valuation.

HMRC guidance on the valuation of assets (tinyurl.com/HMRC-SAV-Goodwill) lists the types of information that should be provided to HMRC in support of goodwill valuations.

Intangible fixed assets

2.71 Historically, a major reform of the tax treatment of intangible fixed assets was introduced in *Finance Act 2002, Sch 29* (subsequently rewritten in *CTA 2009, Pt 8*). To take advantage, it is essential to operate through a corporate medium. Previously, intangible assets fell within the chargeable gains regime. The effect of the current provisions is to take specified intangible assets of companies out of that regime and into the normal trading rules.

In the context of business incorporations, the most common form of intangible asset is goodwill, although the rules also apply to 'intellectual property' as defined (in *CTA 2009, s 712(3)*). If the intangible fixed asset rules apply, the company may normally obtain a deduction for expenditure over a period of time, based on either generally accepted accounting principles, or by election on a fixed rate basis (*CTA 2009, s 726*), and receipts from disposal are treated as taxable.

However, HMRC may challenge tax relief claims for purchased intangible fixed assets if their value appears to be excessive, and there are anti-avoidance rules to prevent the perceived abuse of the intangibles rules.

Furthermore, corporation tax relief is subject to restriction (following changes introduced in *FA 2015*) where a company acquires internally-generated goodwill and customer related intangible assets from a related party on the incorporation of the business generally in relation to transfers from 3 December 2014. However, those restrictions were largely superseded by further changes (introduced in *F(No 2)A 2015*), which (among other things) disallow corporation tax deductions for amortisation under the intangibles regime in respect of goodwill and certain other intangible assets linked to customers and customer relationships, with effect from 8 July 2015 (see **2.74** below).

2.72 As a general rule, the intangible fixed assets provisions broadly apply to assets of a company created on or after 1 April 2002, or where the company acquires such assets on or after that date from an unrelated party. The rules prohibit relief for expenditure on intangible fixed assets in respect of transactions between related parties, subject to certain exceptions (see **2.73**) (*CTA 2009, ss 835, 882*).

A 'related party' includes a participator in a close company (*CTA 2009, s 835(5)(a)*). Thus former sole traders or (say) partners in small partnerships will be related if they were already shareholders when the asset (eg goodwill) was acquired by the company (*Blenheims Estate and Asset Management Ltd v Revenue & Customs* [2013] UKFTT 290 (TC)), or became shareholders upon the goodwill transfer (*HSP Financial Planning v Revenue & Customs* [2011] UKFTT 106 (TC)).

For unincorporated businesses established before the intangible fixed assets rules were introduced (1 April 2002), it is therefore not possible to incorporate the business, have the company make a payment for intangible fixed assets acquired from the former sole trader or partnership and then write off the expenditure for tax purposes in the new company over time.

2.73 However, as indicated above, there are certain exceptions to the general rule prohibiting transfers between related parties from the intangible fixed assets regime, such as upon incorporation.

One such exception is where the related sole trader or partnership acquired the intangible fixed asset after 31 March 2002 from an unrelated third party (*CTA 2009, s 882(4)*).

A further, important exception from the related party prohibition of the intangibles provisions is where the unincorporated business (or any other person) created the asset after 31 March 2002 (*CTA 2009, s 882(5)*).

This exception has become increasingly significant with the passage of time. For example, many sole traders and partnerships commenced trading from 1 April 2002 and will have grown their businesses and enhanced the value of its intangible fixed assets.

Where intangible fixed assets are sold to the company upon incorporation on or after 1 April 2002 and one of the exceptions to the related party rules applies as outlined above, the company's acquisition will therefore normally be subject to the intangible fixed assets regime, rather than under the capital gains rules.

2.74   The availability of corporation tax relief for a company that acquires goodwill (and/or certain other types of 'relevant asset', such as unregistered trademarks) from related party individuals, including partnerships (eg upon incorporation) was restricted by measures introduced in *Finance Act 2015*.

The effect of those measures (in *CTA 2009, ss 849B-849D*) is broadly to restrict debits under the intangible fixed assets regime for internally-generated goodwill and other relevant assets acquired by a company from an individual who is a related party, or from a firm with an individual member who is a related party in relation to the company.

Where the goodwill includes previous third party acquisitions, a measure of deduction is available if certain conditions are met, ie the transferor must have acquired the relevant business (or part of it) in one or more 'third party acquisitions' (ie broadly from an unrelated party, where the acquisition did not have a main purpose of obtaining a tax advantage), and the company must have acquired that business or part from the transferor. The debit that would otherwise be taken into account under *CTA 2009, Pt 8, Ch 3* ('debits in respect of intangible fixed assets') is restricted by an 'appropriate multiplier' (nb the multiplier ensures that the company cannot claim relief for debits in an amount higher than the notional accounting value of the relevant asset acquired from the transferor).

Furthermore, on the subsequent realisation of the goodwill by the company, a debit (ie loss) that would otherwise be taken into account under *CTA 2009, Pt 8, Ch 4* ('realisation of intangible fixed assets') falls to be apportioned, ie between trading debits in respect of third party acquisitions, and non-trading debits in respect of other goodwill.

If no goodwill was acquired by third party acquisitions, the company is not allowed any debit under *CTA 2009, Pt 8, Ch 3* in respect of the acquisition of the goodwill (or other relevant asset). Any debit brought into account by the company on a subsequent realisation of the goodwill (under *Pt 8, Ch 4*), falls to be treated as a non-trading debit.

The above relief restrictions generally apply to transfers of goodwill etc from 3 December 2014 (unless made pursuant to an unconditional obligation entered into before that date). For company accounting periods straddling 3 December 2014, the accounting period is split and the restrictions apply to debits arising from that date.

However, as indicated at **2.71** above, the restrictions introduced in *Finance Act 2015* were largely superseded by further changes announced in *Finance (No 2) Act 2015*, with effect from 8 July 2015.

The effect of those changes is that no amortisation can be claimed by the company under the intangibles regime (under *CTA 2009, Pt 8, Ch 3*) in respect of a relevant asset. A 'relevant asset' includes goodwill, customer information and unregistered trademarks used in the business. In addition, any debit brought into account on the realisation of such assets (under *CTA 2009, Pt 8, Ch 4*) is treated as a non-trading debit (*CTA 2009, s 816A*).

The above changes introduced by *Finance (No 2) Act 2015* generally apply for accounting periods beginning from 8 July 2015. Accounting periods straddling that date are treated as separate accounting periods for the purposes of apportioning debits. However, the changes do not apply to goodwill or other relevant assets acquired by a company before 8 July 2015, or under a contractual obligation that was unconditional before that date. Assets acquired between 3 December 2014 and 8 July 2015 where *CTA 2009, s 849B* applies therefore continue to be subject to the rules in *CTA 2009, ss 849C* and *849D* as outlined above.

The government's explanatory note to the changes states: 'This clause removes this relief with regard to the purchase of goodwill and other intangible assets closely related to goodwill. It will restrict the ability of companies to reduce their corporation tax profits following a merger or acquisition and removes this artificial incentive to buy assets rather than shares.' Whilst not specifically mentioned in the explanatory note, the above measures are also likely to make incorporation a less attractive proposition for some business owners from a tax perspective.

It should be noted that whilst the above restriction applies to goodwill and other relevant assets, corporation tax relief continues to be available for expenditure incurred on other types of intangibles falling within the intangible fixed assets regime in *CTA 2009, Pt 8*.

The government published a consultation document ('Review of the corporate Intangible Fixed Assets regime') in February 2018. The specific areas under consideration included the impact of the 1 April 2002 commencement rule (see **2.72**) and the restriction on goodwill and customer related intangibles on complexity and competitiveness of the regime. The outcome of the consultation is awaited at the time of writing.

For further commentary on the intangible fixed assets regime generally, see *Corporation Tax 2018/19* (Bloomsbury Professional).

Stamp taxes

2.75   Stamp duty is not a tax levied on profits, income or gains. It is not even a tax on transactions. Stamp duty is charged on 'instruments', broadly defined as documents, transferring title to stock or marketable securities (principally shares and securities).

Goodwill ceased to be an asset liable to stamp duty in respect of instruments executed on or after 23 April 2002, and the transfer of debtors ceased to be liable to stamp duty from 1 December 2003.

Assets such as stock or plant and machinery are no longer chargeable to stamp duty. However, the transfer of 'fixtures', ie plant and machinery, which, in law, have become part of the land, is potentially chargeable to stamp duty land tax (or land and buildings transaction tax if the land is situated in Scotland (with effect from 1 April 2015), or land transaction tax if the land is situated in Wales (with effect from 1 April 2018).

Stamp duty now only applies to instruments transferring stock and marketable securities, the issue of bearer instruments and transfers of interests in partnerships which hold stock and marketable securities. As regards bearer instruments, it should be noted that (with effect from 26 May 2015) a UK incorporated company is prohibited from issuing new bearer shares, and from 26 February 2016 all existing bearer shares issued by a UK incorporated company had to be converted into registered shares or cancelled (*Small Business, Employment and Enterprise Act 2015*).

Stamp duty reserve tax is effectively an alternative to stamp duty. It relates to agreements to transfer chargeable securities (eg shares or loan capital), and is generally charged when no document of transfer is presented for stamping.

In the context of incorporation and small owner-managed or family companies, a stamp duty charge may be encountered in some cases, such as when relief is sought under *TCGA 1992, s 162*. However, there is no stamp duty on the issue of shares as such; only in the event that the business assets transferred include shares or securities will there be a stamp duty liability (at 0.5%) on the amount or value of the actual consideration given for the acquisition of the shares or securities. There is no market value rule for the purposes of stamp duty. It should be noted that there is an exemption (*FA 1986, s 79(4)*) for documents transferring certain categories of loan capital.

On 10 July 2017, the Office of Tax Simplification (OTS) issued its report in relation to stamp duty on paper documents and recommended its reform, digitalisation and simplification. In particular, it highlighted two aspects of the stamp duty regime which are out of date and in urgent need of reform.

First, the time-consuming process which requires that a paper document chargeable to stamp duty must be posted to the stamp office in Birmingham, together with a cheque or bank transfer for the duty, in order that a physical stamp can be impressed on the document which is then sent to the relevant company registrar. The OTS's recommendation was that the stamp duty process be digitalised, providing the transferee with a unique transaction reference confirming that the transaction has been notified to HMRC. This would eliminate the need for a physical stamp to be impressed on paper documents. It was also suggested that the legal obligations of company registrars could be changed, allowing them to write up the company's books on receipt of the unique transaction reference or confirmation of notification to HMRC.

Secondly, the current scope of stamp duty is significantly broader than is actually applied in practice as, for example, duty is chargeable on paper documents executed in the UK even if those documents give effect to the transfer of non-UK shares. This results in documents transferring non-UK shares being executed and retained outside of the UK to try to avoid the document being chargeable to stamp duty or to avoid a penalty for late stamping being payable should the document actually have to be stamped because, for example, it is required as evidence in a UK civil court. The OTS stated in its report: 'This is confusing and inefficient'. The recommendations from the OTS were that stamp duty be aligned with SDRT so that broadly it does not apply to paper documents transferring non-UK shares unless those shares are registered in a register kept in the UK. They also suggested making the tax assessable and therefore ending the 'voluntary' nature of the tax.

On 14 August 2017, the Chancellor of the Exchequer responded by letter to the OTS's report and agreed to consider the recommendations carefully, weighing up the benefits of the four main elements of the proposed reforms in the context of the ongoing reforms to the tax system. The four main elements of the reforms identified in the Chancellor's letter were as follows:

● providing taxpayers with a unique transaction reference number;

● amending company registrar's legal obligations in respect of share transfer registrations;

- making stamp duty assessable; and

- aligning the scope of stamp duty with SDRT.

It therefore seems likely that the archaic nature of stamp duty will be the subject of fundamental reform in the near future.

2.76   Stamp duty land tax (SDLT) applies to land transactions, ie broadly to the acquisition or enhancement of interests in UK land and buildings (*FA 2003, s 42*). It has no application to land outside the UK. From 1 April 2015, SDLT ceased to apply to land in Scotland, where it was replaced by land and buildings transaction tax (LBTT), administered by Revenue Scotland, the tax authority with responsibility for the taxes devolved to the Scottish Parliament, including LBTT.

The LBTT legislation borrows heavily from the SDLT regime and therefore in many situations the LBTT implications of a transaction may be the same, or similar, to the SDLT implications which would have arisen had the transaction been subject to SDLT. However, care must be taken as there are some fundamental differences between LBTT and SDLT. It is also possible that Revenue Scotland will take a different view of similar legislation compared to that taken by HMRC. There have been anecdotal instances where Revenue Scotland have, in fact, interpreted similar legislation differently to that of HMRC. Consequently, specific LBTT advice should normally be sought when dealing with a transaction over land in Scotland.

Land transaction tax (LTT) replaced SDLT in relation to land situated in Wales from 1 April 2018, and is administered by the Welsh Revenue Authority, which is the tax authority with responsibility for the taxes devolved to the Welsh Assembly, including LTT. SDLT and LBTT are in point up to 1 April 2018 for, respectively, land in the rest of the UK and Scotland, regardless of whether or not the transactions are effected inside or outside the UK. On or after 1 April 2018, LTT applies to chargeable land interests in Wales (see *s 4* of the *Land Transaction Tax and Anti-avoidance of Devolved Taxes (Wales) Act 2017 (LTTADT(W)A 2017)*) and SDLT applies to chargeable land interests situated in England and Northern Ireland.

The LTT legislation also borrows heavily from the SDLT regime and, therefore, in many situations the LTT implications of a transaction may be the same, or similar, to the SDLT implications which would have arisen had the transaction been subject to SDLT. However, care must be taken as there are differences between LTT and SDLT. It is also possible that the Welsh Revenue Authority will take a different view of similar legislation compared to that taken by HMRC. Consequently, specific LTT advice should normally be sought when dealing with a transaction over land in Wales. For a detailed consideration of SDLT, LTT and LBTT, including statutory compliance obligations such as in relation to tax returns and payments, see *Stamp Taxes 2018/19* (Bloomsbury Professional) and *Land and Buildings Transaction Tax 2018/19* (Bloomsbury Professional). See also **Chapter 11** on Stamp Taxes. Note, in the commentary below, in relation to SDLT, the LBTT and LTT statutory references have been provided for the equivalent legislation.

SDLT, LBTT and LTT are in point regardless of whether or not the transactions are effected inside or outside the UK.

The chargeable consideration for a land transaction is defined in *FA 2003, Sch 4 (LBTT(S)A 2013, Sch 2; LTTADT(W)A 2017, Sch 4)*. In most instances, it will be the consideration given in money or money's worth for the transaction.

However, if land and buildings are transferred to the company upon incorporation, invariably the parties will be connected with each other. If so, the land and buildings are deemed to pass at a chargeable consideration of not less than market value for SDLT purposes (*FA 2003, s 53*). The equivalent LBTT and LTT provisions are *LBTT(S)A 2013, s 22* and *LTTADT(W)A 2017, s 22* respectively.

The rule for connection is found in *CTA 2010, s 1122*. Thus, for example, a controlling shareholder will be connected with the company. Whilst there may be some incorporation cases where the company has diverse shareholdings which will be outside the connection test in *CTA 2010, s 1122*, these are likely to be the exception rather than the rule.

Focus

However, upon the straightforward incorporation of a partnership of individuals, HMRC accept that the SDLT provisions for partnerships (*FA 2003, Sch 15, para 18*) effectively override the market value rule in *FA 2003, s 53* (SDLTM34160). In the Stamp Duty Land Tax manual, HMRC state (at SDLTM34170):

> 'Where the provisions of both *Finance Act 2003, s 53* and *para 18* apply to a transfer of a chargeable interest to a company, the provisions of *para 18* will take precedence to determine the chargeable consideration.'

The HMRC guidance at SDLTM34170 features an example, which indicates that the above SDLT provisions for partnerships will generally be more favourable than the market value rule in *FA 2003, s 53*, such as in circumstances involving the incorporation of a partnership.

As to the application of the SDLT provisions in relation to partnerships, see *Stamp Taxes 2018/19* (Bloomsbury Professional). See also **Chapter 11** – Stamp Taxes.

At the time of writing it is understood that the Welsh Revenue Authority will be updating the draft LTT partnership guidance to reflect the fact that the partnership provisions in *LTTADT(W)A 2017, Sch 7, paras 21, 22* (transfer of land from a partnership) will override the deemed market value rule in *LTTADT(W)A 2017, s 22* where land is transferred out of a partnership and the partners in that partnership are individuals who are connected with the purchaser which is a company.

It is not known whether Revenue Scotland take a similar view regarding the interaction of *LBTT(S)A 2013, Sch 17, paras 20, 21* (transfer of land from a partnership) and the market value rule in *LBTT(S)A 2013, s 22*. It is suggested that until this point is clarified in Revenue Scotland's technical guidance, the views of Revenue Scotland should be sought in relation to any transaction where this is an issue.

2.77 When a partnership acquires or disposes of a property from/to a partner or someone connected with a partner, special rules in *FA 2003, Sch 15* (or *LBTT(S)A 2013, Sch 17*; *LTTADT(W)A 2017, Sch 7*) come into play to determine the amount of tax payable. When a property – possibly forming part of the assets of a business – is transferred from a partnership to a company or vice versa, if the company is owned by one or more of the partners or persons connected with them, actual consideration is irrelevant. The consideration for SDLT purposes (and also for LBTT and LTT purposes) is calculated using a formula which takes account of the market value of the property and the effective change in ultimate ownership. Where there is no change in ultimate ownership, and providing all of the partners are individuals, this can mean that the chargeable consideration for a transfer is zero.

However, the actual calculation can be complex, taking account of proportional partnership shares, other connections between the partners and whether the persons involved are individuals or companies. In relation to disposals of a property from a partnership to a partner or someone connected with a partner, it will also be important to consider relevant historic changes in partnership shares and whether SDLT (or stamp duty), LBTT or LTT was paid on the acquisition of the property from a third party.

Detailed consideration of the various permutations is beyond the scope of this section. Specialist advice will generally be the best course of action.

If property is, for any reason, retained outside the company then rent may be paid. In many cases, this will be in respect of an informal licence without the need for a lease. A licence to use or occupy land is an exempt interest (*FA 2003, s 48(2)(b)*). For LBTT purposes, the grant, assignation or renunciation of a licence to occupy property (which is not a prescribed non-residential licence) is an exempt transaction (*LBTT(S)A 2013, Sch 1, para 3(1)(b)*). Similarly, a licence to use or occupy land is an exempt interest for LTT purposes (*LTTADT(W)A 2017, s 5(1)(b)*).

However, care must be taken to distinguish a licence from a lease, as the distinction is important for SDLT purposes. The Stamp Duty Land Tax Manual states (at SDLTM00320):

> '[N]ote that a document which describes itself as a licence may in fact be a lease, especially if the practical consequence is that the grantee has exclusive occupation.'

This distinction is also important for LBTT and LTT purposes.

2.78   In the case of leasehold property, where an existing lease is transferred SDLT (and LBTT, LTT) is normally chargeable only on any actual consideration given by the transferee for the transfer. This is subject to the substitution of market value for consideration in the case of a transfer to a connected company (see **2.76**). No further SDLT, LBTT or LTT is normally chargeable in respect of rent payable under the lease, nor in respect of any premium previously paid on the original grant of the lease.

However, if the SDLT on original grant has not been finally determined when the lease is transferred (eg because the rent is variable and the transfer occurs during the first five years of the lease), the transferee inherits the ongoing obligations to finally determine the SDLT liability and pay any further tax due (*FA 2003, Sch 17A, para 12*).

If a new lease of commercial property is granted, SDLT is chargeable on both the premium payable, if any, and also on the rent payable (*FA 2003, Sch 5*).

In some circumstances the transfer of an existing lease is treated as the grant of a new lease and SDLT is charged accordingly. This happens when one of a range of reliefs (in *FA 2003, Sch 17A, para 11*) was claimed on the original grant of the lease, and the transfer is the first one since grant which does not qualify for one of the reliefs. The equivalent LBTT and LTT provisions are *LBTT(S)A 2013, Sch 19, para 27* and *LTTADT(W)A 2017, Sch 6, para 22* respectively.

For LTT purposes, the provisions dealing with leases are contained in *LTTADT(W)A 2017, Sch 6* and mirror those for SDLT. Therefore, if the LTT on original grant has not been finally determined when the lease is transferred (eg because the rent is variable and the transfer occurs during the first five years of the lease), the transferee inherits the ongoing obligations to finally determine the LTT liability and pay any further tax due (*LTTADT(W)A 2017, Sch 6, para 23*).

If a new lease of commercial property is granted, LTT is chargeable on both the premium payable, if any, and also on the rent payable (*LTTADT(W)A 2017, Sch 6, paras 29, 33*). However, unlike SDLT, no LTT is charged on so much of the consideration given for the grant of a lease over residential property as comprises rent (*LTTADT(W)A 2017, Sch 6, para 27*).

In relation to LBTT, the special rules for leases can be found in *LBTT(S)A 2013, Sch 19*. In principle, the manner of charging LBTT on the grant of a new lease is similar to that under SDLT. Tax will be calculated separately on the rent and on any premium, and the two amounts added to give the initial tax charge for the grant of the lease. However, unlike SDLT, in calculating the LBTT liability on rent any known increase throughout the life of the lease will have to be taken into account in the initial assessment of the tax payable, apart from increases in line with the retail price index, consumer price index or similar index of inflation. But even then the position will not be finally determined.

In addition, assuming the grant of the lease was notifiable to Revenue Scotland, or became notifiable, the tenant (and any assignee) will be required to review the position every three years during the term of the lease, and again when the lease is assigned or terminates, to determine whether any further LBTT is payable. The aim of the legislation is to charge LBTT on the actual rent paid over the term of the lease. However, the requirement to file multiple returns may prove onerous for some tenants, particularly if they have a number of leased premises.

As to the application of the LBTT provisions in relation to commercial leases, see *Land and Buildings Transaction Tax 2018/19* (Bloomsbury Professional).

2.79   The rate at which SDLT is charged on consideration depends on the amount of the chargeable consideration, and whether the transaction is a residential property transaction or a non-residential property transaction. Historically, until 4 December 2014 the amount of the SDLT payable for both a residential property transaction and a non-residential property transaction was calculated using the so-called 'slab system'. Under that system, the rates were not progressive; rather, the whole consideration was chargeable at a single rate determined by the highest tax band into which the total chargeable consideration fell.

However, the SDLT payable in relation to a residential property transaction, with an 'effective date' on or after 4 December 2014, and in relation to a non-residential or mixed-use property transaction, with an 'effective date' on or after 17 March 2016, is now calculated using a 'progressive system' (like personal income tax). This means that it is only that part of the chargeable consideration falling within each tax band that is taxed at the rate for that tax band.

The rates at which LBTT and LTT are charged on chargeable consideration will also depend upon the amount of the chargeable consideration, and whether the transaction is a residential property transaction or a non-residential property transaction. Like SDLT, the tax rates are applied on a progressive basis similar to income tax.

A 15% slab rate of SDLT (meaning that the whole of the consideration given for the dwelling is charged at a single rate of 15%) may apply to acquisitions of residential properties, for a consideration of over £500,000, purchased by companies and other 'non-natural persons' (see **2.99**), subject to the availability of certain reliefs. There is no equivalent slab rate under either LBTT or LTT.

With effect from 1 April 2016, higher rates of both SDLT and LBTT were introduced for purchases of additional dwellings by individuals and dwellings acquired by companies (whether it is the first such purchase or not). A higher rate of LTT also applies to such purchases. See **2.99** for further commentary.

The rates and bands applicable for each of SDLT, LBTT and LTT are available on the GOV.UK (www.gov.uk/stamp-duty-land-tax), Revenue Scotland (www.revenue.scot/land-buildings-transaction-tax/guidance/calculating-tax-rates-and-bands) and Welsh Government (http://gov.wales/funding/fiscal-reform/welsh-taxes/land-transaction-tax/?lang=en) websites respectively.

Inheritance tax

2.80   Incorporation is a commercial transaction. There should be no gratuitous intent to it. In theory, therefore, there is no charge to IHT, or it should be excluded by *IHTA 1984, s 10* ('Dispositions not intended to confer gratuitous benefit').

Where there is a gratuitous reduction in an individual's estate, most lifetime transfers are potentially exempt transfers (PETs). However, a transfer of value to a company does not constitute a PET (within *IHTA 1984, s 3A(1)(c), (1A)(c)(i)*), and is therefore an immediately chargeable transfer.

In addition, note that if a close company makes a transfer of value and this is apportioned to the participators, this is not a PET and IHT is immediately chargeable (*IHTA 1984, s 94*).

Whilst the interests of the shareholders in the newly formed company will, in most instances, be identical to the interests of the proprietors in the unincorporated business, this is not exclusively the case. To the extent that anyone other than the original business proprietor or spouse takes shares (eg adult children), a potential problem as indicated above is that the transfer of value made in such circumstances is not a PET. It is a chargeable transfer. The recipient of the gift is a company, not an individual, even though the effect of it is to increase the estates of the children. HMRC considers that this is the correct interpretation of *IHTA 1984, s 3A(2)* (see HMRC's Inheritance Tax Manual at IHTM04060, Example 2).

In most instances, the transfer of value in such circumstances will be relatively small. However, the proprietor needs to be aware of the erosion of his IHT nil rate band.

Business property relief

2.81 A separate chapter of this book deals with business property relief (BPR) (see **Chapter 12**). Every business proprietor must be aware of this relief and the impact that incorporation might have on it. For example, the rate could be halved in some cases, and the assets encompassed by it restricted.

2.82 Provided that the business of the sole trader is not excluded by the investment activity test in *IHTA 1984, s 105(3)*, the whole of the value should qualify for BPR in the event of death or a chargeable transfer for IHT purposes, unless there are any 'excepted assets' as defined in *IHTA 1984, s 112*.

As regards the business itself, a partner is in broadly the same position as a sole trader. 100% BPR should be available to a sole trader or partner in respect of a chargeable transfer of the business interest. As *IHTA 1984, s 105(1)(a)* refers only to an interest in a business, the extent of participation is irrelevant. Thus, a partner with (say) a 5% share in a business can obtain exactly the same relief pro-rata to value as a partner with a 90% share.

There is no relief for an asset held outside the partnership, unless the partnership interest itself is relevant business property (*IHTA 1984, s 105(6)*). Again, there is no minimum participation limit in the partnership. So a partner can get BPR in respect of property let to a trading partnership of which he is only a small minority partner. The rate of relief is 50% (*IHTA 1984, s 104(1)(b)*).

However, note that the loan account of a retired partner does not qualify for BPR (*Beckman v IRC* [2000] STC (SCD) 59).

2.83 Shares in unquoted trading companies generally qualify for BPR when there is a chargeable transfer for IHT purposes. BPR is available both to working and passive shareholders. It is not necessary for the shareholder to be a director of the company. There is no minimum size of holding, nor any specification as to the type of share, although there is a minimum ownership period for BPR purposes (see **2.86**). The rate of relief is 100% (*IHTA 1984, s 104(1)(a)*).

If business property is subject to a binding contract for sale at the time of a chargeable transfer, then BPR is not available (*IHTA 1984, s 113*). Beware company articles or shareholder agreements that impose 'buy and sell' arrangements on the members of the company. This pitfall is covered in greater detail in **Chapter 12**.

However, BPR is not denied by *IHTA 1984, s 113* if the reason for the binding contract is the incorporation of a sole trader or partnership in which the sale proceeds are wholly or mainly shares or securities in the company (*IHTA 1984, s 113(a)*). Note that there is no exception from *IHTA 1984, s 113* in the case of a cash sale of the business upon incorporation.

2.84   As with a partnership, a business proprietor who becomes a shareholder may decide to retain property outside the company. The property may qualify for BPR if it is used for the purposes of a business carried on by the company, the shares held are themselves relevant business property, and the transferor controlled the company (*IHTA 1984, s 105(1)(d), (6)*). However, the rate of relief is only 50% (*IHTA 1984, s 104(1)(b)*).

Thus for assets used but not retained within the business vehicle, the situation may worsen. A sole trader would get 100% BPR if the asset comprised part of the business, but a shareholder gets 50% relief, and only if he controls the company.

2.85

Focus

A simple loan to a company does not qualify for BPR. Whilst the incorporation transactions may lead to a positive balance on a director's loan account, this should not be left in place indefinitely. It gives a means of drawing cash from the company without further tax charge but, if it is still in place when the shareholder dies or wishes to make a chargeable transfer of shares, the value is excluded from BPR.

The solution may be, if the funds are required in the company and IHT is a concern, to capitalise the loan for more shares. The freedom to draw down is then, of course, lost. A loan will sometimes be capitalised for more shares if the shareholder's life expectancy is possibly less than the normal two-year ownership requirement for BPR purposes, on the basis that the new shares may be identified with other shares in the company which have been held for at least two years.

For holdings of unquoted shares which would (under the capital gains tax reorganisation rules in *TCGA 1992, ss 126–136*) be identified with other qualifying shares previously owned, for BPR purposes their period of ownership may be treated as including the ownership period of the original shares (*IHTA 1984, s 107(4)*).

However, as illustrated in *Executors of Dugan-Chapman (deceased) v Revenue and Customs Comrs* [2008] SpC 666, it is important that the documentation and implementation is complete and correct, and that the circumstances are suitable (see **12.10**).

2.86   The availability of BPR normally depends on the holding of a certain type of business asset for a minimum period of two years (*IHTA 1984, s 106*). This does not necessarily mean that the same relevant business property must be held throughout. The two-year minimum holding period need not be satisfied by the same relevant business property. It is possible to carry forward the qualifying conditions into replacement property. So, where one item of qualifying business property is replaced by another, the conditions for BPR can remain satisfied. There may even be a gap in ownership. The two-year minimum holding period is satisfied if both assets are held for a total of two years within five years before the transfer of value (*IHTA 1984, s 107(1)*).

The BPR available in respect of replacement property is generally restricted to what it would have been had the replacement(s) not been made. However, this general rule is subject to certain exceptions, one of which is the incorporation of a business, whereby the company is controlled by the former business owner(s) (*IHTA 1984, s 107(3)*).

Incorporation will generally involve a switch from a business held personally (qualifying under *IHTA 1984, s 105(1)(a)*) to shares in a trading company (qualifying under *IHTA 1984, s 105(1)(bb)*). All other conditions being satisfied, one replaces the other and the availability of BPR continues throughout. There is no need to establish a new minimum holding period for the shares.

However, as mentioned, an incorporation involving a business sale (as opposed to an exchange of the business for shares) would not attract BPR to the extent of the sale proceeds. There is also a possibility that HMRC could argue that a company set up in advance of the incorporation has not 'replaced' the unincorporated business in a strict sense, and that the shares are therefore not 'relevant business property'. Such an interpretation would appear harsh, but cannot be completely ruled out.

Agricultural property relief

2.87   A separate chapter of this book includes commentary on agricultural property relief (APR) (see **Chapter 12**). However, in broad terms APR is available in respect of the agricultural value of agricultural property, being the value which it would have if it were to be used perpetually for agriculture.

Much agricultural property will also satisfy the conditions for BPR. Where, on the face of it, both reliefs are available, APR takes precedence (*IHTA 1984, s 114(1)*). However, this does not necessarily prevent a claim for BPR on the excess over the agricultural value.

2.88   If, on incorporation, the land is placed within the company then the business proprietor ceases to own it. Rather, he has shares in the new company, the value of which reflects the value of the land held therein. These shares are clearly not agricultural property in themselves, but their value will reflect the underlying agricultural property. If that is the case, APR may be available on the share value to the extent that that value is attributable to the underlying agricultural land, providing that the shares give the transferor control of the company (*IHTA 1984, s 122(1)*).

The company must also satisfy certain conditions as to the occupation and ownership of the land. In addition, the shareholder must have owned the shares for whichever of the (two-year or seven-year) minimum periods is appropriate to the company, subject to provisions which preserve the relief where the shares replaced other eligible property during the relevant period (*IHTA 1984, s 123*).

Assuming that this will be a trading company, it is more than likely that BPR will be available in respect of the shares as well. This will relieve the excess value of the shares over the agricultural value of the land holding. If the control test is not satisfied, then BPR should be available on the whole value. Loss of APR should therefore be no real disaster.

If the agricultural land is held outside the company, on a new incorporation it is perhaps best to ensure that a formal tenancy is put in place. This would satisfy the conditions of *IHTA 1984, s 116(2)(c)* and, all other things being equal, 100% APR is maintained.

Value added tax

2.89   Most businesses will be registered for VAT. The disposal of the assets of a business is to be treated as a supply made in the course or furtherance of that business. Accordingly, VAT will be chargeable on the sale of such items as stock, plant and machinery, fixtures and fittings (*VATA 1994, Sch 4, para 5*).

HMRC also regard a sale of goodwill as a taxable supply (C&E Press Notice No 790, 10 December 1982).

However, the general rule is that no taxable supply is made and no VAT should be charged where the assets of a business are transferred to another person (eg a successor company) in connection with the transfer of all or part of the business as a going concern.

Therefore, the transfer of a business as a going concern is neither a supply of goods nor a supply of services for VAT purposes (*VAT (Special Provisions) Order 1995, SI 1995/1268, art 5*). This applies where the assets are to be used by the transferee in carrying on the same kind of business as that carried on by the transferor; and where the transferee is a taxable person, or immediately becomes one as a result of the transfer. If only part of the business is transferred as a going concern, the same rule applies where that part is capable of separate operation. The transfer of a going concern (TOGC) rule is mandatory provided all the statutory conditions are satisfied.

In the case of property rental businesses, HMRC accept (following *Robinson Family Ltd v Revenue & Customs* [2012] UKFTT 360 (TC)) that if the transferor of the business retains a small reversionary interest in the property transferred, this does not prevent the transaction from being treated as a TOGC for VAT purposes. Provided the interest retained is small enough not to disturb the substance of the transaction (no more than 1% of the pre-transfer value), the transaction will be a TOGC if the usual conditions are satisfied (Revenue & Customs Brief 30/12).

2.90   There is an exception to the TOGC rules. This is where the assets being transferred include land and buildings which are potentially taxable, ie on which the transferor has exercised the option to tax, or there is a sale of the freehold of a new or incomplete building liable to VAT at the standard rate, and the successor company has not notified HMRC of an election to waive exemption in respect of the property concerned and/or has not notified the vendor that its option to tax of the land and property concerned will not be disapplied (*SI 1995/1268, arts 5(2)–(2B)*). The transferor must then charge standard rate VAT in respect of the supply of the property.

2.91   When the ownership of a business is transferred to a different legal entity it is possible for the transferee to take over the transferor's original VAT registration number. This treatment is broadly available if registration of the original business is cancelled from the date of the transfer, and the new business is not already registered, but is liable or entitled to be registered (*VAT Regulations 1995, SI 1995/2518, reg 6(1)*). The process is effected by completion of form VAT 68, which is available via the GOV.UK website (www.gov.uk/government/publications/vat-request-for-transfer-of-a-registration-number-vat68).

However, it should be noted that transferring a VAT registration number from one business to another transfers the responsibility for any debits and credits both before and after the transfer to the new owner. The decision to transfer a VAT number must be taken in the light of any adverse history or potential liability which may be assumed by the company.

2.92 Alternatively, if it is decided to break the link with the old business, the company may apply for fresh VAT registration. The former business proprietor must deregister immediately after the transfer (unless only part of the business has been transferred and thus the former business owner will continue to trade in some capacity). It is not necessary for the transfer of all the assets of a business to take place for it to be a TOGC. However, what is transferred should be sufficient to enable continued operation of the same business as was carried on by the transferor.

2.93

Focus

It is crucial for all businesses to establish whether or not there is a TOGC. There is no safe option – if VAT is charged on a transaction which turns out to be a TOGC, both parties will have misstated their VAT liabilities, where potentially HMRC can both require the vendor to account for the amount he has incorrectly treated as output tax and deny input tax recovery to the purchaser.

Conversely, if VAT is not charged, but HMRC decide there is no TOGC, the transferor will have a VAT liability which may be impossible to recover from the transferee.

For HMRC's internal guidance, see 'VAT Transfer of a going concern' manual (www.gov.uk/hmrc-internal-manuals/vat-transfer-of-a-going-concern). HMRC will provide clearances on whether a transaction should be treated as a TOGC if its guidance does not cover a particular issue. However, HMRC warns that such clearances may have to be heavily caveated because the enquiry is likely to only come from one party. HMRC will normally only give a clearance in response to an enquiry from the seller (VTOGC2200).

Detailed consideration of the VAT issues surrounding the transfer of a business as a going concern is outside the scope of this chapter, For further commentary, see *Value Added Tax 2018/19* (Bloomsbury Professional).

Investment businesses

2.94   Very often, the nature of an investment business will be the letting of property. Whilst for income tax purposes the receipt of rents from property is treated as a 'property business' (*ITTOIA 2005, ss 264, 265*), the real problem with the tax legislation is that there is no satisfactory definition of a 'business'.

There is abundant case law on activities in the nature of a trade, but very little on activities in the nature of a business. It is clear that a business is rather wider than (but includes) a trade, as well as a profession or vocation. Active management is a characteristic of a business, as is profit motive.

2.95   In any case, would one want to incorporate such an activity? For example, for IHT purposes no BPR would be available in respect of shares in the company. In addition, whilst the commercial letting of holiday accommodation may constitute a business, the business carried on may be mainly that of holding an investment, on which no BPR is due (eg *HMRC v Personal representatives of N Pawson, deceased* [2013] UKUT 050 (TCC)). The same may apply in respect of serviced office accommodation (*The Trustees of David Zetland Settlement v Revenue & Customs* [2013] UKFTT 284 (TC)), or a managed business centre (*Best v Revenue & Customs* [2014] UKFTT 77 (TC)).

Business owners may also perceive that there is a potential double tax charge by operating in corporate form. The company pays tax on its gain; the shareholder pays tax on extraction of the profit.

An unincorporated property letting business will derive gross rents against which may be set various expenses to arrive at a net property business profit. An individual receiving this will be chargeable to income tax at his highest marginal rate as it arises. Getting the profits into a company has the obvious attraction of the ability to withdraw profits by way of dividend rather than salary, just as with a trading company.

2.96   As indicated earlier in this chapter, there are two traditional routes of relieving the capital gains arising on incorporation of a business. These use either the general relief for gifts of business assets in *TCGA 1992, s 165*, or the specific incorporation relief in *TCGA 1992, s 162*.

A claim under *TCGA 1992, s 165* is generally a non-starter. This permits the holdover of a capital gain where an asset is transferred at undervalue and the asset is used for the purposes of a trade, profession or vocation. Whatever property letting may be, it is not a trade (although hotels are generally treated as such), or a profession or vocation. However, see **2.98** below as to the special treatment afforded to furnished holiday lettings.

2.97   By contrast, *TCGA 1992, s 162* provides a mandatory rollover of the gain where a person who is not a company transfers to a company a business as a going concern, together with the whole assets of the business. This must take us back to the question 'what is a business?' As already noted, there is no definition in *TCGA 1992*.

In *Ramsay v HMRC* [2013] UKUT 226 (TCC) (see **2.42**), the taxpayer was the landlord of a large Victorian property which had been converted into ten flats, of which five were occupied by tenants at the relevant time. The taxpayer (and her husband) transferred the property to a company, in exchange for shares in the company. Her tax return for the year of transfer included a claim for incorporation relief under *TCGA 1992, s 162*. Following an enquiry, HMRC issued a closure notice on the basis that *TCGA 1992, s 162* relief did not apply. The taxpayer appealed.

The First-tier Tribunal held that the taxpayer's activities were 'normal and incidental to the owning of an investment property', and dismissed her appeal. However, the Upper Tribunal allowed Mrs Ramsay's subsequent appeal, concluding that the activity undertaken in respect of the property overall was sufficient in nature and extent to amount to a business for *TCGA 1992, s 162* purposes. Whilst the activities could equally have been undertaken by a property investor, where the degree of activity outweighs what might normally be expected to be carried out by a mere passive investor, the tribunal held that this would amount to a business.

HMRC's Capital Gains Manual (at CG65715) tries to extract a meaning from case law. The guidance (rather unhelpfully) states that it is a question of fact whether a particular activity constitutes a business, and that it is not easy to draw the line. Following the *Ramsay* case (in which Mrs Ramsay was found to have worked in the property business for about 20 hours per week), HMRC's guidance instructs their officers as follows: 'You should accept that incorporation relief will be available where an individual spends 20 hours or more a week personally undertaking the sort of activities that are indicative of a business. Other cases should be considered carefully'.

Interestingly, it has been held for VAT purposes that the letting of property can amount to a business activity (see *D A Walker v Customs and Excise Commissioners* [1976] VATTR 10, and *G W and J A Green v Customs and Excise Commissioners* (1992, Decision 9016)). In the former case, the letting of three semi-detached houses on assured tenancies was considered to be a business in VAT terms.

In addition, the Upper Tribunal in the *Ramsay* case (see above) referred to various factors identified in another VAT case, *Customs and Excise*

Commissioners v Lord Fisher [1981] STC 238, and considered that those factors are of general application to the question whether the circumstances describe a business:

(1)   whether the activity is a 'serious undertaking earnestly pursued';

(2)   whether the activity is an 'occupation or function actively pursued with a reasonable or recognisable continuity';

(3)   whether the activity has 'a certain measure of substance as measured by the quarterly or annual value of taxable supplies made';

(4)   whether the activity was 'conducted in a regular manner and on sound and recognised business principles';

(5)   whether the activity is 'predominantly concerned with the making of taxable supplies to consumers for a consideration'; and

(6)   whether the taxable supplies are 'of a kind which … are commonly made by those who seek to profit by them'.

2.98   Incorporation relief in *TCGA 1992, s 162* not only requires a transfer of the business, but of the business 'as a going concern'. The term 'going concern' predicates something more than transfer of a mere collection of assets. There must be an active infrastructure to go with it. On that basis, it seems unlikely in many cases that a property letting business could be transferred to a company with the benefit of *TCGA 1992, s 162* relief. However, some commentators have adopted a more optimistic view that active property letting is arguably a business activity (see, for example, Malcolm Gunn's article 'It's my business' in *Taxation*, 8 November 2007).

A cautious approach is advocated. If incorporation was successfully challenged by HMRC on enquiry, a very large unrelieved gain could ensue with no cash to meet the liability. This uncertainty will clearly be unsatisfactory for those taxpayers seeking to rely on incorporation relief under *TCGA 1992, s 162*. This has resulted in some taxpayers (or their advisers) seeking advance assurance from HMRC under the non-statutory business clearance service that their undertaking amounts to a business for these purposes (and is therefore capable of being transferred as a going concern).

There is no statutory clearance on the availability of *TCGA 1992, s 162* relief. A non-statutory business clearance application to HMRC could be considered (see   www.gov.uk/guidance/non-statutory-clearance-service-guidance)   in advance of the incorporation taking place. HMRC provide a checklist of information ('Annex A') to be included in the clearance application. However, there is anecdotal evidence that HMRC have been unwilling to provide such clearances in some instances where they consider that the incorporation is being undertaken for tax planning reasons.

Where properties meet the conditions to be treated as furnished holiday lettings, they are automatically deemed to be a trade for certain tax purposes. In particular, in the current context, *TCGA 1992, ss 241(3A) and 241A(5)* treat the furnished holiday letting business as a trade for the purposes of *TCGA 1992, s 165*. Therefore, it is possible to transfer a property used for furnished holiday letting at undervalue (to a company) and hold over any capital gain arising by making a claim under *TCGA 1992, s 165*. In other words, it is possible to incorporate a property-letting business which consists entirely of furnished holiday lettings without triggering a taxable capital gain.

However, it should be borne in mind that a furnished holiday letting is unlikely to qualify for BPR for IHT purposes (see **2.95**), unless the level of services offered is exceptionally high.

2.99   One should also bear in mind the impact of SDLT if any land being transferred is situated in either England or Northern Ireland (or LBTT if the land is situated in Scotland, or LTT if the land is situated in Wales) . Where land and buildings are transferred to a company which is connected (*Corporation Tax Act 2010, s 1122*) with the transferor, SDLT (or LBTT, LTT) is normally charged by reference to market value (*Finance Act 2003, s 53; LBTT(S)A 2013, s 22; LTTADT(W)A 2017, s 22*) (see **2.76**).

A higher rate of SDLT applies in respect of additional dwellings and dwellings purchased by companies irrespective of whether it is the first dwelling acquired by the company (*FA 2003, Sch 4ZA* – 'higher rate transactions'). Consequently, the SDLT rates applying to higher rate transactions are 3% higher than the equivalent normal residential rates, subject to certain exceptions including purchases for consideration less than £40,000.

When several properties are transferred in a single transaction (or a series of linked transactions), it is normally necessary to aggregate the consideration for all to determine the SDLT rate, which then applies to all of the transfers (*FA 2003, s 55(4)*). However, where more than one dwelling is transferred in this way, the purchaser(s) may claim for the rate to be determined on the basis of the average consideration per property (ie a claim for 'multiple dwellings relief' – *FA 2003, Sch 6B*). It is not possible for the rate to drop below 1% if the claim is made (*FA 2003, Sch 6B, para 5(2)*). Note that, where a claim to multiple dwellings relief is made, the higher rates of SDLT apply in calculating the SDLT payable if the relevant transaction is a 'higher rates transaction' (*FA 2003, Sch 6B, para 5(6A)*). Any dwellings for which the 15% SDLT 'slab' rate applies (see below) are excluded (*FA 2003, Sch 6B, para 2(4)(aa)*). It should also be noted that, in the absence of a claim for multiple dwellings relief, where six or more dwellings are the subject of a single transaction, they are treated as wholly non-residential property (*FA 2003, s 116(7)*), so that the SDLT rates for non-residential property apply to the transaction.

The 15% 'slab' rate (ie meaning that the whole of the consideration given for the dwelling is charged at a single rate of 15%) of SDLT initially applied to residential properties over £2m purchased by companies and other 'non-natural persons' (NNPs) with effect from 21 March 2012 (*FA 2003, Sch 4A*). However, the threshold for the 15% SDLT rate was subsequently reduced in *FA 2014* to £500,000 for land transactions with an effective date on or after 20 March 2014, subject to transitional rules. There are, however, certain exemptions from the 15% slab rate, including acquisitions by property developers or dwellings acquired for the purposes of a property rental business (*FA 2003, Sch 4A, para 5(1)(a)* and *(b)*) or for a business using the dwelling in the course of a trading activity (*FA 2003, Sch 4A, para 5(1)(ab)*), and so on. There is no equivalent slab rate within the LBTT or LTT regime.

In Scotland, a higher rate of LBTT applies for purchases of additional residential properties, similar to its SDLT equivalent. The 'additional dwelling supplement' applies to individuals acquiring dwellings as second homes etc or as part of a business of investing or dealing in land (either conducting the business as a sole trader or as a partner in a partnership), and first purchases of residential properties (for £40,000 or more) by companies and certain trusts. The additional LBTT is 3% of the relevant consideration. The legislation can be found at *LBTT(S)A 2013, Sch 2A* ('Additional amount: transactions relating to second homes etc'). There are some important differences between the SDLT and LBTT higher rate regimes, which are beyond the scope of this chapter.

In Wales, a 'higher rates residential property transaction' is subject to a higher rate of LTT of 3% on top of the main residential rates, for transactions involving additional dwellings by individuals costing £40,000 or more, and also in respect of the acquisition of dwellings where the buyer is not an individual (such as a company), where the cost of the dwelling is £40,000 or more (*LTTADT(W)A 2017, Sch 5*).

For detailed commentary on this subject, readers are referred to *Stamp Taxes 2018/19* and *Land and Business Transaction Tax 2018/19* (both Bloomsbury Professional). As indicated above, under LBTT there is no equivalent of the SDLT 15% slab rate which applies to residential properties acquired for consideration of over £500,000 purchased by companies and other NNPs.

In addition, legislation in *FA 2013* introduced an 'annual tax on enveloped dwellings' (ATED) worth more than £2m, which are owned by NNPs (ie companies, partnerships with company members and collective investment schemes), subject to a limited range of reliefs (eg for property rental businesses, property developers, etc) (*FA 2013, Pt 3*). The ATED applies in relation to properties under the ownership of the NNP on or after 1 April 2013. The ATED applies to properties situated in any part of the UK notwithstanding the introduction of LBTT and LTT respectively in Scotland and Wales. The threshold of £2m was progressively reduced to £500,000 in *FA 2014*. From 1 April 2015, an annual charge of £7,000 applied for properties within a band with a value greater than £1m but not more than £2m. From 1 April 2016, an annual charge of £3,500 applied to properties within an additional band with a value greater than £500,000 but not more than £1m. Further changes introduced in *FA 2015* increased the annual ATED charges for properties valued at more than £2m, over and above the normal consumer prices index increase. These increased charges applied with effect from the chargeable period beginning on 1 April 2015.

It is specifically provided that the ATED charge will be increased each year in line with increases in the Consumer Price Index to the previous September, rounded down to the next £50 (*FA 2013, s 101*). The rates for the year commencing on 1 April 2018 are as follows:

Value	Tax
More than £500,000 but not more than £1 million	£3,600
More than £1 million but not more than £2 million	£7,250
More than £2 million but not more than £5 million	£24,250
More than £5 million but not more than £10 million	£56,550
More than £10 million but not more than £20 million	£113,400
More than £20 million	£226,950

Furthermore, legislation introduced in *FA 2013* extended the CGT regime to gains on disposals by NNPs of UK residential property or interests in such property from 6 April 2013, where the consideration exceeds £2m (reduced proportionately if the NNP owns or disposes of only part of the property). The charge applies to both resident and non-resident NNPs, and affects those companies or collective schemes within the scope of the ATED (see above). A CGT charge of 28% is imposed (*TCGA 1992, s 4(3A)*). However, gains accruing before 6 April 2013 remain outside the scope of the CGT charge. The ATED-related CGT charge was extended from 6 April 2015 to properties worth more than £1m but not more than £2m, and further extended from 6 April 2016 to properties worth more than £500,000 (*TCGA 1992, s 2D* as amended).

Further provisions (introduced in *Finance Act 2015*) extended the scope of CGT to include gains on the disposal of UK residential property interests by non-UK resident persons (or by individuals in the overseas part of a split year) from 6 April 2015. A restriction in private residence relief was also introduced in *Finance Act 2015* for properties located in a territory in which the individual is not tax resident, broadly where the person does not meet a 90-day test for time spent in the property over the year (*TCGA 1992, s 222C*).

2.100 Historically, care was needed to ensure that a company wholly or mainly in receipt of property rental income was not a close investment holding company (CIHC), which was subject to corporation tax at the main rate (although this would not be the case if, for example, all the properties were let to unconnected third parties).

However, the introduction of a single corporation tax rate and abolition of the small profits rate for companies that do not have ring fence profits (from 1 April 2015) have meant that there is no longer a disadvantage to a company being a CIHC in terms of corporation tax rates.

It should be noted that a potential difficulty arising from CIHC status applies to an investor who borrows to buy shares in, or lend money to, a close company. While relief on the loan interest would normally be due for the shareholder (under *ITA 2007, s 392*), relief is denied where the close company in question is a CIHC. Whilst the CIHC rules were repealed from financial year 2015, *ITA 2007, s 393A* restricts the availability of income tax relief for payments of interest on loans to invest in, or lend to, close companies which are CIHCs.

A close company is automatically treated as a CIHC unless it falls within one of various stated exceptions to CIHC status. The exceptions to CIHC status apply to close companies which exist wholly or mainly, throughout the accounting period under consideration, for one or more permitted purposes, such as carrying on a trade or trades on a commercial basis, or making investments in land (including buildings) which is, or is intended to be, let commercially (see *ITA 2007, s 393A(2)*).

Entrepreneurs' relief and property

2.101 Entrepreneurs' relief is generally not available on disposals of residential property. However, as indicated at **2.98** above, an exception to this general rule applies in respect of commercial furnished holiday lettings in the UK (*TCGA 1992, s 241(3A)*) or elsewhere in the EEA (*TCGA 1992, s 241A(5)*).

The disposal of a commercial property does not of itself qualify for entrepreneurs' relief. However, relief may be available if there is a disposal of the whole or part of a trading business including the premises.

In addition, a measure of relief may apply if the property disposal is 'associated' (within *TCGA 1992, s 169K*) with a disposal of the partnership interest, or a disposal of shares in the company, if certain conditions are satisfied (eg the disposal is associated with a material disposal of the whole or part of the partnership interest or all or some of the company's ordinary shares or securities, it is part of the individual's withdrawal from participation in the business, the property disposed of was used for business purposes throughout a one-year period ending with the material disposal (or cessation of the business, if earlier), and the disposal is of a property owned by the individual throughout the three-year period ending with the date of disposal).

However, it should be noted that entrepreneurs' relief is denied if a market rent is charged for the property, and is subject to restriction (on a 'just and reasonable' basis) if the rent charged is below market value (*TCGA 1992, s 169P*). The entrepreneurs' relief legislation as originally drafted also provided for the restriction or denial of relief if rent had been charged for periods before the relief was introduced. However, this provision was considered by many to be unduly harsh, and a transitional rule was therefore included so that periods prior to 6 April 2008 can be ignored for these purposes (*FA 2008, Sch 3, para 6*).

Employment-related securities

2.102   There is a requirement (in *ITEPA 2003, ss 421J* and *421K(3)(a)*) to notify HMRC when shares in a company are issued to employees (including past or future employees). The relevant return (ie HMRC's 'other' template, previously form 42) must be made to HMRC by 6 July following the relevant tax year.

HMRC guidance states that no report is required where a company is incorporated and all founder shares are acquired at nominal value (NB the other requirements are that no form of security is required; the shares are not acquired by reason of, or in connection with, another employment; and the shares are acquired by a director or prospective director of the company or someone who has a personal family relationship with the director, and the right or opportunity is made available in the normal course of the domestic, family or personal relationship of that person).

Furthermore, no report is required if further shares are allotted after a new company is incorporated, but before the commencement of business or transfer of assets to the company, where certain conditions are satisfied (ie the additional shares are acquired by a founder shareholder or the person is a director or prospective director of the company, the shares are acquired at nominal value, and the shares are not acquired by reason of, or in connection with, another employment).

However, if further shares are allotted after the company has commenced business, HMRC's view is that a return is required, albeit only in respect of those additional shares (see Example 3 at ERSM140040).

HMRC's requirement that the company's shares are acquired at nominal value effectively means that incorporations under *TCGA 1992, s 162* (ie under which the assets of the unincorporated business are transferred to the company wholly or partly in exchange for shares) will require a return to be made to HMRC.

An end of year return template, technical note and guidance notes can be accessed via the GOV.UK website (tinyurl.com/Template-ERS).

DISINCORPORATION

Background

2.103   While there can be clear benefits from operating through a company, and a company may at some stage have been chosen as the optimum operating vehicle for a business, there will be circumstances in which some businesses might benefit from 'disincorporating' and operating through a sole trader or partnership structure instead.

This decision might be prompted by some of the drawbacks of trading through a company, including substantial company car tax liabilities for the business owner (as a director or employee), operating PAYE on their 'drawings' (in the form of salaries and bonuses), additional accountancy fees, *Companies Act* compliance and reporting, etc.

And many businesses which incorporated to take account of the 0%/10% corporation tax rates in effect between the 2000 and 2005 financial years may have subsequently lost much of those tax savings as the corporation tax rate currently stands at 19% (from 1 April 2017).

The incorporation/disincorporation debate has certainly become more relevant as company profit extraction costs have increased as a result of changes to the taxation of dividends from 5 April 2016 (in *Finance Act 2016*) and from 5 April 2018 (in *Finance (No 2) Act 2017*).

And while, as discussed above at **2.41** *et seq*, the legislation provides a specific CGT relief on incorporation – for the transfer of an existing sole trader or partnership business into a company, through the holdover of gains under *TCGA 1992, s 162* (see **2.42**) – there was no equivalent CGT relieving provision for disincorporation until *Finance Act 2013*.

Finance Act 2013 introduced a temporary disincorporation relief for small companies. The effect of this relief was that when a qualifying business disincorporated, and its assets were transferred to individuals, there was no immediate corporation tax on chargeable gains that arose (on qualifying assets) within the company. This relief is explained in more detail in **2.121**. Note that the relief did not prevent potential charges arising on the shareholders/owners of the company.

As the 'disincorporation' legislation applied only to the smallest companies, the next few sections (**2.104–2.120**) deal with the consequences of disincorporation for the majority of companies which were not eligible for disincorporation relief.

Planning a disincorporation

2.104 Disincorporation generally involves the transfer of the assets and liabilities of a business – including its goodwill, property, plant and machinery, stock and creditors – as a going concern to the shareholder(s) who then continue the business in an unincorporated form.

The potential tax charges and events which arise on a disincorporation are similar to those which would occur on any sale of a company's business and assets to a 'third party'. Disincorporation may, therefore, potentially be implemented with minimal tax costs where there are no significant property interests or business goodwill in the incorporated business.

Legal mechanics

2.105 Disincorporation can be implemented through a distribution or sale of the business to the shareholders.

From a company law perspective, the disincorporation of a business is likely to take place by means of a formal winding-up (a members' voluntary liquidation) or an informal winding-up (a simple dissolution or 'striking off').

A distribution may arise through a formal or informal winding up, or it can be made by way of a 'normal' distribution to the shareholders.

Members' voluntary liquidation

2.106 This type of liquidation is largely controlled by the company's shareholders and can be used only where the company being liquidated is solvent (*Insolvency Act 1986, Ch III, Pt IV*). Generally, a special resolution of the shareholders is required to place the company into voluntary liquidation, and the directors must make a statutory 'declaration of solvency' (so that, after having made a full inquiry, they declare that the company will be able to pay its debts within the following 12 months).

The liquidator can then wind up the company which, under a disincorporation, would entail the transfer of the business and assets to the shareholder(s). The liquidator will pay off the creditors and distribute the surplus to the shareholder(s).

The distribution to the shareholder(s) under a formal winding-up should be a capital one (under *TCGA 1992, s 122*).

However, the 'transaction in securities' anti-avoidance provisions contained in *ITA 2007, Pt 13, Ch 1* may need to be considered (see **2.119**). And the targeted anti-avoidance rule in *ITTOIA 2005, s 396B*, introduced by *Finance Act 2016*, may also be in point where a new business is to be started soon after a members' voluntary liquidation, in order to counter any potential 'phoenixism' risk.

The main issue to consider before going down this route is the costs of a 'formal' voluntary liquidation, particularly in relation to the value of the assets within the company.

'Dissolution' or 'striking off'

2.107 Due to the relatively high costs of a formal liquidation, many owner-managers prefer the informal winding-up route – where a company is 'dissolved' by being 'struck off' the Companies House register (*CA 2006, s 1000*).

However, where a company disincorporates by distributing its assets to its shareholders as part of an informal winding up, the shareholders will generally be subject to tax on an income (rather than capital) distribution basis (*CTA 2010, s 1020*). An income distribution will generally be less tax-efficient than a capital distribution in the hands of the shareholders – with entrepreneurs' relief only potentially being available in relation to capital distributions.

The distribution of the assets under an informal winding up may, however, be treated as a capital distribution in the hands of the shareholders where certain conditions are met.

Under a 'dissolution', the company will first transfer its trade and assets to an unincorporated business. (The transfer can be challenged by any minority shareholder or creditor who feels that this is prejudicial to their interests.) Liabilities can either be settled by the company or assigned to the successor business – provided that agreement is obtained from the relevant creditors. The company will then be dissolved under *CA 2006, s 1003*. A dissolution therefore involves fewer legal formalities and minimises costs. However, unlike a liquidation, it is not legally possible for a company to distribute its share capital (or any other non-distributable reserves).

Under Extra-Statutory Concession C16, HMRC were normally prepared to treat a distribution made to the shareholders prior to dissolution as having been made under a formal winding up. The company was required to give certain assurances to the Inspector beforehand. Such a distribution would therefore be treated as a capital distribution (*CTA 2010, s 1030*) for the shareholder, subject again to the 'transaction in securities' anti-avoidance provisions (see **2.119**). The benefit of ESC C16 was that the shareholders could take advantage of the lower tax rates applying to capital distributions.

Until October 2011, any 'unauthorised distributions' (of share capital, for example) could theoretically have been collected by the Office of the Treasury Solicitor. From October 2011, the Treasury Solicitor's Department withdrew its 'Guidelines about the Distribution of a Company's Share Capital', which had stated that the Treasury Solicitor would waive the Crown's right to any funds which a company distributes to its members prior to an informal striking off using ESC C16, where the amount of the 'unauthorised' distribution was less than £4,000.

The Office of the Treasury Solicitor then confirmed that in relation to distributions made from 14 October 2011, it would not seek to recover unauthorised distributions made prior to dissolution (http://webarchive. nationalarchives.gov.uk/20130705010933/http://www.bonavacantia.gov.uk/output/BVC17-FAQS.aspx).

However, from a tax perspective, the House of Lords decision in *R (on the application of Wilkinson) v Inland Revenue Commissioners* [2005] UKHL 30 made it clear that the scope of HMRC administrative discretion to make concessions which depart from the strict statutory position is not as wide as previously thought.

Accordingly, HMRC put ESC C16 on the statute books (*CTA 2010, ss 1030A* and *1030B*), but also took the opportunity to restrict the (favourable) capital treatment to distributions not exceeding £25,000. The legislation took effect from 1 March 2012 and the introduction of this limit has resulted in smaller companies, with relatively few assets, being able to take advantage of the informal winding-up route. Otherwise, many owner-managers may opt for a formal liquidation to take advantage of the beneficial capital gains tax treatment, even if the professional costs of doing so are likely to be significant.

Details of which companies are eligible for disincorporation relief are set out at **2.121** below.

The rest of this chapter assumes that the company is wound up rather than being dissolved.

Case study – B&B Ltd and Richard

2.108   Richard had run his bed and breakfast business for many years through his 100% owned company, B&B Ltd. He decided that he would like to run the business as a sole trader. The disincorporation date was 28 February 2018 (when the trade would be transferred to Richard and the company would be wound up).

The balance sheet at 28 February 2018 (reflecting the estimated trading profits to date) is shown in **Table 2.1**.

Table 2.1

	Note		Book value	Market value
Freehold property	1		120,000	220,000
Goodwill	2		–	20,000
Fittings, plant and equipment	3			
Cost		20,000		
Less: depreciation	4	(8,000)	12,000	15,000
Stock	4		10,000	12,000
Debtors			7,000	
Bank overdraft			(4,000)	
Creditors	5		(9,000)	
Represented by share capital (£100) and reserves			£136,000	

Notes:

1   The freehold property has not been subject to depreciation – and represents the cost of the premises when it was acquired in March 2000.

2   The goodwill value is considered to represent 'free' (pre-1 April 2002) goodwill – and is not attributable to the premises or Richard personally!

3   The tax written-down value of the plant etc at 31 August 2017 was £9,000.

4 Stock and plant, etc will be transferred at their book values.

5 No tax provision has been made in the above figures.

In the six months to 28 February 2018, the tax-adjusted trading profit (before making any cessation adjustments) was expected to be £40,000.

The trade and assets were transferred to Richard on 28 February 2018, so that he could continue to operate the business as a sole trader. Provided the appropriate tax elections are made in relation to trading stock (*CTA 2009, s 167*) and plant (*CAA 2001, s 266*), the corporation tax computation for the six months to 28 February 2018 would be as follows:

Table 2.2

	£
Tax-adjusted trading profit (no cessation adjustments)	40,000
Chargeable gain on sale of freehold property (£220,000 – £120,000) (ignore indexation allowance)	100,000
Chargeable gain on sale of goodwill (£20,000 – £nil base cost)	20,000
Taxable profits for the six months to 28 February 2018	160,000
Corporation tax liability @ 19%	30,400

Hence, B&B Ltd would incur a £30,400 corporation tax charge in its final trading period – of which £22,800 arose as a result of the chargeable gains realised on the transfer of its property and goodwill to the shareholder on disincorporation.

Main corporation tax consequences

Deemed cessation of trade

2.109 There is a deemed cessation of trade for corporation tax purposes on its transfer to Richard, in the case study above, even though the actual trade is continuing (albeit under different ownership) (*CTA 2009, s 41*).

Termination of corporation tax accounting period

2.110 The cessation of trade automatically brings to an end the current corporation tax accounting period (CTAP) of B&B Ltd. The company will therefore have a six-month CTAP to 28 February 2018 (*CTA 2009, s 10*).

Trading losses

2.111   If B&B Ltd incurred a trading loss in its final CTAP, this could be offset against any other corporation tax profits, including chargeable gains, of the current and preceding year (*CTA 2010, s 37(3)*). However, the current trading loss cannot be matched against gains arising from chargeable assets transferred/distributed to the shareholders during the course of the winding-up/dissolution, since these would arise in the subsequent CTAP (see below). In such cases, a sale of the chargeable assets to the shareholders at open market value before 'cessation' should be considered to achieve the appropriate loss offset.

The possibility of making a terminal loss relief claim should only be considered after all other forms of loss relief have been exhausted (*CTA 2010, s 39*).

If B&B Ltd had any unused trading losses, these would effectively be lost on the disincorporation since they cannot be carried forward beyond the deemed cessation of trade (*CTA 2010, ss 45, 45A*). There is no provision for the transfer of trading losses to the unincorporated successor business.

Transfer of closing trading stock

2.112   In the Case Study above, as B&B Ltd (the transferor company) is 'connected' with Richard (see *CTA 2009, s 168*), who will continue to carry on the trade, the deemed 'market value' rule in *CTA 2009, s 166* will apply to the transfer of closing stock.

However, in most cases, it should be possible for the parties to make a joint election under *CTA 2009, s 167* to transfer the stock at its actual transfer value (or, if higher, the book value). In the unlikely event of the company being subject to UK-to-UK transfer pricing, the stock must be transferred at an arm's-length market value (*CTA 2009, s 162*).

Capital allowances: plant and machinery

2.113   The normal 'capital allowance' cessation rules apply. No writing down allowances are given in the final basis period and a balancing adjustment is calculated (*CAA 2001, s 61* and Table Item 6). The balancing adjustment will generally be computed by reference to the actual transfer value, but market value would be applied where the parties are 'connected', as in the Case Study above (*CAA 2001, s 575*).

However, if both parties make an election under *CAA 2001, s 266* the cessation rules will not apply and the plant can be transferred at its tax written-down value (*CAA 2001, s 267*). In this context, an election to transfer the plant at its tax written-down value may not be advantageous if the disincorporating company is going to have unrelieved trading losses. In such cases, a balancing charge could be used to absorb the loss, thus increasing the tax value of the plant for the successor business.

VAT

2.114 Assuming the business is VAT registered, the general rule is that where a trade ceases, the 'registered person' is deemed to make a taxable supply of all the goods then held by the business. However, since the business will be transferred to the shareholder(s) who will continue to carry it on as a sole trader/partnership, there should be no VAT levied on the transfer (by virtue of the 'transfer of going concern' provisions in the *VAT (Special Provisions) Order 1995, SI 1995/1268, art 5*).

To avoid any delays obtaining a new VAT registration it may be considered appropriate to elect to continue to use the business's existing VAT registration number (on form VAT 68), particularly as the history of the business will be well known to the shareholder(s).

Capital gains on transfer of assets

2.115 Chargeable gains will arise when the assets are transferred to the shareholders. The chargeable assets of the company (including goodwill) are deemed to be disposed of at market value for tax purposes (*TCGA 1992, s 17*).

The property held by B&B Ltd in the Case Study above might be distributed *in specie* during the winding-up to avoid SDLT (see **2.116**). This would still trigger a chargeable gain, but in the subsequent CTAP by reference to the property's market value.

Stamp duty land tax

2.116 A stamp duty land tax (SDLT) charge may arise on the shareholders where land or property is transferred to them on disincorporation. SDLT is generally charged on the consideration provided for the transfer so if, in the course of the disincorporation, the shareholders bought the property from the company, SDLT would be chargeable on the purchase price paid.

Where the property is owned by the company, the CGT cost of 'disincorporating' may prove to be prohibitive, particularly if a substantial capital gain is likely to arise. If the decision to disincorporate has been made and the tax cost of transferring the property is manageable, then it may often be preferable to 'distribute' it to the shareholders in specie during the winding-up. This will normally avoid any SDLT charge (see *Finance Act 2003, Sch 3, para 1*) and ranks as a capital distribution in the shareholder's hands. However, any assumption of a property loan/mortgage by the shareholders would represent 'consideration' for the transfer with a consequent SDLT charge.

If the property is sold to the shareholders as, or just before, the trade ceases (this may be done, for example, to access trading losses that might otherwise remain unused), then SDLT will potentially be payable.

Goodwill

2.117 Clearly, business goodwill will follow the transfer of the trade and may trigger a significant capital gain, depending on the market value agreed with HMRC. However, where a business was established after 31 March 2002, the gain will be treated as a taxable (trading) credit under the intangible fixed assets regime in *CTA 2009, Pt 8.*

Given HMRC's recent stance with regard to goodwill valuations on business incorporations (see **2.61** et seq), for example where the trader has opted to sell goodwill to the newly incorporated company at its full market value, it will be interesting to see whether the same approach is adopted on a disincorporation. For many small businesses, HMRC have typically contended that the value of transferable goodwill is low or insignificant. This is because, HMRC argue, most if not all of the goodwill attaches to the proprietor personally and so is not capable of being transferred. (The over-analytical approach adopted by HMRC in relation to goodwill was questioned by the Special Commissioner in *Balloon Promotions v Wilson (Inspector of Taxes)* [2006] STC (SCD) 167.)

Whilst many small 'one-man-band' type businesses might have minimal goodwill, there will be a number of businesses which have built up significant 'free' goodwill attributable to the reputation built up by the business, its name and trade connections, and so on. Any potential uncertainty surrounding the value of goodwill in these cases must be carefully factored into the tax cost likely to arise on the disincorporation. Agreeing the value of goodwill with HMRC Shares and Assets Valuations could well turn out to be a protracted process. In some cases the CGT involved may well make the disincorporation too expensive.

Tax liabilities arising on shareholders

2.118 The company may be wound up as part of the disincorporation and any amounts/assets distributed will normally represent a capital distribution in the hands of the shareholder(s). The amount will therefore be subject to CGT (provided HMRC do not successfully invoke the transactions in securities anti-avoidance legislation (see **2.119**).

Inevitably, a disincorporation will normally involve a classic 'double tax' charge, since the tax suffered by the shareholder on the capital distribution creates a further tax liability on the appreciation in the value of the company's chargeable assets, which has already been taxed in the company.

Entrepreneurs' relief may be available on any capital distributions. Otherwise, the capital distributions will currently attract CGT at either 10% or 20%. The rate applicable will be determined by each shareholder's income and other gains made in tax year of the distribution.

Where a shareholder receives a capital distribution in respect of any shares, he shall be treated as if he had received the consideration for the disposal of his shares (*TCGA 1992, s 122(1)*). This includes any distribution made in the dissolution or winding-up of the company. Therefore, if the conditions for entrepreneurs' relief are met the capital distribution received will suffer a 10% charge on the first £10m of gains (less any entrepreneurs' relief previously claimed). Based on the case study, the estimated CGT payable by Richard on the liquidator's distribution is shown below in **Table 2.3**:

Table 2.3

	£	£
Net reserves at 28 February 2018 (before disincorporation)		136,000
Realisations:		
Goodwill – surplus on transfer		20,000
Freehold property – surplus on transfer/ distribution in specie – £220,000 *less* £120,000		100,000
		256,000
Less: Corporation tax liabilities – (see **Table 2.2**)	(30,400)	
Liquidator's fees and other costs (say)	(8,000)	(38,400)
Surplus available to distribute		£217,600

Based on the above, Richard's estimated CGT liability (ignoring his negligible base cost) would be approximately £20,630 calculated as follows:

	£
Distribution	217,600
Less: Annual exemption	(11,300)
Gain qualifying for entrepreneurs' relief	206,300
CGT liability @ 10%	20,630

Potential impact of anti-avoidance rules

2.119   The 'transaction in securities' provisions now contained (for income tax purposes) in *ITA 2007, Pt 13, Ch 1* must always be considered in relation to transactions involving the company's shareholders.

Following the House of Lords decision in *IRC v Laird Group Plc* [2002] STC 722, the better view was that (by itself) the winding-up and distribution of the company's assets by a liquidator would not fall within the ambit of this legislation. On the other hand, *CIR v Joiner* [1975] STC 657 considered that these provisions would apply where a company's shareholders continue to carry on the trade in a new company *after liquidation*, having extracted the old company's distributable reserves as capital (rather than income). This view is also supported in HMRC's Company Taxation Manual (CTM36850).

Finance Act 2016 widens the 'transaction in securities' provisions in *ITA 2007, Pt 13* to include a distribution on liquidation. However, HMRC confirmed (in their meeting with the ICAEW Tax Faculty on 26 January 2016) that 'there would be no counteraction under the TIS as long as it was a simple liquidation with no successor company or other ancillary issues' (tinyurl.com/ ICAEW-Taxguide02-16).

Even where the disincorporating trade is being transferred into personal ownership (rather than a commonly-owned company), there may in some cases be a risk that HMRC would seek to counteract the 'tax advantage' from the liquidation/dissolution (ie extracting the reserves in an income tax-free form as a capital receipt) under *ITA 2007, s 684*. However, provided it can be demonstrated that the disincorporation was motivated by sound commercial reasons, the normal 'let-out' in *ITA 2007, s 685* should still be available.

2.120   The practical application of *ITA 2007, Pt 13, Ch 1* clearly depends on HMRC's interpretation of the facts in each case. For example, HMRC are likely to challenge those cases where they suspect the shareholders have only disincorporated to extract the company's reserves at a beneficial CGT rate (assisted by entrepreneurs' relief). On the other hand, where all (or substantially all) of the company's funds need to be re-invested in the successor sole trade/partnership business, a more benign approach is likely to be taken. The overall tax costs of the disincorporation may also be an important factor in HMRC's deliberations.

Shareholders requiring certainty on the tax treatment of the capital distribution could consider applying for advance clearance under *ITA 2007, s 701* to confirm HMRC's agreement that the bona fide test is satisfied.

Taxpayers also need to consider the Targeted Anti Avoidance Rule (TAAR) on distributions in the winding up of a UK resident company in *ITTOIA 2005, s 396B* (or *s 404A*, in the case of non-UK resident companies), as introduced by *Finance Act 2016*. Where a number of conditions are satisfied, the TAAR will apply to tax a distribution in respect of share capital on a winding-up as if it was an income distribution. One of those conditions is that the main purposes, or one of the main purposes, of the arrangements is to gain a tax advantage. Hence, tax-motivated disincorporations will potentially be subject to the new TAAR.

There is no formal clearance procedure for the new TAAR, although HMRC have published guidance and examples of what transactions they consider to be caught by the new provisions (https://www.gov.uk/hmrc-internal-manuals/company-taxation-manual/ctm36300).

Disincorporation relief

2.121 Following the recommendations of the Office of Tax Simplification, the *Finance Act 2013* introduced disincorporation relief so that a double tax charge would not arise (on both the company and the shareholders) where the company's business assets were transferred to the shareholder(s) who carried on the business either as a sole trader or within a partnership.

The effect of making a disincorporation relief claim was that the capital gains arising on the transfer of goodwill and land and buildings used in the business would be deferred when these assets were transferred to the shareholders who carried on the business. However, the disincorporation relief only applied where the value of the qualifying assets did not exceed £100,000, so that only the very smallest of businesses could benefit from the relief.

To enable a claim for disincorporation relief to be made five conditions needed to be met:

(1)   The business was transferred as a going concern.

(2)   The business was transferred together with all the assets of the business (other than cash).

(3)   The total market value of the qualifying assets did not exceed £100,000 (as mentioned above, qualifying assets were restricted to goodwill and land and buildings).

(4)   All the shareholders to whom the business was transferred were individuals.

(5)   All shareholders must have held their shares for at least 12 months prior to the date of disincorporation.

The relief claim had to be made jointly by the company and all the shareholders to whom the business was transferred within two years from the business transfer date, and was irrevocable.

The measure was a temporary one and for businesses to qualify the transfer had to take place between 1 April 2013 and 31 March 2018 inclusive. The reasoning behind this was that many businesses incorporated in 2002 when the 0% rate of corporation tax was introduced, and given that the 0% rate had been abolished, the smaller businesses might no longer wish to remain incorporated.

Even if a company met all the conditions listed above there was still likely to be a charge on the shareholders when the assets were transferred to them. If the assets transferred (including non-qualifying assets) were below the £25,000 limit then the company could be dissolved and the shareholders would be subject to a capital gains tax charge. However, if the assets transferred exceeded £25,000 then to obtain the capital gains tax treatment, the business would need to follow the winding-up route and the increased expenses likely to be incurred may have persuaded businesses to remain incorporated.

In its Autumn Budget 2017, the government confirmed that disincorporation relief would not be available beyond 31 March 2018.

Chapter 3

Partnerships

David Whiscombe

SIGNPOSTS

- **Scope** – Partnerships and LLPs are two of the possible structures available when a number of persons come together to carry on a business. Although different legally, partnerships and LLPs are treated in broadly the same way for tax purposes (see **3.1–3.4**).

- **Computational rules** – The same rules generally apply in computing partnership profits as to other traders but their application in particular areas can raise problems or opportunities (see **3.5–3.21**).

- **Profit-sharing** – The basis on which taxable profits are shared between partners may not always be straightforward (see **3.22–3.23**) and disputes may arise (see **3.24–3.29**).

- **Capital gains tax** – Gains may arise not only on actual disposals but also on a change in profit-sharing ratios including on mergers and demergers (see **3.30–3.35**).

- **Entrepreneurs' relief** – Entrepreneurs' relief may be available to partners, former partners and certain trustees (see **3.36–3.40**).

- **Family partnerships** – Care must be taken with the settlements legislation but by no means all family or non-commercial arrangements are vulnerable (see **3.41–3.44**).

- **Salaried partners** – May be treated differently as between ordinary partnership and LLPs, to which a special 'disguised remuneration' regime applies (see **3.45–3.47**).

- **Company partners** – Can be attractive in some circumstances but need to be used with care, especially when alongside connected individuals in the same partnership (see **3.48–3.73**).

- **Stamp Duty Land Tax** – the SDLT regime applying to partnerships is complex but transfers between a partnership and its members can sometimes have a lower tax charge than expected (see **3.74–3.86**).

CHOICE OF MEDIUM FOR CO-OWNED BUSINESSES

3.1   When a number of individuals decide to come together to carry on a business the choice of medium through which to operate raises a number of issues, including commercial, legal and taxation ones, which may be quite different from those which confront a sole trader. The position may be made more complicated by the fact that a structure which suits the personal needs of one of the individuals may not be attractive to the other co-owners and as a result the structure may be a compromise both between the legal commercial and taxation advantages and disadvantages of different structures and the requirements of different members.

Traditionally, the main structures considered by co-owners have been ordinary partnerships governed by the *Partnership Act 1890*, limited liability partnerships and limited companies (ie companies limited by share capital). The various consequences of each of these structures are summarised in **Chapter 1**. In this chapter we look in a little more detail at some specific issues arising with partnerships in the context of tax planning, including partnerships involving companies.

PARTNERSHIPS AND LLPs

3.2   An LLP is not, as a matter of law, a partnership. It is a legal entity which has an existence independent of its members. For certain tax purposes an LLP is treated as if it were a partnership and the members taxed as if they were partners in a partnership: but it is important to bear the limitations and restrictions in mind. More specifically, where an LLP carries on a trade or business with a view to profit, it is treated for income tax and corporation tax purposes as if its activities were carried on in partnership by its members and as if anything done by, to or in relation to the LLP for the purposes of, or in connection with, any of its activities were done by, to or in relation to the members as partners (*Income Tax Act 2007, s 863*; *Corporation Tax Act 2009, s 1273*). For CGT purposes, assets held by such an LLP are treated as held by its members as partners and as if any dealings by the LLP were dealings by its members in partnership (*Taxation of Chargeable Gains Act 1992, s 59A*). Interestingly, by the strict wording of the statute, transparency also extends for income tax purposes (but not for CT or CGT purposes) to an LLP which is carrying on a 'profession'. Since, however, such an LLP will also almost certainly be carrying on a 'business', the difference in wording is probably, in practice, of no significance.

In what follows, when we use the term 'partnership' we mean 'partnership or LLP', except where the context makes it clear that that is not the case.

> **Focus**
>
> In certain circumstances LLPs cease to be tax-transparent – advisers need to be alert to the possibility that CGT charges may arise both at that time and subsequently.

3.3 It is worth bearing in mind both that the tax-transparency of an LLP will come to an end in certain circumstances (the most common being the appointment of a liquidator) and the consequences should that happen. In particular, for CGT purposes the LLP will thereafter be treated as if it were a company rather than as a partnership. This does not retrospectively affect the treatment of gains made before the liquidation, but any chargeable gains arising on disposals of assets after the commencement of the liquidation etc, are computed as if the LLP had never been treated as a partnership. Where business assets roll-over relief has been claimed by rolling over a gain into a share of an asset owned by an LLP, a tax liability (based on an amount equal to the postponed gain which has not come into charge) will arise on the relevant member(s) when the LLP ceases to be tax-transparent. Similarly gains deferred on the gift of business assets under *TCGA 1992, s 165*, or under *TCGA 1992, s 260*, crystallise.

On and from liquidation etc, the interest which each of the members has in the LLP as a member is treated in the same way as a shareholding in a company, the acquisition cost of which is the amount of capital subscribed. Hence the realisation of assets by an LLP which is in liquidation can give rise both to gains subject to Corporation Tax at the LLP level and gains subject to CGT in the hands of members when distributed by the LLP (to the extent that the share of proceeds exceeds the capital contributed by the members).

3.4 In addition to the potential loss of tax transparency, special tax rules apply to LLPs including in regard to:

● treatment of 'salaried members'; and

● availability of relief for trading losses.

COMPUTATION OF PARTNERSHIP PROFITS

3.5 Where all partners in a partnership are individuals, the taxable income of the partnership (whether from trading or from any other source) is computed using the same rules as apply to individuals. Where a partnership includes individuals who are not resident in the UK, income is computed (in relation to those individuals) using the rules applicable to non-UK-residents.

Where a partnership includes one or more companies, the profit share of corporate partners is computed using, broadly speaking, the computational rules applying to companies (which may be different according to whether the company is resident in the UK or not). Often the computational rules for a particular source will be the same for UK resident and non-resident individuals and for UK resident and non-resident companies: but in theory where a partnership includes both resident and non-resident individuals and companies it may be necessary to produce four separate computations of each source of income using four different sets of computational rules.

Focus

Where a partnership has non-resident members and/or corporate members up to four separate computations of tax-adjusted profit may need to be produced and filed with the partnership tax return.

Some specific areas of doubt or difficulty in relation to the computation of profit are considered below.

Indirect and nominee partners

Indirect partners

3.6   The question whether a partnership can itself be a partner in a partnership is complicated. Historically, HMRC guidance (BIM82001) has been clear that it cannot, unless it has distinct legal personality (see PM50800). It was therefore somewhat surprising that one of the areas covered in the Consultation Document 'Partnership taxation: proposals to clarify tax treatment' issued by HMRC in August 2016 was 'The taxation of business structures that include partnerships as partners'.

Following enactment of proposals in the Consultation Document, *Finance Act 2018* introduced the concept of 'indirect partners'. Thus *ITTOIA 2005, s 847(4)* now defines a person as an 'indirect partner' in a partnership ('the underlying partnership') if the person is a partner in: (a) a partnership which is a partner in the underlying partnership; or (b) any partnership which is an indirect partner in the underlying partnership.

Where a partner is an indirect partner, the notional trade that (under the normal partnership rules) he is treated for assessing purposes as carrying on is treated as commencing when he starts to be an indirect partner in the underlying partnership or, if later, when the underlying partnership starts to carry on its trade ('the underlying trade') and as ceasing when he ceases to be an indirect partner in the underlying partnership or, if earlier, when the underlying partnership

154

ceases to carry on the underlying trade. This is the case regardless of whether the cessation arises because he ceases to be a partner in the partnership which is a partner (or indirect partner) in the underlying partnership, or because the partnership in which he is a partner ceases to be a partner (or indirect partner) in the underlying partnership (*ITTOIA 2005, s 852A*).

Similarly, untaxed non-trading income of the underlying partnership is assessed as if it were income of a separate deemed trade which commences when the partner becomes an indirect partner in the underlying partnership (or, if later, when the underlying partnership starts to carry on the underlying trade) and ceases when he ceases to be an indirect partner in the underlying partnership (or, if earlier, when the underlying partnership ceases to carry on the underlying trade).

This presents a difficulty where the partnership filing the return ('the reporting partnership') includes a partner which is itself a partnership (a 'member partnership'). On what basis is the profit allocated to the member partnership to be computed? Before *Finance Act 2018* the answer was unclear, since the legislation did not address the possibility that one partnership might be a partner in another. However, *Finance Act 2018, Sch 6* amended *TMA 1970, s 12AB* (partnership return to include partnership statement) to cover the position. It is now provided that in such a case the reporting partnership must calculate and include in the partnership statement the taxable profit to be allocated to the 'member partnership' on each of the possible bases, namely, that it is:

(a)   a UK resident individual;

(b)   a non-UK resident individual;

(c)   a UK resident company;

(d)   a non-UK resident company.

However, the combined effect of *s 12AB(1C)* and *(1D)* is that if the return gives the name of every of every person who was an 'indirect' partner in the reporting partnership and gives sufficient information to show that one or more of the four bases is not relevant, information on that basis need not be supplied.

Nominee partners

3.7   The position of a person who acts as a partner in a partnership but does so as bare trustee or nominee for others has also historically been less than clear. In the Consultation Document referred to above, HMRC asserted that 'the application of the current law is clear and a partner cannot act in the capacity of a nominee or agent for another person'. Responses to the Consultation Document suggested that the position was not in fact at all clear and that many legal commentators argue that a partner can be a nominee for someone else.

The government's response has been to legislate in *Finance Act 2018* to ensure that the beneficiary of a nominee or bare trust arrangement is treated as a partner for tax purposes. However, the legislation does this by providing (at *ITTOIA 2005, s 848A* for income tax and at *CTA 2009, s 1258A* for corporation tax) that if:

(a)   a partner in a firm is partner as trustee for a beneficiary who is absolutely entitled to the partner's share of the profits of the firm; and

(b)   the beneficiary is chargeable to tax on those profits,

then references in the Act to 'partner' include references to the beneficiary.

The same wording is applied by *TMA 1970, s 12AA(10B)* in relation to the making of partnership returns.

This new legislation presents some difficulties. For one thing, it is by no means certain that the person signing the tax return will necessarily be aware that any of the nominal partners is acting as nominee or bare trustee, much less know the identity of any beneficiary or whether the beneficiary is chargeable to tax on the profits. For another, the use of the word 'include' is unhelpful. The legislation does not require the bare trustee to be ignored and the beneficiary substituted: apparently, they are both to be treated for these purposes as partners and therefore, presumably, both must be included in the partnership statement. Presumably the expectation is that partnership statement will allocate profit to the beneficiary rather than to the bare trustee. It is to be hoped that these matters will be clarified before the first returns affected by the legislation (which will be for 2018/19) have to be made.

These amendments have effect in relation to the tax year 2018/19 et seq.

Drawings and profit share

3.8   Partners' drawings and salaries are an appropriation of profit, not a deduction in calculating it (*PDC Copyright (South) v George* [1997] STC (SCD) 326, SpC 141). However, this does not mean that no payment made by the partnership to a partner is deductible: the true character of the payment must be identified.

For example, it may be that the partnership agreement allocates a slice of profit between partners by reference to the amount of capital each has invested in the partnership. That allocation of profit remains an allocation of profit and not a payment of interest, however it may be described. But it is equally possible for a partner to loan money to the partnership under a separate documented loan agreement providing for the payment of interest. This might be the case if, for example, the arrangements required that the interest was paid by the partnership even if there were no profits out of which to pay it. If that is the case, what has been paid by the partnership and received by the partner will be interest and not profit-share, which will be tax-deductible for the partnership to the same extent and subject to the same rules as any interest paid to any other lender: and taxable on the hands of the partner-lender in the same way as interest received from any other source.

Similarly, the partnership agreement may allocate an enhanced share of profit to a partner who personally owns the property from which the partnership trades. Such an enhanced profit share remains profit share and not rent. But it is equally possible that a partner may enter into a formal lease or licence agreement which requires the partnership to pay rent for occupation of the property. In that case the partner is taxed on the rent like any other landlord, with the partnership having a deduction in calculating its profits in the same way as if the rent had been paid to any other landlord (so long as the rent in relation to the property is not so excessive as to fall foul of the 'wholly and exclusively' rule).

The leading case establishing the principle is *Heastie v Veitch & Co* [1934] 1 KB 535. In this case, a partnership of chartered accountants carried on its business from premises which were owned by the senior partner and for which the partnership paid a rent which was found by the General Commissioners to be a fair and proper rent. It was held by the Court of Appeal that the rent was deductible by the partnership in computing the partnership profit. But it is clear from the judgment in the Court of Appeal that the principle is not limited to rent but extends to any goods or services provided by a partner independently of his position as partner:

> 'suppose two people are carrying on business in partnership as hotel proprietors and it is necessary for the purpose of carrying on that hotel, that business, that they should be supplied from time to time with wine, and suppose one of the partners is carrying on a wholly independent business on his own account in the wine business and supplies wine to the partnership, it would be idle to suggest, would it not, that for the purpose of ascertaining the profits of the hotel you could not deduct the sums paid to the partner who was the wine merchant?' (Romer LJ at p319)

Salaries, fees, etc

3.9   It is not unusual for partners in a professional partnership to hold offices or employments in the course of the partnership business on terms that the income from them is regarded as partnership income and divided between partners in accordance with the partnership profit-sharing arrangements.

Subject to ESC A37 (see below), the income remains taxable as employment income and the normal rules of taxing employment apply to it. It remains taxable as employment income in the hands of the partner earning it and the same limited expenses are deductible for tax purposes as for any other employment income. In particular, costs of travelling to the place of employment are not deductible for tax purposes in computing the amount of employment income, nor are any other incidental expenses such as secretarial or support costs. Where these costs are borne for convenience by the partnership they will not be incurred 'wholly and exclusively' for the purposes of the partnership business and will not be deductible in computing partnership profits. Even if it is clearly demonstrable that the employment itself was undertaken at the instigation of the other partners for reasons closely connected with, and beneficial to, the partnership business, the illogical and unsatisfactory decision by the House of Lords in the case of *Mitchell and Edon v Ross HL* (1961) 40 TC 11 presents an insuperable hurdle to any claim to deduct expenses of the employment in computing the taxable income of that business.

Focus

It is only in certain closely-defined circumstances that salaries and fees received in respect of offices (but not employments) held by partners in connection with the partnership can be treated as partnership income. But VAT may be due even where the income does not pass the test for inclusion in the partnership accounts but remains chargeable as employment income.

3.10   In certain circumstances Extra-Statutory Concession A37 provides that earnings of a partner as director of a company (but, it should be noted, not earnings as an employee) may be treated as part of the professional income of the partnership and brought into the calculation of the profits of the partnership, with expenses incurred being allowed in the normal way. ESC A37 will apply if:

● the fees are only a small part of the profits;

● the directorship is a normal incident of the profession and of the particular practice concerned;

● there is an agreement between the partners that the fees from the appointment are to be treated as partnership income and divided between the partners, and that arrangement actually happens in practice; and

● all the partners agree that the income is to be treated as part of the partnership profits for tax purposes, and written confirmation of this is given to HMRC.

ESC A37 is paralleled by a similar treatment in respect of national insurance contributions (NICs) under *SI 2001/1004, reg 27*.

3.11   Where a person, in the course or furtherance of a trade profession or vocation, accepts any office, services supplied by him as the holder of that office are treated as supplied in the course or furtherance of the trade, profession or vocation (*Value Added Tax Act 1994, s 94(4)*) so will bear VAT. Note that *VATA 1994, s 94(4)* applies only to offices, not employments; but it applies even if the conditions for ESC A37 are not fulfilled (or the benefit of ESC A37 is not taken) such that the income from the office in question is charged to tax as employment income of the individual concerned. In other words, in cases where *VATA 1994, s 94(4)* applies it is not possible to avoid the imposition of VAT by accepting or procuring that the income is treated as employment income rather than as business income of the partnership.

Costs relating to partnership changes

3.12   The costs of drawing up or amending a partnership agreement will usually be disallowable as capital expenditure. This would extend to costs of transferring a partnership's business to a limited company or to an LLP. Similarly, the costs of dissolving a partnership will be capital in nature. However, it is likely that (at least in some circumstances) the legal and professional costs which an ongoing partnership business incurs in getting rid of (or otherwise settling a dispute with) a recalcitrant partner will be revenue in nature and tax-deductible. This is to be contrasted with the position where a partnership dispute is resolved by a splitting of the business, with two or more groups of partners each taking part of the business and going their separate ways: the costs in such a case are likely to be capital in nature.

Focus

Although most costs of dealing with or altering internal partnership arrangements are disallowable, costs of hiring and firing partners (even equity partners) will often prove to be deductible.

3.13   In the past, HMRC have resisted claims to tax relief on the costs of recruiting partners on the basis that they, like the costs of drawing up a partnership agreement, are in the nature of capital costs. HMRC now accept that recruitment costs are normally allowable as revenue expenditure save where there is some additional factor involved. They give as examples of relevant factors (at PM30800) cases where:

● The admission of the partner has a fundamental impact on the structure of the firm's business involving more than a mere expansion of the business.

- The partner is recruited as part of the acquisition of a business.

- The new partner's capital contribution is a material factor in the recruitment.

It is likely that the legal and professional costs which an ongoing partnership business incurs in getting rid of (or otherwise settling a dispute with) a recalcitrant partner will be viewed in the same light as those of recruiting a partner, with similar factors determining the tax-deductibility of the expense.

3.14   The treatment of any payment made to a partner on leaving a partnership depends on its true character. In some circumstances a payment may simply be an additional share of profit which will be taxable on the partner and non-deductible for the partnership in the same way as any other profit share. In others the payment may be in settlement of some alleged grievance which the leaving partner has against the firm which will usually be tax free. Two cases in particular have come before the First-tier Tribunal. In *Self and Morgan v Commissioners of HMRC* [2009] UKFTT 78 (TC) the payments represented allocations of profits to the leaving partners as they were made to them in their capacity as partners and not as an entirely collateral payment made to them otherwise than in their capacity as partners.

However, there are occasions when a payment will not be an allocation of profits, as in *AB v HMRC* [2011] UKFTT 685 (TC). The taxpayer had received termination payments from two unconnected partnerships on two successive occasions. On each occasion the relationship between AB and the partnership had broken down and on each occasion a payment had been made by the partnership on AB's leaving. On the first occasion the payment was described as and held to be a share of profit: in the other it was held to be in the nature of compensation for the adverse treatment AB had suffered at the hands of the partnership. The discussion in the case of the factors to be considered and the reasons why different conclusions were reached in respect of the two payments is well worth reviewing.

Although in the cases cited the tribunal was required only to determine the treatment of the receipts in the hands of the ex-partner concerned (rather than the treatment of the payment in the hands of the partnership), it would seem that the payment would be deductible in computing partnership profits (if, and only if) it had the character of compensation.

Interest paid by a partnership

3.15   Normally interest paid by a partnership is deductible in computing business profits or losses of a business subject to the usual requirements including that it be incurred wholly and exclusively for the purposes of the business. The position may, however, be more complex.

3.16   If a partner's capital account becomes overdrawn, HMRC may argue that part of the partnership's borrowing has been used to fund the overdrawn account such that tax relief for interest on partnership borrowings should be restricted. In the simple case of a sole trader preparing accounts on a cash basis with a bank overdraft, an overdrawn capital account and few business assets, it may be reasonable to say that the overdraft has funded the excess drawings. But things will rarely be that simple, even for a sole trader. If there are both liabilities and assets in the balance sheet, who is to say that the business assets have not been financed by the overdraft and the overdrawn loan account by the business creditors? Or if the capital account has become overdrawn because of losses, how much of the loss is attributable to non-cash items such as depreciation or amortisation?

Focus

Tax relief for interest on third-party borrowings may need to be examined very carefully where one or more partners have overdrawn capital accounts but there are a number of arguments which can be deployed to support a claim for full tax relief.

3.17   The potential complexity of the analysis is apparent from HMRC's somewhat superficial analysis at BIM45690. The Special Commissioners case of *Silk v Fletcher* [1999] STC (SCD) 220 gives some guidance, but not much. In that case the taxpayer was originally in partnership but he then worked as a sole practitioner. His capital account was substantially overdrawn and for many years his drawings exceeded his profits. The taxpayer sought, in calculating profits, to deduct the interest incurred on several loans. The Special Commissioner held that, even if the capital account was not overdrawn, it would not necessarily follow that the interest would be tax deductible. It had to be ascertained how much of the borrowed money was actually used for business purposes. As drawings exceeded profits, the implication was that at least part of the interest was used to fund private expenditure. The taxpayer also argued that his capital account was not overdrawn because the accounts did not reflect goodwill. The former Special Commissioner disagreed with this contention, although the appeal was allowed in part after making adjustments for depreciation, debtors and creditors.

3.18   If the matter is complicated even for a sole trader, it is that much more complicated for a partnership. If one partner's capital account is overdrawn, but others are in credit, it may well be possible to argue that the overdrawn account is being funded not by any partnership bank borrowings but by the positive capital accounts of the remaining partners, such that no restriction to tax relief on interest paid by the partnership should be made. However, each situation will depend on its own facts: at the end of the day the question to be asked is – what was the purpose for which any interest was paid?

3.19   A partner may borrow money to acquire an asset personally but permit the partnership to use the asset on the understanding that the partnership will pay the interest on the loan and charge it in the partnership accounts. The interest payable by the partnership will normally be allowable in this situation as a substitute for payment of rent to the partner. It is a moot point whether strictly speaking the partner should treat himself both as receiving rent equal to the interest paid on his behalf and as paying out the interest which has been paid on his behalf. In practice, HMRC do not seem to take the point. Difficulties will arise if the amount of the interest paid by the partnership exceeds the market value of occupancy of the property or part of the property occupied by the partnership – the excess is in effect a distribution of profit to the partner and is not deductible for the partnership.

Personal expenses of partners

3.20   There is no rule restricting tax-deductible expenses to those incurred by the partnership as a whole. On the contrary, where a partner defrays out of his personal resources some expense which is incurred wholly and exclusively for the purposes of the partnership trade, tax relief for such an expense is available. In the past, one of the most common circumstances in which this arose was in the case of doctors' partnerships. Before the days of self-assessment it was quite common to see a partnership assessment allocating shares of profits to individual doctors and for the statement of partnership share to show further deductions for such personally-incurred expenses as 'use of home as surgery', 'wife's wages', 'conference expenses' and the ubiquitous 'motoring expenses'. Similarly, one would encounter individual capital allowance claims covering assets provided by the doctors individually but used in the partnership business. Such claims were not, of course, restricted to medical practitioners but, in practice, seemed to be most commonly encountered in that context.

Focus

Partnership expenses borne directly by partners are deductible subject to the normal rules for trading deductions but must be deducted in the partnership tax computation and not as a separate adjustment in the partners' personal; self-assessment returns.

Although self-assessment swept away the machinery of such stand-alone expense and capital allowance claims for partners, it changed nothing as regards the tax-deductibility. However, the process now is that any claim for relief for expenditure incurred by partners (as distinct from by the partnership) is nonetheless claimed at the level of the partnership taxation computation. There is no longer any 'second stage' at which individual claims may be made.

Preparing the partnership return correctly therefore involves adding together the partnership expenditure and the expenditure incurred by the individual partners in order to arrive at the total expenditure figure for the partnership. This is then included in the Standard Accounts Information.

HMRC state (at BIM82075) that it is necessary that 'the adjustments are made before apportionment of the net profit between the partners', and they instruct that officers 'should not accept any deductions for expenses from the net profits allocated to a partner'. In practice, HMRC generally accept that tax relief should be effectively given to the partner incurring the relevant expense, by appropriate allocation of the tax-adjusted partnership profit between partners.

Logically, it is difficult to reconcile the deduction of expenses incurred personally by partners with the requirement, at *ITTOIA 2005, s 25*, that profits of a trade must (unless cash basis applies) be computed in accordance with GAAP subject to any adjustment required or authorised by law. If the deduction of an expense incurred by a partner is required in order to arrive at the profit of the trade as computed in accordance with GAAP, it inevitably means that the partnership (or, more particularly, LLP) accounts (which did not include the expense) did not comply with GAAP. However, the practice is long-standing and has long been accepted by HMRC and is, in practice, unchallenged.

One way of avoiding much of the difficulty may be to include all the expenses in the partnership accounts in the first place, with the contra being to the capital or current account of the partner funding the cost of the expense, and adjusting the allocation of partnership profit accordingly.

Overseas aspects

3.21 Care is needed where a partnership either has non-UK-resident members or has trading profits arising outside the UK (or both).

A UK-resident member of a partnership is liable to UK tax on his share of the worldwide income of the partnership. He may also be liable to foreign taxes on any profits of the partnership which arise outside the UK: the UK will give double tax relief for any such taxes either under a treaty or unilaterally.

A partnership is not of itself taxable. The concept of residence status is therefore meaningless in the context of partnerships themselves. It follows that a partnership cannot itself claim any benefits as a 'dual resident' under any Double Taxation Convention ('DTC'), nor will HMRC normally issue a 'certificate of residence' for the purposes of any DTC. A few DTCs do state that a partnership may be regarded as having a residence status and, in those cases, a 'certificate of residence' may be issued. In other cases, partners may be able to claim treaty benefits and HMRC will assist by providing a 'letter of confirmation' confirming UK-residence status where appropriate.

A non-UK-resident member of a partnership is liable to UK tax only on his share of partnership profits arising in the UK. He has no UK tax liability in respect of profits arising outside the UK. For this purpose, where the partnership carries on a single trade in the UK and overseas, HMRC will regard each member's share of profit as arising partly in the UK and partly overseas.

For example, suppose that a UK LLP has members resident in the UK and members resident in Country Y, and branches in both the UK (which makes a profit of £9m) and Country Y (which makes a profit of £1m). Suppose that under the LLP agreement profits are 'streamed' so that the members resident in Country Y share between them the £1m profits arising from the Country Y branch and the members resident in the UK share the £9m profits of the UK branch. Common sense would suggest that UK tax would be payable only by UK members, and on a total of £9m (since the non-resident members take as a matter of fact no share of UK-sourced profits). In fact, HMRC will take the view that profits cannot be 'streamed' in this way for tax purposes (even if they are 'streamed' commercially). They will regard UK members as being entitled to and taxable on 90% of global profits (so £9m) of which £8.1m arises in the UK and £0.9m arises overseas: and the overseas members as being entitled to 10% of global profits (so £1m) of which £0.9m arises in the UK and is taxable in the UK and £0.1m arises overseas and is tax free.

Focus

A non-resident partner is liable to UK tax only on his share of UK income of the partnership which arises in the UK. However, if he fails to pay his tax, the UK-resident partners may be liable to make payment to HMRC as his deemed UK tax agents.

One solution to this difficulty may be to create separate LLPs (or local equivalents) in the UK and overseas, or perhaps to employ the overseas-resident members in Country Y (or even deliberately to arrange matters so as to procure that they are caught by the 'salaried members' legislation described at **3.46** below).

Although a partner resident outside the UK is liable to UK tax on trading profits arising in the UK, there may be obvious practical difficulties in the way of HMRC actually collecting tax from him. For this reason, the *Taxes Acts* make provision (at *ITA 2007, Pt 14, Ch 2C*) for income tax liabilities of a non-resident to be collected from any 'UK representative' of the non-resident. *CTA 2009, Pt 22, Ch 6* makes similar provision in respect of non-resident companies. In relation to partnerships, the partnership itself is treated as the UK representative of the non-resident partners. It may thus be assessed to tax in the name of the non-resident partners. In such circumstances, each of the partners is jointly liable for the non-resident partners' tax – this is the only circumstance in which one partner can be liable for another's tax liability. In the case of an LLP, it is the LLP itself which is liable, but since, in general law, members of an LLP are not personally liable for the LLP's liabilities, no personal liability attaches to members.

In either case, a partnership with UK income and non-resident partners may be wise to take a very close interest in the UK tax compliance arrangements of non-resident partners, including withholding distributions until evidence that all tax liabilities have been met is available.

This is to be distinguished from the case where a UK-resident member of a partnership or LLP leaves the UK, leaving tax debts unpaid. There is, in that case, no UK representative and no liability on the partnership, partners or LLP.

SHARING OF PROFITS AND LOSSES

3.22   Taxable profit is allocated between partners 'in accordance with the firm's profit-sharing arrangements during that period' (*ITTOIA 2005, s 850(1)*). The phrase is simple enough but in some circumstances it may not be clear what it means. Examples in HMRC's guidance notes suggest that the preferred method may be to allocate tax-adjusted profits by applying to them the same formula as has been used commercially. But this can give capricious results – as in **Example 3.1** below where Brown, despite having 50% of the commercial profit, has a smaller tax charge than Smith, who has 31.25% of the commercial profit.

Example 3.1 – Complex profit-sharing ratios

Smith, Jones and Brown share profits as follows:

	Smith	Jones	Brown
First £30,000 (salary)	20,000	10,000	0
Next £50,000 (return on capital)	5,000	5,000	40,000
Balance	45%	45%	10%
Allocation of commercial profit £80,000	25,000	15,000	40,000
Allocation of tax adjusted profit £130,000	47,500	37,500	45,000

3.23   An alternative, which would also arguably meet the statutory requirement of allocation 'in accordance with the firm's profit-sharing arrangements', and which would seem fairer, would be to allocate taxable profits in the same proportion as commercial profits. Probably either method would be acceptable to HMRC if agreed between the partners and applied consistently.

What is clear is that partners cannot agree to allocate profits between them for tax purposes in a way which is different from that in which commercial profits are in fact allocated. Further, 'the allocation of profits or losses for an accounting period cannot be varied retrospectively after the end of that accounting period' (HMRC guidance at BIM82055). While this may be true as far it goes – once profits and their allocation between partners are agreed and the accounts signed off, that is final – it must not be taken too far. In many cases a final decision on dividing up profits is not taken until after the end of the period and the amount of the profit (as well as the relative contributions of the partners) is known. To suppose that this is in any way problematic would be absurd. What is, however, crucial is that the allocation for tax purposes follows the commercial allocation.

Proposal 6 in the Consultation Document, 'Partnership Taxation: proposals to clarify tax treatment' of August 2016, threatened to muddy the water somewhat. This stated that:

> 'Legislation would be introduced to provide that the basis of allocation of tax adjusted profit should be the same as the allocation of the accounting profit or loss between the partners."

How this would work alongside taking deductions in computing taxable profit for expenses incurred outside the accounts in unclear. Revised proposals published in March 2017 following consultation responses stated an intention to proceed by:

> 'clarifying how to apply a firm's profit-sharing arrangements consistently in allocating taxable profits among the partners, including in cases where different partners' taxable profits are computed on different bases'

which is hardly any clearer. Draft legislation published in September 2017 (but which did not appear in *Finance Act 2018*) would have required taxable profits to be allocated in exactly the same ratio as commercial profits. This would have raised further difficulties as to the manner in which 'personal' expenses were allocated and may explain why *Finance Act 2018, Sch 6* (which enacts most of the revised proposals of the Consultation Document) does not enact the provisions of Proposal 6.

One further practical point should be considered. Sometimes one or more partners has his profit share underpinned at a guaranteed minimum figure.

This kind of arrangement, which has historically been fairly common in businesses in the financial dealing sector, can give some anomalous results.

Example 3.2 – Guaranteed profit shares

A is sole trader. He takes B and C into partnership with him. He guarantees that their share of profit in the first year will be not less than their previous salary of £55,000 each.

The partnership loses a large customer and the first year's results show a profit (also the tax-adjusted profit) of only £50,000 in total. Commercially, A suffers a loss of £60,000 (ie the 'guaranteed minima' of £110,000 less the actual profit of £50,000).

B and C will each pay tax on £25,000 of profit. A gets no tax relief for his commercial loss of £60,000 (for there is in fact no partnership loss to be relieved). The planning point here is that any guarantee given by A should be stated in the partnership agreement in terms of after-tax not pre-tax income, or should provide for suitable tax indemnities.

Tax disputes between partners

3.24   A return of partnership profits is required to be made by the nominated partner. The return must show, inter alia, the amount of partnership profit and the allocation between partners. There is no problem if the return is made, it is made on time, and all partners agree with the figures on it. If the return is late, is not made, or is not agreed by all the partners then complexities can arise.

The question of what happens if a partner does not agree with the amount of profit allocated to him in the partnership return was the subject of the First-tier Tribunal decision in *Morgan and Self v CIR* [2009] UKFTT 78 (TC). Although the case was decided on other grounds so that the comments of the tribunal chairman are strictly *obiter dicta*, the judge concluded that the obligation of the member to make his own self-assessment return 'to the best of his knowledge and belief' trumps the requirement to include on the personal return the share of profit allocated on the partnership return. The solution, the judge concluded, was that in cases of dispute the member should include on his personal return the figure which he believes to be the correct share of taxable profit, together with a note explaining that this differs from the figure shown on the partnership return.

3.25   In relation to returns for the tax year 2018/19 et seq, the position is altered by *Finance Act 2018, Sch 6*. This inserts *s 12ABZB* into *TMA 1970* which provides a statutory procedure for dealing with disputes between partners as to profit share. It is important, however, to appreciate before considering the new provisions that they apply only where the dispute is as to the allocation of taxable profit between the partners. They do not apply where the dispute is in substance about the amount (before sharing) of the partnership's profits or losses for a period. For such disputes the principles established in Morgan and Self continue to apply.

Under the new rules, the starting position is that a partnership return is conclusive for tax purposes as to:

(a) whether a person does or does not have a share in the profits or losses or the partnership for any period, and

(b) what the share of any person in those profits or losses is.

(TMA 1970, s 12ABZB(1))

3.26 If there is a dispute between the partners about whether what is given in a partnership return is correct as to these matters (ie what share a person has, if any, in the taxable profits) any party to the dispute may refer it to the tribunal (which means, by *TMA 1970, s 47C*, the First-tier Tribunal or, where determined by or under Tribunal Procedure Rules, the Upper Tribunal). Any such referral must be made, if at all, before the end of the period of 12 months beginning with the day after:

(a) the day on which the partnership return was delivered; or

(b) if the dispute relates to an amendment to the return made under *TMA 1970, s 12ABA*, the day on which the amendment was made.

If no referral to the tribunal is made, the partnership return stands good and is conclusive.

3.27 Where the dispute is referred to the tribunal, the person referring it must at the same time give notice of the referral to the 'reporting partner' (ie the partner who made the disputed return) who must in turn notify every other partner in the partnership and anyone else who appears to him to be a party to the dispute. The referring partner must also at the same time give notice of the referral to HMRC. This extends the time limit for commencing an enquiry under *TMA 1970, s12AC* to the quarter day next following the first anniversary of the day in which HMRC are given notice of the referral; but only in regard to matters to which the dispute relates or which are affected by it.

3.28 The procedure before the tribunal is not set out in detail by the legislation and will presumably be governed by the relevant tribunal rules.

Although the dispute is between the partners, it is assumed that the purpose of requiring notification to HMRC is to allow HMRC to make representations to the tribunal if appropriate.

The tribunal must either confirm that the return as filed is correct or determine how it should be revised; and (if the latter) HMRC must amend the partnership and the partners' returns accordingly. But at any time before the tribunal makes its decision, the partners may notify HMRC that they have agreed the position between themselves in writing. In that case, their agreement is treated as if it were a decision of the tribunal unless within 30 days either one of the partners resiles from the agreement or HMRC give notice that they object to the agreement.

Normally, only one referral may be made in respect of any one partnership return. Thus, if two or more partners are dissatisfied with the share of profit allocated to them on the return, they will need to make a joint referral to the tribunal so that all matters in dispute may be resolved together. However, if a partnership return is, after having been filed, amended under *TMA 1970, s 12ABA* and a dispute arises in consequence of that amendment, that fresh dispute may be referred.

Focus

Where a partner disagrees with the taxable profit or share of disposal proceeds allocated to him on the partnership return he should notify HMRC on his own tax return both of the figures used on the partnership return and the figures which he believes to be correct. The position changes for 2018/19 and later years with the introduction of a statutory procedure for resolving certain inter-partner disputes.

3.29 A similar difficulty may arise if the partner who has been required to make the partnership return fails to do so. The legislation (*FA 2009, Sch 55, para 55*) then imposes penalties not only on the defaulting partner but on all the partners. Thus the law can have the effect of imposing a penalty on a sleeping partner with no practical means of access to the books and records necessary to make the return and no real power either to make the return himself or force the nominated partner to do so. Furthermore, as confirmed in *Dyson v CIR* [2015] UKFTT 131 (TC), it is only the defaulting partner who has the right of appeal against the penalties imposed on himself and on the other partners: if he chooses not to exercise that appeal right the other partners have no recourse. This is, as the judge in the case observed, clearly a breach of Article 6 of the Human Rights Act: but the tribunal was nonetheless bound.

CAPITAL GAINS TAX

3.30   Capital gains tax (CGT) may be relevant to a partnership either in relation to acquisitions or disposals of partnership assets from or to third parties, or in relation to transactions between the partners in those partnership assets which are chargeable assets for CGT purposes. Detailed guidance for partnership capital gains is to be found in HMRC Statement of Practice SP D12.

External disposals

3.31   Partnerships (and, in most circumstances, LLPs) are effectively transparent for the purposes of CGT such that any charge to CGT on the disposal of partnership assets arises in the hands of each individual partner. In so far as the disposal of partnership assets is concerned, the entitlement to the disposal proceeds depends on the agreement between the partners. There is nothing to prevent the partners having a different capital-sharing ratio from that in which trading, professional, or indeed any other income profits are shared. Each partner will have an independent base cost, and each will have the separate ability to roll over or hold over gains through the purchase of qualifying assets within the stipulated time limits.

Focus

Partnerships may share capital profits in whatever way they choose. CGT will follow the commercial allocation. Any change in profit-sharing ratios may give rise to chargeable gains, even where there has been no external disposal. This may apply in particular on mergers and demergers but the possible availability of business asset roll-over relief should not be overlooked.

Transactions between partners

3.32   A change in capital profit-sharing ratios between partners is treated as a disposal for CGT purposes. A partner reducing his share is deemed to make a disposal and a partner increasing his share to make an acquisition. The consideration in each case is deemed to be the relevant proportion of the value at which the asset in question appears in the partnership balance sheet plus any off-balance-sheet payment. Market value is substituted only where the partners are connected other than by being in partnership: even then, market value will be substituted only if it is considered that the transaction would have been undertaken at market value but for the connection.

170

It follows that if assets are carried in the balance sheet at a figure which equates to original cost, any change of capital profit-sharing ratios will (although a disposal) not give rise to any gain or loss for CGT purposes.

It also follows that a revaluation of partnership assets does not of itself amount to a disposal for CGT purposes. This is logical: by simply changing the value at which they choose to recognise an asset in the partnership balance sheet, partners have not changed their financial assets. This remains the case even if the revaluation is used to support further borrowings in the partnership which are then drawn down as additional drawings.

3.33 Thus, there will not be a CGT charge by reason *only* of:

(i)   cash being withdrawn in excess of the capital introduced and retained profits; or

(ii)   assets being revalued and the capital accounts credited with any revaluation surplus in the capital profit-sharing ratio,

or because of a combination of both.

If assets are revalued, however, and a change in capital profit-sharing ratio then takes place, a disposal is deemed to arise in the case of those partners whose shares reduce, whether or not accompanied by a withdrawal of cash. To that extent, the gain on revaluation is regarded as having been realised.

Where partnerships merge, there will normally be a change in the profit-sharing ratios of all chargeable assets held by either of the merging firms. If gains arise (due to an earlier revaluation of assets or payment outside the accounts) each partner may be able to claim rollover relief in respect of shares acquired in the other firm's assets. Similarly, a demerger is likely to involve changes in the profit-sharing ratios. If gains arise on the relinquishment of an interest in some assets (or payment outside the accounts) the partner may be able to claim rollover relief in respect of any enhanced share in other assets; ESC D25 provides that the acquisition of a further interest in an asset already in use for the purposes of a trade is for roll-over relief purposes treated as the acquisition of a new asset.

Writing off goodwill

3.34 Some special care is needed in regard to 'negligible value' claims under *TCGA 1992, s 24* in respect of partnership goodwill. It is not uncommon for partnership agreements to be 'modernised' by providing that all goodwill shall be written out of the balance sheet, and that going forward there shall be neither payment demanded of incoming partners in respect of goodwill nor any payment made to outgoing partners. In these circumstances, partners owning goodwill who have an acquisition cost (or a 1982 value) might consider that since it will be impossible for them to realise any value for goodwill, a 'negligible value' claim should be made so as to crystallise a loss for CGT purposes.

Unfortunately, it is the view of HMRC (see CG28000) that an agreement of this kind does not of itself mean that the goodwill is of negligible value within the meaning of the Act. A claim under *TCGA 1992, s 24* may be made only if the entire goodwill of the partnership as a whole has become of negligible value. This is a question of fact, and is quite different from an agreement between the partners that they will not, as between themselves, attach any value to goodwill. Of course, it may be that the agreement to treat the goodwill as valueless simply reflects the fact that the goodwill has in the real world actually become valueless: but if a negligible value claim is to be sustained it will be necessary to produce evidence to that effect.

As with any revaluation upwards or downwards, the writing off of the goodwill in the balance sheet will affect the consideration deemed to pass on a future change in capital profit-sharing ratios, including on retirement. Thus a partner who, after goodwill has been written off, disposes of his interest in goodwill on reducing his share of capital profits will realise a loss equal to his acquisition cost.

Partners as connected persons and associates

3.35   For the purposes of CGT, partners are 'connected' with each other (and with each other's spouses, civil partners or relatives) except in relation to bona fide acquisitions or disposals of partnership assets (*TCGA 1992, s 286*). Similarly, partners are 'associates' of each other (*CTA 2010, s 448*). These definitions are widely relevant throughout the tax code. Given that for certain tax purposes LLPs are in certain circumstances treated as in the same way as partnerships, the question arises whether the treatment of partners as 'connected' and 'associated' persons also means that fellow members of an LLP are also to be treated in the same way. The answer is probably no.

Focus

The general rule that partners are 'connected persons' for tax purposes probably does not apply to individuals who are fellow members of an LLP and not otherwise connected.

In commercial and legal terms an LLP is, as a body corporate with separate legal identity, quite different from a partnership. Legally the relationship which subsists between fellow members of an LLP is much closer to that which subsists between fellow members of a limited company than to a partnership. HMRC have published no general guidance but it is worth noting that in the specific case of 'association' for the purposes of EIS relief (*ITA 2007, s 253*), which defines 'associate' to include 'partner', HMRC regard 'partner' as meaning 'anyone with whom the individual carries on a business as described in the *Partnership Act, 1890*' – which would, of course, exclude fellow members of an LLP. It seems probable therefore that HMRC would agree that the general rule is that fellow members of LLPs are neither connected persons nor associates.

Entrepreneurs' relief for partnerships

3.36   For the purposes of applying entrepreneurs' relief to the circumstances of a partnership, *TCGA 1992, s 169I(8)* provides that:

- an individual who disposes of (or of interests in) assets used for the purposes of a business carried on by the individual on entering into a partnership which is to carry on the business is to be treated as disposing of a part of the business,

- the disposal by an individual of the whole or part of the individual's interest in the assets of a partnership is to be treated as a disposal by the individual of the whole or part of the business carried on by the partnership, and

- at any time when a business is carried on by a partnership, the business is to be treated as owned by each individual who is at that time a member of the partnership.

Thus, in the context of partnerships, entrepreneurs' relief may potentially be relevant to gains made:

- by a partner on the disposal by the partnership of the whole or part of the partnership business;

- by a partner on the disposal of the whole or part of an interest in a partnership (including on a change of capital profit-sharing ratios);

- by an individual, on actual or deemed disposals when he admits partners into the business for the first time;

- by a partner on a disposal, following the cessation of the partnership business, of assets used by the business at the time of cessation;

- by certain trustees, in relation to 'trust business assets';

- by a partner making an 'associated disposal'; or

- by shareholders of a company which is a member of a partnership in circumstances where the relevant conditions are fulfilled (see **3.53** below).

173

The first three of these are reasonably straightforward, and substantially similar issues arise as arise on the disposal of a business by a sole trader. Note, however, that the requirement that a business must have been carried on for at least one year if relief is to be available is applied separately to each partner. This means that some partners may qualify and others may fail to qualify on the same disposal event.

Example 3.3 – One year of trading required for business to qualify

Rachel and Martyn established a nursery business as a partnership on 1 October 2013. Helen joins the partnership on 1 May 2014, paying £30,000 for her share of the goodwill of the business. Entrepreneurs' relief is not available on the gains realised by Rachel and Martyn, as the business has not been established for at least one year. If Rachel had run the nursery business as a sole trader for some years before Martyn joined as a partner on 1 October 2013, the gains realised by Rachel on 1 May 2014 would qualify for entrepreneurs' relief, but the gain made by Martyn on that date would not qualify.

Cessation of business

3.37 Relief may be claimed by a partner in respect of gains arising on a disposal of assets which were in use for the purposes of the partnership business at the time at which business ceased, provided the partner had been a partner in the business for at least one year before cessation and provided the asset is disposed of within three years of the cessation of the business. The relief applies equally to assets owned by the partnership and to assets owned personally. Although the circumstances in which this relief may be claimed has a superficial similarity to relief under the 'associated disposal' rules, the disposal described here remains a 'material disposal' and, in particular, is not subject to the restrictions on relief which apply to 'associated disposals' (see **3.40** below).

Example 3.4 – Cessation

Mr and Mrs Last have been trading in partnership as shoe repairers for many years from two shops. One of the shops is a partnership asset shown in the balance sheet, and the other is owned personally by Mrs Last. On receiving an offer from a property developer for one of the shops, Mr and Mrs Last decide to close down the business and retire. Assuming both shops are sold within three years of the date the business closes, gains on both the shops will qualify for entrepreneurs' relief.

Trust disposals

3.38 Trustees may, in certain circumstances, claim entrepreneurs' relief.

It is very important to appreciate that, although trustees may be partners in a partnership, the relief is not available in respect of gains made by trustees on the disposal of their interest in a partnership in which the trustees are themselves partners. Nor is it available in respect of gains arising when a partnership in which the trustees are partners makes a disposal of a business or part of a business.

Relief is available only in respect of gains on assets owned by the trustees but used by a partnership in which a 'qualifying beneficiary' is a partner. If there is no 'qualifying beneficiary', there can be no relief. Whether the trustees themselves are partners in the partnership is irrelevant.

The relief is given in respect of gains on disposals of 'settlement business assets'. In the context of a partnership, a trust asset is a 'settlement business asset' if:

- it is used, throughout a period of at least one year ending not more than three years before the date of disposal, for the purposes of a business carried on by a partnership of which a 'qualifying beneficiary' is or was a member; and

- the 'qualifying beneficiary' ceases to carry on the business (either because the partnership ceases to do so or because he ceases to be a partner) on the date of disposal or has done so within three years before that date.

A 'qualifying beneficiary' is one who has an interest in possession (other than for a fixed term) in the 'settlement business asset'. If more than one beneficiary has such an interest, the gain is apportioned and only that part apportioned to the qualifying beneficiary who carries on the business qualifies for relief.

Where the relief is claimed, it counts towards the lifetime limit of the qualifying beneficiary; consequently, any claim must be made jointly by the trustees and the qualifying beneficiary.

Example 3.5 – Trust disposal

Adolphus and his sister Cyrene each have a 50% life interest in a family trust which owns farmland. Adolphus (but not Cyrene) is a partner in the partnership which farms the land. Part of the land is re-zoned for residential development and is sold to a developer for £15m. The partnership continues to farm the remainder of the land.

Provided Adolphus has ceased to be a partner before the land is disposed of, entrepreneurs' relief can be claimed in respect of 50% of the gain (the claim to be made jointly by Adolphus and the trustees).

Note that, if Adolphus is still a partner at the date of disposal, the conditions for relief are not met.

Associated disposals

3.39   Where a partner disposes of the whole or part of his interest in a partnership in circumstances qualifying for entrepreneurs' relief (a 'material disposal'), a disposal of an asset held personally may qualify for entrepreneurs' relief as an 'associated disposal'. There is no requirement that the 'material disposal' actually gives rise to a gain – merely that the circumstances are such that, if there were a gain, it would qualify for entrepreneurs' relief. The conditions for 'associated disposal' relief were significantly restricted by *Finance Act 2015* and again by *Finance Act 2016*, the effect of which is to make rules which were already complex even more so.

The following sets out the position for disposals after 17 March 2015:

- If the material disposal in question is a complete disposal of the partner's interest in the partnership (such as where the partnership business is sold or the partner completely retires), the requirement is that either:

    - the interest disposed of is at least a 5% interest in the partnership; or

    - the partner's interest in the partnership must have been at least 5% throughout a continuous period of at least three years in the eight years ending with the date of the material disposal.

- If the material disposal is a disposal of something less than the partner's complete interest in the business, the material disposal itself must be of at least a 5% interest in the partnership assets.

In each case, there must be no 'partnership purchase arrangements' in existence – that is, arrangements whereby the partner making the disposal (or someone connected with him) can re-acquire an interest in (or increase an interest in) the partnership.

Subject to the above restrictions on which material disposals may be taken into account, entrepreneurs' relief is available on the disposal of an asset which:

- is disposed of as part of the partner's withdrawal from participation in the business carried on by the partnership (*TCGA 1992, s 169K(3),(5)*);

- was used for the purpose of the partnership business for at least one year to the date of disposal of the partnership interest, or the date or cessation of the partnership business if earlier (*TCGA 1992, s 169K(4)*); and

- had (if acquired on or after 13 June 2016) been owned by the partner throughout the period of three years ending with the date of disposal (*TCGA 1992, s 169K(4A)*). Where the asset is or has been jointly owned and the extent of the partner's interest in the asset has changed within the three years ending with the date of disposal, an appropriate apportionment of the gain is made and entrepreneurs' relief is available on the proportion of the gain which corresponds to the smallest share owned in the period.

HMRC manuals give some guidance on the interpretation of the phrase 'part of the partner's withdrawal from participation in the business' – see CG63995. It is explicitly stated that it is not necessary (in the case of a partial disposal) that the individual should actually reduce the amount of work done in the business, but the associated disposal and the material disposal should be 'part and parcel' of one single withdrawal from participation in the business. This means that there should normally be no significant interval between the two disposals. However, where the partnership ceases to trade, HMRC will accept that a disposal is capable of being 'associated' with the material disposal arising on cessation if it takes place within a year after cessation (it may not, by definition, take place before cessation, because of the requirement that it is still in use for the purposes of the partnership business on cessation). It will also qualify if it is disposed of:

- within three years after cessation, provided it has not been leased or used for any other purpose after the cessation of the business; or

- in cases where the partnership business has not ceased, within three years of the material disposal, provided it has not within that period been used for any purpose other than that of the business.

Example 3.6 – Disposal of partnership interest

Graham is in partnership with his son Tristan, sharing all profits: 7/8ths to Graham, 1/8th to Tristan. Graham owns the office from which the partnership has traded for a number of years. On his 60th birthday, Graham gifts the office to his son, and the profit-sharing ratios are changed to 1/4 to Graham and 3/4 to Tristan, but Graham continues to work full-time for the partnership. The disposal of the office to Tristan qualifies as an associated disposal, as Graham has at the same time made a disposal of at least 5% of his interest in the assets of the partnership.

Restrictions

3.40   There are four circumstances in which entrepreneurs' relief on an associated disposal is reduced to such amount as is 'just and reasonable':

(a)   The asset has only been used by the business for only part of the period of ownership by the individual, in which case the gain taken into account will reflect the period of business use.

(b)   Only part of the asset has been used for the purposes of the business, so the gain taken into account will reflect the proportion of the asset used for business purposes.

(c)   The individual has been concerned in the carrying on of the business (whether as sole trader or as a partner of the partnership) for part only of the time during which the asset was used by the business. This is less likely than situations (a) or (b), but is possible where an individual was a salaried partner before becoming a full partner or perhaps where property is owned by a spouse who is subsequently taken into partnership.

(d)   Any payment of rent was made for the use of the asset by the personal company or partnership for a period after 5 April 2008.

The payment of 'rent' in the final restriction means any form of consideration paid for the use of the asset, including licence fees for the use of intellectual property. Where the rent paid is less than a full market rent for the use of the asset, the gain is restricted proportionately.

Note that these restrictions apply only in the context of a claim to 'associated disposal' relief. They are of no relevance where relief is claimed on a 'material disposal' or to a claim by trustees on a disposal of 'settlement business assets'.

FAMILY PARTNERSHIPS

3.41   Family partnerships are often created with a view to spreading income between husband and wife (or more widely within a family) with a view to minimising tax. The first concern in such cases may be whether HMRC are able to challenge the validity of the partnership. Usually, if proper care has been taken with the planning, the answer is no. In HMRC's words:

> 'Where the spouse or civil partner has signed a deed declaring an intention to carry on the business and the deed gives a right to share in the profits, and subsequently accounts of the business show that that person has been allocated a share of the profits, there will not usually be much chance of mounting a successful challenge.' [BIM82065]

There is no reason in law why a child may not be a partner in a business, provided the child has the intellectual capacity to understand the nature of the business and the obligations of partnership. Thus a three-year-old could not be a partner: quite possibly a twelve-year-old could. The law is different in Scotland: there it is very unlikely that a child under the age of 16 could be a partner.

Focus

Partnerships between spouses or civil partners can be an easy and effective way of splitting income for tax purposes though the commercial and legal consequences of entering into partnership (including the exposure to unlimited liability in the case of an ordinary partnership) should be considered very carefully before taking such a step. Partnerships involving minor children (even where the children's capital contribution to the partnership has been funded by, for example, grandparents) are usually best avoided except in very special circumstances.

3.42 Quite separate from the question whether a spouse or other family member can be a partner is that of whether a partnership is capable of amounting to an arrangement conferring bounty and therefore a 'settlement' within the meaning of *ITTOIA 2005, Part 5, Chapter 5*. There are at least three circumstances in which this may be the case.

First, if a parent introduces a minor child into partnership, any share of income awarded to the child will almost always constitute income arising under a 'settlement' made on the child by the parent such that the income remains taxable on the parent. The only exception would be where, despite the minority, the child had genuinely 'earned' the income by his or her efforts: for example where the partnership exists to exploit the talents of a child performer.

Second, a partnership between husband and wife is potentially within the settlements legislation if the 'passive spouse' both (a) has no right to capital but only a right to income and (b) receives a greater share of income than is commensurate with the work done in the partnership. But this will not normally be the case: normally the spouse will share in capital as well as income of the partnership.

Third, a partnership may in some circumstances amount to a 'revocable settlement' and as such caught by the legislation even if the settlement is made on an adult.

Example 3.7 – Revocable settlement

Mr T is in partnership with his wife Mrs T. Their daughter is a university student. The deed is altered to admit the daughter as a partner. All the partners

---

agree that on finishing her course the daughter's interest in the partnership will come to an end. The amendment of the partnership agreement under which the daughter is included without any additional capital or value being added by her is an arrangement with the requisite element of bounty. The gift from the parents is subject to conditions under which the property given will revert to them. The daughter's income is therefore treated as the income of the parents under *ITTOIA 2005, s 624.*

(Based on HMRC guidance at TSEM4215.)

3.43 Although entering into a partnership on favourable terms is likely to amount to the making of a settlement within the definition of the legislation, there are normally no tax consequences where the person benefitted is an adult other than the settlor's spouse or civil partner. In particular, it will not normally be possible for HMRC to challenge arrangements whereby the person benefitted is the settlor's adult child, parent or unmarried cohabitee.

Example 3.8 – Settlement on unconnected adult

Mr S is a tax adviser. He lives with Mr T but they are not in a civil partnership. Mr S and Mr T form a partnership to exploit Mr S's talents as tax adviser, sharing assets, profits and losses of the business equally. Mr T has no knowledge of tax, contributes no capital and does no work in the business. Nonetheless the partnership is not vulnerable to attack under the settlements legislation.

CGT implications of family partnerships

3.44 The introduction of a person into a partnership normally results in a change in the asset profit-sharing ratios and therefore a deemed disposal of chargeable assets held by the partnership. Where the parties are not connected the deemed disposal value will be the value at which the assets are recognised in the partnership balance sheet plus any off-balance-sheet payment. Where the parties are connected other than by being in partnership (as when family members join the partnership) and a different value would have been used had they not been connected, the disposal will be deemed to take effect at the open market value of the interest transferred. Thus, if in a family partnership an adult daughter is admitted to partnership without payment for her share of goodwill and business premises, and it is established that, were it not for the family relationship, values of £20,000 and £50,000 would have been attributed to the interests in the assets transferred to her by the other family members, those values will be used and the CGT consequences will follow.

If the partnership is a trading partnership and the asset is used wholly for the purpose of the trade it will normally be the case that the transferor(s) and transferee may jointly elect for the otherwise chargeable gain to be deducted from the deemed acquisition cost of the transferee (ie the said market value) under the business assets gifts relief provisions of *TCGA 1992, s 165*.

SALARIED PARTNERS

General partnerships

3.45   A person described as a 'salaried partner' may be a true partner; or he may be an employee given the title as matter of prestige. Which he is, is a question of fact.

The question is – is the 'salaried partner' a party to the partnership agreement and entitled under it to participate as principal in the general management and conduct of the business? It is, as HMRC put it at BIM82025, 'inherent in the contract of partnership that a true partner (as opposed to an employee) is permitted, indeed has the right, to participate in the general management and administration of the firm'.

The question of status may arise not only in relation to HMRC but also where a salaried partner, on leaving the firm, seeks to establish that he or she was an 'employee' with full employment rights. This has happened in a number of cases, including *Tiffin v Lester Aldridge LLP* [2012] EWCA Civ 35. The position is now possibly further muddied by the so-called 'gig economy' cases, such as *Aslam, Farrar & others v Uber BV and others, Pimlico Plumbers v Gary Smith, Boxer v Excel Group Services* and *Dewhurst v City Sprint*. The *Employment Rights Act 1996*, the *Working Time Regulations 1998* and the *National Minimum Wage Act 1998* all apply not only to employees but also to 'workers'. This term is defined to mean an individual working under a contract whereby the individual:

> 'Undertakes to do or perform personally any work or services for another party to the contract whose status is not by virtue of the contract that of a client or customer of any profession or business undertaking carried on by the individual.'

Thus, an individual working under a contract may be, depending on the facts:

- employed; or
- self-employed, but a 'worker' entitled to the protections of the *Employment Rights Act* etc; or
- self-employed and not a 'worker'.

Whether this now means that a 'salaried partner' may fall into the third category has not yet been established by the courts.

Limited liability partnerships

3.46   Until *FA 2014* changed the law, it was regarded as impossible for HMRC to challenge the 'employment' status of a member of an LLP: a member of an LLP could not in practice be re-categorised as an employee of it. The obvious scope which this gave for NIC avoidance led to legislation (now *ITTOIA 2005, s 863A et seq*) which treats any member of an LLP as an employee for tax purposes unless at least one of three possible 'escape routes' is satisfied. The legislation in this area is detailed and complex: what follows is a summary highlighting key planning areas. What is important to understand is that these three 'escape routes' are largely mechanistic and are different from the normal tests of employment. It is possible to envisage situations where a person who would not be treated as an employee of an ordinary partnership may be treated as an employee of an LLP and vice versa.

Focus

'Salaried members' of an LLP are subject to a special rule designed to counter 'disguised employment' which does not apply to ordinary partnerships. The special rule differs significantly from the ordinary tests of employment with the result that 'salaried members' who would not be regarded as employees under the ordinary case law tests may nonetheless be caught by the special rule: but some 'salaried members' who have all the normal characteristics of employees may nonetheless be able to take steps to ensure that they are not caught by the special rule.

3.47   The first 'escape route' is that it is reasonable to expect that more than 20% of the member's share of profit from the LLP will be something other than 'disguised salary'. An amount is 'disguised salary' if either: (a) it is fixed; or (b) it varies by reference to something other than the overall profits of the LLP as a whole; or (c) it is not in practice affected by the overall profits of the LLP as a whole. Thus, counter-intuitively, a share of departmental profits, however variable and inconstant, remains 'disguised salary'. A share of profit which is nominally dependent on overall LLP profit but which is subject to underpinning or capping arrangements which mean that the amount actually payable is all but certain will also rank as 'disguised salary'.

3.48   The second 'escape route' is that the member has 'significant influence' over the affairs of the LLP. In small LLPs it is probable that every member has 'significant influence': in larger ones, where management is delegated to a management or executive committee, it is likely that only members of such a committee will have it.

The third 'escape route' is that the member's 'contribution' to the LLP is at least 25% of the amount of the 'disguised salary' which it is reasonable to expect that the member will receive. 'Contribution' means broadly the amount of the member's capital account with the LLP. Artificial arrangements whereby the capital account does not truly represent the amount which the member has at risk are countered by the legislation. Thus a contribution does not count if and to the extent that the 'real' equity members guarantee the LLPs obligations to a 'salaried member' or the contribution is financed by limited-recourse loans or loans guaranteed by the LLP itself.

COMPANIES IN PARTNERSHIP

> **Focus**
>
> There is no reason why a company may not be a member of a partnership, and in some circumstances this may be attractive for tax and other reasons. However, care must be taken with regard to the possible application of anti-avoidance legislation introduced by the *Finance Act 2014*.

Trading status of corporate partners

3.49   Certain tax advantages are afforded to trading companies. The definition may vary according to the relief concerned but one might need to consider, for example, the scope of IHT business property relief (BPR), CGT entrepreneurs' relief or CGT hold-over relief for gifts.

> **Focus**
>
> Is a company whose purpose and activity is to be a partner in a partnership a trading company for tax purposes? On first principles the answer is yes: a corporate partner will as a matter of fact be carrying on in common with the other members of the partnership the business of the partnership; so if the business is a trade, the company is carrying on that trade. It should however be noted that, just like any other trading company which accumulates and invests profits, its status as a trading company may be compromised by its use of the accumulated profits. And, from 18 March 2015, the status of shares in a corporate partner for CGT entrepreneurs' relief requires very careful consideration, having regard to amendments to the definition of 'trading company' made both by *Finance Act 2015* and *Finance Act 2016*.

3.50 Thus, a corporate partner which uses its surplus profits from the partnership business to build, say, an investment portfolio outside the partnership business, may find that, on the facts, the relative sizes of its partnership trading activity and its non-partnership non-trading activity may have the result that IHT BPR or CGT entrepreneurs' relief may be restricted or denied. Overlaid upon that is a special rule applying only to entrepreneurs' relief on which we give further detail at **3.53** below.

Inheritance tax: BPR

3.51 *IHTA 1984, s 105(3)* denies BPR altogether in respect of shares in a company if the company's business is mainly making or holding investments. But even if the company's business is mainly trading so that relief is in principle due, relief may be restricted by virtue of *IHTA 1984, s 112*. This requires relief to be restricted by reference to the value of any assets which are neither used nor required for use in the business ('excepted assets'). HMRC do, however, accept that 'the business' means here the entirety of the company's activities and not just the trading activity (see SVM111220). Hence in the case of a company whose business is mainly trading but which also carries on an investment activity, assets will be 'excepted' only if used for neither the trading nor the investment part of the 'hybrid' business.

Focus

IHT Business Property Relief is denied if the partnership agreement contains obligations and provisions which together amount to a binding contract for sale of a partner's interest in the partnership on death. This can be avoided by careful drafting involving the use of cross-options.

3.52 In HMRC's view, cash which is surplus to the present and future needs of a trading business can almost never be regarded as an asset of a separate investment business (because holding it 'requires no effort and involves no activity') so will almost always constitute an 'excepted asset'. IHT considerations would therefore tend towards recommending investment of surplus cash into other investments so as to demonstrate the existence of an 'investment activity' element to the company's business rather than simply retaining it in cash.

The relief is incidentally denied if, on the death of the shareholder, there are provisions that amount to a binding contract for sale (*IHTA 1984, s 113*). Accordingly, when drafting the partnership agreement, care should be taken regarding the relevant provisions.

Entrepreneurs' relief

3.53   The entrepreneurs' relief position is very different. Shares in a company will qualify for the relief only if the company is a 'trading company' at all relevant times. The basic definition of 'trading company' is at *TCGA 1992, s 165A* – a company which (a) carries on trading activities; and (b) whose activities do not include to a substantial extent activities other than trading activities. 'Substantial' is undefined, but HMRC apply a rule of thumb which treats 'substantial' as meaning more than 20% (see CG64090 for more detail on the application of the 20% test). Thus a company which satisfies the 'wholly or mainly' requirement of IHT BPR may nonetheless fail to meet the stricter test for entrepreneurs' relief. On the other hand, the entrepreneurs' relief test at *TCGA 1992, s 165A* is by reference to 'activities'. It is at least arguable (especially in view of what HMRC say about 'lack of activity' in the IHT context – see SVM111220 above) that the mere passive holding of surplus cash (of whatever amount) can never amount to a non-trading 'activity' so that, while a holding of surplus cash may restrict IHT BPR it can never of itself disqualify a company from entrepreneurs' relief. Thus the best advice if entrepreneurs' relief is to be secured may be diametrically opposed to that which best secures IHT BPR, namely to retain surplus assets in cash and to avoid the further 'activity' implicit in making other investments. Even in this case, the entrepreneurs' relief position is not completely clear: for further guidance on HMRC's current views on the impact on entrepreneurs' relief of the investment of surplus cash, see CG64060.

In summary, a corporate partner which accumulates profits from its partnership trading and either retains those profits in cash or diversifies into other (non-trading) activities may need to take great care lest it be at risk of losing its trading status for the purposes of BPR, entrepreneurs' relief or both.

3.54   It is also necessary to take into account the changes effected first by the *Finance Act 2015* and subsequently by *Finance Act 2016* (with retrospective effect to 18 March 2015). These specify (via *TCGA 1992, Sch 7ZA*) the circumstances in which activities carried on by a company as a member of a partnership are to be treated as trading activities.

Specifically, such activities count as trading activities only if the person disposing of the shares ('P') passes both the 'profits and assets test' and the 'voting rights test' in relation to the partnership. At their simplest, these tests require that P should indirectly possess (via his interest in the corporate member) a right to at least 5% of the profits, assets and votes of the partnership throughout a period of at least one year ending with the disposal. Thus, if the members of a trading partnership comprise four companies all with equal rights, any shareholder who holds at least 20% of one of the companies could potentially qualify for Entrepreneurs Relief on a disposal of his interest in the company (since $20\% \times 25\% = 5\%$).

Focus

The *Finance Act 2015* and *Finance Act 2016* amended the entrepreneurs' relief rules to apply an indirect 5% test to the holding of shares in a company which is a member of a partnership.

There is a sting in the tail of the *Finance Act 2015* change. Normally, when a company ceases for any reason to qualify as a 'trading company', a disposal of shares (including by way of liquidation) can continue to qualify for entrepreneurs' relief if it is made up to three years after the trading status is lost. But where a company loses its trading status as a result of the coming into force of the *Finance Act 2015* change, this 'three-year' rule does not apply.

Capital allowances: annual investment allowance (AIA)

3.55   A partnership consisting of, or including, companies is debarred from claiming AIA.

By *CAA 2001, s 38A* the relief is available only to companies, individuals and partnerships of individuals.

MIXING PERSONAL AND CORPORATE PARTNERS

3.56   It has historically been possible to seek to get the 'best of both worlds' by use of a 'mixed' partnership whereby the members of a trading partnership include both the individual members and one or more companies controlled by the members, either individually or jointly.

With effect from 6 April 2014, *ITTOIA 2005, s 850C* removes virtually all the tax advantages that might otherwise have been expected to flow from mixed member partnerships. From that date mixed member partnerships will seldom be attractive. Nor, unfortunately, is there any 'grandfathering' provision to protect mixed member partnerships already in existence as at the date the law changed.

Focus

Since the enactment of the *Finance Act 2014* the involvement of companies in a partnership should be approached with great care. Existing fully corporate arrangements should normally be safe, but new arrangements may be vulnerable.

Mixed member partnerships: Finance Act 2014 provisions

3.57   Very broadly, *ITTOIA 2005, s 850C* bites where a share of partnership income which would otherwise have arisen to an individual partner in a partnership is in some sense diverted to a company partner in which the individual has some kind of economic interest with a consequent reduction in tax. It operates by re-attributing the income back to the partner from whom it was diverted.

More specifically, the rules apply where one of two conditions ('Condition X and Condition Y') is fulfilled, though there is considerable overlap between the conditions and there are many situations where both conditions will be fulfilled. In each case, the rules apply only if the 'diversion' of profit share from the individual to the company results in a reduction in the overall tax bill. There is no motive test: it is not necessary that the 'diversion' should have been undertaken with the purpose or intention of reducing the tax charge: merely that it does in fact do so.

Condition X

3.58   Condition X is that it is 'reasonable to suppose' that the corporate partner's profit share includes amounts representing the individual's 'deferred profit' – that is, a share of partnership profit which will, or even might, be allocated to the individual in the future. So much of the company's profit share as it is reasonable to suppose is attributable to an individual's 'deferred profit' as determined on a 'just and reasonable' basis is then re-allocated for tax purposes to the individual. The most obvious case will be where profits required for retention as working capital in the business are allocated to a corporate partner but in some way earmarked for individual partners, as in **Example 3.9**.

> **Example 3.9 – Re-allocation of company profit share: Condition X**
>
> Smith, Jones, Green and Brown are in partnership together with SJGB Ltd, a company which they own in equal shares. £100,000 of profit is allocated to SJGB Ltd. In this case the 'deferred profit' is re-allocated equally. More complicated arrangements might involve the use of different share classes with separately designated reserves or simply through a memorandum note; in that case the 'deferred profit' would be reallocated in whatever way is just and reasonable.

3.59   There is no scope for any re-allocation of profit to be retrospectively changed if an individual never receives the 'deferred profit' allocated to him.

Example 3.10 – Non-receipt of re-allocated profit

Following from **Example 3.9**, Brown leaves the partnership some years later and, under the terms of the partnership agreement, his shares in SJGB Ltd are bought back at par value. The law provides no remedy to Brown as against HMRC for the fact that he will have paid Income Tax on £25,000 of profit which he never in fact receives. Any adjustment to be made as between the partners is a matter for private agreement between them, and it would be prudent to cover this in the partnership agreement.

Condition Y

3.60 It is also necessary to consider the alternative condition which may apply to mixed member partnerships, 'Condition Y'. This operates where:

- a corporate member's profit share exceeds the 'appropriate notional profit';

- an individual member of the partnership has 'power to enjoy' any part of the company's profit share; and

- it is reasonable to suppose that the whole or part of the company's profit shares is attributable to the individual's power to enjoy it.

Where these conditions are fulfilled, so much of the company's profit share as exceeds the 'appropriate notional profit' and as, it is reasonable to suppose, is attributable to the individual's power to enjoy (determined on a just and reasonable basis) is re-allocated for tax purposes to the individual. **Example 3.11** illustrates a very straightforward example of the operation of Condition Y.

Example 3.11 – Re-allocation of company profit share: Condition Y

Smith and Jones are in partnership along with Smith Ltd and Jones Ltd (100% owned by Smith and Jones respectively). Profits are allocated 50% to Smith/Smith Ltd and 50% to Jones/Jones Ltd with each individual able to determine how 'his' share of profit is allocated between himself and his company. The effect of *ITTOIA 2005, s 850C* is that (subject to what is said later in this chapter) Smith and Jones will each be assessed to income tax on 50% of the partnership profit.

Appropriate notional profit

3.61   'Appropriate notional profit' is defined as the sum of the appropriate notional return on capital and the appropriate notional consideration for services. The first is, essentially, interest at a commercial rate on any capital which the company has contributed to the partnership. 'Contribution' for this purpose has the same meaning as in *ITA 2007, s 108* – broadly the permanent capital of the partnership as distinct from short-term loans. All relevant circumstances are to be taken into account; these would presumably include the risk profile of the firm's business, what other assets and liabilities the firm had and the rates of interest being paid by the firm on commercial loans from unconnected lenders. HMRC guidance underlines that the rate must be a reasonable rate of interest; it is not relevant that an equity return on the same investment might have been much greater. Thus if, in **Example 3.11**, the partnership was borrowing from commercial lenders at say 6%, and Smith Ltd and Jones Ltd each had capital accounts with the partnership of £100,000, an 'appropriate notional return on capital' might (at least in HMRC's view) be £6,000 per annum for each corporate partner and it would be only the excess of each company's profit share over that amount which would be re-allocated.

3.62   An appropriate notional consideration for services is the arm's length value of services provided to the partnership by the corporate member, but disregarding any services involving other members of the partnership. Thus, in **Example 3.11**, if the only services provided to the partnership by Smith Ltd are the services of Smith himself, the 'appropriate notional consideration for services' would be nil. But if (for example) Jones Ltd owns property which is made available to the partnership rent-free, the 'appropriate notional return for services' would be the market rent of the property.

Power to enjoy

3.63   It is important to appreciate that although the legislation refers to 'mixed membership' it does not attack the mixing of corporate and individual members per se. It is only where an individual partner has 'power to enjoy' all or part of a corporate partner's profit share – very broadly speaking, where he has some sort of connection with the corporate partner – that the legislation comes into play. Thus if, in **Example 3.11**, Mr Smith had been in partnership only with Jones Ltd (a company with which he has no economic interest or connection other than being in partnership), the legislation would not have been relevant. 'Power to enjoy' is, however, very widely defined, with three main branches.

3.64   First, an individual has 'power to enjoy' a company's profit share if he is connected with the company within the meaning of *ITA 2007, s 993* (otherwise, of course, than simply by being in partnership with it). This is itself a very wide-ranging definition and would include the case where the company is controlled (within the meaning of *CTA 2010, s 450*) by the individual or his associates, and can lead to some counter-intuitive results. For example, if Smith is in partnership with a company owned by the trustees of a charitable trust of which his grandfather was the settlor, he has 'power to enjoy' the company's profit share and it will be vulnerable to re-allocation to him.

3.65 Second, there is 'power to enjoy' if any of five specified 'enjoyment conditions' is met. These are, in fact, substantially the same as the notoriously wide enjoyment conditions which apply for the purposes of *ITA 2007, s 723* (the 'transfer of assets abroad' legislation). Thus profits will be vulnerable to re-allocation if:

- the company's profit share is in fact so dealt with as to be calculated at some time to enure to the benefit of the individual; or

- the receipt of the company's profit share operates to increase the value of assets held by or for the benefit of the individual; or

- the individual is entitled to receive any benefit provided out of the company's profit share; or

- the individual may become entitled to the beneficial enjoyment of the company's profit share if one or more powers are exercised by any person; or

- the individual is able to control the application of the company's profit share.

3.66 Third, even if none of these enjoyment conditions is met and the individual is not connected with the company, the legislation provides that the individual will nonetheless be deemed to have 'power to enjoy' if he is a party to any arrangements one of the main purposes of which is to secure that an amount included in the company's profit share is charged to Corporation Tax and not Income Tax. Read strictly, this would seem to put at risk any individual who merely acquiesced in the introduction to the partnership of a corporate partner even though the individual himself derived no direct or indirect benefit from the arrangement, though it is to be hoped that the courts would draw back from such a draconian interpretation of the law.

Attribution

3.67 Having established that the corporate partner's profit share exceeds the appropriate notional profit and that an individual partner has the 'power to enjoy' it in some degree, it remains to determine whether it is reasonable to suppose that any part of the company's profit share is attributable to the power to enjoy. In other words, would the company have received the profit share but for the individual's power to enjoy it? Sometimes the answer to the question will be obvious: in **Example 3.11**, it would defy credibility to suppose that Smith Ltd would have received its profit share had not Smith owned it. In other circumstances there may be a point to be taken. As a rule, it is probably fair to say that the more remote and indirect the individual's 'power to enjoy' interest in the company, the less reasonable it may be to suppose that the company's profit share is attributable to it. It is, however, worth pointing out that one of the odder features of the new law is that it may reallocate to an individual income which would not have been caught by the settlements legislation. For example, if an individual sole trader were to take into partnership his adult children and his spouse, or were to transfer the sole trade to a company in which they were shareholders, neither the profit share nor the dividend income of the family members would normally be within the scope of the settlements legislation and would remain taxable on the recipients. Yet if he were to take into partnership a company in which his family were shareholders, *ITTOIA 2005, s 850C* would be likely to re-allocate the company's entire profit share to him.

Double taxation

3.68   As one would expect, where income of a corporate partner is re-allocated under the new rules to an individual member, a 'just and reasonable' adjustment is made to the corporate partner's taxable profit. Usually this will simply be to reduce the company's taxable profit by the amount taxed on the individual, but in some cases the differing computational rules applying to companies and to individuals will mean that the 'just and reasonable' adjustment is less straightforward.

The other area in which double taxation needs to be considered is in relation to the extraction from the company of amounts representing the re-allocated income. Where income of a company has been taxed on an individual it would plainly be absurd for a second charge to be imposed on the subsequent distribution of that income to the individual. The new rules do indeed provide that any such payment is ignored for tax purposes, but only:

- if there is an agreement in place in relation to the amount re-allocated;

- the payment is made as a result of the agreement; and

- the payment is not made under arrangement one of the main purposes of which is the avoidance of tax.

The legislation is silent as to the form of the agreement or when it must be in place: but best practice may be for the agreement to take the form of a deed and for it to be entered into as soon as it becomes apparent that re-allocation is a possibility.

One possible difficulty may arise where the application of the legislation is not recognised (or not conceded) until some years after the income has arisen in the company and after distributions have been made (whether as salary or as dividend) to the individual in question and after they have been included on that individual's tax return and tax paid on them. Can it really be said either that 'there is an agreement in place in relation to the amount re-allocated' or that the payment is made 'as a result of' that agreement when the payments were in fact made some years before the possibility of re-allocation was recognised? And in such a case can the rule operate to allow a refund to be claimed of the tax previously paid on the relevant remuneration or dividends? One would hope that HMRC would take the same broad and teleological approach to the interpretation of relieving legislation of this kind as to assessing legislation; but there must be a doubt.

And one case in which there would certainly be a difficulty would be if income of a company were to be re-allocated after the company had applied the income in, for example, making pension contributions for the benefit of the individual, as shown in the example below.

Example 3.12 – Inability to distribute re-allocated income

Adam Ltd, controlled by Adam, is a member of a partnership. In the year to 31 March 2015 its share of profit is £100,000. It uses its entire profit share to make a pension contribution to Adam's pension fund. Following enquiry and appeal to the First-tier Tribunal it is held in 2018 that £75,000 of the income of Adam Ltd should be re-allocated to Adam for tax purposes.

The consequence would appear to be that Adam is liable to tax for 2014–15 on the £75,000 even though (a) he has never received it and (b) the company is not able to pay it to him. Logically, the legislation should give him relief against the £75,000 deemed income for the contribution made by the company to the pension fund; but there is no machinery by which this can be done. Adam is therefore significantly worse off than he would have been had he been a member of the partnership personally.

Anti-avoidance, grandfathering and the scope of the new rules

3.69 It might reasonably be supposed that if what is perceived to be objectionable is a 'mixed member' partnership, HMRC would raise no objection to pure corporate partnerships or to the restructuring of existing 'mixed member' partnerships so as to become pure corporate partnerships. That this is not so must be one of the most puzzling features of the legislation.

Yet this is the intention and effect of the anti-avoidance rule introduced as *ITTOIA 2005, s 850D*. This rule applies where a partnership is not in fact a mixed member partnership but:

- an individual personally performs services for the firm;

- a non-individual partner has a share of the firm's profit; and

- it is reasonable to suppose that the individual would have been a partner in the firm but for the new rules introduced by *ITTOIA 2005, s 850C*.

Where *ITTOIA 2005, s 850D* applies, the individual is treated as if he had been a partner in the firm with the result that the main provisions at *ITTOIA 2005, s 850C* potentially apply.

Example 3.13 – Restructuring ineffective in avoiding re-allocation of profit

Smith and Jones are in partnership together with their respective companies Smith Ltd and Jones Ltd. As a result of the new legislation all or part of any profit share allocated to the companies is at risk of being re-allocated by *ITTOIA 2005, s 850C* to the individuals. This remains the case even if Smith and Jones now resign from the partnership leaving only their companies as members, since the anti-avoidance rule will bite: plainly is it 'reasonable to suppose' that Smith and Jones would have continued to be partners alongside their companies but for *ITTOIA 2005, s 850C*.

3.70 In theory, *ITTOIA 2005, s 850D* (and thus *ITTOIA 2005, s 850C*) would not be in point if it could be shown that the motivation of Smith and Jones in resigning from the partnership owed nothing to a desire to avoid the impact of *ITTOIA 2005, s 850C*. In practice, it is difficult to envisage any circumstances in which that could credibly be argued to be the case.

Although in general it is a question of fact whether it is 'reasonable to suppose' that a given individual would have been a member of a given partnership but for *ITTOIA 2005, s 850C*, the legislation at *ITTOIA 2005, s 850D* gives one specific example where it is conclusively deemed to be the case. That is, where the individual is a member not of the partnership itself but of a partnership (or, more likely, an LLP) which is in turn a member of the partnership. Hence structures such as **Example 3.14** will be caught by the new rules.

Example 3.14 – Deemed membership of LLP by individuals

XYZ LLP has as its members X LLP, Y LLP and Z LLP whose members are respectively Mr X and his company X Ltd, Mr Y and his company Y Ltd,

---

and Mr Z and his company Z Ltd. Although XYZ LLP is not a 'mixed member' partnership, it is deemed to be reasonable to suppose that X Y and Z would have been members but for *ITTOIA 2005, s 850C* with the result that the profits of their respective companies are vulnerable to re-allocation.

Grandfathering

3.71 There is no 'grandfathering' for mixed member partnerships which were in existence before the introduction of the new rules: thus, from 6 April 2014, any mixed member partnership must have regard to *ITTOIA 2005, s 850C*.

However, because the anti-avoidance rule at *ITTOIA 2005, s 850D* applies only if it is reasonable to suppose that an individual would have been a member 'but for' *ITTOIA 2005, s 850C*, it logically follows that a pure corporate partnership which antedates *ITTOIA 2005, s 850D* cannot be within its scope. HMRC have confirmed their agreement with that interpretation and accept that it cannot be inferred that an individual would have been a member of a partnership but for the new rules if the individual withdrew from the partnership before the new rules were announced on 5 December 2013. Thus if, in **Example 3.11**, Smith and Jones had by good fortune or by virtue of a reliable crystal ball resigned as individuals before 5 December 2013, leaving a pure corporate partnership as at that date, the profits of their companies would not be at risk of re-allocation to them. HMRC have further confirmed that a change taking place on or after 5 December will be treated in the same way provided the decision to make the change was made before 5 December. One example of this might be where a member who is required to give notice of resignation gave such notice before 5 December 2013 but did not cease to be a member until the expiry of the notice period after that date.

3.72 The position of corporate members joining existing pure corporate partnerships after 5 December 2013 is not completely clear. The key question is whether it is reasonable to suppose that the new member would have joined in an individual capacity if *ITTOIA 2005, s 850C* had not been enacted. In the case of a partnership which has historically been a pure corporate partnership with track record of new members joining as companies, it may be unreasonable to make such a supposition; on the other hand, if a company joins what has historically been a mixed member partnership it may be more likely that *ITTOIA 2005, s 850D* may be in point.

New pure corporate partnerships

3.73 The position of new pure corporate partnerships is even less clear. Where a new pure corporate partnership is created to acquire the business of an existing 'tainted' mixed member partnership it seems likely that *ITTOIA 2005, s 850D* would be in point. But what of a pure corporate partnership created to undertake an entirely new project or trade? It seems to be HMRC's view that it depends on whether the decision to use corporate rather than individual members is driven by tax or by wider commercial considerations, though it must be said that this seems to be a very broad interpretation of *ITTOIA 2005, s 850C* which may not be supported by the courts. Thus if two established companies come together to form a partnership to carry out a particular project – something which is common in, for example, the property development sector – the likelihood that HMRC would seek to invoke *ITTOIA 2005, s 850D* is small. But if a number of individuals wishing to establish a new business form new companies to become members of a new partnership through which the trade is to be conducted, HMRC may feel more confident in seeking to apply *ITTOIA 2005, s 850D*.

STAMP DUTY LAND TAX

3.74   Chargeable interests held by or on behalf of a partnership are treated for SDLT purposes as held by, or on behalf of, the partners, and land transactions entered into for the purposes of a partnership are treated as entered into by, or on behalf of, the partners (and not by the partnership as such). This is the case irrespective of whether the partnership has a legal personality or is a body corporate under the law of the country in which it is formed (*FA 2003, s 104* and *Sch 15, Pt 1*).

The partnership is treated as continuing, regardless of changes in composition, as long as one partner continues.

Focus

Although third-party sales and purchases by partnership are relatively straightforward in SDLT terms, the rules applying to transfers between partnerships and their partners and on sales of interests in a partnership are not only complex but have changed regularly since the introduction of SDLT in 2003. The general rule is now, in essence, to look through to the underlying ownership of the property (but in terms of entitlement to income, not capital). This can create unwelcome charges but is also capable of resulting in a much reduced or zero charge to SDLT on some transfers.

3.75   Purchases and sales of land by the partnership are therefore reasonably straightforward in SDLT terms. The main complexities arise with *Part 3* of *FA 2003, Sch 15* – 'Transactions to which special provisions apply'.

Transactions to which special provisions apply: *FA 2003, Sch 15, Pt 3*

3.76   Special provisions apply to

- the transfer of a chargeable interest to a partnership by a partner or a person connected with a partner;

- the transfer of an interest in a partnership;

- the transfer of a chargeable interest from a partnership to a partner or a person connected with a partner.

Transfer of a chargeable interest to a partnership

3.77   The transfer of a chargeable interest to a partnership by a partner or a person connected with a partner (or a person who become a partner as a result of the transfer) will in principle give rise to a charge to SDLT (*FA 2003, Sch 15, para 10*). The broad aim of the legislation here is to 'look through' the partnership to the partners so as to identify the value that is actually changing hands and to charge SDLT on that amount.

The simplest example is where an individual transfers a chargeable interest to a partnership with whose members he is otherwise unconnected. The amount on which SDLT is charged is in that case the percentage of the market value of the asset which is equal to the percentage which he gives up – that is, the difference between the 100% of the asset which he owns at the outset and the share of the asset which he owns (via his membership of the partnership) after the transfer.

Example 3.15 – Transfer from a partner to a partnership

Smith owns a property. He joins a partnership in which he takes a 25% share and on joining it transfers to the partnership as partner's capital a property worth £400,000.

Smith has effectively given up 75% of the value in the property. SDLT is due on 75% × £400,000 = £300,000. Note that the value which the partners attribute to the property is irrelevant: SDLT will be due by reference to a percentage of the market value.

The same SDLT would be payable if Smith were already a 25% member of the partnership and was selling the property to the LLP for value. Again, he would be giving up a 75% interest and SDLT would be due on 75% of the value (regardless of the selling price).

For this purpose (as for *FA 2003, Sch 15* generally) the shares in which partners are treated as owning partnership assets are determined by reference to the shares in which income profits of the partnership are allocated (*FA 2003, Sch 15, para 34*). This may, of course, be different from the shares in which capital profits are allocated (which is what is relevant for CGT purposes) and may be a trap for the unwary.

Taking a slightly more complex case, where the individual who is making the transfer is connected with other members of the partnership, regard is had not only to share of the asset which he himself owns (via his membership of the partnership) after the transfer but also to that owned by partners connected with him.

Example 3.16 – Effect of connected parties in partnership

If, in **Example 3.15**, Smith's civil partner Jones was also a member of the partnership, with a 15% share of profits, Smith would be regarded as having effectively given up 60% (that is, 100% – 25% – 15%) of the property so that SDLT would be due on 60% × £400,000 = £240,000.

3.78 A charge to SDLT can arise where land has been transferred into a partnership by a partner and within three years of the date of transfer a 'qualifying event' occurs. This is defined as the transferor:

(a) withdrawing from the partnership any money or money's worth other than income profit; or

(b) obtaining repayment of any loan he has made to the partnership.

In such circumstances the 'qualifying event' is treated as a chargeable transaction and the chargeable consideration is taken to be the amount of the withdrawal or repayment up to the market value of the chargeable interest transferred (less any amount previously chargeable).

3.79 If the partnership to which the chargeable interest is transferred is a property-investment partnership (PIP) an election can be made to disapply the treatment described at **3.77** above and instead to pay SDLT by reference to the full market value of the chargeable interest transferred (*FA 2003, Sch 15, para 12A*). Although such an election would initially seem counter-intuitive, the advantage of making the election is that it will avoid any subsequent charge as described under **3.78** above and will also reduce the amount of SDLT payable on a subsequent transfer of an interest in the PIP.

For this purpose, a PIP is not, as might reasonably be supposed, simply a partnership which invests in property. Instead, it is defined (by *FA 2003,*

Sch 15, para 14(8)) as a partnership whose sole or main activity is investing or dealing in chargeable interests (whether or not that activity also involves the carrying out of construction operations on the land in question). A property development partnership and a land dealing partnership will therefore both be PIPs.

Transfer of an interest in a partnership

3.80 SDLT is in principle payable on the transfer of an interest in a PIP where the partnership property includes a chargeable interest. This includes not only the case where a person becomes a partner but also the case where one partner's share reduces (including a reduction to zero on leaving the partnership) and the share of another partner or partners increases. Any person whose partnership share increases (including any new partner) is treated as the 'purchaser' for SDLT purposes and is answerable for the relevant SDLT.

A transfer of an interest in a partnership other than a PIP is not subject to SDLT (regardless of the amount of chargeable property held within the partnership).

3.81 On a transfer of an interest in a PIP, SDLT is chargeable on the proportion changing hands of the market value of 'relevant partnership property'. Thus, if a partner in a PIP having a 10% share in the partnership retires from the partnership, the remaining partners will suffer a charge to SDLT on 10% of the 'relevant partnership property'.

3.82 What is included in (or excluded from) 'relevant partnership property' depends on the type of transfer, styled either a 'Type A' transfer or a 'Type B' transfer.

3.83 A Type A transfer is one where:

- a partner's share is acquired (in whole or part) by another person (either an existing or a new partner) for consideration in money or money's worth; or

- a person becomes a partner; the interest of an existing partner reduces (or ceases) and money or money's worth is withdrawn from the partnership by the existing partner (other than out of resources available to the partnership prior to the transfer).

For a Type A transfer, the 'relevant partnership property' taken into account is every chargeable interest held by the partnership immediately after the transfer of the partnership interest except for:

- any chargeable interest transferred to the partnership in connection with the transfer;

- leases at a market rent; and

- any chargeable interest that is not attributable economically to the partnership interest transferred.

3.84   Any other transfer is styled a Type B transfer. In the case of a Type B transfer, the 'relevant partnership property' excludes (in addition to the exclusions for a Type A transfer):

- any chargeable interest transferred to the partnership on or before 22 July 2004;

- any chargeable interest for which the *FA 2003, Sch 15, para 12A* election has been made; and

- any other chargeable interest which was transferred to the partnership other than by a partner or a person connected with a partner.

Transfer of a chargeable interest from a partnership

3.85   As with a transfer to a partnership, the transfer of a chargeable interest from a partnership to a partner or a person connected with a partner (or to a person who ceases to be a partner as a result of the transfer) will in principle give rise to a charge to SDLT (*FA 2003, Sch 15, para 18*). As with transfers the other way, the broad aim of the legislation is to 'look through' the partnership to the partners so as to identify the value that is actually changing hands and to charge SDLT on that amount.

3.86   Thus on a transfer of land from a partnership consisting of husband and wife (or other connected parties) to a company controlled by those persons (or by any one of them), no SDLT is payable (including in the particular case where a business is incorporated). This may be thought anomalous given that there is no corresponding SDLT relief on the incorporation of a sole trade. Those contemplating taking advantage of the anomaly by converting a sole trade to a partnership shortly before incorporation would, however, be well advised to contemplate the anti-avoidance rules at *Finance Act 2003, s 75A et seq*.

Chapter 4

Company purchase of own shares

Mark McLaughlin CTA (Fellow), ATT (Fellow), TEP, Tax Consultant,
Mark McLaughlin Associates Ltd and The TACS Partnership

SIGNPOSTS

- **Scope** – A purchase of own shares (eg by an owner-managed company) generally falls to be treated as an income distribution. However, there is an exception in respect of unquoted trading companies if certain conditions are satisfied, such that the vendor is normally treated as receiving a capital payment instead. The distinction between income and capital treatment for the transaction can be significant, particularly due to the difference in the rates of income tax and capital gains tax (see **4.1–4.4**).

- **Conditions** – A number of statutory conditions must be satisfied for a company purchase of own shares to be excluded from income distribution treatment and to be treated as a capital payment for tax purposes instead (see **4.5–4.34**).

- **Practical issues** – The transaction may need to be structured and implemented carefully, according to whether capital or income distribution treatment is sought. A clearance application can be made in advance to obtain certainty about HMRC's view of the tax treatment on the company's purchase of its own shares (see **4.35–4.64**).

- **Company law** – A company purchase of its own shares must comply with certain *Companies Act* requirements. Otherwise, the transaction may be void and legally unenforceable, and unforeseen tax implications may result (see **4.65–4.68**).

- **Other points** – Separate tax considerations apply to corporate and trustee vendors. In addition, sundry issues on a company purchase of own shares include returns of share purchases, stamp duty costs and returns, share valuations and the loan relationships 'unallowable purposes' anti-avoidance provisions (see **4.69–4.80**).

INTRODUCTION

4.1 This chapter is mainly concerned with the purchase by an unquoted trading or holding company of its own shares from an individual shareholder, particularly in respect of family and owner-managed companies.

As a general rule, when a company buys back its own shares from a shareholder, any 'premium' (ie payment in excess of the capital originally subscribed for the shares) constitutes a distribution. For tax purposes, the transaction generally falls to be treated as an income distribution (*CTA 2010, s 1000(1)*), such as on a purchase of own shares by a quoted company.

However, there is an exception in the case of unquoted trading companies (*CTA 2010, s 1033*). If certain conditions are satisfied, the transaction is automatically excepted from income distribution treatment. The effect is that the vendor is treated as receiving a capital payment instead (unless the vendor is a share dealer, in which case the receipt is treated as trading income). This treatment provides shareholders with a potentially tax-efficient exit route from the company.

A 20% rate of capital gains tax (CGT) (for 2018/19) makes capital payments less attractive in some cases, where the proceeds are relatively small. The normal lower CGT rate of 10% (for 2018/19) does not apply to the extent that an individual is liable to higher rates of income tax, However, if the conditions for entrepreneurs' relief are satisfied, the first £10m of an individual's qualifying gains are taxable at a rate of 10% (*TCGA 1992, s 169N*). Entrepreneurs' relief has become increasingly valuable over time. The relief limit was increased to £10m from £5m in *Finance Act 2011*, which in turn was increased to £5m from £2m (in *Finance (No 2) Act 2010*), and to £2m from the original ceiling of £1m (in *Finance Act 2010*) with effect from 6 April 2010 (the £1m limit applying in relation to disposals in 2008/09 or 2009/10). For disposals before 6 April 2008 (ie prior to the abolition of taper relief), the position was potentially better, as full business asset taper relief could result in an effective 10% CGT rate with no upper gains limit.

Furthermore, a claim for investors' relief (which was introduced in *Finance Act 2016*) separately provides for a CGT rate of 10% on chargeable gains from the disposal by a qualifying person of shares where certain conditions are satisfied, subject to an overall limit of £10m (*TCGA 1992, ss 169VC, 169VK*). Some shareholders may be eligible to claim investors' relief in due course, although in practice entrepreneurs' relief claims are likely to be more common.

By contrast to the potential CGT rates, the reform of the system of dividend taxation from April 2016 resulted in the removal of the dividend tax credit of 10% and replacement with a dividend nil rate (originally £5,000 a year per individual, but subsequently reduced to £2,000 a year for 2018/19 and subsequent tax years in *F(No 2)A 2017)*. The rate of income tax on dividends (for 2018/19) is 7.5% for basic rate taxpayers, 32.5% for higher rate taxpayers and 38.1% for additional rate taxpayers.

The differential between CGT and income tax rates may vary depending on individual circumstances, but in general terms it is sufficiently wide (in 2018/19) to make capital treatment an important consideration for many individual shareholders.

Conversely, subscriber shareholders in unquoted trading companies may be able to claim a capital loss arising from a purchase of own shares where CGT treatment applies, upon which income tax relief may be available, if certain conditions are satisfied (*TCGA 1992, s 24(2)*; *ITA 2007, s 131*).

A company purchase of own shares can be useful in a variety of situations, particularly in the context of family or owner-managed businesses. For example, a controlling director shareholder may wish to retire and make way for younger management, some or all of whom may be family members. Alternatively, shareholder disputes over the running of the company's trade may be resolved by using a company purchase of own shares to provide dissenting parties with an opportunity to depart from the company and realise the value of their shares. In both cases, this route may seem particularly attractive if a direct purchase of the shares (eg by other shareholders, family members or managers) is not possible due to an insufficiency of funds.

A company purchase of own shares also provides personal representatives or legatees with an opportunity to realise the value of shares following the death of a shareholder. It should be noted that (for 2018/19) the standard rate of CGT for gains accruing to settlement trustees and personal representatives (eg for share disposals) is 20%.

A number of conditions must generally be satisfied in order to qualify for capital gains treatment on a company purchase of own shares, including a 'trade benefit' test, as well as requirements as to residence, length of ownership of the shares and the degree (if any) to which the vendor remains connected with the company. In some cases, it may not be possible to satisfy all the requirements. The business owners may therefore wish to consider alternative exit strategies for the vendor shareholder (eg a management buyout). Such considerations are outside the scope of this chapter.

Employee shareholder shares

4.2 An 'employee shareholder' employment status was introduced from 1 September 2013 (*Employment Rights Act 1996, s 205A*). This status initially offered various tax incentives to encourage employee share ownership, in return for the individual agreeing to forego certain employment rights. Those tax incentives originally included a CGT exemption in respect of qualifying shares issued or allotted to an employee under an employee shareholder agreement with a total 'unrestricted market value' not exceeding £50,000 on receipt (*TCGA 1992, s 236C*). However, this exemption was restricted (in *Finance Act 2016*) to a lifetime limit of £100,000 on the disposal of shares acquired under employee shareholder agreements entered into after 16 March 2016. The CGT exemption was removed completely in *Finance Act 2017*, in relation to shares acquired in consideration of an employee shareholder agreement entered into on or after the 'relevant day' as defined (ie normally 1 December 2016).

There was also specific provision in respect of a company purchase of own shares. No income tax charge originally arose as a distribution (under *ITTOIA 2005, Pt 4, Ch 3*) if shares were sold back to the company (ie the payment was made in respect of shares in the company), those shares were exempt employee shareholder shares (within the meaning of *TCGA 1992, ss 236B–236D*), and the individual was not an employee (or office holder) of the employer company or associated company at the time of disposal (*ITTOIA 2005, s 385A*). However, this income tax relief was also removed in *Finance Act 2017*, once again in relation to shares acquired in consideration of an employee shareholder agreement entered into on or after the 'relevant day' (see above).

The remainder of this chapter deals with the company purchase of shares in an unquoted trading company, which are not employee shareholder shares eligible for the above tax reliefs.

Tax and company law

4.3 The tax legislation on company distributions is contained in *CTA 2010, Pt 23, Ch 3*. This legislation contains provisions specifically dealing with the purchase of own shares by an unquoted trading company (*CTA 2010, ss 1033–1048*). The purchase of own shares rules exclude from distribution treatment payments made by a company on the redemption, repayment or purchase of its own shares, if certain conditions are satisfied.

This chapter outlines those rules, and considers planning points and potential pitfalls in relation to them.

4.4 It is important to note that a purchase of own shares must comply with company law requirements to be valid. In practice, the *Companies Act 2006* requirements are often an after-thought, and have the potential to be overlooked completely by the uninitiated. As this book is mainly concerned with tax law rather than company law, priority is given to tax considerations. However, whilst company law is discussed later in this chapter, strictly speaking it should be the primary consideration. The implications of 'getting it wrong' can be unfortunate to say the least.

A company purchase of own shares should not be confused with a reduction of share capital, for which separate company law provisions apply (*CA 2006, Pt 17, Ch 10*). As to the circumstances in which a reduction of share capital may be appropriate, as well as the company law requirements and tax implications, see **Chapter 5**.

Guidance on the tax treatment of a company purchase of own shares is contained in HMRC's Company Taxation Manual (at CTM17505 onwards), mainly in respect of income distribution treatment, and in the Capital Gains Manual (at CG58600 onwards) relating to capital gains treatment.

Additional commentary on the subject can also be found in *Tax Planning for Family and Owner-Managed Companies 2018/19* by Peter Rayney (Bloomsbury Professional).

MEETING THE CONDITIONS

Checklist

4.5

Focus

Aside from the company law requirements mentioned above, the following checklist is intended as a brief summary of the conditions to be satisfied for a company purchase of its own shares to be excluded from income distribution treatment, and to be treated as a capital payment instead (within *CTA 2010, ss 1033–1048*). These conditions are considered further in this chapter.

Table 4.1: Conditions for company purchase of own shares within *CTA 2010, s 1033(1)*

- **Company status** – the purchasing company must be an unquoted trading company, or the unquoted holding company of a trading group (*CTA 2010, s 1033(1)(a)*).

- **Purpose of the payment** – either the 'trade benefit' (see **4.12**) and 'no scheme or arrangements' (see **4.19**) tests are met, *or* the payment (apart from any amount used in payment of CGT on the transaction) is applied by the recipient in discharging an inheritance tax liability within two years after a death (see **4.7–4.8**) (Note – in the latter case, the further conditions below do not need to be satisfied) (*CTA 2010, s 1033(1)(b)*).

- **Residence** – the vendor shareholder must be UK resident (and for individuals in respect of purchases before 6 April 2013, ordinarily resident) for the tax year in which the purchase takes place (*CTA 2010, s 1034*).

- **Period of ownership** – the shares must have been owned for a minimum of five years ending with the date of purchase. However, if the shares were acquired by will or intestacy, the minimum ownership period is reduced to three years (*CTA 2010, ss 1035–1036*).

- **'Substantial reduction'** – the vendor shareholder's interest in the company must normally be substantially reduced (eg if the vendor retains some shares after the purchase) (*CTA 2010, ss 1037–1041*).

- **No 'continuing connection'** – the vendor must not be connected with the company (or group company) immediately after the purchase (*CTA 2010, ss 1042, 1043, 1062–1063*).

If these conditions are satisfied, capital treatment is automatic. This assumes, of course, that the transaction is valid under company law.

An application can be made to HMRC under *CTA 2010, s 1044* for advance clearance that capital treatment will be available to the vendor shareholder (see **4.59**). This is normally accompanied by an application for clearance under *ITA 2007, s 701* that the anti-avoidance rules regarding 'transactions in securities' in *ITA 2007, Pt 13, Ch 1* do not apply to counteract any income tax advantage (*ITA 2007, s 684*).

4.6   Alternatively, a 'negative' clearance application can be made that the transaction should be treated as an income distribution.

It can be possible to break the conditions for capital treatment, if income distribution treatment is preferable. For example, this could be achieved by the vendor leaving the sale proceeds outstanding as a loan, such that the 'no continuing connection test' is broken. Alternatively, the shares could be bought in stages, so that the 'substantial reduction' test is not met.

Breaching the capital treatment conditions is further considered later in the chapter (see **4.63**).

IHT and 'undue hardship'

4.7   The purpose of the company purchase of its own shares (or redemption or repayment) for which this chapter is mainly concerned is broadly that the payment is wholly or mainly to benefit a trade carried on by the company or group, and is not part of a scheme or arrangement a main purpose of which is to allow the owner to participate in company profits without receiving a dividend, or for tax avoidance.

However, it should be noted that there is a second, alternative allowable purpose. This is that substantially the whole proceeds from the share transaction relating to an unquoted trading company or holding company of a trading group (apart from any payment towards a CGT liability arising in respect of it) are applied in discharging an IHT liability of the recipient on a death, within two years of that event (*CTA 2010, s 1033(3)*).

4.8   If this purpose is relevant, it is not necessary for the vendor to demonstrate that the transaction was for the benefit of the company's trade, and the other conditions which apply to the first purpose need not be satisfied by the vendor of the shares. However, there is a further specific requirement for the second purpose to apply, which is broadly that the relevant IHT liability could not otherwise have been paid without 'undue hardship' (*CTA 2010, s 1033(4)*).

The remainder of this chapter considers the conditions to be satisfied for a purchase of own shares by an unquoted trading company (or unquoted holding company of a trading group) to fall within *CTA 2010, s 1033(2)*.

COMPANY STATUS

4.9   The purchasing company must be an unquoted trading company or the holding company of a trading group (*CTA 2010, s 1033(1)(a)*). The terms 'unquoted company', 'trading company' and 'trading group' (among others) are specifically defined for the purposes of the purchase of own shares rules, and broadly have the following meaning (*CTA 2010, s 1048*):

- An 'unquoted company' is a company which is neither quoted nor a 51% subsidiary of a quoted company. A 'quoted company' is a company whose shares (or any class of them) are listed on the official list of a stock exchange. However, shares listed on the Alternative Investment Market, or dealt in on the Unlisted Securities Market, are regarded as unquoted for these purposes (CTM17507).

- A 'trading company' is a company whose business consists 'wholly or mainly' (ie more than 50%) of carrying on one or more trades (*CTA 2010, s 1048(1)*). This differs from the definition of trading company for entrepreneurs' relief (or investors' relief) purposes, which requires that the company's activities do not include to a substantial extent activities other than trading activities (*TCGA 1992, s 165A(3)*). 'Substantial' in an entrepreneurs' relief context is taken by HMRC to mean more than 20% of certain categories of measure, such as non-trading income (see CG64090).

Hence, it is possible that a company may satisfy the 'wholly or mainly' test of trading status on a purchase of its own shares, and yet a gain on the disposal of those shares may be denied entrepreneurs' relief in the hands of an individual shareholder because the company's non-trading activities are substantial.

- A 'trading group' is one in which the business of its members taken together consists wholly or mainly of carrying on one or more trades (*CTA 2010, s 1048(1)*). In this context 'group' means the company itself and its 75% subsidiaries.

4.10   There is a distinction between 'trade' and 'business' which must be recognised. For example, property investment activities may amount to a business, but on general principles do not constitute a trade. In addition, a 'trade' for the above purposes specifically excludes dealing in shares, securities, land or futures (*CTA 2010, s 1048(1)*).

Finally, in HMRC's view it is not sufficient that the company was formerly trading, or intends trading in the future. It must be a trading company when the transaction takes place (*Tax Bulletin*, Issue 21 (February 1996)).

PURPOSE OF THE PAYMENT

4.11

Focus

The conditions for a company purchase of its own shares to be excepted from distribution treatment include a purpose test containing two separate limbs, both of which must be satisfied (*CTA 2010, s 1033(2)(a), (b)*). These are in addition to a general provision that the other purchase of own shares requirements (in *CTA 2010, ss 1034–1043*) are met, so far as they are applicable (*CTA 2010, s 1033(2)(c)*).

These limbs are considered separately below.

Limb 1: The 'trade benefit' test

4.12   The first limb of the 'purpose' condition mentioned above is that the company's purchase (or redemption or repayment) of shares must be wholly or mainly for the purpose of benefiting a trade carried on by the company, or by any of its 75% subsidiaries. The requirement is referred to in this chapter as the 'trade benefit' test.

As indicated in the Checklist at **4.5**, in addition to the 'trade benefit' condition in *CTA 2010, s 1033(2)(a)*, there are various other conditions for a company purchase of own shares to be excluded from income distribution treatment. Those further conditions are contained in *CTA 2010, ss 1034–1043* (see below), and are relatively unambiguous.

By contrast, a particular difficulty with the 'trade benefit' test is that it is not defined anywhere in the legislation. However, this test was considered in *Allum v Marsh* [2005] STC (SCD) 191, which is discussed at **4.16** below.

STATEMENT OF PRACTICE 2/82

4.13   The 'trade benefit' test is also the subject of guidance by HMRC in Statement of Practice 2/82 ('Company's purchase of own shares: *ICTA 1988*'), which includes examples of situations in which the trade benefit test would normally be regarded as satisfied:

● Disagreements between shareholders over the company's management, which has or could have an adverse effect on the company's trade.

As a general rule, the company must buy back all the dissenting shareholder's shares and remove him entirely. However, there are possible exceptions to this rule, such as if the company cannot afford them all, but buys back as many as it can afford and intends buying the rest as soon as possible, or if the retiring director shareholder wishes to retain up to 5% of the company's issued share capital for sentimental reasons.

● An 'unwilling shareholder' wants to end their association with the company.

The trade benefit test may be satisfied if the purpose of the share buyback is to ensure that the shares are not sold to someone who could be unacceptable to the other shareholders. Statement of Practice 2/82 provides examples of 'unwilling shareholders':

– 'business angels' (ie outside shareholders who wish to withdraw equity finance);

– retiring controlling director shareholders wanting to make way for new management;

– personal representatives of deceased shareholders wishing to realise the shares; and

– legatees of a deceased shareholder not wishing to hold shares in the company.

RETAINING AN INTEREST IN THE COMPANY

4.14 Statement of Practice 2/82 indicates that if the vendor shareholder retains an interest in the company (eg if the company is not buying all the vendor's shares, or if the vendor is retained as a director or consultant) the trade benefit test will probably not be satisfied. However, as indicated above, the possibility of a retained interest is not ruled out as mainly benefiting the company's trade in certain circumstances. For example:

- the company does not currently have the resources to purchase all the shares of a retiring controlling shareholder immediately; or

- a retiring director wishes to retain no more than 5% of the company's shares for sentimental reasons.

It should be remembered that statements of practice only represent the views of HMRC, and are not legally binding. Nevertheless, taxpayers and their advisers should be aware of Statement of Practice 2/82 and its contents.

An Annex to Statement of Practice 2/82 helpfully contains the suggested format of advance clearance applications on a purchase of own shares, including a statement of the expected 'purpose and benefits' of the purchase, trading and otherwise.

HMRC's Help Sheet 'Company Purchase of Own Shares' also contains checklists of information to be provided in clearance applications for a purchase benefiting a company's trade, and a purchase in connection with an IHT liability (tinyurl.com/HMRC-CPOS).

4.15 Despite the non-statutory nature of the trade benefit test, prior to *Allum v Marsh* (see below) case law had not offered much guidance on its meaning. In *Moody v Tyler (Inspector of Taxes)* Ch D 2000, 72 TC 536, the taxpayer resigned as the director of a family company in 1989. The company lent him £50,000. In 1995 the company purchased 2,247 shares from his holding for £50,000. Those monies were offset against the loan. The taxpayer appealed against an assessment to tax as an income distribution, on the grounds that the purchase had been made wholly or mainly to benefit the trade carried on by the company within what is now *CTA 2010, s 1033(2)(a)*.

The General Commissioners dismissed the appeal and the Court of Appeal upheld their decision. Whether the trade benefit test had been satisfied was a pure question of fact, and there was no basis upon which the court could interfere with the Commissioners' decision. In any event, it is interesting to note that the purchase of own shares in this case was in breach of company law, as the proceeds were used to cancel the vendor's outstanding loan account with the company. As noted elsewhere in this chapter, consideration for the transaction must be paid in full, in cash, on completion.

4.16   *Company purchase of own shares*

ALLUM v MARSH

4.16   The subsequent case of *Allum v Marsh* [2005] SpC 446 offers some assistance on the application of the 'trade benefit' test. In that case, the company's purchase of the taxpayer's shares was held not to be for the benefit of the company's trade. The taxpayers, Mr and Mrs A, were the directors of an unquoted trading company. They held all the shares except one held by R, their son. When the taxpayers were approaching age 70, a property developer expressed an interest in purchasing the company's premises. Mr and Mrs A wished to retire from the business and dispose of their shares without selling them outside the company, so that R could run the company and continue trading. The property sale was completed. The company voted to purchase Mr and Mrs A's shares, and to repay an outstanding directors' loan. In the following year, the company's trading operations reduced considerably. Suitable trading premises were not found, and the company's business was carried out from a limited facility shared with another company.

HMRC assessed the taxpayers on the sale proceeds for their shares as an income distribution, on the grounds that the conditions for capital gains tax treatment (in what is now *CTA 2010, s 1033(2)(a)*) were not satisfied. HMRC considered that the company's purchase of its own shares had not benefited the company's trade. The taxpayers appealed.

The Special Commissioner, Dr Brice, dismissed the taxpayers' appeal. In determining whether a company purchase of its own shares had been made 'for the purpose of benefiting a trade', it was necessary to take account of consequences closely linked to the payment, so that unless those consequences were merely incidental, they had to be regarded as a purpose for which the payment had been made. The offer to purchase the property had been made when Mr and Mrs A were approaching age 70, and wished to retire. The company's decision to purchase the taxpayer's shares had been inextricably linked to its need for the sale proceeds from the property to enable it to do so. The company had been left without permanent premises from which to trade, without the benefit of the directors' loan, and without Mr and Mrs A's services. Those consequences were so closely linked to the company's purchase of the shares that they had to be regarded as a purpose for which the payment was made. The purchase of the shares had therefore not been made wholly or mainly for the purpose of benefiting the trade, but to enable the directors to retire.

FACTORS TO CONSIDER

4.17   The Special Commissioner considered a number of principles established in the case *Vodafone Cellular Ltd v Shaw* [1997] 69 TC 376, to decide whether the company's payment for the shares was made wholly and exclusively for the purposes of the trade, or whether there was some element of personal advantage:

- 'For the purposes of the trade' was taken to mean to serve the purposes of the trade, and not for the purposes of the company or for the benefit of the company.

- Was the payment made for the purposes of the taxpayer's trade? To answer this question, it was necessary to discover his object or subjective intentions in making the payment.

- The taxpayer's object in making the payment must be distinguished from the effect of the payment.

- The taxpayer's subjective intentions are not limited to his conscious motives. Consequences which are so inevitably and inextricably linked to the payment must be taken to be a purpose of the payment, unless they are merely incidental.

- The primary question to ask of the taxpayer is 'what was the particular object of the taxpayer in making the payment?'

The Special Commissioner concluded that the purchase of shares was not made 'wholly or mainly' to benefit the company's trade, but to facilitate the retirement of Mr and Mrs A. The purchase allowed the trade to continue, but Dr Brice said that surplus funds could have been paid to Mr and Mrs A, and the trade could still have continued.

4.18 Whilst advance clearance from HMRC on the tax treatment of a purchase of own shares is not mandatory, it will be preferable to make an application in the vast majority of cases, not least in terms of obtaining certainty in cases where the trade benefit requirement is in any doubt.

Limb 2: 'Scheme or arrangement' test

4.19 The second limb of the 'purpose' condition mentioned above is that the company purchase (or redemption or repayment) of its own shares must not form part of a scheme or arrangement, a main purpose of which is either to enable the share owner to participate in the company's profits without receiving a dividend, or the avoidance of tax (*CTA 2010, s 1033(2)(b)*).

'Scheme' or 'arrangement' is not defined for these purposes in the legislation. Both terms require consideration of the motive for the transaction. This is largely a question of fact. However, it may be more difficult to discern whether the 'main purpose' test is breached. It is therefore important that any clearance application made by the company to HMRC in respect of the transaction contains complete and correct details. Otherwise, any clearance given by HMRC cannot subsequently be relied upon.

RESIDENCE OF VENDOR

4.20   A further condition for exception from income distribution treatment on a company purchase of its own shares is that the vendor (and any nominee, if appropriate) must be resident in the UK in the tax year of purchase (*CTA 2010, s 1034(1)*). Prior to changes introduced in *FA 2013*, there was also a requirement to be ordinarily resident in the UK, but this requirement ceased to apply in relation to a purchase of own shares by an unquoted trading company on or after 6 April 2013 (*FA 2013, Sch 46, para 145*).

The statutory residence test (SRT) (in *FA 2013, Sch 45*) generally applies to determine an individual's residence for tax purposes, with effect from 2013/14. For tax years prior to 2013/14, the individual's residence status is determined according to the prevailing legislation and case law at that time.

If it is necessary for SRT purposes (in relation to tax years 2013/14 to 2017/18 inclusive) to determine the individual's residence status for an earlier tax year than 2013/14, an election is available to apply the SRT provisions to determine residence status for the earlier tax year (although the election does not change the individual's actual tax residence status for that year) (*FA 2013, Sch 45, para 154*).

For commentary on residence and the SRT, see **Chapter 9**.

4.21   If the vendors are trustees, the CGT rules for determining their residence status (and ordinary residence status, for tax years before 2013/14) apply (*TCGA 1992, s 69*). A detailed consideration of those rules is outside the scope of this chapter. However, it should be noted that trustees are resident in the UK if all of the trustees are UK resident, or if the following conditions are satisfied (*TCGA 1992, s 69(2)*):

● at least one trustee is UK resident; and

● a settlor was resident, ordinarily resident (for tax years before 2013/14) *or* domiciled in the UK at the 'relevant time' (ie broadly when the settlement was made, or immediately before the settlor's death if the settlement was made by will, intestacy or otherwise). Following changes introduced in *F(No 2)A 2017*, deemed domicile rules (in *ITA 2007, s 835BA*) apply for the purposes of determining the settlor's domicile status (*TCGA 1992, s 69(2F)*), broadly with effect for settlements created on or after 6 April 2017.

4.22   Thus a UK-resident trust may inadvertently become an offshore trust (eg by one of the trustees becoming non-UK resident, and the settlor not meeting the above UK residence or domicile requirements at the relevant time).

The trustees need only be resident in the UK for the purposes of this chapter for the tax year in which the share purchase takes place.

4.23 The residence status (and ordinary residence status, in relation to a purchase of own shares by an unquoted trading company before 6 April 2013) of personal representatives is somewhat more straightforward, as their status follows that of the deceased immediately before death (*CTA 2010, s 1034(3)*).

PERIOD OF OWNERSHIP

4.24 The general rule is that the vendor must have owned the shares throughout the five-year period ending with the share purchase (*CTA 2010, s 1035(1)*). However, this basic requirement is modified in certain respects, depending on the circumstances:

- In the case of transfers to the vendor from a spouse or civil partner, periods of ownership may be combined for the purposes of the five-year test, unless the parties are no longer living together (other than by reason of death) (*CTA 2010, s 1036(1), (2)*).

- If the vendor acquired the shares by will or intestacy, or is the deceased's personal representative, periods of ownership by the deceased (or his personal representatives) may be combined, and the required period of ownership is reduced from five years to three years) (*CTA 2010, s 1036(3)*).

- If the shares were acquired as part of a company reorganisation of share capital (eg the 'stand in shoes' provisions on a share-for-share exchange) within the capital gains tax legislation (*TCGA 1992, Pt 4, Ch 2*), the same treatment applies in terms of the ownership test. However, there are certain exceptions from this relaxation, in respect of allotments for payment and stock dividends within *CTA 2010, s 1049* (*CTA 2010, s 1035(3)*).

If the vendor's shares of the same class were acquired at different times, care may be needed in matching the disposal with those acquisitions. For the purposes of the ownership test a FIFO ('first in, first out') basis applies, so that earlier share acquisitions are taken into account before later ones. This rule is helpful, as it gives the longest possible period of ownership for the purpose of this test.

In addition, any previous share disposals by the vendor are matched with earlier acquisitions on a LIFO ('last in, first out') basis, so that later acquisitions are taken into account first (*CTA 2010, s 1035(2)*).

4.25   Aside from the above exceptions, if the company has been incorporated for less than five years, the shareholder cannot satisfy the five-year ownership test. This includes on the incorporation of a sole trader or partnership business.

THE 'SUBSTANTIAL REDUCTION' TEST

4.26

Focus

Two separate arithmetic tests (referred to below as the 'substantial reduction' test and the 'no continuing connection' test) must be satisfied for the exception from income treatment in *CTA 2010, s 1033(2)* to apply, which are relevant if the vendor retains an interest in the company following the share sale. The interests of 'associates' (see below) are taken into account for these purposes.

The first test is that the vendor's interest as a shareholder in the company must be substantially reduced. The combined interests of the vendor (and any associates) are taken into account for the purpose of this test (*CTA 2010, s 1037(1), (2)*).

The term 'substantially reduced' broadly means that the nominal value of shares owned by the vendor (and any associates) immediately after the purchase, expressed as a fraction of the company's share capital at that time, does not exceed 75% of the corresponding fraction immediately before the purchase (*CTA 2010, s 1037(3)–(5)*). This test is illustrated below.

Example 4.1 – 'Substantial reduction' test

Lee owns 4,000 shares in Quick Retail Ltd, an unquoted trading company. The company's issued share capital is 10,000 ordinary £1 shares. Quick Retail Ltd agrees to purchase 2,000 of Lee's shares. The relevant fractions are as follows:

Before the purchase: 4,000/10,000 (40%)

After the purchase: 2,000/8,000 (25%)

Therefore 75% (the substantial reduction threshold) × 40% = 30%. Lee holds 25% of the company's shares following the purchase.

Lee's remaining holding of 2,000 shares therefore represents a substantial reduction based on his original holding. Note that his interest in the company has actually been reduced by 37.5% (ie (40% – 25%)/40%), but Lee's shareholding in the company has reduced by 50%.

The calculation of the minimum number of shares required for the substantial reduction test to be satisfied can be expressed by formula, as follows:

$$\text{Minimum number} = \frac{nx}{4x - 3n}$$

Where:

n = the number of shares in the vendor's holding (including associates); and

x = the company's issued share capital

Thus in **Example 4.1**, the minimum company purchase of shares required for the above purposes is:

$$\frac{(4{,}000 \times 10{,}000)}{40{,}000 - 12{,}000} = \underline{1{,}429 \text{ shares}}$$

In *Preston Meats Ltd v Hammond; Sharples v Hammond* SpC 2004, [2005] SSCD 90 (SpC 435), the company shareholdings of the taxpayer and his wife amounted to 49.6% of the whole. The taxpayer wished to retire. It was agreed that the company would purchase his shares, with a view to falling within what is now *CTA 2010, s 1033(1)* so that the proceeds would be treated as a capital receipt. However, the company did not have the funds to pay for the shares immediately. The company therefore issued 130,000 £1 redeemable interest-bearing preference shares at par, carrying no voting rights, which were acquired by the taxpayer and his wife. HMRC issued assessments on the taxpayer and the company, on the basis that the taxpayer's shareholding had not been 'substantially reduced', as required by what is now *CTA 2010, s 1037(3)–(5)*. The taxpayer appealed, contending that 100,000 of the preference shares had been acquired for the benefit of his daughter.

The taxpayer's appeal was dismissed. The evidence indicated that the taxpayer had retained ownership of the 100,000 shares. It therefore followed that the condition in *CTA 2010, s 1037(3)–(5)* had not been satisfied. It was held that the taxpayer intended no more than that his daughter should benefit from the money received on redemption of the shares. The taxpayer's holding was also considered to breach the connection test in *CTA 2010, s 1042(1)* (see **4.31**).

4.27   A second 'substantial reduction' test must also be satisfied, broadly in terms of the vendor's interest in the company's profits. Even if the substantial reduction test is met in terms of share capital, it is not regarded as satisfied if the vendor shareholder's interest (expressed as a fractional share) in the company's profits available for distribution exceeds 75% of the corresponding fraction immediately before the purchase.

'Profits available for distribution' has the meaning given in *Companies Act 2006, s 830(2)*, except that the amount is increased by £100 per company plus any fixed distributions to which the shareholder may be entitled. Added to that figure is the excess of all sums payable on share purchases (or redemptions or repayments) over distributable profits available immediately before the purchase (*CTA 2010, s 1038*).

HMRC's Help Sheet 'Company Purchase of Own Shares' (see **4.14**) states in the context of this test: 'Where there are complex profit sharing arrangements, the Clearance Team will be able to advise.'

Groups of companies

4.28   If the purchasing company is a group member, the vendor's interest as a shareholder in the group (together with any associates) must be substantially reduced.

A 'group' is defined as a company (which is not itself a 51% subsidiary) plus its 51% subsidiaries (*CTA 2010, s 1047(1)*). There are two tests to be satisfied.

The first test is a calculation, which involves aggregating the nominal value of shares (expressed as a fraction of the issued share capital) of each company in the group in which the vendor owned shares immediately before or after the purchase, and dividing that aggregate by the number of group companies in which the vendor owned shares immediately before, or immediately after, the purchase. The vendor shareholder's interest in the group is substantially reduced if it does not exceed 75% of the vendor's interest before the purchase (*CTA 2010, s 1040(2)*).

4.29   The second test to be satisfied is expressed in terms of the vendor's entitlement to a share of the group's 'profits available for distribution' (see above). This test involves aggregating the vendor's share of such profits from each group member to which there was a notional entitlement immediately after the share purchase, and dividing that aggregate by each company's profits available for distribution in which the vendor owns shares immediately before, or immediately after, the purchase (including 51% subsidiaries of such companies). The vendor's entitlement to distributable group profits is substantially reduced if it does not exceed 75% of his interest before the purchase (*CTA 2010, ss 1040(1), 1041*).

4.30 There are anti-avoidance provisions to extend the group for these purposes in two specific circumstances.

First, if an unquoted company acquired all or a significant part of the business of the purchasing company (or group member) less than three years before the purchase (or redemption or repayment) of the shares, that outside company (and any 51% subsidiaries) is treated as a member of the same group as the purchasing company (*CTA 2010, s 1047(2), (3)*).

Secondly, a company that has ceased to be a group member continues as such if there are any arrangements under which it could rejoin the group (*CTA 2010, s 1047(4)*).

THE 'NO CONTINUING CONNECTION' TEST

4.31 In addition to the 'substantial reduction' test, there is a further arithmetic test to be satisfied in order to qualify for exception from income distribution treatment on a purchase of own shares. This test requires that the vendor must not be connected with the company (or a group company) immediately after the purchase (*CTA 2010, s 1042*).

4.32 'Connection' is broadly defined in terms of direct or indirect ownership or entitlement to acquire (now and in the future) more than 30% of the company's issued ordinary share capital, loan capital (except in limited circumstances involving money lending companies; see below) and issued share capital, voting power or the entitlement of equity holders to assets available for distribution on a winding-up of the company (*CTA 2010, s 1062(2), (4)*).

However, if the company's loan capital was acquired in the ordinary course of a business carried on by the shareholder that includes the lending of money, and the vendor takes no part in the management or conduct of the company, his interest in the loan capital is disregarded in applying the above 30% test (*CTA 2010, s 1062(3)*).

The rights of associates are also taken into account for these purposes (*CTA 2010, s 1063(4)*). 'Associates' in this context includes spouses or civil partners who are living together, but does not include (for example) adult offspring, or siblings (*CTA 2010, s 1059*).

The vendor is also connected with the company if he controls it (*CTA 2010, s 1062(7)*). 'Control' in this context has the meaning given in *ITA 2007, s 995* for individuals or *CTA 2010, s 1124* for companies (*CTA 2010, Sch 4*), ie broadly a person's power to secure that the company's affairs are conducted in accordance with his wishes, through shareholdings, voting or other powers in respect of the company.

Anti-avoidance

4.33   There are anti-avoidance provisions to prevent the 'substantial reduction' and 'no continuing connection' arithmetic tests being circumvented:

- The purchase must not at any time be part of a scheme or arrangement with a view to the vendor (or an associate) having an interest immediately after the share purchase that would breach the arithmetic tests (*CTA 2010, s 1042(2), (3)*). This condition is subject to the exception at **4.34** below.

- A transaction within one year after the purchase is deemed to be part of a 'scheme or arrangement' for the above purposes (*CTA 2010, s 1042(4)*).

Disposals by associates

4.34   There is a relaxation in the arithmetic tests. An associate may dispose of shares to the company, to enable the vendor shareholder to satisfy the substantial reduction tests (in *CTA 2010, s 1037(2)* or *1039(4)*).

In those circumstances, the arithmetic tests do not apply to the company's purchase of the associate's shares, to the extent that the number of shares purchased enables the vendor shareholder to comply with the test (*CTA 2010, s 1043*).

PRACTICAL ISSUES

Meeting the conditions

4.35   In many cases, in order to satisfy the 'trade benefit' test it may be necessary for the vendor shareholder to dispose of virtually their entire shareholding. However, the purchasing company may have insufficient funds to acquire the vendor's shares without causing cash-flow difficulties. It may therefore be argued that it would be of greater benefit to the company's trade to purchase the shares in tranches.

Focus

However, to avoid income distribution treatment the two arithmetic tests mentioned above (ie the 'substantial reduction' and 'no continuing

---

connection' tests) must be satisfied. In addition, if the shares are being purchased in stages, HMRC clearance should strictly be sought for each transaction.

As well as the 'arithmetic' conditions being met, HMRC would also need to be satisfied that the 'trade benefit' test was passed in each clearance application.

'Loan back' by vendor

4.36 If the company wants to purchase all the vendor's shares but cannot afford to do so, HMRC accept that there is no reason why the vendor should not lend part of the consideration back to the vendor immediately after the purchase. Clearly, the 'substantial reduction' requirement can be satisfied.

However, the 'no continuing connection' test must also be considered, ie the vendor (and any associates) must not have interests in the company of more than 30% of the combined issued share and loan capital (or voting power; see *CTA 2010, s 1062(2)*). A loan back to the company may breach this requirement, particularly if the market value of the shares is relatively high and the remaining issued share capital is relatively small.

4.37 In *Tax Bulletin*, Issue 21, HMRC helpfully point out that it is acceptable for the company to satisfy the connection test by making a bonus issue before the purchase of own shares takes place, in order to increase its issued share capital, as illustrated below.

Example 4.2 – Purchase and loan back to the company

Martin owns 2,500 shares in Express Widgets Ltd, an unquoted trading company. His shareholding represents 25% of the company's issued share capital of 10,000 shares.

Martin wishes to retire, and Express Widgets Ltd therefore agrees to buy Martin's 2,500 shares on 30 September 2018 for their market value of £100,000. Martin has owned his shares for six years, and satisfies the entrepreneurs' relief conditions for CGT purposes. The parties agree that they would like the transaction to fall within *CTA 2010, s 1033*, with the transaction giving rise to a capital gain for Martin, on which full entrepreneurs' relief can be claimed.

However, the company is experiencing temporary cash-flow difficulties. Martin therefore agrees to loan £50,000 of his proceeds back to the company. However, this would mean that Martin held loan capital of £50,000. The company's combined share and loan capital would be £57,500 (ie £7,500 plus £50,000). Martin would therefore be connected with the company (*CTA 2010, s 1062(2)(b)*).

The company's accountants therefore suggest that before the purchase of own shares takes place, the company should make a bonus issue of 20 shares for each share held, out of its distributable reserves. Martin now holds 52,500 shares out of 210,000 in issue. The company then purchases Martin's 52,500 shares for £100,000, and Martin loans £50,000 back to the company.

Martin therefore holds loan capital of £50,000. The company's combined share and loan capital is £207,500 (ie £7,500 original share capital, plus £150,000 bonus share capital, plus Martin's loan of £50,000). Martin's interest in the company is less than 30%.

However, in certain circumstances a bonus issue of shares followed by a repayment of share capital may result in the application of the distribution provisions (see **4.52**).

'Phased' purchases

4.38   For a purchase of own shares to be valid under company law, the company must make full cash payment on purchase. It is questionable whether the transfer of a company asset, or alternatively leaving the proceeds outstanding on loan account, strictly represents 'payment' for these purposes. HMRC's view is that it does not, and that in such circumstances the shares are not treated as cancelled and the vendor retains legal ownership of the shares (CTM17505). The tax implications of any payments already made to the shareholder would then need to be considered, such as whether the proceeds fall to be treated as a loan to a close company participator, within *CTA 2010, s 455*.

However, it should be noted that *Companies Act 2006, s 691* merely requires that 'the shares must be paid for on purchase'.

Note there is a limited relaxation to this rule for private company share purchases in relation to an employee share schemes (see **4.68**).

In the company law case *BDG Roof-Bond Ltd v Douglas* [2000] 1 BCLC 401, the court held (*obiter*) that payment can be made by a transfer of assets *in specie.* The alternative position is that the House of Lords' decision in *CIR v Littlewoods Mail Order Stores* [1965] AC 135 is authority for the proposition that the words 'sale' and 'purchase' require an exchange of property for cash and not for any other form of property (*Taxation* Readers' Forum, 17 December 2009).

4.39   An alternative to the 'loan back' following the purchase of the vendor's entire shareholding is a 'phased' purchase (ie the purchase of shares in tranches). Statutory clearance (if required) should be sought from HMRC in respect of each purchase. HMRC have indicated (subject to the 'trade benefit' test being satisfied) that it is possible for the vendor to make a series of disposals phased over a period (ICAEW Technical Release 745).

However, for the transactions to be eligible for capital gains treatment, the 'substantial reduction' and 'no continuing connection' tests must be satisfied on each occasion. In addition, HMRC may argue that the 'trade benefit' test is not passed on the first disposal, unless there is a clear intention for the company to purchase the remainder of the vendor's shares.

For entrepreneurs' relief purposes, the relevant relief conditions will need to be satisfied if a claim is to be made in respect of each disposal.

Contracts with multiple completion

4.40   As indicated above, a company purchase of its own shares by instalments is prohibited under company law, except in relation to employee share schemes (see **4.68**).

However, a company may enter into a single, unconditional share sale contract with the vendor, with completion taking place on different dates in respect of separate tranches of shares within the agreement. The effect is that the 'substantial reduction' test mentioned above need only be considered once (ie at the contract date), and not at the date of each completion.

The vendor must also satisfy the 'no continuing connection' test. However, if the vendor loses beneficial ownership of the shares at the contract date (see below), he will only remain connected with the company if there is ongoing ownership of, or entitlement to, more than 30% of its issued ordinary shares, loan capital, voting rights and/or assets on a winding-up. The rights and powers of any associates must also be taken into account (see below).

Completion of the contract in stages should not create a debt for connection purposes. In the event that the company defaults on a stage of the purchase, the vendor could sue under breach of contract for the right to enforce specific performance.

4.41   HMRC may be prepared to accept that a multiple completion contract is possible, provided that beneficial ownership passes at the contract date (ICAEW Technical Release 745). This is more a point of non-tax law, but nevertheless HMRC will insist that the contract satisfies this requirement. Whether the beneficial ownership of the shares is lost will depend on the terms of the agreement and how the transactions are undertaken in each case. However, subject to this requirement being satisfied, a claim for entrepreneurs' relief may (subject to the relief conditions being satisfied) be available on the disposal, and subsequent transfers under the agreement would be of legal (as opposed to beneficial) interests and hence would not be disposals for CGT purposes.

HMRC have sometimes argued that until the full purchase price is paid for the shares, the company law position is that the vendor remains on the register and is entitled to vote in respect of the shares without reference to the wishes of the purchaser. Furthermore, HMRC may argue that the seller cannot lawfully give up his voting rights under a contract with multiple completion. Alternatively, if the shares are claimed to be held as nominee for the company, HMRC may contend that this gives rise to a trust, which could make the vendor connected to the company (*CTA 2010, s 1048(3)*).

It may be possible to prevent such arguments by amending the company's articles, to provide that on the company entering into a contract for the purchase of its own shares, the shareholder's rights (including voting rights in relation to the shares) cease with immediate effect. However, such a change to the articles would need to be made before the multiple completion share purchase contract takes effect (*Tax Insight*, March 2011).

Alternatively, after the share purchase agreement has been entered into, consideration could be given to simply re-designating the uncancelled shares as a separate class of non-voting share (see 'Multiple attraction' *Taxation*, 13 October 2011).

The retention of a 'special share' of a separate class following the share repurchase (possibly by re-designating the special share from the vendor's existing holding prior to the proposed repurchase) may be considered if there are 'anti-embarrassment' terms in the contract (eg such that upon a subsequent sale of the company's shares at an enhanced price, the exiting shareholder will become entitled to part of the enhanced share price received by the remaining shareholders). The company's articles would need to reflect that the special share carries no voting or dividend rights, but has capital rights on a subsequent share sale to reflect the anti-embarrassment terms in the contract. The various conditions for capital gains treatment would need to be considered (eg the 30% connection test in *CTA 2010, s 1062(4)*), and the arrangements should be fully disclosed in a clearance application to HMRC under *CTA 2010, s 1044* (see *Taxation* Readers' Forum response by Peter Rayney, 23 January 2014).

The above argument about beneficial ownership may be avoided if it is possible to structure the share tranches in such a way that the arithmetic tests mentioned in the preceding paragraph are satisfied after completion in respect of the first tranche.

4.42 It should be noted that until the shares are (or are treated as) cancelled, they remain part of the company's issued share capital, and (for example) may need to be taken into account for entrepreneurs' relief purposes in determining whether the company's other shareholders satisfy the 'personal company' requirement in *TCGA 1992, s 169S(3)*. It may therefore be relevant to consider the time when the shares are (or are treated as) cancelled in this context (see below).

It has commonly (but not universally) been assumed that the date of disposal for CGT purposes under a company purchase of own shares is determined in accordance with *TCGA 1992, s 28* ('Time of disposal and acquisition where asset disposed of under contract'). The date of disposal under an unconditional contract according to those provisions is when the contract is made (*TCGA 1992, s 28(1)*), notwithstanding that payments are made at later dates. This means that the tax liability arising from the disposal could fall due before the consideration for all the shares is received. However, this may not be a significant problem where, for example, entrepreneurs' relief applies to the entire gain on the disposal. In addition, if the consideration is payable over a period exceeding 18 months, the capital gains legislation allows tax on a chargeable gain to be paid by instalments over a period of up to eight years, if appropriate (*TCGA 1992, s 280*).

In the event that the company fails to complete on one or more outstanding tranches of shares, it may be necessary to consider whether relief can be claimed in respect of the unpaid consideration for the shares (under *TCGA 1992, s 48*).

As indicated above, the time of disposal under a company purchase of own shares is not necessarily straightforward. The above provision setting the time of disposal in relation to contracts (in *TCGA 1992, s 28*) generally applies where an asset is disposed of and acquired under the contract. However, upon a company acquiring its own shares, any shares that are not cancelled on acquisition are treated as cancelled (*FA 2003, s 195(4)(b)*). Thus, shares (including those held in treasury; see **4.66**) that are not cancelled are generally treated as such for tax purposes. Furthermore, the acquisition by a company of its own shares is not treated as the acquisition of an asset (*FA 2003, s 195(2)*). In the case of contracts with multiple completion, there is anecdotal evidence of HMRC sometimes contending that the time of disposal is determined under *TCGA 1992, s 22(2)* (instead of *TCGA 1992, s 28*), being the dates when each capital sum is received. This is understood to be on the basis that there is a disposal under the contract, but no corresponding acquisition as required by

TCGA 1992, s 28(1). Where an entrepreneurs' relief claim is potentially in point, it would therefore be prudent to consider ensuring that the relevant relief conditions are satisfied when each capital sum is received (see **4.46**).

4.43 It should be noted that loss of beneficial ownership of the shares effectively means that the vendor shareholder is unable to participate in dividends paid after the contract date, or exercise voting rights in relation to the shares during the completion period. The vendor shareholder would need to consent to the loss of rights to any dividends or other shareholder rights as a result of entering into the agreement and will therefore probably wish to take legal advice in advance, to ensure that the contract offers appropriate safeguards to protect his position. A contract with multiple completion normally only requires a single clearance application to HMRC under *CTA 2010, s 1044.*

There is also anecdotal evidence of HMRC previously taking the position that although the date of disposal for CGT purposes is the date of the unconditional contract, the other conditions for a purchase of own shares not to be a distribution must be satisfied at the date of acquisition, ie the completion date. On that basis, the five-year ownership condition and the residence requirement etc would need to be met at the date of completion (*Monthly Tax Review* by Matthew Hutton, January 2010).

INCOME OR CAPITAL?

4.44 This chapter has so far mainly been concerned with the conditions to be satisfied by the individual shareholders of unquoted trading companies for a purchase of own shares to be excluded from income distribution treatment, and to be treated as a capital payment instead. This emphasis on capital treatment is understandable. For example, entrepreneurs' relief, if available, can result in a CGT rate of 10% on gains of up to £10m for qualifying business disposals (see **4.1**). Entrepreneurs' relief can apply after a qualifying period of only one year subject to the other relief conditions being satisfied, although in the context of a purchase of own shares the qualifying period of ownership for capital treatment should be noted (see **4.24**).

However, even if the CGT rate of 10% is not available, it may still be preferable for the transaction to be treated as a capital distribution. Income treatment was generally more desirable for disposals during earlier tax years in which the CGT rate exceeded the effective income tax rate on company distributions.

A CGT rate of 10% (for 2018/19) applies where an individual is not liable to income tax at the higher rate; there is also a CGT rate of 20% if the individual is a higher rate taxpayer, or to the extent that chargeable gains exceed the unused part of the individual's basic rate band (although these rates are subject to certain exceptions, such as in relation to chargeable gains accruing on disposals of residential property (that do not qualify for private residence relief) and carried interest; the corresponding CGT rates in those cases are 18% and 28% instead).

Following the reform of dividend taxation in *Finance Act 2016* including the abolition of the 10% tax credit, for 2018/19 the rate of income tax on distributions (subject to a £2,000 nil rate) is 7.5% for basic rate taxpayers, 32.5% for higher rate taxpayers and 38.1% for additional rate taxpayers.

Focus

Thus, if (for example) the shareholder was ineligible for entrepreneurs' relief, a CGT rate of 20% (for 2018/19) will often be more attractive than income treatment, particularly where the individual is a high earner, and/or substantial sums are involved.

However, there may occasionally be cases where income treatment is preferable, such as if the disposal proceeds are relatively small and/or the shareholder's income and gains remain within the basic rate income tax threshold.

It will generally be prudent to compare the relative tax costs of income and capital distributions respectively as a preliminary measure.

4.45   In the case of an income distribution, a purchase of own shares by a company with surplus advance corporation tax (ACT) at 5 April 1999 will give rise to notional (or 'shadow') ACT, which must be taken into account before any offset of actual ACT, in accordance with the shadow ACT provisions (*SI 1999/358*).

STATUS OF THE SHARES

4.46   Under the entrepreneurs' relief provisions, a 'material disposal' of shares in the company can be subject to relief. The rules broadly require that, for a qualifying period of at least one year ending with the date of disposal, the company is the shareholder's personal company and is either a trading company or the holding company of a trading group, and that the individual is an officer or employee of the company or a trading group member (*TCGA 1992, s 169I*).

'Personal company' in this context requires ownership of at least 5% of the company's ordinary share capital and voting rights (*TCGA 1992, s 169S(3)*). However, the 'personal company' requirement does not apply in relation to disposals of relevant EMI shares, and the above one year requirement runs from the date on which the EMI option was granted, rather than exercised (*TCGA 1992, s 169I(7A)*).

Care should be taken to avoid the inadvertent loss of entrepreneurs' relief, such as by the vendor's resignation as a director prior to the date on which the share purchase contract becomes unconditional (under *TCGA 1992, s 28(2)*), which may be determined by the date on which company law requirements were met (*Moore v Revenue and Customs* [2016] UKFTT 115 (TC); see **4.68**), although if there is an employment relationship with the company following the vendor's resignation, entrepreneurs' relief is not necessarily lost (see *Corbett v Revenue & Customs* [2014] UKFTT 298 (TC); *Hirst v Revenue & Customs* [2014] UKFTT 924 (TC)). The availability (or otherwise) of entrepreneurs' relief is likely to have a significant impact on the effective CGT rate on a share disposal to which capital treatment applies, and the relief conditions therefore need to be followed closely.

Furthermore, as indicated at **4.42** above in the context of contracts with multiple completion, for entrepreneurs' relief purposes it would be prudent to ensure that the relief conditions continue to be satisfied (eg the individual vendor continues to be an officer or employee of the company) when each capital sum is received under the contract for the purchase of own shares.

Following the introduction of investors' relief (in *Finance Act 2016*), a CGT rate of 10% also applies (subject to a lifetime cap of £10m) if the relevant conditions (in *TCGA 1992, Pt 5, Ch 5*) are satisfied and a claim is made. Those conditions include that the shares have been held for a period of at least three years starting from 6 April 2016 (that were acquired on or after 17 March 2016). This minimum ownership period is in contrast to the normal five-year minimum ownership period for CGT treatment on a company purchase of own shares (see **4.24**).

As noted elsewhere in this chapter, capital gains treatment in *CTA 2010, s 1033* applies automatically if the relevant conditions are satisfied. However, a claim is required for entrepreneurs' relief (and investors' relief) purposes (*TCGA 1992, ss 169M, 169VM*).

COMPANY STATUS

4.47   The definition of 'trading company' for the purposes of a company purchase of own shares requires that the company is 'wholly or mainly' trading (*CTA 2010, s 1048(1)*).

This is a less stringent test than for CGT purposes in respect of entrepreneurs' relief, which generally requires that the company's activities must not include non-trading activities to a substantial extent (*TCGA 1992, s 165A(3), Sch 7ZA, para 1(2)*). For investors' relief purposes, the definitions of 'trading company' and 'holding company of a trading group' in *TCGA 1992, s 165A* are applied (*TCGA 1992, s 169VV*).

HMRC consider 'substantial' in the context of entrepreneurs' relief to mean more than 20% (see CG64090).

4.48   The circumstances in which HMRC will provide a ruling on the status of a company for entrepreneurs' relief purposes is set out in the Capital Gains Manual. If the company has genuine doubt or difficulty over its trading status, it can seek an opinion under HMRC's Non-Statutory Business Clearance Service to assist the individual taxpayer. A firm opinion should normally be provided on the status of a company for periods that have ended, where all the relevant facts have been provided (CG64100). The company's request for an opinion should be in the format, and contain the material, prescribed in HMRC's Non-Statutory Business Clearance Guidance manual. Guidance is also available on the GOV.UK website (www.gov.uk/guidance/non-statutory-clearance-service-guidance).

It is possible to apply for a 'negative clearance' from HMRC that the conditions for capital treatment on a purchase of own shares are not satisfied (see **4.62**).

Even if the disposing shareholder's genuine concerns over the trading status of the company for entrepreneurs' relief purposes prove to be well founded, capital treatment is still likely to be more beneficial in most circumstances.

Example 4.3 – Company status

Edward has owned 20% of the shares in Dotcom Accessories Ltd, an unquoted company, for nearly six years. The company traded very successfully and quickly grew during that time, accumulating a significant amount of surplus cash at bank, most of which was invested. In May 2018, Edward wished to retire, and it was agreed that Dotcom Accessories Ltd would purchase his shares, realising proceeds of £500,000. Edward's taxable income for 2018/19 was £125,000 (NB: his dividend nil rate has been used).

Edward is concerned that Dotcom Accessories Ltd is not a 'trading company' for entrepreneurs' relief purposes, and asks the company to apply to HMRC for an opinion on its trading status. Unfortunately, HMRC's opinion is that the company is not a trading company for entrepreneurs' relief purposes, on the grounds that its non-trading activities are 'substantial'.

Nevertheless, the company is a trading company in terms of a company purchase of own shares, as it is 'wholly or mainly' trading (*CTA 2010, s 1048(1)*). The CGT rate of 20% is still preferable to the tax liability on an income distribution (ignoring the original cost of the shares, and any reliefs and exemptions available):

Capital payment: CGT liability

£500,000 × 20%	£100,000

Income distribution: income tax liability

	£
£25,000 × 32.5%	8,125
£475,000 × 38.1%	180,975
	189,100

However, where the vendor's income will be modest following the purchase of own shares (eg following retirement), income distribution treatment may be preferable. Consideration could be given in such cases to disposing of the shares over a number of years instead, and possibly seeking 'negative clearance' from HMRC, if appropriate, that income distribution treatment applies. Alternatively, it may be relevant to consider whether the transactions in securities anti-avoidance provisions (*ITA 2007, s 684*) apply for income tax purposes.

Comparing tax rates

4.49   As indicated above, for higher rate or additional rate taxpayers who do not qualify for entrepreneurs' relief (and ignoring the annual CGT exemption), a CGT rate of 20% (for 2018/19) compares favourably with the 32.5% rate on an income distribution for a higher rate (40%) taxpayer, and/ or the 38.1% rate faced by an additional rate (45%) taxpayer on an income distribution (see **4.50** below).

Income tax rates may apply if the company does not qualify for capital treatment on a purchase of own shares, as illustrated in the example below.

Example 4.4 – Income distribution treatment

Sarah is a 45% taxpayer. She owns 20% of the shares in Alpha Buckets Ltd. She wished to retire, and the company bought back her shares on

30 September 2018 for £250,000. Sarah originally subscribed for the shares at par in 1990, at a cost of £100. The conditions for capital treatment are not satisfied.

Her income tax liability on the disposal is calculated as follows (NB: Sarah's dividend nil rate is assumed to have been used):

	£
Proceeds	250,000
Less: Subscription cost	(100)
Amount of distribution	249,900
Income tax liability:	
£249,900 × 38.1%	95,212
Effective income tax rate (rounded): (£95,212/£250,000)	38.08%

Note – the effective rate is slightly lower than the rate of 38.1% mentioned above, due to the subscription cost of the shares.

4.50 For individual shareholders who are 40% taxpayers, the income tax position (for 2018/19) is potentially more complicated. Personal allowances are gradually reduced (by £1 for every £2) to nil to the extent that the individual's adjusted net income exceeds £100,000 (*ITA 2007, s 35(2)*).

In addition, as illustrated in **Example 4.3**, an additional income tax rate of 45% applies to taxable income over £150,000, with an additional tax rate of 38.1% applying to distributions otherwise taxable at the 45% rate. An income distribution to a shareholder on a purchase of own shares may result in a higher rate taxpayer falling partly within the 32.5% dividend rate in respect of the distribution, and partly within the 38.1% dividend additional rate.

If the consideration for the shares is relatively low and/or their base cost is relatively high, the individual vendor shareholder may not be liable to higher rate tax. In such circumstances, income distribution treatment may be more beneficial. However, in practice, such cases are likely to be relatively few.

Income distribution treatment

4.51 As indicated in the above example, the amount of the income distribution is broadly the consideration for the shares, less the original subscription price (*ITA 2007, s 989*; *CTA 2010, s 1000(1)*, category B).

It should be noted that, if the vendor shareholder did not originally subscribe for the shares, but instead bought them for a premium from another shareholder, the original subscription price is taken into account in calculating the amount of the distribution, as opposed to the higher sum actually paid for the shares. Thus a tax charge could arise on a deemed distribution even though the shareholder may have disposed of the shares for no actual profit.

In some cases, share capital may be issued at a premium, representing new consideration (eg following a share exchange on a previous company takeover). The amount of such a premium is generally treated as part of the share capital when considering the amount of any repayment of share capital (*CTA 2010, s 1025*; see CTM17510–CTM17520).

4.52   There are potential traps to avoid in the distributions legislation:

- A previous bonus issue of shares followed by a repayment of share capital may result in the application of the distribution rules in certain circumstances (see *CTA 2010, s 1026(1), (2)*). This applies to the purchase of own shares by a 'relevant company' (broadly a closely controlled or unquoted company) at any time after an earlier issue of bonus shares, but for other companies it only applies to repayments of share capital within ten years of the bonus issue (*CTA 2010, s 1026(3)*).

  The effect is that on a subsequent purchase of own shares, share capital is only treated as repaid to the extent that the repayment exceeds the earlier bonus issue. Thus if (for example) the amount of earlier bonus issues exceeds the amount that would otherwise be treated as a repayment of share capital on the purchase of own shares, HMRC guidance points out that the whole payment for the purchase of own shares will be treated as an income distribution (see CTM17530).

- If a purchase of own shares satisfies the conditions for capital gains treatment (in *CTA 2010, s 1033*), it will not give rise to an income distribution. HMRC accept that exemption from income distribution treatment includes the amount that would otherwise be a distribution because of the earlier bonus issue.

  However, different treatment applies in the case of repeat bonus issues. HMRC considers that if a company makes a bonus issue followed by a purchase of own shares, and then another bonus issue, the provisions of *CTA 2010, s 1026* dealing with distributions following a bonus issue are considered to apply before *CTA 2010, s 1033* (see CTM17550).

- A purchase of own shares followed or accompanied by a bonus issue of shares can result in the latter being treated as an income distribution in certain cases, including close companies, irrespective of capital treatment having applied to the share repurchase, or clearance having been given under *CTA 2010, s 1044* (*CTA 2010, s 1022*). This applies to bonus issues by 'relevant' companies (see above) at any time after the purchase of own shares, but for other companies it only applies to bonus issues within ten years of a repayment of share capital (*CTA 2010, s 1023(1), (2)*).

The effect is that a distribution can arise up to the amount of share capital repaid from the purchase of own shares. HMRC guidance states that this will be the case even if the recipient of the bonus issue is not the same as the vendor on the company purchase of own shares (see CTM17540).

4.53 As a result of income distribution treatment, the proceeds received by an individual vendor shareholder may partly represent a return of share capital for capital gains tax (CGT) purposes, and partly an income distribution. The fact that the transaction is an income distribution does not prevent it from being a disposal for CGT purposes as well. The amount charged to income tax is excluded from the taxable consideration when calculating the CGT position (*TCGA 1992, s 37(1)*).

The net proceeds in the CGT computation would be matched with the original amount paid for the shares. This will often mean that no capital gain or loss arises, as illustrated below.

Example 4.5 – CGT position where income treatment applies

In January 2014, Jason subscribed for 10,000 ordinary £1 shares in Delta Bags Ltd, an unquoted trading company, representing 50% of the company's share capital. The company is successful.

On 30 September 2018, Delta Bags Ltd agrees to purchase Jason's shares for £500,000. Unfortunately for Jason, the company's purchase of his shares does not qualify for capital gains treatment, as the five-year ownership condition has not been satisfied. The transaction is therefore treated as an income distribution.

His CGT computation for 2018/19 is as follows:

	£
Proceeds	500,000
Less: Treated as a distribution (£500,000 – £10,000)	(490,000)
Net proceeds	10,000
Less: Cost	(10,000)
Chargeable gain/(allowable loss)	Nil

4.54 However, in some situations (eg if the vendor shareholder held the shares at 31 March 1982, and the shares had a high value at that time) an allowable capital loss may be generated.

Example 4.6 – Income treatment and capital loss

Gerald subscribed for 100 ordinary £1 shares in Beta Cycles Ltd in 1980, representing 75% of the company's share capital. The company's trade is successful, and Gerald's shares are worth £200,000 at 31 March 1982.

On 31 August 2018, Beta Cycles Ltd agrees to purchase Gerald's shares for £1.4m. The conditions for CGT treatment in *CTA 2010, s 1033* are not satisfied in respect of the transaction.

Gerald's tax position (for 2018/19) is as follows:

	£
Income distribution	
Proceeds	1,400,000
Less: Subscription cost	(100)
Amount of distribution	1,399,900
CGT computation	
Proceeds	1,400,000
Less: Charged to income tax	(1,399,900)
	100
Less: Value at 31 March 1982	(200,000)
Allowable loss	(199,900)

4.55 The rule regarding disposals between connected persons (ie which restricts loss relief to transactions with the same connected person) in *TCGA 1992, s 18(3)* does not apply in the above example. This is because the 'connected persons' rule is engaged when a person 'acquires' an asset, whereas in the above example for company law purposes Beta Ltd cancelled the shares, so in that sense would not 'acquire' anything (*FA 2003, s 195(2)*).

As indicated at **4.42**, there is anecdotal evidence that HMRC sometimes use similar reasoning to contend that the date of disposal on a purchase of own shares under a multiple completion contract is when each capital sum is received (within *TCGA 1992, s 22(2)*), and not the date of the contract (within *TCGA 1992, s 28(1)*), as the latter provisions require that an asset is 'acquired' under the contract. On that basis, the conditions for entrepreneurs' relief would need to be considered when the proceeds are received, as opposed to the date of the contract.

The tax treatment for company or trustee vendor shareholders is considered later in this chapter.

4.56   If an individual vendor subscribes for ordinary shares in an unquoted trading company and a capital loss arises such as in the circumstances outlined above, it may be possible to offset the loss against the taxpayer's total income for the same and/or the preceding year, subject to any restriction in the amount of such 'sideways' loss relief, if the capping of such losses to the greater of £50,000 and 25% of adjusted total income applies for the tax year (*ITA 2007, ss 24A, 131*).

This income tax loss relief is subject to a number of conditions (in *ITA 2007, Pt 4, Ch 6*), consideration of which is outside the scope of this chapter. However, there appears to be no reason why an eligible loss cannot relieve total income, including the distribution arising from the company purchase of its own shares.

Capital gains treatment

4.57   The conditions for automatic capital gains treatment were described earlier in this chapter. If those conditions are satisfied, the income distribution rules are disapplied, and the entire proceeds are treated as a capital receipt instead. For individual vendor shareholders, this presents an opportunity to claim CGT reliefs, allowances and exemptions, if applicable.

For example, the CGT liability of an individual shareholder may be reduced or extinguished by a high base cost (or March 1982 value, if the shares have been held for a sufficient time), capital losses, entrepreneurs' relief and the annual CGT exemption.

Even if the CGT liability is not completely extinguished, capital treatment can result in a relatively low effective tax rate, as illustrated below.

Example 4.7 – Effective rate of CGT

The facts are as in **Example 4.6** above, except that the conditions for capital gains treatment in *CTA 2010, s 1033* are satisfied in relation to Gerald's disposal of 100 ordinary £1 shares to Beta Cycles Ltd for £1.4m on 31 August 2018. In addition, the conditions for entrepreneurs' relief have been satisfied throughout Gerald's relevant ownership period.

His CGT position for 2018/19 is as follows:

	£
Proceeds	1,400,000
Less: Section 104 holding (value at 31 March 1982)	(200,000)
	1,200,000
Less: Annual exemption	(11,700)
Chargeable gain	1,188,300
CGT at 10% (entrepreneurs' relief rate)	118,830
Effective CGT rate (rounded)	8.5%

4.58   If entrepreneurs' relief applies to reduce the gain without restriction, the effective CGT rate (ie the CGT rate as a percentage of disposal proceeds) can be considerably lower than the special 10% rate. This is because the effective CGT rate is subject to additional factors including allowable costs, capital losses and the annual exemption (if available). Capital gains treatment will therefore be the preferred path for many vendor shareholders of unquoted trading companies.

It should be remembered that capital treatment under *CTA 2010, s 1033* is mandatory if the relevant conditions are satisfied. Otherwise, income tax distribution treatment will automatically apply instead.

CLEARANCE APPLICATIONS TO HMRC

4.59

Focus

As noted above, the legislation on the purchase (or redemption or repayment) by an unquoted trading company of its own shares in *CTA 2010, ss 1033–1048* contains various conditions which must be satisfied before the tax treatment allowed by *CTA 2010, s 1033* can apply. Provision is made (in *CTA 2010, s 1044*) for the company (or its agent) to make a written clearance application in advance to HMRC.

It is worth noting the following general points in relation to clearance applications:

- A clearance application is not necessarily required in order for *CTA 2010, s 1033* to apply (ie the application of *CTA 2010, s 1033* is mandatory; either the conditions for capital treatment are satisfied, or they are not). However, if a complete and accurate clearance application is submitted to HMRC, this does provide certainty of tax treatment.

- Clearances applications can either be 'positive' under *CTA 2010, s 1044(2)* (ie that *CTA 2010, s 1033* does apply), or 'negative' under *CTA 2010, s 1044(3)* (ie that it does not). 'Negative' clearance applications are discussed further below (see **4.62**).

- Clearance by HMRC under *CTA 2010, s 1044* differs from certain other statutory clearances, such as under *ITA 2007, s 701* in respect of transactions in securities. Clearance under the latter provisions merely confirms that the proposed transactions are not considered to be undertaken for a main purpose of obtaining an income tax advantage (see **4.61** below). Clearance under *CTA 2010, s 1044* confirms that *CTA 2010, s 1033* will (or will not) apply to the purchase of own shares. Thus, provided that the clearance application correctly and fully discloses all material facts, it should be possible to rely on the clearance given by HMRC, even if it transpires that capital treatment was not technically in point for some reason.

4.60   To assist companies and agents in preparing clearance applications under what is now *CTA 2010, s 1044*, HMRC included as an Annex to Statement of Practice 2/82 pro forma applications for clearance for the purchase of own shares under what is now *CTA 2010, s 1033(2)* (ie relating to the benefit of a trade), and *CTA 2010, s 1033(3)* (ie relating to the payment of inheritance tax).

In more recent guidance, as indicated at **4.14**, HMRC's Help Sheet 'Company Purchase of Own Shares' also contains separate checklists of information to be provided in clearance applications for a purchase benefiting a company's trade, and a purchase in connection with an IHT liability (tinyurl.com/HMRC-CPOS). The pro forma clearance application relating to a purchase benefiting a company's trade is included below.

The application must give particulars of all 'relevant transactions' (*CTA 2010, s 1045(1)(b)*), and must fully and accurately disclose all material facts and circumstances. Otherwise, any resulting clearance given by HMRC is void (*CTA 2010, s 1045(6)*).

4.61 An application to HMRC under *CTA 2010, s 1044* for advance clearance that capital treatment will be available to the vendor shareholder is normally accompanied by an application for clearance under *ITA 2007, s 701* that the 'transactions in securities' anti-avoidance rules do not apply.

Those provisions (in *ITA 2007, Pt 13, Ch 1*) are of relevance to most owner-managed businesses, as they relate to close companies (ie generally those under the control of five or fewer persons, or participators who are directors). They broadly apply to company distributions not otherwise taxable as income (*ITA 2007, s 685*, referred to in the legislation as condition 'A' or 'B') unless HMRC are satisfied that obtaining an income tax advantage was not a main object of the purchase of own shares and no counteraction adjustment (under *ITA 2007, s 698*) ought to be made in respect of the transaction.

Where a joint clearance application is made under *CTA 2010, s 1044*, and also *ITA 2007, s 701* concerning the transactions in securities provisions, a single letter can be used for both clearances, which should be sent to HMRC's Clearance & Counteraction Team. Contact details can be obtained from the GOV.UK website (www.gov.uk/guidance/seeking-clearance-or-approval-for-a-transaction#3). No extra copy is required as the same person will deal with each of the clearances asked for. A single response will be given covering all of them.

'Negative' clearance applications

4.62 As mentioned elsewhere in this chapter, capital gains treatment in *CTA 2010, s 1033* applies automatically if the relevant conditions are satisfied. This will normally be the preferred tax treatment for vendor shareholders if entrepreneurs' relief is due, or otherwise if the CGT rate (20% in most cases) is lower than the effective rate of income tax on an income distribution (eg 38.1% for a 45% taxpayer in 2018/19).

Historically, in the case of family or owner-managed companies before 6 April 2008, it was often desirable to structure the company purchase of own shares so that the relevant conditions for capital gains treatment were breached (eg if little or no taper relief was available for CGT purposes). Income tax treatment also became potentially more attractive in some cases following the introduction of a 28% CGT rate for higher rate taxpayers in respect of gains accruing from 23 June 2010. However, due to the general reduction in CGT rates and increase in tax rates for income distributions (from 2016/17), breaching the conditions for capital gains treatment will be even less of a consideration than before in most cases.

Of course, it is also important to be aware of circumstances in which capital treatment can be lost, to ensure that an inadvertent breach of the rules does not occur.

BREACHING THE CONDITIONS FOR CAPITAL TREATMENT

4.63   A breach of the rules for capital gains treatment can be caused in various ways. For example:

- The vendor selling the shares in stages under separate contracts, or immediately lending the sale proceeds back to the company for a time, such that the 'substantial reduction' and/or the 'no continuing connection' tests are not satisfied.

- The vendor breaching the residence condition, such as by transferring the shares to a nominee who is not resident or ordinarily resident in the UK in the tax year of purchase. The acquisition of shares by the nominee does not trigger a disposal by the vendor for CGT purposes, as transactions between them are specifically disregarded (*TCGA 1992, s 60(1)*). However, the rules for capital treatment on a purchase of own shares require that both the vendor and nominee must be resident in the UK (and ordinarily resident in the UK, for share purchases before 6 April 2013) (*CTA 2010, s 1034(1), (2)*). The transfer of shares to a nominee prior to a company purchase of own shares could also be challenged by HMRC, based on *Furniss v Dawson* [1984] AC 474 principles.

- It may be the case that the purchase of own shares was not wholly or mainly for the benefit of the company's trade. For example, the vendor may be retained as a full-time working director. Alternatively, it may be that the transaction wholly or mainly benefited the vendor shareholder as opposed to the company, eg on the basis that the transaction was undertaken wholly or mainly to provide funds to facilitate the retirement of a director shareholder (as was held by the Special Commissioner in *Allum v Marsh*; see **4.16**), rather than to benefit the company's trade.

There is a 'negative' advance clearance application procedure available to the company by virtue of *CTA 2010, s 1044(3)*, ie to the effect HMRC are satisfied that the transaction is *not* one for which capital gains treatment in *CTA 2010, s 1033* applies.

HMRC are required to give their decision within 30 days of receiving the application, or to request further particulars.

APPLICATION FOR CLEARANCE UNDER *CTA 2010, s 1044* – PURCHASES WITHIN *CTA 2010, s 1033(1), (2)*

4.64

Focus

It should be clearly stated at the top of the letter what clearances are requested (eg *CTA 2010, s 1044* and *ITA 2007, s 701*). It should also be confirmed whether the purchase of shares is regarded as falling within *CTA 2010, s 1033(1)* by virtue of *CTA 2010, s 1033(2)* or *(3)*.

If the purchasing company has previously made an application under *CTA 2010, s 1044* it will be helpful if HMRC's reference can be quoted.

---

1. **Information about the company**

   1.1 The name of the company making the purchase

   1.2 The company UTR

   1.3 Confirmation that the company is unquoted

   1.4 Confirmation that the company is a trading company or the holding company of a trading group

   1.5 Where the company is a member of a group, the names of the group companies together with their UTRs

2. **Information about the payment**

   2.1 Details of the shares to be purchased, the name of the present owner, the purchase price and the number of shares to be bought

   2.2 Details of any other transactions taking place between the company and the seller at or about the same time

   2.3 Confirmation that the company's Articles of Association allow it to purchase its own shares

   2.4 Details of how the payment will be made

3. **Information about the shareholders**

   3.1 A list of the current shareholders in the purchasing company, showing for each person their current holdings including amount, class and dividend rights. Where appropriate include details for each company in the group (as per 1.5)

   3.2 Details of any relationships between the shareholders

3.3 Where the shareholder is the son or daughter of another shareholder, confirmation that he or she is over 18 or else details of their age

3.4 Where the shareholder is a trust please provide details of the names of the trustees, the settlors, and the beneficiaries of the trust

4. Information about the purpose

4.1 A statement of the reasons for the purchase, including the trading and any other benefits expected to accrue from it, whether or not to the purchasing company

4.2 Confirmation that the purchase does not form part of a scheme or arrangement where the main purpose or one of the main purposes is to enable the owner of the shares to participate in the profits of the company without receiving a dividend, or for the avoidance of tax

4.3 Confirmation that the seller will receive no other payment from the company, or details of any such payment to be made

4.4 Particulars of any prior transactions or arrangements to be carried out in preparation for the purchase

5. Information about the seller

5.1 The present residence status of the seller and any intended change

5.2 The UTR or NI number of the seller, or if not known, his or her private address

5.3 The period of beneficial ownership by the seller of the shares to be purchased and any other relevant holdings

5.4(a) Confirmation that the combined interests of the seller and any associates in the company will be substantially reduced, or,

5.4(b) If the company is a member of a group, confirmation that the combined interests of the seller and any associates in the group will be substantially reduced

5.5 Confirmation that the seller (after including any interests held by his associates) will not, immediately after the purchase, be connected with the company making the purchase or with any company which is a member of the same group as that company

6. Accounts and other financial information

The application should be accompanied by:

6.1 Copies of the latest available financial statements for the purchasing company

6.2 If appropriate, copies of the latest financial statements for the group and for any group companies

6.3 A note of any material relevant changes since the balance sheet date or confirmation that there are no changes

6.4 Details of any loan or current account which the seller maintains with the company or with any group company

COMPANY LAW

4.65 A company purchase of its own shares must comply with certain *Companies Act 2006* requirements. HMRC can only consider a request for clearance on a transaction which appears to be a valid purchase of own shares (*Tax Bulletin*, Issue 21 (February 1996)).

Focus

A detailed consideration of company law issues is outside the scope of this chapter. However, compliance with the law is fundamental to the transaction, and the tax treatment is dependent on the legal analysis. The main company law considerations (ie for an unquoted or 'off market' purchase) are therefore outlined below.

Professional advisers who are unfamiliar with company law should obtain the necessary legal advice. Failure to comply with the legal requirements could make the transaction void and legally unenforceable, and render the company and its officers liable to sanctions (*CA 2006, s 658(2), (3)*).

In *Baker v Revenue & Customs* [2013] UKFTT 394 (TC), a company purchase of own shares was held to be void by reason of the failure to comply with Companies Act requirements, which included an insufficiency of distributable profits. The appellant was therefore under an obligation to return funds to the company. This meant that those proceeds did not (as HMRC contended) amount to an income distribution for tax purposes. Thus the appeal was allowed.

The facts in *Baker* were distinguished from an earlier (non-tax) case, *Kinlan & Anor v Crimmin & Anor* [2006] EWHC 779 (Ch). In that case, the company (in liquidation) was seeking the repayment of proceeds paid to a departing shareholder on a purchase of own shares. The court held that the transaction was void as it breached company law (ie by reason that part of the consideration for the shares was deferred). However, it was also held that the shareholder was entitled to keep the money received from the

---

company, based on certain 'important and unusual features of the case'. The tax implications of the decision were not addressed.

The rationale applied in the *Baker* case suggests that HMRC's approach in similar situations would be to treat such funds retained by departing shareholders as liable to income tax as a distribution.

4.66 Shares purchased by an unquoted company are normally treated as cancelled. However, as indicated at **4.68** below, the company may, if authorised to do so by its articles, make a company purchase of own shares out of distributable profits (or the proceeds of a fresh share issue for the purpose of financing the purchase), or alternatively out of capital up to an aggregate purchase price in a financial year of the lower of £15,000 and the nominal value of 5% of the company's fully paid share capital as at the beginning of the financial year (*CA 2006, s 692(1)-(1ZA)*).

If the company purchases its own shares in accordance with *CA 2006, Pt 18, Ch 4* (*ss 690–708*), such shares may be held as treasury shares if the purchase is made out of distributable profits (*CA 2006, s 724(1)*). Shares held in treasury are not actually cancelled, and are retained by the company. However, the rights attaching to the shares are effectively suspended whilst they are held in treasury (ie the company may not vote in respect of the shares or receive distributions in respect of them) (*CA 2006, s 726(2), (3)*).

The purchase by a company of its own shares is not treated as the acquisition of an asset (*FA 2003, s 195(2)*). See **4.42**.

Requirements

4.67 *Companies Act 2006* gives a company power to purchase its own shares, if certain conditions are satisfied (*CA 2006, s 690(1)*). Otherwise, the shares are not treated as cancelled and legal ownership remains with the vendor (CTM17505). The tax implications of the company's payment to the shareholder would then need to be considered. For most owner-managed companies, this would include a potential liability for the company under the 'loans to participators' provisions (*CTA 2010, s 455*), and for the vendor as a taxable benefit under the beneficial loan rules (*ITEPA 2003, s 175*).

Companies Act 2006 specifies a procedure for share buy-backs, which restates some provisions of its predecessor (*Companies Act 1985*), and changed others.

4.68   The following is a brief outline of the main company law requirements.

● **Power to purchase own shares**

A company is not required to have the power in its Articles of Association to purchase its own shares, although the members may restrict or prohibit a purchase of own shares through the company's Articles if they wish. This provision is helpful, because the Articles of some older companies do not contain an authority.

The share purchase must not leave the company with only redeemable and/or treasury shares (*CA 2006, s 690*).

● **Authority for purchase**

A contract for an 'off-market' company purchase of own shares is generally required to be approved in advance (*CA 2006, s 693*). (Note: separate conditions apply if the purchase is for the purposes of or pursuant to an employee share scheme (*CA 2006, 693A*)).

However, the Act allows a company to enter into a contract to purchase its own shares, on condition that the shareholders approve the contract terms by an ordinary resolution, which requires a majority of over 50% (*CA 2006, ss 282, 694(2)*). (Note: prior to changes introduced by the *Companies Act 2006 (Amendment of Part 18) Regulations 2013, SI 2013/999* with effect from 30 April 2013 a special resolution was necessary, which required a majority of not less than 75% (*CA 2006, s 283*)).

If the contract (or its terms) is not approved, the company may not purchase the relevant shares and the contract lapses.

The purchase authority requirements in *CA 2006, ss 693, 694* were considered in the context of an entrepreneurs' relief claim on a company purchase of own shares in *Moore v Revenue and Customs* [2016] UKFTT 115 (TC). In that case, a director shareholder who was employed under a contract of employment agreed that the company would purchase his shares following a dispute with the other director shareholders, and would leave the business. At a general meeting of the company on 29 May 2009, it was resolved that the company would purchase 2,700 out of the taxpayer's 3,000 shares. On the same day, the taxpayer signed a compromise agreement for the termination of his employment, and the company purchase of shares agreement. All Companies House papers concerning the taxpayer's resignation as a director were also signed on that day. However, those documents stated that the effective date of his resignation as a director was 28 February 2009.

Following an enquiry into the taxpayer's return, HMRC concluded that the taxpayer was not entitled to entrepreneurs' relief, because he was not an officer or employee of the company throughout the period of one year ending with the disposal of his shares (as required by *TCGA 1992, s 169I(6)(b)*). The taxpayer appealed. He accepted that he had ceased employment with the company and was no longer an office holder from 28 February 2009. However, it was contended that the completion of the negotiations resulted in a binding contract for sale in February 2009, and it followed that this was the date of disposal for CGT purposes (*TCGA 1992, s 28*). However, the First-tier Tribunal noted that company law (*CA 2006, ss 693, 694*) required a contract for a company's own purchase of shares to be approved in advance by a special resolution. That resolution was not passed until 29 May 2009. Accordingly, the company was incapable of entering into a valid contract to purchase the shares until the resolution had been passed. Even if there had been a contract, it had to be conditional on approval by special resolution. The date of disposal under a conditional contract would (by virtue of *TCGA 1992, s 28(2)*) be the date on which the condition was satisfied, ie 29 May 2009. The appellant's appeal was dismissed.

- **Disclosure of contract details**

  A copy of any written contract (or a memorandum of its terms) must be made available to the members. For resolutions at meetings, it must be available for inspection at the company's registered office for at least 15 days prior to the meeting, and also at the meeting itself (*CA 2006, s 696(2)*).

- **Payment for the shares**

  The shares purchased must be fully paid. In addition, the company is generally required to pay for the shares on completion (*CA 2006, s 691*). However, the latter condition is subject to an exception allowing private companies to purchase shares for the purposes of or pursuant to employee share schemes by instalments (*CA 2006, s 691(3)*, as amended by *SI 2013/999, reg 3*).

- **Distributable profits**

  Subject to certain exceptions (see below), a company must purchase its own shares out of distributable profits, or out of the proceeds of a fresh share issue to finance the purchase (*CA 2006, s 692(2)*). An amount equal to the par value of the shares bought back must be transferred to a capital redemption reserve account.

  However, a private company may purchase its own shares out of capital subject to conditions in *CA 2006, s 692(1ZA)* (see **4.66**), or under *CA 2006, Pt 18, Ch 5* (*ss 709–723*) ('Redemption or purchase by private company out of capital'), consideration of which is outside the scope of this chapter.

- **Cancellation of shares**

  Following the company share repurchase, the relevant shares are treated as cancelled. The company's share capital is reduced by the nominal value of the cancelled shares (*CA 2006, s 706*). This rule does not apply to treasury shares (see above).

- **Return to Companies House**

  A return must be made to Companies House within 28 days of the transaction, stating the number of shares purchased, their nominal value and the date of purchase (*CA 2006, s 707*).

  Except in the case of treasury shares which are not cancelled, the company must also give notification of the cancellation of the shares within 28 days, normally with a statement of the company's share capital (except where it would be the same as a statement required under *CA 2006, s 720B* in relation to an employees' pension scheme) (*CA 2006, s 708*).

- **Inspection of contract**

  The company must keep a copy of the contract (or a memorandum of its terms) available for inspection at its registered office for a period of at least ten years from conclusion of the contract (*CA 2006, s 702*). Alternatively, a copy of the contract (or any variation) may be kept for inspection at a specified place (in regulations made under *CA 2006, s 1136*).

  The company must notify the registrar of the place where the contract is available for inspection, unless it has always been kept at the company's registered office. A contract (or memorandum of terms) relating to a private company must be made available for inspection by any of its members.

CORPORATE VENDORS

4.69   Whilst this chapter is mainly concerned with individual owner-managers of unquoted trading companies, it should be noted that a company purchase of own shares by a UK company from another UK company has potentially different tax implications.

In those cases, if the purchase gives rise to a distribution, the disposal proceeds are not reduced by the amount of the distribution for the purposes of calculating corporation tax on chargeable gains. HMRC originally adopted this approach on the basis that the distribution does not suffer a tax charge as income within *TCGA 1992, s 37(1)* (Statement of Practice 4/89). The distribution is included in the computation of corporation tax on chargeable gains. HMRC guidance states that this treatment only applies to a purchase of own shares, not to a redemption or reduction in share capital (CG58623).

The above approach by HMRC is based on previous distributions legislation (*ICTA 1988, s 208*), which stated: 'except as otherwise provided by the *Corporation Tax Acts*, Corporation Tax shall not be chargeable on dividends and other distributions of a company resident in the United Kingdom, nor shall any such dividends or distributions be taken into account in computing income for corporation tax'. This legislation was subsequently replaced by *CTA 2009, s 1285*, which was itself subsequently repealed (see below).

4.70 HMRC's view on the treatment of a purchase of own shares from a corporate shareholder in Statement of Practice 4/89 was upheld by the Court of Appeal in *Strand Options and Futures Ltd v Vojak* [2003] EWCA Civ 1457. In that case, HMRC had previously confirmed that chargeable gains treatment under what is now *CTA 2010, s 1033* (previously *ICTA 1988, s 219*) did not apply to the taxpayer company, but considered that Statement of Practice 4/89 applied with the effect that not only would the proceeds from the purchase of part of its shareholding in another company be treated as a distribution for tax purposes, but the distribution must also be included in the chargeable gain computation in respect of the shares. The Court of Appeal considered that a true interpretation of the effect of *ICTA 1988, s 208* (except where otherwise expressly provided by the Tax Acts) was that it related directly to dividends and other distributions, rather than indirectly as part of the computation of a taxable amount. If it had been intended to exclude the distribution from the capital gains computation, a specific reference could have been made in *ICTA 1988, s 208*. Accordingly, it was held that the distribution element should be brought into account in computing the taxpayer's chargeable gains.

The above legislation on UK company distributions in *ICTA 1988, s 208* was subsequently replaced by *CTA 2009, s 1285*, which expressly provided that UK dividends and other distributions were not prevented from being taken into account in the calculation of chargeable gains. This provision therefore made the decision in the *Strand Options* case explicit in statute.

However, *CTA 2009, s 1285* was also replaced by legislation (introduced by *Finance Act 2009*, for distributions paid on or after 1 July 2009) which removes the general exemption for UK company distributions. The current provisions (*CTA 2009, Pt 9A*) determine the scope of the corporation tax charge on both UK and foreign company distributions. A detailed consideration of those rules is outside the scope of this chapter. However, it is perhaps worth noting that although, in the majority of cases, company distributions will be exempt from corporation tax, this is not automatically the case.

Unlike the previous legislation in *CTA 2009, s 1285*, the rules in *CTA 2009, Pt 9A* as originally enacted did not expressly state the treatment of distributions in the company's calculation of chargeable gains. However, legislation introduced in *F(No 3)A 2010* explicitly preserves the corporation tax charge on chargeable gains resulting from share capital. It broadly provides that whilst a distribution may be exempt from tax as income, this does not prevent the amount of the distribution from being taken into account in computing a company's chargeable gains (*CTA 2009, s 931RA*). This amendment to *CTA 2009, Pt 9A* applies to distributions from 1 July 2009, and hence the treatment of repurchases of share capital effectively remains unchanged from HMRC's previous position and the decision in the *Strand Options* case, as outlined above.

Whilst a chargeable gain may therefore arise for a corporate vendor on a purchase of own shares, the substantial shareholding exemption (SSE) may apply to the disposal if certain conditions are satisfied (*TCGA 1992, Sch 7AC*). Commentary on the SSE is included in **Chapter 6**.

TRUSTEE VENDORS

4.71   As explained in this chapter, a company purchase of own shares is generally treated as a distribution for tax purposes. Under trust law, such a transaction usually gives rise to a capital receipt. Certain types of capital receipts by trustees are treated as income receipts in their hands, and are liable at 'special trust rates', ie the rate applicable to trusts of 45% or the dividend trust rate of 38.1% (for 2018/19). This includes the receipt from a company which is buying back its own shares from the trustees.

The tax treatment of such a disposal by trustees is stated in *ITA 2007, s 482* ('Types of amount to be charged at special rates for trustees'). A distribution for the purposes of that legislation broadly includes a payment made on the redemption, repayment or purchase of shares in the company. However, a company purchase of own shares which satisfies the conditions for capital treatment is specifically excluded from the meaning of 'distribution' for the purposes of the *Corporation Tax Acts* (*CTA 2010, s 1033(1)*), and the same treatment is applied for income tax purposes by virtue of the definition of 'distribution' in *ITA 2007, s 989*. Hence a capital payment under trust law, and for tax purposes by virtue of *CTA 2010, s 1033*, on a company purchase of own shares should not be subject to income tax as a distribution.

HMRC's Trusts Manual confirms (at TSEM3205):

> 'Where CTA 2010, s 1033 applies a sale of shares is not treated as a distribution. So if the conditions in s 1033 are satisfied, ITA Sections 481 and 482 will not apply to a company purchase of own shares. You should not apply ITA Sections 481 and 482 if the company in question has received 'clearance' that s 1033 does apply.'

4.72   There was some concern that where the vendors of shares are trustees, a 'double' charge to income tax and CGT could arise effectively on the same transaction, for reasons other than those outlined above. For CGT purposes, *TCGA 1992, s 37(1)* provides that disposal proceeds are excluded from the chargeable gains calculation if '… charged to income tax as income of, or taken into account as a receipt in computing income of, *the person making the disposal* …' (emphasis added).

In the case of a settlor-interested trust, the person making the disposal will be the trustees, but the income tax liability will arise on the settlor. In strictness, relief under *TCGA 1992, s 37* would therefore be unavailable in the CGT computation, as the person making the disposal would be different than the person incurring the income tax charge. However, it is understood that HMRC have accepted that a relief claim is available to vacate the CGT assessment (under *TMA 1970, s 32(1)*).

A similar problem potentially arises in respect of life interest trusts which are not settlor-interested, whereby the trustees are liable to CGT on the gain, but the income tax liability otherwise belongs to the life tenant. HMRC are reported to consider that because a purchase of own shares is generally capital under trust law, the income tax liability will not usually belong to the life tenant. The trustees would therefore be liable to income tax instead, and the protection of *TCGA 1992* would then be available. However, as a precaution, the trust deed should not define the life tenant's entitlement to income by reference to 'taxable income' (see 'A problem of trust' by John Barnett, *Taxation*, 9 June 2005).

OTHER POINTS

Associated persons

4.73   For the purposes of the company purchase of own shares rules providing for capital treatment if the conditions in *CTA 2010, ss 1033–1048* are satisfied (eg in respect of the 'substantial reduction' and 'no continuing connection' tests), the interests of associated persons need to be considered. Such interests are added to those of the vendor for these purposes.

'Associated persons' include the following (*CTA 2010, ss 1059–1061*):

- spouses or civil partners living together;

- parents and minors under the age of 18;

- a person connected with a company is associated with that company, and with any other companies which it controls;

- if a person connected with one company controls another, the two companies are associated;

- if a person is accustomed to acting on the directions of another person in respect of the company's affairs, the two persons are associated;

- settlement trustee shareholders are broadly associated with any settlor(s), their associates and with any person who has an actual or potential beneficial entitlement to a significant interest in the shares (subject to certain exceptions relating to pension schemes and employee trusts); and

- the personal representatives of a deceased shareholder are associated with any person who has an actual or potential beneficial entitlement to a significant interest in the shares.

An interest is 'significant' in the context of trustees and personal representatives, broadly, if its value exceeds 5% of the beneficial interest in the settlement or estate concerned (*CTA 2010, ss 1060(4), 1061(2)*).

Returns of own share purchases

4.74

Focus

The company must submit a return to HMRC within 60 days of making a payment for the purchase of own shares to which capital treatment is considered to apply (*CTA 2010, s 1046*).

This requirement applies whether or not clearance was requested and obtained from HMRC that capital gains treatment applies to the payment (CTM17580).

In practice, if a clearance application was made this requirement can often be satisfied in a short letter to HMRC drawing the officer's attention to the clearance letter and outlining any changes between the proposed transactions in the letter and the actual transactions that took place.

If a clearance application was not made, HMRC will need to know the date of the purchase, the name of the vendor, the number of shares, the amount of consideration, and the grounds on which the 'trade benefit' test are considered to be satisfied.

A person connected with the company must give notice to HMRC if the company treats a purchase of own shares as satisfying 'Condition A' in *CTA 2010, s 1033*, within 60 days of becoming aware of any scheme or arrangement within *CTA 2010, s 1042* that affects the payment. *CTA 2010, s 1042(2)* broadly states that the purchase must not be part of a scheme or arrangement which may result in the seller or associate having a disqualifying interest in the company (*CTA 2010, s 1046(3), (4)*).

4.75 HMRC can apply their information and inspection powers (in *FA 2008, Sch 36*) if necessary.

In addition, from 1 April 2012, HMRC's data-gathering powers (in *FA 2011, s 86(1), Sch 23*) broadly provide that HMRC can by written notice require relevant data to be provided by a relevant data holder (as widely defined), subject to penalties for non-compliance. A 'relevant data holder' for these purposes includes a person who receives a payment from the company within *CTA 2010, s 1033 (FA 2011, Sch 23, para 14(1)(c))*.

For notices given or requests made prior to 1 April 2012, if a payment for a purchase of own shares within *CTA 2010, s 1033* is received on behalf of another person, HMRC can require the recipient to disclose the name and address of that other person. HMRC can also require the other person to state the name and address of any other person on whose behalf the payment was received (*CTA 2010, s 1046(5)–(7)*).

4.76 Vendor shareholders will need to ensure compliance with statutory requirements in connection with a company purchase of their shares. For example, they should ensure that the disposal is properly notified and returned to HMRC, and that any tax liabilities are duly paid, within the appropriate time limits. Consideration should also be given to the level of tax return disclosure required to minimise the possibility of an HMRC enquiry, and reduce the risk of a discovery assessment by HMRC outside the normal enquiry window (*Brown & Anor v Revenue & Customs* [2012] UKFTT 425 (TC)).

If an advance clearance application was made and HMRC gave clearance that capital treatment applied, consideration should be given to submitting a copy of the application and HMRC's clearance letter with the tax return, or at least making reference to them in the white space on the return (of course, this assumes that the clearance application fully and accurately discloses all material facts and circumstances).

If a clearance application was not submitted to HMRC but capital gains treatment is still sought, the tax return should disclose all the information that a full and accurate clearance application would have contained, and highlight any areas of uncertainty or potential disagreement on the tax treatment (eg the grounds on which the 'trade benefit' test are considered to be satisfied).

Stamp duty

4.77 The purchasing company is generally liable to a stamp duty charge of 0.5% on a return to Companies House under *CA 2006, s 707*, as if it were an instrument transferring the relevant shares on sale to the company pursuant to a purchase agreement *(FA 1986, s 66)*. This stamp duty liability is rounded up to the nearest multiple of £5.

However, if the consideration is £1,000 or less, the return does not need to be stamped by HMRC before being sent to Companies House, although the company must certify that the transaction does not form part of a larger transaction the consideration for which is more than £1,000 *(FA 1999, Sch 13, para 1(3A))*.

The return (Form SH03) provides details of the share buyback. This form can be downloaded from the GOV.UK website: www.gov.uk/government/publications/notify-a-purchase-of-own-shares.

As indicated above, Form SH03 is a stampable return, and the duty is charged on the consideration for the shares. Note that the return itself is stampable, rather than the share transfer form. If no stamp duty is payable, due to the above consideration threshold of £1,000, it must be certified on the form that this is the case, and it should be sent directly to Companies House.

The company must deliver the return to Companies House within 28 days from the first date on which the shares were delivered to the company.

Professional fees

4.78 Professional costs incurred by the company on the purchase (or redemption or repayment) of its shares are generally not an allowable deduction from trading profits for corporation tax purposes. This is on the basis that such fees are capital expenditure in respect of the company's share capital, and/or that they are excluded from relief under the 'wholly and exclusively' rule *(CTA 2009, ss 53, 54)*.

It may seem anomalous that HMRC can give clearance that a purchase of own shares is wholly or mainly for the benefit of the company's trade, and yet deny a deduction for the professional costs of securing that benefit. However, it does not automatically follow (at least in HMRC's view) that the related professional costs of a purchase of own shares are considered to be 'wholly and exclusively' for the purposes of the trade (see CTM17600).

Professional advisers may therefore wish to word their fee notes carefully, to distinguish between allowable and non-allowable services, with a view to minimising any disallowance for the latter.

For the vendor, if capital gains treatment applies, a deduction for professional fees is available if directly related to the cost of acquiring or disposing of the shares (*TCGA 1992, s 38(2)*). HMRC regard the reasonable professional fees of valuing the shares for the purpose of making a capital gains computation as allowable (CG15260). However, fees incurred in computing the tax liability are not considered by HMRC to be allowable (CG15280).

Valuation of shares

4.79 For valuation purposes, the market value rule for transactions between connected persons for CGT purposes in *TCGA 1992, s 18* does not generally apply to a company purchase of own shares, such as in the case of a family company, as there is no acquisition by the company corresponding to the disposal by the shareholder.

However, market value may still be substituted if the purchase is not considered to be at arm's length (*TCGA 1992, s 17*; see CG58645).

A purchase at what HMRC consider to be overvalue may be referred to HMRC Shares and Assets Valuation. The end result may be that HMRC seek to tax the excess over an arm's-length value, perhaps as an income distribution (within *CTA 2010, s 1020*), or possibly as employment income within *ITEPA 2003, s 446X* ('Securities disposed of for more than market value').

However, reports by HMRC officers to Shares and Assets Valuation on this basis are understood to be rare.

Loan relationships

4.80 The loan relationships regime for companies (*CTA 2009, Pt 5*) includes anti-avoidance provisions that can restrict debits (eg loan interest payments) to the extent that the loan relationship has an 'unallowable purpose' as defined (*CTA 2009, ss 441–442*).

HMRC guidance in their Corporate Finance Manual (at CFM38180) lists transactions that they consider will not normally fall within the unallowable purposes anti-avoidance provisions. In the context of a company purchase of own shares, HMRC state that *CTA 2009, ss 441–442* will not normally apply to loan relationship debits 'that relate to a straightforward borrowing by a UK plc in order to fund a repurchase of its shares provided that there are no attempts to structure the arrangement in such a way as to provide a tax advantage for any other person and/or the amount borrowed (the level of gearing up) is dictated by market forces and hence is at arm's length'.

However, it should be noted that HMRC's guidance specifically refers to a purchase of own shares by a public limited company, as opposed to companies in general.

Chapter 5

Reduction of capital

Pete Miller CTA (Fellow), Partner, The Miller Partnership

SIGNPOSTS

- **Reduction of capital simplified** – The new rules in *Companies Act 2006* make reducing a company's capital simpler and cheaper (see **5.1–5.3**).

- **Reduction of capital cannot be used for takeover schemes under CA 2006, s 899** – Changes were made by secondary legislation in March 2015 to prevent perceived avoidance of stamp duty (see **5.4**).

- **Enhancing distributable reserves** – A reduction of capital can eliminate negative reserves and allow a company to pay dividends (see **5.5–5.7**).

- **Repayment of cash** – The cash subscribed for shares can be returned to shareholders using a reduction of capital (see **5.8–5.13**).

- **Transactions in securities** – Reductions of capital were added to the list of transactions in securities potentially subject to counteraction of an income tax advantage, with effect from 6 April 2016 (see **5.14–5.19**).

- **Forming a group** – Reductions of capital are another useful way to group companies together, and can save stamp duty in contrast with a share exchange (see **5.20–5.23**).

- **Demergers** – Reductions of capital are a helpful mechanism for demergers and other schemes of reconstruction, and should be added to every adviser's toolkit (see **5.24–5.27**).

REDUCTIONS OF CAPITAL – COMPANY LAW

5.1 The reduction of capital of a company is a potentially useful mechanism for a number of transactions, including both merging companies into groups and for demergers. Furthermore, a reduction of capital can potentially be a useful way of returning cash to shareholders.

Although the facility for reducing capital has existed for some time, until recently this was a complex, time-consuming and expensive process, in particular because it required a Court Order (under *CA 1985, s 135*). However, for private companies the process is substantially simplified by the new rules in *CA 2006, Pt 17, Ch 10*.

5.2   The main provision is *CA 2006, s 641(1)(a)*, which states that a limited company with share capital may reduce that capital by a special resolution supported by a solvency statement, where the company is a private company. It may reduce its capital in any way it wishes, subject only to the restriction that there must always be at least one member holding at least one non-redeemable share (*CA 2006, s 641(2), (3)*).

The rules for the statement of solvency are at *CA 2006, s 642*. The statement must be signed by all of the directors of the company, no more than 15 days before the date of the special resolution reducing the company's capital. Both the resolution and the solvency statement must then be registered with Companies House. The solvency statement itself must state that each director considers the company able to pay, or otherwise discharge, all its debts on the date of the statement, along with any debts as they fall due in the year immediately following. If it is intended to wind the company up within 12 months, the company must be able to pay, or otherwise discharge, all of its debts in full within 12 months of the commencement of the winding up (*CA 2006, s 643*).

5.3   Once the special resolution has been passed, a copy of that resolution, of the solvency statement and also a statement of capital must be delivered to Companies House (*CA 2006, s 644*). The statement of capital must state the total number of shares of the company, the aggregate nominal value and details of each class of share, along with the amounts paid up or unpaid on each share. The special resolution only takes effect when the registrar has registered the relevant documents.

The statement of solvency must then be sent to each member of the company before, or at the same time, as the proposed special resolution is sent. If a solvency statement is delivered to the registrar but has not been provided to the members, this is an offence by the officers of the company who are in default and they are potentially liable to a fine.

5.4   A reduction of capital cannot be used to facilitate a takeover of one company by another, if the takeover is the subject of a court order under *CA 2006, s 899* (*SI 2015/472*, with effect from 3 March 2015). The stated purpose of the new regulation is that using a reduction of capital for a takeover constitutes avoidance of stamp duty, as there is no stamp duty on either the cancellation or the issue of shares, only on the transfer of shares.

Takeovers that do not rely on *CA 2006, s 899* are not affected, so it is unlikely that the new regulations will have any effect on transactions involving owner-managed businesses.

COMPARISON WITH PURCHASES OF OWN SHARES

5.5 A reduction of capital is a different transaction from a company purchase of own shares, for which the relevant provisions are at *CA 2006, Pt 18, Ch 4* (see **Chapter 4**). Essentially, a reduction of capital involves reducing the company's capital base, and the maximum amount that can be repaid or otherwise transferred to reserves is the nominal share capital plus any premium originally paid on the shares.

ENHANCING DISTRIBUTABLE RESERVES

Reduction of capital is usually distributable

5.6 When a company reduces its capital under *CA 2006, Ch 10*, whether using the simplified process for private companies or by a court order, available to both public and private companies, the amount concerned must be transferred to a non-distributable reserve, by *CA 2006, s 654(1)*. This reserve is not the same as a capital redemption reserve, which arises under the very different provisions of *CA 2006, s 733*.

However, *CA 2006, s 654(2)* gives the Secretary of State the power to suspend the application of *CA 2006, s 654(1)*, which was done by the *Companies (Reduction of Share Capital) Order 2008, SI 2008/1915*. This states that, where a private company limited by shares reduces its capital, the reserve is to be treated as a realised profit and, hence, as a distributable reserve. Indeed, the statutory instrument gives the same result for reductions of capital by unlimited companies and also where companies with share capital have used the court order route, unless the court orders otherwise. In effect, this appears to render *CA 2006, s 654(1)* somewhat otiose.

Thus, one of the most common use of a reduction of capital is for a company to enhance its distributable reserves. That is, if a company has negative reserves, or insufficient reserves to pay out the dividends that it would like to pay, a reduction of capital might be an appropriate way to enhance the reserves to allow the payment of the required dividends.

Example 5.1 – Eliminating a profit and loss deficit

Acer Limited has been trading at a loss for some time, and the profit and loss account deficit is £63,000. The company has recently had an injection of capital from new investors and is starting to make profits. However, the new investors are keen to have a return on their investment as soon as possible, and do not wish to wait for the profit and loss deficit to be eliminated before they can start to receive dividends. The company has £100,000 of share capital.

Using the provisions of *CA 2006, s 641* onwards, the company resolves to reduce its capital by £65,000, leaving a profit and loss account in credit by £2,000. Future profits from the trading activities can then be paid out to the shareholders by way of dividends.

5.7   In many cases, the company does not have sufficient share capital to allow this approach to creating distributable reserves. However, it is possible that the company has other, non-distributable reserves that might be capitalised, to create share capital that can then be reduced to create distributable reserves. For example, it is common for a company to have a valuable property and, therefore, possibly a revaluation reserve.

Example 5.2 – Property revaluation and share capital reduction

Beech Limited has a profit and loss deficit of £173,000 but only £100 of share capital. However, Beech Limited has a property which stands on the balance sheet at its historical cost of £30,000. This is estimated to currently be worth £400,000. The profit and loss deficit can be resolved by taking the following steps:

1.   Carry out a formal revaluation of the property and create a revaluation reserve of £370,000. This is not a distributable reserve.

2.   Use the revaluation reserve to pay up £200,000 of new share capital.

3.   Reduce the company's capital by £200,000, so that the profit and loss account is in credit by £27,000.

Tax analysis

5.8   The use of the profit and loss account for this purpose should not be a taxable event. No cash is actually returned to the shareholders, so there should be no capital gains or distribution charge on them. In many cases, a straightforward reduction of capital constitutes a reorganisation (by virtue of *TCGA 1992, s 126(1)*), which is specifically removed from the charge to capital gains tax for the shareholders by *TCGA 1992, s 127*.

Nor is there any provision to charge any corporation tax on the company in respect of such transactions.

There is a theoretical possibility that the shares issued in a capitalisation of a revaluation reserve might be employment related securities. However, where it is intended that the shares be cancelled almost immediately afterwards, it seems unlikely that the shareholders could be seen as having any benefit from holding those shares ephemerally, and the author is not aware of HMRC ever taking this point.

RETURNING CAPITAL TO SHAREHOLDERS

5.9   A reduction of capital can also be used to return cash to shareholders. In effect, the reduction of share capital is balanced by a payment of cash to the shareholders.

Similarly, the reduction of capital could be used to reduce an outstanding balance on a shareholder's loan account.

Tax analysis

5.10   As far as the company is concerned, there are no tax consequences. No deduction is allowed for the payments to reduce the share capital.

5.11   As far as the shareholders are concerned, there would, *prima facie*, be a disposal of some or all of their share capital. Therefore, one would expect a capital gains computation to be necessary.

In simple cases, however, what is being returned to the shareholders is no more nor less than what they originally subscribed for the shares, so there should be no gain and no loss. This arises generally out of the share pooling rules.

> **Example 5.3 – Capital reduction resulting in no gain**
>
> Barbie and Ken each subscribe £50,000 for shares in their new company JK Enterprises Limited. Some years later, they decide the company does not need a £100,000 capital base and that £75,000 should be returned to them as shareholders, £37,500 each.
>
> In capital gains terms, we would expect the computation to match the £37,500 share capital originally subscribed with £37,500 share capital returned, leaving a zero gain.

The computation would be different if they had bought the shares from a third party, rather than having subscribed the share capital themselves, as the base cost of the shares and the amounts originally subscribed would not be the same in such cases, so a capital gain or allowable loss might accrue.

5.12   There is a possible concern that the actual market value for the shares should be substituted in the capital gains computation. This arises from *TCGA 1992, s 17*, which states that a bargain otherwise than on arm's-length terms should be adjusted to arm's-length terms, so the question revolves around whether a reduction of capital is a disposal of the shares for an arm's-length price.

Taking the previous example, suppose at the time of the reduction of capital the company was actually worth £1m. If 75% of the share capital were sold to a third party, clearly the shareholders would expect to realise something closer to £750,000 for that disposal. The counter-argument, of course, is that on a reduction of capital, they have not, in fact, made an arm's-length disposal, and they have only diminished the value of the company by the £75,000 cash extracted. There is no obvious conclusion to this discussion, except to note that HMRC must be aware of the point, as it has been raised several times in the tax press, but to date HMRC have not been seen to argue the point.

In this author's view, however, the better argument is that the arm's-length price for a reduction of capital is, in fact, the original capital subscribed, so that there is no adjustment to be made under *TCGA 1992, s 17*.

5.13   It is also worth noting that a reduction of capital can be, and often is, a reorganisation, under *TCGA 1992, s 126(1)*. Technically, this means that the amounts received are taxed under the provisions of *TCGA 1992, s 128*, not the normal disposal provisions. However, this is not of any practical significance.

5.14   So far, this looks like a relatively tax-efficient way of returning cash to shareholders, as they do not pay any tax on the amounts returned to them. If there is a chargeable gain, for example because the shares were acquired by purchase, rather than subscription, it may well be that entrepreneurs' relief is available and that capital gains tax is only due at 10%.

Conversely, an allowable loss may arise, where there is a reduction of capital in respect of purchased shares, if the amounts returned are less than the purchase price per share.

Transactions in securities

5.15   The 'fly in the ointment' of repaying capital to shareholders is the transactions in securities legislation in *ITA 2007, Pt 13, Ch 1 (ss 682–713)*. Very broadly, this legislation is designed to prevent shareholders accessing the company's distributable reserves in a capital form, so that they pay less in capital gains tax than they would otherwise have paid in income tax on a dividend. This legislation only applies where the transaction or transactions in securities are carried out with the intention of obtaining an income tax advantage *(ITA 2007, s 684(1)(c))*. It is unfortunate that HMRC have taken the view that a reduction of capital in return for cash is likely to be income tax avoidance and therefore susceptible to challenge under this legislation.

HMRC legitimised their position by adding the repayment of share capital or share premium to the list of transactions in *ITA 2007, s 684(2)* that are specifically deemed to be transactions in securities for the purposes of this legislation, with effect from 6 April 2016.

The sanctions that HMRC possess effectively involve 'counteracting' the tax advantage. So, to extend **Example 5.3** further, the reader will recall that Barbie and Kenneth have each received £37,500 tax free, being the return of the capital they originally subscribed into JK Enterprises Limited. If HMRC decided that this transaction was carried out for tax avoidance purposes, then an assessment can be raised, under *ITA 2007, s 698*, to charge tax as if the £37,500 each of them had received had been a distribution from the company and was therefore chargeable to income tax at the relevant rate for distributions (credit is given for any capital gains tax already paid or due, by virtue of *ITA 2007, s 687*, although in the example, there was no capital gain).

The transactions in securities rules can only apply if, and to the extent that, the company concerned has distributable reserves *(ITA 2007, s 684)* or, from 6 April 2016, if there are distributable reserves in any companies it controls (see **5.19**). So, if JK Enterprises Limited in **Example 5.3** does not have any reserves, HMRC are powerless.

5.16   There are a number of reasons why the author, and many other observers, consider HMRC's approach to be incorrect. Firstly, one thing that many tax avoidance arrangements have in common is a degree of complexity or artificiality. While this is not a universal rule, it is suggested that in situations like this the shareholders have a simple choice between taking a distribution from the company or reducing its capital. They both require a certain degree of process and pre-transaction scrutiny (for distributions, it is important to ensure that the company has sufficient distributable reserves, for example), they are both relatively straightforward transactions, and neither of them involves any degree of artificiality or contrivance. The main difference, of course, is that a reduction of capital actually has a permanent effect on the company's capital base, for which there might, in any case, be commercial reasons. In this context, a straightforward choice between two relatively straightforward transactions does not seem to the author to constitute the avoidance of income tax.

There is also support for this approach in decided tax cases. In *Duke of Westminster v CIR* 19 TC 490, Lord Tomlin said in the House of Lords that:

> 'Every man is entitled if he can to order his affairs so that the tax attaching under the appropriate Acts is less than it otherwise would be. If he succeeds in ordering them so as to secure this result, then, however unappreciative the Commissioners of Inland Revenue or his fellow taxpayers may be of his ingenuity, he cannot be compelled to pay an increased tax.'

Similarly, in *Ayrshire Pullman Motor Services and Ritchie v CIR* 14 TC 754, Lord Clyde said that:

> 'No man in this country is under the smallest obligation, moral or other, so to arrange his legal relations to his business or to his property as to enable the Inland Revenue to put the largest possible shovel into his stores.'

Of course, these cases date from 1936 and 1929, respectively, and things have moved on since then. However, the comments remain good law in most people's views, and certainly apply where there is no contrivance or artificiality. So we have judicial assurance that we are entitled to make decisions about how we order our financial and commercial affairs, taking the likely tax bill into account. In the author's view, none of this constitutes tax avoidance (unlike the planning in *Duke of Westminster* which was clearly egregious).

5.17 In the context of the transactions in securities legislation itself, there was a similar comment in the case of *Brebner v CIR* 43 TC 705. In this case, a group of trawlermen had arranged their financial affairs in order to finance the acquisition of a coal supplier, which was accepted to have been a wholly commercial reason, despite the fact that a tax advantage was obtained. In terms of the tax avoidance test, Lord Upjohn, in the House of Lords, said this:

> '… When the question of carrying out a genuine commercial transaction, as this was, is considered, the fact that there are two ways of carrying it out – one by paying the maximum amount of tax, the other by paying no, or much less, tax – it would be quite wrong as a necessary consequence to draw the inference that in adopting the latter course one of the main objects is, for the purposes of the section [ie the transactions in securities legislation, then in *FA 1960, s 28*], avoidance of tax.'

In summary, therefore, not only does general case law support the proposition that straightforward tax planning is acceptable, but so does a decided case relating specifically to the transactions in securities rules themselves.

5.18 Finally, for transactions completed before 6 April 2016, the reduction of capital transaction may be outside the scope of the transactions in securities rules, as *ITA 2007, s 685(6)* states that the legislation does not apply to the return of sums paid by subscribers on the issue of securities. This seemed to be a relatively straightforward technical point, and it is hard to see why HMRC do not accept, therefore, that the transactions in securities legislation cannot apply to a reduction of capital.

This provision was repealed for all transactions taking place on or after 6 April 2016. Also, a reduction of share capital or share premium was added to the list of specific transactions in securities to which these rules apply, in *ITA 2007, s 684(2)*, also for all transactions taking place on or after 6 April 2016.

Even under the old rules, HMRC stated in a number of cases that they would consider counteraction on the basis that there were distributable reserves and, therefore, paying out the share capital, and only paying capital gains tax, if that, must be the avoidance of income tax. In discussion of the *FA 2016* proposals, HMRC's view was that there was scope for tax avoidance by reducing capital and returning cash to shareholders, even where the cash represented the amounts originally subscribed by those shareholders out of their own taxed income.

As a result, it is recommended that, if a client wishes to reduce their capital in this way, they should not apply for clearance under *ITA 2007, s 701*. Instead, if they are prepared to take the risk that there may be counteraction and that the sums concerned might be taxed as a dividend, they should merely complete the relevant self-assessment returns in the proper way, noting, if appropriate, any capital gains consequences on the disposals of the shares. However, they are not required to state the possible application of the transactions in securities rules on their tax returns, as these rules are outside self-assessment, a view which has been specifically published by HMRC (in *Tax Bulletin 46*, July 2000). Although this was some years ago, the administrative status of the transactions in securities rules has not changed in the interim and HMRC have never suggested that their view of the interaction between these rules and self-assessment has changed.

In these cases, if HMRC subsequently form the view that the transactions in securities rules may be in point, the author believes there is substantial ammunition to argue against any counteraction proceedings or to win a case in front of the tribunals or courts. In the final analysis, if the company was potentially going to pay out the amounts, anyway, as a distribution, then the clients are no worse off (apart from relevant professional fees).

5.19   There are, also, circumstances where HMRC will not be able to challenge the reduction of capital under these rules. Firstly, if there are no distributable reserves, no lawful distribution could have been paid, so the transactions in securities legislation cannot apply. Strictly, therefore, HMRC should grant clearance in advance in these cases, although personal experience is that they refuse to grant clearance. Instead, they merely confirm that, in the absence of distributable reserves, no counteraction is possible.

There will also be cases where the recipient of the cash would not, in any case, have paid UK income tax, for example where the shareholder is either a non-UK resident individual or company, or indeed a UK company. While there is a corporate equivalent of the transactions in securities rules (*CTA 2010, Pt 15*), they very rarely apply, largely because UK companies are effectively exempt from corporation tax on distributions received, anyway (see *CTA 2009, Pt 9A*). So it is hard to see how a reduction of capital to a corporate shareholder could constitute the avoidance of corporate tax on dividend income.

There are also cases where the commercial drivers for reducing capital are sufficiently strong that HMRC accepts that these commercial reasons demonstrate that the income tax advantage was not one of the main reasons for entering into the transactions. For example, in a case where a reduction of capital was used to facilitate a shareholder exit, HMRC accepted that no counteraction was required.

5.20 In summary, therefore, it is entirely acceptable for a company to reduce its capital and return that capital to the shareholders. HMRC may consider counteraction under the transactions in securities rules, although it is hoped that this would fail for the reasons detailed above.

While this is not a strategy for the faint-hearted, a reduction of capital remains an option, particularly where there are no distributable reserves or the shareholders cannot be avoiding income tax.

FORMING A GROUP

5.21 The previous section might lead to the impression that reductions of capital, while having been simplified, are relatively useless. This is, however, not the case and the rest of this chapter looks at two areas in which they can lead to substantial tax savings, stamp duty and demergers.

When a new company is inserted over an existing company, this is usually done by way of a share exchange. That is, a person will exchange their holdings of shares in company A by transferring those shares to company B which, in turn, will issue shares to that original shareholder. These forms of share exchange are generally free of capital gains tax, by virtue of the share exchange rule at *TCGA 1992, s 135* (see **7.12** *et seq*).

Stamp duty savings

5.22   The other tax charge that might arise on such transactions is the stamp duty charge, at 0.5% of the value of the consideration, for the transfer of the shares in company A. In general, of course, the market value of the shares issued by company B in consideration will be the same as the market value of company A, so essentially the stamp duty charge is at 0.5% on the market value of the shares of company A. This sounds like a low rate but can, of course, be a large amount when the companies are very valuable.

There is a relief from stamp duty at *FA 1986, s 77*. The relief is available so long as the transaction is for *bona fide* commercial reasons and not part of a scheme or arrangement for the avoidance of tax. For the relief to apply, the shareholdings of company B must be of the same class and in the same proportions as the shareholdings of company A immediately prior to the exchange.

The availability of relief under *FA 1986, s 77* is complicated by *FA 1986, s 77A*, introduced for instruments executed on or after 29 June 2016. *FA 1986, s 77A* denies stamp duty relief under *FA 1986, s 77* where it is reasonable to assume that one of the purposes of the transaction is to secure a change of control of the original company to a specified person. However, there is an exemption for mergers, which would normally apply to mergers such as we are discussing here (*FA 1986, s 77A(3), (4)*). This provision will be more relevant for certain demergers (see also **5.25**, and **Example 5.5** at Step 1).

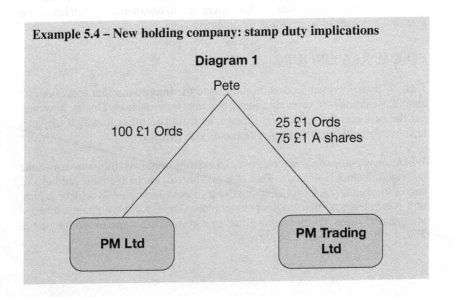

Example 5.4 – New holding company: stamp duty implications

Diagram 1

Pete

100 £1 Ords

25 £1 Ords
75 £1 A shares

PM Ltd

PM Trading Ltd

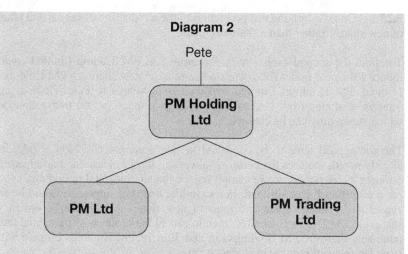

Diagram 2

Pete holds the 100 £1 ordinary shares of PM Limited. For commercial reasons he decides a new holding company is required and exchanges all his shares in return for 10,000 £1 shares in PM Holdings Limited. Stamp duty relief under *FA 1986, s 77* should be available, as Pete holds 100% of the ordinary shares prior to the transaction and 100% of the ordinary shares of PM Holdings Limited immediately afterwards.

Pete also holds all of the share capital of PM Trading Limited and wishes to exchange that company too, so that it is also a subsidiary of PM Holdings Limited. Pete's holding of shares in PM Trading Limited is 25 £1 ordinary shares and 75 £1 A shares. He proposes to transfer these to PM Holdings Limited in return for the issue of 5,000 more £1 ordinary shares by PM Holdings Limited.

While Pete will remain the 100% shareholder of PM Trading Limited, directly before the transaction and indirectly afterwards, his shareholding in PM Holdings Limited will not exactly mirror his shareholding in PM Trading Limited, as all the shares will be ordinary shares, so no relief from stamp duty is available for this transfer.

In the above example, while this does not matter if the company is only worth £50,000 (as the stamp duty would only be £250), it is clearly much more material if the company is worth, say, £5m, so that the stamp duty is £25,000.

5.23   One way around this problem is to use a reduction of capital and issue of new shares, rather than a share exchange.

To effect the second exchange in **Example 5.4**, PM Trading Limited could reduce its capital under *CA 2006, s 641* and issue new shares to PM Holdings Limited. PM Holdings Limited will then issue shares to Pete. There is no transfer of shares from Pete to PM Holdings Limited, so no transaction on which stamp duty can be charged.

The shares will have to be cancelled in two tranches. *CA 2006, s 641*, as already noted, requires the company always to have at least one participating ordinary share issued, so we cannot reduce the share capital to nothing, even for a scintilla of time. Instead, in a case like this, one approach would be to cancel the A share capital and issue of new shares (which can be ordinary shares) to PM Holdings Limited, then to cancel the ordinary share capital and issue new shares to PM Holdings Limited. Finally, PM Holdings Limited will issue the relevant number of shares to Pete.

Clearly this transaction is not a share exchange within *TCGA 1992, s 135*. It is, however, a scheme of reconstruction (see **7.22** *et seq*), so that shareholder level relief under *TCGA 1992, s 136* should be available and clearance under *TCGA 1992, s 138* can be sought, just as it would have been for the share exchange. The restriction at *TCGA 1992, s 137(1)* requires that the transactions be carried out for *bona fide* commercial reasons, which will almost always be the case, and it also requires that the transaction not be part of a scheme or arrangements with a major purpose of avoiding corporation tax or capital gains tax. Therefore, if you take the view that the structuring of the proposed transaction this way is to avoid stamp duty, HMRC are not allowed to refuse the capital gains relief, as *TCGA 1992, s 137(1)* does not refer to stamp duty.

5.24   This is the acceptable structuring of a transaction in a way that carries a lower tax bill than it might have had it been structured another way, squarely within the parameters of the *Duke of Westminster* and *Ayrshire Pullman* cases referred to above, and not, it is ventured, tax avoidance at all.

In any case, the practical experience is that HMRC have never refused clearance for any of the author's clients on these cases. When first using this technology, HMRC tended to ask why the transaction was not carried out by way of share exchange, but they seemed perfectly comfortable with the response that we did not wish to incur a stamp duty charge on the transactions.

That said, however, it is important to remember the restriction for schemes of arrangement under *CA 2006, s 899* (see **5.4** above).

DEMERGER MECHANISM

Demergers

5.25   A demerger is a method of splitting up a company or group into more than one company or group, sometimes owned by the same shareholders and often partitioned between the shareholders. There are several ways that the split can be achieved but most of them required the transfer of assets from the original single company to one or more successor companies, as part of a scheme of reconstruction.

For this to be a tax-free transfer, it has to be for no consideration (see **7.29**), so the question that arises is what mechanisms are available to a company to transfer their assets in this way, without any consideration being given.

5.26   There are three mechanisms available in most cases:

- **Distribution**: the original company distributes assets *in specie* to one or more successor companies.

- **Liquidation**: the original company distributes assets *in specie* to one or more successor companies, under the provisions in *Insolvency Act 1986, s 110*.

- **Reduction of capital**: the original company distributes assets *in specie* to one or more successor companies, as consideration for a reduction of capital.

All of these are used in schemes of reconstruction, particularly demergers. The distribution *in specie* route, however, is only available for trading companies, as there is a specific relief from the income tax charge on a distribution *in specie* where trading activities or groups are being split up (*CTA 2010, Pt 23, Ch 5*). This relief does not apply where trades are being separated from non-trading activities or where non-trading activities are being split.

The liquidation route has been the most common alternative to the distribution *in specie*, simply because of the complexities of a reduction of capital prior to the enactment of *Companies Act 2006*. Reductions of capital were usually only used as a mechanism for demergers of large or public companies, for which the extra fees to obtain a Court Order (required under *CA 1985, s 135*, the predecessor rule to *CA 2006, s 641*) were not a major issue. However, liquidation demergers are not always desirable, as it can be commercially difficult to put a company into liquidation, the liquidator's fees can be quite high and there can be a substantial charge to SDLT in some cases.

5.27 Consider, for example, the division or demerger of a business comprising a portfolio of investment properties. Let us work through the differences between a liquidation demerger and a reduction of capital.

Example 5.5 – Demerger of property investment company

Bill and Ted own PropCo, a property investment company with investment properties. They wish to separate the business between themselves.

The first steps are common to both transactions:

Diagram 3

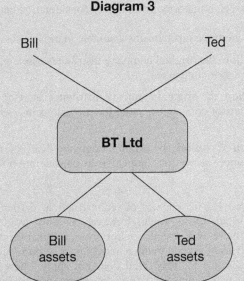

Step 1

Insert a new holding company, HoldCo by way of a tax free share-for-share exchange. *Prima facie*, we would expect the relief from stamp duty at *FA 1986, s 77* to apply. However, one problem with demergers is that the insertion of a new holding company at Step 1 can fall foul of the stamp duty rule in *FA 1986, s 77A*, because a demerger separating a company between two equal shareholders will perforce mean that one company changes control when it ceases to be controlled by two people and becomes controlled by just one of them.

As a result, we can replace Step 1 with a transaction whereby the shares of PropCo are cancelled under *CA 2006, s 641* and new shares are issued to HoldCo, which in turn issues shares to Bill and Ted. Since neither the cancellation nor the issue of new shares carry stamp duty, no stamp duty arises in the first place, so the relief at *FA 1986, s 77* is simply not in point.

See **5.23** for a more detailed technical analysis.

Diagram 4

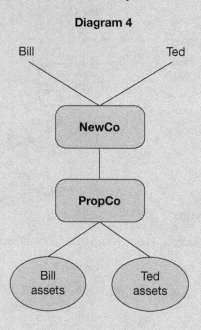

Step 2

Transfer, say, Bill's property portfolio from PropCo to HoldCo.

Generally speaking, it is preferable to do this by way of distribution in specie, which should then be free of SDLT by virtue of *FA 2003, s 54* ('Exceptions from deemed market value rule').

Where this is not possible, or not possible with the whole of the portfolio, usually due to an insufficiency of distributable reserves, the transfer can be done for book value consideration, in which case it will be necessary to rely on the SDLT group relief in *FA 2003, Sch 7*. This does introduce commercial complexities, which is why it is preferable to use a distribution in specie for this step.

5.27 *Reduction of capital*

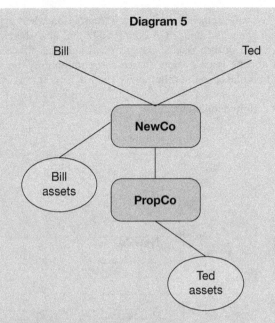

Diagram 5

Liquidation demerger

In a liquidation demerger, HoldCo will then be liquidated.

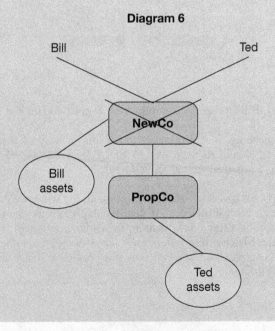

Diagram 6

268

The shares of PropCo, containing Ted's portfolio, will be transferred to TedCo, which will issue shares only to Ted. Bill's portfolio will be transferred from HoldCo to BillCo, which will issue shares only to Bill.

Diagram 7

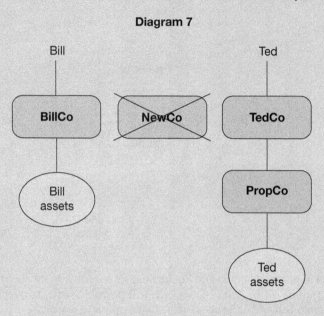

As a result, Bill and Ted will each hold their own separate portfolio of properties and both sets of transactions should be free of capital gains tax, as a scheme of reconstruction.

However, the transfer of Bill's portfolio from HoldCo to BillCo gives us a problem for SDLT purposes. This transfer is, prima facie, a distribution in the winding up of HoldCo, so we would expect the SDLT exemption at *FA 2003, s 54* to apply. However, HMRC's view, and that of a number of other commentators, is that the issue of shares by BillCo is the consideration for the transfer of the portfolio, so that SDLT will be due on the market value of those shares issued. This will, of course, usually be the same as the market value of the properties transferred, so the SDLT charge can be very substantial in such cases.

Reduction of capital demerger

Let us now look at what happens if we use a reduction of capital to effect the demerger. The first two steps are the same as for a liquidation demerger, so our starting point is HoldCo owning Bill's portfolio and PropCo (as above).

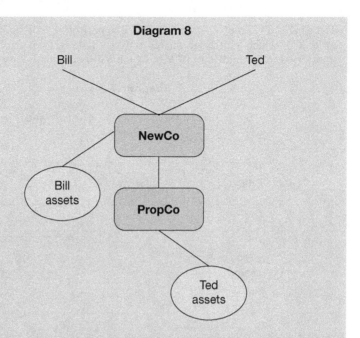

Diagram 8

Instead of putting HoldCo into liquidation, we reduce the capital of HoldCo by cancelling all of Ted's shares (we will probably have reorganised the shares into Bill and Ted classes immediately prior to that step).

In consideration of the reduction of Ted's share capital, PropCo is moved to TedCo which issues shares to Ted only.

Diagram 9

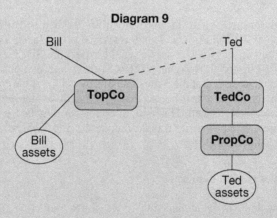

Thus we have effected the demerger, with Bill owning HoldCo with his portfolio and Ted owning TedCo which owns PropCo and his portfolio.

By avoiding a liquidation of HoldCo we have avoided the necessity to transfer Bill's portfolios out of one company and into another, so there is no SDLT as there is no transfer, which represents a substantial saving on the liquidation demerger route. Furthermore, we have not had to put a company in liquidation, with all the commercial consequences of this, and we have saved the fees of an insolvency practitioner.

5.28   The author has carried out a number of these transactions and HMRC are clearly comfortable with the technology. Pre-transaction clearances under *TCGA 1992, s 138* and, where appropriate, *TCGA 1992, s 139* have always been obtained.

When asked why the transaction is being carried out this way, the fact was highlighted that it is actually structurally simpler than a liquidation demerger, commercially more desirable than putting a company into liquidation, and saves the liquidator's fees.

To the extent that this can be seen as planning to prevent a charge to SDLT arising, it is important to highlight the fact that the relevant anti-avoidance provisions only apply to the avoidance of corporation tax and capital gains tax (for *TCGA 1992, s 138*) or those taxes plus income tax (for *TCGA 1992, s 139(5)*).

271

Chapter 6

Groups and substantial shareholdings

Pete Miller CTA (Fellow), Partner, The Miller Partnership
Based on chapter originally written by John Baldry LLB, LLM (London)

SIGNPOSTS

- **Different definitions of 'group'** – The definition of a 'group' of companies is different for different parts of the *Corporation Tax Acts*.

- **Definition of group relief group** – A group for group relief purposes requires one company to be a 75% subsidiary of the other, or both to be 75% subsidiaries of a third company (see **6.9** *et seq*).

- **Anti-avoidance** – *CTA 2010, Pt 5, Ch 6* contains anti-avoidance rules common to most of the definitions of a 'group' (see **6.4** *et seq*).

- **EEA group relief** – Group relief can be given for losses on non-UK subsidiaries resident in the EEA in restricted circumstances (see **6.21** *et seq*).

- **Group relief for carried forward losses** – This is now available in many cases. This applies to losses arising on or after 1 April 2017 only (see **6.20**). This does not apply to EEA group relief.

- **Definition of capital gains group** – A group for capital gains purposes comprises a 'principal company' and its 75% subsidiaries, together with their 75% subsidiaries, and so on, so long as all the companies are 'effective 51% subsidiaries' of the principal company (see **6.25** *et seq*).

- **SSE groups** – For the purposes of the substantial shareholdings exemption, a group comprises a 'principal company' and its 51% subsidiaries, together with their 51% subsidiaries, and so on, so long as all the companies are 'effective 51% subsidiaries' of the principal company (see **6.58** *et seq*).

- **Substantial shareholding exemption** – The exemption is now much more widely available as there are no longer any conditions attached to the vendor company or group. Thus, for disposals on or after 1 April 2017, any disposal of a substantial shareholding in a trading company may qualify for the exemption (see **6.62**).

- **Substantial shareholding exemption** – A new version of the exemption was introduced for disposing companies that are partly owned by qualifying institutional investors (pension funds, sovereign wealth funds and the like) (see **6.66A**).

- **Degrouping** – A degrouping charge arises where a company leaves a group holding assets transferred to it from another group company within the previous six years. This charge is treated as part of the disposal proceeds for most disposals where the transferred asset is a chargeable asset, so that it arises on the vendor company (see **6.33** *et seq*). The degrouping charge for intangible assets arises on the company leaving the group (see **6.75**).

- **Transfers of trades** – There are special rules for transfers of trades between companies under 75% common ownership, preserving losses and capital allowances on the trade transfer (see **6.40** *et seq*).

- **Loss-buying, etc** – There are targeted anti-avoidance rules which prevent buying in capital losses and gain washing transactions, and to prevent the artificial reduction of gains or creation of losses (see **6.47** *et seq*).

- **Group payment arrangements** – There are administrative arrangements whereby all payments of corporation tax by a group can be carried out through a single group company (see **6.76**).

INTRODUCTION

6.1   This chapter deals with the principal considerations which arise for companies which fall to be treated (under tests which differ according to the tax in question) as members of a group for one or more corporation tax purposes. This brings with it both benefits and opportunities for the careful and less desirable consequences for the unwary.

Unlike some other taxing jurisdictions, such as the US, the UK does not operate a consolidated system of group taxation, at least for corporation tax. Rather, the UK tax system respects each company within the group as a distinct legal entity, each subject to the general tax regime, but then overlays various rules in order to take into account the fact that the companies are in reality part of one economic unit.

The principal day-to-day issue for a group of companies will be how to deal with situations where certain members of the group are making profits and others losses. This is dealt with through the group relief rules. Companies may also be concerned about the transfer of assets or businesses, or assignments of debts between members of the group. The tax code attempts to provide for all these scenarios, but in doing so also requires a number of anti-avoidance rules which must be carefully negotiated in order not to cause immediate or future tax concerns.

That is not to say, however, that the rules achieve, or even attempt to achieve, neutrality between the position where an economic entity operates through one company (or 'divisions'), and where it operates through more than one company. Inefficiencies may arise because the group has many companies (eg losses may become stranded by being carried forward in a loss-making member of the group when other members are profitable), or fortuitous planning using subsidiaries may lead to tax advantages not available if the enterprise had been carried on through a different corporate structure (eg a business to be sold is carried on in a separate subsidiary so that substantial shareholding relief is available on the sale).

The tax consequences of a particular group structure are myriad and infiltrate through every area of tax. The main focus of this chapter is on the basic rules which a practitioner or in-house tax adviser to a group is likely to come across, both in the operation of the group and in transactions undertaken by it. It therefore deals principally with group relief, capital gains tax groups, transfers of trades, pre-entry loss provisions, depreciatory transactions and the substantial shareholdings exemption. On the administrative side, group payment arrangements are also dealt with.

There are also numerous anti-avoidance rules which are applicable to groups in a number of areas of corporate tax legislation, including the various specialist regimes, for example those relating to intangible property or loan relationships and derivatives. Detailed consideration of those rules is outside the scope of this work, and is best dealt with in those works which consider the areas concerned. Some of the rules in those regimes which apply specifically to groups are, however, noted in this chapter.

DEFINITIONS

75% subsidiary

6.2   For the purposes of most group tests, *CTA 2010, s 1154(3)* provides the definition for one body corporate being a 75% subsidiary of another. A body corporate will be a 75% subsidiary of another body corporate if and so long as 75% of its ordinary share capital is owned directly or indirectly by that other body corporate.

The 75% subsidiary test is an indirect one. Therefore if A owns 100% of B and C, each of which owns 50% of D, D will be a 75% subsidiary of A, even though it is not a 75% subsidiary of B or of C.

The basic tests of capital ownership for grouping purposes are often referred to as the 'nominal' ownership requirements, referring to the 'nominal' amount of share capital which is required to establish the group, as contrasted with the economic tests discussed below (see **6.4**).

Ordinary share capital

6.3   Ordinary share capital is defined in *CTA 2010, s 1119* and means all share capital of the company, whatever it is called, other than capital the holders of which have the rights to a dividend at a fixed rate but have no other rights to share in the profits of the company. Essentially, therefore, this removes fixed-rate preference shares from the test. Other preference shares, however, count as ordinary share capital. It is also commonly assumed that shares that do not carry dividends are part of the ordinary share capital of a company. This might seem odd at first glance, but the reason for this interpretation is that shares that do not carry dividends do not have a right to a dividend at a fixed rate, as they do not have a right to a dividend at all. This view has recently been upheld by the Upper Tribunal in the case of *McQuillan* (UT/2016/0141). It is understood that the case may be subject to an appeal to the Court of Appeal, so this decision may not be final.

CTA 2010, Pt 5, Ch 6

6.4   *CTA 2010, Pt 5, Ch 6* provides what are often referred to as the 'economic' tests for ownership. Without these, it would obviously be easy to manipulate the ownership of companies so that they fell within a particular group, but where the real economic interest in the company lay elsewhere.

Equity holders

6.5   The basic premise of *CTA 2010, Pt 5, Ch 6* is to establish what an equity holder would receive by way of share of profits or assets if all the profits or assets were distributed by the company. For these purposes, equity holder is a more extensive class than simply shareholder. It means any person who holds ordinary shares in the company, with an extended definition of the meaning of ordinary shares for this purpose (*CTA 2010, s 160*), or who is a loan creditor of the company, where the loan is not a 'normal commercial loan' (*CTA 2010, s 162*).

Ordinary shares

6.6   For *CTA 2010, Pt 5, Ch 6* purposes there is a self-contained definition of ordinary shares, which is not the same as that in *CTA 2010, s 1119* referred to above. The definition of ordinary shares is 'all shares other than restricted preference shares'.

The definition of restricted preference shares is that they must satisfy conditions A to E in *CTA 2010, s 160*. In summary:

A   the shares must be issued for 'new consideration';

B   they must not carry conversion rights, except into (broadly) other restricted preference shares or quoted shares in the company's parent;

C   they must not carry any right to the acquisition of shares or securities;

D   they must carry no right to dividends or a restricted right to dividends;

E   they must not carry rights to repayment of an amount exceeding the new consideration given, except in so far as those rights are comparable with those for fixed dividend shares listed on a recognised stock exchange.

CTA 2010, s 161 then provides the meaning of 'restricted right to dividends' which includes fixed amount or fixed rate shares and 'fluctuating percentage rate' shares, the latter being shares linked to a published rate of interest, the retail prices index, or a similar prices index of the country or territory in whose currency the shares are denominated. The requirement that the dividends must represent no more than a reasonable commercial return on the consideration received by the company for the issue of the shares is also now included in *CTA 2010, s 161*.

The overall impact is that certain fixed rate shares are treated as ordinary shares for the purposes of this test, even they are not part of the ordinary share capital of the company for the purposes of the nominal tests. These shares are essentially seen as having characteristics more akin to participating equity, because of their special properties.

Normal commercial loans

6.7   The definition of 'normal commercial loan', is contained in *CTA 2010, s 162*. In summary, the loan must have been for 'new consideration' and satisfy the following conditions:

A   it must not carry conversion rights except (broadly) those which could be carried by a restricted preference share within *CTA 2010, s 160*;

B   it must not carry any right to the acquisition of shares or securities;

C   it must not carry interest which depends on the results of the company's business, or the value of its assets, or which exceeds a reasonable commercial return on the consideration lent;

D   it must not carry a right to repayment in excess of the amount of new consideration lent, except in so far as that right is comparable with those for debt listed on a recognised stock exchange.

For loans made on or after 21 March 2012 condition A is not breached if the loan is convertible into shares of an unconnected company that is listed on a recognised stock exchange.

Condition C is not breached if the interest rates decrease as the company's results or asset values increase, or *vice versa* (*CTA 2010, s 163(1), (2)*). Nor is condition C breached if a loan is used to buy land by the company and is secured on that land, so that the creditor can enforce payment by exercising rights over the land (*CTA 2010, s 163(3)–(6)*).

Once again, the holders of loans that have equity-like characteristics are equity holders for the purposes of the economic tests.

6.8   In order to deal with situations where shares carry rights to dividends which are limited or which may change by reason of arrangements which exist, or which may change because of the existence of options which may be exercised, *CTA 2010, Pt 5, Ch 6* contains a number of provisions which provide for the recalculation of the distribution of profits. Not all of these apply to all group tests; in particular the group relief test is more stringent than the capital gains tax test. Further reference is made to the differences in these tests in the relevant sections below (see, in particular, **6.28**).

Focus

These anti-avoidance rules apply with modifications across many of the definitions of a group for the purposes of the *Corporation Tax Acts*.

GROUP RELIEF

6.9   The group relief rules allow the transfer ('surrender' in the statutory terminology) of various types of losses, including but not limited to trading losses, from one member of a group (the 'surrendering company') to another (the 'claimant company'). The rules are concerned with income-type losses rather than capital losses (which are dealt with in a different way, see further below). One consequence of the introduction of the various specific regimes over the last decade or so (loan relationships, intangibles, etc) has been that the non-trading losses under such regimes also fall to be dealt with under the group relief regime.

6.10   Until 31 March 2017, group relief operated on an annual basis. It is this fact that caused many inefficiencies to arise in groups of companies. A company could only claim losses in any year to the extent that it has profits to absorb them. If, therefore, a company in a group had surplus losses in a year which could not be surrendered to other members of the group, its only option will be to carry those losses forward to use against its own profits. This resulted in the losses being stranded and becoming more or less worthless.

Focus

For losses arising on or after 1 April 2017, new legislation, introduced by *F(No 2)A 2017, Sch 4*, introduced *CTA 2010, Pt 5A*, which allows a variety of carried forward losses to be used in group relief claims in periods after the losses arose.

Qualifications for membership of a group

6.11   The group relief provisions occupy the seven chapters of *CTA 2010, Pt 6*. For the purposes of the group relief provisions (which apply to all types of losses available for group relief), two companies are members of a group of companies if one is the 75% subsidiary of another, or both are 75% subsidiaries of a third company (*CTA 2010, s 152*). *CTA 2010, s 151(4)* introduces the economic tests of ownership referred to in the discussion on *CTA 2010, Pt 5, Ch 6* above, so that a company will not be treated as a subsidiary of another company at any time where the parent company would not be entitled to 75% of the profits available for distribution to equity holders or 75% of the assets of the company available for distribution to equity holders on a winding-up. For these purposes, the full provisions of *CTA 2010, Pt 5, Ch 6* apply, so the effect of options will need to be taken into account.

6.12   In addition, *CTA 2010, Pt 5, Ch 5* has its own anti-avoidance provision in *CTA 2010, s 154* where there are arrangements under which the relationships between two group members (the 'first company' and the 'second company' may change. In particular the section applies where there are arrangements in existence whereby they may have any of the following effects (referred to as Effects 1 to 3):

- the first company (or any successor company under *CTA 2010, Pt 22, Ch 1*; see further the discussion at **6.40** below) could cease to be a member of the same group of companies as the second company and could become a member of the same group of companies as a third company; or

- any person or persons together have or could obtain control of the first company but not of the second; or

- a third company could begin to carry on the whole or part of a trade which is carried on by the first company either as successor to the first company or as successor to another company which has begun to carry on part of that trade.

6.13 The most obvious application of *CTA 2010, s 154* is when a group member is being sold to a third party. In such a case, there will come a point where the transaction between the seller and purchaser is sufficiently advanced that arrangements will be considered to have come into place, and group relief will no longer be possible. It is not always easy to determine at exactly what time that will be.

Although the terminology of *CTA 2010, s 154* is very broad, there is a necessity for 'arrangements' to exist, and it is accepted generally that this means arrangements with another party or parties. There is some guidance to be found in HMRC manuals, in particular at CTM80165 (and the other paragraphs referred to therein) and SP 3/93 as to HMRC's view, which is that such arrangements do not need to be legally binding and do not need to be in writing.

It is often the case that it is unclear where a sale of a group member will take place until very shortly before signing, the parties' negotiations being continuous until that point with the prospect of no transaction taking place at all. In that case, it would usually be relatively safe to conclude that there were no arrangements in place until agreement had been reached. Obviously once a written agreement is reached, even though it may be conditional, there will be arrangements in place, and group relief will not be possible during a period between sale and completion. In many cases, HMRC will also take the view that arrangements are in place if a potential sale has been ratified by the shareholders of a company.

In joint venture arrangements, ESC C10 provides HMRC's practice in relation to arrangements between joint venture parties which might otherwise fall foul of *CTA 2010, s 154* and also deals with share mortgages.

Residence qualifications for group relief

6.14 Since the *Finance Act 2000*, it is possible for members of a group to be resident outside the UK and to 'trace' groups through ownership of foreign bodies corporate. However, it is obviously not the intention of the legislation to give worldwide relief for losses, and therefore *CTA 2010, s 131* provides that the surrendering company (the group member with the loss) and the claimant company (the group member with the profit against which the loss is to be offset) must either be resident in the UK, or carry on a trade in the UK through a permanent establishment (this is referred to as being 'UK related', which is defined in *CTA 2010, s 134*).

From 1 April 2006 this was extended for certain cases involving companies in the European Economic Area following the *Marks & Spencer* group relief case. The conditions for relief in cases involving companies resident in EEA Member States are dealt with separately in *CTA 2010, Pt 5, Ch 3* (see further **6.21** below).

Types of loss available for group relief

6.15 The types of loss which may be surrendered by way of group relief are set out in *CTA 2010, s 99(1)* and are trading losses, excess capital allowances, non-trading deficits on loan relationships, qualifying charitable donations, UK property business losses (formerly Schedule A losses), management expenses and non-trading losses on intangible fixed assets.

6.16 It should be noted that trading losses, excess capital allowances and non-trading deficits on loan relationships may be surrendered even where the surrendering company has other profits against which they could be set (*CTA 2010, s 99(3)*). However, charges on income, UK property business losses, management expenses and non-trading losses on intangibles may only be group relieved to the extent they exceed the surrendering company's gross profits for the period (see *CTA 2010, s 105*), and are subject to further restrictions (see *CTA 2010, s 99(5)*).

Limits on group relief

6.17 *CTA 2010, s 137* provides for the amount of group relief to be given and deals with the limits on group relief. The basic limitation is the lower of the amount of the loss (the 'surrenderable amount' as defined in *CTA 2010, s 99(7)*) and the claimant company's total profits. The limitations are applied by reference to the 'overlapping period', which is the part of the accounting period which is common to both the surrendering company and the claimant company in relation to the claim in question (*CTA 2010, s 142*).

Overlapping period

6.18 If all members of the group have the same accounting period, then such complications do not arise, but otherwise it is necessary to apportion amounts of profits and losses between accounting periods of the claimant and surrendering companies. The basic rule is that this is to be done on a time basis (*CTA 2010, ss 139(2)* and *140(2)*). However, where that would give rise to a result which is 'unjust or unreasonable', then the apportionments may be made on such other basis as may be just and reasonable (*CTA 2010, s 141(3)*). It is worth bearing this provision in mind where a business is very seasonal or where unusual events during an accounting period have given rise to particular losses, and it would be more advantageous to the taxpayer to attribute those losses to a particular part of an accounting period. Further guidance may be found in the HMRC manuals at CTM80260. It should be noted however, that HMRC interpret this provision as including the position where a time apportionment would be unjust to HMRC.

Restrictions for dual-resident investment companies

6.19 If, in any period, a company is a 'dual-resident investing company' then that company may not surrender any amounts by way of group relief (*CTA 2010, s 109*). This is an anti-avoidance provision which is intended to prevent the double usage of losses by companies which are resident in more than one country; see HMRC manuals at CTM34500 and following paras for history and HMRC's view. The legislation contains restrictive provisions on the types of trading company which fall outside the provision. Trading companies which have as their main function or one of their main functions the activities set out in *CTA 2010, s 109(4)* will still be considered to be investment companies (mainly holding company, finance company and analogous activities).

They may, however, have unexpected application to certain companies which are incorporated in tax-haven jurisdictions, but which may technically be considered within the charge to tax of that territory, and which are also tax resident in the UK by reason of their management and control being exercised in the UK. This is particularly the case in jurisdictions which apply tax to certain types of companies but exempt others. In such cases it may be wise to seek guidance from HMRC if group relief is to be of particular significance in the group in question. There is nothing to prevent such companies being claimant companies for group relief purposes.

Group relief using carried forward losses

Relief for overseas losses of non-resident companies

6.20 As noted above, *F(No 2)A 2017, Sch 4*, introduced *CTA 2010, Pt 5A*, which allows a variety of carried forward losses to be used in group relief claims in periods after the losses arose. The losses to which these new rules apply are:

- non-trading loan relationship deficits;
- non-trading losses on intangible fixed assets;

- expenses of management of an investment business;

- trading losses;

- losses of a UK property business.

However, the new regime only applies to losses that arise on or after 1 April 2017.

In general, if any of the above are available to set off against total profits of a company in any year after they arose, the losses will also be available to surrender by that company, subject to a valid claim by a claimant company.

The detailed rules largely mirror the 'same year' group relief rules in *CTA 2010, Pt 5*, but there are some subtle differences, so practitioners are advised to review the new legislation carefully.

Focus

In *Marks & Spencer plc v Halsey (Inspector of Taxes)* Case C-446/03 [2006] STC 237, Marks & Spencer successfully claimed before the ECJ that as a matter of principle the UK group relief laws breached EU law as, whilst they would allow losses of a UK company arising from a branch in France (for example) to be relieved against another UK group member's profits, it would not allow relief if, as in the case of Marks & Spencer, those losses arose in a French company.

6.21   In response to the *Marks & Spencer* decision, provisions were introduced to permit losses from companies resident in the European Economic Area (or EEA permanent establishments of non-EEA resident companies) to be surrendered to other members of a UK group. Those provisions are in *CTA 2010, Pt 5, Ch 3*. Apart from the conditions therein, it is also subject to its own anti-avoidance provision in *CTA 2010, s 127* where arrangements are entered into to ensure that losses would be available for group relief (eg by taking certain corporate actions to ensure that the conditions discussed below were satisfied). If that is the case, the amount of loss is excluded from relief.

The availability of overseas losses of EEA subsidiaries was highly restricted and was reviewed by the ECJ as potentially being too restrictive for EU purposes. As a result, changes were made in *Finance Act 2013* to make the losses less restrictive and, therefore, possibly more compliant with EU legislation.

6.22   The four conditions for group relief to be permitted in this situation are:

- the equivalence condition: *CTA 2010, s 114*;

- the EEA tax loss condition: *CTA 2010, ss 115* and *116*;

- the qualifying loss condition: *CTA 2010, ss 117–120*; and

- the precedence condition: *CTA 2010, s 121*.

All four conditions must be satisfied in order for a loss to be relieved. In broad terms the principles of the conditions are as follows.

The loss must be equivalent (ie it must correspond in all material respects) with a type of loss which would be surrendered under the domestic rules (the equivalence condition).

It must be calculated in accordance with the relevant rules under the relevant territory for the calculation of losses or other amounts eligible for relief (the EEA tax loss condition).

From 1 April 2013, EEA-resident companies can surrender losses from their UK permanent establishments as group relief in the UK, even if that loss can also be used against the profits of the surrendering company or of any other person (the qualifying loss condition). Where a loss that has been surrendered is later used against non-UK profits, then the benefit of the UK group relief will be withdrawn to the extent that the loss has been used elsewhere. This ensures that the losses are not relieved twice, once as group relief in the UK and then again in another country. This change will not apply to non-UK resident companies which are resident outside the EEA.

Until *FA 2013*, the legislation required that the loss must not have been relieved or be able to be relieved in previous, current or future periods whether against profits of the surrendering company or of any other person (the qualifying loss condition). It was this condition which effectively reduced the use of the overseas loss to cases where the loss has become legally (and not just practically) impossible to use. This rule was challenged by the European Commission in Case C-172/13 *European Commission v UK* (3 February 2015). The challenge was unsuccessful, however, finding that the Commission's examples did not demonstrate that the legislation was unnecessarily restrictive.

This test, whether the losses can be used in the non-UK jurisdiction, must be considered at the end of the accounting period in which the losses arose (*CTA 2010, s 119(4)*). However, in May 2013 the Supreme Court decided (in *R & C Comrs v Marks and Spencer plc* [2013] BTC 162) that this was incompatible with EU law and that the test should be considered at the time that the claim is made, instead. So far, however, no legislative changes have been proposed. So the Supreme Court decision will only apply to what we might call Marks & Spencer claims, ie those pre-dating the UK legislation.

The final qualification is that there is no other territory (not limited to EEA countries) in which effective relief could be given for the relevant loss.

Once those conditions have been satisfied, *CTA 2010, ss 123–126* provide for rules for the recalculation of the amount of the loss in accordance with UK tax rules and the assumptions to be made in making the surrender as regards accounting periods etc.

Administrative requirements for group relief

6.23   Claims for group relief are part of the corporation tax self-assessment regime (CTSA) and are dealt with by *FA 1998, Sch 18, para 66*ff. A claim must be made in the CTSA return or in an amendment to that return. The surrendering company must give its consent to the claim, and consent must be given at or before the time of the claim and the claim must contain a copy of that consent, otherwise the claim for group relief will be ineffective (*FA 1998, Sch 18, para 70*) Revised claims may only be dealt with by amendment of the CTSA return, and strictly this is by withdrawal of one claim and resubmission of another rather than by amendment of the claim (*FA 1998, Sch 18, para 73*).

There are separate time limits for the claiming or withdrawal of a claim for group relief from the general CTSA return amendment rules, which are set out in *FA 1998, Sch 18, para 74*. The basic rule is that the claim must be made by the first anniversary of the CTSA filing date for the company, but this is extended if there is an enquiry into the return or an appeal in relation to the return up to 30 days after the completion of the enquiry or the final determination of the appeal. This obviously gives time for consequential amendments to the group relief claims which may be affected by other matters which are the subject of the enquiry or appeal.

Payment for group relief

6.24   Payments for group relief are ignored for corporation tax purposes provided they do not exceed the amount of the loss (*CTA 2010, s 183*). Obviously, the benefit to the claimant company is that amount multiplied by the effective corporation tax rate for the period in question, and so it will usually be that, lesser, amount which is paid, if any payment is made. The company law relating to corporate benefit and maintenance of capital should be taken into account when deciding whether or not and how much to pay for group relief.

CHARGEABLE GAINS GROUPS

6.25 The provisions relating to corporation tax on chargeable gains in groups principally deal with the transfer of assets from one company in a group to another, and provide for the transfer to be on a 'no-gain-no-loss' basis. The corollary of this is that a potential 'exit charge' is created if the transferee company leaves the group within six years of the transfer, subject to certain exceptions which are discussed further below.

Qualifications for membership of a group

6.26 The primary qualification for being a member of a group is to be a 'company', as defined by *TCGA 1992, s 170(9)*. For these purposes, 'a company' is:

(a) a company as defined in *CA 2006, s 1(1)*;

(b) a company which is constituted under any other Act or a Royal Charter or letters patent or is formed under the law of a country or territory outside the United Kingdom, but not an LLP;

(c) a registered industrial and provident society (under the *Co-operative and Community Benefit Societies and Credit Unions Act 1965*, formerly the *Industrial and Provident Societies Act 1965* until renamed in 2010;

(d) an incorporated friendly society within the meaning of the *Friendly Societies Act 1992*;

(e) a building society.

6.27 Grouping for capital gains tax purposes is dealt with in a conceptually different way to groups for group relief purposes (which, after all, only looks for 75% relationships between companies, rather than a group per se). The legislation works by determining a particular capital gains tax group with one parent company. This is principally so that it can then be determined whether a company has left a particular group for the purposes of applying the exit charge. However, this way of viewing the group does create complications in trying to determine whether a group is the same group or not, for example if a new parent company is formed and the existing parent company transferred to it.

6.28 A group for chargeable gains purposes is defined with dual tests: a nominal test and an economic test. The nominal test defined a group as comprising a company (the 'principal company of the group') and all its 75% subsidiaries, all their 75% subsidiaries, and so on (*TCGA 1992, s 170(3)*). The economic test then tells us that a group does not include any company which is not an 'effective 51% subsidiary' of the principal company. *TCGA 1992,* *s 170(7)* defines an 'effective 51% subsidiary' in terms of profits available for distribution to equity holders and beneficial entitlement of equity holders to assets on a winding-up. *TCGA 1992, s 170(8)* brings in the tests in *CTA 2010, Pt 5, Ch 6* (see **6.6** and **6.7**). For these purposes, *CTA 2010, Pt 5, Ch 6* is modified so that loans from banks in the normal course of their business are excluded from the meaning of 'loan creditor' for the definition of equity holders, and the 'arrangements' and options provisions are also ignored for the purposes of the chargeable gains group tests.

These rules were tested in the case of *Gemsupa and Another v RCC* [2015] UKFTT 97 (TC), where the existence of options was specifically held not to be relevant in determining whether the companies were members of a group. As a result, transfers of properties were accepted as being tax free, under *TCGA 1992, s 171(1)* (see **6.31**), even though the vendor companies' shares were the subject of call options allowing the previous owners to reacquire the companies immediately after the property transfers.

6.29   Because the definition of a group revolves around identifying a particular group rather than simply the relationship between two companies, it is necessary to identify when the group has remained the same group. *TCGA 1992, s 170(10)* provides that a group will remain the same group for as long as the principal company of the group is the same. If the principal company becomes a member of another group, then the two groups are also regarded as the same group.

Residence qualifications

6.30   As with the group relief provisions discussed above, *FA 2000* introduced changes to the definitions of chargeable gains groups so that it is possible for the principal company of a group to be a company resident outside the UK, and for members of the group to be non-UK resident companies. This can give rise to issues where the constitution of groups changes by reason of a transaction taking place entirely outside the UK, and the parties involved overlook a charge to capital gains tax because no-one envisages that such a transaction would cause a UK tax effect. At the same time as the *FA 2000* amendments to the constitution of groups, residence qualifications were inserted into the transfer provisions in *TCGA 1992, s 171* to ensure that the provisions did not permit transfers outside the UK tax net on a tax-free basis.

Transfer provisions

6.31   The principal provision on transfers is *TCGA 1992, s 171*, which provides that where a transfer is made between two members of a chargeable gains group, and they are either resident in the UK, or the asset is (or will be) a chargeable asset in relation to them, then the transfer is deemed for corporation tax to be one at a consideration which will give rise to neither a gain nor a loss.

The use of the phrase 'disposes of an asset to another company', as well as the general framework of the provisions, means that there must be both a disposal and an acquisition of an asset for the provisions to apply, and a disposal without an acquisition (such as the redemption of shares), or an acquisition without a disposal (such as the subscription for shares) will not be within *TCGA 1992, s 171*. There are also some specific exclusions in *TCGA 1992, s 171(2)* and *(3A)*. Of note is the exclusion for transfers to (but not from) dual-resident investing companies. The point made at **6.19** above in relation to unexpectedly dual-resident companies is worth remembering.

Appropriations to or from trading stock

6.32   It may be the case that the assets which are the subject of the transfer are trading assets for one of the companies but capital assets for the other. If the transferee is acquiring the asset as part of its trading stock, then *TCGA 1992, s 173(1)* deems it to have acquired it as a capital asset and then immediately appropriated it to trading stock. This will give rise to a charge under *TCGA 1992, s 161* either as a capital gain, or, by election, by an adjustment to the trading profits of the acquirer.

If the transferor is the trader, then *TCGA 1992, s 173(2)* deems the transferor to have appropriated the stock from trading stock immediately before the transfer. *TCGA 1992, s 161* treats the transferor as having acquired it for the value which is taken into the accounts in respect of it, and *TCGA 1992, s 171* then applies to the transfer. There is no specific statutory provision which provides the figure to be placed in the trading accounts on the deemed appropriation from trading stock in such a case, although in practice market value has been used, on the basis of the principle in *Sharkey v Wernher* (1955) 36 TC 276. There are relatively new provisions introduced by *FA 2008, Sch 15, Pt 2* and now in *CTA 2009, Pt 3, Ch 10* which apply market value to appropriations in general, although their interaction with *TCGA 1992, s 173(2)* is still not entirely clear because *TCGA 1992, s 173(2)* only deems there to have been an appropriation for the purposes of *TCGA 1992, s 161*. However, use of any other figure is likely to lead to an argument with HMRC.

Although the provisions of *TCGA 1992, s 173* open up the possibility of planning by, for example, the triggering of losses, it should be borne in mind that attempts to rely on trading or non-trading status have not received much sympathy before the courts when taxpayers have sought to rely on different group members having a different status. See, in particular, *Reed v Nova Securities Ltd* [1985] STC 124, although the taxpayer company obtained a better result in *New Angel Court Ltd v Adam (Inspector of Taxes)* [2004]

All ER 294 (Mar) where the company won in the Court of Appeal, despite losing in front of the Special Commissioner and the High Court.

Company ceasing to be a member of a group

6.33

Focus

These rules were substantially amended for capital gains purposes by *Finance Act 2011*. Of particular practical importance is that the degrouping charge takes on the character of the associated share disposal, if there is one, and there is a facility to require a degrouping charge to be reduced or eliminated where it is just and reasonable to do so.

These new rules do not apply to degrouping charges applicable to chargeable intangible assets, under *CTA 2010, Pt 8*. However, a parallel change to the rules for intangible fixed assets was the subject of a consultation process between February and May 2018.

Without anti-avoidance measures, the intra-group transfer provisions would obviously be open to abuse as assets could effectively be transferred to third parties by the mechanism of a company. However, rather than adopt any mechanism which depends on there being arrangements in place at the time of the transfer, or any reliance on any motive test, the chargeable gains legislation imposes a charge when a transferee company leaves the group within six years of the transfer under *TCGA 1992, s 179*.

6.34   The basic rule is that if a company, Company A, leaves the group and either it, or an associated company also leaving the group, owns the asset (or an asset into which a gain on the asset has been rolled under the replacement of business assets rules) otherwise than as trading stock, then company A is deemed to have sold and immediately reacquired the asset on its acquisition from Company B. How this gain is then taxed depends on when and how Company A leaves the group, and is covered below.

There are several points worth making in relation to the basic application of *TCGA 1992, s 179*. First, as mentioned above, it is a blanket charge and does not depend on the circumstances of the original transfer being tax motivated or carried out at otherwise than market value. Secondly, the asset may no longer be owned by Company A but may have been transferred on to another company leaving the group at the same time (leading to the mistaken conclusion that *TCGA 1992, s 179(2)* applies (see further below)). Finally, the asset which was the subject of the original transfer to Company A may no longer be owned by the group at all, but *TCGA 1992, s 179* will still impose a charge if a gain on the disposal of the asset has been rolled into another asset under *TCGA 1992, s 151*.

The conditions for the charge (commonly referred to as an 'exit charge') are:

- there has been a transfer from Company B to Company A when both were members of a group;

- at the time of the transfer Company A and Company B were either resident in the UK or the asset was a chargeable asset in relation to them;

- within six years of the time of the acquisition, Company A ceases to be a member of the group.

If company A ceases to be a member of the group by virtue of a disposal of shares (a 'group disposal'), the chargeable gain computed in respect of the asset is not charged on Company A. Instead, the gain is treated as further consideration accruing to the vendor company. This means, first, that the charge falls on the vendor company and not in Company A, which simplifies due diligence and warranty issues in transactions. And secondly, it means that any reliefs or exemptions that apply to the group disposal, such as the substantial shareholding exemption (*TCGA 1992, Sch 7AC*) or the reorganisations provisions (*TCGA 1992, s 135*), will also apply to the degrouping element.

This rule also applies where there is no taxable group disposal but an exit charge still arises, to which the substantial shareholding exemption would apply. For example, if Company A, a member of a trading group, holds shares in a trading company that were transferred to it within the previous six years, and Company A is sold by a non-UK vendor, the gain is added to the consideration received by the vendor and, since the vendor is outside the scope of UK corporation tax, no charge arises. In many cases, the gain on the deemed disposal by Company A would anyway have been exempt under the substantial shareholding exemption, but the degrouping provisions apply anyway, even if the substantial shareholding exemption does not.

6.35   If the exit charge arises other than through a disposal (eg where a new investor subscribes for more than 25% of the enlarged share capital), the charge arises as a chargeable gain in Company A, instead, as there is no vendor company to which it can be applied. Where this happens, the company may be able to transfer the charge to another company in the vendor group by an election under *TCGA 1992, s 171A* (see **6.39**).

Companies leaving a group at the same time

6.36   The primary exemption from the charge under *TCGA 1992, s 179* is contained in *TCGA 1992, s 179(2)* which prevents a charge arising on a transfer between two companies when those companies leave the group together. No exit charge arises in respect of a transfer from one company to another if either:

- both are 75% subsidiaries and effective 51% subsidiaries of another company on the date of the acquisition, and they remain both 75% subsidiaries and effective 51% subsidiaries of that other company until immediately after the degrouping event, or

- one is a 75% subsidiary and an effective 51% subsidiary of the other on the date of the acquisition, and remains both a 75% subsidiary and an effective 51% subsidiary of the other until immediately after the degrouping event.

These are very restrictive rules, as they permit very little intra-group movement in respect of the transferee and transferor companies.

Claim for 'just and reasonable' adjustments

6.37 One problem with the exit charge rules was always the potential for double taxation, inherent in there being a charge in respect of the disposal of the shares and another in respect of the deemed disposal of an underlying asset owned by a company whose shares were being sold. In such cases, the company making the disposal may claim to have the degrouping charge reduced or eliminated (the reduction must be specified in the claim), and HMRC are required to reduce the gain 'by such amount (if any) as is just and reasonable', taking into account the transaction whereby the asset-holding company acquired the asset.

Where a reduction is made, the base cost of the asset concerned is also reduced by the same amount. This prevents the double relief that might accrue if the asset were to be rebased without the commensurate exit charge.

Merger exemption: *TCGA 1992, s 181*

6.38 The merger exemption in *TCGA 1992, s 181* is sometimes overlooked, but it can be useful. The exemption applies where Company A (the transferee) leaves the group as part of a merger carried out for bona fide commercial reasons and the avoidance of tax is not the main or one of the main purposes of the merger. This principally assists in cases where two groups exchange interests in each other's businesses, either via the transfer of business to a new company, or to one of the group companies involved in the transaction. The value of the interests acquired by each group must be substantially the same as the value of the business interest given up (ie this relief is not restricted to 50:50 joint ventures), and the consideration must be substantially in the form of the acquisition of the interest in the business, or applied in acquiring such an interest (ignoring any small amounts) (*TCGA 1992, s 181(4)*).

Notional transfers prior to a sale: *TCGA 1992, s 171A*

6.39   Prior to the introduction of *TCGA 1992, s 171A*, it was common for groups to marshal their gains and losses by the transfer of assets intra-group prior to their disposal to third parties. This type of planning was generally accepted by HMRC, and effectively allowed group relief for allowable (capital) losses. *TCGA 1992, s 171A* is restated by *FA 2009* to dispense with the need actually to deem an intra-group transfer of the relevant asset, which had given rise to issues in some circumstances. Under the new drafting, there is simply an election to transfer the gain or loss between group companies. It should, however, be noted that the gain or loss must be made in respect of an asset to which a transfer under *TCGA 1992, s 171* could have applied.

TCGA 1992, s 171A also permits an exit charge gain to be transferred within a group, so that, if an exit charge arises on a company leaving a group (see **6.35**), that charge can be transferred to another company in the vendor group.

TRANSFERS OF TRADES UNDER *CTA 2010, PT 22, CH 1*

6.40   The transfer of a business between members of the group will of course have more tax implications than just tax on chargeable gains. There may be brought forward trading losses in the transferring trading company which may be lost, or there may be capital assets on which capital allowances have been claimed where a disposal would lead to a balancing charge or a balancing allowance. *CTA 2010, Pt 22, Ch 1* aims to avoid those events where a trade is transferred between parties under common ownership, and avoids the effects of the statutory discontinuance of the trade under *CTA 2009, s 41*. It is subject to its own anti-avoidance provisions.

Common ownership requirements

6.41   The common ownership requirement in *CTA 2010, s 941* is stated in a different way to the grouping tests. *CTA 2010, Pt 22, Ch 1* is intended to be broad in application, and can itself be viewed as an anti-avoidance provision. The terminology of the common ownership test has been somewhat re-written, but the principle is the same, and requires a 75% common interest. The test compares the ownership of the company at the time of the transfer or at any time within the subsequent two years with the owners at any time within the year prior to the transfer. If there is a 75% commonality of ownership between the two dates, the common ownership requirements are met.

Although *CTA 2010, Pt 22, Ch 1* itself only applies to transfers between companies (as it applies for corporation tax), the 'common ownership' requirement can be traced through persons other than companies. *CTA 2010, s 942* sets out the options by which the ownership condition may be satisfied Basically, ownership is traced through the ordinary share capital of the company carrying on the trade. 'Ordinary share capital' for this purpose bears its *CTA 2010, s 1119* meaning discussed above in relation to group relief (see **6.3**). A trade is therefore regarded as belonging to the persons owning the ordinary share capital of the company carrying on the trade, or if it is carried on in a subsidiary, by the persons owning the ordinary share capital of the parent.

There is also a rule, in *CTA 2010, s 941(7)*, which treats for this purpose persons who are related (being husbands, wives, civil partners, ancestors or lineal descendants, and brothers and sisters) as the same person. Shares owned by non-charitable trusts are treated as owned by the persons entitled to the income under the trust (*CTA 2010, s 941(5)*), and for these purposes if there is more than one such person, they are treated as the same person (*CTA 2010, s 941(7)*).

Effect of application

6.42   *CTA 2010, Pt 22, Ch 1* applies for two specific purposes only. First, it prevents a disposal event under the capital allowances legislation, and effectively gives future allowances to the purchaser in the same amounts as would have been given to the seller (*CTA 2010, s 948*). Secondly, it allows the carry forward of losses in the trade under *CTA 2010, Pt 4, Ch 2* to continue to be carried forward by the purchaser (*CTA 2010, s 944*).

Anti-avoidance

6.43   *CTA 2010, s 948* (the capital allowances provision) does not apply if the transferee company is a dual-resident investing company (see the discussion at **6.19** above).

Where liabilities of the transferor company are not assumed by the transferee, and these exceed the value any assets of the transferor not transferred, the loss carry-over under *CTA 2010, s 944* is restricted to the amount of losses over and above that excess (*CTA 2010, s 945*). This provision is designed to prevent the hiving down of trades and associated losses where the liabilities of the trade remain with the transferor (eg in an insolvency proceeding), and the subsequent sale of a company with those losses.

Finance Act 2013 also introduced a further restriction on the transfer of trading losses under this legislation, relating to the interaction with the rules for a change of ownership of a company (*CTA 2010, Pt 14, Ch 2*). The new anti-avoidance rule is designed to stop any device whereby the trade is transferred to another group company. Before this amendment, the effect of

CTA 2010, s 676 was to restrict the carry forward of losses by a successor company where the loss had been sustained by a predecessor if the transfer of the trade occurred before the change in ownership (of the successor). The effect of the new legislation is to extend the restriction of carried forward losses by a company even if the transfer of the trade occurs after the change in ownership (ie where the successor company has not itself undergone a change in ownership). The new rules apply to all changes of ownership on or after 20 March 2013.

Other issues on a transfer of trade

6.44   It should be noted that *CTA 2010, Pt 22, Ch 1* makes no provision about trading stock. The basic provisions in *CTA 2009, Pt 3, Ch 11* will therefore apply by reason of *CTA 2009, s 41* and an amount will have to be brought into account in respect of the disposal of it, which is either the value obtained on transfer, or the market value if the parties are connected (subject to the ability to elect otherwise).

6.45   If only part of a trade is transferred under *CTA 2010, s 951*, a question arises as to whether the transferor continues to carry on the remaining trade as part of the previous trade, or whether there has been a discontinuance of that part (which will not be assisted by *CTA 2010, Pt 22, Ch 1* unless that part is also transferred); see *Rolls-Royce Motors Ltd v Bamford* [1976] STC 162.

This point was further considered in *Leekes Ltd v RCC* TC04298, where a trading company, Coles, was acquired by Leekes and the trade hived up to Leekes, which was agreed to be a succession. Leekes therefore claimed the losses of the acquired trade under what is now *CTA 2010, s 944* (previously *ICTA 1988, s 343(1)* and *(3)*) and HMRC contended that they could only be used against the future profits of the acquired trade, not against the full profits of the combined trade. The First-tier Tribunal found for the company but there was (and remains) some confusion as to whether *CTA 2010, s 944* applies, as accepted by both parties, or whether *CTA 2010, s 951* should apply, in which case HMRC would be correct in their analysis. The Upper Tribunal overturned the First-tier Tribunal decision, deciding that *ICTA 1988, s 343(3)* implicitly required streaming of losses, because it referred to loss relief for 'for any amount for which the predecessor would have been entitled', which necessarily restricted the loss relief to the amount that Coles would have been entitled to. The current legislation, at *CTA 2010, s 944(3)*, is probably clearer in allowing this interpretation, as it refers to 'relief that would have been given ... to the predecessor had it continued to carry on that trade'. As the Coles trade continued to be loss making, no relief could be given for past losses, as that trade had no profits to shelter.

6.46   If the transferee already carries on a trade, the transfer of the new trade may be an expansion of the existing trade, it may result in two separate trades being carried on by the transferee, or it may represent a discontinuance of the previous trade (which, again, will not be assisted by *CTA 2010, Pt 22, Ch 1*).

PRE-ENTRY GAINS AND LOSSES

6.47

Focus

These rules are very effective at preventing the buying in of allowable losses from another company. It is therefore highly unlikely that the losses in a recently acquired company will be available to use in the wider group.

These rules were substantially amended by *Finance Act 2011*. The old rules apply for degrouping events prior to Royal Assent to *FA 2011* and can be found in *Tax Planning 2016–17* (Bloomsbury Professional).

It will be obvious from the discussion above in relation to chargeable gains groups that there is room for manipulation of the rules by reason of companies joining groups having either made a gain or loss in the accounting period in which they join (which is then offset by a later disposal of an asset in the acquiring group or used to offset a gain on an asset about to be disposed of in the acquiring group), or by the acquisition of companies with assets which have inherent unrealised gains or losses. These are referred to as pre-entry (ie into the new group) gains and losses.

The provisions which have been enacted to counter various sorts of these activities have changed over time. The main provision in *TCGA 1992, Sch 7A* (given effect by *s 177A*) (loss buying) was enacted by *FA 1993*, and remains in force. It was joined in 1998 by *TCGA 1992, Sch 7AA* (gain buying). *FA 2006* inserted two new provisions, *TCGA 1992, s 184A* (loss buying avoidance schemes) and *TCGA 1992, s 184B* (gain buying avoidance schemes) (these are referred to as 'targeted anti-avoidance rules'). *FA 2006* also repealed *TCGA 1992, Sch 7AA*, as it was felt to have been superseded by *TCGA 1992, s 184B*. The same was not felt to be true of *TCGA 1992, Sch 7A*, and therefore that provision now exists in tandem with *TCGA 1992, s 184A* (which takes precedence over *TCGA 1992, Sch 7A*). *TCGA 1992, Sch 7A* was amended by *FA 2011*.

Pre-entry losses: *TCGA 1992, Sch 7A*

6.48   *TCGA 1992, Sch 7A* restricts the use of allowable losses which accrued to a company before it became a member of a chargeable gains group (a 'pre-entry loss'). There is no motive or commerciality test in *TCGA 1992, Sch 7A*. The provisions are therefore commonly applicable to groups of companies, and can therefore result in a significant compliance burden in relation to the second leg of the restriction.

6.49   Pre-entry losses which have accrued prior to the time the company joined the group may be deducted from chargeable gains which have arisen on:

- a disposal by the company before the date on which it became a member of the relevant (new) group;

- the disposal of an asset which was held by the company before it became a member of that group; or

- the disposal of an asset which was acquired after the date the company became a member of the group from a person who was not a member of that group at the time of the acquisition, and which was used in a business carried on by that company before it joined the group and continued to be carried on by that company or by another member of the group until the time of the disposal of the asset.

The order in which losses are to be offset against gains is set out in *TCGA 1992, Sch 7A, para 6*.

6.50   The rules which apply when companies join capital gains tax groups, including where *TCGA 1992, s 170(10)* deems there to be a continuity of groups, would undermine the efficacy of these anti-avoidance rules, so *TCGA 1992, Sch 7A, para 1(6)* disapplies *TCGA 1992, s 170(10)* generally. *TCGA 1992, Sch 7A, para 1(6)* works by treating all the members of the first group as becoming members of the second group at the time they actually joined the second group, and not, by reason of *TCGA 1992, s 170(10)*, when they joined the first group.

There is an exception in *TCGA 1992, Sch 7A, para 1(7)*, whereby *TCGA 1992, s 170(10)* may not be disapplied where the transaction is simply the insertion of a new holding company with the same shareholders.

Pre-entry losses: *TCGA 1992, s 184A*

6.51   *TCGA 1992, s 184A* is a broader provision than *TCGA 1992, Sch 7A*, in that it is drafted to apply in wider circumstances. It does, however, contain a motive test, and so to that extent is likely to apply in a much more restricted range of circumstances than *TCGA 1992, Sch 7A. TCGA 1992, Sch 7A* remains in force. Note, however, that the tax advantage in question does not have to be secured for the company making the loss.

TCGA 1992, s 184A applies wherever there has been a 'qualifying change of ownership' and a 'qualifying loss' arises in relation to a 'pre-change asset'. A qualifying change of ownership includes where a company has joined or left a group of companies and also where a company becomes subject to different control (*TCGA 1992, s 184C(6)* – control for this purpose bearing its wider meaning in *CTA 2010, s 450* (formerly *ICTA 1988, s 416*); *TCGA 1992, s 288(1)*). If the provisions apply, a qualifying loss may not be deducted from gains accruing to the company other than those on pre-change assets.

Pre-entry gains

6.52   As mentioned above, *TCGA 1992, Sch 7AA* was repealed by *FA 2006*, and replaced by *TCGA 1992, s 184B. TCGA 1992, Sch 7AA* is not dealt with further in this chapter.

TCGA 1992, s 184B applies in the same circumstances to *TCGA 1992, s 184A*, save that there must have been a 'qualifying gain' made on a pre-change asset rather than a qualifying loss. Again, the motive test should mean that this will not apply otherwise than in avoidance cases, subject to the usual questions of interpretation as to what is meant by tests encompassing 'one of the main purposes' language, as is the case in both *TCGA 1992, ss 184A* and *184B*.

DEPRECIATORY TRANSACTIONS

6.53   The fortunate aspect of these parts of the tax legislation is that it is now irrelevant for disposals to which the substantial shareholding exemption in *TCGA 1992, Sch 7AC* applies. Its existence should not, however, be forgotten. The two sets of provisions are *TCGA 1992, ss 176* and *177* on the one hand, and *TCGA 1992, s 30* onwards on the other.

TCGA 1992, ss 176 and *177*

6.54   *TCGA 1992, s 176* is an anti-avoidance provision which aims to restrict the creation of losses by the reduction in the value of shares or securities prior to their disposal by means of a 'depreciatory transaction'. It only restricts the creation of losses, and does not result in a gain being imposed.

For the purposes of *TCGA 1992, s 176*, a depreciatory transaction is either a disposal of assets between two group members at an undervalue, or any other transaction which involved the company to be disposed of, or one or more of its 75% subsidiaries, where that transaction involved two or more group members. The classic application of *TCGA 1992, s 176* is squarely within the main heading and occurs where assets are transferred intra-group at an undervalue, and the transferor company is then sold at a loss.

Where the section applies, any allowable loss is reduced to the extent 'just and reasonable'.

6.55   *TCGA 1992, s 177* is aimed at the reduction in the value of a target by basic dividend stripping in the form of a payment of a dividend by the target company. It applies where the recipient has a holding of 10% or more of any one class of shares. The consequences are the same as the application of *TCGA 1992, s 176*.

Before 22 November 2017, these rules only applied to depreciatory transactions in the six years immediately preceding the disposal. For disposals made on or after 22 November 2017, or treated as made at an earlier time specified in a claim under *TCGA 1992, s 24* (negligible value claims) made on or after that date, no such time limit applies (change made by *FA 2018, s 28*).

TCGA 1992, s 30 onwards

6.56

Focus

This rule is of wide application as there is no description of the types of transaction that might be caught. Instead, the rules concentrate on their effect.

These rules were substantially amended by *Finance Act 2011*. The old rules apply for degrouping events prior to Royal Assent to *FA 2011* and can be found in *Tax Planning 2016–17* (Bloomsbury Professional).

Unlike *TCGA 1992, s 176*, *TCGA 1992, s 30* can result in the imposition of an actual charge to tax, and has historically therefore given more concern to tax advisers than *TCGA 1992, s 176*. This is partly because the provisions are drafted generally, and then further refined in the context of groups. Approached in this way, they are slightly easier to understand.

The basic criteria for *TCGA 1992, s 30* to apply are that in the context of a disposal of an asset:

- the value of the asset (or of a 'relevant asset') has been materially reduced; and

- a tax-free benefit has been or will be conferred on the person making the disposal, a connected person, or, where there is an avoidance motive, any other person.

For this purpose 'relevant asset' means an asset owned by a company associated with the disposing company. This only applies in limited circumstances, and if there is a charge under *TCGA 1992, s 179*, this element of the provision is excluded.

6.57 Where arrangements have been made materially to reduce the value of those shares or securities, or of a relevant asset, and the arrangements are intended to create a tax advantage, the consideration for the gain or loss on the disposal is adjusted by an amount which is 'just and reasonable', taking into account the arrangements themselves and any tax otherwise payable. This rule does not apply if the arrangements are simply the making of an exempt distribution, being broadly a distribution that would not be taxed under *CTA 2009, Pt 9A*.

For these purposes, a relevant asset is an asset owned by a member of the same group as the disposing company.

SUBSTANTIAL SHAREHOLDING EXEMPTION (SSE)

6.58 The scope of the capital gains tax charge was radically changed for companies under *FA 2002* by the introduction of the substantial shareholding exemption. As mentioned above, this made many of the loss-buying and depreciatory transactions effectively redundant, certainly as far as M&A practitioners were concerned. The regime had some uncertainties, usually largely factual, as the regime only applied to disposals of shares of trading companies or groups by trading companies or groups, although these rules were considerably eased by the amendments introduce by *F(No 2)A 2017*, for disposals on or after 1 April 2017. The 'trading' issue nevertheless remains of paramount importance.

It should be noted that the exemption is not limited to actual disposals to third parties; it applies to disposals for chargeable gains purposes in general. As a corollary, any losses arising on such transactions are correspondingly unallowable.

Basic application

6.59 Despite the drafting of *TCGA 1992, Sch 7AC, Pt 1*, the basic exemption is very simple. There are requirements to be met as regards the shareholding, the disposing company (referred to unhelpfully as the 'investing company' in the legislation), and the company whose shares are being disposed of (the 'company invested in').

6.60   A 'substantial shareholding' is where a company has a holding of not less than 10% of the company's ordinary share capital, is beneficially entitled to at least 10% of the profits available for distribution to equity holders, and is beneficially entitled to 10% of the assets available for distribution to equity holders on a winding-up. *CTA 2010, Pt 5, Ch 6* (as modified for capital gains) applies for the purposes of these tests (*TCGA 1992, Sch 7AC, para 8*, and see **6.6** and **6.7**). The holdings of groups are generally aggregated for this purpose (*TCGA 1992, Sch 7AC, para 9*).

The shareholding must have been held throughout a 12-month period beginning not more than two years before the day on which the disposal takes place, for disposals up to 31 March 2017. For disposals on or after 1 April 2017, the shareholding must have been held throughout a 12-month period beginning not more than six years before the day on which the disposal takes place.

The original one-year run-off period was intended to give some leeway where companies were selling off shareholdings piecemeal. A sale of a small final tranche of shares could qualify for the exemption, even if it were less than 10% (see below), as long as the sale was within a year of the last qualifying disposal. However, this period was never adequate and it seems likely that the government realised this from the results of the Summer 2016 consultation, so decided to extend the run-off period to five years.

Of course, this might also be seen as an anti-avoidance provision, as it also means that any losses arising from disposals out of a sub-10% holding in these circumstances would not be an allowable loss.

Investing company requirements

6.61   For disposals up to 31 March 2017, the disposing company had to be a sole trading company or a holding company of a trading group in order for the exemption to apply. This criterion had to be satisfied from the beginning of the 12-month period during which the substantial shareholding requirement was satisfied to the time of disposal. In most cases, this meant for the 12 months to the date of the disposal, but in cases where shares were sold out of a sub-10% holding within a year of the company having a substantial shareholding, the condition also had to be satisfied for the whole of the run-off period.

The trading condition also had to be satisfied immediately after the disposal.

Therefore, a disposal of its sole trading subsidiary by a non-trading holding company could not satisfy the exemption, because the vendor company was not a trading company or the holding company of a trading group immediately after the disposal. Conversely, the disposal of such a subsidiary by a trading holding company would satisfy the exemption. The lessons for group structuring could hardly be clearer.

The provisions imposing requirements on the investing company were completely repealed for disposals on or after 1 April 2017, by *F(No 2)A 2017*.

Investee company requirements

6.62   The requirements for the company invested in are that it must be a sole trading company or a holding company of a trading group or subgroup in order for the exemption to apply. (This is really due to the fact that the concept of group in *TCGA 1992, Sch 7AC* is by reference to chargeable gains tax groups, so there can be only one group, hence the adoption of the subgroup.)

This criterion has to be satisfied from the beginning of the 12-month period during which the substantial shareholding requirement is satisfied to the time of disposal. In most cases this means for the 12 months to the date of the disposal, but in cases where shares are sold out of a sub-10% holding within five years of the company having a substantial shareholding, the condition also has to be satisfied for the whole of the run-off period.

Until 31 March 2017, the condition also had to be satisfied immediately after the disposal. For disposals on or after 1 April 2017, the investee company does not have to satisfy the condition immediately after the transaction, unless the disposal is to a connected party or it is a disposal that relies on *TCGA 1992, Sch 7AC, para 15A* (see **6.66**), by virtue of the changes made by *F(No 2)A 2017*.

Meaning of trading

6.63   'Trading company', 'trading group' and 'trading subgroup' are defined in *TCGA 1992, Sch 7AC, paras 20, 21* and *22* respectively, but the essence of the primary definition in each is the same – the company (or group or subgroup as a whole) means 'a company carrying on trading activities whose activities do not include to a substantial extent activities other than trading activities'. There is an extended meaning of 'trading activities' which is expressed to include preparatory activities and activities in preparing for acquiring a trade or a company which carries on a trade, as well as activities in the course of or in furtherance of a trade.

In practice, it is usually obvious which activities of a company, group or subgroup are or are not trading, the most frequently seen non-trading activities being property leasing (including intra-group of course), financing (by companies other than those which can qualify as financial traders), and the holding of large amounts of cash (perhaps arising from a disposal) on a temporary basis. What is often less obvious is whether those activities will be 'substantial' to the extent that they taint the rest of the activities of the company, group or subgroup. In the case of the wider group, intra-group activities can usually be ignored (on the basis that the provisions refer to the activities of the members of a group 'taken together'), and the problem usually arises where there is intra-group activity between a company or subgroup which has to be examined, and other members of a wider group.

In relation to non-trading activities, and whether they are substantial, HMRC take a similar approach to that taken for taper relief. For these purposes 'substantial' means more than 20%. HMRC have published guidance on their approach at CG53116 and the following paragraphs. The 20% test is applied to turnover, the value of assets, management time spent and the company's history. The latter test is intended to avoid a 'snapshot' approach to the tests, by looking at them over a period of time.

Because of the difficulties in applying the trading tests, it had become fairly standard practice to seek a ruling from HMRC under Code of Practice 10. Code of Practice 10 rulings are usually available for up to four Finance Acts, and thereafter the legislation is no longer considered new enough to warrant the system being available. However, HMRC relaxed this approach in relation to substantial shareholdings and introduced a new facility in June 2007. This system has now been replaced in effect by the non-statutory clearance procedure; see HMRC's Non-Statutory Business Clearance Guidance Manual for details on how to make an application.

The subsidiary exemptions

6.64   *TCGA 1992, Sch 7AC, paras 2* and *3* contain subsidiary exemptions. *TCGA 1992, Sch 7AC, para 2* deals with disposals of 'assets related to shares' (see *TCGA 1992, Sch 7AC, para 30*), which is intended to cover disposals of options and convertible securities where the main exemption would be met. As the HMRC manuals state, this is effectively to ensure that companies do not have a choice as to whether to dispose of assets which are within the capital gains tax charge or those which are not (and indeed, the same applies generally to the legislation, as otherwise companies would have the choice of creating capital losses).

6.65   *TCGA 1992, Sch 7AC, para 3* contains a further subsidiary exemption. If the substantial shareholding condition is met but the disposal otherwise does not qualify for the exemption, *TCGA 1992, Sch 7AC, para 3(2)(d)* applies a 'look back' provision to the previous two years as regards the exemption to find a time when it would have been satisfied (ie applying all the tests of the exemption at that time). *TCGA 1992, Sch 7AC, para 3(2)(e)* then looks to the two years before disposal and tests the 'company invested in' requirement, and deems that requirement satisfied if that company was controlled by the disposing company or companies connected with the disposing company.

TCGA 1992, Sch 7AC, para 3(3) then limited the application of the *TCGA 1992, Sch 7AC, para 3* exemption in cases where the investing company requirement immediately after disposal was not met, where the failure to meet that requirement was due to the disposing company being wound up or dissolved or the fact it was about to be wound up or dissolved. This provision was repealed for disposals on or after 1 April 2017, by *F(No 2)A 2017*.

In practice, therefore, *TCGA 1992, Sch 7AC, para 3* applies particularly where the status of the company invested in (or indeed the group, but this may be less likely) has changed prior to the disposal, or where the disposing company is in the process of being wound up.

Packaging trades for disposal

6.66   The substantial shareholdings exemption also applies to situations where a company is disposing of a trade or part of a trade and wishes to do so by transferring that trading activity into a new company which can be sold as a clean vehicle to the purchaser. This is intended to ensure that the disposal of the new company by the vendor will, itself, be exempt, subject to certain conditions being satisfied (*TCGA 1992, Sch 7AC, para 15A*).

The conditions are that:

- immediately before the disposal the vendor company holds a substantial shareholding in the new company;

- an asset which, at the time of the disposal is being used for the purposes of a trade carried on by the new company has been transferred to it by the vendor or another company in the group at a time when all the relevant companies were members of the same group; and

- the asset was previously used by a member of the group, other than the new company, for the purposes of a trade carried on by that company.

If these conditions are satisfied the vendor company is treated as having held the substantial shareholding in the new company for the period of 12 months ending with the time of the disposal, so long as, during the whole of that period, the relevant asset had been in use for the purposes of a trade carried on by a company in the group. Furthermore, if the conditions are met, then *TCGA 1992, Sch 7AC, para 19* treats the new company as having been a trading company throughout that 12-month period.

As a result, the substantial shareholdings exemption is available for the 'packaging' of trading activities by a vendor company without the vendor suffering an exit charge.

It is very unfortunate that the change in the exit charge rules is not mirrored in the degrouping rules for chargeable intangible assets under *CTA 2009, Pt 8*. This means that the exemption will be of no use to trades with material amounts of intellectual property created or acquired since 31 March 2002 or where the trade started after that date and a major asset is goodwill. However, an HMRC consultation between February and May 2018 may result in the CGT and intangibles rules being realigned to resolve this issue.

Furthermore, HMRC's stated view is that this extension to the exemption only applies where the vendor company is a member of a group (see HMRC's Capital Gains Manual at CG53080C), which means that the exemption is not available to single companies with several trades. This is an odd interpretation of the legislation, as these new rules were specifically designed with single companies in mind, and not everyone agrees with HMRC's interpretation.

Companies owned by qualifying institutional investors

6.67   A new version of the exemption was introduced with effect from 1 April 2018 by *Finance (No 2) Act 2017*. This exemption is to allow companies held by qualifying institutional investors to dispose of qualifying shareholdings in non-trading companies free of corporation tax (*TCGA 1992, Sch 7AC, para 3A*). The main policy reason is that, in most cases, a direct portfolio holding by the qualifying institutional investor (such as a pension fund) would be exempt, because the fund is exempt from tax. But if the fund chooses to invest through a holding company, a UK-resident holding company would be subject to UK corporation tax on any gains on disposals of shares in non-trading companies. So this exemption is to allow such investment through holding companies on similar terms to a direct holding by the fund.

The conditions for the exemption are as follows:

- There must be a substantial shareholding (**6.60**). Alternatively, a sub-10% shareholding can also qualify, so long as that holding cost a minimum of £20m, including acquisition costs (*TCGA 1992, Sch 7AC, para 8A*).

- The company must fail the tests at *TCGA 1992, Sch 7 AC, para 19*. Broadly, this means that the investment must not be in a trading company (as a substantial shareholding investment in a trading company would qualify for the main exemption, anyway). Technically, the conditions in *para 19* may also be failed if the investment was in a trading company, either to a connected party or through the *TCGA 1992, Sch 7AC, para 15A* route, and the requirement to trade immediately after the transaction is not satisfied. However, we consider this a highly unlikely scenario.

The mechanism for relief is that, if at least 80% of the shares of the vendor company (ie the investor company) are held by qualifying institutional investors, then the gain is wholly exempt. If at least 25% of the shares are held by qualifying institutional investors, but not 80%, then the gain is exempt to the extent of that shareholding (*TCGA 1992, Sch 7AC, para 3A(3)* and *(4)*). For example, if the vendor or company is 40% owned by qualifying institutional investors, the gain on disposal of shares in a non-trading company will be 40% exempt. There is no exemption if the holding by qualifying institutional investors falls below 25%.

The exemption does not apply if the investing company is a disqualified listed company (*TCGA 1992, Sch 7AC, para 3A(2)(c)* and *(5)*). This is a company any of whose ordinary share capital is listed on a recognised stock exchange, unless the company is itself a qualifying institutional investor or a qualifying UK REIT.

For the purposes of this legislation, qualifying institutional investors fall into one of the following seven categories (*TCGA 1992, Sch 7AC, para 30A*):

(1)   Trustees or managers of certain pension schemes;

(2)   A company carrying on life assurance business, so long as the interest in the investing company is part of the long-term business fixed capital;

(3)   Sovereign wealth funds, ie persons who cannot be liable for corporation tax or income tax because of their sovereign immunity;

(4)   Charities;

(5)   Investment trusts;

(6)   Authorised investment funds which meet the genuine diversity of ownership condition throughout the accounting period of the fund in which the disposal is made;

(7)   Exempt unauthorised unit trusts where the trust meets the genuine diversity of ownership condition throughout the accounting period of the trust in which the disposal is made.

Interaction with other provisions

6.68   The application of *TCGA 1992, Sch 7AC* is more complicated in group situations where there has been a reorganisation prior to sale. The overall aim of the legislation is to ensure that ownership which is split between different members of a group, whether in amount or in time, is taken together for the purposes of the Schedule (*Sch 7AC, paras 9* and *10*).

TCGA 1992, Sch 7AC does not displace *TCGA 1992, s 171*, and that provision operates in its usual way as a disposal for a consideration which results in neither a gain nor a loss accruing (*TCGA 1992, Sch 7AC, para 6*).

The application of *TCGA 1992, s 135* to intra-group share exchanges and reconstructions can be complex. *TCGA 1992, Sch 7AC, para 4(1)* effectively gives priority to the substantial shareholdings rules over *TCGA 1992, s 127*. However, removing *TCGA 1992, s 127* leaves one with a transaction under *TCGA 1992, s 171*, over which the exemption does not have priority.

HMRC's view is that there is a disposal for substantial shareholdings purposes, with the result that on a disposal by company A to company B of company C in return for an issue of shares by company B to company A, company A has a substantial shareholdings exempt disposal, company B acquires company C at market value, and company A acquires the shares in company B at the value it held the shares in company C (ie *TCGA 1992, s 127* does apply for that purpose). That is a sensible result, but it is difficult to reach that conclusion on the wording of the legislation.

This does, however, mean the position remains the same as if *TCGA 1992, Sch 7AC, para 4(1)* had not prevented *TCGA 1992, s 127* applying to the transaction as a whole, and means that companies which carry out such internal share-for-share reorganisations should ensure that clearance is obtained so that they know what their base costs in the various subsidiaries are. The previous position, where companies can, to at least a limited extent, indulge in base cost planning in the context of reorganisations (subject to the commercial purpose test) remains the same.

Anti-avoidance

6.69 *TCGA 1992, Sch 7AC* has its own anti-avoidance provision, contained in *TCGA 1992, Sch 7AC, para 5*, which is perhaps considered less than it should be in practice. It is necessary for it to apply that the sole or main benefit that could be expected to arise be that a gain which would otherwise have accrued be exempt, but note that this is not a motive test, rather it is an objective test based on the facts of the case.

The other conditions in *TCGA 1992, Sch 7AC, para 5* are that the disposing company 'acquired' control of the target and there was a significant change in trading activities of the target company when the disposing company controlled the target. The main target of this provision can therefore be seen as artificial manipulation of the trading requirement for the company invested in.

OTHER RELEVANT PROVISIONS FOR GROUPS

6.70   The aim of this section of the chapter is to provide an overview of other provisions which are relevant to groups, although detailed consideration of the regimes is outside the scope of this chapter.

Transfer pricing

6.71   The amendment of the transfer pricing legislation in *TIOPA 2010, Pt 4*, to include transactions between UK companies rather than just between UK and overseas companies has undoubtedly increased the burden on many groups. The pricing of each transaction between group members needs, strictly, to be justified on the basis of arm's-length principles. It should be remembered that this applies in relation to all sorts of transactions, including loans.

There is an exemption for small and medium-sized companies in *TIOPA 2010, s 166*, which applies to transactions between companies resident in the UK and between companies resident in the UK and companies resident in a territory which is party to a double tax treaty with an anti-discrimination provision and subject to certain designation powers of HM Treasury.

Should an adjustment under the transfer pricing provisions apply, then there is the possibility of a compensating adjustment under the provisions. Obviously, all of these provisions need to be considered in the context of the wider tax attributes of the companies concerned and the group as a whole.

Loan relationships

6.72   The loan relationships legislation contains a number of provisions which apply between connected parties and/or members of groups of companies.

The provisions in *FA 2006* were substantially amended by *FA 2004* to cope in particular with the introduction of International Accounting Standards (IAS) accounting, and have now been re-written into *CTA 2009, Pt 6*. *Finance Act 2009* has amended the provisions relating to late-paid interest and accrued discounts between connected parties in an attempt to bring them into line with EU law. *FA 2010, Sch 19* has inserted provisions into both the loan relationships and derivative provisions in *CTA 2009* enabling the provisions to be amended by statutory instrument to deal with changes in accounting rules.

6.73   The rules in *CTA 2009, Pt 5* require careful examination where groups and connected companies are concerned. The main provisions are as follows:

CTA 2009, ss 373–379 may apply to delay an interest deduction where the payee does not accrue the interest under the loan relationships regime and it is not paid within 12 months of the accounting period in which it would have otherwise accrued. The impact of this is much reduced by the amendments made by *FA 2009*, the effect of which is to allow deductions on an accruals basis where the counterparty to the debt is (broadly speaking) in a territory with which the UK has an appropriate double taxation treaty.

CTA 2009, s 361 may cause there to be a deemed release by a creditor company of an amount where it acquires a loan relationship for less than its face value and the debtor is a connected party. The debtor company may therefore suffer a tax charge on that deemed release. Note that these rules have been substantially amended by *FA 2010, Sch 16*.

CTA 2009, s 358 may prevent a charge arising between connected companies on the release of a debt.

CTA 2009, Pt 5, Ch 6 contains the rules for impairment losses between parties having a connection or becoming connected. *CTA 2009, Pt 5, Ch 4* provides for the continuity of treatment where a loan relationship is transferred between members of a group of companies (within the capital gains tax meaning). It is broadly intended to provide for a tax-neutral transfer, whatever the actual value paid on the transfer.

CTA 2009, ss 373–379 has a provision which is very similar to *TCGA 1992, s 179*. It provides for a deemed assignment and reacquisition at market value where a company has acquired a loan relationship within a group and leaves the group within six years. This will obviously only give rise to a charge in practice where the value of the loan relationship was not equal to the carrying value at the time of the transfer.

CTA 2009, s 407 applies to deeply discounted securities, and provides for a deferral of the discount accrual where the parties are connected until the time of redemption of the security. There are equivalent amendments to the late-paid interest rules made by *FA 2009* in this provision.

Derivative contracts

6.74   The derivative contracts regime formerly in *FA 2002, Sch 26* and now re-written to *CTA 2009, Pt 7*, also contains provisions which apply between connected parties and groups. In particular, *CTA 2009, Pt 7, Ch 5* contains provisions on continuity within groups and transferees leaving groups which are modelled on the equivalent loan relationships provisions.

Intangibles

6.75   *CTA 2009, Pt 8* contains its own particular group regime in relation to intangible assets, which is similar to the chargeable gains tax system. The provisions provide for tax-neutral transfers within a group and for a degrouping charge, and there is an exemption for companies leaving the group together in the same way as for chargeable gains (see *CTA 2009, Pt 8, Chs 8* and *9*).

Note that there is an important difference between the degrouping charge for chargeable assets, under the capital gains regime, and for chargeable intangible assets, under *CTA 2009, Pt 8*. The new rules for the degrouping charge for chargeable assets do not apply to chargeable intangible assets, so that the degrouping gain for chargeable intangible asset still arises in the company leaving the group, not in the disposing company, as for chargeable assets. This difference in treatment is part of the subject matter of a consultation between February and May 2018, so it is possible that changes in this area may be made.

CTA 2009, Pt 8, Ch 13 provides for general rules in transactions between related parties, and *CTA 2009, s 851* provides for deferral of accrual of debits if they are not paid within 12 months of the accounting period in which the debit would otherwise accrue (whether or not the recipient accrues the receipt within the charge to corporation tax).

GROUP PAYMENT ARRANGEMENTS

6.76   *FA 1998, s 36* permits HMRC to enter into 'arrangements' for the payment of tax for a group to be made by one designated member. This is done by way of contract with HMRC, and the standard form contract is published on HMRC's website, together with guidance notes.

The arrangements are purely administrative, and *FA 1998, s 36(3)* specifically provides that it shall not affect the liability of any company for corporation tax. The group payment arrangements (GPA) contract provides that HMRC will not pursue individual companies for tax until after the final filing date for corporation tax for all the companies in the group.

The contract only provides for arrangements between the companies and HMRC, and does not deal with arrangements between the companies themselves. It is obviously necessary for there to be some arrangements between the group members and the representative member for the payment of tax. Tax advisers need to take account of these arrangements in the context of company sales and purchases and ensure that agreement is reached, and/or an indemnity obtained in respect of the apportionment of payments under the GPA.

Chapter 7

Reorganisations and reconstructions

Pete Miller CTA (Fellow), Partner, The Miller Partnership

SIGNPOSTS

- **Reorganisations** – A reorganisation of a company's share capital is effectively tax free. It is not treated as a disposal or an acquisition and the new shares/securities effectively stand in the shoes of the original shares (see **7.3** *et seq*).

- **Conversions of securities** – The treatment of conversions of securities is similarly tax free (see **7.8** *et seq.*).

- **Share exchanges** – Share exchanges, schemes of reconstruction and conversions of securities are treated in the same way, so far as possible (see **7.12**).

- **Cash consideration given** – Any cash given is taken into account for capital gains tax purposes as further consideration enhancing the base cost of the new shares or securities (see **7.6**).

- **Cash received** – Any cash received in such transactions is treated as a part disposal of the holdings (see **7.6**).

- **QCB exchanges** – In share exchanges for debentures, where the debenture is a qualifying corporate bond, the gain is computed at the time of the exchange and comes into charge when the bonds are redeemed or otherwise disposed of (see **7.17** *et seq*).

- **Different rules for stamp taxes** – The rules for stamp taxes do not follow those for capital gains, although there are acquisition reliefs and reconstructions reliefs available (see **7.34**).

INTRODUCTION

7.1   This chapter covers a number of transactions, collectively referred to as 'reorganisations' or 'reconstructions', which are largely tax free. These include actual reorganisations of a company's share capital, certain transactions that are treated as if they were reorganisations of share capital and more complex schemes of reconstruction, such as mergers and demergers.

This chapter perforce is only an overview of complex legislation. For a more detailed discussion of most of the issues, consult *Taxation of Company Reorganisations* by Pete Miller and others (Bloomsbury Professional).

REORGANISATIONS OF SHARE CAPITAL

Effect of the legislation

7.2   The effect of the legislation is best summed up by quoting the provision directly: 'a reorganisation shall not be treated as involving any disposal of the original shares or any acquisition of the new holding or any part of it, but the original shares (taken as a single asset) and the new holding (taken as a single asset) shall be treated as the same asset acquired as the original shares were acquired' (*TCGA 1992, s 127*).

In other words, the 'original shares' and the 'new holding' (see below) are treated as being the same asset for capital gains tax purposes and there is no disposal or acquisition. So the new holding is treated as having been acquired at the same time and for the same price as the original shares. This is often referred to as the 'no disposal fiction'.

Meaning of 'reorganisation'

7.3   The relevant provisions apply to a reorganisation or reduction of share capital. The shares held before the reorganisation are referred to as the 'original shares' and the shares or debentures held afterwards are called the 'new holding'. In *Unilever (UK) Holdings Ltd v Smith* 76 TC 300 a class of preference shares was cancelled and the shareholders were paid off. The company argued that this was a reorganisation but the court held that there was no identifiable new holding when an entire class of shares is cancelled, so the transaction was not a reorganisation.

It is clear, however, that a reorganisation can also include converting share capital into other securities (*TCGA 1992, s 126(1)*). The conversion of other securities into share capital is also treated as a reorganisation by virtue of *TCGA 1992, s 132* (see below).

'Reorganisation' is not specifically defined in either tax law or company law. On the plain English approach, it is taken to refer to a company organising its share capital differently.

Example 7.1 – Reorganisation of share capital

Albert subscribed for the issued share capital of Company A, 100 £1 shares, in June 2008. In April 2018, Company A reorganises the £1 shares into 10p shares, so that the issued share capital now comprises 1,000 10p shares.

Since this is a reorganisation, Albert's shareholding still has a capital gains base cost of £100 and the shares are treated as having been acquired in June 2008. The reorganisation of the share capital is not treated as a disposal.

Increases in share capital

7.4   In *Dunstan v Young, Austen & Young Ltd* 61 TC 448, the company successfully argued that an issue of shares to its parent was a reorganisation within the general meaning of the word and it is now accepted that the general meaning of a reorganisation can include share increases. However, a reorganisation requires the continued identity of the shareholders (of each class) holding their shares in the same proportions.

Focus

Not all changes to a company's share capital will be a reorganisation. The transaction must fall within the general meaning of 'reorganisation' or one of the specific inclusions.

Increases in share capital by, for example, bonus issue or rights issue are specifically deemed to be reorganisations for these purposes, as long as the allotments of shares or debentures are in proportion to the original holdings (*TCGA 1992, s 126(2)(a)*).

The alteration of rights of any class of shares, where there are more than one class, are also deemed to be reorganisations (*TCGA 1992, s 126(2)(b)*).

Example 7.2 – Bonus issue of shares

Basil and Claude bought the shares of Company B for £1,500 each in August 2001. They each own 50 £1 shares. In May 2017, to increase its capital, it issues 450 £1 bonus shares to each shareholder, so that they each have 500 £1 shares.

Since this is a reorganisation, Basil and Claude are not treated as having disposed of their original shares (which they clearly have not, anyway), nor as having acquired the new shares. Their capital gains base cost is still £1,500 each, treated as having been incurred in August 2001.

It is not immediately obvious from the legislation whether changing the rights on shares to increase the number of classes of share capital necessarily constitutes a reorganisation, such as a company converting its single class of ordinary shares into A and B shares prior to a demerger. An example might be a company that has two shareholders, each with 50 £1 ordinary shares, which reorganises its capital so that one shareholder now had 50 £1 A shares and the other has 50 £1 B shares, which is a common change as part of many demergers.

Following the principle established in *Dunstan v Young, Austen & Young Ltd*, we would say that the same shareholders hold the capital of the company in the same proportions, which indicates that the transaction is a reorganisation on first principles. This is an important step in many demergers and we are not aware that HMRC have ever questioned this analysis.

Reductions of share capital

7.5   Not every reduction is a reorganisation. Specifically, the paying off of redeemable share capital is not a reduction of share capital that is treated as a reorganisation. Instead, it is treated as a disposal for tax purposes and reorganisation treatment is not available.

The exception to this rule is where the consideration for the redemption of the redeemable shares is newly issued shares or debentures, so the 'redemption' of redeemable shares by issuing new share capital or debentures will be a reorganisation. Similarly, this rule does not apply where the shares are redeemed in a liquidation (*TCGA 1992, s 126(3)*).

It is not clear whether all other reductions of capital are reorganisations, or whether they are required to satisfy the principle established in *Dunstan v Young, Austen & Young Ltd* (above). The uncertainty is because *Dunstan v Young, Austen & Young Ltd* applied to the definition of a reorganisation on first principles, as in *TCGA 1992, s 126(1)*, which refers to 'a reorganisation or reduction of a company's share capital'. So the principles may only apply to a reorganisation and not to a reduction of share capital.

Consideration given or received

7.6   The basic tax treatment of a reorganisation is based on the policy that the shareholder has not actually given or received any value in respect of the reorganisation. If value is given or received, the policy requires adjustment.

Where additional consideration, such as payment for a rights issue, is given for a new holding on a reorganisation, that extra consideration is to be treated as having been given for the original shares (as part of the composite asset fiction). This includes incurring the liability to give additional consideration. However, the surrender, cancellation or other alteration of the original shares or the rights attached to them is not consideration, and nor is the application of value which is, in effect, derived from the assets of the company itself, such as profits or revaluation reserves used to pay up new share capital (*TCGA 1992, s 128(1), (2)*).

The consideration given cannot increase the base cost of a new holding by more than the actual increase in value achieved by an injection of capital on an arm's-length transaction. This amendment was following the *Young, Austen & Young* case, as the consideration given for the new shares was greatly in excess of the market value of the shares issued, which was nil (*TCGA 1992, s 128(2)*).

Where new consideration is given, any indexation allowance will run from the time at which the consideration is given or becomes liable to be given (*TCGA 1992, s 131*).

Where a shareholder receives consideration on a reorganisation, apart from the new holding itself, the shareholder is treated as having made a part disposal of the original shares in return for that consideration. This means that the base cost of the original holding is reduced, as for any part-disposal computation, although for all other purposes the no-disposal and composite asset fiction is maintained.

The receipt of consideration includes consideration from other shareholders for surrendering rights derived from the original shares, as well as any consideration deemed to have accrued on a capital distribution under *TCGA 1992, s 122* (*TCGA 1992, s 128(3)*).

Example 7.3 – Rights issue

Company C has 100,000 issued £1 shares. In order to increase its capital, it offers shareholders a 1 for 1 rights issue (ie each current shareholder can subscribe for 1 new share for each share they already hold). The price is £2.50 a share.

A corporate shareholder, Desmond Ltd, holds 1,000 shares, for which it was an original subscriber at £1 per share. Desmond Ltd takes up its rights, paying £2,500 for the 1,000 extra shares in January 2016. Desmond now has 2,000 shares with a total base cost of £3,500. However, indexation allowance for the recently paid £2,500 only runs from January 2016 to 31 December 2017, when indexation allowance was frozen for companies.

Apportionment of base cost

7.7   Where any part of a new holding is disposed of or deemed to be disposed of by this provision, the base cost of the shares or securities comprising the new holding must be apportioned by reference to the market value of the shares or securities at the date of disposal. HMRC's view is that this means that the base cost is apportioned by reference to the market value of the part disposed of divided by the market value of the entire holding (*TCGA 1992, s 129*; see also CG51892).

There are special computational rules for the apportionment of base costs where the new holding consists of more than one class of shares or debentures, or more than one class of rights in a unit trust, and one or more of those classes or shares or units are quoted on a recognised stock exchange (in the case of shares or debentures) or have published prices (in the case of units) and the listings occurred within three months of the date of the reorganisation. In these cases, the base cost of the different classes of share, debenture or unit is by reference to the market value on the first day on which market values or prices were quoted, whether or not the reorganisation has taken place at that time (*TCGA 1992, s 130*).

HMRC say that this 'gives the taxpayer the advantage of knowing the base cost of his shares in advance of any disposal' and that it also avoids 'difficulties with the interaction between the reorganisation provisions and the pooling rules of section 104 TCGA'.

Conversions of securities

7.8   Broadly, a conversion of securities should be treated as a reorganisation for tax purposes, with 'necessary adaptations' to the rules in *TCGA 1992, ss 127–131*. This deemed equivalence to a reorganisation of share capital tells us that the securities held before the conversion should be treated as if they were the 'original shares' and the securities held after the conversion should be treated as the 'new holding'. Therefore, the converted securities are treated for capital gains purposes as having been acquired at the same time and at the same cost as the original securities (*TCGA 1992, s 132(1)*).

The legislation gives a non-exhaustive list of the transactions to which this rule will apply (*TCGA 1992, s 132(3)*):

- a conversion of securities of a company into shares in the company;

- a conversion of a security which is not a qualifying corporate bond into a security of the same company which is such a bond;

- a conversion of a qualifying corporate bond (QCB) into a security which is a security of the same company but is not such a bond;

- a conversion at the option of the holder of the securities converted as an alternative to the redemption of those securities for cash;

- any exchange of securities effected in pursuance of any enactment (including an enactment passed after this Act) which provides for the compulsory acquisition of any shares or securities and the issue of securities or other securities instead (this is rare these days but this occurred when an industry or business was taken into public ownership (such as nationalisation of an industry) and the shareholders were given government bonds in exchange).

The conversions of a non-QCB into a QCB or vice versa are dealt with by *TCGA 1992, s 116*, but a transaction only gets into that provision by being a transaction to which *TCGA 1992, s 135* would otherwise apply. So conversions to or from a QCB are deemed to be within *TCGA 1992, s 135* so that *TCGA 1992, s 116* can then apply. In the case of *Hancock* [2016] UKUT 81 (TCC), it was decided that *TCGA 1992, s 132* applies to each conversion of a type of security separately. Thus, if *TCGA 1992, s 116* is in point, that provision also applies to each separate type of security, not to a mixed portfolio of securities (as was argued by Mr and Mrs Hancock) (see **7.21**).

The rules apply regardless of whether the conversion is effected by a transaction or occurs in consequence of the operation of the terms of any security or debenture. This change followed the case of *Harding v HMRC* 79 TC 885. Mr Harding purported to have a security that changed its status without a transaction, by the use of a clause that expired after a set period of time, and claimed that the redemption of the bond escaped taxation altogether. HMRC won the case, but the legislation was amended to avoid further doubt.

For the purposes of this legislation, 'security' includes any loan stock or similar security whether of the government of the UK or of any other government, or of any public or local authority in the UK or elsewhere, or of any company, and whether secured or unsecured (*TCGA 1992, s 132(3)*).

Certain debentures, issued on or after 16 March 1993, are deemed to be securities (*TCGA 1992, s 251(6)*). The rules for conversions of securities apply to these, too, so that a conversion of such debentures into QCBs, or a conversion of a QCB into a debenture that is deemed to be a security, are also treated as reorganisations (*TCGA 1992, s 132(4), (5)*).

Premiums received on conversions of securities

7.9   The normal case is to tax the premium as a part disposal of the securities under *TCGA 1992, s 128* (with any 'necessary adaptations').

When the premium received is small compared to the value of the securities, there is a mandatory alternative approach, whereby the premium is deducted from the base cost of the converted securities. In effect, this defers any gain until the securities are disposed of (*TCGA 1992, s 133(2)*).

The meaning of 'small' in this context is not defined but HMRC will usually accept that 'small' means less than 5% of the value or less than £3,000, even if that exceeds 5% of the value of the securities. There may be cases where a premium in excess of 5% of the value of the securities should be treated as being small or where a premium of less than 5% should not be treated as small. These cases will be decided on their merits (see CG57836 and RI 164 (February 1997)).

Where the premium exceeds the allowable expenditure (ie the base cost), this provision does not apply so the premium would be charged to tax in the normal way. However, the recipient can elect that only the excess of the premium over base cost is to be charged, instead. If this election is made, then no base cost of the securities is available to set against the proceeds of any subsequent disposal (*TCGA 1992, s 133(4)*).

There are similar provisions for any cash received on the redenomination of a security into euros from the original currency in which it was denominated on issue (*TCGA 1992, s 133A*).

Compensation stock

7.10   There are special rules for the compulsory acquisition of shares in return for gilt-edged stock, which was most likely to occur on a nationalisation. This legislation requires a gain or loss to be computed as if the shares had been sold at the exchange value deemed by the enabling (nationalising) legislation. The gain (or loss) will then come into effect when the gilt-edged securities are eventually disposed of by sale, redemption, etc. A disposal of only part of the holding of gilt-edged securities will bring into charge an appropriate part of the gain (*TCGA 1992, s 134*).

Stamp duty and reorganisations of share capital

7.11   In general, a reorganisation of share capital does not carry a charge to stamp duty, as there is no transfer of a security. However, a company purchasing its own shares under *Companies Act 2006, s 690* is chargeable to stamp duty under *FA 1986, s 67*.

SHARE EXCHANGES

Introduction

7.12   The issue of shares or debentures in one company in exchange for the shares or debentures in another is not a reorganisation of share capital. However, it is treated as one for capital gains tax purposes, with the necessary adaptations, so long as the appropriate conditions are satisfied. The treatment of such transactions as reorganisations is mandatory and there is no option for a shareholder to choose to have the transaction treated as a disposal (*TCGA 1992, s 135(1), (3)*).

Generally, the treatment of share-for-share exchanges as if they were reorganisations of share capital will only apply if the transactions are carried out for bona fide commercial reasons and not for the avoidance of capital gains tax or corporation tax (unless the members concerned, along with persons connected with them, do not hold more than 5% of the relevant class of shares or debentures of the original company). Pre-transaction clearance to that effect can be obtained from HMRC (*TCGA 1992, ss 135(6), 137(1), (2), 138*). A sample letter applying to HMRC for pre-transaction clearance is attached at the end of this chapter.

Transactions affected

7.13   The fundamental requirement is that there be a disposal by a person of shares or debentures to a company, which then issues shares or debentures as consideration (or as part of the consideration) for the acquisition. It does not matter whether this is an intra-group transaction or an acquisition (*TCGA 1992, s 135(1)*).

There are three circumstances to which the reorganisations treatment applies (*TCGA 1992, s 135(2)*):

Case 1 – Where the acquiring company holds, or in consequence of the exchange will hold more than 25% of the ordinary share capital of the target company. If the acquiring company already holds at least 25% of the ordinary share capital of the target, any further transfer of shares or debentures in the target company to the acquiring company in exchange for the issue of shares or debentures will satisfy Case 1.

The ordinary share capital of a company is defined in *CTA 2010, s 1119* ('all the company's issued share capital (however described), other than capital the holders of which have a right to a dividend at a fixed rate but have no other right to share in the company's profits'). For the purposes of this rule, however, it also includes units in unit trusts and, for companies without share capital, it includes any interests in the company possessed by members of the company (*TCGA 1992, s 135(4), (5)*).

Case 2 – Where the acquiring company issues the shares or debentures in exchange for shares as a result of a general offer made to members of the target company or any class of them (with or without exceptions for persons connected with the acquiring company). The offer must be made in the first instance on a condition such that if it were satisfied the acquiring company would have control of the target company. This Case is more relevant to takeovers of public companies or other companies with many shareholders. Usually, the offer is conditional upon the acquiring company receiving sufficient acceptances to give it control of the target company. The initial terms of the offer are the critical factor here and CG52525 clarifies HMRC's view that Case 2 is satisfied even if the condition is dropped whilst the offer is still open. If the condition were to be dropped and the acquiring company did not receive sufficient acceptances to give it control, Case 2 would nevertheless have been satisfied in respect of any shares exchanged as a result of the offer.

Case 3 – Where the acquiring company holds or in consequence of the exchange will hold the greater part of the voting power in the target company. This Case was introduced to comply with EU law following the introduction of the EU Mergers Directive (Council Directive 90/434/EEC of 23 July 1990 on the common system of taxation applicable to mergers, divisions, transfers of assets and exchanges of shares concerning companies of different Member States (as amended)).

There is no requirement that either party involved in the transaction be UK resident. So, subject to the anti-avoidance provisions, neither the acquirer nor the target company need be UK resident. Obviously, the vendor must be UK resident for there to be a charge to tax in the UK to which the provision can apply.

Focus

Not all share-for-share exchanges will satisfy these conditions and it is important to ensure that the vendor does not have an unexpected tax charge.

Effect of share exchanges

7.14   If there is an exchange that satisfies one of the Cases, the shares issued by the acquiring company are to be taken as being the same as the shares that it acquires in the target on the exchange. So the original shareholders of the target company are treated as having acquired their shares in the acquiring company at the same time and for the same cost as their original shareholdings in the target company. The effect of the legislation is to roll over any gain arising on the disposal of the target company shares until there is a disposal of the shares issued by the acquiring company (*TCGA 1992, s 135(3)*).

In essence, the legislation applies the two fictions of the reorganisation provisions: the no-disposal fiction and the single composite asset fiction.

All the other consequences of *TCGA 1992, ss 127–131*, such as consideration received or given as part of the exchange transaction, will also apply as appropriately adapted.

The legislation is silent as to what 'necessary adaptations' are required to enable a share-for-share exchange to be treated as a reorganisation.

Example 7.4 – Share-for-share exchange

Fred owns Company D and Company E and had paid £100,000 for each company. He decides that he wants to form a group with them, so he sells Company D to Company E and, as consideration, Company E issues more shares to Fred. This is a share-for-share exchange and Company E now owns all the shares of Company D, satisfying Case 1 and Case 3.

Fred is therefore treated as not having disposed of Company D. The capital gains base cost of his shares in Company E is £200,000, being the combined original base cost of the companies.

Incidentally, Company E is treated as having the market value base cost in Company D, by virtue of *TCGA 1992, s 171(3)*. (See also *Westcott v Woolcombers Ltd*, 60 TC 575 and *NAP Holdings (UK) Ltd v Whittles*, 67 TC 166.)

Where the consideration is an issue of debentures, we have two possibilities, depending on whether the debentures are qualifying corporate bonds or not (QCBs or non-QCBs) (see **7.19** below).

In general, therefore, a disposal of shares by a company in return for debentures will be dealt with under *TCGA 1992, s 116* (see below), as will a disposal of shares by an individual in return for debentures that are QCBs. For the corporate shareholder, any future gain or loss on the QCB will be dealt with under the loan relationships legislation (**6.72** *et seq*).

A disposal of shares by an individual in return for non-QCBs will be treated as a reorganisation of share capital, so that the shareholder (now a bondholder) is treated as not having made a disposal. The QCBs will have a capital gains base cost the same as the original shares.

Interaction with capital gains degrouping charge

7.15 Where a target company leaves a group as a result of a share-for-share exchange, it may be holding assets transferred to it within the last six years, and so be potentially subject to the capital gains degrouping charge (**6.33** *et seq*). Under the rules introduced by *FA 2011, Sch 10*, the gain on the deemed disposal and reacquisition of those assets is to be held over until there is a chargeable disposal of the new holding, ie the shares issued by the acquiring company on the exchange (*TCGA 1992, s 179(3E)*).

Stamp duty and share exchanges

7.16 In general, an exchange of shares will carry a charge to stamp duty at 0.5%. However, there is a relief for acquisition of the whole of the share capital of a company, at *FA 1986, s 77*, subject to the conditions for relief being satisfied. Broadly, those conditions are:

- the acquisition is effected for bona fide commercial reasons and does not form part of a scheme or arrangement of which the main purpose, or one of the main purposes, is avoidance of liability to stamp duty, stamp duty reserve tax, income tax, corporation tax or capital gains tax;

- the consideration for the acquisition consists only of the issue of shares in the acquiring company to the shareholders of the target company, so that after the acquisition each person who immediately before it was made was a shareholder of the target company is a shareholder of the acquiring company;

- after the acquisition has been made, the shareholdings in the acquiring company are proportionately identical to the shareholdings in the target company.

This relief clearly does not apply to exchanges in return for debentures, as it fails the initial test of involving an issue of shares.

There is no formal clearance for the availability of this relief. In practice, HMRC will usually accept that it applies in cases where they also accept the bona fide commercial reasons for the transaction for capital gains tax purposes. But this cannot be relied upon. For example, the transaction may have a component involving avoidance of stamp duty reserve tax, which would mean that the stamp duty relief would not be available but would have no bearing on the availability of the capital gains relief (which is only restricted where there is an intention to avoid capital gains tax or corporation tax).

The position is complicated further by *FA 1986, s 77A*, introduced by *FA 2016, s 136* for documents executed on or after 29 June 2016. *FA 1986, s 77A* denies stamp duty relief under *FA 1986, s 77* where it is reasonable to assume that one of the purposes of the transaction is to secure a change of control of the original company. There is an exemption for mergers but this provision will be important for share exchanges that precede certain demergers (see **5.22** and **5.25**, and **Example 5.5** at Step 1).

Where the relief from stamp duty is not available, the transaction may be carried out by a reduction of capital, instead (see **5.21**).

EXCHANGES INVOLVING QUALIFYING CORPORATE BONDS (QCBs)

Introduction

7.17   QCBs are exempt from capital gains tax under *TCGA 1992, s 115* (the same provision that takes gilt-edged securities out of the scope of capital gains tax). Where there is a conversion to which *TCGA 1992, s 132* applies, or an exchange to which *TCGA 1992, s 135* applies, the normal reorganisation rules will not work without special provision. For example, in the absence of specific rules, shares standing at a large gain could be converted (actually or by exchange) into QCBs, which would then be exempt from tax, offering a major avoidance opportunity.

The rules apply to any transaction that would otherwise be or be treated as if it were a reorganisation of share capital, where either the original shares or the new holding, but not both, would be or contain a QCB. A transaction in this context includes a conversion of securities as defined by *TCGA 1992, s 132*, even if this is effected without a transaction (*TCGA 1992, s 116(1), (2)*).

Where these rules apply, the reorganisation provisions are disapplied from any transaction which involves a QCB and the new asset is treated as having been acquired when it actually was acquired, rather than when the original asset was acquired (*TCGA 1992, s 116(5), (6)*).

What is a QCB?

7.18   For the purposes of corporation tax (ie for a corporate bond-holder), a QCB is any asset representing a loan relationship of a company (*TCGA 1992, s 117(A1)*).

Broadly speaking, for any other tax purposes (ie a non-corporate bond-holder) a corporate bond is a security that has at all times represented a normal commercial loan (as defined by *CTA 2010, Ch 6, Pt 5*) and which is expressed in sterling with no provision made for conversion or redemption into any other currency. Generally, a non-convertible debenture denominated in sterling and issued on normal commercial terms will be a QCB (*TCGA 1992, s 117(A1), (1)*).

The important issue here is that the status of an instrument as a QCB depends on the holder. Since 'any asset representing a loan relationship of a company' is a QCB, any security issued in a reorganisation or deemed reorganisation will be a QCB if it is issued to a company.

If it is issued to an individual, as is common, particularly in the private equity field, then the status of an instrument as a QCB or not will depend on its terms. This was important as individuals were often concerned to ensure that they had an adequate holding period for the purposes of business asset taper relief, in which case they would want to receive non-QCBs in a share-for-debenture exchange, so that the instrument would continue to qualify for the relief. However, since business asset taper relief was abolished in 2008, and entrepreneurs' relief operates rather differently, these considerations are likely to be less relevant in future transactions.

There are two common methods of ensuring that the loan notes do not constitute QCBs. One is to incorporate a provision into the loan note instruments enabling them to be converted into a currency other than sterling at a date prior to the redemption date, which would mean that the loan note fails the condition of *TCGA 1992, s 117(1)(b)* that it be expressed and redeemable in sterling. This was challenged in the case of *Nicholas Trigg*, where the First-tier Tribunal decided ([2014] UKFTT 967 (TC)) that clauses allowing conversion into Euro-denominated bonds did not mean that certain bonds were non-QCBs. While this decision was overturned by the Upper Tribunal ([2016] UKUT 165 (TCC)), the Court of Appeal has recently restored the original decision ([2018] EWCA Civ 17) and the case looks set to go to the Supreme Court.

The other method is to incorporate a provision into the loan note instruments enabling the holder to subscribe for additional shares or securities, which would mean that the QCBs do not represent a 'normal commercial loan' as defined in *CTA 2010, Ch 6, Pt 5*.

Focus

HMRC scrutinise the terms of corporate bonds and may challenge whether the terms are sufficiently robust to ensure that a corporate bond is not a qualifying bond. Proper legal advice on the terms of the bond is essential.

Exchanges of QCBs for non-QCBs

7.19   If the original holding consists of QCBs, the exchange, conversion or reorganisation is treated as a disposal of the QCBs, exempt from tax on gains, and the shares or debentures issued in the transaction are treated as being acquired at market value, ie the reorganisation provisions are disapplied and there is a market value acquisition of the new holding. So the no-disposal fiction and the single composite asset fiction do not apply in these circumstances (*TCGA 1992, s 116(9)*).

If, on the exchange, some cash consideration is also given by the vendor, the total cost of the non-QCB for capital gains tax purposes, ie its base cost on a future disposal, is the market value of the QCB plus the cash consideration given (*TCGA 1992, s 116(8)*).

If cash consideration is received on the exchange, this is deducted from the base cost of the non-QCB. This is completely logical: the vendor has disposed of an asset worth £X for consideration with a total value of £X. If he receives £Y in cash, the deemed cost of the new asset must be £(X–Y) (*TCGA 1992, s 116(7)*).

Exchanges of shares or of non-QCBs for QCBs

7.20   If, on the other hand, shares or non-QCB debentures are exchanged for or converted into QCBs, the original securities are treated as not having been disposed of, but the gain that would otherwise have accrued at the time of the exchange is held over. That gain (or loss) then comes into charge when there is an actual disposal of the QCB. If only part of the QCB holding is disposed of, then an appropriate part of the gain or loss is deemed to accrue.

If cash consideration is also given in a non-QCB for QCB transaction, this is taken into account to reduce the held-over gain under *TCGA 1992, s 116(10)* (*TCGA 1992, s 116(6), (8)*).

If cash consideration is received by the vendor in such an exchange, this is charged to tax on the basis of the proportion of the market value of the old asset represented by the cash consideration. So, for example, if the cash represents half the value of the old asset, half the chargeable gain is chargeable immediately and the other half is rolled over to come into charge on disposal of the QCBs.

If there is such a charge on cash received, this gain is then deducted from the gains coming into charge when there is a disposal of the whole or part of the QCB, to prevent double taxation.

323

However, if the cash receipt is small in comparison to the market value of the old asset, this provision is not applied, 'to avoid the delay and expense of a full computation where this would be disproportionate, and to avoid the need for assessments in trivial cases' (RI 164). In such a case, therefore, the entire gain is rolled over into the new QCBs, and the sum received appears to escape taxation. In most cases, HMRC will accept that 'small', for these purposes, means less than 5% of the value or less than £3,000, even if that exceeds 5% of the value of the securities (see above) (*TCGA 1992, s 116(7), (12), (13), (14)*).

In this context, 'disposal' of the QCB is wider in meaning than just a sale. In particular, redemption or waiving of the security will also constitute a disposal in this context.

These provisions only apply to gains held over in the relevant transaction. So if the QCB increases or decreases in value before eventual disposal, that increase or decrease is outside the scope of capital gains tax, although it may be chargeable on a company under the loan relationships legislation (*TCGA 1992, s 116(10)*). One impact of this is that the charge comes into force even if the QCB is subsequently worthless. There is no capital loss relief for any reduction in value of a QCB (unless the QCB was issued before 17 March 1998 and the now repealed provisions of *TCGA 1992, s 254* apply (*TCGA 1992, s 116(15)*).

Focus

Where a gain is held over into a QCB, but the borrower becomes insolvent, it is very difficult to avoid the gain coming into charge. It might be worth considering insurance or a bank guarantee of the bonds so the vendor does not end up with a 'dry' tax charge.

A held-over gain does not come into charge if the disposal is within one of the following categories:

- husband and wife transfers (*TCGA 1992, s 58(1)*);

- transfers to a legatee on death (*TCGA 1992, s 62(4)*);

- intra-group transfers between UK-resident companies (*TCGA 1992, s 171(1)*);

- incorporation of a UK permanent establishment of a company resident in another Member State (*TCGA 1992, s 140A*);

- merger to form a company which is UK resident or has a UK permanent establishment (*TCGA 1992, s 140E*).

In each of these cases, however, the recipient under any of these provisions will suffer the held-over tax charge on the eventual disposal of the securities (*TCGA 1992, s 116(11)*).

Example 7.5 – Conversion of QCBs

Gregory holds loan notes of F Plc, a listed company. The loan notes are QCBs and are currently worth £10,000. The company decides to capitalise its debt by conversion into shares and issues Gregory with 173 shares, which have a market value of £10,200 at the date of issue.

For the purposes of capital gains tax, the 173 shares of F Plc have a base cost of £10,200, ie market value. The disposal of the loan notes is outside the scope of capital gains tax.

Example 7.6 – Redemption of QCBs

Harvey Ltd, an investment company, has a wholly-owned, non-trading subsidiary, Impasse Ltd, which it sells for £15m on 1 April 2017. All of the consideration is in the form of loan notes, which are therefore QCBs for Harvey Ltd. The loan notes will be redeemed at £1m a year starting on the 5th anniversary of the sale.

On the disposal the putative gain is computed. As each tranche of loan notes is redeemed, one-fifteenth of the gain comes into charge on Harvey Ltd.

Note that the charge arises on disposals of the loan notes. So an appropriate proportion of the charge would arise if Harvey Ltd were to sell any of them or if any of the loan notes were to be extinguished, eg on a liquidation of the issuer.

Note also that, had Impasse Ltd been a trading company, the substantial shareholding exemption would have been available and the reorganisations provisions would not have applied (*TCGA 1992, Sch 7AC, para 4(3)*).

7.21   *TCGA 1992, s 116(1)(b)* applies, *inter alia*, where '... the original shares would consist of or include a qualifying corporate bond and the new holding would not ...'. This implies that *TCGA 1992, s 116* cannot be applied to a situation where the starting point is a mixture of QCBs and non-QCBs and the portfolio is wholly converted into QCBs. This analysis was successfully relied upon by the taxpayers (or non-payers) in *Anthony and Tracy Lee Hancock*, where the First-tier Tribunal decided ([2014] UKFTT 695 (TC)) that a mixed holding was converted into all QCBs, then redeemed free of capital gains tax by virtue of the exemption in *TCGA 1992, s 115*. This decision was overturned by the Upper Tribunal ([2016] UKUT 81 (TCC)), and the Court of Appeal upheld the Upper Tribunal's decision ([2017] EWCA Civ 198) (see **7.8**).

SCHEMES OF RECONSTRUCTION

Introduction

7.22 Schemes of reconstruction can also be treated as if they were reorganisations of share capital. Broadly, the principles are the same as for exchanges, with the new holding being treated as if it were the same as the original shares, acquired at the same time and at the same price.

Definition of a scheme of reconstruction

7.23 Broadly, a scheme of reconstruction requires the business carried on by one or more original companies to be carried on by one or more successor companies and it requires the shareholders of the original company or companies, taken together, to be the same as the shareholders of the successor company or companies, taken together.

The definition refers to any 'scheme of merger, division or other restructuring', and so attempts to cover every possible restructuring of corporate-owned businesses. So it covers the situations where:

- one company splits into more than one company, each carrying on part of the business carried on by the original (a demerger);

- two or more companies merge all their businesses into one company (a merger or amalgamation);

- two or more companies mix and merge their businesses into more than one company.

At the same time, the definition of 'reconstruction' requires the shareholder base to be essentially maintained, even if it is split between more than one company.

There is no requirement that a scheme of reconstruction involves only UK companies. Although the tax consequences of a scheme of reconstruction will only be relevant to a company or shareholder that is UK resident for tax purposes, the other companies involved in the scheme need not be UK resident. Indeed, for there to be any such restriction might offend against some of the fundamental freedoms required by the EU, such as freedom of establishment and free movement of capital. So it is entirely possible to have, say, a scheme that involves all non-UK companies where the only person to whom the tax consequences matter is a UK-resident individual shareholder, but so long as the appropriate conditions are satisfied for the scheme to constitute a scheme of reconstruction, the shareholder should be able to claim the benefits of the relevant exemptions.

Essentially, the definition has four conditions, of which the first two, along with one other must be satisfied. However, preliminary reorganisations of share capital and subsequent issue of shares or debentures are disregarded, so in deciding whether the conditions are satisfied, we look at the position after any preliminary reorganisation and before any subsequent issues of shares or debentures (*TCGA 1992, Sch 5AA, paras 1, 6, 7*).

First and second conditions: pro rata issue of ordinary share capital

7.24 The scheme must involve the issue of ordinary share capital of one or more 'successor companies' to the shareholders of one or more 'original companies'. Alternatively, the scheme can involve the issue of shares to the shareholders of one or more classes of share of the original company or companies, so a scheme of reconstruction can be carried out without involving all the shareholders of the original company. The issue of shares must also be pro rata to the shareholders' rights as shareholders of the original company.

The ordinary share capital of a successor company or companies can only be issued to the holders of ordinary share capital of one or more original companies and to no one else, so a reconstruction is not a way of bringing new shareholders into a company or companies. It may well be possible to introduce new shareholders to a company either before or after carrying out a scheme of reconstruction, but the scheme of reconstruction itself requires that shares of the successor company or companies are only issued to shareholders of the original company or companies (*TCGA 1992, Sch 5AA, paras 2, 3*).

Issues of fixed rate capital or of debentures, which are less concerned with proprietary rights over the issuing companies, are excluded from the definition of reconstructions. This does not mean that fixed rate shares or debentures cannot be issued in a scheme of reconstruction, however, merely that there must be an issue of ordinary share capital for the scheme to qualify as a scheme of reconstruction in the first place.

Ordinary share capital means issued share capital other than fixed rate shares with no other rights of participation, as well as units in unit trust schemes and the interests of members in companies that do not have share capital (*TCGA 1992, Sch 5AA, para 8*).

Both the first (issue of ordinary share capital) and second (pro rata) conditions must be satisfied.

Third condition: continuity of business

7.25   The third condition has several alternative components:

- A single original company can be reconstructed into one or more successor companies. The condition is that the business or substantially the whole of the business carried on by the original company must, after the reconstruction, be carried on by a new company or by two or more successor companies, which may include the original company.

- There may be more than one original company, being reconstructed into a single company (a merger). Here the condition is that the businesses or substantially the whole of the businesses carried on by the original companies must, after the reconstruction, be carried on by the successor company, which can also be one of the original companies.

- Less commonly, there may be more than one original company being reconstructed into several successor companies. Here the condition is that the businesses or substantially the whole of the businesses carried on by the original companies must, after the reconstruction, be carried on by different successor companies, some or all of which can also be one of the original companies. That is, the businesses must have moved companies to be a scheme of reconstruction.

The activities of the successor companies are to be considered altogether in considering whether those activities constitute the whole or substantially the whole of the activities carried on by the original company or companies prior to the reconstruction. CG57027c gives a very simple example: imagine an original company with a retail and a manufacturing trade. This company is subject to a scheme of reconstruction whereby one successor company carries on the retail trade and another carries on the manufacturing trade. Taking the overall activities of the successor companies together, they constitute the whole of the activities of the original company.

Where groups of companies are involved, the group structure is largely ignored and the activities of a controlled company are treated as being the activities of the controlling company.

If any original companies retain assets to distribute as share capital on being wound up, this is ignored in considering whether the third condition is satisfied (*TCGA 1992, Sch 5AA, para 4*).

If the third condition is not satisfied, a transaction can still qualify as a scheme of reconstruction if the fourth condition is satisfied, instead.

Fourth condition: compromise or arrangement with members

7.26 This condition requires that the scheme be carried out pursuant to a compromise or arrangements under the 'arrangements and reconstruction rules' of *Companies Act 2006, Pt 26* in the UK or similar provisions applicable in other jurisdictions. No one, apart from the company or companies subject to the compromise or arrangements, can acquire any part of the business or businesses of the original company or companies (*TCGA 1992, Sch 5AA, para 5*).

Focus

HMRC will challenge transactions that they do not think qualify as schemes of reconstruction. It is imperative to take advice and to ensure that the appropriate conditions are satisfied.

THE RECONSTRUCTION RELIEFS

Introduction

7.27 Where there is a scheme of reconstruction, certain reliefs are available to both the shareholders of the companies concerned and, where appropriate, to the companies themselves. To see why these reliefs are necessary, let us look at a simple reconstruction.

Example 7.7 – Simple reconstruction

Company A is liquidated and transfers all its assets to a new company, company B, in consideration for which company B issues shares to the shareholders of company A.

So far as the shareholders of company A are concerned, they still own a company carrying on the same business as before, they have not taken any money out of the corporate structure and nothing material has changed, but the capital gains legislation says that the shareholders have disposed of their shares in company A and received in consideration the shares in company B. Therefore, absent the exemption, the shareholders of company A would suffer a chargeable gain.

Furthermore, company A has disposed of all its assets to company B, which should give rise to a chargeable gain, too.

The reconstruction reliefs at *TCGA 1992, ss 136* and *139* prevent either charge applying (see **7.28** and **7.29**).

Shareholder and creditor reconstruction relief

7.28   The relief for shareholders treats the scheme of reconstruction as if it were a share exchange to which the reorganisation provisions can apply with 'necessary adaptations' (*TCGA 1992, ss 136(2), 135(3)*).

The relief requires an arrangement between a company and its shareholders or debenture holders, in connection with a scheme of reconstruction, whereby another company issues new shares or debentures to those shareholders or debenture holders pro rata to their holdings. There is also provision for the arrangements only to affect specific classes of share or debenture. This is similar in approach to *TCGA 1992, Sch 5AA*, with the added ability to involve debentures as well as shares (but not instead of shares or the transaction would fail Condition 1 in *TCGA 1992, Sch 5AA*).

This provision applies regardless of whether the originally held shares or debentures are retained or cancelled – in a simple reconstruction. In the example in the Introduction, where company A is liquidated, the shares would obviously be cancelled, whereas on a merger or a demerger it is likely that the original shares will be retained (*TCGA 1992, s 136(1)*).

Remember, however, that an issue of loan notes that are qualifying corporate bonds will invoke the hold-over provisions of *TCGA 1992, s 116*.

Note, also, that there is no requirement for the companies involved to be UK resident for tax purposes. The exemption relates to the tax charge on the shareholders and is not concerned with the residence status of the companies.

Preliminary reorganisations of the shareholdings of the original company are permitted and the relief applies *mutatis mutandis* to companies without share capital (but not to units of unit trusts, for some reason) (*TCGA 1992, s 136(3), (5)*).

The relief only applies if the scheme of reconstruction is carried out for bona fide commercial reasons and not part of a scheme or arrangement to avoid capital gains tax or corporation tax (unless the members concerned, along with persons connected with them, do not hold more than 5% of the relevant class of shares or debentures of the original company). Pre-transaction clearance to that effect can be obtained from HMRC (*TCGA 1992, ss 136(6), 137(1), (2), 138*). A sample letter applying to HMRC for pre-transaction clearance is attached at the end of this chapter.

Company reconstruction relief

7.29   Referring back to the example in the Introduction to this section, we see company A passing assets to company B. The reconstruction relief treats this transfer as being at no gain and no loss, so the successor company effectively inherits the original base cost, plus indexation, of the original company (*TCGA 1992, s 139(1)*).

The relief only applies if the scheme of reconstruction is carried out for bona fide commercial reasons and not part of a scheme or arrangement to avoid capital gains tax or corporation tax. Pre-transaction clearance to that effect can be obtained from HMRC (*TCGA 1992, ss 139(5), 138*). A sample letter applying to HMRC for pre-transaction clearance is attached at the end of this chapter.

For the exemption to apply there must be a transfer of a business or part of a business for no consideration from the perspective of the transferring company, except for taking on any of the debts of that business. The word 'business' is much wider than a trade and a transfer of a business is apt to include a wide range of activities. HMRC accept that the holding of subsidiaries is a 'business' for the purposes of this legislation, too, so the relief is available for the transfer of subsidiaries in a reconstruction, as well as for the transfer of businesses per se.

HMRC have always taken the view that 'a company's business' means a business (or subsidiary) that is at least 75% owned by the transferor company, although there is nothing in the statute to support this interpretation.

Both companies involved must be UK resident or carrying on a trade in the UK through a permanent establishment. That said, this provision is clearly contrary to EU legislation (The Treaty for the Functioning of the European Union prescribes the fundamental freedom to establish in any Member State and to move capital freely between Member States) and may be invalid, at least for transactions between EU Member States (*TCGA 1992, s 139(1A)*).

The relief does not apply to assets held as trading stock or to the transfer of a business into an authorised unit trust, a venture capital trust or an investment trust (*TCGA 1992, s 139(2), (4)*).

Interaction with capital gains degrouping charge

7.30 Where a company leaves a group as a result of a transfer under a scheme of reconstruction, it may be holding assets transferred to it within the last six years, and so be potentially subject to the capital gains degrouping charge (see **6.33**). Under the rules introduced by *FA 2011, Sch 10*, this charge would prima facie be treated as consideration received by the transferor company, which would breach the no consideration rule for this relief to apply. However, such deemed consideration is ignored for the purposes of that rule (*TCGA 1992, s 139(1B)*).

HMRC have also stated in correspondence that, in these circumstances, the degrouping charge just disappears. It does not fall on the transferor company and it is not held over until some later event. While this might appear to be a potentially useful tax-planning opportunity, it is important to remember that this relief only applies if the reconstruction is not part of a scheme for the avoidance of corporation tax, so clearance might be refused if a scheme of reconstruction were seen by HMRC as being intended to achieve a tax-free degrouping using this mechanism.

Interaction with the substantial shareholdings exemption

7.31 Where the business transferred is the holding of trading subsidiaries, the substantial shareholdings exemption might prima facie apply. However, that exemption specifically does not apply where there is a no gain, no loss transfer, such as under this reconstruction relief (*TCGA 1992, Sch 7AC, para 6(1)(a)*).

Tax liabilities

7.32 If a business transfer was not for bona fide commercial reasons or was for the avoidance of tax, and the transferor company has been wound up, the tax can be collected from the transferee company. If the tax is not paid within six months of the assessment, HMRC can claim a corresponding part of the unpaid tax from any other person who holds any of the assets in respect of the disposal of which the tax is charged, in so far as that person has acquired those assets through another scheme of reconstruction or by an intra-group transfer. Any person so charged to tax is entitled to try and recover both the tax and any interest charged from the original transferee company (*TCGA 1992, s 139(6), (7), (8)*).

Reconstructions and intangible fixed assets

7.33 The regime for intangible fixed assets (*CTA 2009, Pt 8*) effectively takes intangible fixed assets, created or acquired by a company since 31 March 2002, outside the capital gains regime (*CTA 2009, s 906(1)*).

Such assets, where a disposal would give rise to a credit or debit under *CTA 2009, Pt 8*, are referred to as 'chargeable intangible assets' (*CTA 2009, s 741(1)*).

A transfer of a business in a scheme of reconstruction can include the transfer of chargeable intangible assets, so *CTA 2009, Pt 8* contains a relief designed largely to mirror the provisions of *TCGA 1992, s 139*, with appropriate modifications for the different type of asset (*CTA 2009, s 818*).

The relief applies where there is a transfer of a business as part of a scheme of reconstruction and there is no consideration, apart from the assumption of debt (*CTA 2009, s 818(1)*).

The relief does not apply to intra-group transfers, or if either company is a qualifying friendly society entitled to exemption from tax or a dual-resident investing company (there is no obvious policy reason for the fact that these exclusions are very different from those for chargeable assets) (*CTA 2009, s 818(3), (4)*).

The relief also does not apply unless the transactions have been carried out for genuine commercial reasons and not as part of a scheme or arrangements for the avoidance of corporation tax, capital gains tax or income tax. Pre-transaction clearance that this is so can be obtained from HMRC (*CTA 2009, ss 818(5), 831, 832, 833*).

The transfer must include intangible fixed assets that are chargeable intangible assets to both the transferor and transferee companies, which mirrors the potentially unlawful residence requirements of *TCGA 1992, s 139(1A)*, as assets can only be chargeable intangible assets of UK-resident companies and UK trading permanent establishments (*CTA 2009, s 818(2)*).

Where the relief applies, the transfer is deemed to be tax neutral, meaning that the transfer is deemed not to be a realisation (ie disposal) or acquisition and anything done by the transferor while owning the asset is deemed to have been done by the transferee (*CTA 2009, ss 776, 818(2)*).

Stamp duty and schemes of reconstruction

7.34   The definition of a scheme of reconstruction for capital gains purposes does not apply to either stamp duty or stamp duty land tax. There is no statutory definition of a scheme of reconstruction for stamp taxes, so these taxes use the definition developed by company law, requiring substantially the same business to be carried on after a reconstruction as before, with substantially the same shareholders (see, for example, *Re South African Supply and Cold Storage Co* [1904] 2 Ch 268 and *Brooklands Selangor Holdings Ltd v IRC* [1970] 2 All ER 76).

The practical effect of this is that transactions that are exempt from capital gains tax as schemes of reconstruction might still carry charges to stamp duty or SDLT.

A transfer of shares under a scheme of reconstruction may qualify for the relief at *FA 1986, s 77* (see **7.17** above) if the conditions are satisfied and if *FA 1986, s 77A* does not apply.

A transfer of assets under a scheme of reconstruction may qualify for the relief at *FA 2003, Sch 7, Pt 2*, subject to satisfying the conditions for that relief. These are:

- The consideration for the acquisition consists wholly or partly of the issue of non-redeemable shares in the acquiring company to all the shareholders of the target company.

- After the acquisition has been made each shareholder of each of the companies is a shareholder of the other and the proportion of shares of one of the companies held by any shareholder is the same, or as nearly as may be the same, as the proportion of shares of the other company held by that shareholder.

- The acquisition is effected for bona fide commercial reasons and does not form part of a scheme or arrangement of which the main purpose, or one of the main purposes, is the avoidance of liability to stamp duty, income tax, corporation tax, capital gains tax or stamp duty land tax.

There is no statutory right to a pre-transaction clearance as to the availability of this relief. As noted previously, however, HMRC will, in many cases, accept that the relief applies if they are also satisfied for the purposes of the capital gains reliefs that the transaction is for bona fide commercial reasons and not part of a scheme or arrangement to avoid tax.

APPENDIX – SAMPLE CLEARANCE LETTER

7.35   Dear Sirs

We are writing on behalf of the shareholders of [*name the company or companies involved*] to seek formal clearances under [*statutory provisions*] in respect of the proposed transaction(s) below.

Parties involved

List all the relevant shareholders and companies (this can be in an appendix to the main letter). For individuals, always provide:

- national insurance numbers

- unique taxpayer references

- home addresses

- shareholding(s) in relevant companies

- residence status.

For companies or LLPs, always provide:

- company registration numbers
- unique taxpayer references
- registered office addresses
- residence status.

This will help HMRC identify the parties and ensure that the relevant tax offices are sent details of the application and whether clearance was granted or refused.

History and background

Brief history of the company or companies involved, their business(es), etc. This helps put the whole transaction into context for HMRC.

Bring it up to date with an explanation of the current position and what the transactions are meant to achieve.

Prior transactions

It is sensible to mention any previous transactions that may be relevant within, say, the last five years.

Proposed transactions

Describe these in detail, together with the reasons behind each element of the transactions. Either here, or in the History and background section, you need to explain why the transactions are being carried out and why in this particular way, to demonstrate the commercial drivers and the lack of any tax-avoidance motives.

For more technically based clearances, such as for demergers, it is also important to demonstrate that all the relevant technical conditions are satisfied.

Commercial reasons for the transaction

Some applicants like to spell out the commercial drivers as a separate section of the letter.

Future transactions

For completeness, you should cover any other transactions in contemplation for the near to medium term. This should cover both definite transactions and transactions that have been thought about, albeit they are not definitely going to happen.

Examples might be:

- After a demerger, one of the new companies will be offering shares or share options to key employees. The ability to do this may, indeed, have been one of the reasons behind the demerger.

- Following a reconstruction, it is possible that one of the businesses or companies in a group would be sold, were an appropriate offer to be made. This will probably not affect whether HMRC grant a clearance.

- Following a reorganisation, one of the businesses or companies in a group will definitely be sold. This may affect whether HMRC grant a clearance, depending on the circumstances, such as whether HMRC see the reorganisation as reducing the tax liability on the subsequent disposal, which might be seen as tax avoidance.

Clearance sought

Specifically request the clearances sought and the statutory references.

Enclosures

Always enclose the latest statutory accounts of all the companies involved.

Contact details

If you require any further details concerning the transactions please contact Mr J Smith by email (email address) or by telephone (telephone number). It is relatively uncommon for HMRC to do this but it can help to ensure that minor queries can be dealt with quickly and efficiently.

Chapter 8

Selling or winding-up an owner-managed company

Partha Ray, Cameron & Associates Ltd

SIGNPOSTS

- **Scope** – There are two possible methods of selling a business, either by selling the shares of a company or by a company disposing of its assets. Selling a trading business might entitle a vendor to entrepreneurs' relief resulting in a favourable CGT rate.

- **Entrepreneurs' relief (ER)** – To be eligible for ER, certain conditions need to be met and the main qualifying conditions are set out in **8.5**.

- **Consideration satisfied by shares or loan notes** – Purchasers may not wish to pay for the business by all the cash upfront, and part of the arrangement may be to settle this deferred consideration. We look at the rules for QCBs and non-QCBs although these are now similar (see **8.11–8.25**).

- **Practical issues** – There are corporation tax consequences on a winding-up, including the sale of trading stock and how best to use trading losses (see **8.28–8.38**).

- **Anti-avoidance provisions** – There are restrictions on the surplus available for distribution to shareholders on an informal winding-up (see **8.47–8.49**), and for businesses which are wound up and then continue to trade under a new company (phoenix companies – see **8.59–8.62**).

- **Other points** – There is tax relief for shareholders of insolvent companies who can either make a negligible value claim or it may be possible to obtain income tax relief for capital losses on certain shares (see **8.65–8.77**).

SALES UNDER THE CGT REGIME

8.1   Most owner-managers selling their businesses are likely to qualify for entrepreneurs' relief (ER), which provides the benefit of a 10% CGT rate. However, ER is restricted to the first £10m of eligible share sale gains. Any gains in excess of the £10m limit (which is a cumulative lifetime allowance) are, from 6 April 2016, chargeable at a CGT rate of either 10% or 20%. The rate which will apply is determined by an individual's income and other gains which arise during the tax year in which the disposal is made.

If ER has already been fully utilised then any capital gains, in 2018/19, are taxable at either 10% or 20% depending on the vendor's other income. Where an individual's total taxable income and gains are below the upper limit of the basic rate income tax (£34,500) then the gains will be taxable at 10% (the same rate as ER). Any gains (or part of the gains) which are above this threshold will be taxable at 20%. In this chapter, it is assumed that all gains, for which ER is not available, are taxable at 20%. Under the CGT rules, an important planning consideration will be to ensure that maximum possible use is made of ER, and some owner-managers may wish to fragment their shareholdings to other family members to achieve this.

The table below shows how an owner-manager's CGT liability rises on larger gains.

Gains on shares	CGT payable 2018/19 (with ER)
£000	£000
100	10
1,000	100
5,000	500
10,000	1,000
15,000	2,000

Focus

ER continues to be a very valuable relief for entrepreneurs as the disposal of their business should, in most cases, be subject to capital gains tax at 10% rather than the standard 20% capital gains tax rate for higher and additional rate taxpayers (the gains arising from the disposal of residential property are taxed at 28%). Therefore, advisers should ensure that, where possible, all qualifying conditions are met.

When calculating the gain on a disposal there are a couple of points that individuals and trustee shareholders need to consider:

- Indexation relief is no longer available. For those shareholders who acquired their shares (well) before April 1998 the loss of indexation may prove to be costly in terms of additional CGT.

- March 1982 rebasing is now compulsory for shares held at 31 March 1982. In many cases, this should not affect the shareholder's capital gain (since the March 1982 rebasing value will be used in any case). However, it will no longer be possible to use the original cost of the shareholding, even if that produces a *lower* gain.

All shares in a particular company (of the same class) are generally treated as a single 'pooled' asset, regardless of when they were actually acquired.

HMRC used to apply the 'Transaction in Securities' anti-avoidance rules in *ITA 2007, s 684* more vigorously. It was therefore very important for the vendor shareholders to make use of the statutory clearance procedure under *ITA 2007, s 701*. Provided the main aspects of a transaction have been fully disclosed, the vendor can obtain some certainty before the sale that HMRC are satisfied that the transaction is being made for genuine reasons and will not subsequently be challenged under this legislation.

However, the application of *ITA 2007, s 684* should not apply for sales to unconnected third parties (*ITA 2007, s 686*). The new exemption provides greater clarity and certainty and, targets the application of the rules to transactions which are *mainly* motivated towards obtaining a tax advantage.

BASIC DEAL-STRUCTURING ISSUES

8.2   Generally, vendors can sell either their shares in the company or arrange to sell the trade and assets out of the company. In the majority of cases, the vendor shareholders will seek to structure the deal as a sale of their shares (which is the main focus of this chapter). This is attractive for a number of reasons. The sale proceeds are received directly in the hands of the vendor and would normally be subject to a lower CGT rate (with the benefit of ER). For any disposals in 2018/19, the marginal income tax rate of 45% will mean that, for vendors, obtaining the capital gains tax treatment becomes even more imperative.

A share sale also limits the vendor's commercial exposure, subject to the protection obtained by the purchaser through warranties and indemnities under the sale agreement.

In contrast, an asset deal frequently gives rise to an element of double taxation. This is because capital gains and 'clawbacks' of previously claimed capital allowances typically arise within the company on the sale of the assets (such as goodwill and plant). A further tax charge then arises when the company's post-tax sale proceeds are extracted by the shareholders from the company. Vendors generally tend to be 'forced' to sell the trade and assets out of their company in 'distress' sale situations. Companies that are very small can now take advantage of the disincorporation relief. This is covered in detail in **Chapter 2**.

Purchasers have tended to prefer to acquire the trade and assets since this involves less commercial risk and, for acquisitions until 7 July 2015, the prospect of obtaining tax relief (against trading profits) on the assets purchased, such as on goodwill and other intangible assets. However, in recent years, asset deals are likely to be more expensive in terms of stamp duty land tax (SDLT), where the acquisition contains a substantial element of UK land and property. For example, if the amount paid for (say) trading premises is £1m, the SDLT cost (from 17 March 2016) would be £2,000 on the first £250,000 and £37,500 on the remaining £750,000 (£750,000 × 5%). Goodwill and all transfers of intellectual property or debts no longer attract any stamp taxes.

On the other hand, share purchases only attract stamp duty at 0.5% but this is levied on the *total* value of the company (reflecting the value of non-dutiable assets but reduced by the company's debt and liabilities).

The rest of this chapter concentrates on the CGT consequences and planning opportunities of selling shares in an owner-managed company.

BASIC CAPITAL GAINS TAX (CGT) RULES ON SHARE SALES

Date of disposal

8.3   The vendor will normally generate a capital gain when they sell their shares. The nature of the contract will determine the date of disposal:

(a)   A disposal of an asset will be recognised for CGT purposes when an unconditional contract is executed for its sale (*TCGA 1992, s 28(1)*).

(b)   In the case of a conditional contract, the date of disposal is deferred until the relevant condition precedent is satisfied (or waived) (*TCGA 1992, s 28(2)*). A condition precedent refers to an event which is outside the control of the contracting parties – for example, obtaining satisfactory tax clearances or relevant regulatory approval etc. (On the other hand, a 'condition subsequent' is merely a term of the contract required to be fulfilled by one of the parties and does not create a conditional contract for CGT.)

Cash consideration is immediately chargeable to CGT in the tax year of disposal (*TCGA 1992, s 28*). Tax must be paid on any *fixed* (ie ascertainable) deferred consideration, even it if is conditional, although HMRC will refund the tax when they are satisfied that the conditional amount will not be paid. Instalment relief may be available for the tax payments; given the difficulty of paying the tax before the full cash proceeds are received (*TCGA 1992, ss 48* and *280*). However, fixed deferred consideration is usually best structured through the use of loan notes, as this enables the relevant tax to be held over (see **8.15**).

Calculation of capital gain

8.4   In broad terms, an individual or trustee vendor's capital gain is calculated as the amount by which the sale proceeds (net of allowable incidental costs of disposal) exceeds the amount they originally paid for the shares – often referred to as the 'base cost'.

Where a vendor held his shares at 31 March 1982, he must deduct the market value of the shareholding at 31 March 1982 as his base cost (instead of his pre-March 1982 acquisition cost).

Example 8.1 – Comparative CGT computation for sale of shares (under taper relief and entrepreneurs' relief regimes)

For some months, James has been in serious negotiations for the sale of 'his' company, Anderson Ltd. He expects to sell his company for a cash consideration of £12m (net of legal and professional costs). James acquired his 100% shareholding in June 1996 for £100,000. Anderson Ltd has always been a trading company.

The CGT liabilities for a sale made during 2018/19 is set out below:

	2017/18
	£
Net sale proceeds	12,000,000
Less: Acquisition cost (June 1996)	(100,000)
Chargeable gain	11,900,000
Less: Annual exemption	(11,700)
Taxable gain	11,888,300
CGT @ 10% (first £10m) & @ 20% (on balance)	1,377,660

ENTREPRENEURS' RELIEF

Main qualifying conditions

8.5   For normal share sales the following conditions must be met throughout the one year before the disposal (*TCGA 1992, s 169I(1), (2)(c), (5), (6)*). The vendor shareholder must:

- hold shares in a trading company or holding company of a trading group (see **8.8**); and

- be a director or employee of that company (or fellow group company) and it must be their 'personal company' – ie they must own at least 5% of the ordinary share capital (carrying at least 5% of the voting rights).

Most owner-managers should have little difficulty in satisfying the relevant tests. However, the 'director/employee' requirement should not be that onerous, since there is no requirement to work on a 'full-time' basis – part-time working would therefore suffice. The 5% 'shareholding/votes' test must be satisfied by the individual vendor alone (eg there is no attribution of a spouse's or any relatives' share).

The favourable 10% rate is potentially also available to shareholders who are not connected with the company (investor relief) but this chapter only focuses on the tax aspects of owner-managed companies.

Relaxation of conditions for EMI share options

8.6   The tax advantages of the EMI scheme were enhanced by allowing gains made on shares acquired through exercising EMI qualifying options to be eligible for the beneficial 10% entrepreneurs' relief rate.

The effect of the rules is that an individual will be entitled to entrepreneurs' relief in respect of EMI shares as long as the qualifying option was granted a year before the date of disposal of the shares. There will not be a requirement for the company to be their personal company (ie holding at least 5% of the ordinary share capital), so that entrepreneurs' relief is now more easily available to those who exercise their EMI share options.

The main reason for the change is that the government recognised that EMI options are typically exercised just before the employing company is taken over. This means that the shares would not be owned by the employee for one year and would, therefore, be ineligible for entrepreneurs' relief.

ER must be claimed (broadly) within 22 months after the end of the relevant tax year in which the share sale is made. Thus, for example, an ER claim on a qualifying gain in 2018/19 must be made by 31 January 2021. Once claimed, ER is applied to the complete eligible gain (up to the maximum £10m cumulative threshold) – it cannot be restricted in any way. However, some flexibility could be provided by selling shares in separate tranches, with an ER election being made against specific disposals.

The ER conditions are more restrictive than those which applied to the business taper regime. For example, a large number of minority and employee shareholders will be unable to meet the conditions necessary to secure ER. They will therefore suffer CGT rate of either 10% or 20% under the new regime.

Trustees can also claim ER in certain special cases where their trust has one or more beneficiaries holding an 'interest in possession' (see **8.8**).

Basic mechanics of ER

8.7   To obtain ER, the shares only need to be held on a qualifying basis for at least one year to obtain ER.

ER provides that the first £10m of 'qualifying business gains' are taxed at a lower rate of 10%. This £10m ER allowance is available, separately, to both husband and wife which may be an important consideration when structuring shareholdings.

In 2018/19, gains qualifying for ER are taxed at 10%. The following example shows the computation of ER for different levels of qualifying business gains:

Example 8.2 – ER available on varying levels of eligible gains

	£000	£000	£000
Eligible gain	1,000	10,000	15,000
CGT @ 10% (first £10m) & 20% (on balance)	100	1,000	2,000

Trading company/group test

8.8   The ER 'trading company/group' test is relatively stringent (*TCGA 1992, s 165A*). Broadly, the relevant company/group must be wholly engaged in carrying on trading activities, subject to the *de minimis* rule for 'substantial' non-trading activities.

HMRC's practice is to interpret this rule as permitting non-trading activities, provided they do not exceed 20% of the company's/group's total activities (although this is not a statutory test). Vulnerable *non-trading* activities would include property letting to third parties, investment in shares etc, loans to shareholders/connected companies, and surplus cash not required for future trading activities which is actively managed as an investment activity.

HMRC generally test whether non-trading activities are within the 20% benchmark by looking at a range of measures, such as:

- turnover;

- the asset base of the company;

- expenses;

- time spent by management and employees.

Thus, for example, the turnover/sales income from a company's non-trading activities would be compared with the total turnover generated by the company and so on. It may be necessary to build up the correct picture over time and this may involve striking a balance between all these factors.

Although many considered that substantial surplus cash could invalidate a company's trading status, HMRC now seem to take a more relaxed approach in this area. It would appear that provided the cash had been generated from a company's trading operations and it has not been applied for an investment purpose, then it should be treated as a trading asset.

When determining whether a company/group satisfies the 'trading' status test for ER, qualifying equity investments in joint venture trading companies (which would otherwise be regarded as investment activities) are deemed to represent an appropriate part of the trading activities of a trading company/ group. A shareholding in a 'joint-venture' company qualifies for 'trading' treatment provided the participating company (or group) holds at least 10% of its ordinary shares and:

(a)   the joint-venture company is a trading company or holding company of a trading group; and

(b)   at least 75% of the joint-venture company's equity share capital is held by five or fewer participating shareholders (irrespective of their tax residence status).

It might be possible to obtain an advance (non-statutory) clearance from HMRC as to whether the company satisfies the relevant 'trading' company/ group criteria for ER.

Disposals by trustees

8.9   Trustees can also claim ER in certain special cases where their trust has one or more 'qualifying' beneficiaries holding an 'interest in possession' (over the entire trust fund or the relevant part (such as a 'sub-fund') containing the shares) (*TCGA 1992, s 169J*).

The main trust conditions are directed at the 'qualifying beneficiary' rather than the trustees. Thus, the trustees can make a claim for ER provided the *qualifying beneficiary*:

- is a director or employee of the company (or any fellow-group company); and

- holds at least 5% of the ordinary shares in the company (carrying at least 5% of the voting rights) in their own right.

There is no minimum shareholding condition for the trustees. These 'trust' conditions must be satisfied throughout a period of *one year* ending within the *three years* before the sale. The company must also be a trading company or a holding company of a trading group (see **8.8**) throughout this period.

The conditions mean that to facilitate a potential ER claim by a trust, the (qualifying) beneficiary must have a personal holding of at least 5% of the shares (carrying at least 5% of the votes). However, the trustees do *not* have their own separate £10m ER allowance. The qualifying beneficiary effectively assigns to the trustees all or part of their unused ER allowance (by entering into a joint election). Therefore, if the beneficiary has used all of their £10m allowance, this will preclude any ER claim by the trustees.

Entrepreneurs' relief on associated disposals of personally held property

8.10   Where an individual qualifies for the relief on the disposal of shares, they can also obtain relief on an associated disposal of an asset that has been used by the company (*TCGA 1992, s 169K*). This would typically be a property that is personally owned by a shareholder/director which has been used by the company for its business, but it might also cover the sale of intellectual property that is personally held (outside the company) by the vendor shareholder.

The relief is only allowed for 'associated' disposals so they must therefore take place at the same time as (or shortly after) the share sale – an isolated disposal of personally held property will not qualify for any relief.

TCGA 1992, s 169K requires the following conditions to be satisfied for a qualifying 'associated disposal' (in the context of an ER-related share sale):

- The vendor shareholder must make the 'associated disposal' as part of their 'withdrawal from participation' in the business carried on by the company. (This appears to imply a 'hands-on' working test, so if the vendor continues to work in the target company post-sale, they may not satisfy this condition.)

- Throughout the *one-year* period (normally) prior to the sale of the shares, the relevant property is used for the purposes of the company's trade.

The conditions for associated disposal relief are therefore quite restrictive in terms of timing. For example, the sale of the property some time before the share sale would not qualify (since it would then not have been used for the purposes of the company's trade up to the date of the share sale).

The ER on an associated disposal can also be scaled down on a 'just and reasonable' basis (under *TCGA 1992, s 169P*) to reflect cases where (among other things):

- the property has only been *partly* used for the purposes of the company's trade throughout the vendor's period of ownership;

- a rent has been charged by the 'vendor' to the company for its use of the property.

This means that the gain eligible for 'associated disposal-ER' would now have to be reduced to the extent that a rent had been charged for the property over its entire period of ownership. Thus, if (say) only 40% of the market rent had been charged throughout this period, then 60% of the property gain would be eligible for 'associated disposal' relief. However, there is a provision whereby the restriction, to an individual who has charged rent for the use of an asset by the company, will only apply for rents charged after 5 April 2008.

Focus

Many businesses keep the property, from which the business trades, outside the company as it may belong to one of the directors. In these situations rent is paid for use of the property but the downside is that it may affect eligibility to ER when the property is subsequently disposed of.

TREATMENT OF SALE CONSIDERATION SATISFIED BY SHARES/LOAN NOTES IN THE ACQUIRER

Different types of consideration

8.11 Vendors may sell their shares for a consideration satisfied in cash, loan notes or shares issued by the acquiring company. Very often the vendor is likely to be offered a combination of cash and loan notes/shares. In some cases, vendors may also be given additional deferred consideration in the form of an 'earn-out'.

Consideration shares in the acquirer

8.12 Many private company takeovers, particularly by quoted companies, will entail the purchaser issuing new shares to the vendor shareholders as part of the sale consideration.

Many company takeovers, particularly by listed companies, will entail the purchaser issuing new shares to the vendor shareholders as part of the sale consideration. This enables the vendor to defer their capital gain until the shares are sold. The CGT reorganisation rule in *TCGA 1992, s 127* is applied here so that the vendor is treated as not having made any disposal of his old shares. Instead, he is treated as receiving the new 'consideration' shares at the same time and at the same cost as his old shares.

The share-for-share exchange 'reorganisation' rules are circumscribed by the 'commercial purpose' test in *TCGA 1992, s 137*. Consequently, the beneficial CGT treatment will only apply where the transaction is being undertaken for bona fide reasons *and* where one of the main purposes is not to obtain a tax advantage. Advance clearance should generally be applied for under *TCGA 1992, s 138* to obtain certainty that HMRC agree that these requirements are satisfied in relation to the proposed deal.

The 'commercial purpose' test in *TCGA 1992, s 137* does *not* apply to very small minority shareholders (ie those holding no more than 5% of the target company), presumably because they are not in a position to influence the structure of the transaction (*TCGA 1992, s 137(2)*).

Special election to obtain entrepreneurs' relief on share exchange

8.13 As the 'reorganisation' rule provides that there is no CGT disposal, the vendor would normally be unable to claim ER on the value of the acquirer's shares received as part of their sale consideration. This would be unfortunate if the vendor was unable to claim ER on a later sale of their 'consideration' shares – for example, because they did not possess the requisite 5% shareholding in the acquiring company.

The ER legislation recognises this problem and provides that the vendor can make a special election (under *TCGA 1992, s 169Q*) to opt out of the normal share-for-share exchange treatment. By making a *TCGA 1992, s 169Q* election the vendor is treated as having made a normal CGT disposal with the value of the acquirer's shares being reflected as all/part of their overall sale consideration. In such cases, the benefit of the ER would be reflected in the (higher) market value base cost of the shares in the acquiring company.

Example 8.3 – Effect of special ER election on share exchanges

Sue has been a 'management' shareholder since June 2003 and holds 10% of the equity share capital of Cook Ltd (a successful music publishing and recording company). She acquired her 10,000 £1 shares at their full market value of £20,000.

In August 2018, Cook Ltd was taken over by Stokes Plc. As part of this transaction, Sue received sale consideration of £600,000, which was satisfied as follows:

	£
Cash	200,000
Shares in Stokes Plc, valued at	400,000

Sue's shares in Stokes Plc represented a 3% shareholding (with commensurate voting rights). She is therefore unlikely to qualify for ER on their subsequent sale. However, by making a *TCGA 1992, s 169Q* election, she could benefit from ER on the *total* consideration received on the August 2018 sale, as shown below:

		£
Sale consideration	Cash	200,000
	Stokes Plc shares	400,000
		600,000
Less: Base cost		(20,000)
		580,000

	£
Less: Annual exemption	(11,700)
Taxable gain (qualifying for ER)	568,300
CGT @ 10%	56,830

Sue's base cost of her Stokes Plc shares would be their full market value of £400,000 (as opposed to £13,333 (4/6 × £20,000), being the pro-rata original cost of her Cook Ltd shares if the reorganisation rules had applied).

Making a *TCGA 1992, s 169Q* election

8.14   The *TCGA 1992, s 169Q* election is made on an 'all or nothing' basis. Therefore, it is not possible to restrict its application to gains of £10m. Such elections must be made within 22 months after the end of the tax year in which the sale occurs.

The potential consequences of making a *TCGA 1992, s 169Q* election should always be considered when structuring any deal. Because the reorganisation rule is disapplied, the vendor would generally incur a CGT liability on the 'ER-relieved' gain. The vendor would, therefore, need to ensure they had sufficient cash consideration to fund the tax liability. Furthermore, the timing of any future tax liability (when the higher base cost comes into play) must also be considered.

Clearly, such an election would not be appropriate where the 'cash' element of a company share sale produced chargeable gains exceeding the ER limit of £10m.

> **Focus**
>
> Before making a *TCGA 1992, s 169Q* election, make sure there is sufficient cash to pay the upfront CGT liability.

Consideration satisfied in loan notes (up to 22 June 2010)

8.15   In many deals, the vendor may agree to accept deferred payment for part of the sale consideration by taking loan notes in the acquiring company. As a general rule, where the purchaser satisfies part of the consideration by issuing loan notes, an appropriate part of the vendor's gain is deferred until the loan note is redeemed for payment. The precise mechanics of the deferral depended on the tax status of the loan note, as until 22 June 2010, this varied between Qualifying Corporate Bonds (QCBs) (see **8.16**) and non-QCBs (see **8.20**).

This CGT deferral rules are subject to HMRC being satisfied that the loan note has been issued for genuine commercial reasons and not mainly to avoid tax (*TCGA 1992, s 137*) (see **8.11**). The vendor would normally apply for a *TCGA 1992, s 138* clearance to seek advance confirmation of this point from HMRC.

Dealing with QCBs

8.16 Broadly, most 'non-convertible' loan notes will represent QCBs. The capital gains deferral mechanism for a QCB is governed by the rules in *TCGA 1992, s 116(10)*. These provide that the *chargeable gain* on the loan note consideration is computed at the date of sale. This gain is then postponed and becomes taxed only when the loan note is encashed (or disposed of *outside* the cases specified in *TCGA 1992, s 116(11)*).

Where QCBs were received on a post-6 April 2008 (but before 23 June 2010) share sale, any available ER was deducted in arriving at the gain held over under *TCGA 1992, s 116(10)*. Until 23 June 2010 this meant that the 'carried-forward' gain reflected any ER that was available and claimed at the original sale date.

From 23 June 2010, if there is an exchange of shares for QCBs and no *TCGA 1992, s 169R* election is made to bring the gain immediately into charge, it is likely that when the gain subsequently comes into charge, it will not qualify for ER.

Example 8.4 – Claiming ER on QCBs (up to 22 June 2010)

In May 2010, John sold his 40% shareholding in Arthur Ltd to Lehmann Plc for £2.5m, of which:

- £500,000 was paid in cash on completion; and

- £2m was satisfied by the issue of a QCB loan note (bearing interest at 5%, bank guaranteed and redeemable after 12 months).

John subscribed for his 40,000 £1 shares in Arthur Ltd at par in May 2002.

John would incur a CGT liability on the cash consideration and would be able to defer the capital gain on the part satisfied in QCBs.

2010/11 – CGT on cash consideration

Cash	£
Sale consideration – Cash	500,000
Less: Base cost $£40,000 \times \dfrac{£500,000}{£500,000 + £2,000,000}$	(8,000)
Capital gain	492,000
Less: ER – £492,000 × 4/9	(218,667)
Gain after ER	273,333
Less: Annual exemption	(10,100)
Taxable gain	263,233
CGT @ 18%	47,382

Postponed QCB gain (with ER)

	£
QCB consideration	2,000,000
Less: Base cost $£40,000 \times \dfrac{£2,000,000}{£500,000 + £2,000,000}$	(32,000)
Capital gain	1,968,000
Less: ER – £1,508,000 (£2,000,000 *less* £492,000) × 4/9	(670,222)
Postponed gain	1,297,778

QCB gains and *TCGA 1992, s 169R* elections to gain the benefit of ER (disposals after 22 June 2010)

8.17   The *Finance (No 2) Act 2010* changed the way ER is dealt with on QCB gains held over from 23 June 2010. This follows the change in ER to a straight 10% CGT charge. In such cases, any available ER is no longer factored into the held-over gain, so that now it is the 'gross' gain which is postponed.

If the seller wishes to claim ER on their QCB gain, they must make a special election under *TCGA 1992, s 169R*. This treats the QCB gain as being a chargeable disposal at the time of the share sale (ie the original shares are treated as sold for the QCB consideration), against which the ER CGT 10% rate can be claimed. By making an election, the normal QCB hold-over rules in *TCGA 1992, s 116(10)* do not apply. The *TCGA 1992, s 169R* election must be made by the 31 January following the tax year of the share sale.

This change therefore gives rise to a dilemma for sellers – should they elect under *TCGA 1992, s 169R* and pay 10% ER CGT 'upfront' on the share gain or defer their share gain under *TCGA 1992, s 116(10)* and (probably) pay CGT at 20% on the full held-over gain on redemption (with no ER)?

If a seller wishes to tax the QCB gain upfront to obtain a low ER CGT 10% rate, they would need to ensure that the deal structure provides sufficient cash funds to pay the CGT liability on the 31 January following the tax year of the sale. Where the *TCGA 1992, s 169R* election is made, there is no QCB hold-over and thus the redemption does not trigger any taxable gain.

Example 8.5 – Treatment of QCB gains and ER (post-22 June 2010 share sale)

In May 2018, Mark sold his 40% shareholding in Green Ltd to Blues Plc for £2.5m of which:

- £500,000 was paid in cash on completion; and

- £2m was satisfied by the issue of a QCB loan note (bearing interest at 9%, bank guaranteed and redeemable after 12 months).

Mark subscribed for his 40,000 £1 shares in Green Ltd at par in May 2004.

Mark's CGT position is as follows:

2018/19 – CGT on cash consideration

	£
Cash	
Sale consideration – Cash	500,000
Less: Base cost $\quad £40,000 \times \dfrac{£500,000}{(£500,000 + £2,000,000)}$	(8,000)
Capital gain	492,000
Less: Annual exemption	(11,700)
Taxable gain	480,300
ER CGT @ 10%	£48,030

If Mark does *not* make an election under *TCGA 1992, s 169R*, all the QCB gain is held over (without the benefit of ER).

Postponed QCB gain

		£
QCB consideration		2,000,000
Less: Base cost	£40,000 *less* £8,000	(32,000)
Postponed gain		1,968,000

The postponed gain is likely to become taxable on redemption at 20%, being £393,600 (ignoring the annual exemption).

2018/19 – Taxable QCB gain at ER CGT rate

If Mark makes an election under *TCGA 1992, s 169R* for the QCB consideration to be taxable in 2018/19, he can obtain a 10% ER CGT rate on the QCB gain.

	£
QCB consideration	2,000,000
Less: Base cost	(32,000)
Capital gain	1,968,000
ER CGT @ 10%	196,800

An election to benefit from ER would give Mark a substantial tax saving provided he can manage the acceleration of his tax liability.

Transitional ER for pre-6 April 2008 QCBs

8.18   Special rules apply to QCB loan notes that were acquired as consideration for a pre-5 April 2008 share sale. Taper relief ceases to be relevant where QCB gains are crystallised under the new CGT regime. However, the benefit of any indexation allowance that was built into the held-over gain is retained on a post-5 April 2008 redemption.

Special rules enable ER to be claimed against the QCB gain becoming chargeable on a post-5 April 2008 redemption (*FA 2008, Sch 3, para 7*). Clearly, the QCB holder must have unused ER available to offset against the crystallised gain. However, relief is only given provided the vendor would have been entitled to ER on the original pre-6 April 2008 share sale (on the assumption that the ER legislation had been in force at that time). ER relief will not always be available – for example, the vendor may have sold a very small (less than 5%) holding on the original sale.

For these purposes, the transitional ER claim must be made within 22 months following the tax year in which the held-over gain crystallises.

QCB loss problem

8.19   No capital loss relief is available as a QCB is not a chargeable asset for CGT (*TCGA 1992, s 115*). Furthermore, any capital gain deferred under *TCGA 1992, s 116(10)* can also be triggered if the purchasing company defaults on a QCB loan note which is cancelled or settled via a 'compromise arrangement'. In these dire circumstances, HMRC generally permit the worthless loan note to be 'gifted' to a charity without triggering the held-over gain. Having said that, vendors should always seek to obtain 'commercial bank' guarantees for their loan notes to avoid these types of nightmare scenarios!

Non-qualifying corporate bonds (non-QCBs)

8.20   Where the purchaser issues non-QCB loan notes, the terms of such loan notes will be designed so as to fall outside the criteria for a QCB. Thus, for example, a non-QCB loan note would be one which is convertible into the acquirer's shares or contains the right to subscribe for additional shares or securities. Where such notes are issued in exchange for shares they are deemed to be a security (and therefore do not necessarily have to be 'marketable', readily transferable and so on) (*TCGA 1992, s 251(6)*).

Non-QCB loan notes represent a security for CGT purposes and their receipt falls to be treated as a share reorganisation under *TCGA 1992, s 127* (by virtue of the share exchange rules in *TCGA 1992, s 135*) (see **8.11**). The appropriate part of the vendor's original base cost in the target company's shares is therefore treated as given for the non-QCB security at the original acquisition date(s). (Non-QCBs were often used under the taper relief regime to extend the vendor's taper relief period, but these taper relief issues ceased to be relevant after 5 April 2008.)

Since the CGT deferral in relation to the sale consideration satisfied by non-QCBs is governed by the CGT reorganisation rules in *TCGA 1992, s 127*, it is possible for ER to be claimed on the non-QCB consideration (assuming the relevant ER conditions are satisfied) by making a *TCGA 1992, s 169Q* election). By making this election, the value of the non-QCB consideration is brought into the vendor's CGT computation at the date of the sale (as explained in **8.12**). Before structuring any deal or deciding whether an election would be beneficial, the relevant factors in **8.13** should be considered.

Where the vendor is unable to obtain a commercial bank guarantee for the loan note, many feel that a non-QCB would be a more prudent alternative – this avoids the QCB-type risk of triggering a CGT charge on the cancellation of the loan note (eg where the acquiring company becomes insolvent) (see **8.19**).

EARN-OUT DEALS

Basic tax treatment of 'cash-based' earn-outs

8.21   Owner-managed companies are sometimes disposed of on an 'earn-out' basis with deferred consideration being provided, calculated on a formula basis relating to the post-sale profits, over (normally) the next two or three years. This will generally enable the vendor to enjoy extra consideration, calculated by reference to a formula based on the level of profits achieved by the target company in the two or three years following the sale. An earn-out also limits the purchaser's 'downside' risk as the vendor will receive little or nothing if the anticipated profits are not met.

Under the principles established in the case of *Marren v Ingles* [1980] STC 500, the expected net present value of the earn-out right falls to be included as part of the vendor's taxable consideration for the disposal of the shares. Thus, where the vendor's share sale gain qualifies for ER, the value of the earn-out right will effectively attract the relief (subject to the £10m threshold).

As and when the earn-out payments are received, further CGT charges will arise in respect of the earn-out *right* itself (representing capital sums derived from the right to receive the earn-out (under *TCGA 1992, s 22*) and *not* the disposal of shares). Thus, assuming the vendor had unused ER relief, this would not be available against the disposals of the earn-out right (since these do *not* constitute a disposal of shares). Capital gains on the earn-out payments (taxed under *TCGA 1992, s 22*), which are based on the earn-out payments received less the appropriate deductible base value of the right, will therefore attract CGT at either 10% or 20%.

One of the main potential problems arising from the '*Marren v Ingles*' treatment is the risk of being taxed on an unrealised gain, ie the vendor would suffer tax on the *value of the right* (when their shares are sold). Where the earn-out falls (well) below expectation, this could result in a capital loss arising on the disposal of the right in a subsequent tax year. In such cases, it is now possible to make an election under *TCGA 1992, s 279A* to carry the subsequent loss back to reduce the vendor's original capital gain.

Earn-outs satisfied in shares/loan notes under *TCGA 1992, s 138A*

8.22   An earn-out may also be structured so that it must be satisfied in the form of shares and/or loan notes in the acquiring company (when the relevant earn-out consideration is determined). This enables the 'deferral' mechanism in *TCGA 1992, s 138A* to apply (automatically without the need for an election) and thus avoids the 'upfront' tax charge based on the value of the right. Broadly speaking, provided the original share sale could meet the conditions for a *TCGA 1992, s 135* share exchange (but there does not necessarily have to be one), the vendor is *automatically* treated as (partly) exchanging their original shares for the deemed *TCGA 1992, s 138A* security.

This treatment was particularly beneficial under the (pre-6 April 2008) taper relief regime. Since the vendor was in effect 'rolling-over' into a non-QCB, their taper relief would continue to accrue (normally) at the business rate. This treatment generally enabled vendors to obtain full business taper on their earn-out payments (when they redeemed their actual loan notes). Thus, even where an earn-out was originally proposed to be settled in cash, vendors were advised to amend its terms so as to require the purchaser to satisfy the agreed earn-out amounts in the form of short-dated loan notes. Typically, the sale agreement would require the purchaser to issue these loan notes once the earn-out profits had been computed and the vendor's entitlement had been agreed. After a minimum six-month redemption period, the vendors would encash their loan notes and pay the relevant CGT on their earn-out 'gains' at an effective CGT rate of around 10%.

Treatment of *TCGA 1992, s 138A* earn-outs after 6 April 2008

8.23   When the earn-out is quantified, the acquiring company will issue the relevant loan note or shares for the agreed amount.

QCB loan notes

8.24   Where the earn-out consideration is satisfied in the form of a QCB loan note, this will be dealt with under the company security conversion/exchange rules in *TCGA 1992, s 132*. This treats the event as a CGT reorganisation and therefore brings the QCB rules in *TCGA 1992, s 116(10)* into play.

Broadly, the gain held over against the QCB would be the amount of the relevant earn-out consideration less the pro-rata base cost. (The pro-rata base cost is derived from the original cost of the shares that was carried into the deemed security when the vendor sold their original shares: see **8.2**.) The postponed gain would generally be taxed at the 10%/20% CGT rate when the QCB is finally encashed (HMRC require a minimum redemption period of six months from issue).

From 23 June 2010, if there is an exchange of shares for QCBs and no election is made to bring the gain immediately into charge, it is likely that when the gain subsequently comes into charge, it will not qualify for ER.

Shares/non-QCB loan notes

8.25   In some cases, the acquiring company satisfies the earn-out in the form of a fresh issue of its shares (or a non-QCB). The number of shares issued would generally depend on the earn-out consideration and the (agreed) prevailing market price/value of the acquirer's shares. In such cases, a combination of the *TCGA 1992, s 132* exchange and *TCGA 1992, s 127* CGT reorganisation rules will apply to treat the new shares/security as having been acquired at the same time (and pro-rata) base cost as the vendor's original shares. Any subsequent gain on sale/encashment would generally attract CGT at 10%/20%.

Exceptionally, there may be cases (assuming the vendor has unused ER relief available) where the subsequent disposal of the shares/non-QCB securities could attract ER. However, the vendor would generally need to have satisfied the relevant ER conditions from the time the shares/securities were issued as part of the earn-out. This is because (assuming they remain employed in the target company) it is only from this date that they would generally be able to satisfy the 5% ordinary shares/voting rights test: see **8.5**.

APPLICATION OF *ITA 2007, s 684* ANTI-AVOIDANCE RULES

8.26   As there is a significant difference between the rates of income and capital gains tax, HMRC may invoke the anti-avoidance provisions found in *ITA 2007*. The 'Transactions in Securities' (TiS) anti-avoidance rules (as they apply for income tax purposes) in *ITA 2007, s 684* can potentially apply to counter the tax advantage obtained by selling family or owner-managed (ie 'close') companies in such a way so as not to suffer income tax.

Whilst all owner-managed company sales can, potentially, be caught by the provisions of the TiS legislation, most should be exempted under the 'fundamental change of ownership' rules (see **8.27**). The intention of the revised TiS provisions is mainly aimed at cases where the seller benefits from receiving the (net of tax) ER proceeds, but maintains a significant interest in the business after the sale (eg by selling to a 'connected' company).

The Transactions in Securities legislation will now apply only where all the following conditions are met:

- the shareholder is a party to a Transaction in Securities;

- broadly, they must receive relevant (non-income taxable) consideration in connection with the distribution, transfer or realisation of assets of a close company;

- the shareholder does not fall under the 'fundamental change of ownership' exemption;

- the shareholder's main purpose of the Transaction in Securities is to obtain an income tax advantage and an income tax advantage is obtained.

Fundamental change of ownership

8.27 *FA 2010* substantially relaxed the application of *ITA 2007, s 684* by introducing a 'carve-out' exemption for sales to unconnected third parties, which applies from 24 March 2010. This represents a fundamental and significant shift in HMRC's approach. The new exemption provides greater clarity and certainty and carefully targets the application of the TiS rules to transactions which are *mainly* motivated towards obtaining a tax advantage.

The refocused TiS legislation should only catch those who enter into a relevant transaction with a tax-avoidance objective.

A key component of the revised TiS regime is 'the fundamental change in ownership' exclusion rule, since sales which meet the relevant conditions are completely exempt from the TiS legislation. The conditions are (*ITA 2007, s 686*):

- Before the transaction a person holds shares in a close company and Conditions A, B and C are met for at least two years after the change in ownership.

- Condition A – after the sale at least 75% of the ordinary shares are held by persons who are not connected with the vendor.

- Condition B – the shares above must carry at least a 75% entitlement to any distributions.

- Condition C – the shares must carry at least 75% of the voting rights.

Focus

The introduction of the fundamental change of ownership criteria is a welcome piece of legislation as it should provide greater certainty for genuine business sales as the legislation is intended to catch transactions with a tax-avoidance motive.

WINDING-UP THE FAMILY OR OWNER-MANAGED COMPANY

Background

8.28   If the asset sale route is taken, the shareholders of a family or owner-managed company may decide to wind it up voluntarily. In such cases, there will often be a surplus available for distribution to the shareholders after the interests of the creditors have been satisfied. It will be essential to ensure that the surplus funds are distributed in a tax-efficient manner (see **8.47–8.56**). Where a company is wound up voluntarily, there may be time to implement appropriate corporate tax planning measures to increase the amount ultimately available to the company's shareholders.

In some cases, the existing shareholder(s) may simply wish to 'disincorporate'. This would normally entail winding the company up and transferring its trade and assets to the shareholder(s). The shareholders would then continue to carry on the trade through a sole trader or partnership structure (see **Chapter 2**).

8.29   If the company is wound up by a receiver or creditor, then the shareholders are likely to lose most if not all of their capital stake. It will then be necessary to consider what tax relief can be claimed in respect of their shares and any irrecoverable shareholder loans (see **8.68–8.79**). If the company is insolvent, the actions of the receiver/liquidator will be dictated by commercial requirements but, where possible, these should be conducted in the most tax-efficient basis to enhance the amount available for both creditors and shareholders. However, there is no point in planning to reduce tax liabilities that are never going to be paid due to insufficiency of funds.

CONSEQUENCES FOR THE COMPANY

Pension provision

8.30   Before the company ceases trading the proprietors'/directors' pension provision should be considered. Unless full provision has been made, there will be a tax advantage in making 'top-up' payments to an approved scheme. Provided the pension contributions are *paid* in the final corporation tax accounting period (CTAP) (ie up to cessation of trade), a trading deduction can normally be claimed with no spreading of contributions. This will have the effect of reducing the funds remaining for distribution and hence the shareholder's exposure to tax. However, care needs to be taken where pension contributions exceed the annual allowance of £40,000 (in 2018/19 subject to any unused allowance from earlier years) as the director/proprietor is likely to be subject to an additional tax liability.

Where a company has not made any pension provision for its proprietors/ directors, it may be possible for it to enter into a Hancock annuity arrangement. The company would purchase an annuity from an insurance company before the trade ceases. Following the case of *Hancock v General Reversionary & Investment Co Ltd* (1918) 7 TC 358, the purchase of an annuity to fund a future pension was held to be deductible against profits – it was not a capital payment. The insurance company would then be responsible for paying the pension.

8.31   HMRC have confirmed that Hancock annuities can still be purchased post-A Day as long as they comply with the new pension rules. A specially purchased Hancock annuity for a retiring employee would normally be set up through a registered scheme in the same way as any other pension scheme, especially if a tax-free lump sum is to be provided. Tax relief for the employer contribution is subject to the 'wholly and exclusively' rule. (It is also possible for the company to purchase a Hancock annuity through a registered scheme.)

Under a Hancock-type arrangement, all benefits will have vested, so it does not have to satisfy the annual allowance rules. The lifetime allowance does apply.

Termination of CTAP and closure costs

8.32   The company's trade will usually have ceased before it is wound up and this will have a number of important tax consequences.

The cessation of the company's trade will bring about a termination of the company's current CTAP (*CTA 2009, s 10*). Generally, this will accelerate the date on which the company pays its tax liability. Companies which do not pay their tax in instalments must pay the corporation tax for the final CTAP within nine months following the end of that period. For other companies, the final instalment date is effectively brought forward, being due three months and 14 days after the end of the CTAP. Any unprovided expenses incurred after the cessation of trade (known as 'post-cessation' expenses) can only be offset against post-cessation receipts (see **8.38**), which reduces the prospect of obtaining relief (*CTA 2009, s 197*).

In drawing up the tax computation to cessation, particular care must therefore be taken to ensure that specific provisions are made for all known trade expenses that have been incurred up to the date of cessation. This will include provisions for warranty claims and bad and 'impaired' trading and loan relationship debts.

8.33   HMRC will disallow any expenses incurred in connection with the cessation of trade. However, following the Privy Council's decision in *IRC v Cosmotron Manufacturing Co Ltd* [1997] STC 1134, HMRC will normally allow relief for contractual redundancy or severance payments made on the cessation of trade. The rationale for allowing relief is that the payment is made under a pre-existing contractual or statutory obligation incurred as a consequence of the employees being employed for the purposes of the trade (*Tax Bulletin*, Issue 39).

Termination payments that do not qualify under the above principle, such as *ex gratia* payments, can be specifically relieved under the statutory trading deduction rules. Specific statutory relief is given for statutory redundancy payments and any additional redundancy payments (up to three times the amount of the statutory redundancy payments). Such payments are treated as paid on the date of cessation *if* they are paid after the trade ceases (*CTA 2009, ss 77(4), 79(2)*).

Sale of plant and industrial buildings

8.34 The cessation of trade will give rise to a deemed disposal of plant and machinery for capital allowance purposes, resulting in a balancing adjustment (*CAA 2001, s 61(2)*, Table, item 6). If the plant is sold either before or shortly after the trade ceases, the disposal value will generally be the net disposal proceeds (*CAA 2001, s 61(2)*, Table, item 1).

The sale of an industrial building no longer gives rise to any balancing adjustment. For a post-20 March 2007 disposal, the vendor avoids any recapture of industrial buildings allowances (IBAs) where the building is sold for an amount exceeding its tax residue. However, as part of the phasing out of IBAs, the purchaser could have claimed IBAs on the building (on the transitional basis) until the abolition of IBAs on 31 March 2011.

Capital gains on property sale

8.35 The sale of the company's chargeable assets may also produce capital gains, giving rise to a significant tax liability. Broadly, the disposal of a property etc is recognised for capital gains purposes when an unconditional contract for the sale is made (*TCGA 1992, s 28*). If the company has significant trading losses in the final CTAP, the company should enter into the sale contract for the property on or before it closes down the trade (although completion can take place afterwards). This would enable any gain on the property sale to be sheltered by the current trading losses (that might otherwise be forfeited on cessation).

Inevitably, there will be situations where it is not possible to sell the property until some time after the trade has ceased so that any gain cannot be offset by the trading losses generated in the final CTAP to cessation. Furthermore, the gain will be taxed at the full 19% corporation tax rate (for the year ended 31 March 2019). In these cases, it may be beneficial to crystallise the gain before the trade ceases by arranging for the property to be sold to the owner-manager and then possibly licensed back to the company. The sale of the property would attract SDLT. Where appropriate, it might be possible for the property to be distributed *in specie* to the owner-manager. This would be treated as a distribution (taxable at an effective rate of 32.5%/38.1% in the owner-manager's hands), but would be exempted from any SDLT charge. The company's disposal would be deemed to take place at market value.

Sale of trading stock

8.36 Where the company's trading stock and work in progress is sold to an *unconnected* UK trader, the actual sale proceeds will be credited in the trading account for tax purposes. In such cases, HMRC cannot impute a market value for tax purposes (*CTA 2009, s 165*).

Trading losses

8.37 The liquidator must consider how to make best use of any remaining tax-adjusted trading losses. Trading losses can only be carried forward for offset against profits of the same trade (*CTA 2010, s 45(4)*). Consequently, any unrelieved tax losses cannot normally be carried forward beyond the date of cessation except where they can be offset against post-cessation receipts.

The main reliefs which are likely to be relevant for (tax-adjusted) trading losses are as follows:

- The offset of trading losses for the final CTAP to cessation against the company's other profits (before charges on income) of that period (*CTA 2010, s 37(3)(a)*).

- The offset of any remaining trading losses by carrying it back against the total profits (after deducting trading charges on income) for the previous year (*CTA 2010, s 37(3)(b)*)).

- Tax-adjusted trading losses arising in the final 12 months before cessation of trade can be carried back against the company's total profits (*after* deducting trading charges on income) against the CTAPs falling within the *three* previous years on a LIFO basis (*CTA 2010, s 39(2)*). A company's CTAP terminates on cessation of trade – if an earlier CTAP straddles and ends in the final 12-month period, any trading loss for that CTAP is time apportioned and added to the terminal trading loss claim.

- Trade charges for the final 12-month period can be used to augment the terminal loss claim.

Trade charges for CTAPs partly straddling the final 12 months are apportioned. However, trade charges are now likely to arise only in rare cases. Patent royalties recognised for accounting purposes are now normally included within the trading loss calculation (under the *CTA 2009* intangible fixed assets regime).

Setting off trading losses against post-trading receipts

8.38 Income receipts arising after a company has ceased to trade are assessable as 'non-trading' post-cessation receipts (*CTA 2009, ss 188–190*). This would include the write-back of excessive provisions (upon which tax relief was originally claimed), the unanticipated recovery of a bad debt that had been provided against or written-off and the release of trading liabilities after the trade has ceased.

Post-cessation expenses can be deducted against post-cessation receipts. However, if the company had unused trading losses at the date of cessation, HMRC accept that they can (exceptionally) be carried forward and offset against post-cessation receipts (see HMRC Business Income Manual (at BIM80535) which indicates that 'any unrelieved losses and unused capital allowances of the discontinued business' can be deducted for the purposes of *CTA 2009, s 196*).

A company may make an election (*CTA 2009, s 198*) which enables post-cessation receipts, received within six years of cessation, to be carried back and treated as received *immediately prior* to the cessation. This enables such receipts to be offset, for example, by trading losses brought forward under *CTA 2010, s 45*. The election must be made within two years of the end of the accounting period in which the receipt is received.

Close investment holding company status

8.39 Where a close company ceases to carry on a trade or property investment business, it will usually be treated as a close investment holding company (CIHC) (*CTA 2010, s 34*). The company's post-cessation income and gains would be taxed at the main corporation tax rate of 19% (for the year ended 31 March 2019).

If the company is not a CIHC throughout the CTAP which ends on the commencement of its winding-up, it will not be treated as a CIHC for the next CTAP (*CTA 2010, s 34(5)*). However, where the company has ceased trading before it is wound up, this exemption is unlikely to apply. However, there is an HMRC concession whereby they might still allow the exemption.

Pre-liquidation tax liabilities

8.40 The liquidator will need to take account of pre-liquidation tax liabilities as either preferential or ordinary claims (*Insolvency Act 1986, ss 175, 386*). Broadly, preferential creditors have the right to repayment of their debts ahead of the *unsecured* creditors. Since 15 September 2003, preferential creditors have been confined to liabilities broadly representing unpaid employee remuneration, etc for the four months before the winding-up. Previously, certain 'government' debts were also counted as preferential debts which included unpaid PAYE and national insurance contributions, etc for the 12 months prior to the receiver's/liquidator's appointment and unpaid VAT arising within the previous six months. However, unpaid PAYE and NIC has ceased to be a preferred creditor.

8.41 Assessed taxes are not preferred debts, so any unpaid pre-liquidation corporation tax would rank as an unsecured creditor. Corporation tax arising during the liquidation is, however, normally treated as a liquidation expense (*Re Toshoku Finance UK Plc, Kahn (liquidators of Toshoku Finance UK Plc) v IRC* [2002] STC 368).

A practical approach will normally be required by the liquidator of the insolvent company when dealing with the company's tax affairs. He must inform HMRC of his appointment and determine the outstanding corporation tax position. Where the company is insolvent or has substantial brought-forward tax losses, HMRC may be prepared to agree a 'nil liability' position without the need to submit detailed tax computations (but a CT 600 must be submitted). However, if the liquidator wishes to agree an amount of trading losses for the purposes of a loss relief claim, HMRC will require detailed computations and accounts.

Post-liquidation tax liabilities

8.42 The commencement of a winding-up terminates the company's current CTAP and a new accounting period will begin. Each successive accounting period will last for 12 months, with the final accounting period ending on the date the winding-up is completed (*CTA 2009, s 12*). Similar rules now apply where a company goes into administration.

Corporation tax liabilities which arise during the course of the winding-up would be treated as an expense or disbursement of the liquidation (see *Re Beni-Felkai Mining Co Ltd* (1933) 18 TC 632). In most cases, the only taxable income received during the winding-up period is interest receivable on realised funds. However, interest received from HMRC, by companies in liquidation, on overpaid corporation tax is exempt from tax where the amount is less than £2,000 (*CTA 2010, s 633*).

As a necessary disbursement of the liquidation, the tax liabilities must (together with any overdue tax) be met in priority to the claims of all creditors and the liquidator's remuneration. However, where appropriate, the liquidator can apply to the court for an Order of Priority to be made to ensure that his remuneration and expenses can be dealt with equitably.

Legal formalities

Members' voluntary liquidation

8.43   The shareholders of a solvent company can proceed to wind up the company voluntarily. Generally, a special resolution of the shareholders is required to place the company in voluntary liquidation. Before this is done, the directors must make a statutory declaration of solvency. After having made a full inquiry, the directors must declare that the company will be able to pay its debts within 12 months following the commencement of the winding-up.

A member's voluntary liquidation must be dealt with by a licensed insolvency practitioner. Under a liquidation, a company can only be restored to the Register within a period of two years after the winding-up has been completed (although claims for death or serious injury can be made at any time). Such an order can be brought by a member or creditor or any other interested person. It therefore provides greater protection as regards dealing with creditors. The creditor who surfaces after the company has been liquidated has only two years to put the company back on the register and even then can only overturn distributions made if the liquidator did not take proper steps to contact creditors. Quite often, the costs of a formal voluntary liquidation may seem relatively high compared to the value of the company's assets.

Dissolution under *CA 2006, s 1000*

8.44   A solvent company may also be dissolved as a result of the company's name being struck off the register by the Registrar of Companies under *Companies Act 2006, s 1000*. This route is sometimes preferred to a liquidation. HMRC are prepared to treat a dissolution under *CA 2006, s 1000* as a 'winding-up' for tax purposes (see **8.47**).

8.45   Where the dissolution route is used, there is now less reason for concern where the share capital exceeds £4,000. This follows the Treasury Solicitor's withdrawal of its 'Guidelines about the Distribution of a Company's Share Capital', which stated that the Crown would be entitled to any funds which a company distributes to its members prior to an informal striking-off (unless the share capital was below £4,000). The main reason for the withdrawal of the Guidelines is that Companies Act 2006 makes it relatively easy to reduce capital below the £4,000 limit (see below).

8.46   A (private) limited company can reduce its share capital by a special resolution which is supported by a solvency statement. The amount by which the share capital is reduced is treated as a distributable reserve. Therefore, if the share capital exceeds £4,000, a company can reduce its share capital (below this amount) and distribute all assets before applying for dissolution.

In contrast to the 'two-year' period allowed for liquidations, a dissolved company can be restored by a court order within six years from the publication of the striking-off notice in the Gazette (*CA 2006, s 1024*). Any member or creditor who 'feels aggrieved' can apply to the court for such an order. It would therefore be possible for a creditor to come forward at any time during the six-year period to overturn a transfer of assets to the members.

DEALING WITH SURPLUS AVAILABLE TO SHAREHOLDERS

Capital distributions

8.47   Where a company has surplus funds (ie after its creditors have been paid), it is necessary to decide how these can be extracted for the shareholders' benefit in the most tax-efficient manner.

Distributions made in the course of dissolving or winding up the company are treated as 'capital distributions' (subject to distributions not exceeding £25,000) and are therefore chargeable to CGT (*TCGA 1992, s 122*). A distribution made to shareholders during the course of the winding-up does not count as an 'income' distribution for tax purposes and therefore no tax credit is available to the recipient shareholder (*CTA 2010, s 1030*).

For CGT purposes, a shareholder is treated as making a disposal of an interest in the relevant shares when he becomes entitled to receive the capital distribution from the company (*TCGA 1992, s 122(1)*). The commencement of the liquidation does not trigger any deemed disposal for the shareholder.

Capital distributions under an informal winding-up

8.48   Previously it was preferable for a solvent company to be struck off the Register of Companies under, what is now *CA 2006, s 1000*, as the costs of winding-up are much lower. However, since 1 March 2012 when ESC C16 was put on a statutory footing within *CTA 2010, ss 1030A and 1030B*, most owner-managers prefer the route of a formal liquidation in order to obtain the benefit of the capital gains tax treatment.

The informal winding-up route still works for businesses where the amount available for distribution does not exceed £25,000. Where it still applies, HMRC will treat a distribution made prior to a dissolution as having been made under a formal winding-up, and therefore as a capital payment. Certain assurances must be given to the Inspector beforehand. Normally, the Inspector will require that any remaining tax liabilities are paid and also confirm that, once the assets have been distributed, the company will request the Registrar of Companies to strike the company off the register.

Focus

This route no longer provides the favourable capital treatment where the reserves of a company exceed £25,000. In such cases, especially where the company is a husband and wife company, it is possible to formally liquidate the company for relatively little cost.

CGT on capital distributions

8.49   In many cases, capital distributions may be entitled to entrepreneurs' relief (ER) (see **8.50**). Such capital distributions do not carry any indexation allowance or taper relief entitlement as the legislation for both reliefs has been repealed. ER enables the gain arising on the capital distribution to be taxed at a rate of 10%, up to the maximum 'lifetime' limit of £10m or, if lower, the shareholder's unused ER.

From 23 June 2010, any gain qualifying for ER is taxed at 10%. Other gains are taxable, from 6 April 2016, at either 10% or 20%. This is dependent on whether an individual's income and gains exceed the upper limit of the basic rate income tax band. Any gain (not qualifying for ER) is taxable at 10% if it falls within the basic rate band (£31,500 for 2017/18). If the gain, or part of a gain, falls above that limit it will be taxable at 20%.

Entrepreneurs' relief on post-5 April 2008 capital distributions

Qualifying conditions for entrepreneurs' relief

8.50   Capital distributions made during a winding-up (or distributions treated as capital under *CTA 2010, ss 1030A and 1030B*) are eligible for ER, since they are treated as a disposal of an interest in shares under *TCGA 1992,* *s 122 (TCGA 1992, s 169I(2)(c))*. ER is given in such cases provided the conditions in *TCGA 1992, s 169I(7)* are satisfied:

(1) The company must be a trading company (or holding company of a trading group) in the *one year* before it *ceases* to trade (or ceases its 'holding company of a trading group' status).

(2) Throughout the *one year* before the company ceases to trade (or be a qualifying holding company), the recipient shareholder is required to have:

  – held at least 5% of the ordinary share capital (carrying at least 5% of the voting rights) in the one year;

  – served as a director or employee of the company (or fellow group company).

(3) The relevant capital distribution must be made within *three years* after the date the trade ceases (or the company ceases to be a qualifying holding company). HMRC have no discretion to extend this 'three-year' period.

Planning considerations

8.51 These special ER rules are based around the date the company ceases to trade (or loses its qualifying 'holding company' status without becoming a trading company).

Particular care must be taken to ensure that the company is in a position to pay a capital distribution within the three years after it has ceased to trade. The liquidator must therefore endeavour to realise the company's assets within this time frame.

Example 8.6 – Calculation of taxable gain on capital distribution

White Ltd ceased trading on 30 May 2018 after selling its trade and assets. The company was then immediately wound up with a capital distribution of £25,000 being paid on completion of the winding-up on 6 December 2018.

Mr Jones incorporated White Ltd with 1,000 £1 ordinary shares and his shareholding was worth £2,000 at 31 March 1982.

Mr Jones's capital gain on the capital distribution would be calculated as follows:

	£
Capital distribution	25,000
Less: March 1982 value	(2,000)

	£
Chargeable gain	23,000
Less: Annual exemption	(11,700)
Taxable gain	11,300
CGT at 10%	1,130

* Mr Jones has been a director of White Ltd since its incorporation holding 100% of the shares and voting rights in the company. He therefore qualifies and claims ER on the capital distribution (which is made within three years of the company's ceasing to trade).

Taper relief on pre-6 April 2008 capital distributions

8.52   Under the pre-6 April 2008 taper relief rules, the shares in a company were deemed to have become 'non business assets' from the date it ceased to trade. The gains on such distributions would therefore usually have been subject to time apportionment for business/non business taper relief periods. With ER there are no such restrictions.

Multiple capital distributions

8.53   If a shareholder receives more than one capital distribution, all but the last one will be treated as a part disposal in respect of the shares. The normal

$$\frac{A}{A + B}$$

part disposal formula in *TCGA 1992, s 42* will be used to apportion the base cost of the shares where:

A = the amount of the interim capital distribution;

B = the residual share value at the date of the interim distribution.

In practice, a relatively relaxed approach is taken with regard to agreeing interim valuations of shares (for the purpose of calculating 'B') where the liquidation is expected to be completed within two years of the first distribution (SP/D3). For example, if all the distributions are made before the CGT is calculated, HMRC will normally agree that the residual share value at the date of any interim distribution equals the total amount of subsequent distributions, without any discount for the delay in the receipt of the subsequent payments.

8.54   Depending on the amounts involved it may be beneficial to phase the timing of the capital distributions over as many tax years as possible. This will enable the shareholders to benefit from more than one annual exemption. Although all parties may be anxious to conclude the liquidation as quickly as possible, by timing the liquidation shortly before the start of the tax year, it may be possible to pay capital distributions over three separate tax years (but paid over a period of only (say) 18 months). Where there are a number of shareholders, the benefits from using multiple annual exemptions may be considerable.

Example 8.7 – Tax treatment of multiple capital distributions

Black Ltd went into (a Members' Voluntary) liquidation on 10 March 2018, having ceased trading on 6 February 2018. After the trade ceased, the company leased out its trading premises on a short lease until the property was sold during the liquidation. Entrepreneurs' relief is available on the capital distributions.

Mr Root formed the company in September 1990, subscribing for all the 2,000 ordinary £1 shares at par.

The liquidator made the following distributions to Mr Root from the residual profits and initial capital:

	£
6 July 2018	15,000
31 March 2019 (final)	4,000
CGT at 10%	£530 (see below)

ER is available and claimed by Mr Root on the capital distributions which are made within three years of the company ceasing to trade.

Mr Root's CGT computations would be as follows:

2018/19:	£	£
6 July 2018		
Capital distribution	15,000	
Less: Part disposal cost		
£2,000 × £15,000/(£15,000 + £4,000)	(1,579)	
Chargeable gain		13,421

2018/19:	£	£
31 March 2019		
Final capital distribution	4,000	
Less: Cost: £2,000 *less* £1,579 used in July 2018	(421)	
Chargeable gain		3,579
Total chargeable gains		17,000
Less: Annual exemption		(11,700)
Taxable gain		5,300

Small capital distributions

8.55   'Small' interim distributions are deducted against the shareholder's base cost, effectively postponing any gain (*TCGA 1992, s 122(2)*). For these purposes, a distribution not exceeding £3,000 is always taken as small. In all other cases, the distribution is accepted as 'small' provided it does not exceed 5% of the value of the relevant shareholding at the relevant date. However, HMRC do not insist on deducting the small proceeds against the cost where it is beneficial for the shareholder to crystallise a capital gain, for example, if it can be covered by an otherwise unused annual CGT exemption (*Tax Bulletin*, Issue 27).

Where the capital distribution exceeds the allowable CGT base cost, the 'small proceeds' rule does not apply. Instead, the shareholder can elect to offset the capital distribution against his base cost (*TCGA 1992, s 122(4)*). Once the base cost has been fully used, the balance of proceeds and any subsequent distributions will be fully chargeable to CGT.

Distributions in specie

8.56   If a liquidator distributes assets to the shareholders in lieu of their entitlement to a cash distribution, this will still constitute a capital distribution for tax purposes (*TCGA 1992, s 122(5)*). *In specie* capital distributions can rank for ER in the usual way.

Capital distributions of assets are always treated as a transaction at market value because the shareholders are connected with the company (*TCGA 1992, s 17(1)(a)*).

In contrast to a capital distribution for cash, a distribution *in specie* involves two disposals – one by the company in respect of the asset disposed of (which should be exempt from stamp duty or stamp duty land tax (as appropriate)) and one by the shareholder in respect of his shares. As there is no tax credit available on a capital distribution, this gives rise to an acute form of the 'double charge' effect.

PRE-LIQUIDATION/DISSOLUTION DIVIDEND VERSUS CAPITAL DISTRIBUTION

Benefits of CGT treatment

8.57   Most capital distributions made by owner-managed companies should be eligible for ER although care is needed to ensure that the relevant conditions are satisfied in the 12 months before the trade ceases (see **8.49**). There is an added advantage in that payments paid out up to three years after the cessation of trade will still qualify for ER. Provided the individuals have not used any of their ER, they will pay a CGT rate of 10% on gains (of up to £10m on disposals). On substantial gains (over £10m), their averaged CGT rate will exceed 10% (due to gains over £10m attracting tax at 20%).

Certain groups of shareholders will *not* benefit from ER (such as small minority shareholders holding less than 5% of the voting equity, and 'non-working' passive shareholders) and will therefore pay CGT at either 10% or 20% on their capital distributions (subject to any annual exemption).

In contrast, pre-liquidation dividends received by a higher rate taxpayer would be subject to income tax at the rate of 32.5%/38.1% on the amount received. In such cases, it will always be preferable to wait until the company is wound up before extracting its retained profits as a capital distribution (which is taxed at a lower rate). Similarly, where a company with assets in excess of £25,000 is being liquidated (see **8.43**), the liquidation should be carried out under a members' voluntary liquidation to obtain 'capital' treatment.

Dividends taxed at basic rate

8.58   There may be some cases where it would be advantageous to extract the company's reserves as a (pre-liquidation) income distribution. For example, if the amounts to be distributed (perhaps over several years) could be paid within the shareholders' 'basic rate' income tax bands the dividends would be taxed at 7.5% assuming the dividend allowance is utilised. Such planning must be considered and implemented before the company is wound up, since *income* dividends can only be paid before the company is placed into liquidation.

LIQUIDATION AND *ITA 2007, s 684* ISSUES

Phoenix company arrangements

8.59   The availability of an effective 10% CGT rate under ER may tempt some owner-managers to retain profits in their companies with a view to subsequently liquidating them and extracting the reserves as a capital payment. It would be feasible to extract fairly significant sums in this way.

8.60   The business could subsequently be carried on under identical or similar ownership via a new company – often called a 'phoenix company'. There may of course be tax charges and stamp duty land tax arising on the transfer of the assets to the new company.

HMRC felt they needed more legal teeth to catch this kind of arrangement so the *Finance Act 2016* intends to amend the Transactions in Securities legislation so that distributions on a winding-up which would otherwise be treated as capital will be caught by the TiS provisions.

A new Targeted Anti Avoidance Rule (TAAR) will apply to distributions in respect of share capital in a winding up where the following conditions are met:

- an individual holds at least 5% of the company;

- upon receiving a distribution he continues to be involved, directly or indirectly, with the carrying on of a similar trade; and

- the main purpose of the winding up is to obtain a tax advantage,

ITA 2007, s 684 and the *Joiner* case

8.61   Previously, it was firmly established that *ITA 2007, s 684* could apply where a company (with retained profits) is liquidated with its business being sold to another company under the same or substantially similar ownership. This is broadly what happened in *IRC v Joiner* [1975] STC 601. However, in that case, the House of Lords held that the arrangement was only caught by the 'transactions in securities' legislation because an agreement which varied the shareholders' rights to a capital distribution on a winding-up constituted a 'transaction in securities'.

8.62   The *Joiner* case also concluded that simply putting a company into liquidation was not sufficient (by itself) to be a transaction in securities. HMRC subsequently issued a statement that *ITA 2007, s 684* would *not* be applied to an 'ordinary liquidation'. This effectively means a genuine winding-up of a company, whether it comes to an end or its business is taken over by another entity that is under substantially different control, is unlikely to be vulnerable to a challenge.

On the other hand, HMRC are likely to challenge the transfer of a business to another 'commonly controlled' company in the course of a winding-up. A similar stance may be taken where the shareholder(s) seek(s) to 'disincorporate' their company to enable them to continue to carry on the trade as a sole trade or partnership.

In contrast, HMRC are likely to accept cases where the businesses are being transferred as part of a genuine reconstruction operation within *TCGA 1992, ss 136* and *139* using *Insolvency Act 1986, s 110*.

ENTREPRENEURS' RELIEF ON ASSOCIATED DISPOSALS OF PERSONALLY HELD PROPERTY

Conditions for associated disposal relief

8.63   Some owner-managers prefer to hold the company's trading premises personally (away from the clutches of the company's creditors). In such cases, it is likely that the owner-manager may wish to sell the property to a third party at the same time or shortly after the company has ceased trading.

There are special rules which extend the availability of ER to mitigate the gain arising on such disposals (known as 'associated disposals') where the shareholder makes a qualifying disposal for ER (*TCGA 1992, s 169K(1), (2)*). In the context of a disposal arising on a capital distribution, the vendor shareholder must meet the conditions summarised in **8.50**.

Furthermore, to obtain ER under the 'associated disposal' rules, two additional conditions must be satisfied:

● The associated disposal must be made as part of the 'withdrawal from participation' in the company. In HMRC's view, this is taken to mean the individual reducing their shareholding in the company (rather than scaling down the amount of work they do for the company). Since a capital distribution creates a disposal of an interest in the relevant company's shares, this test should normally be met (*TCGA 1992, s 169K(3)*). Broadly, HMRC would expect the associated disposal to be triggered by the liquidation/dissolution of the company (giving rise to the shareholder's exit).

● The property (or other personally owned asset) disposed of must have been used in the company's trade throughout the one year before it ceased trading (*TCGA 1992, s 169K(4)*). It is therefore important to ensure that the property etc is used in the trade right up to the cessation of that trade.

Restrictions on gain qualifying for associated disposal entrepreneurs' relief

8.64   As a general rule, associated disposal relief only comes into play if the shareholder has unused ER remaining after calculating their taxable gains on the capital distributions. Associated disposal relief is relatively restrictive and the gain on the associated disposal qualifying for relief may be restricted under *TCGA 1992, s 169P*. The main areas in which relief may be restricted and the basis on which this is done (on a *'just and reasonable'* basis) is summarised below:

Circumstances	TCGA 1992 reference	Restriction to relief
Property only used for the purposes of the company's business for only part of the period of ownership.	s 169P(4)(a)	Relief restricted to period of business use only.
Only part of the property is used for the purposes of the company's business.	s 169P(4)(b)	Relief is given on a pro rata basis for the time that it was used for business purposes.
Company pays rent to shareholder for using the asset.	s 169P(4)(d)	No relief is available if a full market rent was received. Partial relief is available where the rent received was less than the full market rent.
		For these purposes, no account is taken of rent received relating to a pre-6 April 2008 period (*FA 2008, Sch 3, para 6*)

Any restriction of the gain qualifying for associated disposal relief is made on a 'just and reasonable basis' by reference to the full ownership period of the relevant asset (subject to the special 'transitional' rule noted above which prevents any pre-6 April rent receipts restricting relief). However, where the shareholder continues to charge a full commercial rent to the company for its use of 'their' asset after 5 April 2008, HMRC will deny relief for the period the asset is held after 5 April 2008 (since it will be regarded as an investment asset as opposed to a trading one).

The restriction in respect of rental income is likely to cause particular difficulties to individuals who borrowed to acquire a commercial property and let it to their company. They will generally wish to charge a rent to the company to fund their personal loan interest payments.

RELIEF FOR SHAREHOLDERS OF INSOLVENT COMPANIES

Negligible value claim

8.65   Where the shares are worthless, a shareholder can make a 'negligible value' claim. There is no specified form for making the claim, but it should clearly identify the shareholding which is claimed as becoming of negligible value, the date on which the capital loss is deemed to arise (see below), and the claim is being made under *TCGA 1992, s 24(2)*.

HMRC should accept a 'negligible value' claim where the shares are 'worth next to nothing' (see Capital Gains Manual at CG13124). This will enable the shareholder to be treated as disposing of their holding for no or virtually no consideration. Where a capital loss is deemed to arise before 6 April 2008, any available indexation cannot be used to increase or create a capital loss.

The deemed disposal does not take place until the claim is made (*TCGA 1992, s 24(2)(a)*). However, *TCGA 1992, s 24(2)(b)* permits a negligible value 'capital loss' claim to be backdated to an earlier date specified in the claim, which must be within two years before the start of the tax year in which the claim is made. Importantly, a 'backdated' claim can only be made if the shares were (held by the claimant and) also worthless at that earlier date.

8.66   Sometimes, negligible value claims are negated because HMRC successfully show that the shareholder's base cost is substantially less than the amount paid for the shares. This is often the case where the shares have been subscribed for shortly before the date of the negligible value claim and are deemed to have been acquired at a (low) market value either by way of the 'non arm's length bargain rule' in *TCGA 1992, s 17(2)*, or on a share reorganisation within *TCGA 1992, s 128(2)*.

It is perhaps worth noting that the Inspector has the discretion to accept certain types of negligible value where the claim is free from any doubt or difficulty (such as the need to agree share valuations). These are for capital losses of under £100,000 on shares in UK unquoted companies which, at the date of the claim or any earlier specified date:

- were in an insolvent liquidation; or

- had ceased trading with no assets.

8.67   If a shareholder does not make a negligible value claim, their capital loss will then be deemed to arise when the company is finally dissolved. In practice, this would be when the liquidation is completed or when the company is finally dissolved – a disposal arises for CGT purposes when the shares are finally extinguished (*TCGA 1992, s 24(1)*).

Example 8.8 – Backdated negligible value claim

Mr Khan's company, Craven Cottage Ltd, went into liquidation in July 2017. The liquidation was completed in July 2018 without Mr Khan receiving any distributions from the liquidator.

Mr Khan formed the company in June 1988 subscribing for 10,000 £1 ordinary shares.

A negligible value claim is made in January 2019, which backdated the deemed disposal of his shares to March 2018 (ie 2017/18).

The calculation of the allowable loss arising in 2017/18 is as follows:

	£
Capital distribution	–
Less: Cost	(10,000)
Allowable loss	(10,000)

Income tax relief for capital losses on shares

Application of *ITA 2007, s 131* relief to companies in liquidation

8.68   In certain circumstances, shareholders may be able to make a claim to offset the capital loss arising on their shares against their other *taxable* income (under the share loss relief provisions in *ITA 2007, s 131*.

For shares issued after 5 April 1998, *ITA 2007, s 131* relief is only available if the company is a qualifying company for EIS purposes. Income tax relief is particularly valuable, as capital losses cannot be relieved unless and until the shareholder makes a capital gain.

In relation to liquidations, income tax relief can be claimed in respect of a capital loss arising on:

● a capital distribution during a winding-up;

- the cancellation (extinction) of the shares under *TCGA 1992, s 24(1)*; or

- a negligible value claim under *TCGA 1992, s 24(2) (ITA 2007, s 131(3))*.

8.69 In many cases, it may be beneficial to establish that a deemed capital loss has arisen by making a negligible value claim. This treats the shares as having been disposed and immediately reacquired at their negligible value. As far as timing is concerned, the deemed capital loss can be specified to arise at the date of the claim or at any time within the two years before the start of the tax year in which the claim was made (provided the shares were also 'negligible' at that time). Where *ITA 2007, s 131* is claimed for a deemed 'negligible value' loss, a clear claim must also be made under *TCGA 1992, s 24(2)*. This was confirmed by the Special Commissioner's decision in *Marks v McNally* (2004) SSCD 503, where a share loss relief claim was denied because of the failure to show unambiguously that the capital loss was being claimed under *TCGA 1992, s 24(2)*.

8.70 Strictly, *ITA 2007, s 131* relief cannot be claimed for a capital loss arising on the dissolution of the company. However, by concession, the relief can be claimed where:

(a) the company has no assets and is dissolved; *and*

(b) the shareholder has not received a capital distribution in the course of the dissolution or winding-up of the company *or* where an anticipated final distribution has not been made; *and*

(c) a negligible value claim has not been made under *TCGA 1992, s 24(2)*.

If reliance cannot be placed on the concession to obtain relief on a dissolution, then a negligible value claim must be made while the shares still exist.

'Subscriber share' requirement

8.71 Shareholders can only obtain share loss relief (against their taxable income) if they originally *subscribed* for the shares. Therefore, relief cannot be claimed for shares acquired 'second-hand'.

Special identification rules deal with cases where the claimant shareholder has a 'mixed' shareholding (ie has 'subscriber' shares qualifying for *ITA 2007, s 131* relief and other shares acquired by purchase, gift, etc). However, these are unlikely to be necessary on a liquidation since all the shares would generally be treated as disposed of at the same time.

Where the shareholding is made up of BES shares, EIS 'income tax' relief shares and EIS 'CGT deferral' shares, these 'subscription' shares are broadly identified on a FIFO basis.

Operation of *ITA 2007, s 131* relief

8.72   *ITA 2007, s 131* relief for disposals (or deemed 'negligible value' disposals) is claimed against the shareholder's income for the tax year of the disposal *and/or* the previous tax year. Where a claim is made for both years, the claim must specify the year against which the *ITA 2007, s 131* deduction is to be claimed first. Otherwise, the claim must specify the relevant year being claimed (*ITA 2007, s 132*). Under self-assessment, any carry-back claim is treated as a claim for the later year. The relief is calculated as the reduction in the previous year's tax liability as a result of the claim. The consequent reduction in the previous year's tax liability is treated as an additional 'payment on account' of the later year (*TMA 1970, Sch 1B, para 2*).

The claim must be made within 12 months after the 31 January following the tax year in which the loss is incurred (*ITA 2007, s 132(4)*).

RELIEF FOR SHAREHOLDER LOANS

Capital loss relief for irrecoverable loans

Outline of *TCGA 1992, s 253* relief

8.73   Generally, a simple debt is outside the scope of CGT and therefore if it becomes irrecoverable, relief would not be available for the creditor's loss. However, an individual shareholder (or indeed any other individual lender) can make a claim under *TCGA 1992, s 253* to obtain a capital loss equal to the *principal* element of their irrecoverable loan (which can include credit balances on current accounts). Corporate lenders generally obtain relief under the loan relationship regime unless they are 'connected' with the borrowing company.

The claimant will receive a capital loss equal to the amount that the Inspector has agreed is irrecoverable. The capital loss *cannot* be offset against income under *ITA 2007, s 131* (as it does not relate to shares).

The capital loss on an irrecoverable loan arises when the claim is made. However, it is also possible to establish the loss at an earlier time, being within the two previous tax years before the start of the tax year in which the claim is made, provided the loan was also irrecoverable at that earlier date (*TCGA 1992, s 253(3), (3A)*).

Conditions for *TCGA 1992, s 253* relief

8.74   To make a competent claim under *TCGA 1992, s 253*, a number of conditions must be satisfied, the most important of which are:

(a)   The loan must be irrecoverable and the claimant must not have assigned their right of recovery.

(b)   The amount lent must have been used wholly for the purposes of a trade (which can include capital expenditure and trade setting-up costs) carried on by a UK-resident company. This trade application test is also satisfied where the borrowing company has lent the monies to another 'fellow' group company for use in its trade. The fellow group company must be in a 75% group relationship – the wider 'group' definition (which includes non-resident companies) applies for loans made after 31 March 2000. Since 6 April 2003, that group company must be a 'trading company'. (Relief is also available where the borrowed amount is used to repay a loan that would have qualified.)

The relief is not therefore available for loans to investment companies or to purchase 'investment' assets.

(c)   The loan must not constitute a 'debt on security' (broadly, a debt on security represents a loan held as an investment which is both marketable and produces a return or profit to the holder) (*TCGA 1992, s 253(1), (3)*).

8.75   In judging whether a loan has become 'irrecoverable' at the date of the claim (or earlier date), HMRC are likely to examine the prospects of its recovery based on relevant balance sheets and other information. The Inspector would seek to determine whether there is a reasonable likelihood of the loan (or part of it) being repaid, having regard to the borrowing company's current and probable future financial position. In practice, where the borrower is insolvent and has ceased trading and it is clear that the loan (or part of it) would not be repaid, a *TCGA 1992, s 253* claim would usually be accepted for the relevant amount. On the other hand, relief may be denied where the borrowing company is still trading (albeit making losses). Similarly, if the borrower was in a parlous state when the loan was made, the Inspector may refuse the claim on the grounds that the loan had not *become irrecoverable* as required by *TCGA 1992, s 253(3)(a)*.

8.76   In *Crosby (Trustees) v Broadhurst* [2004] STC SSCD 348, the Special Commissioners agreed that relief was available on an irrecoverable loan that had (as part of the terms of the borrowing company's sale) been waived before the formal claim was submitted to the Inspector. They did not accept the Inspector's view that the loan had to be in existence at the time the claim was made.

Any subsequent recovery of part or all of the debt will be treated as a chargeable gain arising at the date of repayment. Capital loss relief cannot normally be claimed on intra-group loans under *TCGA 1992, s 253*.

Guarantee payments

8.77   Where an *individual* shareholder has provided a personal guarantee which is called in by the lender, they will be able to claim capital loss relief on any payment made under the guarantee. Claims for guarantee payments made by an individual must be made within four years of the end of the year of assessment in which the payment is made.

Capital loss relief may also be available where a group company makes a payment under a guarantee in relation to a borrowing by a fellow group company. The claim must be made within four years of the accounting period end in which the payment is made. The group guarantor company would become entitled to the rights of the original lender and can therefore claim capital loss relief if it is prevented from claiming a deduction under the loan relationship legislation (*TCGA 1992, s 253(3), (4)(c)*).

Example 8.9 – Capital loss relief for irrecoverable loan

Wright Ltd has traded profitably for a number of years. However, the company has experienced a downturn in trading during the last three years. In May 2007, Mr Billy, the controlling shareholder, had to make a cash injection of £80,000 to the company to ease its ailing finances. However, in December 2018, the company's bankers called in the receiver and the company was subsequently wound up. No part of Mr Billy's loan account was repaid.

Mr Billy can therefore claim under *TCGA 1992, s 253* for the £80,000 to be treated as an allowable loss for CGT purposes.

If Mr Billy realises a capital gain of, say, £50,000 in 2018/19, he should be able to relieve it with his capital loss on the loan, provided he makes the claim by 5 April 2023. To do this, Mr Billy must be able to satisfy the Inspector that the full amount of the loan (or substantially all of it) was irrecoverable by 5 April 2019.

CONVERTING LOANS INTO NEW SHARES

8.78 Given the potential advantages of income tax relief by making a claim under *ITA 2007, s 131* shareholders may be tempted to 'capitalise' their loans by subscribing for further shares. However, if the company is *insolvent*, the amount subscribed for the new shares is unlikely to be reflected as part of the shareholder's CGT base cost. This is because *TCGA 1992, s 17(1)* deems the shares to be acquired at their (negligible) market value (where the amount subscribed is greater than market value).

Alternatively, the capitalisation of the loan for new shares may constitute a 'reorganisation' for CGT purposes. This would be the case where, for example, all shareholders subscribe for additional shares in proportion to their existing holdings. On a 'reorganisation', *TCGA 1992, s 128(2)* effectively provides that the amount subscribed will only be reflected in base cost to the extent that the relevant shareholding increases in value, which in such cases is unlikely.

Given the above difficulties in securing a CGT base cost, it will normally be disadvantageous to substitute share capital for shareholder loans (where the company has a deficiency of net assets). The shareholder should be able to claim capital loss relief for his irrecoverable loan under *TCGA 1992, s 253*, whereas if it is 'converted' into shares there is unlikely to be any relief.

Losses incurred on qualifying corporate bonds (QCBs)

8.79 In some cases, the shareholder may hold a loan note evidencing the debt. This will invariably constitute a qualifying corporate bond (QCB) and represent a 'debt on security'. However, provided the loan was made *before 17 March 1998*, an allowable capital loss can still be claimed for the irrecoverable part of the debt under the provisions of *TCGA 1992, s 254* for CGT loss relief.

However, to qualify the QCB must comply with the 'qualifying loan' rules and the funds concerned must have been lent wholly for the purposes of a trade carried on by the borrower. It follows that if the holder received the QCB as consideration for the acquisition of shares relief will not be available (*TCGA 1992, ss 253, 254*).

No CGT loss relief is available for QCB loans made after 16 March 1998.

Loans made by companies

8.80 Capital loss relief under *TCGA 1992, s 253* is not available where the lender is able to claim a deduction under the loan relationship rules

(TCGA 1992, s 253(3)). In many cases, a corporate lender should be able to claim a 'non-trading' loan relationship deduction for an impairment loss on a 'non-trading' loan (ie where the loan is effectively written off or provided against as an irrecoverable bad debt). A trading deduction would only be available where the loan was made in the course of a trade.

However, if the borrower is a *connected person*, such as a fellow group member or a 'parallel' company under common control, then it is not generally possible to claim a tax allowable impairment loss *(CTA 2009, s 354)*. In this context, *CTA 2009, s 355* provides a mechanism for a lender to obtain relief *only* on amounts which become subject to an impairment 'write-off' after it ceases to be 'connected' with the borrowing company. This means that amounts remaining outstanding when the borrower goes into liquidation cannot be relieved. It should be noted that GAAP usually requires impairment of debts that are not expected to be recovered. Hence the lender is likely already to have impaired most, if not all, of the loan balance prior to the commencement of liquidation, etc. Relief will only be available on such amounts that remain 'unimpaired'.

8.81   The legislation in *CTA 2009, s 355* works by preventing any tax deduction being taken for impairment losses that were denied relief whilst the companies were 'connected'. It is helpful to understand why the 'connection' test in *CTA 2009, s 466* would be broken where the 'connected party' debtor goes into insolvent liquidation or administration. In broad terms, *CTA 2009, s 472* provides that a person has control of a company for this purpose if they are able to conduct the company's affairs in accordance with their wishes through holding the requisite shares, voting power or powers conferred by the Articles of Association or any other documents (such as a shareholders' agreement). Where the borrowing company goes into liquidation or administration, this 'control' nexus would be broken since the liquidator/administrator would take over the management of the company's affairs. A parent company would therefore lose its ability to control the affairs of its subsidiary (eg by appointing and removing directors) and hence would no longer 'control' the company within *CTA 2009, s 472*.

Exceptionally, where the lending company is able to deduct an impairment loss for amounts becoming impaired post-liquidation, it will be allowed as a non-trading (or trading) deduction by virtue of *CTA 2009, s 355*.

Chapter 9

Tax planning for the non-resident and non-domiciled

Robert Maas FCA, FTII, FIIT, TEP, Consultant, CBW Tax Ltd

SIGNPOSTS

- **Concepts** – From 2013/14 onwards there is a statutory definition of residence. For earlier years the concept was not defined.

- **Planning to emigrate** – There are various ways that a person can cease to be UK resident. However, the absence of a statutory definition of residence prior to 2013/14 made it uncertain whether a person had achieved this (see **9.7–9.29**).

- **The concept of domicile** – A person's tax position can be affected by his domicile. This again is not defined. However, it is a concept of general law, not a tax concept, so there is a lot of judicial guidance on its meaning (see **9.30–9.32**).

- **The tax significance of the two concepts** – Why do these concepts matter? What taxes depend on each concept? (see **9.33–9.35**).

- **The remittance basis** – A person who is resident but not domiciled in the UK can claim to be taxed on overseas income and gains only to the extent that they have been brought into the UK. Where a person has been resident in the UK for over seven years a fee of £30,000 to £90,000 has to be paid to HMRC if it is wished to use the remittance basis. This fee is in addition to the tax on remittances. The legislation contains some detailed rules to treat money as being remitted if it is economically used here (see **9.36–9.55**). The rules altered significantly from 6 April 2017. The remittance basis no longer applies to a person who was born in the UK with a UK domicile of origin and ceases to apply to others once they have been UK resident for 15 years.

- **Employment income** – Special rules apply to employment income (see **9.46–9.54**).

- **Taxation of non-UK residents** – Non-residents are not normally taxed in the UK on investment income other than property income.

They are, however, taxed on employment income, trading income and property income where the employment or trade is exercised in the UK (including partly in the UK) or the property is here. Non-residents are not normally taxed on UK capital gains. From 2014/15 (in some cases from 2013/14) this exclusion does not apply to UK residential property. Inheritance tax depends primarily on domicile. A non-resident who is domiciled in the UK or has assets in the UK is within the scope of inheritance tax (see **9.57–9.89**). From 6 April 2017, shares in, and certain loans to, overseas companies that own UK residential property are also brought into inheritance tax.

- **Company residence** – A company is normally resident where its central control and management takes place. The courts have laid down principles to determine how to identify this place. A UK-incorporated company is normally UK resident, even if it is controlled and managed from elsewhere. A non-UK resident company does not wholly escape UK tax; it is taxable here if it carries on a trade in the UK or has property income here (see **9.90–9.103**).

INTRODUCTION

9.1   Chargeability to UK tax depends on two concepts:

- residence; and

- domicile.

Up to 5 April 2013, there was a third, ordinary residence, but this concept was abolished by the *Finance Act 2013* (*FA 2013*) as part of the introduction of a statutory residence test (or in reality a number of such tests). Prior to 2013/14 residence and ordinary residence were concepts of general law that were left to be formulated for tax purposes by the courts. In practice most people relied on the HMRC guidance as set out in the booklet IR20 and its more recent replacement HMRC6. HMRC claimed to base this guidance on the decided cases, but it was often difficult to reconcile the two. HMRC6 seemed to be largely concessionary in parts and more rigid than the court decisions in others. The statutory residence test fundamentally altered the concept of residence. The previous tests are, however, still of relevance in two circumstances. The first is that they apply for all years up to 5 April 2013 and HMRC have until 5 April 2017 (5 April 2019 if they can show a failure to take reasonable care and 5 April 2033 if they can show fraud) to challenge a person's residence status for 2012/13. Secondly, the statutory residence test is actually a series of tests. One of these takes account of whether the taxpayer was UK resident in either of the two previous tax years. This looks at residence under the rules that applied at the time (subject to a right to elect to use the new rules instead), so if one of those years was 2011/12 or 2012/13 it may still be necessary to look at the old rules to determine residence up to 2015/16. Accordingly, the previous residence tests are reproduced below as a separate self-contained section following the review of the current residence test.

A person who is resident and domiciled in the UK is liable to UK tax on worldwide income and assets. If a person does not meet both of these tests then some of his income or assets may well escape UK tax.

The starting point is accordingly these two concepts.

RESIDENCE FROM 6 APRIL 2013

9.2

Focus

From 5 April 2013 a person is UK resident for a tax year if either:

(1)   He is present in the UK for more than 183 days in the tax year (*FA 2013, Sch 43, para 7*).

(2)   He has a home in the UK during the tax year, he spends some time there (however short) on at least ten days in the tax year, and for a period of at least 91 days (30 of which fall in the tax year) either he has no home outside the UK or, if he does, he spends time there on fewer than 30 days in the tax year (*FA 2013, Sch 43, para 8*).

(3)   He works 'sufficient hours in the UK' over a 365-day period (all or part of which falls into the tax year), during that period there are no significant breaks from UK work, and more than 75% of the total number of days in the 365-day period on which he does more than three hours' work are days of work in the UK (*FA 2013, Sch 45, para 9*). Whether a person works sufficient hours in the UK is calculated by reference to a formula. Start from 365. Deduct disregarded days, ie days on which the person works at least three hours overseas (even if he does three hours here as well). Deduct annual leave, parenting leave, sickness, and non-working days embedded in a block of such days. Divide the resulting figure by seven and round down to the nearest whole number (or round up to 1). Ascertain the total hours that the person works in the UK (other than on disregarded days) during the 365-day period. Divide that by the number previously calculated. If this gives 35 or more, the person worked sufficient hours in the UK for the tax year.

Example 9.1 – Working in the UK

Johann comes to the UK from Belgium to work on an installation project in 1 January 2015. He works seven hours a day, five days a week for six months. He then takes four weeks' holiday. He works four hours a day for the next six weeks. He is off sick for the next eight days, after which he resumes work for another 32 days (of which 24 are work days). Johann then returns to Belgium where he works seven hours a day for six weeks. He comes back to the UK for a day to sort out a problem. On that day he works four hours in Belgium and 3.5 in the UK. He then returns to Belgium. Of the first 30 days in Belgium, ie the number required to bring the total days up to 365) Johann works on 20.

From 365 deduct the disregarded days, ie days working in Belgium = 30 + 1 + 20 = 51. From the resultant 314 deduct holidays, etc (28 + 8 = 36) giving 278. Divide by 7 = 39. Ascertain Johann's total hours worked in the UK (26 weeks × 5 days × 7 hours (910) + 6 × 5 × 4 hours (120) + 24 × 4 (96) = 1,126. Divide by 39 = 28.8. As that is less than 35 Johann has not worked sufficient hours in the UK, so is not UK resident under this test.

(4) The person dies during the tax year, was UK resident for each of the previous three years under one of the above tests, had a home in the UK during the tax year and, if he were not resident in the tax year, the previous year would not have been a split year (*FA 2013, Sch 45, para 10*).

(5) He was resident here in any one of the previous three tax years, spends at least 15 days in the UK in the tax year and satisfies one or more of five connecting factors (see below). The number of factors that count vary with the time spent in the UK, namely:

Days spent in UK	*Impact of connection factors on residence status*
Fewer than 16 days	Always non-resident
16–45 days	Resident if individual has 4 factors or more (otherwise not resident)
46–90 days	Resident if individual has 3 factors or more (otherwise not resident)
91–120 days	Resident if individual has 2 factors or more (otherwise not resident)
121–182 days	Resident if individual has 1 factor or more (otherwise not resident)
183 days or more	Always resident

The five connecting factors are:

- **Family** – the individual's spouse or civil partner (or common law equivalent) or minor children are resident in the UK.

- **Accommodation** – the individual has accessible accommodation in the UK and makes use of it during the tax year (subject to an exclusion for a short stay with a relative).

- **Substantive work in the UK** – The individual does substantive work in the UK (but does not work here full time).

- **UK presence in the previous year** – The individual spent more than 90 days in the UK in either of the previous two tax years.

- **More time in the UK than in other countries** – The individual spent more days in the UK in the tax year than in any other single country.

(*FA 2013, Sch 45, paras 17, 18*).

(6) If the individual was not resident in the UK in any of the previous three tax years, he is present here for more than 45 days in the tax year and meets one or more of the first four of the above five factors. Again the number of factors that count vary with the time spent in the UK but the table differs from that at above. The rules are as follows (*FA 2013, Sch 45, para 19*):

Days spent in UK	Impact of connection factors on residence status
Fewer than 46 days	Always non-resident
46–90 days	Resident if individual has 4 factors or more (otherwise not resident)
91–120 days	Resident if individual has 3 factors or more (otherwise not resident)
121–182 days	Resident if individual has 2 factors or more (otherwise not resident)
183 days or more	Always resident

The connecting factors appear to apply throughout the year if they apply on a single day in the year, although split-year treatment (see **9.5**) will often apply in the year that a person comes to, or leaves, the UK. Split-year treatment will not apply where a person ceases to be, or becomes, UK resident because of a change in the number of factors taken into account under (5) or (6) above.

9.3   Even if he would be UK resident under one of the above tests, a person is not UK resident for a tax year if either:

(1)   He was UK resident in at least one of the previous three tax years, spends less than 16 days here in the tax year concerned and does not die in that year (*FA 2013, Sch 45, para 12*).

(2)   He was not UK resident in any of the previous three tax years and spends less than 46 days here in the tax year concerned (*FA 2013, Sch 45, para 13*).

(3)   He works sufficient hours overseas in the tax year, there are no significant breaks from overseas work in that year, he does more than three hours' work in the UK on no more than 30 days and he spends no more than 90 days here in the tax year (ignoring days on which he is deemed to be in the UK) (*FA 2013, Sch 45, para 14*). Sufficient hours overseas is calculated in the same way as sufficient hours in the UK (see above) but by reference to the tax year, not by reference to any 365-day period.

(4)   He dies during the tax year, he was not UK resident for either of the previous two years (or was not UK resident for the previous year and the year before that was a split year) and he spent less than 46 days in the UK in the tax year (*FA 2013, Sch 45, para 15*).

(5)   He dies during the tax year, was not UK resident in either of the previous two years by virtue of head 3 above (or was not UK resident in the previous year by virtue of that head and the year before that was a split year) and he would have been non-UK resident under head three if it applied only by reference to the part of the tax year up to the date of his death (*FA 2013, Sch 45, para 16*).

9.4   For the above purposes a person is normally present in the UK on a day if he is here at midnight on that day. However, a day on which he is in transit as a passenger is ignored provided that he does not engage in activities that are to a substantial extent unconnected with his passage through the UK. HMRC seem to interpret this last condition as meaning that any activities entered into must not be pre-planned. This looks at social activities as well as business ones. The intention seems to be to exclude the day only if the sole reason for being in the UK overnight was because travel connections made it impossible or difficult to travel onwards on the day of arrival (HMRC6, para 2.3).

Up to 60 days on which he would not have been present here but for exceptional circumstances beyond his control that prevent him leaving the UK can also be ignored provided that he intends to leave the UK as soon as circumstances permit (*FA 2013, Sch 45, para 22*). In addition, if (ignoring this special rule) a person has at least three UK connecting factors (see **9.2**), was UK resident in one of the previous three tax years and is present in the UK at some point in the day (but not at midnight) on more than 30 days, every extra day over that 30 on which he is present in the UK (for however short a time) is deemed to be a day of presence in the UK (*FA 2013, Sch 45, para 23*). This prevents a person who lives overseas but works in the UK from avoiding UK residence by coming here early on a Monday morning and leaving late on Wednesday and counting only two days of presence, when the reality is that he is here for virtually three days. This restriction does not apply for the purpose of determining whether the automatic UK resident tests (items (1)–(4) in **9.2** above) and the automatic overseas resident tests (**9.3** above) are met (*FA 2013, Sch 45, para 23(5)*). HMRC indicate in RDR3 that this means that it does not affect the 91-day test (see **9.3**(3)).

If the only reason for a family connection is that the taxpayer's infant child is resident in the UK, that tie can be ignored if the taxpayer sees the child in the UK for less than 61 days in the tax year (*FA 2013, Sch 45, para 32*). If the child is UK resident only because he is in full-time education here, the child can be treated as non-UK resident if he spends less than 21 days here outside term time (*FA 2013, Sch 45, para 33*). Term time for this purpose includes half-term breaks and other breaks during a term when education is not provided.

Accommodation is accessible only if it is available to the taxpayer to live in when in the UK for a continuous period of at least 91 days and he spends at least one night there in the tax year (*FA 2013, Sch 45, para 34*). If the accommodation is the home of a parent or grandparent, a sibling or an adult child or adult grandchild of the taxpayer (or of the spouse or civil partner of such a person) it is only accessible accommodation if the taxpayer spends at least 16 nights there during the tax year.

A person does substantive work in the UK only if he works here for at least three hours a day for at least 40 days (*FA 2013, Sch 45, para 35*).

Where residence for any year up to 2017/18 depends on whether the individual was resident in the UK in 2012/13 or earlier, residence for those earlier years is determined on the basis of the rules that applied at the time (*FA 2013, Sch 45, para 154(2)*). However, the individual can elect for residence for all or any of those earlier years to instead be determined on the basis of the new statutory residence rules (*FA 2013, Sch 45, para 154(3)*). Such an election must be made within 12 months of the end of the tax year concerned and is irrevocable.

Split-year treatment

9.5   There are eight circumstances (or 'cases') in which the tax year can be split, ie the taxpayer is regarded as UK resident only for the part of the year in which he is living in the UK. These are:

(1)   The taxpayer was UK resident in the previous tax year, is non-resident during the following year by virtue of **9.3**(3), and in the current year

there is a period that begins within the tax year on a day on which the taxpayer does more than three hours' work overseas, ends at the end of the tax year, and during which the taxpayer works sufficient hours overseas, has no significant breaks from overseas work, works in the UK for no more than the permitted limit and does not spend more than the permitted number of days in the UK (*FA 2013, Sch 45, para 44*). Sufficient hours overseas is calculated in a similar way to that at **9.2**(3). The permitted limit is 30 days reduced proportionately for the number of whole months in the tax year prior to the start of the non-resident period. The permitted number of days in the UK is 90 reduced for the number of whole months in the tax year prior to the start of the non-resident period.

(2)   The taxpayer was UK resident for the previous tax year, is not UK resident in the following year, has a spouse or partner who meets the above condition, moves overseas during the current tax year so that they can continue to live together, and for the remainder of the year has no home in the UK (or if he does, spends more time in an overseas home than in the UK one) and spends no more than the permitted number of days in the UK (calculated as above) (*FA 2013, Sch 45, para 45*).

(3)   The taxpayer was UK resident for the previous tax year, is non-UK resident for the following year, had a home in the UK at the start of the current tax year but ceases to do so during the year (and has no home here thereafter in the tax year) and following that cessation spends no more than 15 days in the UK and establishes a sufficient link with an overseas country within six months of ceasing to have a UK home (*FA 2013, Sch 45, para 46*). For this purpose a person establishes a sufficient link with an overseas country if either he is treated as a resident there, he has been present there at midnight on every day in the six-month period, or his only home (or homes) is in that country.

(4)   The taxpayer was non-UK resident for the previous tax year, did not have his home (or all of his homes) in the UK at the start of the current year but comes to do so during the year and, for the part of the year prior to that time did not have sufficient UK ties (ie the four connecting factors but with the figures pro rated by reference to the number of months in the part of the year following the acquisition of the UK home) (*FA 2013, Sch 45, para 47*).

(5)   The taxpayer was non-UK resident in the previous tax year, there is a period of 365 days beginning in the current year (on a day on which the taxpayer does more than three hours' work in the UK) before the start of which the taxpayer did not have sufficient UK ties, the taxpayer works sufficient hours in the UK (calculated as above), has no significant breaks from UK work and in that 365-day period at least 75% of the days on which the taxpayer did more than three hours' work were days working in the UK (*FA 2013, Sch 45, para 48*).

(6)   The taxpayer was non-UK resident in the previous year by virtue of the test at **9.3**(3), is UK resident for the following tax year, and there is a period beginning at the start of the current year and ending during the current year on a day on which the taxpayer does more than three hours work overseas, and the taxpayer satisfies the overseas work criteria (*FA 2013, Sch 45, para 49*). A period satisfies the overseas work criteria if the taxpayer works sufficient hours overseas (see earlier), there are no significant breaks from overseas work, the number of days on which the taxpayer does more than three hours' work in the UK does not exceed the permitted limit (see earlier) and the total number of days spent in the UK does not exceed the permitted number of days (see above).

(7)   The taxpayer was non-UK resident for the previous year, is UK resident during the following year, in the current year he moves to the UK so that he can continue to live with his spouse or partner (who satisfies head 6 above), and in the part of the year before coming to the UK the taxpayer had no home in the UK (or if he did, spent more of his time in a non-UK home) and the number of days he spent in the UK does not exceed the permitted number of days (as defined earlier) (*FA 2013, Sch 45, para 50*).

(8)   The taxpayer was non-UK resident for the previous tax year, is UK resident for the following year (and that is not itself a split year) and in the current year had no home in the UK but acquired one during the year and continues to have a home in the UK for the remainder of that year and the whole of the following year, and in the period before acquiring the UK home the taxpayer did not have sufficient UK ties (as defined earlier) (*FA 2013, Sch 45, para 51*).

It will be seen that split-year treatment is more limited than under the old rules. Split-year treatment on coming to the UK can apply only if the taxpayer (or spouse) is coming to the UK to work or had no home in the UK and acquires one here during the tax year. Split-year treatment on leaving the UK can apply only if the taxpayer (or spouse) goes abroad to work or he disposes of his UK house (or does not do so but acquires an overseas property and spends more time in that than in the UK one).

Temporary non-residence

9.6   In the same way as for capital gains tax (see **9.62**) a person who ceases to be non-UK resident and becomes UK resident again within five years can be taxed on certain types of income that arise during his period of non-residence. A person is a temporary non-resident if he is solely UK resident for a complete tax year (or the UK part of a split tax year), following that period one or more tax years (or parts of a split tax year) occur for which he does not have sole UK residence, the temporary period of non-residence is five tax years or less, and at least four out of the seven tax years immediately preceding the tax year in which he ceased to be solely UK resident were tax years for which he had sole UK residence (or a split year for part of which he had sole UK residence) (*FA 2013, Sch 45, para 110*). An individual has sole UK residence for this purpose if he is resident here under UK domestic law and is not treated as non-resident under a double tax treaty (*FA 2013, Sch 43, para 112*). The temporary period of non-residence is, of course, the period between ceasing to be UK resident and again becoming UK resident.

Where a person is temporary non-UK resident:

(1)   Withdrawals from a registered pension scheme or a non-UK pension scheme under a flexible drawdown arrangement paid in the period of temporary non-residence are treated as paid in the period of return, ie the first tax year (or taxable part of a split year) following the individual's return to the UK (*ITEPA 2003, ss 576A, 579CA inserted by FA 2013, Sch 45, paras 116, 117*).

(2)   Relevant foreign income (ie foreign investment income) taxed on a remittance basis received prior to the individual's departure from the UK and remitted during the period of temporary non-residence is treated as remitted in the period of return (*ITTOIA 2005, s 832A inserted by FA 2013, Sch 45, para 118*).

(3)   Employment income which is not earnings or share-related (and as such is taxable in the year of receipt under *ITEPA 2003, s 394*) which is in the form of a lump sum and is received during the period of temporary non-residence is treated as received in the period of return (*ITEPA 2003, s 394A inserted by FA 2013, Sch 45, para 125*).

(4)   A relevant step under the rules in relation to employment income provided by third parties which consists of the payment of a lump sum in the period of temporary non-residence is treated as having been received in the period of return (*ITEPA 2003, s 554Z4A inserted by FA 2013, Sch 45, para 126*).

(5)   A relevant benefit provided under an EFURBS in the form of a lump sum and remitted to the UK in the period of non-residence is treated as having been remitted to the UK in the period of return (*ITEPA 2003, s 554Z11 inserted by FA 2013, Sch 45, para 127*).

(6)   A UK pension paid in the form of a lump sum which accrued in the period of temporary non-residence is treated as having accrued in the period of return (*ITEPA 2003, s 572A inserted by FA 2013, Sch 45 para 129*).

(7)   A dividend or other distribution by a close company to a material participator in the company (or an associate of his) in the period of temporary non-residence must be treated as received in the period of return (unless it is a cash dividend paid out of trading profits arising

after the start of the period of temporary non-residence) (*ITTOIA 2005, s 401C* inserted by *FA 2013, Sch 45, para 133*). A material participator is one who has a material interest in the company (ie over 5%).

(8) Such a dividend from a non-UK company which would be a close company if it were UK resident is similarly treated as received in the period of return (*ITTOIA 2005, s 408A* inserted by *FA 2013, Sch 45, para 134*).

(9) A stock dividend paid by a UK company to a material participator during the period of temporary non-residence is similarly treated as received in the period of return (*ITTOIA 2005, s 413A* inserted by *FA 2013, Sch 45, para 135*).

(10) If a loan or advance by a close company to an individual is written off by the company during the period of temporary non-residence it is treated as having been written off in the period of return (*ITTOIA 2005, s 420A* inserted by *FA 2013, Sch 45, para 136*).

(11) Any other distribution by a close company (or an overseas company that would be close if it were UK resident) to a material participator (or associate) in the period of non-residence is treated as made in the period of return if it would be taxable in the UK if it were made in that period (*ITTOIA 2005, s 689A* inserted by *FA 2013, Sch 45, para 137*).

(12) If an individual's UK tax liability in a period of temporary non-residence is limited under *ITA 2007, s 811* and his income includes dividends or other distributions made by a close company to a material participator, the individual's total income for the period of return must be increased by the amount of such income (unless the distribution is out of trading profits arising in the period of temporary non-residence) (*ITA 2007, s 812A* inserted by *FA 2013, Sch 45, para 138*).

(13) If in the period of temporary non-residence an individual receives a chargeable event gain from an insurance policy issued before the start of that period and no one is liable to UK income tax on that gain, the chargeable event is treated as having occurred in the period of return (*ITTOIA 2005, s 465B* inserted by *FA 2013, Sch 45, para 140*).

CEASING TO BE UK RESIDENT

9.7 Under the statutory residence test it is relatively easy for a person to become non-UK resident for a tax year. He can:

(1) Limit his visits to the UK in that tax year to 15 days (45 days if he was UK resident for only one tax year).

(2) Take up full time work overseas throughout that tax year and not work in the UK at all (or work here for less than 31 days) and limit his visits

to the UK in the tax year to 90 days. Full-time work for this purpose aggregates all employments and self-employments and any day on which more than three hours' work is done counts as a working day.

(3)   Arrange his life to seek to minimise the number of connections that he has with the UK and keep his visits to the UK within the appropriate trigger point for his remaining connections. A point to watch is that one of the connecting factors is that the person spent over 90 days in the UK in one of the previous two tax years. Accordingly it might in some cases be necessary to keep visits to 90 days even though the test may allow a longer period in the UK. This is because if the 90 days is exceeded that might not make the individual resident for the year concerned, but will create an extra connecting factor for the following two years.

An individual can also be treated as non-UK resident under a double tax agreement. Most such agreements provide that where a person is UK resident under UK tax rules and also resident in the other country under its tax rules, a series of tests must be applied to determine which country is to treat him as a resident. If those tests result in his being treated as a resident of the other country, he cannot be taxed (to income tax and capital gains tax) as a UK resident.

A point to watch is that a double tax treaty does not prevent a person being UK resident; it simply taxes him as if he were non-UK resident. Accordingly using a double tax agreement will not break the 15-year period of residence under the deemed domicile test for inheritance tax or the seven or more years of residence for the remittance basis rules.

Deemed non-residence

9.8

Focus

Remember that a client might be dual-resident as a result of being also resident in another country at the same time as he is resident in the UK. If the UK has a double taxation agreement with the other country that agreement will contain a tie-breaker clause to determine which country is entitled to treat the client as a resident, rather than both doing so. Claiming the benefit of the agreement may make the client non-UK resident even though he is UK resident under the UK domestic rules.

However, this deemed non-residence applies only to taxes covered by the agreement. In particular it will not necessarily apply to income arising in third countries.

As indicated above, most, but not all, of the UK's full double tax agreements contain a 'tie-breaker' clause to treat an individual as resident in only one of the countries concerned where he would otherwise be treated by each as resident there under its domestic laws. A fairly standard example is that with the US which provides that where an individual is both resident in the UK under UK law and resident in the US under US law then:

- He is deemed to be resident only in the country in which he has a permanent home available to him.

- If he has a permanent home available in both countries he is deemed to be resident only in the country with which his personal and economic relations are closer (often called his 'centre of vital interests').

- If either his centre of vital interests cannot be determined or he does not have a permanent home available to him in either country he is deemed to be resident only in the country in which he has a habitual abode.

- If he has a habitual abode in both countries (or neither) he is deemed to be resident only in the country of which he is a national.

- If he is a national of both (or neither) the tax authorities of the two countries must endeavour to settle the question by mutual agreement.

(Article 4(4), US/UK Double Tax Agreement)

9.9   The notes to the OECD model double tax convention expand on the second point above:

> 'It is necessary to look at the facts in order to ascertain with which of the two States his personal and economic relations are closer. Thus, regard will be had to his family and social relations, his occupations, his political, cultural or other activities, his place of business, the place from which he administers his property, etc. The circumstances must be examined as a whole, but it is nevertheless obvious that considerations based on the personal acts of the individual must receive special attention. If a person who has a home in one State sets up a second in the other State while retaining the first, the fact that he retains the first in the environment where he has always lived, where he has worked, and where he has his family and possessions, can, together with other elements, go to demonstrate that he has retained his centre of vital interests in the first State.'

Some double tax agreements include a provision that relief from UK tax is due to a resident of the other country only to the extent that the person is liable to tax on the income in that other country. This particularly applies where the other country taxes the income on a remittance basis. Such countries include Australia, Canada, Ireland and Jamaica. Conversely, the US agreement does not grant exemption from US tax where the income is taxed in the UK on a remittance basis and has not been remitted.

RESIDENCE UP TO 5 APRIL 2013

9.10   As indicated earlier, for 2012/13 and earlier years the concept of residence relied on a large number of court decisions but it was difficult to draw much firm guidance from them. HMRC sought to do so in their booklet HMRC6, 'Residents and non-residents – Liability to tax in the UK' (which replaced IR20). This was an extremely useful booklet. It is unwise to seek to decide a person's residence under the pre-5 April 2013 rules without first becoming familiar with this booklet, not only because it highlights areas to which HMRC attach particular importance but also because the HMRC interpretation is to an extent concessionary.

Broadly speaking, a person was resident in the UK if he normally lived here; whether or not he did so was a question of fact.

The HMRC view seemed to be that in order for a UK resident to cease to be resident here he needed to go abroad permanently or for a settled purpose. Once he was accepted as having left the UK he would become UK resident again only if he returned to the UK for more than 90 days a year on average.

In deciding whether or not a person had left the UK, HMRC consider all the relevant evidence, including the pattern of presence in the UK and elsewhere (Revenue & Customs Brief 01/07). It is not wholly clear what this means. Prior to the issue of this statement in January 2007, most people thought that HMRC's approach to residence was an arithmetical one, ie that a person was UK resident if he was physically present in the UK for 183 days or more in a tax year or if he was physically present here for more than 90 days a year on average.

HMRC6 gave the following guidance:

- There are many different factors which will determine whether a person is resident in the UK during a tax year. It is not simply a question of the number of days the person is physically present in the UK during a tax year although this is an important consideration (para 2.2).

- Different considerations apply depending on whether the person is arriving in the UK for the first time from another country or whether he has been resident in the UK in earlier years (this is not in the latest version of HMRC6 but is implicit in the text of para 2.2).

- Residence in the UK will depend on how often and for how long a person is here, the purpose and pattern of his presence and his connections with the UK. These might include the location of his family, his property, his work life and social connections (para 2.2).

- From 6 April 2008 when considering days of presence in the UK, all of the days in which the person is present at the end of the day (ie at midnight) must be included (para 2.2.1).

- A person will always be resident in the UK in any tax year in which he is physically present in the UK for more than 183 days. There are no exceptions to this (para 2.2).

- It is possible to be resident in the UK and some other country (or countries) at the same time (introduction to Chapter 2). However, if the other country is one with which the UK has a double taxation treaty the agreement is likely to contain a 'tie-breaker clause' which might prevent the UK from treating the individual as UK resident for the purpose of the agreement. Double tax agreements do not usually deal with income from third countries.

- Strictly speaking, a person is UK resident for the whole of a tax year if he is resident here for any part of it (para 2.4). However, Extra-statutory Concession A11 provides that if an individual ceases to reside in the UK and he has left for permanent residence abroad (or comes to the UK to take up permanent residence or to stay for at least two years) he will be taxed only for the part of the year up to the date of his departure (or from the date of his arrival). This is known as the split-year concession. It will not apply if the individual remains ordinarily resident in the UK (see below) after his departure or was ordinarily resident in the UK prior to becoming resident here. HMRC6 states that ESC A11 applies if a person has been resident in the UK and 'leaves to live abroad permanently or for a period of at least three years'. There is a further concession (ESC A78) which allows split-year treatment for a person accompanying a spouse or civil partner when they leave the UK to work full-time abroad, or in the year of return to the UK (para 2.4). There is a corresponding CGT concession (ESC D2) but this is much more limited. It does not apply where a person leaves the UK (unless he was not resident and not ordinarily resident here for the whole of at least four out of the last seven tax years preceding that in which he leaves the UK). It applies to a person coming to the UK only if he has not been either resident or ordinarily resident in the UK at any time during the five tax years preceding that in which he becomes resident here.

- If a person comes to the UK to live here permanently or to remain here for three years or more, he will be resident and ordinarily resident from the date of arrival (para 7.2).

- If a person whose home has been abroad comes to the UK as a student for less than four years for a period of education or study he will be resident here, but not ordinarily resident as long as he does not own or buy (or rent for three years) accommodation here and when he leaves the UK he is not planning to return here regularly for visits that average over 90 days in a tax year (para 7.3).

- If a person whose home has been abroad comes to the UK intending to remain for less than three years, he may simply be visiting (para 7.4).

Such a person will be resident and ordinarily resident in the UK from the fifth year he visits if his visits average over 90 days or from such earlier year as he realises that his visits will exceed a 90-day average (para 7.5).

- A person is not regarded as simply visiting if he comes to the UK for a purpose which means that he will be remaining here for at least two years (eg an employment). Such a person may well be resident (but not necessarily ordinarily resident) from the day of his arrival (para 7.4).

- If a person comes to the UK voluntarily and for a settled purpose, he will be ordinarily resident from the time he comes to the UK. If he owns or buys (or rents for over three years) accommodation in the year of arrival, that *may be* an indication that his presence in the UK forms part of the regular and habitual mode of his life for the time being and so he is ordinarily resident from when he arrives (but if he already owned accommodation here and sells it within three years of his arrival he will not be ordinarily resident here) (para 7.7.3). He will also not normally be regarded as ordinarily resident if he actually leaves the UK within three years of arrival (para 7.7.3).

- If a person does not become ordinarily resident when he first comes to the UK he will do so from the beginning of the tax year in which the third anniversary of his arrival falls (eg a person who comes to the UK on 4 April 2010 will become ordinarily resident from 6 April 2012 as 4 April 2013 falls in 2012/13) (para 7.7.3). He can become ordinarily resident here earlier (from the beginning of the tax year in which the trigger event falls) if he makes a decision to stay for three or more years or buys a property here (para 7.7.4).

- If a person leaves the UK permanently (ie to live abroad and not return) or indefinitely (ie to live abroad for at least three years but acknowledging that he might eventually return to live here) the act of going abroad does not mean that he will automatically become non-resident or non-ordinary resident. This depends on a number of factors including:

  - the reason he has left the UK (eg to work or live abroad permanently);

  - what visits he makes to the UK after he has left; and

  - what connections he keeps in the UK such as family, property, business and social connections (para 8.1).

- If a person leaves the UK permanently or indefinitely he will become non-resident and non-ordinarily resident from the time of his departure only if he has physically left the UK for the purposes stated. If he goes abroad on holiday until he moves into his new home or begins his overseas employment, he is regarded as remaining resident here during his holiday period (para 8.2).

- Even if a person has left the UK permanently or indefinitely he will remain resident and ordinarily resident in the UK if his visits back are not such as to show that he has made a definite break with the UK (para 8.2). Prior to the issue of the 2010 version of HMRC6, HMRC accepted that a person would not again become UK resident if his visits back did not exceed an average of 90 days but while this test is still included in the 2010 version its significance has been reduced.

- A person will be ordinarily resident in the UK if:

  (a) he has come to the UK voluntarily (which would include at the request of his employer); and

  (b) his presence here has enough continuity to be properly described as settled (business, employment and family all provide a settled purpose); and

  (c) his presence in the UK forms part of the regular and habitual mode of his life for the time being (para 3.2).

- A person who leaves the UK to work full-time abroad under a contract of employment is treated as not resident and not ordinarily resident in the UK if his absence from the UK and the employment abroad both last for at least a whole tax year (and visits back do not breach the 183- or 91-day rule) (para 8.5). This is considered further below.

- In applying the 90-day and 183-day tests a day must be counted as a day of presence in the UK if the individual is physically present here at midnight on that day. There is an exception if the individual is in transit (ie he arrives in the UK as a passenger and departs from the UK on the next day) and while in the UK he does not engage in activities that are to a substantial extent unrelated to his passage through the UK. HMRC appear to consider that any activity that the individual plans to carry out while he is in transit will prevent the exception applying.

The tests formulated by the courts

9.11

Focus

HMRC claimed to base their approach on court decisions. It should be borne in mind that was simply HMRC's view. In the event of a dispute there is no reason to assume HMRC's interpretation of the court decisions is superior to yours. Consider how the facts of your client's case conform with the principles laid down by the courts.

The above guidance represents HMRC's views only – although, of course, where possible it is sensible to plan on the basis of HMRC's views as to ignore them invites challenge. HMRC do stress that HMRC6 'only offers general guidance ... and does not have legal effect. Whether this guidance is appropriate in a particular case will depend on all of the facts of that case'.

The tests that the courts have laid down to determine residence were summarised by Lewison J in *HMRC v Grace* ([2009] STC 213) as follows:

'(i)   The word "reside" is a familiar English word which means "to dwell permanently or for a considerable time, to have one's settled or usual abode, to live in or at a particular place": *Levene v Commissioners of Inland Revenue* (1928) 13 TC 486, 505. This is the definition taken from the Oxford English Dictionary in 1928, and is still the definition in the current on-line edition;

(ii)   Physical presence in a particular place does not necessarily amount to residence in that place where, for example, a person's physical presence there is no more than a stop gap measure: *Goodwin v Curtis* (1998) 70 TC 478, 510;

(iii)   In considering whether a person's presence in a particular place amounts to residence there, one must consider the amount of time that he spends in that place, the nature of his presence there and his connection with that place: *Commissioners of Inland Revenue v Zorab* (1926) 11 TC 289, 291;

(iv)   Residence in a place connotes some degree of permanence, some degree of continuity or some expectation of continuity: *Fox v Stirk* [1970] 2 QB 463, 477; *Goodwin v Curtis* (1998) 70 TC 478, 510;

(v)   However, short but regular periods of physical presence may amount to residence, especially if they stem from performance of a continuous obligation (such as business obligations) and the sequence of visits excludes the elements of chance and of occasion: *Lysaght v Commissioners of Inland Revenue* (1928) 13 TC 511, 529;

(vi)   Although a person can have only one domicile at a time, he may simultaneously reside in more than one place, or in more than one country: *Levene v Commissioners of Inland Revenue* (1928) 13 TC 486, 505.'

It may be helpful also to set out the tests adopted by the Special Commissioner in *Shepherd v HMRC* ([2006] STC 1821), which Lewison J in *Grace* commended as 'impeccable conclusions that represent the correct approach to be adopted':

'From these authorities I derive the following principles: (i) that the concept of residence and ordinary residence are not defined in the legislation; the words therefore should be given their natural and ordinary meanings (*Levene*); (ii) that the word "residence" and "to reside" mean "to dwell permanently or for a considerable time, to have one's settled or usual abode, to live in or at a particular place" (*Levene*); (iii) that the concept of "ordinary residence" requires more than mere residence; it connotes residence in a place with some degree of continuity (*Levene*); "ordinary" means normal and part of everyday life (*Lysaght*) or a regular, habitual mode of life in a particular place which has persisted despite temporary absences and which is voluntary and has a degree of settled purpose (*Shah*); (iv) that the question whether a person is or is not resident in the United Kingdom is a question of fact for the Special Commissioners (*Zorab*); (v) that no duration is prescribed by statute and it is necessary to take into account all the facts of the case; the duration of an individual's presence in the United Kingdom and the regularity and frequency of visits are facts to be taken into account; also, birth, family and business ties, the nature of visits and the connections with this country, may all be relevant (*Zorab*; *Brown*); (vi) that a reduced presence in the United Kingdom of a person whose absences are caused by his employment and so are temporary absences does not necessarily mean that the person is not residing in the United Kingdom (*Young*); (vii) that the availability of living accommodation in the United Kingdom is a factor to be borne in mind in deciding if a person is resident here (*Cooper*) (although that is subject to *s 336*); (viii) that the fact that an individual has a home elsewhere is of no consequence; a person may reside in two places but if one of those places is the United Kingdom he is chargeable to tax here (*Cooper* and *Levene*); (ix) that there is a difference between the case where a British subject has established a residence in the United Kingdom and then has absences from it (*Levene*) and the case where a person has never had a residence in the United Kingdom at all (*Zorab*; *Brown*); (x) that if there is evidence that a move abroad is a distinct break that could be a relevant factor in treating an individual as non-resident (*Combe*); and (xi) that a person could become non-resident even if his intention was to mitigate tax (*Reed v Clark*).'

9.12   *Tax Bulletin*, Issue 52 dealt with the position of mobile workers, namely people such as lorry or coach drivers who drive their vehicles to and from the Continent, those who work on cross-channel transport and salesmen who make frequent short business trips abroad.

HMRC did not accept that such people had gone abroad for full-time work, even where they did little work in the UK. They considered that even though such a person may have been here for less than 91 days on average he was resident and ordinarily resident here if he usually lived in the UK and made frequent and regular trips abroad in the course of his employment or business.

They regarded a person as usually living in the UK if his home and settled domestic life remained here. It is probable that this was the test that they also applied to decide whether a person who went abroad for a longer period had left the UK. It should be particularly noted that HMRC regarded someone 'travelling to France most Sundays or Mondays in connection with their employment but returning to the UK by or at the following weekend' as a mobile worker (*Tax Bulletin*, Issue 52).

Leaving the UK

9.13   There were four ways that a person who was UK resident could cease such residence:

- leaving to go abroad for one tax year under a contract of employment (or a self-employed assignment);

- leaving the UK permanently or indefinitely for at least three tax years;

- not being physically present in the UK at all during a tax year;

- as now, becoming resident in a country with which the UK has a double tax agreement and being deemed to be non-tax resident for the purpose of that agreement.

Contract of employment

9.14   The individual needed to work full-time abroad under a contract of employment spanning at least one complete tax year (HMRC6 para 8.5). If this condition was met he was regarded as ceasing to be both resident and ordinarily resident in the UK from the date of his departure (or such later date as his employment actually began).

HMRC gave guidance on what they meant by 'full-time' for this purpose in *Tax Bulletin*, Issue 6 (February 1993). In general where a job involves a standard pattern of hours they expected the individual to put in what a layman would clearly recognise as a full working week.

They said that 'there is no fixed minimum number of hours for this purpose but 35–40 hours is obviously a typical UK working week'. However, it is probable that it was sufficient to look at a normal working week in the country where the person was working if this was less than the norm in the UK.

9.15   Where a job did not have a straightforward structure they looked at the nature of the job and, where appropriate, took account of local conditions and practices in that particular occupation. This probably meant that they would expect the individual to put in the number of hours that a person doing a similar job would normally be expected to work.

HMRC also said that where a person had several part-time jobs overseas concurrently, particularly if they were with the same employer or group of companies, it might be reasonable to aggregate the time spent on them. This might also be done where the person simultaneously worked abroad both as an employee and as a self-employed person.

They also warned that where a person had a main employment abroad but also worked in the UK in some unconnected occupation (eg he had a directorship of a UK company), they would want to consider whether the extent of the UK activities might cast doubt on the full-time nature of the overseas employment.

9.16   If the employment was terminated prematurely and a new employment contract entered into with someone else, HMRC reviewed the position but were normally prepared to aggregate the two employments. It is conceivable that they might aggregate them even if the individual returned temporarily to the UK between the employments, planning to go abroad again.

A person was also regarded as having ceased to be UK resident and ordinarily resident if he left the UK to work full-time in a trade, profession or vocation and he met conditions similar to those in HMRC6, paragraph 8.5 (para 8.8). It is not clear what this meant. Did it merely mean that the self-employment overseas must span a complete tax year or might it mean that there needs to be a contract requiring the person to be abroad for such a period?

9.17   If a person was treated as non-resident under either para 8.5 (employed) or 8.8 (self-employed) of HMRC6 his spouse was also treated as non-resident if she accompanied him (or later joined him) even though the spouse was not in full-time employment – provided that the spouse was abroad for at least a complete tax year (para 8.9 and ESC A78).

Where a person was regarded as non-UK resident under this test he could still visit the UK for up to an average of 90 days. However, it is hard to envisage a genuine full-time employment that allowed three months holiday every year.

Leaving the UK permanently or indefinitely

9.18   HMRC said in the original version of HMRC6:

'If you say that you are no longer resident and ordinarily resident in the UK, we might ask you to give some evidence that you have left the UK permanently or indefinitely. For example, we would expect you to show that when you left the UK you had acquired accommodation to live in as a permanent home. The act of leaving the country is not likely to be sufficient evidence that you have left the UK permanently and have become non-resident and not ordinarily resident. If you still have property in the UK which you can use after you leave, we might want you to explain why you are retaining that property when you say you have left the UK' (para 8.2).

9.19   HMRC's Inspector's Manual (IM) (which has been withdrawn) stated:

'If an individual goes to live outside the UK, acquires a permanent home abroad, has a reason for having accommodation for use in the UK which is consistent with the aim of permanent residence abroad, [and] returns to the UK only on visits which do not average 91 days or more a tax year, he will be regarded as having ceased to be resident and ordinarily resident. For tax years before 1993–94 an individual also had to cease to retain accommodation in the UK.

Where an individual claims that he had ceased to be resident and ordinarily resident in this country, his claim may be admitted on a provisional basis at the outset … if the grounds on which it is based are adequately proved, but in no circumstances can a final decision be made until the individual's absence from the UK has extended over a period which includes a full tax year. If adequate proof is not immediately available a decision on the claim is postponed for up to three years from the date of departure and the position is determined by reference to what has actually happened since the date of departure.' (IM41)

These quotations suggest that HMRC were likely to regard a person as ceasing to be UK resident from the time of his departure if he went abroad with an intention to live outside the UK for three years or more (and in fact fulfilled that intention) and did not retain significant ties with the UK. However, he had to go abroad 'for a settled purpose'. This probably required an identifiable change in the person's lifestyle and possibly a specific reason for going abroad. There was no statutory basis for adopting a three-year period. That was simply HMRC's longstanding practice. Indeed the one-year full time work route was undoubtedly based on a presumption that where a person is working full time overseas that is of itself normally sufficient evidence that the person has left the UK for a settled purpose if that purpose lasts for at least one complete tax year. It is easy to overlook that a person is taxed by reference to the law and is entitled to challenge an HMRC practice that he feels does not reflect the application of the law to his particular circumstances.

No presence in UK during tax year

9.20   If a person did not set foot in the UK at all during a tax year it is unlikely that he would have been resident here for that year. He could well have been ordinarily resident though – but see *Reed v Clark* below.

There are two early cases, *Re Young* (1875) 1 TC 57 and *Rogers v CIR* (1879) 1 TC 255, in which the taxpayer was held to be resident in the UK even though they did not set foot here at all during the tax year. These cases involved master mariners, whose voyages lasted for over a year and whose home and family were in the UK. As the taxpayers lived in the UK when not on a voyage these decisions are understandable. In the former case the Lord President commented that 'every sailor has a residence on land'.

9.21   In *Reed v Clark* (1985) 58 TC 528, Nicholls J said that:

'The word "reside" is a familiar English word and is defined in the Oxford English Dictionary as meaning "to dwell permanently or for a considerable time, to have one's settled or usual abode, to live in or at a particular place" and that "the task of the fact finding tribunal … was to consider and weigh all the evidence and then, giving the word 'residing' its natural and ordinary meaning, reach a conclusion on the factual question of whether or not the taxpayer was residing in the UK in the year of assessment".'

In that case he felt that:

'I am in no doubt that the true and only reasonable conclusion from the primary facts found by the Commissioners was that Mr Clark was not residing in the UK in the tax year 1978/79. For the whole of that year his home and place of business was in Los Angeles.'

This suggests that it was possible for a person to be UK resident in a tax year in which he did not set foot in the UK if he is normally resident here and does not have a settled abode somewhere else during that year.

HMRC6 gave no indication that this escape route existed. That is probably because HMRC did not like it. Clearly, though, HMRC guidance cannot override court decisions.

The 91-day test

9.22   Where a person had left the UK (or had never been UK resident) HMRC practice was to treat him as UK resident in any year in which he was physically present here for 183 days or more, or for any year in which his visits to the UK exceeded on average 90 days (the 91-day test).

This average was calculated over the period from a day of departure using the formula:

$$\frac{\text{Days in the UK}}{\text{Total days since leaving the UK}} \times 365$$

If the period since the person left the UK exceeded four years (or the person had never been UK resident) the calculation was done by reference to the last four years only.

9.23 For the purpose of the 91-day test (but not the 183-day one) HMRC were prepared to ignore days spent in the UK because of exceptional circumstances beyond the individual's control such as the illness of himself or a member of his immediate family (Statement of Practice 2/91 and HMRC6 para 2.2). Statement of Practice 2/91 states that 'each case where this relaxation of the normal rules may be appropriate will be considered in the light of its own facts'. In the self-assessment era the notes to the non-residence page of the tax return indicated that it was for the taxpayer to make this judgement himself. It would probably be sensible to flag up in the 'white space' on the return what days have been ignored and why.

IR20 added a caveat that: 'If during your absence the pattern of your visits varied substantially year by year, it might be appropriate to look at the absence as being made up of separate periods for the purpose of calculating average visits. This might be necessary if, for example, a shift in the pattern of your visits suggested a change of circumstances, which altered how we viewed your residence status.' This appears to have been dropped in HMRC6.

9.24 In calculating the days in the UK a day was normally counted only if the taxpayer was in the UK at midnight (HMRC6 para 2.2). This was probably concessional. In *Wilkie v IRC* (1952) 32 TC 495, Donovan J concluded: 'there is nothing in the language ... to prevent hours being taken into the computation, but that ... since what has to be determined is the period of actual residence it is legitimate to do so'. In that case Mr Wilkie arrived in the UK around 2pm on 2 June 1947. He intended to leave on 30 November 1947 but owing to the cancellation of his plane was compelled to remain until he was able to fly out around 10am on 2 December. HMRC claimed that he had been in the UK for more than 182 days as both 2 June and 2 December were days in the UK. Mr Wilkie was held to be non-resident for 1947/48 as he was in the UK for only 182 days and 20 hours, which is less than 183 days.

Although there was no statutory definition of residence, the test of presence at midnight reflected the amendment to *ITA 2007, s 831* (foreign income of individuals in UK for temporary purpose) made by *FA 2008, s 24*. It is likely that HMRC will in practice apply the whole of this amendment in determining residence; it also provides that a day can be ignored if the individual arrives in the UK as a passenger on that day, leaves the UK on the following day and during the time between arrival and departure does not engage in activities that are to a substantial extent unrelated to the individual's passage through the UK. HMRC seem to interpret this last condition as meaning that any activities entered into must not be pre-planned. This looks at social activities as well as business ones. The intention seems to be to exclude the day only if the sole reason for being in the UK overnight was because travel connections made it impossible or difficult to travel onwards on the day of arrival (HMRC6, para 2.3).

HMRC say that they derived the 91-day test from decided cases. However, it seems to give a generous interpretation to such decisions. In *Cooper v Cadwalader* (1904) 5 TC 101 the taxpayer was held to be resident even though he was here for only about two months a year. In *Lowenstein v De Salis* (1926) 10 TC 424 he was here on average for between two and three months a year. In *Lysaght v IRC* (1927) 13 TC 511 the taxpayer was here for 101 days in one year and 94 in the next.

Available accommodation

9.25   Up to 1992/93, a person was regarded as resident in the UK in any year in which he visited the UK, however short the period, if he had accommodation available for his use in the UK. This 'available accommodation' rule was excluded for the purpose of *ICTA 1988, s 336* (now *ITA 2007, s 831*) by *F(No 2)A 1993*. At that time the Minister indicated that the available accommodation rule had been abolished completely as: 'it has been held in the courts in the case of *Lysaght v IRC* (1927) 13 TC 511 … that the language of *s 336* has "illustrative value" in relation to the definition of residence elsewhere in the *Taxes Act 1988*'.

However, the view of HMRC was that this did not mean that the existence in the UK of accommodation available for the person's use was no longer relevant. They still regarded both the existence of available accommodation in the UK and whether or not the taxpayer had accommodation overseas as relevant in relation to the question of whether or not he has left the UK for a settled purpose. It was not, however, decisive; it was simply one of the factors to be taken into account. Accommodation did not have to be owned by the taxpayer for it to be available for his use. It was a question of fact whether it was so available.

Ordinary residence

9.26   HMRC said that the word 'ordinary' indicates that a person's residence in the UK is typical for him and not casual. A person would be ordinarily resident here if his residence had all of the following attributes:

- he had come to the UK voluntarily;

- his presence here had a settled purpose;

- his presence in the UK formed part of the regular and habitual mode of his life for the time being. This pattern could include temporary absences from the UK. They considered that if a person came to live and work in the UK for three years or more he would have established a regular and habitual mode of life here.

HMRC also considered that the pattern of a person's presence, both in the UK and overseas, was an important factor. So were the person's reasons for being in the UK, his intentions when coming to or leaving the UK and his lifestyle and habits.

HMRC practice was to treat a person who came to the UK intending to live here permanently or to remain here for at least three years (four if he came to study) as being ordinarily resident from the date that he arrived in the UK. They treated someone who came here without such an intention as ordinarily resident from the beginning of the tax year after the third anniversary of his arrival or, if earlier, the beginning of the tax year in which the person decided to stay in the UK for three years or more.

If a person already owned accommodation in the UK or acquired accommodation (bought or took a lease of three years or more) in the year of arrival he was again treated as ordinarily resident from the date of his arrival (assuming that he became resident here). If he disposed of the accommodation and left the UK within three years he could, however, be treated as not ordinarily resident. A person who acquired accommodation after his arrival (and not in the same tax year) was treated as ordinarily resident from the beginning of the year in which he acquired such accommodation. However, paragraph 3.2 of HMRC6, after using a three-year period in an example, stated: 'This example looks at a period of three tax years as the appropriate period. This in no way indicates that you can be in the UK for three years before you have to consider whether you are ordinary resident.'

9.27   In *Reed (Inspector of Taxes) v Clark* (1985) 58 TC 528, Nicholls J said:

'The approach which I have found most helpful is to start from the contrast, which has been commented upon more than once, drawn in *s 49* itself (now *ITA 2007, s 829*) between ordinary residence and departure abroad for occasional residence. In the section occasional residence is the converse of ordinary residence. This seems to me to conform to the common usage of the phrase "occasional residence" – a person's occasional residence is contrasted with his usual (or ordinary) residence.

For the meaning of ordinary residence one need look no further than the recent decision of the House of Lords in (*Shah v Barnet London Borough Council* [1983] 2 AC 309). In that case the issue was the meaning of the phrase "ordinary resident" in the context of a student's entitlement to receive an educational grant under an Act and regulations excluding a local authority from being under a duty to bestow an award upon a person who had not been ordinarily resident in the United Kingdom throughout a specified period of three years. In delivering the leading speech, with which Lord Fraser, Lord Lowry, Lord Roskill and Lord Brandon concurred, Lord Scarman observed that "ordinary residence" was not a term of art in English law and that in *Levene v IRC* (1928) 13 TC 486 and *Lysaght v IRC* (1927) 13 TC 511 the House of Lords construed those words in their tax context as bearing their natural and ordinary meaning as words of common usage in the English language. Lord Scarman said (at pages 343–344) "Unless, therefore, it can be shown that the statutory framework or the legal context in which the words are used requires a different meaning, I unhesitatingly subscribe to the view that 'ordinary resident' refers to a man's abode in a particular place or country which he has adopted voluntarily and for settled purposes as part of the regular order of his life for the time being, whether of short or of long duration". He added that a settled purpose did not require an intention to stay indefinitely, but that the purpose, while settled, might be for a limited period only: "all that is necessary is that the purpose of living where one does have a sufficient degree of continuity to be properly described as settled."

On that basis it seems to me plain that a British resident's departure abroad for a period of a few weeks or months with the firm intention of returning at the end of the period to live here as before would be likely always to be for the purpose only of occasional residence. At the opposite end of the scale, it seems to me equally plain that the departure of such a resident abroad for a limited period of (say) three years would not necessarily be for the purpose only of occasional residence just because from the outset he had a firm intention of returning at the end of the period to live here as before ... For my part I think this latter conclusion is also true of residence abroad for just over one year in duration. The difference between these examples is one of degree, and there is an area in which different minds may reach different conclusions. In my view a year is a long enough period for a person's purpose of living where he does to be capable of having a sufficient degree of continuity for it to be properly described as settled. Hence, depending on all the circumstances, the foreign country could be the place where for that period he would be ordinarily and not just occasionally resident.'

Accordingly, the HMRC three-year rule was not necessarily correct.

The tests formulated by the courts

9.28   The tests of ordinary residence adopted by the courts were summarised by Lewison J in *HMRC v Grace* ([2009] STC 213) as follows:

'(i)   "Ordinarily resident" refers to a person's abode in a particular place or country which he has adopted voluntarily and for settled purposes as part of the regular order of his life, whether of short or long duration: *R v Barnet LBC ex p Shah* [1983] 2 AC 309, 343;

(ii)   Just as a person may be resident in two countries at the same time, he may be ordinarily resident in two countries at the same time: *Re Norris* (1888) 4 TLR 452; *R v Barnet LBC ex p Shah* [1983] 2 AC 309, 342;

(iii)   It is wrong to conduct a search for the place where a person has his permanent base or centre adopted for general purposes; or, in other words to look for his "real home": *R v Barnet LBC ex p Shah* [1983] 2 AC 309, 345 and 348;

(iv)   There are only two respects in which a person's state of mind is relevant in determining ordinary residence. First, the residence must be voluntarily adopted; and second, there must be a degree of settled purpose: *R v Barnet LBC ex p Shah* [1983] 2 AC 309, 344;

(v)   Although residence must be voluntarily adopted, a residence dictated by the exigencies of business will count as voluntary residence: *Lysaght v Commissioners of Inland Revenue* (1928) 13 TC 511, 535;

(vi)   The purpose, while settled, may be for a limited period; and the relevant purposes may include education, business or profession as well as a love of a place: *R v Barnet LBC ex p Shah* [1983] 2 AC 309, 344;

(vii)   Where a person has had his sole residence in the United Kingdom he is unlikely to be held to have ceased to reside in the United Kingdom (or to have "left" the United Kingdom) unless there has been a definite break in his pattern of life: *Re Combe* (1932) 17 TC 405, 411.'

HMRC seemed to have clearly changed their approach to both residence and ordinary residence in recent years, albeit that they denied having done so. Their new approach was to require a person who claimed to have ceased to be UK resident to demonstrate that he had left the UK before he could be regarded as non-resident. It is only after they had accepted that he had become non-resident that the 91-day test applied.

The *Gaines-Cooper* case

9.29   In *R Gaines-Cooper v CIR* [2008] STC 1665, HMRC claimed that, in applying the 91-day test, the Commissioners should look at nights in the UK, whereas their previous approach had been to count a day only if the person was in the UK throughout that day. Furthermore, Mr Gaines-Cooper was held to be resident in the UK in some years even though he spent well under 90 days in the UK. This is what prompted HMRC to state in Revenue & Customs Brief 01/07 that they had not adopted a new approach and to seek to justify their approach in that case.

The facts of that case are complex and it is not intended to consider them here. The case emphasises that much of IR20 (the predecessor to HMRC6) was concessional. The courts and the Commissioners must apply the law. They cannot take any account of HMRC concessions (other than in the context of judicial review). In such circumstances it is not surprising that HMRC should argue the case on the basis of the law where this conflicts with their normal practice. An unfortunate side effect of relying on HMRC concessions is that if agreement cannot be reached with HMRC, an appeal to the Commissioners inevitably carries with it a need to forfeit the benefit of such concessions.

It should also be noted that both parties asked the Commissioners to look at the overall position over a period of 11 years, so it is not surprising that they did not hold him to be non-resident in years when his visits to the UK were minimal. Indeed HMRC view this as a case where the taxpayer, although living part of his time abroad and part of his time in the UK for over 20 years, had never left the UK, so the length of his visits were irrelevant. The High Court agreed with the Commissioners and the Court of Appeal refused leave to appeal. Mr Gaines-Cooper also sought judicial review of HMRC's approach on the basis that IR20 gave him a legitimate expectation that if he limited his time in the UK to under 91 days on average he would not be resident here. High Court, Court of Appeal and Supreme Court all held that he did not meet the precise wording of IR20 and thus could not rely on it ([2009] EWHC 2617 (Ch)).

DOMICILE

9.30

Focus

It is not easy to change one's domicile. Unlike with most tax issues it is for a person alleging a change of domicile to prove it. This means that if someone starts with a non-UK domicile, it is for HMRC to show that this has changed. Unless the person has stated on an HMRC form that he intends to live in the UK indefinitely, it is virtually impossible for HMRC to do this while the individual is still alive and able to go to the Tribunal and tell it what his intention is.

Where a client comes to the UK, take care with the completion of form P86 as completing it carelessly can seriously damage his domicile position.

There is no statutory definition of domicile. It is not a tax concept. It is a general legal concept. It ties a person to a system of law. It is accordingly an important concept in matrimonial and family law.

Domicile is largely a question of intention. It is the country (or state in the case of a country with a federal system where each state has its own legal system) that a person regards as his homeland.

A person starts life with a 'domicile of origin'. This is not the place where he was born. It is his father's domicile at the time of his (ie the son or daughter's) birth. If the father is not known it will be the mother's domicile.

A person's domicile can change during their lifetime. However, it is a fairly enduring concept. It is not easy to change one's domicile. If a person does acquire a new domicile and subsequently abandons his new country, his domicile of origin will revive.

9.31 There is an inference that a person retains his original domicile. It is for the person who alleges a change of domicile to prove it. This differs from the normal tax approach where it is for the taxpayer to disprove HMRC's contention.

To change one's domicile one must go to a new country with the intention of living there permanently or indefinitely. It is obviously difficult to prove intention. Indeed there are no published tax cases where HMRC have sought to show that a person who started life with a non-UK domicile of origin has become UK domiciled and that person is still alive. This is because if the individual can go before the First-tier Tribunal and give evidence of his intention, HMRC know that it is virtually impossible for them to show a change of domicile.

This does not mean that HMRC do not challenge domicile; it means that they defer doing so strongly until after a person's death as at that stage he is no longer able to say what his intention was, so the Tribunal has to discern that from the surrounding facts.

9.32   A person who starts life with a non-UK domicile of origin does not become UK domiciled merely by living in this country for many years. This is a common misconception. Many people who have lived in the UK even for 40 or 50 years are not domiciled here because they have retained an intention to return to their home country. Indeed, the probability is that a person who started life with a foreign domicile and came to the UK for a specific purpose, such as to study, to work or to marry, has retained his domicile of origin as it is unlikely that such a person has formed a decision never to return to his home country. Indeed such a person does not even need to show an intention to return to his home country; an intention to go somewhere else is sufficient as the test is whether or not he has ever had an intention to remain permanently in the UK.

Conversely, of course, a person who started life with a UK domicile of origin will have difficulty in convincing HMRC that he has obtained – and retained – a foreign 'domicile of choice', particularly if the claim to be non-UK domiciled is made at a time when he is living in the UK. That is not to say that it is not possible to do so. It depends on the facts. A UK-domiciled person who goes to, say, the US to study and while there marries and decides to stay there may well acquire a US domicile of choice. If his employer were later to send him to the UK to work, or he takes a job in the UK, he will retain his US domicile whilst he is in the UK provided that his intention is always to return to the US at some stage.

Whilst the UK and the US are referred to above, this is a form of shorthand. They are in fact both federal countries. A person cannot actually be domiciled in the UK. He must be domiciled in one of England and Wales, Scotland or Northern Ireland. It is important to realise that. If the hypothetical taxpayer envisaged above had gone to New York to study and now feels that when he retires he will not return to New York as it is too cold but will retire to Florida, his English domicile of origin will have revived when he made the decision not to return to New York as he would have abandoned his intention to live permanently in New York and could not have acquired a Florida domicile of choice as he would have to actually live there for a period before he could do so.

Although a person may retain his non-UK domicile, that does not necessarily mean that he retains the tax benefits of being non-domiciled. From 6 April

2017, a non-domiciled person who has been resident in the UK for all or part of 15 of the previous 20 tax years will be fully taxable here for all of income tax, capital gains tax and inheritance tax in the same way as a UK domiciled individual. Currently such 'deemed domicile' applies only for inheritance tax and only where the person has been UK resident for 17 of the previous 20 years. In addition, an individual, who both was born in the UK and has a UK domicile of origin, will be taxable on worldwide income and gains (and within the scope of inheritance tax on UK assets) for any tax year in which he is resident in the UK.

The UK has a small number of double tax agreements in relation to inheritance tax. In some of those agreements the reference to UK domicile includes deemed domicile but the older agreements refer only to domicile. Those agreements can protect from inheritance tax a person who is domiciled in the other country and deemed domiciled in the UK.

The tax significance of the two concepts

9.33   The most important concept for income tax is residence. A person is taxable on world-wide income if he is resident in the UK. He is taxable only on UK income – and even then there are some exemptions – if he is not resident here. This is subject to a major caveat. A person who is resident in the UK but not domiciled here (or, up to 5 April 2013, was not ordinarily resident here) is often taxable on non-UK source income only to the extent that it is brought into the UK.

From 6 April 2017, this remittance basis can apply only if:

(1)   the individual has been resident in the UK for less than 15 of the previous 20 tax years, and

(2)   he was not born in the UK with a UK domicile of origin.

If these two tests are met, the individual can use the remittance basis if either:

(a)   the individual has been UK resident for less than seven of the previous nine tax years;

(b)   the individual is under 18;

(c)   the individual pays a fee (albeit called a tax charge) to be able to use the remittance basis. The amount of the fee depends on the number of years that the taxpayer has been UK resident. It is £30,000 if he has been resident for at least seven of the previous nine tax years, and £60,000 if he has been resident for at least 12 of the previous 14 tax years;

   or

(d)   the individual's unremitted overseas income for the year is under £2,000.

415

Heads (a), (b) and (d) above also applied prior to 6 April 2017. In addition, the individual had to have been UK resident in at least 17 of the previous 20 years and had to pay a £90,000 fee for the year to purchase the privilege of using the remittance basis (nil if he has been resident less than seven of the previous nine years, £30,000 if he had been resident for less than 12 years but for at least seven of the previous nine tax years, and £60,000 (£50,000 for 2012/13 and 2014/15) if he has been resident for less than 17 years but for at least 12 of the previous 14 years). The £90,000 figure applied only for 2015/16 and 2016/17, the £50,000 figure applying to earlier years.

A person who is entitled to use the remittance basis under (a) to (c) above must complete a tax return and claim that basis in the return, unless (a) or (b) applies and he has both no UK income or gains and no remittances of overseas income or gains. Where (c) above applies the individual can choose year by year at the time he completes his tax return whether to claim the remittance basis and pay the fee. This is nominally tax on specified unremitted overseas income. The taxpayer must nominate at least £1 of such income and can nominate sufficient income and gains to cover the £30,000, £60,000 or £90,000. However, HMRC recommend that people should nominate only £1 unless they intend to claim double tax relief in an overseas country. This is because the nominated income is deemed to be the last amounts remitted and if such income is accidentally remitted the identification of remittances in subsequent years becomes a nightmare!

It is not at all clear that nominating overseas income will enable the £90,000 (or £60,000 or £30,000) to be treated as a 'tax' qualifying for double tax relief. That is up to the overseas country. It cannot be expected to take kindly to the UK introducing a device to seek to shift such money from the overseas treasury to the UK one. However, the nomination requirement was introduced primarily to seek to achieve relief against US tax, and the US tax authority has accepted that it does so. Indeed it is understood that they accept that it does so irrespective of the amount of income that is nominated, although that seems counter-intuitive so it would be safer to nominate sufficient to cover the whole of the taxable US income.

Up to 5 April 2013, one of the main income tax anti-avoidance provisions, *ITA 2007, ss 714–730* (transfer of assets abroad), only applied if a person was ordinarily resident in the UK.

9.34   Capital gains tax is also triggered by residence. Again, capital gains on overseas assets realised by a person who is not domiciled in the UK are taxable here only to the extent that they are remitted to the UK. Prior to 6 April 2013, capital gains tax was also triggered by ordinary residence here.

The restrictions on the use of the remittance basis rules from 2017/18 does not, of course, make unremitted income or gains of years up to 2016/17 freely remittable. Such income and gains will continue to be taxed on the remittance basis and will trigger tax here for the year in which they are remitted if the funds are brought into the UK.

9.35   Inheritance tax depends almost wholly on domicile. A person who is domiciled in the UK is taxable here on world-wide assets. A person who is not domiciled here is taxable only on UK assets. Residence is irrelevant with one exception. If, at the time of death or an *inter vivos* gift, the decedent or donor has been resident here during more than 15 of the previous 20 tax years (17 out of 20 prior to 6 April 2017) or, from 6 April 2017, is deemed domiciled because he was born here, he is chargeable to inheritance tax as if he were domiciled here.

A point to watch is that a person who is resident here at any time in the tax year is treated as resident throughout that year for this purpose. Accordingly, a person who comes to the UK on 5 April and makes a gift on 7 April 15 years later is deemed domiciled in the UK even though he has only been resident here for 15 years and three days.

The remittance basis

9.36

Focus

The key to the remittance basis is to ensure that the client has sufficient overseas bank accounts that he does not need to mix income with capital – and, of course, training him (and his overseas bank) to operate those accounts properly.

Where income and gains are taxable on a remittance basis it is up to the taxpayer to demonstrate that he has not remitted income or gains. If he cannot do so statutory rules apply to determine what has been remitted in relation to receipts into the account after 5 April 2008 (see **9.40**). The legislation is silent as to what happens after all such receipts have been identified. HMRC are likely to regard remittances as representing overseas income on a first-in, first-out basis up to the amount of such income that has arisen since the individual came to the UK. They will probably then treat further remittances as a mixture of capital gains and capital in proportion to the amount of gains and capital in the bank or other account from which the funds were remitted. That was their approach before 6 April 2008.

To avoid these presumptions a non-UK domiciled individual should maintain a number of overseas bank accounts and should take care to ensure that the money in the separate accounts is not mixed. In this context it is important to realise that income does not lose its nature by being invested.

For example, suppose a person has £100,000 of income overseas which he invests in overseas shares and that five years later he sells the shares for £150,000. The £150,000 is £100,000 of income and £50,000 of capital gain, not £100,000 of capital and £50,000 of capital gain. Accordingly, an individual who wants to avoid remitting capital needs to monitor very carefully what is paid into his overseas bank accounts.

9.37   At a minimum a non-domiciled individual needs to maintain two overseas bank accounts, one for income and the other for capital. He then needs to ensure that all income arising overseas is paid into the income account. It can be difficult to convince some overseas banks of the importance of keeping a rigid separation between the two. In particular it is unwise to credit the interest on a capital deposit account to that account and then immediately transfer it to the income account. This is not necessarily fatal, as it may well be possible to convince the First-tier Tribunal that what has been transferred out is the same funds as were paid in. However, it becomes more difficult to do this if other transactions take place in the account between the time of the credit and the time of the transfer out, particularly if the account is overdrawn. It also, of course, needlessly presents HMRC with the opportunity to argue the point.

9.38   If a person generates capital gains overseas, he also ideally ought to have one or more capital gains accounts. It needs to be appreciated though that the sale proceeds of an asset is itself a mixed fund. It is not possible to demonstrate which part is the original capital and segregate it from the gain. The whole of the sale proceeds need to be paid into the capital gains account. There are two caveats to this. The first is that if a share is sold at a loss no part of the proceeds can be gain; the whole amount must be original capital (unless, of course, the initial purchase price represented income or earlier capital gains). Accordingly, where a share or other asset is sold at a loss the whole of the proceeds ought to be paid into the capital account (which represents freely remittable funds). The second is that it probably does not matter if small gains are paid into the capital account. This is because if capital gains are remitted the amount remitted is deemed to be gains of the year they are remitted.

A person is not taxable on (and does not need to declare) capital gains which total in aggregate less than £11,700 pa. Accordingly, if the total capital gains paid into the capital account are below this figure it is irrelevant whether or not they are remitted (unless the taxpayer has already utilised his annual allowance against UK gains). If they exceed that figure there is a problem particularly if the gains form a large proportion of the capital in the account.

9.39   If a person makes a large number of disposals of overseas assets it may be sensible to pay the disposal proceeds into one capital gains account where the taxable gain element of a disposal is high in proportion to cost, into a different bank account where the proportion is relatively low and perhaps into the capital account where it is small. Remittances would be made from the capital account until it is exhausted; then from the second capital gains account (as the taxable proportion is lower); then from the first capital gains account; and finally from income.

HMRC take the view that it is impossible to remit a loss. Accordingly, a person who is taxed on the remittance basis obtained no relief for losses prior to 5 April 2008. From that date it is possible to make an irrevocable election to qualify such losses for relief. Such an election normally needed to be made by 5 April 2012. It is not necessarily beneficial. This is because the taxpayer's UK losses are then set against unremitted overseas gains in preference to UK gains. That makes the election unattractive if the taxpayer has significant UK assets and is unlikely to remit overseas gains.

Remittances from mixed funds

9.40   The legislation spells out in detail how remittances from mixed funds are to be identified. A mixed fund for this purpose covers two things. Anything which contains both income and capital, or capital gains and capital, or all three, is a mixed fund. As indicated above, the sale proceeds of an asset will automatically constitute a mixed fund under this test. In addition a single fund, such as an income bank account, which contains items arising in more than one year, is also a mixed fund.

The order of remittances is:

(a)   employment income that is taxable in the UK whether remitted or not and that is not liable to foreign tax;

(b)   employment income for non-UK duties (if not ordinarily resident) or from a separate overseas employment and which is not liable to foreign tax;

(c)   income from employment-related securities that is not liable to foreign tax;

(d)   overseas investment income that is not liable to foreign tax;

(e)   overseas chargeable gains that are not liable to foreign tax;

(f)   employment income liable to a foreign tax;

(g)   overseas investment income liable to a foreign tax;

(h)   overseas chargeable gains liable to a foreign tax; and

(i)   income or capital not falling within any other head.

The tests are applied first to the amounts of income, capital gains or other items for the tax year in which the payment out occurs that have been paid into the mixed fund in the same tax year prior to the date of the remittance. They are then applied to the income or gains of the previous year, and so on until the whole of the amount remitted has been identified. Curiously, if overseas income of year 1 is invested overseas and the investment is realised in a later year the capital gain element is identified against remittances in priority to the income element, which is the reverse of the rule that applied before 6 April 2008.

The above identification rules apply to all remittances in 2008/09 or later. However, if remittances exceed the post 5 April 2008 income and gains, so that earlier income or gains are deemed to be remitted, the previous 'rules' apply to determine what income or gains have been remitted. That is a bit of a misnomer. Prior to 6 April 2008, the legislation was silent on the order of remittances. HMRC practice was to identify remittances against income as far as possible and then against a mixture of income and capital, in both cases on a first in, first out basis. As it is for the taxpayer to demonstrate that the HMRC identification is incorrect it is difficult to challenge this.

Up to 5 April 2019, a person to whom the remittance basis applied for any year up to 2016/17 (whether or not it still applies) by virtue of his having paid the remittance basis charge and who was not born in the UK with a UK domicile of origin can rearrange money held in a mixed fund by segregating each element into separate overseas bank accounts (*Finance (No 2) Bill 2017*). However, he can only do this once in relation to a particular bank account. This is a potential problem because it is only money that can be recategorised; if an investment derived from a mixed fund is held, this cannot be recategorised, albeit that the proceeds can be if the investment is sold during 2017/18 or 2018/19. Accordingly, the timing of the reallocation can be important in individual cases. The taxpayer must, of course, also have maintained records to be able to demonstrate the source of the balance on the bank account. If he cannot do so, back to the opening of the account, he can at least segregate the funds for the part of the period for which he has records. For pre-6 April 2008 balances, the legislation allows for a rough and ready split in certain circumstances, but that does not apply to post-5 April 2008 deposits. Even where a taxpayer kept separate overseas bank accounts for different types of receipt, this is an important relief because it allows capital gains to be segregated from the original cost price of the asset, which was not possible under the normal remittance basis rules.

Example 9.2 – Identification of account balance

Carl is Canadian domiciled. He was born in Canada but has lived in the UK for 25 years. He has a bank account in Jersey on which the balance at 31 December 2018 is £80,000. He analyses the make-up of the account (applying the above rules to payments out of the account since 5 April 2008) and discovers that the balance is made up as follows:

Income	£20,000
Capital gains element of sales of assets	£25,000
Original capital	£35,000
	£80,000

Carl moves £35,000 to a new capital account in Jersey and £25,000 to a new capital gains account. Following the transfers (and probably the notification to HMRC of the segregation), Carl can remit the £35,000 to the UK without tax and, if he remits the £25,000, it will be taxed wholly as a capital gain. Carl can, of course, split the existing balance into nine separate overseas accounts if he has amounts in the account falling into each of the categories (a) to (i) above.

What is a remittance?

9.41

Focus

In looking at whether funds have been remitted it is not sufficient to look only at what the client has done. You need to identify all of his relevant persons (specified associates) and ensure that the client's overseas income has not been indirectly remitted by a relevant person. In particular it is usually unsafe to allow an overseas company to invest in the UK if it has been funded by the client.

Money or property is remitted to the UK if it is brought to, or received or used in, the UK by or for the benefit of a 'relevant person' and the property is or derives from overseas income or gains of the taxpayer. There is also a remittance if a service is provided in the UK to, or for the benefit of, a 'relevant person' and the property is, or derives from, overseas income or gains. There can also be a remittance if property gifted to a third party is brought to, or received or used in, the UK and enjoyed by a relevant person. It is important to realise that bringing assets into the UK that have been purchased overseas out of foreign income or gains can trigger a remittance. There are some limited exceptions including a £1,000 *de minimis* exemption. It should particularly be stressed that the quantum of the remittance where goods are brought to the UK is their cost, not their value at the time they come into the UK.

There is also a remittance if the funds are used (directly or indirectly) outside the UK in respect of a 'relevant debt'. A relevant debt is, of course, one that relates to property or services that would have triggered a remittance had it been financed otherwise than by the borrowing. Unlike under the previous legislation, the payment of interest on a relevant debt outside the UK constitutes a remittance. There is an exception for interest on a mortgage made before 12 March 2008 for the purpose of enabling the individual to acquire an interest in residential property in the UK (and for no other purpose). This exception will cease if terms of the loan (or any supporting guarantee) are varied, the loan ceases to be secured on the property, any other debt is secured on the property or the property ceases to be owned by the individual.

Relevant persons

9.42   A relevant person is:

(a)   the individual;

(b)   the individual's spouse or civil partner;

(c)   a person living with the individual as if they were their spouse or civil partner;

(d)   a child or grandchild of a person within (a) to (c) who is under 18;

(e)   a close company (or one that would be close if it were UK resident, or a 51% subsidiary of such a company) in which a relevant person is a participator (however small the shareholding may be), or a 51% subsidiary of such a company;

(f)   the trustees of a settlement of which a relevant person is a beneficiary, or a body connected with such a settlement.

This can create extreme difficulties in determining what is a remittance. For example, suppose that the individual makes a gift out of a capital gain to his adult son in France. The son later visits the UK with his young children and uses his credit card to pay for a family meal in the UK. The credit card is settled from the French bank account into which the gift was deposited. The cost of the meal for the son and his wife is not a deemed remittance of the capital gain but the cost of his children's meal is as they are relevant persons in relation to the donor under (d). It is unclear how the donor is expected to obtain the information that he needs to complete his tax return.

The government view is that:

> 'individuals giving unremitted money or assets offshore to a relevant person would need to make arrangements with that person, to enable them to keep track of any remittances to the UK. I acknowledge that there is a complexity for the taxpayer' (Jane Kennedy PBC, 19 June 2008 Col 830).

Unfortunately, she did not mention the added complexity of a gift to a non-relevant person who might use some of it to benefit a relevant person.

Exemptions

9.43   The following do not constitute a remittance:

(a)   the payment of the £30,000 or £60,000 fee, but only if it is made direct to HMRC from an overseas bank account;

(b)   clothing, footwear, jewellery and watches that are acquired out of foreign income or gains and are both the property of a relevant person and for the personal use of a relevant person;

(c)   any other property that derives from foreign income or gains where its cost is under £1,000;

(d)   any other property that derives from foreign income or gains that is temporarily imported into the UK, ie that is here in aggregate for not more than 275 days (counting from 6 April 2008 onwards indefinitely, so that track will need to be kept of each such item, perhaps over a 20- or 30-year period until the 275-day figure is breached, making the cost taxable);

(e)   property that derives from foreign income or gains that is brought into the UK solely for repair or restoration and taken out again once it has been repaired;

(f)   items that are brought to the UK for public display at an approved museum, gallery or other establishment approved by HMRC (this used to be restricted to works of art and collectors pieces and antiques but this limitation no longer applies from 6 April 2013);

(g)   payments outside the UK (ie to a non-UK bank account) in consideration of services provided in the UK which relate wholly or mainly to property situated outside the UK (unless they fall within anti-avoidance rules).

None of these exemptions (other than (g)) can apply to money. Furthermore, if the property ceases to qualify for the exemption there is a deemed remittance at that time. Again, it should be stressed that if the property is sold in the UK the deemed remittance is of the cost not of the sale proceeds. A deemed remittance can arise in some unexpected circumstances. For example, if an expensive dress is gifted to a UK charity shop it will cease to meet the exemption (but if it is gifted to a foreign charity shop no tax charge should arise). If an expensive dress is brought into the UK for use by a mother and while in the UK is gifted to her 17-year-old daughter that will not trigger a tax charge as the daughter is a relevant person. However, it will trigger a tax charge on the daughter's 18th birthday, as she will then cease to be a relevant person (but if on that day the dress is outside the UK, no tax charge will arise).

From 6 April 2013, the exemption will not be lost if the property is lost, stolen or destroyed unless compensation, such as insurance proceeds, is received in respect of it. From 6 April 2012, the tax charge on a sale of exempt property can be avoided by taking the sale proceeds overseas. The proceeds are then not treated as having been remitted provided that the sale is not to a relevant person, it is by way of a bargain at arm's length, once the property is sold no relevant person has an interest in it or can benefit from it, the whole of the sale proceeds are received by the seller within 95 days of the sale date, the sale is not made as part of (or as a result of) a scheme or arrangement one of the main purposes of which is the avoidance of tax, and the whole of the sale proceeds are taken out of the UK (or used to make qualifying investments) within 45 days of the receipt of the proceeds (or of the receipt of the last instalment of them). It should particularly be noted that the whole amount must be taken overseas – except to the extent of fees deducted before the consideration is paid to the seller. If the asset is sold at a gain, that will, of course, be a UK chargeable gain. Similarly from 6 April 2013 compensation received for the loss, theft or destruction of the property will not trigger a tax charge if the compensation is taken overseas within 45 days of its receipt.

CGT rebasing

9.44   A person who paid the remittance basis fee for any tax year from 2008/09 to 2016/17, was not born in the UK with a UK domicile of origin, meets Condition B in *ITA 2007, s 835BA*, remains non-UK domiciled (albeit excluded from use of the remittance basis) and was not born in the UK with a UK domicile of origin, can rebase CGT assets that he personally held at 5 April 2017 (and did not transfer overseas after 16 March 2016) (*F(No 2)A 2017, Sch 8, para 41*). This is an attractive concession because it will enable the entire gain on the asset to be remitted, with no UK tax being payable on the pre-6 April 2017 element of the gain.

> **Example 9.3 – Rebasing at 5 April 2017**
>
> Jay is domiciled in India. He was born in India but has lived in the UK for the last 20 years. He owns a house in New York which cost £400,000, but was worth £2 million at 5 April 2017. Jay sells the house for £2.2 million in 2018/19. Although he will realise a capital gain of £1.6 million, Jay is taxed as if it were £200,000 (£2.2 million less £2 million). Assuming that the initial £400,000 was capital, Jay can remit the whole of the £2.2 million and pay tax of only £40,000 (20% of £200,000).

No election is required. The rebasing is automatic. However, if an asset is disposed of for which the taxpayer would prefer not to use the 5 April 2017 value, he can elect to calculate the tax by reference to the figure that would otherwise have applied. He might want to do this if the asset fell in value between the acquisition and 5 April 2017. Such an election is irrevocable. However, it applies only to that asset; the election does not affect disposals of other assets either in the same, or a later, tax year. The effect of rebasing is to exclude the part of the gain that accrued before 6 April 2017 from UK tax, even if it is remitted.

It should particularly be noted that this rebasing applies only to assets held personally. It will not apply to assets held within an overseas company or trust. Also the asset must remain outside the UK until it is sold (subject to the same exemptions as are set out above).

Relief for remittances for investment purposes (business investment relief)

9.45   From 6 April 2012, a taxpayer can make a claim to treat income or chargeable gains as not having been remitted if they are either used by a relevant person to make a qualifying investment, or brought to the UK in order to be used to make such an investment. An individual makes a qualifying investment if either shares in a company (or securities of a company) are issued to the individual, or the individual makes a loan (secured or unsecured) to the company and Conditions A and B are met when the investment is made.

Condition A is that the company is either an eligible trading company or an eligible stakeholder company. An eligible trading company is a private limited company which carries on one or more commercial trades (or is preparing to do so within the next two years), and carrying on commercial trades is all or substantially all of what it does (or what it is reasonably expected to do once it begins trading). An eligible stakeholder company is a private limited company which exists wholly for the purpose of making investments in eligible trading companies (ignoring any minor or incidental purposes), and holds one or more such investments or is preparing to do so within the next two years. For this purpose, a private limited company is a body corporate whose liability is limited, which is not an LLP, and none of whose shares is listed on a recognised stock exchange. A trade includes anything that is treated for corporation tax purposes as if it were a trade, and also a business carried on for generating income from land. Carrying on research and development activities from which it is intended that a commercial trade will be derived, or will benefit, is treated as the carrying on of a commercial trade but preparing to carry on such R & D activities is not.

Condition B is that no relevant person has (directly or indirectly) obtained (or become entitled to obtain) any related benefit, and none expect to obtain any such benefit. For this purpose a benefit includes the provision of anything that would not be provided to the relevant person in the ordinary course of business or would only be so provided on less favourable terms. A benefit excludes anything provided to the relevant person in the ordinary course of business and on arm's length terms. A benefit is a related benefit if it is directly or indirectly attributable to the making of the investment (whether it is obtained before or after the investment is made), or it is reasonable to assume that the benefit would not be available in the absence of the investment. The provision of a benefit includes any arrangements that allow a person to enjoy any benefit from the thing in question (either temporarily or permanently) and covers things provided in money or money's worth including property, capital, goods or services of any kind.

The investment must be made within 45 days of the money being brought into the UK. This could cause a problem if a loan is to be drawn down over a period. The election cannot be made where exempt property is brought into the UK and is subsequently used to make the investment, even though *ITA 2007, s 809Y* treats the property as triggering a remittance charge when the investment is made.

There is a tight time limit for the claim; the first anniversary of 31 January following the tax year in which the income or gains are remitted to the UK. It does not appear that the company needs to be a UK company or that its trade needs to be in the UK. The relief does not apply if there is a scheme or arrangement the main purpose of which, or one of the main purposes of which, is the avoidance of tax. From 6 April 2013, compensation received in the UK for the loss, theft or destruction of property brought into the UK from overseas can also be invested in such qualifying investments rather than having to be taken overseas to avoid a tax charge. It must be invested within 45 days of receipt.

The amount will be treated as remitted at a later date if:

(a)   the target company ceases to be an eligible trading company or an eligible stakeholder company and the entire shareholding is not sold and the money taken out of the UK within 45 days of the relevant person becoming (or ought to become) aware of that fact;

(b)   the relevant person who made the investment ceases to be a relevant person and the entire shareholding is not sold and the money taken out of the UK within 45 days of the relevant person becoming (or ought to become) aware of that fact (remember that a child ceases to be a relevant person on his 18th birthday);

(c)   the relevant person disposes of all or part of the holding and does not take the money out of the UK (other than the amount needed to pay the CGT on the gain) within 45 days of receiving the disposal proceeds;

(d)   value is received by (or for the benefit of) a relevant person from an involved company/the target company, an investee company or a connected company (other than by a disposal of all or part of the holding) and the money is not taken out of the UK within 45 days of the value being received; or

(e)   the two-year start-up rule is breached and the entire shareholding is not sold and the money taken out of the UK within 45 days of the relevant person becoming aware of the fact.

There is no deemed tax charge if the company takes an insolvency step for genuine commercial reasons (except to the extent of money received from that step). As an alternative to taking the money overseas, it can be reinvested in another qualifying investment. It is only necessary to take the income or gains amount out of the UK. If part of the investment was capital that does not need to be taken overseas again – but the entire holding still needs to be sold. The sale proceeds must be taken out of the UK 'in the form in which they are received'. That is a potential problem as it is not always possible to take an IOU out of the UK as its *situs* is normally treated as being in the UK. Curiously, although the legislation requires a disposal of the entire holding, it seems to allow the proceeds to be reinvested in the same company. If a disposal is not by way of a bargain at arm's length, it is deemed to be made at market value – and it is that market value amount that needs to be taken outside the UK. It is not clear how this can be done if it exceeds the actual proceeds. Where investments are made at different times in the same company, disposals are deemed to take place on a first in, first out basis. There are special rules for mixed funds (*ITA 2007, ss 809VA–809VN*).

Employment income

9.46

Focus

Where a client will work partly in the UK and partly overseas consider whether a dual-contract structure is appropriate. However, to do this the work must be capable of being compartmentalised. It is not sufficient for one contract to cover UK work and the other non-UK as HMRC contend that any UK work that is integral to the overseas work prevents that work being carried out wholly outside the UK. If a job involves some pure overseas tasks and some where the work will be partly done in the UK and partly overseas, consider putting the pure overseas tasks into an overseas employer and leaving the mixed ones to be performed under the UK employment contract.

Employment income is taxable on a remittance basis only if the employee is resident but not domiciled in the UK, the employment is with a foreign employer and the duties of the employment are performed wholly outside the UK (*ITEPA 2003, ss 21–23*). (Prior to 6 April 2013 he also had to be not ordinarily resident here.) For this purpose, duties performed in the UK can be treated as performed outside the UK if they are 'merely incidental' to the performance of overseas duties (*ITEPA 2003, s 39*). In practice, HMRC tend to ignore less than ten days of UK duties as *de minimis*.

9.47   In *Robson v Dixon (Inspector of Taxes)* (1972) 48 TC 527, Pennycuick V-C observed that the words 'merely incidental' are upon that ordinary usage apt to denote an activity (here the performance of duties) which does not serve any independent purpose but is carried out in order to further some other purpose'. In that case an airline pilot who was based in the Netherlands made 38 take-offs and landings in the UK out of 811 in the year. The UK landings were held not to be merely incidental to the Netherlands ones. HMRC interpret this as meaning that duties performed in the UK that are of the same type as those performed overseas are not merely incidental even if performed for only a very short time (*Tax Bulletin*, Issue 76). Visits to the UK to report to a group's head office are likely to be merely incidental to the overseas performance of the subject of the report.

9.48   A non-UK domiciled employee should consider whether he can use a dual-contract arrangement under which he is employed by an overseas company for non-UK duties and a UK company for UK ones. However, *ITEPA 2003, s 24A*, which was inserted by *FA 2014, Sch 3, para 3*, makes this very difficult although not wholly impossible. HMRC do not like such arrangements and are likely to look at them closely. HMRC have said that:

> 'Given the way in which modern business operates and the ease and speed of communication, some employees may find it increasingly difficult to avoid performing substantive UK duties under their overseas contracts. For example, an employee who is responsible under their overseas contract for servicing the business of overseas clients may have to respond to a telephone call or e-mail from a worried overseas client with an urgent problem when the employee is in the UK. Formulating and communicating a response to such a problem would be regarded as a fundamental duty under the overseas contract. It follows that the performance of such duties in the UK will not be merely incidental to the performance of duties outside the UK as they will be of equal importance to the overseas duties. It is the quality of the UK duties and not the time devoted to their performance that determines whether they are merely incidental' (*Tax Bulletin*, Issue 76).

9.49   It is questionable whether that is wholly correct. For example, if a person carries out overseas duties and sends a report to his UK office and next time he is in the office he responds to a telephone call from the client and the response could have been equally made by someone else in the office who had read the report, answering the telephone is unlikely to be a duty of the overseas employment. In other words, the duties are normally segregable if the employee can deal with the UK and overseas aspects wearing two different hats, but would not be segregable if the only person who can perform the UK activity is the person who performed the overseas one, eg because it requires information that is in his head or they are both part of an ongoing negotiation.

9.50   It is generally sensible to list the duties of the overseas employment in detail in the employment contracts. This not only makes clear what those duties are but it highlights when the contract is drawn up the extent to which segregation is practical. Where some duties can be segregated and some cannot, it is advisable to limit the overseas employment to the segregable ones and leave the remaining duties in the UK employment. It does not matter that that includes overseas duties; the key thing is that the overseas employment should not include any UK duties.

9.51   Where a dual-contract arrangement is used it also needs to be borne in mind that the remuneration for the overseas employment needs to be paid outside the UK (as payment in the UK is equivalent to a remittance).

Care also needs to be taken with expenses. If the UK company reimburses expenses incurred on the overseas contracts, HMRC are likely to contend that the arrangements are a sham. If a group has a policy of channelling all expenses through the UK and recharging them to the appropriate company there should be no problem though.

9.52   Where an employee has two or more employments with the same employer or with associated employers (ie under common control), and any of the duties are performed in the UK the emoluments must be aggregated and re-apportioned between the UK and overseas duties in such manner as is reasonable having regard to the nature of, and time devoted to, the UK and overseas duties respectively, and all other relevant circumstances (*ITEPA 2003, s 24*).

Accordingly, if a dual-contract arrangement is used, the split of the salary between the two needs to be done on a basis that can be justified. HMRC's starting point is likely to be to expect the split to reflect the time involved in the respective duties. They are unlikely to accept that overseas work deserves a higher daily rate because it is inconvenient, but should accept that it does so because the employee works longer hours when he is overseas.

9.53   In addition to the rules on UK-linked debts referred to earlier, earnings are treated as remitted to the UK if they are paid, used or enjoyed in the UK or transmitted or brought to the UK in any manner or form (*ITEPA 2003, s 33*). Accordingly, if the employee uses overseas earnings to purchase assets such as a car or a painting and brings them into the UK the earnings used to purchase the assets are regarded as remitted to the UK (Employment Income Manual at EIM40302). HMRC indicate that in general the purchase of investments abroad should not be regarded as a remittance even if the share certificate is brought into the UK, as they will not be enjoyed here, but the sale of such investments in the UK will constitute a remittance.

Travelling expenses

9.54   An employee who is non-UK domiciled is not taxed on travelling expenses (including accommodation) from and to his home country in the five years from the date he comes to the UK (not any later date on which he starts the employment) provided that the cost of the travel is either borne by his employer or is paid by the employee and reimbursed to him by his employer (*ITEPA 2003, s 379*). This relief applies only if the employee did not visit the UK in the two years prior to coming to the UK to work and was not resident in the UK in the two years preceding that in which he came to the UK. There is no limit on the number of journeys qualifying for relief in the five-year period.

Where this relief applies it also extends to the costs of two return journeys per year made by each of the employee's spouse and his infant children, either accompanying him when he came to the UK or to visit him in the UK (*ITEPA 2003, s 374*). Again, the cost must either be borne by the employer or paid by the employee and reimbursed to him by his employer.

Self-employment income

9.55   It is virtually impossible for a person who is resident in the UK to carry on a trade outside the UK as a sole trader. This is because a trade is carried on where its control and management takes place. If the proprietor is UK resident the trade will inevitably be controlled and managed from the UK. In such circumstances overseas income will simply be a receipt of the UK trade.

It is possible for a trade carried on in partnership to be controlled and managed outside the UK if one of the partners is non-UK resident. In such circumstances the UK-resident partners' share of profits will be taxed on a remittance basis.

Overseas workday relief

9.56   Where a person comes to the UK and works both in the UK and overseas a special relief applies for the first three tax years of UK residence (provided that he has not been UK resident for any of the three tax years prior to coming here). Provided that such a person is non-UK domiciled and entitled to use the remittance basis (as will normally be the case), he can use the remittance basis for those three years in respect of overseas earnings from an employment with a non-UK resident employer even if that employment is not carried on wholly outside the UK. The earnings are apportioned between UK and overseas work on a just and reasonable basis (*ITEPA 2003, ss 15, 23, 26A, 41ZA* as amended or inserted by *FA 2013, Schs 6* and *44*).

In practice HMRC are likely to contend that this requires the apportionment to be made on a time basis. The proportion attributed to UK work is taxed irrespective of whether or not it is remitted but the part attributed to overseas work is taxed here only if and when it is brought into the UK. The operation of this rule creates an identification problem with remittances to ensure that the part attributable to UK work is not taxed twice.

Accordingly, a taxpayer who wants to use this relief can nominate a separate overseas bank account into which his earnings will be paid and to which simplified identification rules can apply. Such a nomination must be made by 31 January following the end of the first tax year to which it applies. The account must be an ordinary bank account. It cannot be the nominated account of more than one person (so spouses cannot use a joint account).

Nothing must be paid into the nominated account other than earnings from the employment, disposal proceeds of employment-related securities and interest on the account. If something else is accidentally paid into the account it must be transferred out within 30 days of its being discovered (together with any later prohibited receipts). However, this applies only to the first two mistakes. A third mistake cannot be remedied; the account will cease to be a nominated account. Where an individual has such a nominated account special identification rules apply. The total amount remitted to the UK in the year is first identified and treated as a single transfer made at the end of the tax year. All other transfers out of the account are treated as a second single transfer made immediately after the first. The normal mixed account rules are then applied to those two deemed single transfers. These treat employment income (ie UK earnings) for a tax year as being remitted in priority to foreign employment income for that year. Having determined the deemed make up of the two deemed single payments, each individual transfer is treated as containing the same proportions of the different types of income (*ITA 2007, ss 809RA–809RD* inserted by *FA 2013, Sch 6, para 6*).

TAXATION OF NON-UK RESIDENTS

Investment income

9.57 As indicated above, the UK charges non-UK residents to income tax only on income arising in the UK. Even then not all UK income is taxable. The tax chargeable on a non-UK resident is limited to the tax that would be payable on the individual's UK employment income, trading income and property income (plus, where applicable, deemed income from the release of a loan to a participant of a close company, gains from certain UK insurance policies, disposals of futures and options involving guaranteed returns, non-trading income from intellectual property and film and sound recordings) if he were not entitled to personal allowances, plus any tax deducted at source from other types of income (*ITA 2007, ss 811–814*).

This means that the following types of UK income are not taxable except to the extent of any withholding tax (*ITA 2007, s 813*):

- interest (there is a 20% withholding tax unless the interest is bank interest;

- purchased life annuity payment;

- profits from deeply discounted securities;

- distributions from unauthorised unit trusts;

- transactions in deposits;

- royalties and other income from intellectual property (there is a 20% withholding tax);

- certain telecommunication rights;

- annual payments not otherwise chargeable to tax (there is a 20% withholding tax);

- dividends from UK companies;

- UK social security pensions;

- certain other UK pensions and employment-related annuities;

- social security income (other than income support or jobseekers allowance, although these are unlikely to be paid to non-residents);

- some trading transactions carried out by an independent broker in the normal course of his business;

- any other types of income tax that the Treasury may exclude by regulation.

The above types of income are, however, taxable if they are received through a UK representative of the non-resident who is carrying on a trade in the UK on behalf of the non-resident through a branch or agency (*ITA 2007, s 814*).

Employment income

9.58 A person who is not UK resident is taxable on employment income only to the extent that it relates to duties performed in the UK. The applicable earnings are obviously calculated by apportioning the person's salary between that attributable to UK and non-UK work. Up to 5 April 2008, this limitation also applied to an individual who was resident in the UK but not ordinarily resident here in the tax year in which it was earned (*ITEPA 2003, s 25*). This relief has been preserved as overseas workday relief (see **9.56**).

Most of the UK's double tax agreements prevent the UK from taxing the UK earnings of a resident of the other country if that person is present in the UK for 183 days or less in any 12-month period commencing or ending in the year of assessment concerned, the employer is not UK resident and the remuneration is not borne by a UK permanent establishment. This exclusion does not normally apply to entertainers and sportsmen.

If a person is resident in the UK he is also taxable here on earnings for duties performed outside the UK to the extent that they are remitted to the UK (*ITEPA 2003, s 26*).

Trading income

9.59 A non-resident who carries on a trade in the UK through a branch or agency is taxable on the profits of that branch or agency. It is unclear whether it is possible for a non-resident to carry on a trade here as a sole trader other than through a branch or agency. This is because a trade is normally carried on at the place from which it is controlled and managed, and it would be fairly unusual for that not to take place where the proprietor is resident.

It used to be thought that a trade could not be carried on in the UK if all of its sales contracts were made outside the UK. However, the courts now tend to look at the overall substance of the trade. Where the substance of the trade is primarily in the UK – such as a trade of dealing in UK property – it is sensible for a non-resident to seek to ensure that all contracts are entered into outside the UK and also to evidence that he makes decisions in relation to the trade in his home country.

Property income

9.60 The basic rule is that the rental agent (or the last agent in the chain if there is more than one) must deduct tax at 20% from the rent and account for it quarterly to HMRC (*ITA 2007, ss 971, 972* and the *Taxation of Income from Land (Non-Residents) Regulations 1995, SI 1995/2902*). He can calculate this deduction on the rents that he receives less any expenses he pays on the landlord's behalf during the quarter that he reasonably believes are deductible in calculating the taxable income of the UK property business. He cannot deduct expenses paid direct by the landlord. In most cases the largest expense is likely to be loan interest and this is normally either paid by the landlord or the rents are paid into a bank account with the lender. It is rare for it to be paid by the agent.

Accordingly, where there are borrowings the tax deduction is likely to exceed the tax actually due on the profits of the UK property business. Where there is no agent the tenant is obliged to deduct tax at 20% from the rent and to account for it to HMRC.

9.61 Alternatively, the non-resident can elect to be taxed directly under the Non-Resident Landlord's Scheme. This requires the approval of HMRC. When approved, HMRC will authorise the agent or tenant not to deduct tax from the rents. Until he receives such authorisation the agent must deduct tax. Most non-resident landlords opt to use this scheme. It ensures that only the right amount of tax is paid. The non-resident has to file an annual tax return and must pay tax in accordance with the normal self-assessment rules, which, of course, require interim tax payments to be made based on the previous year's income.

A non-resident individual should normally consider holding UK property through a non-UK company. There are two reasons for this. The individual will pay tax on rental income at rates of up to 45% if the income exceeds the basic rate tax band, whereas an overseas company pays income tax at the 20% basic rate. The second is that as the property is situated in the UK it is within the scope of UK inheritance tax if it is held by the individual but will be outside the scope of IHT if held through an overseas company. This exception does not apply from 6 April 2017 to the extent that the property is residential property.

Capital gains tax

9.62 An individual is normally chargeable to CGT only if he is resident in the UK at some time during the tax year in which the gain is realised. Prior to 6 April 2013 the tax also applied if he was ordinarily resident here. Split-year treatment can apply in the circumstances set out in the statutory residence test (see **9.2**).

9.63   There are three important exceptions to this basic rule. The first is that if a non-UK resident is carrying on a trade, profession or vocation in the UK through a branch or agency he is liable to tax on gains on the disposal of UK assets which are used in (or held for the purpose of) the branch or agency at the time the gain accrues, or were used (or held for) such a purpose at an earlier time or have been acquired for use for such a purpose. For the charge to apply the trade must be carried on at the date of the disposal (*TCGA 1992, s 10*). The provision can be overridden by double tax agreements. The same rule applies for corporation tax (*TCGA 1992, s 10B*).

9.64   The second is that a taxpayer who is a temporary non-resident (see **9.6**) is chargeable to CGT in the period of return on some gains realised during his period of non-residence (*TCGA 1992, s 10A* as amended by *FA 2013, Sch 43, para 117*).

9.65   Where *TCGA 1992, s 10A* applies, the individual is treated as realising in the year of return capital gains equal to the aggregate of the gains that arose to him during his period of temporary non-residence and gains that would have been deemed to arise to him during that period under *TCGA 1992, s 13* (gains of overseas company with a UK shareholder) or *TCGA 1992, s 86* (gains of overseas settlement with a UK settlor). He is similarly treated as realising any losses that accrued to him during the period of non-residence (or would have been deemed to so accrue under *TCGA 1992, s 13*) (*TCGA 1992, s 10AA(3)* inserted by *FA 2013, Sch 43, para 117*). It should be noted that if losses actually realised by the taxpayer exceed the taxable gains, the excess loss is an allowable loss deemed to accrue in the year of return.

There is an exception for assets that were acquired during the period of temporary non-residence and disposed of during that period. This exception does not apply if the asset was acquired under a no gain, no loss acquisition, it was an interest created by (or arising under) a settlement, or a gain on another asset was rolled over into that asset (*TCGA 1992, s 10A(3)*).

The third is residential property in the UK. From 6 April 2015, non-residents are liable to capital gains tax on the disposal of (or of an interest in) UK residential property (see **9.73** below).

9.66   Where an individual would have been resident in the UK but was excluded from doing so by a double tax treaty, deemed gains taxable on the individual under *TCGA 1992, s 13* or *TCGA 1992, s 87* or *89(2)* (gains of overseas settlement) are not taxable on him. However, the double tax treaty is to be interpreted so as to permit actual gains arising to the individual in the period of non-residence to be taxed on his return (*TCGA 1992, s 10(9B), (9C)*).

This prevents an individual seeking to establish residence in a treaty country which did not itself tax capital gains for a year, realising a large gain, and then returning to the UK in the following year. Belgium was a popular country. It is questionable whether that device was in any event effective. It is hard to see why another country should want to argue that a person was resident there in circumstances where it would collect no tax by doing so and could see that the reason for claiming residence there was to seek to avoid UK tax. Furthermore, it is by no means clear that taxing an amount equal to a gain is the same thing as taxing the gain.

9.67   To prevent a non-resident being able to escape a CGT charge under *TCGA 1992, s 10* where he carries on a trade in the UK, there is a deemed disposal if he takes the asset outside the UK or ceases the UK trade prior to selling the asset. Where an asset held by a non-resident for the purpose of a UK trade is removed from the UK, and so ceases to be a chargeable asset, it must be treated as being disposed of and re-acquired at its market value immediately before it left the UK *(TCGA 1992, s 25(1))*. This does not apply if the asset is taken outside the UK contemporaneously with the person ceasing to carry on his UK trade (or if it is an oil exploration asset) *(TCGA 1992, s 25(2))*.

9.68   If an asset ceases to be a chargeable asset by virtue of the owner ceasing to carry on a trade, profession or vocation in the UK through a branch or agency he is deemed to have disposed of the asset and re-acquired it at its market value immediately before the trade ceased *(TCGA 1992, s 25(3))*. This does not apply if the asset again becomes a chargeable asset in the same tax year or accounting period *(TCGA 1992, s 25(5))*. For example, it would not apply if the non-resident set up a new UK trade before the end of the tax year. In the case of a company the charge also does not apply if the trade is transferred to another company by way of an intra-group transfer within *TCGA 1992, s 139* or *171 (TCGA 1992, s 25(5))*.

This provision will, of course, also prevent a UK resident who carries on a trade in the UK from emigrating and avoiding tax on the trading assets by ceasing the trade and selling the asset after he becomes non-UK resident. However, this is a question of timing. Neither *TCGA 1992, s 10* nor *s 25* will apply if a person ceases to carry on the trade while UK resident but defers selling the assets previously used for the trade until he becomes non-resident. *TCGA 1992, s 25(3)* will not apply in such circumstances as, if the owner is UK resident when the trade ceases, the asset will not cease to be a chargeable asset as it is still within the scope of CGT by virtue of the owner being resident and ordinarily resident in the UK.

9.69   Provided that a person intends to remain non-resident for more than five tax years, it is still possible to emigrate while owning UK assets which are not trading assets of a UK branch or agency by deferring a sale until after the owner has become non-resident. Where a person carries on a business in the UK as a sole trader or in partnership and he intends to become non-resident, consideration should be given to incorporating the business for shares under *TCGA 1992, s 162. TCGA 1992, ss 10* and *25* will not apply to a subsequent sale of the shares.

Alternatively, such a person could cease to use the asset in the trade while he is UK resident. For example, at a time when he is UK resident he could transfer the trade to a company but keep the asset personally. After emigration he could then sell both the shares and the asset.

9.70   An individual who is domiciled outside the UK but resident here and has claimed the remittance basis for income tax is also liable to CGT on that basis in relation to gains on overseas assets (*TCGA 1992, s 12(1)*). As with income, the charge can be avoided by spending the sale proceeds outside the UK. The rules considered above in relation to deemed remittances of investment income also apply to capital gains (*TCGA 1992, s 12(2)*).

The gain is deemed to arise when it is remitted. HMRC consider that if a person becomes domiciled in the UK and subsequently remits gains arising at a time when he was non-domiciled they can still tax the remittance under *TCGA 1992, s 12*. It is not wholly clear that this view is correct but anyone who wished to challenge it would need to litigate the point. The wording of the legislation is ambiguous.

9.71   Where an individual intends to become non-resident and sell an asset after he has ceased to be UK resident it needs to be borne in mind that the date of disposal for CGT is the date of contract, not that of completion. A contract does not need to be a formal written document. An offer to sell and the acceptance of that offer creates a contract. HMRC may well want to review all of the correspondence in relation to the sale to look for evidence that a contract came into existence at a time when the individual was still UK resident (or before the end of the tax year in which he ceased to be resident here).

9.72   A conditional contract does not create a disposal until the condition is satisfied. However, it is often difficult to be sure whether the contract is conditional. Lawyers draw a distinction between a condition precedent (ie one the non-fulfilment of which will mean that the contract never became enforceable) and a condition subsequent (ie one which does not destroy the contract but the non-fulfilment of which will give rise to a claim for damages). It is only the former that can qualify as a conditional contract for CGT purposes.

It is accordingly safest to use options if it is wished to make a contract conditional. An option does not create a contract until the option is satisfied. There is a risk with cross-options (ie where the prospective vendor has an option to require the other person to acquire the asset and the proposed purchaser has an option to require the other person to sell it to him). HMRC have been known to contend that cross-options are equivalent to a contract as both parties are able to enforce the bargain. Accordingly, if cross-options are used it is safest for both not to be exercisable at the same time. For example, the vendor could have an option to require the purchaser to buy the asset from him exercisable only during the following May and the prospective purchaser could have an option to require the vendor to sell the company to him exercisable only during the following July. There would then be no time at which both parties could bring the bargain into existence.

Capital gains tax – UK residential property

9.73   As indicated at **9.65**, from 6 April 2015, non-residents have to pay capital gains tax (NRCGT) on the disposal of (or of an interest in) UK residential property (*FA 2015, s 37* and *Sch 7*). They are taxable only on the part of the gain that arises after 6 April 2015. This is normally achieved by revaluing the property at 6 April 2015 and treating that value as the cost of the property. Alternatively the taxpayer can elect to time apportion the gain, ie to calculate the gain over the entire period of ownership and exclude the proportion of that gain that the part of that period ending with 5 April 2015 bears to the entire period of ownership.

A residential property for this purpose includes a property which is only partly a dwelling (such as a shop with a flat above) and a property which has been a dwelling at any time during the owner's period of ownership, but the calculation of the gain limits the charge to tax on only the residential element. The definition also includes an off-plan purchase of a yet-to-be constructed residence.

An NRCGT loss is ring-fenced. It can be used against NRCGT gains but nothing else. If a non-resident who incurs an NRCGT loss subsequently becomes UK resident, the loss becomes a normal CGT loss available to be utilised against any capital gains.

A non-resident who realises an NRCGT gain must submit a tax return for the disposal and pay the tax due within 30 days of the disposal.

9.74   There are few exclusions. It applies to disposals by individual trusts and companies. It applies to let properties and other investment properties. It does not apply to properties included in the stock of a property dealing trade though. The tax does not apply to disposals by widely-held companies (one not under the control of five or fewer people, but shares held by certain connected persons are treated as owned by one of the five or fewer for this purpose) or widely marketed unit trust schemes or OEICs.

There is an exemption for an individual's principal private residence, but this will rarely apply to non-residents. Where a non-resident individual has residences in several countries, his UK property can be regarded as his principal residence only if he occupies it for at least 90 days during the tax year, and anyone who does so risks becoming UK resident for the year under the statutory residence test.

9.75 The normal tax rates apply. This means that an individual is entitled to his £11,700 annual allowance and to his 18% tax band (the amount of which, if any, depends on the size of his UK taxable amount) with the balance being taxed at 28%. A trust pays a flat rate of 28%. A company is taxable at 20% and is entitled to deduct the indexation allowance (to reflect inflation) in calculating the gain.

9.76 A non-resident company can also be liable to CGT on ATED-related gains. ATED (annual tax on enveloped dwellings) is a special tax on high-value residential property held by a company or by a partnership which includes a corporate partner. Where ATED applies to a property, ATED-related CGT applies on its disposal. This is at the rate of 28% on the entire gain, with no deduction for the annual allowance or the 18% lower rate.

There are a great number of exemptions from ATED. The intention is that it should apply only to UK residences available for occupation by shareholders of the owning company or connected persons of theirs.

ATED was introduced from 1 April 2013 for residential properties worth over £2m. It was extended from 1 April 2015 to include those worth over £1m and from 1 April 2016 to residential properties worth over £500,000. These limits are based on the value of the property at 1 April 2012 or, if later, the date of acquisition. Only the part of the gain applicable to the period after 1 April 2013 (or 1 April 2015 or 1 April 2016 as appropriate) is taxable. As with NRCGT, the taxpayer can achieve this by either revaluing the property at the time it comes within the NRCGT net or using time apportionment.

9.77 If the disposal of a property by a company attracts both ATED-related CGT and NRCGT, the two gains must be calculated separately and the tax due aggregated. The part of the ATED-related gain attributable to the period after 6 April 2015 can be deducted in calculating the NRCGT gain. This avoids double taxation, but ensures that the ATED-related gain is taxed at 28% (and without indexation) rather than at the lower rate that applies to disposals by a company.

When ATED and ATED-related CGT was introduced, the government anticipated that properties within the tax would be taken out of the company, so that little tax would actually be collected. This has been proved wrong.

Many non-residents are prepared to accept ATED rather than own the property direct. One of the reasons for this is that ownership of the property by a non-UK company can take the property out of the scope of CGT, whereas ownership direct by an individual subjects it to CGT. Although this ceased to apply to residential property from 6 April 2017, many feel that the stamp duty land tax and capital gains tax charges on de-enveloping the property are too high to contemplate doing so.

9.78   Curiously, although ATED was introduced to discourage ownership of residences through a company (and has to an extent done so as there are other ways of avoiding or minimising IHT if a property is held by an individual or a trust), the NRCGT rules encourage ownership through a company because the 20% corporate rate is significantly lower than the 28% rate potentially payable by individuals and trusts. This anomaly is a by-product of the UK being a member of the EU. ATED applies to ownership by both UK and non-UK companies and both are taxed at 28%. NRCGT does not apply to UK companies and the European rules do not permit the UK to impose a higher tax on EU companies than on a UK company, so the rate of NRCGT for companies has to match the corporation tax rate that a UK company pays on its capital gains.

Inheritance tax

9.79   Inheritance tax is based partly on domicile and partly on the location of the assets. Residence is irrelevant – except to the extent that continuous residence can create a deemed UK domicile (see below). A person is liable to inheritance tax on UK assets irrespective of where he is domiciled or resident. A person who is domiciled in the UK (or to be precise in one of the countries that constitute the UK) is chargeable to IHT in relation to worldwide assets.

From 6 April 2017, some overseas assets are within the scope of IHT to the extent that their value derives (directly or indirectly) from UK residential property. The assets concerned are:

(a)   an interest in a close company, or one that would be a close company if it were UK resident,

(b)   an interest in a partnership,

(c)   a loan that was made to finance (directly or indirectly):

    (i)   the acquisition by an individual, a partnership or a settlement of an interest in a UK residential property or of an interest in a company or partnership within (a) or (b),

    (ii)   the acquisition of an interest in a UK residential property by a close company (or foreign equivalent) or partnership,

(iii) the maintenance or enhancement of a UK residential property interest, and

(iv) any money or other asset held as security, collateral or guarantee for such a loan.

(*IHTA 1984, Sch A1* inserted by *F(No 2)A 2017, Sch 10*)

Heads (a) and (b) do not apply if the interest in the company or partnership is less than 5%. A loan ceases to be a UK asset when the UK residential property is sold. However, if a UK property (or any other asset) is sold and the proceeds are used to buy another UK property, a loan to acquire the first asset is treated as being to indirectly acquire the second.

It should be noted that what falls to be treated as UK property is the value of the shares or partnership interest, and not the value of the UK property.

Example 9.4 – Valuing the shares

Jack and Jill and their daughter Jenny are all non-UK domiciled. They each own one-third of a Jersey company that owns their UK house. The house is worth £900,000.

On Jack's death, his one-third interest in the Jersey company is treated as a UK asset. Its value will be significantly less than a third of £900,000, because it is a minority interest in an unquoted company. If Jill has been UK resident for less than 15 years and pays the remittance basis charge, she might consider gifting her shares in the Jersey company to grandchildren or others, so as to create smaller minority interests, which will have a lower value per share.

Example 9.5 – IHT on loans

Ali, a non-domiciled individual, owns 100% of a Guernsey company that hold six UK residential investment properties. The company owes Ali £100,000, which was used towards the purchase of the first property. The other properties all have bank mortgages to finance 80% of their cost, the other 20% having been financed out of the company's rental income.

On Ali's death, his shares in the Guernsey company are a UK asset. Their value is probably the net asset value of the company. As the company has been largely financed by borrowings, this is probably 20–30% of the value

---

of the properties. In addition, Ali's £100,000 loan is treated as a UK asset; in theory, so are the bank loans but, as the bank is not within the scope of IHT, that is irrelevant. Curiously, if during his lifetime the company had re-mortgaged its first property and repaid Ali, the only taxable item would have been the shares.

Example 9.6 – Treatment of borrowings

John, a non-domiciled individual, owns 100% of a Guernsey company that owns six residential investment properties, one in the UK and the other five in Germany. There are bank mortgages on the German properties, but not on the UK one.

A proportion of the value of the shares will be regarded as a UK asset on John's death. This has to be arrived at on a just and reasonable basis. Bearing in mind that the mortgages have to be allocated rateably to all of the properties, this is probably the proportion of the net asset value that the value of the UK property bears to the total value of all of the properties. Curiously, re-mortgaging the German properties will reduce the value of the deemed UK proportion of the value of the shares.

It is not wholly clear what the position would be if John had lent the company funds to finance the acquisition of the German properties. The attribution of part of the loan to the UK property in valuing the shares probably does not mean that the loan has indirectly financed the acquisition of the UK property.

9.80   Where a person is non-UK domiciled, a holding in an authorised unit trust, a share in an open-ended investment company and a number of UK government securities are excluded from inheritance tax even though they are UK assets (*IHTA 1984, s 6(1A), (2)*). If the individual is domiciled in the Channel Islands or the Isle of Man, Ulster savings certificates, national savings certificate, premium bonds and certified SAYE saving arrangements are also excluded from IHT (*IHTA 1984, s 6(3)*). So are emoluments from the foreign government and tangible moveable property of members of visiting forces if the presence of the property in the UK is due to the individual being in the UK as a serving member of such an overseas military force (*IHTA 1984, s 155*). There is also an exclusion from IHT on death for a foreign currency account with a UK bank where at the time of his death the holder is domiciled outside the UK and neither resident nor ordinarily resident here (*IHTA 1984, s 157*).

9.81   A person who is not domiciled in the UK is treated, for IHT purposes only, or if he were domiciled here (and not elsewhere) at any time if either:

- he was domiciled here at some time within the previous three years; or

- he was resident in the UK for income tax purposes in at least 15 of the 20 tax years ending with the year in which that time falls (17 out of 20 prior to 6 April 2017) and was UK resident for at least one of the four years preceding that time, or he is resident in the UK and was born in the UK with a UK domicile of origin.

(IHTA 1984, s 267(1))

This deeming does not apply for the purpose of *IHTA 1984, s 6(2)* and *(3)* (which deems certain securities etc to be outside the scope of IHT if they are held by a person who is not UK domiciled), *s 48(4)* (which applies *IHTA 1984, s 6(2)* to settlements) or *s 158(6)* (double tax relief) *(IHTA 1984, s 267(2))*. The change in the deemed domicile rules from 6 April 2017 can extend the first of these periods to up to five years where the individual was deemed domiciled at the time of his emigration.

9.82   The IHT exemption for transfers between spouses or civil partners is limited to £325,000 (£55,000 for disposals before 6 April 2013).where the transferor is domiciled in the UK but the transferee is not *(IHTA 1984, s 18(2))*. This provision might well be overridden by the non-discrimination clause of a double tax agreement. It also needs to be borne in mind that any lifetime transfer of value to an individual is a potentially exempt transfer which will be taxable only if the transferor dies within seven years of making the gift *(IHTA 1984, s 3A)*. Accordingly, a lifetime gift to a non-domiciled spouse – or indeed any other non-UK domiciled individual – is exempt, whatever the amount, if the donor survives for the seven-year period.

9.83   Where one spouse or civil partner only is UK domiciled, consideration accordingly ought to be given to putting the majority of the family assets into the ownership of the non-UK domiciled spouse (or into a trust for the benefit of the non-UK domiciled spouse if this can be done without a significant entry charge) during the lifetime of the UK-domiciled spouse.

Where one spouse is UK-domiciled and the other is not, the non-domiciled spouse can elect to be treated as domiciled for IHT purposes. That will avoid the limitation on spousal gifts, but will also bring the spouse's worldwide assets into the scope of IHT, so is not necessarily desirable. The election can be made at any time and can be backdated by up to seven years. The election can be made by the personal representatives of a deceased spouse but such an election must be made within two years of the death. Accordingly, there is no need to elect until the domiciled spouse dies and it can be seen that the election will avoid tax on a failed PET by the deceased to the spouse (made after 6 April 2013) or on a transfer to the spouse on death.

The election is irrevocable but if the individual ceases to be UK resident it ceases to have effect once the individual has been non-resident for four tax years (*IHTA 1984, ss 267ZA, 267ZB*).

9.84 Non-UK property included in a settlement is outside the scope of IHT if the settlor was non-UK domiciled (and not deemed to be UK domiciled) at the time of the creation of the settlement (*IHTA 1984, s 48(3)*). So are units in a UK-authorised unit trust and shares in a UK open-ended investment company which are held by such a settlement (*IHTA 1984, s 48(3A)*). This does not apply if an interest in possession in the property is held by a UK-domiciled person and that interest was acquired for a consideration in money or money's worth (*IHTA 1984, s 48(3B)*).

UK government securities within *IHTA 1984, s 6(2)* are also exempt if they are held by such a settlement and either a non-domiciled person has an interest in possession in them or all possible beneficiaries of the settlement are non-UK domiciled (*IHTA 1984, s 48(4)*).

9.85 If an interest in possession in a pre-22 March 2006 settlement comes to an end there is a deemed disposal of the settled property for IHT purposes. However, no tax is chargeable if, when that interest in possession comes to an end, the settlor's spouse or civil partner becomes entitled to the property, provided that he is domiciled in the UK (*IHTA 1984, ss 53(4), 54(2)*).

Again, this is not necessarily a problem if the interest in possession terminates during the beneficiary's lifetime as the deemed disposal is deemed to be a potentially exempt transfer by the person with the interest in possession so it does not matter that the spouse is not UK domiciled provided that the beneficiary survives for seven years.

A transfer of value made by a close company is apportioned amongst its participators and treated as a transfer of value by the participators (*IHTA 1984, s 94*). However, if a participator is non-UK domiciled this does not apply to the extent that the value apportioned to him relates to non-UK property held by the company (*IHTA 1984, s 94(2)*).

Double tax treaties

9.86 The UK has only ten tax treaties in relation to inheritance tax. Those that it does have fall into two categories, namely those that were entered into pre-1975 and originally related to estate duty (which was payable only on death) and those entered into after 1975 which originally related to capital transfer tax (the original name of inheritance tax) and thus also cover lifetime gifts.

The first category comprises the agreements with France, Italy, India and Pakistan. These treaties now apply to IHT on death only (*IHTA 1984, s 158(6)*).

The second category comprises the agreements with Ireland, Netherlands, South Africa, Sweden, Switzerland and the US.

9.87   Clearly, the individual agreement needs to be looked at in a particular case. However, they normally apply where a person is domiciled in both countries under their domestic law. The category two agreements refer to a person being domiciled in the UK in accordance with its law or treated as domiciled for the purposes of IHT. This raises an interesting question as to the application of the category one agreements where a person is not domiciled in the UK under UK law but is deemed domiciled here for IHT purposes. The probability is that such a person is automatically regarded as French (or Italian, Indian or Pakistani) domiciled for the purposes of the treaty. Where a person is domiciled in a category two country, such as the US, and deemed domiciled in the UK, then the tie-breaker clause of the agreement will apply in the same way as if he was domiciled in both countries.

9.88   The category one agreements (other than that with Italy which is more limited) prevent the UK charging IHT on property situated outside the UK where the decedent was domiciled in the other country and not in the UK for the purpose of the agreement. They also contain rules to determine the *situs* of specific assets. However, these agreements also allow the UK to charge IHT on property which 'passes under a disposition or devolution regulated by the law of some part of Great Britain'. This will allow the UK to tax non-UK property if it passes under a UK will or is held in a UK settlement. Where the other country imposes tax on assets situated in that country, the UK has to give credit for such tax in determining the UK tax payable. This is subject to an important proviso from 6 April 2017: a UK residential property interest held by the non-domiciled individual is brought within the scope of IHT, unless a similar tax to IHT is chargeable on its value under the law of the other country (*IHTA 1984, Sch A1, para 7*).

The category two agreements normally lay down more detailed rules as to what can be taxed by each country. They determine the *situs* of property and normally allow the UK to tax land and business property situated in the UK.

Where the UK does not have a double tax agreement with the other country it allows a credit for foreign tax paid both on death and on lifetime gifts (*IHTA 1984, s 159*).

Use of overseas trusts

9.89   An overseas trust can be an attractive vehicle in which to hold assets where the taxpayer is resident but not domiciled in the UK. Such a trust does not have income tax advantages (unless it is a 'protected trust') but can be attractive from both a CGT and IHT point of view.

It enables CGT to be deferred whilst the funds remain within the trust. The tax charge on the settlor under *TCGA 1992, s 86* does not apply where the settlor is non-UK domiciled. Accordingly, capital gains are taxed only under *TCGA 1992, s 87* when they are distributed from the settlement. This applies to gains on both UK and non-UK assets. On distribution a surcharge is however payable. This is 10% per annum up to a maximum of 60% (giving an effective CGT rate of 32% where the 20% rate of CGT applies). However, if the gain will be retained within the settlement for significantly more than six years the cash-flow benefit is likely to outweigh this disadvantage. A protected trust is one created before 6 April 2017 by a non-UK domiciled (and non-deemed domiciled) settlor (other than one born in the UK with a UK domicile of origin). Such a trust will cease to be protected if any value (other than income) is added to it after 5 April 2017. Income of a protected trust is normally outside the scope of income tax while it is retained in the trust. The charge under *TCGA 1992, s 87* and protected trusts are considered in **Chapter 14**.

Non-UK assets held in a trust are normally outside the scope of IHT if the settlor was non-UK domiciled (and not deemed domiciled) at the time he created the trust. This exemption continues to apply even if the settlor subsequently becomes deemed domiciled in the UK (except where the settlor was born in the UK with a UK domicile of origin). The general IHT benefits that can be obtained from the use of trusts in relation to UK assets are considered in **Chapter 14**.

The residence of trusts and settlements is dealt with in **Chapter 14**.

COMPANY RESIDENCE

9.90   A company is domiciled where it is incorporated, but domicile is rarely important in a corporation tax context.

A company is resident in the country in which its central control and management takes place. This was established by the House of Lords in a commendably brief judgment in *De Beers Consolidated Mines Ltd v Howe (Surveyor of Taxes)* (1906) 5 TC 198. De Beers was incorporated in South Africa where it operated diamond mines. Its head office was in South Africa. The company held weekly board meetings in both London and South Africa. The majority of the directors lived in the UK. Attendance at the London meetings was far greater than at the South African ones and in practice the major decisions were taken at the London meetings. The Lord Chancellor, Lord Loreburn, opined:

> 'In applying the conception of residence to a company, we ought, I think, to proceed as nearly as we can upon the analogy of an individual. A company cannot eat or sleep, but it can keep house and do business. We ought, therefore, to see where it really keeps house and does business. An individual may be of foreign nationality, and yet reside in the United Kingdom. So may a company. Otherwise, it might have its chief seat of management and its centre of trading in England, under the protection of English law, and yet escape the appropriate taxation by the simple expedient of being registered abroad and distributing its dividends abroad. The decision of Chief Baron Kelly and Baron Huddleston, now thirty years ago, involved the principal that a company resides, for purposes of income tax, where its real business is carried on. Those decisions have been acted upon ever since. I regard that as the true rule; and the real business is carried on where the central management and control actually abides. It remains to be considered whether the present case falls within that rule. This is a pure question of fact, to be determined, not according to the construction of this or that regulation or bylaw, but upon a scrutiny of the course of business and trading.'

As the Commissioners had found as a fact that 'the head and seat and directing power of the affairs of the Appellant Company were at the office in London from whence the chief operations of the Company, both in the UK and elsewhere, were, in fact, controlled, managed and directed', the company was held to be resident in the UK.

9.91 HMRC say that 'Although central management and control depends ultimately on the facts, a review of residence normally starts with the question of law. A company is governed first by the law of the country in which it is incorporated and second by its constitution … In the UK, management is normally entrusted to the directors, although it can be given to a single individual such as a managing director who has exclusive authority under the terms of the Articles. Where the company is incorporated abroad, it will be necessary to take into account the system of company management under the law of the country of incorporation' (International Tax Manual, ITM120180).The company law cases have held that normally this is the Board of Directors.

However, as residence is a question of fact it is possible that the people legally charged with the management and control of the company did not in fact exercise it. In *Bullock (Inspector of Taxes) v Unit Construction Co Ltd* (1959) 38 TC 712, the issue in dispute was the residence of a number of Kenyan subsidiary companies of Unit Construction. These were incorporated in Kenya and their Boards of Directors met only in Kenya. In 1950, the parent company directors decided that they would in future make all the major decisions in relation to the operation of the subsidiaries, and the Boards of the subsidiaries acquiesced in this. The East African companies were held to be resident in the UK. In the House of Lords, Lord Radcliffe said:

> 'Ought we, then, to adopt this principle that evidence of what has happened in fact must be excluded by a rule of law if what has been done is inconsistent with the regulations of a company? In my opinion it would be wrong to do so. I cannot see how the corollary of such a principle could fail to be that, if you cannot look beyond what the regulations of the company provide for, it is only those regulations which need to be or indeed can be referred to when a question of residence arises. Companies could be equipped with the most comprehensive sets of constitutions providing for management to be located in this or that selected taxing jurisdiction, and, however much the written requirements were in fact departed from for reasons of convenience or otherwise, all efforts to establish the true facts relating to the actual seat of management would founder on the ground that what had been done was merely "unconstitutional" ... I cannot think that such considerations are sufficient to introduce an important qualification upon this accepted test by which you try to ascertain what are the real facts about the seat of management and control and to put in its place what seems to be the merely formal device of studying a set of written regulations. I do not believe that this would conduce to the health of revenue administration. I think it much better to adhere to the approach laid down by Lord Loreburn, LC, in the De Beers case. "This is a pure question of fact, to be determined, not according to the construction of this or that regulation or by-law, but upon a scrutiny of the course of business and trading".'

9.92   HMRC are very alert to the risk that the decisions might in reality not be made by the Board of Directors. They tell their staff, under a heading 'what is the reality', that:

> 'it has been said that the management and control test is bad because it leads to the nonsense of directors flying to Jersey for board meetings ... It is quite easy for a company operating here to incorporate in Jersey and claim to be managed and controlled there with only a minimal tax cost in Jersey provided the shareholders are not resident there.
>
> On the face of it the point is a valid one. But criticism of that kind is concerned as much with questions of fact as of concept and the two things must be kept separate in our minds. There is, in principle at any rate, no reason why a business which is visibly in this country should not be managed and controlled from, let us say, Jersey. But if the directors of that company are working in this country on a regular basis and probably living here as well, it may be highly unlikely that they will be doing anything

448

more in Jersey than reaffirming decisions already taken here. If that is so the mere fact of having board meetings in the Channel Islands is irrelevant. The question is, where do the people concerned exercise management and control. If they really do it in this country and go through a meaningless form of words in Jersey, that will achieve nothing for them' (International Manual ITH334).

9.93   HMRC have given guidance on residence in Statement of Practice 1/90 where they emphasise:

'In general the place of directors' meetings is significant only insofar as those meetings constitute the medium through which central management and control is exercised. If, for example, the directors of a company were engaged together actively in the UK in the complete running of a business which was wholly in the UK, the company would not be regarded as resident outside the UK merely because the directors held formal meetings outside the UK. While it is possible to identify extreme situations in which central management and control plainly is, or is not, exercised by directors in formal meetings, the conclusion in any case is wholly one of fact depending on the relative weight to be given to various factors. Any attempt to lay down rigid guidelines would only be misleading.

Generally, however, where doubts arise about a particular company's residence status, the Revenue adopt the following approach –

(i)   they first try to ascertain whether the directors of the company in fact exercise central management and control;

(ii)   if so, they seek to determine where the directors exercise this central management and control (which is not necessarily where they meet);

in cases where the directors apparently do not exercise central management and control of the company, the Revenue then look to establish where and by whom it is exercised.'

They also warn:

'In outlining factors relevant to the application of the case law test, this statement assumes that they exist for genuine commercial reasons. Where, however, as may happen, it appears that a major objective underlying the existence of certain factors is the obtaining of tax benefits from residence or non-residence, the Revenue examine the facts particularly closely in order to see whether there has been an attempt to create the appearance of central management and control in a particular place without the reality.'

9.94   Another important case is *Wood v Holden* [2006] STC 443, which was heard by the Court of Appeal in January 2006. This is a significant case partly because it relates to a tax-avoidance scheme, so the courts might be expected to seek to interpret the law so as to thwart the scheme, and partly because it draws a clear distinction between simply implementing decisions of someone else and considering what that other person proposes and deciding that it is in the best interest of the company to adopt that proposal.

9.95   A CGT avoidance scheme was formulated by Price Waterhouse Corporate Finance Ltd in the UK which involved one non-UK company, CIL, being gifted shares in a UK company, Holdings, CIL selling those shares to its wholly owned Dutch subsidiary, Eulalia, at market value and Eulalia subsequently selling the shares in Holdings to an arm's-length purchaser. The Special Commissioners decided that CIL was non-UK resident but that Eulalia was UK resident. They felt that the taxpayer had failed to satisfy them that Eulalia was not UK resident (and both HMRC and the Woods had claimed that CIL was non-resident). This received short shrift from Park J in the High Court:

> 'There plainly comes a point where the taxpayer has produced evidence which, as matters stand then, appears to show that the assessment is wrong. At that point the evidential basis must pass to the Revenue. ... In this case ... Mr and Mrs Wood had to show to the civil standard of proof that the adjustment was wrong. I accept that the onus was on them to show that Eulalia was not resident in the United Kingdom, but rather was resident in the Netherlands. They showed that Eulalia was incorporated in the Netherlands. They showed incontrovertibly that it had been resident only in the Netherlands until it was acquired by CIL. They showed that CIL was not itself a United Kingdom company, and indeed was a company which the Revenue asserted to have been resident outside the United Kingdom. They showed that, from the time when Eulalia was acquired by CIL, its managing director was [ABN AMRO] Trust, a large Dutch company with offices in Amsterdam. They showed resolutions and consequential actions being taken in the offices in Amsterdam. They accepted that what Eulalia was doing was part of a tax scheme which was being superintended by Price Waterhouse in their Manchester offices. They called evidence from the Price Waterhouse partners who at the time were heads of the firm's departments for corporate finance and for tax in Manchester. They produced a witness statement from the head of the legal department at [ABN AMRO] Trust. They were willing for the appeal to be adjourned in order that the witness could attend in person to be available for cross-examination. They produced all the documents which existed (so I assume, and no one has suggested that any documents were suppressed). The documents showed guidance and influence coming from Price Waterhouse, but no more than that. Mr and Mrs Wood were able to point out that the Netherlands Revenue had stated to the United Kingdom Revenue that the actual management of Eulalia was carried out by [ABN AMRO] Trust, "meaning that the taxable domicile of Eulalia

Holding BV is located in the Netherlands". Surely at that point they can say: "We have done enough to raise a case that Eulalia was not resident in the United Kingdom. What more can the Special Commissioners expect from us? The burden must now pass to the Revenue to produce some material to show that, despite what appears from everything which we have produced, Eulalia was actually resident in the United Kingdom.'"

He also thought it was not enough for HMRC to demonstrate that the steps taken were part of a single tax scheme, that there were overall architects of the scheme in Price Waterhouse Corporate Finance Ltd and that those involved all shared the common expectation that the various stages of the scheme would in fact take place. These matters were not denied. However, he felt that, taken together they did not, of themselves, lead to the conclusion that Eulalia was resident in the UK.

9.96   The Court of Appeal agreed with the judge. Furthermore, Lord Justice Chadwick added that:

> 'A further flaw in the Special Commissioners' approach was to treat the decisions which were made by ABN AMRO as not "effective decisions" because they were reached without proper information or consideration. But a management decision does not cease to be a management decision because it might have been taken on fuller information; or even, as it seems to me, because it was taken in circumstances which might put the director at risk of an allegation of breach of duty. Ill-informed or ill-advised decisions taken in the management of a company remain management decisions.'

Companies incorporated in the UK

9.97   From 15 March 1988, a company that is incorporated in the UK must be regarded as UK resident for tax purposes (*CTA 2009, s 14*).

This can, of course, be overridden by double tax treaties (*CTA 2009, s 18(4)*). As with individuals, double tax treaties normally contain a tie-breaker clause to treat a company as resident in one only of the two countries which are party to the treaty. This normally provides that the company is deemed to be a resident only of the country in which its place of effective management is situated. This is probably the same test as central management and control.

Non-resident company trading in the UK

9.98   A non-UK resident company will, of course, be taxable in the UK to the extent that it has taxable income arising here. A non-UK resident company is within the charge to corporation tax if, and only if, it carries on a trade in the UK through a permanent establishment in the UK. It is so taxable on all profits, wherever arising, that are attributable to its permanent establishment in the UK, including income from property or rights used by, or held by or for, the establishment, and on chargeable gains falling within *TCGA 1992, s 10B* (see above) by virtue of assets being used in or for the purposes of the trade carried on through the establishment or being used or held (or acquired for use) for the purposes of the establishment (*CTA 2009, s 19*). From 5 July 2016, it is also taxable on profits from dealing in or developing for sale UK land, even where these do not arise through a UK permanent establishment.

9.99   A company has a permanent establishment in the UK if, and only if, it has a fixed place of business here through which its business is wholly or partly carried on, or an agent acting on behalf of the company has, and habitually exercises in the UK, authority to do business on behalf of the company (*CTA 2010, ss 1141–1145*).

For this purpose, a fixed place of business includes a place of management, a branch, an office, a factory, a workshop, an installation or structure for the exploration of natural resources, a mine, an oil or gas well, a quarry or any other place of extraction of natural resources, a building site and a construction or installation project (*CTA 2010, s 1141(2)*). A company cannot have a permanent establishment in the UK by reason only of the fact that it carries on business here through an agent of independent status acting in the ordinary course of his business (*CTA 2010, s 1142(1)*). A company is not regarded as having a permanent establishment if the activities carried on in the UK are only of a preparatory or auxiliary character, such as the use of facilities for the purpose of storage, display or delivery of goods or merchandise belonging to the company, the maintenance of a stock of goods or merchandise belonging to the company for the purpose of storage, display or delivery or of processing by another person, or purchasing goods or merchandise for the company, or collecting information (*CTA 2010, s 1143*).

The legislation lays down rules for attributing profits to a permanent establishment (*CTA 2009, ss 20–24*).

Where a company is not within the charge to corporation tax it will be chargeable to income tax at the basic rate on UK source income. It is not clear if it can be chargeable to income tax on trading income which does not arise through a permanent establishment. It can, of course, also be chargeable to CGT in relation to UK residential property both under the ATED-related CGT and the NRCGT regimes. These are considered at **9.73–9.78**.

Change of residence

9.100   There is no bar on a UK company changing its residence, although if the company is incorporated in the UK it can do so only by becoming dual resident or being deemed to be non-resident under a double tax agreement, as a UK-incorporated company is treated as resident here (with some exceptions where a company ceased to be UK resident before 1988).

9.101 There are a number of provisions that can impose a tax charge where a UK-resident company ceases to be resident here or which relate to non-resident companies. The main ones are *CTA 2009, ss 41(2)* and *289* (company beginning or ceasing to be within the charge to corporation tax), *TMA 1970, s 109B* (provisions for securing payment by company of outstanding tax), *TMA 1970, s 109E* (liability of other persons for unpaid tax), *TCGA 1992, s 14* (non-resident groups of companies), *TCGA 1992, s 185* (deemed disposal of assets on company ceasing to be resident in the UK), *ITA 2007, ss 835C–835S* (UK representatives of non-residents), *CTA 2010, ss 973–980* (recovery of tax payable by non-resident company), *CTA 2010, ss 969–972* (non-resident companies: assessment, collection and recovery of corporation tax (non-resident companies: extent of charge to income tax), *CTA 2010, s 1142* (non-resident companies: transactions carried out through broker, investment manager or Lloyd's agent), *CTA 2010, ss 107–110* (group relief where surrendering company not resident in UK) and *ITA 2007, s 5(1)* (companies within the charge to income tax).

Dual-resident companies

9.102 As with an individual, it is possible for a company to be resident in two or more countries simultaneously, because the test for residence is different in each country. Where this occurs the legislation can restrict the deductibility of specified expenditure and capital allowances to prevent double relief being obtained. Accordingly, it is normally best to seek to avoid such a status.

Companies treated as non-resident

9.103 Where a UK-resident company is treated as non-resident under a double tax treaty, it is treated as non-resident for all the purposes of the *Taxes Acts* (*CTA 2009, s 18*). For this purpose a company is regarded as treaty non-resident if it meets the appropriate conditions, even if it has not claimed the benefit of the treaty (*CTA 2009, s 18(4)*).

Chapter 10

Agency workers and intermediaries

Originally written by David Heaton FCA, CTA, David Heaton Tax Ltd
and updated by Kye Burchmore LLB, RIFT Legal Services

SIGNPOSTS

- **Background** – Agency workers have been a feature of the economy
  for many years and most have been deemed to receive employment
  income. However structures had developed enabling them to be paid
  gross by intermediaries, without PAYE or NIC, on an increasingly
  widespread basis because they were technically self-employed and
  outside the scope of the agency provisions in *ITEPA 2003* and the
  NIC *Categorisation Regulations 1978*. The government reacted by
  changing the deeming rules in 2014 and the reporting arrangements
  in 2015 (see **10.1–10.3**).

- **Status** – Workers supplied by third parties to work for a client are
  technically self-employed unless they are deliberately given a contract
  of employment (see **10.4**).

- **Liabilities** – The government attempted in April 2014 to counteract
  avoidance via intermediary self-employment, and evasion via
  offshore intermediaries, by changing the deeming rules and
  imposing new liabilities on businesses within the UK, by removing
  the requirement for a personal service obligation from the agency
  provisions and adding new targeted anti-avoidance rules and transfer
  of debt provisions (see **10.5–10.23**). In addition to this, from April
  2017, liabilities for IR35 for public sector work moved from the PSC
  to the public sector body or agency engaging the PSC (see **10.12**).

- **Reporting obligations** – From April 2015, intermediaries paying
  gross for the services of workers who are self-employed or supplied
  by another business must submit quarterly reports of their payments so
  that HMRC may identify and penalised abuse of the 2014 provisions
  at an early stage (see **10.24–10.37**).

- **Restrictions on travel and subsistence expenses** – From April
  2016, umbrella companies and personal service companies supplying

agency workers lost the right to pay tax- and NIC-free travel and subsistence expenses for home-to-work travel to any employee subject to supervision, direction or control as to the manner of carrying out the work, which undermined the business model of most umbrella employers (see **10.38–10.42**).

INTRODUCTION

10.1   This chapter examines the changes made between 2014 and 2017 to the tax and national insurance contribution (NIC) rules for agency and 'temporary' workers and their 'intermediary' suppliers.

Agency workers have been a feature of the economy for many years and according to the Office for National Statistics (ONS) just over 1.5 million people were classed as 'temporary workers' in the first quarter of 2018.

Agencies have been supplying workers for many years, to cover for permanent staff who are absent and to deal with peaks and troughs in demand, but it is not the classic 'temp' who was the target of the changes made in 2014. The mischief at which those changes were aimed has been developing since before the introduction of IR35 in 2000. The problem, as perceived by HMRC, was that the agency worker provisions for PAYE and NIC were being abused so as to save tax and NICs for employers, and payroll deductions were in danger of becoming optional as the problem grew.

The nub of that problem lies in the categorisation of workers as employed or self-employed. Agency workers have for many years been treated as receiving employment income, despite the fact that they are not employees, but certain providers had established alternative employment models that enabled agencies, acting fully within the law, to supply nominally temporary workers as if they were self-employed contractors, thereby saving the employer NICs that would ordinarily be paid in respect of the earnings of agency workers, and deferring the tax for the individual workers by moving the income from the PAYE regime to the self-assessment regime.

An associated but fundamentally different problem was also addressed by changes in 2014. UK NIC law does not levy secondary contributions on employers who have no presence in the jurisdiction (although the jurisdiction now – at least until formal 'Brexit' – extends technically to the whole of the European Economic Area (EEA) when dealing with migrant workers). The jurisdiction normally extends only as far as the 12-mile limit (and beyond the limit is not classed as EEA territory), so employers of workers operating on the UK Continental Shelf have for many years avoided having an onshore presence that would attract a secondary contribution liability. The government identified this as an unacceptable anomaly and created a new system of levying contributions in respect of Continental Shelf workers.

The third problem, addressed by the *Finance Act 2016* changes, centres on intermediary workers employed under 'umbrella' contracts who have been receiving part of their pay as tax- and NIC-free commuting and subsistence expenses. Typical agency workers have been deemed for many years to have a new permanent workplace for each assignment, so they have never been able to receive tax-free commuting expenses. This led to the growth of an 'umbrella' employment industry, in which workers were deliberately given a single, overarching or 'umbrella' employment contract covering all their assignments, rather than an agency contract for services. The same principle applied to workers who set up their own personal service company (PSC) to cover all their assignments. This arrangement meant that they were being sent to a series of temporary workplaces in a single employment, with relief due under *ITEPA 2003, s 338*. Umbrella employers reduced taxable pay and substituted tax-free expenses under 'payday-by-payday' relief models. *ITEPA 2003, s 339A* blocks this approach by deeming each engagement to be a separate employment, putting umbrella employees on the same footing as agency workers and the clients' employees alongside whom they work.

The relevant law

10.2   The tax rules relevant to agency workers and the changes made to them are found in *ITEPA 2003, Pt 2, Ch 7 (ss 44–47)*, with a new record-keeping requirement in *ITEPA 2003, s 716B* and the addition of *ITEPA 2003, ss 61K–61X* to address the perceived non-compliance with IR35 in the public sector. The record-keeping requirement provides power to extend the PAYE record-keeping requirement to cases of self-employed workers supplied by intermediaries.

The NIC rules and changes made to them are found in the *Social Security (Categorisation of Earners) Regulations 1978, SI 1978/1689* (the '*Categorisation Regulations*') and the *Social Security (Contributions) Regulations 2001, SI 2001/1004* (the '*Contributions Regulations*').

The 2014 and 2017 changes were aimed at ensuring that agency workers who work in a similar way to ordinary employees of the client businesses are subjected to the same PAYE and NIC obligations as those ordinary employees, irrespective of their contractual terms. Why this was necessary is explained below (see **10.4**).

For cases where this was (for perfectly valid reasons) not achieved, HMRC also introduced, with effect from 6 April 2015, a new reporting regime so that it at least has visibility over the businesses continuing to use workers supplied by intermediaries, and over which of them are paid gross. The *Income Tax (Pay As You Earn) (Amendment No 2) Regulations 2015, SI 2015/171* added *Regulations 84E–84H* into the *Income Tax (Pay As You Earn) Regulations 2003, SI 2003/2682* to create a new quarterly reporting regime for those intermediaries who contract with end users, referred to as 'clients' in the regulations. The reporting requirements and mechanics are discussed below (see **10.24**).

For oil and gas workers, any employment on the UK Continental Shelf has for many years been treated as employment within the UK and therefore subject to primary NIC liability (*SSCBA 1992, s 120* and *Contributions Regulations, reg 114*), but this deeming rule does not extend to employers of such workers. To impose a secondary contribution liability on such employers or intermediaries (or their clients, if the employers do not pay) for the first time, *NIC Act 2014, s 12* and *Social Security (Contributions) (Amendment No 2) Regulations 2014, SI 2015/572* added new *regs 114A–114D* to the *Contributions Regulations* from 6 April 2014. There is now a licensing and certification regime to provide rig operators with a safe way to hire workers through intermediaries, without exposing themselves to potential NIC obligations.

The reliefs for expenses for necessary travel to a temporary workplace are found in *ITEPA 2003, ss 338–339*. They were created to allow a measure of relief for journeys other than ordinary commuting but were being exploited by the umbrella employment sector in a way that Parliament never envisaged. From 6 April 2016, *FA 2016, s 14* introduced two sections to counter the use of 'salary sacrifice' in connection with this relief:

- *ITEPA 2003, s 339A* restricts *ITEPA 2003, ss 338* and *339* relief by treating as a separate employment each engagement of a worker personally providing services through an intermediary (umbrella or PSC) while under some right of supervision, direction or control. This has the effect of turning more journeys into ordinary commuting, for which no relief is due.

- *ITEPA 2003, s 688B* creates new powers to recover unpaid PAYE in certain circumstances from directors and officers of companies where:

  (i)   fraudulent documents have been provided that purport to evidence an absence of supervision, direction and control, or

  (ii) the intermediary has no evidence to support a claim that there is no supervision, direction or control, or

  (iii) the intermediary is an 'IR35' personal service company without being a managed service company (MSC).

The four mischiefs

10.3 The main target of the changes in 2014, 2015 and 2017 was avoidance by means of ensuring that agency workers were legally classed as self-employed. The change in statutes and regulations now deem many of these workers to be employed by the agency or intermediary supplying them to the client.

The second target in 2014 was employers of offshore workers in the oil and gas industry who previously had had no liability to pay secondary contributions if they had no place of business within the UK. The regulations now deem the secondary contributor to be:

● the employer, if it has a presence or place of business in the UK, or in the absence of such an employer;

● an associated company of the employer that is present in the UK, or in the absence of either of these:

● the oilfield licensee.

The third target in 2014 and 2015 was evasion rather than avoidance. Some intermediaries had deliberately set themselves up outside the jurisdiction so that they were under no obligation to comply with UK law. The law has for many years included 'host employer' provisions for both income tax (*ITEPA 2003, ss 687, 689*) and NIC (*Categorisation Regulations, Sch 3, para 9*), imposing a liability, broadly on somebody within the jurisdiction against whom HMRC could take enforcement action. However, that UK person was unable to comply if the overseas intermediary refused to supply the relevant information, and HMRC was powerless to penalise the UK client who had an obvious 'reasonable excuse' for non-compliance. The new regulations attempt to ensure that the liability for PAYE and NIC in respect of workers supplied by such intermediaries is transferred to the agency in the UK that has the contract with the client.

The fourth target is the exploitation of the temporary workplace provisions to pay what are effectively agency workers a tax-free travel payment in substitution for part of their true pay. *FA 2015* made changes that would catch all expenses paid under salary sacrifice arrangements from 6 April 2016, making them subject to PAYE but leaving open the possibility of a claim by the employee for retrospective relief under *ITEPA 2003, s 338*. *FA 2016, s 14* turns most temporary workplaces for intermediary workers into permanent workplaces, thereby preventing relief under *ITEPA 2003, s 338*.

AGENCY WORKERS' EMPLOYMENT STATUS

10.4 A full analysis of the employment status of agency workers is beyond the scope of this brief chapter, but the principles may be stated succinctly.

It has been established for many years (see *Ready Mixed Concrete (South East) Ltd v Minister of Pensions and National Insurance* [1968] 2 QB 497, page 515) that, for there to be a contract of service, three conditions must be fulfilled:

- the servant agrees to provide his own work in exchange for a wage;

- he agrees to accept the master's control; and

- the other provisions of the contract are consistent with its being a contract of service.

MacKenna J noted that 'Freedom to do a job either by one's own hands or by another's is inconsistent with a contract of service, though a limited or occasional power of delegation may not be ...'.

In the context of a typical agency worker, these conditions may never be fulfilled, even if the worker is supplied by the agency to the same client for many years. The worker contracts with the agency or intermediary and is paid by him, but control is exercised by the client, who is not a party to that agreement, having entered into a separate bilateral agreement with the agency. The tripartite arrangement therefore automatically falls outside the scope of a contract of service (see **Figure 10.1**). The typical agency worker therefore works in law under a 'contract for services', ie as a self-employed contractor.

The government is currently consulting on how to make employment status clearer and all possible options and solutions are up for consideration including bringing in detailed legislation, changing the tests entirely from those identified above or even introducing a type of employer's national insurance for self-employed individuals. It is unlikely that any potential change from this consultation will be directed towards agency workers, but agency workers could still find themselves within the remit of any broad changes. If there were to be a fundamental shift in employment status legislation it would most likely result in further consultations with sufficient lead time before implementation to enable taxpayers to be made aware of and understand any future changes.

Focus

Employment contracts have only two parties, so agency workers are self-employed on common law principles. Tax law applies different rules.

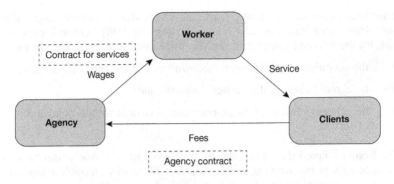

Figure 10.1: The tripartite relationship for agency work

It has been recognised for a long time that agency workers who work alongside permanent staff, doing the same work, broadly in the same circumstances, should be taxed and subjected to NIC deductions just like those permanent staff. This was originally achieved by *ITEPA 2003, s 44* and the *Categorisation Regulations* deeming them to receive employment income if three conditions were fulfilled:

- their income was not already employment income (some agency workers do in fact have a contract of employment, as do almost all 'umbrella' company workers);
- they were obliged to provide personal service; and
- they were subject to supervision, direction or control as to the manner of carrying out the work.

In other words, they were de facto employees, even if they could never be employees in law because they were working via an agency.

A number of activities were specifically excluded for historical reasons. Services as an actor, singer, musician or other entertainer or as a fashion, photographic or artist's model have traditionally been provided via agencies but it has been accepted that the workers concerned ought to be genuinely self-employed. Also excluded were services provided wholly in the worker's own home or at other premises which were neither controlled nor managed by the client nor prescribed by the nature of the services (see *ITEPA 2003, s 47*).

Focus

Not every agency worker is deemed to fall within PAYE and Class 1 NIC: there are a number of exceptions.

There have been occasional examples of agency workers being able to establish that they were employed under a contract of service by the agency (see, eg *McMeechan v Secretary of State for Employment* [1996] EWCA Civ 1166), but the normal position has been and remains that the typical agency worker is self-employed on basic principles (see, eg *Dacas v Brook Street Bureau (UK) Ltd* [2004] EWCA Civ 217). Most agencies therefore pay their temporary workers through payroll, subject to deduction of PAYE and Class 1 NIC.

There were two major exceptions to this: 'umbrella' company workers and those workers who did not meet the three conditions stated.

Firstly, umbrella companies emerged after 1998 as a way of exploiting the tax-free and NIC-free status of expenses for employees travelling between home and a temporary workplace (see **Figure 10.2**). Workers were deliberately given employment contracts for what was, in essence, agency work (with all jobs carried out under the 'umbrella' of a single 'over-arching' contract) and were paid at a lower rate than normal. This was topped up by expenses payments for home-to-work travel that would not be paid to a normal employee of the business. Since only part of the remuneration package was taxable, the actual gross pay required to keep the workers' net pay at the same level as that enjoyed by agency workers was lower than otherwise would have been the case. This enabled the employer, or often a related employment agency, to reduce the rate charged to its clients for supplying the workers' services, giving it a competitive edge. Clearly, no deeming rules were required to bring their income within PAYE and Class 1 NIC. Umbrella workers were therefore very attractive to employment agencies, as costs were lower and payroll administration was undertaken by the umbrella business.

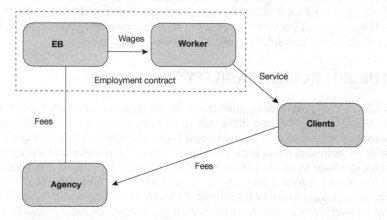

Figure 10.2: The classic umbrella-agency structure

Secondly, some intermediaries began, with those temporary workers who went on to their books, to enter into contracts for services that explicitly permitted the worker to send a substitute rather than commit to carrying out the work personally. Agencies often ensured that actual substitution took place from time to time so that it could be demonstrated that the right was genuine. This had the effect of ensuring that the second condition set out above could not be met, and that the workers would therefore be outside the PAYE and NIC deeming provisions. Here again, a cost saving arose (ie due to the absence of employer contributions) that could be passed on to clients in the form of lower hourly rates.

These structures first became widespread in the construction industry, but the imposition of a 20% deduction under the Construction Industry Scheme meant that HMRC had few concerns about delayed or reduced remittances. However, when the use of self-employed agency contracts began to spread to other industries where there was no similar requirement for deduction at source, and to businesses that moved their entire workforce onto an intermediary's books, HMRC's concerns grew. In *Commissioners for HMRC v Talentcore Limited (t/a) Team Spirits* [2011] UKUT 423 (TCC) the tribunals found against HMRC in a challenge to the arrangements for the company's self-employed sales 'consultants', supplied like ordinary agency staff to work in airport duty-free shops over an eight-year period but not subjected to payroll deductions for tax and NIC.

The intermediary businesses using these arrangements had developed a way of working that threatened the Exchequer, as more employers began to transfer their workforce to an intermediary, sometimes known as a 'payroll company', who was not obliged to make deductions, or to pay employer NICs. The adoption of this type of arrangement was entirely legitimate, provided the freedom to send a substitute was genuine, but the government dubbed it 'false self-employment'. It was of course not false: it was inconvenient that the law made these workers self-employed, so the law had to be changed.

THE 2014 RULES: LIABILITY

10.5   The government announced in its Autumn Statement 2013 that it would tackle the use of employment intermediaries facilitating false self-employment to avoid employment taxes. The results of its consultations, with the amendments to legislation, are noted in the introduction above. New rules deeming most workers supplied by intermediaries to be employees of those intermediaries were in place by 6 April 2014, although the reporting requirements could not be introduced at the same time because of the lead time for software development, so the reporting elements of the legislation were delayed until 2015–16.

FA 2014, ss 16–21 and the matching NIC regulations (*Social Security (Categorisation of Earners) (Amendment) Regulations 2014, SI 2014/635*) changed the basis of deeming workers engaged through intermediaries to be employees for tax and NIC purposes. The NIC equivalent of the anti-avoidance rule in the new *ITEPA 2003, s 46A* required primary legislation, which appeared in *NIC Act 2015, s 6*, adding a new *reg 5A* into the *Categorisation Regulations*.

What is now caught?

10.6   Whereas the old agency rules had set a personal service obligation as one of the conditions for their application, the new version in *ITEPA 2003, s 44(1)* looks simply for:

- actual personal service (other than the traditionally excluded services such as acting, entertaining, modelling and home working) by a worker; together with

- a contract involving the end client (or a person connected to that client) and a third party (ie the 'agency', which need not necessarily be a recognised employment agency, and certainly is not a person connected with the client).

The 2014 rules apply where, under or in consequence of this contract between client and agency:

- the worker's services are provided; or (NB: the draughtsman deliberately did not choose the word 'and' at this point, as the net is to be cast widely)

- the client or a connected person pays or provides consideration for those services.

This defeats the device of creating a contractual structure that avoids the direct provision by the agency of the worker's services, or direct payment by the client for those services, which will not suffice to sidestep the new rules: both conditions must be met if the parties are to escape *ITEPA 2003, s 44*.

10.7   Having noted that the net has been cast widely, it must also be said that HMRC's ambitions are not unlimited: it would make no sense for the rules to encompass every working relationship involving a third party because most of them do not involve any kind of avoidance and many of the workers involved are indeed genuinely self-employed or already on somebody's payroll. *ITEPA 2003, s 44(2)* therefore disapplies the deeming rule so that neither PAYE nor Class 1 NICs are due if:

- it is shown that the manner in which the worker provides the services is not subject to (or to the right of) supervision, direction or control by any person (see further below); or

- remuneration receivable by the worker in consequence of providing the services constitutes employment income of the worker apart from under the agency provisions (which means that umbrella companies supplying their own payrolled employees as temporary workers are out of scope).

Disregarding the personal service obligation and instead relying on seeking actual personal service prevents the simple use of a substitution clause as an escape route from PAYE and Class 1 NIC liability. Many temporary workers who previously worked under a contract with a substitution clause will meet these revised conditions, because the new focus is on the work they do personally, rather than whether they are obliged to do it personally, so they will be deemed to be employees of the agency for PAYE and NIC purposes.

Focus

Anyone working through a one-man personal service (PSC) and finding work through an agency is automatically outside the scope of the PAYE and NIC deeming (but not necessarily the reporting regime).

The impact of *ITEPA 2003, s 44(2)(b)* is that anyone working through a one-man personal service (PSC) and finding work through an agency is automatically outside the scope of the PAYE and NIC deeming (but not necessarily the reporting regime – see **10.29** below). Salary drawn from the PSC is employment income, but dividends paid to the director-shareholder will not be 'remuneration receivable by the worker', as it is classed as investment income. Any salary drawn by the director-shareholder will therefore fall within *ITEPA 2003, s 44(2)(b)* and the arrangement will not require the agency to operate payroll deductions.

Those working for an umbrella company under an overarching contract, whose wages are subject to PAYE and Class 1 NICs, are also excluded from the scope of *ITEPA 2003, s 44* by this rule, although the agency that places the worker (if it is not the umbrella company itself) will still have a reporting obligation (see further below).

10.8   Where the conditions are indeed met, *ITEPA 2003, s 44(3)* provides that the work for the client is treated as an employment of the worker with the agency, and all remuneration received by the worker, from anybody, in respect of the work is treated as earnings from that deemed employment with that intermediary. Where intermediaries work in a chain, so that the final agency in the chain with the contractual relationship with the client does not pay the worker directly, this rule means that this final agency is responsible for the PAYE and NIC obligations if other intermediaries or employers in the chain default. The same intermediary is also obliged to make reports under the 2015 changes (see further below).

Chains are not uncommon, and sometimes it is not easy to identify the end of a chain. While the typical agency temp (an office worker, a fruit picker, an event steward, etc) works under a simple contract for services with an agency (as in **Figure 10.1** above), many thousands of temporary workers are now employed by umbrella companies who supply their services to agencies for onward supply to the agencies' clients (as in **Figure 10.2** above).

In some cases, there is even a chain of businesses recognisable as employment agencies: a UK agency may, for example, have a contract to supply workers to a UK construction business that is a subcontractor to a large building company that is in turn working for a utility that is building a power station, and the UK agency may source its workers from an agency in, eg, Poland that takes on the job of finding enough workers to staff the contract. Less obviously perhaps, in the context of major projects, a main contractor will usually let contracts for elements of the project to a number of subcontractors, who may deliver the services with their own staff, supplemented by expertise bought in from elsewhere, such as specialists working through their own PSCs. An example might be a quantity surveyor (QS) with his own PSC who works on a project basis for a QS practice, which is not obviously an employment agency but may fall within the definition of *ITEPA 2003, s 44* in appropriate circumstances. The QS practice might supply his services to one of the subcontractor businesses on a major construction site, and in reality he may be working for the main contractor on that site, whose client will pay for and use the facility that is eventually constructed. In these circumstances, it is often difficult to identify exactly who is the client and who is the last intermediary in the chain with a contract to supply the individual's personal services.

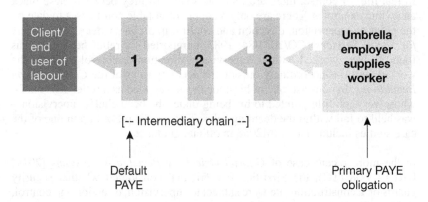

Figure 10.3: The agency supply chain and default responsibilities

Supervision, direction or control

10.9   Note the retention of the second condition from the old rules, the existence of a right of supervision, direction or control as to the manner of doing the work, in *ITEPA 2003, s 44(2)(a)*. This ensures that genuinely self-employed tradesmen and professionals will not be dragged into the deductions net even if they find work through agencies – the rules are intended to collect PAYE and Class 1 NICs from those who are working like employees without meeting all the conditions for a contract of employment. One of the examples issued in HMRC's early guidance on the new rules (now incorporated into the Employment Status Manual at ESM2060) illustrates the point.

Example 10.1 – Agency construction worker

Joiner John, who is supplied by an agency to work on a building project, is asked to build an oak-panelled door from a drawing, and then hang it. He is free to work as he sees fit, using his own workshop at home. He is not supervised as to how he carries out the contracted task, and is not caught by Class 1 NIC or PAYE.

In an alternative scenario, joiner John turns up on site and is allocated to the existing joinery team, working under the contractor's supervisor/foreman, who will direct, oversee and provide guidance over his work. He is also shown how to complete the work where necessary. The *Categorisation Regulations* and *ITEPA 2003, s 44* are clearly in point.

In real life, of course, there are multiple shades of grey between these black and white examples. There are only a couple of notable court cases to date on the point of supervision, direction and control. In *Staples v Secretary of State for Social Services* (CO/1073/84, 1985, unreported), a relief head chef was found to have worked without supervision, direction or control over how he worked, and was accordingly outside the deeming rules of the *Categorisation Regulations*. In contrast, one of his colleagues, supplied as a relief sous chef – whose very job title pointed to his being under the head chef's supervision – was held to fall within the deeming rules. This case is picked up in one of the case studies included as ESM2058 in official guidance.

In the more recent case of *Gabriel Oziegbe v Revenue & Customs* [2014] UKFTT 608 (TC), the First-tier Tax Tribunal considered whether security guards on a construction site were subject to supervision, direction and control, and Nowlan J commented as follows at paragraph 14:

> 'The most obvious situation in which the "control" requirement will not be satisfied is where the particular service being rendered is one that is extraneous to the basic activity of the client, such that it is entirely natural that the client will have no control or right of control over the way in which the services are provided.'

This approach is entirely logical: there would not usually be any control over how an independent contractor works if they are engaged specifically for their expertise in a field where the client lacks the knowledge or specialism. Another noteworthy point highlighted in this case is that the question to be asked is whether there is supervision, direction or control over how the work is done, not what job is to be done. This is only a First-tier Tribunal case but it does at least start the process of shaping the boundaries of when an individual is subject to supervision, direction or control.

In view of the absence of reported cases, HMRC issued 19 pages of guidance and examples to elaborate on their view of how supervision, direction or control might look in a range of industries, such as IT consulting, restaurants, haulage, security, pharmacy, care work, market research, etc (see http://bit.ly/1jnTcah and now ESM2037 and ESM2057–ESM2068). The fact that HMRC's example of a site security operative reaches the opposite conclusion, as was seen in Gabriel Oziegbe, illustrates how complicated this area can be and just how many shades of grey there are.

Focus

HMRC has added guidance to the Employment Status Manual to explain 'supervision, direction or control'.

Some of the agencies targeted by the change in the *Categorisation Regulations* have responded by arguing that most of their temporary workers are too experienced and too qualified to need supervision, and those who are not have been moved onto a subcontractor payroll subject to PAYE, so it remains to be seen how effective the change will be in imposing Class 1 NIC and PAYE on workers who are technically self-employed on basic principles. It is easy to foresee HMRC experiencing the same difficulties with this supervision rule as they have faced for many years with IR35: every individual case is different, and every single one needs a full investigation, for which resources do not exist in HMRC. HMRC are known to have created a number of dedicated compliance teams in late 2015 and an employment status and intermediaries team in 2016 to focus on intermediary workers, using the intelligence gathered via the quarterly returns described below (and on the absence of such returns from some businesses from which they were expected) to identify targets for compliance interventions.

Use of personal service companies

10.10   Other suppliers of self-employed temporary workers responded to the changes by ensuring that the *ITEPA 2003, s 44(2)(b)* escape route is followed: the deeming rules do not apply if the workers are already employees. As noted above, those who wish to avoid liability are free to work through their own PSC and pay themselves principally by dividend, provided that, in the process, they do not fall within the IR35 or managed service company rules. It is not entirely clear why the *FA 2014* rules did not forestall this entirely predictable turn of events, since HMRC knew in advance of the likely response by the temporary employment industry.

The Budget report in July 2015 promised measures to prevent or discourage this type of 'avoidance', if the structures adopted may legitimately be so described, given the limited savings to be made after the introduction of the dividend tax in April 2016. In particular, small companies have been disqualified for 2016–17 onwards from claiming the employment allowance (£3,000 pa from April 2016) if there is only one recipient of NICable earnings and that person is a director. That said, the one-man company need only employ and pay a single casual worker for a few hours to protect its entitlement to the allowance, but most will have simply appointed and paid a second director, so the value of the restriction is doubtful and seems unlikely to raise the £70m–£80m pa scheduled in the Budget Red Book. In addition, the new dividend tax is clearly aimed at narrowing the gap between taking remuneration and dividends from close companies, but the rates may have to be increased if it is to be effective. From April 2018 the dividend allowance will reduce from £5,000 to £2,000, as seen in *Finance (No 2) Bill 2017*.

10.11   HMRC consulted in July 2015 on potential new rules that would make the engager or client responsible for making the decision about whether a PSC worker is engaged like an employee, and transfer any overlooked IR35 liability for PAYE and NICs to the engager or client if the worker is found to have been in disguised employment but to have failed to comply with the IR35 rules. HMRC estimate (albeit on the basis of unpublished evidence and assumptions) that only 10% of PSCs who are within IR35 rules comply with those rules. The aim of the change was to collect money from engagers, who are more likely to be in existence and traceable several years down the line than are PSCs, although the problem of policing their decisions as to whether an individual could be deemed an employee is likely to be no less acute than the present HMRC problem with IR35 non-compliance. The idea was considered and rejected as impractical when IR35 was conceived, and little has changed apart from the government's need for more taxes.

Many informed parties told HMRC that the proposals were impractical. The ICAEW's published comments included this:

> 'how would "earnings" be calculated so as to exclude agents' profit margins, which PAYE code would apply, how would engagers know that they were dealing with a PSC, and which earnings periods and limits would apply for NIC? The plan is impracticable, even if the engager has enough knowledge of the contractor's circumstances to be certain that

the worker is employed by a PSC, which may not always be the case, especially where workers are supplied up a chain of intermediaries.'

The government response in May 2016 was another consultation entitled 'Off-payroll working in the public sector: reform of the intermediaries legislation', which set out proposals, that were ultimately introduced in April 2017, to make public sector bodies and agencies responsible for operating the tax rules that apply to off-payroll working in the public sector. The rules are to remain unchanged in the private sector for the time being although the government is consulting on whether to align the legislation and introduce similar provisions in the private sector.

'Responsible' means going further than the existing Whitehall procurement rules, under which many public sector bodies are already required to check that some of their off-payroll workers are paying the correct taxes. The new rules:

> 'move the liability to make the determination about whether the intermediaries rules apply, and the associated tax liability if so, from the PSC to the public sector end-client or agency or other third party closest in the chain to the PSC if there is one.'

The scope of the term 'public sector' is to be based on the definition in the *Freedom of Information Act 2000* and its Scottish equivalent. This includes 'educational establishments' without differentiating between state and private sector institutions, but the latter logically cannot be in scope.

The change in legislation will not apply if the work is deemed to be 'fully contracted out' of the public sector. This term has not been defined any further and so there will still be cases where it is unclear whether it has been fully contracted out or not but it does at least ensure that not all projects that stem from a public sector entity will be deemed to be public sector work.

Example 10.2 – Fully contracted out

A hospital ward is in a dilapidated state and requires significant redevelopment to be fit for purpose. ABC Construction tenders for and is appointed to redevelop the ward and engages numerous companies and tradesmen to undertake the work, including Malcolm, who provides his services through his own PSC. The work carried out by the PSC would not be deemed to be in the public sector because although the end client is the hospital, the work is not public sector work as it was fully contracted out to ABC. The private sector rules for IR35 would therefore apply and the PSC would continue to be responsible for ensuring compliance with IR35.

10.12 Agencies (and other businesses that are not registered employment businesses but act as intermediaries) supplying PSC contractors to any public sector organisation, and paying them, will be expected to have systems in place to determine in conjunction with the public sector client if an engagement is in scope, collect the necessary standing data (eg name, address, NINO) and to operate PAYE and NIC deductions and make RTI reports as if they are the employer. The normal 5% reduction when calculating the deemed payment for IR35 will not be available to those working within the public sector and within the scope of IR35.

The detail over how payments would be made to a PSC through RTI were half-baked at best and seem not to have been thought through (or, more accurately perhaps, not set out in the proposals), and HMRC have all but said that software developers will have to find solutions as to how this will work. To ensure there is no double taxation, the intermediary will get relief for tax and national insurance but only insofar as it has distributed the net deemed payment to the worker. In respect of the payments from the PSC to the individual, HMRC have stated that an undeclared dividend can be paid to the individual so as to not attract dividend tax, this also has the appearance of a half-baked way around the problem rather than a legitimate solution.

There was no explanation from HMRC of how the RTI system will issue a correct PAYE code to the agency when the system will still show the PSC as the employer. To date, HMRC have been unable to ensure that duplicate employments are not created when a person with one job moves to another and is paid (with the timeous submission of a Full Payment Submission (FPS)) before the old employer submits its final FPS (eg because payday is at the end of the month after the month of leaving, once commissions have been calculated). The deliberate creation of a double employment record in a public sector PSC case is yet another complexity that the RTI system may struggle with but is something that software developers have had to deal with. Many companies simply ignore the PSC and employ the individual directly under PAYE.

The change in legislation assumed that public sector engagers and agencies would simply be able to operate the proposed new system from 6 April 2017, despite the fact that HMRC did not even know what that system would look like.

10.13 Where agencies and other intermediaries are in a contractual chain, the new IR35 legislation is to apply to the agency that contracts directly with the PSC, which the government believes to be best placed to collect the personal details and deduct the tax and NICs. The public sector body will, however, be required, if asked, to provide its opinion within 31 days as to whether the work is caught by the IR35 legislation or not, as they will be the entity that will have a working knowledge of how the individual works and whether it is akin to an employment relationship. If the public sector body confirms that the individual is outside IR35 and the agency or intermediary relies on that information in good faith, or if the public sector body fails to provide an opinion, the public sector body will be the party that is liable to HMRC. This approach has unfortunately led to the unsurprising result of many public sector bodies opting for a cautious approach and simply saying that all individuals are within IR35, without any actual assessment of how the individuals work.

Anti-avoidance and anti-evasion

10.14   The *FA 2014* changes attempted to forestall both of these approaches (ie non-supervision and working via a PSC) by introducing both transfer of debt provisions and a Targeted Anti-Avoidance Rule (TAAR).

Transfer of debt

10.15   The obligation to deduct PAYE in a simple agency situation under *ITEPA 2003, s 44* falls on the agency (*ITEPA 2003, s 44(3)*), which is deemed to be the employer. *Categorisation Regulations, Sch 3, para 2* places the NIC obligation in the same hands.

Logically, an agency seeking to avoid having to operate PAYE would seek evidence from the client that the worker was under no right of supervision, direction or control. The temptation for the client is clear: a worker who is free to work without supervision is outside Class 1 NIC liability, so the hourly rates charged by the agency can be lower. An unscrupulous client under pressure to meet a contractual budget might be tempted to simply tell the agency that there is no right of supervision. However, if an agency is provided with a fraudulent document by the client that dishonestly purports to evidence the fact that there is no supervision, direction or control as to the manner of working, or by any other party to the contractual relationship purporting to show that the worker is already an employee and therefore outside the scope, the provider of the fraudulent document (if he is resident or has a place of business in the UK) becomes the deemed employer (*Categorisation Regulations Sch 3, para 2*, and *ITEPA 2003, s 44(5)*).

It remains to be seen how this rule might be applied in practice, and whether an employee of a client issuing such a document without authority to do so, and without full knowledge of the facts, can validly be accused of 'fraud' as opposed to carelessness or recklessness. Fraud generally requires mens rea (*Fraud Act 2006, s 2* refers to dishonestly making a false representation) so the provision may prove difficult to enforce and time-consuming even to argue (which has long been HMRC's major problem with IR35). An agency open to being pursued for PAYE, that intends to rely on a document purporting to evidence freedom from supervision, would arguably be well advised to ensure that the letter has been signed by someone with clear authority to do so, such as a director of the client. Unconfirmed reports suggest that the special intermediary compliance teams set up in late 2015 are focussing on false claims of a lack of supervision as their first foray into countering the perceived avoidance and evasion.

TAAR

10.16   The TAAR in *ITEPA 2003, s 46A* was added in an attempt to catch any third person entering into 'arrangements' (a term defined widely in *ITEPA 2003, s 46A(2)*), the main purpose, or one of the main purposes, of which is to sidestep *ITEPA 2003, s 44*. That third person is to be treated as the agency under the new *ITEPA 2003, s 44*.

HMRC originally saw this rule being used where, for example, an agency insists that all workers are supplied via their own PSCs so as to avoid the agency rules. Their guidance currently states clearly that the TAAR will not apply to people who set up a PSC for a reason other than reducing tax, such as the limited liability protections provided by incorporation (para 3.69, Onshore Employment Intermediaries: False Self-Employment, summary of responses, 13 March 2014, and ESM2041).

NIC law changed in the same way as the tax rules for agencies, albeit somewhat belatedly, because it (rather inexplicably) required primary legislation: *NIC Act 2015, s 6* added a new *reg 5A* to the *Categorisation Regulations* to do the same job, with its effect backdated to 6 April 2014, except for the elements related to foreign employers and agencies within paras 9(a)–(d), which took effect from 12 February 2015 when *NIC Act 2015* was passed.

PAYE personal liability notices

10.17   To prevent evasion of responsibility by corporate deemed employers being liquidated with unpaid PAYE debts, the government added *Ch 3A* into the *Income Tax (PAYE) Regulations 2003, Pt 4*. This will allow HMRC to issue personal liability notices to the directors of the deemed employer when 'relevant' PAYE debts (ie those transferred under the fraudulent documents or TAAR provisions) remain unpaid at the due date, although the actual timing will of course be some years later when HMRC has (a) identified the default and (b) exhausted other avenues to collect from the entity that is primarily liable.

Directors of employment businesses are ordinarily open to personal liability notices only for unpaid NICs (*SSAA 1992, s 121C*), but not for PAYE. The new *Ch 3A* is aimed directly at countering PAYE avoidance and evasion in the context of the new rules, but *SSAA 1992, s 121C* may conceivably be used against those to whom liability for NICs is transferred under the new *Sch 3, para 2* rules in the *Categorisation Regulations* if the companies concerned fail to pay their NIC debts and cannot do so.

10.18   The *Finance Act 2016* also added *ITEPA 2003, s 688B* and introduced additional PAYE regulations (*Pt 4, Ch 3B, regs 97ZG–97ZM*) to extend the transfer of PAYE debt provisions to arrears arising from any failure to deduct PAYE from non-allowable home-to-work travel expenses of intermediary workers who are subject to supervision, direction or control or work through IR35 companies. The liability may be transferred to the directors of the company that provides fraudulent documents purporting to evidence a lack of supervision, direction or control, or to the directors of the intermediary where it holds no reasonable evidence of an absence of a right of supervision.

Offshore intermediaries

10.19   UK intermediaries exploiting the gaps in the agency rules outlined above were not the only focus of HMRC's efforts to increase NIC revenues. There were also two perceived major problems with offshore intermediaries: failure to comply with existing 'host employer' rules for workers supplied by overseas employers, and an absence of secondary Class 1 NIC liability for non-EEA employers of workers active on the UK Continental Shelf in the oil and gas sector. Both were addressed by the 2014 and 2015 changes.

When a UK worker is employed by an EEA-based employer, normal UK and EEA NIC rules apply, with the employer liable (since 1 May 2010, when EU social security rules were updated by the introduction of Regulations (EC) No 883/2004 and 987/2009, and until the UK leaves the EU) to register in the UK and pay both primary and secondary Class 1 NICs under Real Time Information (RTI) rules.

It is debatable whether HMRC is correct in asserting that the provisions of the EC regulations are of relevance where a worker is a UK resident working on the UK Continental Shelf, since he will have done nothing to bring himself within the scope of the European migrant worker rules, but that is an argument beyond the scope of this chapter.

When a worker is supplied by a non-EEA employer, with no UK place of business, the foreign employer is not generally so liable, but the 'host employer' rules in *Categorisation Regulations, Sch 3, para 9* place the employer's obligations (payment and reporting) on the UK host employer to which the services of the individual are supplied. However, this latter approach requires cooperation between the supplying employer and the host employer, and if the offshore agency or intermediary refuses to supply the relevant information, the UK host cannot comply and has a reasonable excuse for not doing so (assuming no collusion or fraud).

10.20   A small number of offshore employment businesses outside EEA territory were abusing this position to supply tens of thousands of temporary workers to public sector employers (eg supply teachers and nurses) with no secondary NICs being paid, despite the host employer rules. The 2014 offshore intermediary rules collect the NICs from any onshore agency that facilitates the supply of the worker or, in the absence of any such agency, the end client. The target is plainly to put non-compliant offshore suppliers out of business, but this type of evasion is not easy to stop.

Example 10.3 – Host employers

Chrissie, a qualified nurse, signed up with Warezatkair, an online agency based in Niue, a Pacific territory that has no tax or social security treaties with the UK but good internet services. W maintains a database of nursing personnel and has contracts with a number of nursing agencies and nursing banks in the UK for the supply of agency nursing services. It agrees fees with the UK agencies who source their staff via Niue but does not disclose financial details, so the UK agencies do not know how much the agency nurses are paid per shift. The UK users and agencies could not comply with the host employer rules without information from Niue, which was never forthcoming.

UK agencies are now explicitly liable for the PAYE and NIC obligations, but still have the same problem of lacking the necessary information.

To counter both evasion and avoidance, changes were also made to *Categorisation Regulations, Sch 3, para 9* from 6 April 2014 (under the *Social Security (Categorisation of Earners) (Amendment) Regulations 2014, SI 2014/635*) to create a secondary Class 1 NIC liability, where none existed or was enforceable before, in respect of workers provided by foreign employers.

Under the new provisions, the end client may be liable where there is a foreign, but no UK, agency. Where there is a foreign employer or agency, but also a UK agency, the UK agency that has the contractual relationship with the end client may be liable. This is represented in **Figure 10.4** below.

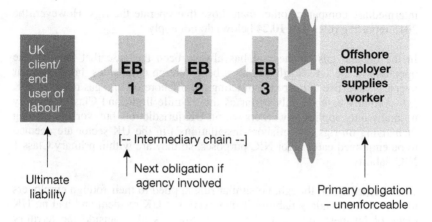

Figure 10.4: Liabilities of Employment Businesses (EB) for workers employed from outside the UK

The liabilities for NICs (other than for pure oil & gas workers offshore) after the introduction of the 2014 offshore intermediary changes may be summarised in the following table:

Table 10.1: Liable employers where workers employed via intermediaries from outside the UK

Mr X working for	Deductions due by
UK host employer via foreign employer	UK host employer
UK client of foreign agency	UK client
UK client of UK agency but via overseas employer or agency	UK agency ('EB1' in **Figure 10.4**)
UK employer, but X works outside UK for UK agency, selling to foreign client, X 'eligible' for UK NIC	UK employer or UK agency with contract with foreign purchaser of services
Foreign employer, but X works outside UK for UK agency, selling to foreign client, X 'eligible' for UK NIC	UK agency with contract with foreign purchaser of services

Oil and gas

10.21   The offshore intermediary rules apply if the worker is engaged to work on an offshore oil and gas installation on the UK Continental Shelf. Many employments carried out on oil and gas rigs are under contracts with intermediary companies other than those that operate the rigs. However, the 2015 reporting rules (see **10.24** below) do not apply.

In the oil and gas business, it has always been the case that most of the operators in the UK North Sea have been foreign companies, bringing their overseas expertise to bear on extracting the offshore oil and gas reserves. UK law normally extends only as far as the 12-mile limit, and Class 1 liability normally only applies to workers within UK jurisdiction, but workers earning their living on rigs (or 'offshore installations') in the UK sector are deemed to be employed earners for NIC purposes, so they are within primary Class 1 NIC liability.

Until 6 April 2014, though, no similar rule applied to their foreign employers to impose a secondary liability if they were not UK resident and had no UK place of business. The UK Continental Shelf is also outside the territory of the EEA, so the foreign employers could not be treated as having a UK place of business even under Regulation (EC) No 883/2004 unless they were established onshore in an EEA state. Many workers were therefore supplied to rig operators by non-EEA operators or agencies (typically in Jersey, Guernsey, Panama, the United Arab Emirates (UAE) or Singapore) so as to avoid the secondary Class 1 NIC liability.

Focus

The wages of oil and gas workers on the UK Continental Shelf now attract a secondary NIC liability even if their employer is outside the UK.

Changes were therefore made to the *Contributions Regulations, reg 114* from 6 April 2014 (empowered by *NICA 2014, s 12*) to create a secondary Class 1 NIC liability where none existed or was enforceable before in respect of workers on 'offshore installations'. The liability may be paid by the legal employer offshore, but if it is not, it falls on an associated company present in the UK, and if there is more than one, on the group company with the largest corporation tax profits in the UK for the accounting period which precedes the tax year in which the contributions are due. If there is no such onshore company, the liability moves to the licensee of the field.

The potential for transfers of secondary NIC liability means that oilfield operators will be justifiably concerned about hiring workers supplied by an overseas business that may or may not have paid the requisite secondary NICs, so in addition to the *Categorisation Regulations*, we now also have, in *Contributions Regulations, regs 114A–114D*, a new certification process. It gives hirers certainty over the credentials of their labour suppliers in Continental Shelf operations. The new provisions provide for the issue of certificates to offshore labour suppliers and licensees who use their labour, excluding the licensees from any NICs liability in respect of the supplied workers. Certification is handled by an HMRC office in Edinburgh – see NIM33800.

Mariners

10.22 The new offshore intermediary rules do not extend to mariners working on ships (as opposed to vessels qualifying as offshore installations, now defined in *Contributions Regulations, reg 114D*), to whom the normal mariner provisions of *Contributions Regulations, reg 115* continue to apply and who may still be employed in appropriate circumstances without a UK secondary NIC liability. The new oil and gas rules are excluded in respect of certain mariners on board vessels that qualify as offshore installations if they fall within certain grade descriptions that relate to marine rather than oil and gas activities (see below).

Meaning of 'at sea' and 'offshore installation'

10.23 *Contributions Regulations, reg 114* deems employment 'at sea' in any designated area of the UK Continental Shelf in connection with oil and gas operations to be work carried out in the UK, even if the contributor does not satisfy the conditions of residence and presence in the UK prescribed in the *Contributions Regulations, reg 145*.

The term 'at sea' could present a conflict with *Contributions Regulations, reg 115* – a worker on a ship in the UK North Sea could potentially fall under either regulation – but the scope of the Continental Shelf rule is limited by *Contributions Regulations, reg 114(4)* so that it applies only to work on or in connection with an 'offshore installation', with the exception of certain grades of mariner set out in a table at the foot of *Contributions Regulations, reg 114*, who will still be treated as mariners within *Contributions Regulations, reg 115* even when working on such structures. The table essentially identifies certain types of worker on board ships or vessels that may be classed as offshore installations (eg, jack-ups or semi-submersibles) whose job is essentially that of a mariner rather than a rig worker and whose duties are covered by the *Merchant Shipping (Safe Manning, Hours of Work and Watch Keeping) Regulations 1997, SI 1997/1320*.

As ever, there are grey areas. For example, *Contributions Regulations, reg 114D* includes a definition of 'offshore installation' specific to these provisions. The term means 'a structure which is, is to be, or has been, put to a relevant use while in water'. The regulation includes a list of relevant uses, all related to exploitation of oil and gas reserves, and defines 'put to use while in water' to mean while standing in any waters, stationed (by whatever means) in any waters, or standing on the foreshore or other land intermittently covered with water. Fixed rigs, and jack-ups that are working, clearly 'stand' on the seabed, while semi-submersibles, flotels (accommodation vessels) and FPSOs (floating production, storage and offloading units) are 'stationed'. The regulation specifically excludes ships or vessels used for the transport of supplies, or as safety/standby vessels, or for the laying of cables, but ships that work while stationary but move around could fall either side of the line (eg, dive support vessels, inspection/construction support vessels and subsea pipe-laying vessels that remains stationary using dynamic positioning while working). As a rule of thumb, HMRC will regard any such ship that remains stationary for no longer than five days as falling outside the definition of offshore installation, which is the same basis it uses for claims to seafarers' earnings deduction (EIM33108–EIM33109).

Note that the *Contributions Regulations, reg 114* rules do not apply to offshore wind and wave farms and vessels that install and maintain them, as exploiting the wind and waves is not a 'relevant use'. These workers, if they are within UK jurisdiction, may therefore fall within the scope of *ITEPA 2003, ss 44–47* and the *Categorisation Regulations*.

THE 2015 RULES: REPORTING

10.24   The problem of allegedly false self-employment will clearly not have disappeared with the introduction of the anti-avoidance changes in 2014. There will still be a significant number of workers who are outside the scope of PAYE and Class 1 NIC because they do not fall within *ITEPA 2003, s 44* and the *Categorisation Regulations*. Some of the escapees will be legitimate (ie there is genuinely no right of supervision, direction or control, or they are already employed by an umbrella company or a PSC), but HMRC needed a way of checking that payments made gross by agencies (and anyone else falling within the scope of the intermediary rules) are indeed legitimate. There is therefore a quarterly online reporting obligation from 6 July 2015 for any payments made by 'agencies' outside the RTI system, intended to alert HMRC to any possible disregard shown for the rules by intermediaries. Where workers are still being paid gross despite the new rules, HMRC wants to know why, from the intermediary with the contract for the supply of the worker to the client.

Example 10.4 – Who has control?

Bean & Co offers bookkeeping services to numerous clients. At times of high demand, it subcontracts work to Jackie, a freelancer who is highly experienced, has her own self-employed business and does not normally take on supervised engagements.

A client, Stalker, has a problem when its financial controller goes off on long-term sick leave and asks Bean if it can supply a temporary replacement for a month. Bean subcontracts the work to Jackie. No PAYE or NICs are due because Jackie is not subject to supervision, direction or control, so Bean pays her gross. A quarterly report is required from Bean, though, because Jackie is supplying her personal services to Stalker via an intermediary.

Any new returns designed by HMRC will now always be digital by default, but there was insufficient time between the conception of the 2014 changes and their introduction for the relevant software to be developed. Design and implementation of the reporting regime required a delay until 6 April 2015.

Where a worker meets the revised conditions in *ITEPA 2003, s 44*, the 'agency' must operate PAYE and Class 1 NICs and make online reports under the RTI rules. HMRC will therefore have information about payments made to these workers and be able to check that the deductions have been paid over.

However, many temporary workers will be outside the scope of PAYE, so intermediaries may not pay wages under deduction, perhaps because they do not pay workers directly (eg, they are sourced from an umbrella company), or they pay workers gross because they are not subject to supervision, direction or control as to the manner in which they work.

HMRC can see both the financial accounts and the RTI returns but has no further information, so it may look as if significant sums are being paid to agency workers without deduction of PAYE and NICs, which would call for compliance action. There would be little point in investigating compliant umbrella company structures, but those agencies paying workers gross are seen as a real compliance risk.

10.25   The quarterly reporting rules from 6 April 2015 are found in the *Income Tax (Pay As You Earn) (Amendment No 2) Regulations 2015, SI 2015/171* which inserted new *regs 84E–84H* into the *PAYE Regulations*. These require specified information from 'specified employment intermediaries' and impose record-keeping requirements on those intermediaries.

Details must be reported even if the workers are paid (by someone else) under deduction of PAYE and NICs. Oddly, their 'employers' may not be the ones doing the reporting.

The reporting requirements depend on the type of worker and the structure in which the engagement is made.

> **Focus**
>
> RTI deductions for umbrella workers are reported by their employers, but agencies must still make quarterly reports of payments to the umbrella companies.

The major exception from the new reporting regime is the classic 'temping' structure: the intermediary must deduct and account for PAYE and Class 1 NICs using the RTI system. This type of engagement is of little interest to HMRC's compliance teams, as there is less likelihood of avoidance of deductions, so nothing is required beyond the normal RTI reporting.

This exception applies equally to businesses that would ordinarily not be classed as agencies or labour providers: for example, an accountant sending an employee on secondment to a client continues to process the earnings through payroll. The client pays the accountant's fee without deducting PAYE or NICs, but the new quarterly reporting requirements are irrelevant.

10.26 In contrast, where temps are actually employees of an umbrella company under an overarching contract of employment, and PAYE and NICs are deducted, with a full payment summary (FPS) for every payment, a report may nevertheless be required by the agency if the umbrella company is not the person who has the contract with the client.

If the umbrella company contracts directly with the client, it accounts for PAYE and NIC and need not file quarterly reports. However, if the umbrella company merely acts as a provider of labour to an agency, and it is the agency that has the contract with the client, the agency will be paying gross fees for the workers' services. Without the full picture, this looks to HMRC as if the agency is paying the workers gross, so the agency must make quarterly reports.

The new rules began to apply from 6 April 2015, with the first reports due between 6 July and 5 August for the quarter to 5 July 2015. HMRC received many more reports in the first quarter than in later quarters, which gave an instant target list for its compliance teams. HMRC believes that the drop in the number of returns signifies a problem with non-compliance, but it seems much more likely that the initial absence of comprehensive guidance about the new rules, especially about what did not have to be reported, led to intermediaries reporting for the first quarter payments that were not in fact in scope. The correct analysis followed in the second quarter, with the help of better guidance, which was issued only on 30 July 2015.

Who reports?

10.27 An 'employment intermediary' is within the new reporting rules if specified in *PAYE Regulations, reg 84E*. The definition of 'employment intermediary', for the purposes of the agency rules only, is now found in *ITEPA 2003, s 716B(2)*:

'a person who makes arrangements under or in consequence of which –

(a) an individual works, or is to work, for a third person, or

(b) an individual is, or is to be, remunerated for work done for a third person.'

ITEPA 2003, s 716B(3) states that:

'an individual works for a person if –

(a) the individual performs any duties of an employment for that person (whether or not the individual is employed by that person), or

(b) the individual provides, or is involved in the provision of, a service to that person.'

10.28 The latter definition appears to be very wide in scope, which is unsurprising in view of the fact that the 2014 changes were intended as an anti-avoidance measure. However, it is doubtful that HMRC intended the reporting obligation to encompass every subcontract arrangement involving an individual worker. The obligation will clearly apply to any organisation, large or small, in any sector, supplying workers to an end client to work *for that client*, but it will be of no relevance where the worker works for the contracting business itself.

HMRC has still, despite this being a real problem, issued no guidance on where the dividing line is between working for a client and working for a supplier to the client, so each case will depend on its facts, which is not very helpful to employers and agencies trying to understand their obligations. The guidance on GOV.UK simply assumes that a supplier will know it is an intermediary and will know when it is in scope.

If an accountant subcontracts work to a self-employed freelancer (see **Example 10.4** above), it should be reasonable to assume that the accountant charging a flat fee for the provision of, eg, a quarterly VAT return would involve the freelancer working for the accountant rather than for the client, so the accountant would not be an employment intermediary. In contrast, if the accountant arranged for the freelance bookkeeper to cover for somebody in-house who was absent, paying the bookkeeper and charging the client a fee for the services, it would perhaps be difficult to avoid characterising the accountant as an employment intermediary.

The specific conditions

10.29   The intermediary will be 'specified', and therefore required to fulfil the reporting obligations, if it meets four conditions set out in *PAYE Regulations, reg 84E*:

(i)   it is an agency (as defined in *ITEPA 2003, s 44*, ie not just a registered employment agency);

(ii)   more than one individual provides services to a client under or in consequence of a contract between the intermediary and one or more clients (this excludes PSCs from scope if they simply sell their director's services direct to a client without involving an agency);

(iii)   the services are not provided exclusively on the UK Continental Shelf (so oil and gas workers are out of scope because they are certified under the *Contributions Regulations, regs 114A–114D* arrangements instead); and

(iv)   the intermediary makes one or more payments in respect of, or connected with, the services provided by one or more individuals that is subject to RTI reporting (ie PAYE under *PAYE Regulations, reg 67B*) but has been omitted from the intermediary's FPS, or is not subject to PAYE under RTI because the worker is neither an employee nor treated as an employee under *PAYE Regulations, reg 10* (ie PAYE for agency workers).

Note that a PSC that subcontracts its work to another PSC will be an 'agency' for these purposes. If the first PSC holds a direct contract with the client, it will have a reporting obligation, because it will be paying gross for what is, in effect, agency work. In contrast, if the first PSC has found its work through an agency, it will not hold the contract with the client and will have no reporting obligation: that will fall on the agency.

Example 10.5 – PSC obligations

Daisy is a marketing consultant operating through her own personal service company, Chain Ltd. When she finds work directly, without agency involvement, Chain is not an intermediary: it is her employer. She can draw salary under PAYE and NIC deduction, or dividends out of distributable profits.

When her work comes via Buttercup, an agency, Buttercup must pay Chain gross and report the payments quarterly.

Occasionally, Daisy wins several contracts in quick succession, and rather than disappoint clients, she subcontracts some of the work to a former colleague, Rose, who also operates via a PSC, Garland Ltd. When Chain pays Garland for Rose's services, Chain can pay gross but it is an intermediary in the context of the transaction and must include the payment on the next quarterly return.

As of April 2017, if Daisy is seen to be working under an IR35-type contract for a public sector organisation, Buttercup will have to put Daisy on its payroll and deduct tax and NICs from the fees paid. If her contract with the public sector organisation explicitly and genuinely allows her to subcontract any of her work to someone like Rose, via Garland or otherwise, Buttercup should not have to worry about the new IR35 rules, as the absence of a personal service obligation should preclude the application of *Chapter 8*, but Buttercup would still have to report quarterly the gross payments made to Chain.

Making returns

10.30   *PAYE Regulations, reg 84F* provides that the specified intermediary must, for each quarter, provide specified information by the 5th of the month following the end of each quarter. Errors in returns may be corrected before the reporting deadline for the next quarter. Agencies need not make just one submission for each quarter if it is more convenient to report weekly or monthly.

The return must be made online (using the reporting intermediary's Government Gateway account – see http://bit.ly/1FEYFmR), in accordance with a specified HMRC template (http://bit.ly/1B5ZKnT), and it must include a declaration of correctness and completeness by the person submitting it. An agent may make reports on behalf of a client by whom it is authorised to file PAYE returns (http://bit.ly/1ItWO2w). Any self-employed person acting as an employment agency without himself being an employer will have to register as an employer so as to obtain a PAYE reference for this purpose, and then make clear to HMRC that it is not in fact an employer and will not be submitting FPS, EPS or P11D returns. HMRC has recognised this problem and advises such agents to send an email to mailbox.employmentintermediariesunit@hmrc.gsi.gov.uk, which suggests that an internal protocol has been agreed for these unusual cases.

The submission (quarterly or more frequent) must be in the form of an open document spreadsheet (.ODS) file or a comma-separated values (.CSV) file in the exact format set out in the template. Data validation rules are set out in a document for software developers at http://bit.ly/1g4eUBm.

Reporting must continue every quarter until the agency has not fallen within the definition of specified intermediary for four consecutive quarters, or has notified HMRC that it is no longer in business as such.

Overseas aspects

10.31   The reporting requirement applies to agencies in the UK who are specified employment intermediaries. However, many UK agencies also have contracts to find workers for overseas projects, and since many applications will now be processed wholly online, not requiring the presence in the UK of the worker, it may be that non-residents, be they British or foreign, are engaged to work on those overseas projects.

The reporting requirements apply only to workers subject to UK tax (if the workers are non-resident and not working in the UK, HMRC has no interest), so agencies in the UK taking on self-employed workers overseas to work for clients solely overseas should not include them in their reports, provided the workers are not UK resident for tax purposes (see ESM2180).

It is unclear how an intermediary is to know or assess the residence status for tax purposes of any such worker, since the statutory residence test requires much information that is not available to an employer (and the NIC rules are different in any case, so an intermediary would need to assess under two sets of criteria, if aware of the distinction and capable of making such a judgment). Sometimes a worker's residence status will be immediately clear: if a UK business wins a contract to build a desalination plant in the Persian Gulf and the UK staffing agency contracted to find the workers recruits them from, eg, India, they are non-UK residents working overseas. The position will be less clear-cut when the new recruits are expatriate British citizens or other nationalities who have lived and worked in the UK in the past and may or may not be UK resident for tax purposes at the time of recruitment or at some point during the contract period.

10.32   When proposals were mooted in 2014 to withdraw personal allowances from non-residents, they were dropped because there was no practical way for an employer reliably to identify a new worker's residence status when first applying PAYE to their remuneration, or for HMRC to assess the worker's residence status without imposing a requirement for a new return of personal information outside the requirements of a tax return. Where an employer takes on a worker, it at least has the advantage that the employer has a direct relationship with the worker, but where an agency is recruiting over the internet for overseas jobs, and the worker is supplied by an offshore employer, the question of residence is much harder to establish reliably. HMRC has not yet indicated how it expects intermediaries to approach the question of a worker's residence status when recruiting for work outside the UK.

Required information

10.33   *PAYE Regulations, reg 84G* sets out the information requirements, which are straightforward provided the agency has a direct relationship with the worker. The intermediary must:

- identify itself by giving specified details:
  - name;
  - address;
  - postcode; and
  - employer PAYE reference (if it has one);
- identify each worker:
  - full name;
  - address;
  - postcode;
  - NI number *or* gender and date of birth if the worker has no NI number; and
  - unique taxpayer reference (UTR) *if* the worker is self-employed or a member of a partnership;
- state the start date of the relevant services for *each worker* in the period;
- state the end date of the relevant services for *each worker* in the period.

As issue occurs when foreign workers who work temporarily in the UK, have no permanent UK address or postcode, no NI number and no UTR. A NI number is of course required by anyone liable to NICs, and a UTR is required by anybody within self-assessment, but many new arrivals looking for work through agencies will have neither or if they have only just started to work under self-assessment, and it is unlikely that a temporary UK address will be of use to HMRC. As soon as a new hire moves home while still on the payroll, HMRC's database will be instantly out of date. The address on the NI and PAYE System (NPS) database is updated from FPS data only when a new worker's record is added to the payroll for the first time, not when a subsequent FPS reports a changed address.

10.34   Where a payment is made to an individual outside the RTI regime (or someone who should have been paid under PAYE but was not), further details are required by *PAYE Regulations, reg 84G(c)*:

- the full name and address of the recipient if paid to someone other than the individual worker whose details are included above, and if the recipient is a partnership, the name under which it trades;

- the total of the payments to that person in the quarter (in either £ or €, indicating which currency has been used, although that is not explicit in the regulations);

- a reason code for why no tax was deducted;

- if the reason is that the recipient is a limited company, the full name of the company and its registration number; and

- an indication of whether the payment included any VAT.

PAYE Regulations, reg 84G(c) is arguably incoherent, as it could be read as not requiring these further details where a payment is made to a company, partnership or LLP in respect of the services to clients. However, it must clearly be read as a payment made by *anybody* to an individual in respect of that individual's services to a client, otherwise bullet point four would be nonsensical: paying outside the RTI regime is clearly not limited to paying a self-employed individual without PAYE; it applies equally to paying an umbrella company or PSC for the individual's services.

Gross payment reason codes

10.35   There are six possible circumstances and reason codes listed in the guidance why PAYE might not have been deducted:

A   the payee is self-employed

B   the worker is a member of a partnership

C   the worker is a member of an LLP

D   the worker is supplied by a limited company (including personal service companies)

E   the worker is on a non-UK engagement and is supplied from a company, partnership or person outside the UK

F   PAYE has already been applied by someone else

One of the reasons for falling into the intermediary reporting regime, namely omitting to apply RTI to the earnings of an agency worker who is subject to PAYE, does not appear in the above list. The obvious corrective action would be to file an FPS (or earlier year update (EYU) if there is significant delay) and account for the PAYE.

The specified intermediary is instructed in the guidance to use the reason that comes first in the above list, even if more than one reason applies. This demonstrates further incoherence, because many workers are supplied to the agency by an umbrella company, which will typically be employing the worker. It will apply PAYE, but reason D will have to be used when reason F is more logical.

Information and record-keeping obligations

10.36   *PAYE Regulations, reg 84H* requires the specified employment intermediary to keep and preserve information, records and documents which evidence the specified information when the details are not already required to be sent to HMRC under any other provision of the regulations.

Agencies putting workers on their own payroll will keep RTI records, but where they have no PAYE obligation, the normal PAYE and NIC record-keeping requirements would not apply.

Under *PAYE Regulations, reg 84H*, relevant information, records and documents must be retained for not less than three years after the end of the tax year to which they relate, although it is specifically provided that they may be kept in any form or by any means, so a digital archive should be acceptable.

It should be noted that the record-keeping requirement is imposed only on the 'specified employment intermediary'. Where workers are supplied along a chain of contracts, via a number of intermediaries, only the last intermediary in the chain must make the reports and keep the records. It is not clear how that specified intermediary is to enforce the requirement for items of personal data that it may not hold and that it may not be able to access if the employer or intermediary higher up the chain is outside UK jurisdiction and subject to foreign data protection laws.

Penalties

10.37   Unsurprisingly, late returns, non-submission and inaccuracies will be subject to penalties, although there is nothing specific in the regulations, so the PAYE penalty regime in *TMA 1970, s 98* (as amended by *FA 2015, s 18*) applies.

HMRC guidance (http://bit.ly/1SHnsQo) states that the first offence in a 12-month period will attract an automatic penalty of £250, the second offence

£500, and further offences £1,000, all of which are below the statutory maximum in *TMA 1970, s 98* and the guidance at ESM2190. It also threatens daily penalties for continued failure to submit a report. *TMA 1970, s 98* does not impose automatic penalties, so the guidance must be taken merely as a statement of HMRC's intentions.

HMRC's guidance (ESM2190) states that penalties will be imposed proportionately, and will be used where:

- the payments declared for workers contained in the return are significantly incorrect and understated;

- workers have been omitted from the return;

- identity details have been omitted on a significant number of occasions; or

- the return uses reason F (PAYE under RTI already applied by somebody else) to justify gross payment when in fact no PAYE has been accounted for.

TRAVEL AND SUBSISTENCE RESTRICTIONS – APRIL 2016

10.38   As noted above, workers supplied to agencies through 'umbrella' companies have typically been given permanent employment contracts so that they can legitimately claim to have a series of temporary workplaces and legitimately claim a tax- and NIC-free amount of commuting costs between home and those temporary locations.

Historically, umbrella employers obtained dispensations for paying the expenses of travel and subsistence for their workers, and they have exploited this by reducing taxable pay and exchanging it for tax-free expenses. Sometimes part of the tax saving has been passed to the workers by increasing their net take-home pay including expenses, but some umbrella employers have simply protected net pay and used the tax and NIC savings to reduce their rates to clients, arguing that the workers are no worse off because they would in any event have been incurring the relevant commuting costs out of their own pocket.

Contracts often allowed for variable gross pay but protected net pay, at a known hourly rate. HMRC warned that this type of 'payday-by-payday' relief structure was ineffective, but in the only case so far to have been considered by the courts (*Reed Employment plc and Others v HMRC* [2015] EWCA Civ 805) the (losing) employer's problem was a failure to implement permanent contracts (and thereby create a series of temporary workplaces for the 'temps' in question) rather than any salary sacrifice or exchange, so HMRC's opinion is still open to question.

Example 10.6 – Workplace type: 2015/16 rules

Roy needed to assemble a team of workers in 2015/16 for a temporary project in Wembley. He sourced the workers from elsewhere, as he had few resources of his own and needed workers who knew what they were doing.

If the workers had been hired via an agency, the Wembley site would have become their permanent workplace for the duration of the contract and their commuting costs would not have been deductible, so Roy sourced them from a range of umbrella employers, with whom they already had permanent employment contracts and who sent them to various sites around the UK every week. The Wembley site was therefore just another temporary workplace for them, and their expenses of travelling between home and the site were therefore generally deductible where the journey to the site was not substantially the same as ordinary commuting for them.

Raheem, one of the workers who is an additional rate taxpayer, travelled to Wembley from his home in Cheshire every week, and chose to stay in an hotel, at a total cost of £1,000 per week. Raheem's employer, Sky Blue plc, in order to minimise its employment costs, agreed with him that it would reduce his pay and reimburse his travel and subsistence expenses instead, for which it held a P11D dispensation, but it would ensure his net pay was protected.

Switching £1,000 from pay to expenses would have increased net pay by the income tax and primary NIC liability saved (£470 per week), so Raheem's revised taxable pay was agreed to be £1,886 lower (ie £1,000 for the expenses and £470 ÷ (100% – 47%) for the grossed-up tax saving). This saved tax and NIC of £886, so Raheem was only £1,000 out of pocket, which was covered by the tax-free expense reimbursement. Sky Blue also saved £260 in employer NICs, so its employment costs were reduced by £1,146 (£1,886 + £260 – £1,000), some of which it chose to pass on to Roy to make the contract price more attractive, some of which it retained to cover administration costs and make a contribution to profit.

Raheem's friend Harry, who lives near Wembley, and his umbrella employer were also spurred on by Roy's agency to use the same salary exchange arrangement, but they couldn't, as Harry's travel to Wembley was very similar to his normal commute to a permanent site in North London, only a few miles from Wembley.

Tackling the tax loss

10.39 Whether or not HMRC could have blocked this structure by litigating its view that 'payday-by-payday' salary sacrifice was ineffective, the government chose instead to tackle the perceived loss of tax and NICs at the root by yet more legislation, blocking the temporary workplace rule for intermediary workers who are, in effect, working in exactly the same way as an ordinary employee of the client, alongside whom they work, and who cannot claim tax relief for their ordinary commuting costs.

With retrospective effect from 6 April 2016, *Finance Act 2016, s 14* introduced *ITEPA 2003, s 339A* to achieve this, together with a new *ITEPA 2003, s 688B* and new PAYE personal liability notices for the directors of companies who disregard the new rules or who provide fraudulent documents in an effort to sidestep the block.

In summary, *ITEPA 2003, s 339A* blocks any claim under *ITEPA 2003, ss 338* and *339* by a worker who is supplied by an intermediary or PSC (other than a managed service company, which is taxed under existing rules) by deeming each engagement to be a separate employment. This has the effect of applying the normal travel and subsistence rules to such workers: they cannot claim relief for travelling to the base for that assignment, but they can still claim if the client sends them to a temporary location in the course of carrying out the duties of the assignment.

Example 10.7 – Workplace type: 2016/17 rules

Roy's successor, Sam, needs to assemble a new team of workers in 2016/17 for a different temporary project based in Wembley. He again sources the workers from a series of umbrella employers.

Raheem again commutes from his home in Cheshire every week, and again stays in a hotel, at a total cost of £1,000 per week. Raheem's employer, Sky Blue plc, can no longer pay Raheem's expenses of travel and subsistence tax-free for the Wembley contract, because the Wembley engagement is treated as a new, separate employment, which means that Wembley becomes his permanent workplace for the duration of the engagement. Its price to Sam increases accordingly to cover the costs of Raheem's extra salary, the associated employer NICs and pension costs, and its profit margin.

In the middle of this contract, Sam decides that the team all need a few days at specialist training facilities at Lilleshall in Shropshire, so Raheem incurs the expense of travelling to a temporary workplace, just like the permanent members of Sam's staff at Wembley. These expenses may be reimbursed

---

tax-free. The same applies to Harry and his employer, as he incurs expenses in travelling from London to Shropshire for a temporary, wholly business purpose.

Scope

10.40   Not every worker finding work through an intermediary is caught by the 2016 changes. The government's aim was to raise more taxes by curbing relief to umbrella and PSC employees who work just like the client's own staff, since it is unfair that an employer can outsource its workforce to an agency and an umbrella employer and pay less because some of the pay is called travel and subsistence expenses and is paid tax-free.

For the purposes of *ITEPA 2003, ss 338* and *339* ('travel for necessary attendance') only, *ITEPA 2003, s 339A* therefore deems each engagement to be a separate employment if the worker provides personal service (other than solely in the home of the client, which means that domestic cleaners, in-home carers, etc are not caught) under an intermediary contract rather than under a direct contract with the client or a connected person of the client. Note that the restriction to *ITEPA 2003, ss 338* and *339* means that the normal rules in *ITEPA 2003, ss 336* (expenses incurred wholly, exclusively and necessarily in the performance of the duties) and *337* (travel in performance of duties, which generally applies to travelling appointments such as meter readers, district nurses and salesmen) are unaffected.

To ensure that only quasi-employees are in scope, and that genuine freelance contractors hired in for their expertise rather than as a cheaper employee-substitute are not, the block on claiming relief for travel and subsistence expenses does not apply 'if it is shown that the manner in which the worker provides the services is not subject to (or to the right of) supervision, direction or control by any person' *(ITEPA 2003, s 339A(3))*.

However, this exclusion cannot apply where the engagement is through a PSC within the *Chapter 8* IR35 rules *(ITEPA 2003, s 339A(4))*. Managed service companies are excluded from the exclusion (Tax Law Rewrite principles appear to have been forgotten by the draughtsman), but for this purpose the definition of MSC is extended beyond that in the *Chapter 9* MSC rules to include not only those companies within the meaning given by *ITEPA 2003, s 61B*, but also companies that would be classed as such if they were not avoiding classification as an MSC by virtue of paying the whole of the worker's income out as employment income *(ITEPA 2003, s 339(11))*.

10.41   There is a further exclusion from *ITEPA 2003, s 339A* for engagements where the *Chapter 8* IR35 rules do not apply because there is no disguised employment (ie the circumstances in *ITEPA 2003, s 49(1)(c)* are not met), but the intermediary otherwise meets the conditions for IR35 in *ITEPA 2003, s 51, 52* or *53*, and the intermediary is not an MSC (applying the extended MSC definition above) (*ITEPA 2003, s 339(5)*). In determining whether a corporate intermediary meets the *ITEPA 2003, s 51* conditions, it is only necessary to consider whether the worker has a material interest in the intermediary company, and any link between payments from client to PSC and from PSC to worker is regarded as irrelevant (*ITEPA 2003, s 339(6)*).

There are special provisions to guard against abuse and attempts to evade liabilities by somebody providing fraudulent evidence purporting to show that the exclusion for absence of supervision in *ITEPA 2003, s 339(3)* applies: where the client or some other person (other than the worker or a person connected with the PSC) who is resident or has a place of business in the UK and is involved in the relevant services contract provides the intermediary with a fraudulent document intended to constitute such evidence, and as a result the intermediary fails to account for PAYE that should have been due, the worker is then treated as having an employment with the client or other person who provided the document and the PAYE liability is transferred to that client or other person, who is then treated as the employer and payer of the earnings (*ITEPA 2003, s 339A(7), (8)*).

There is also a catch-all targeted anti-avoidance rule intended to forestall attempts at circumventing *ITEPA 2003, s 339A*: no regard is to be had to any arrangements the main purpose, or one of the main purposes, of which is to secure that the denial of a deduction for the expenses is not to apply (*ITEPA 2003, s 339A(10)*).

Deterrence: transfer of liability

10.42   As is the case with the reformed 2014 agency provisions, the directors and officers (ie any manager, secretary or other similar officer, or any person acting or purporting to act as such) of companies involved in the provision of services through intermediaries are also threatened with personal liability notices in respect of amounts of PAYE, interest and penalties that their company is to account for under the *ITEPA 2003, s 339A* provisions.

ITEPA 2003, s 688B provides power for PAYE regulations to specify rules for the issue of personal liability notices. These may be issued in a number of cases to:

- persons providing fraudulent documents (ie the directors of the companies that issue such documents);

- the directors of the intermediary companies or LLPs who have failed to deduct PAYE from non-deductible travel expenses on the basis that the worker was not subject to supervision, direction or control without holding evidence on the basis of which it would be reasonable in all the circumstances to conclude that *ITEPA 2003, s 339A(3)* applies; and

- the directors of PSCs (other than MSCs) within IR35.

Chapter 3B (regs 97ZG–97ZM) was also added to *Part 4* of the *Income Tax (Pay As You Earn) Regulations 2003, SI 2003/2682* setting out the details of the recovery mechanisms for such 'relevant PAYE debts'. They are broadly similar to the personal liability notice rules for NICs and a group of directors is jointly and severally liable for any amounts due, but there are also key differences. The accelerated payment notice provisions have clearly affected the draughtsman's approach: the only grounds of appeal are that the specified amount does not represent the amount of relevant PAYE debt or that the person served with a notice was not a director of the company on the relevant date. The possibility that a director or officer might not be culpable, which is recognised in the NIC legislation, does not appear to have been contemplated.

Chapter 11

Stamp taxes

Ken Wright BA, CA, CTA, Group Tax Manager, John Menzies plc

SIGNPOSTS

- **Introduction** – From 1 April 2018 there are three land transaction taxes in the UK – Stamp Duty Land Tax (SDLT) (England and Northern Ireland), Land and Buildings Transaction Tax (Scotland) and Land Transaction Tax (Wales). In addition, stamp duty, or stamp duty reserve tax when no document is presented for stamping, apply UK wide and are charged on transfers of shares or securities. A brief outline is given of each of these taxes covering when a charge arises, who is liable for the tax and the amount upon which the charge is levied (see **11.1–11.7**).

- **SDLT Planning – Anti-avoidance provisions** – The anti-avoidance provision in *FA 2003, ss 75A–75C* makes it extremely difficult to find 'off the shelf' planning approaches which can be applied to a range of transactions to reduce the SDLT liability below the expected level. The best approach, therefore, is to have the fullest possible knowledge of the various statutory reliefs, exemptions and treatments which are available, so that these can be applied to each individual transaction in the most favourable way. This section considers the circumstances in which *FA 2003, ss 75A–75C* might apply to increase the SDLT liability. There is no equivalent anti-avoidance provision to *FA 2003, ss 75A–75C* within either of the Land and Buildings Transaction Tax (LBTT) or Land Transaction Tax (LTT) regimes. However, there are general anti-avoidance rules, ie the Scottish 'GAAR' (*Revenue Scotland and Tax Powers Act 2014, ss 62–72*) and the 'Welsh GAAR' (*Tax Collection and Management (Wales) Act 2016, ss 81A–81I*). Within the LTT regime there is also a general anti-avoidance provision which applies to any claim for an LTT relief (*LTTADT(W)A 2017, s 31 – 'Reliefs TAAR'*) (see **11.8–11.29**).

- **Pitfalls** – At least as important as tax planning is the need to be aware of the pitfalls waiting to trap the unwary. This section lists some of the more common pitfalls arising in relation to SDLT, LBTT and LTT (see **11.30**).

- **Group relief** – Group relief provides a complete exemption from SDLT, LBTT and LTT provided that certain conditions are satisfied and no disqualifying arrangements are in existence. This section considers both the conditions which must be satisfied, and the disqualifying arrangements which must not exist, if the relief is to be available. The relief can be clawed back if the purchaser ceases to be a member of the same group as the vendor within three years of the original transaction. The circumstances in which the relief will, and will not, be clawed back are considered (see **11.31–11.37**).

- **Partnerships** – Special rules apply where an interest in land is transferred to a partnership by a partner (current, departing or joining) or a person connected with such a partner, or where an interest in land is transferred from a partnership to a partner or to a person who has been one of the partners or to a person connected with a partner or a person who has been one of the partners. Where those special rules apply to a transfer of an interest in land to a partnership, this starts a three-year period within which certain events can lead to a further tax charge. In certain circumstances where the special rules have applied to the transfer of an interest in land to a partnership, a subsequent transfer of an interest can give rise to a tax charge. There may be no tax charge where a partnership of individuals is incorporated (see **11.38–11.54**).

- **Leases** – On the grant of a new lease, the SDLT, LBTT or LTT liability must be calculated separately on any rent payable, and on any premium payable, and then added together to get the total tax liability. There are differences between SDLT/LTT and LBTT in calculating the tax liability on the grant of a new lease. For all three taxes break clauses are ignored in determining the length of a lease and this can lead to a tax deferral opportunity. In certain circumstances, tax liabilities in relation to rent may fall on the assignee of an existing lease (see **11.55–11.67**).

- **Acquisition of dwellings – higher rate of tax** – With effect from 1 April 2016, higher rates of SDLT apply to purchases of additional residential properties (referred to in the legislation as 'dwellings'), such as second homes and buy-to-let properties. In fact, the legislation is much wider than the original policy description and, for example, applies to first purchases of residential properties by companies and other non-individual purchasers. If the higher rate legislation applies it imposes an additional 3% SDLT charge on chargeable transactions falling within its provisions. This section provides an outline of when the higher rate charge applies, the implications of acquiring more than one dwelling under a single transaction and the interaction of the higher rate with a claim for 'multiple dwellings relief'.

495

There are also equivalent higher-rate regimes under LBTT and LTT (see **11.68–11.75**).

• **Annual tax on enveloped dwellings (ATED)** – This annual tax applies when an interest in a single dwelling situated in the UK, with a value of more than the threshold (the lowest threshold is now £500,000), is held by a company, partnership or collective investment scheme at any time in the 'chargeable period'. It applies to a partnership only if the partners include one or more companies. Reliefs are provided for dwellings held by property traders and developers or properties held for the purposes of a property rental business etc. To avoid the charge to ATED the property may be transferred out of the company etc, however, if there is debt outstanding, care must be taken to avoid a charge to SDLT, LBTT or LTT (see **11.76–11.77**).

• **Sale (or lease) and leaseback relief** – Where a vendor (A) sells or leases a 'major interest' (freehold or leasehold interest) in a property to a purchaser (B) and, in consideration (wholly or partly), B grants a lease (the 'leaseback') to A out of that major interest, the leaseback may be exempt from SDLT, LBTT or LTT. If the requirement to grant back the lease reduces the value of the interest transferred it may be that reduced value which is taxed. The relief may not be available in a development situation (see **11.78**).

• **Stamp duty planning** – Stamp duty is currently chargeable only on documents effecting transfers of 'stock and marketable securities' and interests in partnerships owning stock and marketable securities. It is usually only necessary to stamp a transfer document for stock and marketable securities, if they are chargeable securities, so that the stamp duty reserve tax (SDRT) charge is cancelled and any registration formalities may be completed. Planning for transfers of both shares and securities, and partnership interests is considered together with certain pitfalls. Detailed consideration is given to the relief for the insertion of a new holding company (*FA 1986, s 77*). Following a report from the Office of Tax Simplification on 10 July 2017, it seems likely that the archaic nature of stamp duty will be the subject of fundamental reform in the near future (see **11.79–11.91**).

INTRODUCTION

Focus

Whilst the LBTT and LTT tax regimes borrow heavily from the SDLT legislation, it should be borne in mind that Revenue Scotland (LBTT) and the Welsh Revenue Authority (LTT) may take a different view, compared to HMRC, of the same or similar legislation. Specific LBTT or LTT advice should therefore be taken where a transaction involves, respectively, land situated in Scotland or Wales.

11.1 This chapter looks at some of the practical issues, pitfalls and planning in relation to SDLT and stamp duty which, together with SDRT, are often referred to as 'stamp taxes'. SDRT is mostly administered and paid by professionals in the financial services industry, often operating on the basis of rules and arrangements negotiated directly with HMRC. These rules and arrangements are beyond the scope of this chapter.

With effect from 1 April 2015, SDLT ceased to apply to transactions over land situated in Scotland being replaced, from that date, by LBTT.

Similarly, but with effect from 1 April 2018, SDLT ceased to apply to transactions over land situated in Wales being replaced, from that date, by LTT.

Both the LBTT and the LTT regimes borrow heavily from the SDLT legislation and in many cases the legislation is the same, or at least very similar. This chapter therefore concentrates on SDLT but quotes the corresponding LBTT and LTT statutory references where appropriate and highlights any significant differences between the taxes. It should, however, be borne in mind that Revenue Scotland (LBTT) and the Welsh Revenue Authority (LTT) may take a different view, compared to HMRC, of the same or similar legislation, and therefore the author would always advise taking specific LBTT or LTT advice where a transaction involves, respectively, land situated in Scotland or Wales.

The bulk of the legislation covering the three taxes can be found in the following acts:

SDLT – *Finance Act 2003 (FA 2003)*

LBTT – *Land and Buildings Transaction Tax (Scotland) Act 2013 (LBTT(S)A 2013)*

LTT – *Land Transaction Tax and Anti-avoidance of Devolved Taxes (Wales) Act 2017 (LTTADT(W)A 2017)*

SDLT

11.2 SDLT is charged on land transactions, whether effected by a document or not . Neither the places of residence of the parties, nor the place where any documents are executed, are relevant to the charge (*FA 2003, s 42; LBTT(S)A 2013, s 1; LTTADT(W)A 2017, s 2*). SDLT is under the control of HMRC, LBTT is under the control of Revenue Scotland and LTT is under the control of the Welsh Revenue Authority.

A land transaction for these purposes means the acquisition of a chargeable interest (*FA 2003, s 43(1); LBTT(S)A 2013, s 3; LTTADT(W)A 2017, s 3(1)*). Acquisition may include not only a straightforward sale and purchase of land, but also the creation, surrender, release or variation of an interest in land. SDLT will therefore not only apply to the purchase of land/assignment of an existing lease but also to the grant of a new lease, the surrender to the landlord of an existing lease and the variation of the terms of an existing lease (*FA 2003, s 43(3); LBTT(S)A 2013, s 6; LTTADT(W)A 2017, s 3(1)*). The acquisition (which is widely defined as discussed above) may occur under the terms of a court order, a statutory provision or by operation of law, as well as, as is more common, by agreement between the parties (*FA 2003, s 43(2); LBTT(S)A 2013, s 6(5); LTTADT(W)A 2017, s 3(2)*). A complex and indirect definition makes clear the intention that any party whose interest in land benefits under the transaction is to be regarded as the purchaser. However, a person will only be treated as a purchaser if he has either given consideration for, or is a party to, the transaction (*FA 2003, s 43(5); LBTT(S)A 2013, s 7(2); LTTADT(W)A 2017, s 7(1)*).

Obligation to file a land transaction return and pay the tax

Focus

Under current law SDLT, LBTT and LTT obligations to file a land transaction return and pay the respective taxes arise 30 days after the 'effective date' of the transaction. However, for SDLT, the period by which the filing and payment obligations have to be fulfilled is reducing to 14 days for transactions with an 'effective date' on or after 1 March 2019. There are currently no plans to reduce the filing and payment window for either LBTT or LTT. At the latest, the 'effective date' is the date of 'completion', however, it can be earlier if the contract is 'substantially performed' before 'completion' of the transaction.

11.3 In general, SDLT, LBTT and LTT obligations (by which is meant the obligation to file a land transaction return and pay any tax due) arise 30 days after the 'effective date' of the transaction (*FA 2003, ss 76(1) and 86(1); LBTT(S)A 2013, ss 29(3) and 40(2); LTTADT(W)A 2017, ss 44(2) and 57(1)*). At the latest, the 'effective date' is the date of completion. For the purposes of SDLT and LTT, the word 'completion' is not defined and, therefore, bears its normal legal meaning, broadly summarised as the final action required to give the transaction full legal effect. For LBTT purposes 'completion', in relation to the grant of a new lease means when it is executed by the parties or constituted by any means, and in relation to any other transaction, it means the 'settlement' of the transaction *(LBTT(S)A 2013, s 64)*. The term 'settlement' is not itself defined in the legislation and, therefore, bears its normal legal meaning, broadly summarised as completion of the transaction when the price is paid by the buyer to the seller in return for the land being acquired.

However, in some cases, the 'effective date' is triggered by substantial performance (see below for the meaning of this term) of the transaction before completion.

The government confirmed in the November 2017 Budget that the SDLT filing and payment window will be reduced from 30 days to 14 days for any land transaction with an 'effective date' on or after 1 March 2019. Therefore, from that date, SDLT obligations will arise 14 days, rather than 30 days, after the 'effective date'. Improvements are planned to the SDLT return with the aim of making compliance with the new time limit easier. There are currently no plans to reduce the filing and payment window for either LBTT or LTT.

Substantial performance is defined using a combination of terms such as 'possession' and 'occupation', which are themselves not clearly defined, together with measurement of the proportion of any consideration actually paid. In any dispute as to whether an agreement has been substantially performed, expert legal advice may be required as to the meaning of terms. However, in general, a contract is substantially performed where either the purchaser takes possession of substantially all of the property passing under the contract, or substantially all of the consideration is paid or provided *(FA 2003, s 44(5); LBTT(S)A 2013, s 14(1); LTTADT(W)A 2017, s 14(1))*. In relation to SDLT, HMRC have indicated that they will regard 90% or more as substantially all, but SDLTM07950 indicates they will not consider themselves tied to this figure if they detect an attempt to exploit it for avoidance. *Any* payment of rent under the terms of a lease will be regarded as substantial performance of the lease, as will the purchaser becoming entitled to receipt of *any* rent etc from a tenant *(FA 2003, s 44(6) and (7); LBTT(S)A 2013, ss 29(3) and 14(2), (3); LTTADT(W)A 2017, s 14(2) and (3))*.

This gives rise to a potential issue for the purposes of SDLT and LTT – Standard Terms and Conditions for land transactions may entitle the purchaser to rent from a tenant or sub-tenant earlier than the time of payment for the property, which may trigger early substantial performance. It is always worthwhile reviewing the terms and conditions carefully to avoid such problems. The Standard Terms and Conditions do not apply in Scotland.

In LBTT Technical Bulletin 1 (para 6.2) Revenue Scotland make it clear that what constitutes a 'substantial amount' of the consideration paid or provided for the purposes of LBTT will be considered on a case-by-case basis. They specifically state that the Scottish Parliament did not set a specific amount, that an amount less than 90% might be substantial in this context, and that the words must take their plain English meaning. Consequently, if there is doubt as to whether the quantum of the chargeable consideration given for a transaction over land in Scotland, in advance of completion, might cause a contract to be 'substantially performed', it is suggested that an opinion be sought from Revenue Scotland.

It should, however, be noted that for LBTT purposes (unlike SDLT and LTT) the assignation of a contract (which is to be completed by a conveyance), before its 'substantial performance' and completion, triggers 'substantial performance' of that contract (*LBTT(S)A 2013, s 14(1)(c)*). As a consequence, the contract is treated as if it were the transaction provided for in the contract, and the 'effective date' of the deemed land transaction is the date of 'substantial performance' (*LBTT(S)A 2013, s 10(1) and (2)*).

The Welsh Revenue Authority manuals confirm that, in determining whether a contract has been 'substantially performed' for the purposes of LTT, the 90% threshold applied by HMRC in relation to SDLT will also be applied in relation to LTT.

If a contract for a land transaction is entered into and is completed by a formal conveyance not later than the time of 'substantial performance', the contract and conveyance are treated as a single land transaction, taking effect at the date of completion (*FA 2003, s 44(3)*; *LBTT(S)A 2013, s 9*; *LTTADT(W)A 2017, s 10(3)*). Submission of a return and payment of the tax will be due 30 days from that date (in relation to SDLT it will be 14 days for land transactions with an 'effective date' on or after 1 March 2019). Where, however, the contract is entered into and substantially performed before completion, the contract itself is treated as a land transaction, the effective date being that of substantial performance (*FA 2003, s 44(4)*; *LBTT(S)A 2013, ss 29(3) and 10(1) and (2)*; *LTTADT(W)A 2017, s 10(4)*). The return and tax payment are due 30 days from that date (14 days for SDLT land transactions with an 'effective date' on or after 1 March 2019). If such a transaction is later completed by a formal conveyance, that conveyance will be a separate land transaction (in some circumstances, but not always, requiring submission of a further return), but SDLT, LBTT or LTT will only be payable to the extent that the tax payable on the conveyance is greater than the tax paid on 'substantial performance' of the contract – there should be no overall 'double charge' (*FA 2003, s 44(8)*; *LBTT(S)A 2013, s 10(3)*; *LTTADT(W)A 2017, s 10(5)*). However, care is needed where reduced or zero SDLT is paid at the time of substantial performance because of a relief or exemption – in some circumstances, the later completion can trigger further liability because conditions for the relief or exemption are not satisfied at that time.

It is the purchaser's obligation to file the land transaction return and pay the tax

11.4   SDLT, LBTT and LTT obligations (to file a land transaction return and pay any tax due) fall on the purchaser, identified in the legislation as the person who acquires the interest in land, or whose existing interest is enlarged or enhanced. The identity of the purchaser is obvious in straightforward transfers and grants of leases, but less obvious in some other cases. In particular:

• if a chargeable interest is transferred or granted to the trustees of a settlement, the trustees are jointly purchasers (*FA 2003, Sch 16, para 4*; *LBTT(S)A 2013, Sch 18, para 10*; *LTTADT(W)A 2017, Sch 8, para 4*);

• if an existing chargeable interest is transferred to bare trustees or nominees, the beneficial owner is the purchaser (*FA 2003, Sch 16, para 3(1)*; *LBTT(S)A 2013, Sch 18, para 5*; *LTTADT(W)A 2017, Sch 8, para 3(1)*);

• if a lease is granted to bare trustees, those trustees are (jointly, if more than one) purchasers of the whole interest (*FA 2003, Sch 16, para 3(3)*; *LBTT(S)A 2013, Sch 18, para 8*; *LTTADT(W)A 2017, Sch 8, para 3(3)*);

• if a lease is surrendered or the term shortened, the landlord is the purchaser (*FA 2003, s 43(3)(b), Sch 17A, para 15A(2)*; *LBTT(S)A 2013, s 6(3)(b), Sch 19, para 29(3)*; *LTTADT(W)A 2017, s 6(3)(b), Sch 6, para 24(3)*);

• if the rent under a lease is reduced, the tenant is the purchaser (*FA 2003, Sch 17A, para 15A(1)*; *LBTT(S)A 2013, Sch 19, para 29(1)*; *LTTADT(W)A 2017, Sch 6, para 24(1)*); and

• if any chargeable interest other than a lease (eg for the purposes of SDLT an easement) is varied, whoever benefits is the purchaser (*FA 2003, s 43(3)(c)*; *LBTT(S)A 2013, s 6(3)(c)*; *LTTADT(W)A 2017, s 6(3)(c)*).

SDLT, LBTT and LTT are payable by the purchaser (buyer in Scotland) (*FA 2003, s 85(1)*; *LBTT(S)A 2013, s 28(1)*; *LTTADT(W)A 2017, s 56*). The rates and bands applicable for each of SDLT, LBTT and LTT are available on the GOV.UK (www.gov.uk/stamp-duty-land-tax), Revenue Scotland (www.revenue.scot/land-buildings-transaction-tax/guidance/calculating-tax-rates-and-bands) and Welsh Government (http://gov.wales/funding/fiscal-reform/welsh-taxes/land-transaction-tax/?lang=en) websites respectively.

Chargeable consideration

Focus

SDLT, LBTT and LTT are generally charged on the actual consideration given under the transaction, however, in certain circumstances, the tax can be charged by reference to market value. In particular, when land is transferred to a company which is 'connected' with the transferor, the taxes are charged on the higher of (a) the market value and (b) the actual consideration, including any VAT chargeable. However, the market value rule does not apply in the case of some transfers to trustees or where the transfer is a distribution out of the assets of a company, unless group relief has been claimed in the last three years.

11.5 SDLT, LBTT and LTT are generally chargeable by reference to the value of the actual consideration, but in some circumstances this is substituted by the market value of the property acquired. One example is where land is transferred in payment of a debt exceeding the value of the property (*FA 2003, Sch 4, para 8(2)*; *LBTT(S)A 2013, Sch 2, para 8(4)*; *LTTADT(W)A 2017, Sch 4, para 8(6)*); another is where properties are exchanged and actual consideration is less than the market value of the property acquired (*FA 2003, Sch 4, para 5*; *LBTT(S)A 2013, Sch 2, para 5*; *LTTADT(W)A 2017, Sch 4, para 5*).

However, the main relevance of market value is when land is transferred to a company which is connected with the transferor. When this happens, the consideration is to be taken as not less than the market value of the interest transferred (plus any rent where the transaction is the grant of a lease) (*FA 2003, s 53*; *LBTT(S)A 2013, s 22*; *LTTADT(W)A 2017, s 22*). For these purposes, 'connected' is as defined in *Corporation Tax Act 2010 (CTA 2010), s 1122*. If the actual consideration, including any VAT chargeable on the transaction, is greater than market value, tax is chargeable by reference to the actual consideration, unless a relief or exemption is available.

The market value rule does not apply in the case of some transfers to trustees. Nor does it apply where the transfer is a distribution out of the assets of a company. However, an anti-avoidance rule re-applies the market value rule if group relief has been claimed on the property (or on a superior interest, if the property is a lease) within the previous three years (*FA 2003, s 54*; *LBTT(S)A 2013, s 23*; *LTTADT(W)A 2017, s 23*).

Further reading on SDLT, LBTT and LTT

11.6 For a detailed consideration of SDLT, LTT and LBTT, including statutory compliance obligations such as in relation to tax returns and payments, see *Stamp Taxes 2018/19* (Bloomsbury Professional) and *Land and Buildings Transaction Tax 2018/19* (Bloomsbury Professional).

Stamp duty and stamp duty reserve tax

Focus

Stamp duty is charged on 'instruments' (broadly documents) transferring title to stock or marketable securities (principally shares and securities). Stamp duty reserve tax is effectively an alternative to stamp duty and is generally charged when no document of transfer is presented for stamping. Following the Office of Tax Simplifications' report dated 10 July 2017 it is likely that stamp duty will be digitalised and simplified in the near future.

11.7   Stamp duty is not a tax levied on profits, income or gains. It is not even a tax on transactions. Stamp duty is charged on 'instruments', broadly defined as documents, transferring title to stock or marketable securities (principally shares and securities).

Stamp duty only applies to instruments transferring stock and marketable securities, the issue of bearer instruments and transfers of interests in partnerships which hold stock and marketable securities. As regards bearer instruments, it should be noted that (with effect from 26 May 2015) a UK incorporated company is prohibited from issuing new bearer shares, and from 26 February 2016 all existing bearer shares issued by a UK incorporated company had to be converted into registered shares or cancelled (*Small Business, Employment and Enterprise Act 2015*).

Assets such as stock or plant and machinery are no longer chargeable to stamp duty. However, the transfer of 'fixtures', ie plant and machinery, which, in law, have become part of the land, is potentially chargeable to SDLT, or LBTT if the land is situated in Scotland (with effect from 1 April 2015), or LTT if the land is situated in Wales (with effect from 1 April 2018).

There is no stamp duty on the issue of shares nor is there any market value rule for the purposes of stamp duty. It should also be noted that there is an exemption (*FA 1986, s 79(4)*) for documents transferring certain categories of loan capital.

Stamp duty is generally paid by the transferee (purchaser) as it is the transferee who normally wants to register the change of ownership and cancel any SDRT charge which may arise.

SDRT is effectively an alternative to stamp duty. It relates to agreements to transfer chargeable securities (eg shares or loan capital), and is generally charged when no document of transfer is presented for stamping (*FA 1986, s 87*). The purchaser is liable for the tax (*FA 1986, s 91*).

On 10 July 2017, the Office of Tax Simplification (OTS) issued its report in relation to stamp duty on paper documents and recommended its reform, digitalisation and simplification. In particular, it highlighted two aspects of the stamp duty regime which are out of date and in urgent need of reform.

First, the time-consuming process which requires that a paper document chargeable to stamp duty must be posted to the stamp office in Birmingham, together with a cheque or bank transfer for the duty, in order that a physical stamp can be impressed on the document which is then sent to the relevant company registrar. The OTS's recommendation is that the stamp duty process be digitalised, providing the transferee with a unique transaction reference confirming that the transaction has been notified to HMRC. This would eliminate the need for a physical stamp to be impressed on paper documents. It is also suggested that the legal obligations of company registrars could be changed, allowing them to write up the company's books on receipt of the unique transaction reference or confirmation of notification to HMRC.

Secondly, the current scope of stamp duty is significantly broader than is actually applied in practice as, for example, duty is chargeable on paper documents executed in the UK even if those documents give effect to the transfer of non-UK shares. This results in documents transferring non-UK shares being executed and retained outside of the UK to try to avoid the document being chargeable to stamp duty or to avoid a penalty for late stamping being payable should the document actually have to be stamped because, for example, it is required as evidence in a UK civil court. The OTS states in its report that 'This is confusing and inefficient'. The recommendations from the OTS are that stamp duty be aligned with SDRT so that broadly it does not apply to paper documents transferring non-UK shares unless those shares are registered in a register kept in the UK. They also suggest making the tax assessable and therefore ending the 'voluntary' nature of the tax.

On 14 August 2017, the Chancellor of the Exchequer responded by letter to the OTS's report and agreed to consider the recommendations carefully, weighing up the benefits of the four main elements of the proposed reforms in the context of the ongoing reforms to the tax system. The four main elements of the reforms identified in the Chancellor's letter were as follows:

- providing taxpayers with a unique transaction reference number;

- amending company registrar's legal obligations in respect of share transfer registrations;

- making stamp duty assessable; and

- aligning the scope of stamp duty with SDRT.

It therefore seems likely that the archaic nature of stamp duty will be the subject of fundamental reform in the near future.

Focus

The best approach to SDLT mitigation is to have the fullest possible knowledge of the various statutory reliefs, exemptions and treatments which are available, so that these can be applied to each individual transaction in the most favourable way. However, in virtually every case, it remains essential to consider carefully whether the combination of steps required to complete the transaction bring it within the scope of *FA 2003, ss 75A–75C*, whether any disclosure responsibility arises under the DOTAS rules or whether the general anti-abuse rule (the GAAR) in *FA 2013, ss 206–215* could apply to increase the charge to SDLT.

SDLT PLANNING

Background

11.8 Historically, SDLT mitigation has generally involved one or more of four general approaches as follows:

(1) Arrange to have the benefit of a relief or exemption, or a combination of two or more reliefs or exemptions.

(2) Avoid transferring the land. This may be achieved either by transferring something else (for example, shares in a land-owning company) or by entering into a commercially different transaction.

(3) Reduce the value of the land transferred (with most of the consideration paid for something else).

(4) Arrange to fall within a specific statutory treatment which gives rise to a low or zero SDLT charge. For example, structuring a transaction so that it falls within the specific provisions of *FA 2003, Sch 4, para 17 (LBTT(S)A 2013, Sch 4, para 17; LTTADT(W)A 2017, Sch 4, para 18)* which removes certain amounts from the calculation of the consideration chargeable to SDLT in relation to certain transactions between public bodies and the private sector (eg PFI type contracts).

However, specific anti-avoidance legislation and *FA 2003, ss 75A–75C* makes it extremely difficult to find 'off the shelf' combinations of these approaches which can be applied to a range of transactions to reduce the SDLT liability below the expected level. New versions of old ideas emerge from time to time, but the Disclosure of Tax Avoidance Schemes (DOTAS) rules allow HMRC to block them quickly with new legislation when necessary. HMRC now also have the benefit of the general anti-abuse rule in *FA 2013, ss 206–215* to deploy against any unacceptable arrangements which escape more specific anti-avoidance measures.

The best approach to SDLT mitigation is therefore to have the fullest possible knowledge of the various statutory reliefs, exemptions and treatments which are available, so that these can be applied to each individual transaction in the most favourable way. However, in virtually every case, it remains essential to consider carefully whether the combination of steps required to complete the transaction bring it within the scope of *FA 2003, ss 75A–75C*, whether any disclosure responsibility arises under the DOTAS rules or whether the general anti-abuse rule (the GAAR) in *FA 2013, ss 206–215* could apply to increase the charge to SDLT.

There is no equivalent general anti-avoidance provision to *FA 2003, ss 75A–75C* within the LBTT regime, however, there is a general anti-avoidance rule (the Scottish 'GAAR') (*Revenue Scotland and Tax Powers Act 2014, ss 62–72*) which is specifically designed to be broader in scope than the UK general anti-abuse rule found in *FA 2013, ss 206–215*. The objective of the Scottish GAAR is to counteract 'tax advantages' arising from a 'tax avoidance arrangement' which is 'artificial'. The Scottish GAAR does not contain the safeguards of an advisory review panel (see **11.29**), and the so-called double reasonableness test, which apply to the UK general anti-abuse rule.

Similarly, the LTT legislation does not include a general anti-avoidance provision equivalent to *FA 2003, ss 75A–75C*. There is, however, an anti-avoidance provision which applies to any claim for an LTT relief (*LTTADT(W)A 2017, s 31 – 'Reliefs TAAR'*) and a general anti-avoidance provision (*Tax Collection and Management (Wales) Act 2016, ss 81A–81I – the 'Welsh GAAR'*). Similar to the Scottish GAAR the objective of the Welsh GAAR is to counteract 'tax advantages' arising from a 'tax avoidance arrangement' which is 'artificial'.

Consequently, when considering any planning in relation to LBTT or LTT, the potential application of the anti-avoidance provisions detailed above should always be considered.

SDLT general anti-avoidance provision

11.9

Focus

The SDLT general anti-avoidance provision does not include a motive test and therefore it potentially applies to all transactions in relation to land in

---

England and Northern Ireland other than those consisting of simple single steps, unless they are specifically excluded under the legislation. However, in published guidance, HMRC state that in their view the provision only applies where there is avoidance of SDLT and that they will not seek to apply the provision where they consider the transaction has already been appropriately taxed. The difficulty is that in many instances it is not clear when HMRC will consider that a transaction has been appropriately taxed and therefore the potential application of the anti-avoidance provision should be considered where a transaction consists of more than a single step.

FA 2003, ss 75A–75C constitutes a general anti-avoidance rule specifically aimed at SDLT and introduced more than six years before the GAAR. It potentially applies to all transactions in relation to land in England or Northern Ireland other than those consisting of simple single steps, unless they are specifically excluded under the legislation. The legislation operates by comparing the total SDLT actually paid on all steps with the SDLT which would be payable on a 'notional transaction'. If the SDLT actually paid is less, any real land transactions are disregarded and, in their place, the notional transaction becomes chargeable. Credit is given for any SDLT paid on real transactions, and further SDLT is payable to bring the total up to that on the notional transaction.

11.10 As set out in the legislation, the test is completely objective – that is, there is no need to consider the motives of the parties. This means that a series of transactions which are not entered into with any intention of avoiding tax, but which happen to reduce the SDLT bill below that implied by the notional transaction, could still be caught. For this reason, it is not safe to ignore the rules merely because there is no avoidance motive; their application must be considered in all multi-step transactions.

11.11 HMRC guidance on the application of *FA 2003, ss 75A–75C* is not consistent with the case law on the subject, nor is it clear when HMRC will take the view that the anti-avoidance provision will apply. At SDLTM09175, HMRC state their view that, because *FA 2003, s 75A* is an anti-avoidance provision, it is considered that it only applies where there is avoidance of tax, and HMRC specifically state that they will not seek to apply the provision where they consider the transaction has already been taxed appropriately. The problem is that it can often be difficult to decide whether HMRC are likely to consider that a particular transaction has been appropriately taxed. This therefore appears to be an example of possibly unnecessarily draconian legislation which HMRC will not apply rigorously if they feel happy with the actions of the parties.

Although that may be a reasonable approach, it is not supported by the legislation nor by the decisions of the First-tier Tribunal, the Upper Tribunal and the Court of Appeal. The First-tier Tribunal decision in *Project Blue Limited v HMRC* [2013] UKFTT 378TC states:

> 'Whilst it is clear that the purpose of section 75A is to counteract the avoidance of SDLT, the provision contains no requirement that the taxpayer should have a tax avoidance motive or purpose as a precondition or defence to the application of the provision ... Parliament obviously intended that the provision should apply regardless of motive'.

This is quoted, apparently with approval, in HMRC's note on de-enveloping transactions issued on 20 December 2013 (see www.hmrc/gov.uk/so/stamps-de-enveloping.htm). In the decision of the Upper Tribunal ([2014] UKUT 0564 (TCC)), the presiding judge Mr Justice Morgan held that whilst there was no specific avoidance motive test in *FA 2003, s 75A,* a requirement that SDLT has been avoided is implicit as the section only applies if the tax saving test in *FA 2003, s 75A(1)(c)* is satisfied. However, this contention is open to debate as it is possible (and perhaps even common) for there to be a number of ways of structuring a transaction each of which may result in a different amount of SDLT being payable, and for a particular structure to be pursued, for wholly commercial reasons, but in circumstances where an SDLT saving is achieved. In such circumstances it is arguable that there is no SDLT avoidance, however, *FA 2003, s 75A* could still apply. The decision of the Court of Appeal ([2016] EWCA Civ 485), given on 26 May 2016, supports the view that *FA 2003, s 75A* can apply in the absence of an SDLT avoidance motive. Lord Justice Patten states at 39:

> 'The first is that Mr Thomas was wrong in my view in his submission that *s 75A* has no operation unless it can be shown that the object of the relevant scheme transactions was the avoidance of tax. Although, as the side-note to *s 75A* makes clear, the provisions were clearly introduced to combat the avoidance of SDLT, they operate according to their terms and nowhere in *s 75A* is there any reference to the purpose of the scheme transactions being tax avoidance or any requirement to establish the existence of such a purpose or objective as a pre-condition to the operation of the section. The UT [Upper Tribunal] was right in my view to reject Mr Thomas's construction of *s 75A* and to treat avoidance as spelt out by the conditions for the application of *s 75A* contained in *s 75A(1)*.'

It therefore seems clear that there is no requirement that an SDLT avoidance motive exist before *FA 2003, s 75A* can apply. If the actual liability to SDLT on a transaction is less than the liability which would arise under the notional transaction fiction of *FA 2003, s 75A* (see *FA 2003, s 75A(1)(c)*), then the anti-avoidance provision is in point, assuming that the other conditions in *FA 2003, s 75A(1)* are satisfied. This makes advising on the potential application of *FA 2003, s 75A* very difficult because on the one hand you have HMRC stating that they will not apply *FA 2003, s 75A* if they consider that a transaction has been appropriately taxed and on the other hand you have the case law telling the adviser (or purchaser) that if there is an SDLT saving, compared to the notional transaction under *FA 2003, s 75A*, then the anti-avoidance legislation can apply, and a significantly higher SDLT liability may arise.

The SDLTM guidance may therefore no longer be current. For what it is worth, it gives examples of where HMRC considers that the rules do not (normally) or do apply (SDLTM09225 and SDLTM09250). These are helpful so far as they go but the examples do not amount to a 'white list' since HMRC only say that the rules are 'unlikely' to apply. Most of the examples in the guidance where it is stated the rules will apply involve partnerships and/or the grant, variation or termination of leases. This confirms the nature of the avoidance against which the legislation is primarily directed.

When do the rules apply?

11.12 The rules apply where one person (V) disposes of a chargeable interest, and another person (P) acquires it or a chargeable interest deriving from it. It does not matter that there may be various steps between the disposal and the acquisition, nor does it matter if the chargeable interest goes through various transformations between the disposal and the acquisition. The legislation was introduced to deal with schemes which involved precisely that kind of step and transformation. If the asset disposed of or acquired is not a chargeable interest, the rules do not apply.

Example 11.1 – No transfer of a chargeable interest

X Ltd owns 100% of the shares of Y Ltd. Y Ltd owns a valuable property. X Ltd makes a loan to Y Ltd, allowing Y Ltd to pay a cash dividend to X Ltd, thus reducing the value of Y Ltd to £1. X Ltd then sells the shares of Y Ltd to unrelated party Z Ltd. Assuming there are no other steps, *FA 2003, s 75A* does not apply to the transaction, because there has been no disposal or acquisition of a chargeable interest, ie an interest in land. There may have been a saving of stamp duty on a transfer of the shares, but stamp duty is not within the ambit of *FA 2003, s 75A*. Shares in a company are not 'chargeable interests', even if the company's only asset is property. However, this may change in future – from time to time, the government has threatened to introduce land-rich company rules, which may deem shares in such a company to be chargeable interests. It is also unlikely that this arrangement would fall foul of the GAAR in respect of stamp taxes, as stamp duty is not within the scope of that rule. However, such an arrangement may give rise to advantages in relation to other taxes and it would be important to consider the possible impact of the GAAR in this respect.

11.13   The rules only apply if there are 'a number of transactions' (which may include non-land transactions) involved in the disposal and acquisition. To make sense of this provision, 'a number' must be taken to mean more than one. However, 'transaction' includes an agreement, offer or undertaking not to take a specified action, and any kind of arrangement, even if it would not normally be described as a transaction (*FA 2003, s 75A(2)*). In other words, apparently unilateral acts and failures to act may be regarded as transactions. It does not matter when the transactions occur – they merely have to occur 'in connection with' the disposal and acquisition. The transactions are referred to as 'scheme transactions' (*FA 2003, s 75A(1)(b)*).

11.14   The legislation (*FA 2003, s 75A(3)*) lists examples of 'scheme transactions' as follows, but makes it clear this is not an exhaustive list:

- acquisition of a lease derived from a freehold formerly owned by the vendor;

- sub-sale to a third party;

- grant of a lease to a third party subject to a right to terminate;

- exercise of a right to terminate a lease or take some other action;

- agreement not to exercise a right to terminate a lease or take some other action; and

- variation of a right to terminate a lease or take some other action.

It is clear from this list that transactions involving the grant and termination of leases were foremost in HMRC's collective mind when the rules were written. Although not exhaustive, this list is important when considering 'incidental transactions' (see **11.16**).

Example 11.2 (part 1) – Scheme caught by *s 75A*

Scott owns a freehold residential property worth £2.1m. He grants a lease to Cameron to hold as nominee for himself. Cameron is a friend but not otherwise connected with Scott. The terms of the lease are as follows:

- yearly rent, one peppercorn, no premium; and

- term one month, but with an option (exercisable before the end of the month) to extend to 100 years in return for payment of £1.

There is no SDLT on the grant of the lease because it is treated as granted beneficially to the nominee (see **11.4**), and there is no reason to substitute the actual consideration with market value or any other figure. However, on the assumption that the option is likely to be exercised, the value of

---

the freehold interest is now minimal. Scott sells the freehold to Rory for £1. Again, there is no SDLT on this sale as there is no reason to substitute anything else for the actual consideration.

Scott then undertakes to refrain from exercising the option to extend the lease if Rory pays him £2.15m. There could possibly be an argument that this is a land transaction subject to SDLT, but in real, slightly more complicated, arrangements based on this general structure, it was considered that this was not a land transaction. The overall result then is that Rory has spent £2.15m to acquire a property but paid no SDLT.

There are a number of transactions, comprising the grant of the lease, sale of the freehold and undertaking not to exercise the option, so this series of transactions is potentially caught by *FA 2003, s 75A*.

The notional transaction

11.15   The rules only apply if the total SDLT paid on all transactions in the scheme is less than the amount which would be payable on a 'notional land transaction' (*FA 2003, s 75A(1)(c)*). This notional transaction is defined as a transaction effecting the transfer from V to P, for consideration (*FA 2003, s 75A(5)*) equal to the largest amount (aggregated if more than one):

• given by or on behalf of any one person; or

• received by or on behalf of V (or a person connected with V),

by way of consideration for the scheme transactions. Reference to a notional land transaction sometimes causes confusion, because the legislation does not specify the nature of the transaction. However, this is unimportant. All that matters in this regard is that there is deemed to be a chargeable transaction for a specified amount of chargeable consideration, which determines the minimum SDLT charge.

Incidental transactions and reliefs

11.16   In measuring the chargeable consideration for this notional land transaction, certain amounts must be left out of account. The amounts are:

• the consideration for any transaction which is merely incidental to the transfer of the chargeable interest (*FA 2003, s 75B(1)*); and

• any consideration paid in respect of a transaction covered by the following reliefs in *FA 2003 (FA 2003, s 75C(4))*:

   –   *s 60* (compulsory purchase facilitating development);

   –   *s 61* (compliance with planning obligations);

511

- *ss 63, 64* (demutualisation of insurance company or building society);
- *s 65* (incorporation of limited liability partnership);
- *s 66* (transfers involving public bodies);
- *s 67* (transfer in consequence of reorganisation of parliamentary constituencies);
- *s 69* (acquisition by bodies established for national purposes);
- *s 71* (acquisition by registered social landlord);
- *s 74* (collective enfranchisement by leaseholders);
- *s 75* (crofting community right to buy);
- *Sch 6A* (relief for acquisition by housing intermediaries etc); and
- *Sch 8* (charities relief).

Without these exclusions, many of the reliefs would become relatively useless in real-life transactions which often involve multiple steps for entirely innocent reasons. Perhaps of more importance are the reliefs which are not listed above, the most important of which are the group, reconstruction and acquisition reliefs set out in *FA 2003, Sch 7*. HMRC are concerned that these reliefs may be exploited in ways which were not intended, and are not keen to facilitate such exploitation.

Example 11.2 (part 2) – SDLT payable under *FA 2003, s 75A*

The total SDLT paid on the basis of the scheme transactions is nil. The consideration for the notional transaction is £2.15m (plus £1), being the aggregate amount given by Rory. Therefore, *FA 2003, s 75A* applies and the SDLT payable is calculated as follows (assuming that the additional rate of SDLT (see **11.68** et seq) does not apply):

Chargeable consideration	Rate	SDLT
£	%	£
125,000	0	Nil
125,000	2	2,500
675,000	5	33,750
575,000	10	57,500
650,001	12	78,000
2,150,001		171,750

This scheme is precisely the kind of arrangement that *FA 2003, s 75A* appears to be designed to block.

Effective date

11.17 The effective date of the notional transaction is the last date of completion of a scheme transaction or, if earlier, the last date of substantial performance of a scheme transaction (*FA 2003, s 75A(6)*). In the example above, this is likely to be the date on which Rory pays Scott £2.15m. If the transaction was a simple sale for £2.15m, the effective date would typically be the date on which the consideration was paid, so this appears reasonable.

Exclusions from *FA 2003, s 75A*

11.18 The potential scope of *FA 2003, s 75A* is very wide. In particular, it could inhibit a legitimate arrangement of transactions in order to come within the terms of a relief or favourable treatment. To guard against this, there are two specific exclusions in *FA 2003, s 75A* itself, and some general restrictions on application set out in *FA 2003, ss 75B* and *75C*.

11.19 *FA 2003, s 75A* does not apply if the only reason for the reduced SDLT is that *FA 2003, ss 71A–73* (alternative property finance reliefs) or *Sch 9* (right to buy etc, reliefs) apply (*FA 2003, s 75A(7)*). It is important to remember that the exclusion only applies if these reliefs are the *only* reason for the SDLT saving. A combination of steps which qualify for one of the reliefs with other steps risks losing the protection of the exclusion and bringing the whole transaction within the scope of *FA 2003, s 75A*.

FA 2003, s 75B – incidental transactions

11.20 Consideration for a real transaction in a series may be ignored in calculating the consideration for the notional transaction, if the real transaction is 'merely incidental' to the transfer of the chargeable interest from V to P. There is no comprehensive definition of 'merely incidental'. The legislation gives three examples of transactions which may be incidental (*FA 2003, s 75B(3)*), as follows, but the list does not claim to be exhaustive:

● a transaction undertaken for the purpose of constructing a building on the land;

● a transaction for the sale of anything other than land; and

● a loan or other provision of finance to enable someone to pay for part of the process by which the land transfer takes place.

Since the legislation only says these transactions 'may' be incidental, the list is of very limited use. It is further limited by the statement that transactions in the list (at **11.14**) are not incidental (*FA 2003, s 75B(4)*). A transaction cannot be regarded as incidental if it forms part of the process by which the transfer of the chargeable interest is effected, or if the transfer is conditional on completion of the transaction (*FA 2003, s 75B(2)*).

Example 11.3 – Incidental transactions

The facts are as in **Example 11.2** above, but Rory also pays Scott £25,000 for the furniture and other chattels in the house. This is a payment for something other than land. Subject to confirmation that this represents a 'just and reasonable' allocation of the overall amounts paid, this will be regarded as an incidental transaction, and the amount paid will not be taken into account in determining the consideration for the notional land transaction.

FA 2003, s 75C – other exclusions and conditions

11.21 A transfer of shares or securities is ignored for the purposes of *FA 2003, s 75A* if (but only if) it would otherwise be the first of a series of scheme transactions (*FA 2003, s 75C(1)*). This allows a degree of corporate reorganisation in order to permit a claim to relief on a subsequent land transaction.

11.22 If a real transfer equivalent to the notional transaction would have been eligible for a relief, the relief applies to the notional transaction (*FA 2003, s 75C(2)*).

11.23 If the notional transaction is a transfer to a company which is connected with the vendor, *FA 2003, s 53* applies to deem the consideration to be at least equal to market value (*FA 2003, s 75C(6)*).

11.24 If there are two notional transactions which, together, amount to an exchange, *FA 2003, Sch 4, para 5* applies to deem the consideration for each notional transaction to be equal to the market value of the interest deemed transferred under that notional transaction (*FA 2003, s 75C(7)*).

Example 11.4 – Exclusion of first step, transfer of shares

Henry owns all of the shares in two companies (Anne Ltd and Jane Ltd). Anne Ltd owns the freehold of a property which is let to Jane Ltd at a rent

---

which is below the market rate. The lease held by Jane Ltd therefore has a capital value. Henry wants to put the value of the property into a single company, partly to extract cash and, later, to raise finance. Henry transfers the shares of Jane Ltd to Anne Ltd for payment in cash. He then arranges for Anne Ltd to transfer the freehold property to Jane Ltd as a contribution to capital (claiming group relief from SDLT), at which point the lease held by Jane Ltd collapses into the freehold by operation of law.

This is a series of transactions forming part of a single scheme. There is a transfer of property from Anne Ltd to Jane Ltd. This is for no consideration, but as a transfer to a connected company it is deemed to be for market value consideration. The notional transaction is the transfer from Anne Ltd to Jane Ltd, which is deemed to be for market value consideration by virtue of the application of *FA 2003, s 53* as noted above. The SDLT paid (nil) is less than would be payable on this notional consideration, so *FA 2003, s 75A* potentially applies. However:

(1) as the first step in the series, the transfer of shares of Jane Ltd to Anne Ltd is ignored. There is, therefore, only one step in the transaction (the transfer of the property to Jane Ltd), so *FA 2003, s 75A* does not apply;

(2) if there were other steps such that this was not enough to disapply *FA 2003, s 75A*, the notional transfer (being a transfer from Anne Ltd to Jane Ltd) should qualify for group relief just as the real transfer does. So, even if *FA 2003, s 75A* does apply, the SDLT charge could be removed by a claim to group relief.

11.25 It should be noted that the application of a relief to the notional transaction is subject to the normal conditions and restrictions which would apply in relation to that relief for a real transaction.

11.26 Other provisions which are applied to the notional transaction as they would apply to a real transaction are as follows:

• an interest in a property-investment partnership is treated as a chargeable interest (*FA 2003, s 75C(8)(a)*); and

• if any of the scheme transactions is entered into in connection with a transfer of an undertaking (such that *FA 2003, Sch 7, paras 7–8* apply), the notional transaction is also treated as entered into in connection with the same transfer (*FA 2003, s 75C(3)*).

11.27 Where V or P is a partnership, the normal partnership rules were originally applied in relation to a notional transaction which comprises a transfer of land to or from the partnership, from or to a partner or someone connected with a partner. However, HMRC concluded that this might allow avoidance. *FA 2003, s 75C(8A)* therefore provides that the rules in *FA 2003, Sch 15, Pt 3* do not apply to any notional transaction which consists of a transfer to or from a partnership. As a result, any such notional transaction will be subject to SDLT as if it was a transfer between two ordinary persons. This may produce an unfair result where an actual transfer to a partnership involves more than one step, thus bringing *FA 2003, s 75A* into play.

Example 11.5 – Potentially unjust result from application of *FA 2003, s 75A*

RST is a partnership of three otherwise unconnected individuals R, S and T, who share partnership profits equally. The partnership requires further premises. R's wife owns a suitable building which is currently vacant and in need of refurbishment. R's wife leases the building to R for 10 years for no premium and a peppercorn rent. In turn, R sub-lets the building to the partnership for 10 years at a market rent, but with the first year rent-free to reflect the cost of refurbishment which the partnership will incur.

If the transactions are regarded separately, no SDLT arises on the lease from R's wife to R, and SDLT will be chargeable on the partnership in respect of only 67% of the NPV of rents on the lease to the partnership: 33% of the NPV represents the interest effectively retained by R through his membership of the partnership (see **11.47** et seq).

If the transactions are regarded as a series within *FA 2003, s 75A*, the notional transaction will be the grant of a lease at rent from R or R's wife (it does not matter which, for these purposes) to the partnership. The normal partnership rules will not apply, and the full NPV of rents under the lease to the partnership will be subject to SDLT. The SDLT cost will, therefore, be increased by the application of *FA 2003, s 75A*, even though there was no avoidance in the original series of transactions. In this situation, the taxpayers would hope to rely on HMRC's assertion that *FA 2003, s 75A* will not be applied where there is no avoidance – but it would be far better to have this explicit in the legislation.

11.28   *FA 2003, s 75C(5)* and *(10)* makes it clear that any apportionment of amounts for the purpose of measuring consideration on the notional transaction must be on a just and reasonable basis, and that any SDLT paid in respect of an actual transaction which is ignored under *FA 2003, s 75A* is to be treated as paid in respect of the notional transaction. This, therefore, should avoid any element of double charge. However, it is possible that *FA 2003, s 75A* could apply to more than one group of steps in a complex series of transactions. This could lead to more than one charge under *FA 2003, s 75A*, even where a 'simple' transfer of the property from the original vendor to the ultimate purchaser would only have led to a single charge.

General anti-abuse rule

Focus

HMRC guidance states that the primary policy objective of the general anti-abuse rule ('the GAAR') is to deter taxpayers from entering into arrangements which are abusive and to deter would-be promoters from promoting abusive arrangements. There are a number of safeguards built into the GAAR provisions to ensure that any reasonable course of action chosen by a taxpayer should not fall within the regime. However, where the SDLT charge on an arrangement is less than that which might be expected, the potential application of the GAAR, to counteract the 'SDLT saving', should be considered.

11.29 The GAAR is set out in *FA 2013, ss 206–215* with procedural rules in *FA 2013, Sch 43*. HMRC guidance on the application of the GAAR can be found at www.hmrc.gov.uk/avoidance/gaar.htm. The rule applies to a wide range of taxes including SDLT and so is couched in fairly general terms. It applies to any arrangements, a main purpose of which is the obtaining of a tax advantage. 'Tax advantage' is not comprehensively defined but stated to include relief from, or repayment of, tax, reduction, avoidance or deferral of a tax liability, or avoidance of an obligation to deduct or account for tax. Where HMRC consider that the rule may apply, they will seek to make adjustments to counter the tax advantage. The taxpayer may then make a claim for 'consequential adjustments', effectively to relieve any cases of multiple taxation caused by the initial adjustments. The making of adjustments is governed by the procedural rules in *FA 2013, Sch 43*. These require HMRC first to give written notice to the taxpayer, setting out what arrangements are considered to be abusive and the reason. The taxpayer has the opportunity to respond and refute HMRC's view. If HMRC are not satisfied with the response, they must refer the matter to the GAAR Advisory Panel for an opinion. After receiving representations from both the taxpayer and HMRC, the GAAR Advisory Panel must express an opinion on the matter. In the light of this, HMRC may then make adjustments, or instruct the taxpayer as to what adjustments must be made, to counter the tax advantage. Although the GAAR provisions do not specifically cover the matter, it appears to be assumed that adjustments made by way of assessment or refusal of a claim are potentially subject to appeal to the Tax Tribunals and beyond in the normal way.

SDLT differs from other taxes covered by the GAAR in that it is a transaction tax. It is perhaps less clear which arrangements have the saving of tax as a main objective when, in the absence of the transaction there would be no tax.

PITFALLS

11.30 At least as important as tax planning is the need to be aware of the pitfalls waiting to trap the unwary. In relation to SDLT, LBTT and LTT, such pitfalls would include the following:

- clawback of group relief previously claimed where the purchaser ceases to be a member of the same group as the vendor within three years of the date of the original transaction (see **11.35–11.37**);

- transfer to a company which is connected with the transferor, but does not fulfil the precise and strict conditions to be treated as in a group with the transferor. Mere common ownership is not enough to qualify for group relief. In such circumstances, tax is charged by reference to the market value of the land interest transferred (see **11.5**);

- informal arrangements for occupation of a property, which continue for long enough to give rise to a tenancy on which SDLT, LBTT or LTT arises. In these circumstances, the obligation to file a land transaction tax return and pay the tax is often missed;

- transfer of a lease when a relief was claimed on grant which may then be taxed as the grant of a new lease (see **11.63–11.66**);

- transfer of property by operation of law, especially in non-UK mergers etc, which may still be treated as a transfer for consideration for SDLT, LBTT or LTT purposes. Again, in these circumstances the obligation to file a land transaction tax return and pay the tax is often missed;

- withdrawal of cash or other value from a partnership after the transfer of property to the partnership from a partner or connected person (see **11.50**); and

- timing issues, being unaware of factors which can lead to SDLT, LBTT or LTT becoming payable much earlier than commercial completion of a transaction or can lead to the expiry of time limits to claim relief or deferment of tax earlier than expected (see **11.3**).

The remainder of this chapter looks at some of these pitfalls in more detail and considers some of the planning opportunities which might arise.

Focus

Group relief removes any SDLT, LBTT or LTT charge on land transactions between companies (ie bodies corporate) which are members of the same group. However, the relief will be withdrawn (clawed back) if the

---

purchaser, while it or a 'relevant associated company' still owns the property (or an interest derived from it), ceases to be a member of the same group as the vendor, either within three years of the effective date of the property transfer, or later but under arrangements entered into within that three-year period. It is the purchaser's obligation to detect and disclose to the relevant tax authority any situation in which a claw-back arises. If the relief is clawed back, tax is charged on an amount equal to the market value of the property at the time of the original transfer and, if the acquisition was the grant of a lease at rent, that rent. Where group relief has been claimed, it is therefore important to put in place arrangements to monitor ownership of the property, and of the companies involved in the original claim, for an appropriate period, which is generally three years.

GROUP RELIEF

11.31 Group relief removes any SDLT, LBTT or LTT charge on land transactions between companies (ie bodies corporate) which are members of the same group (*FA 2003, Sch 7, para 1*; *LBTT(S)A 2013, Sch 10, para 2*; *LTTADT(W)A 2017, Sch 16, para 2*). To be members of the same group, one company must be the 75% subsidiary (direct or indirect) of the other, or each must be the 75% subsidiary of a third company. For A to be the 75% subsidiary of B, B must be:

(a)   the beneficial owner of not less than 75% of the issued ordinary share capital of A;

(b)   beneficially entitled to at least 75% of any profits of A available for distribution to equity holders; and

(c)   beneficially entitled to at least 75% of any assets of A available for distribution to equity holders on a winding up.

Where ownership is indirect, proportions are to be calculated in the normal algebraic manner under *Corporation Tax Act 2010 (CTA 2010), ss 1155–1157*. Rights of equity holders are measured in accordance with *CTA 2010, Pt 5, Ch 6* (omitting references to arrangements which might affect future rights if put into effect). If shares in a particular company are not identical as to par value and rights, or if creditors have greater rights than payment of the relevant debts, it will be necessary to consider the impact of this Chapter.

Example 11.6 – What constitutes a group for group relief purposes?

Fred, an individual, owns 100% of the shares of Gill Ltd and 100% of the shares of Irene Ltd. Gill Ltd owns 90% of the shares of Jack Ltd and 75% of the shares of Kerri Ltd. Irene Ltd owns the other 10% of Jack Ltd and 20% of Harry Ltd. Jack Ltd owns the remaining 80% of Harry Ltd. Fred's business partner Leo owns the remaining 25% of shares in Kerri Ltd. All shares are ordinary, same class and denomination, and there are no share options or other instruments which might change relative entitlement to dividends or asset distribution in a winding up. The structure is therefore as follows:

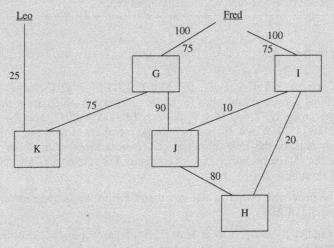

Clearly, Fred ultimately controls all of the companies, so they are connected for the purposes of *Corporation Tax Act 2010, s 1122*. This has implications for the measurement of consideration for any land transactions between them (see **11.5**). However, they are not all members of the same SDLT, LBTT or LTT group. J and H form a group, so transfers between them are capable of qualifying for group relief. Equally G, J and K form a group, and transfers between them may qualify for relief. However, H is not grouped with G or K. This is because G has (indirect) beneficial ownership of only 72% (90% × 80%) of H, the other 28% being owned directly and indirectly by I (and I is not grouped with any of the other companies). Note that J is separately grouped with both H, and G and K. In contrast with some direct tax provisions, it is acceptable for SDLT purposes for a company to be a member of more than one group in this way. Although H and G (or K) are not directly grouped, it appears at first glance that it should be possible to transfer land between them free of SDLT, for example, by G making the transfer first to J, and then J transferring onwards to H. However, SDLT, LBTT and LTT group relief is surrounded by anti-avoidance provisions, and it is possible that these would apply to such a sequence, potentially denying relief on both transfers and leading to a higher charge than would have applied to a direct transfer.

11.32   In accordance with *FA 2003, Sch 7, para 2*, (*LBTT(S)A 2013, Sch 10, paras 3–8*; *LTTADT(W)A 2017, Sch 16, para 4*) group relief is not available if, at the time of the transfer, there are 'arrangements' under which:

• at that or a later time, a person could obtain control of the purchaser but not the vendor. This condition may be breached if a third party has options to acquire or subscribe for shares of the purchaser, for example. However, if the arrangements are part of a scheme of reconstruction which itself will qualify for stamp duty relief under *FA 1986, s 75*, relief will not be denied; or

• any part of the consideration is to be provided or received by someone other than a group member. In principle, this could lead to denial of relief where, for example, the purchaser borrows funds from a bank. In Inland Revenue *Tax Bulletin* Issue 70 (April 2004), in relation to SDLT, HMRC state that borrowing on ordinary commercial terms to fund an intra-group transfer will not normally lead to a denial of the relief (para 29). In addition, HMRC indicate that they will consider all of the facts and interpret this provision as not denying relief unless loan finance is provided as part of a scheme to save SDLT when the property leaves the SDLT group (para 27); or

• the companies are to cease to be members of the same group by reason of the purchaser leaving the group. It is not generally a problem if there are arrangements under which the vendor is to leave the group. However, arrangements even for this must not be too far advanced, or beneficial ownership of the relevant shares may already be lost and the group broken before the time of the transfer.

11.33   Group relief is additionally subject to the condition that the transaction must be for bona fide commercial purposes, without the avoidance of tax forming a main purpose (*FA 2003, Sch 7, para 2(4A)*). In relation to SDLT, 'Tax' means stamp duty, SDLT, income tax, corporation tax and capital gains tax. In relation to LBTT it only means LBTT itself so that an arrangement to avoid any other tax is not caught (*LBTT(S)A 2013, Sch 10, para 8*). For the purposes of LTT group relief the Reliefs TAAR (see **11.8**) applies and 'Tax' means LTT, income tax, corporation tax, capital gains tax, SDLT, SDRT and stamp duty (*LTTADT(W)A 2017, s 31*). For each of the three taxes this condition is effectively a general anti-avoidance provision. There is no legislative guidance within any of the three taxes as to its scope, and doubt over this has led, and will continue to lead, to significant uncertainty as to whether relief is due. In response to widespread disquiet in relation to SDLT, HMRC produced a 'white list' of transactions which would not normally be regarded as falling foul of this condition. The list can be found at SDLTM23040. However, the list itself contains a number of caveats and gives limited comfort in the context of real commercial transactions. After a meeting between HMRC and representative bodies, including the Chartered Institute of Taxation, HMRC confirmed in August 2013 that group relief would not be denied merely because one company obtained a tax advantage by:

(1)   acquiring another company which held property; then

(2)   transferring the property elsewhere within the purchaser's group.

(See http://www.hmrc.gov.uk/so/bulletin02-2013.pdf, item 3.)

Claw-back of group relief

Focus

SDLT, LBTT or LTT group relief may be clawed-back if the purchaser ceases to be a member of the same group as the vendor within three years of the effective date of the transaction which qualified for the relief (or later, but under an arrangement entered into within that three-year period) and the purchaser (or a 'relevant associated company') still owns the property (or an interest derived from it) which was the subject of the transaction. It is therefore important to put in place arrangements to monitor ownership of the property, and of the companies in the original claim, for an appropriate period, which is generally three years. There are, however, circumstances in which group relief is not clawed-back even though the conditions for claw-back appear to be satisfied.

11.34   Even where a transaction initially qualifies for SDLT, LBTT or LTT group relief, in certain circumstances the relief may be retrospectively withdrawn, leading to crystallisation of the tax charge originally relieved. Because each of SDLT, LBTT and LTT are self-assessment taxes, it is for the taxpayer to detect and disclose any situation in which a claw-back arises (*FA 2003, s 81*; *LBTT(S)A 2013, s 33(1)(d)*; *LTTADT(W)A 2017, s 49(1)(c)* – 'Further return where relief withdrawn'). Where one of these reliefs has been claimed, it is therefore important to put in place arrangements to monitor ownership of the property, and of the companies involved in the original claim, for an appropriate period, which is generally three years.

11.35   Group relief is clawed back if the purchaser, while it or a 'relevant associated company' still owns the property (or an interest derived from it), ceases to be a member of the same group as the vendor, either within three years of the effective date of the property transfer, or later but under arrangements entered into within that three-year period. A 'relevant associated company' is any other member of the group which leaves the group 'in consequence of' the purchaser leaving. This provision prevents an otherwise simple avoidance arrangement, under which the purchaser transfers the property to a wholly-owned subsidiary before both purchaser and subsidiary leave the vendor's group and the purchaser is thus able to claim that it no longer holds any interest in the property. If the interest which the purchaser (or a relevant associated company) still holds is less than the interest originally transferred, a pro rata amount of the relief is withdrawn (*FA 2003, Sch 7, para 3*; *LBTT(S)A 2013, Sch 10, paras 13–19*; *LTTADT(W)A 2017, Sch 16, para 8*).

Example 11.7 – SDLT chargeable when group relief is clawed-back

Morgan Ltd (M) owns 100% of the shares of Ross Ltd (R) and Smith Ltd (S). On 2 March 2018, R transfers to S a freehold interest in a commercial property which is situated in England, and which is worth £800,000, and group relief from SDLT is claimed. In September 2018, S grants a capital lease of part of the property to a third party, in return for a premium of £600,000 and a peppercorn rent. It is agreed that the value of the part thus disposed of is three-quarters of the value of the whole property. On 24 February 2019, M sells 50% of the shares of S to another third party, in the course of setting up a joint venture. S therefore leaves the M group while still holding an interest in the property with a value of one-quarter of the value of the whole property. The SDLT payable is, therefore, one-quarter of the SDLT which would have been payable on the original transfer on 2 March 2018, if group relief had not been claimed. The SDLT on the original transfer would have been calculated as follows:

Purchase price	Rate	SDLT
£	%	£
150,000	0	Nil
100,000	2	2,000
550,000	5	27,500
800,000		29,500

Consequently, the amount chargeable under the claw-back is one-quarter of £29,500 or £7,375.

Note: the SDLT is *not* calculated as if there was a transfer of a property with a value of one-quarter of the original; in the present case, such a calculation would give a liability of £1,000 – but, sadly, this is not how the claw-back operates! However, even if SDLT rates or thresholds have subsequently changed, the claw-back is still calculated on the basis of rates and thresholds which applied at the time of the original transfer.

11.36 Group relief is not clawed back where the purchaser leaves the vendor's group (*FA 2003, Sch 7, para 4*; *LBTT(S)A 2013, Sch 10, paras 21 and 22*; *LTTADT(W)A 2017, Sch 16, para 9*):

- as a result of the winding up of the vendor or a company above the vendor in the group;

- in the course of a reconstruction which itself qualifies for relief under *FA 1986, s 75*, as a result of which the purchaser becomes a member of the same group as the 'acquiring company'; or

- in the course of a qualifying demutualisation of an insurance company.

11.37 In addition, group relief is not clawed back if it is the vendor which leaves the group rather than the purchaser. This allows a group to remove property, which it wishes to keep, from a subsidiary which is to be disposed of. However, if there is subsequently a change of control of the purchaser within three years of the original transfer, the purchaser is at that time treated as leaving the vendor's group, and claw-back applies accordingly (*FA 2003, Sch 7, para 4ZA*; *LBTT(S)A 2013, Sch 10, para 28*; *LTTADT(W)A 2017, Sch 16, para 10(4)*). There are complex anti-avoidance provisions designed to ensure the 'change of control' rules apply as intended, where successive transfers of the property might otherwise lead to doubt as to their application. Although the reasoning is not clear, the winding up of the purchaser is also treated as a change of control (*FA 2003, Sch 7, paras 4ZA and 4A*; *LBTT(S)A 2013, Sch 10, paras 32–39*; *LTTADT(W)A 2017, Sch 16, para 12*).

However, if the purchaser ceases to be a member of the same group as the vendor as a consequence of the vendor being wound up, or a company above the vendor being wound up, so that group relief is not clawed back, it is understood that HMRC accept that a subsequent change of control of the purchaser will not cause the group relief to be clawed back under *FA 2003, Sch 7, para 4ZA*. It is not known whether Revenue Scotland and the Welsh Revenue Authority take the same view as regards LBTT and LTT respectively.

Focus

Special rules apply where a property is transferred to or from a partnership and there is a connection between the partnership and the other party, ie where the other party is a partner (current, departing or joining) or is connected with a partner. Generally, in these circumstances, SDLT, LBTT and LTT are charged by reference to the market value of the property interest in question and the proportion of the property which is deemed to be transferred to or from the partnership (see **11.47**). A transfer of a property interest to a partnership from a partner (current, departing or joining) or a person connected with such a partner starts a three-year period during which certain other events can lead to a further charge to SDLT, LBTT or LTT (see **11.50**). A transfer of an interest in a 'property-investment partnership' (PIP) can lead to a charge to SDLT, LBTT or LTT, as can a transfer of an interest in a partnership which is not a PIP if it is part of an arrangement under which a property interest was transferred to the partnership (see **11.52**). The incorporation of a partnership, which holds property interests, in which all of the partners are individuals, may not give to a charge to tax (see **Example 11.14**).

PARTNERSHIPS

11.38 The main legislation specifically dealing with partnerships is in *FA 2003, Sch 15 (LBTTA(S)A, Sch 17; LTTADT(W)A 2017, Sch 7)*.

The UK tax system has always had difficulty working out how to deal with partnerships – in particular, whether to treat them as separate entities distinct from their members or as mere aggregations of separately taxed members – and SDLT, LBTT and LTT continue that uncertainty.

Three types of UK-based partnership are recognised:

(1)   a (general) partnership within the *Partnership Act 1890*;

(2)   a limited partnership (LP) registered under the *Limited Partnerships Act 1907*; and

(3)   a limited liability partnership (LLP) formed under the *Limited Liability Partnerships Act 2000* or the Northern Ireland equivalent.

The SDLT, LBTT and LTT rules seek to treat all three types of entity in the same way; they also apply the same treatment to any 'firm or entity of a similar character' formed under the laws of another country. Difficulties arise because the three types of entity listed above and many equivalent overseas entities have quite different legal and commercial characteristics. As a result, the treatment of a particular transaction may be logical in one case (say, involving a general partnership) but less so in another (say, involving an LLP). These differences have in the past been a factor in the use of partnerships to mitigate SDLT costs, and many of the special rules which now apply to partnerships for the purposes of all three taxes were originally intended to combat perceived avoidance.

Particular issues arise from the fact that LLPs (together with Scottish LPs and many overseas equivalents) are bodies corporate for the purposes of general law and many other tax purposes (LLPs) and/or have separate legal personality (Scottish LPs), but are treated as 'transparent' as regards ownership of land for SDLT, LBTT and LTT purposes.

General principles in relation to a partnership

11.39   Property held by or on behalf of a partnership is treated as held by or on behalf of the partners (and not the partnership); a land transaction entered into for the purposes of a partnership is treated as entered into by or on behalf of the partners (and not the partnership); this is so even if the partnership is regarded as a body corporate or other legal entity for other purposes, such as the ability to enter into contracts and to own property (*FA 2003, Sch 15, para 2*; *LBTT(S)A 2013, Sch 17, para 3*; *LTTADT(W)A 2017, Sch 7, para 4*). However, the partners at the effective date of the transaction have joint and several liability for payment of any tax. They also have responsibility, in some circumstances together with any partners who join after the effective date, for payment of any penalty, for example for failure to make a return or notify liability (*FA 2003, Sch 15, para 7*; *LBTT(S)A 2013, Sch 17, para 10*; *LTTADT(W)A 2017, Sch 7, para 11*). Although this means all partners have responsibility for compliance, they may nominate 'representative partners' to act on behalf of the partnership. Any such nomination must be notified to HMRC, Revenue Scotland or the Welsh Tax Authority as appropriate (*FA 2003, Sch 15, para 8*; *LBTT(S)A 2013, Sch 17, para 9*; *LTTADT(W)A 2017, Sch 7, para 10*).

11.40   If there is a change in the membership of a partnership, it is nonetheless treated as the same continuing partnership, provided at least one member before the change remains a member afterwards (*FA 2003, Sch 15, para 3*; *LBTT(S)A 2013, Sch 17, para 5*; *LTTADT(W)A 2017, Sch 7, para 6*). Thus, despite the assertions in **11.39**, there are ways in which a partnership is treated as a separate entity.

Partnership share

Focus

In order to determine the chargeable consideration for many transactions entered into by a partnership, or even in some cases to determine whether a chargeable transaction has occurred, it is necessary to know the *share* (as defined in the legislation) which each partner has in the partnership. Normally, a partner's share in the partnership is determined by their percentage right to share in the income profits of the partnership for the accounting period in which the 'effective date' of the transaction falls.

11.41   In order to calculate the chargeable consideration for many partnership transactions, or even in some cases to determine whether a chargeable transaction has occurred, it is necessary to know the shares which the different partners have in the partnership. For most SDLT, LBTT and LTT purposes, a partner's share in a partnership is defined as the proportion in which he is entitled to share in the income profits of the partnership at the effective date of the transaction (*FA 2003, Sch 15, para 34(2)*; *LBTT(S)A 2013, Sch 17, para 44*; *LTTADT(W)A 2017, Sch 7, para 45(2)*). When property is transferred out of a partnership, a more complicated definition applies, although in many cases it produces the same result (*FA 2003, Sch 15, paras 21* and *22*; *LBTT(S)A 2013, Sch 17, paras 25* and *26*; *LTTADT(W)A 2017, Sch 7, paras 26* and *27*). Entitlement to capital, or to capital profits, does not enter into the calculation. The definition causes practical difficulties – partnerships often decide the precise sharing of profits after the year-end, once total profits and the contribution of each partner to them are known. In such cases, it may be necessary to complete an SDLT, LBTT or LTT return and pay tax based on estimated shares, then amend the return once profit shares are finally settled. Since profit shares do not normally vary from day to day, the reference to the 'effective date' is usually taken to mean the accounting period containing the effective date.

Ordinary transactions

11.42   If a partnership (or a partner on behalf of a partnership) enters into a land transaction with a person who is completely at arm's length, that transaction is treated in the same way as an equivalent transaction not involving a partnership. The only modification is that the partners have joint and several responsibility for any compliance matters. A person is completely at arm's length to the partnership if he is neither a partner (whether current, joining or departing) nor connected with a partner. Connected for these purposes is as defined by *s 1122* of the *Corporation Tax Act 2010 (CTA 2010)*, although the automatic connection of partners with each other is omitted. It follows that, for such an arm's-length transaction, SDLT, LBTT or LTT is generally chargeable by reference to the value of the actual consideration, and it is only necessary to consider the market value of the property itself where that would be required for a non-partnership transaction (eg for exchanges of property interests).

Special provisions

11.43   The application of the SDLT, LBTT and LTT rules to arm's-length transactions is relatively straightforward. Complications arise when there is a connection between the partnership and the other party, ie where the other party is a partner (current, departing or joining) or is connected with a partner. It is necessary to consider separately the implications of the partnership acquiring or disposing of property, including modification of an existing interest where that would be treated as an acquisition or disposal under general SDLT, LBTT or LTT rules. It is also necessary to consider the implications of changes in the membership or relative interests of the members in a partnership which owns property; in certain cases, such changes are deemed to give rise to a corresponding transfer of property interests between partners.

11.44   Generally, if partnership transactions are subject to the 'special provisions', SDLT, LBTT and LTT is charged by reference to the market value of the property interest in question and the proportion of the property which is deemed to be transferred. Actual consideration (other than any change in partnership share) is irrelevant. However, there are many anti-avoidance rules; in some circumstances, amounts which are commercially equivalent to consideration may trigger these.

11.45   The legislation sets out formulae which must be applied to the market value of the property in question to determine the deemed consideration for the transaction. The formulae appear complex, but are generally seeking to achieve a relatively simple overall effect, which is to ensure that tax is charged on the economic transfer of value which takes place.

Example 11.8 – Simple partnership case

Cameron and Stewart are in a general partnership, sharing income and capital profits equally. They agree to admit Scott as an equal partner (so each partner has a one-third share in profits, losses and assets) in return for Scott agreeing, inter alia, to contribute freehold premises situated in England to the partnership. The property is transferred to Cameron and Stewart jointly to hold on trust for the partnership (this is a normal arrangement, because a general partnership is not a body capable of holding the title to land). In the absence of any other complicating factors, SDLT is chargeable by reference to two-thirds of the market value of the property contributed by Scott. This is the proportion which has economically changed hands by transfer to the other partners; Scott still has a one-third interest in the property through his membership of the partnership, so no SDLT is charged on that proportion.

11.46   Inevitably, real transactions do include complicating factors, and the relevant tax authorities are keen to minimise avoidance. Therefore, the basic formulae are supplemented by definitions and rules for special cases which must be taken into account. It would not be safe to assume that the simple apportionment set out above gives the correct tax charge, without checking the specific facts of the case against the detailed rules.

Acquisition by a partnership from a partner (current, departing or joining)

> **Focus**
>
> In these circumstances, SDLT, LBTT or LTT will be charged by reference to the market value of the property interest being transferred to the partnership and the proportion of that property interest which is effectively transferred to the other partners within the partnership. The actual consideration given by the partnership is irrelevant in determining the tax liability.

11.47 Under *FA 2003, Sch 15, para 10 (LBTT(S)A 2013, Sch 17, para 14; LTTADT(W)A 2017, Sch 7, para 13(3))*, when a chargeable interest is acquired by a partnership from a partner, or from a person who becomes a partner as a result, or from a person who is connected with either, SDLT, LBTT or LTT is charged on deemed consideration equal to:

$$MV \times (100 - SLP)\%$$

where MV is the market value of the chargeable interest at the effective date of the transfer, and SLP is the 'sum of the lower proportions'. A five-step calculation is required to determine SLP, set out in the legislation (*FA 2003, Sch 15, para 12; LBTT(S)A 2013, Sch 17, para 13; LTTADT(W)A 2017, Sch 7, para 14*) as follows:

(1)   Identify the 'relevant owner(s)'. These are persons who have an interest in the property immediately before it is transferred and are partners or connected with partners immediately after the property is transferred.

(2)   For each relevant owner, identify the 'corresponding partner(s)'. These are persons who are partners immediately after the transfer and who are relevant owners or are individuals connected with relevant owners. For these purposes, a company may be regarded as an individual connected with a relevant owner *only* if it holds property as trustee and is connected by virtue of *CTA 2010, s 1122(6)* (trustee connected with settlor etc).

(3)   For each relevant owner, take the proportion of the property to which he is entitled immediately before the transfer and apportion it between any one or more of his corresponding partners. Where a relevant owner has more than one corresponding partner, the apportionment may be performed in whatever manner gives the best result.

(4)   Find the 'lower proportion' for each person who is a corresponding partner in relation to one or more relevant owners. The lower proportion is the lower of:

    (a)   the proportion apportioned to him under (3) above; and

    (b)   his partnership share immediately after the transfer.

(5)   Add together the lower proportions for each partner who is a corresponding partner. This is the SLP.

Example 11.9 – Calculating the sum of the lower proportions

Alfred, Betty and Carl are in partnership, sharing 40%, 40% and 20% respectively. Betty and Carl are sister and brother; apart from the partnership, Alfred is not related to or connected with Betty or Carl. The partners agree to buy a building situated in England from Danielle, who is Betty and Carl's sister, for £500,000. The calculation steps are as follows:

(1)   The only relevant owner is Danielle, because she owns 100% of the property before the transfer.

(2)   Betty and Carl are corresponding partners because they are individuals connected with the only relevant owner, their sister Danielle.

(3)   Danielle was entitled to 100% of the property before the transfer. We choose to apportion this 50% to each corresponding partner, Betty and Carl.

(4)   For Betty, her partnership share immediately after the transaction is 40%, and the proportion apportioned to her under (3) is 50%, so her lower proportion is 40%; for Carl, his partnership share immediately after the transaction is 20%, and the proportion apportioned to him under (3) above is 50%, so his lower proportion is 20%.

(5)   The sum of the lower proportions is 40% (Betty) plus 20% (Carl), which is 60%.

The consideration for SDLT purposes is therefore MV × (100 – 60)%, or 40% of the market value, ie £200,000. In this relatively simple case, it can be seen that this represents the proportion of the property effectively transferred to Alfred, the partner who is not connected with the original owner of the property.

11.48   In most cases before the transfer, the property will be owned by one person, so there will be only one relevant owner. If two or more persons own a property as beneficial joint tenants, they are treated as owning as tenants in common, in equal shares.

Connected companies

11.49 The restriction to individuals in step (2) detailed in **11.47** is designed to prevent the use of a partnership arrangement to transfer property to a connected company without suffering SDLT (or LBTT, LTT) on the full market value of the property.

Example 11.10 – Partnership including connected company

Derek sets up a company, Fiddler Ltd, in which he is the sole shareholder. Derek and Fiddler Ltd form a limited partnership in which Derek is the limited partner with a 1% share and Fiddler Ltd is the general partner with a 99% share. Derek transfers a valuable property situated in England to the partnership. The steps to calculate the proportion of market value on which SDLT is charged are as follows:

(1)   Derek is the only relevant owner with 100%.

(2)   Derek is also the only corresponding partner. Fiddler Ltd cannot be a corresponding partner, as it is not an individual.

(3)   Therefore, Derek's 100% ownership before the transfer must be apportioned 100% to Derek as corresponding partner after the transfer.

(4)   Derek's partnership share immediately after the transfer is only 1%, so his lower proportion is 1%; Fiddler Ltd is not a corresponding partner, so it does not figure in the calculation.

(5)   The SLP is therefore 1%, and SDLT is chargeable on the 99% of the market value effectively transferred to Fiddler Ltd.

Three-year period during which certain events can lead to a tax charge

Focus

When a partnership acquires a property interest from a partner (current, departing or joining), this starts a three-year period during which a withdrawal of money or money's worth from the partnership by that partner, which does not represent income profit, can lead to a further charge to tax. Similarly, if the partner who transferred the property interest to the partnership has made a loan to the partnership (or where the transfer to the partnership was from a person connected with a partner, that person has

> made a loan to the partnership) any repayment of that loan, or a withdrawal of any amount which does not represent income profit, may also give rise to a charge to tax. It will therefore be important to monitor withdrawals of money or money's worth from the partnership, and any loan repayments, during that three-year period to avoid triggering a tax charge.

11.50   The transfer of property from a partner or person connected with a partner to a partnership marks the start of a three-year period within which certain other events can lead to a further SDLT, LBTT or LTT charge (*FA 2003, Sch 15, para 17A*; *LBTT(S)A 2013, Sch 17, para 18*; *LTTADT(W)A 2017, Sch 7, para 19*).

- *Withdrawal of money or money's worth*

  If, during that three-year period, the partner concerned withdraws from the partnership money or money's worth which does not represent income profit, but:

  - is capital withdrawn from the partners' capital account; or

  - arises from the partner reducing his interest or ceasing to be a partner,

  the withdrawal is treated as a chargeable land transaction. Where the original transfer was from a person connected with a partner, withdrawal of value by either the partner or any person connected with the partner is treated as a chargeable transaction. However, presumably, the connected person would have also to be a partner to be able to legitimately withdraw capital etc.

- *Repayment of a loan or withdrawal of any amount not representing income profit*

  If the partner (or, where the original transfer was from a person connected with a partner, the partner or a person connected with the partner) has made a loan to the partnership, the repayment of any of the loan or a withdrawal of any amount by that person which does not represent income profit of the partnership is also treated as a chargeable land transaction.

In either case, the chargeable consideration is the smaller of:

(a)   the amount withdrawn from or repaid by the partnership; and

(b)   the market value of the land at the date of the original land transfer, reduced by any amount which has already been charged to SDLT, LBTT or LTT.

If the withdrawal of money or money's worth is also subject to SDLT as a transfer of an interest in a 'property-investment partnership' (PIP), the SDLT charged under the 'withdrawal of money' provision is reduced by the amount of any charge under the 'transfer of an interest in a PIP' provision (*FA 2003, Sch 15, para 17A(8)*; *LBTT(S)A 2013, Sch 17, para 18(9)*; *LTTADT(W)A 2017, Sch 7, para 19(9)*). A PIP is defined as a partnership whose sole or main activity is investing or dealing in chargeable interests, whether or not the activity includes the carrying out of construction activities on the land (*FA 2003, Sch 15, para 14(8)*; *LBTT(S)A 2013, Sch 17, para 31*; *LTTADT(W)A 2017, Sch 7, para 33*). So, a partnership which invests in property in order to receive rent, or buys and sells property in order to make a profit (whether as a trade or an investment activity), is a PIP if this is its sole or main activity.

Example 11.11 – Repayment of loan after transfer

Using the facts as in **Example 11.9**, the partnership does not have enough ready cash to pay the whole price of the building purchased from Danielle, so it is agreed that £350,000 will be left outstanding as a loan from Danielle to the partnership, with interest being charged at 2% above the Bank of England base rate, payable monthly in arrears. The loan arrangement has no effect on the SDLT charge on the initial transfer of the property to the partnership. One year later, after a purge on debtors, the partnership has enough cash and pays off the loan. The loan repayment is taken to be a land transaction, and SDLT is chargeable on the partnership. However, SDLT was paid on £200,000 when the property, with a value of £500,000, was transferred to the partnership. The chargeable consideration for the deemed land transaction cannot exceed the part of that market value which has not yet been taxed. So, SDLT is chargeable on £300,000, and not on the full £350,000 loan repayment. Note that this limitation is assessed by considering the market value of the property when it was transferred, and not the value at the time of the loan repayment or other withdrawal of value.

Had the partnership borrowed from a bank at the outset and paid Danielle in full, the SDLT charge on the original land transfer would still have been based on £200,000, but the subsequent repayment of the bank debt would not have given rise to an SDLT charge. It is difficult to see any policy reason for this discrimination, which therefore looks rather like a poorly directed anti-avoidance provision.

Transfer to a PIP may also involve transfer of partnership interest

11.51 The charge on the partnership when a new or existing partner (or someone connected with him) transfers a chargeable interest to the partnership does not depend on the amount or form of consideration given by the partnership. As suggested in **Example 11.8**, the consideration could take the form of admitting a new partner or increasing a partner's share. This acquisition of, or increase in, partnership share will be regarded as a transfer of an interest in a partnership. If the partnership is a PIP (see **11.50** for the definition of a PIP), this transfer will be separately subject to SDLT, LBTT or LTT, chargeable on the new partner or the partner whose share has increased. This is in addition to the charge on the partnership arising from the acquisition of the property. The transaction is an exchange. This fact should not affect the calculation of the tax payable because, both in transactions between a partnership and its partners (or persons connected with them) and in an exchange, the tax is calculated by reference to the market value of the chargeable interests acquired (albeit indirectly, where a partnership interest is acquired) rather than the consideration given. The newly transferred property is not taken into account in determining the tax charge on transfer of the partnership interest, so there is no double charge.

Example 11.12 – Admission of partner, transfer of property

X Ltd and Y Ltd are limited partners in Spendit LP, a limited partnership which owns shopping centres and is clearly a PIP. The general partner is a Jersey-registered company with a negligible partnership share. X Ltd has a 40% partnership share, and Y Ltd has 60%. The shopping centres are worth £100m. It is agreed that Z Ltd will be admitted as a limited partner with a partnership share of 30%, so that X Ltd's share drops to 28% and Y Ltd's to 42%. By way of payment, Z Ltd will transfer a further shopping centre to Spendit LP, with a value of £45m. Apart from membership of Spendit LP, there are no other connections between X Ltd, Y Ltd and Z Ltd.

- **Transfer of property to Spendit**: The calculation set out at **11.47** shows that Spendit LP is liable for SDLT on 70% of the £45m value of the property brought to the partnership by Z Ltd.

- **Transfer of partnership share to Z Ltd**: Z Ltd is deemed to have acquired an interest in the 'relevant partnership property' owned by Spendit before Z Ltd joined. The consideration is the market value of the property multiplied by the partnership interest acquired, ie 30%. Whether the shopping centres already owned by Spendit are 'relevant partnership property' will depend on their history, and the question of whether the transfer to Z Ltd is 'Type A' or 'Type B'.

Two situations give rise to a Type A transfer (*FA 2003, Sch 15 para 14(3A), (3B); LBTT(S)A 2013, Sch 17, para 32(8); LTTADT(W)A 2017, Sch 7, para 34(8)*).

The first occurs when the whole or part of a partner's interest as partner is transferred to another person (whether or not an existing partner) in return for consideration in money or money's worth. For the legislation to make sense, this must mean consideration given to the partner whose interest reduces (or to someone else at that partner's behest). The mere contribution of capital to the partnership by the person who gains partnership share does not amount to the giving of consideration for these purposes.

The second occurs when a new partner joins and an existing partner withdraws money or money's worth from the partnership, thereby reducing or extinguishing his partnership share. However, this is not a Type A transfer if the withdrawal of money or money's worth comes from resources available to the partnership prior to the transfer. Any transfer of an interest in a PIP which is not a Type A transfer is a Type B transfer (*FA 2003, Sch 15, para 14(3C)*; *LBTT(S)A 2013, Sch 17, para 32(9)*; *LTTADT(W)A 2017, Sch 7, para 34(9)*).

The transfer of the partnership interest in this example would therefore be a Type B transfer as neither of the two situations giving rise to a Type A transfer are present.

It is important to note that the distinction between Type A and Type B transfers is relevant only for deciding whether the partnership holds 'relevant partnership property' and, if yes, its value. Both types of transfer are potentially subject to SDLT, LBTT or LTT. However, in many Type B transfers, there will be no 'relevant partnership property' and so no SDLT, LBTT or LTT liability. Relevant partnership property in relation to a Type A transfer is defined in *FA 2003, Sch 15, para 14(5)*, (*LBTT(S)A 2013, Sch 17, para 32(6)*; *LTTADT(W)A 2017, Sch 7, para 34(6)*) and in relation to a Type B transfer is defined in *FA 2003, Sch 15, para 14(5A)*, (*LBTT(S)A 2013, Sch 17, para 32(7)*; *LTTADT(W)A 2017, Sch 7, para 34(7)*).

Transfer pursuant to earlier arrangements

Focus

A transfer of an interest in a partnership, which is not a PIP (see **11.50** for the definition of a PIP), may give rise to a charge to SDLT, LBTT or LTT if that transfer is part of an arrangement under which a property interest was first transferred to the partnership by a partner. This anti-avoidance provision therefore prevents the special rules for the transfer of a property interest to a partnership by a partner being used to avoid a charge to tax on the subsequent transfer of an interest in that property by means of the transfer of a share in a partnership which is not a PIP.

11.52 If:

- a chargeable interest, ie an interest in land is transferred to a partnership from a partner or person connected with a partner,

- that person or partner then transfers any or all of his partnership interest under arrangements which were in existence at the time of the land transfer, and

- the partnership transfer would not otherwise be a chargeable transaction ie the partnership is not a PIP (see **11.50** for the definition of a PIP),

the partnership transfer is a chargeable land transfer (*FA 2003, Sch 15, para 17*; *LBTT(S)A 2013, Sch 17, para 17*; *LTTADT(W)A 2017, Sch 7, para 18*). The partners are treated as the purchaser under this deemed transaction, and the chargeable consideration is the market value of the land at the date of the land transfer multiplied by the proportionate share in the partnership transferred under the arrangements. However, this treatment does not apply if an election is made by a PIP in respect of the land transfer under *FA 2003, Sch 15, para 12A* (*LBTT(S)A 2013, Sch 17, para 35*; *LTTADT(W)A 2017, Sch 7, para 36*). For these purposes 'arrangements' are defined as including any scheme, agreement or understanding, whether or not legally enforceable.

11.53 The practical implication is that, if a partner transfers a chargeable interest to a partnership and shortly after transfers his partnership interest, HMRC, Revenue Scotland or the Welsh Revenue Authority as appropriate are likely to question whether the transactions are part of a single arrangement. The deemed land transaction arising as a result of such a transfer of an interest in a partnership is notifiable (by completion of a land transaction tax return) only if the deemed consideration is sufficient for tax to be payable (*FA 2003, Sch 15, para 30*; *LBTT(S)A 2013, Sch 17, para 41*; *LTTADT(W)A 2017, Sch 7, para 44*). For example, in relation to SDLT, if the initial property transfer to the partnership did not involve the grant of a lease at rent and if there are no linked transactions, the subsequent transfer of the partnership interest will not be notifiable unless the deemed consideration exceeds the zero rate limit of £125,000 or £150,000 for residential or non-residential/mixed property respectively. In relation to the £125,000 limit this assumes that the additional rate of SDLT does not apply (see **11.68** et seq) since, if it did apply, a 3% SDLT charge would arise if the property had a value of £40,000 or more.

Disposal by a partnership to a partner or a person who has been one of the partners (or person connected with a partner or a person who has been one of the partners)

Focus

In these circumstances, SDLT, LBTT or LTT will be charged by reference to the market value of the property interest being transferred out of the partnership and the proportion of that property interest which the acquiring partner and/or connected individual partners did not already own indirectly through their membership of the partnership. The actual consideration given for the property interest is irrelevant in determining the tax liability.

11.54   A disposal of a chargeable interest by a partnership should not directly give rise to any SDLT, LBTT or LTT obligations for the partnership; it is for the purchaser to deal with any tax charge. If the disposal is to an unrelated third party, the purchaser will be liable for the tax in the normal way, based on the actual consideration given. However, if the disposal is to a partner or a person who has been one of the partners or to a person connected with a partner or a person who has been one of the partners, special rules come into play (*FA 2003, Sch 15, para 18*; *LBTT(S)A 2013, Sch 17, paras 20–26*; *LTTADT(W)A 2017, Sch 7, paras 20–27*). These are similar to those outlined in **11.47**; their purpose is to ensure the purchaser pays tax only on the proportion of the property which he and/or connected individual partners did not already own indirectly through membership of the partnership. SDLT, LBTT or LTT is charged on deemed consideration equal to:

$$MV \times (100 - SLP)\%$$

where MV is the market value of the chargeable interest at the effective date of the transfer, and SLP is the 'sum of the lower proportions'. Again, a five-step calculation is required to determine SLP, set out in the legislation (*FA 2003, Sch 15, para 20*; *LBTT(S)A 2013, Sch 17, para 22*; *LTTADT(W)A 2017, Sch 7, para 22*) as follows:

(1)   Identify the 'relevant owner(s)'. These are persons who have an interest in the property immediately after it is transferred and are partners or connected with partners immediately before the property is transferred.

(2)   For each relevant owner, identify the 'corresponding partner(s)'. These are persons who are partners immediately before the transfer and who are relevant owners or are individuals connected with relevant owners. For these purposes, a company may be regarded as an individual connected with a relevant owner *only* if it holds property as trustee and is connected by virtue of *CTA 2010, s 1122(6)* (trustee connected with settlor etc).

(3) For each relevant owner, take the proportion of the property to which he is entitled immediately after the transfer and apportion it between any one or more of his corresponding partners. Where a relevant owner has more than one corresponding partner, the apportionment may be performed in whatever manner gives the best result.

(4) Find the 'lower proportion' for each person who is a corresponding partner in relation to one or more relevant owners. The lower proportion is the lower of:

(a) the proportion apportioned to him under (3) above, and

(b) his partnership share immediately before the transfer.

(5) Add together the lower proportions for each partner who is a corresponding partner. This is the SLP.

Example 11.13 – Transfer of property to a partner

Alfred, Betty and Carl are (still) in partnership, sharing income profits 40%, 40% and 20% respectively. Betty and Carl are siblings, Alfred is not related to them. Betty decides to withdraw from the partnership and it is agreed she will take one of the properties, which is situated in England, in satisfaction of her entitlement to partnership capital. The calculation of Betty's SDLT liability is as follows:

(1) The only relevant owner is Betty, because she owns 100% of the property after the transfer.

(2) Betty and Carl are corresponding partners because they are, or are connected with, the only relevant owner, Betty.

(3) Betty is entitled to 100% of the property after the transfer. We choose to apportion this 50% to each corresponding partner, Betty and Carl.

(4) For Betty, her partnership share immediately before the transaction is 40%, and the proportion apportioned to her under (3) is 50%, so her lower proportion is 40%; for Carl, his partnership share immediately before the transaction is 20%, and the proportion apportioned to him under (3) above is 50%, so his lower proportion is 20%.

(5) The sum of the lower proportions is 40% (Betty) plus 20% (Carl), which is 60%.

The consideration for SDLT purposes is therefore MV × (100 − 60)%, or 40% of the market value. In this simple case, it can be seen that this represents the proportion of the property effectively transferred from the partner who is not connected with the final owner of the property. Again, the same principles apply in relation to rent if the 'transfer' is the grant of a lease at rent.

Example 11.14 – Transfer of property to a connected company

The initial facts are as in **Example 11.13**, but it is Alfred who wishes to withdraw from the business. It is decided to wind up the partnership and transfer the properties and other assets to a newly formed company, BC Ltd, in which Betty and Carl are equal 50% shareholders. It is agreed that BC Ltd will pay for the business and properties by paying Alfred an agreed amount of cash and by issuing shares to Betty and Carl. The calculation of BC Ltd's SDLT liability is analogous to that in **Example 11.13**:

(1)   The only relevant owner is BC Ltd, because it owns 100% of the property after the transfer.

(2)   Betty and Carl are corresponding partners because they are individuals connected with the only relevant owner, BC Ltd. This is on the basis that both Betty and Carl will be treated as being connected with BC Ltd by virtue of *Corporation Tax Act 2010, s 1122(3)(b)* which states: 'A company is connected with another person ("A") if– … (b) A together with persons connected with A have control of the company'. As Betty and Carl are both connected with each other, as they are siblings, they are both treated as controlling BC Ltd (*Corporation Tax Act 2010, s 1122(5)(b)*).

The question which then arises is whether Alfred is also treated as having control of BC Ltd, even though he has no equity interest in BC Ltd. *Corporation Tax Act 2010, s 1122(3)(a)* states that: 'A company is connected with another person ("A") if– (a) A has control of the company …'. Control for these purposes is defined in *Corporation Tax Act 2010, s 450*, which broadly provides that a person has control of a company if he exercises direct or indirect control over the company's affairs. For these purposes the rights of any 'associate' of a person are attributed to that person in determining whether that person has control of a company (*Corporation Tax Act 2010, s 451(4)(c)*). *Corporation Tax Act 2010, s 448(1)(a)* provides that any partner of a person is an 'associate' of that person. Consequently, as Alfred is in partnership with Betty and Carl he will be an 'associate' of both, and attributing the rights and powers of Betty and Carl in relation to BC Ltd to Alfred would mean that Alfred would be treated as possessing the whole of the share capital of BC Ltd, and therefore he would be treated as controlling BC Ltd. Therefore, Alfred is connected to BC Ltd by virtue of *Corporation Tax Act 2010, s 1122(3)(a)*, and is consequently a corresponding partner in relation to BC Ltd.

(3)   BC Ltd is entitled to 100% of the property after the transfer. We choose to apportion this 40% to Alfred, 40% to Betty and 20% to Carl.

539

(4)   Alfred's partnership share immediately before the transaction is 40%, and the proportion apportioned to him under (3) above is also 40%, so his lower proportion is 40%. For Betty, her partnership share immediately before the transaction is 40%, and the proportion apportioned to her under (3) is 40%, so her lower proportion is 40%; for Carl, his partnership share immediately before the transaction is 20%, and the proportion apportioned to him under (3) above is 20%, so his lower proportion is 20%.

(5)   The sum of the lower proportions is 40% Alfred plus 40% (Betty) plus 20% (Carl), which is 100%.

The consideration for SDLT purposes is therefore MV × (100 − 100)%, which is nil. It can therefore be seen that where all of the partners in a partnership are individuals the incorporation of the partnership should not give rise to a charge to SDLT.

In these circumstances there is an apparent conflict with the rule in *FA 2003, s 53* that a transfer to a connected company is deemed to be at not less than market value. However, HMRC have confirmed at SDLTM 34170 that the partnership rules override *s 53*.

It might seem attractive for a sole proprietor, who wishes to incorporate his property business, to seek an escape from the SDLT market value rule in *FA 2003, s 53* (see **11.5**) by (say) introducing one or family members as partners in the business, prior to its incorporation, in the hope of obtaining the SDLT result outlined in **Example 11.14**. However, it may be expected that HMRC will look carefully at any attempt to exploit these provisions to avoid an SDLT charge. For example, HMRC, as a matter of principle, may challenge whether there is a genuine partnership. There is also no 'safe' period between the sole proprietor introducing a partner to the business and the incorporation of the business. Although the partnership rules contain no specific anti-avoidance rules which would impact such arrangements, it is possible that either the SDLT general anti-avoidance provision in *FA 2003, ss 75A–75C* (see **11.9** et seq) or the GAAR (see **11.29**) could be applied.

At the time of writing (June 2018), it is understood that the Welsh Revenue Authority will be updating the draft LTT partnership guidance to reflect the fact that the partnership provisions in *LTTADT(W)A 2017, Sch 7, paras 21, 22* (transfer of land from a partnership) will override the deemed market value rule in *LTTADT(W)A 2017, s 22* where land is transferred out of *a* partnership and the partners in that partnership are individuals who are connected with the purchaser which is a company.

As the LBTT technical guidance is silent on the matter, it is not known whether Revenue Scotland take a similar view regarding the interaction of *LBTT(S)A 2013, Sch 17, paras 20, 21* (transfer of land from a partnership) and the market value rule in *LBTT(S)A 2013, s 22*. It is suggested that until this point is clarified in Revenue Scotland's technical guidance, the views of Revenue Scotland should be sought in relation to any transaction where this is an issue.

Focus

When a new lease is granted SDLT, LBTT or LTT must be calculated separately on any rent, and on any premium or deemed premium, which is payable. The two components are then simply added to give the tax liability. When calculating the tax liability on the grant of a lease the length of the lease is taken as the term specified in the lease, ignoring any break clauses, other right to terminate early, or any right to extend or renew. In circumstances where successive leases of substantially the same premises are granted, and those leases are linked (see **11.56**), the second and subsequent leases are effectively treated as extending the earlier lease (see **Example 11.15**). In certain circumstances, the assignee of an existing lease may inherit the obligation to pay future tax or the assignment of the existing lease may be taxed as the grant of a new lease (see **11.61–11.66**). Anyone acquiring a second-hand lease should therefore check whether it will be subject to these special rules and seek protection from unexpected tax liabilities by way of warranties, indemnities, retentions, etc. Where a new lease is granted which supersedes a previous lease of substantially the same premises, which itself was subject to the SDLT, LBTT or LTT regime, overlap relief may be available (see **11.67**).

Leases

11.55   When a new lease is granted or deemed to be granted, SDLT, LBTT or LTT must be calculated separately on any rent, and on any premium or deemed premium, which is payable (*FA 2003, Sch 5*; *LBTT(S)A 2013, Sch 19, Parts 2 and 3*; *LTTADT(W)A 2017, Sch 6, paras 28–36*). The two components are then simply added to give the SDLT, LBTT or LTT liability. As in other cases, any VAT chargeable must be included in both rent and premium. However, if VAT arises as a result of the landlord exercising the 'option to tax' *after* the effective date of the transaction, this does not have to be taken into account (*FA 2003, Sch 4, para 2*; *LBTT(S)A 2013, Sch 2, para 2*; *LTTADT(W)A 2017, Sch 4, para 2*).

11.56   To calculate the SDLT, LBTT or LTT on the rent, it is first necessary to establish the amount of rent to be taken into account for each year of the lease. Once the rent for each year is determined (or estimated if uncertain at the outset), the net present value (NPV) of that rent over the life of the lease must be calculated, using the formula and discount rate specified in the legislation (*FA 2003, Sch 5, paras 3, 8; LBTT(S)A 2013, Sch 19, Part 2; LTTADT(W)A 2017, Sch 6, paras 29–32*). The discount rate is 3.5%.

Under SDLT and LTT the tax liability on rents payable under a lease is finally determined by reference to the rent payable during the first five years of the term of the lease, with the rent payable in relation to year 6, and subsequent years, deemed to be the highest rent for any consecutive 12-month period in the first five years (*FA 2003, Sch 15, para 7(3); LTTADT(W)A 2017, Sch 6, para 10(3)*).

There is no such rule in relation to LBTT – any known increases throughout the life of the lease will have to be taken into account in the initial assessment of tax, apart from increases in line with the retail price index, consumer price index or similar index of inflation. But even then the position will not be finally determined. In addition, assuming the grant of the lease was notifiable to Revenue Scotland, or becomes notifiable, the tenant will be required to review the position every three years during the period of the lease, and again when either the lease is assigned or the lease comes to an end, to determine the tax due (*LBTT(S)A 2013, Sch 19, Part 4*). The intention under the LBTT legislation is to adjust the tax payable at these three-yearly intervals to take account of increases in rent or other changes to the terms of the lease. The requirement for submission of new returns every three years (whether or not there is additional LBTT to pay) may be an onerous obligation for some lessees, especially those that have numerous leased premises. This is a fundamental difference between the taxation of leases under SDLT/LTT and that under LBTT.

When calculating the tax liability on the grant of a new lease for the purposes of each of SDLT, LBTT and LTT, the length of the lease is taken as the term specified in the lease, ignoring any break clauses, other right to terminate early, or any right to extend or renew (*FA 2003, Sch 17A, para 2; LBTT(S)A 2013, Sch 19, para 19; LTTADT(W)A 2017, Sch 6, para 2*). However, if any right to extend or renew is subsequently exercised, the resulting further lease or extension may be linked with the original lease, whether successively or not (see **11.57**).

Mitigating or deferring the tax liability on the grant of a new lease

---

Focus

A tenant being granted a new lease may defer part of the charge to SDLT, LBTT or LTT by entering into a lease for a shorter period but with an option to renew which, if exercised, would extend the lease to the desired term.

11.57   It is important to note that break clauses are ignored. This means that if a tenant enters into a ten-year lease with a right to break after five years, the right to break is ignored and the lease is taxed as a ten-year lease. In contrast, if that same tenant enters into a five-year lease with an option to renew after five years the tenant should be in the same commercial position, as he can choose whether or not to exercise the right to renew after five years, however, in this case, initially, the lease will be taxed as though it were a five-year lease, rather than a ten-year lease, resulting in a reduced tax liability. However, if the option to renew is exercised, the planning will likely only give rise to a deferral of tax, rather than an absolute saving, as the original five-year lease and the new five-year lease are likely to be treated as successive linked leases (see **11.57**). Lease transactions may be 'linked' with other land transactions (whether or not involving other leases) if they form part of a single scheme, arrangement or series of transactions between the same vendor and purchaser or persons connected with them (*FA 2003, s 108; LBTT(S)A 2013, s 57; LTTADT(W)A 2017, s 8*).

Successive linked leases

Focus

A subsequent lease of substantially the same premises will be treated as being 'linked' with the grant of the earlier lease if, at the time the earlier lease was granted, there was an agreement (explicit or implied) that the next lease would be granted. In these circumstances the subsequent lease is treated as extending the earlier lease. If the earlier lease contained an option for the grant of a further lease the leases are probably linked.

11.58   In circumstances where successive leases of substantially the same premises are granted, and those leases are linked (see **11.56**), the second and subsequent leases are effectively treated as extending the earlier lease (*FA 2003, Sch 17A, para 5; LBTT(S)A 2013, Sch 19, para 23; LTTADT(W)A 2017, Sch 6, para 6*). As each lease in the series after the first is granted (or substantially performed), any SDLT, LBTT or LTT return made in respect of the earlier lease must be amended to show details for what is now deemed to be a longer lease, and any additional tax must be paid. Additional tax may arise in relation to rent (the NPV of the rent will have increased because the deemed lease is for a longer period) and/or premium (if a further premium is paid, the premiums must be aggregated both to determine the rate of tax and to calculate the amount of tax).

Example 11.15 – Successive linked leases

Harriet granted Ian a five-year lease of a warehouse situated in England commencing 1 September 2013 for a premium of £130,000 and a yearly rent of £50,000. The lease was executed on the start date without prior substantial performance. The lease agreement included an option for Ian to take a further five-year lease commencing on 1 September 2018 at the same rent, on payment of a further premium of £130,000. Ian exercises the option; the second lease is executed on 1 August 2018 (ie one month before commencement) and the additional premium is paid on 1 September 2018.

During September 2013, Ian submitted a SDLT return for the five-year lease, with premium £130,000 and yearly rent of £50,000. The total SDLT paid was £2,057, comprising £1,300 on the premium (charged at 1% because the rent is £1,000 or more) and £757 on the rent. A further SDLT return is needed in respect of the second lease. The leases are linked, so there is deemed to be a ten-year lease at a flat rental of £50,000 per annum and a premium of £260,000, commencing 1 September 2013. The SDLT on such a lease is £10,458, comprising £7,800 on the premium (at 3%) and £2,658 on the rent. The SDLT paid on the original lease is deducted, leaving £8,401 payable as a result of the second lease. Although the second lease is not 'substantially performed' early, it is executed one month before commencement, so the further SDLT return and payment are due 30 days after execution, that is no later than 31 August 2018. As the leases are linked, such that there is deemed to be a single lease, for a term of 10 years, commencing on 1 September 2013, it is the SDLT bands and rates which applied on 1 September 2013 which are used to calculate the SDLT on the 'extended' lease, and not those which applied on 1 August 2018 when the second lease was granted.

Successive leases are not necessarily linked. If, when the first lease was granted, there was no agreement (explicit or implied) that the next lease would be granted, and if the next lease was negotiated independently of the first, they are not likely to be linked. However, if the first lease contained an option for grant of a further lease, they probably are linked. HMRC, Revenue Scotland or the Welsh Revenue Authority are likely to assume that successive leases are linked unless there is clear evidence to the contrary.

Tax charge on rent

11.59 To calculate the SDLT, LBTT or LTT charge on rent, in simple terms, the rent for the first 12 months is divided by 1.035 to give its discounted value, the rent for the second 12 months is divided by (1.035)2, and so on to the end of the term of the lease. The discounted rent figures for all years are then totalled. If this total does not exceed the relevant threshold (for SDLT these are currently £150,000 for non-residential or mixed property, or £125,000 for residential property: *FA 2003, Sch 5, para 2*), no SDLT is chargeable on the rent. The threshold for both LBTT and LTT for non-residential or mixed property is also £150,000.

Under LBTT the grant of a lease over residential property is an exempt transaction and no LBTT is therefore payable on rent or any premium payable under a lease of residential property (*LBTT(S)A 2013, Sch 1, para 3*).

Under LTT no tax is chargeable on rent on the grant of a lease over residential property, however, tax is chargeable on any premium payable in the normal way (*LTTADT(W)A 2017, Sch 6, para 27*).

11.60 It should not be unduly difficult to set up a spreadsheet to perform the tax calculation for the grant of a new lease. However, each of the tax authorities provide a calculator for this purpose on their respective websites. The calculators work for most cases, provided the correct information is input, and its use is recommended. However, it is purely a mechanical aid. It will not detect whether the correct information is entered, and the taxpayer will be held responsible if the calculator gives incorrect answers because incorrect information has been entered. Therefore, it is important to have a full understanding of the nature of the transaction when entering information into the calculator, to guard against errors. A copy of the output (printed or electronic) should be retained in case of any future query.

Example 11.16 – Calculation of NPV

On 1 May 2018, Jeremy agrees to grant Kate a 10-year lease of a hotel situated in England at an annual rent of £25,000, including VAT, and for a premium of £250,000. There is an upwards-only rent review on the fifth anniversary. The lease is granted on 1 July 2018 without previously having been substantially performed. The effective date is therefore 1 July 2018, and the rent review is due on 1 July 2023. The SDLT can be calculated manually as follows:

Year	Actual rent for SDLT purposes	Discounted rent
1	£25,000	£24,154
2	£25,000	£23,337
3	£25,000	£22,548
4	£25,000	£21,786
5	£25,000	£21,049

Year	Actual rent for SDLT purposes	Discounted rent
6	£25,000	£20,337
7	£25,000	£19,649
8	£25,000	£18,985
9	£25,000	£18,343
10	£25,000	£17,722
Total discounted rent		£207,910
Less zero rate band		(£150,000)
SDLT charged at 1% on		£57,910
SDLT on rent		£579
SDLT on premium: £250,000 (£150,000 at 0% + £100,000 at 2%)		£2,000
Total SDLT (on rent and premium)		£2,579

Assignment of a lease

11.61 In a straightforward case, the transfer of an existing lease to a new tenant (with no other change in terms and conditions) will be subject to SDLT, LBTT or LTT in the same way as the transfer of any other interest in land. The new tenant will be subject to tax on any consideration given: (a) to the outgoing tenant; and (b) to the landlord (apart from ordinary rent) – for example, a lump sum paid to persuade the landlord to consent to the transfer. However, neither the rent payable under the lease nor any premium paid to the landlord by the outgoing tenant (for example, in return for the landlord agreeing to release the tenant from the lease) will figure in the new tenant's SDLT, LBTT or LTT liability. Equally, the assumption of normal tenant's obligations and undertakings (such as to maintain the property) do not count as consideration (*FA 2003, Sch 17A, para 17; LBTT(S)A 2013, Sch 19, para 16; LTTADT(W)A 2017, Sch 6, para 18*).

Liabilities which fall on transferee

Focus

For the purposes of SDLT and LTT, if, during the first five years of the term of the lease, the rent payable was uncertain or variable, then the new tenant (the assignee) inherits the obligation to file any further land transaction returns, and to pay any additional SDLT or LTT due, once the uncertainty is resolved.

11.62 However, many cases are not straightforward, and it is always necessary for the new tenant to understand the full history of the lease, in order to determine whether the transfer, or the nature of the lease itself, may give rise to other tax liabilities and obligations. Additional obligations may arise in two situations. The first, which only applies in relation to SDLT and LTT, is where during the first five years of the term of the lease the rent was uncertain or variable when the lease was granted. If the lease is transferred to a new tenant before the SDLT or LTT liability is resolved, the new tenant inherits the obligation to make any necessary disclosures or further returns and to pay any additional SDLT or LTT once the uncertainty is resolved.

In relation to LBTT, as discussed at **11.56**, on the assumption that the grant of the lease was notifiable to Revenue Scotland, or becomes notifiable, the existing tenant will be required to review the position when the lease is assigned to determine the tax due (*LBTT(S)A 2013, Sch 19, para 11*). The subsequent three-yearly reviews of the tax payable in relation to the lease must then be done by the assignee (*LBTT(S)A 2013, Sch 19, para 28*).

Relief claimed on original grant of lease

Focus

If, on the grant of a new lease, one of a number of reliefs was claimed (see **11.66**), the first assignment of that lease, which does not itself qualify for one of those reliefs (not necessarily the same relief as applied on the grant of the lease), will be taxed as the grant of a new lease for the remaining term of the actual lease and at the rent payable by the transferee. It is, therefore, important that any person acquiring an existing lease understands the history of that lease and, in particular, whether any of the specified reliefs were claimed when the lease was granted.

11.63 The second situation where the new tenant may incur unexpected liabilities is where one of a specified list of reliefs (see **11.66**) was claimed when the lease was granted (*FA 2003, Sch 17A, para 11*; *LBTT(S)A 2013, Sch 19, para 27*; *LTTADT(W)A 2017, Sch 6, para 22*). If nothing has already happened to cause claw-back of that relief, the first transfer of the lease which does not itself qualify for one of the specified list of reliefs is treated as the grant of a new lease for the remaining term of the actual lease and at the rent payable by the transferee. This means, for example, if there has been any rent increases between the dates of original grant and transfer, the current (higher) rent will be taken into account in calculating any SDLT or LTT payable. SDLT, LBTT or LTT is also payable, in the normal way, on any premium which the new tenant pays to the landlord. In relation to SDLT, HMRC consider that any amount paid by the new tenant to the outgoing tenant in respect of the transfer is also within the charge to SDLT, as would be the case for a straightforward transfer of a lease on which no relief had previously been claimed. It is logical that this should be the case, but it is by no means clear that the wording of the legislation supports this view. It is considered likely that Revenue Scotland and the Welsh Revenue Authority will take a similar view in relation to LBTT and LTT.

11.64 SDLT, LBTT or LBTT is chargeable on the transferee, and not on the original lessee who claimed the relief. Therefore, strictly, this is not a claw-back, it is merely a modification of the normal rules for determining a purchaser's tax liability. However, as **Example 11.17** below demonstrates, in practice the rules do lead to an effective claw-back of part of the relief previously claimed, even though it is the new owner/tenant who has responsibility for the resulting SDLT, LBTT or LTT which is payable.

11.65 The rules are not subject to any kind of time limitation: they apply on disposal of the lease at any time in its life. Anyone acquiring a second-hand lease should therefore check whether it will be subject to these special rules and seek protection from unexpected tax liabilities by way of warranties, indemnities, retentions or whatever other protection which may be thought appropriate.

11.66 For SDLT, the special rules apply where any of the following has been claimed on the grant of a lease:

(1)   group, reconstruction or acquisition relief;

(2)   sale and leaseback relief;

(3)   charities relief;

(4)   relief for transfers involving public bodies; or

(5)   any relief brought forward from the stamp duty rules by regulations under *FA 2003, s 123(3)*.

Care must be taken in relation to the last of these as there are many specialised reliefs, for acquisitions by certain bodies, which are provided in legislation other than *Finance Acts* and which fall within category (5).

However, the special rules do not apply if the transfer itself qualifies for any of the reliefs in the list (not necessarily the same relief as that previously claimed), provided the transferee claims the relief in an SDLT return.

In relation to both LBTT and LTT the list of reliefs is similar but there are some differences and the relevant legislation should therefore be checked (*LBTT(S)A 2013, Sch 19, para 27; LTTADT(W)A 2017, Sch 6, para 22*).

Example 11.17 – Transfer of lease after relief claimed

On 1 March 2011, V plc granted a 25-year lease over commercial property situated in England to its subsidiary, W Ltd, at a rent of £100,000 per annum, subject to five-yearly upwards-only rent reviews. Group relief was claimed. On 1 March 2016, the scheduled rent review leads to the rent being increased to £110,000. On 1 June 2018, W Ltd transfers the lease to an unrelated company X Ltd. X Ltd pays W Ltd £180,000 for the transfer and takes over all of the other terms and conditions of the lease.

X Ltd is not entitled to any of the reliefs in the list detailed at **11.66** above, so the transfer is treated as the grant of a new lease for the remaining 17 years 9 months of the term, at an initial yearly rent of £110,000. This charge effectively claws back part of the relief claimed by W Ltd when the lease was first granted. In this example, it is worse than a simple claw-back because it also takes account of the new, higher rent. In addition, in this example, X Ltd pays a sum to W Ltd for the transfer, and this will be subject to SDLT as if it was a premium. The SDLT chargeable on the premium would be £600 (£150,000 at 0% plus £30,000 at 2%). This particular example is worse than that. When X Ltd takes on the lease, a further rent review is due in less than five years. Therefore, the acquisition is treated as a grant of a lease for uncertain or variable rent. It will be necessary for X Ltd to review the position when the rent review occurs, submitting a further SDLT return and paying further SDLT as appropriate.

Overlap relief

Focus

Where a new lease is granted which supersedes a previous lease of substantially the same premises, and that previous lease had not reached the end of its term, then it may be possible to reduce the SDLT, LBTT or LTT charge on the grant of the new lease by claiming credit for any tax paid on the grant of the previous lease to the extent it related to rent arising in the period of overlap, that is, the period which would have been covered by the previous lease but is now covered by the new lease.

11.67 Where a new lease is granted which supersedes a previous lease of substantially the same premises, which itself was subject to the SDLT regime, overlap relief may be available. In calculating SDLT on the new lease, the rent for the 'overlap period' (that is, the period which would have been covered by the old lease but is now covered by the new lease) is reduced by the rent which would have been paid under the old lease if that lease had been left to run its course (*FA 2003, Sch 17A, para 9*). This is not strictly a relief, it is a statutory treatment. Therefore, it is not necessary to claim the 'relief' by answering 'yes' to question 9 of the SDLT1 return form and entering a code. It is sufficient, when calculating SDLT on the new lease, to reduce the rent by the amount of the rent which would have been paid under the old lease. The relief may also apply where the new lease is granted to someone who acted as guarantor under the original lease, or in certain circumstances where the new lease is granted to someone who was a sub-tenant of the original lessee.

This relief is in addition to the general principle set out in *FA 2003, Sch 17A, para 16* that, where a lease is surrendered in consideration of the grant of another, neither the surrender nor the grant counts as consideration for the other.

A similar statutory treatment applies under LBTT (*LBTT(S)A 2013, Sch 19, para 24*) and under LTT (*LTTADT(W)A 2017, Sch 6, para 7*).

Focus

Higher rates of SDLT, LBTT and LTT apply to purchases of additional residential properties (dwellings) such as second homes and buy-to-let properties. However, the legislation is much wider than that and, for example; the higher rates apply to first purchases of residential properties by companies and other non-individual purchasers. Where the higher rate applies, 3% is added to each of the residential property tax rates for SDLT, LBTT and LTT. Where two or more dwellings are acquired under a *single transaction* the SDLT and LTT legislation does not allow there to be a combination of higher rate and 'normal' residential rate transactions, and the transaction will either be a 'higher rates transaction' or it will not. Thus, if two or more dwellings are to be acquired from the same vendor, and those dwellings satisfy the conditions for the higher rate of SDLT to apply, and one of the dwellings to be acquired is replacing, or may become a replacement for, the individual's only or main residence, that dwelling should be acquired under a separate contract to avoid a charge to the higher rate. However, if, as part of a single transaction, six or more dwellings are acquired, the SDLT/LTT rates for non-residential or mixed use transactions will apply (*FA 2003, s 116(7); LTTADT(W)A 2017, s 72(9)*). In such circumstances, the purchaser can therefore choose whether to apply the non-residential rates by *not* making a claim for multiple dwellings relief. If a claim for multiple dwellings relief is made, the higher rates of SDLT and LTT will apply if the conditions are satisfied (see **Example 11.16**).

Acquisition of dwellings – higher rate of tax

11.68 With effect from 1 April 2016, higher rates of SDLT apply to purchases of additional residential properties (referred to in the legislation as 'dwellings'), such as second homes and buy-to-let properties. In fact, the legislation is much wider than the original policy description and, for example, applies to first purchases of residential properties by companies and other non-individual purchasers. The legislation can be found in *FA 2003, Sch 4ZA* ('Stamp Duty Land Tax: Higher Rates for Additional Dwellings and Dwellings Purchased by Companies') and it imposes an additional 3% SDLT charge on chargeable transactions falling within its provisions.

A transaction which falls within the legislation is referred to as a 'higher rates transaction' (*FA 2003, Sch 4ZA, para 2(1)*).

The higher rates of SDLT are as follows:

Consideration (£)	Rate of SDLT on additional dwellings – 'effective date' on or after 1 April 2016
Not exceeding £125,000	3%
£125,001 to £250,000	5%
£250,001 to £925,000	8%
£925,001 to £1,500,000	13%
Exceeding £1,500,000	15%

The legislation which imposes the higher rate of SDLT (*FA 2003, Sch 4ZA*) is complex and a full explanation of the regime can be found in *Stamp Taxes 2018/19* (Bloomsbury Professional). Reference should also be made to the HMRC Guidance Note (November 2016), which is headed 'Stamp duty land tax: Higher rates for purchases of additional residential properties'. The guidance includes some helpful examples and a series of 'Questions and Answers'.

A calculator is available at https://www.tax.service.gov.uk/calculate-stamp-duty-land-tax which will calculate the SDLT chargeable on a 'higher rates transaction'.

Meaning of 'higher rates transaction'

11.69 Where there is only one purchaser, a transaction will be a 'higher rates transaction' if it falls within any of the five scenarios detailed in the legislation by reference to that single purchaser (*FA 2003, Sch 4ZA, para 2(2)*).

Where there are two or more purchasers it is necessary to take each of the purchasers in turn and determine whether, by reference to any of those purchasers, the transaction falls within any of the five scenarios detailed in the legislation; if so, then it is a 'higher rates transaction' (*FA 2003, Sch 4ZA, para 2(3)*).

Which of the five scenarios a transaction falls within is generally determined by three factors as follows:

(a)   whether or not the purchaser is an individual;

(b)   whether a single 'dwelling' or multiple 'dwellings' are being acquired; and

(c)   where multiple 'dwellings' are being acquired whether the 'chargeable consideration' for only one of the dwellings, or for more than one of the 'dwellings', amounts to £40,000 or more.

Broadly, if the purchaser of the dwelling is an individual, and after the acquisition the purchaser, or his or her spouse or civil partner, own another dwelling, the transaction is likely to be a higher rates transaction unless the individual is replacing his or her sole or main residence, the consideration given for the dwelling is less than £40,000 or the interest acquired in the dwelling is subject to a lease which at the 'effective date' of the transaction has an unexpired term of more than 21 years. Alternatively, if the purchaser of the dwelling is not an individual, for example, it is a company, the transaction will be a higher rates transaction provided the consideration given for the dwelling is £40,000 or more and the purchased dwelling is not subject to a lease which at the 'effective date' of the transaction has an unexpired term of more than 21 years. Where the purchaser is not an individual, it is therefore irrelevant whether the purchaser owns another dwelling at the time the dwelling is acquired or whether a sole or main residence is being replaced. It should be noted that this is a high-level summary of complex legislation and the detailed legislation should always be considered to determine whether the acquisition of a dwelling is a higher rates transaction.

11.70   The higher rates of SDLT will not apply to the acquisition of the following:

- **Non-residential or mixed use properties.** For example if, as a single transaction, an individual is acquiring a house with a garden and grounds together with some agricultural land close by, but clearly not part of the garden and grounds of the house, and not required for the proper enjoyment of the house and its gardens and grounds, then that transaction should be treated as the acquisition of mixed-use property (ie both residential and non-residential property is being acquired) and the SDLT higher rates should not apply to any part of the transaction.

- **Transactions for which the 'chargeable consideration' given for the acquisition of the single dwelling is less than £40,000.** It should, however, be noted that the £40,000 amount is not a 0% band and, if the transaction is chargeable to the SDLT higher rates, it is chargeable on the whole of the consideration and not only the amount in excess of £40,000.

- **Caravans, houseboats and mobile homes.** This is on the basis that these items are moveable and payments in relation to such items are not generally chargeable to SDLT. However, if the moveable asset became sufficiently fixed to the land so as to become a fixture (ie in law the item has become part of the land), SDLT may be chargeable and the SDLT higher rates may apply if the relevant conditions are satisfied.

- **Enveloped residential properties.** The higher rates of SDLT will not apply to the acquisition of a single dwelling for more than £500,000 if the single rate of SDLT of 15% applies to that transaction by virtue of *FA 2003, Sch 4A*. However, where such a transaction also includes the acquisition of a dwelling to which the 15% rate does not apply, the deemed separate transaction may be subject to the higher rates of SDLT if it meets the conditions in any of the five scenarios set out in the legislation.

The 15% single rate of SDLT applies where an interest in a single dwelling is acquired, for actual or deemed chargeable consideration of more than £500,000, either by a company, by a partnership whose partners include one or more companies, or on behalf of a collective investment scheme. 'Dwelling' is defined so as to exclude buildings such as student halls of residence, care homes and the like. There are provisions for apportionment where a single transaction includes interests in dwellings and other properties. It is not possible to take advantage of the relief for transfers of multiple dwellings (see **11.72**) to reduce the rate charged. Anti-avoidance provisions seek to prevent avoidance of the higher rate by fragmenting the purchase (*FA 2003, s 55A* and *Sch 4A*). There are, however, a number of reliefs available from the 15% single rate including:

(a) properties used in the course of 'a qualifying property rental business'; and

(b) properties used for the purposes of a trade that is run on a commercial basis with a view to a profit.

(*FA 2003, Sch 4A, para 5(1)(aa) and (1)(ab)*)

FA 2003, s 116(7) – reclassification of residential property as non-residential where six or more properties are transferred in a single transaction (see **11.71**) – has no application in determining whether the 15% rate applies to a transaction. This is because the 15% single rate of SDLT applies to the acquisition of an interest in a single dwelling for a chargeable consideration of more than

£500,000, and it is irrelevant whether the acquisition of that single dwelling is part of a single transaction under which five or more other separate dwellings are acquired, such that *FA 2003, s 116(7)* would reclassify the transaction as an acquisition of non-residential property.

The stated purpose of the 15% single rate of SDLT is to discourage the 'enveloping' of high value residential properties within corporate shells, a practice which allows future transfers to be made free of SDLT by transferring the interests in the corporate shell rather than the property. As such, it may be regarded as an anti-avoidance provision.

There is no similar punitive rate of tax within either the LBTT or LTT regimes, presumably on the basis that house prices in Scotland and Wales are lower, and there is little evidence of high value residential properties being transferred to corporate entities to avoid a future charge to tax.

A number of dwellings acquired under a single transaction

Focus

Where two or more dwellings are acquired under a single transaction, the legislation does not permit there to be a combination of higher rate and 'normal' rate transactions, and the transaction will either be a 'higher rates transaction' or it will not. Therefore, if two or more dwellings are to be acquired from the same vendor, and those dwellings satisfy the conditions for the higher rate of SDLT to apply, and one of the dwellings to be acquired is replacing, or may become a replacement for, the individual's only or main residence, that dwelling should be acquired under a separate contract. Provided that separate contract is legally independent from any of the other contracts, the higher rate of SDLT should not apply to its acquisition, or in due course, on a disposal of the previous only, or main, residence, a claim can be made that the higher rates do not apply.

11.71 Where two or more dwellings are acquired under a *single transaction* the legislation does not allow there to be a combination of higher rate and 'normal' residential rate transactions, and the transaction will either be a 'higher rates transaction' or it will not. Thus, if two or more dwellings are purchased in the same transaction, and at least two of those dwellings satisfy the relevant conditions, the transaction will be a 'higher rates transaction', and the higher rates will apply to all of the dwellings acquired under the transaction. This is irrespective of whether the individual owns an interest in another dwelling at the end of the day on which the acquisition is made, or whether one of the purchased dwellings replaces an individual's sole or main residence.

The legislation does not define what is meant by 'a single transaction' but it is considered that it means one contract between the same vendor and purchaser (and not including parties connected with the vendor and purchaser) for the acquisition of the agreed number of properties. Thus, if two or more dwellings are to be acquired from the same vendor, and those dwellings satisfy the conditions for the higher rate of SDLT to apply, and one of the dwellings to be acquired is replacing, or may become a replacement for, the individual's only or main residence, that dwelling should be acquired under a separate contract. Provided that separate contract is legally independent from any of the other contracts, the higher rate of SDLT should not apply to its acquisition, or in due course, on a disposal of the previous main residence, a claim can be made that the higher rates do not apply.

Interaction with multiple dwellings relief

Focus

The higher rates of SDLT will apply to any claim for multiple dwellings relief if the relevant conditions for that regime to apply are satisfied. However, even if the higher rates of SDLT do apply, a claim for multiple dwellings may still be worthwhile and may reduce the SDLT liability. If, as part of a single transaction, six or more dwellings are acquired, the SDLT rates for non-residential or mixed use transactions will apply. A purchaser can, therefore, choose to apply the non-residential rates by *not* making a claim for multiple dwellings relief where six or more dwellings are acquired as part of a single transaction.

11.72 Where two or more dwellings are acquired as part of a single transaction, or under a number of 'linked transactions', it may be possible to reduce the aggregate SDLT liability by making a claim for multiple dwellings relief. The higher rates of SDLT will apply to claims for multiple dwellings relief if the relevant conditions in any of the five scenarios set in the legislation are satisfied. However if, as part of a single transaction (see **11.71**), six or more dwellings are acquired, the SDLT rates for non-residential or mixed use transactions will apply (*FA 2003, s 116(7)*). In such circumstances the purchaser can therefore choose whether to apply the non-residential rates by *not* making a claim for multiple dwellings relief. However, see **Example 11.17** where a claim for multiple dwellings relief is made in relation to linked transactions.

Example 11.18 – Acquisition of six or more dwellings as part of a single transaction

Ewan purchases a block of eight flats situated in England for £750,000. If a claim for multiple dwellings relief is made, the average consideration per flat would be £93,750 (£750,000/8) and the SDLT payable would be £22,500 (average price of £93,750 × 3% × 8 flats – a 3% SDLT rate applies to the purchase of a dwelling for £93,750 as the additional SDLT rate applies). If no claim is made for multiple dwellings relief then the non-residential SDLT rates will apply (six or more dwellings are being acquired as part of a single transaction) as follows:

Purchase price	Rate	SDLT
£	%	£
150,000	0	Nil
100,000	2	2,000
500,000	5	25,000
750,000		27,000

In this case it would be beneficial to make a claim for multiple dwellings relief as this would reduce the SDLT liability from £27,000 to £22,500.

Linked transactions

Focus

Neither the legislation nor the HMRC guidance makes it clear how linked transactions are to be taxed if one transaction is chargeable at normal SDLT rates and a second transaction is to be taxed at the higher rate. The calculation is further complicated if a claim for multiple dwellings relief is made in relation to the linked transactions. **Example 11.19** below sets out the author's understanding as to how the SDLT liability should be calculated in these circumstances.

11.73 Transactions are linked if they form part of a single scheme, arrangement or series of transactions between the same vendor and purchaser or, in either case, persons connected with them (*FA 2003, s 108*). Connected persons are as defined in *CTA 2010, s 1122*. As discussed in **11.71**, if an individual acquires two or more dwellings in a *single transaction* the legislation does not permit the acquisition of one dwelling to be charged at the normal rates and the acquisition of another dwelling to be charged at the higher rates. However, neither the legislation nor the HMRC Guidance Note (November 2016 – 'Stamp duty land tax: Higher rates for purchases of additional residential properties') makes it clear how *linked transactions* are treated if, for example, one transaction is chargeable at normal SDLT rates and the second transaction at the higher rate. The calculation is further complicated if a claim for multiple dwellings relief is made in relation to the linked transactions. It is understood, however, that the SDLT liability should be calculated as set out below in **Example 11.19**.

Example 11.19 – Linked transactions where one is taxed at normal SDLT rates and the second is taxed at the higher SDLT rates

On 11 March 2018, under *separate contracts*, Campbell agrees to acquire two houses from a developer, one of which he intends to use as his main residence and the other he will let out to third parties. On 14 August 2018, Campbell sells his previous main residence and completes the contract for the purchase of his new main residence for a consideration of £450,000. On 24 November 2018, Campbell completes the purchase of the buy-to-let property for a consideration of £550,000.

Campbell must file a land transaction return, and pay the SDLT, on the acquisition of his new main residence by 13 September 2018. As Campbell is replacing his main residence the normal SDLT rates apply and the liability is calculated as follows:

Purchase price	Rate	SDLT
£	%	£
125,000	0	Nil
125,000	2	2,500
200,000	5	10,000
450,000		12,500

Following completion of the acquisition of the buy-to-let property on 24 November 2018 Campbell must file a land transaction in relation to that transaction, by 24 December 2018, and pay SDLT at the higher rates as the dwelling is being acquired to let and Campbell is not replacing his main residence. As the purchase of the main residence and the buy-to-let properties are 'linked transactions', the SDLT liability is calculated as follows:

Aggregated purchase price	Rate	SDLT
£	%	£
125,000	3	3,750
125,000	5	6,250
675,000	8	54,000

Aggregated purchase price	Rate	SDLT
£	%	£
75,000	13	9,750
1,000,000		73,750

The SDLT payable in relation to the buy-to-let property would therefore be £40,562 (£550,000/£1,000,000 × £73,750).

The revised calculation of the SDLT liability in relation to the new main residence, using the normal rates of SDLT, would be as follows:

Aggregated purchase price	Rate	SDLT
£	%	£
125,000	0	Nil
125,000	2	2,500
675,000	5	33,750
75,000	10	7,500
1,000,000		43,750

The amended SDLT liability in relation to the acquisition of the new main residence would therefore be £19,687 (£450,000/£1,000,000 × £43,750). The total SDLT payable would therefore be £60,249 (£40,562 + £19,687).

However, if Campbell makes a claim for multiple dwellings relief it is understood that the SDLT liability should be calculated as set out below.

The average consideration per house would be £500,000 and the SDLT payable at the higher rates would be as follows:

Purchase price	Rate	SDLT
£	%	£
125,000	3	3,750
125,000	5	6,250
250,000	8	20,000
500,000		30,000

The total SDLT payable would therefore be £60,000 (£30,000 × 2 houses) and the amount payable on the buy-to-let property would be £33,000 (£550,000/£1,000,000 × £60,000).

The SDLT payable at the normal rates based on an average consideration per house would be as follows:

Purchase price	Rate	SDLT
£	%	£
125,000	0	Nil
125,000	2	2,500
250,000	5	12,500
500,00		15,000

The total SDLT payable would therefore be £30,000 (£15,000 × 2 houses) and the amount payable on the replacement main residence would be £13,500 (£450,000/£1,000,000 × £30,000).

The total SDLT payable if a multiple dwellings relief claim is made would therefore be £46,500 (£33,000 + 13,500), which compares to a liability of £60,249 if no claim for multiple dwellings relief is made. It is therefore beneficial for Campbell to make a multiple dwellings relief claim.

Campbell must file an amended land transaction return by 24 December 2018, in relation to the purchase of his new main residence and pay the additional SDLT due of £1,000 (£13,500 – £12,500).

He must also file a land transaction return by 24 December 2018 in relation to the purchase of the buy-to-let property and pay the SDLT due of £33,000.

The author understands that this is how the calculation should be carried out in relation to linked transactions however it is suggested that confirmation of the calculation methodology be obtained from HMRC.

LTT – higher rates for residential property transactions

11.74 The rate applied to each of the LTT bands, on a purchase of additional residential properties, and the purchase of first residential properties by companies and other non-natural persons, is increased by 3% under a regime which mirrors the higher rates of SDLT provisions described in **11.68** et seq (*LTTADT(W)A 2017, Sch 5*).

LBTT – additional dwellings supplement

Focus

There are some significant differences between the 'additional dwellings supplement' regime which applies for the purposes of LBTT and the higher rates of SDLT regime.

11.75   In response to the introduction of the higher rate of SDLT on purchases of additional residential properties, and ostensibly to avoid distortions in the property market between Scotland and the rest of the UK, the Scottish Government also introduced a higher rate of LBTT for the purchase of additional residential properties. The higher rate of LBTT, which is referred to as the 'additional dwellings supplement', applies from 1 April 2016. Like its SDLT equivalent, it is also much wider than the policy description and it applies to first purchases of residential properties by companies and other non-individual purchasers. There are, however, some important differences between the two regimes. As discussed above in **11.70**, under SDLT the higher rate does not apply to the acquisition of mixed-use properties whereas under LBTT, the higher rate would apply, with a just and reasonable apportionment of the consideration being made between the residential and non-residential elements of the property. Under SDLT an individual has 36 months to sell his old sole or main residence and claim a refund of the additional rate of SDLT paid, whereas under LBTT, the period is 18 months. Where the LBTT additional rate applies, it adds 3% to each of the LBTT rates, including the 0% rate. The LBTT additional rate, however, does not apply if the chargeable consideration for the transaction is less than £40,000.

Focus

Annual tax on enveloped dwellings (ATED) applies when an interest in a single dwelling, with a value of more than £500,000, is held by a company, partnership with a corporate partner or a collective investment scheme, in any chargeable period beginning on each 1 April. The tax applies to dwellings situated in any part of the UK. A specified amount of tax is payable dependent upon the value of the property. A number of reliefs are available from the tax including where the dwelling is held by a property trader, property developer or for the purposes of a property rental business. If a property is to be transferred out of a company etc, to avoid an ongoing charge to ATED, care should be taken if debt is involved as a charge to SDLT, LBTT or LTT may arise.

Annual tax on enveloped dwellings

11.76 *Finance Act 2013, Pt 3 (ss 94–174* and *Schs 33–35)* introduced a new tax known as annual tax on enveloped dwellings, or ATED.

A detailed, in-depth explanation of the tax may be found in *Property Taxes 2018/19* (Bloomsbury Professional).

The key attributes of ATED are as follows:

(1)　the tax applies when an interest in a single dwelling, with a value of more than the threshold, is held by a company, partnership or collective investment scheme at any time in the 'chargeable period'. It applies to a partnership only if the partners include one or more companies;

(2)　the tax applies to 'chargeable periods', being years from 1 April to 31 March. The first chargeable period for properties with a value of more than £2m was that commencing 1 April 2013. The first chargeable period for lower value properties commenced on 1 April 2015 in relation to properties with a value of more than £1m but not more than £2m and from 1 April 2016 to properties with a value of more than £500,000 but not more than £1m;

(3)　the amount of tax payable for each chargeable period depends on:

(a)　the value of the interest in the dwelling; and

(b)　whether the interest is held for the whole chargeable period;

(4)　it is a self-assessment tax;

(5)　there are reliefs for properties held by certain entities;

(6)　there are anti-avoidance provisions; and

(7)　interest, penalty and enforcement rules apply and are similar to those applying to SDLT.

The amounts of tax shown in the table below are those which apply for the years commencing 1 April 2017 and 2018.

Despite the introduction of LBTT in relation to land situated in Scotland, and LTT in relation to land situated in Wales, the ATED regime continues to apply to properties situated in Scotland and Wales if the relevant conditions are satisfied.

Value	Tax	Tax
More than £500,000 but not more than £1m	£3,500	£3,600
More than £1m but not more than £2m	£7,050	£7,250
More than £2m but not more than £5m	£23,550	£24,250

Value	Tax	Tax
More than £5m but not more than £10m	£54,950	£56,550
More than £10m but not more than £20m	£110,100	£113,400
More than £20m	£220,350	£226,950

11.77 It may be decided to transfer the property out of the company to prevent future liability to ATED. Care is needed if this is to be done without creating a liability to SDLT, LBTT or LTT depending upon the location of the property. Provided that the company is debt-free, the property can be transferred as a distribution in the winding up of the company and no SDLT, LBTT or LTT charge will normally arise. However, if the company has debt – typically in the form of a mortgage secured on the property – transfer in return for the shareholder taking on the debt will be a transfer for consideration and liable to SDLT, LBTT or LTT.

In relation to SDLT, HMRC have confirmed that, where the debt is owed to the shareholder so that it simply disappears when the company is wound up and the property transferred to the shareholder, this will not be regarded as giving consideration. However, if there is a third party debt and the shareholder provides funds for it to be paid off (whether by loan, gift or by subscription for further shares), HMRC will consider whether *FA 2003, s 75A* applies (see **11.9** et seq). If they consider that the provision of funds to pay off third party debt is 'involved in connection with the disposal' of the property to the shareholder, HMRC will seek to apply *FA 2003, s 75A* and charge SDLT as if the third party debt had been assumed by the shareholder. See SDLTM04042 for details of HMRC's views on this matter.

Focus

Where a vendor (A) sells or leases a 'major interest' (freehold or leasehold interest) in a property to a purchaser (B) and, in consideration (wholly or partly), B grants a lease (the 'leaseback') to A out of that major interest, the leaseback may be exempt from SDLT, LBTT or LTT. The relief has no impact on the tax payable by B on the acquisition of the freehold or leasehold interest. However, if the original transfer agreement requires the leaseback to be granted and if this requirement reduces the value of the interest originally transferred, SDLT on that original transfer will only be charged on the reduced value. The only consideration permitted for the initial sale/lease (which must not be a sub-sale), other than the grant back of the lease, is cash and/or the assumption, satisfaction or release of a debt; A and B must not be companies in a group relationship, such that they could qualify for group relief.

Sale (or lease) and leaseback relief

11.78   Where a vendor (A) sells or leases a 'major interest' (freehold or leasehold interest) in a property to a purchaser (B) and, in consideration (wholly or partly), B grants a lease (the 'leaseback') to A out of that major interest, the leaseback may be exempt from SDLT, LBTT or LTT (*FA 2003, s 57A; LBTT(S)A 2013, Sch 3; LTTADT(W)A 2017, Sch 9*). The only other consideration permitted for the initial sale/lease (which must not be a sub-sale) is cash and/or the assumption, satisfaction or release of a debt; A and B must not be companies in a group relationship, such that they could qualify for group relief.

The purpose of the relief is to facilitate the transfer of properties from occupiers to investors. Absent the relief, it might be possible for the same effect to be achieved by A first granting a lease to a group company, with SDLT, LBTT or LTT group relief being claimed on the grant of the lease, then transferring the property, subject to this lease, to B. However, the relief allows a simpler process and resolves doubts as to whether anti-avoidance provisions might otherwise apply.

The relief itself does not reduce the SDLT, LBTT or LTT charge on the original transfer from A to B. However, if the original transfer agreement requires the leaseback to be granted and if this requirement reduces the value of the interest originally transferred, SDLT on that original transfer will only be charged on the reduced value. HMRC's agreement with this analysis is confirmed at SDLTM04020a Example 3. It is not known whether Revenue Scotland or the Welsh Revenue Authority agree with this analysis.

A fairly commonplace commercial arrangement is for an owner to transfer a property to a developer in return for the developer redeveloping the site and granting the owner a long lease of part of the new development. The developer recoups his cost and makes a profit by selling the rest of the development to third parties. It is understood that HMRC consider that the lease back to the owner does not qualify for sale and leaseback relief, because the developer's agreement to redevelop the site amounts to non-qualifying consideration (ie it is not cash or the assumption, satisfaction or release of a debt). SDLT is therefore due on both the original sale to the developer and the lease back to the owner. It is likely that Revenue Scotland and the Welsh Revenue Authority will also deny the relief in these circumstances, however, their view should be confirmed if the point is relevant to any transaction.

Focus

Stamp duty is only chargeable on documents effecting transfers of 'stock and marketable securities' and interests in partnerships owning stock

---

and marketable securities. It is usually only necessary to stamp a transfer document for stock and marketable securities, if they are 'chargeable securities' for the purposes of SDRT, so that the SDRT charge has to be cancelled or to ensure that any registration formalities can be completed. The simplest form of planning is, therefore, to structure a transaction so that there is a transfer of securities which are not chargeable securities for SDRT purposes – for example, shares in a non-UK incorporated company – and then choose not to present the transfer document for stamping (see **Example 11.20**). A major pitfall in relation to stamp duty concerns the measurement of consideration and, more specifically, the impact of the contingency principle. Under this principle, any ascertainable consideration which may be payable on the happening of a particular contingency is regarded as payable and subject to stamp duty. In contrast with SDLT, LBTT or LTT, there is no relief or adjustment if the consideration eventually proves not to be payable (see **Example 11.22**). A stamp duty relief is available for the transfer of all of the shares in one company (T) to another company (A) in return for A issuing shares *pro rata* to the shareholders of T in circumstances where the shareholdings in A immediately after the acquisition mirror those in T immediately prior to the acquisition. In addition, the acquisition of T by A must be effected for bona fide commercial reasons, must not have a tax avoidance motive and must not be part of an arrangement to secure that a particular person obtains control of A (*FA 1986, s 77*).

Stamp duty planning

11.79   Stamp duty is currently chargeable only on documents effecting transfers of 'stock and marketable securities' and interests in partnerships owning stock and marketable securities.

11.80   In relation to transfers of partnership interests, the simplest planning is to choose not to present any transfer document for stamping. This is effective provided the parties are satisfied that there is no need for a stamped document. A stamped document is normally only required if it is to be produced in evidence or used for other official purposes. Therefore, the most likely occasions on which a stamped document may be needed are in relation to a dispute between the parties or in order to prove to HMRC that the transfer has taken place. In practice, it appears to be rare for transfers of partnership interests to be stamped. An alternative approach is to structure the transaction so that there is no transfer document which may require to be stamped. For example, an effective transfer of a partnership interest might be achieved by the outgoing partner withdrawing capital from the partnership, and the incoming partner introducing the same amount of capital. This may be regarded as a transfer for some purposes. However, it should not be necessary to execute a transfer and no stamp duty liability should arise.

11.81   It is usually only necessary to stamp a transfer document for stock and marketable securities, if they are chargeable securities, so that the SDRT charge is cancelled and any registration formalities may be completed. The simplest form of planning is, therefore, to transfer securities which are not chargeable securities – for example, shares in a non-UK incorporated company – and then choose not to present the transfer for stamping (but beware the risk of making them chargeable securities by keeping the share register in the UK).

11.82   Some planning has taken the form of attempting to make the consideration wholly unascertainable, but there are risks in such an approach. In particular, in the case of *L M Tenancies 1 plc v IRC* [1996] STC 880, HMRC succeeded in arguing that linking consideration to the price of a publicly traded security, when that price was not likely to change much, did not make the consideration wholly unascertainable. It is safer to make the consideration ascertainable but low.

Example 11.20 – Minimising consideration for stamp duty purposes

Non-UK company Foreign SA owns UK company Reid and Wright Ltd (current value £9m) and non-UK company Investment Sarl (current value £1m). Foreign SA has agreed to sell both companies to Conglomerate Pty Ltd for £10m. A direct transfer of the Reid and Wright Ltd shares for £9m would cost Conglomerate Pty Ltd £45,000 stamp duty (£9m × 0.5%). However, Foreign SA first transfers Reid and Wright Ltd to Investment Sarl in return for the issue of two shares by Investment Sarl. Investment Sarl already has 1,000 shares in issue, all held by Foreign SA. Further (and this is very important), under the company law and constitution governing Investment Sarl, all shares are identical, giving shareholders identical rights in all respects. Foreign SA then transfers Investment Sarl to Conglomerate Pty Ltd for £10m.

For stamp duty purposes, the consideration given by Investment Sarl for the shares in Reid and Wright Ltd is simply the value of the two shares issued. This will be 2/1002ths of the £10m value of Investment Sarl after the transfer of the Reid and Wright Ltd shares, or £19,960. Most of the value of Reid and Wright Ltd flows into the Investment Sarl shares already held by Foreign SA, but this value shift does not count as consideration for stamp duty purposes. The stamp duty on this transfer will be £100 (after rounding – £19,960 × 0.5%). The SDRT, on the other hand, would probably be £45,000 (£9m × 0.5%) based on the increase in the value of Foreign SA's holding of shares in Investment Sarl, ie £9m. It is therefore essential that the transfer of Reid and Wright Ltd shares to Investment Sarl is submitted for stamping, in order to cancel the SDRT charge which otherwise arises.

It is unlikely to be necessary to pay stamp duty on the transfer of the shares in Investment Sarl to Conglomerate Pty Ltd because the shares of Investment Sarl are not UK registered.

This planning technique can also be used where the transaction is a sale of the shares in a UK incorporated company.

Cameron owns all of the shares in Blue Skies Ltd, an unlisted UK incorporated company with a market value of £20m. Cameron agrees to sell all of his shares in Blue Skies Ltd to Stewart for £20m. A direct sale of the shares in Blue Skies Ltd for £20m would result in a stamp duty liability of £100,000. Instead of a direct sale, the following transactions are entered into:

- Cameron incorporates a company in Jersey (Newco) and subscribes £999 for 999 shares of £1 each.

- All of the legal formalities in relation to the issue of the shares by Newco, and registering Cameron as the owner of those shares, are completed.

- Cameron transfers Blue Skies Ltd to Newco in return for the issue of one share of £1 by Newco.

For stamp duty purposes, the consideration given by Newco should be the value of the one share issued. This will be 1/1000ths of the £20,000,999 value of Newco after the transfer of the Blue Skies Ltd shares, or £20,001. Most of the value of Blue Skies Ltd flows into the Newco shares already held by Cameron but this value shift does not count as consideration for stamp duty purposes. The stamp duty on this transfer will be £105 (after rounding – £20,001 × 0.5%). The SDRT, on the other hand, would probably be £100,000 (£20m × 0.5%) based on the increase in the value of Cameron's holding of shares in Newco, ie £20m. It is therefore essential that the transfer of the Blue Skies Ltd shares to Newco is submitted for stamping, in order to cancel the SDRT charge which otherwise arises. It is unlikely to be necessary to pay stamp duty on the transfer of the shares in Newco to Stewart because the shares of Newco are not UK registered.

Stamp duty pitfalls

11.83　A major risk in relation to stamp duty is linked with the SDRT risk identified in **Example 11.20**. Transfers of many shares and securities may theoretically be within the charge to stamp duty but, if the securities are outside the charge to SDRT, there is normally no imperative to stamp the transfers. If shares or debt instruments unintentionally become chargeable securities, an SDRT charge will arise on an agreement to transfer for valuable consideration. This may be cancelled by stamping a transfer, but that in itself will require payment of stamp duty unless the transfer qualifies for a relief. In either case the transfer must be stamped within six years of the agreement to transfer, or it becomes impossible to cancel the SDRT charge.

11.84   A related difficulty arises where different assets are transferred by means of the same document. This is unlikely to be a problem where UK shares are transferred by means of a stock transfer form, because that form is normally only valid to transfer UK shares. However, where the transfer takes the form of, say, a declaration of trust, it would be possible for a single document to transfer UK and non-UK shares. This should generally be avoided.

Example 11.21 – Mixed assets in a single transfer

Reptile plc, a UK company, agrees to pay market value to buy the shares of two companies, Lizard Ltd and Gecko Ltd, from Reptile's 51% shareholder, Zoo Inc. Lizard is a UK company worth £100,000, Gecko is a Cayman-registered company worth £1m. The agreement gives rise to an SDRT liability of £500 (£100,000 at 0.5%). Reptile intends immediately to carry out a reorganisation which will involve further transfers of the shares of these companies, so it is agreed that Zoo Inc will execute a declaration of trust in favour of Reptile in relation to the shares. Zoo Inc will then eventually transfer the shares to the final shareholder within Reptile's group. Because Reptile is a UK company and makes payment out of a UK bank account, it is likely that any transfer will relate to 'any matter or thing to be done' in the UK and so will be liable to stamp duty. If a single declaration of trust is executed, it will be necessary to pay stamp duty in relation to both the Lizard and the Gecko shares – a total of £5,500 (£1,100,000 at 0.5%) – before the transfer can be regarded as 'duly stamped' thus cancelling the SDRT charge. To avoid the problem, separate declarations of trust should be completed for the two companies, allowing Reptile to stamp only the one relating to the Lizard shares. Alternatively, the SDRT could be paid on the Lizard shares and the declaration of trust could be left unstamped, but only if Reptile is happy it will never be necessary to produce the declaration of trust for any UK official purpose.

11.85   Many other risk areas relate to specific reliefs (especially group and reconstruction reliefs). It is important to note that the restrictions which may lead to denial of these reliefs only apply at the time of the transaction in respect of which relief is claimed. There is no question of stamp duty reliefs being clawed back as a result of subsequent events, although relief may be denied if there were arrangements for those subsequent events at the time of the original transaction. This is in contrast to the equivalent reliefs under SDLT, LBTT and LTT, where a change in control too soon after the original transaction, even if unrelated to that original transaction, may lead to retrospective disallowance of the relief.

11.86 The other major pitfall in relation to stamp duty concerns the measurement of consideration and, more specifically, the impact of the contingency principle. Under this principle any ascertainable consideration which may be payable on the happening of a particular contingency is regarded as payable and subject to stamp duty. In contrast with SDLT, LBTT or LTT, there is no relief or adjustment if the consideration eventually proves not to be payable.

Example 11.22 – Contingency principle

David buys the shares of a trading company from Goliath for consideration of £1m payable now, plus further consideration equal to 20% of the company's trading profits for the next two years. The further payment is subject to a ceiling of £2m. Meanwhile, Saul buys a similar company from Goliath for consideration of £1m, plus 20% of the company's trading profits for the next two years with no ceiling specified. David will have to pay stamp duty of £15,000 (£1m certain plus £2m contingent, at 0.5%) but Saul will only have to pay £5,000 (£1m at 0.5%), because the further consideration is wholly unascertainable.

Unfortunately, there is often a conflict between the desire to minimise stamp duty and the commercial need to limit the contingent consideration. As a result, David's fact pattern is perhaps seen more often than Saul's.

Relief for insertion of new holding company

11.87 In the heading to the legislation (*FA 1986, s 77*), this is described as relief for acquisitions, but the paragraph heading above is more accurate. No stamp duty is chargeable on a transfer of shares in one company (T) to another company (A) where the transfer forms part of an arrangement for A to acquire all of the shares in T, provided certain conditions are satisfied. The conditions which must be satisfied are as follows:

(1)   the transfer forms part of an arrangement under which A acquires the whole of the issued share capital of T;

(2)   the acquisition is effected for bona fide commercial reasons and does not form part of a scheme or arrangement of which the main purpose, or one of the main purposes, is avoidance of liability to stamp duty, stamp duty reserve tax, income tax, corporation tax, or capital gains tax;

(3)   the only consideration for the acquisition is the issue of shares in A to the shareholders of T;

(4)   every shareholder of T immediately before the acquisition is a shareholder of A after the acquisition, and holds the same proportion of shares in A as previously held in T;

(5)   if T has shares of different classes, the classes and relative proportions by number of each class are replicated in A; and

(6)   the proportion of shares of A of any particular class, in issue or held by any particular shareholder, is the same as the proportion of shares of that class in T, in issue or held by that shareholder, immediately before the acquisition.

(7)   at the time the instrument transferring the shares in T to A is executed there are no 'disqualifying arrangements' (as set out in *FA 1986, s 77A*) in existence (*FA 2016, s 137(5)*). This additional condition only applies to instruments executed on or after 29 June 2016, however, the 'disqualifying arrangement' could have been entered into at any time, including before 29 June 2016.

The reference to different share classes relates to the rights and characteristics of the shares, not particularly how they are labelled. So, if shares are labelled class A and class B purely to identify by which member of a consortium they are held and if they have identical rights etc, they will not be regarded as being of different classes. But shares which have different voting or dividend rights or different nominal values will be regarded as being of different classes.

The legislation specifically provides that the references to 'shares' and 'share capital' also include a reference to 'stock' (*FA 1986, s 77(4)*). For these purposes, 'stock' takes its meaning from the *Stamp Act 1891, s 122* by virtue of *FA 1986, s 114(4)*. The *Stamp Act 1891, s 122* definition of 'stock' refers not only to shares or share capital but also includes the *funded debt* of any county council, corporation, company, or society in the UK, or of any foreign or colonial corporation or society. Although not clear from this definition, HMRC Stamp Taxes takes the view that for these purposes 'funded debt':

'... means "debt instruments" *issued* by the target company such as bonds and loan notes (irrespective of whether the note is exempt or chargeable to stamp tax if transferred independently) which can be traded separately in a manner akin to that of equities.'

They go on to state:

'We would not expect "funded debt" to include mortgages, bank loans, financing and overdrafts within the meaning because these are not normally issued and tradeable instruments with the characteristics of equity' (STSM042415).

Consequently, for an arrangement to qualify for relief under *FA 1986, s 77*, A must not only acquire all of the shares in T, it must also acquire any 'funded debt' issued by T, and A must then issue 'funded debt' which mirrors that issued by T. Therefore, if T, for example, has issued loan notes to a shareholder or a third party, A must acquire those loan notes, along with all of the shares in T, and A must then itself issue identical loan notes to the shareholder or third party. However, mortgages, bank overdrafts, bank term loans, etc can be ignored.

11.88   Prior to 29 June 2016 there was no denial of the relief under *FA 1986, s 77* if the control of A changed shortly after the share-for-share exchange transaction took place. However, HMRC's view is that the purpose of *FA 1986, s 77* relief is to ensure that there is no stamp duty charge where there is no real change of ownership of T following its acquisition by A. Consequently, a new condition was introduced in relation to instruments executed on or after 29 June 2016 which requires that, at the time the instrument transferring the shares in T to A is executed, there must be no 'disqualifying arrangements' in existence.

The term 'arrangement' is widely defined as including '… any agreement, understanding, or scheme (whether or not legally enforceable)' *(FA 1986, s 77A(6))*.

An arrangement will be a 'disqualifying arrangement' if it is reasonable to assume that the purpose, or one of the purposes, of the arrangement is to secure that *(FA 1986, s 77A(2))*:

● a particular person obtains control of A; or

● particular persons together obtain control of A.

For these purposes, 'control' is defined in *Corporation Tax Act 2010, s 1124* and means the power of a person (P) to secure by the means of holding shares or the possession of voting power in relation to A (or any other body corporate) so that the affairs of A are conducted in accordance with P's wishes. In addition, 'control' can be exercised as a result of any powers conferred by the articles of association or other document regulating the affairs of A (or any other body corporate). Consequently, any arrangement under which a person or persons could acquire the majority of the shares in A, or the majority of the voting power in A, would be a 'disqualifying arrangement'. In the author's view, for such an arrangement to exist, the particular person or persons would have to have been identified at the time the relevant transfer is executed.

11.89   It is specifically provided that the following are not 'disqualifying arrangements' *(FA 1986, s 77A(3) and (4))*:

● any issue of shares by A as consideration for the acquisition of T within *FA 1986, s 77(3)*; and

- 'relevant merger arrangements' – such an arrangement will exist where the share-for-share exchange transaction between the shareholders of T and A is followed by a second share-for-share exchange between the shareholders in a second company (B) and A. The second share-for-share exchange transaction must meet the following conditions (*FA 1986, s 77A(4)*):

(1) the only consideration given by A for the acquisition of the whole of the share capital of B must be the issue of shares to the shareholders of B;

(2) the acquisition of B must be for bona fide commercial reasons and must not form part of an arrangement with a main purpose of avoiding a liability to stamp duty, stamp duty reserve tax, income tax, corporation tax or capital gains tax;

(3) after the acquisition of B has been made each person who was a shareholder of B must be a shareholder of A;

(4) after the acquisition of B the shares in A must be of the same class as were the shares of B immediately prior to the acquisition and the relative proportions by number of each class of shares in B must be replicated in A; and

(5) the proportion of shares of A of any particular class held by any particular shareholder, must be the same as the proportion of shares of that class in B held by that shareholder, immediately before the acquisition of B.

In assessing whether conditions (4) and (5) above are satisfied, the shares issued by A for the acquisition of T are ignored since, if this were not done, the conditions could never be satisfied. (*FA 1986, s 77A(4)(c)(i)*).

As for *FA 1986, s 77*, the definition of 'shares' and 'share capital' within the meaning of 'relevant merger arrangements' includes 'funded debt' (see **11.87**). This means that A must not only acquire all of the share capital of B but must also acquire any 'funded debt' issued by B, and must then issue identical 'funded debt' to the persons who previously held the 'funded debt' in B (*FA 1986, s 77(4)*).

The exception of 'relevant merger arrangements' from 'disqualifying arrangements' means that *FA 1986, s 77* relief will still be available in relation to A's acquisition of T even if there is an 'arrangement' for A to acquire the whole of the share capital of another company (B), provided that under that 'arrangement' all of the shareholders of B are to become shareholders of A, the shareholdings (class and proportion of shares held) in A are a mirror image of the shareholdings in B immediately before the acquisition of B (ignoring the shares issued by A to acquire T), and the acquisition of B is for bona fide commercial reasons and not part of a scheme to avoid any of the taxes listed in point (2) above.

If the 'relevant merger arrangements' or the share for share exchange within *FA 1986, s 77(3)*, which are excluded from 'disqualifying arrangements', are part of a wider scheme or arrangement which has a purpose of securing that a particular person(s) obtains control of A (see **11.88** for the meaning of control), but those wider arrangements do not fall within *FA 1986, s 77A(3)*, then the 'relevant merger arrangements' or share for share exchange are treated as 'disqualifying arrangements' *(FA 1986, s 77A(5))*. See HMRC commentary on this point at STSM042470.

11.90   The introduction of the additional condition that there must be no 'disqualifying arrangements' in existence at the time the instrument transferring T to A is executed will prevent the insertion of a new holding immediately prior to a sale to a third party (or the introduction of a new controlling shareholder). However, in these circumstances, it should still be possible to claim the relief provided the new holding company is inserted before any third party purchaser (or new controlling shareholder) is identified, and therefore before any 'arrangement' to sell A to a particular person (or to introduce a new controlling shareholder into A) has come into existence. This is confirmed by HMRC at STSM042480 where it is stated:

> 'A reorganisation in advance of a potential future sale where no purchaser(s) has been identified will not be disqualifying arrangements for the purposes of *FA 1986, s 77A*. For example, there may be a reorganisation of a group of companies to make the group better structured for sale in the future.'

It has been suggested by various commentators that *FA 1986, s 77A* was introduced to prevent the avoidance of stamp duty on the takeover of a UK company. This could be achieved by A, a non-UK incorporated company, being placed on top of T in such a way that no stamp duty was payable as relief was available under *FA 1986, s 77*, with a third party purchaser then acquiring A free of UK stamp taxes, as no UK stamp tax is generally payable on the acquisition of shares in a non-UK incorporated company. However, in the author's view, it is unlikely that *FA 1986, s 77* relief would have been available in any event as *FA 1986, s 77(3)* provides that the relief is not available if the main purpose, or one of the main purposes, of A's acquisition of T is the avoidance of stamp duty.

At STSM042470, HMRC give their views on arrangements which would not constitute disqualifying arrangements for the purposes of *FA 1986, s 77A*. They make the point that for *s 77A* to apply:

> 'there have to be arrangements where it is reasonable to assume that a purpose or one of the purposes of the arrangements is for a particular person or persons together to obtain control of the acquiring company.'

They go on to say that:

> 'In respect of "particular persons together" this is more than a numerical test. It must be reasonable to assume that the parties to the arrangements intend to act in such a way that particular persons together obtain control of the acquiring company.'

This means that in **Example 11.23** below there should not be a disqualifying arrangement for the purposes of *FA 1986, s 77A* provided the incoming shareholder is not acting together with one of the existing shareholders to control the new holding company.

Example 11.23 – No disqualifying arrangement for the purposes
FA 1986, s 77A

Cameron and Rory own 50% each of a trading company ('Tradeco'). Craig agrees to invest cash into Tradeco in return for a 10% shareholding. It is decided to create a new holding company ('Holdco') with a significant share capital to enable Craig to subscribe for shares in Holdco at par. Holdco is incorporated and acquires the existing shares in Tradeco in return for an issue of shares to Cameron and Rory. The shares issued to Cameron and Rory are of the same class as the shares they previously held in Tradeco and the shares are held in the same 50:50 proportion. Shortly after this reorganisation is completed, Craig subscribes cash to Holdco in return for a 10% shareholding. It could be said that there is a change of control of Holdco in these circumstances as following the new investment, Cameron (45%) and Craig (10%) could be said to control Holdco, as could Rory (45%) and Craig (10%). However, provided Craig is not acting together with either Cameron or Rory to control Holdco there should be no disqualifying arrangement for the purposes of *FA 1986, s 77A*.

11.91 The transaction must be part of the acquisition of all of the target company's share capital. If A already holds some shares in T (for example, after stake building in a quoted company) or if any shares of T remain with another shareholder (for example, a dissenting shareholder), the relief will not be available. In practice, therefore, the relief is only of use for insertion of a new holding company by a 100% shareholder or by agreement amongst a group of shareholders with 100% between them. This is most commonly done as a first step in a further reconstruction or reorganisation, or perhaps to put a 'clean' company at the top of a group prior to a stock market initial public offering. However, as discussed above, at the time that T is acquired by A there must be no disqualifying arrangement within the meaning of *FA 1986, s 77A*.

FUTURE REFORM OF STAMP DUTY

11.92   As outlined in **11.7** above, on 10 July 2017 the Office of Tax Simplification (OTS) issued its report in relation to stamp duty on paper documents and recommended its reform, digitalisation and simplification. On 14 August 2017, the Chancellor of the Exchequer responded to the OTS's report and agreed to consider the recommendations carefully, weighing up the benefits of the four main elements of the proposed reforms in the context of the ongoing reforms to the tax system. It therefore seems likely that the archaic nature of stamp duty will be the subject of fundamental reform in the near future. Some of the planning ideas discussed above may be impacted by any such reform.

Chapter 12

Business and agricultural property relief and woodlands relief

Mark McLaughlin CTA (Fellow), ATT (Fellow), TEP, Tax Consultant, Mark McLaughlin Associates Ltd and The TACS Partnership

Chris Erwood CTA, ATT, TEP, Erwood & Associates Ltd

SIGNPOSTS

- **Business property relief (BPR)** – BPR reduces the value of transfers of relevant business property by a specified percentage. The rate of relief depends on the type of business property. BPR must be claimed, and is subject to certain conditions (see **12.1–12.3**).

- **Business carried on** – BPR does not generally apply in respect of businesses wholly or mainly carrying on certain types of activity, such as making or holding investments (see **12.4–12.8**).

- **Ownership** – No BPR is generally due unless the transferor has owned the relevant business property for a minimum period of two years before the transfer. However, this general rule is subject to certain exceptions, such as for replacement property (see **12.9–12.12**).

- **Practical issues** – Various issues may need to be addressed in respect of BPR. For example, BPR is subject to restriction for 'excepted assets'. In addition, groups of companies may need to structure their activities and assets carefully to ensure that BPR is not inadvertently lost or restricted. BPR is not normally available if the business property is subject to a binding contract for sale at the time of the transfer. Business property transferred within seven years before death may affect the availability of BPR unless certain conditions are satisfied (see **12.13–12.46**).

- **Other planning** – BPR planning opportunities and pitfalls exist in respect of the death estate. Other planning has sometimes included the use of multiple ('pilot') trusts and 'placing' debt to maximise the relief, although the former arrangement was affected by provisions

> (introduced in *F(No 2)A 2015*) on 'same day additions', and the latter is subject to anti-avoidance rules on liabilities (introduced in *FA 2013*). BPR clearance applications may be made to HMRC in some cases (see **12.47–12.61**).
>
> - **Agricultural property relief (APR)** – APR operates to reduce the value of transfers of qualifying property by either 50% or 100%, dependent on the terms of occupation (see **12.62–12.64**).
>
> - **Time qualification** – Unlike its BPR sibling, APR is subject to a two-tier time test which pivots on end use and ownership of the underlying farming activity (see **12.70–12.73**).
>
> - **The 'piggy back' facility** – The landowner can gain access to APR by reference to the qualification of the underlying farmer tenant (see **12.73** and **12.81**).
>
> - **Complexity** – The complex rules surrounding the scope and application of APR should not be understated and as a consequence it remains a risk area for the professional practitioner tempted to 'dabble' (see **12.70–12.71**, **12.85–12.86**, **12.102**).

BUSINESS PROPERTY RELIEF

INTRODUCTION

12.1   Business property relief (BPR) is an important and valuable relief from inheritance tax (IHT). It reduces the value transferred by a transfer of value of certain types of business or business property by a specified percentage. The current rates of BPR are 100% and 50% respectively. The actual rate of relief applied to a transfer depends on the type of business property.

The relief applies to actual or deemed transfers. It is available for lifetime transfers, or to relevant business property included in an individual's estate on death. There are no territorial limits to the relief, so it can apply to business property situated worldwide. BPR also applies to settled property included in the death estate, and is available to trustees in respect of the periodic and exit charges that apply to discretionary trusts, and to most other types of trust following changes introduced in *FA 2006*.

The law on BPR is contained in *IHTA 1984, ss 103–114*. The relief must be claimed. The claimant must therefore be aware of the categories of business property that qualify, and the correct rate of BPR applicable. A number of conditions must be satisfied before the relief is available, and a number of potential traps exist for the unwary.

The first part of this chapter outlines the conditions for BPR, and highlights some planning points and possible pitfalls in connection with the relief.

Conditions

12.2   BPR applies if the value transferred by a transfer of value relates to relevant business property. The categories of business property, and the rates of BPR attributable to them, are broadly as listed below (see *IHTA 1984, ss 104, 105(1)*):

- a business or an interest in a business – 100%;

- control holdings of unquoted securities in a company – 100%;

- unquoted shares in a company – 100%;

- control holdings of quoted shares in a company – 50%;

- land, buildings, plant and machinery used by a company controlled by the transferor, or by a partnership of which the transferor was a member – 50%;

- land, buildings, plant and machinery of a settlement in which the transferor was beneficially entitled to an interest in possession and was used in his business – 50%.

12.3   In the context of companies, the term 'unquoted' applies for BPR purposes to shares listed on the Alternative Investment Market (AIM).

However, shares traded on NASDAQ are currently treated as listed for IHT purposes, and BPR does not apply except (rarely) for controlling shareholdings.

HMRC accepts that many shares traded on the ICAP Securities & Derivatives Exchange Ltd (ISDX) will qualify for BPR, although some shares on the ISDX Main Board will be regarded as listed and so will only qualify for BPR if the transferor had control of the company (and then only at 50%) (see HMRC's Inheritance Tax Manual at IHTM18333).

In general, if a company is not listed on the UK Stock Exchange, or any foreign recognised Stock Exchange, its shares and securities will be unquoted (*IHTA 1984, s 105(1ZA)*). However, in relation to those companies and in general, it is necessary to consider whether the business carried on makes the shares or securities (or a business interest) eligible for BPR. Furthermore, a company that is initially treated as unquoted for BPR purposes (eg by only being listed on the AIM) should be monitored regularly to ensure that it does not subsequently obtain a secondary listing on (for example) a foreign recognised stock exchange.

It is worth noting that securities forming part of a controlling holding in an unquoted trading company (ie securities that give control either by themselves or together with other securities owned by the transferor and any unquoted shares so owned) are eligible for BPR at the 100% rate (*IHTA 1984, s 105(1)(b)*), such as loan notes with rights in general meetings of the company forming part of a single holding giving the holder control.

In the case of land, buildings, plant and machinery used by a company, it is important to note the requirement that the company must be controlled by the transferor. 'Control' for these purposes is defined in *IHTA 1984, s 269*, broadly in terms of the exercise of a majority of voting power on all matters affecting the company as a whole. In *Walding and others (Walding's Executors) v CIR* [1996] STC 13, Mrs Walding held 45 out of 100 shares in a company on her death. Her executors claimed that the deceased had control of the company for BPR purposes, on the basis that 24 shares were in the name of her four-year-old grandson, but the court dismissed the executors' appeal against the Revenue's refusal of a BPR claim on factory units owned by the deceased and occupied by the company.

However, note that a company chairman with a 50% shareholding and a casting vote under the company's articles has been held to have control for these purposes (*Walker's Executors v IRC* [2001] STC (SCD) 86).

It should be noted that the 'related property' provisions (*IHTA 1984, s 161*) apply for the purposes of determining control (*IHTA 1984, s 269(2)*). This can be helpful if, for example, spouses or civil partners each hold shares in the company which are not controlling holdings in isolation, but are deemed to give control as related property. This situation will sometimes be encountered in unquoted companies in particular.

A group structure (see **12.23**) may be considered in appropriate cases, such as to hold the shares in a trading company and also the trading premises, with a view to securing BPR at 100% on the business premises (and shares), as opposed to only 50% if the premises is owned by a controlling shareholder (or no BPR at all, if the shareholder does not hold a controlling interest in the company).

A beneficiary with a qualifying life interest in trust property is treated for IHT purposes as owning the underlying assets. A qualifying life interest for these purposes means an interest in possession within *IHTA 1984, s 49(1)*. If those assets were used in the beneficiary's business on death, they will normally qualify for 100% BPR (*Fetherstonaugh and others v IRC* [1984] 3 WLR 212). As to HMRC's view in relation to lifetime transfers, see **12.12**.

The *Fetherstonaugh* (or '*Finch*' as HMRC refer to it at IHTM25154) case was successfully relied upon by the executor in *Revenue and Customs v Brander (personal representative of the Fourth Earl of Balfour)* [2010] UKUT 300 (TCC), in terms of satisfying the two-year ownership test for BPR purposes (in *IHTA 1984, s 106*; see **12.9** below).

What is a 'business'?

12.4 'Business' has a wider meaning than 'trade' for BPR purposes; it specifically includes a profession or vocation. However, it does not include a business carried on otherwise than for gain (*IHTA 1984, s 103(3)*; see, for example, *Grimwood-Taylor and another (executors of Mallender, deceased) v Inland Revenue Commissioners* [1999] SpC 223). A hobby activity is therefore likely to be excluded unless it can be demonstrated that it has been run in a proper, business-like manner.

Prior to the decision in the *Nelson Dance Family Settlement Trustees* case (see below), it was commonly thought that the transfer of business *assets* (as opposed to a transfer of the business itself) did not qualify for BPR. The *Nelson Dance* case concerned the transfer of some farmland with development value to the trustees of a family settlement. The trustees claimed BPR on the basis that there had been a transfer of value which resulted in a reduction in the value of 'relevant business property' within *IHTA 1984, s 105*. HMRC sought to disallow the BPR claim, but the trustees' appeal was successful. The Special Commissioner ([2008] SpC 682) held that BPR was due on the basis that: 'all that is required is that the value transferred by the transfer of value is attributable to the net value of the business.'

HMRC's subsequent appeal (*Revenue and Customs Commissioners v Trustees of the Nelson Dance Family* [2009] EWHC 71 (Ch)) was dismissed. The High Court held that it was sufficient for BPR purposes that the diminution in value of the transferor's estate by reason of the transfer was attributable to the value of relevant business property. As the land had been used in the farming business, its transfer could be regarded as attributable to the value of the business, and BPR was therefore available on the transfer.

The *Nelson Dance* decision would therefore seem to offer an opportunity for sole traders and partners wishing to transfer business assets (ie not 'excepted assets' – see **12.14**) into trust with the benefit of BPR (and CGT holdover relief in most cases), whilst continuing to carry on the business. Particularly in the case of trading assets, the decision whether to transfer them into trust must be considered carefully if the business interest would qualify for 100% BPR in any event. The same might be said of the investment assets of a 'mixed' trading and investment business which is mainly trading, although a transfer may be attractive if, for example, the business owner wishes to secure CGT entrepreneurs' relief on all assets of the business, on the basis that 'substantial' investments would preclude any relief (*TCGA 1992, s 169L(4)(b)*).

It should be remembered that relevant property trusts are liable to periodic and exit charges for IHT purposes. There are traps for the unwary. For example, on an exit charge in the first ten years of the trust, BPR is ignored when determining the initial value of the asset. This can be problematic if BPR is not available on exit. In addition, a transfer to a relevant property trust of (for example) land with development value could (following *Nelson Dance*) attract BPR, but at the next ten-year anniversary the trustees might be found to hold a mere business asset or a mere investment, in respect of which no relief would be available.

The decision in *Nelson Dance* does not seem to accord with HMRC's interpretation of the BPR rules. HMRC guidance states (at IHTM25152): 'Refer any transfers of value where this case is relied on to Technical'. A future change in the law is possible, so any planning opportunities may be limited.

Focus

Business property is generally precluded from relief if the business consists wholly or mainly of dealing in securities, stocks or shares or land or buildings, or in making or holding investments (*IHTA 1984, s 105(3)*).

There are some limited exceptions, in respect of market makers or discount house businesses carried on in the UK. This exception for market makers was extended with effect from 31 December 2012, to apply BPR if the business concerned is a market maker within the EEA (other than the UK) in a recognised regulated market (*The Inheritance Tax (Market Makers and Discount Houses) Regulations 2012, SI 2012/2903*).

There is also an exception in group situations, if a company's business is wholly or mainly to be the holding company of one or more companies whose business is not an excluded one (*IHTA 1984, s 105(4), (4A)*).

Groups of companies are discussed later in this chapter (see **12.23–12.29**).

Property consisting of farmland, which was let for grazing under seasonal grazing arrangements described as conacre (ie a temporary easement creating a licence to use land) but which, more precisely, were agistment agreements (ie the letting of land for grazing) in Northern Ireland was held to be enough to constitute a business within *IHTA 1984, s 105(1)* on the facts in *McCall and another (Personal Representatives of McClean, dec'd) v Revenue and Customs Commissioners* [2009] NICA 12.

However, the Court of Appeal upheld the conclusion of the Special Commissioner ([2008] SpC 678) that the arrangements could not be viewed as a business of providing grass, but rather as a business of holding an investment, such that BPR was not due. Girvan LJ stated:

> 'The agisting farmer had exclusive rights of grazing; he was entitled to exclude other graziers including the deceased; the deceased could not use the land for any purpose that interfered with the grazing and the letting for grazing was the way in which the deceased decided that the grasslands could be used and exploited as uncultivated grassland short of the creation of a lease. The deceased's business consisted of earning a return from grassland whose real and effective value lay in its grazing potential. The activities which were regarded as just sufficient to lead to the lettings of the land being regarded as a business were all related to enabling that potential value to be released.'

Thus although there was sufficient activity to constitute a business, that business was held to be excluded from BPR, on the grounds that it consisted wholly or mainly of making or holding investments, within *IHTA 1984, s 105(3)*. The Court of Appeal supported the view of the Special Commissioner that the activities of the business consisted in making available its major asset (ie the farm fields) to others for payment, without the separate provision of other goods or services to any substantial degree. The deceased had made the land available, not to make a living on it, but from it; the management activities related to letting the land; it was unlike 'hotel accommodation for cattle' as argued by the taxpayers (as to investment businesses, see **12.15** below). Thus although the letting of land does not necessarily constitute an investment business, the availability of BPR is likely to depend on the nature and extent of other services also provided.

By contrast, in *Vigne Deceased, Personal Representative of the Estate of v Revenue and Customs* [2017] UKFTT 632 (TC), a livery business was held to be a business which was not wholly or mainly one of holding investments (within *IHTA 1984, s 105(3)*), and was therefore eligible for BPR.

Caravan parks

12.5   A number of cases have considered what constitutes a 'business' for BPR purposes. This is particularly so in relation to caravan park businesses, for the purposes of determining whether they were substantially investment in nature due to rental receipts, or whether the trading (eg sales and service) components of the businesses were sufficient to enable them to qualify for BPR.

In *IRC v George and another (executors of Stedman, dec'd)* [2003] EWCA Civ 1763, Lord Justice Carnwath accepted on the facts that a caravan site qualified, commenting that it was '… difficult to see why an active family business of this kind should be excluded from business property relief, merely because a necessary component of its profit-making activity is the use of land'.

HMRC's Inheritance Tax Manual (IHTM) provides a useful insight into its approach following the decision in *George*, and commentary is therefore repeated below. In practice, HMRC are likely to refer caravan park cases in which BPR is claimed to their Technical Group.

'Caravan sites and furnished lettings' (extracts from IHTM25279)

'The judgment in *George* is helpful in clarifying what is to be regarded as either investment or non-investment activity. It makes clear that the provision of services to owner occupiers under the terms of a pitch agreement is largely a non-investment activity. This means that in cases where a large part of the business's activities (measured in both time and money) consists of providing services to residents, we would be more likely to consider that the business was neither wholly or mainly investment in nature. However, we need to be satisfied that the figures for pitch fees, for instance, are not artificially depressed in the accounts in favour of inflated figures for wages or other non-investment expenses.'

'Note also that payments paid by non-owner occupiers may well be primarily rental payments to occupy the caravan/mobile home/chalet, rather than for the provision of services.'

'The judgment in *George* also recognises that the time and money spent on maintaining amenity areas is in part designed to maintain the value of the owner's investment. It follows that the taxpayers are entitled to return a reduced level of investment income by offsetting against it part of the maintenance costs. As this could lead to the net investment income being, proportionally, a smaller part of the overall income of the business we might well conclude in a particular case that the business was neither wholly or mainly one of holding investments.'

'On the other hand, we would also need to take into account the time spent by the owner and/or his employees in the maintenance work. When taken together with other work carried out in the business, the evidence might lead us to conclude that the majority of work done is involved in maintaining the value of the owner's investment. If so, then we would seek to deny the claim under *s 105(3)*.'

'The judgment in *George* also suggests that the holding of land as an investment is separate and distinct from the service element of the business. Finally, when looking at the facts "in the round", trading figures are only a part of the overall picture.'

'When dealing with a claim for business relief on a caravan park, you will need to obtain detailed business accounts, including breakdowns

---

> of both the income and expenditure between the investment and non-investment elements of the business. In addition, you should ask the taxpayers to state precisely what services were provided to the park residents and how long was spent by the deceased (as park owner) and his partners and/or employees providing those services.'

The 'right' business?

12.6 A detailed consideration of what constitutes an eligible business for BPR purposes is outside the scope of this chapter. However, the following points are worthy of note:

- *Property construction* – the restriction on dealing in land and buildings does not prevent a property construction business from qualifying for BPR, such as a building company holding houses or plots as stock in trade for development. However, if a house builder has not built any houses recently and is selling off its land, in HMRC's view the business will not qualify for BPR at the time of the business transfer, on the basis that it consists wholly or mainly of dealing in land and buildings, for which relief is precluded by *IHTA 1984, s 105(3)* (IHTM25266).

  However, in *Executors of Piercy (dec'd) v Revenue and Customs Commissioners* [2008] SpC 687, a property development company owned land on which it had built workshops for letting. The executors of a major shareholder claimed BPR, but HMRC denied it on the ground that the company received substantial investment income and its business was therefore mainly making or holding investments. The executors claimed that the company was still trading: it still held undeveloped land that it wished to develop for housing but had to wait for uncertainty to be resolved concerning proposals for a new railway line.

  The Commissioner found that the land was still held as trading stock, not as an investment, and allowed the appeal. A land-dealing company will not qualify for BPR if it is a speculative trader or dealer, but land-dealing companies that actively develop land or build on land are outside the exclusion. For a company to be wholly or mainly holding investments, the Commissioner held that it must actually have investments: thus holding the land as trading stock was highly relevant.

- *Hotels, nursing homes, etc* – other property-backed businesses such as hotels and nursing homes will also usually qualify for relief, in view of the level of services provided. However, HMRC guidance (at IHTM25277) indicates that BPR in respect of certain types of hotel (ie the 'self-service/

583

budget hotel industry') may be susceptible to challenge: '… you should also ascertain the nature of a "hotel" business to establish whether on the facts it actually falls at the investment end of the spectrum'.

- *Holiday lettings, etc* – HMRC have tended to examine BPR claims in respect of holiday lettings relatively closely, presumably to establish if the activity constitutes a 'business', and if so, whether it is wholly or mainly one of holding investments.

In *HMRC v Personal Representatives of N Pawson, Deceased* [2013] UKUT 050 (TCC), Mrs Pawson owned an interest in a large bungalow ('Fairhaven') on the Suffolk coast at the time of her death. Her executors claimed BPR in respect of the property. Their claim was on the basis that Fairhaven had been used for a holiday letting business, and that it was not disqualified (by *IHTA 1984, s 105(3)*) from being relevant business property on the basis of being a business consisting wholly or mainly of making or holding investments. The First-tier Tribunal (FTT) allowed the executors' appeal ([2012] UKFTT 51 (TC)), finding that the exploitation of Fairhaven had constituted a business, which did not consist wholly or mainly of holding an investment. HMRC appealed.

The Upper Tribunal noted that some business activities carried on at Fairhaven naturally fell on the investment side of the line, but that certain additional services were provided to occupants as part of the holiday letting business. Those additional services comprised: a cleaner/caretaker to clean the property between each letting and carry out regular inspections of the property; space heating and hot water; a television and telephone at the property; being on call to deal with queries and emergencies; and minor matters such as the replenishment of cleaning materials as and when necessary, and the provision of an up-to-date welcome pack (laundry services were also provided, but only after Mrs Pawson's death).

The Upper Tribunal considered that the critical question was whether those additional services prevented the business from being mainly one of holding Fairhaven as an investment. The Upper Tribunal noted that the judgment in *IRC v George* (see **12.5**) made it clear that the provision of such services is 'unlikely to be material' in the case of a property letting business because they were not enough to prevent the business remaining 'mainly' one of property investment. The services provided were considered to be of a relatively standard nature. Looking at the business in the round, in the Upper Tribunal's view there was nothing to distinguish it from any other actively managed furnished holiday letting business, and there was certainly no basis for concluding that the services comprised in the total package were such that the business ceased to be one which was mainly of an investment nature. HMRC's appeal was allowed.

The decisions in *Pawson* (and *George*) were subsequently considered in *Green v Revenue and Customs* [2015] UKFTT 236 (TC), where it was held that lifetime transfers of interests in a furnished holiday lettings business to a settlement were not eligible for BPR, as the First-tier Tribunal decided that the business consisted mainly of making or holding investments.

Similarly, in *Ross v Revenue and Customs* [2017] UKFTT 507 (TC), it was held that a two-thirds share of a partnership that carried on a business of running and managing eight holiday cottages plus two staff flats in Cornwall and a property in Weymouth consisted mainly of making or holding investments, and hence BPR was precluded by *IHTA 1984, s 105(3)*. The First-tier Tribunal referred to the above decisions in *Pawson* and *Green*, and held that (despite the high level of services provided to holiday cottage guests in the present case) the business activity nevertheless consisted mainly of investing in property.

HMRC's guidance in the Inheritance Tax Manual previously indicated that BPR would normally be allowed if the lettings were short term (eg weekly or fortnightly) and there was substantial involvement with the holidaymakers, both on and off the premises. This applied even if the lettings were for only part of the year.

However, HMRC's guidance (IHTM25278) was amended in late 2008 and subsequently. At the time of writing, it states the following:

'HMRC's view is that furnished holiday lets will in general not qualify for business property relief. The income derived from such businesses will largely consist of rent in return for the occupation of property. *There may however be cases where the level of additional services provided is so high that the activity can be considered as non-investment, and each case needs to be treated on its own facts*' (emphasis added).

HMRC's revised approach suggests that the active involvement of the holiday lettings proprietor is of less importance than the degree of service and nature of services offered to guests. In the absence of more specific guidance from HMRC, it would seem logical to assume that the closer the comparison between the holiday accommodation and a traditional hotel in terms of services provided, the better would appear the prospect of securing BPR.

Other types of lettings involving land may fall foul of *IHTA 1984, s 105(3)* in HMRC's view. Their guidance states (at IHTM25280): 'You will need to consider whether the exploitation of land ownership in other ways, such as self-storage, car parks, business parks, DIY livery, moorings or beach huts, is an investment activity'. However, in

Vigne Deceased, Personal Representative of the Estate of v Revenue and Customs [2017] UKFTT 632 (TC) (see **12.4**), the level of services provided to horse owners prevented HMRC's assertion that the livery business in that case was mainly one of holding investments from succeeding.

- *Property lettings* – difficulties can arise with property lettings. For example, in *Clark and another (executors of Clark, dec'd) v HMRC* [2005] SpC 502, a company's business comprised rents from properties it owned (ie investment income), plus trading income from management charges in respect of a number of dwellings owned by family members. Viewed 'in the round', the company's business was held to consist mainly of investments. The company's maintenance of the rented properties was held not to constitute the separate provision of services, but was inherent in the property ownership.

- *Loans* – In *Phillips and others (Executors of Rhoda Phillips, dec'd) v HMRC* [2006] SpC 555, shares in a company which made informal, unsecured loans to related family companies were held to be relevant business property, on the basis that the company's business was making loans, and therefore did not consist wholly or mainly of making or holding investments within *IHTA 1984, s 105(3)*.

'Wholly or mainly'

12.7 The 'wholly or mainly' business test (see also **12.4**) applies to a business, business interest or company shares or securities. For the purposes of determining whether a company satisfies this test, it is necessary to consider all the company's activities 'in the round'. HMRC state the following (at SVM111150):

'It is not possible to lay down any precise ground rules. Each company has to be looked at in the round. It may however be readily accepted that, where the majority of both the tangible asset value and profit of the company is attributable to trading activities, relief is available.'

HMRC's guidance adds that the 'wholly or mainly' test should be considered over a reasonable period prior to the transfer in case of temporary fluctuations in activity and performance.

The likely approach by HMRC in appropriate cases will therefore be to consider the company's activities, assets and income or gains, not only when business property is transferred, but also over what they regard as a 'reasonable period' leading up to it (IHTM25265).

In *Brown's Executors v IRC* [1997] STC (SCD) 277, HMRC refused a BPR claim on shares, on the grounds that the business consisted wholly or mainly of making investments at the date of death. The company had traded as a nightclub, but the business was sold before the shareholder's death and the proceeds held on a short-term bank deposit pending the acquisition of a new nightclub. However, the executors' appeal was upheld.

12.8

Focus

An important point to note is that BPR is only denied if the business activities mentioned in *IHTA 1984, s 105(3)* (ie dealing in securities, stocks and shares, dealing in land or making or holding investments) represent more than 50% of all business activities.

Thus, for example, the shareholder of an unquoted company undertaking 51% trading activities and 49% investment business activities can benefit from full BPR if the other relief conditions are satisfied. Conversely, if trading activities represent 49% and investment business activities 51%, no BPR is due at all.

In practice, it may be difficult to measure the respective activities accurately. The Special Commissioner's decision in *Farmer and another (executors of Farmer, dec'd) v IRC* [1999] SpC 216 offers some guidance on the possible approach to this problem.

In *Farmer*, the deceased carried on the business of farming and letting properties which were surplus to the requirements of the farm. The net rental profits were greater than the net farming profits, but the farming assets had a higher value at death than the properties used for letting. HMRC denied BPR on the basis that the business consisted mainly of making or holding investments.

However, the executors' appeal was upheld. The Special Commissioner held that it did not follow that the level of net profit was the only or principal test in *IHTA 1984, s 105(3)*. The business and its activities had to be looked at 'in the round'. The letting of properties was subsidiary to the main farming activity, and although they were more profitable in the overall context of the business, this was not conclusive. The overall context of the business, capital employed, the time spent by employees and consultants and the levels of turnover supported the conclusion that the business consisted mainly of farming.

Subsequently, in *Executors of Piercy (dec'd) v Revenue and Customs Commissioners* [2008] SpC 687 (see **12.6**), the Special Commissioner held that a property development company whose land was stock did not thereby hold investments, such that its business could not be excluded for BPR purposes by *IHTA 1984, s 105(3)* as consisting wholly or mainly of making or holding investments. This was notwithstanding that slow trading meant that some of the development sites could not be sold and had to be leased, thereby generating substantial investment income for the company.

The issue of mixed usage was considered in *Revenue and Customs v Brander (personal representative of the Fourth Earl of Balfour)* [2010] UKUT 300 (TCC), in the context of a landed estate. In that case, the Earl of Balfour inherited a life rent interest in the family estate in 1968, including land used for farming. The activities carried on included in-hand farming and management of commercial woodlands, but there was also substantial letting activity. He entered into a farming partnership with his nephew in November 2002. In June 2003, he died. HMRC considered that BPR was not due. However, the First-tier Tribunal held that the ownership requirements of *IHTA 1984, s 107* as to replacement property were satisfied, and that *IHTA 1984, s 105(3)* did not apply to deny BPR.

The Upper Tribunal dismissed HMRC's subsequent appeal. In deciding the meaning of 'the business of holding investments' the tribunal said the test to be applied is that of the intelligent businessman who would be concerned with the use to which the asset is being put and the way it was being turned to account. Furthermore, the question of whether a business consists wholly or mainly of making or holding investments is a decision of fact for the decision-maker, who should look at the business in the round to form an overall picture of the relative importance of the investment and non-investment activities in that business. This exercise involves looking at the business over a period of time.

Looking at the overall context of Lord Balfour's business in operating a unitary landed estate with in-hand farming, forestry/woodland, sporting activities and the letting of farms, the First-tier Tribunal was entitled to treat that context as a factor which pointed towards a business that was mainly a trading business. It was also entitled to conclude that the turnover and net profit figures supported the conclusion that management of the estate was mainly a trading activity. The Upper Tribunal agreed that *IHTA 1984, s 105(3)* did not apply. BPR was therefore available.

In *The Trustees of David Zetland Settlement v Revenue and Customs* [2013] UKFTT 284 (TC), HMRC refused a BPR claim in respect of an IHT charge arising on the ten-year anniversary of a settlement. The trustees appealed. The BPR claim had been made in respect of (among other things) a commercial building divided into units let to tenants. The trustees contended that the services provided to the tenants were such that its business activities were prevented from being 'mainly' one of making or holding investments within *IHTA 1984, s 105(3)*.

The tribunal noted from the Upper Tribunal decision in the *Pawson* case (see **12.6**) that the relevant test is the nature of the activities carried out, not the level or degree of activity, and commented: 'In the *Pawson* case the bar has been set quite high. The facts do not get the Appellants over the bar. The services provided were mainly of a standard nature aimed at maximising income through the use of short term tenancies.' The trustees had pointed towards various services and facilities as being additional over and above those normally provided to tenants (eg a café, communal events, internet services, cleaning services, a gym, hair salon). However, the tribunal concluded that the non-investment activities were primarily concerned with increasing the return on the building, and were not sufficient to tip the balance in favour of obtaining BPR. The trustees' appeal was dismissed.

In *Best v Revenue and Customs* [2014] UKFTT 77 (TC), a claim for BPR in respect of unquoted company shares was denied by HMRC, on the basis that the business of the company consisted wholly or mainly of holding investments. The deceased shareholder's executor appealed. The company owned a business centre, which provided industrial and warehouse space for small to medium-sized businesses. The tribunal noted the authorities (in *George* (see **12.5**), *McCall* (see **12.4**) and *Pawson* (see **12.6**)) in the context of land and whether a business consists wholly or mainly of holding investments. The tribunal held that the nature and extent of additional services provided by the company did not predominate when considering its activities as a whole, and that the company's business was mainly holding investments. The executor's appeal was dismissed.

PERIOD OF OWNERSHIP

12.9 The general rule is that no BPR is due unless the relevant business property has been owned by the transferor for a minimum period of two years immediately preceding the transfer (*IHTA 1984, s 106*).

In terms of IHT lifetime planning, this two-year minimum holding period compares favourably with the seven-year period required for potentially exempt transfers to become exempt. It makes investment in (for example) unquoted trading company shares (see **12.3**) potentially more attractive to individuals whose life expectancy is likely to exceed two years but is uncertain to exceed seven years due to age or ill health, particularly while BPR is available at the 100% rate. However, such investments are generally risky in nature, and their commercial implications must therefore be carefully considered.

HMRC appear to apply the ownership test to businesses as a whole, rather than individual assets of the business. It therefore follows that capital and assets introduced into a business less than two years before death or transfer will qualify for BPR as part of the net value of the business (within *IHTA 1984, s 110*), provided that they were used in the business at the relevant time (IHTM25342).

12.10

Focus

Changes in the business during the two-year period are not necessarily fatal for BPR purposes. The nature of the business need not be the same, but there must have been a business throughout that period (IHTM25303).

There are also certain exceptions to the basic two-year ownership requirement, in connection with replacement property, acquisitions on death and successive transfers respectively.

These exceptions broadly apply as outlined below.

- *Replacement property* – the ownership test is treated as satisfied if the property replaced other business property eligible for relief, provided that the combined period of ownership is at least two years out of the preceding five years (see, for example, *Revenue and Customs v Brander (personal representative of the Fourth Earl of Balfour)* [2010] UKUT 300 (TCC)).

  However, the BPR available is restricted to what it would have been had the replacement or any one or more of the replacements not been made (*IHTA 1984, s 107(2)*), subject to the exceptions below.

  The replacement property rule may be helpful in certain circumstances:

  - *incorporation of a business* – the acquisition of the business by a company controlled by the former business owner(s);

  - *partnerships* – changes resulting from the formation, alteration or dissolution of a partnership (eg retiring from one partnership to form another);

  - *company reorganisations, etc.* – holdings of unquoted shares which would (under the capital gains tax rules in *TCGA 1992, ss 126–136*) be identified with other qualifying shares previously owned may treat their period of ownership as including the ownership period of the original shares (*IHTA 1984, s 107(4)*).

In *Executors of Dugan-Chapman (deceased) v Revenue and Customs Commissioners* [2008] SpC 666, a BPR claim relied on the company reorganisations exception to the two-year ownership rule. Mrs Dugan-Chapman was allotted one million ordinary shares in the company on 27 December 2002, two days before her death. The issue was broadly whether those shares could be identified for BPR purposes with other shares in the company which she had held for at least two years prior to her death. The Special Commissioner dismissed the executors' appeal against HMRC's determination that the value of those shares could not be reduced by BPR. HMRC had contended that the shares were issued as the result of a simple subscription for shares. There was insufficient evidence or documentation to support the executors' argument that a reorganisation had actually taken place.

As a postscript, subsequently in *Vinton and others v Fladgate Fielder* [2010] EWHC 904 (Ch), the executors, trustees and residuary beneficiaries of Mrs Dugan-Chapman's estate sued the solicitors for damages to recover the IHT that became payable and the costs of the above unsuccessful tax appeal. The solicitors applied to have the claim struck out as 'fanciful', but the court refused to strike out the claim.

Although a BPR claim was unsuccessful in the above case (albeit that 300,000 shares allotted to Mrs Dugan-Chapman on 23 December 2002 pursuant to a valid rights issue did qualify for BPR), there is still a potential planning opportunity available in 'deathbed' situations (eg where a shareholder has a life expectancy of less than two years). However, as the *Dugan-Chapman* case illustrates, it is important to get the facts and the paperwork right. For example:

–   There should be a commercial need for cash, since otherwise the money used to acquire the new shares will be an excepted asset (within *IHTA 1984, s 112*).

–   The directors should record the need for funds for the purposes of the business of the company.

–   The rights issue should be executed correctly (eg so that all shareholders can participate (and several should actually do so), in addition to the 'target' shareholder).

–   If possible, the balance of voting rights should be left as it was before the share arrangement.

–   No attempt should be made to 'water down' the arrangement in any way. For example, the new money must not be a mere loan, nor be seen as such by attempting to distinguish between one class of share and another.

The above BPR limit for replacement property in *IHTA 1984, s 107(2)* does not apply to changes in value resulting from the formation, alteration or dissolution of a partnership, nor from the acquisition of a business by a company controlled by the former owner of the business. Thus, in the case of the first two instances listed above, the potential restriction in BPR mentioned earlier is disregarded (*IHTA 1984, s 107(3)*).

● *Successions* – for the purposes of the two-year ownership requirement and the replacement property rule, business property inherited on death is generally treated as owned from the date of death. However, if the deceased was a spouse or civil partner, the ownership periods of both individuals are combined (*IHTA 1984, s 108*). This applies irrespective of how long they have been married (IHTM25321). However, note that this provision applies to business property acquired on the death of another person, and not where that other person made a lifetime gift.

● *Successive transfers* – BPR is broadly available for relevant business property if that property was eligible for relief when it was originally transferred to its owner (or their spouse or civil partner), and that (or replacement) property would be relevant business property on the later transfer (but for the two-year rule), provided that either the original or later transfer was made on death (*IHTA 1984, s 109(1)*). However, BPR can be subject to limitation in certain specific circumstances (in *IHTA 1984, s 109(2), (3)*), broadly relating to replacement property and to earlier partial acquisitions (see IHTM25333).

For the purposes of the ownership requirement in *IHTA 1984, s 106* (and *IHTA 1984, s 107*), it would seem that shares are owned when they are acquired, whether they are issued fully or partly paid up, as there are no specific BPR provisions regarding partly paid shares. Acquiring shares on that basis may therefore seem attractive in terms of starting the ownership 'clock'.

What if some of an individual's shares meet the two-year ownership requirement, but other shares do not? In terms of identifying the shares for BPR purposes, HMRC's approach is stated to be as follows (SVM111090):

'Where the transferor acquired additional shares during the 2 years prior to the transfer and it is claimed that the shares transferred derived from the holding acquired earlier, the agents should be asked to provide the necessary evidence – such as a copy of the relevant entries in the register of transfers or of the relevant share certificates. However if, exceptionally, firm evidence does not exist (for example because, following a reorganisation of the share capital, a fresh certificate was issued to cover the whole of the transferor's holding) relief may be given to the extent that it would be available **on the basis of a "first in-first out" assumption**' (emphasis added).

BPR and interests in possession

12.11 In the context of BPR, 'ownership' generally applies in terms of beneficial entitlement.

HMRC consider ownership in relation to settled property to mean legal ownership by the trustees of a settlement in which there is no interest in possession (IHTM25302).

Beneficial entitlement includes a beneficiary's beneficial entitlement to an interest in possession in the settled property (*IHTA 1984, s 49(1)*). The IHT regime for interests in possession was changed significantly by *FA 2006*, and only certain post-22 March 2006 interests in possession (eg immediate post-death interests) are subject to this treatment.

If an unadministered residuary estate includes business property, the residuary beneficiary is treated as owning the business property (or an appropriate share of it) (*IHTA 1984, s 91*).

12.12 As indicated at **12.2** above, land, buildings, plant and machinery of a settlement in which the transferor had a beneficial entitlement to an interest in possession and was used in his business qualify for BPR at the 50% rate.

However, if the transferor has a qualifying interest in possession in the assets used for his business, those assets will normally be treated as part of his business upon the life tenant's death and will be entitled to 100% relief (*Fetherstonaugh v IRC* [1984] 3 WLR 212; see **12.3**).

HMRC consider that there is 'some doubt' whether the *Fetherstonaugh* decision can apply to lifetime as well as death transfers, and will refer claims for 100% BPR on lifetime transfers to their Technical Group (IHTM25154).

PRACTICAL ISSUES

Value of the business

12.13 BPR is available in respect of the net value of the business. 'Net value' is the value of business assets (including goodwill) less business liabilities (*IHTA 1984, s 110(b)*). Any assets not used in the business cannot qualify for relief. In addition, BPR is not available for assets not used wholly or mainly for business purposes throughout the preceding two years, nor required for future business use (*IHTA 1984, s 112(2)*; see **12.14**).

In *Hardcastle and another (executors of Vernede, dec'd) v IRC* [2000] SpC 259, the Lloyd's assets of a non-working name was accepted to qualify as business property eligible for 100% relief. Uninsured underwriting losses were held to be liabilities deductible from the value of the deceased's other estate rather than the deceased's underwriting interests. The losses were not considered to be liabilities incurred for the purposes of the business under *IHTA 1984, s 110(b)*.

In *IRC v Mallender* [2001] STC 514, the deceased's Lloyd's underwriting business was also considered to be business property eligible for relief. However, a tenanted investment property used to support a security for a bank guarantee did not qualify as business property. The land was worth considerably more than the maximum sum guaranteed. The court held that the bank guarantee was the asset used in the business rather than the investment property itself.

Subsequently, in *Seymour (Ninth Marquess of Hertford) v IRC* [2005] SpC 444, a stately home (Ragley Hall) was operated as a business. 78% of Ragley Hall was open to the public, and 22% was occupied as a private residence. The deceased's executors claimed BPR on the value of the building as a whole, as being one of the assets of the business within *IHTA 1984, s 110(b)*. They appealed against HMRC's refusal to allow relief for 100% of the property value. The Special Commissioner held that the asset attracting business property relief was Ragley Hall in its entirety, not just 78% of it.

Unfortunately, HMRC appear to view this case as an 'unusual' one, on the basis that '… it was the nature of the business in this particular case and the part that the physical structure of the hall played in that business that most influenced the Commissioner's decision'. BPR claims on buildings based on the decision are therefore likely to attract the attention of HMRC's Technical Group (see IHTM25342).

Excepted assets

12.14   There is a potential restriction of BPR in respect of 'excepted assets', ie assets not used wholly or mainly for business purposes for at least the last two years, nor which are required for future business use (*IHTA 1984, s 112*). This provision therefore has the potential to restrict BPR such as, for example, in relation to surplus cash held by an unquoted trading company (see **12.17**).

The 'future use' requirement offers a useful let-out in cases where an asset has not been used wholly or mainly for business purposes throughout the last two years. If the asset is in actual business use at the relevant point in time, it will probably be required for future business use as well.

Different rules apply to land or buildings, plant or machinery used wholly or mainly for the business of a company controlled by the transferor, or by a partnership of which he was then a partner, for which 50% BPR is available. The description of relevant business property in *IHTA 1984, s 105(1)(d)* only requires that the asset is in business use immediately before the transfer. However, the excepted asset provisions broadly require business use throughout the preceding two years, subject to relaxations for replacement property and under the rules in *IHTA 1984, s 109* for successive transfers (*IHTA 1984, s 112(3)*).

A helpful relaxation in the excepted asset rules applies to land and buildings, where part is used exclusively for business purposes but the whole of the land or building is not used wholly or mainly for business purposes (eg it was used for the benefit of a transferor or a connected person). In those circumstances, the part used exclusively for business purposes, and the rest of the property, are treated as separate assets and BPR is applied accordingly to the business part. The value of the entire land or building is apportioned between those parts for this purpose (*IHTA 1984, s 112(4)*).

Example 12.1 – Partial BPR

Stanley owned a three-storey building on his death. The ground floor was a shop from which he operated a confectionery business. He used the second and third floors for his living quarters. The value of the whole building is £600,000, of which the upper floors are valued at £350,000.

The ground floor shop is treated as a separate asset, which is not an excepted asset.

In the case of property subject to a mortgage (or other loan), prior to changes introduced in *FA 2013*, BPR could be maximised if the mortgage was secured on the non-business part of the property. However, this planning strategy has been blocked in relation to mortgages or loans taken out on or after 6 April 2013 (see **12.56**).

Investment 'business'?

12.15

Focus

Investment assets will not necessarily be excepted assets. A trading company that includes a 'business' of making or holding investments may qualify for BPR, provided that the investment business does not predominate. A 'wholly or mainly' test applies for these purposes (*IHTA 1984, s 105(3)*).

HMRC accept that a 'hybrid' company that is mainly trading will not be subject to the excepted assets rule in respect of assets used in the investment element of the business (see Shares and Assets Valuation Manual at SVM111220).

However, HMRC consider that a 'business' involves a degree of activity. In *American Leaf Blending Co v Director-General of Inland Revenue (Malaysia)* [1978] 3 All ER 1185 (a Malaysian tax case) (see **12.20**), Lord Diplock held: 'The carrying on of "business", no doubt, usually calls for some activity on the part of whoever carries it on, though, depending on the nature of the business, the activity may be intermittent with long intervals of quiescence in between.'

In the case of surplus cash, the company's holding of it generally requires no effort and involves no activity. In *Jowett v O'Neill and Brennan Construction Ltd* Ch D 1998, 70 TC 566 (a corporation tax case), the holding of cash on interest-bearing deposit was held not to constitute a business. On the other hand, a holding of investment shares or securities may constitute a business, depending on the size of holdings, the degree of active management and the reason for acquiring them.

12.16   Another corporation tax case (*Revenue and Customs Commissioners v Salaried Persons Postal Loans Ltd* [2006] EWHC 763 (Ch)) gives rise to the possibility that a company owning property and deriving a rental return from it may be considered not to be carrying on an investment business.

In that case, the company's only source of income was rental income from a former business premises. HMRC contended that the company was carrying on a business, but the Special Commissioner allowed the taxpayer's appeal, and HMRC's subsequent appeal was dismissed. It was relevant to consider why the company received income and what it actually did to receive the income. The company had merely continued letting its old trading premises, which it had done for nearly 30 years. The circumstances in which a company letting property is found not to be carrying on a business are likely to be exceptional. However, the possible application of the decision in the *Postal Loans* case in a BPR context should be borne in mind.

In *McCall and another (Personal Representatives of McClean, dec'd) v Revenue and Customs Commissioners* (discussed at **12.4** above) the Special Commissioner ([2008] SpC 678) considered that the business in that case consisted wholly or mainly of the making of investments, on the basis that:

> 'the activities of the business consisted of the making available of its major asset to other persons for payment without the separate provision of any substantial other goods or services.'

He added:

> 'The activities surrounding the letting (except perhaps the provision of water) were not so substantial as to constitute themselves a part of the business distinct from holding the land: this was not like a car hire business where income derives from the letting of a car but where the cleaning, servicing, insuring and dealing in the cars may be such a large part of what is done to say that it is not just a business of holding cars; instead the major part of what was done was letting the land and the other activities a necessary part of that or small in comparison.'

The Special Commissioners' decision was upheld in the High Court ([2009] NICA 12). It would therefore seem that, whilst the letting of land does not necessarily constitute an investment business, the availability of BPR is likely to depend upon what other services are provided as well, and the extent of those services.

'Surplus' cash

12.17

Focus

It may be relevant to ask: is surplus cash 'surplus' at all? For example, what is the company's working capital requirement? Could the funds be applied towards repaying creditors? Or expanding the company's trade?

In the context of the 'future use' test in *IHTA 1984, s 112(2)(b)*, HMRC have stated that, unless there is evidence that cash is held for an identifiable future purpose, it is likely that the surplus cash will be treated as an excepted asset. Thus the holding of funds as an 'excess buffer' to weather an adverse economic climate is not considered by HMRC to be a sufficient reason for it not to be classed as an excepted asset (*ICAEW Taxguide 1/14*).

HMRC's Shares and Assets Valuation Manual states (at SVM111220):

'[Surplus cash] cannot be regarded as a separate investment business nor as part of the hybrid business, as it requires no effort and involves no activity. It is a factual test.'

The guidance then lists the following questions, which may provide a helpful checklist (or at least a useful insight into HMRC's approach) when considering if cash is indeed 'surplus':

- Was the cash used for the business?

- Was the cash used to finance the business carried on by the company?

- How much cash did the company use regularly?

- What were its short-term cash requirements?

- Does the amount of cash fluctuate?

The excepted assets restriction for BPR purposes (see **12.14**) can apply to assets which are not wholly or mainly required for future business use. This condition was considered in *Barclays Bank Trust Co Ltd v IRC* [1998] SpC 158.

In that case, the deceased had been a shareholder in a company operating the business of selling bathroom and kitchen fittings. At the date of the deceased's death, the company held £450,000 in cash. Turnover was around £600,000. HMRC accepted that £150,000 of that cash was required by the company at that time, but maintained that the remaining £300,000 was an excepted asset. The Special Commissioner accepted HMRC's view, and dismissed the appeal against the BPR restriction. The possibility of using the money at some future point if a suitable opportunity arose was not sufficient. To be required for future use, there must be some evidence that the money will be required for a specific project or business purpose.

The *Barclays* case perhaps provides a helpful 'rule of thumb', on the footing that a cash balance equivalent to 25% of turnover was accepted as being required for the day-to-day running of the business. However, it may be possible to justify a higher proportion in practice, subject to the working capital requirements of the particular business. For example, some trades may be subject to seasonal fluctuations, which could perhaps mean that a larger proportion of cash is required.

12.18 By contrast, in *Brown's Executors v IRC* [1996] SpC 83, the deceased owned shares in an unquoted trading company which operated a nightclub. The nightclub was sold to third parties. Proceeds from the sale of the nightclub were held in a short-term interest-bearing deposit account with a bank pending acquisition of a new nightclub business. The deceased investigated the possibility of acquiring other nightclubs, but then died suddenly. The executors appealed against HMRC's refusal of a BPR claim on the shares. HMRC claimed that the company's business consisted wholly or mainly of making or holding investments, within *IHTA 1984, s 105(3)*. However, the Special Commissioner accepted the executors' evidence that the company had been actively seeking alternative sites for another nightclub, and allowed the appeal.

The issue in the *Brown's Executors* case differs from the *Barclays Bank* case, but it does illustrate two points. First, the question of excepted asset status is only relevant if the shares are relevant business property. Secondly, in the context of excepted assets and generally, it is important that clear evidence of future trading requirements for apparently 'surplus' cash is available. HMRC guidance states (at SVM111230):

> '**[T]he future use should clearly be in contemplation at the valuation date**. In other words, as regards capital expenditure, there has to be some positive decision or firm intention existing at that time. The mere toying with an idea or some distant thought should circumstances change cannot suffice' (emphasis added).

Thus formal business plans and meeting minutes may be helpful in this context.

12.19 As mentioned (see **12.14**), in the case of land and buildings, the excepted assets rule also contains an apportionment provision (*IHTA 1984, s 112(4)*). This rule applies if part of the asset is used exclusively in the business, where the whole of the land and buildings would otherwise be an excepted asset because it was not used wholly or mainly for business (or would be excluded from relief under a separate provision relating to land and buildings, machinery and plant in *112(3)*). Its effect is that the part used exclusively for business purposes and the rest of the property are treated as separate assets, and the value of the land or building as a whole is apportioned between them.

This apportionment may apply where, for example, a dentist operates a practice from home. The house is mainly the dentist's residence, but rooms on the ground floor are used for a surgery, office and waiting room.

Investment 'business'

12.20 The BPR restriction for surplus cash as an excepted asset can be overcome by applying those funds towards an investment 'business'. However, care is needed to ensure that the company's trade remains the dominant business.

599

In addition, the question arises as to what constitutes a 'business' for these purposes. In the case of shares and securities, HMRC's Shares Valuation Manual suggests that some caution is required (SVM111220):

'... much will turn on the size of the holdings, the time spent on their management (including buying and selling) and the reason for their acquisition. You should however, bear in mind the conclusion of the Privy Council in *American Leaf Co v Director General* [1979] AC 676 that "in the case of a company incorporated for the purpose of making profits for its shareholders any gainful use to which it puts any of its assets prima facie amounts to the carrying on of a business." If a company does carry on an investment business ancillary to its trading business, it cannot be said that the investments made have not been used for the purposes of the hybrid (mainly trading, partly investment) business. Thus those investments cannot be regarded as excepted assets.'

12.21   If the asset was used wholly or mainly for the personal benefit of the transferor or a person connected with him (eg a yacht), it is deemed not to have been used wholly or mainly for the purposes of the business concerned (*IHTA 1984, s 112(6)*).

However, what is the practical effect of excluding the excepted asset? HMRC accept that, in some cases (eg minority shareholdings), the exclusion of an asset would make little or no difference to the value transferred (SVM111220). This will particularly be the case if shares are valued on a capitalisation (or 'earnings' basis) as opposed to an 'assets' basis, as the existence of an excepted asset may only have a minor effect on value. However, HMRC guidance states:

'Where, however, shares are being valued by reference to the capitalisation value of a company, you should remember that the value of any substantial non-business asset ought to be added to the capitalisation value of the company. The added value of the non-business asset will clearly have to be excluded from relief.'

12.22   The BPR restriction for surplus cash as an excepted asset can also be mitigated by repaying trade and other creditors (eg hire purchase liabilities, long-term loans).

In addition, following *Phillips and others (Executors of Rhoda Phillips, dec'd) v HMRC* [2006] SpC 555 (see **12.6** above), BPR can seemingly be secured by engaging in the business of making loans (eg to related businesses).

Groups of companies

12.23   Without a special rule for holding companies in group situations, their shareholders would be denied BPR under the general rule in *IHTA 1984, s 105(3)*, which excludes shares (and also businesses or business interests) from relief if the company's business is wholly or mainly dealing in securities, stocks or shares, land or buildings or making or holding investments.

The exception for shares or securities in holding companies applies if the company's business is wholly or mainly as a holding company of at least one subsidiary whose business does not fall into any of the excluded categories mentioned above (*IHTA 1984, s 105(4)(b)*).

A group may be considered as an appropriate structure for BPR purposes in certain circumstances, such as to allow a group member to hold the premises of a trading group member (*IHTA 1984, s 111b*), if it is desired to keep the trading company and premises separate (eg for asset protection reasons).

By contrast, where an individual holds shares in an unquoted trading company and personally owns the business premises, the latter attracts BPR (at 50%) only if he has control of the company (*IHTA 1984, s 105(1)(d)*).

12.24   The value of a company's shares or securities is reduced for BPR purposes if it is a holding company and one or more group members is not within the definition of relevant business property.

A company is treated as not being a group member in a valuation context unless it either satisfies the conditions for being wholly or mainly a trading company (subject to exceptions for a market maker or discount house business carried on in the UK (or in an EEA state, with effect from 31 December 2012 (*IHTA 1984, s 105(4), (4A); SI 2012/2903*)) or holding companies, as described above), or unless its business is wholly or mainly of holding land or buildings mainly occupied by group members whose business would not preclude its shares from being relevant business property (*IHTA 1984, s 111*).

Thus on a transfer of shares in the holding company, the value of any 'excluded' subsidiaries would not be taken into account when considering how much of the transfer of value is eligible for BPR.

There is also an exclusion from the excepted asset rules in the case of groups. An asset will not be an excepted asset in a group situation provided that the company using it was a member of the group at the time of use and immediately before the transfer, and that the use is in a company not excluded by virtue of *IHTA 1984, s 111* as outlined above (*IHTA 1984, s 112(2)*).

12.25

Focus

Where a group of companies carries on investment business activities, some care may be required to prevent the restriction or denial of BPR.

Example 12.2 – BPR planning: group investments (1)

(a)   Holdco owns investment properties

Holdco Ltd has three wholly-owned subsidiaries, A Ltd, B Ltd and C Ltd. Each of the subsidiaries is trading. However, Holdco owns a valuable portfolio of investment properties. The value of those properties is such that Holdco is not 'mainly' a holding company within *IHTA 1984, s 105(4)(b)*. Consequently, the shareholders of Holdco would not be entitled to BPR on their shares under the existing structure.

(b)   Subsidiary owns investment properties

Alternatively, suppose that one of the subsidiaries (say, A Ltd) owned all the investment properties, Holdco may qualify as a holding company as the trading nature of the group as a whole predominated. However, for the purposes of calculating BPR on the Holdco shares, the value of A Ltd's shares would be excluded, as though it was not a group member.

(c)   Trading premises

By contrast, if the assets were not investments but properties from which A Ltd and the other group members traded, the value of the A Ltd shares (in (b) above) could be taken into account for BPR purposes as a qualifying company (*IHTA 1984, s 111(b)*).

12.26   It might be possible to arrange for an alternative allocation of investments between group members, which could result in BPR being available to the Holdco Ltd shareholders.

Example 12.3 – BPR planning: group investments (2)

Following on from **Example 12.2**, the investment properties are divided so that Holdco Ltd, A Ltd, B Ltd and C Ltd each hold their own separate, smaller investment property portfolios, which are carefully structured so that each subsidiary is mainly trading.

Each property portfolio constitutes a business, so there is no BPR restriction in respect of their value. Similarly, Holdco is mainly carrying on the activities of a holding company. The investment property portfolios do not cause BPR to be denied, and there is no 'excepted asset' restriction because the property holdings represent a smaller business on which BPR also falls to be due.

If it is not possible to spread investments between group members in such a way, consideration could be given to extracting the investments from the group, although this may have other tax implications, such as corporation tax for the company in respect of chargeable gains.

12.27 Care is needed. The 'wholly or mainly' test in terms of qualifying activities should ideally be considered before the group asset structure is put in place. The test is particularly important in the case of the holding company, as the availability of BPR for the entire group may depend on it. The test should be measured on any appropriate basis (eg turnover, profitability or asset values), and also 'in the round' to take account of the overall nature of the group.

For further guidance on the potential approach and the categories of measure to consider (albeit in a different context), see **12.8** above and the Special Commissioner's decision in *Farmer and anor (executors of Farmer, dec'd) v IRC* [1999] SpC 216.

The position should be monitored on an ongoing basis, as trading activities may fluctuate and property values may increase, to the point where the 'wholly or mainly' test ceases to be met.

Intra-group loans

12.28 What is the position if intra-group loans are made by the holding company to one or more subsidiaries? If a loan falls to be treated as part of the holding company's business of being a holding company (within *IHTA 1984, s 105(4)(b)*), BPR status should not be adversely affected. However, it is necessary to consider not only whether the holding company's business consists mainly of being a holding company, but also whether providing loan finance to subsidiaries can properly be treated as forming part of that business.

HMRC confirmed (in a letter to the Chartered Institute of Taxation in January 2011) that, whilst all cases depend on their own facts, the provision of loan and other finance to subsidiaries is an activity which is indicative of the business of a holding company.

Thus, if the subsidiaries are themselves qualifying (ie non-investment) companies, and if the holding company's business as a holding company predominates, BPR would normally be available for the shares in the holding company. Intra-group loans are regarded as non-investment if the subsidiaries use them for the purposes of their non-investment business, and if the amounts are reasonable in the context of the group's business as a whole.

In correspondence with the Institute of Chartered Accountants in England and Wales (ICAEW), HMRC subsequently confirmed that the BPR implications depend on where the funds are held within the group, and the purpose for any loans. A loan made to support non-investment business activity would not of itself be regarded as an investment. However, each case will depend on its own facts. HMRC would look critically at any loans with an apparent non-commercial purpose, but these would still be viewed in the context of the group as a whole.

The correspondence between the above professional bodies and HMRC on intra-group loans is contained in ICAEW Taxguide 5/11, to which reference should be made for detailed guidance on BPR and groups of companies. Subsequent correspondence between Society of Trusts and Estates Practitioners member, Emma Chamberlain, and HMRC in 2015 (which was reconfirmed in 2017) clarified some points in relation to groups and intra-group activities (see www.step.org/sites/default/files/Policy/BPR_Correspondence.pdf).

'Deep' group structures

12.29   In some cases, the group may be deeper than a single holding company with one or more direct subsidiaries. More than one layer of holding company and subsidiary may exist. The legislation provides for the availability of BPR for a group parent company holding shares in a qualifying trading company (*IHTA 1984, s 105(4)(b)*). However, it may be necessary to carefully consider the availability of BPR for group structures involving a second layer of holding company.

It was initially thought that HMRC may be prepared to accept that a group structure with up to six levels of holding company potentially falls within the BPR regime, subject to meeting the general criteria regarding qualifying activities and not having excepted assets (see *Taxation*, 1 October 2008).

However, in subsequent correspondence with the ICAEW, HMRC have indicated that there is no limit to the number of intermediate holding companies (provided that Companies Act requirements are met – see, in particular, the definition of 'holding company' in *CA 2006, s 1159*), but that such companies cannot be ignored or looked through (see IHTM25263). In practice, HMRC will look at the group as a whole to determine whether it is mainly investment or non-investment in nature, before considering each individual company separately within the group structure to determine whether any relief restriction is necessary in accordance with *IHTA 1984, s 111*.

See **12.28** above on the correspondence between professional bodies and HMRC and subsequent guidance regarding BPR issues in connection with group structures and financing, particularly in the context of a complex holding company structure (which is common in large privately-owned groups) with a number of different ('intermediate') underlying holding companies, each effectively being its own separate group.

OTHER POINTS

Company liquidations, reorganisations, etc

12.30   When a company is no longer required, the business owners may decide to liquidate or informally wind up the company. The company's shares or securities generally cease to be eligible for BPR when the decision is made to end the company (eg when a winding-up order or resolution has been passed).

However, there is an exception from this general rule if the company's business is to continue after a reconstruction or amalgamation. This exception applies either if the reconstruction or amalgamation is the reason for the winding-up, or if the reconstruction or amalgamation takes place no more than a year after the transfer of value (*IHTA 1984, s 105(5)*).

With regard to company reorganisations, as indicated at **12.10** above for the purposes of the two-year ownership requirement in *IHTA 1984, s 106*, holdings of unquoted shares which would (under the capital gains tax rules in *TCGA 1992, ss 126–136*) be identified with other qualifying shares previously owned may treat their period of ownership as including the ownership period of the original shares (*IHTA 1984, s 107(4)*).

605

Partnerships

12.31   There is no general requirement for an asset to have been eligible for BPR throughout the period of ownership. However, it must be relevant business property immediately before the chargeable event. For example, a partner's interest in a partnership is property which is relevant business property *(IHTA 1984, s 105(1)(a))*. Upon retirement, the partner's capital account is converted into a debt, and the retiring individual becomes a creditor of the partnership. The debt is not relevant business property *(Beckman v IRC* [2000] SpC 226).

To preserve entitlement to BPR, the partner may wish to make a gift of the capital before retiring (ie an interest in the business, as opposed to a simple gift of cash; see IHTM25250), or possibly to delay retirement by taking a lesser role on the business in return for a reduced partnership share.

BPR may be available to a business partner under two separate headings:

- an interest in a business *(IHTA 1984, s 105(1)(a))* – eligible for 100% BPR;

- land, buildings, plant and machinery used by a partnership of which the transferor was a member *(IHTA 1984, s 105(1)(d))* – eligible for 50% BPR.

In the latter case, consideration could be given to restructuring the partnership agreement in appropriate circumstances, with the asset (eg land and buildings) becoming part of the partnership's assets (see 'Staying alive' by Kevin Slevin, *Taxation,* 21 November 2013).

If the partnership holds the land and buildings (or plant and machinery) and the partner retains an interest in the business until death, HMRC are understood to accept BPR claims on the partner's interest in the land and buildings at the 100% (not 50%) rate, on the basis that the interest is comprised in the notional transfer of his business interest within *IHTA 1984, s 105(1)(a)*. The position is thus distinguishable from the notional transfer on death of land owned outside the partnership, on which only 50% BPR is due within *IHTA 1984, s 105(1)(d)*.

12.32   However, what is the BPR rate on a lifetime transfer of the partner's interest in land and buildings held by the partnership? Unless the transfer is of the partner's interest in the partnership as a whole, it cannot fall within *IHTA 1984, s 105(1)(a)*, so would fall within *IHTA 1984, s 105(1)(d)* instead, giving BPR of 50%. On that basis, in terms of the BPR rate it makes no difference whether the partner's lifetime transfer is of land and buildings held within the partnership or outside it, as the BPR rate in both cases is 50% (IHTM25225).

However, in the case of a retiring partner, it would seem at least arguable that the transfer of an interest in land and buildings held by the partnership as part of the partner's overall withdrawal from the business and the transfer of his qualifying interest to another partner falls within *IHTA 1984, s 105(1)(a)* and is therefore eligible for 100% relief. Unfortunately, there is no indication that this view is accepted in HMRC's guidance on partnerships (at IHTM25250).

Limited liability partnerships

12.33 Limited liability partnerships (LLPs) are not normally treated as owned by the individual partners, in the same way that shareholders own shares in a company. Instead, a business carried on by the LLP is treated as carried on by the partners. The LLP's property is treated as that of the partners. Property occupied or used by the LLP is treated as occupied or used by the partners. The incorporation (ie. formation) of an LLP is treated as the formation of a partnership, and a transfer of value by or to an LLP is treated as made by or to its members (*IHTA 1984, s 267A*).

For BPR (and APR) purposes, there is no change in the treatment of assets held outside, but used in, the partnership. The incorporation of a partnership into an LLP is not treated as interrupting a partner's period of ownership in terms of BPR (see *Tax Bulletin,* Issue 50).

There is a difference between loans to, and interests in, an LLP. Thus, BPR will be available only on the capital, not on any loans, in line with the rule in *Beckman v IRC* (see **12.31**, and also below).

HMRC's view is that LLPs differ from other partnerships, on the basis that an LLP interest is deemed to be an interest in every asset of the partnership, whereas an interest in a 'traditional' partnership is a 'chose in action'. However, when considering if an LLP is an investment business, HMRC will look at the nature of the LLP's business, rather than the nature of the LLP's assets.

For example, HMRC guidance indicates that, in the case of an LLP investing in unquoted shares in a trading company (and nothing else), BPR is not available on an interest in the LLP. This appears to be on the basis that the LLP's business is investment in nature if its activities consist wholly or mainly of holding shares in the company, notwithstanding that the underlying assets constitute business property (IHTM25094).

HMRC subsequently affirmed the view set out in IHTM25094, stating that, if an LLP simply takes the place of a holding company, the effect of *IHTA 1984, s 267A* is that BPR (within *IHTA 1984, s 105(4)(b)*) is prevented from applying in respect of its holding of shares in the unquoted trading company (*ICAEW Taxguide 1/14*).

However, HMRC also state:

> 'in cases where the LLP also carries on a qualifying business, the business may be regarded as a hybrid, and if the shares in the subsidiary companies are used in the business (rather than being held as investments), then it is possible that the interest in the LLP may qualify for BPR if it does not fail the "wholly or mainly" test (IHTM25264). The question of whether an asset is used in the business or held as an investment will be highly fact specific.'

This view by HMRC is reflected in their responses to two hypothetical scenarios (ie examples 2 and 5) in the above ICAEW guidance, which indicate that BPR may be available in respect of interests in LLPs in certain specific circumstances.

HMRC's view is not universally accepted. For example, in 'A merry dance' (*Taxation,* 20 March 2014), James Kessler QC and Oliver Marre consider that HMRC's view is incorrect, on the basis that it is necessary to consider the relevant statutory provision for BPR (*IHTA 1984, s 104(1)*), and ask whether the value transferred by a transfer of value is attributable to the value of any relevant business property.

Where BPR is available (under HMRC's approach) on the basis that the LLP is itself trading, it may be necessary to consider whether the shares in subsidiaries are excepted assets within *IHTA 1984, s 112*.

Retirement of a partner

12.34   The timing of lifetime transfers of land or buildings, plant or machinery used by the partnership is important in terms of qualifying for any BPR at all. As noted above in relation to partnership interests, the asset must have been wholly or mainly used for business purposes immediately before the transfer, by a partnership of which the transferor was then a partner. A transfer after retirement therefore attracts no BPR.

This point was illustrated in *Beckman v IRC* [2000] STC (SCD) 59. The deceased (H) and her daughter (B) had been business partners until H's retirement. H's financial interest in the business immediately before her retirement, represented by her capital account, remained the same after her retirement.

However, the Special Commissioner held that her legal interest was radically changed on her retirement. Previously, she had all the rights of management conferred by the *Partnership Act 1890* and all the liabilities of a partner. Following retirement, in the absence of any agreement to the contrary, she became simply a creditor of B. Accordingly, on H's death four years later, business property relief on the sum due to her was denied. For the purposes of *IHTA 1984, s 105*, H's interest in the business ceased when she retired from the partnership that carried on that business.

In terms of BPR planning, as indicated at **12.31**, partners wishing to avoid a similar outcome could consider making a gift of the capital prior to retiring, or alternatively remaining a partner with a reduced profit share.

Contracts for sale

12.35 BPR is not normally available where the subject matter of the transfer is itself already subject to a binding contract for sale at the time of the transfer (*IHTA 1984, s 113*).

This may result in a loss of relief, in that the owner of the property can no longer claim the relief on a transfer made after a 'buy and sell' agreement has been entered into. However, arrangements between partners and shareholders can often be structured in such a way that BPR is not jeopardised.

Focus

It is important to recognise the types of agreement that constitute a 'binding contract for sale'. HMRC identify three key elements (see IHTM25292) (emphasis added):

- an *agreement* for the deceased partner's business interest or shareholder's shares to pass to his personal representatives;

- a *requirement* for the personal representatives to sell to the surviving partners or shareholders; and

- an *obligation* for the surviving partners or shareholders to buy the asset under the terms of the agreement (funds for the purchase often being provided by life assurance policies).

HMRC's stated view is that such terms (referred to as 'buy and sell' agreements) prevent BPR from being due on the business interest or shares (Statement of Practice 12/80).

However, BPR is not prevented by *IHTA 1984, s 113* from applying to company shares or securities, if the company's articles of association require the personal representatives to offer his shares for sale to the company, or to other shareholders or directors. However, there should be no obligation to buy; nor should there be a mutually binding obligation to buy and sell (SVM111120).

12.36 The types of agreement which are not 'caught' by *IHTA 1984, s 113* include:

- *'Accruer'* clauses – the deceased's interests pass ('accrue') to the surviving partners, who are required to pay the personal representatives a particular price (eg based on a valuation or formula). The agreement in these circumstances will generally be at arm's length.

- *Options* – the deceased's interest falls into the estate, but with an option for the surviving partners to purchase it. Agreements sometimes provide for a two-way (or 'cross') option. There is (in principle, at least) an argument that cross-options are not materially different in substance to a binding contract for sale. This argument seems unlikely in the case of genuine options, but in any event such concerns could be set aside by using a single option (ie put or call), or by providing for successive put and call options with their own separate and distinct exercise periods.

12.37 HMRC are alert to planning involving lifetime transfers of unquoted shares, shortly followed by a sale of the company (IHTM25291). They are likely to investigate such transfers (in the context of a possible binding contract for sale within *IHTA 1984, s 113*) if, for example, the company is sold within six months of the transfer, or possibly longer if the circumstances suggest that a sale was in prospect when the lifetime transfer was made (SVM111120).

However, it should be noted that BPR is not denied by *IHTA 1984, s 113* if the reason for the binding contract is the incorporation of a sole trader or partnership in which the sale proceeds are wholly or mainly shares or securities in the company, or in the case of company shares or securities if the purpose of the sale is a reconstruction or amalgamation (*IHTA 1984, s 113(a), (b)*).

Lifetime gifts and BPR

12.38 An important point to consider for IHT planning purposes is whether to make gifts during lifetime, or to leave assets in the estate until death. In the case of assets eligible for 100% BPR, there are potential benefits to delaying gifts until death. These include a possible CGT-free uplift in value on death, no concerns about the possible clawback of BPR on lifetime gifts, and the retention of control over the asset in question.

On the other hand, there is the constant danger that BPR rates may be reduced, or that the relief may be abolished altogether. These concerns may make transferring business property into a relevant property trust to 'bank' BPR seem an attractive proposition, with the donor retaining a degree of control over the asset as a trustee.

However, this type of planning needs to be considered 'in the round', taking account of factors including the loss of CGT-free uplift on death.

Avoiding a clawback of BPR

12.39   IHT charges can arise on a transferor's death if, for example, the transferee has disposed of the business property without replacement, or if the asset is no longer relevant business property. A gift of business property from one individual to another generally constitutes a potentially exempt transfer, in which case BPR is not an immediate issue. However, the availability of BPR will need to be considered in the event of the transferor's death within seven years.

Alternatively, if a chargeable lifetime transfer (eg a gift to a discretionary trust) was reduced by BPR and the transferor dies within seven years, the additional IHT on death is calculated as if the transfer had not been reduced by BPR unless certain conditions are satisfied, as outlined below (*IHTA 1984, s 113A(1), (2)*).

12.40   The BPR clawback provisions do not apply if the following conditions are satisfied (*IHTA 1984, s 113A(3), (4)*):

● the transferee continued to own the business property until the donor's death (or until the transferee's death, if earlier); and

● the original property is still relevant business property at that time (but see below). The two-year ownership test does not apply for the purposes of this rule.

The first condition above is relaxed if the transferee has replaced the original asset with other business property. BPR may still be available, subject to further conditions (*IHTA 1984, s 113B*; see below).

The second condition above does not have to be satisfied for lifetime transfers of shares or securities which were quoted at the time of the transfer, or of unquoted shares which remained as such until the transferor's death, or of unquoted securities which, either by themselves or together with other such securities owned by the transferor and any unquoted shares so owned, gave the transferor control *(IHTA 1984, s 113A(3A))*.

12.41   A potential trap exists in the meaning of transferee. A 'transferee' is defined as the person who became the owner of the original property on the transfer, or where on the transfer the property became (or remained) settled on discretionary trusts, the trustees of the settlement *(IHTA 1984, s 113A(8))*.

For example, if the original transfer was to the trustees of a discretionary trust, the first condition above will not be satisfied if, before the transferor's death, a beneficiary becomes absolutely entitled to the trust property (eg following an appointment by the trustees, or the termination of the trust). HMRC guidance warns that the meaning of transferee is precise in this context (IHTM25367).

12.42   If the BPR clawback rules apply to an immediately chargeable lifetime transfer, only the additional IHT on that transfer is affected by the loss of BPR. The additional tax on the transferor's death is calculated on the basis of no BPR (ie the additional tax payable on death is the difference between the IHT at death rates (after taper relief, if appropriate) on the value excluding BPR and the tax paid at lifetime rates on the reduced value). However, for the purposes of cumulating the lifetime transfer with subsequent transfers within the seven-year period before death (including the death estate), the value transferred by the transfer remains as reduced by BPR.

Therefore, it can be advantageous to make chargeable lifetime transfers of business property subject to 100% BPR, compared with making potentially exempt transfers which become chargeable on death (ie where the transfer must be aggregated in full) *(IHTA 1984, s 113A(1), (2))*.

For example, if an individual dies within seven years of settling shares worth up to his available nil rate band on a discretionary trust (on which 100% BPR was claimed), the effect of a clawback of BPR is that the chargeable transfer is of an amount that falls within the individual's nil rate band. The individual's cumulative total is unchanged. Thus the clawback of BPR in this case does not result in an IHT liability.

It should be noted that if the BPR clawback provisions only apply to a part of the gifted property, BPR may still apply to the balance *(IHTA 1984, s 113A(5))*.

For example, if the original transfer was a potentially exempt transfer (PET) of 1,000 unquoted shares worth £100,000, and the transferee sells 500 shares for £25,000 without replacement, BPR of £50,000 remains available on the other half of the shares.

Replacement property

12.43   As indicated above, the condition that the transferee must generally own the original property at the transferor's death is relaxed in the case of replacement property.

The 'replacement property' rules apply if the transferee has sold all or part of the original property before the transferor's death and invested the whole of the proceeds in the purchase of other qualifying property. The conditions are broadly as follows (*IHTA 1984, s 113B(1), (2)*):

- the whole of the consideration must be reinvested in the replacement property (HMRC consider 'whole of the consideration' to mean the proceeds net of any professional costs and CGT; see IHTM25369);

- the replacement property must be acquired (or a binding contract for its acquisition entered into) within the 'allowed period' of three years (or such longer period as HMRC may allow) after the disposal of the original property; and

- the disposal and acquisition must both be made in transactions at arm's length, or on arm's length terms (eg exchanges of business property).

12.44   If the above conditions are met, the basic conditions for BPR on lifetime gifts within seven years of the transferor's death in *IHTA 1984, s 113A(3)* (see above) are taken to be satisfied in relation to the original property, provided that the following conditions are also met in relation to the replacement property (*IHTA 1984, s 113B(3), (4)*):

- the replacement property is owned by the transferee immediately before the transferor's death (or until the transferee's death, if earlier);

- throughout the period from the date of the chargeable transfer until death (disregarding any period between the disposal and acquisition) either the original property or the replacement property was owned by the transferee; and

- the replacement property is relevant business property immediately before the death (or would be, apart from the minimum period of ownership requirement in *IHTA 1984, s 106*).

It should be noted that if the transferor has died (before the transferee) after disposal of all or part of the original property by the transferee, but before the replacement property is acquired, BPR remains available if the replacement property is acquired (or a binding contract for its acquisition entered into) within the 'allowed period' mentioned in **12.43** (see *IHTA 1984, s 113B(5)*).

12.45 A special rule applies where shares owned by the transferee immediately before the transferor's death (or before the transferee's earlier death) represent the original property received from the transferor. This rule may apply if, for example, the transferee holds shares following a company reorganisation (within *TCGA 1992, ss 126–136*), or if the shares were issued to the transferee in consideration of the transfer of business property consisting of the original property. The effect is that the shares are treated for replacement property purposes as the original property (*IHTA 1984, ss 113A(6), 113B(6)*).

Interestingly, where the replacement property treatment in *IHTA 1984, s 113A(6)* is claimed, HMRC guidance indicates that the claim will be referred to their Technical Group for adjudication (IHTM25370).

The order of gifts

12.46 The making of lifetime gifts of business assets should be considered carefully, as the availability of BPR may depend upon the order of such gifts.

For example, BPR (at the 50% rate) applies to land and buildings, machinery or plant used wholly or mainly in a business carried on by a company of which the transferor then had control (*IHTA 1984, s 105(1)(d)*).

The controlling shareholder of an unquoted trading company who owns its business premises may wish to make gifts of shares and the premises at different times. It is important that he retains the controlling interest in the company when the property is given away. Otherwise, BPR at 50% may be lost on the subsequent gift of the premises. See **12.3** above on the meaning of 'control' in this context.

A loss of BPR in the above circumstances is not necessarily fatal for IHT purposes if the gifts are to another individual, as the gifts (including the property) are potentially exempt transfers which become exempt after seven years. It may be possible, and desirable, to insure against the risk of the donor's death within that time. However, if the gift is chargeable when made (ie as for most lifetime transfers into trust), the non-availability of BPR could result in an immediate, and perhaps unnecessary, IHT charge.

OTHER PLANNING

Maximising BPR

12.47 Planning involves not only taking advantage of possible tax savings, but also avoiding potential pitfalls which could, for example, result in the loss of an available relief or allowance.

For example, BPR is generally wasted if qualifying assets are left to the spouse or civil partner, because such legacies are normally exempt in any event. There is also a danger that BPR may not be available on the spouse's later death (eg due to a change in law).

Assets that may qualify for 100% BPR could therefore possibly be given to a future generation (eg the grandchildren), or to appropriate trusts. However, consideration should be given to whether the surviving spouse requires the business assets (eg shares in the family trading company, which could provide income through future dividends).

Avoiding the loss of BPR

12.48

Focus

If an estate includes assets eligible for BPR and other assets, and the deceased's will provides for both chargeable beneficiaries (eg adult children) and an exempt beneficiary (eg a UK-domiciled spouse, civil partner or a charity), it is important to ensure that specific business property (eg unquoted trading company shares) is left to chargeable beneficiaries, if possible.

If an estate includes property attracting BPR (or APR), special provisions apply for the purposes of valuing specific and residuary gifts where part of the estate is exempt. The provisions can result in an apportionment of relief between the chargeable beneficiaries and exempt surviving spouse or civil partner (*IHTA 1984, s 39A*).

If any residuary gifts (after 17 March 1986) include business (or agricultural) assets, any specific gifts of non-business assets (eg cash gifts) will be entitled to a due proportion of BPR. The value of such specific gifts is the 'appropriate proportion' of their value (*IHTA 1984, s 39A(3), (4)*).

This apportionment of BPR can have unfortunate consequences.

Example 12.4 – BPR and a partly exempt estate

Scott died on 10 May 2018. His estate of £1,625,000 consists of shares in an unquoted trading company worth £800,000, and other assets (ie cash,

---

shares and an investment property) worth £825,000. Scott's nil rate band (£325,000 for 2018/19) is available in full on his death.

Scott's will leaves cash and specific other (non-business) assets amounting to £500,000 to his spouse. The residue of Scott's estate, including the trading company shares (eligible for 100% BPR) is left to his adult children, together with the remaining other non-business assets worth £325,000.

The value of Scott's estate (net of BPR) is £825,000. As he left £500,000 to his spouse, his personal representatives assume (incorrectly) that the remaining £325,000 will be covered by Scott's nil rate band, and that no IHT will be payable. However, the result of applying the 'appropriate proportion' (see above) to the spouse's exempt legacy is:

$$£500,000 \times \frac{£825,000}{£1,625,000} = £253,846$$

The residue (ie the chargeable free estate) is (£825,000 – £253,846) = £571,154. The decrease in the amount subject to the spouse exemption has resulted in a significant (and unexpected) IHT liability.

12.49 As the above example illustrates, if an exempt legacy receives a proportion of BPR, the relief is effectively wasted because the legacy is subject to IHT exemption (ie the spouse exemption) in any event. On the death of an individual with business (or agricultural) property, a will which provides for a 'nil rate band' legacy in non-specific terms (eg words such as 'the maximum amount of funds without incurring a liability to IHT on my death') will probably not have the intended effect. However, if the business property is given by a chargeable, specific gift, its value is reduced by BPR (*IHTA 1984, s 39A(2)*).

BPR (or APR) can be optimised by ensuring that specific gifts of business (and agricultural) assets which attract 100% relief are made to chargeable parties in addition to the nil rate band, if appropriate. If the deceased's will does not provide for such specific legacies, it may be possible to vary the dispositions in the will using a deed of variation within two years of the deceased's death, and including a statement in the deed that it is to apply for IHT purposes (*IHTA 1984, s 142;* see **Chapter 15**).

12.50 The rates of BPR available may be 100%, 50%, or some other effective rate due to the operation of the excepted assets rule in *IHTA 1984, s 112*. A married (or civil partner) testator with business (or agricultural) property may therefore wish to consider a chargeable legacy comprising all business property qualifying for 100% relief, plus property qualifying for less than 100% relief (see below). The remainder may be left to the surviving spouse or civil partner absolutely, or possibly as an immediate post-death interest (*IHTA 1984, s 49A*).

If the nil rate band legacy comprises (say) business property qualifying for 50% BPR, the maximum specific legacy to a chargeable party without giving rise to an IHT liability is equal to twice the available nil rate band.

Example 12.5 – BPR at the 50% rate

Mr A dies on 10 July 2018, owning a controlling interest in quoted trading company shares, and had made no gifts in the preceding seven years. The maximum 'nil rate band' legacy is £650,000, calculated as follows:

	£
Shares	650,000
Less: BPR (50%)	(325,000)
	325,000
Less: nil rate band (2018/19)	(325,000)
Chargeable	Nil

12.51   An alternative form of chargeable legacy has traditionally been to a discretionary trust. BPR is available to the trustees of such a settlement (*IHTA 1984, s 103(1)(b)*). In addition, lifetime gifts to the trustees of most types of settlement are (following *FA 2006*) immediately chargeable transfers for IHT purposes (*IHTA 1984, s 3A(1), (2)*), and therefore the availability of BPR in connection with trusts has assumed added importance generally.

A trust to which the rules for 'relevant property' (as defined in *IHTA 1984, s 58*) apply, which consists entirely of business property eligible for BPR at the 100% rate, can avoid ten-yearly or exit IHT charges. BPR does not necessarily reduce the IHT rate for trusts, but it can apply to reduce the value transferred to nil.

'Doubling up' BPR

12.52   BPR can effectively be obtained twice on the same property in certain circumstances.

For example, the first spouse (or civil partner) to die leaves business property on discretionary trusts in favour of the survivor and issue. BPR (and a CGT-free uplift of the business property's base cost to market value) is obtained on the first death. The surviving spouse subsequently purchases the business property from the trustees at arm's length (under an option granted on the first death). Subject to surviving the required two-year period, BPR may be secured on that property for a second time, whether on death or on a lifetime transfer.

Example 12.6 – Two bites of the cherry

Mr Smith died on 31 August 2018, having made no lifetime gifts and owning the following assets:

	£
Family home	600,000
Shares in the family trading company	1,000,000
Investment properties	450,000
Building society and bank deposits	1,225,000
Portfolio of quoted shares	550,000
	3,825,000

In his will, Mr Smith leaves the family company shares to a discretionary trust in favour of Mrs Smith, his adult children, and grandchildren. He also leaves cash from his bank and building society accounts to the trust, up to the nil rate band (£325,000 for 2018/19), which is available in full. The residue of his estate is left to Mrs Smith absolutely, which is made up as follows:

	£
Family home	600,000
Investment properties	450,000
Building society and bank deposits (£1,225,000 – £325,000)	900,000
Portfolio of quoted shares	550,000
	2,500,000

The legacy into the discretionary trust amounts to £1,325,000. This comprises the family trading company shares worth £1,000,000, on which

BPR of 100% is available, plus cash of £325,000, which utilises Mr Smith's nil rate band. Hence no IHT is payable on Mr Smith's death.

Mrs Smith buys the family company shares from the trustees for £1,000,000, which equates to market value in this example. The purchase is financed partly in cash of £300,000. The balance is financed by selling the investment properties for £450,000, plus part of the portfolio of quoted shares for £250,000 (no CGT liabilities arise on the properties or shares, the values of which were uplifted to market value on Mr Smith's death).

If Mrs Smith survives for at least two years following the share acquisition, and assuming that BPR at 100% is then available in respect of her family company shares, only her remaining estate would be liable to IHT, comprising (based on current values):

- the family home (£600,000);

- building society and cash deposits (£600,000); and

- the portfolio of quoted shares (£300,000).

After deducting the available nil rate band, the IHT liability on her death estate is significantly reduced (the residence nil rate band is ignored in this example). In addition, she may have benefited from the income generated by the funds held by the discretionary trust in her capacity as a beneficiary.

Protecting against future BPR changes

12.53 Given the undoubted generosity of BPR (particularly at the 100% rate), it is open to speculation how long the BPR rates will remain at their present levels. It may therefore be considered prudent to 'bank' the relief to protect against future changes in BPR.

This could be achieved by making a lifetime transfer of the business property to (say) a discretionary trust (or, following *FA 2006*, to most other types of trust).

Prior to anti-avoidance legislation introduced in *Finance (No 2) Act 2015* (see **12.54**), if the value of business property exceeded the nil rate band, the use of a number of trusts was a potentially attractive strategy.

Example 12.7 – Multiple trusts (I)

Mrs Jones had business property worth £975,000. She created three 'pilot' discretionary trusts early in 2014/15 with nominal amounts at staggered intervals, and subsequently added (on 30 November 2014) business property so that each settlement was worth £325,000. There was no IHT liability on the transfers into the trusts, as BPR applied at the 100% rate.

Following the transfers, each trust should be protected by a nil rate band, even if the BPR rates are changed in the future, and even if the assets cease to be relevant business property.

12.54 Even before the anti-avoidance rules (outlined below) were introduced, this strategy carried potential risks. First, the arrangements could be challenged on the grounds of artificiality. Second, HMRC could seek to invoke the 'associated operations' rule (*IHTA 1984, s 268*), although this risk was lessened somewhat following the decision in *Rysaffe Trustees (CI) Ltd v IRC* [2003] EWCA Civ 356.

These risks were arguably reduced by ensuring that each trust was properly and separately administered. It may also have been preferred if there were genuine differences between the trusts (eg different trustees and beneficiaries), that the trusts were created as far apart as practicable in terms of time periods, and that they were not pre-ordained.

The implications for other tax purposes (eg capital gains tax – see below) must be considered as well.

Anti-avoidance legislation (*IHTA 1984, ss 62A–62C*) was introduced (in *Finance (No 2) Act 2015*) with effect from 18 November 2015 to counter the use of multiple pilot trusts, through a 'same day addition' rule. The legislation broadly provides that where a transfer of value is made to one settlement ('Settlement A') and on the same day the same settlor adds value to one or more other settlements ('Settlement B'), in calculating the rate of tax for the purposes of relevant property trust IHT charges in Settlement A (eg ten yearly and exit charges) the added value in Settlement B and (if Settlements A and B are not 'related settlements') the original value of Settlement B is taken into account under these provisions.

A 'same-day addition' (as defined in *IHTA 1984, s 62A*) can include a transfer of value on the creation of a settlement, but not if Settlement A and Settlement B are 'related settlements' (ie settlements created by the same settlor on the same day (*IHTA 1984, s 62A(4)*)).

Example 12.8 – Multiple trusts: same day additions (II)

The facts are in **Example 12.7**, except that Mrs Jones added the business property to the three pilot trusts after the anti-avoidance legislation in *IHTA 1984, s 62A* was introduced.

In calculating (for example) the rate of IHT on a distribution from one of the trusts before its first ten-year anniversary (under *IHTA 1984, s 68*), the value of the 'same-day additions' must be taken into account.

The trusts are not related settlements in this instance (ie they were created on different days), so the value of the relevant property in those settlements immediately after they were created is also taken into account in the *IHTA 1984, s 68* calculation (*IHTA 1984, s 68(5)(e)–(f)*).

The above anti-avoidance legislation is aimed at same day additions to other relevant property trusts (*IHTA 1984, s 62A*), subject to some limited exceptions (see *IHTA 1984, s 62B*), including a *de minimis* provision for lifetime transfers to exclude same-day additions of £5,000 or less where certain conditions are satisfied, and for transfers of value to charitable trusts.

Furthermore, the same day addition provisions do not apply if either or each of Settlement A and Settlement B is a protected settlement (*IHTA 1984, ss 62B(1)(c), 62C*). A settlement is a 'protected settlement' if it commenced before 10 December 2014 and either of two conditions (A or B) is satisfied.

Condition A is broadly that the settlor has not added value to the settlement since 10 December 2014. Thus, in **Example 12.7**, the settlements created by Mrs Jones will not be affected by the above anti-avoidance provisions, provided she makes no further transfers resulting in the value of the settled property being increased.

Condition B is that the settlor makes a transfer on or after 10 December 2014 resulting in the value of the property being increased, where the transfer arises (under *IHTA 1984, s 4*) on the settlor's death before 6 April 2017 by reason of a 'protected testamentary disposition' (ie under the settlor's will, where its provisions are substantially the same as they were immediately before 10 December 2014).

Whilst there is an exception from the same day additions rule for transfers of value of £5,000 or less (under *IHTA 1984, s 62B*), transfers of value of *any* amount by the settlor from 10 December 2014 can result in protection from the same day additions provisions for a protected settlement (under *IHTA 1984, s 62C(3)(a)*) being lost (eg a settlor's payment of trust professional fees may be caught).

It should be noted that it remains possible for the settlor to create a new settlement every seven years, each with its own nil rate band (assuming that no other chargeable transfers or potentially exempt transfers have been made in the intervening periods). Consideration could also be given to adding business property to existing pilot settlements on different days. The additions would fall to be aggregated with earlier transfers, but the aggregation is of the values transferred by any chargeable transfers made by the settlor (*IHTA 1984, s 67(3)*), and BPR operates to reduce the value transferred by a transfer of value (*IHTA 1984, s 104*).

BPR and CGT

12.55 A disadvantage of making lifetime gifts of assets eligible for 100% BPR is often the CGT position. Whilst hold-over relief may be available in many cases under *TCGA 1992, s 165* (eg on a gift of unquoted trading company shares to a UK-resident individual), a tax-free uplift to market value on the death of the owner will often be preferable.

One possible solution in appropriate cases would be to gift the business asset to an elderly relative (eg a grandparent). The gift to the elderly relative would be free of IHT, and a CGT hold-over relief claim may be considered. On the elderly relative's death, 100% BPR should be available (the normal minimum period of ownership being relaxed because the conditions in *IHTA 1984, s 109* are satisfied). The property may then pass under the relative's will to the intended beneficiaries with the benefit of the CGT uplift to market value.

Example 12.9 – BPR and CGT uplift on death

Donald is a shareholder of Titanic Ltd, an unquoted trading company. The shares currently qualify for 100% BPR. He wishes to gift the shares to his son Michael during 2018/19. The shares are worth £1.4m, and there is an inherent capital gain on them, on which the potential CGT liability is approximately £250,000. Entrepreneurs' relief is not available.

Donald gives the shares (ie his desired gift to Michael) to his father Edward, who is in his late eighties. The gift is a PET, which would otherwise be subject to full BPR. The chargeable gain is held over under *TCGA 1992, s 165*. Donald hopes that Edward will leave the shares to his grandson Michael in his will (note there must be no prior agreement or arrangement).

On Edward's death, there is no IHT as 100% BPR is available. However, there is a CGT free uplift in the base cost of the shares to market value as at Edward's death. A CGT saving of £250,000 has therefore been achieved.

If Edward's will did not leave the shares to Michael, a deed of variation could achieve the same result, subject to the co-operation of the beneficiary under the will.

BPR, debt and charging business property

12.56 The value of relevant business property for BPR purposes is its net value (*IHTA 1984, s 110(a)*). 'Net value' is broadly the value of business assets, less any liabilities incurred for the purposes of the business (*IHTA 1984, s 110(b)*). For example, a sole trader's fixed and current business assets (eg plant and machinery and stock) are reduced by business liabilities (eg a bank overdraft) in determining the net value of the business.

The business property itself may be acquired with a mortgage or other loan. In such cases, the general rule for a debt (or 'incumbrance') charged on property is that it reduces the value of that property as far as possible (*IHTA 1984, s 162(4)*). This treatment applies to the extent that the liability is not already taken into account under *IHTA 1984, s 162B*, which is an anti-avoidance provision introduced in *FA 2013*. It broadly provides that if a liability was incurred (directly or indirectly) to acquire, maintain or enhance assets on which BPR (or agricultural property relief, or woodlands relief) is due, the liability reduces the value of those assets. BPR then applies to the resulting net value. However, this provision does not apply if a liability has already been taken into account under *IHTA 1984, s 110(b)* in arriving at the net value of the business (*IHTA 1984, s 162B(2)(a)*).

If any excess liability remains, it may be allowable as a deduction against the estate in general, subject to another anti-avoidance rule (in *IHTA 1984, s 175A*) regarding unpaid liabilities after death.

For example, a sole trader may have had a loan secured on his house, the funds from which were applied in financing the business. Prior to the introduction of *IHTA 1984, s 162B*, as the borrowings were charged on the house, *IHTA 1984, s 162(4)* provided that the 'incumbrance' on the house should be taken to reduce its value for IHT purposes. However, for mortgages and loans incurred on or after 6 April 2013, such borrowings would be deducted from the value of the business, before BPR is applied (*IHTA 1984, s 162B(2)*).

If a liability financed a mixture of business property and investment asset, and the liability has been partially repaid before an IHT charge arises, supplementary provisions set out the order in which the liability is treated as having been discharged (see *IHTA 1984, s 162C*).

As stated earlier in this chapter, 'business' has a wider meaning than 'trade' and can include the making or holding of investments. However, in determining whether a business interest or company shares are relevant business property, the investment 'business' must generally not predominate (*IHTA 1984, s 105(3)*).

12.57

Focus

Investors can no longer use BPR and the mortgage or charging provisions to their advantage as before, such as by borrowing on non-business assets (eg the home) and investing the proceeds in assets giving entitlement to BPR (eg AIM listed shares in trading companies), or possibly subscribing for shares in an unquoted family trading company. The borrowing must first be applied to the business property as opposed to the home, resulting in a loss of BPR. This treatment applies to liabilities incurred on or after 6 April 2013 (*FA 2013, Sch 36, para 5(2), (3)*).

In any event, the commercial risk generally inherent in such investments must be measured against any potential IHT benefit.

BPR and gifts with reservation

12.58 A lifetime transfer of business property may be treated as remaining comprised in the donor's estate, if the 'gifts with reservation' (GWR) rules apply (in *FA 1986, s 102* and *Sch 20*). An asset subject to the GWR rules can qualify for BPR, broadly if the following conditions are satisfied:

- the asset was relevant business property at the time of the gift; and

- the asset would qualify for BPR at the time of the GWR charge (ie on the donor's death or earlier release of the reservation) if the donee made a notional transfer of it.

The BPR conditions will generally need to be considered at the date of gift, and also when the GWR charge arises (ie on the death of the donor, or when the benefit ceases).

For the purposes of the two-year ownership test, any period of ownership by the donor before the gift is treated as that of the donee (*FA 1986, Sch 20, para 8(2))*. If the donee dies before the GWR charge, the period of ownership of the personal representatives or beneficiaries is also treated as that of the donee (*FA 1986, Sch 20, para 8(5)*).

A GWR is not generally a problem for IHT purposes if BPR at 100% is available and maintained, but there are specific circumstances where reservation can be fatal. For example, where BPR is at 50% on an asset used by a company controlled by the transferor, and the asset passes to a minority shareholder such that clawback is in point, the donee cannot satisfy the requirements of the relief (*FA 1986, Sch 20, para 8(1A)(b)*). Such a lifetime disposal can also be disadvantageous for CGT purposes, as it sacrifices the market value uplift on death.

If BPR is claimed on the basis that the original property has been sold and the proceeds used to buy other property which would (on a notional transfer of value by the donee immediately before the donor's death, apart from the ownership tests) qualify for BPR, HMRC guidance indicates that the replacement property provisions are 'complicated' and cases will be referred to their Technical Group (IHTM25384).

BPR and APR

12.59   Agricultural property relief (APR) is considered in the second part of this chapter (see **12.62** *et seq*). APR also applies automatically, and for the purposes of this chapter it should be noted that if the same property qualifies for both BPR and APR in respect of a transfer, APR takes precedence (*IHTA 1984, s 114(1)*).

However, the agricultural value may be lower than its value for BPR purposes (eg farmland with planning permission or development value), in which case if both reliefs are in point it may be possible to claim APR on the agricultural value, and BPR on the excess.

BPR clearances

12.60   It can often be difficult to know whether property qualifies for BPR. However, HMRC provide a BPR clearance procedure. It was initially described in HMRC Brief 25/08, and is a non-statutory clearance as to the application of the tax law to a specific transaction or event.

HMRC will give a view of the tax consequences of a transaction or event in the following circumstances (www.gov.uk/guidance/non-statutory-clearance-service-guidance):

- the relevant HMRC guidance has been fully considered, and/or the relevant helpline has been contacted; and

- the information needed could not be found; or

- there is remaining uncertainty about HMRC's interpretation of tax legislation.

Conversely, HMRC will not provide guidance or advice in some cases. On 13 June 2017, HMRC updated their general online guidance and also their BPR checklist (Annex C). The section 'When HMRC will not provide advice under this service' was amended to state that HMRC will confirm the reason why the advice requested has not been provided, if appropriate; listed examples include:

- Where all necessary information has not been provided.

- HMRC do not consider that there are genuine points of uncertainty.

- The advice requested amounts to asking HMRC to give tax planning advice or to approve tax planning products or arrangements.

- The application is about the treatment of transactions that HMRC consider are for the purpose of avoiding tax.

- HMRC are already checking the tax position for the period in question.

- Any related return for the period in question has become final (except for clearance applications in connection with an offshore disclosure being made via HMRC's digital disclosure service).

- There is a statutory clearance procedure applicable to the transaction.

- The advice sought relates to the application of the settlements legislation (in *ITTOIA 2005, Pt 5, Ch 5*) or the tax consequences of executing non-charitable trust deeds or settlements.

Annex C (BPR checklist) was updated to make clear that it may not be used for gifts to individuals, ten-year anniversary charges, conditional dispositions of property under a will, deeds of variation, the tax consequences of executing a trust deed, the application of *ITTOIA 2005, Pt 5, Ch 5*, valuations, or general confirmations of the status of businesses for BPR purposes.

The clearance facility is available if the transfer involves an immediately chargeable transfer. This means that (for example) a share transfer to a discretionary trust is possibly eligible for a clearance application as to the availability of BPR in respect of the shares, but (as indicated above) a potentially exempt transfer, such as a gift from one individual to another, is not.

The clearance facility is potentially helpful. However, for BPR applications involving a change of ownership of a business (succession), any clearance given will only remain valid for six months.

A checklist and guidance on HMRC's BPR clearance service (Annex C) is available via the GOV.UK website (tinyurl.com/HMRC-BPR-Clearance-App).

Testing for BPR

12.61 In cases where the BPR clearance service is not appropriate, it may be possible to 'test' the availability of BPR. There is a specific problem where a will has created, or has been varied so as to create, a nil rate band discretionary trust and the executors wish to put into it property that qualifies for relief.

Consider the following, which has previously been suggested by Emma Chamberlain and Chris Whitehouse as a possible solution to the problem:

- set up the discretionary will trust;

- transfer from the estate of the deceased to the will trust substantial value in the form of specific 'target' property which (it is hoped) qualifies for BPR, but without making the transfer dependent on its availability; and

- transfer to the will trust such cash sum as would not attract a tax charge (eg the available nil rate band, ignoring the target property).

The thinking is that the transfer to such a trust will prompt HMRC to adjudicate the BPR issue, since unless the trustees within two years of death appoint property to an exempt beneficiary such as the spouse there has been a chargeable transfer. If BPR is allowed, fine: the trust can roll forward or can perhaps be the vehicle for further IHT saving, such as where the spouse buys the business property so as to recycle the relief.

If relief is denied, provided the decision is reached quickly enough, the trustees have the option of appointing the 'failed' assets to the spouse within two years under *IHTA 1984, s 144* to avoid paying the tax.

AGRICULTURAL PROPERTY RELIEF

AGRICULTURAL ASSETS: PROPERTY

12.62 Agricultural property relief (APR) is, as the name implies, a relief not an exemption and that distinction is important. APR operates by reducing the value transferred by a reduction set at 100% or 50% dependent on determinative tests. The code is set out in *IHTA 1984, ss 115–124C* and is very similar to that for business property relief (BPR), but there are important differences of detail.

HMRC have published their guidance on the entire APR section of the Inheritance Tax Manual and reading is strongly recommended – it is generally well expressed and carefully written (see IHTM24000 et seq.).

The HMRC website also contains a short but readable 'Customer Guide' to APR (see www.hmrc.gov.uk/cto/customerguide/page17.htm), which contains useful and helpful information aimed at both the professional adviser and the client. Accordingly, as clients become better informed and seek, naturally, to keep the cost of advice to a minimum, it is not unreasonable for them to expect practitioners to know at least as much as, but preferably much more than, is available in that HMRC Customer Guide.

APR is available on 'agricultural property' (ie primarily agricultural land or pasture used for agricultural purpose), but with such term also extended to include:

- woodland and buildings used for the intensive rearing of livestock or fish, *but* only if the occupation of that woodland or those buildings is ancillary to the occupation of the agricultural land or pasture: see *Williams v HMRC* [2005] STC (SCD) 782;

- cottages, farm buildings and farmhouses and the land occupied with them, but only if of a *character appropriate* to the property;

- stud farms. HMRC consistently argue that for APR purposes the stud farm must be 'viable', hence run for profit along established business lines and not a mere hobby enterprise, but there is scant authority for that former view. Running a stud can be a business but one difficulty is enthusiasm and an absence or lack of a business approach: a person who loves horses and spends all their time caring for them, showing them and talking to like-minded people who may occasionally buy horses, may have little time or interest in keeping detailed stock records or year-end valuations and the like so as to prove that their passion is actually also a trade. It is therefore necessary if not critical to demonstrate that the stud farm is run on business lines and has the attributes and makings of a business.

IHTA 1984, s 115(5) used to restrict APR to property located in the UK, the Channel Islands and the Isle of Man but this was amended by *FA 2009, s 122* with effect from 23 April 2009 – the relief is now extended to land within the European Economic Area (note that, for BPR purposes, relief was always operative on a worldwide basis).

12.63 Following the well-publicised Lands Tribunal decision in *Lloyds TSB Private Banking Plc (personal representative of Rosemary Antrobus, dec'd) v HMRC* DET/47/2005 (known as *Antrobus II*), the distinction between the purchasing power (and attributes) of a 'working' and 'lifestyle' farmer may be significant when considering the agricultural value of agricultural property. Another difficulty is the link, or nexus, between land and a farmhouse since often the main value of APR will be not be in the land but in the farmhouse. If that link between the land and the farmhouse is not strong enough, APR will be denied on the latter. HMRC are also leaning more actively toward initial denial of APR on the farmhouse where the supporting land is subject to grazing licences, which is often the case where the farmer has scaled down his farming activities by reason of old age and infirmity – the HMRC argument presented pivots on the notion that merely allowing others to use the land for grazing does not in itself amount to farming and as such it cannot be said that the farmhouse is the centre of farming operations. Even so, this does not mean that the HMRC view should prevail – much will depend on the history of the farm, the nature of the terms of that grazing licence and, in particular, the activities carried out by the farmer land owner in tending, maintaining and nurturing that grazing land.

12.64   In broad terms, APR at 100% applies to vacant property, or property subject to a lease created or succeeded to on or after 1 September 1995; else APR at the reduced rate of 50% applies otherwise unless vacant possession can be obtained within 12 months (or within 24 months under ESC F17) or the property is broadly valued at market value. Importantly, the value to which APR attaches is not market value but the value which the property would carry if subject to a perpetual covenant prohibiting its use otherwise than as agricultural property. As a consequence, this latter value will typically be less than the open market value, and this disparity will be greater to the extent there is development potential or where the land, for any reason, commands a premium. Accordingly, even APR at 100% will often fail to eliminate the entire transfer of value attributable to the agricultural property in question. Examples include:

- small areas of grassland that would attract indulgent parents of pony-riding offspring;

- agricultural land bought at a premium price as a 'safe haven' investment by non-farmers; and

- areas of land of particular beauty that command a 'leisure' or 'vanity' premium in excess of their agricultural value.

Some factors may now limit this trend – in recent years there has been some resurgence in the value of farmland, perhaps driven by better commercial yields; indulgent parents and others may now have less spare liquidity as a consequence of the far-reaching shadow of the past recession, the legacy of which still persists. In the light of this and where supported by relevant facts, HMRC's standard opening argument that not all of that value should qualify for agricultural relief should be strongly resisted.

However, such a resistant approach should be distinguished from the situation where it is clear there is a dominant development value, as demonstrated in the BPR case of *McCall and Keenan (personal representatives of McLean, dec'd) v Revenue and Customs* [2009] NICA 12 (see **12.4**), a decision of the Court of Appeal in Northern Ireland. In that case the land had an agricultural value of £165,000, but was zoned for redevelopment and was thus worth an impressive £5.8 million at the date of death. It was accepted that the owner, having lost her mental faculties, could not be said herself to be carrying on a business, but her son-in-law looked after the land on her behalf.

The Court of Appeal confirmed the view of the Special Commissioner that there was a business (just) but it was held to be an investment business; the test applied was that of an intelligent businessman; a landowner who derives income from land is an investor if he carries out only incidental maintenance work. The use of the land by graziers was sufficiently exclusive for the land to be an investment. The agisting farmer could exclude other graziers, including the landowner, which prevented the owner from using the land in a way that interfered with the grazing. The case is a useful and detailed reconsideration of the BPR issues considered earlier in this chapter.

CLAWBACK

12.65 Where a donor makes a PET of a lifetime gift of agricultural property (or business property qualifying for BPR) potentially qualifying for APR at that time but dies within seven years such that the PET fails, there is a risk that APR potential attaching to the original gift will be clawed back. That clawback can be avoided if the donee retained the original property from the date of the transfer until the date of death and it continued to qualify at that latter point (by reference to the donee) or if he disposed of it during that period he reinvested the net proceeds of sale in qualifying replacement property. In the latter scenario, the reinvestment must take place within three years post the sale of the original property (*IHTA 1984, s 118(1)*). In contrast to the position for CGT rollover relief, 'reinvestment' during the 12 months before the disposal of the original property is not permitted.

It is generally accepted that professional costs and CGT may be deducted in computing the net proceeds of sale before reinvestment; importantly, reinvestment into business property is permitted even when the original property was agricultural property (see RI95).

Can the donee of a PET of a qualifying business or agricultural property safely dispose of it four years after the gift, thus before expiry of the donor's seven-year survival window? Yes, but only if it is the donor who dies within the next three years (the replacement window), because the donee can smartly reinvest the net proceeds in qualifying replacement assets – there is no requirement to retain the reinvested assets for a minimum period (*IHTA 1984, s 124B*). If, however, the *donee* dies within the seven-year period, the opportunity to reinvest and thereby prevent clawback is lost. Reinvestment by the donee's personal representatives will not prevent clawback.

Use of chargeable transfer to limit clawback

12.66   If the death of the donor (or donee) within seven years is likely, then the classification of the lifetime gift as a chargeable transfer may be preferable to PET status. This is so since in the case of a failed PET, there may be full clawback which would impact on the donor's cumulative clock whilst for the chargeable transfer there is only a clawback on the death rate uplift – it does not affect the seven-year cumulation principle of the donor's lifetime clock.

For a PET, once the seven years have elapsed the donee may sell the asset without risk of clawback. Likewise, APR is still available on death even though the inheritor may sell the very next day.

INVESTMENTS IN THE CONTEXT OF FARMING

12.67

Focus

The *Farmer* case (below) is critical in its demonstration of the overlap and interaction of APR and BPR in a business context. The established principles have been soundly reinforced by later case decisions, notably *Brander*, but *Farmer* remains the main reference point where there is any element of diversification away from the central farming activity.

In *Farmer and another (executors of Farmer dec'd) v IRC* [1999] STC (SCD) 321 (see **12.8**), the deceased was a shareholder in a company that carried on the business of letting properties as well as the business of farming. The profits of the letting business were greater than the farming profits, but the farming assets, which admittedly included the farmhouse itself, were (at death) more valuable than the properties used for letting. HMRC refused BPR arguing that since the profits of the letting business were greater than those derived from the farming activity, the business was wholly or mainly one of making investments.

The executors appealed to the Special Commissioners, who found in their favour. It was held that the nature of the business had to be considered in the round and that no single factor – such as profitability – should be determinative. On the facts, although the lettings were more profitable than the farm, the overall context of the business, the capital employed, the time spent by the employees/consultants and the levels of turnover supported the conclusion that the business consisted mainly of farming.

It should be noted that *Farmer* was a case on BPR rather than APR but, until the decision in *McCall* noted above, it was helpful and a point of reference for those borderline cases where BPR, as is nearly always the case, might be more valuable than APR, ie where agricultural land has development value but APR, even at 100%, is restricted to the lower agricultural value as noted at **12.64** above.

The 'fallout' from *McCall* has had a significant impact and local HMRC Inspectors are not shy of relying on it to deny relief on initial application, as noted at **12.64** above.

The principles drawn from the *Farmer* case were further underpinned in *Brander (personal representative of the fourth Earl of Balfour v Revenue and Customs* [2009] UKFTT 101. Here the First-tier Tribunal had to consider the replacement property provisions of *IHTA 1984, s 107*; but in doing so found it necessary to decide whether farming and related operations fell within the 'wholly or mainly' exclusion from business relief under *IHTA 1984, s 105(3)*. The tribunal followed the *Farmer* case in allowing that the running of a typical Scottish landed estate, consisting mainly of farming and of management of cottages (that were often let to people whose expertise could benefit the estate), was not an investment business. HMRC failed in their appeal to the Upper Tribunal heard in May 2010 (*Revenue and Customs v Brander (personal representative of the Fourth Earl of Balfour)* [2010] UKUT 300 (TCC)) (see **12.8**).

FARMING PARTNERSHIP

12.68   For a fuller discussion of partnerships, please refer to the first half of this chapter which considers the BPR perspective (see **12.31** and following).

In relation to a limited liability partnership (LLP), under the *Limited Liability Partnerships Act 2000* the LLP is not treated as owned by the individual partners. For APR there is no change in the treatment of assets held outside, but used in, the partnership, nor is incorporation into an LLP regarded as an interruption for APR and/or BPR.

Partnership farmland

12.69   The old rule that treated partnership property as personal or moveable property was repealed by the *Trusts of Land and Appointment of*

Trustees Act 1996. Land held outside a partnership (or company controlled by the taxpayer) and used for an agricultural purpose attracts 100% APR (*IHTA 1984, s 116*). If held as another business asset, 50% BPR is available (*IHTA 1984, s 105(1)(d)*), but free of the restriction as to agricultural value imposed by *IHTA 1984, s 115(3)*.

PERIOD OF OWNERSHIP OR OCCUPATION

Minimum period of ownership

12.70

Focus

Access to APR pivots on satisfying the minimum ownership period of two or seven years but critically this rule is modified in two key circumstances where death is a common factor.

Unlike BPR where a single ownership period test applies, for APR there are two alternative time rules which must be considered, namely the owner occupier and the landlord tenant occupier. Under *IHTA 1984, s 117(a)*, APR is available where the transferor has occupied and farmed the land for the purposes of agriculture (farmed in hand) for *two years*, whilst under *IHTA 1984, s 117(b)* that period is extended to *seven years*, during which the transferor has owned the land and it has been occupied (by anyone) for the purposes of agriculture (the landowner).

Contrast these rules with those for BPR, where a period of ownership will count towards the qualifying period even though the asset may not have been used for business until just before the transfer (note that in Scotland the relevant date for ownership may be that of execution of the disposition, not the later recording in the Register of Sasines: see *Marquess of Linlithgow v HMRC* [2010] CSIH 19).

Slightly amended rules apply to farming companies: see below. The quality of occupation is considered towards the end of **12.111**: it is always wise to document the basis on which land is being used, to support the claim when the time comes. As will be seen in the commentary below on the case of *Atkinson v HMRC* (see **12.111**), the precise basis of occupation can determine the tax analysis.

Spouses and civil partners: a special succession rule

12.71   The minimum period of ownership requirement is modified where the transferor who acquired the APR property did so on the death of his spouse or civil partner. *IHTA 1984, s 120(1)(b)* deems such a transferor to have owned the property for the combined period of his own and deceased spouse's ownership and where that aggregate is equal to or greater than two years then the ownership test is satisfied.

Importantly, this aggregation applies only to periods of ownership falling either side of a transfer on the death of the first spouse. It does not apply where the first spouse made a lifetime gift of the land to the second spouse who later dies, and the author is aware of many cases where flawed reliance has been placed on the misunderstanding of the rule. This point demonstrates the sheer complexity of APR, which underpins the need of the professional advisor to continually review and consider the applicable rules pertinent to the individual facts in each case.

Successions

12.72　Under *IHTA 1984, s 120(1)(a)*, a legatee is deemed to own an inherited asset from the date of death and where the legacy was from his spouse, the spouse's period of ownership is also deemed to be counted for the purpose of determining the qualifying ownership period – see **12.71** above.

However, a lesser-known provision will also assist the legatee who has inherited agricultural property from a person (whether his spouse or not) who satisfied the minimum period of ownership requirement, where the ownership requirement is effectively waived on a subsequent transfer by the legatee: see **12.73**.

Successive transfers

12.73　Where there are two successive transfers, of which at least one was on death, and the earlier transferor satisfied the ownership or occupation requirements, these time requirements (subject to certain conditions) are waived for the transferee (*IHTA 1984, s 121*).

Example 12.10 – Legacy of agricultural land

A owns agricultural land which qualifies for APR in all respects including minimum period of ownership and, on his death in September 2018, he leaves that agricultural land to B. The land can still qualify for APR on a later transfer by B, even if that transfer occurs less than two years after A's death – B can 'piggyback' on A's time qualification. Furthermore, as the transfer by A to B ('the earlier transfer') was on A's death, the transfer by B ('the subsequent transfer') can be either a lifetime or a death transfer.

> ### Example 12.11 – Lifetime gift of farming company shares
>
> On 30 September 2018, C, who also owns land which qualifies for APR in all respects including minimum period of ownership, makes a lifetime gift of his majority shareholding in a farming company to D. That land will qualify for APR on a transfer by D on his later death by 'piggybacking' on C's qualification even if D's death is within two years of the gift. Since the original transfer by C to D ('the earlier transfer') was a lifetime transfer, the transfer by D ('the subsequent transfer') will benefit from *IHTA 1984, s 121* only if it is on D's death. If D wishes to make a lifetime transfer which qualifies for APR, he will need to build up his own period of ownership.

In both of the examples above, it is irrelevant whether A and B or C and D are spouses/civil partners because in each case, A and C had owned the shares for the required period. The special treatment given to spouses/civil partners would only be relevant if:

- the earlier transferor had not satisfied the minimum period; and

- the earlier transfer was on death.

Revisiting the example of A and B above, consider that A and B were married/ civil partners and that A had owned the land for one year only – B could benefit from APR on a subsequent transfer by holding the land for a further year after A's death in order to achieve the minimum two-year combined ownership period (*IHTA 1984, s 120(1)(b)*). The rule would be dis-applied if the transfer had been made during lifetime – see **12.71** above.

Replacements

12.74 Consider the case of a farmer, who having owned agricultural property and occupied it for qualifying agricultural purposes for the requisite period, is now minded to sell. If he reinvests no more than the (net) proceeds of sale of his original farm in the purchase of new agricultural assets, there is no need to re-qualify under the ownership and occupation tests as *IHTA 1984, s 118(1)* credits him with his past occupation period. However, if the farmer invests additional funds perhaps to buy a larger unit, *IHTA 1984, s 118* relief will extend only to the replacement proportion of the new farm and a fresh qualification period will apply to the excess (*IHTA 1984, s 118(3)*), but note that this restriction does not apply if the replacement was brought about by the formation, alteration or dissolution of a partnership (*IHTA 1984, s 118(4)*).

Residuary estates

12.75 A legatee or transferee whose minimum period of ownership has been waived or reduced by *IHTA 1984, s 120* or *IHTA 1984, s 121* (see **12.72** and **12.73** above) must nevertheless hold that property as qualifying agricultural property in order to access APR. That relief would not be compromised if the legatee died or made a gift before the administration of the estate has been completed.

IHTA 1984, s 91(1) treats the legatee as being *entitled as from the date of the death*, and therefore the administration period will count as time during which the legatee could occupy or own the land. However, as soon as the complexities of administration of this estate will allow, and liquidity is assured, the personal representatives should assent or appropriate the agricultural assets to the legatee.

AGRICULTURAL VALUE

Introduction

12.76

Focus

It is critical to be aware that APR, if in point, is restricted to the agricultural value of the asset alone – this may not be and, certainly in the case of realty, is unlikely to be the same as market value, which may be significantly higher.

As was noted at **12.62** above, APR is available on only so much of the value transferred as is attributable to the agricultural value of the property, which is the value that it would have if it were subject to a perpetual covenant prohibiting its use otherwise than as agricultural property (*IHTA 1984, s 115(3)*).

In the case of an attractive farmhouse or of land with development potential, this will normally be much less than its value in the open market without such a restriction; and (as noted in the leading case next mentioned) lower than property that is merely subject to a planning tie. A restriction in a planning permission can, and quite often is, varied after a number of years.

Often in the case of small parcels of land there will be a transfer of value equal to the excess of market value over agricultural value, but as noted this should not apply to larger parcels of bare land sold as farms in the present economic climate.

12.77 In the landmark case of *Lloyds TSB (personal representative of Antrobus, dec'd) v IRC* [2002] STC (SCD) 468 (known as '*Antrobus I*'), a farmhouse, Cookhill Priory, attracted APR, as being of a 'character appropriate' to the agricultural land and pasture forming part of the estate, within *IHTA 1984, s 115(2)*.

Subsequently, in *Lloyds TSB Private Banking Plc (personal representative of Rosemary Antrobus, dec'd) v HMRC* DET/47/2005 (known as '*Antrobus II*'), the Lands Tribunal was required to consider the 'agricultural value' of Cookhill Priory for the purposes of *IHTA 1984, s 115(3)*. The tribunal concluded that the agricultural value should be determined on the basis that the assumed perpetual covenant in *IHTA 1984, s 115(3)* would have prohibited use of the land in any other way and, after excluding 'lifestyle' farmers from the theoretical market, the open market value was eventually set at £608,475 and the agricultural value set at 70% thereof, at £425,932. This was a point that HMRC pursued vigorously, so the practitioner should allow for it in valuing a transfer of land as well as farmhouses, as noted at **12.62** above but that does not mean that the discount will apply in all cases.

Availability of relief since *Antrobus II*

12.78 The question 'what is a farmhouse?' had been discussed in *Antrobus II* even though, strictly, it was of no concern of the Lands Tribunal, having already been determined in *Antrobus I*. It was noted, in *McKenna v HMRC* [2006] SpC 00565, that the test in *Antrobus II* should be approached with caution, though in *McKenna* that was not enough to secure APR for Rosteague House, a fine house by the sea (a house with land rather than the more accepted view of land with a house).

The test that has emerged with some strength is that a farmhouse is the dwelling, the hub, the centre from which the farmer manages the farm, so where the land is actually all subject to a contracting agreement and the landowner does virtually no farming himself it is more difficult to sustain that argument. This is an area of prime interest for HMRC and, in the author's experience, there is clear evidence that HMRC are sharpening their attack by probing closely into the depth and nature of the farming activities undertaken. The moral is clear in that relief for the farmhouse should never be assumed, but rather should be carefully reviewed in anticipation that any claim may need to be robustly defended.

Special valuation issues

12.79   Where a person has both freehold land and a share in a partnership to which the land is let on an agricultural tenancy, there is a natural question as to whether the two interests should be valued on the assumption that they are sold together, and if so, how that valuation should be calculated.

In *IRC v Gray (Executor of Lady Fox)* [1994] STC 360, the testatrix was the freeholder and had a 92.5% interest in the partnership which held the tenancy of that freehold estate. The Court of Appeal decided that, for valuation on death purposes, a freehold reversion in land *must* be aggregated with a partnership interest which holds a tenancy of that land (following the principle of realising the maximum realisable price without undue expenditure of time and effort: *Duke of Buccleuch v IRC* [1967] 1 506, HL). In other words, it is a single 'natural unit'. The existence of a tenancy can therefore bring about the worst of both worlds. The valuation will be initially on vacant possession principles notwithstanding the tenancy, but, by virtue of *IHTA 1984, s 116(2)(c)*, only a 50% agricultural property discount may be available (where tenanted prior to 1 September 1995) rather than 100%.

12.80   *Walton's Executors v IRC* [1996] STC 68, CA, concerned the valuation of an agricultural tenancy for capital transfer tax (CTT) purposes, where the W family were the freeholders which had let the farm to a partnership of Mr W and son. On Mr W's death, HMRC claimed that the capital transfer tax value of the lease was the difference between the value of the freehold with vacant possession and its value subject to the lease. HMRC's reasoning was that, on Mr W's death, there was a hypothetical sale of the tenancy valued at £70,000.

The taxpayer's claim, accepted by the Land Tribunal and the Court of Appeal, was that there was no hypothetical sale, as the son did not wish to sell but to continue the farming. Therefore, the value of the tenancy was based on a potential profit rental basis (£6,300), ie a real-world situation. This was typically a small value in the absence of any special purchaser, who did not exist in this case.

THE LEVEL OF RELIEF

Assets qualifying for 100% relief

12.81

Focus

The landowner can secure APR on agricultural land and buildings used in the farming activity carried on by the underlying tenant by '*piggy backing*'

---

on the qualification of that tenant. However, be aware of the denial of APR for the farmhouse where the latter and the land are not in common tenant occupation.

The circumstances in which 100% APR is available are set out in *IHTA 1984, s 116(2)(a)–(c)*, namely:

- *Transferor has vacant possession or the right to obtain it within 12 months (IHTA 1984, s 116(2)(a))*

  This provision covers owner-occupied farms and farms where the transferor's interest entitles him to vacant possession or will do within the next 12 months (by concession, extended to 24 months (ESC F17)). It is important to note that a partnership could, according to the terms of its agreement, have occupation rights but these must not prejudice the landowner's right to vacant possession.

- *Transferor has held his interest since before 10 March 1981 (IHTA 1984, s 116(2)(b))*

  'Working farmer' relief is still available under this heading and is still seen occasionally in practice. It applies where the transferor held his beneficial interest since before 10 March 1981 where had he given away that interest before then and made an appropriate claim, *FA 1975, Sch 8, para 2* would have applied in computing the value transferred without limitation by *FA 1975, Sch 8, para 5*. The main elements of these pre-1981 rules are:

  - a limit of £250,000 in value and 1,000 acres in area; and

  - the requirement that the transferor was wholly or mainly engaged in farming during five out of the previous seven years. The latter test is deemed to be satisfied if not less than 75% of his income was derived from agriculture.

  Relief will be denied if at any time between 10 March 1981 and the transfer of value in question the transferor acquired the right to vacant possession, acquired the right to obtain vacant possession within 12 months, or failed to acquire either such right by reason of an act or deliberate omission.

  Relief may be cut down in certain circumstances: see *IHTA 1984, s 116(4)*.

- *The property is let on a tenancy beginning on or after 1 September 1995 (IHTA 1984, s 116(2)(c))*

  This relief, designed to encourage the granting of fresh agricultural tenancies, coincided with the introduction of the *Agricultural Tenancies Act 1995* which deregulated the market for let farmland.

Where a tenant dies on or after 1 September 1995 and his tenancy vests under his will or intestacy in another person, that other person's tenancy is deemed under *IHTA 1984, s 116(5A)* to commence at the date of the earlier death for the purposes of determining whether 100% APR is available. Similar provision is made (although this is not applicable to property in Scotland) where, on the death of the surviving tenant on or after 1 September 1995, another person obtains a tenancy under a legislative right.

Where the tenant has given notice to retire in favour of a new tenant, but before such retirement takes place the landlord dies, then the new tenant is deemed to have commenced his tenancy immediately before that latter death, so the estate of the landlord benefits from 100% APR under this head as if the new tenancy had already commenced. This extension of the relief is subject to the condition that the tenant does indeed retire in favour of the new tenant after the landlord's death and within 30 months of the giving of notice.

Landlords and tenants may work together to bring an old arrangement under the post 31 August 1995 rules (surrender and re-grant), ie the landlord might add land to the tenancy, making it a new one. There are two points to consider:

(1)   The surrender of an existing lease followed by a re-grant on a non-arm's length basis undertaken purely in order to obtain 100% APR in the future might amount to a PET by the tenant but this is thought unlikely through absence of gratuitous intent (*IHTA 1984, s 10*).

(2)   The surrender of the old lease could constitute a CGT disposition by the lessee under either the value-shifting provisions in *TCGA 1992, s 29* or by reason of valuable consideration (re-grant). There is a strong argument that this might be avoided if a new lease is granted in an arm's-length transaction on the same property at a different rent but otherwise on the same terms, but only if that could be justified commercially. Further relief is also available under the lesser-known ESC D39 ('Extension of leases'). If the surrender is regarded as a chargeable disposal, it is HMRC's view that the gain on the extinguishment of the old lease cannot be the subject of holdover on grounds that the new lease is a separate asset.

Assets qualifying for 50% relief

12.82   50% APR is available on agricultural property which qualifies in all other respects but which does not fall within any of the three heads of 100% APR. This will mainly comprise property which has been let since before 1 September 1995 and there is no right to vacant possession within the next 12 (or 24) months.

Concessionary reliefs

12.83 Two Extra-statutory Concessions are relevant here:

(1) ESC F17 treats the condition in *IHTA 1984, s 116(2)(a)* as satisfied where the transferor's interest in the property, immediately before the transfer, carried the right to vacant possession within 24 months (as opposed to 12 months) of the date of the transfer (see **12.81** above). It also treats the conditions as satisfied where, notwithstanding the terms of the tenancy, the transferor's interest is valued at an amount broadly equivalent to the vacant possession value. See *IRC v Gray (Executor of Lady Fox)* [1994] STC 360, CA – see **12.79**.

(2) ESC F16 also gives 100% APR in respect of transfers of agricultural property which include a cottage occupied by a retired farm employee or spouse. This is subject to the occupier being a protected tenant or having a lease for life as part of his contract of employment. In practice, as fewer people actually work on the land and, of those who do, fewer are employed but rather are contractors, this relief will eventually become obsolete.

THE MAIN ESTATE-PLANNING LESSONS

12.84 APR in its current form is very generous to the non-farmer investment landowner and for that reason its continued existence will always be the subject of debate and concern. Since APR is available on lifetime gifts as well as transfers on death, those who currently qualify for relief might wish to consider making lifetime gifts to insulate themselves as far as possible against future changes in the law which would deny/restrict relief. On the other hand, there are some advantages in delaying making gifts, which need to be considered too.

Shareholdings and partnerships (LLP)

12.85

Focus

BPR and APR work closely together where there is central farming business activity but there can be complications where that activity is incorporated.

The real difficulty with a limited farming company is (see *IHTA 1984, s 122*) that only a majority shareholding qualifies for APR. If the company qualifies in all respects for BPR then that will not matter, but if it does not, then a minority shareholder may find that his asset is in a mere investment company carrying no access to relief. Subject to that, several issues must be considered:

- Selling the shares or retiring from the partnership could cause significant loss of relief. Not only will the possibility of 100% APR on the shares or partnership interest themselves be lost, but so will the 50% BPR on assets belonging to the individual and used in the business of the company or partnership.

- If it is likely that shares, which qualify for APR now, will in the future cease to do so, consider making a lifetime gift now. It may be possible to hold over CGT under *TCGA 1992, s 165*. The downsides to this are:

  - the possibility of clawback (see **12.65** above);

  - the lack of CGT uplift on death;

  - the gift with reservation provisions are still relevant even where a lifetime gift of business or agricultural property is made. *FA 1986, Sch 20, para 8* modifies the gifts with reservation provisions. In general terms, if the donor reserves a benefit, then the conditions for relief must continue to be met by reference to the donor until the donor's death in order to preserve the relief and reduce the charge on death. However, by *FA 1986, Sch 20, para 8(1A)(b)* the rate at which relief is given is calculated by reference to the donee; thus these provisions cause difficulty where a transferee, for some reason, does not have that control.

The rules as to gifts with reservation contain several complexities. One of them is illustrated with agricultural land.

Example 12.12 – Gift with reservation of agricultural land

On 31 October 2014, Boris made a gift of the land but continued to occupy and farm it until his death on 30 September 2018 such that the transfer fell within the gift with reservation rules. For APR purposes, the donor farmer was in occupation at death so APR should be available under *FA 1986, Sch 20, para 8*; but will BPR be available in respect of any 'premium' value not qualifying for APR?

FA 1986, Sch 20, para 8(1A)(b) provides a 'piggyback' quality by treating the deemed transfer as being made by the donee of the land, disregarding the shortness of period of ownership if less than two years. Thus, if the donee qualifies for BPR, there will be no clawback.

Use of 'relevant property' trusts

12.86

Focus

Be aware of the conflicting APR application to the value of non-qualifying assets leaving the confines of a relevant property trust before and after the first ten-year charge.

APR can reduce IHT otherwise chargeable under the IHT regime applicable to 'relevant property' trusts which, since *FA 2006*, now comprises nearly all lifetime settlements. In determining whether certain conditions, such as the minimum period of ownership, are met, references to the transferor are treated as references to the trustees (*IHTA 1984, ss 103(1)(b)* and *115(1)(b)*).

A trust in which the assets comprise only property that qualifies for 100% APR, with no market value premium, can neatly sidestep the impact of any ten-yearly or exit charges. Although APR does not reduce the effective rate at which tax is charged on an exit before the first ten-year anniversary, this is not a problem provided the value transferred is, post application of APR, reduced to nil – in other words, the asset subject to the exit charge, with identical agricultural and market value, qualifies for 100% APR in its own right (see **12.87** below).

12.87   The position is not so simple where:

- APR is at 50% (ie on let land pre-1 September 1995); or
- APR is given against part of the actual value (ie a farmhouse).

In these cases the impact of APR on both the ten-yearly charge and exit charges *after* the first ten-yearly charge can reduce both the rate of tax and the value transferred.

However, it is important to be aware that a different rule applies during the first ten years of the trust's life. In this period, APR operates to reduce only the initial value transferred into trust (thus from the settlor's perspective) or else to attach to the exiting asset if it qualifies for APR in its own right. Its impact is ignored in arriving at the exit charge itself of which the principal component is the value of trust property on creation/added later ignoring APR. Accordingly, to obtain maximum benefit from APR, it is recommended that distributions during the first ten years are, where possible, avoided.

12.88 The transfer of farming assets into a trust, whether by lifetime gift or on death, is often one of the best estate-planning methods available due to the availability of APR of a maximum 100%. Subject to any premium over agricultural value, agricultural assets can be held in such a trust almost indefinitely without attracting any ten-yearly charges or exit charges after that first ten-year anniversary.

It is therefore critical that the trustees fully satisfy the relevant APR conditions at each ten-year anniversary. Assuming that the 100% rate applies and that any other assets in the trust fall within the nil rate band (to include any premium over agricultural value) – the effective ten-year anniversary charge rate will be nil%. A curious feature of the regime is that this nil rate will continue to apply until immediately prior to the next ten-year anniversary, even if the assets comprised within the trust are no longer business or agricultural assets (ie because the trust fund consists of the proceeds of sale). This provides ample scope for tax planning.

APR 'recycled'

12.89 In certain circumstances, APR can effectively be obtained twice on the same property. This is also considered in the context of business property (see **12.52**). Assume that, on the death of the first spouse/civil partner, agricultural property is left on discretionary trust in favour of the surviving spouse and issue. APR and a CGT uplift of the base cost to market value should be obtained on that first spouse's death.

The surviving spouse/civil partner has the option to purchase the agricultural property from the trustees at its market value. Subject to surviving the requisite two-year period (note that the benefit of the aggregation period under *IHTA 1984, s 120* is not available here, since the asset did not pass directly from spousal partner to partner but from spousal partner into trust), the spouse may then obtain APR a second time – either on their death or on a lifetime transfer. The CGT-free uplift should also be available a second time.

12.90 Life assurance is worth considering where, as in this example, the effectiveness of a plan to minimise IHT is dependent on a particular individual's survival for a specific period. One option would be to purchase term cover for the surviving spouse for at least two years, and this would be appropriate if the matter is being considered at or after the date of the first spouse's death.

Alternatively, even before the death of the first (business-owning) spouse, life assurance could be taken out to cover the risk of the second spouse dying first.

Obviously, if that risk materialised, it would prevent the plan for double relief from working. In this case, the cover should be against:

- the risk of the second (non-business owning) spouse dying first; *and*

- the risk of that second spouse dying within two years of the first spouse. This would be a form of term assurance, but that term would be dependent on the date of death of the first spouse, ie the life of X + two years.

Example 12.13 – 'Doubling up' on APR/BPR

Celia Johnson was married with children and grandchildren. Her estate (after allowing for funeral and debts) comprised net liquid assets and savings, of £2,325,000; 30% of the family trading company, Johnson Knitwear Ltd, which makes socks, and is worth £500,000; and Hill Top Farm which Mrs Johnson farmed under an agreement with her neighbour. The farmhouse is worth £500,000 and the land and other buildings £780,000.

By her will made in August 2016, Mrs Johnson left, to a discretionary trust for close family members:

- the shares in the knitwear company; and

- the farmland (but not the house); and

- cash equal to the nil rate band at her death.

The drafting of the will made it clear exactly how much passed to the trust, avoiding the difficulties noted in *RSPCA v Sharp* [2010] EWHC 268 (Ch). The remaining assets were left to her widower. He was also given an option to buy the business and agricultural assets from the trust at market value.

30 April 2018: death of Mrs Johnson

There is no IHT due to the interaction of APR, BPR, spousal exemption and the nil rate band. There will also be a CGT-free uplift to market value of the base cost of all the assets. The nil rate band for 2018/19 is £325,000 so, on the basis that Mrs Johnson had made no chargeable lifetime gifts, the amount of cash that would go into the trust would be determined by any adjustments, as for example 30% of the value of the farmhouse not qualifying for APR. Of the cash, therefore, up to £325,000 would go into the trust but about £2m would go to Mr Johnson absolutely. He also, of course, acquired the option to buy the business and agricultural assets from the trust at market value.

Mr Johnson promptly (ie in May 2018) buys the business and agricultural assets from the trust using £1,280,000 from the cash that he inherited absolutely. Having little else to do, he takes a more active interest in running the farm than his late wife had done, using the farm kitchen as the place from which he works. The trustees made substantial distributions to the family. Mr Johnson survives a further two years from the exercise of the option.

31 May 2019: Death of Mr Johnson

The assets in his estate would be:

- the farmhouse (inherited by him in April 2018);

- the land, with 100% APR (owned since May 2018);

- the shares, with 100% BPR (also owned two years); and

- cash (about £720,000 less any living expenses and small gifts).

There was never any need for the trustees to pay income to Mr Johnson: he had sufficient in his own right.

The IHT taxation of the trust created under the will of Mrs Johnson is complex. There is a single transfer on death under *IHTA 1984, s 4*, of which the transfer of the nil rate band is only part, with the balance comprising property qualifying for APR/BPR. However, the general rule for relevant property trusts is that, even though they may be established within the nil rate band that is ignored when calculating the exit charge in the first ten years. This is because what is measured is the transfer itself and not the value transferred as reduced by reliefs such as, in this case, APR/BPR. Thus, unless the exit is a distribution *in specie* of property qualifying for APR/BPR such that it is itself reduced to nil, an exit charge may still trigger.

The business and agricultural property will benefit from a second capital gains tax-free uplift of their base costs to market value on Mr Johnson's death. Although the introduction of the transferable nil rate band in *FA 2008* reduces the necessity for its use on the first death, this example demonstrates how it can still be helpful to utilise the nil rate band on that first death.

It should be noted that when dealing with relevant property trusts the capital gains tax position is different if they are created on death rather than in lifetime. There was some uncertainty about the availability of holdover relief under *TCGA 1992, s 260* on non-business assets, on the basis that, if 100% APR/BPR applied, there was no chargeable transfer. However, HMRC have confirmed that, in their view, a gift qualifying for 100% BPR/APR is nonetheless treated as a chargeable transfer for the purposes of *TCGA 1992, s 260* (see CG67041). That must be right: it is chargeable, but at 0%.

Creation of several lifetime trusts to achieve protection against future changes in the reliefs

12.91 A specific and popular arrangement involved the use of a number of small relevant property trusts (pilot trusts) to maximise the respective trust's nil rate band. It could be adapted where 100% BPR or APR applies see – *Trust and Estates 2018/19* (Bloomsbury Professional) for more detail.

Example 12.14 – Multiple trusts

Fred owns farmland with an agricultural value in excess of £2m. He created six relevant property trusts at staggered intervals over the course of 2018/19 each with a nominal amount of cash. He later transfers assets (all carried out on the same day) carved out of the landholding which, applying the 'loss to estate' principle, amounts to less than £325,000 each, thus leaving Fred with only nominal value at the end.

Provided (see below) that 100% APR applies, all of the transfers will escape exposure to IHT, and a CGT liability can be avoided by use of holdover relief under *TCGA 1992, s 260*: the terms of the changes introduced in *FA 2008* do not restrict the operation of *TCGA 1992, s 260*.

Under current law each trust should be protected by the nil rate band rule even if:

- the BPR/APR rules are altered in the future (unless in the extremely unlikely event that retrospective legislation is introduced); or

- the assets cease to be relevant business property or agricultural property (ie they are sold).

However, there are, as always, several risks associated with this type of scheme:

First and foremost there is its artificiality.

Second, HMRC could invoke the associated operations rule, although this risk was severely curtailed following the decision in *Rysaffe Trustees (CI) Ltd v IRC* [2003] STC 536. The risk could be further reduced by ensuring that there are genuine differences between the trusts (ie different trustees and beneficiaries), whilst the staggered intervals are as far apart as practicable and are not preordained (it should be noted that HMRC were successful in invoking *IHTA 1984, s 268* to show that life policies, when taken out with annuities, constituted associated operations: see *Smith and others* [2008] STC 1649). This landmark case decision did provide good protection from HMRC attack and was further reinforced by inclusion of the same in an HMRC publication of illustrative situations not considered to be tax abusive and hence outside the reach of the general anti-abuse rule (GAAR).

However, this route (which was first thought to have been negated through HMRC's proposal to introduce a settlement nil rate band, which was itself later withdrawn) has nonetheless been overshadowed by targeted anti avoidance legislation contained in *Finance (No 2) Act 2015* aimed at the use of multiple trusts. The rules (*Finance (No 2) Act 2015, ss 62A–62C*), effective from 10 December 2014, provide that, where property is added to two or more relevant property settlements on the same day and after the commencement of those settlements, the value of the added property together with the value of property settled at the date of commencement (that is not already in a related relevant property settlement) will be brought into account in calculating the rate of tax for the purposes of trust IHT charges (eg ten years and exit charges).

Third, where land is carved up into smaller lots, valuation issues become complicated. The value of a lifetime transfer is the loss to the donor's estate measured on a pre/post transfer basis, thus if the third trust included part of two 'natural letting units' it might depress the value of retained land. If it did, the value transferred (subject to APR) might well be different from the value of the actual parcel of land. This issue is even more important where a share or interest in land is transferred, rather than merely the separation of an enclosure from neighbouring land.

Fourth, there is the possible loss of CGT rollover relief under *TCGA 1992, s 152*.

Fifth and finally, consideration should be given to the potential loss of entrepreneurs' relief, which might otherwise be available on a material disposal of business assets such as the whole or part of a farming business (*TCGA 1992, s 169H*). The disposal of an asset is not necessarily a disposal of the whole or part of a business (CG64015). In addition, HMRC's view appears to be that a claim for holdover relief takes precedence over a claim for entrepreneurs' relief (CG64137), although this has yet to be established at tribunal level: see *Capital Gains Tax 2018/19* (Bloomsbury Professional) for more detail.

OTHER WAYS OF USING APR

Gifts to elderly relatives

12.92   The main disadvantage to a lifetime gift of valuable assets eligible for 100% APR/BPR, is the CGT position, albeit of lesser importance given the current low 10/20% rate (18/28% rate for residential property/land). Whilst holdover relief may be available under *TCGA 1992, s 165*, the tax-free uplift to market value on the death of the owner is clearly a much better alternative.

Consider the position of an asset given to a trusted but elderly relative, ie grandparent. The gift, as a PET, would be potentially free of IHT and normally holdover relief would be available to avoid exposure to CGT. On the grandparent's death, 100% APR/BPR should be available and the normal minimum period of ownership may also be relaxed under the succession provisions of *IHTA 1984, s 109* (BPR) or *121* (APR), discussed at **12.72**, such that the IHT exposure is effectively reduced to nil. The property may then pass under the grandparent's will to the intended beneficiaries, but with the added benefit of the CGT uplift to market value.

WILL PLANNING

12.93

Focus

Be aware of the impact of the *IHTA 1984, s 39A* rule resulting in a dilution of APR (and BPR) on a gift of qualifying property where the spousal exemption is in point. This little-known but so damaging provision can lead to a wholly unexpected tax outcome.

Some aspects of planning through wills rely on detailed consideration of the special rules which apply to APR/BPR relieved property and thus are dealt with in this chapter. Leaving agricultural property to a spouse/civil partner may suit family purposes but will waste APR which is traded away against the spousal exemption. From a purely tax perspective, agricultural property that may qualify for 100% APR should be given to the lower generations (children and grandchildren) or to appropriate trusts.

Key to the choice is the running of the farming business: a careful balance must be struck between fairness, as between siblings, and the need for 'those who work the land to own it'. Will an agricultural asset retain its character in the hands of a family member who treats it as a mere investment? Will APR continue or remain at its present level? A gift to the next generation may 'lock into' the reliefs at present levels. Frequently, a surviving spouse does not need the business assets, such as shares in the family company, which may be illiquid, but would prefer (or need) the liquid or cash assets instead.

12.94   If the surviving spouse/civil partner does need the agricultural assets, those assets can be placed into a 'wait and see' two-year discretionary trust and, if needed, distributed to the surviving spouse at a later point: previously if the distribution was absolute then this had to take place more than three months but not later than two years after the first spouse's death (*IHTA 1984, s 144*) – see *Frankland v IRC CA* [1997] STC 1450. However, *Finance Act (No 2) 2015* removed this three-month stipulation where such appointment is made to a surviving spouse and this mirrors the existing approach applied where the distribution is on IPDI terms (*IHTA 1984, s 144(3)(c)*).

A word of warning – if the testator wants to give agricultural assets to chargeable beneficiaries to supplement a nil rate band gift, and leave the residue to the surviving spouse, he must ensure that the specific property, ie the farm, is given to the non-exempt beneficiaries to avoid an apportionment (and hence dilution) of APR between them and the exempt surviving spouse under *IHTA 1984, s 39A*.

The burden of IHT can create unfairness between chargeable beneficiaries, ie a gift of shares qualifying for 100% BPR to the testator's daughter and a gift of an equivalent cash sum to the testator's son would result in an effectively exempt gift to the former while the son's gift would be subject to IHT.

OTHER ADVANTAGES OF DELAYING SUCH GIFTS UNTIL DEATH

12.95   If an estate owner is reasonably confident that 100% APR/BPR will be available on his death, there is little incentive to relinquish control or reduce a substantial minority holding by making lifetime gifts. Indeed, there can even be a disadvantage by reason of the clawback operation. The case of *Rosser v IRC* [2003] STC (SCD) 311 illustrates a situation where, for IHT purposes, it would have been preferable to defer gifting agricultural property until death.

12.96   The advantages of delaying gifts until death are as follows:

● There is no question of clawback of APR/BPR as this only applies to lifetime gifts (*IHTA 1984, ss 124A and 124B*). It should be noted that there is a specific problem in relation to business property that falls within *IHTA 1984, s 105(1)(d)* where the donor had the necessary control but the donee does not but this has no exact parallel for APR.

- There will be full CGT exemption and tax-free uplift on death, which is more favourable than CGT holdover relief, itself more akin to a deferral. This matter has perhaps become more of an issue since the CGT overhaul in *FA 2008* when rebasing, indexation and taper relief ceased to apply, although entrepreneurs' relief may provide some shelter. In relation to business assets and farming assets qualifying as business assets, the change in tax burden could be dramatic.

- The estate owner can retain control of his shareholding and for many 'self-made' individuals, this advantage will be hard to resist: they may feel that their children should earn their own living, rather than rely on an inheritance.

- If the estate owner would really like to tie up the land for successive generations, this is best done by creating an immediate post-death interest (IPDI) by will which thus becomes effective on their death – the same form of trust if created in lifetime would enter the relevant property regime and hence the value of lifetime gifted assets therein would be treated as a chargeable transfer. However, the creation of an IPDI trust on death whilst carved out of the chargeable estate would not enter the relevant property regime but would continue to be treated as an old-style interest in possession (IIP) as a qualifying interest.

12.97   In the past a common alternative saw the estate owner create a settlement in which he retained a lifetime interest but with capital appointment at trustee discretion. If the settlor wanted his children to have control of decisions in the meantime, this could be achieved by their appointment as trustees. The creation of such a trust in this post-21 March 2006 era would be a chargeable transfer (rather than PET under the pre-22 March 2006 regime) and, whilst the value transferred would still benefit from APR, the CGT-free uplift on the life tenant's death would no longer apply as the trust would be within the relevant property regime. Notwithstanding, the IHT analysis would conclude that, by reason of the potential for the trustees to exercise discretion over capital in favour of the life tenant, a benefit in the gifted trust assets had been reserved under *FA 1986, s 102*, but that APR would be available to cushion its impact.

The obvious flaw in the plan is that holdover relief would not be available at the time of making the post-21 March 2006 lifetime settlement, as the trust would be settlor interested (*TCGA 1992, s 169B*). Until 6 April 2008, this restriction was not considered a real concern in practical terms as the gain could benefit from a substantial amount of taper relief accrued during the settlor's personal ownership, thus softening the CGT exposure. However, the *FA 2008* CGT rules (with its repeal of taper relief in favour of the more restrictive entrepreneurs' relief) did not replicate the favourable pre-6 April 2008 regime. During the lifetime of the settlor, the trust would be of 'relevant property'. Periodic charges to IHT would be mitigated by APR or BPR, but cash in the trust could suffer IHT charges.

DEEDS OF VARIATION (*IHTA 1984, s 142*)

12.98 In the context of APR where death occurred less than two years ago, consideration should be given to the redirection of gifts of agricultural property attracting 100% APR from the exempt spouse to non-exempt persons, such as children, grandchildren or discretionary trusts. This would make good use of nil rate band trusts that are no longer needed by virtue of the transferable nil rate band introduced with effect from 9 October 2007.

MORTGAGING OR CHARGING AGRICULTURAL OR BUSINESS ASSETS

12.99 The placing, moving or rearrangement of debt to achieve instant tax savings has been dealt a severe blow as a result of *IHTA 1984, s 162B* as introduced in *FA 2013*, and its impact should be studied in detail.

Avoid mortgaging or charging a farm?

12.100 In the past there were two situations to consider when securing debt:

- charge the farm;
- charge non-APR assets.

In the first, the pre-*IHTA 1984, s 162B* prevailing wisdom dictated that this should be avoided wherever possible since on a transfer of value, APR would be restricted to the net value of the farm namely the value of the farm less the mortgage. Thus the second option was the preferred route since it maximised the APR and reduced the chargeable value of the non APR asset against which secured, but this was subject to the approval of the mortgagor which gave rise to practical rather than tax difficulties.

However, the *FA 2013* introduction of *IHTA 1984, s 162B* demands that irrespective of the actual asset against which the borrowing is secured such borrowing must first be attributed to relievable agricultural property to the extent that the borrowing (directly or indirectly) has been used to finance the acquisition, maintenance or enhancement of that agricultural property. This has the effect of reducing the value of the asset otherwise attracting the benefit of APR and instantly thwarts any attempt to maximise APR through repositioning of the charge. See **12.56** for a more detailed discussion of *IHTA 1984, s 162B*.

12.101 In the BPR case of *IRC v Mallender and others (executors of Drury-Lowe, dec'd)* [2001] STC 514 (see **12.13**), the deceased had given security to a bank over some land in return for a bank guarantee to Lloyd's which was lodged as part of the deceased's underwriting business. Initially, the Special Commissioners had held that the land itself was business property, albeit that its value was several times the value of the guarantee, but this decision was swiftly overturned by the High Court.

Remember that a guarantee that has not been called-in may not be allowed by HMRC at its full value for the purposes of deduction. It may be necessary to negotiate a value to be deducted, to take account of the likelihood, at the date of death, that the guarantee would be called in. For this purpose an unsecured guarantee might carry a lower valuation for deduction purposes than a secured guarantee. Alternatively, it might even lapse with the guarantor and not be deductible at all.

TAX PLANNING FOR AGRICULTURAL PROPERTY: AGRICULTURAL COTTAGES AND THE FARMHOUSE

12.102

Focus

The APR qualification of the farmhouse remains one of the most contentious areas and HMRC challenge can and should be anticipated in any case where values are significant. The availability of the relief is very much driven by case law and thus heavily dependent on the precise facts in each case. This is a fluid area subject to constant testing by both HMRC and the taxpayer and as a consequence it is vital to remain abreast of current developments in this area.

IHTA 1984, s 169 is a little-known provision which provides that, whether or not the ownership conditions for APR are satisfied, where farm cottages are occupied by persons employed in agriculture, their valuation will be on the basis that they are only suitable for that purpose. Accordingly, they command a lower transfer value for gifting purposes.

The difficult case of *Starke (Brown's Executors) v IRC* [1995] STC 689, CA suggests that reference in *IHTA 1984, s 115(2)* to 'agricultural land or pasture' should be given the narrow meaning of the bare land, not the wider meaning under the *Interpretation Act 1978* which automatically includes buildings on the land. As a consequence, HMRC argue that, for IHT purposes, a farmhouse or building will qualify for APR only if its occupation is ancillary to that of agricultural land.

On the facts in *Starke*, a six-bedroom farmhouse on 2.5 acres did not qualify for APR. *Starke* is a special case, decided on the basis of an undertaking given during the proceedings that limited the scope of the judgment. However, some weight should be given to the observations of Morritt LJ that some nexus, other than ownership of land, might link a house to the farmland.

12.103 In *Williams (personal representative of Williams, dec'd) v HMRC* [2005] STC (SCD) 782, it was held that broiler houses situated on land leased to a company and used for the intensive rearing of birds were not agricultural property within *IHTA 1984, s 115(2)*. The broiler houses were not 'ancillary' to the deceased's farm but instead dominated it. They were not a subsidiary part of the purpose of an overall agricultural activity carried out on the land.

Example 12.15 – APR on a retained interest

An estate owner gave 85% of his farm to his daughter and retained 15% together with the farmhouse.

If the estate owner continues to be involved in the farming business (ie through a partnership) the farmhouse may be eligible for 100% APR but it is a question of degree – it is possible to have a 100% interest in the farmhouse and a 15% interest in the partnership. It is also suggested that a service contract be entered into between the partnership and the 'farmhouse' owner setting out the specific administration and other farming duties he must satisfy.

The judgment in *Starke* (see above) contains *dicta* that admit the possibility that land may be agricultural property by virtue of some nexus other than direct unity of ownership. This was challenged in *Rosser* (see below), but here the taxpayer acted in person and in a review of the case report, the case was not fully argued. Interestingly, the point is still not formally decided and a further test case is anticipated.

12.104 In *Harrold v IRC* [1996] STC (SCD) 195, APR was in point in considering the clawback provisions. APR was claimed under the seven-year occupation test but as the house in question, though qualifying in other respects as a farmhouse, was unoccupied at the donor's death, APR was denied on the basis it was not occupied for the purposes of agriculture since it was not occupied at all.

In *Dixon v IRC* [2002] STC (SCD) 53, a claim for APR failed through lack of substance – the agricultural use was derisory, comprising only an orchard of 0.6 acres.

The farmhouse must be of a 'character appropriate' to the agricultural property (*Lloyds TSB (personal representative of Rosemary Antrobus, deceased) v IRC* [2002] SSCD 468 (known as *Antrobus I*)). In that case, a six-bedroom country house situated in approximately 126 acres of agricultural land and pasture, which had been farmed by the Antrobus family since 1907 and had been a working farm, was held to be of a character appropriate to the agricultural land and pasture within *IHTA 1984, s 115(2)*.

12.105 By contrast, in *Higginson's Executors v IRC* [2002] STC (SCD) 483, the deceased lived in a lodge in a landed estate but that lodge was not a typical farmhouse. The Special Commissioner held that the lodge was not a farmhouse within *IHTA 1984, s 115(2)*. For that purpose, the land and house must be part of an agricultural unit, in which the land dominated. However, in this case the lodge dominated evidenced by the fact that when sold, it commanded a substantial price, far more than a 'real' farmer would pay for an agricultural investment. In essence this was a house with land and not land with a house.

In *Rosser v IRC* [2003] STC (SCD) 311 the estate owners/farmers made lifetime gifts of some 39 out of 41 acres of farmland, but retained the 'farmhouse' and a barn which were still held on the relevant death. The claim for APR on the home failed on grounds that it had clearly become merely a 'retirement home'. The moral emerging is to leave such gifting until death which also then benefits from the CGT death exemption and market value uplift (*TCGA 1992, s 62*).

12.106 The determination of whether a farmhouse is agricultural property is largely driven by the purpose of occupation, rather than the actual use put to it by the owner or occupier. In an article written for *Taxation,* published on 15 June 2000, the late Peter Twiddy (Assistant Director, HMRC Capital Taxes Office), described the test adopted by the then Capital Taxes Office (CTO) as follows:

'... The CTO asks the District Valuer to consider the appropriate test through the eyes of the rural equivalent of the reasonable man on the Clapham omnibus ...'

The CTO in its previous guidance applied eight tests when determining whether a farmhouse is of a 'character appropriate' to the agricultural property. These were replaced in subsequent HMRC guidance by the following (IHTM24051):

- 'Is the farmhouse appropriate when judged by ordinary ideas of what is appropriate in size, layout, content, and style and quality of construction in relation to the associated land and buildings?

- Is the farmhouse proportionate in size and nature to the requirements of the agricultural activities conducted on the agricultural land? You should bear in mind that different types of agricultural operation require different amounts of land. This is an aspect on which the VOA will be able to give advice.

- Within the agricultural land does the land predominate so that the farmhouse is ancillary to that land?

- Would a reasonable and informed person regard the property simply as a house with land or as a farmhouse?

- Applying the "elephant" test, would you recognise this as a farmhouse if you saw it? Although this test involves some subjectivity it can be useful in ruling out extremes at either end of the scale.

- How long has the farmhouse and agricultural property been associated and is there a history of agricultural production? The matter has to be decided on the facts as at the date of death or transfer but evidence of the farmhouse having previously been occupied with a larger area of land may be relevant evidence.

- Considering the relationship between the value of the house and the profitability of the land, would the house attract demand from a commercial farmer who has to earn a living from the land, or is its value significantly out of proportion to the profitability of the land? If business accounts have been supplied, copies should be forwarded to the VOA. Business accounts can give a useful indication of the extent of the agricultural activity being carried on, although a loss-making enterprise is not on its own considered to be a determinative factor.

- Considering all other relevant factors, including whether land is let out and on what terms, is the scale of the agricultural operations in context?

- There must be some connection or nexus between "such cottages, farm buildings and farmhouses, together with the land occupied with them" and the property to which they must be of a character appropriate. The argument that the nexus must be derived from common ownership rather than common occupation was accepted by the Special Commissioner in *Rosser v Inland Revenue Commissioners* [2003] STC (SCD) 311.'

12.107 It is worth noting that in HMRC's revised guidance (see **12.62**) the original eight tests were extended to nine, the seventh and ninth bullet points above were added, and the following instruction (in IHTM24052) inserted:

'... It is not a question of "how many factors have to be failed" in any given case before a house is judged not to be of a character appropriate to the property. It is necessary to consider all the various factors about the house and the land and come to a judgement ...'

The notorious 'elephant test' relates to something which is difficult to describe, but is nonetheless recognised on sight. However, whereas there may be a consensus as to what an elephant is and what is not, an equivalent measure of certainty will not always be present when dealing with a question of fact and degree. A particular area of difficulty is in deciding to what extent any of the reported cases merely turn on their own unique facts.

Whilst the bullet points set out above are still part of the guidance, it is clear that a 'points test' as such does not apply: it must be stressed that each case must be considered on its own merits whilst accepting as a general premise that large houses on small estates and houses on estates that are largely let, will not easily qualify for relief.

12.108 The case of *Executors of D Golding Deceased v Revenue & Customs Commissioners* [2011] UKFTT 351 (TC) produced a very interesting outcome in favour of the taxpayer and introduced a bold view, namely that profitability and scaling back of active farming due to age or infirmity are not necessarily a determining factor when considering the 'character appropriate' test.

In that case, the deceased had for many years until his death at age 81, farmed a smallholding of just 16.29 acres – the diverse farming trade comprised some 600 chickens, seven to ten cattle, harvesting of fruit from trees and growing vegetables. The farm produced milk and crops of wheat and barley were produced for sale. It was accepted that old age and infirmity led to scaling back of activities confined to selling of eggs, fruit and vegetables which produced a net profit of approximately £1,500 pa on average over the last five years – equal to less than 25% of the deceased sustainable income. Even so in the early years the farm had been sufficient to sustain a family albeit not to any great state of luxury. The farmhouse was small in size, without electricity in parts and in a very poor state of repair. HMRC had implied acceptance that the house in which the deceased lived and from which he carried out his farming activities, was a farmhouse for agricultural purposes but disputed that the property was of 'character appropriate' – the argument rested to a great extent on the profitability of the farm.

In a refreshingly simple and clear analysis of the facts as presented, the tribunal in finding for the taxpayer stated '... we do not accept that the lack of substantial profit is detrimental to the decision that the farmhouse was of character appropriate ...'.

12.109   HMRC did not like and have not warmed to the decision in *Golding* (although this is now referred to in HMRC's Inheritance Tax Manual at IHTM24053) and HMRC subsequently warned taxpayers seeking to rely on *Golding* that 'each case is judged on its own particular facts. It is unlikely that the facts will be the same as those of *Golding* in many cases and as the decision is not of binding precedent the decisions in the cases of *Rosser*, *Higginson*, *Dixon*, *Antrobus 1* and *2* and *McKenna* are still relevant'.

12.110   Case authority, as opposed to HMRC Guidance, on what constitutes a farmhouse is *McKenna v HMRC* [2006] SSCD 800 (SpC 00565), where an estate comprised Rosteague House, a lodge, a cottage and a stable flat and 188 acres. Some 52 acres were coastal slope and 100 acres were agreed to be agricultural land. HMRC denied APR on the house and the taxpayer's appeal from the decision failed.

The case is worth reading in full but as a broad summary, the property title went back to the 13th century. The house was part Elizabethan, part 18th century, listed Grade II but at the relevant time, it had fallen into dilapidation and needed very considerable repair. There was evidence of farming from 1365 onwards but during the 20th century farming was mainly done by others, the owner living in London until retirement to Rosteague in 1978. As long as his health allowed, the estate owner ran the farm from the house but eventually it was managed by an agent and over time the extent of agricultural activities declined. Mr McKenna relied on a pension and not on the farm for his living.

The estate was eventually sold, and, importantly, not as a farm but as residential property. The land was incidental, being mentioned only briefly in the sales literature and of the sale price of £3.05m as much as £2.03m might fairly be attributable to the house alone.

The Special Commissioner held that:

- the decision in *Antrobus II* as to what constitutes a farmhouse should be approached with some caution;

- it was necessary to decide on the basis of the words of *IHTA 1984, s 115(2)* rather than apply general principles, though the idea that a farmer is the person who farms the land on a day-to-day basis was a helpful one;

- a farmhouse is a dwelling from which the farm is managed;

- the farmer is the person who farms the land on a day-to-day basis, rather than the person who is in overall control;

- it is not occupation that matters so much as the purpose of that occupation;

- if the premises are 'extravagantly large for the purpose for which they are being used' then even though used for farming they may have become 'something much more grand';

- each case turns on its own facts, to be judged by ordinary ideas of what is appropriate in size, content and layout.

On the facts as presented and evidenced, the farming activity had been reduced and was no longer conducted from the house. The house was considered too grand for the level of farming activity carried out.

Critically, it was recognised that a farmer need not make a profit (and this lack of profitability has been reaffirmed in the *Golding* case – see above), but it certainly did not help the taxpayer on the facts in this case. It was held that it was not a farmhouse. However, even if it had been accepted as a farmhouse it was not of a character appropriate: it was 'at the very top end of the size of a farmhouse in Cornwall'. Applying the tests of *Antrobus I* in turn, it failed. It also failed the occupation test: neither Mr nor Mrs McKenna occupied for the purpose of farming: they were prevented by ill health from farming. This particular aspect, where the occupier of the house does little active farming, forms a central plank in the HMRC argument to deny relief.

Notwithstanding the judgment, there are still some issues unresolved, which the following example may illustrate:

Example 12.16 – Gift of farmhouse

On 30 June 2018, Mr and Mrs Gilliam, lifelong farmers, retire and, as in *Rosser*, give their farm to their daughter who takes over the farming. Mr and Mrs Gilliam continue to live in the farmhouse and the daughter lives elsewhere.

In those circumstances, the farmhouse ceases to be agricultural property because there is no common occupation by the same person who farms the land (the daughter runs the farm from other premises). The solution may be for the Gilliam's to retain some partnership interest in the overall farm.

Example 12.17 – Life interest in farmhouse

Consider instead that Mr and Mrs Gilliam occupied a farmhouse as life tenants under a pre-*FA 2006* qualifying life interest trust. The land is separated from the trust interest and is now held by the daughter in her own right. The Gilliam's give up occupation of the farmhouse to their daughter, retiring into a bungalow nearby. The daughter moves into the farmhouse and runs the farm from there.

The daughter is a farmer of the type favoured by *Antrobus I* she actually farms the land from the farmhouse. It is arguable that there is such a close connection between the house and the land that, on the death of Mr Gilliam or of Mrs Gilliam, APR should be given on the house (this very point was discussed in the *Hanson* case below).

Consider then the decision in *Joseph Nicholas Hanson as Trustee of the William Hanson 1957 Settlement v Revenue & Customs* [2012] UKFTT 95 (TC). In this case, the First-tier Tribunal held that when determining whether a farmhouse qualifies for APR, both it and the land (to which the farmhouse is of 'character appropriate') must be in the same occupation but not necessarily in the same ownership.

The facts of the case were straightforward. Immediately before his death in December 2002, Joseph Charles Hanson was the life tenant of a trust created by his father in 1957. The trust held a property which HMRC agreed was a 'farmhouse' for APR purposes with an agreed market value in December 2002 of £450,000. Mr Hanson's son lived in the farmhouse which he had occupied since 1978 under a rent-free licence and from there he farmed 215 acres of land of which 128 acres was owned by him personally and 25 acres was part owned by Mr Hanson. The remainder of the 215 acres comprised 20 acres rented by the son from a third party and a further 42 acres whose ownership was unspecified. The only land in common ownership and common occupation with the farmhouse was the 25 acres part owned by Mr Hanson and farmed by the son.

Following Mr Hanson's death his executors claimed APR on the value of his interest in the farmhouse. HMRC denied the relief on the basis that there was insufficient agricultural land in both common ownership and common occupation with the farmhouse for the farmhouse to pass the 'character appropriate' test. The son appealed the decision in his capacity as sole trustee of the trust arguing that common occupation was the only connecting factor required between the farmhouse and the agricultural land to which it was of a character appropriate. The Tribunal agreed.

However, HMRC made it clear at the outset in the hearing before the First-tier Tribunal that this was, for them, an important point and thus it was inevitable that HMRC would look to the Upper Tribunal on appeal. The Upper Tribunal (*HMRC v Hanson* [2013] UKUT 0224 (TCC)) in finding for the taxpayer delivered a resounding judgment of strong common sense based on intricate academic examination of the statute, relevant case discussion and of analytical construction of all the arguments brought to the appeal. It was particularly encouraging that the Upper Tribunal did not lose sight of the fact that the Hanson land was very much a working farm, with livestock, and had little reliance on outside contractors. It was the exact sort of operation that 'ought' to qualify for APR. HMRC leave to appeal was denied.

This welcome decision is of significance in situations where a downsizing farmer has moved out of the farmhouse and gives away much of the agricultural land.

12.111 Following *IRC v Forsyth-Grant* [1943] 25 TC 369, if the grant of a farm business tenancy gives the owner a grant of herbage ('profit a prendre') but with responsibility for mowing, seeding and fertilising the land which is actually carried out, then 100% APR will apply to both the land and the farm buildings including the farmhouse (but of course subject to the 'character appropriate' tests set out above).

The potential availability of relief for short-term grazing lets or licences is referred to in the Inheritance Tax manual's APR guidance (see **12.62**). However, that guidance also includes the following note of caution in relation to farmhouses (IHTM24074):

> '… It is unlikely that a landowner who has allowed most or all of the agricultural land to be occupied on a grazing licence agreement where he does nothing but collect the rent and maintain boundaries, will be considered to be in agricultural occupation of that land. Consequently, as there is no farming activity actually being carried out, any associated house cannot be considered to be a farmhouse and therefore would not be eligible for APR ….'

The matter of whether pasture land was truly 'occupied for the purposes of agriculture' was considered by the Special Commissioner in *Re Executors of Walter Wheatley (dec'd)* [1998] STC (SCD) 60. It was held that grazing by horses such as draught animals could qualify because the horses would have a 'connection with agriculture' and by the same token grazing by horses used for leisure pursuits did not so qualify. Arguably, the issue is the exact basis of occupation. If there is a tenancy, the *dicta* in *Wheatley* should apply; but if there is a licence, the owner-occupier is producing an agricultural crop, grass, whatever eats it. However, in the light of the *McCall* case, this will seldom amount to a business, so only APR will be available.

To avoid the house being treated as an excepted asset within *IHTA 1984, s 112(2)*, by reason of its use wholly or mainly for the personal benefit of the transferor (*IHTA 1984, s 112(6)*), an arm's-length contract of employment should be considered. It is strongly recommended that the exact basis of occupation of the land is formally recorded. However, it is accepted that, in real life, land is often occupied by the neighbouring farmer or grazier who has known the landowner for many years such that there is no commercial reason to produce and sign a contract. In such a case the test is one of fact: what is the land used for? In completing IHT400 and its supporting schedules, the more precise the detail of occupation and use that can be given, the better – but be prepared for HMRC challenge.

The precise terms of conacre or agistment agreements were considered in detail in *McCall and Keenan (personal representatives of McLean, dec'd) v Revenue and Customs Commissioners* [2009] NICA 12, where it appeared that some of the agreements were negotiated orally and only later, if at all, recorded in writing.

In an interesting case, a special and technical rule was initially thought to have come to the aid of the taxpayer in *Atkinson and Smith (Executors of Atkinson Deceased) v HMRC* [2010] UK FTT 108 (TC). It concerned occupation of a farm bungalow that had been the residence of a farmer for many years but in which he was not living at the time of his death, being then in a nursing home. This is a common problem and, in the past, HMRC had been successful in their argument that lack of occupation for the purpose of agriculture by its owner at the chargeable event date denied access to APR.

The distinguishing feature in *Atkinson* was that the land on which the bungalow stood was, with other land, let to a family partnership of which the deceased was still a partner at his death. It was established that he had originally occupied the bungalow and the partnership occupied all the land for the purpose of agriculture. Thus at the death, although he was not in residence, he was still taking an interest in the family business; his personal belonging and furnishings were still there; no-one else moved in and he wanted to go back there but as he aged that became less likely. The occupation was by the partnership as a whole but that was thought sufficient.

However, the success was short lived and the case was overturned on appeal by HMRC ([2011] UKUT B26 (TCC)), although it should be noted that the taxpayer was unrepresented due to lack of financial resources such that HMRC succeeded as much by default than by persuasive argument. Notwithstanding this, it does demonstrate the continued aggressive stance taken by HMRC as they continue to rebut any and all challenge to their interpretation of the qualifying farmhouse.

TAX PLANNING FOR AGRICULTURAL PROPERTY: FALLOW LAND AND OTHER FARMING ASSETS

12.112   Fallow land (ie under an EEC set-aside scheme) qualifies for APR provided that it is not used for another business purpose. Until recently much arable land was not actively farmed, because the return was far less attractive than doing nothing and relying on entitlement under the Basic Payment Scheme (as to which see below). Accordingly, the question arose whether such land was truly occupied for the purpose of agriculture, or whether its nature had changed by reason of the passive purpose of drawing subsidy. As a consequence the farmer did well to take seriously his duties to keep the land in good order, even if he did not grow a crop.

Holiday lettings are not agricultural property and are unlikely in the main to qualify for BPR either (see below), unless the landlord contributes active management and services. In other words, it is necessary to show that the activity in question constitutes 'trading' and not 'a mere investment'. See the Special Commissioners' decisions in *Martin (Moore's Executors) v IRC* [1995] STC (SCD) 5 and *Burkinyoung (Burkinyoung's Executors) v IRC* [1995] STC (SCD) 29.

12.113   HMRC's original guidance on furnished holiday lettings indicated that BPR would normally be allowed if the lettings were short term (ie weekly or fortnightly) and there was substantial involvement with the holidaymakers both on and off the premises. This applied even if the lettings were for only part of the year. However, HMRC subsequently revised their guidance (IHTM25278), which now indicates that close attention will be given to the level and type of services, rather than who provided them.

The issue was highlighted following the initial unexpected First-tier Tribunal decision in the then much-publicised case of *Pawson (deceased) v Revenue & Customs* [2012] UKFTT 51 (TC). Its swift reversal in favour of HMRC on appeal (as discussed earlier (see **12.6**)) was perhaps to be expected, given the weakness of the case, but the summary analysis and judgment was so damning as severely to dampen optimism that BPR could ever be applied to furnished holiday lets. The position was further damaged by the later case of *Green v Revenue & Customs* [2015] UKFTT 0236 (TC) (see **12.6**), which again made specific reference to the importance of and in this case the lack of 'extra services' so needed to support the reality of a trading business. What must be considered as the final death knell was sounded in the case of *Marjorie Ross (dec'd) v HMRC* [2017] UKFTT 507 (see **12.6**). The case of *Farmer and another (executors of Farmer, dec'd) v IRC* is often quoted in support of claims to BPR where the landowner puts his land to mixed use. That case concerned an estate of over 400 acres, but there is little case law or HMRC direction which definitively confirms the smallest acreage that may qualify for BPR by applying the *Farmer* principles – perhaps that is not perceived as an issue, provided it constitutes a 'landed estate' and is managed as such.

12.114 Diversification within the same ownership to non-agricultural use (eg a golf course) will deny access to APR but may well attract BPR in its place such that all is not lost. As previously stated, in that circumstance there is no requirement to own such business property for two years in order to gain access to BPR, provided it was previously owned as qualifying agricultural property and the aggregate is at least two years.

In past times, it was common to create tenancies to achieve substantial tax savings by reason of the double discount namely the capital transfer tax agricultural property discount plus the reduction in value from open market vacant possession value. However, since 1 September 1995, there is little point as land let on new tenancies qualifies for APR at 100%. This situation is dependent on maintaining the current generous APR rate. Thus, if the 100% APR rate is reduced in the future, the double discount plan might revive.

12.115 In an era where vacant possession gives access to full 100% APR, the continuing grant of a tenancy is not generally advisable for IHT purposes. Instead of family-type tenancies, consider a partnership with vacant possession (or at least vacant possession within 12 or 24 months). Licensing arrangements that do not constitute leases or tenancies are also acceptable, for example for grazing, provided that vacant possession can be obtained within only 12 months. However, in this context it should be noted that ESC F17 (which extends the vacant possession period to 24 months) is restricted to 'tenanted' land and does not extend to land under licence.

The case of *Lubbock Fine & Co v Customs and Excise Commissioners* Case 6-63/92 [1994] STC 101 reinforces that surrenders of leases are exempt from VAT. However, it must be borne in mind that tenants who currently have security of tenure may be reluctant to agree to a surrender. Furthermore, the income tax and capital gains tax implications of retaining a tenancy should also be factored in as part of the overall review.

TENANT FARMERS

12.116

> **Focus**
>
> The more onerous seven-year landlord ownership rule can be replaced by the lesser two-year test where the underlying tenant later acquires the freehold. In such circumstances there is no requirement to restart the clock as the earlier tenancy period may count towards the two-year qualification.

A cash-rich tenant farmer perhaps should consider purchasing the freehold title in order to acquire exempt IHT assets thereby reducing his liquid estate not otherwise eligible for APR/BPR. This is because a tenant who has been in occupation as tenant for a minimum of two years prior to acquisition of the freehold will qualify for 100% APR immediately without a further waiting period.

Example 12.18 – Tenant purchase of freehold

Evan and Ifor are brothers who inherited farms from their father some years ago. Evan farmed until his health failed at which point he let his farm to Ifor, advising that he would be happy to sell any time it suited Ifor to buy. Ifor carried on farming.

Road widening in their Welsh Valley consumed part of Ifor's farm and provided a welcome cash payment of £300,000 into his bank account. This event, occurring shortly before his 75th birthday, provided some consolation not only for the loss of the land but also for the doctor's advice that for health reasons he should now cut back on his workload and perhaps give up the land he rented from his brother.

Ifor took advice from both his doctor and his lawyer. The former told him he had at most 18 months to live; the latter that he should buy the freehold of Evan's land nonetheless. He did, dying much sooner than predicted. No tax fell due on the value of Evan's land by reason of APR/BPR.

The arrangements for occupation of farmland are often informal, as was recognised when considering agistment in the Northern Ireland case of *McCall* (see **12.64**). Be aware that HMRC guidance urges Inspectors to call for evidence of the terms of occupation and, for example, to ask for substantive evidence that consideration has been given for occupation – such HMRC approach is now becoming increasingly routine in practice.

In real life, a landowner in later years may not be well enough to care for livestock or to manage crops and may enter into a quite genuine, but oral arrangement under which he retains occupation but another, whom he may have known all his life, carries out the necessary agricultural operations on their behalf. This practical and workable arrangement may cause problems through lack of formal evidence of that intention. What did the parties intend? Were they related? Was the consideration shown on the landowner's tax return? Informed practitioners should seek both to resolve and record the issues between the parties. Despite its failure on appeal the *Atkinson* case described at **12.111** might well have fallen at the first fence, but for the existence of a tenancy agreement.

FARMING COMPANIES

12.117   Farming companies (*IHTA 1984, s 122*) are at a clear disadvantage since 100% APR is only available if the transferor controls the company (but note the use of the related property rules in *IHTA 1984, s 161*, which may serve to preserve control in a spousal/civil partner scenario) – no relief is available to the minority shareholder.

Contrast this with BPR, where a 100% 'discount' is currently available whatever the size of the shareholding in an unquoted trading company. A shareholding in a farming company of 50% or less will be denied APR, but if it can be proved that the farm is a business, 100% BPR should be available to restore the status quo. Timing here is not critical, since control need exist only at the moment of transfer.

However, the company must fulfil the same requirements and minimum periods for APR as an individual. The shareholder transferor must (*IHTA 1984, s 123(1)*) have owned the shares for whichever of the two or seven year minimum periods is appropriate to that company.

Example 12.19 – Gift of farm or farming company shares?

On 31 October 2017, Angela, a widow whose late husband had fully utilised his nil rate band, gave her farm to her niece – that was a PET and thus was not formally tested for APR at that point. The farm consisted of a house worth £350,000 and 450 acres worth £5,000 per acre (ie £2,250,000) resulting in a total value of £2,600,000.

Assuming that 70% of the value of the farmhouse qualifies for APR, the part not so qualifying is £105,000 (£350,000 @ 30%). The agricultural value of the property given was therefore £2,495,000 ((£350,000 @ 70%) + £2,250,000). Angela had already used both her own nil rate band and her annual exemptions and prior to the gift she had occupied the farm and farmed it herself for 20 years.

The niece farmed the land until Angela's unexpected death on 28 February 2018, with the PET (which became a chargeable transfer with no tapering relief), of £105,000 attracting at 40% a tax charge of £42,000 payable over ten years by instalments. Interest (see *IHTA 1984, s 234(1)*) runs only from the due date of each instalment.

The wording of *FA 2009, Sch 53, para 7* is somewhat convoluted. It first appears to impose late interest charges from the due date for payment of an instalment on woodland (here meaning the timber, not the underlying land); or on business interests; but then excludes from the extra charge (see *FA 2009, Sch 53, para 7(4)* onwards) shares in a 'genuine' trading business, ie not one that fails the 'wholly or mainly' test. The legislation could have been more simply drafted to specify what does attract the charge rather than what does not. Farmland is excluded under *FA 2009, Sch 53, para 7(3)*.

If Angela had rolled over her farming business (including the land) into a company, A Ltd, a year before the transfer, that transfer of her shareholding to her niece, instead of the farm itself, would still qualify for relief if the niece kept the shares at least until Angela's death. The niece could add together the separate periods of occupation of both Angela and A Ltd. IHT would similarly be payable by instalments which, if paid on time, would carry no interest.

HABITAT SCHEMES

12.118 Land that is subject to habitat schemes, for the protection of the environment and preservation of the countryside, qualifies for APR even though the land is not 'occupied' for the purposes of agriculture (*IHTA 1984, s 124C*).

SPECIAL TYPES OF FARMING

Farm sharing

12.119 Farm sharing is very popular with those land investors who do not have the time or inclination to do any actual farming. The arrangement involves:

- a joint contractual venture between the owner of the farmland and the operator (who actually farms the land);

- provision by the owner of land, and sometimes fixed equipment and machinery;

- the supply by the operation of working machinery and labour;

- the purchase and supply by the owner of seed etc (but this is usually organised by the operator); and

- the sharing of gross outputs.

The outcome of that arrangement may be summarised as follows:

- there is no partnership established;

- the owner and operator have separate businesses;

- there is no landlord/tenant relationship;

- for IHT purposes 100% APR should be available on any farmland, though it is perhaps harder to secure a claim on the farmhouse.

Both parties should have vacant possession rights. In particular, the owner should be involved in policy-making decisions and exercise rights of inspection: this becomes particularly relevant in supporting the APR claim on the farmhouse, where it must be shown that the 'farmer' physically lives there.

HMRC appear to agree with some reluctance that farm-sharing arrangements qualify for capital gains tax reliefs such as rollover relief, and constitute trading as farmers for income tax purposes (*ITTOIA 2005, ss 9* and *859(1)* for income tax purposes, and *CTA 2009, s 36* for corporation tax).

Contract farming

12.120 It is also necessary to consider contract farming where the estate owner owns the farm but the actual farming activity is subcontracted out and usually to someone who is self-employed. In their guidance, HMRC state that contract farming may perhaps be better viewed as 'farming with contractors' (IHTM24082). Again, 100% APR should normally be available.

However, great care must be taken over the invoicing arrangements. Thus, for example, the purchase of seed and fertiliser should be done by the owner of the land. The same issue arises over the eligibility of the farmhouse, particularly in the light of *McKenna v HMRC*. HMRC's guidance states the following in relation to farmhouses:

'... While the existence of a Share or Contract Farming agreement is unlikely to affect the availability of agricultural relief on the farmland, it may have an impact upon any the relief available on the farmhouse. This is a question of fact and degree to be decided in each case and may involve consideration of aspects such as:

– The degree of financial risk for the deceased

– The deceased's involvement in the day to day agricultural activity including the regularity and scope of any meetings with the share/ contract farmer

– The deceased's involvement in decisions relating to the selection of crops, sowing, harvesting, sales, and so on ....'

The sale of grasskeep or agistment or (in Northern Ireland) conacre can give rise to special problems. Properly drafted, it was previously thought that such arrangements left the landowner in occupation of the land and thereby still engaged in the business of producing the agricultural crop (grass) to which the other party is entitled to take by means of grazing animals. However, this view has been challenged in light of case law – for a detailed review of the principles, see the decision of the Court of Appeal in *McCall and Keenan (personal representatives of McClean, dec'd) v Revenue and Customs Commissioners* [2009] NICA 12, considered in detail earlier in this chapter (see **12.4**) and the contrasting distinction between whether a taxpayer is a farmer or landowner for general tax purposes in *John Carlisle Allen* (TC5100).

The *Allen* case also involved a conacre arrangement where the debate centred on the 'occupation' of land for the purposes of agriculture. The taxpayer (and his brother) grew the grass which was eaten by the tenant's stock as permitted under the conacre agreement under which the taxpayer received £1,000 per annum described as 'a licence fee'. The taxpayer maintained the right to temporarily house animals on that land, supplied fertiliser when required, maintained fences and drainage, supplied water and undertook the weeding of the hedges. In addition to grazing access, the tenant was also permitted to remove silage at certain times and claim part of the farming subsidy. However, crucially the tenant was not able to spread artificial fertiliser but could only use farmyard manure or that supplied at no cost by the taxpayer when the grass became under nourished.

It was held that the land was occupied by the taxpayer for the purpose of husbandry and a key point in that decision was recognition that the taxpayer managed the land in such a manner as to maximise and maintain the quality of the grass crop.

BASIC PAYMENT SCHEME

12.121   The Basic Payment Scheme (formerly known as the Single Farm Payment Scheme) effectively separated farming subsidies from production. Entitlement potentially arises in the hands of farmers and non-farmers but is subject to various conditions and standards, such as keeping the land in good agricultural and environmental condition. A substantial payment of the entitlement in 2005 was expected to provide income support for the following eight years but, thereafter, anyone wishing to receive the subsidy could only do so through acquisition of an entitlement from someone entitled to receive it.

For IHT purposes, the entitlement is subject to the normal IHT rules concerning transfers of value and the death estate and thus the transfer of the entitlement may attract IHT as with any other asset. It is, though, a separate asset falling outside the definition of 'agricultural property' in *IHTA 1984, s 115(2)*, and cannot therefore qualify for APR, although BPR may be available. However, transfers of entitlement as an individual asset by non-traders (as opposed to a business or interest in a business) will not qualify for BPR.

'BUY AND SELL' AGREEMENTS/ARRANGEMENTS

12.122   APR and BPR (see **12.35**) are not available if the partners or company directors or shareholders have entered into a 'buy and sell' agreement under which, on the death of one of them before retirement, his personal representatives are obliged to sell and the others are obliged to buy his interest or his shares. Such an agreement, being more than a mere option, is regarded as a binding contract for sale within *IHTA 1984, s 124.*

However, in practice, an option arrangement can achieve the desired result without penalty. In theory cross-options (ie a put and call) are equivalent in substance to a binding contract for sale, on the grounds that the terms will be beneficial to one party or the other and thus a sale is inevitable, but the argument is seldom seen or tested in practice. If cross-options are used, they should be made successive in time and carry different exercise periods.

12.123 Automatic accrual arrangements between members of a partnership may seem similar to binding sale contracts, but IHTM25292 states:

'... agreements under which the deceased's interest passes to the surviving partners, who are required to pay the personal representatives a particular price ... do not constitute contracts for sale. So they do not prevent the interest from qualifying from business property relief by reason of *IHTA 1984, s 113.*'

WOODLANDS RELIEF

INTRODUCTION

12.124

Focus

Albeit descriptive, the use of the term 'relief' is misleading. Woodlands relief operates as a deferral mechanism and should not be confused with or regarded as full exemption akin to APR or BPR. Accordingly, it must be recognised that the deferred liability will spring back into charge at some later point.

Forestry used to be a very popular investment by reason of the favourable income tax treatment, but those advantages have been seriously eroded over time. Nevertheless, it is still seen as a good investment, especially for small 'amenity' parcels that might not qualify for APR or BPR.

The principal IHT relief provisions for woodlands are contained in *IHTA 1984, ss 125–130* and apply only to trees and underwood but not the land on which they stand. Although the underlying land is excluded, its value will usually be relatively low and will be eligible for APR if occupied with, and ancillary to, agricultural land or pasture: see the detailed discussion of the need of cattle for shade in *Williams v HMRC* [2005] SSCD 782 (SpC 500).

The word 'woodland' is defined as a wood of sizeable area and to a significant extent covered by growing trees capable of being used as timber. Accordingly, a plantation of Christmas trees, which does not have the maturity, the height or the size to be useful as timber, and which resembles bushes rather than trees, does not constitute woodland (as discussed in *Jaggers v Ellis* [1997] STC 1417). The analysis in that case provides useful guidance on the meaning of woodland in the context of IHT legislation. Thus, a small remnant of ancient woodland (and known by that title), useful for walking a dog or for watching wildlife, whilst no doubt a delightful investment, is unlikely to qualify for relief because the timber is not felled but merely preserved. Furthermore, its value will be in the land rather than in the timber and, of course, it is only the latter which qualifies for the relief, as discussed below.

It should be noted that woodlands relief is potentially affected by changes introduced in *FA 2013*, where there is a liability attributable (directly or indirectly) to financing the acquisition of land, trees or underwood, or planting the trees or underwood, or maintaining or enhancing the value of the trees or underwood (*IHTA 1984, s 162B(5), (6)*).

The effect of the changes is that the liability must (as far as possible) reduce the value of the trees or underwood, so as to prevent the liability being secured against other assets on which no woodlands relief (or APR or BPR) is due.

NATURE OF RELIEF

12.125 IHT relief is only applicable on death and is subject to a claim made by *notice in writing* within two years of death, or such longer period as HMRC will allow. It applies to woodlands other than agricultural property to which APR may attach. The value of the timber is left out of account at death but IHT may be payable on later disposal (*IHTA 1984, s 126*). In this way, it must be recognised that woodlands relief is a deferral mechanism and not a complete exemption.

The deferred IHT is eventually payable on a disposal in relation to the last death on which the timber passes and it is the person entitled to the sale proceeds, or who would be entitled if the disposal were a sale, who is liable for the tax (an inter-spouse/civil partner disposal is ignored). IHT is only charged on the first disposal of the trees or underwood following the death (*IHTA 1984, s 126(3)*).

IHT is calculated on the net sale proceeds or, if not a sale, on the net value at the date of disposal. Importantly, the tax rate scale is the one which would have applied if the chargeable value had been included in the estate in relation to the latest death on which it passes and represented the highest part of that estate (*IHTA 1984, s 128*). If the IHT charge crystallises after a reduction in the rates, the reduced rates apply (*IHTA 1984, Sch 2, para 4*).

12.126 Where the woodlands are being managed commercially (ie would have qualified for BPR), the amount on which IHT tax is charged under *IHTA 1984, s 126* is reduced by 100% (50% for years prior to 6 April 1992). However, if there is a woodland election under *IHTA 1984, ss 125–127* (see below), only 50% BPR will be available on a later sale.

Where woodland relief has been claimed on death, and the later disposal is itself subject to IHT as a chargeable transfer, there will be two IHT computations – the first (the deferred charge) will relate to the earlier death and the second to the later chargeable transfer. However, the amount of the deferred charge may be deducted from the value of the chargeable transfer to arrive at the IHT liability on the latter (*IHTA 1984, s 129*). This treatment will also be the case should a PET fail by reason of the donor death within seven years of death (*IHTA 1984, s 3A(4)*).

CONDITIONS OF RELIEF

12.127 Relief is only available if the deceased held the woodland beneficially throughout the five years preceding his death, or acquired it otherwise than for money or money's worth. In tandem with APR, the restriction that the land must be situated in the UK was partly lifted with effect from 22 April 2009 (*FA 2009, s 122*) such that woodland which is within the European Economic Area, Channel Islands and Isle of Man at the time of the transfer may also qualify for the relief: see *IHTA 1984, s 115(5)(b)*.

Net values are after deduction of sale costs and expenses of replanting incurred within three years, or such longer period as the Board may allow (*IHTA 1984, s 130(2)*), except to the extent that these expenses are allowable for income tax (*IHTA 1984, s 130(1)(b)*).

Where the woodlands are being managed commercially and would qualify as relevant business property for BPR under *IHTA 1984, ss 103–114*, the amount on which IHT is charged is reduced by 100%, as was noted above. However, if there is an election under *IHTA 1984, ss 125–127* to leave the value of the woodlands out of account in determining the value of the estate on death, only 50% BPR will be available on an eventual sale (*IHTA 1984, s 127(2)*).

Obviously, if at all possible, it is sensible for the owners of woodland to endeavour to manage the woodlands in a commercial and active manner in order to preserve access to the more valuable 100% BPR. To assist this treatment, separate accounts should be kept in relation to the woodlands and these accounts should not be included in the overall farming accounts.

Example 12.20 – Woodlands relief claim

Ethan Hawker died on 30 September 1991 and left the following estate, there having been no lifetime transfers. The timber qualified for 50% BPR relief (the rate in force at the time of death):

	£
Sundry assets	285,000
Value of timber	80,000
Estate total	365,000

If no claim had been made for woodland relief, IHT on death would have been calculated as follows:

	£
Estate	365,000
BPR @ 50% on timber	(40,000)
	325,000
Nil rate band (1991/92)	(140,000)
Chargeable	185,000
IHT @ 40% thereon	74,000 (A)

On the basis that Ethan's executors made the woodland relief claim, IHT on death would have been calculated as follows:

	£
Estate	365,000
Value of timber	(80,000)
Adjusted estate	285,000
Nil rate band (1991/92)	(140,000)
Chargeable	145,000
IHT @ 40% thereon	58,000 (B)

IHT 'saving' on Ethan's death by reason of the woodlands election would be as follows:

	£
No woodlands election – IHT due Estate (A)	74,000
Woodlands election – IHT due on estate (B)	(58,000)
IHT 'saving' as a result of the election	16,000

On 1 May 2018, the timber was sold for £200,000 (on which 50% BPR is due) net of selling and replanting expenses, so that IHT is payable on Ethan's estate is recalculated as follows:

	£	£
Value of timber (net of BPR @ 50%)	200,000	
BPR @ 50%	(100,000)	
	100,000	
Sundry assets	285,000	
	385,000	
Nil rate band (2018/19)	(325,000)	
Chargeable (which all relates to the woodland as the top slice)	60,000	
IHT thereon @ 40%		24,000
Original estate excluding woodland	285,000	
Nil rate band at trigger date (2018/19)	(325,000)	
Chargeable	Nil	
IHT thereon @ 40%		Nil
Deferred IHT charge due following sale of timber		24,000

The impact of claiming the woodland relief on Ethan's death leading to a deferred charge on the later sale of the timber in May 2018 is calculated as follows:

	£
Original IHT due on estate net of woodlands relief (B)	58,000
Deferred charge due on 2018 sale of timber	24,000
	82,000
IHT on estate if no woodlands election made(A)	(74,000)
Increase in IHT due to woodlands election*	8,000

* Representing the 40% IHT charge on the increase (net of BPR) in the chargeable woodland value ((£200,000 @ 50%) – (£80,000 @ 50%) @ 40%).

As stated in **12.125** a two-year time limit does apply to claims in connection with woodland relief but this may be extended at HMRC's discretion.

TRANSFERS OF WOODLANDS SUBJECT TO A DEFERRED ESTATE DUTY CHARGE

12.128   Under the estate duty regime, death duties on woodlands could be deferred until the legatee felled or sold the timber. If the legatee died before the timber was sold, estate duty on his death replaced the earlier deferred charge and could itself again be deferred. Under *FA 1986, Sch 19, para 46* any transfer which includes woodlands subject to a deferred estate duty charge is denied PET treatment so that there is an immediate lifetime chargeable transfer and the deferred estate duty is treated as discharged.

The problem with that, taken literally, would be that any single large transfer which included some small part of woodlands subject to deferred estate duty would be refused PET treatment. Extra-statutory Concession F15 restricts the denial of PET treatment only to such part of the transfer as consists of the woodlands subject to the deferred estate duty. Thus, there is an immediate IHT charge on the woodlands subject to the deferred estate duty, but the remaining part of the transfer constitutes a PET.

Chapter 13

Private residence relief

Jackie Anderson LLB, ACA, CTA, LHA Consulting Ltd

SIGNPOSTS

- **Introduction** – Private residence relief, available on the disposal of a taxpayer's main residence, is an extremely valuable relief which generates ongoing case law and legislative developments, and plenty of planning opportunities and pitfalls too (see **13.1–13.4**).

- **What constitutes a residence?** 'Dwelling house' – and 'residence' are not defined in the legislation, so guidance must be taken from the decided cases. The nature of the property, the 'curtilage', the quality of occupation, and the 'permitted area' are all factors which need to be considered in this context (see **13.5–13.9**).

- **Other uses of a residence** – The impact on private residence relief of other property uses – for business purposes, as a property let, for adult care and dependent relatives, and in relation to employer purchases – also need to be considered (see **13.10–13.17**).

- **Periods of occupation** – In determining periods of occupation for the purposes of private residence relief, there are provisions covering a delay in taking up occupation, deemed occupation (for the final few months), periods of absence due to work, and job-related occupation (see **13.18–13.22**).

- **Two or more residences** – There are provisions for the taxpayer to nominate (or 'elect' for) one of two or more properties to be regarded as their 'main residence', and to vary the notice (see **13.23–13.28**).

- **Trusts and estates** – Private residence relief may be claimed by trustees – of interest in possession and discretionary trusts – and by personal representatives (see **13.29–13.33**).

- **Marriage, separation and divorce** – Spouses and civil partners (living together) can only have one main residence for private residence relief purposes, with the facility to make an election where they own more than one residence between them. Transfers of

---

677

property, separation and divorce also need to be considered in this context (see **13.34–13.40**).

- **Administration** – Private residence relief is automatic and does not require a claim, with disclosure in the taxpayer's tax return only required in certain circumstances. Proper documentation, however, should always be kept where HMRC might contest the nature of the taxpayer's residence at a property (see **13.41–13.43**).

- **Planning opportunities and pitfalls** – The potentially significant value of private residence relief means that consideration needs to be given to the planning opportunities and pitfalls, particularly in relation to the main residence election, and the development and sale of land (see **13.44–13.49**).

INTRODUCTION

13.1   The relief from capital gains tax (CGT) on any profit arising on the disposal of the taxpayer's main private residence, commonly known as 'private residence relief', is an extremely valuable relief for homeowners in the UK (although many won't be aware of it as they will simply assume that they can profitably sell their family home without a tax charge arising!).

The corollary of CGT relief for a gain is, of course, that private residence relief prevents the taxpayer from claiming tax relief for any capital loss incurred on the disposal of their main private residence.

Key features of private residence relief

13.2   Private residence relief (*TCGA 1992, ss 222–226B*) is available where the taxpayer meets all of the following conditions:

- the 'dwelling house' has been their 'only or main residence' (see **13.5–13.8**) throughout their 'period of ownership';

- the 'garden or grounds' (including the buildings on them) are not greater than the 'permitted area' (see **13.9**);

- no part of the home has been used exclusively for 'business purposes' during their period of ownership (see **13.11**);

- they have not been absent, other than for an allowed period of absence or because they have been living in 'job-related accommodation', during their 'period of ownership' (see **13.18–13.22**).

Whilst let properties do not generally qualify for private residence relief – as a let property cannot also be the taxpayer's main residence at the same time – there is a form of relief where the taxpayer lets their main residence (see **13.14**).

Planning aspects of private residence relief

13.3   Private residence relief commonly provides planning opportunities and pitfalls in relation to the following areas:

- main residence elections (see **13.44**);
- development of land – in particular:
  - – trading transactions (see **13.45**);
  - – intention to reside (see **13.46**);
  - – surplus land (see **13.47**);
  - – residual building plot (see **13.48**); and
  - – enhancing the value of the property (see **13.49**).

Recent developments

13.4   Some recent case law and legislation developments in relation to private residence relief include the following:

- A new charge of non-resident capital gains tax (NRCGT) applies from 6 April 2015 to gains made on the disposal of UK residential property owned by non-resident taxpayers. Non-resident individuals may be eligible to claim private residence relief for their UK property in certain circumstances (see **13.24**).

- The *Finance Act 2014* reduced the deemed period of occupation for taxpayers who have been resident in their dwelling house at some point in their period of ownership from 36 months to the last 18 months for properties disposed of after 5 April 2014 (see **13.20**).

- In *Hartland v Commissioners for Revenue and Customs* [2014] UKFTT 1099 (TC), the intention of the taxpayer to reside in the property was helpfully considered and was proved to be sufficient in relation to one property, but not in relation to a second property (see **13.8**).

- The case of *Wagstaff and another v HMRC* [2014] UKFTT 43 (TC) confirmed that a right to occupy the property under the inferred intention to create a trust could create an entitlement to private residence relief (see **13.31**).

- The First-tier Tribunal ruled that the quality of occupation had an insufficient degree of permanence, continuity or expectation of continuity to justify describing that occupation as 'residence' in *Iles & Kaltsas v HMRC* [2014] UKFTT 436 (TC) (see **13.8**).

- In *John Arthur Day and Amanda Jane Dalgety v HMRC* [2015] UKFTT 139 (TC), the First-tier Tribunal similarly confirmed that private residence relief was not due where the taxpayer had no intention of occupying the property as his main residence (see **13.8**).

- The recent case of *Oates v Revenue & Customs* [2014] UKUT 409 (LC) considered the 'just and reasonable' apportionment of sales proceeds between a house and land for the purposes of private residence relief (see **13.13**).

- The case of *Fountain v HMRC* [2015] UKFTT 419 (TC) decided that, whilst it is possible for a garden detached from a residence to be covered by a private residence claim, in this case the taxpayer had not provided any evidence in support of this contention (see **13.9**).

- The nature and quality of the taxpayer's residence, for private residence relief purposes, was considered by the First-tier Tribunal in the recent cases of *Richard James Dutton-Forshaw v HMRC* [2015] UKFTT 478 (TC) and *Kothari v HMRC* [2016] UKFTT 127 (TC) (see **13.8**).

- A recent development which further enhances the value of private residence claims, which arises from an Autumn Statement 2015 proposal, is that from April 2020 there will be an accelerated payment date for CGT due on the sale of residential property, so that the tax will be due within 30 days of completion – except where there is no CGT liability due to private residence relief. HMRC has issued a Consultation (in April 2018) on the calculation and administration of tax liability, and on changes to the CGT payment on account system for non-residents disposing of UK residential property.

- The recent case of *Desmond Higgins v HMRC* [2017] UKFTT 236 (TC) demonstrated that the period of ownership for private residence relief purposes began and ended with the dates of the contracts to acquire and sell the property (see **13.19**).

- In *Paul Munford v Revenue and Customs Commissioners* [2017] UKFTT 19 (TC), the burden of proof as to whether the property had been occupied as his main residence fell on HMRC, which they could not discharge (see **13.8**).

- *Oliver v Revenue and Customs Commissioners* [2016] UKFTT 796 (TC) considered the quality of the taxpayer's 'residence', concluding that there was no indication of an intention to permanently reside (see **13.8**).

- And the First-tier Tribunal in the case of *Stephen Bailey v HMRC* (2017) UKFTT 658 (TC) confirmed that relatively short periods of occupation could still provide a sufficient degree of permanence in this context (see **13.8**).

- In *W&H Ritchie v HMRC* (2017) UKFTT 449, the permitted area argument focused on what is necessary, and found that some areas were, and some were not (see **13.9**).

WHAT CONSTITUTES A RESIDENCE?

'Dwelling-house' and 'residence'

13.5 Private residence relief is provided by *TCGA 1992, s 223* which states that: 'No part of a gain to which section 222 applies shall be a chargeable gain if the dwelling-house or part of a dwelling-house has been the individual's only or main residence throughout the period of ownership ...'.

Focus

The legislation does not define 'dwelling house', 'residence' nor 'only or main residence', so guidance must be taken from the decided cases. HMRC's views on what constitutes a 'dwelling house' (at CG64230–CG64328) and 'only or main residence' (at CG64420–CG64555) should also be considered.

There are three key issues to consider as to what constitutes a 'dwelling house', a 'residence' and the 'only or main residence' in this context:

- the nature of the property (see **13.6**);

- the 'curtilage' (see **13.7**) and 'permitted area' (see **13.9**);

- the quality of occupation (see **13.8**).

The nature of the property

13.6 A 'dwelling house' can include a house or a flat, and certain other structures not commonly regarded as dwelling houses – for example, rooms within a factory or hotel (CG64320).

There must be an element of permanence, hence a mobile caravan does not qualify for relief (*Moore v Thompson* 61 TC 15) – but may be exempt from CGT as a tangible moveable wasting asset anyway – but a static one connected to the mains services may qualify (*Makins v Elson* 51 TC 437). Similar principles would apply to yachts and houseboats, etc.

The 'curtilage'

13.7   Private residence relief can extend to other properties within the 'curtilage' of the house (CG64245). The 'curtilage' is a legal concept which helps to define the extent of the dwelling house, and whether it includes outbuildings, etc. The curtilage is the house, not the grounds, but can include any unconnected buildings that have a residential purpose and obviously 'go with' the house.

Case law has established two principal tests to determine whether a separate building qualifies with the main part of the dwelling, namely:

- The building must be used in conjunction with the enjoyment of the main dwelling to form part of one residence. Thus a cottage to house a caretaker and another for a gardener were held to be occupied for the benefit of the main house and so formed part of the main residence (*Batey (Inspector of Taxes) v Wakefield* [1981] STC 521).

- The building must be adjacent or at least quite close to the main house. For this reason, a cottage on the opposite side of a large estate to the main house (175 metres away) was considered not to be part of the main residence (*Lewis (Inspector of Taxes) v Rook* [1992] STC 171). Whereas in *Batey v Wakefield,* a cottage built for the caretaker which was separated from the main house by a narrow strip of land was eligible for relief.

The quality of occupation

13.8   Occupation of the dwelling house is a key factor which turns a house into a home, and thus a 'residence' for relief purposes. There are many cases which concern the redevelopment of a property, or the temporary occupation of a property.

Private residence relief was denied in *Goodwin v Curtis (Inspector of Taxes)* [1996] STC 1146 where a director purchased a newly developed farmhouse from his company for his own use. He took up occupation and had the services and telephone connected. The property was offered for sale within a matter of days, and soon after contracts were exchanged to sell the property at a very substantial profit. There was little evidence that he intended to make the property his permanent home – he lived in the property for only five weeks. It was held that it was necessary for the occupation to have 'some degree of permanence, some degree of continuity or some expectation of continuity'.

In this context, the following facts will be relevant to indicate where the taxpayer resides:

- where he is registered to vote;
- where the children of the family go to school;

- where the family spends most of its time;

- the correspondence address for bank accounts, credit cards, etc;

- where his main place of work is;

- where he is registered with a doctor or dentist;

- where the individual's car is registered and insured; and

- which property is the main address for council tax.

The quality of the occupation was examined in *Harte v HMRC* [2012] UKFTT 258 (TC). The Hartes inherited the property which was close to their own home. They elected for the property to be treated as their main residence for a short period before sale, but this claim was rejected on the basis that the taxpayers did not demonstrate any degree of permanence or expectation of continuance and, in particular, did not:

- take any personal possessions to the property;

- acquire a TV licence at the property;

- have a computer or internet connection at the property;

- entertain there or have anyone to stay; or

- change the name on the bills from 'occupier'.

In the cases of *Anthony Metcalf* [2010] TC753, *Malcolm Springthorpe* [2010] TC 832 and *Alison Clarke v HMRC* [2014] TC4062, the courts referred to the low level of power consumption in electricity bills in concluding that there was insufficient occupation to be eligible for the exemption.

In the case of *Hartland v Commissioners for Revenue and Customs* [2014] UKFTT 1099 (TC), the taxpayer contested HMRC's refusal to allow the appellant's claim for CGT private residence relief under *TCGA 1992, s 222* in relation to two properties. Private residence relief was allowed for *Primrose Cottage* – despite quite extensive works being undertaken – supported by the facts that the property was used as the appellant's correspondence address, he paid for energy supplies, the building and its contents were insured and the cottage contained furniture. However, relief was denied for *Grey Cottage*, where the First-tier Tribunal was satisfied that the acquisition, demolition, rebuilding and sale were undertaken in the course of a property development trade. The property was not fit for family occupation when the appellant purchased it, and there was no evidence he ever lived there. It was sold almost as soon as it had been rebuilt, and the appellant's mortgage application for the property described him as a self-employed builder with an income well over double that declared on his tax return for the relevant year. A different address was used on his mortgage application and no letter or other communication addressed to the appellant at *Grey Cottage* was produced.

And, in *Iles & Kaltsas v HMRC* [2014] UKFTT 436 (TC), the First-tier Tribunal examined the intention of the taxpayer to make the property a permanent or long-term home, as opposed to a temporary residence. The taxpayers occupied a small flat for 24 days after it had been let for some time and just prior to its sale. The Tribunal ruled that the quality of occupation had an insufficient degree of permanence, continuity or expectation of continuity to justify describing that occupation as 'residence'.

However, in *David Morgan v HMRC* [2013] UKFTT 181 (TC), the taxpayer bought a property to occupy with his fiancée, but she broke off the engagement. Mr Morgan occupied the property for only 10 weeks before it was let. The Tribunal decided that he had intended the property to be his home, and accepted the private residence relief claim.

Whereas in *John Arthur Day and Amanda Jane Dalgety v HMRC* [2015] UKFTT 139 (TC), the First-tier Tribunal confirmed that private residence relief was not due where the tax payer had not occupied the property, and whilst he might have had a row with his partner, they had not split permanently and he had no intention of occupying the property as his main residence.

In *Richard James Dutton-Forshaw v HMRC* [2015] UKFTT 478 (TC), the property in question was only occupied by the taxpayer for two months out of a total ownership period of 44 months, but still judged to be the taxpayer's only residence as he had no other residence during that two-month period.

In the recent First-tier Tribunal case of *Kothari v HMRC* [2016] UKFTT 127 (TC), the decision went against the taxpayer on the basis that his six-month period of occupation did not have a sufficient degree of permanence or continuity, as he put the property on the market just one month after moving in.

In *Paul Munford v Revenue and Customs Commissioners* [2017] UKFTT 19 (TC), HMRC challenged a private residence relief claim, but because a discovery assessment was made outside the normal time limits, the burden of proof as to whether the property had been occupied as his main residence moved from the taxpayer to HMRC, and HMRC could not discharge that burden. *Oliver v Revenue and Customs Commissioners* [2016] UKFTT 796 (TC) was another case in which the taxpayer's quality of 'residence' was considered. Here, although the taxpayer may have stayed at the property, there was no indication of an intention to permanently reside there – including no telephone or internet connection.

And the First-tier Tribunal in the case of *Stephen Bailey v HMRC* (2017) UKFTT 658 (TC) allowed a private residence relief claim where the taxpayer had two relatively short periods of occupation, but there was a sufficient degree of permanence for the property to be his 'residence' in this context.

The 'permitted area'

13.9   The CGT relief for the gain on a taxpayer's main residence extends to 'land which he has for his own occupation and enjoyment with that residence as its garden or grounds up to the permitted area' (*TCGA 1992, s 222(1)(b)*) (CG64800 *et seq*).

The permitted area is defined as being an up to 0.5 of a hectare (including the house), and being the part of the grounds that is 'the most suitable for occupation and enjoyment with the residence'.

TCGA 1992, s 222(3) states that a larger area may be recognised where it is 'required for the reasonable enjoyment ... having regard to the size and character of the dwelling-house'. This is a stricter test than for areas of less than 0.5 of a hectare where it is sufficient to show that the land was part of the garden or grounds of the house.

Land that is physically separated from the house by a road, fence or other houses, can qualify for exemption; HMRC recognise that cottage gardens may lie across the village street (CG64367).

It is not sufficient for this purpose that the property owner has his or her own special requirements. For instance, an individual may use extra grounds to keep horses or vintage cars. That does not mean that area is necessary for the reasonable enjoyment of the property, as other occupiers may not have this requirement (*Longson v Baker (Inspector of Taxes)* [2001] STC 6).

The case of *Fountain v HMRC* [2015] UKFTT 419 (TC) decided that, whilst it is possible for a garden detached from a residence to be covered by a private residence claim, in this case the taxpayer had not provided any evidence in support of this contention. He had built a new property which was then sold, with private residence relief being claimed on the sale of a separate plot which the taxpayer argued was the garden of the sold property.

In the recent case of *W&H Ritchie v HMRC* (2017) UKFTT 449, the First-tier Tribunal decided that the permitted area required for reasonable enjoyment of a residence should be based on what is necessary, and in this case found that a shed and path that approached the house qualified, but not land lying on the other side.

OTHER USES OF A RESIDENCE

13.10   Full private residence relief will completely eliminate any chargeable gain arising on the sale of the taxpayer's 'dwelling house'. However, relief may be restricted, and the chargeable gain apportioned according to qualifying and non-qualifying elements of the gain, where there are 'other' uses.

Focus

The main 'other' uses of a residence to be considered in this context are:

- business purposes (**13.11**);

- property lets (**13.14**);

- adult care (**13.15**);

- dependent relatives (**13.16**); and

- employer purchases (**13.17**).

Note that, where an individual lets out a room under the 'rent-a-room' scheme (where a lodger shares the house), private residence relief is still available for the whole house (including the room let out).

Business purposes

13.11 Private residence relief is available in respect of the entirety of a dwelling house or of a part only. However, a separate apportionment is recognised by *TCGA 1992, s 224(1)* for dwelling houses or parts of dwelling houses which are exclusively used for a trade, business, profession or vocation (CG64660). This will be the case where a person works from home and either has an annex or outbuilding designated as an office, or has a room within his property which is exclusively used for office work.

Example 13.1 – Property partly used for business

Alice lives in a small house from which she runs a business. She also owns a small row of lock-up garages adjoining her home. Alice uses one garage for her domestic car, one for her delivery van, one for the stock of finished goods, and she lets the remainder. She uses the dining room to make curtains, but there is just enough room to have family meals in there as well.

On disposal of the house and the garages at a gain, Alice must apportion the gain between the different parts of the property. The garages that were let are a simple investment and taxable as such, with no relief under *TCGA 1992, s 222*. The garages used for the storage of stock and to house the delivery van have been used exclusively for the business and not for any domestic purpose, and are therefore also outside the scope of *TCGA 1992, s 222*.

The remainder of the property qualifies for private residence relief, even though Alice may have claimed a proportion of the costs of services etc

---

against her business profits. There is only one dining room and the family spends considerable time in there; it is not used exclusively for the business. The garage for the family car is not used for business.

Alice would need to agree a reasonable apportionment of the gain with HMRC between the qualifying and non-qualifying elements.

'Just and reasonable' apportionments

13.12   As indicated at **13.11**, an apportionment is required for the purposes of establishing private residence relief if there is 'mixed' (ie residential and exclusively trade or business use) of the dwelling house. In certain circumstances (eg a change of use), the relief is adjusted on a 'just and reasonable' basis (*TCGA 1992, s 224(2)*).

A 'just and reasonable' approach may also be necessary (under *TCGA 1992, s 52(4)*) if, for example, an individual's only or main residence forms part of a larger disposal of land, some of which does not constitute the residence. In such cases, the sale proceeds may need to be apportioned to determine the amount attributable to the residence for private residence relief purposes.

13.13   In *Oates v Revenue & Customs* [2014] UKUT 409 (LC), the taxpayers sold a house with adjoining land for development. HMRC issued a determination to the taxpayers, apportioning the sale proceeds of £725,000 as to £170,000 for the house and £555,000 for the land. The taxpayers appealed, on the grounds that the correct apportionment should be £325,000 for the house and £400,000 for the land.

The Upper Tribunal (Lands Chamber) noted that the Valuation Office Agency's (VOA's) Capital Gains and Other Taxes Manual (at para 8.61; see http://app. voa.gov.uk/corporate/publications/Manuals/CapitalGainsTaxManual/sect8/b-cgt-man-s8.html#P75_1171) used a formulaic approach to find constituent values for apportionment purposes. Whilst finding the formula in the VOA manual to be 'less than satisfactory', the Tribunal decided to adopt it. The Tribunal concluded that a 'just and reasonable' apportionment of the sale proceeds was £325,000 for the house and £400,000 for the adjoining land. The taxpayers' appeals were therefore allowed.

Property lets

13.14   Let properties do not qualify for private residence relief as a let property cannot also be the taxpayer's main residence at the same time. However, there is a specific relief in *TGCA 1992, s 223(4)* which can apply where a person lets all or part of his own home, either while he also occupies the property (see **Example 13.2**), or during another period of the ownership when the property is fully let (see **Example 13.3**). (See CG64700 *et seq.*)

The tax relief is limited to the lowest of the following amounts:

- the part of the gain which is exempt because it was used as the taxpayer's main home;
- the gain attributed to the let period; and
- £40,000 per owner.

Example 13.2 – Letting part of the home

Henry bought an urban terraced property for £480,000 of which 25% is represented by the value of accommodation in the basement that could be occupied separately; the remainder relates to the ground floor and upper floor. He lives there, allowing a lodger to occupy the basement, and later sells the entire property for £660,000.

There is valuation evidence that the basement flat is still worth 25% of the whole.

The gain from the upper 75% of the property of £135,000 (75% × 180,000) is exempt under *TCGA 1992, s 222*. The gain on the basement is £45,000, of which £40,000 is exempt under *TCGA 1992, s 223(4)(b)* (being the lowest figure of £135,000, £45,000 and £40,000).

Example 13.3 – Letting the second home

Jane bought her cottage in Dorset on 1 June 2004 and owned it for exactly 14 years. She occupied it as her sole residence for the first three months, let it for eight years, and used it as a second home for the remainder of the period. The gain is £280,000 or £20,000 per year of ownership.

The taxable gain of £210,000 is calculated by reducing the capital gain of £280,000 before tax relief by £35,000 (being the main home exemption for 3 months, plus the last 18 months of ownership – £280,000 × 21/168 months – see **13.18**) and a further £35,000 (being the relief for letting restricted to lowest of (i) the gain exempt because it was used as the taxpayer's main home – £35,000, (ii) the gain attributed to the let period – £160,000 (8 months × £20,000), and (iii) £40,000).

Adult care

13.15 Under the adult placement scheme, a carer provides accommodation for the adult who needs care in the carer's home, and the carer is regarded as carrying on a caring business from that property. The adult who needs care will normally require exclusive use of part of the property. Where these circumstances apply, the exclusive use of the property for the caring business is disregarded for the purposes of the relief for disposals made on or after 9 December 2009 (*TCGA 1992, s 225D*) (CG64695).

Dependent relatives

13.16 Property owned by a taxpayer and occupied rent-free by a dependent relative on or before 5 April 1988 is treated as if it had been the only or main residence of the taxpayer (regardless of the fact that the taxpayer may have had another residence qualifying for relief) for as long as the dependent relative lived there (*TCGA 1992, s 226*) (CG65550).

Employer purchases

13.17 As part of an employment relocation, the employer may agree to buy the employee's home, thereby providing the employee with the capital to purchase a new home in the new area. In some cases, the employer (or a company acting on behalf of the employer) and employee enter a 'home purchase agreement', under which they agree to share any profit made on the disposal of the old home when it is eventually sold to a third party. In this situation, CGT relief is given to the employee on his share of the profit under that agreement (*TCGA 1992, s 225C*).

PERIODS OF OCCUPATION

13.18 To benefit from the relief in *TCGA 1992, s 222*, the dwelling house must be the taxpayer's only or main residence throughout the period of ownership. Otherwise, subject to the concessions and reliefs discussed below, some apportionment of the gain may be required between different periods of ownership.

Delay in taking up occupation

13.19 HMRC will, under concession ESC D49, ignore a short delay in taking up occupation, when considering whether *TCGA 1992, s 222* relief applies to the full gain on disposal of the property. For example, delays might arise where the taxpayer has acquired land and is having a house built on the land, or where the taxpayer has acquired a property but alterations and decorations are being carried out before the taxpayer occupies that property.

Provided that the delay is no more than one year, this period of non-residence is treated as if it were a period of residence (provided that the taxpayer moves in within that time). If a taxpayer needs more than one year, he may have a second year if there are good reasons for delay.

In *Henke v HMRC* [2006] SSCD 561, a married couple purchased land in 1982 with planning permission for the construction of a house, which commenced in December 1991. The couple took up residence in the house in June 1993. The Special Commissioner held (among other things) that the 'throughout the period of ownership' condition (in *TCGA 1992, s 223(1)*) was not met. An apportionment was therefore required (under *TCGA 1992, s 223(2)*), limiting private residence relief to the period of ownership from the first occupation of the house as the taxpayers' private residence in 1993.

The recent case of *Desmond Higgins v HMRC* [2017] UKFTT 236 (TC) considered the impact of a delay in taking up residence of a new flat which was being built. The First-Tier Tribunal decided that the period of ownership for private residence relief purposes began when the purchase had been physically and legally completed, and when the taxpayer had the right to occupy.

Deemed occupation

13.20   Homeowners may experience significant delays in finding purchasers, whilst personal circumstances compel them to move into a new residence before disposing of the old. *TCGA 1992, s 223(2)(a)* provides that if the taxpayer has been resident in the dwelling house at some point in his period of ownership, the last 18 months of ownership will qualify to be treated as a period of occupation as the main residence 'in any event'.

For properties disposed of before 6 April 2014, this deemed period of occupation was 36 months. This period was reduced to 18 months by *Finance Act 2014, s 58*.

Apart from that deemed period of occupation, the basic rule is that private residence relief is calculated on a time-apportionment basis and is allowed in respect of periods of occupation but not of periods of absence.

Since the last 18 months of ownership of a main residence will always qualify for exemption, even if it has not been occupied as such in that period, two properties may qualify at the same time.

Finance Act 2014, s 58 also introduced *TCGA 1992, s 225E*, to provide for a 36-month final exempt period where the disposer or their spouse is a disabled person or is a long-term (three months) resident in a care home. The additional period only applies where the disposer or their spouse have a single private residence relief, and does not extend the period for those with more than one home.

'Sandwich' reliefs

13.21 A person may be unable to continue to live at a property throughout his period of ownership but, if the dwelling house was the only or main residence of the taxpayer both before and after the period of absence, the following periods of absence can be deemed to be periods of occupation under *TCGA 1992, s 223(3)*:

- any length of time during all of which the taxpayer worked outside the UK;

- a period, up to four years, or periods together not exceeding four years, during which the taxpayer could not live at the residence because of where he was working or as a result of any condition imposed by his employer that required him to live elsewhere;

- any other period of absence up to three years, or periods together not exceeding three years.

Example 13.4 – Periods of absence

Hosking buys a house in July 2000 for £180,000. After living there for three years, in July 2003 he and his family are sent abroad by his employer.

On his return in July 2017, it was valued at £600,000.

Hosking sold the house in August 2017, without resuming occupation. The CGT position in 2017/18 would be:

		£
Sale proceeds		600,000
Cost – July 2000		(180,000)
Total gain		420,000
Exempt		
Occupation as main residence	36 months	
Last 18 months	18 months	
	54 months	
Total ownership	204 months	

691

	£
Exempt 54/204 × £420,000	(111,176)
Gain before annual exemption	308,824
Annual exemption – 2017/18	(11,300)
Chargeable gain	297,524
Tax at 28%	83,307

If Hosking had resumed ownership for a short period, the entire gain would have been exempt.

Job-related accommodation

13.22 If a property or part of it has been purchased with the intention that it should eventually be a residence, but the owner for the time being lives in job-related accommodation, the owner is deemed to occupy the property. It does not matter that the house is never, in fact, occupied, provided that the intention to occupy can be proved (CG64555).

Accommodation is job-related where a person or his spouse or civil partner has some kind of employment that meets the following conditions (*TCGA 1992, s 222(8A)(a)*):

- it is necessary for the proper performance of the work to live in specific accommodation;

- it is provided by the employer for the better performance by the employee of his duties and it is customary in that trade or employment to provide living accommodation for employees; or

- it is provided as part of special security arrangements, as there is a special threat to the security of the employee.

Where the taxpayer, his spouse or civil partner is self-employed, two conditions must be satisfied (*TCGA 1992, s 222(8A)(b)*):

- the worker is required as part of the contract to carry on the work on premises that are provided by another person (who may, but need not, be the other party to the contract); and

- it is a term of the contract that the contractor should live on those premises or on some other premises provided by the other party to the contract.

TWO OR MORE RESIDENCES

Nomination of a property as the main residence

13.23   Where the taxpayer has two or more residences, they may nominate, by notice (or 'election') to HMRC which of those residences is to be treated as his main residence for the purposes of private residence relief (*TCGA 1992, s 222(5)(a)*).

The election must be made within two years of the date on which the second or subsequent residence became available. (Note that it is not the date of acquisition of a second or subsequent property which triggers the need for this notice, but the date the second property is first used as a residence (CG64495).)

Focus

The taxpayer does not have to nominate the property which has the greatest use as a residence (being the one which is factually his main residence). The nomination can apply to any property which is actually a residence (CG64485).

If no action is taken by the taxpayer to nominate a residence as the main residence, the question of which property is the main residence is one of fact (CG64575).

Example 13.5 – Main residence elections

Renee has several houses outside the UK in which she spends five months of the year, with the rest of the time in the UK. On 1 September 2010 she acquires a London flat and makes a main residence election in respect of it. On 31 January 2011, she acquires a country house in Surrey and makes a main residence election in respect of that instead. On 1 September 2012 she decides to acquire a Scottish estate as many of her friends enjoy countryside pursuits. She makes a main residence election in respect of the Scottish property. She divides the seven months she spends in the UK between her various residences, spending the week in London and the weekend in her Surrey home and holidays in Scotland. Hence, all of them are occupied as a residence.

Dissatisfied with the London flat, she sells it in August 2013 and buys a larger house in Chelsea, again making a main residence election in respect of that property. Shortly afterwards, fed up with the British weather, she sells the Surrey home and purchases a property in the south of France instead. However, she does not make a main residence election in respect

---

of the French property. By September 2015, she decides that she prefers France and sells all her properties in the UK.

All of Renee's UK properties have been nominated as her main home for some period, so the last 36 months of ownership of each property, or 18 months for properties sold after 5 April 2014, will qualify for the CGT exemption.

Non-resident capital gains tax

13.24   The *Finance Act 2015* introduced a new charge of non-resident capital gains tax (NRCGT) from 6 April 2015 which applies to gains made on the disposal of UK residential property owned by non-resident taxpayers. Where a loss arises on a disposal potentially subject to NRCGT, that loss can only be set against gains arising on disposals of other UK residential property.

For further commentary on the NRCGT provisions, see **9.73–9.78**.

13.25   Non-resident individuals may be eligible to claim private residence relief for their UK property, but only in relation to qualifying tax years in which:

● the taxpayer (or spouse or civil partner) satisfies a residence requirement for these purposes; or

● the taxpayer satisfies a 'day count' test (within *TCGA 1992, s 222C*), ie broadly by spending at least 90 days in the property in the tax year (or 90 days spread across all the properties the person owns in the country where the property is located). This day count test is adjusted in respect of 'partial tax years' (ie where only part of a tax year falls within the individual's period of ownership).

If neither of the above conditions is satisfied, the tax year broadly falls to be treated as a 'non-qualifying tax year'. The dwelling house is treated as not having been occupied as the individual's residence at any time within that tax year (or a 'non-qualifying partial tax year'). This rule does not apply for tax years before 2015/16, except in the case of NRCGT disposals (*TCGA 1992, s 222B*).

Note that UK residents who want to nominate a property located in another country (where they are not tax-resident) as their main home, will have to meet the 90-day requirement for that overseas property from 2015/16 onwards.

13.26   Where an individual disposes of a dwelling house that was occupied as a residence at any time during their period of ownership, and it is a NRCGT disposal (within *TCGA 1992, s 14B*), an election is available to nominate which of two or more residences (one of which was the dwelling house) was their main residence for any period within its ownership period.

The election must be given in the NRCGT return in respect of the relevant disposal, and cannot subsequently be varied (*TCGA 1992, s 222A*).

Varying the notice

13.27 The taxpayer may vary a notice given under *TCGA 1992, s 222(5)(a)* by giving further notice to HMRC. The statute does not require any minimum period during which a person must reside at a property in order to claim relief. However, the quality of occupation in the nominated property must be such as to constitute 'residence'. The nomination may be varied to apply to a second home for very short period, even a few days, which will give that second home a CGT exemption for gain arising in respect of the last 36 or 18 months of ownership (CG64510) (see **13.20**).

Focus

It is essential to file the notice under *TCGA 1992, s 222(5)* within the set two-year period and to submit any variation of that notice within the same time period.

Licence or tenancy

13.28 It was originally thought that any residence could trigger the need for an election under *TCGA 1992, s 222(5)* but, since October 1994, HMRC interpret *TCGA 1992, s 222(5)* purposively so that it is not appropriate to consider notice of election where the second residence is merely occupied under licence and the taxpayer has neither a legal nor an equitable interest in it (CG64536).

TRUSTS AND ESTATES

Trusts

13.29 Where a beneficiary occupies a trust property under the terms of the trust as their main residence, then on a disposal private residence relief should be available where the trustees make a claim in accordance with *TCGA 1992, s 225*.

13.30 Most trusts are created by a formal written trust deed (ie an 'express trust'). These are considered further below. However, HMRC acknowledge that trusts can sometimes be created by operation of the law (ie 'implied trusts') as opposed to creation by the express intention of the settlor. Furthermore, HMRC recognise that relief under *TCGA 1992, s 225* may be available in such cases to the legal owner of the property, as they hold the property as trustee.

HMRC sub-divides these implied trusts into resulting and constructive trusts. A 'resulting trust' can broadly arise where someone other than the legal owner has made a material contribution to the acquisition of a property. A 'constructive trust' can arise if a person has agreed with the legal owner that the property should be held in some particular way and the person has acted on that agreement.

In practice, a lack of evidence as to the existence of an implied trust is often an impediment to claims for private residence relief under *TCGA 1992, s 225* on the subsequent disposal of the property. However, successful claims can be possible depending on the particular circumstances and the documentary and/ or other evidence available (see, for example, *Wagstaff and another v Revenue & Customs* [2014] UKFTT 43 (TC)).

Constructive and resulting trusts are beyond the scope of this chapter. Detailed commentary on HMRC's view and approach in relation to such trusts is included in its Capital Gains Manual (at CG65406 *et seq*).

Interest in possession trusts

13.31   Although a trust may have multiple life tenants, only one life tenant needs to occupy a property as their main residence in order for the trustees to obtain private residence relief. In other words, relief is not restricted to the extent that the occupying life tenant has an interest in the trust fund (so, for four equal life tenants, relief is not restricted to 25%). This can produce some helpful planning opportunities where a trust owns a property but not all the life tenants can occupy the property.

Where there is more than one residence held by the trustees for the use of the beneficiary, the trustees and the beneficiary can jointly elect under *TCGA 1992, s 222(5)(a)* as to which property is to be treated as the main residence for CGT purposes.

Similarly, where a beneficiary occupies a trust property as a residence but also occupies their own residence, private residence relief will only be available in respect of one property, but this can be decided by a joint election made by the trustees and the beneficiary.

The recent case of *Wagstaff and another v HMRC* [2014] UKFTT 43 (TC) confirms that, where property is held subject to certain legal obligations, the intention to create a trust may be inferred. In this case, the property was purchased by Mrs Wagstaff's son at an arm's length price, subject to an underlying written agreement that Mrs Wagstaff had a right to occupy the property at no cost for the remainder of her life or until she remarried. A private residence relief claim under *TCGA 1992, s 225* was allowed on the subsequent sale of the property.

Discretionary trusts

13.32   Where a trust instrument gives the trustees complete discretion over what benefit may be enjoyed by any of the objects of the trust, the effect is that, until the trustees take action, none of the beneficiaries actually has a right to any of the trust assets. Hence, no private residence relief would be available under *TCGA 1992, s 225*, because they do not have a right to occupy as required by that section.

In *Sansom v Peay* [1976] STC 494, the discretionary trust allowed the trustees 'to permit any beneficiary to reside in any dwelling house or occupy any property or building … for the time being subject to the trust hereof upon such conditions … as the trustees … think fit'. Beneficiaries occupied a trust property and it was held that the occupations resulted from the exercise by the trustees of their powers under the deed. When the beneficiaries moved into the house, they were entitled to stay there unless and until permission was withdrawn by the trustees. As at the date of the disposal of the house, the beneficiaries were still entitled to occupy it and were occupying it under the terms of the trust deed. The gain was therefore sheltered by private residence relief.

Estates in administration

13.33   Sometimes there will be a substantial increase in the value of a dwelling house from the date of the death of its owner to the date on which the property can be sold. Delays can arise where there is a dispute about the terms of a will or where a claim is made under the *Inheritance (Provision for Family and Dependants) Act 1975* or where, quite simply, everything takes rather longer than it should.

Where an individual occupies a property and then the owner dies, but under their will the individual is entitled to at least 75% interest in the property either absolutely or as an interest in possession, then any gain made by the personal representatives will be eligible for private residence relief. This may occur where the deceased spouse owned the home but jointly occupied it with their spouse, and they then leave it to the surviving spouse absolutely or via an interest in possession trust. See *TCGA 1992, s 225A* for further details.

MARRIAGE, SEPARATION AND DIVORCE

Spouses and civil partners

13.34   An individual living with his spouse or civil partner can have only one main residence for both of them as long as they are living together (*TCGA 1992, s 222(6)*). A couple must nominate a residence jointly.

> **Focus**
>
> Where each party to a relationship has a residence, each may claim private residence relief unless and until they begin to be treated as living together within the context of marriage or a civil partnership.

Two or more residences

13.35   The taxpayer has an opportunity to make or vary a notice each time another property becomes a residence, or from the date of a marriage/civil partnership when the partner to the marriage already owns a residence (*Griffin v Craig-Harvey* [1994] STC 54).

Example 13.6 – Only one private residence relief for a married couple

Liz owns a flat in London whilst her fiancé Phil owns a house in the country. They both work in London during the week, so live in Liz's flat during the week, before they both return to Phil's cottage to enjoy weekends.

Prior to their marriage, both properties will qualify for private residence relief, but following their marriage, they have two years to jointly elect for one of their properties to be treated as their main residence, otherwise HMRC will base this on the facts of the case.

However, where one party to the marriage owns two or more residences, but the other does not own any property, then HMRC take the view that the marriage does not provide a new two-year opportunity to make an election, as a joint election is only required where it affects both parties.

Transfers of property

13.36   When a property or an interest in a property is transferred between spouses (or civil partners) who are living together, the transfer is treated as taking place on a no gain, no loss basis (*TCGA 1992, s 58*).

However, where an interest in the sole or main residence is transferred, the recipient spouse's period of ownership is deemed to commence at the date of the original acquisition by the transferor spouse, and not at the date of transfer of the interest between the spouses (*TCGA 1992, s 222(7)*). Similarly, on a death, the surviving spouse inherits the period of ownership of the deceased spouse.

Where one spouse is eligible for private residence relief under *TCGA 1992, s 223(3)*, as a result of living in work-related accommodation elsewhere in the UK, the other spouse is also treated as satisfying the condition provided they are living together.

Year of separation

13.37   A common feature of the breakdown of marriage or of civil partnership is the disposal, by one party, of an interest in the residence that was formerly shared. Timing is everything, because a disposal between the parties that takes place within the tax year of separation is treated by *TCGA 1992, s 58* as if made on a no gain, no loss basis; whilst a disposal delayed into the following or even a later year may attract CGT.

Example 13.7 – Transfer within year of separation

Selena and Richard decide to divorce. They bought their flat for £500,000 on marriage, 75% with Selena's money, with Richard taking a mortgage for the balance. It is worth £900,000 on 31 December 2016.

Richard leaves the flat on 31 December 2016. Selena pays him £225,000 to go, completing the arrangement on 31 March 2017. This is treated as the disposal by Richard of his share to Selena for £125,000 (on a no gain no, loss basis) and his true gains of £100,000 are sheltered, not by private residence relief but by *TCGA 1992, s 58*.

Selena is treated as acquiring Richard's share at an undervalue, but that does not worry her: even if she later sells that share of the flat for more than the deemed acquisition value of £125,000, that gain will be sheltered by private residence relief.

Mesher orders

13.38   *TCGA 1992, s 225B* (formerly ESC D6) provides relief on disposals in connection with divorce (or dissolution of a civil partnership) etc. The relief seems to acknowledge that divorce may result in a court order that is often referred to as a *Mesher* order (so-called after a case of that name), under which the house is broadly occupied by one of the spouses for a limited period.

For example, a *Mesher* order may provide that upon the spouse ceasing to occupy the matrimonial home (the husband, in this example), his interest is held on trust until the couple's youngest child reaches the age of 18 or ceases full-time education, and that the other spouse shall continue to occupy the home during the trust period.

HMRC guidance (at CG65365) points out that the *Mesher* order results in a transfer into trust, which constitutes a disposal for CGT purposes (within *TCGA 1992, s 70*) by the husband in the above example. However, if the conditions in *TCGA 1992, s 225B* are satisfied, private residence relief is available.

When the trust period comes to an end (ie when the youngest child ceases full-time education in the above example) there is a deemed disposal of his property interest as a trustee (*TCGA 1992, s 71(1)*), but private residence relief under *TCGA 1992, s 225* ('Private residence occupied under the terms of settlement') should then apply. However, the husband in this example is still potentially liable to CGT on any increase in value between the trust ending and the property being sold.

13.39   It should be noted that relief under *TCGA 1992, s 225B* is subject to certain conditions being met, one of which is broadly that the individual potentially seeking to claim the relief has not made a main residence election under *TCGA 1992, s 222(5)* (see **13.44**). The individual will therefore need to consider whether or not relief under *TCGA 1992, s 225B* will be beneficial, compared to a possible loss of private residence relief on his or her new home. Interestingly, HMRC makes this planning point in its own guidance (see CG65375).

It should also be noted that private residence relief under *TCGA 1992, s 225B* requires a claim by the individual concerned (*TCGA 1992, s 225B(5)*).

13.40   For detailed commentary on separation and divorce, the matrimonial home and the CGT main residence exemption, together with *Mesher* orders (including the possible IHT implications of trust arrangements), see **16.39–16.61**.

ADMINISTRATION

How the relief takes effect

13.41

Focus

Private residence relief arises under *TCGA 1992, s 222* and is automatic (ie it does not have to be claimed by an individual).

Tax returns

13.42 Taxpayers do not need to complete the capital gains pages of their tax returns in relation to homes disposed of with private residence relief. However, if not all of the conditions are met, and a claim for partial relief is being made, then the relevant tax return pages do need to be completed.

Proper documentation

13.43 In any event, it is essential to ensure that an individual's 'residence' of a property is properly documented.

The case of *Paul Favell* [2010] TC00642 is an illustration of a decision being found in HMRC's favour, purely due to there being a 'complete absence of objective documentary evidence' to support the taxpayer's claim that he resided at the property in question.

PLANNING OPPORTUNITIES AND PITFALLS

Main residence elections

13.44 Where a taxpayer varies (see **13.27**) a notice given under *TCGA 1992, s 222(5)(a)* (see **13.23**) by giving further notice to HMRC, the variation may apply to a second home for very short period, even a few days, which will give that second home a CGT exemption for gain arising in respect of the last 36 or 18 months of ownership (see **13.20**).

This is the process known as 'flipping', and is considered to be 'acceptable' tax planning by the GAAR guidance, which states: 'Buying properties that are occupied as residences and then using the main residence election is using a relief afforded by statute and is not an abusive arrangement. The legislation places no limit on the number of times the election may be swapped'. The scenario outlined at **Example 13.5** is based on GAAR guidance.

Development of land

Trading transactions

13.45 Private residence relief will be denied where the property was acquired wholly or partly for the purpose of making a gain from the disposal where there was no intention that the house would be occupied as a main residence (*TCGA 1992, s 224(3)*). This is in contrast to the position

701

where an individual genuinely intends to occupy the property as their main residence but also naturally hopes it will appreciate in value over time.

Hence, cases where renovation of the property is followed by a quick sale may be vulnerable to HMRC challenge. In such cases, HMRC may not only deny the private residence relief, but they might also seek to treat the gain as arising from 'trading' transactions and so subject to income tax (and not CGT). This vulnerability could also extend to the conversion of a house into flats, the conversion of outbuildings into dwellings, or the acquisition by a leaseholder of a superior interest in the property.

In *Lynch v Edmondson (Inspector of Taxes)* [1998] STI 968, a bricklayer purchased two plots of land, developed them into two flats, and immediately let one of the flats at a premium for a term of 99 years. The Special Commissioner summarised the various tests that led to the final decision to deny private residence relief with the transaction instead considered to be consistent with a trading transaction:

- land is a commodity in which it was possible to trade;

- the taxpayer realised substantial money from one of the units by letting it as soon as it was built;

- much of the cost of the development was repaid from the premium that was taken on the grant of the lease of the first unit to be finished;

- the original purchase of the land was divided up into units for sale; and

- the taxpayer had told the bank that had lent him the money that he would sell one of the flats.

Where a clear pattern of dealing can be discerned, for example, where a person buys properties, renovates them and resells them on a regular basis, HMRC may well regard this as trading.

This can give rise to some cause for concern. A house purchaser often expects that the property value will increase over a period of time and there is an anticipation of gain on a future sale. Many individuals and couples acquire properties which they know they will be selling in, say, two or three years' time to buy larger properties.

The exclusion of the main residence exemption is clearly not aimed at normal home purchases and sales. The fact that the house has been purchased because it may have been a 'bargain' or was expected to appreciate in value does not itself prevent the exemption from applying.

Intention to reside

13.46   Where a residence is purchased and sold at a profit within a short period, it may be necessary to demonstrate the following facts to the Inspector:

- That the intention was to occupy the property as a main residence. This might be evidenced by reasons as to why the house and location, together with any local amenities, were particularly desirable. It may also be useful to give positive reasons for leaving the previous residence.

- That the property was actually occupied as a main residence. Whilst intention to occupy will help refute any contention that the property was bought with the objective of selling at a profit, no exemption will be available unless the property is actually occupied as a main residence (*Goodwin v Curtis* [1998] STC 475). Apart from the family's furniture being moved there, it should also be seen that the family slept in the house; cooked and entertained there; received mail there; the address was used for local amenity purposes (eg with libraries); and the occupants were registered there in the electoral register.

- The intention to sell should have arisen after the property was acquired. It may be necessary to demonstrate special reasons for a short-term sale such as financial problems, job requirements, problems with neighbours or any other reasons why the location or house may have become unsuitable.

- The timing of any advertising of the property for sale or its placement with estate agents should be consistent with the facts referred to in the points above.

Where the relief under *TCGA 1992, s 222* applies to any gain arising on the main residence, any loss made on the disposal of the same property is not an allowable loss for CGT purposes. The taxpayer in *Jones v Wilcox (Inspector of Taxes)* [1996] STI 1349 was unsuccessful in their attempt to use *TCGA 1992, s 224(3)* to create an allowable loss from disposal of his own home (to set against a separate and unconnected gain).

Surplus land

13.47   Private residence relief extends to 'up to the permitted area' (*TCGA 1992, s 222(1)(b)*), which is an area of up to half a hectare, or more where appropriate to the size and character of a dwelling house.

Where the grounds exceed half a hectare, HMRC must be satisfied that the extra area is required for the reasonable enjoyment of the property (*TCGA 1992, s 222(3)*). In that case, it may be crucial that the land is bought and sold with the house. If it is bought or sold separately, this would indicate that a previous or subsequent owner did not 'require' this land for the 'reasonable enjoyment' of the residence, so the gain would not be covered by private residence relief.

Example 13.8 – Selling part of the grounds

Belinda lives in the Old Coach House, built in 1850 as part of a much more extensive property. The Old Coach House has 1 hectare of garden which includes a former stable block and access to a side road. Belinda secures planning permission to convert the stable block into a mews residence, which she sells with 0.25 of a hectare of land.

It is difficult for Belinda to resist the HMRC argument that, if she is now selling the stable block and a parcel of land, that land is not 'required for the reasonable enjoyment of the (retained) dwelling house'. Clearly, if Belinda goes on living at the Old Coach House, the land is not now so required.

Residual building plot

13.48   At the time when land is sold, it must have been owned and used for enjoyment with the house. This condition cannot have been met where any portion of the land had been kept after the sale of the house – even if the original total area was less than half a hectare.

This common pitfall is illustrated by the case of *Varty v Lynes* [1976] STC 508. In that case, Mr Lynes sold his home and retained part of the garden which he sold at a later date. The High Court found that the relief in *TCGA 1992, s 222* could not apply to the later sale of the garden, as at the date of the sale it was no longer part of the residence occupied by Mr Lynes. The wording in *TCGA 1992, s 222(1)(b)* is precise in distinguishing the house from its grounds on this point (CG64377).

The above technically applies regardless of whether the gap between the sale of the house and the land was several years or one day. HMRC have confirmed this view in CG64377–64387.

Example 13.9 – Sale of land after sale of the home

Charles owned and occupied a large property with a 5-hectare plot. He obtained planning permission for a single dwelling on the plot. He then put both his home and the plot with planning permission on the market. In the end, the contracts for sale of his former house were exchanged before

---

the sale of the adjoining plot. Any gain on the sale of the house itself, after apportionment, is covered by private residence relief.

Unfortunately for Charles, in general there can be no CGT relief on the eventual sale of the building plot. It would have been better for Charles to have sold the house and the plot together but with the benefit of the planning permission.

HMRC are prepared to relax the strict rule in CG64377 where all the land was formerly occupied as garden, and the land is disposed of between the date the contracts are exchanged on the house and the contracts are completed with conveyance of the house to the new owner. In that situation, the relief under *TCGA 1992, s 222* is given in respect of the land sold separately, but not if the land is sold after conveyance of the former home (CG64385).

Enhancing the value of the property

13.49 If any construction, refurbishment or improvement work is carried out on a main residence to enhance its value on sale, part or all of the gain arising may not be eligible for private residence relief.

Gains attributable to expenditure incurred wholly or partly for the purpose of realising a gain on the sale of the property are excluded from the main residence CGT exemption (*TCGA 1992, s 224(3)*). Therefore, any development and building profit arising from applying for planning permission and incurring construction costs could be fully assessable to CGT. The related provision is also sufficiently wide to catch any improvements that increase the value of the property on sale. This includes the acquisition of the freehold reversion by a leaseholder. Note that simply incurring expenditure on planning permission, or having a restricted covenant released, will not itself result in any loss of the exemption (CG65243).

Improvements may well be carried out with the expectation that the value of the house will be increased as a result. Any such expenditure could, technically, result in a restriction of the exemption. Accordingly, it may be necessary to demonstrate, where appropriate, that the whole or main objective of any work done was to improve the amenities of the property for the owner's benefit and not to realise a profit.

If the property is sold shortly after any work is carried out, this must add support to a possible argument that the expenditure was incurred with a profit motive. Where this inference is incorrect, the taxpayer may have to be prepared to present to the Inspector evidence that the intention to sell arose after the work commenced.

13.49   *Private residence relief*

Where an opportunity arises to commercially develop a main residence, it might be appropriate to transfer the property to a company or partnership before any work is carried out. This could help ensure that the gain to the date of transfer will be exempt from tax. The further gain on the property in the hands of a company or partnership would almost certainly be taxable as income. This would most likely be as trading income (under *CTA 2009, s 201*).

Chapter 14

Tax planning with trusts

Robert Maas FCA, FTII, FIIT, TEP, Consultant, CBW Tax Ltd

SIGNPOSTS

- **Introduction** – Trusts have a long history. Despite a large number of attempts by successive governments to limit their use, they can still be an important tax-planning tool (see **14.1–14.7**).

- **Types of trust** – There are two basic types of trust: interest in possession and discretionary trusts. There are, however, a large number of variants on these basic models (see **14.8–14.20**).

- **Taxation of UK-resident settlements** – A UK-resident settlement is fully within the charge to UK tax. In some circumstances income (but not capital gains) can be treated as income of the settlor instead of that of the trust (see **14.21–14.41**).

- **Taxation of non-UK resident trustees** – A non-UK trust is outside the scope of UK tax except in relation to certain types of UK income and in some circumstances where there was a UK settlor. For 2015/16 onwards the trustees are liable to CGT on the disposal of UK residential property. However, income can be taxed on the settlor, and so can gains unless the settlor was non-UK domiciled. Both income and gains can alternatively be taxed on a beneficiary who receives a distribution or, in some cases, a benefit from the settlement (see **14.42–14.58**). A new type of protected settlement has been introduced from 6 April 2017 to cater for the situation where the settlor was non-UK domiciled when he created the trust but subsequently becomes deemed domiciled in the UK (see **14.59–14.60**).

- **Inheritance tax** – A special IHT regime applies to trusts. Under this an IHT charge can occur on the creation of the settlement, on each tenth anniversary and on property leaving the settlement. A different regime applies to some interest in possession trusts (see **14.61–14.88**).

- **Tax planning with trusts** – There is still a lot of scope for the use of trusts in IHT planning, however, there are a number of pitfalls that need to be considered (see **14.89–14.91**).

INTRODUCTION

14.1　Trusts have always been an important tool in tax planning. They can be very flexible vehicles. They effectively allow assets to be held in suspense and for the three main attributes of an asset, capital value, income and control, to be separated out.

Not surprisingly, tax authorities do not like trusts because these attributes facilitate tax planning. There are, accordingly, many anti-avoidance provisions in relation to trusts. One of the earliest UK anti-avoidance provisions was the *Statute of Uses 1535*. A use was an early form of trust. A landowner would transfer his land jointly into the name of two or three friends, for the benefit (or use) of either himself or his children. The feudal dues would then not be payable on the death of the original landowner (as he no longer owned the land) or on the death of one of the title holders, as on his death the land passed to the others (and a new title holder could be added to ensure that the ownership never reverted to a sole name).

The *Statute of Uses* deemed the land to belong to the person for whose use it was held. The statute was nominally introduced to protect the interests of the user as instances occurred where on the original landowner's death the title holders simply disinherited his children. It is generally accepted though that the real reason was to protect the royal revenues and other feudal dues that fell due to the king or a local lord on the death of a landowner.

14.2　A trust is a development of the medieval use. A settlor transfers assets to trustees to be held on the terms laid down by the settlor for the benefit of a beneficiary or a number of beneficiaries.

No formalities are needed to create a trust (other than whatever is needed to transfer legal title of the asset to the trustees, although even that is not strictly necessary as direct tax depends on beneficial ownership, and not legal title). A trust can be oral unless land is involved. However, it is obviously sensible to have a formal trust deed. This both evidences the creation of the trust and avoids misunderstandings as to both the terms of the trust and the identity of the beneficiaries.

14.3　A trust can have a single trustee. However, this creates a problem if the trustee dies, as someone will need to apply to the court to appoint a new trustee. Furthermore, a trust cannot dispose of land unless there are at least two trustees, which again would require the expense of an application to the court if there is a single trustee. It is accordingly normal to have a minimum of two trustees. There is no upper limit on the number of trustees but, as trustees must act unanimously unless the trust deed specifies otherwise (and even where it does all of the trustees are entitled to be involved in decision making), a large number of trustees can make operating the trust unwieldy.

14.4   Many people are suspicious of trusts. There are too many anecdotal horror stories in circulation of where things have gone wrong. Many of these date from times when trusts were far less flexible than a modern trust and it was common to have as the trustees one's solicitor and accountant – so a lot of such stories are actually instances of professional trustees declining to follow the wishes of a settlor because the trust deed did not give them the necessary power to do what the settlor was asking them to do.

14.5   There is actually no need to have any professional trustees (although that is obviously desirable for a charity or other public trust). There is no reason – either under trust law or tax law – why the settlor and his spouse should not be the sole trustees of a family trust. Indeed, as the settlor and his spouse might be expected to be uniquely placed to determine what is in the best interests of their own children, this would in many cases be the sensible thing to do.

One situation where some people think this may not be desirable is if the settlor and/or his spouse are amongst the beneficiaries of the trust, as there would be a potential conflict between their duty as a trustee to consider the needs of all of the beneficiaries and their interest as beneficiaries. There could then be a risk that a beneficiary could successfully challenge decisions of the trustees through the courts unless there is an independent trustee who was involved in the decision making. Many parents are happy to accept the risk of being sued by their children though, as they view such a possibility as remote.

14.6   Another deterrent from the use of trusts is that a trust deed looks complicated. The average trust deed runs to 20 or 30 pages. However, this is not because the trust is complicated (although obviously some are), but because a trust is a creature of statute. As such the trustees are entitled to do only what either trust law or the trust deed itself permits them to do. If the law or deed is silent on what they need to do – such as insure the trust assets – they need either to apply to the court to approve the proposed action or to go ahead and risk challenge by a beneficiary. Accordingly, only two or three pages of a typical trust deed actually set out the terms on which the trustees hold the trust property. The rest contains rules for administering the trust, such as the means for appointing and removing and remunerating trustees (a trustee is not entitled to be paid for his services unless the deed authorises it) and a long list of powers to enable the trustees to operate sensibly in relation to the trust assets and obviate the need to obtain court approval for a whole range of things that experience has taught the draftsman trustees frequently need or want to do.

14.7   Many trusts are created by a person's will to take effect on their death. Curiously, such trusts are normally expressed fairly briefly and most seem to operate effectively even though the will does not contain the numerous pages of powers that solicitors write into lifetime settlements. A trust created in a will is often called a will trust.

14.8   *Tax planning with trusts*

Trusts are, of course, not simply, or even primarily, tax-avoidance devices. What they actually do in many cases is remove an obstacle that stands in the way of arranging ownership of family assets in a sensible manner. This obstacle is normally either a reluctance by the settlor to give up control over an asset in circumstances where he does not believe that his children have the expertise to exercise such control properly, or a reluctance to give a child a large amount of either income or capital at the stage where his parents do not think he has the maturity to handle such funds sensibly.

The term 'trust' (ie the terms on which property is settled) and 'settlement' (the act of creating a trust) are generally used interchangeably to refer to a trust. 'Settlement' has a different specific meaning in land law in relation to certain trusts of land but is used in the tax legislation to mean a trust as commonly understood.

Types of trust

14.8

Focus

Trusts can be very flexible provided that the necessary powers are contained in the trust deed. When setting up a trust, understand what the client wants to achieve and discuss with them whether they might need greater flexibility in the future. However, some clients are wary of too much flexibility if this requires giving to trustees who may be strangers to them a lot of discretion over the use and distribution of the funds. It is not necessarily sensible to give the trustees powers that they do not need to meet the client's objectives 'just in case' things change in the future.

There are two main types of trust; interest in possession (IIP) and discretionary. Under an IIP trust someone has an entitlement to the income. Under a discretionary trust no one is entitled to the income; it is at the discretion of the trustees (within the terms of the trust deed) how the income is dealt with.

There are a number of other types of trust that have been created as such by the inheritance tax legislation. These are either hybrids of IIP and discretionary trusts, or are IIP trusts which must also meet specific statutory conditions.

14.9   An 'accumulation and maintenance trust' is a discretionary trust for the benefit of an infant or infants which automatically converts to an IIP trust for the benefit of the infant when they reach 18 or an earlier age specified in the trust deed.

14.10   A 'trust for bereaved minors' is a will trust for the benefit of an infant child or children of the deceased settlor under which the minor must become absolutely entitled to the assets at or before age 18 and until then it is either an IIP trust of which the minor is the principal beneficiary or a discretionary trust where the discretion of the trustees is limited to paying the income to or for the benefit of the minor or accumulating it.

14.11   An 'age 18-to-25 trust' is similar to a trust for bereaved minors and, like it, can be created only by will and only by a deceased parent for his own children, but the child need not become entitled to the assets (or attain an IIP) until age 25.

14.12   An 'employee benefit trust' is, as the name suggests, a discretionary trust for the benefit of the employees of a particular employer or persons engaged in a particular trade or profession (and their spouses or civil partners and dependants).

14.13   A 'newspaper trust' is a type of employee benefit trust which can also include UK newspaper publishing companies or newspaper holding companies amongst its beneficiaries and whose only or principal asset are shares in a newspaper publishing company or newspaper holding company.

14.14   A 'trust for a disabled person' is a discretionary trust which includes a disabled person (as defined in the legislation) as a beneficiary and provides that the settled property is applied during his lifetime for that person's benefit, subject to relatively small monetary limits.

14.15   Mention should also be made of a 'charitable trust' which is a trust whose income and assets can be used only for charitable purposes (although the special tax rules relating to charities are not dealt with in this chapter) and a protective trust. This is an IIP trust which automatically becomes a discretionary trust, the beneficiaries of which are the person with the interest in possession and his family, if the person with the interest in possession does or tries to do anything which divests him of his right to the income. For example, he becomes bankrupt or tries to sell his interest.

Although there is a basic distinction between an IIP and a discretionary trust it is possible for a person to have an interest in possession in only some of the income of a trust with the trustees having discretion over the remainder, or for sub-trusts to exist within a trust under which some of the assets are held on different trusts to the remainder. In addition, many IIP trusts give the beneficiary a right to income only, leaving the destination of the capital to the discretion of the trustees.

Residence of trustees

14.16

Focus

It is important to realise that having one UK trustee is sufficient to make the trust UK resident even if there are five non-UK trustees and all decisions are taken overseas. In particular, a UK resident settlor cannot be a trustee of his offshore trust.

Like an individual a trust can be UK resident or non-UK resident. The residence determines which tax rules apply to the trust – and which anti-avoidance provisions might apply to the settlor or beneficiaries.

For income tax and capital gains tax purposes a trust is resident in the UK (and prior to 6 April 2013, also ordinarily resident) if either:

- all of the trustees are UK resident; or

- at least one of the trustees is UK resident and at the time of creation of the settlement (or immediately before his death in the case of a will trust or other trust arising on death such as on an intestacy) the settlor was either resident, ordinarily resident or domiciled in the UK.

(*ITA 2007, ss 475, 476; TCGA 1992, s 69*)

14.17   In applying these tests a person who acts as trustee in the course of a business which he carries on in the UK through a branch, agency or permanent establishment in the UK must be treated as if he were UK resident if he is not (*ITA 2007, s 475(6); TCGA 1992, s 69(2D)*).

If neither of these conditions is met the trust is neither resident nor ordinarily resident in the UK (*ITA 2007, s 475(3); TCGA 1992, s 69(2E)*).

Different rules applied before 5 April 2007 but the above rules apply from that date irrespective of when the trust was created. Under the old rules, the test for CGT was where the majority of the trustees were resident. Accordingly, trusts with one UK trustee and the majority non-UK would have been non-UK resident but will automatically have become UK resident on 6 April 2007.

Extended meaning of settlement

14.18   A settlement is not defined as such for income tax and capital gains tax. The legislation states that (unless the context otherwise requires) 'settled property' means any property held in trust and that references to property comprised in a settlement are references to settled property (*ITA 2007, s 466(2), (4)*; *TCGA 1992, s 68*).

However, property held by a person as nominee for another person or as trustee for another person absolutely entitled as against the trustee, or for another person who would be so entitled but for being an infant or other person lacking legal capacity, is not settled property (*ITA 2007, s 466(3)*; *TCGA 1992, ss 60, 68*). Such a trust is called a bare trust.

For most tax purposes the assets and income of a bare trust are treated as that of the beneficiary, not the trustee. A person is absolutely entitled to property as against the trustee if he has the exclusive right to direct how the property is to be dealt with (subject to the trustees' right to use the property for the payment of duty, taxes, costs or other outgoings) (*ITA 2007, s 466(5)*; *TCGA 1992, s 60(2)*). Where a person becomes absolutely entitled to property as against the trustees, the trustees cease to be trustees and become nominees for the beneficiary if they do not transfer the assets to him.

14.19   For the purpose of *ITTOIA 2005, s 619* (amounts treated as income of settlor) a settlement is defined to include 'any disposition, trust, covenant, agreement, arrangement or transfer of assets' (*ITTOIA 2005, s 620*). However, the courts have cut down the very wide scope of this wording a little by requiring there to be an element of bounty. This was affirmed by the House of Lords in *IRC v Plummer* (1979) 54 TC 1, where Lord Wilberforce said:

> 'These sections, in other words, though drafted in wide, and increasingly wider language are nevertheless dealing with a limited field – one far narrower than the field of the totality of dispositions, or arrangements, or agreements which a man may make in the course of his life. Is there any common description which can be applied to this? The courts which, inevitably, have had to face this problem, have selected the element of "bounty" as a necessary common characteristic of all the "settlements" which parliament had in mind.'

The *Plummer* case was a tax-avoidance scheme which involved the sale of an annuity to a charity. This was held not to create a settlement.

14.20   Transactions which have been held to create a settlement include:

●   The allotment of shares at a low price to children of the directors of a company coupled with the payment of a dividend on those shares (*Copeman v Coleman* (1939) 22 TC 594).

●   An outright gift of shares by a father to his minor children (*Hood Barrs v IRC* (1946) 27 TC 385).

- Payments into a savings account in the name of minor children (*Thomas v Marshall (Inspector of Taxes)* (1953) 34 TC 178).

- The allotment of shares in a new company to children of a director, coupled with the payment of dividends and the parent providing the company with the opportunity to earn profits (*Butler (Inspector of Taxes) v Wildin* (1989) 61 TC 666).

- The surrender by a life tenant of his interest in a settlement so that the right to income passed to his children under the terms of the settlement (*IRC v Buchanan* (1957) 37 TC 365).

- The creation of a settlement by a grandparent for the benefit of a child coupled with its subscribing for shares in a company and the child's father generating income for the company by working for it at a very low salary (*Crossland v Hawkins* (1960) 39 TC 493).

- A loan by a settlement to the beneficiary's father carrying interest coupled with the father re-lending the money interest free to a company and the settlement distributing the interest to the beneficiary (*IRC v Leiner* (1964) 41 TC 589).

- A covenant to make annual payments to a company controlled by the covenanter until such time as the company was wound up with the payments being used by the company to pay dividends to a third party (*IRC v Payne* (1940) 23 TC 610). The transfer was similarly held to be a settlement in *IRC v Morton* (1941) 24 TC 259 and *Dalgety v IRC* (1941) 24 TC 280, where assets were transferred to the company instead of covenanting annual payments.

- The assignment of a life policy to trustees and covenanting with the trustees to continue paying the premium (*IRC v Tennant* (1942) 24 TC 215).

- A reorganisation of share capital so that trustees ended up with preference shares carrying high dividend rights for five years (*IRC v Prince-Smith* (1943) 25 TC 84).

- The issue of preference shares to the wives of the controlling shareholders combined with the declaration of substantial dividends on those shares (*Young (Inspector of Taxes) v Scrutton* (1996) 70 TC 331).

- A gift of shares to a charity with an option to repurchase, combined with the declaration of substantial dividends (*Vandervell v IRC* (1976) 43 TC 519).

- The guarantee of a bank overdraft secured by the deposit of cash, with the bank agreeing to pay no interest on the deposit and charge only 1% pa on the overdraft and dividends being paid by a company to enable the overdraft to be repaid and the deposit to be released (*IRC v Wachtel* (1970) 46 TC 543).

- An actress entering into an agreement with a company to render her services at a nominal salary combined with a settlement by her father for her benefit of the shares in the company (*Mills v IRC* (1972) 49 TC 367).

Although some of these transactions involved the creation of formal settlements, it was not that settlement that was discerned by the court but a separate deemed settlement resulting from the overall arrangement.

THE TAXATION OF UK-RESIDENT SETTLEMENTS

Income tax

14.21   The normal rule is that income of trustees is chargeable at the 20% basic rate, the savings rate or the dividend ordinary rate, as the case may be (*ITA 2007, ss 11, 12, 14*).

However, if accumulated or discretionary income arises to the trustees (and the trust is not a charitable trust) it is instead charged either at the trust rate, which is 45%, or the dividend trust rate, which is 38.1% (*ITA 2007, ss 9, 479*).

Income is accumulated or discretionary income if either it is required to be accumulated or it is payable at the discretion of the trustees or of any other person (*ITA 2007, s 480(1)*). In particular income is payable at a person's discretion if he has discretion over whether, or the extent to which, it is to be accumulated, the persons to whom the income is to be paid, or how much is to be paid to any person (*ITA 2007, s 480(2)*). Income is excluded from being accumulated or discretionary income if it is deemed to be the income of some person other than the trustees, it is held for the purpose of a superannuation fund relating to undertakings outside the UK (and not held as a member of a property investment LLP) or is income from residential property service charges (*ITA 2007, s 480(3)–(6)*).

The income of an IIP trust belongs to the person with the interest in possession and is taxable on him. Accordingly, in practice, the 20% rate applies only where the trustees are taxable as being the person in receipt of the income and the trust is an IIP trust. If it is not an IIP trust, the 45% trust rate applies.

14.22   Deemed income under the following provisions are also taxable at that rate (unless they are already so taxable) even if the trust is an interest in possession trust so that actual income is taxable on the beneficiaries. The reason is probably because under trust law these items are capital so would not be taxed as income at all unless they are taxed at trust level:

(1)   a payment by a company on the redemption or purchase of its own shares;

(2)   accrued income profits under *ITA 2007, s 628(5)* or *630(2)*;

(3)   offshore income gains under *Offshore Funds (Tax) Regulations 2009 (SI 2009/3001), reg 7.*

(4)   deemed income of employee share ownership trusts under *FA 1989, s 68(2) or 71(4)*;

(5)   the income element of premiums on leases under *ITTOIA 2005, ss 276–307*;

(6)   profits from deeply discounted securities under *ITTOIA 2005, s 429*;

(7)   gains from life insurance contracts under *ITTOIA 2005, s 467*;

(8)   gains on transactions in deposits under *ITTOIA 2005, s 554*;

(9)   gains on disposals of options under *ITTOIA 2005, s 557*;

(10)   proceeds of sale of foreign dividend coupons under *ITTOIA 2005, s 573*;

(11)   deemed income from transactions in land under *ITA 2007, ss 752–772*.

Amounts within 1 above are taxed at the dividend trust rate, but that under the other heads (including, curiously, head 10) is taxed at the 45% trust rate (*ITA 2007, ss 481, 482*).

14.23   Where the trust rate or the dividend trust rate applies, a deduction is allowed for expenses of the trustees which are properly chargeable to income (ie legally chargeable ignoring the express terms of the settlement) (*ITA 2007, s 484*).

Broadly speaking, expenses are properly chargeable to income only if they solely benefit the income beneficiaries (although the appropriate part of an expense where some of the cost can meet this test is also allowable) (*HMRC v Peter Clay Discretionary Trust* [2009] STC 469).

Any unrelieved expenses can be carried forward to subsequent years (*ITA 2007, s 485*). Expenses are set first against dividend income from UK companies (and stock dividends or the release of a loan to a participator in a close company). Any excess is set against other dividend income, then against savings income and finally against other income. The relievable expenses must be grossed-up, so relief is not obtainable at the basic rate, dividend rate or savings rate (*ITA 2007, s 486*).

14.24   The trust rates and dividend trust rates do not apply to the first £1,000 pa of income. Where the settlor has created more than one settlement, the £1,000 figure is divided by the number of settlements but if there are more than five the first £200 in each settlement is taxable at the basic rate, savings rate or dividend rate as the case may be (*ITA 2007, ss 491, 492*).

Where the trustees make a discretionary payment to a beneficiary the payment is grossed-up at the trust rate and the beneficiary (or the settlor if the payment is made to a minor child of the settlor) is treated as having paid tax at that rate – and so can claim a refund if he is not taxable or is taxable at the basic rate only (*ITA 2007, s 494*).

14.25   The trustees must account to HMRC for the grossing-up amount to the extent that it exceeds the balance of their tax pool. This is the accumulated tax suffered by the trustees. However, notional tax, including tax credits in respect of dividends up to 2015/16 is not included in the tax pool.

It will be seen that an interest-in-possession trust is taxed more lightly than a discretionary trust. The income is treated as that of the beneficiaries, with the trustees being liable to tax at the basic rate only as the person in receipt of the income. Accordingly, where the beneficiaries of a trust are not higher rate taxpayers it is preferable from an income tax point of view to use an interest-in-possession trust. There are inheritance tax consequences in doing so where the trust was created before 22 March 2006, but for trusts created after that date this is no longer a problem in most cases.

A discretionary trust used to be particularly disadvantageous where the main assets of the settlement were UK shares, because the loss of the tax credit meant that the balance of the tax pool was often less than the tax payable on distributions to beneficiaries, but this problem has disappeared with the abolition of tax credits.

14.26   Using an interest-in-possession trust does mean having to fix the division of income amongst the beneficiaries in advance. However, a well-drawn trust is a very flexible entity. There is no reason why the trustees should not have power to revoke all or part of an interest in possession and instead grant an interest in possession in that part of the income to a different beneficiary. By this means it should be possible to divide the income broadly as the trustees would have done with a discretionary settlement, but using future rather than past income to adjust the share going to each beneficiary. However, it will not allow income to be accumulated instead of distributed, unless the power includes turning the trust into a discretionary one.

Charge on settlor

14.27   In some circumstances trust income is treated as income of the settlor (and not of the trust). This can happen in three circumstances (*ITTOIA 2005, s 624*):

- where the settlor retains an interest in the settlement;

- where income is paid to an unmarried minor child of the settlor;

- where the settlor receives a capital sum from the settlement or a body connected with the settlement.

14.28 A settlor has an interest in the settlement if there are any circumstances in which the settled property or any related property (which includes the income from the settled property) is payable to the settlor or to his spouse or civil partner, or is applicable for the benefit of any such person (or will or may become so payable or applicable) (*ITTOIA 2005, s 625(1)*).

There are a number of exceptions:

- If the only circumstance in which that can happen is:

    - the bankruptcy of a beneficiary (or a potential beneficiary);

    - the assignment or charging of the trust property by a beneficiary (or potential beneficiary);

    - in the case of a marriage (or civil partnership) settlement, the death of both parties to the marriage and of all or any of the children of one or both of them;

    - the death at or before age 25 of a child of the settlor who had become beneficially entitled to the property or any related property.

- If the only circumstance in which that can happen is the bankruptcy of a beneficiary or the assignment or charging of the beneficiary's interest in the trust, whilst that person is alive and under 25.

- The settlor does not have an interest in the trust property if his spouse or civil partner dies and they are separated under an order of the court or a separation agreement, or in circumstances that the separation is likely to be permanent.

- The settlor does not have an interest in the trust property merely because his widow or surviving civil partner may do so at a future time.

- The settlor does not have an interest in the settled property at a time when he is unmarried merely by virtue of the fact that he may subsequently marry (or become a civil partner of) a beneficiary.

- For income arising after 21 March 2012, the settlor does not have an interest in the settled property if the settlor is not an individual (*ITTOIA 2005, s 625*).

An outright gift of property from one spouse (or civil partner) to the other is not a settlement provided that:

- the gift carries a right to the whole of the income from the property gifted; and

- the property gifted is not wholly or substantially a right to income.

(*ITTOIA 2005, s 626(1)–(3)*)

A gift is not an outright gift for this purpose if it is subject to conditions or if there are any circumstances in which the property gifted (or any related property) is payable to the donor, or is (or will or may become) applicable for the benefit of the donor (*ITTOIA 2005, s 626(4)*).

14.29 It is important to realise that, as an arrangement can constitute a settlement, the property gifted by the donor is not necessarily the settled property; that may simply be part of the machinery making up the settlement. Thus, the fact that a gift of shares carries with it the right to dividends will not necessarily take the dividends out of the section if the arrangement is that the donor will work for the company for a nominal salary and the company will use the income generated by his work to pay dividends.

That was HMRC's contention in *Jones v Garnett (Inspector of Taxes)* [2007] STC 1536. The House of Lords rejected the argument in that case on the basis that ordinary shares carry a bundle of rights and are not substantially a right to income. However, the HMRC argument would be likely to prevail if the shares are preference shares or are a special class of shares with limited voting rights or rights to capital. It should also be borne in mind that the case concerned the exclusion for gifts which are not wholly or substantially a right to income and that this exclusion applies only to gifts to a spouse or civil partner; there is no corresponding exemption for gifts to infant children.

14.30 The settlor is not taxable under these provisions in relation to income which:

- arises under a settlement made by one party to a marriage (or civil partnership) by way of provision for the other after the dissolution or annulment of the marriage (or civil partnership) or while they are separated under an order of a court, under a separation agreement, or where the separation is likely to be permanent, where the income is payable to (or applicable for the benefit of) the other party;

- consists of annual payments made by an individual for commercial reasons in connection with the individual's trade, profession or vocation;

- consists of qualifying donations to charity (within *ITA 2007, s 416* (gift aid));

- consists of a benefit under a registered pension scheme (or other specified pension scheme) (*ITTOIA 2005, s 627*); or

- is donated by the trustees to a charity in the tax year in which it arises (and it is income to which a charity is entitled under the terms of the trust) (*ITTOIA 2005, s 628*).

14.31 Income is also treated as income of the settlor (and not of any other person) if it is paid to, or for the benefit of, a child of the settlor (including a stepchild) who is under 18 and unmarried (and not in a civil partnership) (*ITTOIA 2005, s 629(1), (7)*). This does not apply if the total amount of income paid to (or for the benefit of) the child during the tax year does not exceed £100 (*ITTOIA 2005, s 629(2)*). As with *ITTOIA 2005, s 624*, there is also an exception for income donated to charity by the trust (*ITTOIA 2005, s 630*).

If the trustees retain or accumulate income as an addition to capital and a payment is subsequently made in connection with the settlement to (or for the benefit of) a minor unmarried child of the settlor, that payment must be treated as a payment of income up to the amount of income retained or accumulated (*ITTOIA 2005, s 631*).

14.32   Any capital sum paid directly or indirectly in any tax year by a settlement to the settlor (or to his spouse or civil partner) is treated as income of the settlor for that year, up to the amount of 'income available' up to the end of that year. This is the income of the settlement from inception which has neither been distributed nor treated as income of the settlor under some other provision (and less tax at the trust rate on that undistributed income less any part taxed on the settlor under *ITTOIA 2005, s 624 or 629*) (*ITTOIA 2005, s 635*).

The capital sum is treated as a net amount from which tax has been deducted at the trust rate, so the taxable amount is the grossed-up figure (*ITTOIA 2005, s 640*).

If the capital sum exceeds the income available, the excess is carried forward and taxed as income of the settlor in future years (up to a maximum of ten future years) (*ITTOIA 2005, s 633(3), (4)*).

14.33   A capital sum for this purpose is:

- a loan;

- a loan repayment;

- any other payment which is made otherwise than as income and not for full consideration in money or money's worth; and

- any sum paid by the trustees to a third party either at the settlor's discretion, or as a result of the assignment by the settlor of his right to receive that sum, or which is otherwise paid or applied for the benefit of the settlor.

(*ITTOIA 2005, s 634*)

References to the settlor include his spouse and the settlor (or his spouse) jointly with some other person (*ITTOIA 2005, s 634(7)*).

Trust expenses which, in the absence of any express provision of the settlement, would be properly chargeable to income are deducted in calculating the available income (*ITTOIA 2005, s 636*).

14.34 If this charge is triggered by the making of a loan, and the loan is subsequently repaid, income arising after the date of repayment is not taxed on the settlor (*ITTOIA 2005, s 638(1)*).

If the settlement makes a loan to the settlor, and there have been previous loans to him that have been wholly repaid, the new loan attracts the tax charge only to the extent that it exceeds the amount previously taxed on the settlor by reference to the earlier loan (*ITTOIA 2005, s 638(2), (3)*).

If the capital sum is the repayment of a loan by the settlor and he subsequently makes a fresh loan which is at least equal to the capital sum, the income arising after the date of the fresh loan is not caught by the section (*ITTOIA 2005, s 638(4), (5)*).

If the capital sum is a loan and a tax charge has been triggered on the settlor on the release of that loan under *ITTOIA 2005, s 416* (release of loan to participator in close company) the amount taxed is not also taxable under *ITTOIA 2005, s 633* (*ITTOIA 2005, s 639*).

14.35 If a capital sum is paid to the settlor by a body corporate connected with the settlement and an associated payment has been, or is, made (directly or indirectly) to that body by the settlement, the capital sum is treated as having been paid to the settlor by the settlement (*ITTOIA 2005, s 641*).

There is an exception where the whole of the loan is repaid within 12 months and no loans to or by the settlor to the body corporate within the previous five years have been outstanding for more than 12 months (*ITTOIA 2005, s 642*). This will ensure that a director's loan account which is cleared regularly by voting remuneration or dividends will not trigger the charge.

A body corporate is connected with a settlement if it is a close company (or would be if it were UK resident) in which the trust is a participator or if it is controlled by such a company (*ITTOIA 2005, ss 637(8), 643(2)*). An associated payment is a capital sum paid to the body corporate by the trust and any other sum paid, or asset transferred by the trust other than for full consideration in money or money's worth in the five years preceding or the five years following the payment of the capital sum to the settlor (*ITTOIA 2005, s 643(3)*).

Although the provision refers only to the settlor, HMRC consider that it applies also to a payment to his spouse (Company Taxation Manual CT61060). It is not clear why. The extension of *ITTOIA 2005, s 633* to a spouse is contained in *ITTOIA 2005, s 634(7)*, but that provision is expressed to apply only for the purpose of *ITTOIA 2005, ss 633–638*. It may be because *ITTOIA 2005, s 643* provides that any question in *ITTOIA 2005, s 641* or *642* whether a capital sum has been paid to the settlor by a body corporate is determined in the same way as any question under *ITTOIA 2005, s 633* whether a capital sum has been paid to the settlor by the trustees, although it seems doubtful whether such wording is apt to import *ITTOIA 2005, s 634(7)* into *ITTOIA 2005, s 641*.

It should particularly be noted that these provisions cannot apply to an interest in possession settlement as the income of such a settlement belongs to the beneficiaries and so cannot be retained or accumulated by the settlement.

Capital gains tax

14.36 Capital gains of trusts are taxable at the full 20% or 28% rate depending on the type of asset (28% on disposals before 5 April 2016) irrespective of whether the trust is a discretionary one or there is an interest in possession (*TCGA 1992, s 4(1AA)*).

The CGT annual exemption for a trust is lower than that for an individual. For 2018/19, it is a maximum of £5,850. However, where a person is a settlor of more than one settlement (ignoring one created before 6 June 1978), the £5,850 figure is divided by the number of such settlements to determine the annual exemption of each, subject to a minimum exemption of £1,170 per settlement (which will apply where there are more than five) (*TCGA 1992, Sch 1, para 2*).

Accordingly, a settlement can be unattractive from a CGT point of view if the beneficiaries do not normally utilise their annual exemption in full or if their personal taxable income and capital gains are under £34,500 (for 2018/19) so that they would pay CGT at only 10% or18% if they were to realise the gain personally.

14.37 There are two exceptions. In arriving at the annual allowance of a settlement, no account is taken of any other settlement for a disabled person (see below), any settlement that is non-UK resident throughout the tax year or of any charitable settlement or sponsored superannuation scheme (*TCGA 1992, Sch 1, para 2(7)*).

A settlement for a disabled person attracts the full £11,700 annual exemption (for 2016/17). The settlement must secure that during the lifetime of the beneficiary all of the settled property which is applied (or all other than £3,000 or 10% of the value of the trust property if smaller) is applied for the benefit of that beneficiary.

The definition of a disabled person in *FA 2005, Sch 1A* (see **14.41**) applies If a person creates more than one such settlement by the same settlor the annual exemption must again be divided by the number of settlements subject to a minimum of £1,170 per settlement – but disabled persons' settlements are not aggregated with other settlements for this purpose (*TCGA 1992, Sch 1, para 1*). A non-resident settlement does not attract any annual exemption but when its gains are taxed on a UK-resident beneficiary or settlor the individual can utilise his own annual allowance against the trust gains.

14.38   The transfer of property into a settlement is a disposal by the settlor and will trigger CGT on the settlor by reference to the market value of CGT assets put into the settlement (*TCGA 1992, s 70*). It will also trigger IHT, as a lifetime gift to a trust is not a potentially exempt transfer.

If the asset settled is a business asset (within *TCGA 1992, s 165*) the settlor can elect to treat the disposal as being at a no gain, no loss price in which case the settlement will be deemed to have acquired the asset at that price for CGT purposes (*TCGA 1992, s 165*). A similar election can be made by the settlor in relation to other assets if the settlement is within the IHT discretionary trust regime (*TCGA 1992, s 260*). Virtually all settlements created after 22 March 2006 (other than some will trusts) will come within this regime.

If the gift to the settlement is covered by an IHT exemption – as opposed to being within the nil rate band – hold-over relief will not apply (unless the exemption is that for transfers to political parties, to maintenance funds for historic buildings or of heritage property) (*TCGA 1992, s 260(2)(b)*).

14.39   There is a deemed disposal by the trust (and a reacquisition by the trustees as nominee for the beneficial owner) at market value where a beneficiary becomes absolutely entitled to any settled property as against the trustee, ie where he became entitled to the asset or would do so but for being an infant or other person under a disability (*TCGA 1992, s 71(1), (3)*). Again, the tax can sometimes be deferred by making an election under *TCGA 1992, s 165* or *260*. Such an election can also reduce the tax rate if the beneficiary is taxable at only 10% or 18% on the gains or is able to utilise entrepreneurs' relief against them.

It needs to be realised that a beneficiary can become entitled to assets as against the trustees automatically as a result of a provision of the trust deed. For example, if the deed provides that the assets shall be held in trust for A whilst he is under 30 and that when he reaches 30 A will become entitled to the assets, A will become beneficially entitled to the assets as against the trustee on his thirtieth birthday, so triggering a tax charge, without the need for any decision by the trustees.

14.40   If a loss accrues to the trust on a person becoming absolutely entitled to an asset as against the trustees and the trust cannot utilise that loss in relation to disposals of other assets before that time, the loss is treated as accruing to the beneficiary but can only be utilised by him against gains from the same asset (or, if the asset is an interest in land, from that interest or any other asset deriving from it) (*TCGA 1992, s 71(2)*).

If on the death of a life tenant IHT is payable in relation to the settled property (as will apply to a pre-22 March 2006 IIP settlement and many post-22 March 2006 will trusts) the assets in which the interest subsisted are deemed to be disposed of and reacquired at their market value at the date of death – but no chargeable gain is treated as accruing to the settlement, ie there is simply an uplift in the settlement's CGT base cost of the assets (*TCGA 1992, s 72*).

If a beneficiary disposes of his interest in a settlement that disposal is exempt from CGT provided that the interest was created by, or arose under, the terms of the settlement and the settlement has never been non-UK resident. The exemption extends to a disposal by any other person, other than one who acquired (or derived his title from someone else who acquired) his interest in it for a consideration in money or money's worth.

Trusts with a vulnerable beneficiary

14.41   Special rules apply to trusts with a 'vulnerable beneficiary'. This is a disabled person or a relevant minor. A disabled person is one who is incapable of administering his property or managing his affairs by reason of mental disorder (within the Mental Health Act 1983); a person in receipt of attendance allowance; a person in receipt of disability living allowance by virtue of entitlement to the care component at the highest or middle rate or the mobility component at the higher rate; a person in receipt of personal independence payment; a person in receipt of (armed forces) constant attendance allowance; or a person in receipt of armed forces independence payments (*FA 2005, s 38* and *Sch 1A* inserted by *FA 2013, Sch 44, paras 19, 18* and amended by *FA 2014, s 284*). The definition was slightly different prior to 6 April 2013 and, in some respects, prior to 5 April 2014 also.

A non-resident disabled person can qualify for the relief provided that he shows that he would have been entitled to the appropriate allowance had he met the requirements for that allowance but does not do so only because he does not meet the UK residence and UK presence requirements. A person who ceases to be entitled to attendance allowance, disability living allowance or personal independence payments because her or she is in receipt of alternative benefits is treated as continuing to qualify.

A relevant minor is a person who is aged under 18 and at least one of whose parents has died (*FA 2005, s 39*).

The trustees of such a trust can make a claim to reduce their income tax liability to what the liability on the income would have been had it arisen directly to the vulnerable person. Such an election can be made even if the trust is non-UK resident, but only in relation to UK income. The claim is an annual one.

If the trust is UK resident (and the vulnerable beneficiary does not die during the tax year) and the vulnerable beneficiary election is made for the tax year, the CGT payable by the trust is similarly reduced to the amount that would have been payable by the beneficiary had he realised the gain direct (*FA 2005, ss 30–32*).

The property of the trust (or of a sub-trust) must be applicable only for the benefit of the vulnerable beneficiary and no part of the income can be distributable to anyone else. From 6 April 2013, this latter requirement is relaxed to allow up to £3,000 of income and capital gains (or, if less, 3% of the maximum value of the trust assets during the tax year) to be applied to other beneficiaries (*FA 2005, ss 25, 28, 34, 35* as amended by *FA 2013, Sch 44, paras 14, 15*).

THE TAXATION OF NON-RESIDENT TRUSTEES

Focus

There are a large number of anti-avoidance provisions in relation to overseas trusts with UK resident beneficiaries. If the settlor is UK domiciled these are likely to apply even where the funds remain in the trust. If the settlor is non-UK domiciled (and not deemed-domiciled) they generally apply only where funds are distributed or a benefit is provided by the trust.

It is important to consider the impact of these provisions before making a distribution from the trust. If there are both UK and non-UK beneficiaries the order in which distributions are made can alter the tax charges.

Income tax

14.42 The normal rule is that non-UK residents are chargeable to income tax only on UK earnings and property income and on other income only to the extent that tax is deducted at source (*ITA 2007, ss 811–814*).

However, this rule does not apply to a non-resident trust if it has a beneficiary who is either an individual who is resident in the UK (ordinary resident prior to 6 April 2013) or a UK-resident company (*ITA 2007, s 812*). A beneficiary for this purpose includes an actual or potential beneficiary who is (or will, or may, become) entitled under the trust to receive some or all of any income of the trust (or capital which represents amounts originally received as income) or to whom some or all of any income of the trust may be paid or for whose benefit such income might be used in the exercise of a discretion conferred by the trust (*ITA 2007, s 812(2)–(5)*).

It should be noted that the provision does not apply if all of the income beneficiaries are non-resident but trust capital can be paid to a UK resident. Accordingly, a trust with a non-resident life tenant and a resident remainderman would not be caught. Where a trust falls within *ITA 2007, s 812*, it will, of course, be taxable on UK-source income only, as the territoriality principle will prevent the UK taxing a non-resident on non-UK source income.

14.43   The provisions in relation to UK settlements that attribute income of a settlement to the settlor in certain circumstances (*ITTOIA 2005, ss 624–629*) apply equally to non-resident settlements. So do the provisions that tax the income of a settlement (other than an interest-in-possession settlement) at the trust rate (*ITA 2007, ss 479–482*).

Where a non-resident settlement has both UK and non-UK source income the deduction for trustees' expenses is restricted in the proportion that non-UK (or other non-taxable) income bears to the total trust income (*ITA 2007, s 487*).

It also needs to be borne in mind that the anti-avoidance rules in relation to the transfer of assets to a non-resident as a result of which a person who is resident (or, prior to 6 April 2013, ordinarily resident) in the UK has power to enjoy the income of the non-resident or receives a benefit from the non-resident (*ITA 2007, ss 714–751*) apply to non-UK trusts and, where relevant, their underlying companies, in the same way as with other non-residents.

Capital gains tax

14.44   A non-UK settlement, like any other non-UK resident, is not liable to UK capital gains tax (except in relation to assets used for the purpose of a trade) (*TCGA 1992, s 2(1)*). For 2015/16 onwards, this does not apply to gains from UK residential property which are chargeable to NRCGT, a special version of CGT applying only to non-residents. The application of NRCGT is dealt with at **9.73–9.78**.

However, the gains of a non-UK settlement can be attributed to either the settlor or to beneficiaries.

Trust gains can be taxed on the settlor (as such) only if he is domiciled (or in some cases, deemed-domiciled) in the UK at some time during the tax year in which the gain accrues and he is resident here at some time during that year

(TCGA 1992, s 86(1)(c)). In addition, the settlement must be a 'qualifying settlement' and the settlor must have an interest in the settlement at some time during the tax year concerned *(TCGA 1992, s 86(1)(a), (d))*.

14.45 A settlement is a qualifying settlement if it was created after 18 March 1991 or if it was created before that date and subsequent to 18 March 1991 one of the following applies *(TCGA 1992, Sch 5, para 9(1)–(6A))*:

- property or income is provided directly or indirectly for the purpose of the settlement otherwise than under a transaction entered into at arm's length (and otherwise in pursuance of a liability incurred before 19 March 1991) – but any additions solely to meet a deficit on the trust expenses can be ignored;

- the trust became non-UK resident (or fell to be regarded as non-resident under a double tax agreement);

- the terms of the settlement are varied so that either the settlor, a spouse or civil partner of the settlor, a child or grandchild of the settlor or the settlor's spouse, the spouse or civil partner of a child or grandchild, or a company controlled by any such person or persons (or associated with a company so controlled) becomes for the first time a person who will or might benefit under the settlement (and under the terms of the settlement as they stood at 18 March 1991 that person would not have been capable of enjoying a benefit from the settlement after that date); or

- the settlement ceases to be a 'protected settlement' at a time after 5 April 1999.

14.46 A settlement is a protected settlement if it was formed before 19 March 1991 and at 5 April 1999 (and at all times thereafter) the only beneficiaries of the settlement were:

- children of the settlor (or of a spouse or civil partner of the settlor) who are under 18 (at the end of the tax year immediately preceding that in which the gain arises);

- unborn children of the settlor (or of a spouse or civil partner of the settlor or of a future spouse or civil partner of the settlor);

- future spouses or civil partners of any children (or future children) of the settlor or a spouse or future spouse (or civil partner or future civil partner) of the settlor;

- a future spouse or civil partner of the settlor; or

- persons outside these defined categories (ie he is not a person whose relationship to the settlor (or any of the settlors if there is more than one) would give the settlor an interest in the settlement *(TCGA 1992, Sch 5, para 9(10A), (10B))*).

In applying these tests a person is a beneficiary if there are any circumstances whatsoever in which any of the settled property (or income therefrom) is, or will or may become, applicable for his benefit or payable to him or he enjoys a benefit directly or indirectly from any of the settled property or the income therefrom (*TCGA 1992, Sch 5, para 9(10C), (10D)*).

14.47   The settlor has an interest in the settlement if any of the settled property, or income therefrom, is (or will or may become) applicable for the benefit of (or payable to) a defined person in any circumstances whatsoever, or any defined person enjoys a benefit directly or indirectly from any of the settled property or income therefrom (*TCGA 1992, Sch 5, para 2(1)*).

The defined persons are:

(a)   the settlor;

(b)   the spouse or civil partner of the settlor;

(c)   a child of the settlor (or of the settlor's spouse or civil partner);

(d)   the spouse or civil partner of any such child;

(e)   any grandchild of the settlor (or of the settlor's spouse or civil partner);

(f)   the spouse or civil partner of any such grandchild;

(g)   a company controlled by one or more of the above; and

(h)   a company associated with a company controlled by one or more of the above.

(TCGA 1992, Sch 5, para 2(3))

14.48   There are the usual exceptions where the defined person can benefit only in the event of the bankruptcy or similar event of someone who is not a defined person (*TCGA 1992, Sch 5, para 2(4)(5)*).

Heads (e) and (f) do not apply to a settlement created before 17 March 1998 unless property is added to it after that date, it becomes non-resident after that date, its terms are varied after that date, or a grandchild (or spouse) receives a benefit after that date he could not have received under the terms of the settlement as they stood at 17 March 1998 (*TCGA 1992, Sch 5, para 2A*).

It will be seen that this provision is significantly wider than the corresponding income tax provision, which does not include either grandchildren or adult children of the settlor.

14.49   If the settlor does not have an interest in the settlement the trust gains are attributed to beneficiaries. The amount to be attributed in a tax year is of course the trust gains for the year plus any unattributed gains (after taper relief where appropriate) of earlier years (*TCGA 1992, s 87(1), (2)*). NRCGT gains or losses (ie on UK residential property – see **9.73**) are excluded from the calculation as they will already have been taxed on the trustees (*CTGA 1992, s 87(5A)*).

The amount so calculated is attributed to UK resident beneficiaries who receive capital payments from the settlement in the tax year or who received capital payments in earlier years which have not yet been matched with gains. The gains are then attributed to those beneficiaries in proportion to their capital payments up to the amount of such payments. Any unattributed part of the gains is carried forward to the next tax year (*TCGA 1992, s 87(4), (5)*). From 2018/19 onwards, payments to non-resident beneficiaries are normally ignored in making this attribution (*TCGA 1992, s 87D inserted by FA 2018, Sch 10, para 1*).

Gains attributed to a beneficiary who is not domiciled in the UK are taxable here but subject to any application of the remittance basis. The domicile of the settlor does not affect the taxability of the beneficiary. Gains attributed to beneficiaries who are UK resident and domiciled are treated as gains realised by the beneficiary.

14.50 If the settlement migrates to the UK without all of the past gains having been attributed to beneficiaries the attribution continues so as to attribute those gains to beneficiaries who receive capital payments from the settlement in subsequent years (*TCGA 1992, s 89*).

To the extent that gains are not matched with capital payments in the same tax year or the year following that in which the gain arises, the beneficiary is also liable to a surcharge on the tax. The surcharge is 10% pa for the period from 1 December following the tax year in which the gain arose to 30 November in the tax year following that in which the capital payment is made. The surcharge cannot run for more than six years though, so it is effectively limited to 12% of the gain (60% of the 20% tax rate) (*TCGA 1992, s 91*). This gives an effective CGT rate of 32%.

14.51 If the settlement distributes assets to another settlement the unallocated trust gains of the first are treated as trust gains of the second settlement and allocated to beneficiaries who receive capital payments from the second settlement. If part only of the settled property is transferred then only a proportionate part of the unallocated gains of the first settlement is transferred to the second (*TCGA 1992, s 90*).

The normal exemption for a disposal by a beneficiary of his interest in a settlement does not apply to an interest in a non-resident settlement (*TCGA 1992, ss 76(1A), 85*). Such a disposal is accordingly chargeable to CGT.

In addition, where the interest is disposed of for consideration and the trustees were UK resident at any time in the tax year in which the disposal occurs, the settlor was UK resident or ordinarily resident in that year or in any of the five previous tax years, and the settlor has an interest in the settlement in that or in the previous two tax years, the trustees must be treated as having sold and immediately reacquired the relevant underlying assets of the settlement, ie the part of the assets in which the beneficiary's interest subsisted (*TCGA 1992, Sch 4A, paras 1–8*). *TCGA 1992, Sch 4A* displaces the charge on the beneficiary, unless that would be greater than the charge on the trustees (or there would be a lower loss on the disposal) under *TCGA 1992, Sch 4A* – in which case, *TCGA 1992, s 76(1A)* displaces the *TCGA 1992, Sch 4A* charge (*TCGA 1992, Sch 4A, para 10(2)*).

14.52 If a UK-resident settlement ceases to be UK resident at any time, the migration triggers a deemed disposal and reacquisition of all of the trust assets at the time of the migration so as to create a taxable gain while the settlement is UK resident (*TCGA 1992, s 80*). There is an exception where the migration occurs because of the death of a trustee provided that the settlement becomes UK resident again within the following six months (and the assets have not been disposed of during the period of non-residence) (*TCGA 1992, s 81*).

If the tax due on the migration of a settlement is not paid within six months of the due date, HMRC can recover it from anybody who was a trustee at any time in the 12 months prior to the migration. They cannot recover the tax from a person who ceased to be a trustee some time before the migration and can show that at the time that he ceased to be a trustee there was no proposal that the trust should emigrate (*TCGA 1992, s 82*).

14.53 If it is wished to migrate a settlement, it needs to be borne in mind that *Trustee Act 1925, s 37(1)(c)* provides that a trustee should not be discharged from his trust unless there will be either a trust corporation or at least two individuals to act as trustees to perform the trust. In most cases a trust corporation is a company incorporated in either the UK or another EU country.

In *Jasmine Trustees Ltd v Wells & Hind (a firm)* [2007] STC 660, UK trustees resigned and were replaced by an Isle of Man company. It was held that the resignation was ineffective, with the result that the previous UK trustees were still the trustees, so the trust remained UK resident and all of the acts of the new trustees must have been entered into as agent for the real trustees.

14.54 If the trustees of a non-resident settlement with a UK-resident beneficiary or a UK resident and domiciled settlor makes a transfer of value and that transfer is linked with trustee borrowing, the trustees are deemed to dispose of and immediately reacquire the whole (or a proportion of) the chargeable assets of the settlement (*TCGA 1992, Sch 4B, para 1*).

For this purpose trustees make a transfer of value if they:

- lend money or any other asset to any person;

- transfer an asset to any person either for no consideration or at an undervalue; or

- issue a security of any description to any person either for no consideration or at an undervalue.

14.55 The transfer of value is treated as made when the loan is made, the transfer is effectively completed (ie the transferee becomes for practical purposes unconditionally entitled to the asset) or the security is issued, as the case may be (*TCGA 1992, Sch 4B, para 2*).

A transfer of value is linked with trustee borrowing if at the time of the loan or transfer there is outstanding trustee borrowing, ie either:

- any loan obligation is outstanding; or

- there is trustee borrowing that has not been either applied for normal trust purposes or triggered a tax charge under *TCGA 1992, Sch 4B* in relation to an earlier transfer of value.

(*TCGA 1992, Sch 4B, para 5*)

14.56 A borrowing is applied for normal trust purposes if it is used to acquire a trust asset either at arm's length or at no more than an arm's-length price, is used to repay an earlier borrowing for such a purpose, or is used to meet bona fide current trust management expenses (*TCGA 1992, Sch 4B, para 6*).

The deemed disposal is of the whole of the trust assets unless the amount of value transferred is either:

- less than both the amount of outstanding trustee borrowing and the effective value of the remaining chargeable assets, in which case the deemed disposal and reacquisition is of the proportion of each of the remaining chargeable assets given by:

$$\frac{\text{amount of value transferred}}{\text{effective value of the remaining chargeable assets}}$$

- less than the effective value of the remaining chargeable assets (but not less than the outstanding trustee borrowing) in which case the deemed disposal and reacquisition is of the proportion of each of the remaining chargeable assets given by:

$$\frac{\text{amount of outstanding trustee borrowing}}{\text{effective value of the remaining chargeable assets}}$$

14.57 The effective value of the remaining chargeable assets is their aggregate market value less so much of that value as is attributable to trustee borrowing (*TCGA 1992, Sch 4B, para 11*). The value of an asset is attributable to trustee borrowing to the extent that the trustees applied the borrowing to acquire or enhance the value of the asset (or the asset represents directly or indirectly an asset whose value was attributable to the trustees having so applied the proceeds of trustee borrowing) (*TCGA 1992, Sch 4B, para 11*).

14.58 Where *TCGA 1992, Sch 4B* applies the gains are, of course, attributed to the settlor (if he has an interest in the settlement) or to beneficiaries who receive capital payments from the settlement (if he does not) (*TCGA 1992, Sch 4C*).

This provision prevents avoidance of the tax charge by the trustees borrowing against the trust assets and distributing the money borrowed instead of selling the assets and distributing the proceeds. It was aimed against what was known as the 'flip-flop' scheme under which trust 1 would borrow and distribute the amount borrowed to trust 2 and in the next tax year sell the assets and use the gain to repay the borrowing. As trust 1 made no capital payment to beneficiaries and trust 2, which did make capital payments, realised no gains this was thought to avoid the tax charge.

In fact, in the light of the subsequent decision in *West (Inspector of Taxes) v Trennery* (2003) 76 TC 713, the scheme probably did not work but the very complex legislation in *TCGA 1992, Schs 4B* and *4C* nevertheless remains.

Settlements with non-UK domiciled settlors

14.59 Broadly speaking, the non-UK income and gains of a settlement with a non-UK domiciled settlor and non-UK domiciled beneficiaries were outside the scope of the anti-avoidance rules on both income tax and capital gains tax up to 5 April 2017, provided that, if the income or gain was distributed to the beneficiary, it was not remitted to the UK. Following the changes to the domicile rules, such an overseas settlement, where the settlor is resident in the UK and was born in the UK with a UK domicile of origin, is brought fully within the anti-avoidance rules from 6 April 2017 (although prior income and gains of the settlement continue to be tax-free while they remain in the settlement, and any distribution of them to UK resident beneficiaries continues to be taxed in the UK on a remittance basis).

However, *F(No 2)A 2017, Sch 8* created a new form of protected settlement. The CGT settlor charge (see **14.44**) does not apply where the settlor was non-UK domiciled and remains non-UK domiciled (or deemed domiciled until he has lived in the UK for 15 out of 20 tax years). It also does not apply where the settlor has become deemed domiciled under the '15 out of 20 years' rule, provided that he does not (directly or indirectly) add any property to the settlement after 5 April 2017 (*TCGA 1992, Sch 5, para 5A*, inserted by *F(No 2)A 2017, Sch 8, para18*). There are exemptions: for added property or income that is provided on arm's length terms (ie the settlor sells something to the settlement at market value); for a loan on arm's length terms (including a pre-5 April 2017 loan, if the terms are amended to provide for a market rate of interest), provided that the interest is actually paid annually; for a loan repayment by the trustees to the settlor; and for property or income provided to meet the trust's expenses of administration (or taxation), to the extent that such amounts exceed the trust's income for the year (*TCGA 1992, s 86(5B)*).

14.60   There is a similar exemption for protected foreign source income of a non-UK settlement. This is income that: would be relevant foreign source income (as defined in *ITTOIA 2015, s 830*) if it were income of a UK resident; is derived from property originating from a non-domiciled settlor (and non-deemed domiciled, if the settlement is created after 5 April 2017); arises in a year in which the settlor is a non-domiciled person (and is not deemed domiciled under the '15 out of 20 years' rule); and is not provided (directly or indirectly) to the settlement by the settlor (or by another settlement of which the settlor is settlor or a beneficiary) at a time when the settlor is UK domiciled or deemed domiciled under the '15 out of 20 years' rule (*ITTOIA 2005, s 628A*, inserted by *F(No 2)A 2017, Sch 8, para 22*). The same exceptions for added property or income as apply for CGT purposes also apply for this purpose (*ITTOIA 2005, s 628B*). The exemption is, of course, carried through to the tax charge on the settlor that applies where the trust distributes income to his minor child (*ITTOIA 2005, s 630A*) and to the charge on capital payments to the settlor (*ITTOIA 2005, s 635(3)*). *ITA 2007, ss 721* (undistributed income which the settlor has power to enjoy) and *729* (capital receipts) are similarly amended to exclude protected foreign source income from being taxed on the settlor under that provision (*ITA 2007, ss 721(3B), 721A, 721B*). The rules on capital receipts are also amended so that a capital payment to a non-domiciled settlor after 5 April 2017 cannot be matched with protected foreign source income (*ITA 2007, ss 728(1A), 729A*).

However, such a settlor is brought within *ITTOIA 2005, s 731* (receipts by persons other than the settlor), so that an actual distribution to the non-domiciled settlor will attract income tax in the same way as distributions to other beneficiaries.

The effect of these changes is to keep income and gains of a qualifying settlement with a non-UK domiciled settlor out of the scope of both UK income tax and capital gains tax while it remains within the settlement. This applies to both pre- and post-6 April 2017 income and gains. However, a distribution from the settlement of the income or gains to the settlor will trigger both income tax and CGT in the same way that a distribution to a beneficiary previously did.

Inheritance tax

14.61   Trusts are within the scope of inheritance tax (IHT) but are taxed under a special IHT regime – or to be more precise a number of different IHT regimes. The residence or domicile of the settlor is irrelevant, except to the extent that non-UK assets of a settlement are excluded property (and therefore outside the scope of IHT) if the settlor was non-UK domiciled (and not deemed UK domiciled) at the time that the settlement was made (*IHTA 1984, s 48(3)*).

There are two main trust regimes, the interest-in-possession regime and the relevant property regime. Relevant property simply means property not falling into the IIP regime. The relevant property regime applies to all trusts created after 22 March 2006 including *inter vivos* interest-in-possession trusts (but excluding special forms of will trust). The interest-in-possession regime applies to interest-in-possession trusts created before 22 March 2006 and to some will trusts created after that date.

The relevant property regime

14.62   There are three possible occasions of charge to IHT:

- on the settlor on creation of the settlement (the 'entry charge');
- on the settlement on each tenth anniversary (the 'ten-yearly charge');
- on distributions from the settlement or the termination of the settlement (the 'exit charge').

The entry charge

14.63   Transferring assets into settlement constitutes a gift. A gift into settlement is generally not a potentially exempt transfer, so it attracts IHT but at 50% of normal rates, ie the tax charge is 20% of the value of the assets put into the settlement in excess of the £325,000 nil rate band (for 2018/19). As with other gifts, prior gifts within the seven years prior to the gift into settlement are aggregated with the gift into settlement to determine how much, if any, of the nil rate band is available to utilise against the gift.

The entry charge does not apply in the case of a will trust, as the death of the deceased will have triggered IHT and the creation of the trust is simply the disposition of part of the assets on that death.

The ten-yearly charge

14.64   The ten-yearly charge is imposed on each tenth anniversary of the creation of the settlement (*IHTA 1984, s 64*). If extra assets are added to the settlement the addition is not treated as a separate settlement; there is only one anniversary date for the entire settlement.

The charge is at a special rate of 30% of half the normal IHT rate. This gives a maximum rate of 6% of the value of the assets in the settlement at the anniversary date (30% of 50% of 40% = 6%) (*IHTA 1984, s 66(1)*). In most cases the charge is significantly less than 6% as the nil rate band applies in the normal way.

14.65   The tax rate is based on the tax that would be payable on a gift equal to the value of the trust assets at the anniversary date by a deemed donor who had made gifts in the prior seven years equal to the gifts made by the actual settlor in the seven years prior to the initial gift into settlement (*IHTA 1984, s 66(3)*).

Accordingly, if the actual settlor had made no gifts in the seven-year period the full £325,000 nil rate band would be available in calculating the tax payable under the ten-yearly charge. If assets have been added to the settlement in the ten-year period the gifts in the seven years prior to that addition are used as the starting point if they are greater than those in the seven years prior to the creation of the settlement (*IHTA 1984, s 67*).

The tax is calculated by computing the average rate and applying that to the value of the relevant property, ie the capital assets held by the settlement. However, if assets have been added to the settlement since the previous ten-year anniversary, the tax attributable to such assets is pro-rated by reference to the number of quarter years that the assets were in the settlement (*IHTA 1984, s 66(2)*). This reduction does not apply to uncapitalised income which is deemed to be capital under *IHTA 1984, s 64(1A)* (*IHTA 1984, s 66(2A)*).

This provides that income received is treated as relevant property, ie as capital, for the purpose of the 10-yearly charge if it arose more than five years before the anniversary date, arose (directly or indirectly) from property comprised in the settlement which at the time was relevant property, and at the time it arose no one had an IIP in the property from which the interest derives (*IHTA 1984, s 64(1A)* inserted by *Finance Act 2014, Sch 21, para 4*). This is intended to prevent trustees with a power to accumulate income from delaying a decision to capitalise the income until after the next 10-year anniversary. It is, however, a somewhat odd provision as it applies only to income generated by the trust capital (including income that has been actually accumulated). It will not affect income under, say, a deed of covenant or income from the investment of past income that has not been formally capitalised. The reason for this distinction is not readily apparent.

Where the settlor was not UK domiciled at the time the settlement was made, income which arises outside the UK or which is represented by a holding in an authorised unit trust or a share in an OEIC is disregarded for this purpose. So is income represented by IHT on exempt gifts provided that all known persons for whose benefit the capital or income might be applied meet the terms of the exemption.

Example 14.1 – Ten-year anniversary charge

Joe created a settlement on 1 June 1976. On 1 June 2016, the value of the assets in the settlement was £2,025,000. £400,000 of those assets were added by Joe to the settlement on 31 December 2014. Joe had made no gifts in the seven years prior to the creation of the settlement or in the seven years prior to 31 December 2014.

The tax on £2.025m is	£325,000 @ nil%	£ nil
	£1,700,000 @ 40%	£680,000
		£680,000
The average rate is		33.56%
30% of 50% of 33.56% is		5.03%
The tax payable is		
5.03% of £1,625,000		£81,737.50
6/40 × 5.03% of £400,000 (as the property was in the settlement for only six quarters in the ten-year period)		£3,018.00
Tax payable		£84,755.50

The exit charge

14.66 If there is other property in the settlement which is not subject to the ten-yearly charge, such as property in which there is an interest in possession, the value of that property at the time that it was put into the settlement does not have to be brought into account in calculating the effective rate of tax on the relevant income. The value at the date of the settlement of relevant property put into a related settlement (one made by the same settlor on the same day) does have to be added however (*IHTA 1984, s 66(4)*).

The exit charge is similar to the ten-yearly charge. It is payable when assets are distributed from the settlement. It is in effect the proportion of the ten-yearly charge attributable to the number of quarters (or part quarters) for which the property was in the settlement since that charge last arose (*IHTA 1984, s 69*).

14.67 The rate of tax used for the exit charge is, however, based on the average rate at the previous ten-year anniversary (*IHTA 1984, s 69(1)*). On a distribution before the first ten-year anniversary the rate is that payable by a notional transferor at the time of the creation of the settlement who had made transfers equal to the value of the property settled (at the time it was settled) plus the value of any gifts made by the settlor in the seven years prior to the creation of the settlement (*IHTA 1984, s 68*).

The effect of this is that if no tax was payable on the creation of the settlement nothing is payable on a distribution of the assets prior to the first ten-year anniversary, however high the value of those assets might be at the time of the distribution. That is not wholly correct. There is a tax trap if the assets settled qualified for business property or agricultural property relief. The notional transfer by the deemed transferor is not a transfer of such property. Accordingly, it is only if the value before business or agricultural property relief fell within the nil rate band that the tax payable on a distribution will be nil. Of course, this may not matter if the property that is distributed itself qualifies for 100% business property relief as, in such a case, the value to which the rate is applied is nil, so the rate does not matter.

No exit charge is payable if the distribution takes place within three months after a ten-year anniversary (*IHTA 1984, s 65(4)*).

The interest-in-possession regime

14.68 The interest-in-possession (IIP) regime applies to:

- interest-in-possession trusts created before 22 March 2006;

- some accumulation and maintenance trusts created before 22 March 2006;

- will trusts with an 'immediate post death' interest;

- trusts for disabled persons;

- protective trusts.

It should be borne in mind that where property is added to an existing settlement that addition is actually a separate settlement held on the trusts of the existing one (except for the purpose of the ten-yearly charge) (*IHTA 1984, s 43(2)*).

Accordingly, property added to a pre-22 March 2006 IIP trust after that date will be governed by the relevant property regime not the IIP one.

Pre-22 March 2006 IIP trusts

14.69   The settled property is treated for IHT purposes as belonging to the life tenant (or other person with the IIP) even if he has no right to capital (*IHTA 1984, s 49(1)*). There is no ten-yearly charge on such a settlement but IHT at the full rates is payable on the death of the life tenant, treating the settled property as the top slice of his estate. The trustees are liable for payment of the tax, but if they do not pay it the tax can be collected from the deceased's estate, any person who receives a benefit from the settlement after the death or, in the case of a non-resident settlement, the settlor (*IHTA 1984, s 201*).

If the interest in possession terminates during the life of the beneficiary with the IIP he is treated as making a gift of the settled property. The effect is that if the property remains in the settlement, eg it becomes a discretionary settlement or an IIP is created in relation to someone else, he is treated as creating a new discretionary settlement, thus triggering an entry charge liability, but if the property passes to an individual the deemed gift will be a potentially exempt transfer on which IHT will be payable only if the beneficiary dies within the next seven years.

14.70   Prior to 22 March 2006, if the property remained in the settlement but a different beneficiary became entitled to an IIP this was also treated as a PET. This treatment continued to apply if the IIP came to an end before 6 October 2008 (*IHTA 1984, s 49C*). This effectively gave a short window within which the identity of the person with the IIP could be altered. For example, an IIP in favour of a parent could be terminated by creating a new IIP in favour of his child (provided, of course, that the trust gave the power to do so).

It also continues to apply if the IIP comes to an end by the death of the beneficiary after 5 April 2008 and the spouse or civil partner of the beneficiary becomes entitled to an IIP on the death of the beneficiary (*IHTA 1984, s 49D*).

It also continues to apply where the settled property is an insurance contract, the person with the IIP dies after 6 April 2008 and a different person acquires an IIP on the death. This treatment will continue if a new beneficiary takes over the IIP on the second beneficiary's death and so on, provided that there is an unbroken sequence of IIPs from 22 March 2006 (*IHTA 1984, s 49E*).

14.71   Where a beneficiary has an IIP in only part of the trust assets the IIP treatment obviously applies only to that part (*IHTA 1984, s 50(1)*). If the interest is a right to a fixed annual sum (or to the trust income less a fixed annual sum) special rules apply to determine the amount in which the IIP is deemed to exist (*IHTA 1984, s 50; CTT (Settled Property Income Yield) Order 2000, SI 2000/174*).

If an IIP beneficiary disposed of his IIP (and the trust is within the IIP regime at the time) the disposal is not charged to CGT but the interest of the beneficiary is instead deemed to terminate so triggering the IHT charge that would arise on a termination of the IIP (*IHTA 1984, s 51*). No charge arises if the disposal is a gift for the maintenance of the life tenant's family (*IHTA 1984, s 51(4)*).

If the IIP beneficiary sells his interest (or otherwise disposes of it for money or money's worth) the consideration is deducted from the value of the settled property in calculating the IHT (presumably because the sale proceeds remain in the beneficiary's estate) (*IHTA 1984, s 52*). No tax is of course chargeable in relation to any of the trust assets which are excluded property (non-UK assets of a settlement created by a non-UK domiciled settlor) (*IHTA 1984, s 53(1)*).

14.72 There is also an exception if the trust property reverts to the settlor or his spouse or civil partner (or to his widow or surviving civil partner if he died within the previous two years) on the termination of the IIP and the settlor or spouse, etc is alive at that time and (except in the case of a revertor to the settlor) domiciled in the UK (*IHTA 1984, s 53(3), (4)*). The exemption does not apply if the settlor or spouse, etc acquired the reversionary interest for a consideration in money or money's worth (*IHTA 1984, s 53(5)*).

The revertor to settlor exemption also applies if the reversion is brought about by the death of the life tenant (*IHTA 1984, s 54*).

Accumulation and maintenance settlement

14.73 An accumulation and maintenance (A&M) settlement is a cross between a discretionary trust and an IIP trust. The settlement must have been created before 22 March 2006, and the settled property must be held for one or more persons who will become entitled to an interest in possession in it on or before age 18, and while no interest in possession subsists the income must be either accumulated or applied to, or for the benefit of, such beneficiaries (*IHTA 1984, s 71(1)*).

In addition either all of the beneficiaries must be grandchildren of a common grandparent (or surviving children of a deceased grandchild) or all of the beneficiaries must acquire their IIP within 25 years of the creation of the settlement (*IHTA 1984, s 71(2)*). No IHT charge arises on the death of a beneficiary before he obtains his IIP or on the attainment of the IIP, and after he does so the normal IHT rules apply (*IHTA 1984, s 71(4)*).

14.74 Prior to 6 April 2008, the IIP could be deferred until age 25. The *FA 2006* change gave a short window in which to amend existing A&M

settlements to preserve the tax benefits. However, most people do not want children to acquire substantial assets at 18 for fear that the child may be financially immature at such a comparatively young age. Accordingly, it is unlikely that many people will have taken the opportunity to amend their A&M settlements in this way. An A&M settlement that does not meet the new rules came into the discretionary trust regime from 6 April 2008 (except, of course, to the extent that any beneficiary may have already become entitled to an IIP in part of the settled property). Where this happened there was, however, no IHT charge by reference to that event (*FA 2006, Sch 20, para 3(3)*).

14.75 If the settled property ceases to qualify as an A&M settlement in any other circumstances (other than by being used to meet trust expenses) IHT is chargeable at a special rate (*IHTA 1984, s 71(5)*). This is based on the period during which the property was held on A&M trusts (but ignoring any period before 13 March 1975). It is:

- 0.25% for each of the first 40 quarters;

- 0.20% for each of the next 40 quarters;

- 0.15% for each of the next 40 quarters;

- 0.10% for each of the next 40 quarters;

- 0.05% for each of the next 40 quarters.

(*IHTA 1984, s 70(6)*)

For example, if a property is held in A&M trusts for 22 years and the assets are then distributed to an adult beneficiary (other than the one with the IIP) the charge would be 4.8% of the value of the asset (0.25% for ten years plus 0.20% for ten years plus 0.15% for two years).

Immediate post-death interests

14.76 An immediate post-death interest is an interest in possession in settled property where the settlement was created by will or under the laws of intestacy, the beneficiary became entitled to the IIP on the death of the testator or intestate and he has remained entitled to it since that time (*IHTA 1984, s 49A*).

As with pre-22 March 2006 IIP trusts, the beneficiary is treated as owning the assets for IHT purposes, so the discretionary trust regime will not apply even though the testator's death occurred after 22 March 2006 (*IHTA 1984, s 49*).

14.77 This provision was introduced to preserve the IHT exemption where an IIP in the testator's estate is left to his surviving spouse on his death. As the surviving spouse is deemed to beneficially own the assets, on the death the exemption for a gift to the spouse applies to the assets in which the IIP is created.

However, an immediate post-death interest is not limited to assets passing to the surviving spouse or civil partner; such an interest can be created in favour of anybody. If the beneficiary is someone other than the surviving spouse or civil partner, IHT will, of course, be payable on the death, but no further IHT charge will arise until the termination of the IIP.

Trusts for disabled persons

14.78   A trust for a disabled person is one under which during the life of the disabled person no interest in possession in the settled property exists but the trusts secure that during the disabled person's life any distribution is applied for the benefit of the disabled person.

For money put into the settlement prior to 8 April 2013 only, at least half of the settled property that is applied by the trustees during that person's life must be applied for his benefit (*IHTA 1984, s 89(1)* as amended by *FA 2013, Sch 44, para 6*).

In relation to property transferred to the settlement after 7 April 2013, the trust can still qualify as one for a disabled person if the trustees have power to pay up to £3,000 of income and capital gains (or 3% of the maximum value of the trust property during the tax year, if less) otherwise than for the benefit of the disabled person. They can also have the power of advancement under *Trustee Act 1925, s 32* (including with a less restrictive limitation than the Act allows) (*IHTA 1984, s 89(3), (3A), (3B)* as substituted by *FA 2013, Sch 44, para 6*).

A disabled person has the same meaning as in *FA 2005, Sch 1A* (see **14.41**). In relation to property transferred into the settlement before 8 April 2013, a disabled person is one who, when the property was settled, fell within one of the following categories:

(a)   incapable by reason of mental disorder (within the meaning in the *Mental Health Act 1983*) of administering his property or managing his affairs;

(b)   in receipt of attendance allowance under *SSCBA 1992, s 64*;

(c)   in receipt of a disability living allowance under *SSCBA 1992, s 71*, by virtue of entitlement to the care component at the highest or middle rate or the mobility component at the higher rate;

(d)   a person who would have met (b) or (c) but for the exceptions for persons in a hospital undergoing treatment for renal failure or for whom certain accommodation has been provided; or

(e)   any other person who satisfies HMRC that he would have met (b) or (c) had he met the prescribed conditions of residence under *SSCBA 1992, s 64(1)* or *71(6)*, and had the provisions made by regulations under *SSCBA 1992, s 67(1), (2)* or *72(8)* been ignored (these conditions require the person to be resident in the UK, so this head will cover trusts for non-UK resident disabled persons).

(IHTA 1984, s 89(4)–(6))

Where these conditions are met the disabled person is deemed to have an interest in possession in the settled property and the IIP regime accordingly applies to the settlement even if it is created after 22 March 2006 (*IHTA 1984, s 71(2)*). The qualifying conditions for trusts created before 10 March 1981 are slightly different (*IHTA 1984, s 74*).

Settlement by a person with a condition likely to lead to disability

14.79   If a person creates a settlement for his own benefit at a time (after 21 March 2006) when he can satisfy HMRC that he has a condition that is likely to lead to him becoming a disabled person within the meaning of *FA 2005, Sch 1A* (see **14.41**) (or would be one if he were resident in the UK), he is treated as being beneficially entitled to an interest in possession in the property (*IHTA 1984, s 89A*).

The property must be held on trusts under which the individual does not have an interest in possession in the settled property and which secure that, during his lifetime, the settled property (and the income from it) can only be used for his benefit and, if the trust is terminated, either he will become absolutely entitled to the settled property or a disabled person's interest will subsist in the settled property. As with a trust for a disabled person, this applies the IIP regime to the trust. A disabled person's interest is an interest in possession to which a disabled person (or a person within *IHTA 1984, s 89A*) is treated as beneficially entitled; an interest in possession in settled property to which a disabled person becomes beneficially entitled after 21 March 2006; or an interest in possession in settled property to which the settlor is entitled and for which the settlor satisfies HMRC that the conditions of *IHTA 1984, s 89A* (other than the requirement for no interest in possession) exist (*IHTA 1984, s 89B*).

As with a disabled person's settlement, for assets settled after 7 April 2013 the trust can still qualify if the trustees have power to pay up to the £3,000 or 3% of assets limit to someone else (*IHTA 1984, s 89A(6A)–(6C)* inserted by *FA 2013, Sch 44, para 7*).

Where a person is or is likely to become disabled, it is clearly sensible to ensure that any trust meets the conditions to qualify for this special treatment.

Protective trusts

14.80   Property is held on protective trusts if it is held on trusts to the like effect as those specified in *Trustee Act 1925, s 33(1)* (*IHTA 1984, s 88(1)*). This is a trust in which a person ('the principal beneficiary') has an IIP but if the principal beneficiary does, or attempts to do or suffers, any event or thing whereby he would be deprived of the right to the trust income (eg he becomes bankrupt or tries to sell his interest in the trust) the income instead comes to be held on discretionary trusts for the maintenance or support (or otherwise for the benefit of) the principal beneficiary and his spouse, children or remoter issue (or for the principal beneficiary and the persons who would become entitled to the trust property on his death if he has no spouse or descendants).

The principal beneficiary is treated for IHT purposes as continuing to have an IIP in the settled property even if the trust has become discretionary. The IIP regime will accordingly continue to apply if the trust was created before 22 March 2006. It will not, however, apply if the trust was created after that date unless the beneficiary's interest is an immediate post-death interest, a disabled person's interest or a transitional serial interest (ie a post-21 March 2006 IIP arising in succession to a pre-22 March one) (*IHTA 1984, s 88*).

Special trusts

14.81   Special rules apply to:

- trusts for bereaved minors;
- age 18-to-25 trusts;
- charitable trusts;
- employee trusts and newspaper trusts;
- maintenance funds for historic buildings.

Trusts for bereaved minors

14.82   A trust for a bereaved minor is one established under the will of a deceased parent of the minor or under the Criminal Injuries Compensation Scheme and which provides that:

- the bereaved minor will become absolutely entitled to the settled property (and any accumulated income) at or before age 18;

- any income applied for the benefit of a beneficiary whilst the minor is under 18 is applied for the benefit of the bereaved minor; and

- any other benefit provided out of the settled property whilst the minor is under 18 is applied for the benefit of the bereaved minor.

(IHTA 1984, s 71A(1)–(3))

The statutory trust created on the intestacy of a parent for the benefit of a bereaved minor also qualifies *(IHTA 1984, s 71A(1))*. A bereaved minor is a person who is under 18 and at least one of whose parents had died *(IHTA 1984, s 71C)*.

No IHT charge arises on the bereaved minor obtaining his right to the settled property, or dying under 18, or on any capital distribution to the bereaved minor while he is under 18 *(IHTA 1984, s 71B(2))*. The special tax charge described above in relation to A&M settlements applies if the settled property ceases to be held for the benefit of the bereaved minor in any other circumstance (other than it being used to meet trust expenses) *(IHTA 1984, s 71B(3))*.

In relation to property transferred into a settlement after 7 April 2013, a trust can still qualify as one for a bereaved minor if it allows up to £3,000 of income and capital gains (or 3% of the maximum value of the settled property in the trust during the tax year, if less) to be applied otherwise than for the benefit of the bereaved minor *(IHTA 1984, s 71A(4), (4A) inserted by FA 2013, Sch 44, para 2)*. There is also no tax charge on a distribution other than to the bereaved minor provided that it falls within the £3,000 or 3% of capital figure *(IHTA 1984, s 71B(2A), (2B) inserted by FA 2013, Sch 44, para 3)*.

Age 18-to-25 trusts

14.83 An age 18-to-25 trust is similar to a trust for a bereaved minor, and like it can only be created by will or under the Criminal Injuries Compensation Scheme, but the beneficiary need not become entitled to the asset until age 25 *(IHTA 1984, s 71D)*. Many people are unwilling to take the risk that a child may be financially immature at age 18 and thus are unlikely to be attracted to a trust for a bereaved minor. Some such people may be more willing to create such a trust if the beneficiary does not take the assets until age 25.

The trust must provide that the beneficiary will become absolutely entitled to the capital, any income arising from it and any accumulated income on or before age 25, that any distribution while he is under 25 is applied for his benefit and that any distributions are applied for his benefit (*IHTA 1984, s 71D(6)* as amended by *FA 2013, Sch 44, para 2*).

The income can be held on protective trusts but only for the beneficiary (*IHTA 1984, s 71D(6A)* inserted by *FA 2013, Sch 44, para 4*). As with trusts for deceased minors, in relation to property transferred into the settlement after 7 April 2013, a trust can still qualify if up to £3,000 or 3% of the capital value is applied for a different beneficiary (*IHTA 1984, s 71D(7)(za), (7A)* inserted by *FA 2013, Sch 44, para 4*).

As with a trust for a bereaved minor, IHT is not charged on the death of a beneficiary under the age of 18 (not 25), or on a distribution of capital to the beneficiary at or under the age of 18. Nor is it charged in respect of assets used to meet trust expenses, or to make distributions to other beneficiaries within the £3,000 or 3% of assets limit (*IHTA 1984, s 71E(2), (3), (4A)* as amended by *FA 2013, Sch 44, para 5*).

14.84   There is, however, a tax charge on the death of the beneficiary over the age of 18, on the distribution of assets to the beneficiary after that age, and on the beneficiary becoming entitled to the assets. The charge is calculated in the same way as the exit charge on a discretionary settlement but on the assumption that the settlement started on the beneficiary's eighteenth birthday (*IHTA 1984, s 71F*).

Accordingly, the maximum charge is 4.2% of the value of the assets, ie 7/10ths (or 28/40ths) (as the assets can be held for a maximum of seven years out of the ten-year period) of the value of the settled property multiplied by 30% of the rate payable on a chargeable lifetime gift (a maximum rate of 20%) by the notional transferor.

If the property ceases to be held for the benefit of the beneficiary in any other circumstances the special charge described earlier in relation to A&M settlements applies.

Charitable trusts

14.85   A charitable trust is outside the scope of IHT. The transfer of property to such a trust is exempt from IHT (*IHTA 1984, s 23*).

If settled property held in an A&M trust, a trust for a bereaved minor, an age 18-to-25 trust, an employee or newspaper trust, an old protective trusts or trusts for a disabled person, is transferred to a charity or comes to be held on charitable trusts without limit of time, the normal IHT charges that would otherwise have arisen do not apply (*IHTA 1984, s 76*).

If property is held in a temporary charitable trust, ie where the property is held for charitable purposes only until the end of a period (whether deferred by date or in some other way), a tax charge at a special rate applies when it ceases to be charitable. This is the special rate outlined at **14.75** in relation to A&M settlements. This charge does not arise if the property is transferred to a permanent charity (or the limitation on the charitable period is removed) or to the extent that the funds are used to meet trust expenses (*IHTA 1984, ss 70, 76(1)*).

Employee trusts and newspaper trusts

14.86   An employee trust is one where the settled property is held on trusts which do not permit it to be applied otherwise than for the benefit of persons of a class defined by reference to employment in a particular trade or profession or employment by, or office with, a body carrying on a trade, profession or undertaking (or spouses, civil partners or dependants of such persons) or for such a purpose and charitable purposes. If the trust applies to employees of a particular body the class must comprise all or most of the persons who work for that body (or it must be for the purpose of an approved profit-sharing scheme or approved share-incentive plan) (*IHTA 1984, s 86*).

A newspaper trust is an employee trust whose class of beneficiaries also includes a newspaper publishing company or a newspaper holding company (*IHTA 1984, s 87*).

Such trusts are outside the scope of IHT. However, if any of the assets cease to be subject to the trusts the special tax charge described at **14.75** applies (*IHTA 1984, s 72*).

Maintenance funds for historic buildings

14.87   Such funds are outside the scope of IHT. The relevant conditions are contained in *IHTA 1984, Sch 4*. If any part of the funds ceases to be held for the qualifying purposes, the special tax charge described at **14.75** applies.

Other points

14.88   If property is transferred from one settlement to another it is treated for IHT purposes as remaining comprised in the first settlement (unless in the interim some person has become beneficially entitled to the property, eg it has been distributed to a beneficiary and remitted by him (*IHTA 1984, s 81*)).

Tax planning with trusts

14.89

Focus

Trusts are still very useful tax planning tools in the right circumstances. However, they are hedged around with anti-avoidance rules and undistributed income and gains can be taxed at a higher rate than if the income or gain arose direct to the beneficiary. These higher rates can often be avoided, but only by structuring things right before they arise.

The changes made to the IHT trust regime by the *Finance Act 2006* mean that, in some cases, trusts will be used in different ways in future to those in the past. The following principles now apply to such IHT planning:

- It no longer makes any difference for IHT purposes if a new lifetime trust is a discretionary trust, an accumulation and maintenance trust or an interest-in-possession trust. This decision can now be based solely on family considerations. However, income tax considerations may affect the decision. The income of an IIP trust is taxed as income of the beneficiary so may attract tax at a lower rate than the 45% one which applies to a discretionary trust.

- It is still worth putting business assets into a trust if they attract 100% BPR and are likely to be sold at some stage. There is no IHT on the initial transfer and when the assets are sold and replaced by non-business assets the only IHT is the future ten-yearly charges and exit charge.

- Similarly, it is still worth putting into trust assets worth less than the £325,000 IHT nil rate band, which are likely to increase in value. Again this avoids the entry charge and gets the assets out of the settlor's estate subject only to the ten-yearly and exit charges.

- When the value exceeds £325,000 it may be worth selling the asset to a trust at a £325,000 undervalue leaving the sale proceeds outstanding. The outstanding amount remains in the donor's estate but the growth in value is in the trust and subject only to the ten-yearly and exit charges.

- The creation of a trust to hold non-UK assets is still virtually a must for those who are non-UK domiciled and not yet deemed domiciled here. And remember that if a person is deemed domiciled here his infant children may well not be, as they must themselves meet the '15 out of 20 years' test to be deemed domiciled. Of course, a very young child probably does not have the legal capacity to create a settlement but a teenager is likely to be competent to do so. Such trusts also give capital gains tax exemption while the gain remains in the trust, even for gains on UK assets (other than residential property), in most cases.

- Where a deemed domiciled individual created a protected trust (see **14.59**) care needs to be taken not to lose the protected status by adding further property to the trust. In this context it should be borne in mind that an interest free loan to the trust or most other transactions that adds value to the trust is regarded by HMRC as an addition of property to the trust.

- Bare trusts can still be used where the beneficiary is under 18 and unmarried as the beneficiary is deemed to be beneficially entitled to the assets in the trust.

- If the main concern that prevents a gift direct to the beneficiary is a fear that the beneficiary might squander the money, a gift subject to a condition, eg that management of the money is carried out by a specified third party and that the beneficiary will not call on the fund until he is 25 or 30 or whatever, is worth considering. However, that would not protect the assets from creditors of the beneficiary.

- The strategy for wills is likely to be:

  – A trust for the surviving spouse (or civil partner) should be an interest-in-possession trust with power to advance capital to the spouse or to pay capital to a second class of beneficiary. There will then be no IHT on the death and any capital appointed to someone other than the spouse will constitute a potentially exempt transfer by the surviving spouse (or civil partner) so there will be no IHT if the spouse survives for seven years after the appointment.

  – Assets put into trust for an infant child should go into a trust for a bereaved minor or an age 18-to-25 trust provided that it is intended that the child should become entitled to the assets at or before age 25.

  – If, as is likely to be the case, it is not wished to give an infant the assets at age 25 then a discretionary trust should probably be used. There is no charge on creating such a trust by will (as IHT already has to be paid on death where the assets go to someone other than the surviving spouse or civil partner and no trust creation charge arises in addition) so the only additional IHT will be the ten-yearly charge and exit charge, which could well be acceptable if the child is to take the assets at say, age 35.

  – Trusts for adult children should be discretionary trusts. Again there is no trust creation charge. Depending on the age of the child, the total ten-yearly charges and exit charge may well be less than the 40% that would be payable on the child's death.

  – Trusts for other people who would in the past have been given a life interest should probably now be discretionary trusts.

It can be sensible to put assets into trust even if this triggers the entry charge, as the £325,000 nil rate band can have a significant impact on the effective tax rate. For example:

Value of asset	tax on settling		ten-yearly charge		Reduction in tax on death
£250,000	–	–	–	–	£100,000
£500,000	£35,000	7.00%	£10,500	2.1%	£200,000
1,000,000	£135,000	13.50%	£40,500	4.05%	£400,000
1,500,000	£235,000	15.67%	£70,500	4.70%	£600,000
2,000,000	£335,000	16.75%	£100,500	5.03%	£800,000

A 40% rate on death has been assumed as the individual normally has sufficient assets to use up his nil rate band. The tax under the ten-yearly charge assumes that the settlor had made no gifts in the seven years prior to the creation of the settlement.

If a person aged 60 creates a settlement of £1,000,000 now there is likely to be a maximum of four ten-yearly charges during his lifetime. Accordingly, the total IHT will be:

Entry charge	£135,000
Four annual charges	£162,000
	£297,000

This is a saving of over 25% of the £400,000 tax that would be payable on death if he were to retain the asset. In reality, of course, the asset is likely to increase in value so the saving will be greater as the entry charge and the first couple of ten-yearly charges are likely to be payable on a significantly lower amount than the value of the assets at the time of the settlor's death.

14.90 For older settlors the saving is greater. If an 80-year-old creates a settlement of £2m and dies at age 91, the total charge will be £435,500 (plus an exit charge of around £10,000 if the assets are then distributed), compared with the £800,000 that would otherwise have been payable on death.

It should also be borne in mind that, if assets pregnant with CGT are put into a trust that is governed by the IHT relevant property regime, the CGT can be deferred until the trustees sell the asset concerned (and can be deferred again if they distribute it to a beneficiary).

Things to avoid

14.91

- It no longer normally makes sense to create a trust of which the settlor is a beneficiary. This triggers the initial IHT charge but the property remains in the settlor's estate under the reservation of benefit rules so it creates double taxation. There are no longer income tax or CGT benefits in creating such a trust, unless the settlor is non-UK resident or is taxable on the remittance basis and will not breach the '15 out of 20 years' rule for several years. Even in such cases, for a UK resident the IHT on creation of the settlement needs to be weighed against the anticipated income tax and CGT advantages.

- Similarly, it will normally no longer make sense to create a lifetime trust of which the settlor's spouse or civil partner is the main beneficiary, as a gift direct to the spouse avoids the trust creation charge of up to 20%.

- Careful thought needs to be given to the use of a trust for CGT planning where a person is non-UK domiciled but deemed domiciled; in such a case, it has been sensible in the past to set up an offshore IIP trust for the settlor's own benefit to obtain the CGT and income tax advantages of such a trust. This may no longer make sense if it will trigger an immediate IHT charge – although it might still be worth selling the assets to the trust rather than gifting them.

- Where an individual is deemed domiciled under the '15 out of 20 years' rule, great care needs to be taken to avoid adding anything to pre-5 April 2017 trusts. Provided that such a trust remains untainted, it is a 'mini tax haven' for the UK resident family while the funds remain in the trust.

- A similar issue arises where a person wants to let his principal private residence but wants to stop time apportionment eroding the exemption already achieved. In such cases, putting the property into trust for oneself has achieved that objective in the past. Again, a sale to a trust rather than a gift may still be viable.

- There is no longer any benefit in holding a UK residential property through an overseas trust structure.

Chapter 15

Payments made on the termination of employment

Donald Pearce-Crump BA (Hons), LLB, CTA (Fellow), ATT

SIGNPOSTS

- **Scope** – A discussion of the main tax issues that arise when a lump-sum payment or benefit is made to an employee on the termination of his employment and how planning in this context is geared towards structuring a termination payment, as far as the rules allow, so that it is a residual termination payment, ie one that falls within *ITEPA 2003, Pt 6, Ch 3* in order to access the tax advantages accorded such payments (see **15.4**).

- **Conditions** – The main condition that a payment has to meet in order that it falls within the above legislation is that it must not otherwise be charged to income tax. Avoiding the other four heads of charge that might apply to a termination payment (see **15.3**) makes planning in this context a complex matter. Even where the other heads of charge are successfully avoided, the division of a chargeable residual termination payment into earnings and non-earnings components may result in less tax being saved than may have been anticipated.

- **Practical issues** – Adopting the correct approach to analysing a termination package (see **15.5**) is fundamental to identifying the correct tax treatment of its constituent payments and benefits. Navigating a payment away from the other four heads of charge requires a detailed consideration of the documents and other evidence that govern the relationship between an employer and an employee generally and which relate to the making of the termination payment in particular. In some cases it may be possible to get assurance from HMRC that a payment will be afforded the favourable treatment sought (see **15.111**). It is important to analyse and categorise correctly the elements of a termination package as those elements that are treated as residual termination payments may benefit from the exemptions accorded only to such payments so that it is not always the case that the exercise is futile (which it may sometimes be

---

751

> if a chargeable residual termination payment comprises an earnings component only).
>
> - **Employment law** – The common law and employment law treatment of termination payments may be determinative of their tax treatment and a sound understanding of these matters should not be overlooked.
>
> - **Structure** – This chapter starts with the identification of the legislative provisions dealing with termination payments (see **15.2**) and how termination packages are analysed (see **15.5**). It then identifies the types of termination payment that benefit from the advantageous tax and NIC treatment intimated above (see **15.8**) and discusses the many exceptions from tax afforded such payments (see **15.23**). Termination payments within the other categories of employment income are then identified (see **15.68**), concentrating on those payments that are charged to tax in full as earnings (see **15.69**). The discussion concludes with a number of miscellaneous planning points (see **15.108**).

INTRODUCTION

15.1   This chapter will examine the main tax issues that typically arise when a lump-sum payment or benefit ('termination payment') is made to an employee (or officer) on the termination of his employment (or the vacation of his office). However, there will be excluded from the discussion lump-sum payments made by any type of pension fund established for an employee as part of his service agreement or to which an employee may belong as part of his terms of service. The discussion applies primarily in relation to the 2018/19 tax year. With effect from 6 April 2018, substantial changes have been made to the tax treatment of termination payments by *Finance (No 2) Act 2017* and *Finance Act 2018*. However, where appropriate, comparisons are drawn with the rules that applied in 2017/18 and earlier tax years to enhance understanding of the changes that have been made. There are further proposals for changes to the rules and they are set out in **15.113**.

Tax planning in this context is, usually, planning to secure an advantage, namely that a termination payment should be structured so that it falls within *ITEPA 2003, Pt 6, Ch 3* (all statutory references in this chapter are to *ITEPA 2003*, unless otherwise stated). This is still the case notwithstanding the enactment of the changes referred to above, and those advantages are listed in **15.4** below.

However, as is the case for much tax planning, a taxpayer who is leaving his employment should primarily ensure that his legal and financial position is secured and only then seek to find a tax-efficient way of structuring a termination payment. It may not always be the case that the two objectives coincide, but to the extent that they can the best tax outcome is achieved if the payment falls within the scope of the above legislation. Indeed, seeking this tax-driven outcome may, in some cases, coincide with securing a sound financial outcome for an employee given the benefit of the reliefs available to such payments.

THE SCHEME OF LEGISLATIVE PROVISIONS DEALING WITH TERMINATION PAYMENTS

15.2   As intimated above, the optimum tax treatment of a termination payment is that found in *ITEPA 2003, Pt 6, Ch 3* which is entitled 'Payments and benefits on the termination of employment etc'. However, the title is misleading. The true nature and scope of that part of the legislation is dictated by *ITEPA 2003, s 401(3)* which reads as follows: 'This Chapter does not apply to any payment or other benefit chargeable to income tax apart from this Chapter'. This clearly indicates that *ITEPA 2003, Pt 6, Ch 3* is a residual category of employment income within *ITEPA 2003*. By implication, therefore, termination payments (whether made in cash or kind) may fall within other categories of employment income set out in *ITEPA 2003*.

15.3

Focus

It is essential to know the categories of employment income within which a termination payment may fall in order to appreciate how many hurdles, practically speaking, need to be considered before concluding that the payment falls within the favourable residual category.

The categories of employment income within which a termination payment might fall are the following:

(a)   earnings from employment;

(b)   the benefits-in-kind code;

(c)   restrictive undertakings;

(d)   employer-financed retirement benefits scheme (EFRBS);

(e)   termination payments within *ITEPA 2003, Pt 6, Ch 3* ('residual termination payments').

Together these categories are, in this chapter, called the scheme of legislative provisions dealing with termination payments. The residual category of termination payments applies to payments and other benefits received directly or indirectly in consideration or in consequence of, or otherwise in connection with, the termination of a person's employment by the person, or the person's spouse or civil partner, blood relative, dependant or personal representatives (*ITEPA 2003, s 401(1)*).

15.4   It is important to note the order in which the categories of employment income are set out in the above list. If more than one of the categories prima facie applies in relation to a termination payment, priority sections in the legislation dictate that a category mentioned earlier in the list has priority over a category mentioned later in the list. So for example, if a lump sum payment made to an employee on the termination of employment is for his giving an undertaking not to divulge his former employer's industrial know-how after he leaves his employment, then the payment is charged to income tax as a payment for a restrictive undertaking (category (c)) and not as a residual termination payment (category (e)), even though the payment may satisfy the conditions for the application of the residual category as set out above. If the employee and employer are going to plan for the tax-efficient treatment of a termination payment, they are going to have to avoid its falling within categories (a) to (d). In some cases, however (as will be discussed later), the circumstances of their employment relationship or the nature of the payments made are such that they have no choice in the matter, in which case their planning opportunities in the sense described above will be limited. It should be appreciated that they may not always be able to pick and choose which category of employment income is applicable given the terms of their relationship which were agreed upon at the time their relationship commenced (see **15.6**).

There is a number of misconceptions about the tax treatment of termination payments following the enactment of the changes referred to in **15.1** above. A main misconception is that termination payments no longer have to be analysed into their constituent categories because, even if they do fall within the residual category, they are taxable in any event. There are several reasons why it is still important to go through the often difficult exercise of correctly classifying termination payments. They are as follows:

(a)   Only payments that fall in the residual category can benefit from the total exemptions from tax that are accorded to such payments (provided, of course, the conditions for the availability of the exemptions are met). Unless the payment is correctly classified, the exemptions will not be available.

(b)   Even though a non-exempt residual termination payment must be divided into an earnings component and a non-earnings component (the former not benefitting from the well-known £30,000 exemption), the application of the relevant computational may result in the earnings component being nil.

(c)   The non-earnings component of a chargeable residual termination payment is, for 2018/19, not liable to national insurance contributions. Although from 6 April 2019, it is anticipated that the non-earnings component will attract employer's national insurance contributions to the extent that it exceeds £30,000, none of the non-earnings component will attract employee's national insurance contributions. The other categories of termination payments attract a charge to national insurance contributions on the full amount of the payment.

ANALYSING TERMINATION PACKAGES

Focus

It is essential to have an informed understanding of the process to follow in analysing a termination package so that the correct tax treatment of its constituent payments and benefits may be identified. Particular attention has to be paid to locating and analysing the myriad documents and other pieces of evidence that govern the relationship between an employer and an employee as the content of that relationship is often determinative of the tax treatment of the elements of a termination package. Parties must guard against jumping to conclusions and determining the tax treatment of a payment merely by what it is called.

15.5   A contract of employment may end for a variety of reasons and when it does, an employee may receive a package comprising a variety of payments and benefits. In order to identify the tax treatment of the component elements of the package two steps have to be taken:

(a)   First the nature of each component within the package has to be determined (but without having undue regard to the label attached to the component by the parties as their descriptions may not always be accurate).

(b)   The next step is to match the scheme of legislative provisions dealing with termination payments to the component so analysed in order to ascertain the correct tax treatment of that component. Each category of employment income in the scheme charges income tax but each has its own set of exemptions and other relieving provisions associated with it. Only some of the categories of employment income in the scheme are subject to national insurance contributions. The application of the appropriate provision in the scheme on termination payments will depend on the occasion on which a payment or benefit is made and upon its nature.

15.6   *Payments made on the termination of employment*

15.6   If the parties are in the position where they are able to plan for the making of a tax-efficient termination payment, they should appreciate that each component of the package must be analysed separately: they must understand in substance and in truth the bargain that they are making in the context of their existing relationship and understand what each payment is for (*Henley v Murray (HM Inspector of Taxes)* 31 TC 351).

In achieving this level of understanding it is necessary for the parties to know the parameters in which they are able to work:

(a)   They may be constrained by their existing relationship (*Henry v Foster* 16 TC 605). They will have to consider their conduct and all the documents and other evidence which govern their relationship generally and which relate to the making of the termination payment in particular.

(b)   They must understand that the language used by them to describe a constituent element of a termination package (eg 'compensation for loss of office') is not the factor that determines its tax treatment. Rather they have to decide the nature of the payments made (*Henley v Murray (H M Inspector of Taxes)* 31 TC 351).

(c)   They will be able to take comfort in the fact that HMRC must analyse any termination package as put together by the parties themselves (*Chappell & Co Ltd v Nestle Co Ltd* [1960] AC 87) and it is not open to HMRC to re-arrange a package genuinely agreed. Consequently, where the parties identify a number of components of a package and allocate a consideration to each or some of those components, generally speaking, HMRC will analyse the package in accordance with the agreed terms (EIM12805–EIM12810).

(d)   In drawing up a termination package, the parties should consider carefully whether a single, lump sum payment should be agreed for all or a number of the elements comprised in the package. Depending upon the construction of the terms of the package (as contained, for example in a compromise agreement), it may be that a single sum that is payable for two or more separate and identifiable considerations is properly apportioned between to the two (*Wales (HM Inspector of Taxes) v Tilley* 25 TC 136; *A G Reid v RCC* [2016] UKFTT 79 (TC)). In such a case an apportionment may give rise to an outcome not expected by the parties (as was the case in *Carter v Wadman* 28 TC 41 – see **15.12**), although it may be that an apportionment can fall in the taxpayer's favour (see *Johnson v RCC* [2013] UKFTT 242 (TC) in **15.14**). In other cases an apportionment may not be possible and valuable tax reliefs may be lost as a result. For example, in *Owolabi v RCC* [2012] UKFTT 334 (TC), although the taxpayer argued that part of her payment for loss of office (as sub-postmaster) was a payment of capital and compensation for the expenditure she had originally incurred in buying and adapting her post office business (which was now ceasing), there was no evidence showing that the payment had a character of something other than compensation for loss of office and hence a residual termination payment, taxable as such.

Example 15.1 – Components of a termination payment

A payment of £66,000 is paid to an employee on the termination of his employment by reason of redundancy. This comprises the following elements:

- £5,000 as a contractual payment in lieu of notice

- £15,000 as a bonus owing at the time of termination

- £20,000 for an undertaking not to disclose confidential information after termination

- £26,000 on account of redundancy

On a proper analysis only the final amount falls to be treated as a residual termination payment. The first two amounts are earnings and the third amounts falls to be treated as a payment for a restrictive undertaking.

15.7   As already intimated in **15.1** above, a taxpayer who has secured his legal and financial position on the termination of employment, may be able to plan (in conjunction with his former employer) his termination package in such a way that most (if not all) of the components are treated as residual termination payments.

This chapter will develop along the following lines:

- It will discuss the types of payment within the residual category of termination payments so that it will be understood by the parties whether their circumstances are such that it is possible for them to take advantage of that category.

- It will then discuss the exceptions and reliefs associated with that category.

- It will then discuss the circumstances in which payments fall within the other categories of employment income comprising the scheme of legislative provisions dealing with termination payments so that the parties will understand when they cannot take advantage of the residual category; suitable planning opportunities will then be highlighted in these cases.

- Finally, it will discuss a number of miscellaneous planning and other points.

THE TYPES OF TERMINATION PAYMENT THAT FALL IN THE RESIDUAL CATEGORY

Introduction

15.8 The types of termination payment that fall in the residual category are set out in **Table 15.1**.

Table 15.1 – Residual termination payments

- Redundancy payments
- Payments made under compromise agreements
- Payments in lieu of notice (PILONs)
- Payments to compromise legal action generally
- Damages for breach of contract
- Payments made under employment protection legislation
- Payments made under anti-discrimination law
- Ex gratia payments

Redundancy payments

Focus

If a termination payment is paid by reason of an employee being made redundant, its categorisation as a residual termination payment is assured (even if it is paid under the contract of employment between the parties). It is essential to ensure though that the termination of employment occurs by reason of redundancy and that the payment is made to alleviate only the consequences of redundancy and is not made for some other work-related reason. UK legislation provides a specific definition of redundancy and, unless the reason for a dismissal satisfies it, the process is not a redundancy dismissal at all and payments made on the termination of employment will not be redundancy payments.

Statutory redundancy payments

15.9 A contract of employment will come to an end by reason of redundancy if the dismissal is attributable to:

(a) the fact that his employer has ceased, or intends to cease, to carry on the business for the purposes of which the employee was employed by him, or has ceased, or intends to cease, to carry on that business in the place where the employee was so employed; or

(b) the fact that the requirements of that business for employees to carry out work of a particular kind, or for employees to carry out work of a particular kind in the place where he was so employed, have ceased or diminished or are expected to cease or diminish.

It is clear from this definition that redundancy involves a reduction in an employer's need for employees because of, for example, the disposal of part of his business, its relocation or the introduction of new methods of work that reduces the number of employees needed. It includes the case of a 'bumped redundancy' where employee A's job disappears but it is employee B who is made redundant because the employer wants to retain employee A. Such redundancies may be common in large-scale redundancy programmes.

The *Employment Rights Act 1996 (ERA 1996), s 136* provides that, if a qualifying employee (basically one who has been employed for at least two years) is made redundant, then he is entitled to a redundancy payment (quantified in accordance with the Act) which is compensation for the loss of the particular job from which he is being dismissed. Such a payment is not taxed as the employee's earnings from his employment (*ITEPA 2003, s 309(1)*), but it does count as a residual termination payment and hence uses up part of the £30,000 threshold (*ITEPA 2003, s 309(3)*) (see **15.24**). Statutory redundancy payments can never be categorised as deemed earnings within the residual category (*ITEPA 2003, s 402C(2)*) (see **15.25**).

Non-statutory redundancy payments

15.10 It is not unusual for employers to make additional payments upon the termination of an employee's employment by reason of redundancy. Such payments can be determined and paid at the time of the redundancy in question or they may be made in accordance with the conditions under which an employee has given service during the subsistence of his contract (eg under a non-statutory redundancy scheme which may be provided for in the employee's contract of service or some other work-related document such as a staff handbook, a letter of appointment, a side letter to the main employment contract or an employer-trade union agreement).

Such non-statutory redundancy payments are charged to tax as residual termination payments (*Mairs (Inspector of Taxes) v Haughey* [1993] STC 569; *Colquhoun v RCC* [2010] UKUT 431, [2011] STC 394). This treatment is so even where the payment is made under the terms of an employee's contract (or other work-related document) and so is an important exception from the general treatment (as earnings) of termination payments made under a contract of employment (see **15.71**). Further, in *Colquhoun v RCC* [2010] UKFTT 34 (TC) it was held that a payment to buy out contractual redundancy rights was a residual termination payment even where the employment did not end until several years after the payment. However, it must be a non-statutory redundancy payment that is made in order for it to be categorised as a residual termination payment; a contractual payment in lieu of notice made on an employee's redundancy is (correctly) treated as earnings despite it being paid on the occasion of an employee's redundancy (*Andrew v RCC* [2015] UKFTT 514 (TC)) (see **15.12** and **15.74**).

HMRC Statement of Practice 1/94 confirms this treatment and acknowledges that the scheme may be a standing one which forms part of the terms on which the employees give their services or it may be an ad hoc scheme to meet a specific situation such as the imminent closure of a particular factory (see SP 1/94, para 2). The statement is restricted to payments 'genuinely made solely on account of redundancy' and paragraph 4 of the Statement states that HMRC are:

'... concerned to distinguish between payments under non-statutory schemes which are genuinely made to compensate for loss of employment through redundancy and payments which are rewards for services in employment or more generally for having acted as or having been an employee.'

In paragraph 3 of the Statement, HMRC say that where payments made under a non-statutory redundancy scheme do not compensate for the loss of employment through redundancy, then *ITEPA 2003, Pt 6, Ch 3* may not apply, and quote as an example a case where a terminal bonus is disguised as a non-statutory redundancy payment. The statement gives as examples payments made for meeting production targets or doing extra work in the period leading up to redundancy. Also included are payments which are conditional on continued service in the employment for a time if they are calculated by reference to any additional period served following the issue of a redundancy notice. In the case of *Allan v CIR* [1994] STC 943, payments were made to all employees in a company only some of whom were made redundant. The payments to those employees whose employments continued were held to be taxable in full as earnings from their employments.

Care must always be taken to ensure that a payment is actually made under a non-statutory redundancy scheme if it is to be treated as a residual termination payment. For example, a contractual term may provide that an employer must make a payment to an employee on the termination of his employment 'for any reason'. If a termination of employment occurs on account of the redundancy of the employee, then any payment made by the employer will not count as a non-statutory redundancy payment. At EIM13765, HMRC explain that redundancy may have triggered the payment, but any type of termination would have done so and the character of the payment (as earnings – see **15.71**) remains the same whatever the trigger.

HMRC go on to say, however, that if the contractual terms specify redundancy (eg the contract provides that a payment be made on the termination of employment 'for any reason (including redundancy)'), then it may be accepted that the intention of the employer is to pay compensation for loss of employment by reason of redundancy. In this case the payment made on redundancy will be treated as a residual termination payment.

If an employer who operates a non-statutory redundancy scheme wants to be certain that a payment made under the scheme is to be treated as a residual termination payment, then he may make an application in writing to HMRC for clearance (see **15.111**). Such an application must be accompanied by the scheme document together with the text of any intended letter to employees which explain its terms. The clearance procedure is available only in respect of a scheme in its final documented form, and is not available for schemes in the process of development and cannot be used to assist in that development (see EIM13190).

Other comments regarding redundancy payments

15.11 Provided that a redundancy is genuine, subsequent re-engagement by the same employer or an associated employer does not normally affect the treatment of a redundancy payment. This will also be the case where an employer outsources part of the business so that the employees working in that part are made redundant and those same persons become employees of the concern that takes on that business. Again the tax treatment of their redundancy payments should not be affected where the arrangement is genuine.

Payments made under compromise agreements

Focus

Always read (or draft) compromise agreements carefully, as any part of any termination payment made under the agreement in full and final settlement of an employee's unpaid remuneration is taxable otherwise than as a residual termination payment. It will not benefit from the benign treatment afforded such payments. Be particularly wary of compromise agreements that fructify the terms of an employee's contract of employment and avoid altering an employee's contract of employment by way of a compromise agreement.

Compromise of employees' contractual rights

15.12   A compromise agreement in this context is one made between an employer and employee whereby they agree to end their relationship under a subsisting contract of service. In consideration of entering into the agreement and giving up his employment, the employee receives a lump sum payment. In practice, this most commonly occurs where an employee is serving under a fixed-term contract (usually one that does not provide for notice) or where he is serving his contractual notice, be it indefinite or one for a fixed term. It is agreed that the contract of service should be brought to an end before the expiry of the respective periods. This compares with a garden leave situation where a contract of employment is not ended but allowed to run its course; rather the employer waives his right to call on the employee to work during the period concerned (ie the period of garden leave). A payment made during a period of garden leave is the salary due to the employee for the period and is taxable as earnings (see **15.71**).

A payment made under a compromise agreement (which may be labelled a payment in lieu of notice) falls within the residual category of termination payments where it is attributable wholly to the loss of employment occasioned by the total abrogation of the employee's contract of employment (*Henley v Murray (H M Inspector of Taxes)* 31 TC 351; *Clayton v Lavender* 42 TC 607; *Essack v RCC* [2014] UKFTT 159 (TC); *Michael Phillips v RCC* [2016] UKFTT 174 (TC); *Tottenham Hotspur Ltd v HMRC* [2016] UKFTT 389 (TC)). It is not necessary that there has to be a breach of the employment contract in order for a payment made under a compromise agreement to be so categorised (*Tottenham Hotspur Ltd v HMRC* [2016] UKFTT 389 (TC)). Whether an employment contract has been terminated following a breach of contract or whether the contract has been terminated by mutual consent, a payment made under a compromise agreement which abrogates entirely the contract of employment falls within the residual category.

An element of care must be exercised here, however, as a payment made under a compromise agreement entered into in the above circumstances may satisfy some other right in an employee's contract (eg a right to a bonus not yet paid) in addition to being compensation for the loss of employment. Where this is the case, a part of the payment will be attributed to that right and be taxed accordingly (probably as earnings) (*Carter v Wadman* 28 TC 41). So care must be exercised where a compromise agreement is stated to be 'in full and final settlement of all claims' that an employee may have against his employer at the time of the termination of his employment. This issue is forcibly illustrated in *Andrew v RCC* [2015] UKFTT 514 (TC) where the taxpayer was made redundant. His employer exercised his power under the contract of employment to terminate the contract without notice and the taxpayer entered into a compromise agreement which was expressed to be in full and final settlement of all and any claims the employee had in respect of his contract of employment and its termination. The payment made under the compromise agreement was then expressed to a payment of the salary and benefits which would have been paid during the notice period to which the taxpayer was entitled and was being paid instead of giving notice. It was held, that despite his redundancy, the payment under the comprise agreement, described as it was, was a payment made in lieu of notice in accordance with the right given to the employer to do so by the employment contract itself. Consequently the payment was the taxpayer's earnings and did not fall within the residual category (see **15.74**). The exception for non-statutory redundancy payments (see **15.10**) did not apply in this case as no redundancy payment was in fact made under the compromise agreement.

Care must also be exercised where a compromise agreement fructifies (ie gives effect to) the terms of an employee's contract of employment, that is to say where the compromise agreement is the mechanism by which the terms of a contract of employment are effected (see **15.84**).

The case of *Hill v RCC* [2015] UKFTT 295 (TC) illustrates other circumstances where a payment made under a compromise agreement may not be treated as falling in the residual category. In that case the taxpayer was paid a sum as a result of a change in the terms of his contract of employment. The taxpayer's contract of employment had been transferred from one employer to another under the *Transfer of Undertakings (Protection of Employment) Regulations 2006, SI 2006/246* (the '*TUPE Regulations*'). Whereas his contract stipulated that he was not required to work more than 10 miles from an address in Luton, his new employer required him to work in London. The taxpayer complained and under a compromise agreement he was paid a sum for agreeing to the change to his contract of employment. He argued that he was being paid a sum on the termination of his employment with his former employer for agreeing not to pursue a claim for damages in respect of a breach of the terms of his contract (rather than simply for agreeing to work for his new employer on varied terms). The judge refused to accept that distinction and held that the tax treatment of the payment would be the same in both cases. He stated that in both cases the effect of the compromise agreement was that the taxpayer was paid a sum of money in return for agreeing that he would work for his new employer at a place more than 10 miles from Luton. Consequently, in accordance with the principles laid down in *Hamblett v Godfrey (Inspector of Taxes)* [1987] STC 60 and *Kuehne & Nagel Drinks Logistics Ltd v RCC* [2012] EWCA Civ 34, it was held that the taxpayer received a payment from his employer as compensation for a change in the terms of his employment contract and the payment was properly characterised as earnings from employment.

The judge stated that he did not need to decide the case on the basis of the effect of the *TUPE Regulations* (see **15.112**); the case was decided simply on the point that, on the facts, the payment was made by the taxpayer's new employer for the taxpayer agreeing to a change in the terms of his employment following the transfer of his employment contract. He pointed out, interestingly, that the outcome may have been different if there had been no transfer under the *TUPE Regulations* and instead the taxpayer had, following the termination of his employment, been paid a sum by his former employer for a breach of its obligations during the time the employee was employed by it. In such a case, the payment made may have come within the residual category (although it should be pointed out that such a payment would have to be connected with the termination of the employment (see **15.109**)).

Compromise of legal action

15.13   A compromise agreement in this context is also one whereby an employee, having been wrongfully dismissed, agrees to refrain from instituting or continuing legal proceedings against his former employer in consideration of receiving a payment (ie he gives up his cause of action to sue for wrongful dismissal). The agreement may be reached where there is a threat of court proceedings or court proceedings have started but not completed. 'Tomlin orders' (ie an order which records that an action is stayed by the agreement of the parties on terms set out in a schedule) are also included within this category of payment.

Compensation paid under such agreements is taxed as a residual termination payment (*Du Cros v Ryall (H M Inspector of Taxes)* 19 TC 444; *Wilson v Clayton* [2005] STC 157). However, in certain respects care must again be exercised. A principal feature of a compromise agreement is the employee's undertaking to give up his right to sue his employer. Indeed, although the consideration for the payment is most likely to be his giving up the pursuit of his cause of action, any amount specifically paid for this restriction in the employee's future behaviour may be charged to tax in full under the restrictive covenant category of employment income (*ITEPA 2003, s 225*) (see **15.97–15.99**).

Compromise agreements that vary an employment contract

15.14   In addition to the special case of a compromise agreement that gives effect to the terms of an employee's contract of employment (see **15.12**), care must be exercised where a compromise agreement is made before a termination of employment is in prospect. Such an agreement may amount to a variation of the terms of the employee's contract of employment so that any payment subsequently made will simply be a payment under the employment contract and taxable as earnings (see **15.71**).

Conversely, where compromise agreements are stated to supersede all previous agreements and understandings between the parties, this could have the effect of turning a non-taxable payment to the employee into a taxable one. In *Reid v RCC* [2012] UKFTT 182 (TC), an employer granted his employee an option for a sum of money and agreed to refund the amount should his contract of service be terminated. In the event the contract was brought to an end under a compromise agreement which included a term that declared the compromise agreement to 'constitute the entire agreement between the parties' and to 'supersede' all previous agreements between them. The compromise agreement therefore had the effect of negating the earlier promise to make the refund. As the compromise agreement failed also to mention that a refund was actually being made, it was held that no part of the payment made under the compromise agreement comprised the (tax free) refund; it was held that the payment under the compromise agreement was taxable as a residual termination payment. (Also see *Sjumarken v RCC* [2016] UKUT 568.)

However, it must be emphasised that each case depends on its own facts, as illustrated in *Johnson v RCC* [2013] UKFTT 242 (TC) where a compromise agreement providing for a payment made in full and final settlement of the employee's claims against his employer did include (even though it was not expressly stated) the (tax-free) refund of £30,000 paid during his employment for the grant of an EMI option (which lapsed when his employment ended). The difference between the two decisions lies in the proper construction of the compromise agreements in each case. The case usefully sets out the principles laid down by the House of Lords in *Investors Compensation Scheme v West Bromwich Building Society* [1998] 1 WLR 896 by which contractual documents are construed, namely:

(a)   Interpretation is the ascertainment of the meaning which the document would convey to a reasonable person having all the background knowledge which would reasonably have been available to the parties in the situation in which they were at the time of the contract.

(b)   The background may be referred to as the 'matrix of fact'. Subject to the requirement that it should be reasonably available to the parties and to the exception to be mentioned next, the background includes absolutely anything which would affect the way in which the language of the document would be understood by a reasonable man.

(c)   The law excludes from the admissible background the previous negotiations of the parties and their declarations of subjective intent. They are admissible only in an action for rectification. The law makes this distinction for reasons of practical policy and, in this respect only, legal interpretation differs from the way utterances in ordinary life are interpreted.

(d)   The meaning which a document (or any other utterance) would convey to a reasonable man is not the same thing as the meaning of its words. The meaning of words is a matter of dictionaries and grammar; the meaning of the document is what the parties using those words against the relevant background would reasonably have been understood to mean. The background may not merely enable the reasonable man to choose between the possible meanings of words which are ambiguous but even (as occasionally happens in ordinary life) to conclude that the parties must, for whatever reason, have used the wrong words or syntax.

(e)   The 'rule' that words should be given their 'natural and ordinary meaning' reflects the common sense proposition that it is not easily accepted that people have made linguistic mistakes, particularly in formal documents. On the other hand, if one would nevertheless conclude from the background that something must have gone wrong with the language, the law does not require judges to attribute to the parties an intention which they plainly could not have had. If detailed semantic and syntactical analysis of words in a commercial contract is going to lead to a conclusion that flouts business common-sense, it must be made to yield to business common-sense.

Payments in lieu of notice (PILONs)

Focus

Take care to ensure that the correct type of PILON has been identified before concluding that it falls to be taxed as a residual termination payment. Other types of PILON are discussed at **15.72** (contractual PILONs), **15.80** (so-called auto-PILONS) and **15.83** (garden leave payments).

15.15   In the present context a payment in lieu of notice is one which may be described as follows:

'Without the agreement of the employee, the employer summarily dismisses the employee and tenders a payment in lieu of proper notice … The employer is in breach of contract by dismissing the employee without proper notice.'

In this case the employer tenders the payment in lieu of notice to make good his breach of contract and such a payment is in the nature of damages. The tax treatment of such a PILON (ie as a residual termination payment) follows that for damages as discussed in **15.17**. It does not matter that the payment may be included in a compromise agreement. This position is confirmed in *Rubio v RCC* [2012] UKFTT 361 (TC).

Nothing turns on the label used to describe the payment as defined above. The PILON label is used to describe a range of payments made in a variety of legal situations (*Delaney v Staples (t/a De Montfort Recruitment)* [1992] 1 AC 687). It should be carefully noted that this category of PILON applies only where the contract of employment between the parties makes provision for notice only and not where it allows the employer a choice as to how to end the contract of employment – that is *either* by giving notice *or* by making a payment in lieu of notice (PILON). Such PILONs are taxed as earnings (see **15.72**). Nor does the present category of PILON apply to circumstances properly analysed as garden leave; a PILON made to an employee on garden leave is taxable on him as his earnings (see **15.82**). Neither does the present category apply to a PILON made at the end of an employment where the employer and the employee agree that the employment is to terminate forthwith on payment of a sum in lieu of notice. Such a payment is probably treated in the same way as a payment made under a compromise agreement (see **15.12**). In such a case, the employer is not in breach of contract in dismissing summarily and the payment in lieu is not remuneration for work done during the continuance of the employment.

However, care must be taken where an employer has established a practice of making termination awards which would create an expectation for all employees to receive PILONs on the termination of their employment; HMRC are of the opinion that a payment that is expected and received may be earnings (see **15.80**).

Payments to compromise legal action generally

15.16   This category of payment includes any payment made by an employer to compromise legal action. In *Clinton v RCC* [2009] UKFTT 337 (TC) the employee had been constructively dismissed and a payment made to her by her employer was motivated by the desire to obviate her taking proceedings for wrongful or unfair dismissal so that it did not have to admit that its actions had amounted to constructive dismissal. The payment so made was held to be a residual termination payment. Payments under agreements to compromise legal action (**15.13**) and PILONs within **15.15** are examples of payments within this broader category.

Damages for breach of contract

Unliquidated damages

15.17   A fundamental breach of a contract of service by an employer allows an employee to treat the contract as at an end. A cause of action to sue accrues to him under the common law and, if a tribunal or court gives judgment in his favour, the employer will be under an obligation to pay damages (called unliquidated damages) ordered by the court or tribunal. To constitute damages the lump sum must be awarded unconditionally by the court (including a consent order) as distinct from an amount which a party to a dispute agrees to pay out of court so as to settle the action or threatened action against him. (The tax treatment of compensation received for agreeing to compromise a cause of action is dealt with at **15.15** above.)

Damages compensate for loss suffered owing to breach of contract and seek to ensure that the injured party is put in the same position, so far as money can do it, as if he had not suffered the loss occasioned by the breach. Damages for wrongful termination of a contract of service are residual termination payments (*Du Cros v Ryall (H M Inspector of Taxes)* 19 TC 444; *Henley v Murray (H M Inspector of Taxes)* 31 TC 351).

Liquidated damages

15.18   Although the point has not been settled by the courts, there are *dicta* in *Henley v Murray (H M Inspector of Taxes)* 31 TC 351 and *Clayton v Lavender* 42 TC 607 to the effect that, even though liquidated damages are provided for in a contract of employment, unliquidated and liquidated damages are treated in the same way. Liquidated damages clauses in contracts of employment operate so as to provide a pre-arranged statement of the damages to be paid on termination of employment; provided the clause is properly structured and drafted so that it is enforceable as a matter of law and so that the amount provided for is a genuine pre-estimate of loss, such damages that compensate for that loss will not be treated as earnings but as a residual termination payment even though they are specified in the contract of employment itself. (See *Dale v de Soissons* 32 TC 118 (**15.71**) in which liquidated damages clauses are specifically distinguished from other payments made pursuant to the terms of an employee's service; see **15.71** and **15.76**.) A payment of liquidated damages is not given as a reward for services; it seeks to compensate the employee for the loss suffered as a result of the breach of the employment contract and so it has the same compensatory nature as a payment of unliquidated damages. Consequently, it should be treated no differently.

Comment

15.19   At EIM13922 HMRC sound a warning in relation to payments of damages. They say that damages for a breach of contract may not always be treated as a residual termination payment. They give as an example a failure to pay wages due when an employment ends. This is a breach of contract but the remedy given by the court may be to enforce the contractual terms so that the so-called damages are merely an unpaid debt. In this case the payment will be one of wages paid under the contract of employment and taxable as earnings (see **15.69**).

Payments made under employment protection legislation

15.20   Employment protection legislation in the UK gives an employee a wide variety of rights in relation to the termination of his employment, and regardless of how that legislation describes a payment to which an employee may be entitled under any aspect of that legislation, the tax treatment of such a payment must, as ever, be determined according to its substance (see **15.5**(a)).

The following payments have been treated as falling in the residual category of termination payments:

(a)   Compensation paid for unfair dismissal (*Walker v Adams (Inspector of Taxes)* 2003 SpC 344). An employee who has been employed for at least two years has the statutory right not to be unfairly dismissed. Where he is unfairly dismissed, he may be awarded compensation consisting of a basic award, a compensatory award, an additional (or higher additional) award and a special award (*ERA 1996, s 112*). The same treatment applies to sums payable where the employee is re-instated or re-engaged by the employer. Such payments (although described by the ERA 1996 as remuneration) compensate for any benefits (including arrears of pay) that the employee would have had if he had continued as an employee for the period from the date of dismissal to the date of his re-instatement or re-engagement. However, it is HMRC's view that such a sum is compensation for unfair dismissal and so is taxable only as a residual termination payment (see EIM12960). (It should be noted however the *Social Security Contributions and Benefits Act 1992 (SSCBA 1992), s 112(3)(a)* deems sums payable in respect of arrears of pay in pursuance of an order for re-instatement or re-engagement to be earnings subject to Class 1 national insurance contributions.)

If a tribunal orders a payment of compensation for an employer's failure to comply with a re-instatement or re-engagement order under *ERA 1996, s 117*, that payment too is treated as a residual termination payment. However, HMRC state that where, exceptionally, there is as a matter of fact continuous employment between the two dates, any payment for the period is earnings. They say that this may happen where an employee is dismissed and immediately re-employed to allow a provision to be left out of his contract and the date of re-instatement or re-engagement is later than the re-employment date.

Finally, when making a claim for unfair dismissal an employee may also claim that his employer failed to provide a written statement for the reasons of dismissal. If this claim is upheld, the tribunal may award compensation (*ERA 1996, s 93(2)(b)*) and this too is taxable as a residual termination payment.

(b)   Protective awards under the *Trade Union and Labour Relations (Consolidation) Act 1992, s 189* paid for failure by an employer to follow the consultation process on redundancy *(Mimtec Ltd v IRC* [2001] STC (SCD) 101; *K&N Drink Logistics Ltd v RCC* [2010] UKUT 457). (It should be noted however that *SSCBA 1992, s 112(3)(c)* deems protective awards to be earnings subject to Class 1 national insurance contributions.)

(c)   Statutory redundancy payments (see **15.9** above).

Payments made under anti-discrimination law

> **Focus**
>
> Analyse payments made under anti-discrimination law carefully, as some may be outside the scope of income tax altogether (and hence not taxable).

15.21   Apart from the *Employment Rights Act 1996* and other labour-related Acts, the *Equality Act 2010* (which was enacted to harmonise equality law and restate the greater part of earlier enactments relating to discrimination and harassment related to certain personal characteristics) provides rights to compensation for various forms of discrimination by employers (ie claims in respect of discrimination on the grounds of age, disability, gender reassignment, marriage and civil partnership, pregnancy and maternity, race, religion or belief, sex and sexual orientation). Compensation for such discrimination may be paid under different heads such as for loss of earnings, for injury to feelings, personal injury and so on. The amount of damages awarded in discrimination cases takes into account the guidance given by the Court of Appeal in *Vento v Chief Constable of West Yorkshire Police* [2002] EWCA Civ 1871 (the so-called 'Vento' guidelines). The amount of compensation awarded depends on the seriousness of the circumstances in which the discriminatory behaviour occurred.

The tax treatment of such compensation payments made at the time of termination of employment depends upon whether they have been paid 'in connection with' the termination. If, on the one hand, a payment is not so connected, it will not fall within the residual category of termination payments (*A v HMRC* [2015] UKFTT 189 (TC)). If, on the other hand, a payment is so connected, then it will fall within the residual category of termination payments (*Walker v Adams* [2003] STC (SCD) 269; *Mr A v HMRC* [2009] SpC 734; *Chidi Anthony Oti-Obihara v HMRC* [2010] UKFTT 568 (TC); *Krishna Moorthy v RCC* [2014] UKFTT 834 (TC), [2015] UKUT 13, [2018] EWCA Civ 847). In the last-mentioned case the First-tier Tribunal approached the question of taxability of such payments by reference to the correct principles of statutory construction and provides a rigorous analysis of the law which was lacking in the earlier cases. The tribunal analysed the earlier cases and discussed the deficiencies in the reasoning in them. The Upper Tribunal in that case did not disagree with the reasoning of the First-tier Tribunal and neither did the Court of Appeal which condoned the approach to the enquiry taken by the First-tier Tribunal and the Upper Tribunal.

Any such payment that is attributable to discrimination occurring before the termination of employment and not connected with the termination is unlikely to be a residual termination payment (and indeed is likely to escape income tax altogether, being outside the scope of all the categories of employment income and hence entirely outside the charge to income tax levied by *ITEPA 2003* on employment income – see, in particular, **15.69**). This is illustrated in the case of *A v HMRC* [2015] UKFTT 189 (TC) where a payment was made at the time of an employee's redundancy but in respect of a claim for race discrimination which occurred sometime before the redundancy situation arose.

So if a payment relates only to the consequences of termination (eg loss of future earnings) or is made to compensate for discrimination that occurred at the time of and was connected with the termination of employment (eg compensation for sex discrimination due where an employee is dismissed because she is pregnant), then such a payment will most likely be treated as a residual termination payment. (There is nothing in the legislation that restricts the charge to tax on amounts paid in connection with the termination of employment only to the extent that they represent compensation for financial loss; there is no distinction in *section 401* between non-pecuniary aspects of a termination package, such as injury to feelings, and pecuniary aspects such as financial loss.) By contrast, compensation for sex discrimination occurring over a period leading up to termination and inherent in the termination itself may be reasonably apportioned and only the latter element taxable as a residual termination payment. This is a summary of the law as set out by HMRC in EIM12965. In the Upper Tribunal in *Krishna Moorthy* it was observed that there appears to be an anomalous distinction between payments of compensation for discrimination before termination (which are not taxable as earnings) and such compensation paid in connection with termination which is taxed as a residual termination payment. But that is a consequence of the provisions of *ITEPA 2003, s 401* which deem such payments to be taxable and the Court of Appeal was of the same view.

However, even where a payment pursuant to a claim for discrimination does fall within the residual category of termination payments, it may be that it benefits from one of the exceptions from the charge to tax thereby imposed (see **15.23**). Before 6 April 2018, this included a payment for injuries to feelings as well as bodily or psychiatric injury (*Krishna Moorthy v RCC* [2018] EWCA Civ 847) (see **15.42**).

On a practical level, where a compromise agreement does not apportion an award of damages between taxable and non-taxable elements, it is for the employee (and not the employer) to sort out the position with HMRC. The employer should deduct tax from the entire award of damages (subject to the £30,000 exemption if and to the extent applicable) when they are paid (*Norman v Yellow Pages Sales Ltd* [2010] EWCA Civ 1395). Where possible this situation should be avoided so that the employee does not suffer adverse cash-flow consequences and so that he does not have the extra burden of having subsequently to deal with HMRC to sort out the matter.

Ex gratia payments

15.22   Termination payments that are pure gifts which are not charged to tax as earnings from employment (see **15.88**) or as benefits from an EFRBS (see **15.100–15.107**) are taxed as residual termination payments. It is possible to make tax-efficient gifts when an employee leaves his employment, and the suggested wording for any letter or minute or memorandum conferring such a payment is simply as follows: 'That the payment is made as a mark of the employer's goodwill'. In EIM13914, HMRC give the following example of a payment falling under this head. An employee with nine months' service is made redundant. Because he has worked for less than two years, he has no right to a statutory redundancy payment. But, as a gesture of goodwill, the employer decides to pay £1,000 to the employee on account of redundancy; it is taxable as a residual termination payment.

An example of a case where an ex gratia payment was taxed as a termination payment (rather than as a reward for services) is *Resolute Management Services Ltd v RCC* [2008] STC (SCD) 1202. In that case a company involved in the Lloyd's insurance market was set up with the intention of dealing with a number of liabilities. This entailed it working itself out of business as it settled each problem and claim. The taxpayer was employed by the company as HR director. Once it achieved its objectives the company began to downsize and the taxpayer's job changed from managing high volume of staff recruitment and establishing HR policies for the company to managing a planned redundancy programme over a five-year period. When the taxpayer considered that her task had been accomplished, she resigned from the company and in so doing she forfeited her own redundancy benefit and other long-term incentive payments to which she was contractually entitled. She was motivated to do 'the right thing' by the company. In recognition of this, the company made an ex gratia payment of £150,000 to her. HMRC contended that the payment was the taxpayer's earnings. The company contended that it was a payment made in connection with the termination of the taxpayer's employment.

The Special Commissioner found that the payment was not earnings for the purposes of *ITEPA 2003, s 62*, as it was paid in recognition of the fact that the taxpayer had done the right thing in resigning her position. On the facts the payment was truly a gift. The taxpayer had no contractual entitlement to the payment and had done nothing to earn it. Whilst it is true that had she not resigned the payment would not have been made, yet it was not paid in return for the resignation and neither was it paid in respect of any service that the taxpayer had rendered or was obliged to render. The payment was a residual termination payment. Although it was made 'for doing the right thing', the right thing was resigning and accordingly the payment was in consequence of, or in connection with, the termination of her employment.

EXCEPTIONS FROM THE RESIDUAL CATEGORY OF TERMINATION PAYMENTS

Introduction

15.23   There are several exceptions from income tax in respect of residual termination payments. These exceptions apply only to residual termination payments and are therefore incentives to structuring a termination payment so that it falls in this category of employment income (see **15.1**).

The exceptions in **Table 15.2** are selected for discussion in this chapter (the list not being exhaustive).

Table 15.2 – Exceptions from the residual category of termination payments

- £30,000 threshold
- Payments made on death
- Payments made for injury or disability
- Contributions to registered pension schemes
- Foreign service exception
- Foreign service relief
- Payments of certain legal costs
- Counselling and other outplacement services
- Retraining courses
- Long-service awards

£30,000 threshold

Focus

The application of the £30,000 threshold is quite complicated. First ensure that all residual termination payments received on the termination of an individual's employment (but excluding those that are otherwise fully exempt from income tax) are correctly divided between his deemed earnings ('the earnings component') and a balancing amount ('the non-earnings component'). Only the non-earnings component of the residual termination payment is capable of benefitting from the threshold. Where it is available, ensure that it is correctly applied where employers are associated or where the non-earnings component comprises both cash payments and benefits, especially if they are made or provided over a number of years.

15.24 All residual termination payments that count as the employment income of an employee on the termination of his employment are aggregated and it is the total amount that is considered in relation to the £30,000 threshold. In so far as those residual termination payments are received on or after 6 April 2018 on the termination of an employment that has occurred on or after 6 April 2018, that amount is first split into two parts – an amount not benefitting from the threshold and an amount that does so benefit (*ITEPA 2003, s 402A*). The amount that does not benefit from the threshold is deemed to be the earnings of the employee or former employee (ie it is 'the earnings component of the residual termination payment') and is taxable in full (*ITEPA 2003, ss 7(5)(ca), 402B*). To the extent that the aggregate amount is not treated as deemed earnings (ie 'the non-earnings component of the residual termination payment') and to the extent that it exceeds £30,000, the amount in excess of that threshold is counted as the employee's employment income (*ITEPA 2003, s 403(1)*). Where the aggregate amount that is the non-earnings component of the residual termination payment does not exceed the threshold (or to the extent that it does not exceed it), then, as it is not charged to tax under any of the other categories of employment income, it is free of income tax. Neither is such an amount chargeable to capital gains tax.

It is important to note that, in respect of employments that end on or after 6 April 2018, in considering the availability and application of the £30,000 threshold, the starting point is to take into account *all* the chargeable residual termination payments received on the termination of an individual's employment. Do not just consider certain types of chargeable payment (eg a PILON) within the residual category. The total chargeable amount is sub-divided into the earnings and non-earnings components of the aggregate residual termination payments. This means that chargeable payments other than PILONs (such as gifts made on termination) may be treated as the employee's or former employee's deemed earnings and taxed accordingly. It is also important to note that the amount of either component may be nil; it all depends on the results of the application of the computational rules that determine the amount of the earnings component (see **15.25–15.26**).

It will be noted that the sub-categorisation of an individual's residual termination payments is carried out only in respect of his chargeable residual termination payments; payments that are excepted from the charge to income tax as residual termination payments (see those listed in **Table 15.2**) are fully exempt from income tax and none is deemed to be the earnings of the employee or former employee. The effective exemption from income tax of such payments remains a key incentive to structuring a termination payment so that it falls to be treated as a residual termination payment.

The 'earnings component' of a residual termination payment

15.25　Of the total chargeable residual termination payments received on the termination of an individual's employment on or after 6 April 2018, a certain amount does not benefit from the £30,000 threshold. That amount is deemed to be the earnings of the employee or former employee. In calculating that amount, first exclude any statutory redundancy pay (see **15.9**) (which, therefore, always benefits from the threshold (*ITEPA 2003, s 402C(2)*) and then apply the computational rules to the balance. Consequently, statutory redundancy pay will always be treated as a residual termination payment, none of which can be treated as earnings.

The rules that apply to calculate the amount of deemed earnings comprised in a residual termination payment are complex, but, broadly speaking, so much of the residual termination payment as equates to the individual's 'post-employment notice pay' (if any) is an amount of deemed earnings (*ITEPA 2003, s 402C(3), (4)*).

An individual's post-employment notice pay (PENP) (calculated in accordance with the formulae set out in *ITEPA 2003, ss 402D, 403E*) represents payments in lieu of notice which are not otherwise chargeable to income tax (ie non-contractual PILONs). An amount of PENP will arise where an employee receives no notice or less notice than he is entitled to under his contract of employment or statute. If an employee works his full notice period and is paid accordingly, then the effect of the computational rules is that none of his residual termination payment is accounted for as his deemed earnings and the whole amount may benefit from the £30,000 threshold. Hence, PENP represents the amount of basic pay an employee would have received had he worked the period of notice he was entitled to.

In relation to so much of a residual termination payment that counts as deemed earnings, *ITEPA 2003, s 403(3)* (see **15.34**) does not apply to determine the date on which those earnings are received; rather the general rules on receipt of earnings is applied (*ITEPA 2003, s 18*).

Example 15.2 – Deemed earnings

Louis is an employee whose salary is £60,000 a year payable monthly on the last day of each month. Under his contract of employment he is entitled to one months' notice of termination of employment from his employer. Louis is made redundant and he leaves his employment on 31 August 2018. He has not been required to work his notice period and is paid £2,000 in statutory redundancy pay, £5,000 as a payment in lieu of notice and £4,000 as a gift.

Louis' total residual termination payment is £11,000. Of that, £2,000 cannot be part of the earnings component of the termination payment as it is statutory redundancy pay. The balance of £9,000 is therefore divided into the earnings and non-earnings components of the payment. In accordance with the formula in *ITEPA 2003, s 402D*, his PENP is £5,000 and that comprises the earnings component of the residual termination payment. It is charged to tax as Louis' earnings. The balance of the payment of £4,000 is the non-earnings component of the residual termination payment which, together with the £2,000 statutory redundancy pay, is not charged to tax as together they amount to £6,000 which is less than the £30,000 threshold.

15.26   In ascertaining an individual's PENP, regard is had only to his basic pay (which, in the case of Louis in the previous example, was £5,000, his monthly earnings). An individual's basic pay is his total employment income for his last pay period before his employment ends but excludes any amount received by way of overtime, bonus, commission, gratuity or allowance, benefits in kind, payments for restrictive undertakings, other termination payments and employment related securities. Basic pay also includes salary that would have been received had it not been sacrificed for a benefit in kind. There are anti-avoidance rules which prevent the manipulation of basic pay so as to bring in a lower amount for tax purposes (*ITEPA 2003, s 402C(11)*).

The earnings component of a residual termination payment is also treated as earnings for NIC purposes so that both primary (employee's) and secondary (employer's) Class 1 contributions are payable in respect of it (*Social Security Contributions and Benefits Regulations 2001, SI 2001/1004, reg 22(14)*).

The non-earnings component of a residual termination payments

15.27   The discussion that follows in relation to the £30,000 threshold applies to the non-earnings component of a residual termination payment received on or after 6 April 2018 in respect of a termination of an employment occurring on or after 6 April 2018. (It also applies to all residual termination payments whenever received in respect of the termination of an employment occurring before 6 April 2018.)

Termination packages made by associated employers

15.28 The £30,000 threshold is available to an individual only once in respect of each employment of his that has been brought to an end (*ITEPA 2003, s 404(1)(a)*).

The first implication of this rule is that where a termination package is received by an employee in instalments over a number of tax years, the £30,000 threshold is not available each year; one £30,000 amount applies to the package no matter when it is received.

> **Example 15.3 – The £30,000 threshold**
>
> Charles, having worked and been paid for his notice period, leaves his employment with Greatermans Ltd by reason of redundancy on 30 April 2018. He is eligible for a payment of £46,000 from the company's non-statutory redundancy scheme which is to be paid in two equal instalments on 1 May 2018 (ie in 2018/19) and 1 May 2019 (ie in 2019/20). Only one £30,000 threshold is available and the excess payment of £16,000 falls into charge to tax (in 2019/20).

15.29 The second implication of this rule is that where an employee suffers the termination of more than one employment (whether held by him concurrently or successively), then separate £30,000 thresholds are available in respect of each employment that has been brought to an end.

> **Example 15.4 – Separate £30,000 thresholds**
>
> Albert, having worked and been paid for his notice period, is made redundant on 7 April 2018 and receives a payment of £30,000. This is the non-earnings component of a residual termination payment and is exempt (*ITEPA 2003, s 403(1)*). He finds a new job with a new employer (who is not associated with his former employer) in May 2018, but is made redundant from that job in February 2019 when he is again paid £30,000 (having also worked and been paid for his notice period). This, too, as the non-earnings component of a residual termination payment will be exempt. Consequently, in 2018/19, Albert has, in his circumstances, had the benefit of two £30,000 thresholds.

15.30 It is an important fact that in the immediately preceding example, the two employers are independent of one another (ie they are not 'associated'). Where employers are 'associated' then only one £30,000 threshold is available to an individual. This is also the case where an individual has different employments with the same employer.

Example 15.5 – Same employer

James, having worked and been paid for his notice period, is made redundant on 7 April 2018 and receives a payment of £30,000 (the non-earnings component of a residual termination payment). This will be exempt (*ITEPA 2003, s 403(1)*). He finds a new job with the same employer in May 2018, but is made redundant from that job in February 2019 when he is again paid £30,000 (having also worked and been paid for his notice period). Although this is the non-earnings component of a residual termination payment, it will not be exempt and a charge to tax arises in relation to the whole of the second £30,000 payment. This is because James's employer, in both cases, is the same person and so only one £30,000 threshold is available to James. (This contrasts with the example of Albert above where his successive employers are different persons.)

Example 15.6 – Associated employers

Aragon Ltd owns all the shares of Seymour Ltd. Henry worked for Aragon Ltd from 1 January 2010 until 1 May 2018 when his employment was ended by compromise agreement. A payment was made to him on that date, £27,000 of which was the non-earnings component of the payment. This falls wholly within the £30,000 threshold and is not taxable. Henry then started work with Seymour Ltd but was, after he had worked and been paid for his notice period, made redundant in June 2019 and received £5,000 as an ex gratia payment. This payment is exempt as to £3,000 only – ie the amount of the payment that is equal to the balance of the £30,000 threshold that is left after the payment made in respect of the May 2018 termination. This is because at the time of the termination of his employment with Seymour Ltd (ie June 2019), that company was associated with Aragon Ltd and so only one £30,000 threshold is available in respect of Henry's two employments.

15.31 In the light of the above treatment, it is important to know when two or more employers are associated. There are three alternative tests.

First test. Employers are associated if, on the date of the termination of the employment in question, one of them is under the control of the other

(*ITEPA 2003, s 404(2)(a)*). For example, if A Ltd owns all the share capital of B Ltd and both companies are concurrent or successive employers of Mr X, then A Ltd and B Ltd are associated employers.

Second test. Employers are associated if, on the date of the termination of the employment in question:

(a)   one of them is under the control of a third person, and

(b)   that third person controls the other (first limb of *ITEPA 2003, s 404(2)(b)*).

For example, if Mr X owns all the shares in Y Ltd and Z Ltd and both companies are the concurrent or successive employers of Mr Q, then Y Ltd and Z Ltd are associated employers.

Third test. Employers are associated if, on the date of the termination of the employment in question:

(a)   one of them is under the control of a third person, and

(b)   that third person is under the control of the other (second limb of *ITEPA 2003, s 404(2)(b)*).

For example, if M Ltd owns all the share capital of N Ltd which owns all the share capital of P Ltd, and M Ltd and P Ltd are the concurrent or successive employers of Mr Z, then M Ltd and P Ltd are associated employers.

Composition and terms of payment of a termination package

15.32   The rules on the application of the £30,000 threshold also take on an element of complexity in relation to the possible composition of a termination package and the terms under which the parts of the package may be paid. The non-earnings component of a residual termination package may comprise both cash payments and non-cash benefits which are paid (or given or made available) by instalments either in a single tax year or in two or more tax years.

Instalment payments in a single tax year

15.33   If the non-earnings component of a residual termination payment consists of more than one cash benefit received in a tax year in which the £30,000 threshold is exceeded, the exempt amount (or the balance of it) is set against the amounts of cash benefits as they are received (*ITEPA 2003, s 404(5)(a)*). Cash benefits comprised in the non-earnings component of a residual termination payment are treated as received when payment is made of or on account of them, or when the recipient becomes entitled to require payment of or on account of them (*ITEPA 2003, s 403(3)(a)*).

779

Example 15.7 – Termination package: two instalments

Andrew's termination package (which is a package of residual termination payments) includes a non-earnings component of £40,000 in cash. The amount is to be paid in two equal instalments in July and December 2018, his employment having ended on 30 June 2018. The application of the £30,000 threshold is as follows:

	£
July instalment	20,000
Threshold	(20,000)
	Nil
December instalment	20,000
Threshold (30,000 – 20,000)	(10,000)
	10,000

For 2018/19, therefore, £10,000 of the total non-earnings component of Andrew's termination package is counted as his employment income.

15.34   If the non-earnings component of a residual termination package comprises both cash and non-cash benefits, and if at the end of the tax year in question any amount of the £30,000 threshold (having first been used in relation to any cash benefits) remains unused, then the balance is set against the aggregate amount of non-cash benefits received in that year (*ITEPA 2003, s 404(5)(b)*). Non-cash benefits are treated as received when they are used or enjoyed (*ITEPA 2003, s 403(3)(b)*). This is a question of fact. In the case of corporeal property, mere physical possession constitutes its enjoyment even if the item is not used until a later date. In the case of incorporeal property, the ownership of a right constitutes its enjoyment.

Example 15.8 – Termination package: cash and benefits

Edward's employment ended on 30 June 2018. His termination package (which is a package of residual termination payments) includes a non-earnings component of £24,000 cash to be paid in two equal instalments in July and December 2018 and the transfer of an asset in September 2018 worth £8,000. The application of the £30,000 threshold is as follows:

	£
July instalment	12,000
Threshold	(12,000)
	Nil

	£
December instalment	12,000
Threshold	(12,000)
	Nil
Asset transfer	8,000
Threshold (30,000 – 24,000)	(6,000)
	2,000

For 2018/19 the amount treated as Edward's employment income is £2,000.

15.35 This second rule is of benefit to employees. Since cash payments are treated as exempt in priority to non-cash benefits, the PAYE regime has no application. The former employee thereby achieves a cash-flow advantage. Under the PAYE regime, income tax is deducted from the cash element of the non-earnings component of a residual termination package by the employer making the payment. The rate at which tax is deducted depends upon when a payment is made. If it is made before the end of the employment (usually the date on which the P45 is issued), tax must be deducted in accordance with the employee's notice of coding using the appropriate tax tables. By contrast, if the payment is made after the employment ends, then tax using the 0T code (on a week 1/month 1 non-cumulative basis) must be deducted from the payment and accounted for to HMRC (*Income Tax (Pay as You Earn) Regulations 2003, SI 2003/2682, reg 37*) (see **15.108**). To the extent that cash payments are exempt, no deduction will occur. Non-cash benefits will be returned by the employee himself under the self-assessment regime and tax on them will be due only on the 31 January in the tax year following that in which the non-cash benefit is received. Income tax under the above rules of the PAYE regime will also be deducted by the employer from the cash element of the earnings component of a residual termination package.

Instalment payments in two or more tax years

15.36 If the non-earnings component of a residual termination payment comprises both cash and non-cash benefits which are received in different tax years, the £30,000 threshold is set against the amount of such payments and other benefits received in earlier tax years before those received in later tax years (*ITEPA 2003, s 404(4)*). This rule does not displace the rules on instalment payments made in a single year (as described in **15.33** above) or the rule that allocates the threshold to cash payments in priority to non-cash benefits (as described in **15.34** above); it is applied in addition to them, so that in any one tax year, the £30,000 amount is first set against cash and then against any non-cash benefits.

Example 15.9 – Cash and benefits package: separate years

Elizabeth's termination package (which is a package of residual termination payments awarded under an agreement made on 1 January 2019, the date her employment ended) includes a non-earnings component made up as follows:

(a)   £39,000 to be paid in three equal annual instalments on 1 January 2019, 1 January 2020 and 1 January 2021;

(b)   the use of a car, the cash equivalent of which is £2,000, £7,000 and £7,500 in 2018/19, 2019/20 and 2020/21 respectively.

The total value of the non-earnings component of the package is £55,500 in respect of which only one £30,000 threshold is available. It will be allocated as follows:

(a)   *2018/19:* total taxable value is £13,000 cash plus £2,000 in respect of the car. This £15,000 is within the threshold, leaving a balance of £15,000 to be carried forward to 2019/20.

(b)   *2019/20:* total taxable value is £13,000 cash plus £7,000 in respect of the car. This £20,000 is exempt as to £15,000, £13,000 of the threshold being set against the cash, then the balance of £2,000 being set against the cash equivalent of the car, leaving £5,000 taxable (in respect of the non-cash element of the non-earnings component of the package in this year).

(c)   *2020/21:* total taxable value is £13,000 cash plus £7,500 in respect of the car. This £20,500 is taxable in full, no balance of the threshold being available.

Instalment payments: termination of employment before 6 April 2018

15.37   Where an employment is ended before 6 April 2018 and a residual termination award is made to the employee affected, the award is not subject to the rules that came into effect on that date requiring it to be sub-divided into its earnings and non-earnings components. The £30,000 threshold is available in respect of the full amount of the award and the rules described in **15.27–15.36** above apply to the whole award. Where such an award is paid in instalments and all or some of those instalments are made on or after

6 April 2018, they remain unaffected by the rules that came into force on 6 April 2018. Such instalments of such an award do not need to be sub-divided when they are received. It is reiterated that the employment itself must end on or after 6 April 2018 in order for a residual termination payment made in respect of it to be subject to the rules sub-dividing it into its earnings and non-earnings components.

Example 15.10 – Termination package payable in instalments: termination of employment before 6 April 2018

Elizabeth's termination package (which is a package of residual termination payments awarded under an agreement made on 1 January 2017, the date her employment ended) provides for:

(a)   £39,000 to be paid in three equal annual instalments on 1 January 2017, 1 January 2018 and 1 January 2019;

(b)   the use of a car, the cash equivalent of which is £2,000, £7,000 and £7,500 in 2016/17, 2017/18 and 2018/19 respectively.

The total value of the whole package is £55,500 in respect of which only one £30,000 threshold is available. It will be allocated as follows:

(a)   *2016/17:* total taxable value is £13,000 cash plus £2,000 in respect of the car. This £15,000 is within the threshold, leaving a balance of £15,000 to be carried forward to 2017/18.

(b)   *2017/18:* total taxable value is £13,000 cash plus £7,000 in respect of the car. This £20,000 is exempt as to £15,000, £13,000 of the threshold being set against the cash, then the balance of £2,000 being set against the cash equivalent of the car, leaving £5,000 taxable (in respect of the non-cash component of the package in this year).

(c)   *2018/19:* total taxable value is £13,000 cash plus £7,500 in respect of the car. This £20,500 is taxable in full, no balance of the threshold being available.

The £30,000 threshold and foreign-service relief

15.38   Where an employee's service under his contract of employment includes foreign service which does not, on account of the inadequacy of the duration or timing of that service, qualify for the foreign-service exception (see **15.50**), he will be able to claim foreign-service relief. It must be noted, however, that the £30,000 threshold applies before a deduction is taken for foreign service relief (*ITEPA 2003, s 414(2)*).

In relation to an employment that ends on or after 6 April 2018, however, it must be noted that, unless the employee is a seafarer, foreign service relief applies only if the employee is not resident in the UK in the tax year in which the employment terminates and the residual termination payment is received after 13 September 2017 (*ITEPA 2003, s 414(1)(za); FA 2018, s 10(5)*) (see **15.55**). In that case, the deduction for foreign service relief is given against both the earnings and non-earnings components of the residual termination payment but after the application of the £30,000 threshold to the latter component (see **15.27** above) (*ITEPA 2003, s 414(2)*).

Example 15.11 – Foreign-service relief

Alexandra is employed in an employment for five years. In respect of two of those years, she receives earnings in respect of foreign service. At the end of the fifth year in 2018/19 when she is non-UK resident, she receives a residual termination payment, the earnings component of which is £50,000 and the non-earnings component of which is £100,000. The amount which is counted as her employment income is:

	Earnings Component	Non-earnings Component
	£	£
Termination payment	50,000	100,000
Less: threshold		(30,000)
		70,000
Less: foreign service relief		
50,000 × 2/5; 70,000 × 2/5	(20,000)	(28,000)
Taxable amount	30,000	42,000

Payments made on death

Focus

Take care not to fall into the trap of thinking that termination payments made on death are necessarily not charged to income tax. Ensure that such payments which are ex gratia are not taxed as payments under an employer-financed retirement benefits scheme and so taxable in full (see **15.105**).

15.39 *ITEPA 2003, s 406(1)(a)* provides that a payment or other benefit provided in connection with the termination of employment by the death of an employee does not fall to be taxed as a residual termination payment. All payments, whether ex gratia or made under some form of obligation (whether legal or not), are capable of coming within this exception. Furthermore, in respect of employments that end on or after 6 April 2018, the payment does not have to be sub-divided into its earnings and non-earnings components. The whole payment is exempt and none of it is treated as the employee's deemed earnings.

However, care must be exercised here to ensure that the payment is not chargeable to tax as a payment under an EFRBS (see **15.105**) as the payment will not then be a residual termination payment.

15.40 The rule is drafted very widely and is satisfied if the making of the payment merely has something to do with the termination of the employment which has been brought about by the death of the employee. This should cover all possible circumstances in which a death might arise – be it from natural causes, by accident or otherwise (eg as the result of a criminal act).

15.41 There are no conditions imposed by the exception as to the circumstances in which death occurs. It is not necessary that the employee be carrying out his employment duties at the time of the death. A payment following a fatal car crash, for example, whilst the employee is on holiday would also be within the exception.

Payments made for injury or disability

Focus

Take care not to fall into the trap of thinking that termination payments made on account of injury or disability are necessarily not charged to income tax. There are a number of complex conditions that have to be satisfied for such a charge not to arise.

15.42 *ITEPA 2003, s 406(1)(b)* provides that a payment or other benefit provided on account of injury to, or disability of, an employee does not fall to be taxed as a residual termination payment. Again, all payments, whether ex gratia or made under some form of obligation (whether legal or not), are capable of coming within this exception provided the other conditions for the exception are met. Furthermore, in respect of employments that end on or after 6 April 2018, the payment does not have to be sub-divided into its earnings and non-earnings components. The whole payment is exempt and none of it is treated as the employee's deemed earnings.

15.43   In order to be within the exception, the payment must be provided 'on account of' the injury or disability. In contrast to the exception on death, the condition relating to the provision of the payment in this context is more stringent for it must be established as a subjective fact that the injury or disability is the motive for making the payment (*Horner v Hasted (Inspector of Taxes)* [1995] STC 766). If the employer decides to dismiss an employee on commercial grounds (eg the employee's work has deteriorated and is adversely affecting the performance of the employer's business), then any payment made upon dismissal is unlikely to come within the disability exception even if the reason for the deterioration in the employee's work is, in turn, due to a disability. In order to establish entitlement to the exception, the injury or disability must motivate or induce the employer to make the payment. In *Flutter v RCC* [2015] UKFTT 249 (TC) the taxpayer, who suffered from a hearing disability that impinged on his ability to carry out his employment duties (which involved the extensive use of the telephone), was made redundant and received a termination payment. Although the taxpayer's hearing loss was more likely than not a significant contributory factor to the timing of the termination of his employment, it was found that the payment made by the employer was not motivated by his disability and so the exception afforded by *section 406(1)(b)* was not available in respect of it.

In *Khrishna Moorthy v HMRC* [2018] EWCA Civ 847, the Court of Appeal observed, obiter, that the exception for injury to an employee is not qualified by any words linking it to the termination of employment (as is the exception for death). The injury does not have to be something that immediately leads to the termination of employment. In principle, the injury could be wholly extraneous to the employment, and have no effect on the employee's duties or level of earnings, yet still be relevant if the employer chose, for whatever reason, to make a payment on account of it when the employee eventually retired. So, for example, an employee nearing retirement age might have been injured in a motor accident, but not so seriously as to prevent him from carrying out his duties as before and at the same salary. If, on his retirement, the employer were then to give him an ex gratia payment in recognition of his injuries, there is no reason why such a payment would not qualify for exemption under *ITEPA 2003, s 4016(1)(b)*.

15.44   What type of injury comes within the exception? An injury is a physical injury (eg the loss of a limb or a sense (eg sight) that renders the victim incapable of carrying out the duties of his employment. In EIM13610, HMRC state that a psychological injury is also within the exception. In *Khrishna Moorthy v HMRC* [2018] EWCA Civ 847, the Court of Appeal (reversing the decision of the High Court) held that 'injury' in the context of *ITEPA 2003, s 406(1)(b)* constitutes a recognisable form of personal injury, in accordance with medical science as it develops from time to time. This clearly encompasses physical and psychiatric injuries. However, the Court of Appeal went on to say, having reviewed the development of the law generally, that the term 'injury' also encompasses any other form of injury in the normal sense of that word which is recognised by Parliament as providing a basis for the payment of compensation to an employee. Consequently, it held that an award of damages for injury to feelings, in respect of actionable discrimination on grounds of age, falls within the exception. It expressed no view, however, on the question whether the exception might also apply in principle to payments made in respect of injury to feelings where no statutory basis for such a claim could exist.

The rule laid down in *Moorthy* applies only in respect of 2017/18 and earlier years of assessment. For the tax year 2018/19 and subsequent years of assessment, *ITEPA 2003, s 406(2)* provides that 'although "injury" includes psychiatric injury, it does not include injured feelings' (*FA 2008, s 5(10)*).

However, the injury does not have to be sustained during working hours while the employee is carrying out the duties of his employment. Neither does it necessarily need to be suffered by accident. But the injury must occur to an individual while he is an employee, not after he has ceased to be an employee.

15.45   Understanding what comes within the scope of the term 'disability' is more problematic. In *Horner v Hasted (Inspector of Taxes)* [1995] STC 766 it was held that a disability is a condition that amounts to a total or partial impairment (which may arise from physical, mental or psychological causes) of the employee's ability to perform the functions or duties of his employment.

HMRC in SP 10/81 accept that 'disability' means the incapacity to fulfil the duties and responsibilities of the employment resulting from sudden affliction (eg coronary thrombosis), or arising out of the culmination of a process of deterioration of physical or mental health caused by chronic illness (eg bronchitis). Disability, therefore, encompasses ill health, but it is unclear why HMRC limit their practice to chronic illness only. Certainly, the legislation does not indicate that such a restriction be imposed, and this is in keeping with the definition of the term found in the Shorter Oxford English Dictionary which defines the word as a physical or mental condition (usually permanent) that limits a person's activities or senses, especially the ability to work. HMRC do not regard the normal process of ageing as a disability within the exception (EIM13620). In the *Horner* case, the taxpayer's distress and insomnia caused by his work were not considered to be a disability qualifying for exception even though they affected his work. In that case there was insufficient evidence to show that this caused a medical condition which disabled or prevented the taxpayer from carrying out the duties of his employment.

HMRC will give formal binding answers in relation to the meaning of disability under SP 10/81 and to enquiries on the application of this disability and injury compensation exception in any particular case (see **15.111**).

15.46   EIM13630 makes the following points (based on the *Horner* case) in relation to the disability exception.

First, there must be an identified medical condition that disables or prevents the employee from carrying out the duties of the employment. Any injury or disability must be established as an objective fact. Medical evidence confirming the precise nature of the disability must therefore be provided in all cases, and it must be clear that the nature of the disability prevents the employee carrying out the specific duties of the employment.

Secondly, the payment must be made on account of the disability and on account of nothing else. If, for example, the employer is unaware of the disability when the employee leaves, then the payment cannot be made 'on account of' disability. Similarly, if any part of the payment is a reward for specific services, or due on termination regardless of the cause, it cannot be 'on account of' disability. HMRC will frequently require seeing all documentation to establish why the employer made the payment.

Thirdly, it is important to ensure that the medical condition and its employment consequences are considered by reference to the situation at the point of termination of employment, and not at any other time. For example, evidence of a medical condition existing, say, two years before termination is not determinative.

Contributions to registered pension schemes

Focus

This exception is perhaps the most valuable tool in termination payment planning as it may often be combined with the £30,000 threshold (where it is available) to make larger payments entirely tax free. Take care though not to overfund a pension scheme or exceed an employee's annual allowance.

15.47   *ITEPA 2003, s 408(1)* provides that a contribution to a registered pension scheme (ie under *FA 2004, Pt 4, Ch 2*) or an employer-financed retirement benefit scheme (EFRBS) is not counted as a residual termination payment if the contribution is made:

(a)   as part of an arrangement relating to the termination of the person's employment (*ITEPA 2003, s 408(1)(a)*), and

(b)   in order to provide benefits for that person in accordance with the terms of the scheme or approved personal pension arrangements (*ITEPA 2003, s 408(1)(b)*).

15.48   In respect of employments that end on or after 6 April 2018, it will be noted that the payment to the pension scheme does not have to be sub-divided into its earnings and non-earnings components. The whole payment is exempt and none of it is treated as the employee's deemed earnings.

It will be noted, however, that the contribution must be made as part of an arrangement relating to the termination of the employee's employment (eg under a compromise agreement). It would appear that the exception will not apply where a payment is made to the former employee who then makes a contribution to the pension scheme. The amount of the contribution must be within the limits imposed by the scheme rules, which will have to be checked whenever such a contribution is made. Similarly, care should be taken to ensure that any contribution made to a registered pension scheme is within the employee's cumulated annual allowance to avoid an annual allowance charge arising on him (*FA 2004, s 227*) or that it does not negate any transitional protection regime that he may enjoy on account of the reduction of the pension lifetime allowance to £1m from 6 April 2016 (or any other protection regimes that are in place on account of earlier reductions in the lifetime allowance).

15.49   This exception is a most valuable one and should not be overlooked in planning. For example, where a termination package within the residual category provides that a payment of £50,000 be made to a former employee, it is possible to shelter the whole amount from income tax through a combination of the £30,000 threshold and a contribution to a registered pension scheme (assuming the earnings component of the payment is nil and a £20,000 special contribution to the pension fund is within its funding limits and the individual's current annual allowance). The efficacy of the planning is, of course, compromised to the extent that the part of the residual termination payment that is not made to the pension fund is deemed to be the employee's earnings.

Where a contribution is made to an EFRBS however, although the payment is not regarded as a residual termination payment, consideration must be given as to whether a charge to tax may arise in respect of the contribution in accordance with the rules on employment income provided through third parties (*ITEPA 2003, Pt 7A*).

Foreign service exception

> **Focus**
>
> This exception is another valuable tool in termination payment planning as payments to which it applies are entirely tax free regardless of their amount.

15.50 The normal rules on residence and domicile in so far as they relate to the taxation of general earnings (*ITEPA 2003, Pt 2, Chs 4, 5*) do not apply in relation to the imposition of a charge to UK income tax on residual termination payments and such payments are prima facie within the charge to UK income tax no matter where in the world they are made or to whom they are made (*Nichols v Gibson* [1996] STC 1008). However, this worldwide application of this category of employment income is limited by the foreign service exception.

If the exception for foreign service is to apply in respect of a residual termination payment, the employment in respect of which it is made must include 'foreign service' as defined in *ITEPA 2003, s 413(2)–(6)*. Service in or after the tax year 2013/14 is foreign service to the extent that it consists of duties performed outside the UK in respect of which earnings are not relevant earnings; so if the employee serves abroad for a period but his earnings for that period of service are relevant earnings, then that period will *not* count towards the exception. Relevant earnings are those for a tax year in which the employee is resident in the UK (including overseas earnings in respect of which a claim for the remittance basis has been made, including a claim under the overseas workday relief provisions). In short, therefore, an employee has a period of foreign service for the purposes of this exception only if his duties are performed outside the UK at a time when he is not resident in the UK (as determined using the statutory residence test). If the employee finds himself in any other position, his period of service does not count as foreign service. This will typically be the case where the employee is not resident in the UK and his duties are performed here. Similarly, the UK duties of a UK resident cannot qualify as foreign service even if they meet the overseas workday relief provisions (*ITEPA 2003, s 26A*).

Strictly speaking, the definition of 'foreign service' relates to service in a single employment, although HMRC will treat employments with different group companies as a single employment for the purpose of calculating periods of foreign service, provided that the termination payment relates to the service with those group companies as a whole (EIM13975).

HMRC will give formal binding answers in relation to the application of the foreign service exception in any particular case (see **15.111**).

15.51 A residual termination payment is exempt if paid in respect of an employment in which the employee's service has:

(a)   included foreign service; and

(b)   that foreign service falls within one of three qualifying classes (*ITEPA 2003, s 413(1)*).

An employee's foreign service must satisfy the requirements of any one of the three qualifying classes in order for the exception to apply. Each class requires that a proportion of the employee's period of service be comprised of foreign service. This requires one to ascertain the length of his foreign service and compare this to the length of his total period of service ending with the date of termination of his employment. Where the exception applies, it should be emphasised that the whole termination payment is exempt from tax, not only that part of it which is attributable to the period of foreign service. Furthermore, in respect of employments that end on or after 6 April 2018, the payment does not have to be sub-divided into its earnings and non-earnings components. The whole payment is exempt and none of it is treated as the employee's deemed earnings.

However, where an employment terminates on or after 6 April 2018, it must be noted that, unless the employee is a seafarer, the foreign service exception applies only if the employee is not resident in the UK in the tax year in which the employment terminates and the residual termination payment is received after 13 September 2017 (*ITEPA 2003, s 413(A1); FA 2018, s 10(5)*). In other words, the foreign service exception is not available in respect of termination payments received after 13 September 2017 by an individual who is resident in the UK when his employment ends after 5 April 2018. This means that, from 2018/19, all employees who are UK resident in the tax year when their employment is terminated will be liable to income tax on their terminations payments regardless of whether they have worked abroad. They will be taxed in the same way as those who have not worked abroad. If advantage of the foreign service exception is to be taken, the employee who has qualifying periods of work abroad must be non-UK resident when his employment ends. Although the statutory residence test will be applied to determine whether a person is non-UK resident when his employment ends, this additional requirement for the availability of the foreign service exception reduces its likely availability to those employees who are abroad when their employment ends.

15.52 Foreign service falls within the first qualifying class where:

(a)   the employee's total period of service has exceeded 20 years (a period of 20 years exactly being insufficient); and

(b)   the foreign service:

    (i)   comprises one-half or more of that period; and

    (ii)   includes any ten out of the last 20 years (*ITEPA 2003, s 413(1)(c)*).

It is not necessary that the period of foreign service be continuous, so long as in aggregate all such periods meet the conditions set out in paragraph (b) above.

Example 15.12 – Foreign service: first qualifying class

Suleman and Maria are both employees of Chancellor Ltd. Both of their employments commenced on 6 October 1998 and both were wrongly terminated on 5 April 2019 when each was paid £100,000 in damages

Suleman was in foreign service for two periods, namely 6 October 1999 to 5 October 2002, and 6 October 2011 to 5 April 2019. His period of service comprises 20½ years, and so, prima facie, it is within the first qualifying class. His period of foreign service totals 10½ years which is more than one-half of the total period. The last 20 years of service comprise the period 6 April 1999 to 5 April 2019. The periods 6 October 1999 to 5 October 2002, and 6 October 2011 to 5 April 2019, together comprise a ten-year period falling in the last 20 years during which there was foreign service. Suleman was not resident in the UK in 2018/19 when his employment ended. The first qualifying class applies and his damages are tax free.

Maria was in foreign service for two periods, namely 6 October 1999 to 5 October 2002, and 1 January 2007 to 30 June 2014. Her period of service comprises 20½ years, and so, prima facie, it is within the first qualifying class. Her period of foreign service totals 10½ years which is more than one-half of the total period. The last 20 years of service comprise the period 6 April 1999 to 5 April 2019. The periods 6 October 1999 to 5 October 2002, and 1 January 2007 to 30 June 2014, together comprise a ten-year period falling in the last 20 years during which there was foreign service. However, Maria was resident in the UK in 2018/19 when her employment ended. Although she meets the conditions for the first qualifying class, the damages paid to her are a taxable residual termination payment. The exception does not apply. The payment will have to be sub-divided into its earnings and non-earnings components, and each component will be charged to tax accordingly (see **15.24**).

15.53 Foreign service falls within the second qualifying class where:

(a)   the employee's total service has exceeded ten years (a period of exactly ten years is insufficient); and

(b)   the foreign service comprises the whole of the last ten years of that period (*ITEPA 2003, s 413(1)(b)*).

This class includes periods of total service of 20 years or more. Where the period exceeds 20 years, therefore, *prima facie*, the first and second qualifying classes are in point. The further conditions of each class will then determine which one is applicable (if at all). The conditions in paragraph (b) are met where at least the whole of the last ten years of service are made up of foreign service. In this case though, and by way of contrast to the provisions of the first qualifying class, there must be foreign service continuously throughout the final ten years of service.

15.54 Foreign service falls within the third qualifying class where:

(a)　the employee's total period of service is of any length; and

(b)　the foreign service comprises three-quarters of that period (*ITEPA 2003, s 413(1)(a)*).

The class is not limited to cases where the foreign service is exactly three-quarters of the whole period of service. It is sufficient if at least three-quarters of that period is made up of foreign service. It is also important to appreciate that this qualifying class applies to periods of service of any length, even those contemplated by the other two qualifying classes. Where the additional conditions of those classes are not satisfied it is still possible that the third qualifying class may apply.

Example 15.13 – Foreign service: third qualifying class

Clive is employed by Computer Services Ltd. His employment commenced on 1 January 2006 and was terminated on 31 December 2018 when he received £45,000. During this period he had ten years of foreign service comprising the periods 1 March 2006 to 28 February 2008 and 1 January 2011 to 31 December 2018. Although his period of service was in excess of ten years (but less than 20 years), it does not fall within the second qualifying class as the whole of the last ten years does not comprise foreign service. However, it does fall within the third qualifying class as his period of foreign service represents 76.9% of his total service. The £45,000 is, therefore, not charged to income tax as (it appears) that Clive is not UK resident in 2018/19 when his employment ends.

Foreign service relief

Focus

If a payment does not qualify for complete exception under the foreign service exception, do not overlook foreign service relief, but take care to apply it and the £30,000 threshold correctly (see **15.38**).

15.55 A residual termination payment made in respect of an employment in which the service of the employee includes foreign service may not, on account of the inadequacy of the duration or timing of that service, qualify for the foreign service exception. In such a case, however, a taxpayer will be able to claim foreign service relief (*ITEPA 2003, s 414(1)*). The relief operates by allowing a deduction to be made from the termination payment before it is charged to income tax (*ITEPA 2003, s 414(2)*). If the employee's employment ends on or after 6 April 2018, the deduction for foreign service relief is given against both the earnings and the non-earnings components of the residual termination payment before they are charged to income tax (see **15.38** above).

However, where an employment terminates on or after 6 April 2018, it must be noted that, unless the employee is a seafarer, foreign service relief applies only if the employee is not resident in the UK in the tax year in which the employment terminates and the residual termination payment is received after 13 September 2017 (*ITEPA 2003, s 414(1)(za)*; *FA 2018, s 10(5)*). In other words, foreign service relief is not available in respect of termination payments received after 13 September 2017 by an individual who is resident in the UK when his employment ends after 5 April 2018. This means that, from 2018/19, all employees who are UK resident in the tax year when their employment is terminated will be liable to income tax on their terminations payments regardless of whether they have worked abroad. They will be taxed in the same way as those who have not worked abroad. If advantage of the foreign service relief is to be taken, the employee who has worked abroad must be non-UK resident when his employment ends.

15.56   The amount of any termination payment which is left in charge to tax (ie the 'taxable proportion' (Z)) after the application of the relief is calculated as follows (*ITEPA 2003, s 414(3)*):

	£
Termination payment	P
Less: P × F/T	(X)
Taxable portion	£Z

where:

P   is the amount of the termination payment which is 'chargeable to tax' before the relief is given; in the case of an employment that ends after 5 April 2018, P is the amount of the non-earnings component of the residual termination payment which is 'chargeable to tax' before the relief is given

F   is the length of the employee's period of foreign service

T   is the length of the employee's total period of service before the date of termination.

The amount (P) of the termination payment (or component of the termination payment) which is 'chargeable to tax' before the relief is given is calculated after applying the £30,000 threshold (*ITEPA 2003, s 414(2)*) (see **15.38**). As this deduction is made before the relief for foreign service is given, the effect is that the benefit of the £30,000 threshold is restricted.

It is important to note that the reduction must be claimed within four years after the end of the tax year to which it relates; this must not be overlooked as the other exceptions tend to apply automatically. This is an important point for employers; because the relief has to be claimed by the employee, no account should be taken of it when operating PAYE. However, in practice HMRC may agree that the employer may operate PAYE taking into account foreign service relief where it has requested permission in advance of making a termination payment.

Finally, in the context of a payment qualifying for foreign service relief, it may be the case that a residual termination payment may have suffered tax in the country in which foreign service was rendered. In this case, any double tax agreement with the foreign country concerned should be consulted to see whether relief for that tax is available. The provisions in UK domestic law for unilateral double tax relief should also be considered.

Payments of certain legal costs

Focus

Take care to structure the discharge of an employee's legal fees incurred in connection with a termination of his employment in such a way that the stringent conditions applicable to this exception are satisfied. The same advice goes for payments for outplacement counselling (**15.58**) and retraining courses (**15.61**). In respect of employments that end on or after 6 April 2018, it will be noted that none of these payments has to be sub-divided into its earnings and non-earnings components. Each payment is fully exempt and none of it is treated as the employee's deemed earnings.

15.57 Legal costs paid by an employer on behalf of an employee in connection with the termination of his employment will be regarded as a residual termination benefit received by the employee. An exception is provided however for legal costs that meet two conditions (*ITEPA 2003, s 413A(1)*).

The first is that the payment must meet the whole or part of the legal costs incurred by the employee exclusively in connection with the termination of his employment (*ITEPA 2003, s 413A(2)*). Legal costs are the fees payable for the services and disbursements of a lawyer (as defined below) (*ITEPA 2003, s 413A(4)*).

The second condition is set out in *ITEPA 2003, s 413A(3)* and is in the alternative. It provides that:

(a)   the payment must be made pursuant to an order of a court or tribunal, or

(b)   the termination of the employee's employment results in a settlement agreement between the employer and the employee, the agreement provides for the payment to be made by the employer and the payment is made directly to the employee's lawyer (ie a qualified lawyer as defined in the *ERA 1996, s 203(4)* or the *Employment Rights (Northern Ireland) Order 1996, art 245(5)*).

It is essential that if the second alternative of the second condition is to be satisfied there must be a settlement agreement (ie compromise agreement) and it must contain two terms. First, it must provide that the payment is to be made by the employer; secondly it must make it clear that the payment be made directly to the employee's lawyer by the employer. The agreement should also state that the legal costs concerned relate exclusively to the termination of the employee's contract and not to any other matters. Care must therefore be taken in the drafting of such compromise agreements. The fees of accountants and other professionals must not be settled direct by the employer, otherwise the exception will not apply; such expenses should be billed as the lawyer's disbursements and settled by him out of the payment made to him by the employer. Also the employee should not first pay his solicitor and then seek reimbursement from his employer if the exception is to apply.

Counselling and other outplacement services

15.58   When an employee loses his employment, his employer may pay for him to receive professional advice and assistance designed to help him cope with his new situation and find a new job. Such professional advice is known as outplacement counselling and may consist of anything from a single advisory interview to ongoing assistance for a period of several months. It is a fairly common feature of redundancy packages offered by employers.

15.59   Payments for counselling services which meet certain conditions qualify for exemption from the charge to income tax levied on all categories of employment income comprising the scheme of legislative provisions dealing with termination payments (and so on residual termination payments in particular) (*ITEPA 2003, s 310*). No liability to income tax arises in respect of:

(a)   the provision of services to a person in connection with the cessation of the person's employment; or

(b)   the payment or reimbursement of:

    (i)   fees for such provision, or

    (ii)   travelling expenses incurred in connection with such provision,

if Conditions A to D and, in the case of travel expenses, Condition E are met.

15.60   Condition A is satisfied if the only or main purpose of the provision of the services is to enable the person either to adjust to the cessation of the employment or to find other gainful employment (including self-employment), or indeed both of these matters.

Condition B is met if the services consist wholly of any of the following:

(a)   giving advice and guidance;

(b)   imparting or improving skills;

(c)   providing or making available the use of office equipment or similar facilities.

Condition C is met if the person provided with the services has been employed full time in the employment which is ceasing throughout the period of two years at the time when the services begin to be provided or, if earlier, at the time when the employment ceases.

Condition D is met if the opportunity to receive the services, on similar terms as to payment or reimbursement of any expenses incurred in connection with their provision, is available generally to employees or former employees of the person's employer in that employment or to a particular class or classes of them.

Condition E is met if the travel expenses are expenses in respect of which mileage allowance relief would be available if no mileage allowance payments had been made or which would be deductible as expenses of the employment under *ITEPA 2003, Pt 5.*

Condition E operates off the back of an assumption that receiving the services is one of the duties of the employee's employment, the employee incurs and pays the expenses and the employment continues even though it may, in fact, have ceased.

Retraining courses

15.61   *ITEPA 2003, s 311(1)* provides that no liability to income tax arises under any category of employment income comprising the scheme of legislative provisions dealing with termination payments (and so including the residual category of termination payments in particular) in respect of the payment or reimbursement of retraining course expenses (including certain travel expenses) by a person ('the employer') if a number of conditions are met. There are four categories of conditions that have to be satisfied in order for the exemption to be available:

(a)   conditions relating to the employer;

(b)   conditions relating to the expenses;

(c)   the course conditions; and

(d)   the employment conditions.

Conditions relating to the employer

15.62   The employer must incur expenditure in paying or reimbursing qualifying expenses (see **15.63**). Clearly, such expenditure will have been incurred by him where he has actually paid the expenses or reimbursed someone else. The condition is also satisfied where the employer has the obligation to pay or reimburse the expenses.

There is no bar on who pays the course provider. It could be the employer for he would then satisfy the condition that he pays the relevant expenses. However, if the employee or another person pays the expenses initially, his expenses must be reimbursed by the employer. The employee or other person is not allowed merely to take a deduction from his earnings for his expenditure; reimbursement is essential.

Conditions relating to the expenses

15.63   The expenses to which the exemption relates must be within the following list (*ITEPA 2003, s 311(2)*):

(a)   fees for attendance of the employee at a training course;

(b)   fees for any examination which is taken during or at the conclusion of the course;

(c)   the cost of any books which are essential for a person attending the course; and

(d)   travelling expenses incurred in connection with the course.

Any expenses incurred that do not fall within this list and which are paid or reimbursed by the employer are outside the scope of the exemption and will, in the absence of the application of any of the other categories of employment income comprising the scheme of legislative provisions dealing with termination payments, fall into charge to tax as residual termination benefits or payments.

As regards (d) above, the travel expenses must be expenses in respect of which mileage allowance relief (see *ITEPA 2003, Pt 4, Ch 2*) would be available if no mileage allowance payments had been made or which would be deductible as expenses of the employment under *ITEPA 2003, Pt 5* (*ITEPA 2003, s 311(5)*).

The conditions relating to qualifying expenses operate off the back of an assumption that attendance at the course is one of the duties of the employee's employment, that the employee incurs and pays the expenses, and that the employee continues to be employed by the employer even if his employment has, in fact, ceased (*ITEPA 2003, s 311(6)*).

The course conditions

15.64 *ITEPA 2003, s 311(3)* provides that the course must be a qualifying training course in that it must:

(a) provide training designed to impart or improve skills or knowledge relevant to, and intended to be used in the course of, gainful employment, including self-employment, of any description;

(b) be entirely devoted to the teaching or practical application of such skills or knowledge (or to both such teaching and practical applications); and

(c) not exceed two years in duration.

The employment conditions

15.65 In order to qualify for exemption all the following conditions in *ITEPA 2003, s 311(4)* relating to the employee must be satisfied.

The employee must:

(a) begin the course while he is employed by the employer or within one year of ceasing to be employed by the employer;

(b) either have left the employment before the course begins or have left the employment not later than the end of the period of two years beginning at the end of the course;

(c) not be re-employed by the employer within a period of two years of the employment ceasing;

799

(d)   be employed by the employer throughout the period of two years up to the time he begins to undertake the course or, if it is earlier, at the time he ceases to be employed by the employer; and

(e)   have been given the opportunity to attend the course and have the cost met or reimbursed by the employer on the same terms as offered to employees or former employees generally or to a particular class or classes of employee or former employee.

If an employee's liability to tax has been determined on the assumption that *ITEPA 2003, s 311* applies and subsequently condition (a) is not met because he fails to begin the course within one year after ceasing to be employed or conditions (b) and (c) of the above employment conditions are not met because of his continued employment or re-employment, then HMRC will withdraw the exemption and raise an assessment to collect any tax due (*ITEPA 2003, s 312*). It is HMRC's view, however, that the *ITEPA 2003, s 311* exemption is not withdrawn or withheld if an employee does not find a job or start a business or if the employment or self-employment subsequently undertaken is in a field unconnected with the course, so long as all the other conditions are satisfied.

Example 15.14 – Retraining courses

An individual is employed by Traill Ltd. His employment commenced on 1 April 2016 and was terminated by reason of redundancy on 1 January 2018. As part of the individual's redundancy package, Traill Ltd pays the qualifying costs of a qualifying retraining course. The course began on 1 July 2018 and ended three months' later. The costs incurred by Traill Ltd will not be exempt under *ITEPA 2003, s 311*. Although the course began on 1 July 2018 which was within one year after the end of the employment which occurred on 1 January 2018 and the employee had ceased to be employed before the course began, he was in employment for the period 1 April 2016 to 1 January 2018 (the date of cessation of employment being taken as it is earlier than 1 July 2018 when the course started) and this was not a period of two years' continuous employment. Hence the employment conditions for the application of the exemption are not satisfied.

Long-service awards

15.66   *ITEPA 2003, s 323* provides that no liability to income tax arises under any category of employment income in respect of a long-service award which meets the following conditions:

(a)   The award must be made to an employee to mark not less than 20 years' service with the same employer. Service is treated as being with the same employer if it is with two or more employers, each of whom is a successor or predecessor of the others, or one of whom is a company which belongs or has belonged to the same group as the others or a predecessor or successor of the others. A group comprises a body corporate and its 51% subsidiaries.

(b)   The amount of employment income which would be charged to tax in respect of the award apart from the exemption does not exceed £50 for each year of service in respect of which the award is made. If the amount of the award exceeds this ceiling, then the excess only is outside the scope of the exemption and charged to income tax accordingly.

(c)   The award must take one of the following forms – tangible moveable property, shares in a company which is, or belongs to the same group (as defined above) as, the employer; or the provision of any other benefit except a cash payment, a cash voucher, a credit token, securities, shares other than those just mentioned, or an interest in or rights over securities or shares.

This means that, for example, cash, cheques, premium bonds, National Savings Certificates and options over any shares may not be given as a long-service award; however, non-cash vouchers (eg travel tickets) are not excluded and may be so given, as may most other non-cash awards, including land, intellectual property or other intangible assets (eg the benefit of a contract such as the provision of a holiday). If a non-cash award fails to meet the conditions of the exemption or exceeds the monetary limit, then the employer may be prepared to pay the tax arising under a PAYE Settlement Agreement (treating the award as a minor benefit – see SP 5/96).

15.67   The exemption for long-service awards does not apply to a later award if an earlier award to mark a particular period of service with the same employer has been made to the employee in the period of ten years ending with the date on which the later award is made (*ITEPA 2003, s 323(4)*).

So the first time that a long-service award is made is after 20 years' service. On this occasion the maximum tax-free amount is £1,000. Thereafter, awards may only be made at ten-yearly intervals, but the calculation of the tax-free element of the award may take into account all years of service down to that later anniversary. So, an award made to an employee on the anniversary of 30 years' service may be tax free up to £1,500, even though an earlier award of £1,000 was made to him at the 20-year anniversary.

The time limits imposed by the section mean that it is likely that the exemption will be used only once or twice in a typical working life time. No exemption is due if an employee has received another long service award, for service with the same employer, within the previous 10 years. An employee who receives an award after 25 years and then again after 30 years, cannot benefit from the exemption for the award given on the 30-year anniversary because the 10-year rule is not satisfied. In the application of the 10-year rule it does not matter if the earlier award did or did not qualify for exemption. All earlier awards in respect of service with the same employer are taken into account for the purpose of the 10-year test, whether taxed or not.

Despite its restrictions, this exemption is quite valuable when used in connection with the termination of an employee's employment in the appropriate circumstances.

Example 15.15 – Long service awards (see EIM01510)

An employee receives long service awards from her employer as follows (all the awards being made on or after 13 June 2003):

- after 20 years' service, an article costing £1,000

- after 30 years' service, an article costing £500

- after 35 years' service, an article costing £625

- after 40 years' service, an article costing £1,000

The application of the exemption for long services awards is as follows:

The 20-year award is not taxed. This is the first award received, the 20 year condition is satisfied, and the cost does not exceed £50 for each year of service (20 × £50 = £1,000). If the article had cost £1,500, tax would have been charged on the excess over £1,000.

The 30-year award is not taxed. It satisfies the conditions for exemption and it does not matter that the employee has already received a tax-free award.

The 35-year award is taxed in full. It is within the monetary limit (35 × £50 = £1,750), but no exemption is due because the employee received a similar award within the previous 10 years.

The 40-year award is taxed in full. It is within the monetary limit (40 × £50 = £2,000), but no exemption is due because the employee received a similar award within the previous 10 years. The 35-year award is counted even though it was taxed in full.

TERMINATION PAYMENTS WITHIN THE OTHER CATEGORIES OF EMPLOYMENT INCOME

Introduction

15.68　The other categories of employment income into which termination payments may fall have been listed in **15.3**. Attention now focuses on dealing with each of those other categories in turn in the order in which they should be applied in ascertaining the treatment of a termination payment (see **15.3**) and discussing the types of payments that come within them. As intimated in **15.4**, it may be the case that the terms of the employment relationship between an employer and his employee (which were agreed upon at the time their relationship commenced) are such that the parties have little or no choice as to which category of employment income is applicable to a termination payment made by the employer to his employee. However, even if a payment falls to be treated otherwise than as a residual termination payment, it should not be forgotten to consider whether there are any exemptions available in respect of the category of employment income into which it falls.

Earnings from employment

15.69　Termination payments which are in the nature of rewards for services or which are attributable only to the employer-employee relationship are payments that fall to be taxed as earnings from employment (see *ITEPA 2003, s 9(6)*) notwithstanding the time of making the payment is deferred to the end of the employment or a time following that. The main types of payment within this category that will be discussed in this chapter are set out in **Table 15.3**.

Table 15.3 – Termination payments that are earnings

- Deferred remuneration
- Payments made pursuant to express terms of service
- Contractual PILONs
- Payments made pursuant to implied terms of service
- Payments that are expected on account of employer behaviour
- Payments for employment-related rights
- Payments for garden leave
- Payments under certain compromise agreements
- Termination payments that are inducement payments
- Ex gratia payments

Where, however, a payment is not in the nature of a reward for services or is not one which is attributable only to the employer-employee relationship, it will not be earnings. In *A v HMRC* [2015] UKFTT 189 (TC) a payment which was made to settle a claim for race discrimination was held not to be earnings from employment. Although HMRC had argued that the payment was designed to make good shortfalls in salary and bonus received by the taxpayer and was therefore earnings, the Tribunal found that the payment was made to settle his claim for race discrimination and so was not earnings, being as it was not a reward for services but a sum paid for some reason other than just the employment relationship. This was so even though the payment was calculated by reference to underpaid earnings. The Tribunal stated that while the discrimination may have manifested itself through the way in which the employee was remunerated, the compensation payment arose not because the employee was under-remunerated but because the underpayment was discriminatory.

Deferred remuneration

15.70   Where a contract of service provides expressly or impliedly that a payment is to be made upon the termination of the contract, and the payment is described as (or on a proper construction of the terms of the contract is in substance) a payment of deferred remuneration for services rendered, then such a sum is taxable as earnings 'from' the employment (*Allen and Another (as Murray's Executors) v Trehearne (HM Inspector of Taxes)* 22 TC 15; *Henry v Foster* 16 TC 605). Such a payment cannot therefore be a residual termination payment.

Payments made pursuant to express terms of service

15.71   The terms upon which an employee serves may expressly provide that a payment is to be made to him upon termination of his employment. The source of such terms is not limited to the contract of employment itself, but includes all sources which contain the terms of an employee's engagement, including a company's articles of association, staff handbooks, trade union agreements, oral arrangements and so on.

Payments made pursuant to such express terms are earnings from employment (*Dale (H M Inspector of Taxes) v de Soissons* 32 TC 118; *Williams (Inspector of Taxes) v Simmons* [1981] STC 715). The specific example of a payment falling within this head, namely a statutory PILON, is dealt with separately below.

Excepted from such categorisation is a payment made under a genuine, non-statutory redundancy scheme whether the scheme is brought into existence and the payment is determined and paid at the time of redundancy or whether the payment is made at the time of redundancy but in accordance with a scheme that has been provided for in an employee's contract of employment and so part and parcel of the conditions under which he has given service during the subsistence of his contract (see **15.10**). Such payments may count, however, towards the earnings-component of a chargeable residual termination payment. (see **15.25**).

Contractual PILONs

Focus

It is often assumed that a contractual PILON clause in an employment contract is an absolute bar to the application of the residual category of employment income to a termination payment made under the clause. It is a fundamental misconception that once a contract of employment contains a provision for a PILON, it becomes impossible for there to be a wrongful dismissal and hence a payment that is a residual termination payment (see **15.74**). But care must be exercised here as there may be other adverse employment law consequences where an employer breaches a contract.

15.72 In the present context a payment in lieu of notice is one paid under a contract of service which expressly provides that an employment may be terminated either by notice or, on payment of a sum in lieu of notice, summarily. The following is an example of such a clause:

Pay in lieu of notice

'(1)   One party has the duty to give three months' notice to the other of his intention to terminate the contract.

(2)   However, the employer reserves the right to terminate the contract without giving notice upon the payment of three months' salary in lieu of notice.'

15.73   The clause bestows upon an employer the freedom to choose which of the two methods provided for in the contract he will use to end the contract. When the choice is made there will be no breach of contract, the employer having infringed none of the employee's rights (*Rex Stewart Jeffries Parker Ginsberg Ltd v Parker* [1988] IRLR 483; *Abrahams v Performing Rights Society Ltd, The Times,* 5 June 1995; *Delaney v Staples* [1992] 1 All ER 944). The freedom here is created by the parties themselves and the effect is that it absolves the employer from the duty which he would otherwise have had under clause (1). Once the employer has made his choice, only then does he

15.74 *Payments made on the termination of employment*

fall under a contractual duty. Under choice (1), the employer is obliged to give notice (*Woolridge v Sumner* [1962] 2 All ER 978) and to allow the employment relationship to subsist for the agreed period. Under choice (2) the employer is under a duty to make a payment.

15.74 The payment of a sum in lieu of notice in this context is a payment of earnings from employment (*EMI Group Electronics Ltd v Coldicott (Inspector of Taxes)* [1999] STC 803). Such a payment is made in pursuance of a contractual provision, agreed at the outset of employment (or subsequently by variation of the employment contract), which enables the employer to terminate the employment on making that payment. The employee is entitled under the bargain struck at commencement of employment (or at the time of the subsequent variation of its terms) either to security or continuity of employment – or the security or continuity of salary – for a given period or to an additional payment on summary termination. In both cases the terms are agreed upon as terms under which service will be given by the employee and so the payment made under those terms falls squarely within the tests laid down by the House of Lords in *Hochstrasser v Mayes* 38 TC 673 as a payment made in return for acting as or being an employee and in *Shilton v Wilmshurst* 46 TC 78 as being an emolument from being or becoming an employee. This is the case whether that term was part of the contract of employment from the outset (as in the *EMI Group Electronics Ltd* case itself) or whether it was introduced by a subsequent amendment (for example, as in *SCA Packaging Ltd v RCC* [2007] STC 1640). Although such a clause reduces the scope for dispute where termination of employment occurs, the tax treatment of a payment that might be made under it needs to be understood when the contract is signed as the clause restricts the planning opportunities of the parties when the contract ends (see **15.6**).

The above principle does not apply where a contract contains an express provision permitting early termination of a fixed-term contract by mutual consent and the parties agree that, on the employer making a payment, the contract will be terminated. In such a case the employee is not receiving the security, or continuity, of salary which he required as an inducement to enter the employment. This is because the parties' right to terminate a contract arises as a result of general contract law; it does not come from the contract itself. Moreover, an employee entering into such a contract has no greater security or continuity of salary that he would obtain by entering into a fixed-term contract which did not expressly include a right to terminate by mutual agreement. Therefore, an employee employed under such a contract is in the same position as one employed under a fixed-term contract that is silent as to the circumstances in which it is terminated early (*Tottenham Hotspur Ltd v HMRC* [2016] UKFTT 389 (TC), [2017] UKUT 453). Payments made under compromise agreements that bring to end a contract of employment by mutual consent are payments that fall into the residual category (see **15.12**).

15.75   Even where a contract of employment contains a contractual PILON clause, on the authority of *Cerberus Software Ltd v Rowley* [2001] IRLR 160, it is still open to the employer to breach the term of an employment contract providing for a contractual PILON (although the employer will lose the benefit of any restrictive covenants in the contract). The employer may both dismiss the employee summarily and fail to make the PILON. The Court of Appeal has in these circumstances held that the employee has no automatic right to the payment in lieu of notice; his claim is for damages and he is under an obligation to mitigate his loss. In such a case, any subsequent payment by the employer to remedy such a breach or any payment of damages awarded by a tribunal or court to compensate for such a breach should be treated as a residual termination payment (see **15.16**, **15.18** and **15.19** respectively).

In *Tax Bulletin*, Issue 63 (February 2003), HMRC acknowledge this position but warn that it is crucial to establish and examine the facts in cases where it is claimed a contract with a contractual PILON clause has been breached and that damages have been paid instead of the payment promised in the contract. They list the following factors that need to be taken into account as guidelines in determining the matter.

(a)   Although each case will depend upon its own facts, a settlement that is substantially the same in value as an exercise of the discretion would have produced is likely to be viewed as made by exercise of the discretion. They cite the case of *Richardson v Delaney* [2001] STC 1328 (see **15.84**) as an example of this – that in the absence of an identifiable breach of contract, the source of the payment lies in the employer's discretion to make a payment. They say that the case demonstrates that a payment made by the exercise of the employer's discretion need not be made precisely in either the sum or in the form provided for by the contract.

(b)   A payment resulting from a decision not to exercise discretion could be expected to have characteristics normally associated with compensation or damages for breach of contract rather than those associated with a contract payment.

   (i)   One such characteristic is apparent in *Cerberus* where the payment was reduced (or mitigated) to reflect the fact that the employee had secured alternative employment before the end of the notice period and by doing so had reduced the loss or damage caused by the employer's breach.

   (ii)   Other adjustments are common when calculating such payments, for example, to reflect the difference in tax and NIC consequences between an emolument from employment (taxable and liable for Class 1 NICs) and a payment of damages (taxed and liable to Class 1 NICs according to the rules that apply to the residual category of termination payments – see **15.24**).

(iii) A damages payment will normally take into account all salary and benefits that would have been available in the notice period.

(c) A decision by an employer not to exercise its discretion might be evidenced in writing.

All factors need to be weighed in the balance in deciding whether the discretion has been exercised. Essentially the matter is a question of fact (see **15.84** for cases where the discretion has been treated as exercised). Problems in deciding the correct position are often caused by incomplete documentation of the events surrounding termination and the calculation of the payment made.

Payments made pursuant to implied terms of service

15.76 The above discussion of the tax treatment of payments made pursuant to express terms of service may, of course, apply equally to payments made pursuant to implied terms of service. In this context, an implied term is one properly implied as a matter of contract law.

As a matter of contract law, a term will be implied if a court can presume that it would have been the intention of the parties to include it in the agreement. In order to make such a presumption, the court must be satisfied that:

(a) the term is necessary to give the contract business efficacy; or

(b) it is the normal custom and practice to include such a term in the contract; or

(c) the term is implied by the conduct of the parties; or

(d) the term is so obvious because the parties must have intended it.

15.77 As a matter of contract law, terms may be implied into employment contracts if they are regularly (but not necessarily universally) adopted in a particular trade or industry, in a particular locality or by a particular employer. It will be assumed that the parties were aware of the custom and tacitly agreed that it should be part of their contract without any need to put it in writing (*Sagar v H Ridehalgh & Son Ltd* [1931] 1 Ch 310). So, the usual requirement for a term to be implied by custom and practice is that the custom must be reasonable, notorious and certain. This means it must be fair and not arbitrary, that it must be generally established and well known, and that it must be clear-cut. Where a practice is discretionary, the fact that it had been carried out for a number of years will not necessarily convert it into an implied term. In *Quinn v Calder Industrial Materials Ltd* [1996] IRLR 125 (EAT) it was held that redundant employees had no implied right to enhanced redundancy payments. The employers' policy of making such payments was not incorporated into any agreement and details of the policy had never been communicated to the employees. Although the policy had been followed in every case over a period of years, the payment remained discretionary. In *Pellowe v Pendragon plc* EAT 804/98, the employers had for 20 years given redundant employees a payment greater than their statutory redundancy pay. The chart for calculating the amount was contained in a management manual which was not publicised to staff. An employee who was paid only statutory redundancy pay sued for a larger amount but it was held that he had not acquired a contractual right, through custom and practice, to the enhanced payment. It had not been made known to staff that they would receive enhanced payments and so the term could not be said to be notorious.

Another way in which an implied term might come into being is to look at how the parties have operated the contract of employment in practice. This approach may demonstrate that the contract had been performed in such a way as to suggest that a particular term existed (*Mears v Safecar Security Ltd* [1982] ICR 626).

15.78 HMRC adopt a very robust practice in this regard and seek to treat as earnings any termination payment which an employee expects to receive, without much concern for the detailed application of the presumptions that bring about the existence of an implied term. However, what the above cases show is the high degree of certainty and knowledge required before a term becomes an implied term of a contract, and so practitioners should rely on this to test an allegation by HMRC that a payment is taxable as earnings from employment on the grounds that it is expected. This point was made in *Clinton v RCC* [2010] UKFTT 337 (TC) where HMRC argued that the taxpayer expected a termination payment pursuant to an implied term in her contract of employment and so was taxable in respect of it as her earnings. Judge Aleksander noted that the threshold for custom and practice to have the effect of implying terms into employment agreements is high. 'Expectation' in the context of employment law means more than a mere hope (akin to the expectation of a legacy under a will) – the expectation has to rise to the level of an enforceable contractual certainty. It is submitted therefore that HMRC would have to show that the expectation is held on the part of every employee in the employment of the employer in question because they knew of the practice and that they had a reasonable expectation of receiving the payment upon the termination of their employment. Alternatively, there must be a well-established custom.

15.79 Despite their practice regarding payments that are expected by an employee, it is useful to note that, as stated in *Tax Bulletin*, Issue 63 (February 2003), HMRC accept that it is unlikely that an implied term in relation to payment in lieu of notice can exist. It is stated that contract law suggests that if something conflicts with an express or written contractual term, then it cannot be implied. Since contracts generally include a right to receive notice of termination of employment (whether directly or through the application of the *ERA 1996*), then an implied right to receive a payment in lieu of notice would appear to conflict with the express term that the employee is entitled to receive notice of termination. So where an employer regularly dismisses employees summarily, it cannot be argued that payments in lieu of notice made to compromise actions for breach of contract are made under an implied term of their contracts.

Payments that are expected on account of employer behaviour (auto-PILONs)

Focus

HMRC are very quick to allege (even on the slightest pretext) that a termination payment made to an employee is expected by him and hence is to be taxed as earnings from employment. However, this is not a settled area of the law and careful consideration should be given to this and the preceding paragraphs on implied terms of service.

15.80 Despite acknowledging payments made under an implied term of a contract of employment and the difficulty of identifying such a term, HMRC contend that a termination payment made automatically, habitually or by practice may be chargeable as an employee's earnings otherwise than under an implied term of his employment contract.

At EIM12977 they cite as an example an employer that makes a payment for any notice period that is not worked where nothing is written down about the payment. They say that this may be described as a custom, habit, practice or expectation and that if the payment is made as an automatic response it is arguable that the payment is earnings (although it is acknowledged that damages paid in this way are not treated as earnings).

HMRC go on and say that if the payment is not one of damages then the fact that an individual employee does not know about the practice is not crucial; what is more important is whether it is part of the employment relationship where the individual works, namely whether it is perceived as a normal part of the employer–employee relationship rather than as a specific response to not receiving due notice at that time. It is less important, they say, how long the practice has been in place than whether it is an automatic part of the employment. So where it is clear that an employer intends to follow a particular path in the future, a practice can come into being very quickly.

However, it is not HMRC policy to argue for this treatment where there is a procedure for making a genuine critical assessment in the making of a payment, so that they are not made automatically. They give as an example the case where an employer makes PILONs instead of giving notice, but where each payment is looked at under an internal written procedure that assesses what payment is to be made. The result is that some employees may be forced to sue for compensation or some may receive less than the equivalent gross salary and benefits. HMRC observe that a critical assessment will essentially seek to identify adjustments typical of a damages payment. Such PILONs are dealt with as damages (which are residual termination payments – see **15.17–15.19**), because an individual employee cannot be certain that a payment equal to salary due in the notice period will automatically be made and so is not part of the working relationship between employer and employee. Such adjustments are not mandatory and an employer may have valid commercial reasons not to make them (eg in a large-scale programme where employees predominantly have short notice periods, the gain from making adjustments might be outweighed by the cost of doing so and the potential bad feeling generated in the workforce may also be a factor). Any such reasons must be taken into account when deciding whether the character of the payment is that of damages.

Payments for employment-related rights

15.81   An employee's termination package may contain an amount paid in lieu of holidays to which he was entitled but had not taken by the time he left employment. In some cases this is because the employee had a contractual right to such a payment. Such payments are earnings from employment and taxable as such (*ITEPA 2003, s 9(6)*) because they are payments made to compensate for the loss of a right directly connected with an employee's employment (ie if the employment did not exist there would have been no right to take holidays) (*Hamblett v Godfrey (Inspector of Taxes)* [1987] STC 60). Even where a right to such a payment does not exist, nevertheless, payments made voluntarily by the employer may also be charged as the employee's earnings because they arise from the employer–employee relationship and for no other reason (*Laidler v Perry (Inspector of Taxes)* 42 TC 351).

'Garden leave' payments

15.82   'Garden leave' is a colloquialism used to describe the case where an employer, in fulfilment of obligations under a contract of service, gives due notice of termination to an employee. The employee's right to receive notice will therefore have been observed. The contract remains in force and will come to an end only at the expiry of the notice period. However, at the start of, or during the course of, the notice period, the employee is asked to remain at home and is told that he will not be called upon to render any service until the termination date. This device of garden leave is useful where the employer wishes to keep the employee bound by the covenants of the contract (eg those relating to confidentiality and fidelity) and yet take the employee out of the marketplace for a short period so that he cannot work for competitors. The employer waives the right to call on the employee to render service, but it does not absolve him from the duty to pay the remuneration to which the employee is entitled. At the same time that the employer tells the employee no longer to report for duty, he gives the employee, as a lump sum, the remuneration attributable to the notice period (ie there is an advance payment of remuneration). This is sometimes referred to as a PILON.

15.83   Regardless of the terminology used, viewed from the perspective of the employee, there is no reason for the receipt of the payment other than the employer–employee relationship, and so the payment is earnings from employment and cannot be a residual termination payment (*Ibe v McNally* [2005] STC 1426).

Payments under certain compromise agreements

15.84   This category of earnings arises from the case of *Richardson (Inspector of Taxes) v Delaney* [2001] STC 1328. The taxpayer had been employed under a service agreement which included a contractual PILON clause (see **15.72**). The employer gave the employee notice. Whilst he was serving his notice, an agreement was made by the parties to end the contract of employment before the expiry of the notice period on the payment of an agreed sum. The court held that the payment was taxable as earnings and not taxable as a residual termination payment under a compromise agreement (see **15.12**). The effect of the compromise agreement in this case (and indeed in the later cases of *Goldman v RCC* [2012] UKFTT 313 (TC) and *Manley v RCC* [2013] UKFTT 99 (TC)) was to fructify the terms of the service agreement, in particular the PILON clause. In other words, the compromise agreement was the mechanism by which the PILON clause was effected, or putting it another way, there was effectively the specific performance of the contract of employment. It does not matter that the payment made under the compromise agreement does not equal the amount provided for in the contract of employment if the compromise agreement was aimed at enforcing, to the maximum amount attainable, the employee's contractual entitlement. The fact that an employee is unable as a practical matter to obtain full enforcement of his contractual entitlement and is obliged to settle for less is not a relevant factor in deciding whether the payment is earnings.

15.85   Notwithstanding doubt being expressed both in the courts and by the profession about the correctness of the *Richardson* case, it has not been expressly overruled. So, in order to avoid the decision in *Richardson* applying in any case, it is important that a replication of the precise facts of the case should be avoided where a compromise agreement is used to bring a contract of service to an end. In other words, where an employment contract gives an employer the liberty of choosing to end the contract either by the giving of notice or by the payment of a sum in lieu, a compromise agreement between the parties must be avoided once notice has been given. Unless this is done, then *Richardson* is likely to apply to a payment made under such an agreement, and accordingly it will not be taxable as a residual termination payment.

15.86   The case is, however, unlikely to apply to determine the taxation of payments made in the following circumstances which are distinguishable from the facts of *Richardson*:

(a)   where a contract of service gives an employer the liberty of choosing to end the contract either by the giving of notice or by the payment of a sum in lieu, and a compromise agreement is entered into without the exercise of this liberty at all (see **15.12**) (now confirmed in *Brander v RCC* [2007] STC (SCD) 582, in which case the amounts actually paid under a compromise agreement exceeded the amounts payable under the contract of employment);

(b)   where a contract of service provides only for the giving of notice to bring the contract to an end, and a compromise agreement is entered into whether before or after such notice has been given (see **15.15**);

(c)   where a contract of service has been wrongfully or unfairly ended by an employer, legal proceedings have been initiated by the employee, and a compromise agreement is entered into between the parties to settle the dispute out of court (see **15.16**);

(d)   where a contract of service which gives an employer the liberty of choosing to end the contract either by the giving of notice or by the payment of a sum in lieu, is amended to remove these clauses from the contract, and subsequently a compromise agreement is struck to terminate the employment (see **15.12**). However, the pitfalls associated with compromise agreements that vary an employment contract must be avoided (see **15.14**).

The effect of the case is also avoided if a contract of service is breached and a payment is made by an employer as damages or compensation for that breach (see **15.17** and **15.75**). There may be employment law reasons why, in any particular case, this may not be a viable way of proceeding in order to avoid the effects of *Richardson*, but it is nonetheless a possibility to be considered (but see **15.75** above).

Termination payments that are inducement payments

15.87   Care needs to be exercised where a payment made on the termination of employment is a form of inducement to an employee to take up service with another employer. In *Shilton v Wilmshurst* [1991] STC 88 the taxpayer was employed by a football club which negotiated his transfer to another club. In order to induce the taxpayer to agree to the move, the first club promised to make a payment to him when he left. The payment was held to be a reward for future services and taxable as earnings from his (future) employment. (Also see *Glantre Engineering Ltd v Goodhand (Inspector of Taxes)* [1983] STC 1.)

Particularly vulnerable to this treatment are payments made by a new employer to an employee to compensate him for the loss of rights connected with his former employment (eg loss of deferred remuneration rights contingent on his remaining in employment) (*Teward v IRC* [2001] STC (SCD) 36). By contrast, however, payments that are made to a new employee to compensate him for giving up benefits of a personal nature (unconnected with any service he may render) are not treated as earnings (*Jarrold (HM Inspector of Taxes) v Boustead* (1964) 41 TC 701; *Pritchard (HM Inspector of Taxes) v Arundale* (1971) 47 TC 680).

Ex gratia payments

15.88　It may be the case that an ex gratia payment (ie a gift) made to an employee on the termination of employment is taxable as earnings. In *McBride v Blackburn (Inspector of Taxes)* [2003] STC (SCD) 139, having reviewed the authorities, the Special Commissioner listed the following occasions when this might be the correct treatment of a gift:

(a)　if it is received by an employee in respect of the discharge of his duties;

(b)　if it accrues by virtue of the employment or if it is in return for acting in the employment;

A payment is not taxable however if it retains its characteristics as a gift (ie an exercise of bounty intended to benefit the donee for reasons personal to him), even though it is given in recognition of services rendered. Also a gift is not taxable if it is peculiarly due to the personal qualities of the recipient or if it is to mark his participation in an exceptional event. Relevant factors to be taken into account in determining the tax treatment of a gift are: whether the payment is made by the employer; whether the office is at an end; whether other remuneration is paid; whether the payment is exceptional; whether there is an element of recurrence; and whether the recipient is entitled to the payment (see *Moore v Griffiths (H M Inspector of Taxes)* 48 TC 338).

In *Collins v RCC* [2012] UKFTT 411 (TC), a gift was made by the owner of a company to a former employee four years after he had left employment and about two years after the company had been sold. The payment was expressed to recognise the friendship between the owner and former employee as well as his contribution and dedication to the success of the company.

The First-tier Tribunal held that the payment was not the former employee's earnings. They cited the following reasons for reaching this conclusion: that the payment of $2m was wholly disproportionate to the salary of £150,000 per annum formerly earned by the employee and was not a supplement to an inadequate salary; the former employee had no expectation of receiving the gift; there was no indication that any other payment would be made (ie it would not recur); the payment was not made by the former employer but by a shareholder of the employer; the payment was not made in connection with the termination of the former employee's employment; and the payment was made by a generous person from the proceeds of sale of the shares in the company.

Category (b) above is the category that may be relevant to the discussion on auto-PILONs and holiday pay in **15.80** and **15.81** above.

The benefits code

General

15.89   Benefits given to an employee on the termination of employment will not be treated as residual termination payments where they are taxable under the benefits code. The benefits code in *ITEPA 2003, Pt 3, Chs 2–10* applies, generally speaking, only during the currency of an employment (ie benefits must be received or enjoyed whilst the employee is in employment). Consequently, as a general rule the code does not apply to benefits to be enjoyed after the termination of employment, even though their provision may be agreed upon whilst the employment is still in existence. So, for example, the code will apply where the employee enjoys benefits whilst on garden leave, but will not apply where the benefit in kind is given as part of a compromise agreement to be enjoyed after the termination of his employment.

At EIM12815, HMRC confirm that as a matter of practice benefits that straddle the termination of employment should be apportioned on a time basis, those falling after termination being taxed as a residual termination payment (where appropriate). For example, an employer pays a non-refundable lump-sum premium of £12,000 into a health scheme for his (higher paid) employee on 6 April 2018 to cover the provision of health care until 5 April 2019. That employee is dismissed on 5 January 2019. He will be charged to tax under the benefits code on only three-quarters of the premium.

15.90   The general rule just described is subject to an important exception in the case of the release or the write-off of an employment-related loan (*ITEPA 2003, s 188(2)*) (see **15.92–15.95**).

Benefits as residual termination payments

15.91 Benefits in kind given to employees as part of their termination package that do not fall under the benefits code are likely to be residual termination payments (unless they are given as consideration for the giving by the employee of a restrictive undertaking) (**15.97–15.99**). *ITEPA 2003, Pt 6, Ch 3* contains its own mini benefits code (*ITEPA 2003, s 402*) under which the quantification of benefits follows the benefits code itself. Where a benefit in kind falls to be treated as a residual termination payment on the termination of any employment on or after 6 April 2018, it is aggregated with other residual termination payments made on that occasion and may form part of the earnings component of the residual termination payment (see **15.25**). The legislation does not provide rules for determining to what extent each component should be treated as comprising part of the benefit.

However, it should be appreciated that the mini code is wider than the main code and it is unlikely that something provided as part of a termination package falls outside its scope. For example, in tax years before 2016/17, whereas lower paid employees were outwith the benefits code, benefits provided to such persons on the termination of employment become taxable as residual termination payments. Also, if a benefit is exempt from the benefits code, do not assume that it is exempt from the charge on residual termination payments. It will only be so exempt if an employment-income exemption (as opposed to an earnings-only exemption) applies in respect of it. This will depend upon the wording of each exemption described in *ITEPA 2003, Pt 4*, but typically exemptions for counselling and other outplacement services (**15.58**), retraining courses (**15.61**) and long-service awards (**15.66**) are such exemptions. Additionally, the following benefits are exempt from tax under the mini termination benefits code under *ITEPA 2003, s 402(2), (4)* (the exemption applying in respect of employments ending on or after 6 April 2018 so that none of the benefit is chargeable to tax and it does not have to be sub-divided into its earnings and non-earnings components):

(a)   benefits connected with taxable cars and vans and exempt heavy goods vehicles;

(b)   non-cash vouchers or credit tokens to obtain goods or services (or money to spend on goods or services) in connection with taxable cars or vans or exempt heavy goods vehicles;

(c)   one mobile telephone;

(d)   the right to receive a residual termination payment or benefit.

Employment-related loans

15.92   A director or employee may be given a loan at a beneficial rate of interest by reason of his employment. In such a case (ie of an employment-related loan that is a taxable cheap loan), a benefit in kind arises under *ITEPA 2003, ss 173–175* calculated by reference to the interest that would have been paid by the employee had the loan carried interest at the official rate.

A second, separate benefit arises when any employment-related loan (be it at a beneficial rate of interest or not) is released or written off in a tax year whether in whole or in part. *ITEPA 2003, s 188(1)* provides that, where, at the time of the release or write-off, the employee holds the employment in relation to which the employment is an employment-related loan, the amount released or written off is to be treated as earnings from the employment for that year.

15.93   An employee who leaves employment at a time when such a loan has not been repaid is regarded as in receipt of earnings when the loan is written off or released under the above provision by the operation of *ITEPA 2003, s 188(2)* which provides as follows:

'But if the employment has terminated … and there was a time when –

(a)   the whole or part of the loan was outstanding, and

(b)   the employee held the employment, and

(c)   [before 2016–17] the employment was not an excluded employment [ie held by a lower-paid employee],

subsection (1) applies as if the employment had not ended … '

The effect of this section is to deem the individual's employment to continue. The result is that he will be treated as being in receipt of earnings chargeable to income tax when the employment-related loan is released or written off in an amount equivalent to the amount of the loan released or written off.

15.94   It will be noted that the operation of *ITEPA 2003, ss 173–175* (ie the benefit related to the beneficial rate of interest in respect of taxable cheap loans) is not so preserved on the termination of employment; only

ITEPA 2003, s 188 (ie the benefit related to the release or writing-off of the loan) continues to operate. Since a charge to tax arises otherwise than under the provisions dealing with residual termination payments, the release or writing off of a loan cannot benefit from the exceptions and reliefs that apply to such payments. Neither can the amount written off be treated as forming any part of the non-earnings component of a residual termination payment (see **15.27**).

Example 15.16 – Benefits post-termination of employment

An employee enjoys a remuneration package which includes the provision of a £52,000 loan at a rate of interest of 2.25%. The employee, having worked his notice period, is made redundant on 31 December 2018 and receives a cash payment of £25,000 and the use of a company car until the expiry of the lease in 2020. On 5 April 2019 it is subsequently agreed that the employee will be released from the obligation to repay the loan. The official rate of interest being 2.5%, the taxable amount arising in relation to the redundancy in 2018/19 is:

	£
ITEPA 2003, s 401	
Cash payment	25,000
Loan benefit $(52,000 \times (2.5 - 2.25)\% \times 3/12)$	32
Car benefit (say)	1,675
	26,707
Less: threshold (restricted)	(26,707)
	Nil
ITEPA 2003, s 188	
Loan release	52,000
Taxable amount	52,000

The balance of the threshold of £3,293 will be carried forward to 2019/20 and used in relation to the cash equivalent of the car benefit arising as a residual termination payment in that year; it cannot be used against the charge on £52,000 arising on the release of the loan under *ITEPA 2003, s 188*.

15.95 In order to avoid the operation of *ITEPA 2003, s 188(2)* an employee may wish to pay off the loan using personal funds. Funds could be made available for this purpose by increasing the termination award through an ex gratia payment (which payment is likely to be regarded as a residual termination payment (see **15.22**)).

Also, it must be noted that *ITEPA 2003, s 188* does not apply where a release or writing off of an employment-related loan takes place on or after the death of an employee (*ITEPA 2003, s 190*). Thus, the section does not apply where an employment terminates on account of the death of the employee. In such a case the normal rules apply (see **15.89–15.90**).

Payments for restrictive undertakings

Focus

Take considerable care when drafting compromise agreements that contain restrictive undertakings. Do not inadvertently cause payments made under such agreements to become wholly or partly taxable by falling into the restrictive undertaking category of employment income (see **15.3**). In particular, follow carefully the advice contained in SP 3/96 wherever possible.

15.96   A payment made on termination of employment may be for the giving by the employee of a restrictive undertaking (ie an undertaking whereby the employee agrees to restrict his conduct once he has left employment). Prima facie such payments fall to be charged to income tax under *ITEPA 2003, s 225*. It has to be considered whether such payments can ever be residual termination payments.

Payments for conventional restrictive covenants

15.97   An employee may receive a payment in connection with the termination of his employment for agreeing to restrict his future conduct or activities after the employment comes to an end. Such covenants conventionally fall into the following categories:

(a)   non-competition covenants under which the employee undertakes not to work for a competitor or within a specified area or within a specific time;

(b)   non-solicitation covenants under which the employee undertakes not to contact former suppliers or customers or poach former colleagues;

(c)   confidentiality covenants under which the employee agrees to keep secret privileged information.

These covenants may be contained in an employee's contract of employment or in a compromise agreement made at the time the employment ends. Very often a compromise agreement reaffirms the covenants given in a contract of employment.

15.98   Where an employee receives a specific payment on the termination of his employment for making such an undertaking, that sum will be treated as earnings and not as a residual termination payment (*RCI (Europe) Ltd v Woods* [2004] STC 315).

However, very often no payment is actually allocated for agreeing to the restrictions contained in the covenants. They are merely terms of the agreement in which they are contained. As no part of any termination payment will be attributable to the giving of the covenants, *ITEPA 2003, s* 255 cannot apply (see **15.99**). Also, in some compromise agreements the departing employee is asked to confirm that the restrictions set out in his contract of employment continue to apply. If the employee does so and is given no consideration for that confirmation, then again *ITEPA 2003, s 225* cannot apply (see **15.99** and EIM03605 and EIM03606 and *Vaughan-Neil v IRC* [1979] STC 644). However, HMRC do warn that, where it is not possible to account for all of any lump-sum termination payment under the categories contained in a compromise agreement, it may be possible that an oral agreement beyond the written agreement has been reached and that some of the consideration is given for that oral agreement. In the final analysis, however, the allocation of a consideration to the giving of a restrictive covenant is a question of fact and a matter of evidence.

SP 3/96

15.99   SP 3/96 applies to undertakings contained in a financial settlement relating to the termination of an employment whereby the employee:

(a)   accepts the termination package in full and final settlement of all his outstanding claims relating to the employment; and/or

(b)   undertakes not to commence or, if already commenced, to discontinue, any legal proceedings in respect of those claims; and/or

(c)   reaffirms any covenants about his conduct or activity after termination which formed part of the terms on which the employment was taken up.

HMRC accept that where a sum is paid under a compromise agreement for the loss of employment, no portion of that amount will be attributed under *ITEPA 2003, s 225* to such undertakings.

However, care must still be exercised, as SP 3/96 does not cover the case where a severance agreement is framed in two distinct parts, the one an agreement for the payment of a sum of £X in consideration of the loss of employment, the other an agreement for the giving of a restrictive undertaking in consideration of a separate sum of £Y. The latter amount will still be taxed as earnings (*Appellant v Inspector of Taxes* [2001] STC (SCD) 21).

Compromise agreements often contain a 'repayment clause'. Such a clause provides that if the employee does later initiate proceedings before a tribunal or court – despite giving an undertaking not to do so – then the sum paid under the agreement must be repaid to the employer. HMRC will not argue that such a clause means that a sum is being attributed to the undertaking not to pursue claims. In virtually all cases, the sum paid under the agreement can be fully attributed to the settlement of the claims being dealt with. So there is no sum remaining to be attributed to that undertaking, even where there is a repayment clause. However, it should be noted that if the employee does repay such sums, there is no provision in the legislation that gives any deduction or relief for that payment.

Example 1 (see EIM03626)

An employee is made redundant by his employer. He is advised by a solicitor and enters into a 'compromise agreement' provided by *The Trade Union Reform and Employment Rights Act 1993*. The agreement contains a clause that states that the agreement is 'in full and final settlement of any and all claims that the employee may have against the former employer'. No consideration is attributed for agreeing to the clause. No other restrictive undertakings are contained in the agreement. Consideration of £40,000 is paid to the employee under the terms of the agreement.

The Inspector contends that all of the £40,000 is within *ITEPA 2003, s 225* as nothing would be paid if the employee did not agree to the restriction.

Comment

It is true that the settlement sum of £40,000 would not be paid unless the employee agreed to the conditions set out in the document. However, it is also clear that amounts within the lump sum are paid for other reasons:

- payment in lieu of notice;
- statutory redundancy pay;
- holiday pay.

The only restriction contained in the agreement is the 'in full and final settlement' clause and no consideration is attributed to that. In consequence, Statement of Practice 3/96 applies. Any part of the sum that is not earnings will fall to be treated as a residual termination payment and may attract the exemptions afforded to such payments.

Example 2 (based on EIM03620)

An employee's contract of employment contains a covenant to the effect that he shall not work within a 25-mile radius of the employer's premises or contact any customer or supplier of the employer for a period of 18 months after the termination of his employment. In a subsequent compromise agreement the employee merely confirms the conditions set out in his employment contract. *ITEPA 2003, s 225* does not apply in this case as no consideration has been paid for the giving of the undertaking and no new undertakings were made in the compromise agreement. If the compromise agreement identified a payment of say £25,000 for the re-affirmation of the covenant, then *ITEPA 2003, s 225* would have applied to the payment.

Payments from employer-financed retirement benefits schemes

Focus

The making of a gift on the termination of employment needs careful consideration. It could be taxable as a payment under an employer-financed retirement benefits scheme (especially where the recipient is retiring) or as his earnings (see **15.88**); such a payment is not automatically treated as a residual termination payment (see **15.22**). As to whether an employee is retiring is not an easy question to answer and special regard should be had to HMRC practice in this matter (see **15.107**). HMRC are quick to allege that payments are made under schemes (so as to bring them within this category of employment income) but this should be resisted in appropriate cases (see **15.101–15.103**).

15.100 The recipient of relevant benefits provided under an employer-financed retirement benefits scheme (EFRBS) is charged to income tax (*ITEPA 2003, s 393(1)*). This category of employment income is particularly relevant in the context of a termination payment where an employer makes an ex gratia payment (ie a gift) on the death or retirement of an employee (and the discussion here is limited to this case). In such a case, as the employer is making a payment direct to an employee *under* an EFRBS (and is not giving an undertaking to make a contribution *to* an EFRBS), the rules in *ITEPA 2003, Pt 7A* (Employment income provided through third parties) (the so-called 'disguised remuneration' rules) are not engaged, do not displace the application of the rules on EFRBS and do not have to be considered further.

It will be seen that three alternative arguments can be relied upon to avoid the application of this category of employment income applying to an ex gratia payment on the death or retirement of an employee – that there is no scheme under which it is made, that the payment is an excluded benefit or that the employee has not retired.

An 'employer-financed retirement benefits scheme' is a scheme for the provision of benefits consisting of or including relevant benefits to or in respect of employees or former employees of an employer (*ITEPA 2003, s 393A*). The term 'scheme' is defined as including any deed, agreement, series of agreements or other arrangements (*ITEPA 2003, s 393A(4)*). The scheme does not have to be formally constituted and it does not have to adopt any particular form.

15.101 At EIM15048, HRMC explain that a scheme includes:

(a)   a decision taken at an employers' meeting (to make a payment);

(b)   a decision taken by an employee (eg a personnel manager) with delegated authority or in accordance with a policy (to make a payment);

(c)   the making of a payment under a plan, pattern, policy, practice, decision-making process or custom.

15.102 It is not entirely clear from doubt that a payment made in these circumstances is one paid under a scheme. In *Allum v Marsh* [2005] STC (SCD) 191, the taxpayer and his wife ('the taxpayers') were the directors and shareholders of an unquoted trading company. The company voted to purchase all the shares held by the taxpayers out of distributable profits. Later the same day, the taxpayers resigned as directors leaving their son as the only director. The next day, the board agreed to make voluntary payments of £30,000 each to the taxpayers 'following the resignation due to retirement, in appreciation of their services to the company over many years'. The board also approved the contract to purchase the taxpayers' shares and cheque payments were made accordingly.

HMRC sought to assess the payments contending that the voluntary payments made by the company to the taxpayers after they ceased to be directors were payments under (what is now) an EFRBS. It was held, however, that on the facts, the payments were not paid under a scheme. The Special Commissioner stated that there was no arrangement as there was no prior formal or informal understanding with the taxpayers that the payments would be made. The matter had not previously been discussed with them and they were both surprised and gratified when the company decided to make the payment. There was no expectation of reward. There was no system, plan, pattern or policy connected with the payments. Furthermore, the request by the board to the company's accountant to budget for the payment was not the establishment of a scheme or arrangement but merely a means of ensuring that the decision taken by the board to make the payment could be implemented. Consequently, it was held that the payments were not made under an EFRBS.

15.103   In *Barclays Bank plc v RCC* [2006] STC (SCD) 100, [2007] STC 747 by contrast, the bank made payments to pensioners who had retired from employment with the bank. The payments were made by way of compensation for the termination of an arrangement whereby a subsidiary of Barclays offered to those pensioners (and their widows or widowers) a free service for the preparation of their annual tax returns. The payments were made in order to avoid an adverse reaction from the pensioners similar to one that had occurred at an earlier time when it was mooted that the service be withdrawn. The amount of the compensation was calculated according to the age of the pensioner and the complexity of his affairs. HMRC contended that the payments were benefits provided under (what is now) an EFRBS.

The Special Commissioner commented (*obiter*) that there was an arrangement and hence a scheme under which the payments were made. He made the following observations in relation to the definition of a scheme:

(a)   That arrangements need not be bilateral (as a deed can be a unilateral instrument).

(b)   That since a benefit must be received under the arrangement, the arrangement is distinct from the benefit. The components of an arrangement must have a commercial life separate from the mechanics which merely implement the conferring of the benefit under the arrangements.

(c)   The motivation that informs the conferring of a benefit is irrelevant as to whether there is a scheme. The meaning of scheme or arrangement calls attention to whether there is a construct comprised of one or more elements. The motivation behind the construct plays no part in informing the meaning of scheme or arrangement.

(d)   Whether or not there is an arrangement or scheme is a question of fact. Thus an arrangement must have terms and it must seek to achieve a particular objective. There can be no arrangement in the abstract which cannot be fructified according to its terms. Equally there can be no arrangement which cannot be implemented on its terms because say there is a legal or factual impediment which prevents its implementation.

In this case there was an arrangement and therefore a scheme. The work done to calculate the compensation payments was not the arrangement. However, the letter informing the pensioners that the bank's subsidiary was to be sold, that the tax services would be withdrawn and that one-off payments would be made by the bank to the pensioners constituted the framework, distinct from the mechanics of calculating and implementing the mechanics of the payments, under which the payments were to be made. The letter raised an expectation of payment. It revealed a plan to enable the payments to be made. That plan was distinct from the mere mechanics of the payments. So when the payments arrived, the payments fructified the plan embodied in the letter. That letter articulated and constituted an arrangement. Contrast the position in *Allum* where a voluntary payment out of the blue did not fructify any prior expectation that had been raised through the existence of an arrangement.

In *Moffat v HMRC* [2006] STC (SCD) 380, the taxpayer was a former employee of Scottish Bus Group which was privatised. He received an ex gratia payment from the government on the winding up of the group's pension schemes. A surplus amount had arisen in the pension scheme and it was agreed by the Scottish Executive and the Treasury that the surplus be paid to the United Kingdom Exchequer following the winding up of the schemes. However, when this was done it was understood that a large part of the surplus funds would be paid on an ex gratia basis, calculated by reference to the previous entitlement under the pension scheme and length of service, to members of the pension scheme. Although a legal entitlement to these payments did not exist, the decision was made to make the payments in order to mirror the payments made in relation to a settlement from a court action from the privatisation of the National Bus Company, which had operated in England and Wales. The terms of the payments were broadly similar to those of the payments made to the members of the National Bus Company.

HMRC argued that the payment received by the taxpayer was made under (what is now) an EFRBS and the Special Commissioner agreed. There was a scheme because there existed arrangements providing for relevant benefits. The arrangements stemmed from the agreement between the Scottish Executive and the Treasury that effect would be given in Scotland to the distribution broadly equivalent to what had happened in England and Wales. There was most certainly an expectation that such distribution would be made. The mechanics of payment were distinct from the arrangements enabling the payments.

So it would appear from the above two cases that there cannot be a scheme for the purposes of the rules on EFRBS, unless the employee is aware of the arrangements under which he may benefit.

15.104 In order for a scheme to be an EFRBS it must make provision for benefits consisting of or including relevant benefits. 'Relevant benefits' are defined in *ITEPA 2003, s 393B(1)* as meaning any lump sum, gratuity or other benefit (including a non-cash benefit) provided or to be provided (*inter alia*):

(a)   on the retirement or in anticipation of the retirement of an employee or former employee;

(b)   on the death of an employee or former employee; or

(c)   after the retirement or death of an employee or former employee in connection with past service.

However, excluded benefits are not relevant benefits (*ITEPA 2003, s 393B(2)*). Excluded benefits include benefits in respect of ill health or disablement of an employee during service, benefits in respect of the death by accident of an employee during service, and benefits defined in regulations as excluded (*ITEPA 2003, s 393B(3)(d)*) (see **15.106**).

Benefits in respect of death or early retirement through ill health

15.105   Particular attention needs to be paid to the application of the EFRBS rules to ex gratia payments made on an employee's death or early retirement through ill health. In relation to a payment made on an employee's death, the first point to note is that a 'relevant benefit' does not include any lump sum paid in respect of the death by accident, of a person occurring during his service (*ITEPA 2003, s 393B(3)(b)*). If a payment is not a relevant benefit, the arrangement to pay it alone cannot, by definition, be an EFRBS.

In order to be within the exemption it is necessary to ask whether it was only the accidental death that motivates the making of the payment. HMRC interpret this requirement quite loosely. The condition is regarded as satisfied if the accident occurs during the subsistence of the employment contract. It does not necessarily have to occur during the time that the employee is on duty so that an accident does not have to be workplace-related. For example, an ex gratia lump sum payable following an employee's death while travelling to work would not be a relevant benefit. So the issue is whether the individual was in employment at the time of the death, not whether he was working. The death must, however, occur by accident. Death through natural causes does not fall within the exclusion and a payment made in such a case would be a relevant payment.

As regards lump-sum payments on early retirement through ill health, a payment which is afforded in respect of the employee's ill health or disablement occurring during his service is also, by definition, not a relevant benefit (*ITEPA 2003, s 393B(3)(a)*). It will be noted that the employee's ill health or disablement does not have to occur on account of an accident; disablement that occurs otherwise than by accident (eg the loss of sight through a progressive illness) is also within the scope of the provision. The EFRBS rules cannot, therefore, apply to such payments.

Benefits defined in regulations as excluded

15.106   The *Employer-Financed Retirement Benefits (Excluded Benefits for Tax Purposes) Regulations 2007, SI 2007/3537* provide for certain benefits to be excluded benefits for the purposes of *ITEPA 2003, s 393B(3)(d)*. These benefits fall under the following heads (and the regulations should be referred to for the detailed rules):

(a)   welfare counselling;

(b)   recreational benefits;

(c)   annual parties;

(d)   writing of wills etc;

(e)   equipment for disabled former employees;

(f)   living accommodation and related benefits;

(g)   removal expenses;

(h)   repairs and alterations to living accommodation;

(i)   council tax paid for living accommodation;

(j)   annual health screening and medical check-ups;

(k)   trivial benefits; and

(l)   certain benefits given to armed forces personnel.

15.107   The term 'retirement' is not defined in the legislation, but in the case of *Venables v Hornby (Inspector of Taxes)* [2002] STC 1248 (which had to do with the construction of the terms of the trust deed under which a pension scheme was constituted) it was held in the Court of Appeal that whether a person had retired was a matter of fact and degree to be judged in a common sense and commercial way, and connoted withdrawing from active work. It did not, however, mean or include a mere reduction in workload or a change in the nature of service as an employee (eg by changing roles from managing director to non-executive director). On the other hand, as the case shows, a retirement can occur where the individual concerned continues to be interested to a small degree in the work of his former employer (perhaps by being an unpaid, non-executive director whose experience the employer could draw on from time to time).

In the later case of *Ballard v RCC* [2013] UKFTT 87 (TC) (which had to do directly with the construction of the EFRBS legislation in *ITEPA 2003*) it was again confirmed that the word 'retirement' has no special meaning. In particular, it is not linked with qualifying for a pension of any sort, nor is the individual's age of any relevance (although the older a person is when he leaves employment the more likely it is that he will not seek alternative employment and will effectively retire). Where a person makes a firm decision not to seek further employment he may be said to retire (as happened in the case). The occasion on which the individual concerned makes this decision is not a relevant factor (eg it could be taken during a redundancy consultation process) and making such a decision does not require the agreement of the former employer. The decision to terminate an individual's employment may be taken by an employer but the decision to retire is the employee's alone.

In the light of the *Venables* case, HMRC have (at EIM15300) set out how they regard this decision applying in specific cases (although they do point out that it is only a guide as each case depends on its own facts):

(a) A long-service employee leaves to take a senior executive position in another company at the age of 60. The person has retired from the first employment.

(b) A division of the company is sold and the 55-year-old manager responsible for running it leaves to take a job with the purchaser. Again the employee has retired from the first employment.

(c) A person in his 50s has a heart attack and is advised by his doctor to leave and seek a less stressful position. This is regarded as a retirement. (But if the ex-gratia payment made is purely consolation for loss of health that results in the premature termination of employment, it would not be regarded as made in connection with retirement.)

(d) An employee aged 50 leaves to take a job nearer home to be able to nurse her aged parents. The employee has retired.

However, in the light of the First-tier Tribunal's comments in *Ballard* it appears that these examples are open to doubt. The tribunal dismissed the idea that age was determinative of the question whether an individual had retired (although it did acknowledge that a person's' age affected the burden of proving that he had retired). It observed that a person whose employment comes to an end may make no decision about his future employment at all. He may actively look for further employment; he may wait and see what happens; or he may make a firm decision not to seek further employment – and there are probably other alternatives. In *Ballard* itself the individual had made a firm decision not to seek further employment and made that clear to his employer. It was held that he had retired. In the final analysis it will always be a question of fact whether a person has withdrawn from active work and hence retired.

MISCELLANEOUS PLANNING AND OTHER POINTS

Timing issues

Focus

When making a termination payment take into account the fact that if it is paid after the employee's contract of service has ended, it may (in part)

> have tax deducted from it under PAYE at the additional rate of 45% (or the Scottish top rate of 46% in the case of a Scottish taxpayer).

15.108   When structuring a termination package, consideration should be given to when it should be paid to (ie received by) the employee. If it can be paid by instalments over two or more tax years, that may result in the employee not being a higher rate (or additional rate) taxpayer in either (see **15.36**).

Consideration should be given to making the payment just before the employment ends. If a payment is made after the end of the employment, the employer is obliged under the PAYE rules to deduct tax from the payment using a 0T code (see **15.35**). This means that a taxable payment of more than £12,500 in 2018/19 will have tax deducted from it at the rate of 45% (or 46% as the case may be) to the extent that it exceeds that amount (although of course the employee will be able to claim a refund for any excess tax deducted).

Payments that have no connection with the termination of employment

15.109   In very limited circumstances a termination payment may be entirely tax free because it has no connection with the termination of the employee's employment (but this will not be the case merely because there is an extended period of time between the termination of employment and the making of the payment). A payment is made 'in connection with' the termination of an employment if it really and substantially has something to do with the termination (*Walker v Adams (Inspector of Taxes)* 2003 SpC 344). The test of connection is one of fact and degree (*Barclays Bank plc v RCC* [2006] STC (SCD) 100).

In *Crompton v RCC* [2009] STC (SCD) 504, the taxpayer, an ex-soldier, was enlisted in the Territorial Army and had taken up a post as workshop clerk. When it was decided that he was no longer eligible for that post, he applied for a number of other posts. Due to procedural failures of the selection boards, he was not appointed to any of these posts even though he was correctly qualified and had priority over other candidates. Shortly before he was made redundant from the workshop clerk post, he accepted the post as a store man. However, due to a misunderstanding about the conditions, the taxpayer took up the redundancy and left the army. He received a redundancy payment. He was, after he had complained, also offered compensation for financial losses suffered as a consequence of the selection boards' failings. HMRC alleged that this payment was a payment made in connection with the termination of his employment with the army and charged it to tax as a residual termination payment. The taxpayer argued that the payment was not in fact connected with the termination of his employment. The actual termination was his dismissal by redundancy from the store man position; there was no causative link between that and the selection boards' failures for which he was compensated. The Special Commissioner agreed with the taxpayer, with the result that the payment was not liable to income tax. It was held that a connection had to be some sort of link, joint or bond between two things. There was no such link between the compensation received and the termination of the taxpayer's employment with the army. The payment was for the selection boards' unfair treatment of the taxpayer but that did not lead to his leaving the army. He left the army at the time he left the store man post on account of redundancy and not because of his failure to be selected for the posts for which he had applied. Consequently, the compensation was not a payment made in connection with the termination of his employment.

At EIM13910 HMRC provide the following example of where there is a link between a payment and the termination of employment. An employee is dismissed. The company wants to make sure that there is a complete break and so insists that all the employee's shares in the company are sold. The employee protests about the costs and the possible loss of future gains on the shares. It is agreed that the shares will be sold, but the company will pay £10,500 as compensation. The sale price received by the employee for the shares is not a payment in connection with the termination of his employment. Although the sale was required by the termination agreement, the transfer of ownership of the shares, rather than the loss of employment itself, wholly explains the payment. So none of that receipt came to the employee even indirectly as a payment for the termination itself. The payment arose as a consequence of the sale; all that arose as a consequence of the termination was a requirement to sell the shares, and that requirement of itself yielded no payment. By contrast, the compensation of £10,500 is in connection with the termination. None of this payment represents the value of the shares. Its receipt is wholly explained by the company's decision to make a payment to settle claims arising from the termination agreement.

Recipient of payment

15.110 Generally speaking little planning can be achieved with regard to whom a termination payment is made to. A payment is taxable if it is received by the former employee, or is provided on his behalf or to his order (eg the employee directs his employer to make the payment direct to his bank to discharge his mortgage liability). It is also taxable if it is paid to his spouse or civil partner, blood relative, dependant or personal representatives. The only gap in this list is a cohabitant of the employee who is not also his dependant. But then the payment cannot be made to the order of the employee. So a payment is still taxable if the employee directs that the payment is made to his cohabitant; it is likely not to be taxable however if paid under the direction of a court to the cohabitant of an employee suffering severe psychological problems or to a former cohabitant after the employee's death but these are unlikely to be common occurrences.

Seeking HMRC guidance

Focus

HMRC are committed to giving clearances on many aspects of the tax treatment of termination payments. Follow the guidance below to see where that will be the case.

15.111 EIM12825 sets out HMRC's approach to handling enquiries in relation to termination payments. It states that formal binding answers will be given in relation to the meaning of disability under SP 10/81 (see **15.45**) and to clearances for redundancy schemes under SP 1/94 (see **15.10**). EIM12827 extends formal binding answers to be given to enquiries on the disability and injury compensation exception (see **15.42–15.46**), the foreign service exception (see **15.50–15.54**), how the £30,000 threshold applies to payments from third parties, and non-cash provisions. It may be useful to take advantage of these when structuring termination packages.

Termination of employment

15.112 It is axiomatic that a payment be made on the termination of employment before it can be argued that it falls within the residual category of termination payment as regards its tax treatment. This requires that a contract of employment be brought to an end as a matter of the Common Law. In this regard it is not settled as to how the *TUPE Regulations* operate. Those regulations specifically provide that a transfer of employment under the regulations 'shall not operate so as to terminate the contract of employment of any person employed by the transferor ... but any such contract shall have effect after the transfer as if originally made between the person so employed and the transferee'. In other words, by virtue of the regulations the transferee stands in the shoes of the transferor following the transfer. In the absence of the regulations there would have been the termination of the employee's contract of employment with the transferor and the commencement of another employment with the transferee.

The view taken by the First-tier Tribunal in *Kuehne & Nagel Drinks Logistics Ltd v RCC* [2009] UKFTT 379 (TC) and *A G Reid v RCC* [2016] UKFTT 79 (TC) was that the deeming language of the *TUPE Regulations* were limited to its particular purpose and should not be taken into account in applying *ITEPA 2003*. In other words, the transfer of a contract of employment under the *TUPE Regulations* would nevertheless be treated as being brought to an end for tax purposes. In *Hill v RCC* [2015] UKFTT 205 (TC), however, the tribunal expressed the view that the tax legislation should be applied on the basis of the fiction contained in the regulations (ie that there is no termination of employment and that the employee has a single ongoing employment). However, it was not necessary for the tribunal to decide the case on the basis of the observation (see **15.12**).

CONCLUSION

15.113   The termination of an employee's employment affords an opportunity to the parties concerned to structure a payment in a tax-efficient way should the nature of their contractual relationship allow it. Yet this is an opportunity that arises in the context of an area of tax law where the relevant rules interact in a complex way. Careful consideration has to be given to all those rules and their interaction if satisfactory results are to be achieved.

Although there is an added dimension to that complexity and planning from 6 April 2018 following the enactment of changes to the tax treatment of residual termination payments by *Finance (No 2) Act 2017* and *Finance Act 2018*, structuring payments in such a way that they fall into the residual category of termination payments still brings a number of advantages (see **15.4**). However, one of those advantages – that the non-earnings component of a residual termination payment does not attract a charge to national insurance contributions – will be short-lived. With effect from 6 April 2019, it is expected that a new *National Insurance Bill* will impose a liability to employer's national insurance contributions (ie secondary Class 1 NICs) at a rate of 13.8% in respect of payments in the residual category to the extent that it exceeds £30,000. Employees will continue to enjoy an exemption from national insurance contributions on such payments, but this additional cost will, in particular, need to be factored into the costs of redundancy programmes and employers will have to decide whether to make smaller discretionary awards.

Chapter 16

Separation and divorce

George Duncan Solicitor, CTA, TEP, Partner, Charles Russell Speechlys LLP

SIGNPOSTS

- Tax issues are often thrown up by the financial arrangements made in the context of divorce and relationship breakdown. There are few if any opportunities for achieving an artificial advantage through tax planning. However there are some sensible planning steps that can be taken and many pitfalls to avoid. The main role of the tax adviser will usually be to spot pitfalls in advance and either suggest a way around them or at least quantify them so that they can be taken into account in financial negotiations.

- The UK tax code is wildly inconsistent in the way in which it treats divorce and relationship breakdown. For some tax purposes the key date is the date of permanent separation of the couple, for other tax purposes the key date is the end of the marriage on decree absolute, and for yet others the key date is the end of the tax year of permanent separation.

- The chapter starts with an outline of the steps involved in a divorce where significant financial issues exist. It then looks at the taxes which are most likely to be an issue in the context of divorce and relationship breakdown and examines the main issues which are likely to arise. It then looks at the tax issues which arise in some specific scenarios including dealings with the matrimonial home, the issues raised where beneficial ownership of property differs from the legal ownership and the assignment of life policies. The chapter looks very briefly at pension sharing. At the end of the chapter there is a table summarising some tax consequences of the different stages of the process of separation and divorce.

INTRODUCTION

16.1 This chapter examines the main tax issues typically raised by separation and divorce. The breakdown of civil partnerships will raise the same tax issues.

Tax planning in this context is, usually, planning in the sense of planning to avoid disasters, rather than planning to secure an advantage.

References to family law and trust law and to litigation procedures are to the law and practice in England and Wales.

AN OUTLINE OF THE STEPS INVOLVED IN A DIVORCE WHERE SIGNIFICANT FINANCIAL ISSUES EXIST

16.2 In broad outline the typical pattern will be as follows.

First, sadly, the relationship will break down leading to the permanent separation of the parties. The date of permanent separation is significant for certain tax purposes. It is a question of fact and will be referred to in various documents lodged with the court in the process of the matrimonial proceedings. It is not possible to specify a date of permanent separation for tax purposes different from that which has been acknowledged in documents submitted to the court.

16.3 The question whether a separation is permanent tends to be judged with the benefit of hindsight. However, the test is whether the separation is likely to be permanent, not whether it actually proves to be permanent. In *Bradley v Revenue & Customs Commissioners* – see **16.46** below – the tribunal accepted that a separation had been likely to be permanent even though a reconciliation had unexpectedly taken place. This is very much a question of fact and in *Benford v HMRC* [2011] UKFTT 457 (TC) the tribunal found that the taxpayer had not discharged the burden of proof required to demonstrate that his separation from his wife had been likely to be permanent.

Separation for these purposes is separation in the family law sense. It is possible, though rare, for a couple to be separated in the family law sense if they are living separate lives under the same roof, but also possible for a couple not to be separated if they are resident in different jurisdictions, for example where one of them has gone to live overseas for employment purposes and the other has stayed at home.

For the circumstances where husband and wife may be considered to have separated while still living under the same roof see *Holmes v Mitchell*

(Inspector of Taxes) [1991] STC 25, where the General Commissioners found that a husband and wife were living as separate households under the same roof and Vinelott J as he then was accepted the conclusion that they were living apart with the consequence that the husband was not entitled to the higher personal allowance.

Permanent separation will, typically, be followed by the commencement of court proceedings for the dissolution of the marriage.

Example 16.1 – The difference between separation for tax purposes and in the geographical sense

Mr and Mrs A and Mr and Mrs B are all four resident in the UK. They live next door to each other.

Mr A receives an attractive offer of a job in one of the Gulf states. This is a permanent position and all the duties of his employment will be performed outside the UK. After discussion with Mrs A he decides that he will accept the offer, which he does.

However, Mrs A does not wish to accompany him. She does not like hot climates. Moreover, she has an equally good job in the UK. Therefore, Mr A departs for that Gulf state while Mrs A remains in the UK. Mr A easily satisfies the requirements in the statutory residence test introduced by *FA 2013, Sch 45* so that he ceases to be UK resident. However, Mr and Mrs A remain happily married. Modern technology allows them to keep in regular touch with each other and they spend as much time with each other as they can.

However, sadly, there is a falling out between Mr and Mrs B. Although they continue to live under the same roof, they come to lead quite separate lives and everything indicates that their separation will be permanent.

Therefore Mr and Mrs A are still living together as husband and wife, even though they are resident in different continents, while Mr and Mrs B are permanently separated even though they are living under the same roof.

16.4   The parties and their advisers will then try to agree 'minutes of order'. This is a document that will be submitted to the court by consent of both parties as being a form of order which both parties consider it would be appropriate for the court to make. The minutes of order are *not* a binding contract on which anyone can sue. They are an agreed recommendation to the court. However, it requires unusual circumstances for the parties not to be held to the substance of them: see *Xydhias v Xydhias* [1999] 2 All ER 386. The court said in *Xydhias* that the purpose of negotiation (in the context of an application for ancillary relief) was not to finally determine the payer's liability but to reduce the length and expense of the process by which the court carried out its function.

The judge will often make a consent order in the form of the minutes which have been supplied to him, but only if he considers it just to do so.

16.5   The court has wide powers when dealing with marriage breakdown. The court may order either party to the marriage to make periodical payments to the other party for that party's own benefit or for the benefit of children of the marriage. It can also order the payment of lump sums and the transfer of property between the parties, the settlement of property for the benefit of the other party to the marriage and of the children of the marriage, or either or any of them, and sharing or attachment of pensions. Attachment orders are merely a type of periodical payments or lump sum order. It also has power to vary the terms of pre-existing settlements but only if they are 'nuptial' or 'antenuptial' settlements.

Sometimes the court order will be made on the basis of undertakings given by one or both of the parties that they will do things which the court could not directly order itself.

The making of the court order dealing with financial matters will typically be preceded by the decree nisi and then, on the application of either party, followed by the decree absolute. The decree absolute ends the marriage for all legal purposes and it is then that the court order takes effect. Maintenance pending suit orders can take effect before decree nisi or absolute.

16.6   Property adjustment orders made before decree absolute take effect only on decree absolute.

It is possible under certain circumstances for financial matters to be left unresolved at decree absolute, in which case an order of the court dealing with financial matters may be made after decree absolute. Any order for payment of a lump sum or adjustment of property made after decree absolute will normally come into immediate effect.

There are of course many variations to this general pattern. If agreement cannot be reached on financial matters between the parties then there will be a contested court hearing and the court will make whatever order it thinks just. In some cases the parties will enter into a binding separation agreement which may or may not be followed by divorce proceedings. Couples who separate may make their own financial arrangements independently of the court but, in that case, the court might order different financial arrangements if it deemed it just to do so. Moreover, a reconciliation may take place leading to an abandonment of the court proceedings.

INCOME TAX

Focus

Income tax relief for maintenance payments is now no longer a major issue. Maintenance payments are not subject to income tax in the hands of the recipient. However there are points to watch out for. If one spouse provides for the other by making an outright transfer of capital then the income from that capital will be taxable in the normal way. Interest paid on overdue principal sums will also be taxable. The special rules for property jointly held by husband and wife cease to apply on a permanent separation and in some cases this may make a major change to the income tax position of the parties.

Maintenance payments

16.7　　Tax relief for maintenance payments was at one time a key issue on marriage breakdown. However tax relief was greatly restricted by *FA 1988* and has subsequently become even more restricted so that it is currently seldom an issue. Relief for 'qualifying maintenance payments' survives in a very truncated form in the *Income Tax Act 2007 (ITA 2007), Pt 8, Ch 5*, though only in a case where either of the parties to the marriage or civil partnership was born before 6 April 1935 or, in the case of certain child support maintenance payments, where either the person who made the payment or the person to whom it was made was born before that date. The amount of this truncated relief is a tax reduction of 10% of the lesser of the total amount of qualifying maintenance payments made by the individual in question which fall due in the tax year in question and the minimum specified in *ITA 2007, s 43* (£3,360 for 2018/2019).

16.8　　In other cases although maintenance payments are annual payments for tax purposes they attract no tax relief in the hands of the payer and they are tax free in the hands of the recipient. It is irrelevant whether the maintenance payments are secured or not. This treatment applies also to maintenance payments made by order of an overseas court (though they may attract tax relief overseas).

The statutory basis for this is contained in the Income Tax (Trading and Other Income) Act 2005 (*ITTOIA 2005*), *Pt 6, Ch 8*. *ITTOIA 2005, s 727* provides that no liability to income tax arises under *Pt 5* in respect of an annual payment if it:

(a)   is made by an individual; and

(b)   arises in the UK.

There are certain exceptions to this which are not relevant to maintenance payments.

ITTOIA 2005, s 730 (Foreign maintenance payments) provides that no liability to income tax arises under *Pt 5* in respect of an annual payment if:

(i)   it is a maintenance payment;

(ii)   it arises outside the UK; and

(iii)   had it arisen in the UK it would be exempt from income tax under *ITTOIA 2005, s 727* (certain annual payments by individuals).

The section goes on to explain that a 'maintenance payment' is a periodical payment which meets one of two conditions. Condition A is that the payment is made under a court order or a written or oral agreement. Condition B is that the payment is made by a person:

(1)   as one of the parties to a marriage or civil partnership to, or for the benefit of, and for the maintenance of, the other party;

(2)   to any person under 21 for that person's own benefit, maintenance or education; or

(3)   to any person for the benefit, maintenance or education of a person under 21.

The word 'marriage' is defined as including a marriage that has been dissolved or annulled.

Both *ITTOIA 2005, ss 727* and *730* are extended to certain payments made by an individual's personal representatives.

It should be noted that these exemptions for maintenance payments do not extend to income arising under an outright transfer of capital by one party to the marriage to the other. If there is such an outright transfer of capital then income arising from that capital will be taxed in the hands of the recipient in the normal way.

It should also be noted that these exemptions apply only to maintenance payments made by individuals. Sometimes the financial arrangements made in the context of divorce or relationship breakdown involve the provision of income to one party in the form of payments made by trustees, either of a pre-existing trust or of a new trust established by one of the parties for the purpose. Such trust income will not fall within these exemptions and will be taxable in the hands of the recipient in the normal way unless, exceptionally, it falls within the income tax settlement rule, on which see below, so as to be attributed to the settlor.

Interest payments

16.9   There is no tax exemption for interest received on a principal sum paid under an order of the court made in the context of divorce or marriage breakdown. Such interest will therefore be subject to tax in the hands of the recipient, being caught by the general income tax charge on interest imposed by *ITTOIA 2005, s 369* (see SAIM2070). This is notwithstanding that the payer will obtain no tax relief for the interest payment. If it is envisaged that there will be a delay in the making of a lump sum payment it may therefore be advantageous for periodical payments, which will be tax free in the hands of the recipient, to continue, or to continue at a higher rate, until the lump sum payment is received, rather than interest being paid.

Tax reductions for married couples and civil partners

16.10   The married couple's allowance now survives only in a truncated form (though it has been extended in a similar truncated form to civil partnerships). It is now represented by a tax deduction given under *ITA 2007, Pt 3, Ch 3* and applies where, for the whole or part of a tax year, the couple are living together (although it is reduced in the tax year of marriage or entry into civil partnership). It is therefore available in full for the tax year of permanent separation but not thereafter. It is available only where one of the spouses or civil partners in question was born before 6 April 1935.

The relief is lost if the payer claims the remittance basis of taxation (*ITA 2007, s 809G*). Rather curiously, the relief for maintenance payments does not however seem to be lost in these circumstances.

Transferable tax allowance for married couples and civil partners

16.11   The *FA 2014* introduced a very limited provision enabling the transfer of the personal allowance between spouses and civil partners (*FA 2014, s 11*, inserting *Ch 3A* of *Pt 3* in *ITA 2007*). The broad effect of the new provision is to enable the transfer of a proportion of one spouse or civil partner's personal allowance to the other in a case where neither is a higher rate taxpayer and part of the personal allowance of the one who makes the transfer would otherwise be wasted.

One of the requirements for a transfer to be made is that neither of the spouses or civil partners in question makes a claim for the married couple's allowance in respect of the tax year in question.

If the other conditions for the making of an election are satisfied then an individual may make the election for a transfer if he or she is married to, or in a civil partnership with, the same person for the whole or part of the tax year concerned and when the election is made. Thus the ending of a marriage or civil partnership ends the ability to make the election, even if the intention is to make a retrospective election in respect of a year during which the marriage or civil partnership was subsisting.

An individual is not entitled to more than one tax reduction under this provision for the tax year, regardless of whether the individual is a party to more than one marriage or civil partnership in the tax year.

The provision came into force in the tax year 2015/16 when the maximum transferable amount of the allowance was £1,060. For the tax year 2016/17 and subsequent tax years, the maximum transferable amount is 10% of the individual personal allowance. There is no requirement that the spouses or civil partners should be living together when the election is made, or during the tax year affected by the election. The reduction is lost if the person otherwise entitled to benefit claims the remittance basis of taxation (*ITA 2007, s 809G*).

Jointly held property

16.12 Where income-producing property is held in the joint names of a married couple or civil partners who live together, they are treated for income tax purposes as beneficially entitled to the income in equal shares (*ITA 2007, s 836*), unless they make a joint election of unequal beneficial interests in which case the income will be taxed in accordance with the actual beneficial ownership (*ITA 2007, s 837*). Certain types of income are excluded from these provisions. This presumption of equal entitlement ceases to apply on the date of permanent separation (see TSEM9836). In a case where significant income was involved and there was a marked disparity in beneficial entitlement permanent separation could thus have a significant effect on the income tax position of the parties.

Example 16.2 – Effect of permanent separation upon the tax treatment of income from assets held in joint names

Mr C has a substantial income and is an additional rate taxpayer. He has a substantial portfolio of shareholdings in UK companies and is therefore liable to tax on dividends from those holdings, beyond the first £2,000, at the dividend additional rate. Mrs C, however, has only a very small Stock Exchange portfolio and her income is well under the higher rate threshold.

In order to reduce the family's overall exposure to income tax, Mr C persuades Mrs C that they should combine their portfolios so that they are held in joint names. However, there are limits to Mr C's generosity. He persuades Mrs C to join in a Declaration of Trust recording that the joint portfolio belongs to them beneficially in the proportions in which they had contributed, Mrs C's beneficial interest thus being very small.

Mr and Mrs C deliberately refrain from making an election of unequal beneficial interest. Consequently, the dividends from the joint portfolio are treated for income tax as belonging to them in equal shares. Mrs C's income is still not enough to bring her above the higher rate threshold so she will have no income tax liability on the first £2,000 of the dividends allocated to her and will pay tax at only 7.5% on the excess.

However, the relationship between Mr and Mrs C breaks down and they separate permanently. One consequence of this is that, from the date of their permanent separation, Mr C becomes liable to tax at the dividend additional rate on the proportion of the dividends from the joint portfolio which belongs to him beneficially. Thus his income tax liability significantly increases.

The settlement rules

16.13   The settlement rules are contained in *ITTOIA 2005, Pt 5, Ch 5*. Where these rules apply some or all of the income arising under the settlement will be treated as income of the settlor. For these purposes, 'settlement' is broadly defined (*ITTOIA 2005, s 620(1)*). It is, however, established by case law that the settlement rules can apply only where there is an element of bounty and, in most cases, it will be hard to argue that there is any element of bounty in a settlement made by one party to a marriage or civil partnership under the compulsion of a court order or as a result of arm's length negotiation (or both). There are three limbs of the settlement rules.

16.13 *Separation and divorce*

ITTOIA 2005, s 624 provides that income which arises under a settlement is treated for income tax purposes as the income of the settlor and of the settlor alone if it arises:

(a)   during the life of the settlor, and

(b)   from property in which the settlor has an interest.

ITTOIA 2005, s 625(1) explains that a settlor is treated for the purposes of *ITTOIA 2005, s 624* as having an interest in property if there are any circumstances in which the property or any related property:

(a)   is payable to the settlor or the settlor's spouse or civil partner,

(b)   is applicable to the benefit of the settlor or the settlor's spouse or civil partner, or

(c)   will, or may, become so payable or applicable.

However, *ITTOIA 2005, s 625(4)* provides that, in sub-section (1), 'the settlor's spouse or civil partner' does not include:

(a)   a spouse or civil partner from whom the settlor is separated under an order of the court or a separation agreement, or

(b)   a spouse or civil partner from whom the settlor is separated where the separation is likely to be permanent.

Moreover, *ITTOIA 2005, s 627* (Exceptions for certain types of income) excepts certain types of income from this key rule. One of these exceptions is that the rule in *ITTOIA 2005, s 624* does not apply to income which:

●   arises under a settlement made by one party to a marriage or civil partnership by way of provision for the other:

   –   after the dissolution or annulment of the marriage or civil partnership; or

   –   while they are separated under an order of the court, or under a separation agreement, or where the separation is likely to be permanent; and

●   is payable to, or applicable for the benefit of, the other party.

The second limb is contained in *ITTOIA 2005, s 629* and provides that income which arises under a settlement is treated for income tax purposes as the income of the settlor and of the settlor alone for a tax year if, in that year and during the life of the settlor, it:

(a)   is paid to, or for the benefit of, a relevant child of the settlor, or

(b)   would otherwise be treated, apart from the section, as income of the relevant child of the settlor.

This provision does not apply to income which is treated as income of the settlor under *ITTOIA 2005, s 624*.

For these purposes, 'relevant child' mean a minor child who is unmarried or not in a civil partnership.

ITTOIA 2005, s 631 supplements this by providing that, if the trustees of a settlement retain or accumulate income arising under the settlement and a payment is subsequently made in connection with the settlement to, or for the benefit of, a child of the settlor who is unmarried or not in a civil partnership, the payment is treated for the purposes of *ITTOIA 2005, s 629(1)* as a payment of income, but only so far as there is retained or accumulated income available.

This second limb of the settlement rules could be an issue in a case where a capital settlement is made for the benefit of the children of the marriage as well as, or instead of, one of the spouses.

In *Harvey v Sivyer* [1986] Ch 119, Nourse J explained an earlier decision of the House of Lords on the basis that the natural relationship between parent and young child was one of such deep affection and concern that there must always be an element of bounty by the parent, even where the provision is, on the face of things, made under compulsion.

16.14   It follows, as one would expect, that no income tax advantage may be obtained by maintaining a minor child through the making of a capital settlement on the occasion of a divorce: distributions from such a settlement for the benefit of a minor child would be likely to be caught by *ITTOIA 2005, s 629*.

The third limb of the settlement rules is contained in *ITTOIA 2005, s 633* and applies where a capital sum is paid directly or indirectly in any tax year by the trustees of a settlement to the settlor. Such a capital sum is, broadly speaking, treated as income of the settlor up to the amount of income which has been accumulated within the settlement.

This is supplemented by *ITTOIA 2005, s 638* (capital sums paid by way of loan or repayment of loan) and *ITTOIA 2005, s 641* (capital sums paid to settlor by body connected with settlement).

This third limb will not usually be relevant in the context of the breakdown of marriage, although it could be relevant if one of the spouses sought to raise funds by persuading the trustees of a settlement which was otherwise outside the settlement rules to make a capital distribution to him or her.

The settlement rules will not often be an issue in a financial settlement made on the occasion of marriage breakdown, but the possibility of their application should always be considered where a capital settlement is made, especially where the children of the marriage may benefit. Since tax relief for maintenance payments has almost ceased, the rules could be an issue only in the context of a settlement of capital, rather than of income only.

The transfer of assets abroad rules in *ITA 2007, Pt 13, Ch 2*

Focus

This legislation betrays its age in that it treats a married couple as a unit and contains no concessions for permanent separation. In some cases this might leave one spouse being subject to income tax on income from which he had no prospect of benefiting.

16.15   A transfer of assets made in the context of divorce or relationship breakdown will not often itself be a transfer falling within these rules. However, problems may result from previous transfers, reflecting the fact that the legislation treats spouses, or civil partners, as a unit and there is no relieving provision that applies in the event of permanent separation. This is a feature of the legislation that goes back to its origins in the *FA 1936*. Consider the following example.

Example 16.3 – Permanent separation has surprisingly little effect on the transfer of assets abroad rules

Mr and Mrs D are resident in the UK. Mr D is in the fortunate position of having £1m to invest. He decides to invest it through an overseas company, so he purchases an off the shelf company incorporated in Jersey. (No particular significance attaches to the choice of this jurisdiction.)

Mr D invests his £1m by subscribing for shares in his Jersey company, in which he is the sole shareholder. The company invests the money and income arises to the company as a result. None of the exemptions contained in the legislation apply. The income arising to the company is thus squarely within the transfer of assets abroad rules. Income has arisen to a 'person abroad' as a result of a transfer of assets made by Mr D; Mr D has 'power to enjoy' that income within the meaning of the legislation, an equivalent amount of income is then treated as arising to Mr D under *ITA 2007, s 721* and he is charged to tax on that income under *ITA 2007, s 720*. He does, however, have the consolation that, if the company distributes the income to him, the income received will be treated as not being his income for income tax purposes, under the relieving provision contained in *ITA 2007, s 743* (no duplication of charges) (as amended by *FA 2013*).

Mr D is a generous as well as a wealthy man. He proceeds to make an outright gift of the entire issued share capital in the Jersey company to Mrs D. However, from the point of view of income tax, not much changes as a result of this gift. The gift is not a settlement within *ITTOIA 2005, Pt 5, Ch 5* because it is an outright gift to his spouse and not a gift of property which is wholly or substantially a right to income (*ITTOIA 2005, s 626*). However *ITA 2007, s 714(4)* provides that in that chapter references to individuals include their spouses or civil partners. Thus, although Mr D no longer has power to enjoy the income in question, the fact that his spouse has power to enjoy that income is in itself enough to make him liable. He rather than his spouse is still the transferor. It is not even clear that *ITA 2007, s 743* will apply to any distribution of the income in question by the company to Mrs D, so as to prevent a second charge to tax on Mrs D in respect of the same income. (In practice, it could probably be assumed that HMRC would not seek to charge the same income twice, unless perhaps very aggressive tax avoidance was involved.)

Unfortunately, differences arise between Mr D and Mrs D. They separate permanently. However, neither wishes to divorce. Their separation has no effect upon Mr D's liability under these rules. Mrs D is still his spouse and she still has power to enjoy the income in question. He therefore remains liable to tax on that income. The legislation gives him no right of indemnity against Mrs D, nor even a right to obtain any information from her, or from the company. He would be well advised to negotiate such rights if he can.

The high income child benefit charge

16.16   *ITEPA 2003, Pt 10 Ch 8 imposes an* income tax charge where a person ('P') has 'adjusted net income' for a tax year exceeding £50,000 and one or both of conditions A and B are met.

Condition A is that P is entitled to an amount in respect of child benefit for a week in the tax year and there is no other person who is a partner of P throughout the week and has an adjusted net income for the year which exceeds that of P.

Condition B is that another person ('Q') is entitled to an amount in respect of child benefit for a week in the tax year, Q is a partner of P throughout the week and P has an adjusted net income for the year which exceeds that of Q.

In other words, the legislation asks the question 'are two people partners?' and, if the answer is 'yes', and if either has an adjusted net income exceeding £50,000 and if either is in receipt of child benefit for a week in the tax year in question, there is an income tax charge upon whichever of the partners has the higher income. The charge is a percentage, up to 100%, of the benefit.

For these purposes, two people are 'partners' if they are a man and a woman who are married to each other and are neither:

(a)   separated under a court order, nor

(b)   separated in circumstances in which the separation is likely to be permanent.

A man and woman who are not married but who are living together 'as husband and wife' are also 'partners'. The definition also extends to civil partners unless they are separated, the definition of 'separation' being equivalent to that for husband and wife, and to persons living together 'as if they were civil partners'.

The drafting of this legislation is complicated by the fact that, while income tax works on the basis of the tax year, entitlement to child benefit is calculated on a weekly basis.

It follows that the *beginning* of the week of permanent separation is the key date for these purposes.

It is possible for the person entitled to elect not to receive child benefit so as to avoid this income tax charge. In such a case, it might be worth revoking the election following permanent separation if the spouse or civil partner otherwise entitled to receive the benefit had an 'adjusted net income' markedly lower than that of the other.

Capital gains tax

Focus

This tax is often a major issue in the context of divorce and relationship breakdown. There is no general exemption for gains realised on disposals made in this context.

Disposals made between spouses before the end of the tax year of permanent separation fall within the 'no gain no loss' rule and it will sometimes be advantageous to accelerate the transfer of assets so that they fall within this rule.

Transfers between spouses made after the end of the tax year of permanent separation will usually be treated as made at open market value. However holdover relief may sometimes be available.

The timing of the CGT disposal is crucial. In some cases this will be the date of decree absolute and in some cases it will be the date of actual transfer of the asset. For detailed rules, see below.

16.17 The financial arrangements made in the context of divorce and relationship breakdown will often involve the transfer of assets between the parties. They may also involve the sale of assets to third parties to raise funds and the transfer of assets into or out of a settlement. With two exceptions explained below the legislation contains no specific exemptions and major liabilities often arise. CGT is now generally charged at a flat rate of either 10% or 20% but at 18% or 28% in the case of gains from residential property and carried interests. The rate is 10% where entrepreneurs' relief is available.

For both income tax and CGT, a married couple or civil partners are treated as living together unless:

- they are separated under an order of a court of competent jurisdiction;

- they are separated by deed of separation; or

- they are in fact separated in circumstances in which the separation is likely to be permanent.

See *TCGA 1992, s 288(3); ITA 2007, s 1011.*

Disposals between spouses before the end of the tax year of permanent separation

16.18 Disposals before the end of the tax year of permanent separation take place at 'no gain, no loss' in accordance with *TCGA 1992, s 58* (see CG22202).

Thus it will often be advantageous to accelerate the transfer of assets standing at a gain to a time before the end of the tax year of permanent separation. However, such transfers, while they will avoid any immediate

CGT liability for the transferring spouse, may store up future problems for the recipient spouse who will thus take with a reduced CGT acquisition cost.

Example 16.4 – Advantages of prompt transfer of property following permanent separation

Mr and Mrs E separate permanently early in the 2018/19 tax year. Mr E is the sole owner of a valuable country property which the couple have used but which does not in any way qualify for the principal private residence relief. It shows a gain of £1m.

It is agreed in the course of negotiations that, as part of the financial settlement, Mr E will transfer this property into the outright ownership of Mrs E.

Mrs E intends to move to the country and to occupy this property as her main residence.

If the transfer takes place before 6 April 2019 then 'no gain, no loss' will apply. Mr E will have no CGT to pay. Mrs E will take a reduced CGT acquisition cost, but this is of no concern to her since she intends to occupy the property as her main residence.

If, however, the transfer takes place after 5 April 2019, Mr E will be exposed to CGT on his gain of £1m.

It should be noted that *TCGA 1992, s 58* applies even where the recipient spouse or civil partner is non-UK resident and thus outside the scope of CGT (see CG22300).

Thus, a transfer falling within *TCGA 1992, s 58* could have the effect of removing a gain permanently from the scope of CGT, for example where the recipient spouse goes to live permanently overseas as a result of the breakdown of the marriage.

Transfers between the end of the tax year of permanent separation and decree absolute

16.19   During this period transfers no longer qualify for 'no gain, no loss' treatment. However, the spouses will still be connected persons within *TCGA 1992, s 286* with the result that transfers will be deemed to take place at open market value in accordance with *TCGA 1992, s 18*.

Transfers between spouses after decree absolute

16.20 Following decree absolute the couple will no longer be connected persons for CGT purposes (unless they are connected for some other reason). However, it will be wise to assume that, one way or another, transfers of assets between them made under a court order or as part of the financial arrangements made between them in the context of the divorce will fall within *TCGA 1992, s 17* and thus be treated as taking place at open market value, unless they are, as a question of fact, the result of arm's-length bargains.

Hold-over relief

16.21 The view of HMRC is that where there is a disposal of an asset from one spouse to another after the end of the year of assessment in which they separate but prior to decree absolute this is, where there is no recourse to the courts, usually made in exchange for a surrender by the donee of rights which they would otherwise be able to exercise to obtain alternative financial provision. HMRC thus take the view that the value of the rights surrendered represents actual consideration of an amount which would reduce the gain potentially eligible for hold-over relief to nil. They accept that, exceptionally, there may be a substantial gratuitous element in the transfer so that hold-over relief will be available in the case of an appropriate asset.

16.22 HMRC formerly took this view in the case of transfers under a consent order. However HMRC now accept that, in cases where there is recourse to the courts and a court makes an order:

- for ancillary relief under the *Matrimonial Causes Act 1973* which results in a transfer of assets from one spouse to another; or

- for property adjustment under the *Civil Partnership Act 2004*; or

- formally ratifying an agreement reached by the divorcing parties or by the civil partners of a dissolved civil partnership dealing with the transfer of assets,

the spouse or civil partner to whom the assets are transferred does not give actual consideration, in the form of surrendered rights, for their transfer.

A court order, made in these circumstances, reflects the exercise by the court of its independent statutory jurisdiction and is not the consequence of any party to the proceedings agreeing to surrender alternative rights in return for assets, there is no actual consideration. Thus hold-over relief under *TCGA 1992, s 165* may be available for transfers of assets under a court order, even a consent order. This may be an extremely useful relief in the case of business assets, including shares in unlisted trading companies, and agricultural land. However hold-over relief reduces the acquiring spouse's acquisition cost and may thus store up problems for the future. The relief requires the consent of the acquiring spouse. This approach represents a change in the Revenue's prevailing practice following consideration of judicial observations made in the case of *G v G* [2002] EWHC 1339, [2002] 2 FLR 1143 (see CG67192).

There is some tension between *G v G* and the decision of the Court of Appeal in a non-tax case, *Haines v Hill and Another* [2007] All ER (D) 56 that a wife did give valuable consideration for the transfer of an asset to her by her husband under a court order made in matrimonial proceedings with the result that the court could not set that transfer aside as a transaction at an undervalue under the *Insolvency Act 1986, s 339* on the application of the trustee in bankruptcy of her former husband. However, that decision, which clearly reflects the desire of the Court to achieve a balance between the interests of creditors and those of estranged spouses, seems not to have affected the views of HMRC.

The time of the CGT disposal

16.23   It will be important to establish this. This is not only because disposals made before the end of the tax year of permanent separation will qualify for 'no gain, no loss' treatment but because the timing of the disposal will determine when any CGT has to be paid and the availability of exemptions and reliefs, including the annual exemption and loss relief. Moreover, the value of the asset may change as time goes on.

In the case of assets transferred outside the framework of a court order the normal rules apply. The date of disposal will thus be the date of actual transfer except in a case where the transfer was made in accordance with a binding contract, in which case the date of the contract will be the date of the disposal (unless it was a conditional contract, in which case the date of disposal will be the date when the condition is fulfilled). This is governed by *TCGA 1992, s 28* in the usual way.

16.24   The position is more difficult where the disposal is made in accordance with a court order. The view of HMRC, as set out in CG22423, is as follows:

- **Asset transferred under a court order before the date of decree absolute or before the dissolution of the civil partnership is made final.** Court orders of this type do not take effect until decree absolute has been granted or until dissolution has been made final. It is well established in case law that until the order takes effect, it is contractual in nature. Therefore, where an asset is transferred in pursuance of such an order before the date of decree absolute or the dissolution of the civil partnership is made final, the transfer is treated as a disposal under a contract. The parties are treated as entering into the contract on the date of the court order.

- **Asset transferred after the date of decree absolute or after the dissolution of the civil partnership is made final, in pursuance of a court order made before the date of decree absolute or before the dissolution of the civil partnership was made final.** A court order embodying the terms of the settlement made before the decree absolute or before the date of dissolution of the civil partnership remains contractual in nature until the date of the decree absolute or the date the dissolution is made final. After that date the court order ceases to be contractual and the terms derive their legal effect from the court order itself.

  So where an asset is transferred following the date of decree absolute, or following the date the dissolution is made final, in pursuance of an order made before decree absolute or before dissolution is made final, the date of disposal is the date of decree absolute or the date the dissolution is made final.

- **Asset transferred in pursuance of a court order made after the date of decree absolute or after the date the dissolution of the civil partnership is made final.** Where a court order is made after the date of decree absolute or after the date that the dissolution of the civil partnership is made final and an asset is transferred in pursuance of that order, the date of disposal is the date of the order.

The first part of this guidance is, presumably, contemplating a consent order. One would have thought that, if an asset is actually transferred before a court order comes into effect, the disposal will have taken place on any possible view, unless there was something suggesting otherwise in the particular terms on which the transfer was made.

HMRC expressly reject the view that, where the parties have approached the courts for an order to give effect to a prior agreement between them for the division of the assets of the marriage or civil partnership, and a consent order is obtained, the prior agreement is a binding contract so that the date of the agreement is the date of disposal for CGT purposes. See CG22420 which quotes the following extract from the judgment of Lord Diplock in *de Lasala v de Lasala* [1980] AC 546:

> 'Financial arrangements that are agreed upon between the parties for the purpose of receiving the approval and being made the subject of a consent order by the Court once they have been made the subject of the Court Order no longer depend upon the agreement of the parties as the source from which their legal effect is derived. Their legal effect is derived from the Court Order.'

It should be noted that this guidance attaches no importance to any delay between the coming into force of a court order requiring the transfer of an asset and its actual transfer. This is consistent with the decision of the Court of Appeal in the non-tax case *Mountney v Treharne* [2003] Ch 135 that it is the matrimonial court order, not the subsequent transfer of the asset which transfers the beneficial interest to the recipient spouse.

16.25 It will be seen that there is some scope for planning here. If desired and with goodwill the disposal of an asset could be accelerated by actually transferring the asset in advance of a court order (in which case any subsequent court order could leave its ownership unchanged). Alternatively, the disposal could be deferred by slowing the litigation.

The receipt of lump sums under court orders

16.26 There is no CGT on the receipt of a lump sum under a court order in itself. The authority for the payment of the lump sum comes from the court order, not from the disposal of any asset. HMRC accept that this principle extends to lump sums ordered by the court when discharging previous orders for periodical payments (see RI 227, April 2001).

See below for the special circumstances applying to disposals of the main residence.

Entrepreneurs' relief

16.27 Entrepreneurs' relief is now an extremely valuable relief from CGT, allowing gains of up to £10m to be charged at the rate of only 10%. The relief can be extremely useful when assets are to be transferred in the context of financial arrangements made on divorce or marriage breakdown. However, the relief may easily be lost. Note in particular the position where one spouse owns shares in a family trading company and is also an officer or employee of that company, owning at least 5% of the ordinary share capital and being entitled to exercise at least 5% of the voting rights by virtue of that holding. If the arrangements made on marriage breakdown involve that spouse both transferring his or her shareholding to another family member and resigning from the office or employment then the relief will be available (if its other conditions are satisfied) if the transfer takes place before resignation but will be lost if the order of events is reversed. See *TCGA 1992, ss 169I(6)* and *169S(3)*.

Inheritance tax

Focus

For various reasons an outright transfer of capital between spouses in the context of divorce or relationship breakdown will not usually be a chargeable transfer for IHT purposes. However the circumstances need to be carefully examined in each particular case. One of the protections, that given by *IHTA 1984, s 10*, is in fact relatively restricted.

Although the transfer of capital into settlement will not usually give rise to an immediate IHT charge the settlement will be exposed to the ten-yearly and exit charges following the changes made by *FA 2006*.

Great care should be taken if assets to be transferred qualify, or may qualify, for reliefs or exemptions from IHT, such as business and agricultural property relief. A transfer may well lead to the loss of a relief or exemption. Transfers of assets which have been the subject of a potentially exempt transfer during the seven-year 'waiting period' within which the death of the transferor may trigger an IHT charge are especially hazardous.

For IHT purposes the date of decree absolute is important rather than the date of permanent separation. In particular the spouse exemption will continue to apply to outright transfers of capital made before the date of decree absolute. The ability to transfer the nil rate band is not lost on permanent separation but only on decree absolute.

16.28   Until the enactment of *FA 2006*, IHT was rarely an issue in the context of divorce and relationship breakdown. This was for a number of reasons.

First, dispositions made on divorce for the benefit of a former spouse, whether under a court order or as a result of arm's-length negotiations, are normally accepted as being within *IHTA 1984, s 10* (dispositions not intended to confer gratuitous benefit) even if they would otherwise be transfers of value (see IHTM04165).

It must however be borne in mind that the protection given by *IHTA 1984, s 10* is all or nothing. If a disposition does not fall wholly within *IHTA 1984, s 10* then *IHTA 1984, s 10* gives no protection at all. A disposition cannot fall within *IHTA 1984, s 10* if it is made in a transaction or series of transactions which, with any associated operations, fails to meet the requirements of *IHTA 1984, s 10*. HMRC seem to have developed a more aggressive approach to *IHTA 1984, s 10* at least in the context of contributions to employee benefit trusts. See Revenue & Customs Brief 18/11 (Employee Benefit Trusts: Inheritance Tax and Income Tax Issues), which expresses the view that the slightest possibility of gratuitous intent will take a contribution to such a trust outside the protection of *IHTA 1984, s 10*.

In an interesting First-tier Tribunal decision *Parry (as personal representative of Staveley deceased) and Others v Revenue & Customers Commissioners*

TC3548 [2014] UKFTT 419 (TC), HMRC failed in an attempt to argue that *IHTA 1984, s 10* did not apply to a transfer that formed part of a series of transactions (although they succeeded on another issue). In 2000, following her acrimonious divorce, Mrs Staveley transferred her pension fund from an occupational pension scheme linked to her ex-husband's company to a *Finance Act 1981, s 32* buy-out policy. She was advised that on her death a substantial part of the funds could revert to the company for the benefit of her ex-husband. In order to prevent this, in November 2006 Mrs Staveley, who by then knew she was suffering from terminal cancer, requested that the policy be transferred to a personal pension plan and signed a Statement of Wishes that the death benefit should be paid equally to her two sons, who were beneficiaries under her will. Six weeks later she died, without having drawn any benefits from the plan. HMRC argued that the transfer into the personal pension plan had been a transfer of value for IHT purposes. However, the tribunal rejected that. Part of the tribunal's reasoning was that the transfer had not in itself been intended to confer a gratuitous benefit and, although it had affected the same property as the omission to draw benefits, it was not an associated operation with that omission because there was no connection of intent: operations had to be linked by the intention to confer gratuitous benefit if they were to be 'associated operations'.

The Upper Tribunal upheld the decision on this point and allowed the taxpayer's appeal on the point on which the First-tier Tribunal had found for HMRC ([2017] UKUT 4 (TCC)).

Such dispositions may also fall within *IHTA 1984, s 11* (dispositions for the maintenance of family). This applies to dispositions made by one party to a marriage in favour of the other party or of a child of either party which are either:

- for the maintenance of the other party; or

- for the maintenance, education or training of the child for a period ending not later than the year in which he attains the age of 18 or, after attaining that age, ceases to undergo full-time education or training.

Even in the absence of *IHTA 1984, ss 10* and *11* the straightforward transfer of an asset in pursuance of a matrimonial court order should not represent a transfer of value. The view of HMRC is now that where dispositions are made following a court order under the *Matrimonial Causes Act 1973*, the decision in *Haines v Hill* (see **16.22** above) confirms that the applicant spouse's right to apply for a property order is consideration equal to the value of the money or property that is to be transferred under the court order. As a result, there is no loss to the respondent spouse's estate in the first place and there is no need to rely on any exemption or other exclusion to present a transfer of value arising. See IHTM11032.

The position might, however, be less straightforward if the transferor had given an undertaking as a basis for the court order or if the parties implemented a court order in such a way as to make greater provision for the children of the marriage than would have been required to satisfy the court.

HMRC will allow a deduction, in calculating the value of a person's estate chargeable to IHT on his death, for enforceable financial obligations to a former spouse or civil partner. See IHTM28090 following.

16.29 *IHTA 1984, s 11* expressly extends to dispositions made on the occasion of the dissolution of a marriage. However the provision is still somewhat limited in its effect, especially in the light of the decision of the Special Commissioner in the *Phizackerley case* (2007) SpC 591, [2007] STC (SCD) 328 that the provision of housing, in the context of a transfer from husband to wife, was not the provision of maintenance.

Unlike *IHTA 1984, s 10, IHTA 1984, s 11* can apply to part only of a disposition, as in *McKelvey v Revenue & Customs Commissioners* SpC 694 [2008] STC (SCD) 944 where a daughter had given two investment properties to her elderly and dependent mother and the Special Commissioner held that *IHTA 1984, s 11* applied to part only of the value of the gift.

Dispositions falling within either *IHTA 1984, s 10* or *11* are not transfers of value for IHT purposes.

16.30 In any case, since a married couple are still husband and wife until decree absolute, the spouse exemption will still apply to outright transfers made up to decree absolute, even after permanent separation, unless restricted by the domicile of the recipient spouse. Correspondingly, on decree absolute the related property rule (under which the property of husband and wife is aggregated for valuation purposes) ceases to apply (*IHTA 1984, s 161*).

Major difficulties have, however, been caused by the changes made by *FA 2006* to the IHT treatment of settled property. It often happens that, as part of the financial arrangements made on divorce or relationship breakdown, an interest-in-possession settlement will be established. Typically, this will take the form of a life interest for the spouse/former spouse with remainder to the children of the marriage.

16.31 The difficulty is that, even though the transfer of capital into the settlement may not be a transfer of value, the settled property will, under the post-2006 rules, be 'relevant property' exposed to the ten-yearly and exit charges, notwithstanding the former spouse's interest in possession.

This change discourages the establishment of such settlements and causes particular difficulties in the context of the former matrimonial home, on which see below.

There is some concern that anti-avoidance provisions inserted into *IHTA 1984* by *FA 2010, s 53* may, inadvertently, affect certain settlements made on the occasion of marriage breakdown.

These anti-avoidance provisions were intended to counteract certain tax planning arrangements under which a taxpayer would purchase an interest in possession in a settlement for full value.

The provisions apply where a person is beneficially entitled to an interest in possession in settled property and:

(a)   was domiciled in the UK on becoming beneficially entitled to it; and

(b)   became beneficially entitled to it by virtue of a disposition which was prevented from being a transfer of value by *IHTA 1984, s 10* (*IHTA 1984, s 5(1B)*).

Where the provisions apply, the settled property in which the interest in possession subsists is treated as being in the 'estate' of the person in question, so that it is exposed to IHT on his death or on a lifetime termination of his interest in possession, but *also* subject to the relevant property regime.

However, it seems that, at least under normal circumstances, these anti-avoidance provisions would not apply in the context of marriage breakdown. If property is settled in pursuance of a court order and a person is entitled to an interest in possession under the settlement, then the disposition under which he becomes entitled to it, that is the making of the settlement, is not prevented from being a transfer of value by *s 10*, because it does not in itself reduce the value of the estate of the settlor. He or she is just giving effect to a binding obligation. Nevertheless, the provision should be borne in mind. The view of HMRC is now that a settlement arising under a court order which gives the applicant spouse an interest in possession will be a relevant property trust and the spouse's interest in possession will not form part of their estate in view of *IHTA 1984, ss 5(1B) and 49(1A)* (IHTM11032).

Reliefs and exemptions from inheritance tax: some pitfalls

Business and agricultural property relief

16.32   If the ownership of assets is to change as a result of financial arrangements made in the context of divorce or relationship breakdown, then it is important to find out whether those assets qualify for any relief or exemption from IHT and, if so, whether that relief or exemption will be lost, permanently or temporarily, on the change of ownership.

One difficulty lies in the length of ownership requirement for business property relief (*IHTA 1984, s 106*) and the length of occupation or ownership requirement for agricultural property relief (*IHTA 1984, s 117*). The provisions for replacement (*IHTA 1984, ss 107* and *118*) are unlikely to help in the case of a transfer of property made in the context of divorce or relationship breakdown. The provisions for successive transfers (*IHTA 1984, ss 109* and *121*) may help if assets otherwise qualifying for business property relief or agricultural property relief are transferred in the context of divorce or relationship breakdown and are subsequently the subject of a transfer of value made by the recipient on his death, but not in the event of a lifetime transfer by the recipient. Moreover the provisions for successive transfers only help if there has been an earlier transfer of value, so seem not to help if the only other transfers fell within *IHT 1984, s 10* or *11* in which case they will not have been transfers of value.

There may thus be an IHT exposure on the assets transferred until the transferee has satisfied the length of ownership or length of occupation or ownership requirements in his or her own right.

Another pitfall lies in wait where an asset which is transferred has previously been the subject of a potentially exempt transfer (*IHTA 1984, s 3A*) and the seven-year 'waiting period' following that previous transfer has not yet expired. In that case, should the original transferor die within that seven-year period and the potentially exempt transfer thus become chargeable, relief may be lost.

Even if the asset in question qualified for business property relief or agricultural property relief in the hands of the original donor at the date of the potentially exempt transfer these reliefs will not be available in calculating the tax payable as a result of the subsequent death of the original donor unless (*inter alia*) the asset in question is still owned by the original donee at the date of the original donor's death (or at the earlier death of the original donee) (*IHTA 1984, ss 113A* and *124A*). There are provisions for replacement property (*IHTA 1984, ss 113B* and *124B*), but these help only where the transferee has disposed of all or part of the property in question before the death of the transferor and the whole of the consideration received by him for the disposal has been applied by him in acquiring other property, so they will not help where no consideration has been received by the original transferee on making his disposal.

A further difficulty is that, should a potentially exempt transfer 'fail' because of the death of the transferor within seven years and should the property in question have been transferred in the meantime to the estranged spouse of the original donee for no consideration, then not only would business property relief or agricultural property relief be lost but the estranged spouse would then be one of the persons liable for the tax on the 'failed' potentially exempt transfer (*IHTA 1984, s 199*) because the estranged spouse would be a person in whom the property was vested at any time after the transfer. Even if the transfer to the estranged spouse took place on arm's-length terms the estranged spouse would not be a 'purchaser' and thus protected from liability under *IHTA 1984, s 199* unless he had acquired the property in good faith for a consideration in money or money's worth (*IHTA 1984, s 272*), which would seemingly not be the case if the transfer had been made by order of the court. However the practice of HMRC is to treat the transferee of a 'failed potentially exempt transfer' as primarily liable for tax (IHTM30042).

Example 16.5 – Hazards of transferring business property which has been the subject of a PET

Mr and Mrs F separate and divorce. Mr F transfers to Mrs F, in accordance with a court order, a block of shares in an unlisted trading company worth £1m which would qualify for business property relief at 100% in his hands.

Five years previously that same block of shares had been given outright to Mr F by his father, this transfer being a potentially exempt transfer. At the time of that gift the shares qualified for 100% business property relief in the hands of Mr F's father. The shares were also worth £1m at the date of the gift to Mr F by his father.

One year after the transfer by Mr F to Mrs F, Mr F's father dies and the potentially exempt transfer thus 'fails'.

Since Mr F no longer owns the shares at the date of his father's death and since he had not sold them and applied the proceeds in purchasing replacement business property no business property relief is allowed in calculating the tax payable on the 'failed' potentially exempt transfer. If HMRC encounter difficulties in recovering the tax from Mr F then they may seek to recover it from Mrs F.

Entitlement to business property relief in respect of certain shares and securities of a company depends upon the owner having control of the company in question (*IHTA 1984, s 105(1)(b)* and *(cc)*) with the result that eligibility for further relief may be lost if the result of a transfer is to separate ownership of a block of shares or securities from control of the company in question.

Entitlement to business property relief in respect of certain categories of land or building, machinery or plant depends upon the owner (or beneficial owner if the assets are settled property) having control of a company which uses those assets for the purposes of its business or being a member of a partnership which uses those assets for the purposes of its business in which case entitlement to relief in respect of those assets may be lost if they are transferred separately from control of the company in question or membership of the partnership in question (*IHTA 1984, s 105(1)(d)*).

Example 16.6 – Separation of assets from business ownership

Mr and Mrs G carry on business as retail newsagents in partnership with their son. The partnership business is carried on from a number of different premises, the freeholds of which are held outside the partnership by Mr and Mrs G as beneficial tenants in common in equal shares. Mr and Mrs G have owned the freeholds for many years and they have been used in the partnership business for many years. Thus, as matters stand, the freeholds will qualify for business property relief at the lower 50% rate in accordance with *IHTA 1984, ss 104(1)(b)* and *105(1)(d)*.

The partnership occupies the premises under leases granted by Mr and Mrs G.

Mr and Mrs G separate and divorce. As part of the associated financial arrangements Mrs G resigns from the partnership. However, in order to provide her with a continuing income, Mr G assigns to her his interest in the freeholds so that she becomes the outright owner of them and receives the whole of the rent payable by the partnership. Consequently, the freeholds will no longer qualify for business property relief. The link with the partnership will have been broken. Mrs G will also lose any possibility of obtaining entrepreneurs' relief under *TCGA 1992, Pt V, Ch 3* on a subsequent disposal of the freeholds.

Conditional exemption

16.33 The advantage of owning property which has attracted conditional exemption from IHT usually lies in pride of ownership rather than in any immediate financial returns, so such property is not a natural subject of a financial settlement made on the occasion of divorce or relationship breakdown. However it should be borne in mind that any disposal of such property, whether by sale or gift or otherwise, is prima facie a 'chargeable event' on which tax may be charged (*IHTA 1984, s 32(3)*). A disposal otherwise than by sale is not a 'chargeable event' with respect to any property if:

- the disposal is itself a conditionally exempt transfer of the property; or

- fresh undertakings are given by such persons as the Board thinks appropriate in the circumstances of the case presumably in most cases the transferee (see *IHTA 1984, s 32(5)* and *(5AA)*).

Thus, should conditionally exempt property be transferred otherwise than by sale, in order to avoid a 'chargeable event', either the exemption must be renewed (which could be done only if the disposal was itself a transfer of value and not potentially exempt) or the undertakings must be renewed. In either case the broad effect would be to pass liability for the tax that would be payable when and if the conditional exemption was lost to the transferee, who would be severely inhibited in his use of the property by the undertakings which he would probably have been required to give.

Growing timber

16.34   *Chapter III* of *Part V* of *IHTA 1984* provides that where part of the value of a person's estate immediately before his death is attributable to the value of land on which trees or underwood are growing but which is not agricultural property, the value of the trees or underwood may (subject to certain conditions) be left out of account in valuing that person's estate on death in which case tax is charged on the disposal of the trees or underwood. However there is no tax charge on a disposal made by any person to his spouse or civil partner (*IHTA 1984, s 126(2)*). Thus, in some cases it would be possible to avoid a tax charge on the transfer of trees or underwood by making the transfer before decree absolute.

The transferable nil rate band

16.35   It is a requirement of the provisions for the transfer of unused IHT nil rate bands introduced by the *FA 2008* and now contained in *IHTA 1984, ss 8A, 8B* and *8C* that (*inter alia*) a person has died who, immediately before his death, had a spouse or civil partner and who had unused nil rate band on his death. However it is not necessary that such spouses or civil partners were living together at the time of the first death, or that the second deceased spouse or civil partner benefited from the estate of the first deceased person. This may give rise to unexpected results. The same applies to any transfer of the residential nil rate band introduced in relation to deaths on or after 6 April 2017 under *F(No 2)A 2015*. See *IHTA 1984, s 8G*.

Example 16.7 – Separation and transfer of nil rate band

Mr and Mrs H separate permanently after having been married for a number of years. One of the reasons for the breakdown of their relationship is that Mrs H does not share Mr H's great love for animals. Neither of them wishes to divorce. Mr H changes his will, wholly excluding Mrs H and leaving his entire estate to an animal welfare charity. He then dies and the provisions of this will are implemented. His nil rate band was intact at the time of his death and, since the only gift made by his will qualifies for the charity exemption from IHT, it is not used on his death.

When Mrs H dies (assuming no change in the law), her executors will be able to claim Mr H's unused nil rate band, notwithstanding that they had separated permanently during his lifetime and that she did not benefit from his estate. The beneficiaries of Mrs H's estate may thus be better off (at current tax rates) by £130,000 (£325,000 @ 40%). (This example ignores the residential nil rate band.)

Election to be treated as domiciled in the UK

16.36   *FA 2013, s 177* has made it possible, if certain conditions are satisfied, for a person to elect to be treated as domiciled in the UK for IHT purposes, thus securing the spouse exemption for transfers to that person. Such an election may also be made under certain circumstances by the personal representatives of a deceased person. It should be noted that, although the election is only possible if the person in question had a spouse or civil partner who was domiciled in the UK at the effective date of the election, a subsequent divorce or dissolution of the civil partnership would neither prevent an election nor invalidate one which had been made (*IHTA 1984, ss 267ZA and 267ZB*).

Example 16.8 – Divorce and election for deemed domicile

At the start of the 2013/14 tax year, Mr and Mrs I have been married for a number of years. Both are resident in the UK. Mr I is domiciled in the UK but Mrs I is not, neither does she have a deemed domicile under *IHTA 1984, s 267*.

Mr I is a wealthy man. However, all is not well. Unknown to Mrs I, Mr I is conducting an affair with Miss X. Moved by guilt he decides to make Mrs I an immediate gift of £1m, which he makes on 6 April 2013.

This gift is intended to confer gratuitous benefit so it does not fall within *IHTA 1984, s 10*, nor is it a disposition for the maintenance of Mrs I so it does not fall within *IHTA 1984, s 11*. Mr I has two annual exemptions available so the first £6,000 of the gift is exempt. The spouse exemption is also available but, because of Mrs I's overseas domicile, even with the more generous provision introduced by the *FA 2013* applying to transfers made on or after 6 April 2013, the spouse exemption is still restricted to the amount of the nil rate band, thus £325,000. This is a lifetime limit but suppose that Mr I had not previously used any part of it. Suppose that Mr I has not previously used his nil rate band. Thus the first £331,000 of the gift is exempt but the balance of £669,000 is a potentially exempt transfer that will fall into charge to IHT should Mr I fail to survive for seven years, though the first £325,000 will be taxed at a nil rate.

Mrs I then discovers the relationship between Mr I and Miss X, which leads to a rapid disintegration of the relationship between Mr and Mrs I. This is followed by their permanent separation and divorce. The decree absolute is obtained later in the 2013/14 tax year and this is immediately followed by the marriage of Mr I to Miss X.

Under the financial settlement made on the divorce, Mrs I retains the £1m, this being taken into account in the divorce settlement.

Mr I then dies within the course of the 2018/19 tax year. This means that the potentially exempt transfer has 'failed' and there is an immediate liability to IHT which HMRC may recover from Mrs I.

It is, however, open to Mrs I to make an election under *IHTA 1984, s 267ZA* to be treated as domiciled in the UK from and including 6 April 2013. This is well within the period of retrospection permitted by the legislation. For the making of the election it is sufficient that she was married to Mr I at the effective date of the election: the facts that they were subsequently divorced and that he remarried are irrelevant. Mrs I cannot revoke the election but if she is not resident in the UK for income tax purposes for the period of four successive tax years beginning at any time after the election was made, the election ceases to have effect at the end of that period (*IHTA 1984, s 267ZB(10)*). Mrs I should, however, consider carefully, before she makes the election, whether she has herself made any transfers of value that might become chargeable as a result of the election and whether she might in future make such transfers while the election is in force.

Mrs I would, clearly, have been well advised to obtain an indemnity in respect of the April 2013 gift as part of the financial settlement with Mr I, though even if she did she might reasonably have been expected to mitigate her loss by making the election.

One unintended consequence of the election is that Mr I's nil rate band is no longer set against the April 2013 gift so it will be available either to his executors or, if the spouse exemption is available because he leaves his entire estate to his new wife, to be transferred to the executors of the former Miss X.

Stamp duty land tax and stamp duty

16.37   In the past, SDLT has rarely been an issue in the context of separation and divorce. It has been more common for it to be an issue in the financial arrangements made on the breakdown of a relationship between cohabitees. However, the breakdown of a relationship may well lead to the purchase of a new home bringing with it an SDLT charge and in some circumstances the 3% surcharge introduced by the *FA 2016*.

There is a very wide exemption contained in *FA 2003, Sch 3, para 3*, which provides that a transaction between one party to a marriage and the other is exempt from charge to SDLT if it is effected:

- in pursuance of an order of a court made on granting in respect of the parties a decree of divorce, nullity of marriage or judicial separation;

- in pursuance of an order of a court made in connection with the dissolution or annulment of the marriage, or the parties' judicial separation, at any time after the granting of such a decree;

- in pursuance of:

    - an order of a court made at any time under *Matrimonial Causes Act 1973, s 24A;* or

    - an incidental order of a court made under *Family Law (Scotland) Act 1985, s 8(2)* or by virtue of *Family Law (Scotland) Act 1985, s 14(1)*;

- at any time in pursuance of an agreement of the parties made in contemplation or otherwise in connection with the dissolution or annulment of the marriage, their judicial separation or the making of a separation order in respect of them.

(This statement of the legislation omits some wording which is obsolete because of changes to matrimonial law.)

A similar wide exemption for transactions in connection with the dissolution of civil partnerships is contained in *FA 2003, Sch 3, para 3A*.

16.38   Even in the absence of this exemption, SDLT would not often be an issue because, in the context of separation or divorce, there would usually be no chargeable consideration for SDLT purposes given for the transfer of an interest in land. SDLT would, however, in the absence of this exemption, be an issue if, for example, land was transferred subject to a mortgage. Transfers of mortgaged properties between cohabitees, or changes in the beneficial ownership of mortgaged properties by cohabitees, or indeed exchanges of properties between cohabitees, may well give rise to SDLT issues.

It should be noted that this exemption does not extend to transfers made by or to third parties, for example to a child of the marriage, as part of financial arrangements made on the occasion of separation or divorce.

There is a similar wide exemption from stamp duty contained in *FA 1985, s 83*.

The higher rate SDLT charge for additional dwellings has been introduced by *FA 2016* inserting *Sch 4ZA* into *FA 2003*. In broad outline the effect of the new rules is that if a taxpayer purchases a dwelling and, at the end of the day of completion, owns another dwelling as well, then he will have to pay SDLT on the purchase at higher rates, those higher rates representing a surcharge of 3% on the rates that would otherwise have applied. Dwellings are excluded from this surcharge if they cost less than £40,000 or if they are subject to a lease with an unexpired term of more than 21 years. The surcharge does not apply if the purchased dwelling is intended to be the purchaser's only or main residence and replaces another dwelling which had previously been the purchaser's only or main residence. The precise conditions for this relief for replacements are somewhat technical and the relief does not apply in some circumstances where one might have expected it to.

In deciding whether the surcharge applies, spouses or civil partners are treated as a unit if they are living together for which the same tests apply as for the purposes of income tax. Thus, for example, if husband and wife are living together, the husband alone owns the matrimonial home and the wife purchases a holiday home (or vice versa) the purchase will normally attract the surcharge, even though the spouse who makes the purchase has no interest in the other property.

The surcharge may well apply to a property transaction entered into as a consequence of marriage breakdown.

Example 16.9 – Divorce and higher rate SDLT charge for additional dwellings

Mr and Mrs J occupy a house in London which is their matrimonial home and their main residence. This property is owned solely by Mr J. They also have a holiday home in Cornwall which is owned solely by Mrs J. Both properties are unencumbered freeholds worth considerably in excess of £40,000. They own no other properties at any relevant time.

They separate permanently and commence divorce proceedings. After the date of permanent separation, but before Decree Absolute, Mr J sells the London property. He uses part of the proceeds of sale to purchase a smaller property for his own occupation and transfers the other part to Mrs J, who herself buys a smaller property for her own future occupation.

Mr J is clearly not liable for the surcharge on his purchase since he owns only one dwelling at the end of the day of completion and because of the permanent separation he is no longer 'aggregated' with Mrs J for these purposes.

It is also seems that Mrs J escapes the surcharge. Although she will own two dwellings at the end of the day of completion, the new dwelling seems to qualify as a replacement for the previous matrimonial home for the purposes of *paragraph 3(6)* of the *Schedule*. This requires Mrs J to intend the purchased dwelling to be her only. or main. residence, which she does. It also requires that:

- in another land transaction the purchaser or the purchaser's spouse or civil partner at the time disposed of a major interest in another dwelling which itself had been the purchaser's only or main residence; and

- following an amendment made by *FA 2018*, immediately after the effective date of this transaction neither the purchaser nor the purchaser's spouse or civil partner had a major interest in the sold dwelling; and

- at no time during the period beginning with the effective date of the previous transaction and ending with the effective date of the transaction concerned, that is her purchase, had the purchaser or the purchaser's spouse or civil partner acquired a major interest in any other dwelling with the intention of it being the purchaser's only or main residence. (There are time limits specified in the legislation but assume for the purposes of the example that these are satisfied.)

There is no requirement that the purchaser had any beneficial interest in the previous dwelling nor that, if the sale is undertaken by the purchaser's spouse rather than by the purchaser himself or herself, the couple should have been living together at the time.

The position would, however, be different if Mr J had sold the matrimonial home after the Decree Absolute, when he was no longer a spouse of Mrs J.

In that case, she could not benefit from the replacement relief and would have to pay the surcharge on her own purchase.

The position would also be different if, rather than selling the former matrimonial home, Mr J retained it for his own occupation and instead raised money from another source to pay to Mrs J to finance her purchase of a property for her own occupation.

Although this legislation is new, it is already clear that it will sometimes apply in an unexpected way and that its application is sensitive to the timing of transactions.

Certain modifications were made to the legislation dealing with the surcharge by *FA 2018*. *Paragraph 9A*, inserted into *Sch 4ZA* by *FA 2018*, disapplies the surcharge where, broadly speaking, one spouse or civil partner purchases from the other. However, this relief applies only where, on the effective date of the transaction, the two spouses or civil partners are living together. Thus permanent separation ends this relief.

Paragraph 9B, also inserted into *Sch 4ZA* by *FA 2018*, contains a relief which applies where there is a property adjustment order on divorce, dissolution of civil partnership, etc. The paragraph applies where:

(a)   a person ('A') has a major interest in a dwelling;

(b)   a property adjustment order has been made in respect of the interest for the benefit of another person ('B'); and

(c)   the dwelling:

(i)   is B's only or main residence; and

(ii)   is not A's only or main residence.

Where the paragraph applies, A is to be treated for the purposes of the Schedule as not having any interest in the dwelling. This could relieve him from the obligation to pay the surcharge on the purchase of another dwelling. A 'property adjustment order' is defined as meaning an order under *s 24(1)(b)* of the *Matrimonial Causes Act 1973* and under equivalent provisions in other legislation dealing with property adjustment orders after overseas divorce, property adjustment orders under the matrimonial law of Northern Ireland and property adjustment orders made in connection with the dissolution etc, of civil partnerships.

Note, that since April 2015, SDLT has no longer applied to land transactions in Scotland. These are now subject to Land and Buildings Transaction Tax (LBTT). In the case of Wales, Land Transaction Tax (LTT) has replaced SDLT starting from 1 April 2018.

Pre-owned assets tax

16.39   This is seldom an issue.

The disposal of any property is an 'excluded transaction' in relation to any person if, *inter alia*:

- the property was transferred to his spouse or civil partner (or, where the transfer has been ordered by a court, to his former spouse or civil partner);

- it was a disposal by way of gift (or, where the transfer is for the benefit of his former spouse or civil partner, in accordance with a court order), by virtue of which the property became settled property in which his spouse or civil partner or former spouse or civil partner is beneficially entitled to an interest in possession (see *FA 2004, Sch 15, para 10(1)(b)* and *(c)*).

PARTICULAR ISSUES

The matrimonial home and the CGT main residence exemption

Focus

In a case where a couple own more than one home the application of the main residence exemption may not be straightforward and it is important to establish the facts before any transfer takes place.

The 'three-year rule' was often extremely helpful and its reduction to 18 months has greatly increased the problems in this area. In other cases the former *ESC D6* now *TCGA 1992, s 225B* may be helpful.

16.40   The breakdown of a relationship will almost invariably lead to one or both parties to the marriage leaving the matrimonial home. It will also often lead to the transfer of the former matrimonial home, or of an interest in it, from one spouse to the other, or from one spouse into a settlement for the benefit of the other. Relationship breakdown will also often be followed by the sale of the former matrimonial home to a third party. The situation is even more complicated if the couple have owned or occupied more than one property.

The first step will be to establish to which (if any) of the properties in question the main residence exemption applies. It should be borne in mind that, in the case of an individual living with his spouse or civil partner, there can only be one main residence for both, so long as they are living together, and where a notice as to which residence the exemption is to apply to affects both the individual and his spouse or civil partner, it must be given by both (see *TCGA 1992, s 222(6)*).

16.41   Moreover, in the case of an individual living with his spouse or civil partner, if there is a disposal of, or of an interest in, a dwelling-house which is their only or main residence from one to the other, then the recipient inherits the transferor's history of entitlement to the exemption (see *TCGA 1992, s 222(7)* and CG64950). If the exemption is restricted in the hands of the transferor, this problem thus passes on to the transferee.

There may be scope for planning if a property is to be transferred that has qualified for the exemption during part only of its ownership by the transferor but which will qualify without restriction in the hands of the transferee: if the transfer can be effected within the 'no gain, no loss' rule but outside *TCGA 1992, s 222(7)* the chargeable element of the gain falls away.

Example 16.10 – Transfers where the main residence exemption is restricted

Mr and Mrs K occupy a property which is owned outright by Mr K. Their main residence exemption currently attaches to it but there was a period earlier in Mr K's ownership during which the exemption did not attach to it.

The property shows a gain of £1m. Differences have, unfortunately, arisen between Mr and Mrs K. They are still living together in the property but are contemplating separation followed by divorce proceedings. They envisage that, if they separate, Mr K will transfer the property into the outright ownership of Mrs K who will thereafter occupy it as her only residence while Mr K will live elsewhere.

Mr and Mrs K decide to press ahead with the transfer while they are still living together. Mr K therefore transfers his interest in the property to Mrs K. Soon afterwards they separate permanently. Mrs K continues to occupy the property in question as her only residence while Mr K goes to live elsewhere.

Mrs K will now have her own separate entitlement to the exemption, which will automatically attach to this property since this is her sole residence as a question of fact. However, *TCGA 1992, s 222(7)* applies. The result is that Mrs K's entitlement to the exemption is 'contaminated' by Mr K's

---

history of non-entitlement. Mrs K will inherit Mr K's acquisition cost under the 'no gain, no loss' principle.

Consequently, when Mrs K comes to sell the property a proportionate part of the gain she realises will be taxable, subject to whatever other exemptions and reliefs are then available.

Contrast the position if the transfer of the property was postponed until after the date of permanent separation. In that case, so long as Mrs K occupied the property continuously as her only or main residence until a time within 18 months of her disposing of it, the exemption would apply in full to the gain she realised on its disposal, notwithstanding that there had been restricted entitlement to the exemption before the date of transfer.

In most cases, the main residence exemption will attach to the former matrimonial home, though if the couple have occupied more than one residence they may have made a joint election for the exemption to attach to a residence which is not, on the face of things, their main residence. The restriction upon the ability of non-UK residents to make elections as to which property the exemption attaches to, introduced by *FA 2015, s 37* and *Sch 9* inserting *TCGA 1992, ss 222A–222C*, will now need to be taken into account.

In this context the 'three-year rule' formerly contained in *TCGA 1992, s 223(1)* was extremely helpful and the reduction of the period, in most cases, to 18 months by *FA 2014, s 58* is unhelpful. If the main residence exemption attaches to the former matrimonial home then, if a spouse has ceased to occupy that former matrimonial home as a result of the breakdown of the relationship, he has 18 (formerly 36) months in which to transfer his interest in the property before losing entitlement to the exemption (though bearing in mind that it may be restricted in some other way, for example by a previous period of non-occupation).

Once a couple have separated permanently, each becomes separately entitled to the main residence exemption and may make a separate election for the exemption to attach to a separate property, if otherwise entitled to do so. Prompt action may be needed to make the best use of the exemption.

Example 16.11 – Advantages of prompt election for main residence exemption

Mr and Mrs L own two properties, a house in the country and a flat in London, in each case as beneficial tenants in common in equal shares.

Both have appreciated greatly in value. They divide their time between the two but have made a joint election for the London flat to qualify for the exemption, on the basis that it is increasing in value more quickly and that it is likely to be sold first.

The relationship breaks down and as a result Mr L ceases to occupy the London flat. He acquires rented accommodation in London for his own use. However, he continues to make regular use of the country house at weekends (when Mrs L is not there).

It is less than two years since these changes happened. It is anticipated that, when a settlement is negotiated between the parties, Mr L will assign to Mrs L his interest in both the country house and the London flat. Mr L also intends, at a later stage, to purchase a further London property for his future occupation, in which case he will give up his rented accommodation.

Mr L will probably be well advised to make an immediate election in favour of the country house. This will prevent his exemption from attaching to his rented accommodation where it would be wasted. It will give him at least 18 months' worth of the exemption in respect of the country house, where it will be more useful. This will not prejudice his entitlement to the exemption in respect of the London flat which will continue to apply for up to 18 months after his departure from it. When he acquires his new property in London, he should consider whether to make a fresh election in favour of that property, to make sure that the exemption attaches to that property, if he thinks it will be more useful there.

TCGA 1992, s 225B (formerly Extra-statutory Concession D6)

16.42   In cases where the transfer of a property, or of an interest in it, will not in any case be exempt under the 18-month rule, it may be advantageous to claim the benefit of *TCGA 1992, s 225B* which has replaced ESC D6 for disposals made on or after 6 April 2009. This provides as follows:

'(1)   Where an individual –

    (a)   ceases to live with his spouse or civil partner in a dwelling-house or part of a dwelling-house which is their only or main residence, and

    (b)   subsequently disposes of, or of an interest in, the dwelling-house or part to the spouse or civil partner, then, if conditions A to C are met, *ss 222* to *224* shall apply as if the dwelling-house or part continued to be the individual's only or main residence until the disposal.

(2) Condition A is that the disposal mentioned in *subs (1)(b)* is pursuant to –

    (a) an agreement between the individual and his spouse or civil partner made in contemplation of or otherwise in connection with the dissolution or annulment of the marriage or civil partnership, their judicial separation or the making of a separation order in respect of them, or their separation in other circumstances such that the separation is likely to be permanent, or

    (b) an order of a court –

        (i) made on granting an order or a decree of divorce or nullity of marriage, for the dissolution or annulment of the civil partnership, or for judicial separation,

        (ii) made in connection with the dissolution or annulment of the marriage or civil partnership or the parties' judicial separation and which is made at any time after the granting of such an order or decree,

        (iii) made at any time under *s 22A, 23, 23A, 24* or *24A* of the *Matrimonial Causes Act 1973*,

        (iv) made at any time under *art 25* or *26* of the *Matrimonial Causes (Northern Ireland) Order 1978*,

        (v) made under *s 8* of the *Family Law (Scotland) Act 1985*, including incidental orders made by virtue of *s 14* of that Act, or

        (vi) made at any time under any provision of *Sch 5* to the *Civil Partnership Act 2004* that corresponds to any of the provisions mentioned in paragraphs (iii) and (iv).

(3) Condition B is that in the period between the individual ceasing to reside in the dwelling-house or part of the dwelling-house and the disposal to the spouse or civil partner, the dwelling-house or part continues to be the only or main residence of the spouse or civil partner.

(4) Condition C is that the individual has not given notice under *s 222(5)* that another dwelling-house or part of a dwelling-house is to be treated as the individual's main residence for any part of that period.

(5) *Section 223* (as applied by this section) shall apply only on the making of a claim by the individual.'

16.43 The limitations of this relief should be noted. In particular, it applies only in relation to transfers between spouses or civil partners, thus not to a sale on the open market, and it requires the spouse or civil partner who claims the benefit of the relief to give up the main residence exemption in respect of any other property for the period in question, thereby potentially storing up CGT problems for himself in the future. It is therefore much less beneficial than the 18-month rule, in cases where that rule applies.

16.44 A series of decisions of the courts and tax tribunals have addressed the question of what quality of occupation of a dwelling is needed to turn that occupation from mere occupation into residence so that the dwelling in question becomes the taxpayer's residence, rather than merely a dwelling which he is occupying on a temporary basis, so that he will be entitled to main residence relief on disposing of it if the other conditions of the relief are satisfied. This is a sensitive issue in the context of relationship breakdown which is very likely to lead to upheaval in the lives of those concerned.

In *Goodwin v Curtis* [1998] STC 475, a case where the taxpayer, who was separated from his wife, had occupied the dwelling in question, a farmhouse, for just over one month and it had already been put on the market when he moved in, the Court of Appeal held that the relief was not available. Millett LJ accepted the substance of the Commissioners' finding that the nature, quality, length and circumstances of the taxpayer's occupation of the farmhouse did not make his occupation qualify as residence. Schiemann LJ accepted the Revenue's contention that in order to qualify for the relief the taxpayer must provide some evidence that his residence in the property showed some degree of permanence, some degree of continuity or some expectation of continuity.

The difficulty is that, in the nature of things, the breakdown of a relationship is likely to lead to a lack of continuity and permanence in the lives of those concerned.

16.45 The issues are illustrated by four decisions of the First-tier Tribunal Tax Chamber reported in 2013, *Bradley v Revenue & Customs Commissioners* [2013] UKFTT 131(TC); *Moore v Revenue & Customs Commissioners* [2013] UKFTT 433 (TC); *Wade Llewellyn v HMRC* [2013] UKFTT 323 (TC) and *Morgan v HMRC* [2013] UKFTT 181 (TC). It is worth looking closely at these decisions.

16.46 In *Bradley v Revenue & Customs Commissioners*, Mrs Bradley had at all relevant times been married to Mr Bradley. Until August 2007 they lived together at 118 Ashley Road, which was owned by them jointly. In addition Mrs Bradley owned 124 Exning Road and 68 Weston Way, both of which were normally let to tenants.

In the year or so leading up to August 2007 differences arose between Mr and Mrs Bradley and in August 2007 Mrs Bradley left Ashley Road. As the flat at Weston Way was vacant she moved there. When the tenancy at Exning Road ended she moved from Weston Way to Exning Road.

At that stage her intentions were to separate permanently from her husband with a view to obtaining a divorce following a two-year separation.

Mrs Bradley moved into Exning Road in April 2008. She made certain improvements to make it more a 'home'. However, she had already, in March 2008, placed Exning Road on the market for sale. Although no offers were forthcoming the property was never taken off the market.

During the autumn of 2008 Mr and Mrs Bradley became reconciled and Mrs Bradley moved back to Ashley Road in November 2008. She then sold Exning Road in January 2009. The point at issue was whether the main residence relief applied to Exning Road because of Mrs Bradley's occupation between April and November 2008.

The tribunal decided that Mrs Bradley had not occupied Exning Road in such a way as to qualify for the relief. At the time she moved into Exning Road she had already placed it on the market and she never withdrew her instructions to the estate agents. She never intended to live permanently at Exning Road; it was always only ever going to be a temporary home, and therefore it was never her residence for the purposes of the relief.

It is noteworthy that the tribunal considered the fact that Mrs Bradley had been occupying Exning Road and no other dwelling during the period in question was not in itself sufficient to secure the relief.

Another interesting feature of the decision is that the tribunal accepted the separation of Mrs Bradley from her husband was likely at the time to have been permanent, so that she and her husband were separately entitled to the relief, on the basis of her intentions at the time, even though in the event the separation proved not to be permanent.

16.47 In *Moore v Revenue & Customs Commissioners*, Mr Moore purchased 110 Headlands, a two-bedroom house, on 5 November 2002. This and all the properties concerned were in Huntingdon. He let the property out from November 2002 until November 2006. When the last tenant left, Mr Moore's first marriage was in difficulties. Mr Moore moved out of the matrimonial home, 9 Church Street and into 110 Headlands, his first wife remaining at 9 Church Street.

Mr Moore took some furniture with him from 9 Church Street and bought further furniture for his own use. He also took all his clothes with him as he knew he would not return to 9 Church Street to live there.

Mr Moore had a lady friend, subsequently his second wife on their marriage in January 2011, who lived at 64 Orthwaite. Mr Moore said in evidence that it was around March or April 2007 that his relationship with this lady developed to the point that they decided they would live together.

After Mr Moore had moved to 110 Headlands, some correspondence continued to be sent to him at 9 Church Street and some correspondence to 64 Orthwaite. His evidence was that during the period in which he lived at 110 Headlands, he spent pretty much every night there. His financial circumstances were unsettled because of impending divorce proceedings and his evidence was that he lived at 110 Headlands until his financial circumstances became clearer. However, fairly soon after moving into 110 Headlands, he began to look for another property. At this point, the position is complicated by the fact that Mr Moore produced further evidence to the tribunal after an adjournment: he produced documentary evidence that his estate agents commenced marketing 110 Headlands in April 2007. Contracts were exchanged on the purchase and completion took place in August 2007.

The property of the lady who became Mr Moore's second wife was put on the market by her in May 2007 and sold with completion also taking place in August 2007. Mr Moore and his second wife jointly purchased a further property, 10 Church Close, the purchase being completed in July 2007. This was a four-bedroomed house and, unlike 110 Headlands, had the space needed to accommodate Mr Moore, his second wife and her two sons.

There were produced to the tribunal letters written by Mr Moore to HMRC in 2010 suggesting that during the relevant period he had been living in 110 Headlands only temporarily.

Mr Moore moved money between different building society accounts in February 2007 and the judge concluded that this was preparatory to a move which Mr Moore knew at that time he would be making.

Mr Moore showed that he had been charged council tax on 110 Headlands for the period from November 2006 to July 2007 with a discount appropriate to single occupancy.

The judge accepted that Mr Moore had been living in 110 Headlands between November 2006 and July 2007. The question was whether his occupation had had the necessary degree of permanence, continuity or expectation of continuity.

The judge rejected Mr Moore's argument that when he moved into 110 Headlands he simply did not know how he was placed financially and that he was expecting to live there until his financial affairs were sorted out, which could have taken a long time. He decided that the most important factor which determined Mr Moore's expectation at any time of what the continuity or permanence of his occupation of 110 Headlands would be was the state of his relationship with the lady who subsequently became Mrs Moore. Mr Moore conceded that it was around March or April 2007 that his relationship with Mrs J Moore developed to the point that they decided they would live together. However, the judge had difficulty in accepting he had no serious hope or expectation that he would be able to buy a house with Mrs J Moore before March 2007. In that case, matters had moved on with almost unbelievable speed after that. The judge accepted that in matters of the heart things can move with such rapidity but had to consider that on the balance of probabilities Mr Moore had had such a serious hope or expectation before March 2007. He concluded that Mr Moore had failed to discharge the burden of proof which was on him to satisfy the judge that for any significant period after he moved to 110 Headlands he did not have an expectation of being able to move from there and set up a home jointly with Mrs J Moore. The judge emphasised the fact that post had been delivered during the relevant period to other addresses and the fact that Mr Moore had been unable to show any bills other than council tax documentation recognising his address as 110 Headlands in the relevant period. He concluded that Mr Moore had never envisaged 110 Headlands as a long-term home and that his occupation lacked the necessary degree of permanence, continuity or expectation of continuity.

16.48   In *Wade Llewellyn v HMRC*, Mr Wade Llewellyn had lived with his partner at 10 Netley Terrace, Southsea for a number of years. However, Mr Llewellyn began to experience personal difficulties with his partner. He purchased another property, 10 Henderson Road, which was in a very poor state. He moved into the property with a chair, sleeping bag and kettle. There was no evidence that he had established his base at 10 Henderson Road and he returned to 10 Netley Terrace to pick up his post. The relationship later healed and after about ten months he moved back permanently to Netley Terrace, letting out Henderson Road. The tribunal decided that there was no evidence to show that his occupation of Henderson Road had amounted to residence there with some degree of permanence, some degree of continuity or some expectation of continuity so as to qualify for the relief.

16.49   In *Morgan v HMRC*, Mr Morgan purchased a property intending to live there with his fiancé. Unfortunately for Mr Morgan, shortly before he moved in, his fiancé broke off the engagement and the property could no longer fulfil his intended purpose of being the matrimonial home. Mr Morgan nevertheless moved into the property hoping for a reconciliation. It became clear that this was not going to happen and, in the event, he only lived in the property for some two and half months. The tribunal found the case to be extremely finely-balanced but decided that Mr Morgan had intended when he moved in to make the property his permanent residence and that his occupation of the property did qualify it as a residence for the purposes of the relief.

16.50   Another interesting decision of the First-tier Tax Tribunal came in 2015 in *Dutton-Forshaw v HMRC* [2015] UK FTT 0478 (TC). One interesting feature of this decision is that the taxpayer had again occupied the property concerned for quite a short time, about seven weeks, but the tribunal still found that he had been occupying it as a residence and that the exemption applied.

The facts of this case were rather complicated. During the period of 12 years considered by the tribunal, the taxpayer had occupied nine different properties and also sometimes stayed on his boat moored in Lymington Harbour. He had divided his time in rather a complicated way between Lymington and London. During the period in which he occupied the property in question, 32 Cornwall Gardens, SW7 in August to September 2006, he had had strong ties to London where his business was, but his ex-wife and infant daughter were living in Lymington. After this short period of occupation of 32 Cornwall Gardens he moved back to Lymington, where he had lived previously and where he owned another property. This was because of a concern that his former wife, whose new husband was living in Spain, might herself go to live in Spain and take with her the taxpayer's daughter. The taxpayer was very much against this idea partly because he did not want to be separated from his daughter and partly because of concerns about his former wife's health. He was faced with the possibility that the only way of preventing his daughter's move to Spain would be for him to move back to Lymington to look after her. Cornwall Gardens was then rented out.

The tribunal considered that the question of permanence or continuity should not be over-stated. It was simply one of the factors to be taken into account in weighing up whether the property in question was a 'residence'. The tribunal found that, when the taxpayer moved into Cornwall Gardens, he had hoped to live there on a continuous basis but was aware that circumstances might arise which would require him to move to live full-time in Lymington. In that sense he was in a similar position to that of Mr Morgan (see **16.49** above). Although the taxpayer's bank statements and other formal correspondence continued to be sent to an address in Lymington, it was not essential to change this as the taxpayer could continue to pick up his post from his property in Lymington when he visited Lymington to see his daughter. The tribunal attached more importance to the fact that he registered his car at Cornwall Gardens and obtained a parking permit from Kensington & Chelsea, in the knowledge that the parking permit system in Kensington & Chelsea was policed very carefully. The tribunal found that 'the nature, quality, length and circumstances' of the taxpayer's occupation of Cornwall Gardens did make that occupation qualify as residence for the purposes of the exemption and, since he had had no other residence during the relevant period, Cornwall Gardens had been his only residence during that seven-week period, so the private residence relief and lettings relief were both available.

This decision contains a careful analysis of the earlier case law and the tribunal must be right in its conclusion that the question of whether a person's occupation of a dwelling is mere occupation or residence is a more subtle question than the question whether there is an element of permanence or continuity in his occupation.

16.51 All the above decisions were heavily fact-dependent and some of them were complicated by some dispute over the facts. However, the following lessons may be drawn for the taxpayer who moves to a new home as a result of a relationship breakdown and wishes to demonstrate that his new home is a residence rather than merely somewhere he is occupying on a temporary basis:

– so far as possible, arrange for correspondence to be addressed to that property;

– notify that address as the taxpayer's permanent address for official purposes such as council tax and the electoral roll, notifying HMRC would be a good start;

– move furniture and possessions to the property and try to demonstrate that the taxpayer is not just 'camping out' there; do not just take your chair, sleeping bag and kettle;

– spend as much time in that home as possible, especially nights (to demonstrate that it is a residence);

– formulate no plans for moving elsewhere and, above all, do not place the property on the market – or remove it from the market if it has already been put on the market. It seems to have been this point above anything else which undermined the position of Mrs Bradley and, indeed, Mr Goodwin.

Although some of these cases concerned relatively short periods of time, no doubt they were considered worth fighting because of the extension of the main residence exemption to the last 18 months (formerly 36 months) of ownership and in some cases to periods of letting.

Position where the former matrimonial home is to be retained following separation of the couple for occupation by one spouse only and where the non-occupying spouse wishes to keep a stake in the property

---

Focus

This area has become extremely difficult following the changes to the IHT treatment of settled property made by the *FA 2006*.

An arrangement under which one spouse has the sole right to occupy the former matrimonial home during his life or until the happening of a specified event without being entitled outright to the sale proceeds is likely to constitute a settlement for both CGT and IHT purposes. The CGT position is likely to be favourable but such an arrangement may well lead to IHT charges.

One alternative is to transfer a property into the outright ownership of the occupying spouse but subject to a charge granted to the non-occupying spouse linked to the value of the house. However the tax treatment of a gain realised on the redemption of such a charge is unclear. The intuitive answer is that the gain will be subject to CGT because the gain will be capital in economic terms. However, there are arguments that the gain will be subject to income tax. On the other hand, if tax was paid only when the charge was redeemed there would be funds available to pay the tax.

16.52   Here one enters difficult territory.

One traditional approach is to seek a *Mesher* order. Under this type of order, one spouse will have the sole right to occupy the property (perhaps with the children of the marriage) during his life or until the happening of a specified event, such as all the children of the marriage attaining a specified age or completing their tertiary education, but on the death of the occupying spouse or on the happening of that event, the property is to be sold and the proceeds divided between the two spouses (or their estates).

In such a case, the view of HMRC is that the making of such an order results in the property becoming settled property for CGT (see CG65365).

16.53   There will thus be disposals by both spouses of their entire interests in the property. However, this will usually be of no consequence for CGT purposes. Almost invariably, the occupying spouse will qualify for the main residence exemption and, usually the non-occupying spouse will be protected by the 18-month rule.

Once the property has become settled property then, since usually the occupying spouse will occupy as his main residence, the main residence exemption will apply, subject to the making of a claim as required by *TCGA 1992, s 225*.

16.54 A *Mesher*-type order is thus attractive from the point of view of CGT, except in a case where there has been a long interval since the departure of the non-occupying spouse from the former matrimonial home with the result that he is exposed to CGT on the disposal he is deemed to make on the making of the order.

Once the house is settled property, the interests of the former spouses in the property will be interests in settled property and thus, in a normal situation, exempt from CGT under *TCGA 1992, s 76*.

A similar result follows if the property is expressly settled upon the occupying spouse for life or some lesser period.

16.55 In an interesting First-tier Tax Tribunal decision, *Wagstaff and Another v Revenue & Customs Commissioners* [2014] UKFTT 43 (TC), the tribunal took a broad view of what constitutes settled property for CGT purposes. In that case, a husband and wife had purchased a flat from the wife's mother. The sale was subject to a brief agreement which allowed the mother/mother-in-law to continue to occupy the flat for the remainder of her life or until remarriage, in return for a lump-sum payment. The tribunal concluded that, in acquiring the flat on terms that included the agreement, the husband and wife were assuming the role of trustees and did not become at that time absolutely entitled to the flat with the exclusive right to direct how it should be dealt with. Thus the flat had become settled property and the principal private residence exemption was available.

In other words, if a property becomes subject to a legally binding arrangement which has the characteristics of a trust, then it will become settled property for CGT (and, indeed, for other legal purposes) even if the arrangement is not formally labelled as a trust.

16.56 However, since *FA 2006*, such an arrangement has become unattractive from the point of view of IHT. Although the definition of settled property for CGT purposes is quite distinct from the definition of a settlement for IHT purposes (these definitions being contained in *TCGA 1992, s 68* and *IHTA 1984, s 43* respectively), if property is settled property for the purposes of CGT, it will usually be hard to deny that it is comprised in a settlement for the purposes of IHT. The occupying spouse will normally insist, for his own protection, upon an exclusive right to occupy the property. Any arrangement under which one person has the exclusive right to occupy a property rent free but without being the exclusive beneficial owner seems likely to constitute a settlement for IHT purposes, unless the occupation is under the terms of a lease other than for life.

For a broad view of what can constitute a settlement for IHT purposes see *Smith and Others v Revenue & Customs Commissioners* [2009] SpC 742, [2009] STC (SCD) 386 (building society account in joint names, arrangement that one joint holder would be solely entitled to interest during her life and the other joint holder to the capital on her death).

If the property has become comprised in a settlement for IHT purposes then it will be 'relevant property' and thus exposed to the ten-yearly and exit charges. These charges will, as the law currently stands, be at a maximum rate of 6%. They may, however, be irksome depending upon the value involved, particularly because, by definition, there will normally be no liquid funds comprised in the settlement from which the charges could be paid.

Planning strategies based upon securing multiple nil rate bands would be difficult to deploy in this scenario as they would involve fragmenting the ownership of the property between different settlements when the essence of the arrangement must be that one spouse is entitled to occupy the property as whole.

16.57 Furthermore, although the former matrimonial home will thus be relevant property, the capital interests of the former spouses in it will also be within their estates for IHT purposes as reversionary interests in settled property to which the settlors are entitled (*IHTA 1984, s 48(1)(b)*) (assuming both spouses previously had interests in the property).

One alternative approach would involve the transfer of the property into the outright beneficial ownership of the occupying spouse, the non-occupying spouse being given a deferred charge over the property redeemable only on the happening of the events under which a sale of the property would have been triggered under a *Mesher*-type order. The amount needed to redeem the charge would be linked to the value of the property at that time.

In the author's view, it is important to look at the arrangements, whether or not comprised in a court order, as a whole. The details of the arrangement might well be such as to make the property settled property for CGT, as in the *Wagstaff* case. If, for example, the property is supposed to be in the outright beneficial ownership of the occupying spouse but cannot be sold without the consent of the other spouse, it seems likely that it would be treated as settled property for both CGT and IHT purposes.

If the property is not settled property for CGT, then one enters especially different territory in the tax treatment of the deferred charge. It is reasonably clear, in the author's view, that the 'profit' realised by the non-occupying spouse on the redemption of the charge would be subject, one way or another, either to income tax or to CGT, subject to whatever of the usual reliefs and exemptions were available.

It is, however, harder to see precisely how the gain would be charged to tax, or how any tax would be calculated. The general view seems to be that the gain would be subject to CGT, which seems intuitively the right answer, but the position is far from clear.

One disquieting possibility is that the gain might be subject to income tax as interest. This is counter-intuitive: a gain linked to the growth in value of a capital asset would not normally be characterised as interest. However, the view of HMRC is that, where the trustees of the estate of a deceased person make loans linked to the retail prices index, or a similar index, to the surviving spouse, the uplift in value above the principal sum lent constitutes interest and is taxable as such (HMRC Trusts and Estates Newsletter April 2017). This is not a directly analogous situation (and, in any case, HMRC may well be wrong) but there are points of similarity and the views of HMRC should be borne in mind. In *Pike v Revenue & Customs Commissioners* [2014] All ER (D) 172 (Jun) the Court of Appeal upheld decisions of the First-tier Tribunal and the Upper Tribunal that an additional sum payable on redemption of loan stock was interest, even though it was not payable periodically and was not labelled as interest by the parties.

16.58 Depending upon the drafting of the charge, it might qualify as a 'deeply discounted security' within *ITTOIA 2005, Pt 4, Ch 8*. In that case there would be a charge to income tax on the difference between the redemption proceeds and the amount paid to acquire the security (*ITTOIA 2005, s 439*). However it might, depending upon the drafting, qualify as an 'excluded indexed security' under *ITTOIA 2005, s 433*, on the basis that its value was linked to the value of an asset within the scope of CGT and thus not be a 'deeply discounted security'. This presupposes that a financial instrument issued in a family as opposed to a commercial context can be a security for tax purposes, but this did not seem to trouble the tax tribunal in *Audley v Revenue & Customs Commissioners* [2011] UKFTT 219 (TC).

Another possibility is that *ITA 2007, Pt 9A* might apply on the basis that the charge was land and was acquired with the sole or main object of realising a gain from disposing of the land. *ITA 2007, s 517S* provides that, in that Part, the word 'land' includes *inter alia* any estate, interest or right in or over land.

It is known from *Page v Lowther* [1983] STC 799 that what is now *ITA 2007, Pt 9A* can apply to transactions not specifically designed to avoid tax.

(It would seem very hard to apply *ITA 2007, Pt 9A* to a beneficial interest in the former matrimonial home under a *Mesher*-type order, since this would normally be, in substance, retention of a pre-existing beneficial interest in the property.)

16.59 If the profit realised on redemption of the charge was not subject to income tax then it would, in the writer's view, be subject to CGT.

One of the difficulties would lie in establishing the acquisition cost of the charge since its market value on creation would clearly reflect the delay before it was due to be redeemed and the uncertainty as to when this would happen, as well as the possibility of an increase in value.

Thus, the choice seems to lie between incurring small but recurrent charges to IHT or what might be a more substantial income tax or CGT charge at a future date, but when there would be funds to pay the tax.

Legal and beneficial ownership

Focus

The beneficial ownership of an asset held in the joint names of spouses or in the sole name of a husband or wife may differ from the legal ownership. In most cases it is the beneficial rather than the legal ownership which is important for tax purposes.

The question of beneficial ownership will not usually be litigated in matrimonial proceedings because of the very wide powers the court has to adjust ownership. However it is important to establish the beneficial ownership of an asset for tax purposes.

The beneficial ownership may be difficult to establish except in a case where the parties have clearly recorded this when the asset was acquired. There is a great deal of case law arising from disputes between cohabitees over property held in joint names and an important decision of the Supreme Court seems to give the court more latitude in determining beneficial ownership of jointly held property than was previously the case.

The practice of HMRC in most circumstances is to accept an agreement between the parties as to beneficial ownership of a home held in the sole name of one of the spouses, or a recognition of an equitable interest by the court.

> If both spouses have a beneficial interest in a property it is vital to establish whether they hold as beneficial joint tenants or tenants in common. In the former case the joint tenancy can be severed leading to ownership as tenants in common.

16.60 It is important to bear in mind that, for most tax purposes, it is the beneficial rather than the legal ownership of a property that counts. If a property is held in the sole name of one spouse, then the other spouse may well have a beneficial interest. It is also possible that, where a property is held in joint names, the interests of the spouses are not equal.

This is a complex area and only the barest outline of the issues can be given here.

In general the beneficial ownership of a property will not be an issue in matrimonial litigation because the court has such wide powers to order changes to the beneficial ownership. This, however, does not alter the importance of beneficial ownership in the tax context.

In some cases the intended beneficial ownership of a property will have been recorded at the time of its acquisition, for example by a declaration of trust. In such a case it may be unnecessary to look further.

In the absence of such a written record of the intended beneficial ownership it may be necessary to look at contributions to the purchase price and to consider the application of the equitable presumptions (if English law applies). If a husband funds the acquisition of a property in the name of his wife then there is a presumption of advancement: the husband is presumed to have intended a gift to his wife. If, however, a wife funds the acquisition of a property in the name of her husband then the husband is presumed to hold on resulting trust for her. These, however, are only presumptions which can be readily rebutted by a contrary intention. If a dispute about beneficial ownership comes to court then the court may be expected to look at whatever evidence is available of the express or implied intention of the parties.

The presumption of advancement will be abolished, prospectively, by *Equality Act 2010, s 199* when *Pt 15* of that Act comes into force.

The beneficial ownership of a property is more likely to be litigated when a relationship between unmarried cohabitees breaks down, in which case the court lacks the wide powers it has in the case of the breakdown of a marriage or civil partnership. In *Stack v Dowden* [2007] 2 AC 432 the House of Lords decided, in a case involving the breakdown of a relationship between an unmarried couple, that a conveyance into joint names, in the domestic consumer context, established a prima facie case of joint and equal beneficial interests unless and until the contrary was proved. The contrary could be proved by looking at all the relevant circumstances in order to discern the common intention of the parties. In the particular case, the House of Lords upheld the decision of the Court of Appeal that the beneficial ownership was unequal, while emphasising that this was an unusual conclusion based upon the particular facts.

16.61   The Supreme Court addressed the difficulties raised in ascertaining the beneficial ownership of a property following the breakdown of a relationship between cohabitees, where there was no express declaration of trust, in the case of *Jones v Kernott* [2012] 1 AC 776.

In that case the parties met in 1980 and formed a relationship. They did not marry. They had two children. In 1985 the parties bought a property in their joint names. In 1993 the parties separated. Thereafter, the claimant assumed sole responsibility for the outgoings on the property they had purchased in 1985. In 1995 the parties cashed in a joint life insurance policy and the proceeds were divided between them to enable the defendant to put down a deposit on a home of his own. The claimant had conceded that in 1993 when the couple separated there had been insufficient evidence to displace the presumption that their beneficial interests in the property they had bought in 1985 followed the legal title, so that they were then joint tenants at law and in equity. However, she contended that the purchase of the second property, along with other events since the separation, was evidence that their intentions with regard to the beneficial interest in the first property had changed. Thus, the point at issue was whether, although the couple had originally had equal beneficial interests in the first property, those beneficial interests had subsequently changed, without any express agreement or documentation.

The court held that the following principles were to be applied in cases where the family home was bought in the joint names of a cohabiting couple who were both responsible for a mortgage but without any express declaration of their beneficial interests. The starting point was that equity followed the law and that they were joint tenants both at law and in equity. However, that presumption could be displaced by showing (a) that the parties had had a different common intention at the time when they acquired the home, or (b) that they had later formed a common intention that their respective shares would change. Their common intention was to be deduced objectively from their conduct. In those cases where it was clear either (a) that the parties had not intended joint tenancy at the outset, or (b) that they had changed their original intention, but it was not possible to ascertain by direct evidence or inference what their actual intention had been as to the shares in which they would own the property, the answer was that each was entitled to that share which the court considered fair having regard to the whole course of dealing between them in relation to the property. The 'whole course of dealing' had to be given a broad meaning, enabling a similar range of factors to be taken into account as might be relevant to ascertaining the parties' actual intentions. Each case would turn on its own facts and, whilst financial contributions were relevant, there were many other factors which might enable the court to decide what shares were intended, in a case where it was possible to ascertain their intentions, or fair, in a case where it was not possible to infer what their actual intention had been.

This decision seems to give the courts more latitude in determining what the beneficial ownership of a property held in joint names is than had previously been the case, especially in circumstances where there is a reason to believe that the intentions of the parties as to beneficial ownership have changed since the original acquisition of the property. In such circumstances, there will be more scope for the court to decide what is fair. However, the court still cannot make a finding as to the beneficial ownership of a property contrary to whatever evidence exists showing what the parties actually intended. Thus, the discretion of the court when dealing with disputes as to the beneficial ownership of a property between cohabitees is still very much more limited than in the case of the breakdown of a marriage or civil partnership.

16.62   The practice of HMRC in the situation where it is claimed that a spouse or civil partner has an equitable interest in a home held in the sole name of the other spouse or civil partner is recorded in CG65310. This (sensible) practice is that if there is an agreement between the parties or recognition by the court of such an equitable interest, it should be accepted that the wife or civil partner had an equitable interest in the home from the outset. Moreover, their equitable interest of up to one half should be accepted without investigation, unless exceptionally there is obvious evidence to contradict it. Presumably, the same practice would apply in reverse in the case of a house held in the sole name of the wife where it is claimed that the husband has an equitable interest.

It should also be borne in mind that, under the *Law of Property Act 1925, s 53(1)(c)*, a disposition of an equitable interest subsisting at the time of the disposition must be in writing signed by the person disposing of the same, or by his agent thereunto lawfully authorised in writing or by will. However, this section does not affect the creation or operation of resulting, implied or constructive trusts. Thus, in general, once an equitable interest exists, it can only be disposed of in writing. Note that the *Law of Property Act 1925* applies only in England and Wales.

Where a property is owned by husband and wife beneficially then they will be either equitable joint tenants or equitable tenants in common. If they are equitable joint tenants then their interests will be co-extensive: neither can have a greater beneficial interest than the other. If, however, they are equitable tenants in common then they will hold separate shares in the equity which may be equal or may be of different sizes.

An equitable joint tenancy can always be 'severed' thus converting it into an equitable tenancy in common. If there is initially a declaration of a beneficial joint tenancy which is later severed then the parties will become tenants in common in equal shares, even if the initial contributions to the purchase price were unequal (see *Goodman v Gallant* [1986] 1 All ER 311).

Conventionally, an undivided share in a property is valued for tax purposes at a 10% discount to the corresponding percentage share of the overall value of the property, except where the inheritance tax related property rule applies. However, the extent of the discount and the allocation of value between spouses are now a matter for negotiation if one of the co-owners has occupation rights under the *Trusts of Land and Appointment of Trustees Act 1996*. See *IRC v Arkwright* [2004] STC 1323 and IHTM09737.

PARTICULAR SITUATIONS

Extracting funds from companies and settlements

Focus

Funds often need to be extracted from companies or trusts in the context of divorce and relationship breakdown but there are no special exemptions that apply in such a situation and extraction may well trigger tax liabilities.

16.63   Financial arrangements made in the context of relationship breakdown and divorce will often involve the extraction of funds from companies and trusts. There are no special exemptions which apply in this situation and all of the usual tax difficulties in extracting funds from companies and trusts will need to be considered.

If one spouse has much of his capital tied up in a trust or company structure, and if the other spouse is seeking to obtain a lump sum that can only be paid if funds are extracted from that structure, then the spouse seeking the lump sum can be expected to press for funds to be distributed to the other spouse first. In that case, any adverse tax consequences will fall upon that other spouse and the funds will reach the recipient spouse in a 'clean' form.

In *Ebsworth v Revenue & Customs Commissioners* [2009] UKFTT 199 (TC); [2009] SFT 602, the First-tier Tribunal in allowing an appeal against a notice issued under *TA 1988, s 703* accepted that certain transactions in securities had been undertaken for the purpose of separating the personal and commercial interests of the taxpayer and his estranged wife and none of the main objects of the transactions had been the avoidance of tax.

If funds seem likely to reach the recipient spouse with tax liabilities attached to them then, clearly, those tax liabilities must be quantified in order to ascertain the adequacy of the capital payment.

This will be especially significant if funds are to be extracted from an offshore trust. A capital payment to a beneficiary out of an offshore trust may attract an income tax liability under *ITA 2007, s 731* or a CGT liability under *TCGA 1992, s 87*.

16.64 Permanent separation and decree absolute may have a beneficial effect upon the liability to income tax or CGT of a spouse who is a settlor in relation to a settlement.

Following permanent separation, the fact that the permanently separated non-settlor spouse (or civil partner) may benefit under the settlement will not in itself be sufficient to bring that settlement within the settlement rule (*ITTOIA 2005, s 625(4)(a)* and *(b)*).

The fact that a former spouse or civil partner of a settlor is a beneficiary or potential beneficiary of an overseas settlement will not, in itself, be sufficient to give that settlor an interest so as to bring the settlement within *TCGA, s 86* leading to the attribution of its gains to the settlor. Moreover, the fact that any other person related to the settlor only by a marriage or civil partnership which has ended may benefit will not in itself be sufficient to give the settlor such an interest (even if it would have done before the marriage or civil partnership ended). This applies to the whole of the tax year during which the marriage or civil partnership ends, ie during which decree absolute is obtained or the civil partnership is dissolved (*TCGA 1992, Sch 5, para 4(4)*)).

Close companies

Focus

On decree absolute a husband and wife cease to be 'associates' of each other for the purposes of the close company legislation and this may give rise to a range of consequences which should always be considered in such a situation.

16.65   On decree absolute, a husband and wife cease to be 'relatives' and thus 'associates' of each other for the purposes of the close company legislation (*CTA 2010, s 448*). This could, under certain circumstances mean that a company ceased to be close, because the rights and powers of one spouse could no longer be attributed to the other in determining whether that other spouse had control of the company for the purposes of the close company provisions now contained in *CTA 2010, Pt 10* (see *CTA 2010, ss 450* and *451*). An expense incurred by a close company in providing a benefit to a former spouse could not be treated as a distribution under *CTA 2010, s 1064* as a benefit provided to an associate of a participator (see *CTA 2010, s 1069*). However, a benefit provided to a former spouse of a participator in a close company could still, presumably, be treated as a benefit to that participator if it discharged a financial obligation imposed on that participator under the terms of a court order or agreement reached in the context of the breakdown of the marriage, thus limiting planning possibilities.

One consequence of divorce or the dissolution of a civil partnership is that relief under *ITA 2007, s 383* for interest on a loan taken out to buy an interest in a close company might be lost, either because the company ceased to be close or because the former spouses or civil partners no longer had a 'material interest' in the company as defined in *ITA 2007, s 394* since their interests would no longer be aggregated for the purposes of that definition.

Spouses with non-UK domicile

Focus

Great care must be taken if one or both spouses are remittance basis users, especially in view of the *FA 2008* changes. A spouse is still a 'relevant person' for the purpose of the remittance rules even if permanently separated.

When either spouse has overseas connections it is important to consider the possibility of a charge to tax in another jurisdiction.

16.66   If one or both spouses have non-UK domiciles and are taxable on the remittance basis, then the greatest care should be taken that the financial arrangements made in the context of relationship breakdown and divorce do not involve any remittance of funds to the UK such as to give rise to a UK tax liability unless this is unavoidable.

This area has become more difficult following the changes to the remittance rules made by the *FA 2008*. Under the new rules, which are contained in *ITA 2007, Pt 14, Ch A1*, the overseas income or chargeable gains of an individual taxable on the remittance basis will be treated as remitted to the UK, *inter alia*, if the income or chargeable gains are brought to, or received or used in, the UK by or for the benefit of a 'relevant person'. A husband or wife or civil partner is a 'relevant person' for these purposes even if permanently separated *(ITA 2007, s 809M(2)(b)* and *(c))*. Where spouses are estranged and a spouse who is a remittance basis user makes payments to the other spouse out of funds potentially taxable on the remittance basis, the payer may be in a difficult position as he may become liable to tax as the result of a remittance wholly outside his control and of which he may have no knowledge. If circumstances allow, indemnities should be obtained in such a situation combined with undertakings to notify the paying spouse of any remittance.

Note that even after decree absolute a minor child of the dissolved marriage will still be a 'relevant person' in relation to both former spouses. A former spouse who is a remittance basis user may therefore be liable to tax on funds used in the UK by his or her former spouse for the benefit of a minor child even after decree absolute *(ITA 2007, s 809M (2)(d))*.

Where either spouse has overseas connections, the possibility of financial arrangements or asset transfers triggering overseas tax liabilities should always be borne in mind.

Although overseas taxes are outside the scope of this chapter, it is worth sounding a warning about the special difficulties that may arise if one spouse is a US taxpayer, especially where a spouse who is a US taxpayer is to transfer assets to a spouse who is not.

Liabilities to US tax may arise when there is no liability to UK tax. Since the USA imposes tax upon the basis of citizenship as well as a territorial basis, even a long-term UK resident may remain within the scope of US tax.

The assignment of life policies

> **Focus**
>
> It is common for life policies to be assigned in the context of divorce and relationship breakdown and tax liabilities may arise. There may be advantages in transferring the ownership of policies under the court order rather than by a separate agreement between the spouses.

16.67 The financial arrangements made in the context of relationship breakdown or divorce will often involve the assignment of life policies, or interests in life policies, between spouses.

If a non-qualifying life policy or, in certain limited circumstances, a qualifying life policy is assigned for money or money's worth then there may be a charge to higher rate tax in accordance with *ITTOIA 2005, Pt 4, Ch 9*.

For the purposes of that chapter, however, an assignment of rights under a policy or of a share in such rights is ignored if it is made between spouses or civil partners living together (*ITTOIA 2005, s 487*).

16.68 The Revenue previously took the view that the transfer by one spouse to the other of all or some of the rights under a policy as part of a divorce settlement was invariably for money or money's worth, thus potentially leading to a higher rate income tax charge. However, HMRC now accept that transferring ownership of the rights conferred by a life insurance policy under a court order is not for money or money's worth and no gain can arise because of it (see RI 267 (December 2003)). This change of policy followed the change of policy in relation to CGT hold-over relief.

It follows that, if it is desired to avoid the higher rate income tax charge that may arise on the assignment of a life policy or of an interest in a life policy for money or money's worth, and if such an assignment is intended to take place in the context of a divorce, it would be as well to make sure that the assignment took place in pursuance of a court order.

This HMRC change of practice may enable an immediate tax charge to be avoided but it is not all good news since the recipient spouse is, sooner or later, likely to be faced with an income tax charge when a 'chargeable event' arises in relation to the policy in question, if the policy is of a type subject to this charge.

CGT is seldom an issue on the assignment of a life policy, or of an interest in a life policy, made in the context of relationship breakdown or divorce. *TCGA 1992, s 210* has the effect of taking life policies out of the scope of CGT unless they are 'secondhand policies'. The section provides that a gain accruing on a disposal of, or of an interest in, the rights conferred by any policy of insurance or contract for a deferred annuity is not a chargeable gain unless:

(a) (in the case of a disposal of the rights) the rights, or any interest in the rights; or

(b) (in the case of a disposal of an interest in the rights) the rights, the interest or any interest from which the interest directly or indirectly derives (in whole or in part)'

have or has at any time been acquired by any person for actual consideration. However actual consideration for a disposal which is made by one spouse or civil partner to the other or is an 'approved post-marriage disposal or an approved post-civil partnership disposal' is to be treated as not constituting actual consideration.

For these purposes a disposal is an approved post-marriage disposal or an approved post-civil partnership disposal if:

(a)   it is made in consequence of the dissolution or annulment of a marriage or civil partnership by one person who was a party to the marriage or civil partnership to the other;

(b)   it is made with the approval, agreement or authority of a court (or other person or body) having jurisdiction under the law of any country or territory or pursuant to an order of such a court (or other person or body); and

(c)   the rights disposed of were, or the interests disposed of was, held by the person by whom the disposal is made immediately before the marriage or civil partnership was dissolved or annulled.

See *TCGA 1992, s 210(6)*.

The broad effect of this is that the transfer of a life policy between spouses in the context of divorce will not bring that policy within the scope of CGT, as a second-hand policy acquired for value, even if the assignment was for actual consideration.

FA 2013 imposed a general limit of £3,600 per annum upon the premiums that may be paid under a qualifying policy. All policies under which an individual is a beneficiary are aggregated for this purpose. This limit does not generally affect policies taken out before 6 April 2013. However, the assignment of a pre-6 April 2013 policy in the context of divorce or the dissolution of a civil partnership may bring such a policy within the new rules, either making it non-qualifying or making it a 'restricted relief qualifying policy'. Such a policy is subject to tax charges on the happening of a chargeable event to the extent that, broadly, premiums in excess of £3,600 per annum are paid after it becomes a restricted relief qualifying policy. If a qualifying policy issued on or after 21 March 2012 is assigned in this context and the assignment causes the assignee to breach the annual premium limit, taking his other qualifying policies into account, it will become non-qualifying. See *ICTA 1988, Sch 15, Pt A1, paras A1* and *A2, ITTOIA 2005, ss 463A–463D* and IPTM2081.

Transfers of assets in respect of which tax reliefs have previously been obtained

16.69   Great care needs to be taken if assets which are to be transferred in the context of divorce or relationship breakdown have previously attracted tax reliefs. See above for the issues where assets have been the subject of a potentially exempt transfer or are conditionally exempt from IHT. Another example is EIS relief, which may be clawed back if shares which have attracted the relief are transferred between spouses or civil partners no longer living together, in which case the relief for transfers between spouses or civil partners no longer applies (*ITA 2007, s 209(4)*). There is a similar rule for SEIS relief (*ITA 2007, s 257FA(4)*) and for social investment relief (*ITA 2007, s 257R(1)(d)*). However, holdover relief for gains reinvested in social enterprises is not clawed back on a disposal within marriage or civil partnership (*TCGA 1992, Sch 8B, para 6(1)(a)*).

If an individual subscribes for shares and then transfers them to another individual, at a time when transferor and transferee are living together as spouses or civil partners, the transferee is treated for the purposes of investors' relief as having subscribed for the shares (*TCGA 1992, s 169VU(3)*, inserted by *FA 2016, Sch 14*).

Note that share loss relief may be available if a person subscribes for shares in certain types of trading company and transfers those shares to his spouse or civil partner who subsequently realises a loss on their disposal (*ITA 2007, s 135(3)*). Thus an effect of postponing a transfer of shares between spouses until after decree absolute, in circumstances where the relief is not available to the transferor in relation to the transfer itself, may be to lose the share loss relief that might otherwise have been available on a subsequent disposal to a third party by way of a bargain at arm's length. The spouses or civil partners need not be living together at the date of the transfer.

Statutory residence test

16.70   For the purposes of the statutory residence test, a person has a family tie for a tax year if he has a relevant relationship at any time in that tax year with another person who is resident in the UK for that year and a relevant relationship exists between two people at any time, inter alia, if they are husband and wife or civil partners and not separated, applying the usual income tax test of separation. Under certain circumstances a person would therefore lose a 'family tie' at the end of the tax year of permanent separation which, if he was on the cusp of satisfying the statutory residence test, might result in his ceasing to be UK resident for tax purposes. See *FA 2013, Sch 45, para 32*.

Example 16.12 – Effect of permanent separation on the statutory residence test

Mr M is an international businessman. He has homes and business interests in a number of different countries. He is married to Mrs M.

Mr M regularly spends more than 45 but not more than 90 days in the UK in the course of a tax year. He does not meet any of the automatic UK tests or any of the automatic overseas tests. Therefore his residence status depends upon the number of his ties.

Mrs M has many ties to the UK and is undoubtedly UK resident. Therefore, so long as Mr M is married to Mrs M and they are not permanently separated, he has a family UK tie. He owns a house in the UK which is available for him to live in, so he has an accommodation tie. He regularly spends at least 40 days in the course of a tax year working in the UK, so he has a work tie. However, he has no other UK ties. There are no children of the marriage, so he has no other family ties.

Since Mr M spends more than 45 but not more than 90 days in the UK in the course of a tax year, and since he has three UK ties and (suppose) he has been resident in the UK for a number of years, he is resident in the UK under the statutory residence test.

However, Mr and Mrs M separate permanently early in the 2018/19 tax year. Mrs M ceases to use the UK house which belongs to Mr M, but Mr M retains it and continues to use it. This means that Mr M will continue to be UK resident until the end of the 2018/19 tax year but (assuming nothing else changes) he will cease to be UK resident at the end of that tax year as he will have only two UK ties.

Pension sharing

> **Focus**
>
> A number of issues need to be considered if the court makes a pension sharing order. One of these is the ability of the spouse whose pension rights have been reduced to rebuild his entitlement by making additional contributions. This is a complex area in which care must be taken. The flexibility for members of defined contribution pension schemes aged 55 and over to withdraw funds introduced by the *Taxation of Pensions Act 2014* may provide an alternative to pension sharing, although such withdrawals may give rise to immediate and substantial income tax charges.

16.71 This is a complex subject and only the barest outline will be given here.

The *Welfare Reform and Pensions Act 1999, Pt III* and *Pt IV* (which operate partly by inserting provisions into the *Matrimonial Causes Act 1973*) gives the court power to make pension-sharing orders in connection with proceedings in England and Wales for divorce or nullity of marriage. There are equivalent provisions in Scotland.

This power applies to most though not all forms of pension scheme. It applies not only to registered pension schemes, but also to unapproved schemes and to the earnings-related element of the state scheme. It does not apply to overseas schemes.

Where the court makes an order under this power the entitlement of one spouse under the scheme in question is reduced (a 'pension debit') and the other spouse is given rights of corresponding value (a 'pension credit').

The pension debits and credits must be expressed as a percentage of the cash-equivalent transfer value of the spouse whose rights are reduced.

A pension-sharing order can be made in respect of pensions that are in payment as well as in respect of rights to pension benefits which have not yet been drawn.

Where a pension-sharing order is made in respect of a funded scheme, the rights created for the spouse who acquires a pension credit may be given effect to either by creating rights for that spouse within the scheme or by making a transfer into a separate scheme.

Pension debits and credits will, respectively, reduce and increase the value of the pension rights of the spouses to be set against their lifetime allowances under *FA 2004*. It should, however, be borne in mind that the calculation of the value of pension rights for the purpose of this test is quite distinct from the calculation of the cash-equivalent transfer value.

It may therefore be possible for the spouse whose rights have suffered from the pension debit to make additional contributions, beyond those which would otherwise have been permissible under the *FA 2004*, to rebuild his entitlement. However, the greatest care must be taken in the event of a taxpayer with transitional rights under *FA 2004* wishing to make further contributions. Note in particular the warning set out at PTM029000. If the member has enhanced protection, fixed protection or fixed protection 2014, paying extra contributions may cause the member to lose their protection. See *FA 2004, Sch 36, para 13*.

If the rights of a scheme member with primary protection under *FA 2004* are reduced by a pension debit on or after 6 April 2006, then the value of that member's pension rights under primary pension protection will be recalculated and the member will be given a new personal lifetime allowance.

The reduced personal lifetime allowance applies to all benefit crystallisation events that take place after the member's rights have been reduced by the pension debit. The reduction occurs on the effective date of the pension-sharing order, not when the order is implemented.

Where the pension debit reduces a member's protected pension rights value below £1.5m, the member will lose primary protection and reverts to the standard lifetime allowance. See *FA 2004, Sch 36, para 11* and PTM092300.

If an individual has (at any time after 5 April 2006 but before the benefit crystallisation event) acquired rights under a registered pension scheme by reason of having become entitled to a pension credit, the pension credit derived from the same or another registered pension scheme, and the rights under that registered pension scheme which became subject to the corresponding pension debit consisted of or included rights to a post-commencement pension in payment, then that individual becomes entitled to a lifetime allowance enhancement factor with respect to that benefit crystallisation event. This reflects the fact that the pension credit will already have been tested against the lifetime allowance so it would be unreasonable to test it twice (see *FA 2004, s 220*). This section applies only if notice of intention to rely on it is given to HMRC in accordance with regulations made by HMRC. See PTM095200.

There are similar provisions for pension sharing on the dissolution or annulment of a civil partnership contained in the *Civil Partnership Act 2004, Sch 5, Pt 4*.

Finance Act 2011, Pt 4 made major changes to the taxation of pensions, including reductions to the annual allowance and lifetime allowance. Further restrictions have been introduced by the *FA 2013, FA 2014* and *FA 2016*. In each case there are transitional provisions.

Overview

16.72   In a rational world the breakdown of a relationship would not lead to any windfall tax-planning opportunities; nor would it lead to any windfall receipts for the Exchequer. The existing legislation does, broadly speaking, achieve the former objective, but not the latter! It is especially difficult to see why, as a matter of policy, transfers of assets ordered by the court on the occasion of marriage breakdown should lead to windfall CGT receipts for the Exchequer or why a settlement established for purely asset-protection reasons on the occasion of marriage breakdown should be exposed to the IHT ten yearly and exit charges.

Moreover, in a rational world, tax law would take a coherent and consistent approach to relationship breakdown, avoiding the many anomalies which exist at present. To single out one particular anomaly, it is extremely difficult to see why, under the *FA 2008* changes to the remittance basis of taxation, if a taxpayer who is a remittance-basis user separates from his spouse and cohabits with someone else then both his estranged spouse and the person with whom the taxpayer is cohabiting are 'relevant persons' in relation to the taxpayer. This seems to be having it both ways! Consequently, a remittance to the UK by either the estranged spouse or the cohabitee might impose a tax liability upon the taxpayer, even though a remittance by the estranged spouse might well be completely beyond the control or even the knowledge of the taxpayer.

Table 16.1 – Summary of some tax consequences of the different stages of the process of separation and divorce

Event	Tax consequences
Permanent separation of the couple	One spouse can no longer be liable to the high income child benefit charge by virtue of child benefit to which the other is entitled.
	The transferor spouse's history of entitlement to the CGT main residence exemption will no longer pass to the transferee spouse on a disposal of, or of an interest in, the dwelling-house which is occupied as their only or main residence between the spouses.
	If one spouse is a settlor in relation to a settlement, then the fact that the other spouse may benefit under that settlement will no longer in itself be sufficient to bring that settlement within the settlement rule (*ITTOIA 2005, s 625(4)*).
	An assignment of rights under a policy of life insurance, a contract for a life annuity or a capital redemption policy between the spouses is no longer ignored for the purposes of *ITTOIA 2005, Pt 4, Ch 9* (which charges to tax certain gains arising on such assignments if made for money or money's worth).
	The presumption of equal beneficial entitlement to the income of jointly held property ceases to apply: *ITA 2007, s 836*.
	EIS relief and SEIS relief previously given may be clawed back on a subsequent transfer of company shares between the couple. Social investment relief will be lost on a subsequent transfer of the investment between the spouses.
	Shares subsequently transferred between the spouses cannot entitle the transferee spouse to investors' relief on their disposal by virtue of their having been subscribed for by the transferor spouse.

	If one spouse subsequently purchases a dwelling, any dwellings owned by the other are not taken into account in deciding whether the higher rates of SDLT for additional dwellings apply. However, the relief from the surcharge for purchases by one spouse from the other ceases to apply.
End of tax year of permanent separation	Transfers of assets between the spouses cease to qualify for 'no gain, no loss' treatment for CGT purposes.
	Entitlement to the married couple's allowance for income tax ceases, even if it was previously available.
	The spouses can no longer have family ties to the UK by virtue of their relationship.
Decree absolute	If one spouse is a settlor in relation to an overseas settlement the fact that the other spouse is a beneficiary or potential beneficiary of that settlement will no longer, in itself, be sufficient to bring that settlement within *TCGA 1992, s 86*.
	The couple cease to be 'connected persons' for tax purposes, unless they are so treated for some other reason.
	The inheritance tax spouse exemption ceases to apply to transfers of value between the couple and the inheritance tax related property rule ceases to apply to the valuation of their property. Unused IHT nil rate band can no longer be transferred between them.
	The couple will no longer be 'relatives' and so 'associates' for the purposes of applying the close company legislation: *CTA 2010, s 448*.
	The couple cease to be 'relevant persons' in relation to each other for the purposes of the extended remittance rules introduced by *FA 2008*. Any other persons who were previously 'relevant persons' in relation to one spouse solely through a connection with the other also cease to be 'relevant persons' in relation to that first spouse.
	The possibility of share loss relief will no longer be preserved on transfers of certain shareholdings between the couple.

Chapter 17

Research and development relief

Anne Fairpo Barrister, CTA (Fellow), ATT

SIGNPOSTS

- **Qualifying R&D** – The project must seek an *advance* in overall knowledge in an area of science or technology by resolving an *uncertainty* that is not readily resolved by a competent professional in the field (see **17.1–17.7**).

- **Reliefs** – There are three forms of relief:

    - the small companies' relief – a super-deduction of 230% on qualifying R&D revenue expenditure (see **17.19**);

    - the repayable tax credit – available where the small companies' relief creates or increases a loss, which provides a repayment equivalent to up to 33.35% of qualifying expenditure in exchange for the surrender of the loss (see **17.53–17.56**); and

    - the R&D expenditure credit for large companies (see **17.21** *et seq*);

    The large companies' relief, which was a super-deduction of 130%, has been phased out and replaced with the R&D expenditure credit.

- **Qualifying expenditure** – Relief is available on specific revenue expenditure relating to the R&D activities, including staff costs, costs of consumables (including power and fuel) and subcontracted work for SME relief (see **17.29–17.45**). Receipts of grants or subsidies may affect the amount of expenditure qualifying for relief (see **17.46**).

- **Points to note** – The definition of SME is double the usual thresholds, and there is no geographical restriction on where the expenditure is incurred (see **17.22–17.28**). Similarly, there is no geographical restriction on ownership: provided that the SME criteria are met, the R&D company can be a subsidiary Or permanent establishment of an overseas company. Where an SME does not meet the criteria for SME relief (except on a going concern basis), it can claim a deduction that is equivalent to the large company R&D relief instead of the SME relief.

- **Capital expenditure** – This does not qualify for the R&D reliefs, but there is an R&D capital allowance which provides 100% relief for capital expenditure on qualifying R&D, including expenditure on providing buildings and facilities for such R&D.

WHAT IS 'RESEARCH AND DEVELOPMENT'?

17.1

Focus

R&D (for tax purposes) is not the broad phrase often used in business – covering market research, commercial product development and other such activities that do not qualify as relevant R&D for tax purposes.

In the first instance, R&D for tax purposes has the same meaning that it does in generally accepted accounting practice (*CTA 2009, s 1138(2)*), excluding oil and gas exploration and appraisal. That definition is somewhat too wide for the government's purposes when giving the enhanced reliefs, and so the definition for the purposes of these reliefs is further constrained by the R&D Guidelines (see below).

HMRC now offer an advance clearance process to allow 'smaller' companies making their first R&D claim to apply to HMRC for assurance that their project involves qualifying R&D. In the 2017 Autumn Budget, the Chancellor announced that an advance clearance process is to be introduced for RDEC claimants; this is to start as a pilot with invited companies and, at the time of writing, no timetable for wider access to the process has been announced.

Accounting definition

17.2   The corporate intangibles tax rules outsource the definition of research and development by ensuring that an activity will broadly qualify as research and development for tax purposes if it would be treated as research and development under generally accepted accounting practice (GAAP) for companies in the UK under FRS 102.

17.3 *Research and development relief*

Under UK accounting practice, R&D is defined in FRS 102 as:

- 'research', which is 'original and planned investigation undertaken with the prospect of gaining new scientific or technical knowledge and understanding'; and

- 'development', which is 'the application of research findings or other knowledge to a plan or design for the production of new or substantially improved materials, devices, products, processes, systems or services before the start of commercial production or use'.

The international accounting standards' definition of research and development (IAS 38) is the same as the UK GAAP definition:

- 'research' is original and planned investigation undertaken with the prospect of gaining new scientific or technical knowledge and understanding; and

- 'development' is the application of research findings or other knowledge to a plan or design for the production of new or substantially improved materials, devices, products, processes, systems or services prior to the commencement of commercial production or use.

R&D Guidelines

17.3   For tax purposes, the accounting practice definitions are modified by Guidelines (the 'Guidelines on the Meaning of Research and Development for Tax Purposes') which cover in some detail the meaning of 'research and development' with examples indicating what can and cannot qualify as R&D. HMRC have published their commentary and interpretation of the Guidelines in the Corporate and Intangibles Research and Development (CIRD) Manual, starting at CIRD81900. Given some of the difficulties that can arise with gov. uk, it may be preferable to confirm the Guidelines in the Manual against the Guidelines maintained in PDF format on the BEIS website (https://assets. publishing.service.gov.uk/government/uploads/system/uploads/attachment_ data/file/71260/bis-10-1393-rd-tax-purposes.pdf).

The Guidelines take precedence over accounting definitions for tax purposes; activities that are R&D for accounting purposes may not, therefore, be regarded as R&D for tax purposes.

The principal distinction between the tax definition and the UK accounting definition of R&D are in the area of development: research (as defined for accounting purposes) should qualify as R&D for tax purposes. However, development will only qualify as R&D for tax purposes where it concerns *appreciable* (which may not be the same as 'substantial') improvements to products, materials, and devices, etc. Development related to installation of new processes and systems will generally not be R&D for tax purposes, under the Guidelines, unless there is also a technological uncertainty that needs to be resolved, advancing technology, in the process.

The tax definition of R&D is also considerably narrower than the accounting definition – that has no requirement either that any technological uncertainties be resolved, or that any advance in science or technology is sought.

The focus of the Guidelines is on activity, rather than attempting to formulate a definition of 'research and development'. Instead, R&D is described as activities that take place within a qualifying project.

In the Autumn Statement 2015, the Government announced that it planned to update the Guidelines but, to date, no revision has been published.

Project

17.4   A project is defined by the Guidelines as a collection of '*activities* conducted to a method or plan in order to achieve an *advance* in *science or technology*' (para 19; italicised words defined below). The beginning and end of a project are not always straightforward to determine, as projects may arise out of other projects and activities.

For the project to qualify as R&D for tax purposes the Guidelines state that it must seek to achieve an advance in science or technology (para 3). For example, periodic updating or modification of a product will not be research and development unless that updating or modification involves an appreciable element of innovation.

The project must seek to achieve the advance through resolution of scientific or technological uncertainty (para 4). This point was emphasised in the case of *BE Studios v Smith & Williamson* [2006] STC 358, where the company claiming the relief could not show the necessary advance in scientific or technological knowledge. Merely being 'cutting edge' and 'innovative' was not sufficient; the R&D had to resolve some scientific or technological uncertainty.

Identifying when a project starts is important to ensure that R&D tax relief is maximised: the project begins when the work to resolve an uncertainty begins, once the uncertainty has been identified, and there is no qualifying R&D until that uncertainty has been identified.

The project will end either when the uncertainty has been resolved or the project is abandoned. Uncertainty will, generally, be considered to be resolved when the knowledge obtained from the project can be expressed in a tangible form – perhaps as a prototype, or as a published document.

A project does not need to succeed in order for its activities to qualify as R&D (para 10) – it is the intention of the project that is important, not the outcome.

Arguably, a failure of the project can still be considered to be an advance in science or technology – by failing, the project has expanded the knowledge of what does not work.

Activities

17.5   R&D activities are those which directly contribute to attempting to resolve the underlying *uncertainty* (see below) which would lead to an advance in either science or technology (paras 4, 26). These include:

- scientific or technological design, testing and analysis undertaken to resolve the scientific or technological uncertainty;

- scientific or technological planning activities; and

- activities to create or adapt software, materials or equipment needed to resolve the scientific or technological uncertainty, provided that the software, material or equipment is created or adapted solely for use in R&D (para 27).

The Guidelines also include a list of activities which do not directly contribute to the resolution of scientific or technological uncertainty:

- commercial and financial activities;

- non-scientific or non-technological aspects of a new or appreciably improved process, material, device, product or service;

- production and distribution of goods and services;

- administration and other supporting services;

- general support services; and

- qualifying indirect activities (para 28).

Qualifying indirect activities

17.6   In addition to the activities which directly contribute to resolving the uncertainty, certain indirect activities are also regarded as R&D activities (para 5). The status of qualifying indirect activities has been in doubt from time to time, but HMRC have confirmed that qualifying indirect activities do constitute R&D for relief purposes (see, eg CIRD81300).

The Guidelines provide an exhaustive list (para 31) – if an activity is not on this list, it cannot be a qualifying indirect activity (para 32):

- indirect supporting activities: maintenance, security, administration and clerical activities, and finance and personnel activities, insofar as undertaken for R&D;

- ancillary activities essential to the undertaking of R&D (eg taking on and paying staff, leasing laboratories and maintaining research and development equipment including computers used for R&D purposes);

- training required to directly support an R&D project;

- research by students and researchers carried out at universities;

- research (including related data collection) to devise new scientific or technological testing, survey, or sampling methods, where this research is not R&D in its own right;

- feasibility studies to determine the strategic direction of a specific R&D activity; and

- scientific and technical information services for the purpose of R&D support (eg the preparation of the original report of R&D findings).

It should be noted that the range of qualifying expenditure (see **17.29** onwards) is not altered by the inclusion of qualifying indirect activities: for example, leasing laboratories is a qualifying indirect activity, but rental costs are not qualifying expenditure. In practice, it is likely that only staff time spent on dealing with a laboratory lease would qualify. The indirect activity must relate to the R&D activities: for example, maintenance staff expenditure would only qualify if there is some aspect of the maintenance that relates to the R&D activities.

Science or technology

17.7 Science is defined in the Guidelines as 'the systematic study of the nature and behaviour of the physical and material universe' (para 15), and specifically excludes any study of the arts, humanities and social sciences. Included within science is work in physics, chemistry, engineering (civil, mechanical, etc).

Technology is defined as 'the practical application of scientific principles and knowledge' (para 17).

It is the particular project that is important; the overall business need not be specifically focused on science or technology.

Example 17.1 – Qualifying R&D project

A logistics trucking company develops a new low-cost refrigeration unit for its trucks, subcontracting much of the work. The project requires the resolution of an area of technological uncertainty with regard to the

---

> refrigeration material and the refrigeration material developed represents an advance in scientific knowledge.
>
> The project will be qualifying R&D, although the principal business of the company – logistics, trucking goods around the country – does not initially appear likely to involve R&D.

Advance

17.8   Activities may be research and development if the project of which they form part is concerned with achieving an advance through (paras 6–12):

- the use of new scientific or technological principles in an existing area of investigation; or

- the adaptation of existing scientific or technological principles to a new area of investigation.

Advances in science or technology sought by a project must be advances in *overall* knowledge in that field, not simply in the company's knowledge. Overall knowledge is that which is publicly available or readily deducible by a competent professional in that field; companies are not expected to know their competitors' trade secrets, for example (paras 20–22).

Uncertainty

17.9   The Guidelines do not specifically state what is or is not uncertainty; instead, it is considered to be present when certain factors exist (paras 13–14):

- where the ability to achieve the scientific or technological objective is unknown;

- where the method of achieving that objective is not readily ascertainable;

- where a particular type of method of achieving an objective is not readily ascertainable – for example, producing a low-cost version, or improving reliability.

Uncertainty is more than simply a lack of knowledge; if the competent professional in the field could readily resolve the problem, then that problem is not considered to be uncertainty under the Guidelines.

Commercial development

17.10   Commercial development is excluded under the Guidelines; it may be difficult in some areas to decide whether development is commercial or not and the guidelines suggest that what is important is the motive behind the development; if it is being carried on to test the viability of the R&D then it may be classed as R&D itself.

For example, drug development may involve testing to ensure that the delivery mechanism (the tablet casing or bindings in which the active ingredients are bound to enable a patient to take the drug) does not interfere with the drug itself. The dyes used in a casing could potentially interfere with the drug, for example, so expenditure on establishing the colour of the final product may be qualifying R&D. Expenditure on establishing the best colour for a new type of mobile phone, however, is very unlikely to be qualifying R&D, even where the phone itself contains technology developed through qualifying R&D.

If the scientific or technology uncertainty which the R&D sought to overcome is no longer in question, the continued development is likely to be considered to be commercial; expenditure on commercial development will be dealt with under the general rules.

In some cases, R&D activities may overlap with non-R&D development – for example, where work continues on resolving the scientific or technological uncertainties underlying a project to develop a particular product whilst, at the same time, carrying out market research to support work on the aesthetic development of the product.

Careful analysis of the various activities involved in a project is necessary to be able to support a claim for R&D tax relief; there is no single methodology that can be applied to distinguish qualifying activities from non-qualifying activities, so each project must be considered on its facts.

Particular cases

Prototypes

17.11   The boundary between experimental development (which is R&D for tax purposes) and pre-production activity (which is not) can be extremely grey in respect of prototypes in engineering work. The design, construction and testing of a prototype will generally involve qualifying R&D expenditure.

There can be more than one prototype before the R&D activities of a project are completed; either the initial prototype continues to be modified, or the project generates a series of prototypes. A series of prototypes will be produced where testing renders the previous prototype unusable, or where multiple models are required for field-testing. For example, electronic equipment used in racing cars is likely to need to be tested in races as part of the R&D process – the R&D will not be complete until it has been established that the electronics can perform in the harsh environment of a race; where the cars complete in a race series open to a variety of cars, the equipment will need to be tested in all the cars to ensure that it can operate not only in the conditions but also in each of the types of cars. Each of the prototypes will, at this stage, still be within qualifying R&D if the resolution of uncertainties is being tested (eg to check whether a new type of anti-vibration system functions). It is generally not cost-effective to attempt to reproduce this type of race environment simply for testing purposes!

Once testing is satisfactorily completed and the uncertainty has been resolved, further work will be classed as pre-production and subsequent prototypes will be commercial development, which will not qualify for the enhanced relief.

17.12 This has, historically, been an area of contention between taxpayers and HMRC. Paragraph 28(c) of the Guidelines explicitly excludes production activity from the definition of R&D.

The area of contention is around 'first in class' products and other one-off items that may be produced as prototypes but, if they work, would then be sold to a customer. It is not necessarily economically appropriate to scrap the prototype and rebuild it for sale, particularly where it is a bespoke item and there is no intention to produce any further quantities for sale. HMRC accepted that if the sole aim of producing the prototype was for use in R&D but it was later sold to a customer, this would not change the nature of the activity in constructing the prototype. The particular problem was with projects where the intention was, on creation of a successful version, to sell that version to the customer – ie where the intention to sell arose later, after the R&D.

This did not entirely accord with other areas of the Guidelines, as para 34 states that '… an R&D project ends … when a prototype or pilot plant with all the functional characteristics of the final process, material, device, product or service is produced.' That is, the R&D ends after the prototype/pilot has been produced and not before.

17.13 After much discussion, HMRC have produced a revision to their Manual section CIRD81350 which acknowledges that, if the main aim of creating a prototype is experimentation to resolve an uncertainty, part the costs of producing the prototype can still be part of R&D, even where it is successful and is intended to be sold to a customer in the event of success.

The guidance indicates that HMRC do now accept that 'where production trials are necessary to test whether the scientific or technical advance has been made, the whole or part of the expenditure on such a trial may be on R&D, depending on the degree of uncertainty existing within the process at a particular time'.

As a result, HMRC will be looking for information as to when in the production trial the uncertainty was resolved, for example, so some consideration of the point will need to be made and recorded. This does extend to bespoke products (or 'first in class' products, as HMRC refer to them), where part of the 'costs ... would qualify for R&D relief, even though the total build costs would not'. Again, the company will need to determine where in the process the uncertainty was resolved.

In *FA 2015*, the qualifying expenditure which can be included in an R&D relief claim in respect of such prototypes was amended so that consumables costs relating to a prototype which is sold cannot be included in the claim (*FA 2015, s 28* inserting *CTA 2009, ss 1126A* and *1126B*).

Computer software

17.14   Software development can be either the object of R&D or to produce a tool for use in a research and development project – a modelling system, for example, or data-handling software (CIRD81960).

Qualifying software research and development includes theoretical computer science, the development of new operating systems and new languages, significant technical advances in algorithms, and artificial intelligence investigation.

However, routine software activities are not research and development. These include:

● supporting existing systems;

● converting or translating programming languages;

● de-bugging systems;

● adapting existing software; and

● producing user documentation.

Where software is used to achieve research and development, expenditure on the software element of the project may still qualify for enhanced R&D relief even though there is no technical advance to the software itself involved. The types of project that are likely to qualify would include:

● drug design; and

● aerospace innovation

as both of these fields make extensive use of computer modelling. This will require expenditure on creating computer software to do the modelling and will be part of the qualifying R&D expenditure on the pharmaceutical or aerospace project, even where creating the software alone would not be qualifying R&D.

Using software simply to simulate aerodynamics or fluid dynamics, though, will probably not qualify as R&D expenditure. However, developing new software to provide such 'in silico' simulation might qualify (provided that the necessary advance in scientific or technological knowledge could be shown).

Capitalised software

17.15 Where internally developed software is classed as a tangible asset in the accounts – because it is software included within hardware costs as being 'directly attributable to bringing a computer system or other computer-operated machinery into working condition for its intended use within the business' – then the included software would not be within the intangibles regime and so the expenditure would not be able to be excluded from the regime to fall within the R&D reliefs. The overall capital expenditure on the system as a whole, including the software, would generally be eligible for plant and machinery capital allowances.

Other internal software development (not so linked to hardware) should be within UK GAAP as the result should be an intangible fixed asset.

Expenditure on an intangible fixed asset that is qualifying R&D expenditure is excluded from the intangible fixed asset rules, even where the expenditure has been capitalised (*CTA 2009, s 814*), so that it can come within other tax rules on R&D, including the R&D reliefs.

Capitalisation of R&D under UK GAAP is an option even where the specific conditions are met, rather than a requirement, so it should be possible to ensure that the expenditure is not capitalised in the first place.

Pharmaceuticals

17.16 HMRC have issued additional guidance on the availability of R&D relief for activities in pharmaceutical R&D (CIRD81920).

In practice, HMRC will generally accept that research activities of discovery, pre-clinical development and Phase I to III clinical trials (required for licensing of medicines by a regulator) will usually be concerned with the resolution of scientific and technological uncertainty.

Phase IV clinical trials are carried out post-licensing and are focused on longer term safety and efficacy; the scientific advance has generally been established by the time the licence for the medicine is granted and so HMRC will not expect companies to claim R&D relief for these trials. That said, they accept that in unusual circumstances qualifying R&D may be done in Phase IV trials.

This does not override the general principles of what activities qualify as R&D – brand name research and development work, for example, will not qualify.

Generics

17.17 Once a patent on a pharmaceutical drug has expired, other companies can produce generic versions of that drug. To get a licence for a generic drug, the company generally only needs to demonstrate that their product is bio-equivalent and has equal clinical safety to the previously patented product. Neither of these demonstrations is likely to involve the resolution of any scientific or technological uncertainty and so a generic drug manufacturer is unlikely to have qualifying R&D activities.

RESEARCH AND DEVELOPMENT TAX RELIEF

17.18 There are, in effect, two reliefs – the small- and medium-sized companies' relief and the R&D expenditure credit – and a repayment credit for SMEs. Revenue expenditure of a small and medium-sized enterprise (SME) that does not qualify for the SME relief may, in some circumstances, be eligible for the R&D expenditure credit.

The R&D reliefs are only available for companies, not partnerships, individuals or other non-corporate entities.

SME relief

17.19 The SME R&D relief provides an enhanced deduction for tax purposes of an additional 130% (125% for the period 1 April 2012–31 March 2015, 100% for the period 1 April 2011–31 March 2012, 75% for the period 1 August 2008 to 31 March 2011, and 50% prior to 1 August 2008) of qualifying revenue expenditure on qualifying R&D, in addition to the 100% deduction already available for revenue expenditure under the normal tax rules (*CTA 2009, s 1004(8)*, as amended by *FA 2012*).

Example 17.2 – R&D tax deduction – SME

SMECo carries out qualifying R&D, and its qualifying costs for the accounting period starting on 1 April 2018 are £150,000. It will be able to claim a total deduction in respect of R&D of £345,000:

Expenditure	£150,000
R&D tax relief @ 130%	£195,000
Total deduction	£345,000

909

Large company relief

17.20   The large company R&D relief provided an enhanced deduction of 30% in addition to the standard 100% deduction for revenue expenditure. This relief has been abolished and replaced by the R&D expenditure credit for expenditure incurred on or after 1 April 2016.

R&D expenditure credit

17.21   The R&D expenditure credit was introduced in *FA 2013* as a replacement for the large company relief. It is the only relief available for large companies for expenditure incurred on or after 1 April 2016; between 2013 and 2016, a company could elect to use the R&D expenditure credit instead of the large company relief. The R&D expenditure credit is also available for SMEs in respect of certain expenditure for which the SME relief is not available.

The R&D expenditure credit is calculated in a very different way to the SME relief and large company relief; instead of increasing deductible expenditure, a direct credit of 12% (11% between 1 April 2015 and 31 December 2017, and 10% prior to 1 April 2015) of qualifying expenditure is brought into account and then deducted from tax (repayable for loss-making companies).

SMALL- AND MEDIUM-SIZED COMPANIES' RELIEF

What is 'small and medium-sized' (*CTA 2009, ss 1119–1120*)

17.22

Focus

Before 1 August 2008 the standard EU definition of an SME applied to establish the companies entitled to the SME. From that date, the standard EU thresholds were doubled (for R&D relief purposes only) so that the small- and medium-sized companies' relief is now available to 'larger SMEs' that have:

- fewer than 500 employees in a year and either, or both, of:

- an annual turnover not exceeding €100m; and

- a period-end balance sheet total not exceeding €86m.

The company must also be independent, and must be a going concern: these points are considered below.

Independence

17.23 In all cases, to be an SME or larger SME, the company must be independent: that is, less than 25% of its capital or voting rights can be owned by one or more companies that are not SMEs (unless such companies are venture capital companies or institutional investors and public investment corporations, provided that they do not have actual control of the SME – CIRD91700). This does not mean that the company cannot be a subsidiary of another company, but its parent company must be an SME.

The calculation of these limits may include the employees, turnover and balance sheet total of other enterprises, including linked enterprises and partner enterprises, if the company in question is not a stand-alone company. Note that, although only *companies* may claim R&D tax relief, the tests take into account *enterprises*, which may not be corporate entities – an enterprise is any entity carrying on an economic activity, regardless of its legal form, and so can include even an individual.

Linked enterprises

17.24 Linked enterprises are those in which one enterprise can exercise control, directly or indirectly, over the affairs of the other(s) (CIRD91600) by:

- having more than 50% of the shareholders' or members' voting rights in another enterprise, either directly or as a result of provisions in a shareholder agreement;

- having the right to appoint or remove a majority of the members of the administrative, management or supervisory body of that other enterprise;

- having the right to exercise a dominant influence over another enterprise as a result of the terms of a contract entered into with that enterprise or as a result of a provision in its memorandum or articles of association.

Enterprises can also be linked if a relationship of the sort listed above exists through an individual or group of individuals acting together, but only if the enterprises are engaged (wholly or partly) in the same markets or adjacent markets in a vertical supply chain.

The limits are applied to the aggregate of the figures for *all* the enterprises with which the company under consideration is linked, together with those of the company itself.

Partner enterprises

17.25 Partner enterprises are those in which one enterprise does not control another but where, either alone or in connection with linked enterprises, one enterprise owns 25% or more of the share capital or voting rights of the enterprise under consideration. In this case, the limits are applied to the aggregate of the figures of the enterprise under consideration together with the appropriate percentage of the figures of the partner enterprises. However, note that venture capital companies, business angels, universities and institutional investors (see CIRD91700 for full list) may own more than 25% (but not more than 50%) of the company without being considered to be a partner enterprise of the company.

Subsidiaries

17.26   The independence requirement does not mean that the SME cannot be part of a group; provided that the group as a whole meets the SME criteria, a subsidiary (including a subsidiary of an overseas company) can be within the scope of R&D relief.

Change in size

17.27   The EU definition of an SME provides a 'year of grace' for companies which exceed the SME thresholds. Such a company will not change status from SME to large unless it exceeds the thresholds for two years in a row, in which case it will become large with effect from the second year (CIRD92000).

This 'year of grace' only applies in respect of the staff, turnover and assets thresholds: if a company ceases to be an SME because it has been taken over by another enterprise, the year of grace will not apply and the company will be treated as large from the beginning of the accounting period in which it was taken over.

Going concern

17.28   The accounts of an SME claiming the SME relief or the repayment credit must be prepared on a going concern basis (*CTA 2009, ss 1046* and *1057*), but this must not be only because it is expected that R&D relief will be received. There must be other reasons for enabling the accounts to be prepared on a going concern basis (*CTA 2009, s 1106*).

A company will not be a going concern at any time if it is in administration or liquidation (*CTA 2009, s 1046*; after amendment by *FA 2012, Sch 3, para 10*). This amendment was introduced because a company's going concern status is determined by the most recent set of accounts; these may have been prepared several months ago, and the company's financial position could have changed substantially in the meantime.

Note that where a company fails to qualify for the SME relief on a going concern basis, it will not be able to claim *any* R&D relief, either under the SME relief or the R&D expenditure credit. Where a company fails to qualify for the SME relief for other reasons, it can usually claim the RDEC instead (see **17.45** below). This option is not available to companies that fail on a going concern basis.

Qualifying expenditure

17.29

Focus

The expenditure that qualifies for relief (*CTA 2009, ss 1052–1053*) must be:

- revenue expenditure;

- relevant to the trade of the SME;

- relating to:

    - the cost of qualifying staff involved;

    - software and consumable items used;

    - qualifying subcontractor costs;

    - costs of externally provided workers (for expenditure incurred after 26 September 2003); and

    - payments to the subjects of clinical trials (for expenditure incurred after 1 August 2008).

All these are considered in more detail below.

Note that the expenditure does not need to be incurred in the UK; this is one of the more generous aspects of the UK R&D tax relief – many other countries restrict relief to expenditure incurred in that country alone.

Maximum relief

17.30   There is an overall cap on the amount of relief that can be obtained by an SME under the SME relief (and, prior to 1 April 2012, vaccine research relief) in aggregate on any one project, of €7.5m (*CTA 2009, s 1113*). This cap was introduced in *FA 2008*, following agreement with the EU in order to get approval for the changes in rates and the size of qualifying SMEs for the SME relief, which is an EU State Aid.

A formula is used to test whether the cap has been exceeded in an accounting period. Where an SME exceeds the cap, it can claim the R&D expenditure credit on qualifying expenditure in excess of the cap amount.

Revenue expenditure

17.31　For the expenditure to be eligible for R&D relief, it must be allowable as a deduction in calculating in the profits of the trade (*CTA 2009, s 1044*). It must also be paid before the claim is made and within the statutory time limits for inclusion as a deduction (see *Gas Recovery and Recycle Ltd v HMRC* [2016] UKFTT 746, although note that this case is not, in the opinion of HMRC, entirely correct as to what those time limits are).

UK GAAP – accounting treatment of research costs

17.32　FRS102 generally requires that pure and applied research costs should generally be deducted immediately in the profit and loss account as they are incurred.

Where the outcome of a project can be identified and technical and commercial feasibility established, then it may be possible to capitalise the expenditure on creating the intellectual property rather than writing the expenditure off immediately through the profit and loss account – in practice this will not happen often during the research phase of a project, given the inherent uncertainties over intellectual property research.

UK GAAP – accounting treatment of development costs

17.33　Development activities are considered to be easier to identify for accounting purposes, and easier to match to actual or potential future revenues. However, even at a development stage there can often still be areas of uncertainty over features of a project and so, given the accounting concept of prudence, development costs will still be deducted in the profit and loss account if the future economic benefit is not sufficiently certain.

Note, however, that only development which still relates to scientific or technical uncertainties will be qualifying R&D for tax purposes (see above).

International accounting standards

17.34　The basic principle in IAS 38 is that all research costs should be expensed (IAS 38.54), and that development costs can be capitalised only once the technical and commercial feasibility of the asset for sale or use has been confirmed (IAS 38.57).

Where it is not clear whether the research phase has completed and the development phase has begun, IAS 38 requires expenditure to be expensed and not attributed to an asset; HMRC will not be so forgiving when it comes to R&D tax relief and so the fact that R&D expenditure is expensed under IAS 38 will not automatically mean that the expenditure (assuming it is a qualifying project) will qualify for relief.

An R&D project acquired in a business combination is treated as an asset under IAS, even where part of the cost of the project is research. Any subsequent expenditure on that project is accounted for as any other research and development cost, so subsequent research expenditure will usually be expensed (IAS 38.34).

Capitalised expenditure

17.35   Where development expenditure has been capitalised in the accounts, then it may still be possible to obtain R&D relief for that expenditure. This will usually be where the company has adopted international accounting standards, as IAS38 requires the capitalisation of development costs, but there is still scientific or technological uncertainty so that the activities remain within the scope of qualifying expenditure for R&D relief purposes. This will be unusual; as noted above, IAS 38 requires capitalisation where the technical feasibility of the asset has been confirmed, which would usually be after the point at which scientific or technological uncertainties had been resolved.

In this case, R&D tax reliefs are available for qualifying revenue expenditure on research which is added to the capitalised costs of an intangible asset in the accounts in accordance with UK GAAP or IAS (*FA 2004, s 53*; CIRD98500).

Relevant to the trade (*CTA 2009, s 1042*)

17.36   Research and development expenditure is 'relevant' expenditure in respect of a company if it relates to a trade carried on by the company, including R&D that could lead to an extension of that trade. Broadly, most R&D expenditure incurred by a company is likely to be relevant expenditure as it is unusual for a company to spend money on pure 'blue sky' R&D with no thought as to how that R&D might benefit the trade. An extension of the trade can be the possibility of licensing out any resulting intellectual property – it does not have to be used by the company in producing goods and services directly.

Where the trade of the company is the carrying out of R&D (eg where a single group company provides all R&D functions for the group, creating new intellectual property for the group to exploit), then the R&D carried out is still considered to be relevant to that trade.

Finally, relevant R&D expenditure will also include expenditure on medical research that is particularly relevant to the welfare of workers employed in the trade of the company. This will generally only apply to trades where there are specific risks to workers (eg in the mining sector).

Qualifying staff

17.37   Qualifying staff are employees (generally, someone with whom the company claiming the relief has an employment contract – CIRD83000) and directors who are directly and actively involved in the R&D – researchers, managers, etc, who organise and carry out or support the R&D activity (*CTA 2009, s 1124*).

Any support function must still be directly and actively involved to qualify – for example, directing technical activity will qualify for the relief, but long-term strategic planning and contract administration will not qualify, and neither will equipment maintenance. It is the actual activity that is important and not the title of the individual. The staff costs must be apportioned for staff members who are not involved full time with the R&D activity.

Example 17.3 – Qualifying staff costs

RD Co has three employees, including the managing director. Total staff costs are £110,000 per annum. One employee, a researcher, is paid £30,000 per annum and spends all his time on R&D activities. The managing director is paid £60,000 per annum and spends 50% of her time on R&D activities, 35% of her time maintaining investor relationships and seeking new funding, and 15% of her time on other general administration activities. The third employee, paid £20,000 per annum, supports both of the others and spends around 75% of his time on R&D activities.

The qualifying staff costs are therefore:

Researcher: 100% of £30,000	£30,000
MD: 50% of £60,000	£30,000
Assistant: 75% of £20,000	£15,000
Total qualifying staff costs	£75,000

The allowable staff costs (*CTA 2009, s 1123*) include:

- emoluments paid by the company, including all salaries, wages, bonuses and other perquisites, but not benefits in kind;

- secondary Class 1 NICs paid by the company; and

- pension fund contributions paid by the company.

The exclusion of benefits in kind can be an issue for small technology companies that reward staff with share options, to participate in the growth in the company, and can only afford to pay small salaries – only the salaries will count as R&D expenditure. The share options are benefits in kind and so are not qualifying staff costs.

Note that *CTA 2009, s 1123* also includes expenses paid to staff as qualifying costs; HMRC has stated that, to qualify for R&D relief, such expenses must be attributable to relevant R&D and that the expense must be incurred for the employee to perform the requirements of their job. This interpretation appears to be rather more restrictive than the wording of the legislation, and HMRC's interpretation remains potentially subject to challenge.

Where staff are seconded, intra-group and salary costs incurred by another group company are recharged to the R&D company. These are not qualifying staff costs for the purposes of R&D relief, although they may qualify as costs of externally provided workers (see below).

Software and consumable or transformable material

17.38   Consumable items include supplies directly used up in the R&D activity – essentially materials and equipment, but only where the equipment has a short useful life. Consumable items also include utilities such as power, water and fuel (*CTA 2009, ss 1125–1126*).

Spending on consumables that are only indirectly used for the R&D activity – generally, administration consumables, such as paper – will not qualify for the relief.

HMRC will accept claims for relief on expenditure on materials (such as chemicals) that are recycled provided that the materials are actually used in the first place and (in practice, although not stated in guidance) will generally accept expenditure on catalyst materials which, by their nature, are not transformed or used up (CIRD82400).

If the software, materials or utilities are only partly used for R&D, an apportionment needs to be made – any practical apportionment can be made, such as by floor area or staff headcount, between R&D activity utilisation and non-R&D activity utilisation. Where an R&D function makes heavy use of utilities, it may be cost-effective to have separate metering for the R&D areas to evidence that utilisation.

Example 17.4 – Allowable costs

TechCo has electricity bills of £250,000 per annum for the building in which its offices and labs are based. The labs make up 80% of the area of the building and so TechCo makes an R&D claim for 80% of £250,000 = £200,000 in respect of the power costs.

As noted above, TechCo should consider whether it would be better to have separate meters for the labs are and the administration area if the R&D activity is an intensive user of power, as apportionment by area may not adequately reflect the R&D element of the power costs.

TechCo has also spent £100,000 on a software licence – the software is used by one administration employee and 12 R&D researchers. In this case, one-thirteenth of the licence cost will not qualify, but the balance of £92,308 will qualify for R&D relief.

Capital equipment – R&D allowances only

17.39   Equipment that is expected to have an enduring benefit to the company is capital expenditure and does not qualify for the R&D tax relief – but it should qualify for the 100% R&D allowance.

Subcontracted R&D

17.40   Expenditure on subcontracted qualifying R&D will qualify for R&D relief for an SME, and the subcontractor to an SME cannot claim R&D relief on its costs (*CTA 2009, ss 1065–1068*).

The subcontractor does not have to be a small or medium-sized company for the relief to be available to the claimant and it need not be in the UK. The work done by a subcontractor need not, on its own, qualify for R&D relief provided that it is part of a larger project of the SME that will qualify.

For example, some testing procedures are better outsourced than done in house by a claimant because it would not be cost-effective for the claimant company to purchase the equipment needed for testing. The testing procedure alone would not be considered to be R&D because it does not involve any innovation. However, where it is a part of an activity that does meet the definition of R&D, the costs of the subcontract will be part of the qualifying R&D costs for relief.

Where the company and the subcontractor are connected persons (as defined in *CTA 2010, s 1122*), the company can claim relief on the lower of:

- the costs which the subcontractor includes in his year-end accounts in respect of staff and consumables costs relating to the work done;

- the amount of the company's payment to the subcontractor (*CTA 2009, s 1134*).

If the company and the subcontractor are not connected, they may still elect to use the connected persons treatment (*CTA 2009, s 1135*). The election needs to be made within two years of the end of the accounting period of the company in which the subcontract is entered into. As the election needs to be joint, the company should ensure that any contract relating to the subcontract work requires the subcontractor to sign such an election when requested to do so.

This election also, in effect, requires the subcontractor to disclose to the R&D company information that would indicate the profit being made on the contract: the subcontractor may be reluctant to provide this information and so may not agree to enter into the election.

If the joint election is not made, the company can claim relief on 65% of the payment made to the subcontractor (*CTA 2009, s 1136*).

Example 17.5 – Subcontracted R&D

RD Co subcontracts a specialist testing routine to Sub Co for a payment of £100,000. The two companies are not connected.

Sub Co's accounts show qualifying costs in respect of that subcontracted test of £75,000; the rest of the charge to RD Co reflects the use of equipment, which is not a qualifying cost, and a profit margin.

If no election is made, RD Co can claim 65% of the payment made, ie £65,000.

If RD Co and Sub Co make the election, RD Co can claim the lower of its actual payment (£100,000) and Sub Co's costs (£75,000). RD Co would be better making the election, if it can persuade SubCo to do so, as this will enable it to claim £75,000 rather than being restricted to the 65% (£65,000) otherwise available.

Externally provided workers

17.41   Relief is available for workers who are not employed by the company carrying out the SME but, instead, are employed by an intermediary company to provide services to the SME (*CTA 2009, s 1127*). A staff provider may also include another company within the same group as the company carrying out R&D.

There are strict requirements that must be met for the expenditure to be eligible (*CTA 2009, s 1128*), requiring that the worker:

- must be an individual;

- cannot be a director or employee of the R&D company (confirmed in *Gripple* [2010] STC 2283);

- must provide services through a staff provider;

- must be subject to the control of the R&D company; and

- must personally provide services to the R&D company through a contract between the worker and *someone other than the R&D company* (amendment introduced in *FA 2012, Sch 3, paras 33–37*. Prior to 1 April 2012, the contract had to be directly with the staff provider. This change allows for other intermediaries to be included in the chain, such as a personal service company).

The requirement to provide services personally to the R&D company under the contract means that general temporary staff costs will not usually be eligible, as they are not usually contracted to provide services to a specific company. This can also be an area where group employment companies can fail to qualify, if employee contracts simply require them to work for the group as a whole and not for the specific R&D company.

Relief is available on the expenditure paid by the company to the intermediary in respect of the services supplied by the external workers; it does not include payments in respect of ancillary costs, such as any recruitment costs incurred by the intermediary.

The external workers must be directly and actively engaged in relevant R&D. Where only a proportion of the external workers' time is spent on relevant R&D activities, relief is available for only that proportion of the costs.

Self-employed consultants

17.42   As a result of these requirements, R&D relief is *not* available for the costs of self-employed consultants (although, of course, the normal revenue deduction will still be available), as the staff provider must be a company – this can be resolved if the consultant operates through a personal service company, as the relief should then be available, provided that the contracts are properly structured.

IR35

17.43   Similarly, where the external worker is self-employed through a personal service company, it is unlikely that the requirements will be met where the arrangements are such that IR35 does not apply.

IR35 is a set of rules that are intended to ensure that employment is not disguised by the use of a worker's personal service company; where the rules apply, the worker's personal service company is required to account for PAYE and NICs on 95% of the income from the engagement. The tests as to whether IR35 applies are broadly the same as the normal employment status tests; the detail of these is outside the scope of this chapter but, in brief, where the engaging company (the R&D company in this case) has control over the worker, it is likely that the IR35 rules will apply.

Deduction

17.44   The deduction which can be made for the R&D tax relief in respect of expenditure on externally provided workers is calculated in a similar way to expenditure on subcontractors.

Where the R&D company and the staff provider are not connected, the SME can claim R&D relief on 65% of the qualifying payments to the staff provider (*CTA 2009, s 1131*).

Where the company and the intermediary are connected, the qualifying expenditure is the lower of:

* the costs which the intermediary includes in his year-end accounts in respect of remuneration incurred in providing the company with the staff; and

* the amount of the company's payment to the intermediary (*CTA 2009, s 1129*).

If the company and the intermediary are not connected, they may still elect to use the connected persons treatment (*CTA 2009, s 1130*). The election needs to be made within two years of the end of the accounting period of the company in which the contract is entered into. As the election needs to be joint, the company should ensure that the contract relating to the externally provided workers requires the intermediary to sign such an election when requested to do so.

If the joint election is not made and the parties are not connected, the company can claim relief on 65% of the payment made to the intermediary.

Relief for expenditure on work subcontracted to an SME

17.45 An SME can claim the R&D expenditure credit (RDEC) from 1 April 2016 (or could claim it earlier by election) where the company incurs qualifying expenditure on R&D that has been subcontracted to it by either:

- a large company; or

- any person otherwise than in the course of a UK taxable trade, profession or vocation (broadly, such persons are likely to be foreign companies).

The reason for this exception is that, otherwise, all R&D relief would be lost in respect of such subcontracted R&D because a large company cannot claim R&D relief on work that it subcontracts to others. A foreign company could, in theory, set up a UK subsidiary to carry out R&D; that subsidiary would be able to claim R&D relief on qualifying expenditure. In each case, an SME to which the work is subcontracted can claim the RDEC on its expenditure so that some relief is therefore granted. Large companies, in particular, should take note of this and endeavour to negotiate the costs of the contract accordingly, taking into account the enhanced relief that the SME will receive as a result of the subcontract.

Grants and subsidies

State Aid

17.46

Focus

Where a notified State Aid is received in connection with an R&D project *none* of the expenditure on that project will qualify for the SME R&D tax relief (*CTA 2009, s 1138*; CIRD81670), even if the State Aid grant is intended to cover capital expenditure. This is because the SME R&D relief is a State Aid, and EU rules do not permit the accumulation of State Aid – most government/EU funding is also a State Aid.

Where the receipt of a State Aid grant means that the company cannot claim the SME R&D relief, then the R&D Expenditure Credit can be claimed by the SME for the R&D expenditure on the project instead.

'Project' is not defined and HMRC state that each case depends on its own merits; in practice, good documentation prepared to establish the scope of a project and supporting the independence of that project from others carried on by the company will assist in any queries that HMRC may raise over the allocation of expenditure between grant-supported and non-supported projects.

An SME carrying out qualifying R&D should, therefore, take care to establish the effect of the receipt of a grant as it may be considerably less advantageous to accept the grant. The RDEC is given at a lower rate and does not cover subcontracted expenditure.

Example 17.6 – R&D relief vs government grant

R&D Co has two projects underway. It is considering making an application to the local RDA for a grant for research and development in respect of one of those projects.

The budget for the project in question is £1.5m; the maximum grant for which the company qualifies is £200,000.

If the company does not make the application, it will be able to claim SME R&D relief on the expenditure; assuming that all the expenditure qualifies, the additional R&D relief deduction available during the life of the project will be:

130% of £1.5m = £1,950,000

Assuming that the company is loss-making, this can be surrendered in exchange for a repayable tax credit (see below). The overall repayment available over the life of the project will be:

14.5% of (£1,500,000 + £1,950,000) = £500,250

Net effect if no grant received: £500,250 repayment available, no loss carried forward.

In comparison, if the company decides to apply for – and receives – the grant, it will only be able to claim the R&D expenditure credit in respect of that project (note: any R&D relief claim in respect of the other project, for which no grant is claimed, is *not* affected by the grant received for this project, provided they are independent projects).

The R&D expenditure credit is worth (overall) 8.8% of qualifying expenditure, so that the value of the credit to R&D Co would be £132,000.

This assumes that all of the expenditure is incurred in-house: if, for example, £500,000 of the £1.5m project expenditure is subcontracted costs, the R&D expenditure credit value will only be £88,000.

The R&D expenditure credit can be repaid to loss-making companies, although 20% notional tax will be deducted from the repayment and carried forward as a credit against future tax.

Net effect of receipt of grant: £200,000 immediately available (from grant) and a potential repayment of £105,600, compared with the potential repayment of £500,250 if no grant is claimed.

Not State Aid

17.47　Other grants and subsidies will reduce qualifying expenditure for the purposes of the SME R&D relief but will not disqualify all expenditure on the project (*CTA 2009, s 1052*; CIRD81650).

For that part of the project expenditure that is covered by a grant or subsidy, the R&D expenditure credit will be available; SME relief continues to be available for expenditure on the project that is not covered by the non-State Aid grant or subsidy.

In practice, non-State Aid and subsidies are often given for capital expenditure which is not covered by the R&D relief and, where this is the case, they will have no effect on the R&D relief.

Pre-trading expenditure

17.48

Focus

Where a company is undertaking R&D in order to be able to trade, but is not yet doing so as part of a taxable trade, there are specific rules to allow the company to claim the SME R&D tax relief immediately in respect of qualifying expenditure (*CTA 2009, s 1045*). Without such rules, the company could not claim relief until it began trading, when such expenditure would be treated as having been incurred on the first day of trading.

The company can elect to be treated as having incurred a trading loss for the accounting period equal to 230% (from 1 April 2015; 225% for the period 1 April 2012–31 March 2015, 200% for the period 1 April 2011 to 31 March 2012, 175% for the period 1 August 2008 to 31 March 2011, and 150% before 1 August 2008) of the amount of its qualifying expenditure in that period.

The company can therefore surrender the deemed loss and claim the payable R&D tax credit immediately (see below), to assist with cash flow through the pre-trading period. The usual pre-trading rules are disapplied in respect of that expenditure so that it is not brought into account again on the first day of trading.

The deemed trading loss cannot be carried back against any profits that may have been made by the company in an earlier period, although it can be used for group relief or carried forward if not surrendered for repayment.

If an election is made, it must be made in respect of *all* of the qualifying R&D expenditure for that accounting period. An election cannot be made in respect of part only of that expenditure.

The election must be made in writing to HMRC within two years of the end of the relevant accounting period. The election must specify the accounting period for which it is made, as a separate election is required for each accounting period in which pre-trading R&D expenditure is to be treated as a trading loss.

Where the company does not yet have an accounting period, it is treated for these purposes as though an accounting period began when the relevant R&D activity began.

Form of the SME R&D relief

17.49   Provided that the SME is carrying on a trade, the relief is taken as an expense, a deduction for tax purposes (*CTA 2009, s 1044(7)*) reducing a profit or increasing a loss (to reduce future profits) then, if the business is loss-making, the additional loss arising from the relief can be surrendered in exchange for an immediate repayment from HMRC (see below, repayable tax credit).

Deduction from profits

17.50   The relief is given by allowing a business to deduct 130% (for expenditure from 1 April 2015; see above for rates before that date) of its qualifying expenditure when calculating profits/losses for tax purposes, in addition to the 100% deduction already available under the general rules.

For a tax-paying company, this will reduce the tax liability. For a loss-making company it will increase the loss available to carry forwards or backwards, use against other income of the period, surrender as group relief, or surrender for the repayable tax credit.

Example 17.7 – R&D deduction

Net Co spends £40,000 of qualifying expenditure on relevant R&D activity in a year. The company can deduct £92,000

(£40,000 + (£40,000 × 130%))

from turnover when calculating its profits/losses for that year.

Claiming the relief

17.51 The relief must be claimed within two years of the end of the accounting period to which the claim relates (*FA 1998, Sch 18, para 83B* (as amended)). The relief should be claimed on the company's self-assessment return or by an amended return.

Maximum relief

17.52 An SME can only claim R&D relief to the extent the total combined R&D relief and vaccine research relief claimed for expenditure on a particular project does not exceed €7.5m in total. This is a lifetime limit on relief for each project (*CTA 2009, s 1113*).

There is a formula to calculate the total R&D relief received to date, to identify whether the cap has been reached, and a recalculation is required each year (*CTA 2009, s 1114*).

Where the cap is reached for a particular project by an SME any qualifying R&D expenditure in excess of the threshold may qualify for the R&D expenditure credit on that excess.

PAYABLE RESEARCH AND DEVELOPMENT TAX CREDIT

17.53 If the SME is loss-making once the R&D relief has been deducted, the option of surrendering the loss relating to the SME R&D tax relief and qualifying expenditure and taking the credit as immediate cash is available – but the payment from HMRC is less than the tax ultimately saved if the relief is carried forward as a loss. The repayment option may be preferential for a company that has cash-flow issues, where the longer term financial disadvantage is less important than the short-term need for cash.

In exchange for surrendering the loss relating to the SME R&D tax relief and qualifying expenditure, the company can claim a repayment that is effectively up to 33.35% of the qualifying costs, calculated according to the loss surrendered by the company.

Any trading loss carried forward arising in the relevant accounting period is reduced by the loss surrendered to obtain the tax credit repayment.

Surrenderable loss

17.54   The company can surrender a loss equal to the lower of (*CTA 2009, s 1056*):

- the R&D reduction – 230% (from 1 April 2015) of the qualifying R&D expenditure;

- the total loss of the trade, less;

  - any claim made, or which could be made, to set the loss against other profits or gains of the same accounting period; and

  - any other relief claimed in respect of the losses, including losses carried back to an earlier accounting period or surrendered by group or consortium relief.

Example 17.8 – Loss surrender calculation

LossCo, an SME, spends £250,000 of qualifying expenditure on R&D activity in a year, incurs other losses of £500,000 and has taxable income of £100,000 in that same year from subletting part of its office space.

LossCo's total deduction for R&D is:

£250,000 + (£250,000 × 130%) = £575,000

LossCo can surrender the lower of:

R&D deduction: £575,000

Total losses: £(500,000 + 575,000 – 100,000) = £975,000 (the total loss of the company after setting losses against income)

As the R&D deduction is less than the total losses, LossCo can surrender the whole of the R&D deduction (£575,000) to obtain a repayment.

Once the surrenderable loss has been determined, the company can claim a maximum repayment of (*CTA 2009, s 1058*, as amended by *FA 2014, s 31*) 14.5% of the surrendered loss in respect of expenditure incurred on or after 1 April 2014 (11% for expenditure between 1 April 2012 and 31 March 2014; 12.5% from 1 April 2011 to 31 March 2012; 14% from 1 August 2008 to 31 March 2011; 16% prior to 1 August 2008).

At the 20% corporate tax rate, this equates to 33.35% of the qualifying R&D expenditure (32.625% from 1 April 2014 to 31 March 2014, 24.75% from 1 April 2012 to 31 March 2014; 25% from 1 April 2011 to 31 March 2012; 24.5% from 1 August 2008 to 31 March 2011; 24% prior to 1 August 2008).

The company is not required to surrender the maximum amount possible; part of the loss arising from the SME R&D tax relief can be retained to carry forwards and, where the full R&D relief cannot be surrendered, must be retained to carry forward to set against future profits.

Claiming the repayment

17.55   The repayment credit must be claimed within two years of the end of the accounting period to which the claim relates, and must be made in the company's corporation tax return or by amended return (*FA 1998, Sch 18, para 10(2)* (as amended)). The claim must be quantified when it is made.

Although HMRC generally pay the repayment credit to the company soon after receipt of the claim, that payment can be withheld if the corporation tax return for that period is subject to enquiry before the R&D repayment has been made.

No payment will be made until the company has paid all the PAYE and Class 1 NICs for the accounting period of claim. In addition, HMRC can use the repayment credit to discharge any corporation tax liabilities of the company (*CTA 2009, s 1060*).

Deduction or repayment – which is more useful?

17.56   To make the decision between taking a repayment (potentially equivalent to 33.35% of expenditure) and keeping a deduction (potentially equivalent to 43.7% of expenditure, at the current 19% corporate tax rate), the company will need to consider the cost of the capital employed in the business (ie the interest cost, any returns due on preference shares, etc), and balance that cost against the benefit of a loss going forwards. If a deduction is taken, no benefit as such is received until the business moves into profit, when it will defer the point at which the business exhausts its losses and begins to pay tax on profits.

The company therefore needs to be funded until it moves into profit and becomes self-sustaining; if the deduction is taken more funds (either raised by borrowing or from the sale of equity) will be needed than if a repayment is taken. If the cost of that additional borrowing or equity sale, less the future tax saving, is more than the difference between the repayment and the future tax saving then it is likely to be better to take the repayment and have the cash immediately, reducing the funding requirement.

Group relief

17.57   Alternatively, an SME which is a member of a group may be able to surrender the loss to another, profitable, UK group company by way of group relief (*CTA 2010, Pt 5*).

A surrender of losses through group relief will reduce the profits of the other company so that the group as a whole benefits more than it would have done if the R&D company had surrendered the loss for a repayment. Where there are cash-flow issues for the R&D company, the profitable company to which the loss is surrendered can pay the R&D company for the surrendered loss; such a payment is ignored for corporation tax purposes provided that it does not exceed the corporation tax saved (*CTA 2010, s 183*).

No consortium relief

17.58   An SME may be owned by a consortium rather than a group; a company will be owned by a consortium where at least 75% of its ordinary share capital is owned by two or more companies, each of which owns at least 5% of the share capital (*CTA 2010, s 153*). Provided that such companies were also SMEs, a company could be owned by a consortium and still qualify as an SME itself (see the independence test above).

A company can surrender trading losses to consortium members (*CTA 2010, s 143*) but, where an SME is owned by a consortium, it cannot surrender any R&D relief losses to the consortium members (*CTA 2009, s 1049*).

LARGE COMPANIES' RELIEF

17.59   The large companies' relief was abolished from 1 April 2016; large companies may now only claim the R&D expenditure credit on expenditure incurred on or after that date.

A large company is any company that does not meet the definition of a small- or medium-sized company (*CTA 2009, s 1122*).

Qualifying expenditure

17.60   Expenditure that qualified for the large companies' R&D tax relief is the same as the qualifying expenditure for the R&D expenditure credit (see **17.65**).

Large company relief-equivalent claims by SMEs

17.61   Where an SME could not claim the SME R&D relief because the qualifying R&D expenditure:

● had been subsidised (see **17.46–17.47**); or

● was over the €7.5m project cap (see **17.30**); or

● had been sub-contracted to the SME by a non-SME (see **17.62**),

the SME could claim an additional deduction equivalent to the large company relief for that qualifying R&D expenditure (*CTA 2009, s 1068*).

Subcontracted work

17.62   An SME could claim an additional deduction equivalent to the large company relief for qualifying R&D expenditure where the R&D was subcontracted to the SME by a larger company or a person not carrying on a trade that is subject to UK tax (*CTA 2009, s 1063*). However, the activities subcontracted to the SME still had to be qualifying R&D for the SME on a stand-alone basis.

No repayment credit was available for an SME in respect of the large company relief.

Form of the large company R&D relief

17.63   The research and development tax relief for large companies was given by allowing the company to deduct 30% (25% for expenditure incurred prior to 1 April 2008; *FA 2008, Sch 8, para 2*) of its qualifying expenditure on R&D (in addition to the 100% deduction given under the normal rules) when calculating its profits for tax purposes; this either reduced the tax payable by the company or, if it was loss-making, increased the loss available to the company.

> **Example 17.9 – Large company R&D tax relief**
>
> If a company spent £100,000 on qualifying R&D, it could deduct £130,000 – £100,000 was deducted under the normal rules and £30,000 was deducted under the R&D tax relief:
>
> - if the company was tax paying, this would reduce tax by up to £6,000 (at the 20% rate of corporation tax, on the £30,000 R&D tax relief); or
>
> - if the company was loss-making, the additional loss could be used as a trading loss of the period and either carried forward or, if appropriate, set against other income of the period, carried back to earlier periods or surrendered as group relief.

The large company relief did not provide an equivalent to the SME repayable credit.

Claim for relief

17.64   As with the SME R&D tax relief, a claim had to be made within two years of the end of the accounting period in which the qualifying expenditure was incurred. The claim was made either in the company's corporation tax return or by way of amended return.

R&D EXPENDITURE CREDIT

17.65   The R&D expenditure credit can be claimed by large companies (defined as a company that is not an SME, as above) in respect of their qualifying expenditure (*CTA 2009, Chapter 6A, Pt 3*). For expenditure incurred on or after 1 April 2016, this is the only R&D relief available to large companies. The R&D expenditure credit may also be claimed by SMEs in certain circumstances.

Early election

17.66   For expenditure incurred on or after 1 April 2013 but before 1 April 2016, a large company could elect to claim the R&D expenditure credit rather than the large companies' relief. Such an election was irrevocable; the company had to continue to use the R&D expenditure credit in subsequent accounting periods, even if these were before 1 April 2016.

SME claims

17.67   The R&D expenditure credit can be claimed by an SME company in respect of certain expenditure that does not qualify for the SME relief, specifically (*CTA 2009, s 104A(3)*):

- qualifying expenditure that exceeds the €7.5m cap on total relief for a project (see **17.30**);

- subsidised qualifying expenditures (see **17.46**); and

- R&D subcontracted to the SME by a large company or an entity outside the scope of corporation tax (see **17.62**).

An SME could, similarly to a large company, elect to use the R&D expenditure credit in preference to the large company-equivalent relief for this sort of expenditure incurred on or after 1 April 2013 but before 1 April 2016. For relevant expenditure incurred on or after 1 April 2016, the R&D expenditure credit is the only R&D relief available for such expenditure.

Qualifying expenditure for large companies

17.68   Expenditure that qualifies for the R&D expenditure credit for large companies is similar to that for SME relief, wth some modifications. A company can claim the R&D expenditure credit on (*CTA 2009, s 104A(4)*):

- in-house direct R&D;

- sub-contracted R&D (in very limited circumstances); and

- contributions to independent research.

Subcontracted work

Work subcontracted by a large company

Focus

Expenditure by large companies on R&D that is subcontracted to another party will not be eligible for the R&D expenditure credit, unless the work is subcontracted to one of the following:

- a qualifying body (universities and other higher education institutions; charities; scientific research organisations; NHS bodies); or

- an individual; or

- a partnership of individuals.

17.69   A qualifying body does not have to be based in the UK, but must be approved by HMRC before payments will qualify. A list of already-approved non-UK qualifying bodies is maintained by HMRC (CIRD82250). If the body in question is not on the list then approval should be sought from HMRC for the body to be designated as qualifying; the enquiry can be made to the R&D specialist office, who will refer it to the CT International and Anti-Avoidance (Technical) department.

In each of these cases, if work is subcontracted by a large company, no R&D relief would be available to anyone as the entities carrying out the subcontracted work cannot claim R&D relief.

Where work is subcontracted to an SME, that SME can (if it is qualifying R&D for the SME) claim the R&D expenditure credit on the expenditure it incurs in performing the subcontracted work (see above) and so no R&D relief can be claimed by the large company commissioning the work.

Where the R&D expenditure credit (or, formerly, the large company relief) can be claimed on the costs of subcontracting, the full costs can be eligible for relief: there is no requirement to take only 65%, or use connected parties relief, as there is for the SME relief (*CTA 2009, s 1078*).

Work subcontracted to a large company

17.70   Where a large company has work subcontracted to it, expenditure by the company on the R&D can qualify for R&D relief where the work has been subcontracted by either:

*   another large company; or

*   any person otherwise than in the course of a UK taxable trade, profession, vocation (principally where the work is sub-contracted to the company from overseas).

The activities subcontracted to the large company must still be qualifying R&D (see above) for the company on a stand-alone basis.

This requirement is modified where the work is subcontracted to the company by another group company which pays for the work, the activities of the two group companies are considered together to determine whether the activities are qualifying R&D. Where the aggregate activities are qualifying R&D, the company carrying out the work will be able to claim the R&D expenditure credit (or, formerly, the large company relief), even if the specific activities would not qualify as R&D expenditure on a stand-alone basis (*CTA 2009, s 1082*).

Where work is subcontracted by an SME to a large company, the large company will not be able to claim any relief, to prevent double relief being claimed, as the SME can usually claim the SME R&D relief on some or all of the expenditure it incurs in commissioning that subcontracted work (see above).

Contributions to independent research

17.71 Payments to qualifying bodies in respect of their research will also qualify for relief where the work is not actually subcontracted (ie where the company does not receive the benefit of the work done by the organisation (*CTA 2009, s 1079*)). However, for the expenditure to qualify, the R&D carried out by the organisation must be relevant to the trade of the company. Where the contribution is made to an individual or a partnership, the company must not be connected to the individual or to any member of a partnership.

Going concern

17.72 Note that a large company must be a going concern in order to claim the R&D expenditure credit, as must an SME. The company will be a going concern if its latest accounts are prepared on a going concern basis and the company has not since gone into administration or liquidation. The accounts must not have been prepared on a going concern basis solely because the R&D expenditure credit was expected to be received (*CTA 2009, s 104T*).

Form of the R&D expenditure credit

17.73 The R&D expenditure credit is given in a very different way to the SME relief or the former large company relief.

The R&D expenditure credit amount (12% of qualifying R&D expenditure; 11% between 1 April 2015 and 31 December 2017; 10% from 1 April 2013– 31 March 2015) is first brought into account as a receipt of the trade of the claimant company, increasing the profits of the company (or decreasing a loss). This may affect the quarterly instalment payments of the company. The same amount is then given as a credit against corporation tax. If the amount is more than the corporation tax due (or where the company is loss-making), a repayment may be available to the company.

Note that, as this is a credit, it is not taken into account in calculating quarterly instalment payments so that, overall, the expenditure credit may lead to a slight increase in quarterly instalment payments for a company. The credit may, however, be used to discharge future quarterly instalment payments once a return has been submitted and a claim made for credit (CIRD89870).

Example 17.10 – R&D expenditure credit

A company has taxable profits of £750,000 and spends £100,000 on qualifying R&D and claims the R&D expenditure credit, it must first bring into account £12,000 as a receipt of the trade for corporation tax purposes, so that its taxable profits are increased to £762,000.

Assuming a corporation tax rate of 19%, the corporation tax due on profits of £762,000 would be £144,780. However, a credit of £12,000 is now given against this as a result of the R&D expenditure credit, so that the actual corporation tax due is £132,780.

If the profits of the company had been, instead, £25,000 (with the same qualifying R&D expenditure) then the R&D expenditure credit would have the effect of increasing taxable profits to £37,000. The corporation tax due on £37,000 would be £7,030. After the R&D expenditure credit of £12,000 is given against corporation tax, the company would be potentially entitled to a repayment of £4,026, with a carried-forward tax credit of £944.

Payment of the R&D expenditure credit

17.74 Where a company claims the R&D expenditure credit, the credit against tax is given in accordance with a specific sequence of steps (*CTA 2009, s 104N*):

(1) deducted from any corporation tax liability (as above);

(2) any remaining credit is reduced by the main rate of corporation tax (eg if the main rate of corporation tax is 20%, the remaining credit is reduced by 20%);

(3) the remaining net credit is compared to the company's total PAYE and NIC liabilities for the accounting period. If the remaining net credit is more than the PAYE and NIC liabilities, then the excess over the amount of those liabilities must be carried forward to use as a credit in a future accounting period;

(4) the element of the net credit which is equal to or less than the PAYE and NIC liabilities is then used against any other outstanding corporation tax liability of the company – any excess is carried forwards to get set against tax liabilities in future years;

(5) any remaining net credit can now be (but is not required to be) surrendered to another group company;

(6)   the net remaining net credit is used to reduce any other outstanding tax liability of the company (eg VAT, PAYE etc); and

(7)   finally, any net remaining credit is repayable to the company.

Notional tax availability

17.75   The notional tax deducted at step 2 can be carried forward and will be available to reduce the corporation tax liability of the company in a future accounting period. It can also be surrendered to another group company to reduce its corporation tax bill for the current accounting period.

Example 17.11 – Payment of R&D expenditure credit

Taking the example above, and looking at each of the steps:

(1)   The R&D expenditure credit of £12,000 has been deducted from the company's corporation tax liability of £7,030, leaving remaining credit of £4,970.

(2)   The remaining credit is reduced by the main rate of corporation tax. If this is 19%, then the net remaining credit available is £4,026. The £944 'notional tax' deducted will be carried forward or can be surrendered to a group company.

(3)   Assuming that the company has PAYE and NIC liabilities for the accounting period of £2,500, then £944 is carried forward to use as a credit in a later accounting period.

(4)   Assuming that the company has no outstanding corporation tax liabilities, the remaining £944 continues to be available.

(5)   If the company chooses not to surrender the remaining credit to a group company, then £944 continues to be available.

(6)   Assuming that the company has no outstanding tax liabilities, the net remaining credit of £2,500 continues to be available.

(7)   The net remaining credit of £2,500 will be repayable to the company.

PAYE and NIC liabilities

17.76   The PAYE and NIC liabilities which are taken into account in comparing the repayable credit are the PAYE and NIC liabilities which relate to staff involved directly in R&D activities (*CTA 2009, s 104P*).

In addition, the company can bring into account the PAYE and NIC liabilities (if any) incurred by a group company in providing externally provided workers to the R&D company. This is limited to the percentage of such liabilities which corresponds to the percentage of staff costs for which R&D expenditure is actually claimed; claims for group externally provided workers are generally limited to a proportion of the actual costs (see above).

Claim for the R&D expenditure credit

17.77   As with the other R&D tax reliefs, a claim must be made within two years of the end of the accounting period in which the qualifying expenditure was incurred. The claim is made either in the company's corporation tax return or by way of amended return.

ANTI-AVOIDANCE

17.78   There are anti-avoidance provisions attached to the R&D tax relief (*CTA 2009, s 1084*) and the R&D expenditure credit (*CTA 2009, s 104X*).

If the transaction leading to the relief is connected with arrangements undertaken wholly or mainly for a disqualifying purpose, that transaction is not taken into account when determining the amount of R&D relief (including pre-trading relief).

A disqualifying purpose is one in which the main object, or objects, of the arrangements is to enable the company to obtain an amount (or an increased amount) of R&D relief than that which it would otherwise be entitled to; in other words, the R&D is entered into purely to obtain the tax relief and not for the purposes of the trade.

Chapter 18

The patent box

Anne Fairpo Barrister, CTA (Fellow), ATT

SIGNPOSTS

- **Qualifying patents** – These include UK patents, patents granted by the European Patent Office, and national patents of some EEA countries (see **18.3**).

- **Qualifying companies** – A claimant company must have carried out, or have a group company that carried out, relevant development in respect of the patent or products derived from it. An intellectual property (IP) holding company will usually need to actively manage its patents to qualify for the patent box (see **18.4–18.15**).

- **Points to note** – The patent box calculation can result in a patent box loss as well as a patent box profit; the loss does not affect the corporation tax charge for the accounting period, but it must be set against any patent box profits of the group or the company in that year, or carried forwards (see **18.16–18.43**).

- **Losses** – The relief is being phased in: only 60% of the relief could be claimed in 2013–14, the year of introduction. The amount that can be claimed will be increased by 10% each until the full relief becomes available in 2017–18 (see **18.48** and **18.49**).

- **New rules from 1 July 2016** – In order to comply with the framework for patent box regimes introduced by the OECD's BEPS project, the patent box rules changed for new IP, and new entrants to the regime, from 1 July 2016. The principal difference is to the calculation, introducing a restriction on the patent box benefit where R&D has been substantially outsourced to group companies, or where the claim substantially dependent upon acquired IP. Claimants within the new regime will need to calculate profits at the level of an IP asset, and will need to track R&D expenditure on qualifying IP more closely; the range of claimants and qualifying IP will not change.

WHO CAN CLAIM?

18.1

> **Focus**
>
> The patent box deduction is available to companies within the scope of UK corporation tax which have patent income, regardless of size. It is also available to partnerships in respect of the profits of one or more of the corporate partners of the partnership – it does not provide relief for non-corporate partners.
>
> Where an individual owns the patent used by a company, take care in planning to use the patent box in the company: a sale of patent rights by an individual to a company will give rise an income tax charge on the profit/gain on sale (*ITTOIA 2005, s 587*), and if the patent is a post-1 April 2002 asset for the company, the sale will be deemed to take place at market value (*CTA 2009, s 845*). Where the sale of patents is subject to income tax, the individual will not be able to use capital gains tax reliefs to reduce the tax charge.

Election

18.2   An election is required for a company to use the patent box (*CTA 2010, s 357A*). The election is made by giving notice to an officer of HMRC in writing, specifying the first accounting period to which it applies, and must be given within two years of the end of that accounting period (*CTA 2010, s 357G*). In practice, this means that the election should be sent with the tax return (or amended return) on which the patent box relief is first claimed.

Note that elections could be made within this two year period to elect into the regime in respect of pre-1 July 2016 IP and profits, provided that the company met the conditions for the patent box regime at 30 June 2016; there is no requirement to have made the election before 1 July 2016.

An election by one group company does not affect any other group company – each must make its own election. Similarly, each corporate partner in a trading partnership with relevant income must make a separate election.

An election will apply to subsequent accounting periods unless, and until, it is revoked by notice in writing to an officer of HMRC (*CTA 2010, s 357G(5)*). The notice must specify the first accounting period from which the revocation will have effect, and must be given within two years of the end of that accounting period.

Once a company has revoked an election in respect of the patent box regime, it cannot re-elect into the regime for any accounting period that begins within five years of the day after the last day of the accounting period from which the revocation has effect (ie the company must be out of the regime for at least six years before it can elect back in) (*CTA 2010, s 357GA(5)*).

Under the pre-July 2016 rules, the election applies to all of the trades of the company (*CTA 2010, s 357G(4)*), and the patent box is calculated on a trade-by-trade basis for the company.

Under the new rules, applying from 1 July 2016 to new IP and new entrants, the patent box calculation still applies to all trades and is still operated on a trade-by-trade basis but also requires that the calculation of the patent box profits for each trade be calculated on an asset-by-asset basis for the company (an IP asset will be a patent, a product or a product category, or a process, whichever is most appropriate to the business).

Nevertheless, under the new rules, a small company (see **18.39**) can make a global streaming election (*CTA 2010, s 357BNC*) to opt to calculate the patent box using a single IP stream.

A company which qualifies for the old rules may choose to elect to calculate the patent box on the basis of the new rules from 1 July 2016 (*CTA 2010, s 357A(11)(b)*). This might be beneficial for a company which has carried out its own R&D, where the result is likely to be the same under the new rules, and would simplify the calculations.

QUALIFYING INTELLECTUAL PROPERTY

> **Focus**
>
> Only income from qualifying intellectual property rights will be eligible for the patent box relief. The intellectual property rights which are eligible are (*CTA 2010, s 357BB*):
>
> - UK patents, granted under the *Patents Act 1977*;
>
> - patents granted under the European Patent Convention (ie granted through the European Patent Office, *not* patents of the individual European countries, although some of these may be eligible separately – see below);
>
> - inventions which are not granted a patent solely because the application contains information prejudicial to national security or safety (ie where the inventor is notified under *s 18(4)* of the *Patents Act 1977*);

- plant breeders' rights, granted under the *Plant Varieties Act 1997* or EC Regulation 2100/94;

- Supplementary protection certificates (issued under Regulation (EC) No 469/2009 – medicines – or Regulation (EC) No160/96 – plants);

- EU marketing authorisations (data exclusivity for medicinal products for human use, orphan medicinal products and veterinary products).

Note that there is no change to the range of qualifying intellectual property under the new rules from 1 July 2016, although the range of qualifying intellectual property in the OECD BEPS framework is wider than that in the UK regime.

Foreign intellectual property

18.3 The range of qualifying intellectual property can be extended by Treasury Order and, so far, patents granted by the patent offices of a number of European countries have been included (the *Profits from Patents (EEA Rights) Order 2013, SI 2013/420*):

- Austria;
- Bulgaria;
- The Czech Republic;
- Denmark;
- Estonia;
- Finland;
- Germany;
- Hungary;
- Poland;
- Portugal;
- Romania;
- Slovakia;
- Sweden.

QUALIFYING COMPANIES

Focus

A company must meet the relevant ownership conditions (*CTA 2010, s 357B*) *and* the development condition (*CTA 2010, s 357BC*) in respect of the qualifying intellectual property. These requirements are not changed for the new regime.

Ownership condition

18.4   The company must meet either the current or the prior ownership conditions and a company that is part of a group must *also* meet the active ownership condition.

Current ownership

18.5   A company will meet the current ownership condition for a particular accounting period where, during that accounting period, it either:

● owns qualifying intellectual property rights; or

● has an exclusive licence in respect of qualifying intellectual property rights.

Note that intellectual property acquired by a company on or after 2 January 2016 from certain foreign connected parties, where the main purpose, or one of the main purposes, of the transfer was the avoidance of tax, cannot benefit from the grandfathered rules; any patent box profits for such IP must be calculated using the new rules, even if the company has elected into the patent box for a period prior to 1 July 2016.

Prior ownership

18.6   A company will meet the prior ownership condition for an accounting period where it has income during the accounting period which is derived from a qualifying intellectual property right which the company previously owned, or to which it previously had an exclusive licence.

However, the income must be derived from an event which occurred when the company:

● owned or had an exclusive licence to the intellectual property; *and*

● had elected into the patent box regime.

As a result, the patent box relief will not be available for income from patents which were sold or expired before the patent box rules come into force on 1 April 2013: no election can be made before that date.

Active ownership (group companies only)

18.7   This condition must be met in addition to either the current ownership condition or the prior ownership condition, but applies to group companies only: it is intended to ensure that the company owning the intellectual property is not simply a passive holding company within the group.

In order to fulfil the condition for an accounting period, all, or almost all, of the qualifying intellectual property held by the company must be intellectual property for which the company either (*CTA 2010, s 357BE*):

- carries out a significant amount of management activity; *or*

- carries out the development itself (ie the development condition is not met by attribution of another group company's activity).

'Management activity' means 'formulating plans and making decisions in relation to the development or exploitation of the rights'. 'Significant' is not defined; whether the level of activity is 'significant' will depend on all the relevant circumstances, including the resources and responsibilities of the company within the group. 'Almost all' is also not defined, and there is no information in the HMRC guidance (CIRD210210) as to its meaning. In practice, it likely that this will mean at least 90% of the qualifying intellectual property will need to be actively managed or have been developed by the group company owning it.

Note that, under the post 1 July 2016 regime rules, if a group company meets the active ownership requirement through management activity rather than development activity, it may find that the benefit of the patent box is restricted (see below).

Exclusive licence

18.8   An exclusive licence is a licence which (*CTA 2010, s 357BA*):

- is granted by the person who holds either the qualifying intellectual property rights, or holds an exclusive licence to those rights; *and*

- gives the licensee (alone or with others authorised by the licensee) specific rights over the qualifying intellectual property rights.

These specific rights are:

- rights over the qualifying intellectual property to the commercial exclusion of all others, including the grantor, in a commercially distinct area of business in at least one country; and either

- the right to bring proceedings for infringement of the rights without consent of the grantor or any other person; or

- the right to receive the whole (or greater part) of any damages awarded in respect of any infringement.

Groups

18.9 The requirement to include specific rights is relaxed for licences between group companies (CIRD210120). In particular, where the licence is granted by one group company to another, it will still be regarded as exclusive where the group as a whole has all the necessary rights. This allows the group intellectual holding company, for example, to retain the rights to enforce, assign or licence the intellectual property so that it can continue to manage the intellectual property portfolio of the group as a whole. Note, there must be some evidence as to the intra-group licencing: this can be in the form of a group policy document, but the licence terms must be clear and demonstrate that the requirements of the legislation as to the terms of the exclusive licence are met.

Development condition

18.10 The company must have either (*CTA 2010, s 357BD*):

- created, or significantly contributed to the creation of, the intellectual property; or

- performed a significant amount of activity for the purposes of developing the intellectual property or any item or process incorporating the intellectual property.

'Significant' is, again, not defined but – as for the active ownership condition – all relevant circumstances need to be taken into account. Merely applying for a patent in respect of acquired rights, or acquiring the rights to and marketing a fully developed patent or invention, or product incorporating the invention, will not be 'significant' activity.

Meeting the development condition

18.11 A company can meet the development condition through meeting *one* of four conditions:

- **Condition A:** The company has carried out the qualifying development activity at any time and has not since joined or left a group.

- **Condition B:** The company previously carried out qualifying development activity, has since left or joined a group, but has continued to carry out development activity of the same description for at least 12 months after leaving or joining the group.

- **Condition C:** The qualifying development activity was carried out by another company which was a member of the same group at the time it carried out the development.

- **Condition D:** The qualifying development activity was carried out by another company which at some point in time was a member of the same group and that other company continued to carry out development activities for at least 12 months after joining the group and did not leave the group during that time.

In effect, if a company enters or leaves a group, it must undertake development activity for 12 months after doing so in order to continue to, or start to, claim the patent box – this is a point which should be noted for corporate acquisitions or buyouts from groups, in particular.

Note that meeting the development condition through either Condition C or Condition D is likely to result in a restriction on the benefit of the patent box under the new rules (see below).

Partnerships

18.12 A partnership will meet the development condition in respect of qualifying intellectual property if it has itself carried out qualifying development in relation to the right, or if a relevant corporate partner (one that is entitled to at least a 40% share of profits or losses of the partnership) has done so.

The active ownership condition will be met by the partnership if the development condition is satisfied by the partnership, but not if it is satisfied by a relevant corporate partner only (*CTA 2010, s 357GB*).

GROUP COMPANIES

Focus

The definition of a group for the purposes of the patent box regime is substantially wider than most tax definitions of group: 'a company ("company A") is a member of a group at any time if any other company is at that time associated with company A' (*CTA 2010, s 357GD(1)*). This definition is broad, and has no geographical restriction.

Associated

18.13 A company (A) will be associated with another company (B) at a particular time (the 'relevant time') if *any* of the following applies:

- in the accounting period in which the relevant time occurs, the financial results of the two companies are, or are required to be, consolidated in group accounts (under UK or foreign law) or would be required to be consolidated if an exemption did not apply; or

- for company A's accounting period which includes the relevant time, the companies are connected; or

- at the relevant time, one of the companies has a major interest in the other; or

- in the accounting period which includes the relevant time, the financial results of company A are consolidated in group accounts with the results of a third company, and at the relevant time that third company has a major interest in B; or

- for an accounting period which includes the relevant time, there is a connection between A and a third company, and at the relevant time that third company has a major interest in B.

Connected

18.14 Two companies are connected if they meet the connection tests in *CTA 2009, ss 466–471*.

Major interest

18.15 A company has a 'major interest' in another company if it meets the tests in *CTA 2009, ss 473–474*.

CALCULATING THE PATENT BOX RELIEF

18.16 Under the grandfathered rules, there are two routes through the calculation:

- the standard calculation, using an apportionment method (*CTA 2010, s 357C*); and

- the alternative streaming calculation (*CTA 2010, s 357D*) which may be chosen by a company or required by HMRC in certain circumstances.

A separate calculation is required for each trade of the company.

Under the new rules, the calculation must be done on the streaming basis, and a separate calculation is required for each patent or, where it is not reasonably practicable to stream by patent, then for each product using patents or each product category using patents (each stream then being a IP stream) (*CTA 2010, s 357BF(2)*, inserted by *s 60* of the *Finance Act 2016*).

GRANDFATHERED RULES: THE STANDARD (APPORTIONMENT METHOD) CALCULATION

Focus

There are a number of steps to the calculation, depending on the company's position:

- Steps 1–3 calculate the pro-rata profits of the trade that relate to qualifying intellectual property;

- Step 4 deducts a 'routine return' – if the result at this step is a patent box loss, Steps 5–6 are ignored;

- Steps 5 or 6 (these are alternatives) are intended to eliminate any element of the patent box profit that relates to brand intellectual property (trademarks etc);

- An optional last step, applying only in the year of grant of a patent, allows a company to get some relief for pre-grant qualifying IP profits in the year of grant

Any patent box losses must be taken into account once a patent box profit is calculated, and the final calculated profit is then subject to a formula to determine the deduction from total taxable profits before calculating corporation tax (see **18.48**).

Steps to the standard (apportionment method) calculation

Step 1 – calculate 'TI', the gross trade income for the accounting period

18.17 'Gross trade income' of the trade includes:

- all income which is brought into account in calculating the trading profits for tax purposes; and

- damages, insurance proceeds and other compensation relating to the intellectual property which is not included above; and

- receipts that are brought into account as receipts under *CTA 2009, s181* (ie where there has been a change of accounting policy and an amount falls out of GAAP recognition); and

- amounts brought into account as a credit on the sale of intangible assets under the corporate intangibles tax rules, if not already included; and

- profits from the sale of patent rights held for the purposes of the trade which are not within the corporate intangibles tax rules (ie, pre-1 April 2002 patent rights which have not been acquired since that date from a third party).

'Gross trade income' specifically excludes financial and similar income.

Step 2 – calculate X%, being RIPI/TI × 100

18.18   Having established TI in Step 1, it is now necessary to calculate the trade's relevant intellectual property income (RIPI) and then calculate X% – the percentage of total income that relates to relevant intellectual property income.

Relevant IP income is income falling within any of five specific 'heads':

- Head 1: income from the worldwide sale of:

  - items wholly or partly protected by a qualifying IP right;

  - items which incorporate a qualifying item, or designed to incorporate a qualifying item which is sold with that item at a single price; and

  - items which are wholly or mainly designed to be incorporated in items included above (ie spare parts).

  Where one such item is sold as part of a package with other non-patented items under a single agreement, the income from that sale must be apportioned between the qualifying and non-qualifying items on a just and reasonable basis.

- Head 2: income from licensing qualifying intellectual property for granting rights over:

  - qualifying IP rights (including rights out of an exclusive licence);

  - a qualifying item or process (eg where the non-UK/EPO patents over that item or process are licensed to third parties); and

  - other associated IP rights under an agreement granting one or more of the rights above.

- Head 3: proceeds of sale etc, of qualifying intellectual property

  This covers income from the sale, realisation or other disposal of qualifying intellectual property rights, or from the sale etc of a qualifying exclusive licence.

- Head 4: infringement income

  This covers amounts received by the company as compensation for infringement (awarded by a court) or alleged infringement (under a settlement agreement) of qualifying intellectual property rights.

- Head 5: damages, insurance, etc

  This covers income which is not directly related to infringement of the qualifying intellectual property and so does not fall within Head 4.

Notional royalty: on election

18.19   The notional royalty provisions are available to companies who use patents in their processes, so that such companies can calculate income that can be treated as RIPI for patent box relief purposes. A company that has elected to bring in a notional royalty can include in RIPI an 'appropriate percentage' of the income derived from the use of the qualifying intellectual property.

The 'appropriate percentage' is the proportion of any IP derived income which the company would pay a third party on an arm's length basis for the use of the IP, if it did not already have the right to use the IP. Once established, the appropriate percentage will continue to apply for each following accounting period for which the company holds the rights.

Step 3 – calculate X% of the profits of the trade for the accounting period

18.20   The taxable profits of the trade must be adjusted under the patent box rules, to account for excluded income and to allow R&D relief to be available at the company's normal corporate tax rate.

The following must be added back to to the taxable profits of the trade:

- debits relating to loan relationships and derivative contracts (as these are excluded);

- the *additional deduction* from R&D relief given by superdeduction (ie 130% for SMEs, 30% for large companies or SMEs claiming the 30% relief; see **Chapter 17**);

- any *additional deduction* claimed as relief for production of television programmes, video games or theatrical productions; and

- any R&D shortfall (in first four years – see **18.21**).

18.21 *The patent box*

The following must be *deducted* in calculating the taxable profits of the trade:

- the amount of any R&D expenditure credit brought into account (see **17.65**); and

- any finance income brought into account.

Note that these adjustments are *only* for the purposes of calculating the patent box relief: the actual profits of the trade for tax purposes are not adjusted by these amounts.

R&D shortfall adjustment

18.21 This adjustment relates to actual accounts R&D expenditure of the company, *not* the amounts deducted for tax purposes under the R&D relief rules (CIRD220410).

This adjustment is intended to bring into the patent box expenses relating to earlier R&D costs, where the expenses of the company in the current accounting period do not properly reflect the development costs of the items etc, from which patent box income is derived. This is meant to ensure that the company does not receive disproportionately more patent box relief by electing into the regime only once all R&D has been completed.

The shortfall deduction must be considered in the first accounting period in which the company elects into the patent box regime, and then in each accounting period that begins within the four years that begin with that accounting period.

Shortfall

18.22 There will be a shortfall where the actual R&D expenditure (ie *not* the amount of the R&D relief) in the accounting period in which the patent box relief is claimed is less than 75% of the average annual R&D expenditure over the four years before the company elects into the patent box regime.

Adjustment to deduction

18.23 In calculating the deduction, the actual R&D expenditure during the first four years *after* the company elects into the patent box regime must be considered: any expenditure in those years above the average must be carried forward and used to add to future accounting periods in which expenditure below 75% of average before any adjustment is made.

Deduction

18.24   Where the company's actual R&D expenditure, after adding in any brought-forward above-average expenditure from the first four years within the patent box regime is less than 75% of the average R&D expenditure during the four years before election into the regime, then the amount added back in adjusting the profits to which X% is applied in this step is the difference between:

(a)   the total of actual and any brought-forward; and

(b)   75% of the pre-patent box average.

Where the brought-forward above-average expenditure is more than required to bring up the actual expenditure to 75% of the pre-patent box average, the excess over that requirement is carried forward again.

Where the actual R&D expenditure together with any brought-forward amounts is still less than 75% of the average pre-patent box expenditure, the amount added back is deemed to be 75% of the average R&D expenditure.

Step 4 – deduct the routine return

18.25   The routine return is calculated as X% of 10% of the following expenses:

- capital allowances deducted in calculating taxable profits;

- premises costs (rent, rates, repair, water, fuel, power, etc);

- staff costs (costs of employing directors and employees, and costs of externally provided workers);

- plant and machinery costs (other than capital allowances: includes leasing costs, construction and modification costs, maintenance, services, operations, etc);

- professional services (consultancy, professional fees, administration and management);

- other services (software, telecoms, post, transport, waste, legal, accountancy, etc).

Where some or all of these expenses are incurred by another group company on behalf of the company claiming the patent box, the expenses are included in the calculation as if they had been incurred by the patent box claimant.

R&D expenses excluded

18.26   Any expenditure in these categories which qualifies for R&D tax relief is not included in the calculation of routine expenses, and neither is the R&D tax relief given on that expenditure. R&D capital allowances and patent allowances are also excluded (but *not* know-how allowances).

Deduction

18.27   Once the routine expenses have been established, the routine return is calculated as being 10% of the routine expenses, and then X% of this figure is calculated to arrive at the amount to be deducted from the profits attributed to relevant intellectual property income (calculated at Step 3).

If the result is a profit then this is termed the qualifying residual profit (QRP) of the company, and further adjustments are required to establish the amount of the patent box relief.

Where the result is negative (or nil) then there is a patent box loss (relevant IP loss, or RIPL) and no further adjustment is needed – the next step in the calculation for a patent box loss is Step 7, if relevant.

Steps 5 or 6 – exclude profits relating to trademarks etc

18.28   As the patent box relief is intended to give relief on income from a limited range of intellectual property only, these Steps 5 or 6 (they are alternatives) will deduct an amount intended to adjust for the profits attributable to trademarks and other marketing intangibles included in QRP.

Step 5 is a formula calculation that takes no account of the actual contribution of brand and marketing intangibles. It can be used by election, provided that a company meets specific conditions. Where the company does not meet the conditions, or chooses not to elect to use Step 5, then the more detailed calculation at Step 6 must be used instead. In practice, Step 5 can substantially reduce the benefit of the patent box claim.

Step 5: small claims election

18.29   A company can elect to use the small claims treatment for a trade where it meets *one* of two conditions:

(a)   the RIPP for all the trades of the company in aggregate does not exceed £1,000,000 (patent box losses are ignored in the aggregate); or

(b)   the aggregate RIPP of the trades of the company does not exceed the relevant maximum *and* the company has not used the Step 6 calculation method for excluding non-qualifying intellectual property in the previous four years.

The 'relevant maximum' is calculated as:

$$\frac{£3,000,000}{(1 + N)}$$

where N is the number of associated companies of the company in the relevant period. The maximum is reduced pro-rata where the accounting period is less than twelve months. 'Associated' means that the companies are grouped for patent box purposes and have elected into the patent box regime.

As a result, for a solo company with a single trade, the options are:

- QRP < £1m: can always elect to use Step 5;

- QRP > £3m: can never elect to use Step 5;

- QRP ≥ £1m and ≤ £3m: will be able to elect if it has not used the Step 6 calculation method in the previous four years.

Calculation

18.30   Where the company meets one of the conditions and elects to use the small claims treatment then the patent box profits amount on which the patent box relief is based is the *lower* of:

(a)   75% of QRP for the trade (as calculated in Step 4); and

(b)   the small claims threshold for the company divided by the number of trades of the company.

The small claims threshold is:

$$\frac{£1,000,000}{(1 + N)}$$

where N is, again, the number of companies associated with the company in the relevant period which have elected into the patent box regime. Where the accounting period is less than twelve months, the small claims threshold is reduced pro rata.

In practice, this formula will usually substantially reduce the value of the patent box to a company; it will usually be more appropriate to consider using the provisions of Step 6 instead.

Step 6: marketing assets return

18.31 Where a company does not qualify for Step 5, or does not elect to use Step 5 where it qualifies, the company must calculate a 'marketing assets return' amount to deduct from QRP to establish the relevant IP profits (RIPP) of the trade.

Marketing assets return amount

18.32 The marketing assets return is the difference between:

- the notional marketing royalty of the company; and

- any actual marketing royalty paid by the company.

However, the marketing assets return is deemed to be nil where the difference is:

- negative (ie the actual marketing royalty exceeds the notional marketing royalty); or

- less than 10% of the QRP for the accounting period.

This is supposed to assist companies, so that they are not required to undertake an expensive valuation exercise where the contribution from the marketing royalties is small and HMRC have said that they will take a pragmatic approach (not requiring calculation of the notional marketing royalty; CIRD220490) where the circumstances are such that it is reasonably clear that the trademark and marketing intangibles contribution is less than 10% of QRP (usually in business-to-business situations where the products are sold on the basis of cost or technical specification).

Notional marketing royalty

18.33 This is the percentage of relevant intellectual property income for the accounting period (as calculated at Step 2 of the standard calculation, or Step 1 of the streaming calculation) that the company would pay to a third party on an arm's length basis in order to be able to use the brand/marketing intangibles if the company did not already own those intangibles.

The brand/marketing intangibles which need to be considered are:

- trademarks and design rights (registered or unregistered; UK or foreign);

- signs or indications of geographic origin of goods or services; or

- customer information used for marketing purposes.

The notional marketing royalty should be assessed in each accounting period, although it is likely to stay the same in respect of a stable product. In contrast, where a company is actively promoting a new product which has an associated trademark (for example), the notional marketing royalty in respect of that product is likely to increase year-on-year as the trademark becomes more valuable with the success of the product.

Actual marketing royalty

18.34 In comparison, the actual marketing royalty is reasonably straightforward to calculate: this is a proportion of the royalties actually paid by the company to use brand/marketing intangibles (as defined above).

The proportion is X%, and the amount paid is: the aggregate royalties and other sums paid to acquire or exploit the relevant marketing assets, provided that they have been brought into account in calculating taxable profits. This will include amortisation deductions where the marketing asset was acquired outright and is being amortised over its useful economic life.

Where the streaming calculation has been used, with the alternative Steps 1–4, then there is no need to take X%. Instead, the amount of the actual marketing royalty is that which has been allocated to the RIPI stream on a just and reasonable basis.

Optional, year of grant only – additional relief for pre-grant profits

18.35 This step is another elective step, rather than a compulsory element of the calculation. It is intended to provide a measure of patent box relief for profits which a company makes from a product etc, before a patent over that product is actually granted.

The company can look back up to six years before the grant, but can only take into consideration accounting periods in which it had elected into the patent box regime. The company must also elect to claim the pre-grant relief, and such election should be made with effect from the year of application to ensure maximum pre-grant relief (the election must be made within two years of the end of the accounting period from which pre-grant relief is to be first claimed).

The amount which can be added to patent box profits for relief purposes is the difference between:

- the actual aggregate patent box profits for each accounting period whilst the patent application was pending (to a maximum of six years before grant); and

- the aggregate patent box profits which would been calculated for those accounting periods if the patent had been granted at the date of application.

The effect of this additional amount is (in effect, through the calculation mechanism) a corresponding decrease in the taxable profit of the company, so that less is taxed at the mainstream corporation tax rate – in effect, recovering a proportion of the tax which was paid on the relevant income when it actually arose.

Deduction from tax

18.36 At the end of the calculation, the calculated patent box profit of the trade is adjusted to take into account any patent box losses. If there is still a profit following that adjustment, the patent box relief is given as an additional deduction in calculating the profits of the trade for corporation tax purposes.

This deduction is:

$$\frac{RP \times (MR - IPR)}{MR}$$

where:

- RP is the RIPP of the trade after adjusting for patent box losses;

- MR is the main rate of corporation tax; and

- IPR is the patent box tax rate (10%).

Note that the main rate of corporation tax is used in the formula, even if the company was subject to tax at the small profits rate prior to the abolition of that rate from 1 April 2015.

Where the company has more than one trade, the patent relief must be calculated separately for each trade so there may be a series of deductions (one for each trade).

The relief is given by way of deduction from profits to get around problems that might otherwise arise with losses and other reliefs if, instead, a rate of 10% were to be applied directly.

Phasing in

18.37 The relief was phased in over four years by applying a percentage to the patent box profits (after adjustment for patent box losses) to reduce these before the patent box relief is calculated. The percentages were:

2013–14:	60%
2014–15:	70%
2015–16:	80%
2016–17:	90%

The full relief has been available from 1 April 2017. Where the accounting period straddled a tax year, the relief had to be pro-rated and the relevant percentage applied.

STEPS TO THE STREAMING CALCULATION (PRE JULY 2016 AND UNDER THE NEW RULES)

Focus

In some cases, a company's income and profits are such that a straightforward apportionment of profits between IP income and non-IP income does not give a reasonable approximation of the actual profits that arise from exploitation of qualifying IP rights, so that the profits attributed to qualifying intellectual property in the standard calculation (at Step 3) are much lower than actually is the case.

In this case a company can elect to use streaming to allocate profits, to allocate expenses and profits to income streams on a just and reasonable basis. Once an election is made, it will continue to apply until the company elects otherwise, and the company will use the following Steps 1–4 in place of those in the standard calculation.

Under the new rules, this method of calculation is the only method available.

Grandfathered rules: mandatory streaming

18.38   The streaming calculation *must* be used where any one of three conditions are met:

- **Condition A:** the gross income of the trade includes a substantial amount of credits brought into account in calculating taxable trade profits, but not fully recognised as revenue under GAAP (eg transfer pricing adjustments); or

- **Condition B:** the gross income of the trade include a substantial amount of licensing income that is not relevant intellectual property income (eg trademark licensing etc); or

- **Condition C:** the trade generates income that is not relevant intellectual property income and the company also receives a substantial amount of relevant intellectual property income from licences granted, where those licenses are granted out of exclusive licences held by the company (eg conduit arrangements).

In this case, 'substantial' has been defined – licensing income from non-qualifying IP rights will be substantial if it is more than:

(a)   £2m; or

(b)   (if lower) 20% of the gross income of the trade for that accounting period.

There is a de minimis level so that, if the licensing income from non-qualifying IP rights is no more than £50,000, it will not be regarded as substantial even where it is more than 20% of gross income.

New rules: small claims elections

18.39   Under the new rules, three elections are available to companies with lower levels of patent box profits to simplify the calculation of the patent box for such companies. These are the global streaming election (see **18.40**), the notional royalty election (see **18.19**), and the small claims figure election to calculate the marketing assets return (see **18.44**).

In order to make these elections, a company must calculate its patent box profits using the new rules and must meet the following conditions:

- the company must have only one trade; and
- the company must have qualifying residual profits for the accounting period (see below) of less than:

   (a)   £1,000,000; or

   (b)   the relevant maximum (see below) for the accounting period, if higher.

However, even if a company meets these conditions, it cannot make any of these elections if (*CTA 2010, s 375BN(3)*):

(a)   the company's qualifying residual profits exceed £1,000,000 for the accounting period; and

(b)   the company has calculated patent box profits on the basis of the new rules in any of the previous four years; and

(c)   the company did not make the relevant election in each of the years in that prior four year period in which it used the new rules to calculate patent box profits.

'Qualifying residual profit' for the purposes of establishing eligibility to make these elections, is effectively the aggregate result of the patent box calculation under the new rules, up to and including Step 4, ignoring any sub-stream with a negative result.

The 'relevant maximum' is £3,000,000 where the claimant company has no related 51% group companies. Where it has got related 51% group companies, then the 'relevant maximum' is (£3,000,000) / (1+N), where N is the number of related 51% group companies that are elected into the patent box (whether under the old rules or the new rules).

Step 1 – identify the streams of income

18.40   Grandfathered rules: the taxable income of the trade (ie all amounts brought in as taxable credits), after deduction of finance income, must be apportioned into two streams of income:

(a)   relevant intellectual property (RIPI) income (this is the same as the RIPI established at Step 2 of the standard calculation; and

(b)   all other income.

New rules: the taxable income of the trade (as above) is apportioned between IP and non-income streams. The IP stream is then divided into "relevant IP income sub-streams" so that each sub-stream consists of income attributable to a particular qualifying IP right or to a particular kind of IP item (a product or product category), where it is not practicable to stream on the basis of qualifying IP rights, such as where the claimant company produces products covered by multiple qualifying IP rights.

A company with small patent box profits (see **18.39**) can make a global streaming election (*CTA 2010, s 357BNC*) in order to calculation the patent box on the basis of a single IP stream, as under the grandfathered rules – although note that the R&D fraction is still applied to this stream.

In addition, a company with small patent box profits with IP-derived income which is not in Heads 1–5 of the definition of RIPI (see **18.18** above) can elect to use a notional royalty (as in **18.19**) and further may elect to use a fixed percentage of 75% of the IP-derived income instead of calculating the 'appropriate percentage'.

Step 2 – allocate expenses between the income streams

18.41   Grandfathered rules: the expenses of the trade (ie all debits deducted in calculating taxable profits except finance debits, the additional deductions for R&D relief or television programme relief, video games relief, or theatrical production relief) plus any R&D shortfall amount, are allocated to the income stream to which they relate on a just and reasonable basis. This should result in the RIPI stream having intellectual property-related expenses allocated to it and all other expenses allocated to the non-RIPI stream. All debits must be allocated to one of the two streams.

New rules: the expenses of the trade are allocated on a just and reasonable basis between the "all other income" (non-IP) stream and each of the relevant IP income sub-streams (or to the global IP stream where a company with small patent box profits has elected to use global streaming). Finance debits, the additional deductions for R&D relief or television programme relief, video games relief, and theatrical production relief continue to be excluded, but the R&D shortfall adjustment is not included in the new rules.

What is 'just and reasonable' will depend on the company's particular circumstances and, once established, the same method of allocation must be used in each accounting period unless there is a change of circumstances relating to the trade of the company which makes the method inappropriate.

Under the grandfathered rules, where the allocation method is no longer appropriate, the company can either chose a different method or elect out of the streaming calculation where it is not mandatory. There is no restriction on a company later electing back into the streaming calculation in a later accounting period, if it becomes appropriate again.

Under the new rules (or where HMRC required the use of streaming under the grandfathered rules) the company must amend the methodology if it ceases to be appropriate.

Step 3 – calculate the net relevant intellectual property income amount

18.42   This is straightforward: deduct the amount calculated in Step 2 from the amount calculated at Step 1 in respect of each sub-stream (or from the global IP stream where a company with small patent box profits has elected to use global streaming).

Step 4 – deduct the routine return

18.43   Grandfathered rules: the routine return is 10% of the routine expenses which are included in the RIPI stream.

New rules: the routine return is 10% of the routine expenses which are included in the relevant IP income sub-stream (or in the global IP stream where a company with small patent box profits has elected to use global streaming).

'Routine expenses' are the same as those for the standard calculation (see **18.25–18.27**).

Step 5/6 – deduct marketing assets return

18.44   If the result of the calculation at the end of Step 4 is a figure greater than nil, a marketing return is then calculated and deducted.

The marketing return is calculated as in the apportionment method, using either the small claims figure (calculated as set out in **18.30**, and available by election for company with small patent box profits, for which see **18.39**) or by using the notional marketing royalty as for the apportionment method (see **18.28** onwards), for each trade (pre-July 2016 rules) or relevant IP income sub-stream (or to the global IP stream where a company with small patent box profits has elected to use global streaming) (new rules).

Note that the small claims figure election is not available to a company for qualifying residual profit of more than £1,000,000 which was elected into the patent box under the old rules in any of the previous four years, but did not elect to use the small claims treatment available under the old rules in each such year.

As with the apportionment method, if the marketing assets return is less than 10% of the amount of the relevant IP income stream (grandfathered rules) or sub-stream (or to the global IP stream where a company with small patent box profits has elected to use global streaming) (new rules), or the actual marketing royalty exceeds the notional marketing royalty, the marketing assets return is taken to be nil.

New rules – new Step seven – apply R&D fraction

18.45   The BEPS framework requires that patent boxes be limited by the amount of economic substance/activity in the jurisdiction where the patent box is offered. As there are many ways that economic substance could be measured, the proposals opt for research and development activity as a proxy. Accordingly, patent boxes are required to limit the tax benefit in accordance with the proportion of R&D undertaken by the claimant in respect of the specific patent or product for which the patent box is claimed.

The UK follows the framework closely, setting out an 'R&D fraction' which must be applied to each IP asset's patent box profits (or to the global IP stream where a company with small patent box profits has elected to use global streaming) to establish the deduction that will be available.

This is set out as the lower of:

$$\frac{(D + S) \times 1.3}{(D + S + A + R)} \text{ and}$$

where:

D = direct (in-house) R&D costs

S = costs of R&D subcontracted to third parties

A = IP acquisition/licensing costs

R = costs of R&D subcontracted to related parties

D, S, A and R are calculated on a cumulative basis, over the life of the relevant IP asset; it will be necessary to identify R&D expenditure, and acquisition costs, relating to an IP asset and maintain records of that expenditure for up to 20 years.

In effect, patent box claims will effectively be limited where the company outsources a substantial amount of R&D to related parties – even if those related parties are in the UK. Groups could well need to rethink their R&D arrangements accordingly. The limitation relating to acquired/licensed IP costs may, in practice, be less of an issue – if the company is spending that much, comparatively, on the relevant acquired/licensed IP, it may well not meet the development condition.

The *Finance (No 2) Bill 2017* includes provisions regarding cost-sharing arrangements, to ensure that companies are neither advantaged nor disadvantaged by such arrangements in calculating the nexus fraction. These provisions take effect from 1 April 2017.

In exceptional circumstances, where the R&D fraction is not an accurate reflection of the position, the company can increase the R&D fraction (although it can never increase above 1). This may, for example, arise where a company has acquired intellectual property which later turns out to contribute very little value to the eventual product.

Following the application of the R&D fraction, all the IP sub-streams of the trade are added together (unless the company has elected to use global streaming).

Pre-grant relief and deduction calculation

18.46 The calculation of pre-grant relief and the deduction (and phasing in, prior to April 2017) is the same for the streaming method as for the apportionment method (see **18.35–18.37** above).

Note that the pre-grant relief adjustment is made after the R&D fraction under the new rules; the calculation of the amount of the relief for earlier years will have included the R&D fraction and so it does not need to be applied again when the relief is actually given.

TRANSITION FROM GRANDFATHERED RULES TO NEW RULES

18.47 As noted above, the grandfathered rules continue to apply until 30 June 2021 to existing IP (ie that applied for before 1 July 2016) of companies who have elected into the patent box with effect from a period before 1 July 2016.

For companies that continue to develop intellectual property, it is likely that over that five-year period, new qualifying IP will start to apply to existing products as they continue to be developed. Such products will, therefore, be covered by both new and grandfathered IP. Provided that the core IP of the product is grandfathered (pre-1 July 2016) IP, then the income from that product will continue to be within the grandfathered rules.

Where the core IP underlying the product becomes new IP, but the product remains covered by some grandfathered IP, it will be necessary to apportion the profit from the product between the grandfathered rules and the new rules, following the proportion of grandfathered IP to total qualifying IP.

From 1 July 2021, the new rules will apply to all companies elected into the patent box, in respect of all qualifying IP.

PATENT BOX LOSSES

Focus

18.48 Patent box losses (relevant intellectual property losses, or RIPL) are a product of the patent box calculation, whether standard or streaming, and can arise in otherwise profitable companies – broadly, a patent box loss will arise where the expenses relating to relevant intellectual property income exceed that income.

Where a trade generates a patent box loss, that loss *must* be set against patent box profits of (in order):

(a)   other trades of the company;

(b)   other group companies; and

(c)   future accounting periods of the company or other group companies.

Any patent box loss set off against patent box profits will reduce the amount of the patent box deduction in calculating the taxable profits of the company. Essentially, a company cannot have the benefit of the patent box relief until all patent box losses of that company or any of its group companies have been utilised.

Losing the losses

18.49   The patent box losses of a company are not necessarily extinguished by the company:

● ceasing to trade; or

● revoking its election into the patent box regime; or

● ceasing to be within the corporation tax charge.

If there are any patent box losses in a company when one of these events occurs, those losses must be transferred to any other group company that is a qualifying company at that time. Only if there are no other group companies elected into the patent box are the patent box losses extinguished if the company ceases to trade etc.

ANTI-AVOIDANCE

Principal anti-avoidance rule

18.50   The main anti-avoidance rules applies where a company which has elected into the patent box regime is party to a scheme, one of the main purposes of which is to obtain a relevant tax advantage (*CTA 2010, s 357FB*).

A 'relevant tax advantage' is obtained where patent box profits are increased as a result of the scheme and the scheme is:

● designed to avoid the application of any part of the patent box rules; or

- designed to create a mismatch between expenses and income relating to a qualifying IP right (eg where a company enters a group);

- designed to recognise non-IP income as something other than revenue (to increase the proportion of IP income).

Anti-avoidance – exclusivity

18.51 Where a licence is made exclusive and the main purpose (or one of the main purposes) of the exclusivity is to get the benefit of the patent box, the patent box relief will not be available. That is, exclusivity in a licence should be commercially justifiable for income derived from that licence to qualify for the patent box relief.

Anti-avoidance – incorporation of patented items

18.52 An anti-avoidance rule also applies where a patented item is incorporated into a product simply to bring the sale of the product within the patent box regime – there must be some commercial reason for the inclusion of the patented item within the overall product.

Example calculations

18.53 The examples below illustrate the pre-1 July 2016 rules and the new rules.

Example calculation – pre 1 July 2017 rules

Assume that this relates to a company's accounting period for the calendar year 2018, and that the company has only one (old) patent and no associated companies, and the following financial information:

Trade turnover (from the accounts)	£10,000,000
Of which, IP income is:	
Income from sales of patent product	£6,000,000
Settlement award relating to patent	£1,000,000
Interest income	£1,000,000
Interest expense	£250,000
Routine expenses	£1,250,000

R&D expenses within routine expenses	£300,000
Total R&D tax relief claimed	£450,000 (tax relief only, not including costs)
Taxable profits (before patent box)	£4,000,000

Step one: calculate TI: 'trade income'

Gross trade turnover	£10,000,000
Less finance-related income	(£1,000,000)
TI	£9,000,000

Step two: establish RIPI: 'relevant IP income' and X%

Income from sale of patented items	£6,000,000
Infringement income	£1,000,000
RIPI	£7,000,000

$$X\% = \frac{RIPI}{TI} \times 100$$

$$\frac{£7,000,000}{£9,000,000} \times 100 \qquad 77.78\%$$

(Note: if the company had elected to use the streaming calculation, this would be Step 1 of the calculation. Step 2 would be an analysis of all expenditure, allocating it between IP and non-IP streams, on a just and reasonable basis. For reasons of space, no example of the streaming calculation differences has been given.)

Step three: establish X% of adjusted profits

Taxable profits	£4,000,000
Add back R&D tax relief claimed	£450,000
Add back loan relationship debits	£250,000
Less R&D adjustment	(£200,000) – see below
Less finance-related income	(£1,000,000)
Adjusted profits	£3,500,000
X% of adjusted profits	
77.78% × £3,500,000	£2,722,300

(Note: if the company had elected for the streaming calculation, this step would be simply to deduct the figure in Step 2 from the figure in Step 1.)

Early years R&D average spend adjustment

Assume that in the four years prior to electing into the patent box, the company's average R&D expenditure in the accounts was £1m. Accounts R&D expenditure in each of the accounting periods in the four years following entry into the patent box is (assume 12-month accounting periods):

AP1 (2013):	£1,050,000	>100%, no adjustment and £50,000 c/f
AP2 (2014):	£800,000	>75%, no adjustment but <100% so no additional c/f
AP3 (2015):	£500,000	<75%, use £50,000 b/f to increase, but adjustment of £200,000 still required to match pre-patent box average

The company will need to check R&D expenditure again in AP4, but not thereafter.

Step four: establish QRP: 'qualifying residual profit'

Routine costs (from tax computation)	£1,250,000
Less routine costs on which R&D relief claimed	(£300,000)
Routine expenses	£950,000
10% of routine expenses	£95,000
X% of routine expenses	
77.78% (from step three) × £95,000	£73,891
QRP (X% of adjusted profits less X% of routine expenses)	
£2,722,300 – £73,891	£2,648,409

(Note: if following the streaming calculation, only those routine costs in the IP expenses stream calculated at Step 2 would be taken into account, and QRP would be 10% of those routine costs.)

Step five: establish RIPP by formula deduction of marketing royalty (by election, if qualifying)

Company will qualify as QRP < £3,000,000 and QRP also < £3,000,000/ associates/trades

Adjusted QRP = **lower** of 75% × QRP/associates/trades **or** £1,000,000

75% × QRP/associates/trades   75% × £2,648,409/1/1 = £1,986,307

As this is more than £1,000,000, QRP would be reduced to £1,000,000 if an election to use this step was made.

Step six: establish RIPP by marketing royalty deduction (where step five not used)

Assuming the company does not pay any marketing royalties

Notional marketing royalty (from valuation)	£250,000
Actual marketing royalty	£0
Net marketing royalty	£250,000

This is less than 10% of the QRP calculated above, so no adjustment required

RIPP	£2,648,409

In this case, it would not benefit the company to elect to use the formula in Step 5, as that will more than halve the amount of patent box relief available. Even with the costs of a valuation exercise taken into account, Step 6 would seem more likely to be beneficial.

Step seven: pre-grant relief (by election)

In 2015 the company is granted a patent it applied for in 2010. The company had elected into the patent box when first able to do so, in 2013. The additional RIPP that would have been included in the patent box calculation if the patent had been granted in earlier years is:

2013:	£300,000
2014:	£500,000
Total	£800,000 added to 2015 RIPP if elect to do so

RIPP for 2015, on election

£2,648,409 + £800,000	£3,448,409

Phasing-in adjustment

As the accounting period (calendar year 2018) is not within the phasing-in period, no adjustment to RIPP is required.

Patent box deduction

The deduction from taxable profits is given by the formula:

$$\frac{\text{RIPP} \times (\text{main rate of corporation tax-patent box rate})}{\text{main rate of corporation tax}}$$

Deduction (as 2018 corporation tax rate is 19% and patent box rate is 10%)

$$\frac{£3,448,409 \times (19-10)}{19} = £\,1,633,457$$

Corporation tax

The company's taxable profits before the patent box deduction were £4,000,000 (as at Step 3) so, following deduction of the patent box, total taxable profits are:

£4,000,000 – £1,633,457	£ 2,366,543

and corporation tax payable is reduced from

£4,000,000 @ 19%	£760,000

to

£2,663,741 @ 19%	**£449,643**

Example calculation – new rules

Assume that this relates to a company's accounting period for the calendar year 2018, and that the company has only one (new) IP asset and no associated companies, and the following financial information:

Income from sales of patented product	£6,000,000
Settlement award relating to patent	£1,000,000
Routine expenses	£1,250,000
R&D expenses within routine expenses	£300,000
Taxable profits (before patent box)	£4,000,000

Step one: IP income

Allocate any income taken into account in calculating the profits of the trade (ignoring any finance income) between a non-IP income stream and an IP income stream.

Income from sale of patented items	£6,000,000
Infringement income	£1,000,000
IP stream	£7,000,000

Step two: sub-divide IP streams

For companies with multiple IP assets, the IP income stream will need to be divided into IP sub-streams, one for each IP asset. The non-IP income stream is disregarded for the rest of the calculation. In this example, the company has only one IP asset and so the IP sub-stream is the same as the IP stream above.

Step three: allocate expenditure

Allocate expenditure brought into account in calculating the profits of the trade (ignoring loan relationship debits and additional deductions for R&D relief, television production relief, video game relief or theatrical production relief) relating solely to non-IP income to the non-IP stream. Allocate expenditure relating solely to each IP asset to the IP sub-stream for that IP asset. Establish one or more methodologies for allocating overhead expenses between the IP sub-streams and the non-IP expense stream.

As methodologies will vary substantially between companies, this example does not set out any methodologies

IP income stream	£7,000,000
Allocated expenses (ignoring R&D relief)	(£3,500,000)

Step four: deduct expenses allocated and routine return

For each IP sub-stream, identify the routine expenses allocated to that sub-stream, less any non-routine deductions (such as R&D expenses) and calculate 10% of such expenses to establish the routine return for that sub-stream.

Routine expenses in sub-stream	£1,250,000
Less routine costs on which R&D relief claimed	(£300,000)
Routine expenses	£950,000
Routine return: 10% of routine expenses	£95,000
IP stream income	£7,000,000
Less: IP stream expenses	(£3,500,000)
Less: routine return	(£95,000)
IP stream	£3,405,000

Step five: deduct marketing royalty by formula deduction (by election, if qualifying)

Company will not qualify as QRP > £3,000,000, so no election can be made.

Step six: deduct marketing royalty (where Step five not used)

Assuming the company does not pay any marketing royalties:

Notional marketing royalty (from valuation)	£250,000
Actual marketing royalty	£0
Net marketing royalty	£250,000

This is less than 10% of the QRP calculated above, so no adjustment required

IP stream	£3,405,000

Step seven: apply the R&D fraction

Assume that:

- cumulative direct R&D costs on the IP asset ('D') are £1,500,000
- cumulative third party sub-contracted R&D costs ('S') are £0
- cumulative acquisition costs ('A') are £500,000
- cumulative group R&D costs ('R') are £0

The R&D fraction is the lower of $((D+S) \times 1.3)/(D+S+A+R)$ and 1

Applying the formula gives: $((1,500,000+0) \times 1.3)(1,500,000+0+500,000+0) = 0.975$

As this is lower than 1, this is the fraction used.

Applying this to the IP stream gives: £3,405,000 × 0.975 = £3,319,875.

Step eight: add together IP streams

Having repeated Steps two to seven to establish the IP sub-stream for each IP asset, add together the IP sub-streams to establish the total patent box profits.

In this example, there is only one IP asset, so the total patent box profit is £3,319,875.

Step nine: pre-grant relief (by election)

Assume that the patent for which patent box profits are being calculated was granted in 2018, having been applied for in August 2016. The company had elected into the patent box when first able to do so, in 2016. The additional patent box profit that would have been included in the patent box calculation if the patent had been granted in earlier years is:

2016:	£300,000
2017:	£500,000
Total	£800,000 added to 2018 patent box profits if elect to do so

Additional patent box profits for 2018, on election

£3,319,875 + £800,000	£4,119,875

Patent box deduction

The deduction from taxable profits is given by the formula:

$$\frac{\text{IP stream} \times (\text{main rate of corporation tax-patent box rate})}{\text{main rate of corporation tax}}$$

Deduction (assuming 19% corporation tax rate and patent box rate is 10%)

$$\frac{£4,119,875 \times (19-10)}{19} = £1,951,520$$

Corporation tax

The company's taxable profits before the patent box deduction were £4,000,000 so, following deduction of the patent box, total taxable profits are:

£4,000,000 – £1,951,520	£2,048,480

and corporation tax payable is reduced from

£4,000,000 @ 19%	£760,000
to	
£2,048,480 @ 19%	**£389,211**

Chapter 19

Investors' relief

Chris Williams LLB

This chapter includes material originally adapted from the book
Capital Gains Tax Reliefs for SMEs and Entrepreneurs
(Bloomsbury Professional) by Satwaki Chanda and Chris Williams.

SIGNPOSTS

- **Operation of the relief** – Which disposals qualify, shareholding requirements, interests in shares (see **19.3–19.12**).

- **Comparison with other reliefs** – The differences from entrepreneurs' relief and EIS are handily summarised (see **19.3–19.4**).

- **What companies and shares qualify** – No listing at time of issue, what is an ordinary share, trading requirements (see **19.13–19.21**).

- **Who can claim the relief** – Which individuals, what sort of trusts and what connections they can have with the company, when relief is denied (**19.22–19.26**).

- **Order of disposal** – Qualifying, potentially qualifying and excluded shares, special share identification rules for IR, lifetime limit for IR (see **19.27–19.37**).

- **Share reorganisations** – Reconstructions and share exchanges (see **19.38–19.44**).

- **Overseas matters** – Remittance basis, temporary non-residents (see **19.43–19.45**).

- **Trustees** – Need for a qualifying beneficiary, what are the trust business assets, how much relief can be claimed, how to make that claim, offshore trusts (see **19.46–19.57**).

INTRODUCTION

19.1 *Finance Act 2016, Sch 14* introduced *TCGA 1992, ss 169VA–169VY* and *Sch 7ZB* which add investors' relief (IR) to the range of CGT reliefs. Announced in the 2016 Budget as an extended form of entrepreneurs' relief (ER), investors' relief (IR) shares both the 10% rate of CGT and £10 million lifetime relief limit but little else. In particular, IR only applies to company shares and the provisions are deliberately drafted to ensure that there is minimal overlap between IR and ER; it would be virtually unheard of for a person to be eligible for both IR and ER on shares in the same company.

The discrete nature of the two reliefs is something of a double-edged sword in that they do not overlap and an individual's shareholding that qualifies for IR will not also be eligible for ER and vice versa, so it is essential that the right relief be identified. But this is not all bad news, in fact the separation provides a great advantage because each is subject to a lifetime limit of £10 million, both of which may be used. Thus an individual may be able to take advantage of 10% rates on gains of up to £20 million.

IR can apply to shares:

- subscribed for by the claimant;

- issued on or after 17 March 2016; and

- disposed of on or after 6 April 2019,

subject to the qualifying conditions being met.

Every individual has a lifetime IR allowance (currently £10 million), of gains against which relief may be claimed. Trusts do not have a separate limit but may use a beneficiary's allowance. The IR allowance is separate from and additional to the individual's IR limit.

IR does not apply automatically but must be claimed (see **19.56**). This enables the taxpayer to choose whether claiming the relief is in his best interests, perhaps not to claim in order to use another roll-over or deferral relief, or to preserve the lifetime limit so it can be used for another disposal. Sometimes, a protective IR claim may be advisable, such as where the taxpayer is non-resident or non-domiciled, but there is a possibility that he may resume UK residence within five years, after the time limit for claiming IR has passed (see **19.45**).

Legislation

19.2   The IR legislation is *TCGA 1992, ss 169VA–169VY* and *Sch 7ZB*.

TCGA 1992, s 169VA acts as a contents section for the main IR provisions thus:

- *s 169VB* defines 'qualifying shares', 'potentially qualifying shares' and 'excluded shares';

- *s 169VC* creates the relief, to be known as 'investors' relief';

- *s 169VD* deals with disposals from holdings consisting partly of qualifying shares;

- *ss 169VE* to *169VG* contain rules to determine which shares remain in the holding out of which previous disposals have been made;

- *ss 169VH* and *169VI* make provision about disposals by trusts;

- *s 169VJ* makes provision about disposals of interests in shares;

- *ss 169VK* and *169VL* cap the amount of IR that can be claimed;

- *s 169VM* makes provision about claims for investors' relief;

- *ss 169VN* to *169VT* make provision for IR following a company's reorganisation of its share capital, an exchange of shares or securities or a scheme of reconstruction;

- *ss 169VU* to *169VY* contain definitions; and

- *Sch 7ZB* contains provisions about disqualification of shares where the investor receives value within the 'period of restriction'.

HMRC guidance is provided in CG63500P and following.

COMPARISON WITH ENTREPRENEURS' RELIEF AND EIS/SEIS

Entrepreneurs' relief

19.3   Although the reliefs are superficially similar it cannot be stressed enough that they are designed to operate as separate, mutually exclusive reliefs: hence the duplication of the lifetime limits on gains qualifying for relief. There are numerous differences between the reliefs, reflecting the fact that ER is intended to reward owner-participators whilst IR is specifically intended to act as an inducement to attract investment from participators who will not be involved in the business at all when they invest and are not expected to become involved at the time when they invest.

19.3 *Investors' relief*

The table below summarises key differences

	Investors' relief	Entrepreneurs' relief
Type of business	Company only	Company or partnership
Qualifying activity	Any trade, must be carried on for a qualifying period of at least one year, ending on disposal or ceasing to be a trading company within three years before disposal	Any trade, must be carried on throughout a period of 12 months ending on either the date of disposal or, if the company has ceased to be a trading company, within the three years preceding disposal
Share acquisition	Subscription only: shares may not be acquired by gift except inter-spouse transfers	Any method of acquisition
Ownership period	Minimum ownership period three years Only the original subscriber (or spouse) may claim IR: the shares must be held throughout the period from issue to disposal without any break	One year
Minimum interest	No minimum shareholding requirement	Minimum shareholding 5% of voting and assets except where shares acquired through EMI
Assets used in the business	No relief for any asset other than the IR shares	Associated disposals relief available if the individual is entitled to ER
Trusts	Trustees may hold shares for benefit of any beneficiary	Trustees may hold shares for benefit of any beneficiary who holds the required minimum interest for the company to be his personal company

Activity in the business	Investor may not be an employee or director other than an unremunerated director at the time when the shares are issued. Subject to conditions, an investor may subsequently become an employee or remunerated director without invalidating IR	Shareholder must be an officer or employee of the company

In most cases the would-be investor will not have a choice between IR and ER at the time when the investment is made because of the restrictions relating to employment status:

• an existing employee or office-holder other than an unremunerated director cannot qualify for IR;

• a non-employee cannot qualify for ER at the time of the investment but may find that he can claim ER when he comes to sell his shares if he has become an employee in the meantime and acquired the requisite shareholding interest; and

• an investor who has become eligible for ER may not have shed his entitlement to claim IR when disposing of his shares.

EIS and SEIS

19.4   Unlike entrepreneurs' relief (ER) which is specifically targeted at participators in the business, IR is a relief that competes with the Enterprise Investment Scheme (EIS) and Seed EIS (SEIS) as a means of attracting investment from investors who are not involved in running the business.

The table below summarises key differences

	Investors' relief	EIS/SEIS
Activity	Any trade but the investee company must be a trading company throughout the period of ownership	Restricted to qualifying trades through the three year qualifying period from issue/starting to trade
Nature of relief	Reduced rate of CGT on disposal	• Income tax relief as a percentage of investment • Shares exempt from CGT • Hold-over relief for gains reinvested in shares

Share acquisition	Subscription only: shares may not be acquired by gift except inter-spouse transfers	Subscription only: shares may not be acquired by gift except inter-spouse transfers
Ownership period	Minimum ownership period three years Only the original subscriber (or spouse) may claim IR: the shares must be held throughout the period from issue to disposal without any break	Minimum ownership period three years from later of issue and commencement to trade Only the original subscriber (or spouse) may claim IR: the shares must be held throughout the period from issue to disposal without any break
Minimum interest	No minimum shareholding requirement	No minimum shareholding requirement
Trusts	Trustees may hold shares for benefit of any beneficiary	Trustees may hold shares for benefit of any beneficiary who holds the required minimum interest
Activity in the business	Investor may not be an employee or director other than an unremunerated director at the time when the shares are issued. Subject to conditions, an investor may subsequently become an employee or remunerated director without invalidating IR	Shareholder must be an officer or employee of the company

Investors in companies eligible for SEIS or EIS will generally find that EIS/SEIS is the preferred option because of SEIS and EIS offer much greater advantages than the reduction in CGT rate that is the sole tax advantage of IR.

Planning tip

Shares an EIS/SEIS company may lose their status, so that the EIS/SEIS relief is withdrawn. This is most likely to happen because the investor receives value from the company or the company's trade ceases to meet the strict qualifying trade rules for EIS/SEIS. But there is no provision in *TCGA 1992* that excludes IR where EIS or SEIS relief has been claimed, whether or not the relief has been withdrawn. There is also no need to claim IR at the time of investment, only following disposal. Therefore an EIS/SEIS investor would still be able to claim IR if the IR relief conditions were met in relation to shares on which EIS/SEIS relief had been claimed but on which the relief had been withdrawn.

OPERATION OF THE RELIEF

What disposals qualify

19.5   IR is available on gains made by an individual who disposes of qualifying:

- ordinary shares;

- in a trading company or holding company of a trading group;

- issued to the claimant when none of the company's shares or securities is listed on a recognised stock exchange, on or after17 March 2016;

- held for a minimum period of three years; and

- disposed of on or after 6 April 2019.

Although no claims will be possible until 6 April 2019, it is essential that would-be claimants ensure that the conditions for a claim are observed and maintained throughout the period from issue of the shares until their disposal.

A disposal for IR can be:

- a sale;

- a gift or transfer at undervalue;

- where a capital distribution is received in respect of shares held in a company, for example on the liquidation of that company; or

- a capital sum derived from an asset.

No minimum shareholding required

19.6   In contrast with ER, IR carries no minimum or maximum limit on the size of the qualifying shareholding. This simplifies matters considerably in the sense that investors do not need to be wary of their shareholdings falling below any threshold.

Qualifying shares

19.7   *TCGA 1992, s 169VB* applies the qualifying share (QS) test at the point immediately preceding disposal. However, all but one of the criteria must be satisfied throughout the investor's 'share-holding period'.

The shares must be subscribed for by the investor. The subscription conditions are that:

- the investor subscribes for the shares personally, in his own right;

- the shares are issued to the investor, ie not to a nominee or trustee;

- the only consideration for subscription is cash;

- the shares are fully paid up at the time of issue;

- the shares are subscribed for and issued for genuine commercial reasons and not as part of arrangements the main purpose, or one of the main purposes of which, is to secure a tax advantage to any person; and

- the subscription is an arm's length bargain (*TCGA 1992, s 169VU(1)*).

Married couples and civil partners

19.8   The investor can transfer qualifying shares to their spouse or civil partner, at a time when they are living together as a married couple/civil partnership, without losing the benefit if IR. In this case the transferee is treated as if he had subscribed for the shares on the date on which they were issued to the transferor. Because a transferee spouse is treated as having been the subscriber they too can transfer the shares back to the original subscriber or to a new spouse (*TCGA 1992, s 169VU(3), (4)*).

Planning point

The freedom to transfer qualifying shares between spouses offers more than just flexibility: if one spouse held shares on which the gains would exceed their lifetime allowance, he/she could transfer those shares to their spouse or civil partner at any time up until immediately before disposal so as to take advantage of the transferee spouse's lifetime limit.

Jointly held shares

19.9   IR is available on shares issued to the individual or trustee holder and to interests in shares that they subscribed for within the meaning given by *TCGA 1992, s 169VU*:

'(1) For the purposes of this Chapter (other than this subsection) a person "subscribes for" a share in a company if –

(a)   that person subscribes for the share,

(b)   the share is issued to that person by the company for consideration consisting wholly of cash,

(c)   the share is fully paid up at the time it is issued,

(d)   the share is subscribed for, and issued, for genuine commercial reasons and not as part of arrangements the main purpose, or one of the main purposes, of which is to secure a tax advantage to any person, and

(e)   the share is subscribed for, and issued, by way of a bargain at arm's length.'

However, *TCGA 1992, s 169VJ* explicitly provides for disposals of joint holdings and interests in shares. This creates a mess of confusion because, whilst more than one individual may subscribe jointly for shares (though only the first-named holder may be recorded on the company's statutory register) it is not possible to subscribe for an interest in shares.

Joint ownership

19.10   Unless it is accepted that a joint owner can be treated as a subscriber, even though the shares were not actually issued to them, the provisions allowing for joint ownership appear to be restricted to married couples and civil partnerships. *TCGA 1992, s 169VU* provides specifically for a transferee spouse to be treated as if they were the original subscriber for the shares and so obtain IR. Therefore, the only certainty in relation to joint ownership and interests in shares is that IR will be available to spouses and civil partners who receive their interests from their spouse who was the original subscriber. This will cover shares transferred into joint names and cases where the subscriber spouse does not transfer legal ownership but creates an interest for their spouse in any other way, such as by a declaration that they hold shares on bare trust for themselves and their spouse as joint owners.

If the subscriber creates an interest for a non-spouse that will be a disposal, on which IR may be claimable, but the transferee will not be able to claim IR on their subsequent disposal of the shares.

Interests in shares

19.11   It would appear that the references to disposal of an interest can only apply to a subscriber who makes a part disposal by creating an interest over the shares that they continue to legally own. The one case where an interest in shares will clearly be eligible for IR concerns married couples: if the husband subscribes for shares and subsequently makes a declaration of trust, sharing beneficial ownership with his wife, they will both be able to claim IR.

Continuous ownership from subscription until disposal

19.12 Any shares acquired as qualifying shares will cease to be qualifying shares if they are disposed of, other than to a spouse or civil partner. Therefore, the investor cannot sell and reacquire the shares and hope to obtain IR on their eventual disposal (*TCGA 1992, s 169VB(2)(b)*).

WHICH COMPANIES AND SHARES QUALIFY

No stock exchange listing at time of issue

19.13 The company may not have any of its shares listed on a recognised stock exchange at the time when the IR shares are issued. A recognised stock exchange does not include AIM and the application of this requirement only at the time of issue means that early investors in companies that later become listed will still be able to benefit from IR when they eventually dispose of their shares (*TCGA 1992, s 169VB(2)(d)*).

This continuity of treatment may be affected if there is a reorganisation, reconstruction or disposal of the company in exchange for shares because special rules apply in such cases and continuity cannot always be guaranteed (see **19.38–19.44**).

Shares must be ordinary shares

19.14 This requirement does not apply throughout the share-holding period, only at the times:

- when the share is issued; and
- immediately before disposal.

The definition of an ordinary share has been the subject of a number of legal cases in relation to EIS and ER and there may be problems with shares carrying fixed dividend rights, a specified 'zero-dividend' right or no dividend rights at all (see **19.15**).

Ordinary shares

19.15 Ordinary share capital is defined in *ITA 2007, s 989* as all of a company's issued share capital (however described), other than capital the holders of which have a right to a dividend at a fixed rate but have no other right to share in the company's profits. The interpretation of this apparently simple definition has caused a number of problems and led to tribunal decisions that have not entirely clarified matters.

The latest case to consider this issue was *HMRC v McQuillan* [2017] UKUT 344 (TCC) in which the Upper Tribunal (UT) upheld HMRC's appeal against a decision of the First-tier Tribunal (FTT). The UT accepted HMRC's contention that entitlement to no dividend was the same as being entitled to a fixed dividend of 0% and neither was sufficient to bring the shares within the scope of *ITA 2007, s 989*. In this instance the NV shares had been created for a specific non-tax purpose and were not intended to unbalance the rights and entitlements attaching to the other shares which all the shareholders regarded as the true ordinary share capital. The FTT had decided that, in this respect, *ITA 2007, s 989* was ambiguous and it was just that it should be interpreted in a way that did not create an absurd result. However, in reversing the FTT decision, the UT decided that *s 989* was unambiguous and no alternative interpretation was possible, even though it produced a manifestly unfair result.

This accords with *Castledine v HMRC* [2016] UKFTT 145 (TC) in which the FTT decided that non-voting deferred shares which carried no dividend rights and entitlement to a small share of assets in a winding-up were ordinary share capital. The FTT found that although the chance of those shares participating in the company's profits was vanishingly small, that chance nonetheless existed and so the deferred shares did form part of the company's ordinary share capital. The FTT's view on this occasion was that *ITA 2007, s 989* was unambiguous and had to be followed to the letter.

The uncertainty over the definition of ordinary share capital is unlikely to cause as many problems under IR as it can for ER because investors will normally want shares that participate fully in dividends and capital; care is nevertheless needed to ensure that shares subscribed for in the hope of obtaining IR do meet this criterion.

Fixed rate preference shares do not count as ordinary share capital, but it is not always clear whether the preference shares are fixed rate. The coupon on a preference share can be fixed at the outset, but the actual amount may vary. Where the share has a stepped coupon, such that the actual percentage changes from year to year, HMRC do not regard those shares as being fixed rate. Where shares carry no dividend rights, HMRC consider those shares to be ordinary shares, not shares with a fixed-rate dividend of 0% (see Employee Tax Advantaged Share Scheme User Manual at ETASSUM23160).

Appendix 11 to the HMRC Capital Gains Manual (CG-APP11) provides a discussion of what HMRC consider to be ordinary share capital, which may be particularly helpful when dealing with non-UK companies. Note that there is no requirement for the company to be resident in the UK, or trading in the UK, for the shares to qualify for IR.

Trading company or holding company of a trading group

19.16 This requirement will apply throughout the share-holding period, ie from issue until immediately before disposal which could be a long time. The government is clearly conscious of its need to prevent companies being used at any time as investment-holding vehicles; this requirement is significantly different from the ER requirement that the company should have been a trading company or holding company of a trading group only for a final 12-month period. This is examined further in **19.17**.

Trading activities

19.17 Trading activities are those carried on by the company or group in the course of, or for the purposes of, a trade that it is carrying on, or it is preparing to carry on (*TCGA 1992, s 165A(4)*). HMRC regard trading activities as including those activities that a company or group has to carry out before it can start trading. In such cases, trading activities may include developing a business plan, acquiring premises, hiring staff, ordering materials and incurring pre-trading expenditure (CG64065).

HMRC highlight the distinction between trading and investment activities. HMRC give the example of land bought either as trading stock or as a fixed asset to be used to support the trading business, in which case the buying of the land would be a trading activity. Conversely, the land may be held as an investment to generate rental income, which is not a trading activity (CG64060). In some circumstances, the making and holding of investments may be part of the company's or group's trading activities; whether those activities are trading activities can only be decided on the facts (see **19.19** regarding the letting of surplus business property).

HMRC acknowledge that companies and groups may acquire shares other than for investment reasons. They may be paid in shares in place of cash, or be required to hold shares in a trade organisation. The holding of such shares will be considered to be a trading activity if HMRC can be convinced of the trading reason to hold the shares (CG64080).

It is quite common for a company, which is reaching the end of its useful life for the owners, to hold a significant cash balance that has been generated from trading activities, but has not been paid out as dividends or otherwise invested in business assets. It may not be clear whether such a company has become an investment company, due to the ratio of investment activities (cash balances) to trading activities. The HMRC guidance is that short-term lodgement of surplus funds in a deposit account could count as a trading activity rather than an investment activity. Also, funds retained to distribute as dividends would not be an investment activity. However, the long-term retention of surplus earnings would be considered an investment activity unless those funds had been preserved for a particular trading purpose (CG64060).

Trading activities can include activities undertaken with a view to the company acquiring or starting to carry on a trade, or with a view to its acquiring a 'significant interest' in the share capital of another company that is a trading company or the holding company (see **19.20**) of a trading group (so long as, where the acquiring company is a member of a group of companies, it is not a member of the target company's group). These activities qualify as trading activities only if the acquisition is made, or (as the case may be) the company starts to carry on the trade, as soon as is reasonably practicable in the circumstances (*TCGA 1992, s 165A(5)*). HMRC accept that a company that has disposed of its trade and invested the proceeds and is 'actively seeking' to acquire a new trade or trading subsidiary might still be a trading company if it does not have substantial non-trading activities. What is 'reasonably practicable in the circumstances' will depend on the particular facts of the case (CG64075).

Trade

19.18   Trade means anything which is:

- a trade, profession or vocation within the meaning of the *Income Tax Acts*; and

- conducted on a commercial basis with a view to the realisation of profits (*ITA 2007, s 989*).

The commercial letting of furnished holiday accommodation (FHL) is deemed to be a trade for the purposes of IR and certain other CGT reliefs (*TCGA 1992, s 241(3A)*). The conditions that must be met for a deemed FHL trade are discussed in more detail in Chapter 2 of Chanda and Williams, *CGT reliefs for SMEs 2017/18* (Bloomsbury Professional).

Activities that a company carries on as a member of a partnership may be included in the company's trading activities. There is no exclusion of such activities for IR equivalent to that which applies for ER.

Substantial extent

19.19   Where a company carries on activities other than trading activities, the existence of those non-trading activities will not disturb the trading status of the company if they are not carried on to a substantial extent (*TCGA 1992, s 165A(3)*). This measure of trading activities is the same as used in the substantial shareholding exemption, and is identical to the test previously used for taper relief.

HMRC regard 'substantial extent' as meaning more than 20% (CG64090). However, the legislation only refers to the word 'substantial' and, in the first instance, the normal everyday meaning should be used, being an equivalent word to 'considerable', 'solid' or 'big'. The words of Viscount Simon in *Palser v Ginling* [1948] AC 291 should be heeded:

> 'If the judgment of the Court of Appeal in *Palser*'s case were to be understood as fixing percentages as a legal measure, that would be going beyond the powers of the judiciary. To say that everything over 20 per cent of the whole rent should be regarded as substantial portion of that rent would be to play the part of the legislator.'

Even if the 20% boundary is taken as being reasonable, it is not clear from the legislation which attributes of the business should be categorised into trading and non-trading, to prove that the trading activities of the whole business do exceed 80% of the whole. HMRC indicate the following attributes of the business will be indicators of the trading or non-trading activities:

- income from non-trading activities, such as investment property;

- the company's trading and non-trading asset base, taking account of intangible assets such as goodwill or trademarks;

- expenses incurred, or time spent, by officers and employees of the company in undertaking its trading and non-trading activities; and

- the company's history over several years or seasons.

These measures should not be regarded as individual tests which all need to be passed; they are just factors which may point one way or the other. The HMRC officer is instructed to weigh up the relevance of each measure in the context of the individual case and judge the matter 'in the round', as demonstrated by the approach of the Special Commissioner in *Farmer (Farmer's Executors) v IRC* [1999] STC 321.

Where a company lets property that is surplus to its current requirements, HMRC do not consider that the following activities necessarily indicate non-trading activities (CG64085):

- letting part of the trading premises;

- letting properties that are no longer required for the purpose of the trade, where the company's or group's objective is to sell them;

- sub-letting property where it would be impractical or uneconomic in terms of the trade to assign or surrender the lease; or

- the acquisition of property (whether vacant or already let) where it can be shown that the intention is that it will be brought into use for trading activities.

If the company is uncertain as to whether it does qualify as 'trading', it may ask HMRC for an opinion in accordance with the non-statutory business clearance procedure, as described in the HMRC Non-Statutory Business Clearance Guidance (see checklist at tinyurl.com/NSBCAnnex). HMRC have confirmed that an opinion will be given to the company in these circumstances, but they will not enter into correspondence with the individual shareholders on this matter (CG64100).

Holding company

19.20   A holding company is a company that has one or more 51% subsidiaries (*TCGA 1992, s 165A(2)*).

A 51% subsidiary is defined in *CTA 2010, s 1154* as a company where more than 50% of its ordinary share capital is owned directly or indirectly by another body corporate. Thus, a company where 50.1% of its ordinary shares were held by another company would count as a 51% subsidiary.

Where the group has a number of intermediate holding companies owning trading subsidiaries, and an ultimate holding company at the top of the group, it is not clear whether a shareholding in the intermediate holding company would qualify. In such a situation, a ruling or clearance may be sought from HMRC (see **19.19**).

Trading group

19.21   A group of companies means a company that has one or more 51% subsidiaries.

When looking at whether the group is trading, the activities of all the members of the group are taken together as one business (*TCGA 1992, s 165A(8)*). This allows the group to contain one or more companies that are not trading and still qualify as a trading group. The intra-group transactions are ignored.

However, where a minority individual shareholder disposes of shares in a subsidiary company, that particular subsidiary company must be a trading company in order to qualify for IR.

WHO CAN CLAIM THE RELIEF?

Employees and office holders

19.22   The general rule in *TCGA 1992, s 169VW* is that IR on shares is not available to 'relevant employees'. A relevant employee is a person who is an employee or office-holder of the company or any connected company at any time in the relevant period (ie from issue of the shares until immediately before disposal).

Specific exceptions to this rule apply to people who become employees (see **19.23**) and unremunerated directors (see **19.24**).

Employees

19.23 A person who is already an employee or office-holder, but not a director, cannot subscribe for IR shares but a person who has subscribed for shares may still obtain IR on disposal if:

- he becomes an employee more than 180 days after the shares are issued; and

- at the time when he subscribed for the shares there was not a reasonable prospect of him becoming an employee *(TCGA 1992, s 169VW(5))*.

Unremunerated directors

19.24 Unremunerated directors can qualify for IR if they have never previously been either:

(a) connected with the issuing company; or

(b) involved in carrying on (whether on the person's own account or as a partner, director or employee) the whole or any part of the trade, business or profession carried on by the issuing company or a company connected with that company *(TCGA 1992, s 169VW(4))*.

TCGA 1992, s 169VX defines an unremunerated director as a director who neither receives nor is entitled to receive a 'disqualifying payment' from the company.

A disqualifying payment is defined by *TCGA 1992, s 169VX(2)* as any payment other than:

'(a) a payment or reimbursement of travelling or other expenses wholly, exclusively and necessarily incurred by the person concerned in the performance of his or her duties as a director,

(b) any interest which represents no more than a reasonable commercial return on money lent to the issuing company or a related person,

(c)   any dividend or other distribution which does not exceed a normal return on the investment to which the dividend or distribution relates,

(d)   any payment for the supply of goods which does not exceed their market value,

(e)   any payment of rent for any property occupied by the issuing company or a related person which does not exceed a reasonable and commercial rent for the property, or

(f)   any necessary and reasonable remuneration which is–

(i)   paid for qualifying services that are provided to the issuing company or a related person in the course of a trade or profession carried on wholly or partly in the United Kingdom, and

(ii)   taken into account in calculating for tax purposes the profits of that trade or profession.'

This exclusion applies throughout the relevant period, ie from the date of issue of the shares until immediately before disposal. It includes payments received by the director and any relative or person connected with them.

Receipt of value by investors

19.25   The investor is denied relief if he receives value from the company.

This restriction applies to all investors: any investor who receives a payment in the 'period of restriction' which begins one year before the shares are issued and ends immediately before the third anniversary of their issue has their shares disqualified from IR (*TCGA 1992, s 169VB(5)* and *Sch 7ZB*).

The restrictions take the wide-ranging form that is customary in such cases, extending to any form of uncommercial bargain including loans left unpaid.

Receipt of value

19.26   Receipt of value is defined in *TCGA 1992, Sch 7ZB, para 2(1)* thus:

'(1)   For the purposes of this Schedule the investor receives value from the company if the company –

(a)   repays, redeems or repurchases any of its share capital or securities which belong to the investor or makes any payment to the investor for giving up a right to any of the company's share capital or any security on its cancellation or extinguishment,

(b) repays, in pursuance of any arrangements for or in connection with the acquisition of the shares, any debt owed to the investor other than a debt which was incurred by the company –

  (i) on or after the date of issue of the shares, and

  (ii) otherwise than in consideration of the extinguishment of a debt incurred before that date,

(c) makes to the investor any payment for giving up the investor's right to any debt on its extinguishment,

(d) releases or waives any liability of the investor to the company or discharges, or undertakes to discharge, any liability of the investor to a third person,

(e) makes a loan or advance to the investor which has not been repaid in full before the issue of the shares,

(f) provides a benefit or facility for the investor,

(g) disposes of an asset to the investor for no consideration or for a consideration which is or the value of which is less than the market value of the asset,

(h) acquires an asset from the investor for a consideration which is or the value of which is more than the market value of the asset, or

(i) makes any payment to the investor other than a qualifying payment.'

Qualifying payments

19.27   Qualifying payments to the investor, ie payments that do not create a receipt of value are defined in *TCGA 1992, Sch 7ZB, para 2(4)* thus:

'(4) In this paragraph "qualifying payment" means –

(a) the payment by any company of such remuneration for service as an officer or employee of that company as may be reasonable in relation to the duties of that office or employment,

(b) any payment or reimbursement by any company of travelling or other expenses wholly, exclusively and necessarily incurred by the investor to whom the payment is made in the performance of duties as an officer or employee of that company,

(c) the payment by any company of any interest which represents no more than a reasonable commercial return on money lent to that company,

(d) the payment by any company of any dividend or other distribution which does not exceed a normal return on any investment in shares in or other securities of that company,

(e) any payment for the supply of goods which does not exceed their market value,

(f) any payment for the acquisition of an asset which does not exceed its market value,

(g) the payment by any company, as rent for any property occupied by the company, of an amount not exceeding a reasonable and commercial rent for the property,

(h) any reasonable and necessary remuneration which –

    (i) is paid by any company for services rendered to that company in the course of a trade or profession carried on wholly or partly in the United Kingdom; and

    (ii) is taken into account in calculating for tax purposes the profits of that trade or profession, or

    (iii) a payment in discharge of an ordinary trade debt.'

The £10 million lifetime limit

19.28 The lifetime IR limit is completely separate from the ER limit of the same amount and may be used in addition to the ER limit, allowing for gains of up to £20 million on qualifying investments to enjoy the reduced CGT rate.

As is detailed below, each individual's limit applies to their own IR claims and claims by trustees on shares in which they are interested as an eligible beneficiary (*TCGA 1992, s 169VK*).

ORDER OF DISPOSAL

Excluded shares

19.29 Any share that meets all of the criteria, except for the share-holding period, is a potentially qualifying share (PQS).

Any share that meets all of the criteria including the share-holding period is a qualifying share (QS).

Any share that is neither qualifying nor potentially qualifying is an excluded share (E) and cannot ever become a QS or PQS again, so the opportunity to claim IR on that share is lost.

This distinction will need to be considered whenever a disposal is in prospect, although it will usually be impossible to rectify any defects other than the shares not being ordinary shares immediately before disposal.

Share identification rules for IR

19.30   There are special identification rules that determine which shares are disposed of first for the purposes of IR but not for any other purposes. These rules are benignly drafted, ie they operate in a way that generally gives the best chance of retaining IR on mixed holdings.

Some of the holding qualifies for IR

19.31   When the investor disposes of shares and claims IR it may be necessary to distinguish between shares that do and do not qualify for IR. *TCGA 1992, s 169VD* rules that where IR is claimed and the shareholding out of which the disposal is made consists only partly of qualifying shares, it is the qualifying shares that are deemed to be disposed of first: *TCGA 1992, s 169VD* expresses this simple concept through a clumsy fraction but that is what it means. The fraction of the shares disposed of that qualifies for IR is Q/T where:

- if the number of qualifying shares in the entire holding is less shares than the number disposed of, Q = the number disposed of;

- if the number disposed of is no greater than the number of qualifying shares in the holding, Q = the number of qualifying shares in the holding; and

- T is the total number of shares disposed of.

Therefore, where IR is claimed it is used up to the maximum possible by the current disposal. There are specific rules for subsequent disposals which determine which shares are deemed to be disposed of according to whether IR was claimed on the previous disposal(s).

No claim – no waste of IR

19.32   *TCGA 1992, ss 169VC–169VE* must be read carefully, otherwise the false impression could be gained that qualifying shares are always deemed to be disposed of first. These ordering rules only apply to cases where IR is being claimed because *TCGA 1992, ss 169VD–169VE* refer to cases where 'a disposal' ('the disposal concerned') is made as mentioned in *TCGA 1992, s 169VC(1)*; this refers specifically to a disposal where IR is claimed.

Therefore, if there is a disposal on which IR is not claimed there is no requirement at that time to identify which shares are deemed to be disposed of and in what order: that only becomes relevant when IR is actually claimed on a later disposal.

If IR is never claimed, there is clearly never any need to work out the order of disposal but it is likely to be the case that IR will be claimed at some time, so keeping a record of the 'IR pool' will usually be worthwhile.

IR claimed on previous disposal

19.33

- When IR has been claimed on an earlier disposal, *TCGA 1992, s 169VF* must be applied to the last disposal to work out which, if any, of the shares disposed of in that earlier disposal were excluded shares or potentially qualifying shares. The starting point is the shares on which IR was claimed, ascertained under *TCGA 1992, s 169VD* as above (see **19.31**).

- The next tranche of shares deemed to have been disposed of in the earlier transaction comes out of any excluded shares held at the time of that earlier disposal.

- If those excluded shares do not account for all the remaining shares, the next tranche to be reduced are the shares that were potentially qualifying shares, again, at the time immediately before the last disposal.

This order of set off is the most advantageous to investors in that it means that the potential for an IR claim is not lost.

19.34

Example 19.1 – Some shares are excluded from IR claim

Barney subscribes for 10,000 shares in Pugh Pews Ltd in three tranches:

- 5,000 on 31 March 2017;
- 2,500 on 31 July 2018; and
- 2,500 on 31 January 2019.

On 31 March 2019 he becomes an employee of Pugh Pews which makes shares acquired in the preceding six months (ie those acquired on 31 January 2019) excluded shares (see **19.27**).

He then disposes of 7,000 shares on 31 July 20209 and the remaining 3,000 on 1 August 2021, claiming IR on both occasions.

Disposal 1

At the time of this disposal the only qualifying shares are the initial investment of 5,000 shares which are the only ones that have been held for more than three years: they are deemed to have been disposed of first, so Pugh can claim IR on 5,000/7,000 and the remaining shares (against which he sets his annual exemption) are taxable at the full CGT rate (20% unless rates change).

The question of share identification does not make a difference to Barney's 2020/21 liability but it does become relevant when we come to consider the second disposal.

Disposal 2

When Barney sells his remaining 3,000 shares it is more than three years since he acquired his second tranche, so they are no longer PQS: they are now qualifying shares but the question is how those 3,000 shares are divided between excluded and qualifying shares. This is where *TCGA 1992, s 169VF* applies.

TCGA 1992, s 169VF says that the first shares to be considered after qualifying shares disposed of on 31 July 2020 are the excluded shares. So the 2,000 non-IR shares in that disposal, on which Barney has paid full-rate CGT anyway, are deemed to come out of the 2,500 shares acquired on 31 July 2018 which became excluded shares when Barney became an employee. This benefits Barney because it means that all 2,500 of the shares acquired on 31 January 2018 qualify for IR as qualifying shares and only 500 shares are taxed at the full CGT rate as excluded shares.

IR not claimed on previous disposal

19.35   The rule, in *TCGA 1992, s 169VG*, is simpler than that applying where IR has previously been claimed in respect of holdings in the same company (*TCGA 1992, s 169VF*).

TCGA 1992, s 169VG simply states that the first shares deemed to have been disposed of in the previous disposal are those that were excluded shares at the time of the disposal.

19.36

> **Example 19.2 – No previous IR claim**
>
> Cuthbert subscribes for 10,000 shares in AIM company Dibble & Grubb plc (D&G) in three tranches:
>
> - 5,000 on 31 March 2019;
> - 2,500 on 31 July 2020; and
> - 2,500 on 31 January 2023.
>
> He sells 7,000 shares on 31 August 20212but does not claim IR because he has losses in the same year which are automatically set off against the gains, meaning he has no net chargeable gains for 2020/21.
>
> On 30 September 2022, Cuthbert becomes an employee of D&G which means that the shares acquired in the preceding six months (ie those acquired on 31 July 2020) are excluded shares (see **19.27**).
>
> He then sells the remaining 3,000 on 1 August 2026, claiming IR.
>
> Cuthbert can only claim IR on 500 of the 3,000 shares sold now: the identification rules still help him but in a different way.
>
> He cannot claim that the shares that became excluded when he became an employee should be matched with the earlier disposal as *excluded* shares because they had not become excluded at that point.
>
> Out of the 7,000 shares disposed of on 31 August 2021, 2,000 were part of the 2,500 he acquired on 31 July 2022, meaning they were *potentially qualifying* shares at the time of the earlier disposal; as such they must be matched with the earlier disposal. Those shares subsequently became excluded shares when Cuthbert became an employee.
>
> This means that, as 2,000 of those shares have been treated as part of the earlier disposal, covered by losses, only 500 excluded shares remain in the 'pool', so Cuthbert can still claim IR on 2,500 of the shares sold on 1 August 2026.

19.37 It would be impossible to give examples of all possible permutations but the examples given here show the need to keep a careful check on all shareholdings that may qualify for IR.

REORGANISATIONS, RECONSTRUCTIONS AND SHARE EXCHANGES

19.38 The normal rules whereby, on a reorganisation, reconstruction or takeover the new shares received stand in the shoes of the old, are amended in the case of IR. These rules are applied at the time of disposal but must be considered at the time of the reorganisation to ensure that the investor is not denied IR on ultimate disposal.

Share reorganisation where no new consideration given

19.39 Where the company's share capital has been reorganised within the meaning of *TCGA 1992, s 126* and the investor provided no new consideration for the new shares, those new shares are treated as having the same proportions of qualifying (Q), potentially qualifying (P) and excluded shares (E) as were comprised in the original share-holding before the reorganisation. Shares in the new company are deemed to have been subscribed for at the same date and held continuously for the same period as the corresponding shares in the original company. Therefore, there should be no automatic disqualification from investors' relief, as long as no consideration is given for the new shares.

Share reorganisation where new consideration was given

19.40 Where the investor provided consideration as part of the reorganisation, the position is different. For the purposes of investors' relief, any shares received in exchange for consideration are treated as having been issued when they were actually issued. The holding would therefore need to be split, notionally, between the replacement shares which stand in the shoes of the original shares, and the new shares which may be either excluded or at best potentially qualifying shares which must wait for three years to become qualifying shares.

Take-over or reconstruction

19.41 Following a share exchange within the meaning of *TCGA 1992, s 135* or a scheme of reconstruction in line with *TCGA 1992, s 136*, there are new rules in *TCGA 1992, ss 169VL–169VN* that explain the treatment after those exchanges or reconstructions. These rules include a requirement that the conditions that the conditions in *TCGA 1992, s 169VB(2)(f)* – trading company or holding company of a trading group – and *TCGA 1992, s 169VB(2)(g)* – investor not to be connected with the company – must be met:

- in relation to the original share, from its issue date until the reorganisation or reconstruction; and

- in relation to the new share, from the reorganisation or reconstruction to the disposal.

Whilst this emphasises that great care is needed ensure that access to investors' relief is preserved, it also means that those tests do not need to be applied at times when they are not really relevant.

Investor may elect for *TCGA 1992, s 127* not to apply

19.42   An election can be made to disapply the treatment outlined above. This ensures that investors' relief is not lost if the original share-holding would have qualified at the time of the reorganisation but the new one does not (or might not).

If this election is made, a gain arises on the point the old shares are surrendered for new ones and investors' relief can be claimed. The disadvantage of making this election is that no consideration will have been received with which to pay the tax due.

OVERSEAS MATTERS

19.43   There are three categories of taxpayer who may pay CGT on gains in a current tax period, when the underlying gain actually accrued an earlier tax period. This can cause problems for the calculation of, and elections relating to, IR. The categories of taxpayer are:

- remittance basis users (see **19.44**);
- temporary non-UK residents (see **19.45**); and
- settlors and beneficiaries of offshore trusts (see **19.57**).

The HMRC Capital Gains Manual guidance does not currently consider the position of any of the above taxpayers for either IR or ER. However, ICAEW Tax Guide 1/12 does address some of these issues. Where an unusual situation arises, guidance may be sought from HMRC through the non-statutory clearance service (see **19.19**).

Remittance basis

19.44   IR can apply to gains made on assets situated outside the UK and on shares or securities held in overseas companies.

For a more detailed discussion of the remittance basis, refer to Booth & Schwarz: *Residence, Domicile and UK Taxation* (Bloomsbury Professional).

In brief, CGT is not charged on gains accruing on the disposal of assets situated outside the UK to individuals who claim the remittance basis for the particular tax year in question, and those overseas gains are not treated as being received in the UK.

The general rule is that an amount is treated as received in the UK in respect of a gain if it is:

● an amount paid, used or enjoyed in the UK; or

● an amount transmitted or brought in any manner or form to the UK.

Where a gain is not remitted directly but is invested in other assets, the gain is traced through those assets in order to establish whether the gain has been remitted to the UK. HMRC take the view that such tracing can take place through 'any number of investments, deposits to bank accounts, transfers between accounts etc' (CG25350). Thus, gains may be remitted to the UK many years after they arose.

HMRC may accept that IR can be claimed by remittance basis users and that the delay between the time when the gain arises and when the remittance is made is no bar on the claiming of IR, provided a valid claim is made within the required time limit. This would be consistent with HMRC's view that an ER claim must be made by the first anniversary of 31 January following the tax year in which the gain was realised, not the year in which the gain was remitted (see ICAEW TaxGuide 1/12).

It is understood that HMRC's settled view with regard to ER is that the lifetime limit to apply with respect to remittance basis gains is that limit which was in force when the gains arose, and not the limit that applies when the gains are remitted to the UK. This issue will need to be clarified before the first disposals eligible for IR take place on or after 6 April 2019.

Temporary non-residents

19.45   The definition of 'temporary non-residence' that applies for departures from the UK before and after 6 April 2013 is discussed in detail in Booth & Schwarz: *Residence, Domicile and UK Taxation* (20th edn, Bloomsbury Professional).

In brief, an individual is treated as a temporary non-resident (*TCGA 1992, s 10A*) if his residence status would otherwise mean that he escaped CGT having left the UK, and the following applies:

● the individual was UK resident for at least four of the seven tax years prior to departure; and

- the period of non-residence is less than five years (before 6 April 2013 this period is measured in 'tax years').

In this case, gains arising in the year of departure are chargeable in that tax year, and gains arising during the period of non-residence are chargeable in the year in which UK residence for tax purposes is resumed (*TCGA 1992, s 2*). Gains on assets that are both acquired and disposed of during the period of non-residence, are outside the charge, subject to certain anti-avoidance provisions.

Trustees

19.46   Under *TCGA 1992, s 169VH* trustees are eligible to claim IR in a way that is similar to but not identical with ER. As with ER the trustees do not have an entitlement to IR for the trust itself but only in respect of an 'eligible beneficiary'.

The share acquisition and holding rules apply to trustees in the same way as to individual investors (*TCGA 1992, s 169VH(5)* applies *TCGA 1992, s 169VB(2)(g)*). This means that for trustees to claim IR it is the trustees who must have made the initial investment: IR cannot apply to shares acquired by an individual and then settled on trust.

Qualifying beneficiary

19.47   An eligible beneficiary is a beneficiary who, as against the trust:

- has a life interest in possession in the shares concerned immediately before the disposal;

- held that interest throughout the three years immediately preceding the disposal;

- has not been a 'relevant employee' (see below) of the company at any time in those three years; and

- has elected to be treated as an eligible beneficiary in relation to the disposal.

Eligible interests in possession

19.48   An interest in possession (IIP) cannot be for a fixed time only (*TCGA 1992, s 169VH(4)*). The legislation does not elaborate on how interests subject to reappointment at the trustees' discretion are to be treated. Similarly, where a beneficiary has an interest in shares that have been sold and IR claimed the IIP may be extinguished by the trustees appointing the net sale proceeds to the beneficiary.

Beneficiary needs not own any shares personally

19.49   Unlike ER where the 'personal company' requirement means that a beneficiary must personally own shares, there is no such requirement under IR. This is logical, given that IR carries no minimum interest requirements for individual investors.

Election for treatment as an eligible beneficiary

19.50   The beneficiary may elect to be treated as an eligible beneficiary at any time before the trustees make the IR claim. The claim does not need to be made to HMRC, it is sufficient for the beneficiary to inform the trustees of the election, in writing or orally and the election may be withdrawn and/or reinstated at any time until the trustees make the claim.

Trustees' claims

19.51   Trust claims must be made jointly by the trustees and the beneficiary. The time limit is the first anniversary of 31 January following the end of the year in which the disposal takes place.

Period of share ownership

19.52   Whilst the requirements of *TCGA 1992, s 169VB* must be satisfied by the trustees, where applicable, throughout the trusts period of ownership, ie from issue on subscription until disposal, the beneficiary only needs to satisfy the Eligible beneficiary requirements throughout the three years leading to the disposal. Before then the trustees may hold the shares on any other interest for any other beneficiary.

19.53

Example 19.3 – Trust and beneficiary holdings

Mr Onion died on 1 June 2018 leaving his entire estate on a discretionary trust for the benefit of his grandchildren, Clive and Charlotte.

On 18 March 2019 the trustees subscribed for 100,000 £1 ordinary shares in Scallion plc, an AIM listed trading company.

On 6 April 2021 Garlic plc makes a cash offer for all the shares in Scallion. Considering this to be a good offer the trustees vote in favour of acceptance

---

and on 1 May 2021, before the offer is accepted unconditionally, appoint unlimited interests in possession in the shares; half each to Clive and Charlotte.

This scenario satisfies the conditions for the trustees to claim IR jointly with either or both of Clive and Charlotte, subject to their not having used their lifetime allowances.

Restriction on trustees' relief

19.54   Whilst *TCGA 1992, s 169VH* refers to the beneficiary having a settled interest in possession in the shares, implying that it is not possible to give one beneficiary the IIP in the income but not the asset itself, ie the capital, *TCGA 1992, s 169VI* puts a different slant on things by requiring gains of joint beneficiaries to be allocated to them in proportion to their shares in the *income*, not interests in the capital of the trust. This is not really a restriction on the relief, merely a requirement that joint beneficiaries be treated in the same way as joint owners of shares.

Trustees may claim IR on the aggregate of all eligible beneficiaries' shares in the gain.

Trustees share the beneficiary's lifetime limit

19.55   The amount of IR that can be claimed by the trustees will be restricted by the amount of the unused lifetime limit which is available to the qualifying beneficiary, and this will be reduced by claims for IR already submitted by:

- the qualifying beneficiary for gains made in his own name;
- the trustees in conjunction with the same qualifying beneficiary; or
- the trustees of any other trust in conjunction with the same beneficiary.

The amount of the beneficiary's lifetime limit that is assigned to the trust is controlled by the qualifying beneficiary, not by the trustees and not by the date on which gains are made. The beneficiary may choose to retain all of his lifetime limit to use against personal gains made in the same tax year, or to be made in a later year.

The amount of the trust gains that can be relieved using the qualifying beneficiary's lifetime limit is also limited to that beneficiary's relevant proportion of the gain. If the beneficiary is only entitled to 50% of the income from the trust assets which were disposed of, only up to 50% of the gain can be relieved using that beneficiary's lifetime limit.

Planning point

Trust ownership offers investors flexibility with regard to transferring shares that is not available if shares are held personally.

19.56

Example 19.4 – Flexibility of trust holdings

Anna is interested in investing in Morels and More ltd, but regards this as a long-term investment which may take a long time to bear fruit. She believes the investment will grow rapidly and wants it to benefit her children, Jordan and Nicole. However, Jordan and Nicole are still young and Anna would be reluctant to give them shares outright. She is also concerned that she may need to access the shares, or their sale proceeds, for her own benefit.

Therefore Anna creates a trust which subscribes for the shares using money that she has provided and retains to herself the power to appoint interests to beneficiaries. This enables Anna to take an interest in possession herself for as long as she needs to, but appoint a life interest in possession to Jordan and Nicole once she no longer requires to retain the interest. Provided Jordan and Nicole meet the requirements to be qualifying beneficiaries (see **19.47**) and the shares are not disposed of within three years of the appointment the trustees will be able to make a joint IR claim with the beneficiaries. This option may be particularly beneficial if the shares' value has mushroomed because the IR available to cover the trustees' gains will not be a single £10m, nor will it depend on Anna's lifetime limit. Instead the shares representing each beneficiary's interest will benefit from that beneficiary's lifetime limit. Therefore if the trust's shares produce gains totalling £20m, divided equally between Jordan and Nicole, and they have not claimed any IR already, they may join with the trustees and claim IR on the entire £20m gain.

This arrangement depends on the trustees being the subscribers for the shares and Anna being able to settle cash on trust without incurring a lifetime inheritance tax charge when she creates the trust: settlements that are within her IHT nil-rate band (NRB) or which consist of assets on which IHT is not chargeable (eg business or agricultural assets) may be suitable for this purpose.

Claims

19.57 A claim for IR will need to be made jointly by the trustees and the individual within the same period as a claim made by an individual, ie by the first anniversary of 31 January following the end of the tax year in which the disposal occurred (*TCGA 1992, s 169VM)*).

A problem may arise on the death of the relevant beneficiary who is the sole life tenant of the trust. This death will mean the trust has ceased to exist. Where this life tenant became entitled to the interest in possession on or after 22 March 2006, his death will trigger a deemed disposal of the trust assets (*TCGA 1992, s 71(1)*), which is not exempt from CGT (*TCGA 1992, s 73(2A)*). If the beneficiary met the qualifying conditions for the relief up to the date of death, IR should apply to the trust assets. This would be the same treatment as HMRC have confirmed applies under ER (see ICAEW Tax Guide 1/12). However, a valid claim needs to be signed both by the trustees (who are technically no longer trustees, as there is no trust) and on behalf of the deceased beneficiary. In this situation HMRC will accept a claim signed by the personal representatives of the deceased beneficiary, and the trustees.

Offshore trusts

19.58 The capital gains tax rules that apply to offshore trusts are very complex; for an excellent summary, refer to Chapter 27A of *Revenue Law: Principles and Practice* (Bloomsbury Professional, 32nd edition).

Capital gains realised by an offshore trust may be attributed to the settlor under *TCGA 1992, s 86*, and in some cases to the beneficiaries of the trust under *TCGA 1992, s 87*. In that case no claim for IR would appear to be possible because the taxpayer who is deemed to realise the gain is not the person to whom the shares were issued and so the condition in *TCGA 1992, s 169VB(2)(a)* is not met.

Chapter 20

Extracting funds from the company

Peter Rayney FCA, CTA (Fellow), TEP, Peter Rayney Tax Consulting Ltd

This chapter includes material originally adapted from *Tax Planning for Family and Owner-Managed Companies 2018/19* (Bloomsbury Professional)

SIGNPOSTS

- **Surplus profits: retain or extract?** – There are various potential issues to consider in the decision whether to retain or extract surplus profits from the family or owner-managed company. For example, retaining profits in the company may be attractive to some individual shareholders if entrepreneurs' relief would be available on a disposal of their shares. It is possible to extract funds or value from the company in a number of ways. The overall tax cost of the various extraction methods will vary, and it is important to determine the tax implications and efficiency of each one in advance (see **20.1–20.6**).

- **Capital receipts versus income receipts** – A purchase of the company's own shares, liquidation or sale of a company tend to be the most common 'exit routes' for shareholders of family or owner-managed companies. The tax liabilities under the income and capital routes should be compared well in advance of these transactions, in order to determine the most tax-efficient route (see **20.7–20.8**).

- **Bonus versus dividends** – Factors to consider in the decision whether to extract company profits as bonuses or dividends include the NIC impact on bonuses, the national minimum wage and national living wage rules (where applicable), the level of the company's distributable reserves in relation to dividends, the 'dividend allowance', and whether the company has tax losses (see **20.9–20.20**).

- **Implications of paying a bonus** – These include corporation tax relief (if the bonus is commercial and not excessive), the timing of relief for accrued remuneration, PAYE/NIC and cash flow, and reporting requirements under real-time information (see **20.21–20.25**).

- **Payment of dividends** – Any such payments must comply with company law requirements. The 'bonus versus dividends' decision will often also be influenced by factors including pension provision, protecting the state pension and social security benefits, the effect on share valuations, the spread of shareholdings, and personal borrowing. There is no substitute for doing the relative computations to compare the combined effective tax rates (for the company and its owner-manager(s)) for each extraction method (see **20.26–20.28**).

- **Remuneration paid to other family members** – Tax savings are often possible if income can be paid to other members of the owner-manager's family in order to use their annual personal allowances and benefit from their lower marginal tax rates. However, remuneration payments must be commercial and not excessive in relation to the duties performed, and care is needed to ensure that dividends to spouses (or civil partners) or other family members are not 'caught' by anti-avoidance provisions (see **20.29–20.38**).

- **Charging rent for personally owned assets** – The company's owner-managers will sometimes own the trading property (and/ or other assets used in the company's trade) personally. In such cases, the owner-manager can extract funds from the company by charging it a market rent for the use of the property. In addition to the tax effects of extracting profits via rent, issues to consider potentially include SDLT, the implications for entrepreneurs' relief purposes on any subsequent 'associated disposal' of the property, and VAT (see **20.39–20.43**).

- **Selling an asset to the company** – Owner-managers might consider extracting a capital sum from their company by selling personally owned assets (eg trading premises) to the company. Issues to consider potentially include SDLT for the company, CGT for the vendor on a capital gain, and VAT (see **20.44–20.46**).

- **Charging interest on loans to the company** – Owner-managers who make loans to the company, or have credit balances on their current account, could consider charging the company interest on the loan or credit balance, up to a commercial rate. Corporation tax relief would generally be available to the company under the 'loan relationship' provisions, although the interest deduction may be restricted if the initial recognition of the loan gave rise to a non-taxable credit (see **20.47–20.51**).

- **Loans from the company** – Such loans (including overdrawn director's loan accounts) will generally have implications for closely controlled companies under the 'loans to participator' rules, and benefit-in-kind implications for owner-managers under the 'beneficial loan' provisions. Anti-avoidance provisions aimed at circumventing tax charges under the loans to participator (and also benefits to participators and return payments to the company) rules may also need to be considered. If loans to shareholders are waived, further tax (and NIC) implications potentially arise (see **20.52–20.74**).

- **Benefits-in-kind to non-working shareholders** – Expenses or benefits provided to a close company shareholder (or an associate of a shareholder) may be taxable as distributions, unless the expense or benefit is already taxed under the employment income rules in ITEPA 2003 (see **20.75**).

- **Appendix** – A planning checklist of strategies for extracting funds from the company is included at **20.76**.

SHOULD SURPLUS PROFITS BE RETAINED OR EXTRACTED?

Main issues

20.1

Focus

Family and owner-managed companies can freely decide how much of their profits should be returned to the shareholders or retained within the business. The 'working' shareholders will need to extract a basic level of income from the company to satisfy their personal requirements. Hitherto, the comparatively lower income tax rates tended to encourage companies to extract surplus profits. Companies that relied on bank borrowings or institutional finance may, however, have been prescribed financial limits on the amount of dividends and other payments which can be made to the owner-manager shareholders.

From a commercial perspective, the company's cash flow and working capital requirements must be considered when determining the timing and amount of funds to be taken out. Given that the extraction of funds (see **20.5**) gives rise to a tax charge, which will be particularly expensive where large sums are involved, there is little point in taking them out by bonus, dividend, etc unless they are required by the owner-manager for their personal/family's needs. With the current high levels of income tax rates many owner-managers are likely to retain more profits within their companies. Within these constraints, some owner-managers may still wish to regularly remove 'surplus' cash from the business so as to remove it from any further business risk (subject to the requirements of the *Insolvency Act 1986*, for example, the 'two year' look-back period for 'preferential' or 'under-value' transactions under *IA 1986, ss 238* and *239*).

A further factor to consider is the potential double charge to tax, which arises where profits retained in the company are invested in appreciating assets. The appreciation in asset values could potentially be taxed both in the company and when the value is realised by the shareholders, perhaps on a sale or liquidation of the company. However, if the company is eventually sold for a price based on a multiple of earnings, the value of the shares may bear little relationship to the level of retained profits. Furthermore, the 'double charge' effect would not be a problem where the company's shares are to be passed down as a family heirloom on death. Owners of personal service companies are effectively forced to extract 'tainted' income and additional factors will come into play.

Entrepreneurs' relief (ER) and Investors' relief (IR)

20.2   Owner-managers of trading companies enjoy particularly favourable CGT treatment, with a current 'exit' ER CGT rate of 10% (up to a cumulative lifetime gains, limit of £10m). However, all other 'non-ER' significant gains are now taxable at 20% (except those arising on the sale of residential property).

The *Finance Act 2016* introduced Investors Relief (IR), which provides a 10% CGT-rate of the disposal of qualifying shares after three years. Like ER, the IR 10% CGT rate is subject to a separate £10m lifetime gains limit. As a general rule, 'business angels' should normally be eligible for IR but employees and 'paid' directors cannot qualify.

Retention of profits

20.3   With a current ER limit of £10m, the overall tax costs of realising retained profits as a capital gain (for example, by liquidation or sale – see **20.4**) have remained identical to the pre-6 April 2008 business taper regime (assuming the (cumulative) gains are below £10m).

Retained profits only suffer corporation tax at the company's marginal tax rate and may ultimately be realised at low CGT rates.

The ability to reinvest profits within company structures at relatively low tax rates has encouraged many sole traders and partnerships to incorporate their businesses. For 2018/19, unincorporated businesses earning substantial profits will generally suffer a marginal 47% combined income tax/Class 4 NIC rate on their profits, regardless of whether the profits are 'ploughed-back' within the business or extracted.

All companies pay corporation tax at 19% (reducing to 17% from 1 April 2020). Thus, the total effective rate of taking profits as a capital sum is 27.1% (ignoring the impact of any base cost, etc) calculated as follows:

	£
Profit	100
Corporation tax at 19%	(19)
Retained profit = chargeable gain	81
CGT @ 10% (assuming ER)	(8.1)
Net realisation	72.9
Total effective tax rate	27.1%

If ER is not available at the time the retained profits are taken as a 'capital distribution', the overall effective rate increases to 35.2% (assuming a 20% CGT rate). The rates on retained profits compare very favourably with the current top income tax rates.

Taking profits as capital gains

20.4

Focus

Unless the owner-manager is making a complete, or almost complete, 'exit' from the company, it may be difficult to find an effective method of converting profits into a capital sum. Taking the profits as a capital distribution on a subsequent winding-up is not a realistic option if the business is continuing. This means that the individual will have to sell their shares either back to the company or by way of an external sale.

Given the relatively wide gap between CGT and dividend tax rates, HMRC are likely to use the Transaction in Securities rules where shares in close companies are sold to a commonly controlled company, Employee Benefit Trust, pension fund, etc but not normally on commercially driven sales to third parties. However, unless there is *complete certainty* that the transaction will satisfy the post-sale 'no-connection' test, it is recommended that the advance clearance procedure in *ITA 2007, s 701* is used to obtain assurance that HMRC is satisfied that the transaction is not driven by the avoidance of income tax.

If the company is likely to be sold, the level of its *retained* profits will not normally influence its sale price, which is normally based on a multiple of its post-tax earnings. With the relatively low rates of CGT, however, it is tempting to 'gross up' the price for the retained earnings rather than strip them out as a pre-sale dividend.

Taking all the above factors into account, a balanced approach between retention and extraction of profits will generally be required in practice. Ultimately, the decision must depend on whether the shareholders need the money for their personal requirements and whether they are able to obtain a better 'return' on the funds than the company.

Extracting funds or value from the company

20.5

Focus

It is possible to extract funds or value from the company in a number of ways, although (a) to (c) below are usually available only for those shareholders who work in the company as a director or employee.

The most important methods of extracting value are listed below:

(a)   directors' remuneration or bonuses and paying salaries to other family members (see **20.9–20.38**);

(b)   provision of benefits in kind and company shares;

(c)   pension contributions;

(d)   dividends (see **20.12–20.17, 20.26–20.28**);

(e)   charging rent on personally owned property which is used in the company's trade (see **20.39–20.43**);

(f)   selling assets to the company for value (see **20.44–20.46**);

(g)   charging interest on loans to the company (see **20.47–20.51**);

(h)   loans or advances from the company (see **20.52–20.68**);

(i)   purchase of own shares; and

(j)   Repayment/reduction of share capital.

(k)   liquidation of the company.

The overall tax cost of the various methods of extraction will vary and it is important to determine the tax efficiency for each method of extracting funds/value.

20.6 On an on-going basis, the working shareholders may well, in addition to drawing a normal salary, decide whether to extract surplus profits by means of a bonus or dividend. This aspect is considered in further detail at **20.9–20.38**. In addition, owner-managers will often ensure that adequate provision is made for their future pension and that tax efficacious benefits in kind are provided. Owner-managers may also consider extracting funds through a loan account, but this too involves a tax cost.

CAPITAL RECEIPTS VERSUS INCOME RECEIPTS

Basic planning techniques

20.7 A purchase of the company's own shares, liquidation or sale of a company tend to be the most common 'exit-routes' for shareholders when they wish to leave the company, retire or realise capital value.

In the context of a purchase by the company of its own shares, it is usually possible to structure the transaction either as a capital gains receipt within *CTA 2010, s 1033*, or as a distribution.

Similarly, if the company is about to be wound up, value can be extracted by means of an income dividend if the amount is paid prior to liquidation. Amounts distributed during the winding up should be a capital distribution (liable to CGT) for the shareholder. However, where the liquidation is mainly driven by 'unacceptable' phoenixing to extract the company's retained profits at beneficial CGT rates, the *FA 2016* 'anti–phoenix' Targeted Anti-Avoidance Rule ('TAAR') is likely to apply. If the liquidation falls within the TAAR, the liquidation distributions would be taxed at dividend *income tax* rates (as opposed to CGT).

Comparing income and capital gain positions

20.8

Focus

It is particularly important to compare the tax liabilities under the income and capital route *well in advance* of these transactions in order to determine the most tax-efficient route.

For individual shareholders, an income distribution in 2018/19 will generally carry a tax charge of 32.5% or (where the taxpayer's income exceeds the £150,000 top tax rate bracket), 38.1%.

The tax efficiency of taking a capital gain will therefore depend on the shareholder's potential effective CGT rate (maximum of 20% with reduction to 10% if ER or IR is available).

Any planning steps which are then necessary, for example, to characterise the transaction as income, can then be implemented with minimal risk of an HMRC attack under the *Furniss v Dawson* doctrine (*Furniss v Dawson* [1984] STC 153). The potential application of the GAAR may also be a consideration, where HMRC consider the relevant planning to be abusive or egregious.

BONUS VERSUS DIVIDENDS

Impact of National Insurance Contributions (NIC)

20.9 Although the working shareholders can reward themselves in a number of ways, the main choice often lies between whether to pay a bonus or a dividend. The high levels of NIC rates have meant that more owner-managers tend to draw a substantial part of their profits in the form of dividends. Profits extracted as 'earnings' (ie salary or bonus) are now subject to significant NIC charges. For 2018/19, the first £162 per week (or, if earnings are calculated on an annual basis, £8,424 per year) does not suffer employers' NIC. Above this 'secondary threshold', the company pays NIC on all earnings at 13.8%. Most P11D benefits in kind are subject to a NIC Class 1A charge of 13.8% (without any threshold).

For 2018/19, directors and employees suffer NIC at the rate of 12% on their earnings and benefits between £162 and £892 per week (or, if earnings are calculated on an annual basis, £8,424 and £46,350. An additional employee NIC charge of 2% is levied where the individual's total earnings/benefits exceed the 2018/19 upper earnings limit of £46,350. This means that a 2% employees' NIC charge arises on all earnings, etc above the £46,350 threshold with no restrictions.

For 2018/19, companies will still be able to deduct (up to) £3,000 from their first remittance of employer's NIC's providing the director is *not* the sole employee.

For those owner-managers with the 'work till you drop' ethos, it is perhaps worth noting that employees' NIC ceases to be payable on their earnings after they have reached 'pensionable age'. This is currently 65 years old for men, 60 years old for women born before 6 April 1950, and 65 for women born after 5 April 1955 (with a sliding scale operating between those dates). From December 2018, the state pension age will start to increase for both men and women to reach 66 years by October 2020.

However, employers' (ie secondary) NICs continue to be paid on an individual's earnings beyond their pensionable age.

An employer's NIC charge under Class 1A applies to the majority of benefits in kind, including company cars and private fuel. The Class 1A NIC charge is based on the total benefits taxed as 'employment income' under the *ITEPA 2003* rules.

National Minimum/Living Wage

20.10   Owner-managers will need to adhere to the National Living Wage (NLW) and National Minimum Wage (NMW) legislation. The NLW effectively replaced the NMW on 1 April 2016 for employees aged 25 and over. The NMW continues to apply for those employees who have not reached their 25th birthday. HMRC is responsible for policing the minimum wage legislation on behalf of the Department for Business, Innovation and Skills (BIS).

The NLW and NMW legislation only applies where an individual has a contract of employment. In law, the directors' rights and duties are defined by that office. They can be removed from office by a simple majority of the votes cast at a general meeting of the company. Clearly, if the director *actively* works in the business, receives a salary, and enjoys other rights accorded to employees, an employer/employee relationship will be established.

In contrast, an employee's rights and duties are expressed in a contract of employment, which need not be in writing and can be an implied or oral contract. Due to the informal nature of the arrangements in many small companies, there may be some uncertainty as to whether an employment contract exists between the company and its controlling director. The question of whether an office holder is employed will clearly depend on the facts of each case. Where there is no explicit contract, the NMW and NLW rules are unlikely to apply, even where the director carries out a wide range of activities, which might include 'working in the company's shop'. In such cases, the work would be regarded as done in the director's capacity as an office holder.

Indeed, BIS confirms that if there is no written employment contract or other evidence of an intention to create an employer/worker relationship, it will not seek to contend that there is an unwritten or implied employment relationship between a director and his company.

However, a prudent course of action would be for 'owner-manager' directors to pay themselves (and of course their staff) sufficient remuneration to satisfy the requirements of the NLW and NMW legislation.

The current NLW/NMW rates are as follows:

Age	From 1 April 2018 Hourly rate
Employees aged 25 and over (NLW)	£7.83
Employees aged 21–24	£7.38
Development rate (employees aged 18–20)	£5.90
Young workers rate (aged 16–17)	£4.20
Apprentices under 19, or over 19 and in first year	£3.70

Dividends cannot be treated as remuneration for this purpose, nor can benefits in kind, other than the provision of living accommodation.

Employers that do not comply with the NLW/NMW will have to pay the 'underpaid' amount to its workers at current minimum wage rates. HMRC will issue a Notice of Underpayment (NoU) to start this process.

Breaking the NLW/NMW law can be an expensive business, since non-compliance is subject to penalties of up to 200% of the underpaid amount (with a 50% reduction if paid within 14 days). The overall maximum penalty is 'capped' at £20,000 for each worker.

The government will 'name and shame' the most exploitative employers, which may cause reputational damage to their businesses. For example, nearly 230 of the worst offending employers' details were published on the government's website in August 2017 (350 offenders were published in August 2016) with Argos being revealed as the worst culprit having reportedly failed to pay nearly £1.5m to more than 12,000 staff. Although the tide seems to be turning with a significant reduction in the number of published offenders, compliance with the NLW/NMW should still be taken very seriously!

Determining appropriate amount to extract from company

20.11 Most discussions about profit extraction usually start by focusing on the amount available to be paid out to the owner-manager(s). This is generally influenced by one or more of the following factors:

- the amount required for future retention in the business (to satisfy future working capital or capital investment purposes);

- the level of the company's distributable reserves and 'free' cash flow;

- any provisions or restrictions laid down in Shareholder Agreements or a company's Articles, particularly where venture capital finance has been used;

- the desire to 'de-risk' part of the 'surplus cash' generated by the business by taking it out of the company;

- the shareholders' personal 'income' requirements and tax position (and the impact of the 45% income tax rate!);

- 'one-man-band' type service companies may be affected by IR35 and 'spousal' settlement considerations in fixing the level of 'remuneration' to be paid out, although the House of Lords decision in the *Arctic Systems* case gives potentially vulnerable taxpayers greater comfort in this area.

Having broadly determined the appropriate level of profits that can be 'extracted' by the owner-manager(s), attention then usually shifts to deciding whether the amount should be paid out as a bonus and/or dividend.

Comparison between bonus and dividends

20.12

Focus

If the company pays tax at the small profits' rate it is nearly always beneficial to extract surplus funds by means of a dividend as the now relatively high cost of NICs is avoided.

The substitution of dividends for remuneration is not regarded as an abnormal pay practice for NIC purposes (*Social Security and Benefits Act 1992, Sch 1, para 4(c)*). It is possible, however, that the National Insurance Contributions Office (NICO) may seek to challenge dividends which have not been declared in accordance with the relevant *Companies Act* formalities. If the correct legal procedures are not followed, it can be asserted that a payment is not a 'valid' dividend and hence must be 'NIC-able' earnings.

The recent Court of Appeal ruling in *HMRC v PA Holdings Ltd* [2011] EWCA Civ 1414 demonstrates that the judiciary may seek to treat purported dividend payments as employment income where aggressive tax avoidance schemes have been used.

20.13   For 2018/19 the key aspects for owner-managers are summarised as follows:

- Dividends do not carry any form of tax credit.

- Owner-managers have a £2,000 dividend tax allowance (£5,000 pre-6 April 2018) which essentially represents a 'nil rate' band for their dividend income.

- Dividend income represents the highest slice of income and is allocated to the tax bands *before* the £2,000 dividend 'nil-rate' band.

- Subject to personal allowances and the £2,000 dividend 'nil-rate' band, dividends are taxed at the following rates:

Total taxable income	Tax rate applied
Below basic rate income threshold – £34,500	7.5%
Between basic rate threshold and £150,000	32.5%
Above £150,000	38.1%

20.14   Some owner-managers may be tempted to extract their income entirely in the form of dividends, but it is often sensible to extract a reasonable level of salary. In any event, if the owner-manager has no other taxable income, it is often beneficial to pay at least a sufficient salary to maintain NIC records such that each year is a qualifying year for state pension 'accrual' purposes.

Various tax comparisons between extracting surplus profits as a bonus or a dividend for 2018/19 are shown in the worked examples below. The various factors listed at **20.27** may also influence the decision, depending on the relevant circumstances of each case.

Bonus versus dividend comparison – 2018/19

20.15   **Example 20.1** (assuming a marginal income tax rate of 40%) and **Example 20.2** (assuming a marginal income tax rate of 45%) below illustrate that it will often still be beneficial to extract surplus profits as a dividend for 2018/19 (despite the recent reduction in the dividend allowance). The payment of a dividend is subject to the other factors cited at **20.27**.

It should be noted that, where a company pays a bonus, there is an additional NIC cost – but corporate tax relief is given on the total cost of the bonus and related NIC, ie the company does not pay corporation tax on this part of its profits. On the other hand, a dividend is not tax deductible and hence profits earmarked for a dividend suffer corporation tax.

Example 20.1 – 2018/19: Bonus versus dividend comparison (owner-manager's marginal tax rate of 40%)

Greaves Limited is likely to have surplus profits available of £100,000 for the year ended 31 March 2019, which could be paid to its sole shareholder, Mr Jimmy, as a bonus or dividend. Mr Jimmy already draws a monthly salary of £4,000 (ie in excess of the basic rate threshold upper earnings limit), and therefore his marginal tax rate is 40%.

The relevant tax and NIC effects are compared below.

			Bonus	*Dividend*
	£		£	£
Available profits			100,000	100,000
Less: Employer's NIC –				
£87,873 @ 13.8%			(12,127)	
Corporation tax @ 19%				(19,000)
			87,873	81,000
Income tax thereon				
Bonus	87,873	@ 40%	(35,149)	
Employees' NIC @ 2% (rate on earnings above upper limit)	87,873	@ 2%	(1,758)	
Dividend:				
Tax	79,000*	@ 32.5%		(25,675)
Net cash available			50,966	55,325
Tax and NIC liabilities				
Employer's NIC			12,127	
Corporation tax				19,000
PAYE and NIC (£35,149 + £1,758)			36,907	
Dividend tax liability				25,675
			49,034	44,675
Effective overall tax rate			49.0%	44.6%

Example 20.2 – 2018/19: Bonus versus dividend comparison (owner-manager's marginal tax rate of 45%)

Bonds Limited is likely to have surplus profits available of £100,000 for the year ended 31 March 2019, which could be paid to its sole shareholder, Mr Billy, as a bonus or dividend. Mr Billy already draws a monthly salary of £16,000 and therefore his marginal income tax rate is 45%.

The relevant tax and NIC effects are compared below.

	£		*Bonus* £	*Dividend* £
Available profits			100,000	100,000
Less: Employer's NIC –				
£87,873 @ 13.8%			(12,127)	
Corporation tax @ 19%				(19,000)
			87,873	81,000
Income tax thereon				
Bonus	87,873	@ 45%	(39,543)	
Employees' NIC @ 2% (rate on earnings above upper limit)	87,873	@ 2%	(1,758)	
Dividend				
Tax	79,000*	@ 38.1%		(30,099)
Net cash available			46,572	50,901
Tax and NIC liabilities				
Employer's NIC			12,127	
Corporation tax				19,000
PAYE and NIC (£39,543 + £1,758)			41,301	
Dividend tax liability				30,099
			53,428	49,099
Effective overall tax rate			53.4%	49.0%

Shareholders paying tax at the basic rate

20.16   For 2018/19, where the shareholder only pays tax at the basic rate, their dividend income would simply be subject to income tax at 7.5%. This should still give a reasonable tax 'extraction' rate (especially where the £2,000 dividend nil-rate band is available)

Example 20.3 – 2018/19: Dividend tax and £2,000 nil rate band (basic rate tax payer)

Terry's expected taxable income during the year ended 5 April 2019 is as follows:

- Employment income – £11,850

- Dividend from Blues Ltd – £15,000

Terry's income tax liability is £975, calculated as follows:

	Total	Personal Allowance	Basic rate band
	£	£	£
Employment income	11,850	11,850	
Less: Personal allowance		(11,850)	
Dividend	15,000		15,000
Dividend nil-rate band	(2,000)		(2,000)
Taxable	13,000	nil	13,000
Taxed at 7.5%			975

20.17   The above examples have been simplified to show the relevant tax that would be payable at relevant marginal rates. There will, of course, be many cases where tax/NIC is payable over two or more rate bands and detailed calculations will be required. Under the post-5 April 2016 regime, dividends are still the preferred route, although the tax savings have become smaller.

As a result of the large 'gap' between individual and corporate tax rates, companies will become increasingly attractive as a vehicle to earn and retain income. Many highly profitable sole traders, partnerships and LLPs have either recently incorporated or are considering incorporation in the near future. However, the sale of goodwill of an unincorporated business to a company no longer qualifies for entrepreneurs' relief (ER) (for post-2 December 2014 disposals). Thus, the transfer of goodwill would normally be taxed at 20% (rather than the 10% ER CGT rate).

COMPANIES WITH TAX LOSSES

20.18 If the company has tax losses, the payment of a bonus will increase the tax-adjusted trading loss. If there is scope to carry back the loss against the previous year, corporation tax relief is effectively obtained. The rate of relief would depend on the level of the prior year's profits. If there is no scope to relieve the bonus by loss carry-back (or group relief), then it will be included as part of the company's carried forward trading losses and the tax relief is effectively deferred until the losses are offset against future trading profits.

Carried forward trading losses arising after 1 April 2017 are subject to more generous offset rules. In such cases, companies can offset their unused losses against profits from different types of income (and profits of other group companies). However, 'very large' companies may be subject to certain restrictions in the amount of losses they can offset.

Repayment interest would accrue on tax repaid for the previous year, from nine months after the end of that period.

In contrast, a dividend would not create an additional loss.

The 'bonus versus dividend' equation therefore depends, amongst other things, on the effective rate of company tax relief and the amount of any repayment interest.

WHEN SHOULD THE 'BONUS v DIVIDEND' COMPARISON BE MADE?

20.19 It is generally preferable for the computational 'bonus versus dividend' profit extraction comparison to be made *before* the year end. From the owner-manager's viewpoint, there may of course be a timing point regarding the particular tax year into which the bonus/dividend should fall (particularly if there is a need to avoid the top tax rate).

Focus

The position with bonuses is more flexible since it is also possible to make a provision in the year end statutory accounts and obtain tax relief in that

---

period, provided the bonus is paid within nine months of the year end (see **20.22**). In the vast majority of cases, such a provision must comply with FRS 102/FRS 105, which requires a legal or constructive obligation to pay the bonus to exist at the balance sheet date.

20.20   In practical terms, this means that the anticipated results should be considered before the year end and an agreement should be in place for any required bonuses. It may also be preferable to look at the anticipated results of the company for other reasons. For example, this would enable the directors to consider the amount of any pension contributions which must be paid before the year end to ensure that tax relief is obtained in the current period. This means that reliable management accounting figures should be available.

DETAILED IMPLICATIONS OF PAYING A BONUS

Corporation tax relief

20.21   In the case of a trading company, the remuneration or bonus should be deductible against profits. It is very rare for an Inspector to challenge the level of remuneration paid to working director shareholders. The amounts paid to owner-managers will generally stand up to scrutiny as being a commercial rate, given their role in the company and the responsibility involved. In contrast, HMRC often seeks to limit the tax deduction for directors' fees paid by investment companies to a very modest amount. In such cases, extracting funds via a dividend is likely to be more tax efficient.

If the Inspector challenges the corporation tax deduction for the remuneration and denies relief for the amount considered to be excessive, this amount will still be subject to PAYE tax and NICs. However, by concession, HMRC is prepared to refund the PAYE tax paid on this amount, provided the excess amount is formally waived by the director and the amount is actually reimbursed to the company (see *ICAEW Tax Faculty Technical Release TAX 11/93*). However, any NIC liability will still stand as the NICO does not apply this concession.

Relief for accrued remuneration

20.22   A special rule applies to remuneration which is accrued or unpaid at the end of a company's accounting period, such as a provision for a bonus. Such remuneration can only be deducted against the company's taxable profits for that period if it is paid within nine months after the period end (*CTA 2009, ss 1288 and 1289*). The date when remuneration is deemed to be paid is defined in *ITEPA 2003, s 18* (this rule also applies for PAYE purposes).

In the case of directors, the date of payment will often be the time when payment is actually made, or when the director becomes legally entitled to the amount (although the statutory definition also includes other events). In practice, HMRC will accept that a bonus is 'paid' when it is credited to a director's current account.

Unless a director has a service agreement, his remuneration can only be determined when it is approved by the shareholders at the company's AGM, which will normally be the date on which the company's annual accounts are signed. However, the decision in *Re Duomatic* [1969] 1 All ER 161 (applied more recently in *Cane v Jones* [1981] 1 All ER 533) has often been used to override the need for corporate formalities by allowing shareholders to make decisions informally. This case decided that, where the directors agree in their capacity as shareholders the amount to be paid to them as directors' remuneration, this agreement will have the same effect as a resolution passed at the AGM.

Consequently, where the AGM is likely to occur after the end of the nine-month period, it should still be possible to trigger a 'payment' of the bonus within the nine-month period by agreement of the director shareholders, which should be formally minuted. It will be appreciated that bonuses provide a convenient way of reducing a company's taxable profits after the year end.

However, the recent cases of *Randhawa and Anor v Turpin and Anor* [2017] EWCA Civ 1201 and *Dickinson v NAL Realisations (Staffs) Ltd* [2017] EWCA28 (Ch) demonstrate that the courts have placed some limits on the application of the 'Duomatic principle'. Prudence dictates that it should only be relied on as a last resort and shareholders should seek to adopt the relevant legal procedures.

20.23   If the shareholder director is fortunate enough to have a healthy credit balance on their loan/current account, they can draw amounts from the account during the accounting period without attracting any PAYE or NIC charges. The loan/current account can then be 'topped up' by a bonus following the year end and the exercise repeated next year.

The tax deduction rules for accrued bonus/remuneration may be used to obtain earlier corporation tax relief for amounts to be paid within the nine months following the year end. Provided the statutory accounts have not been signed-off, a provision can be made for bonuses paid (or to be paid) within nine months of the year end. Care must be taken that any such provision is FRS 102/FRS 105 compliant. This would require there to be a 'present obligation' at the balance sheet date to pay a bonus. This could be evidenced by minutes of a board meeting held prior to the year end, or even by the fact that such bonuses are regularly made. A provision written into the accounts after the year end (which does not satisfy current UK GAAP) would be open to challenge from HMRC, since it could seek to disallow the deduction in the year. HMRC are increasingly looking at accounting and accounting treatment under FRA 102/FRS 105 as part of their enquiries.

When providing for accrued directors' remuneration in the accounts, it is normal practice to provide also for the PAYE and NIC (including employer's NIC) liabilities in the accounts to which the remuneration relates. If this practice is not adopted the amount would be provided gross and when the directors' final remuneration is approved (at the AGM, if not earlier), the net remuneration would then be credited to the relevant director's accounts. At that date, the PAYE and NICs must then be accounted for (*ICAEW Tax Faculty Guidance Note TAX 11/93*).

PAYE and cash flow

20.24   The payment of the bonus will, of course, attract a PAYE/NIC liability. PAYE at the basic rate (and higher rate, if applicable) and Class 1 NICs are normally payable 14 days after the end of the month in which the bonus is 'paid' or 'made available' (*SI 2003/2682, reg 69*). If the director receives a relatively low monthly salary and a high bonus payment once a year, further NICs are likely to become due on the annual re-calculation (this is because the NICs accounted for will have been subject to the monthly 'upper earnings limit').

If the tax due on the bonus was incorrect (for example, if the PAYE code was wrong), there may be additional tax to pay when the individual submits their tax return (at the latest by 31 January following the relevant tax year). However, provided the unpaid amount is less than £3,000 and the tax return is submitted early (say) by 31 October after the tax year for a paper return and 31 December after the tax year (if filed online), HMRC will adjust the PAYE code for the following tax year enabling that tax to be collected on a gradual basis over the next tax year.

With a bonus, the owner-manager only receives the net amount after deducting PAYE and NIC. By contrast, where a dividend is paid, the owner-manager receives the full cash amount and does not have to pay the higher rate tax until a later date. Payments of tax on the dividend are made in accordance with the normal self-assessment rules. This requires interim tax payments to be made on 31 January in the tax year and on 31 July following the tax year (based on the previous year's tax liability), with a final payment being due on the following 31 January. Where a regular payment of dividends is established, the tax may become factored into the interim payments. Some owner-managers alternate between bonuses and dividends to prevent tax on dividends being factored into their payments on account.

In some cases, it may be beneficial to defer the payment of a dividend from say March to 6 April or later, as this may defer the higher rate liability (particularly if the director/shareholder's interim tax payments are based on a low prior year tax liability).

The tax cash flow implications therefore need to be considered, which will vary according to the individual circumstances of each case. When interest costs have been taken into account, this may affect the 'bonus v dividend' comparisons considered above.

REAL TIME INFORMATION (RTI)

20.25   Under RTI, details of payments of earnings to directors must now be sent to HMRC every time a payment is made. The report must be made in the form of a Full Payment Submission (FPS).

With the introduction of the RTI system for reporting PAYE it is even more important for owner-managers to be clear about the status of all payments made to them at the time they are made. Furthermore, evidence must be retained to support the relevant treatment.

For example, if amounts drawn by a director (and debited to their loan account) are later considered to be a salary/bonus, they will not have been reported 'on or before the payment is made' in accordance with the RTI rules, which may lead to penalties being imposed by HMRC.

Care must be taken to ensure that amounts drawn by a director and debited to their loan account are *not* regarded as a payment on account of earnings, which would be reportable under RTI. HMRC will not consider such amounts to be earnings in the absence of evidence as to their exact true nature (HMRC EIM 42280). It should also be noted that HMRC appears to be making increased use of the rule in *ITEPA 2003, Pt 3, Ch 3* which provides that any personal expenses paid by the company should be treated as (advance) payments of earnings. If *ITEPA 2003, Pt 3, Ch 3* catches these payments, they would be subject to PAYE and NICs. For owner-managers it is therefore important to place on record that overdrawn loan accounts are to be cleared by dividends or personally by the director and are not paid as expenses.

Under the RTI regime, many owner-managed companies have had to develop greater financial discipline. As part of this process, companies should produce proper *contemporaneous* evidence to support dividends, salaries and bonuses.

One sensible approach is for owner-managers to develop an agreed payment plan at the start of the tax year. Assuming the company has sufficient reserves, it would be sensible to bring the loan account in credit by paying an appropriate dividend at the start of the year. The owner-manager can then draw down regular amounts during the year (whilst keeping their loan account in credit). A one-off salary payment can be made in the last month of the tax year, which would avoid regular monthly RTI reporting. Consideration might also be given to applying for annual RTI reporting.

ICAEW RTI Helpsheet 3 published in April 2013 contains further guidance relating to the impact of RTI on directors' remuneration.

PAYMENT OF DIVIDENDS

20.26   In the context of a family or owner-managed company, the company's directors decide on the maximum level of the annual dividend that should be paid, based on the company's annual accounts and general financial position. Their proposed dividend is then put forward to the shareholders (in many cases, the same or largely the same individuals as the directors), who vote (by ordinary resolution) whether to pay the suggested figure or a *lower* amount.

Dividends are paid proportionately to the number of shares held (of the same class), although it is possible for shareholders to waive all or some of their dividend entitlement. Some companies have different classes of shares enabling them to alter the level of dividend paid on each separate class. It is only possible to pay dissimilar levels of dividend on different classes of shares. Once the vote has been passed, the dividend becomes 'declared' when it is then strictly regarded as having been made for tax purposes.

Directors usually have the power to make interim dividends before the final dividend is made. It is, therefore possible to pay dividends on a regular basis. However, many owner-managers find it easier just to pay one 'large' dividend, which is then credited to their current account with the company, upon which they can draw through the year. In practice, HMRC treats the 'crediting' of a dividend to a loan/current account as having been paid for tax purposes.

BONUS VERSUS DIVIDEND – OTHER FACTORS

20.27   The 'bonus versus dividend' decision will often be influenced by a number of other factors, the main ones being set out below:

(a)   ***Pension provision*** – In the past, owner-managers often enjoyed considerable flexibility regarding the level of contributions they were able to make. However, they can currently only enjoy tax relief on pension contributions of up to £40,000 in the relevant tax year (plus any unused 'allowance' brought forward from the three previous years).

The 'annual allowance' limit applies to both personal and *company* contributions. It cannot therefore be side-stepped by routing pension contributions through the company.

Personal contributions only rank for income tax relief if the payer has sufficient 'relevant earnings' since relief is available on up to 100% of their relevant earnings for the tax year. However, if they have little or no earnings, relief is always given on gross contributions of up to a maximum of £3,600. Thus, where the owner-manager decides to draw little or no salary, they will still be able to fund a personal pension scheme at a rate of up to £3,600 (gross) per year. It should be noted that dividend income does not count as relevant earnings.

Owner-managers will need to have a reasonable level of salary/bonuses/ benefits to make worthwhile (tax relievable) pension contributions. Thus, where additional pension provision is required, it will often be necessary to pay appropriate bonuses. The bonus would not attract any income tax if it can be sheltered by a matching pension contribution (made within the relevant limit). However, a personal pension payment would *not* shelter the employers' and employees' NIC liability on the bonus. These NIC costs can be avoided where the company undertakes to pay the individual's pension contributions (instead of the bonus). Although the company is discharging a pecuniary benefit of the individual, this does not give rise to a taxable benefit.

(b) ***Protecting social security and basic state retirement benefits*** – Dividends do not attract NICs and therefore a certain level of remuneration is required to secure certain earnings-related social security benefits and the National Insurance Retirement Pension ('NIRP'). It is only necessary for an individual's earnings to be above the lower earnings limit (£116 per week for 2018/19) to qualify and, therefore, a small salary should always be paid (also possibly to satisfy the National Living Wage requirements – see **20.10**). In fact, provided the earnings exceed the lower earnings limit but are below the primary earnings threshold (£162 per week for 2018/19) basic state retirement benefits can be protected without incurring any NIC liability.

(c) ***Share valuations*** – A history of dividend payments might increase the value of minority shareholdings for tax purposes. This is because the valuation of a minority shareholding may be determined by the expectation of dividend income. Share valuations for controlling shareholders are unlikely to be affected.

(d) ***Spread of shareholdings*** – as shareholders receive dividends in proportion to their holdings, the amount of dividends received by each shareholder may not provide a fair reward for the working shareholders and may prove too generous for the non-working or 'passive' shareholders. On the other hand a bonus can be a problem where the company's shareholdings have become widely spread over time. A 'dividend waiver' may be the answer here, provided it does not create any 'settlement' problems. Use of a separate class of shares for the non-working shareholders might be a more elegant solution on a long term basis.

(e)   ***Personal borrowing and other issues*** – some lenders may not understand the methodology of profit extraction used by owner-managed companies and only focus on 'remuneration/salary' (as opposed to bonuses and dividends) when providing mortgages, loans, etc. Remuneration is also used to calculate redundancy pay and remains important for income protection plans. PHI cover can be provided to take salary/bonus as well as dividends into account.

EXTRACTING SURPLUS PROFITS – SOME CONCLUSIONS

20.28   The various worked examples in this chapter largely concentrate on the extraction of 'surplus' profits where a reasonable level of salary has already been paid. It is often considered beneficial to pay a modest level of salary. However, where tax-efficiency is paramount, there is no substitute for doing the relative computations to compare the combined effective tax rates (for the company and its owner-manager(s)).

All companies now pay tax at 19% (subject to limited exceptions), reducing to 17% from 1 April 2020. Therefore, based on effective tax rates, the payment of dividends should still be preferable, albeit the tax savings are lower than they were before 6 April 2016. Dividends also offer the added potential of a longer deferment in the payment of income tax.

Where shareholders only pay tax at the lower or basic rates, dividends will invariably be more tax efficient.

However, the above broad generalisations may be overturned by various other factors. Thus, a relatively high bonus payment might be required to enable the owner-manager to augment their personal pension fund with tax allowable contributions (subject to the annual allowance limits). In certain situations, the payment of a bonus may provide a useful way of keeping a company outside the quarterly instalment regime for corporation tax.

In summary, family and owner-managed companies should consider a sensible combination of bonuses and dividends and, in appropriate cases, pension contributions. The precise mix would depend on the particular circumstances of each company and its shareholders.

REMUNERATION PAID TO OTHER MEMBERS OF THE FAMILY

20.29

Focus

As a general rule, tax will be saved if income can be paid to other members of the owner-manager's family in order to use their annual personal allowances and benefit from their lower marginal tax rates. Inspectors are likely to scrutinise salaries paid to members of the family to see whether they are paid at or above the market rate for the duties performed.

Where the amount clearly exceeds the commercial rate, the Inspector will seek to disallow the 'excess' element on the grounds that it has *not* been incurred wholly and exclusively for the purposes of the company's trade. In practice, the agreement of an 'allowable' amount is likely to be negotiated.

TRANSFERRING INCOME TO THE SPOUSE

Income tax for spouse or civil partner

20.30 For the sake of brevity, but at the risk of appearing sexist(!), the following commentary (in particular) is couched exclusively in terms of the husband being the one who owns and runs the company and puts income into his wife's hands. However, the comments below apply equally to those situations where the wife owns the company and the roles are reversed. (The same considerations also apply to same-sex couples, either married or registered as civil partners.)

Under independent taxation, each spouse has their own personal allowance and personal basic rate bands. It is generally beneficial to bring the spouse in as a director or employee and pay them a salary, provided the following conditions are met:

(a) the salary is taxable at a lower rate of tax (than that suffered by the owner-manager on his income);

(b) this income tax saving is not exceeded by the additional NIC liability (see **20.40**); and

(c) the company is able to obtain a tax deduction for the salary (see **20.42**).

In all such cases, it is recommended that the remuneration (or dividend – see **20.44**) should not be paid into a joint bank account, but one in the spouse's sole name. The same benefits may also apply to bringing in a civil partner as an employee/director.

20.31   Many spouses only work on a 'part-time' basis. However, part-time workers also fall within the National Living Wage (NLW) legislation. Hence, the amount paid to the spouse (providing they are over 25 years old) must not be lower than the current rate of £7.83 per hour requirement (see **20.10** for further details). However, if the spouse works for the company without any remuneration at all, she may well not be an employee, and hence the NLW legislation will not apply as the relationship may be explained by a desire to assist the company voluntarily (ICAEW Tax Guide 7/00).

Universal credit

20.32   The 'Universal Credit' system replaces almost all social security benefits and tax credits system.

Details of the Universal Credit are set out in the *Welfare Reform Act 2012*. Universal credit for working people is administered and 'underpinned' by the RTI system (see **20.25**).

Universal credit replaces the following:

- Income-based Jobseeker's Allowance;
- Income-related Employment and Support Allowance;
- Income Support;
- Child Tax Credits;
- Working Tax Credits;
- Housing Benefit.

Universal Credit is firmly targeted at jobseekers and low paid workers and so it offers few benefits to most owner-managers. It will supply a standard allowance plus additional amounts for disability, housing, children and other caring responsibilities. Claimants under the current benefits system are guaranteed to be no worse off under the Universal Credit system.

The amount payable will be restricted by reference to income thresholds for earned and unearned income at rates of 63% to 100% respectively. Most owner-managers would have a withdrawal rate of 100% where they extract profits by way of dividends and thus are unlikely to receive any benefits under the Universal Credit system.

Spouse's NIC liabilities

20.33 The income tax benefits of giving a salary to a spouse are often reduced by the NIC cost. In 2018/19, if the spouse earns £162 or more per week (or more than £8,424 on an annual basis), *employees'* NICs are payable at 12% on earnings between £162 and £892 per week (£8,424–£46,350 per year). The first £162 per week is free of NICs. Contracting out is no longer possible since 6 April 2016.

When the spouse's total annual earnings reach the upper earnings limit of £46,350, a 2% NIC 'surcharge' is levied on any amount exceeding the limit.

For 2018/19, *employer's* NICs are levied at the standard rate of 13.8% for earnings exceeding £162 per week with no maximum limit (the first £162 per week (£8,424 per year) is NIC free).

An annual salary of up to £8,424 can therefore be paid in 2018/19 without any income tax or NIC liability.

TAX DEDUCTION FOR REMUNERATION PAID TO SPOUSE

20.34

Focus

The optimum amount to be paid to the spouse must therefore be carefully considered. Unless the spouse works for the company on a full-time basis, HMRC will require the amount to be substantiated in relation to the duties performed. Inspectors often critically assess the amount of remuneration paid to a wife in relation to the work she performs. It may be helpful to draw up a job specification listing all the wife's duties (for example, secretarial, certain administrative duties, etc) together with some indication of the time commitment.

There must also be some evidence of payment to the spouse. Unsurprisingly, in *Moschi v Kelly* [1952] 33 TC 442, tax relief for the wife's wages was denied since they were charged to the owner's own drawings account!

If the wife is appointed as a director, then the legal obligations and responsibilities assumed in that position alone should justify a reasonable level of remuneration. Provided the amount paid to the wife reflects the work she *actually* carries out, the company should have no difficulty in obtaining a tax deduction. (Similar considerations apply to remuneration paid to a civil partner, etc.)

A further advantage of paying remuneration to the wife is that it can be used to support company pension contributions to provide her with a pension in her own right, subject to the spouse's overall package meeting the 'wholly and exclusively' requirement (and the pension payment being within the annual allowance).

A spouse could also pay tax-deductible personal pension contributions up to 100% of her salary.

The *Copeman v William Flood & Sons Ltd* case

20.35   Where HMRC considers the level of remuneration to be excessive, they will challenge it using the decision in *Copeman v William Flood & Sons Ltd* (1940) 24 TC 53. (Similar issues apply to the tax deductibility of company pension contributions.) This case enables them to disallow the 'excess' part of the remuneration charged in the accounts on the grounds that this element was not paid wholly and exclusively for the purposes of the company's trade (*CTA 2009, s 54*).

In the *Copeman* case, the Revenue contested the deduction for remuneration of £2,600 paid in 1938 to a pig dealer's daughter, for dealing with telephone queries. This would be equivalent to remuneration of well over £75,000 in current day values! The case was remitted to the Commissioners to determine the amount which should be disallowed.

Waiving 'disallowed' remuneration

20.36   If HMRC succeed in substituting a lower figure for the tax deductible remuneration, the wife would strictly be taxable on the *full amount* of the remuneration. However, provided the 'excess' element is formally waived and paid back to the company, HMRC will generally restrict the income tax charge to the *deductible* element of the remuneration (*Employment Income Manual*, para 42730).

If the spouse is also a shareholder, the Inspector may treat any non-waived 'disallowed' amount as a distribution, which should not increase the tax liability. However, HMRC will still retain any NIC liability.

Paying dividends to a spouse

20.37   If the wife does little or no work for the company, no relief can really be justified. In these cases, it is generally better to structure the shareholdings so that the spouse receives dividend income instead. Provided fully-fledged ordinary shares are provided to the spouse, HMRC is unlikely to challenge it now, following its defeat in *Garnett v Jones* [2007] STC 1536 – the so-called *Arctic Systems* case. On the other hand, if the shares issued only contain dividend rights (such as non-voting preference shares), HMRC will probably be able to counter the relevant arrangements, as they successfully did in *Young v Pearce* [1996] STC 743.

Dividend-splitting may also be considered by those owner-managers affected by the 'top' (2018/19) dividend tax rate of 38.1%. In many cases, owner-managers will seek to pay their spouses part of 'their' dividend entitlement to avoid paying this tax rate on their dividends.

HMRC was very keen to introduce legislation to negate these types of income-shifting/income splitting arrangements as soon as the *Arctic Systems* ruling went against it. However, the Treasury seems to have lost the appetite to introduce appropriate new legislation to counter income splitting between married couples. It is recommended that any spousal dividend should be paid into their own bank account (rather than an account in joint names).

Focus

Following the recent changes to the dividend tax regime, spousal dividend planning still remains attractive. For example, for 2018/19, a 'non-tax paying' spouse could take a *tax-free* dividend of £13,850 (ie an amount equal to their personal allowance of £11,850 and dividend nil-rate band of £2,000).

Most owner-managers prefer taking advantage of the 7.5% 'basic-rate' band. Thus, assuming spouses have no other taxable income, they could receive a dividend in 2018/19 of (say) £46,000 at a tax cost of only £2,411, as calculated below:

	£
Cash dividend	46,000
Personal allowance	(11,850)
Taxable dividend	34,150
Basic rate band is £34,500 but	
First £2,000 – nil rate	–
Next £32,150 @ 7.5%	2,411
Tax Liability	2,411

Where spouses take dividends, they would have little or no relevant earnings for pension purposes. However, it is still possible for them to make annual tax-deductible gross pension contributions of up to £3,600 gross (£2,880 net of basic rate tax relief relieved at source), provided this can be justified in terms of their 'commercial' pay package.

Example 20.4 – Salary or dividend for spouse – part 1

Mr Astle is the controlling shareholder of Astle Ltd, which is based in the West Midlands. His wife holds 20% of the ordinary shares in Astle Ltd.

Mr Astle is deciding whether to pay £20,000 to his wife as a salary (before NICs) or dividend for the year to 31 March 2019. She has no other income. Mrs Astle performs secretarial and administrative duties for the company which should be sufficient to justify corporation tax relief for the salary.

	£	Salary £	Dividend £
Available Profits		20,000	20,000
Less Employer's NIC (13.8% on			
(£18,596 – £8,424)		(1,404)	
Gross pay		18,596	
Less Employees' NIC 12% × (£18,596 – £8,424)		(1,221)	
Corporation tax at 19%		–	(3,800)
		17,375	16,200
Less Income tax thereon			
On Salary			
Salary	18,596		
Less PA	(11,850)		
Taxable	6,746		
Income tax (£6,746 at 20%)		(1,349)	
On Dividend			
Cash	16,200		
Less PA	(11,850)		
Taxable dividend	4,350		
Income tax (£4,350 – £2,000 dividend nil rate band at 7.5%)		–	(176)
Post-tax receipt		16,026	16,024

This shows that at this level (ie £20,000) there is no difference between a salary or dividend.

Example 20.5 – Salary or dividend for spouse – part 2

The facts are the same as in **Example 20.4**, except that Mr Astle is proposing to pay £30,000 to his wife for the year ended 31 March 2019.

	£	Salary £	Dividend £
Available Profits		30,000	30,000
Less Employer's NIC (13.8% on (£27,384 – £8,424)		(2,616)	
Gross pay		27,384	
Less Employees' NIC 12% × (£27,384 – £8,424)		(2,275)	
Corporation tax at 19%		–	(5,700)
		25,109	24,300
Less Income tax thereon			
On Salary			
Salary	27,384		
Less PA	(11,850)		
Taxable	15,534		
Income tax (£15,534 at 20%)		(3,107)	
On Dividend			
Cash	24,300		
Less PA	(11,850)		
Taxable dividend	12,450		
Income tax (£12,450 – £2,000 dividend nil rate band at 7.5%)		–	(784)
Post-tax receipt		22,002	23,516

This shows that at this level (ie £30,000), his wife is £1,514 better off.

EMPLOYING THE CHILDREN

20.38   The owner-manager's children may also work for the company at weekends, or in their school/college/university holidays. The company will need to comply with the appropriate legislation and by-laws for employing children aged under 16. Children cannot be employed in a factory and those under 13 cannot be employed except for light duties in limited circumstances.

The National Living Wage (NLW) rules must be adhered to for children aged 25 or over and the National Minimum Wage (NMW) rules for children aged between 16 and 24 (see **20.10** for current applicable rates).

If the children have taken out student loans, then the company may be liable to make appropriate deductions from their salary towards repayment of their loan. No student loan deductions are currently required where the salary is less than £18,330 per year in 2018/19.

The wages received by the children can be paid tax free up to their personal allowance, with any excess being liable at the basic rate or higher rate, as appropriate. Once again, HMRC will seek to establish the commercial justification for the payment in relation to the work done by the children. Payments made to the owner-manager's children which constitute 'disguised pocket money' will be disallowed (see *Dollar v Lyon* [1981] STC 333). There will, of course, be cases where a fairly reasonable amount can be substantiated as a genuine trading expense of the company. For example, the author is aware of a case where a teenage son of an owner-manager was paid a justifiable commercial wage for trial testing computer games that had been developed by the business. In such cases, such amounts will clearly be allowable as a trading expense.

Under the current pension regime, pension contributions of up to £3,600 gross (£2,880 net of the basic rate tax relief contributed at source by HMRC) can be made for each child, even in the absence of any relevant earnings.

CHARGING RENT ON PERSONALLY OWNED ASSETS USED BY THE COMPANY

Rationale for holding property personally and tax treatment of rent

20.39

Focus

A number of owner-managers leave the trading property outside the company to mitigate the effect of the potential 'double-tax' charge and to create wealth outside the company (free from the claims of its creditors

---

> (subject to personal guarantees), etc). In such cases, the owner-manager can extract funds from the company by charging the company a market rent for the use of the property.

The rent may be paid under a formal lease agreement between the owner-manager and the company. If the property is jointly-owned, for example, by the owner-manager and their spouse, then the rent would be paid to both in the appropriate shares.

SDLT is payable where (and to the extent that) the chargeable consideration for the lease exceeds £150,000 (for commercial property). A 2% charge applies for chargeable consideration falling within the '£150,001 to £250,000' band, with any excess over £250,000 being charged at 5%.

In broad terms, the chargeable consideration represents the net present value of the future rental income, with special rules applying to variable and/or contingent rents. It is not possible to mitigate the SDLT charge by charging a low rent, since a deemed market rental value applies where the property is let to a 'connected company' (as will generally be the case). If the SDLT charge is prohibitive, it may be worth considering granting a simple 'licence to occupy' the property since this is an *exempt* interest in land for SDLT purposes. In broad terms, a licence to occupy represents a non-exclusive right of occupation so it is important that any documentation does not grant the company the sole exclusive right to occupy the property (*FA 2003, s 48(2)(b)*).

The rent paid by the company would be deductible against its profits (provided it represents a market rent) and the rent received would be taxable in the owner-manager's hands as property income (but no NIC liability would arise). The owner-manager can deduct, as property business expenses, the normal expenses of running the let property, including repairs (not capital improvements), service expenses, insurance, security costs and relevant professional fees. Interest paid on personal loans taken out to purchase or improve the property will also be tax-deductible (subject to the income tax relief restriction for interest costs which is being phased in from 2017/18).

Where the owner-manager has borrowed money to purchase the property, he would normally charge rent to secure immediate tax relief for the interest (*ITTOIA 2005, s 272*). Clearly, if only part of the building is let, then only a corresponding part of the costs can be deducted as property business expenses.

Where personally held property is subsequently sold alongside a disposal of the owner-manager's shares, it may be possible to claim Entrepreneurs'

Relief (ER) on the property gain under the associated disposal rules. Provided the owner-manager has 'ER capacity' after relief has been claimed against the share sale, a 10% ER CGT rate can be applied to the property gain. Shareholders' must sell at least a 5% stake in the company to qualify for 'associated disposal' relief.

In such cases, the gain qualifying for ER would be denied or restricted where the owner-manager has previously charged a rent for the use of the property.

INTEREST ON BORROWINGS AND CAPITAL ALLOWANCES

20.40   In some cases, the owner-manager may not charge a rent, but will arrange for the company to pay the interest on their personal borrowings that were taken out to purchase or improve the property. Such 'interest' would be deductible in computing the company's trading profits as it represents consideration for occupying the property for trading purposes. Following normal accountancy principles, the company's interest payment on the owner-manager's behalf is counted as a property business receipt in the owner-manager's hands, but this would be offset by the owner-manager's actual obligation to pay the interest (subject to the proposed phasing out of full income tax relief (see **20.39**)). (If the company does not pay rent or interest, the owner-manager cannot secure any income tax relief for the interest.)

Other allowable deductions include capital allowances on integral features and plant attached to the building.

VAT issues

20.41   Provided the property is used for normal commercial (non-residential) purposes, the owner-manager can elect to opt to tax it. Where the owner-manager is personally VAT registered, VAT would be added to the rent charged to the company (as well as on any service charges). An option to tax would almost certainly be required where VAT was charged on the purchase price paid for the property (or on any substantial improvements). Provided the election is in place, this will enable the owner-manager to recover VAT on any expenses incurred in relation to the property in their capacity as a landlord. However, it also means that if the property is sold, VAT would have to be charged on the sale proceeds (unless it was possible to use the 'transfer of going concern' exemption.

Provided the company is fully taxable (for VAT purposes), VAT charged on the rents would be fully recovered. Thus, overall, charging VAT on the rent is likely to be cash neutral whilst enabling VAT to be reclaimed on property improvements and running expenses.

Where the owner-manager is only likely to suffer minimal VAT costs, it may not be worthwhile to opt to tax (unless of course VAT was charged on the original purchase cost which needs to be recovered).

Extraction of profits via rent

20.42   The tax effect of extracting profits via a rent is similar to the payment of remuneration, except that no PAYE or NIC is payable.

Example 20.6 – Rent charged to company for use of owner-manager's property

Mr Downing owns the entire share capital of The Downing Cross Company Ltd. The factory used by the company was, however, purchased by Mr and Mrs Downing in equal shares many years ago.

For the year ended 31 March 2019 the company was charged a rent of £30,000. Mr and Mrs Downing's claim for allowable property expenses were £3,000 each. They had no finance costs.

Assuming that, for the year ended 31 March 2019, the company's taxable profits before charging the rent were £260,000, the tax consequences are as follows:

	Company	Mr Downing	Mrs Downing
	£	£	£
Taxable profits before rent	260,000		
Less: Rent charged	(30,000)	15,000	15,000
Taxable profit (after rent charge)	230,000		
Less: Corporation tax @ 19%	(43,700)		
Post-tax profit	186,300		
Less: Allowable property expenses		(3,000)	(3,000)
Taxable rent		12,000	12,000
Company tax saving on rent			
£30,000 @ 19%	5,700		
Income tax payable:			
Marginal tax rate @ 40%		6,000	
Marginal tax rate @ 20%			3,000

Subsequent sale of property

20.43   If the owner-manager subsequently sells the property, any capital gain will generally be taxed at the main current CGT rate of 20%.

Where the property is being sold along with an ER-eligible disposal of shares in the company, the owner-manager *may* be able to obtain a 10% rate on any unused ER entitlement against the property gain under the 'associated disposal' rules (subject to any restriction for rent charges) (see also **20.39**).

SELLING AN ASSET TO THE COMPANY FOR VALUE

Background

20.44   The controlling shareholder may personally own the company's trading premises. This means that the property should not be exposed to the company's creditors on a winding up, although in many cases, banks or other lenders will secure a charge on the property. Consequently, as far as the commercial risk is concerned, there may be little difference whether the property is owned by the company or shareholder.

Focus

Owner-managers might consider extracting a capital sum from their company by selling the (personally-owned) property to the company. The disposal would generate a capital gain in their hands, which will now generally be taxed at 20%. (Note that 'associated disposal' ER relief is not available for 'separate property sales'.)

SDLT may be payable on the purchase by the company. In such cases, SDLT would normally be levied on the market value of the property irrespective of the actual sale price paid by the company (see **20.46**). The transfer of the property to the company may also improve the owner-manager's business property relief position for IHT purposes.

Care is necessary to ensure that the property is not sold at an over-value, since the excess amount could be taxed as employment income (or as a shareholder distribution) (*CTA 2010, s 1000*).

CGT treatment

20.45   An immediate chargeable gain can be avoided by selling the property to the company at its original base cost (which will be the March 1982 value where the property was held by the owner-manager at that date). Although the disposal computed by reference to market value, the 'unrealised element' of the gain can be held over under the business asset gift relief provisions in *TCGA 1992, s 165* (which must be claimed on form IR295). This relief is not affected by any previous rent charges. By concession, it is not necessary to agree the market value of the gifted asset with HMRC. The 'transferor' owner-manager and the company must request this treatment in writing (SP8/92).

Where the owner-manager sells the asset at its original base cost/March 1982 value, the company will effectively acquire it at that amount.

Where the asset is sold to the company at its original base cost or a lower amount, this will be the acquisition cost on the company's balance sheet. However, it is possible to bolster the company's balance sheet by subsequently revaluing the asset. The uplift in valuation would be credited to a revaluation surplus account within shareholders' funds.

VAT and SDLT

20.46 The owner-manager will normally be connected with the company within *CTA 2010, s 1122*, since they either control it in their own right or together with their family members. Consequently, the 'deemed market value' rule in *FA 2003, s 53* will apply for SDLT purposes, irrespective of the actual consideration paid by the company. The amount of SDLT payable on the acquisition of the property by the company will therefore depend on its market value (which is treated as the 'chargeable consideration'). However, if the property was previously owned by a 'connected' family partnership, the special partnership SDLT provisions take precedence over the deemed 'market value' rule, which may result in a reduction or elimination of the SDLT charge.

The SDLT chargeable consideration normally includes any VAT chargeable on the sale and it appears that HMRC requires any potential VAT to be added to the 'deemed' market value consideration for these purposes.

Where the property is subject to a VAT option to tax (see **20.39**), the owner-manager will need to charge VAT on the purchase price (which is normally recoverable by the company). Some care is required over the timing of the transaction to ensure that the company is able to recover the input VAT before it is paid over by the owner-manager. Although the property may have been previously let to the company at a commercial rent, the sale cannot be treated as a transfer of a going concern since the same letting business would not be carried on by the company (the property would then become 'owner-occupied').

CHARGING INTEREST ON LOANS TO THE COMPANY

Commercial implications

20.47

Focus

Where owner-managers make a loan to the company or have a credit balance on their current account, there is nothing to stop them charging the company with interest on the loan. The interest rate charged should be at a commercial rate, which (depending on the company's financial position and creditworthiness) could be several base points above the bank base lending rate. This would recognise the 'risk' element of non-recovery if the company gets into financial difficulty, although it may be possible to secure the lending (for example) against the company's property.

If the interest charged by a shareholder-director materially exceeds a commercial rate, HMRC may seek to treat the 'excess' amount as a salary (seeking PAYE and NIC) or dividend distribution.

ACCOUNTING FOR OWNER-MANAGER'S LOAN TO COMPANY

FRS 102 requirements

20.48 FRS 102 requires all financing transactions to be accounted for on a consistent basis. Consequently, where owner-managers make an interest-free or below market interest loan to 'their' companies, this is seen as giving additional financial benefits to the company as compared with arm's length borrowing transactions.

Loans with a fixed repayment term (of longer than 12 months) are shown as a non-current liability on the balance sheet. Unless the company is 'small' (see **20.49** below), FRS 102 requires interest-free loans (or loans below commercial interest rates), to be valued at their amortised cost ie, the present value of the future payments discounted at a market rate of interest for a similar debt instrument. Consequently, the loan must be discounted to its present value. In subsequent periods, the interest is unwound by debiting the profit and loss account.

This treatment produces an intial gain and notional finance charges for accounting purposes, which are dealt with through the profit and loss account. There is an exception if the loan is provided from an owner-manager, when the initial gain is recognised as a capital contribution from the owner-manager. This reflects the economic substance of the transaction and would be credited to equity (ie shareholders 'capital').

Tax treatment of interest-free or below market rate loans

20.49 The *F(No 2)A 2015* provides that where the initial credit is taken to equity (as opposed to profit and loss account), this is not taxable under the loan relationship rules.

To achieve tax symmetry, for accounting periods starting after 31 March 2016, the corresponding interest charges that relate to the initial non-taxable credit are not allowable for tax purposes (see **Example 20.7** below). Thus, for loans made in accounting periods starting *after 31 March 2016*, the initial 'credit' and the subsequent notional interest adjustments are effectively completely ignored for tax (*CTA 2009, s 446A*).

These accounting complications do not arise where the loan is repayable on demand, although it would then be recorded under current liabilities (and may therefore weaken the company's financial profile). Alternatively, the owner-manager could charge interest at a commercial rate.

Example 20.7 – Accounting for shareholder's interest-free loan to company under FRS 102

Cyril has owned 100% of Regis (WBA) Ltd for many years.

On 31 December 2017, he advanced an interest-free loan of £500,000 to the company to finance the purchase of a new fleet of lorries. The loan will not be repaid until 31 December 2023.

It is estimated that the company could obtain an equivalent bank loan at 10%.

For the purposes of drawing up the accounts to 31 December 2017, the loan would be discounted by $1/(1.10)^5$. The discount factor is 0.620921.

The intial value of the loan in the 31 December 2017 accounts is therefore £310,460 (£500,000 × 0.620921).

The initial accounting entries at 31 Decmber 2017 would be as follows:

	Dr	Cr
Bank (cash)	500,000	
Shareholder loan		310,460
Capital contribution (equity)		189,540
	500,000	500,000

In the year ended 31 December 2018, the interest charged to profit and loss account would be:

£310,460 × 10% = £31,046

However, since this interest clearly relates to the initial 'non-taxable' credit, it is not allowable for tax purposes.

Shareholder loans that were already in existence when a company moved to FRS 102 had to be valued at a discounted value (if they were interest-free or below-market rate). These are dealt with by the *Loan Relationships and Derivative Contracts (Change Of Accounting Practice) Regulations 2004, 2004/3271*. Broadly, these rules provide that any initial difference is brought into account for tax purposes over a ten-year period.

FRS 102 relaxation for 'small' companies

20.50   Different rules apply where the company is 'small'. For these purposes, a company is 'small' (for accounting periods starting after 31 December 2015), if it falls below at *least two* of the following thresholds for the current/previous year or the previous two years (or for the first year of incorporation):

Turnover	£10.2m	For 12 months or, where appropriate, pro-rata
Total gross assets	£5.1m	
Employees	50	Monthly average of employees
* Parent companies of a group must meet at least two of the above 'net' basis limits *and* turnover (£12.2m) and gross assets (£6.2m) on a 'gross' basis (ie without eliminating intra-group transactions).		

Where a company is small, it can opt to account under FRS 105 which does not require the above 'valuation' treatment.

However, many small companies have adopted FRS 102. Thankfully, in May 2017, the Financial Reporting Council amended FRS 102 enabling *small companies* to report shareholder loans (or loans from any close family member of a shareholder) to be reported at their transaction value (as opposed to the present value)!

Company's tax deduction for interest

20.51   Under the 'loan relationship' rules, the company normally obtains relief for interest charged in its accounts on an accruals basis, ie on the amount charged against its profits. However, any loan to a close company from an individual shareholder (or an associate of a shareholder) is subject to the 'late interest' rule. (Although the *Finance Act 2015* repealed much of the late interest rules, they still apply for loans from owner-managers and other individual shareholders.) Furthermore, the interest deduction may be restricted if the intial recognition of the loan gave rise to a non-taxable credit (see **20.49**).

Under the 'late interest' rules, the corporate tax deduction for any interest that remains unpaid more than 12 months after the accounting period end, is deferred until the interest is actually paid (*CTA 2009, ss 373* and *375*).

A close company therefore only gets relief for the interest on a loan from its owner-manager on an accruals basis provided it is paid in, or within 12 months after the end of, the relevant accounting period.

If the period of the loan exceeds (or can be extended beyond) one year, the interest would be treated as 'annual interest'. Since the interest is paid to an individual, the company must deduct lower rate tax (of 20%) at source when the interest is paid. (Only interest on bank and building society loans can be paid 'gross' from 6 April 2016.) This interest is reported and paid over to HMRC on Form CT 61. The recipient shareholder-director is taxed on the ('grossed up') interest *received* (with credit being given for any tax deducted at source). The interest does not constitute earnings and therefore no NICs are payable.

Focus

In some cases, it may be possible to secure a timing advantage by exploiting the late interest rule within the constraints of the rules.

For example, a company could accrue interest on an owner-manager's loan account in its accounting period ended 31 March 2019 with the interest being paid in (say) June 2019. Thus, the interest would still be deductible against the company's profits for the year ended 31 March 2019 (with the benefit of the tax reduction being obtained on 1 January 2020). On the other hand, the recipient would be taxed on a 'received' basis in 2019/20, with the income tax liability being payable on 31 January 2021.

Example 20.8 – Charging interest on a director's loan account

Mr Cresswell is a 75% shareholder of Aaron 3 Ltd. Over the years, he has ploughed back most of his dividend income to provide additional working capital for the company.

During the year ended 31 March 2019, the balance outstanding on his loan account with the company was £300,000 on which he charged interest at 8% per year.

The company's taxable profits (*before* charging interest on Mr Cresswell's shareholder loan account) for the year ended 31 March 2019 were £780,000.

The tax position for the company and Mr Cresswell is as follows:

Year ended 31 March 2019

Company	£
Taxable profits before interest	780,000
Less: Interest charge	
£300,000 × 8% =	(24,000)
Taxable profit after interest charge	756,000
Corporation tax @ 19%	(143,640)
Profit after tax	612,360
Company tax saving on interest	
£24,000 @ 19%	£4,560

The company will only obtain tax relief in the year ended 31 March 2019 provided the interest is actually paid to Mr Cresswell by 31 March 2020. Relief will not be given if the interest is simply 'rolled-up' as a credit to his loan account and remains outstanding at 31 March 2020.

Mr Cresswell

Interest received net of tax deducted by company	
£24,000 *less* £4,800 (ie 20% × £24,000)	19,200

Less: Income tax payable

£24,000 @ (say) 40% = £9,600 *less* £4,800 (tax deducted at source by company)	(4,800)
Net amount received	14,400

LOANS FROM THE COMPANY

Companies Act restriction

20.52 Private companies can make loans to directors (provided they have been approved by shareholders) (*CA 2006, s 197*). Loans to those connected with the director are also subject to the same 'shareholder approval' rules. (Connected persons under the *CA 2006* include spouses, minor and adult children, parents, and so on.)

The *CA 2006* does not require any approval for small loans/quasi-loans (£10,000) and minor credit transactions (£15,000).

If the company fails to obtain the required resolution of its shareholders, the loan is voidable under *CA 2006, s 213*. This means that the company could rescind the loan and recoup its money.

Scope of *CTA 2010, s 455* charge

20.53 Strictly, the *CTA 2010, s 455* charge only arises on loans made to 'participators' (invariably shareholders) of a *close* company, and the vast majority of owner-managed companies will be 'close' for these purposes.

Consequently, owner-managers will normally be subject to a *CTA 2010, s 455* charge of 32.5% where the company makes a loan or advance to them which is not repaid within nine months of the company's year-end (see **20.56**).

The charge can also apply where a loan is made to an 'associate' of the shareholder, such as a spouse, parent, grandparent, child, grandchild, brother or sister, as well as a business partner (*CTA 2010, s 448(2)*).

For FRS 102-related accounting issues for (overdrawn) directors' loan accounts, see **20.60–20.62**).

Changes introduced in *FA 2013* have widened the scope of *s 455* in relation to loans made to 'related' partnerships and trusts after 19 March 2013 (see **20.54**).

Furthermore, *FA 2013* also introduced:

- special rules to deal with 'bed and breakfasting arrangements (see **20.63**); and

- an anti-avoidance charge on 'benefits' enjoyed by shareholders (under arrangements that would not otherwise be caught by *CTA 2010, s 455)* – see **20.66**.

There is a separate rule which deems a *CTA 2010, s 455* liability to arise where a participator (or associate) incurs a debt to the company – for example, where the shareholder buys a 'personal' asset on credit in the company's name *(CTA 2010, s 455(4))*. This particular trap can also occur with management charges that remain due to a 'parallel' partnership service company (for longer than six months (see exemption (*b*) below)). Any debt incurred by the partnership would fall within *CTA 2010, s 455(4)* (see *Grant v Watton; Andrew Grant Services Ltd v Watton* [1999] STC 330).

There are various exemptions from the *s 455* tax liability, but they are of little assistance to most family and owner-managed companies:

(a) loans up to £15,000 in total are exempt where the borrower works full time for the company and does not own more than 5% of the ordinary share capital *(CTA 2010, s 456(4))*;

(b) indirect loans involving the supply of goods on credit by the close company are exempt provided this is made in the normal course of trade (except where the credit given exceeds six months) *(CTA 2010, s 456(2))*;

(c) the tax charge does not apply where the company is a lending institution which makes the loan or advance in the ordinary course of its business *(CTA 2010, s 456(1))*. HMRC only regards this exemption as being available where the company is carrying on the business of money lending and this is part of its general business activities.

Although *CTA 2010, s 455* is generally regarded as a 'deposit' tax (since it is repayable when the loan/advance is repaid), it is still treated as 'an amount of corporation tax' and thus is liable to interest and penalties in the normal way. It is therefore important that all *CTA 2010, s 455* loans are disclosed on the CT 600 return, even if the relevant tax liability is discharged by repayment of the loan within nine months of the company's year-end (see **20.68**).

Loans to 'related' trusts and partnerships/LLPs

20.54   A *CTA 2010, s 455* charge will now firmly catch loans made to the trustees of a settlement in which at least one of the trustees or beneficiaries (actual or potential) is a participator (or an associate of an individual of a participator).

FA 2013 ensures that 'close company' loans made to a trust are caught by *CTA 2010, s 455*, irrespective of whether the trust holds shares in the company. All that is required is that either:

– (at least) one trustee; or

– a beneficiary of the trust

is a shareholder of the 'lending' company. Thus, loans made to an Employee Benefit Trust to facilitate the purchase of shares for an employee share scheme would be caught, which seems a little harsh!

For loans made after 19 March 2013, the *FA 2013* confirms that a loan or advance to a partnership/LLP in which *at least one* participator (or their associate) is a partner/member is caught by *CTA 2010, s 455*. Furthermore, the new *CTA 2010, s 455(1)(c)* also catches loans made to a partnership/ LLP that includes at least one corporate partner/member. A *CTA 2010, s 455* charge can therefore easily apply where there is no significant overlap between the company's shareholders and the partners/members.

Unfortunately, the *FA 2013* provisions do not include any 'commercial purpose' exemption, which had been widely called for. *CTA 2010, s 455* will therefore apply to commercially based loan arrangements, such as where a 'related' close company makes a loan to a property development LLP to fund a new development.

These rules also catch a loan made by a corporate member of a partnership/LLP where an individual partner/member is a shareholder of that (close) company.

Partners or members often inject funding into the partnership/LLP through their capital accounts, which reflects the nature of their investment or proprietorial interest in the relevant firm. Since partners do not have a right to demand repayment of their capital account, many would strongly argue that this cannot be viewed as a 'loan or advance' within the meaning of *CTA 2010, 455(1)(c)*. Consequently, where a corporate partner/member makes a capital contribution to a partnership/LLP, it should *not* be subject to a *CTA 2010, s 455* charge.

Example 20.9 – Application of *CTA 2010, s 455* to loans made to partnerships/LLPs

Mr Byram is a 60% shareholder in Thurrock Traders Ltd and is also a 50% member of Leeds Property Development LLP ('LLP'), as shown below:

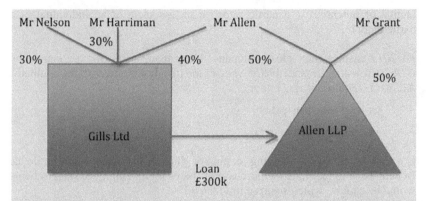

Thurrock Traders Ltd makes up accounts to 31 December each year. In August 2016, it lends the LLP £1,500,000 to held finance a property development project.

However, since Mr Byram is a shareholder in Thurrock Traders Ltd and a member of the LLP, the loan is within *CTA 2010, s 455*.

Therefore, unless the loan is repaid by 30 September 2017, Thurrock Traders Ltd will be liable to a *CTA 2010, s 455* charge of £487,500 (32.5% × £1,500,000).

Beneficial loan charge

20.55 Since owner-managers will also be within the scope of the directors'/employment/benefit, any loan made to them by the company will also fall within the scope of the beneficial loan provisions. Thus, if the company does not charge any interest on the loan (or the interest charge is less than the official rate), a taxable benefit will arise on the 'interest' benefit (*ITEPA 2003, s 175*).

Mechanics of *CTA 2010, s 455* charge

20.56 The aim of this legislation is to levy tax on what would otherwise be an easy method of extracting cash from the close company on a tax-free basis. *CTA 2010, s 455* requires the company to account for tax at the rate of 32.5% on the loan/advance. For loans/advances made before 6 April 2016, *CTA 2010, s 455* tax is charged at 25%.

The *CTA 2010, s 455* tax therefore represents a stand-alone charge which is deposited with HMRC. If the loan or overdrawn account is repaid in whole or in part (or is released (see **20.73**)), the appropriate portion of the *CTA 2010, s 455* tax is discharged or refunded (*CTA 2010, s 458(2)*). Any repayment from HMRC must be claimed within four years from the end of the *financial year* in which the loan is repaid/released.

For companies that are not subject to the Quarterly Instalment Payment (QIP) regime, the *CTA 2010, s 455* liability falls due nine months after the end of their company's accounting period (in line with their normal due date for payment of tax). However, if the company pays its tax under the QIP regime, any (undischarged) *CTA 2010, s 455* liability must be factored into its instalment payments.

Some owner-managers may wish to consider extracting funds from company by making a substantial loan to mitigate their income tax liabilities. There will be a one-off *CTA 2010, s 455* charge equal to 32.5% (25% for pre-6 April 2016 loans/advances) and an annual employment benefit charge based on the official rate of interest.

Thus, the *CTA 2010, s 455* charge on a £100,000 loan advanced on 1 June 2018 would be £32,500 (assuming the amount remains outstanding more than nine months after the company's year-end) and the tax on the 'interest' benefit would be just £1,200 for a 40% taxpayer (ie £100,000 × 3% × 40%).

If the loan is repaid before the *CTA 2010, s 455* tax is due for payment, the liability is discharged and the tax does not have to be paid over. However, if the loan remains outstanding after the nine month due date, HMRC will seek the *s 455* tax and charge interest from the due date until the tax is paid.

When the loan is subsequently repaid, the repayment of the *CTA 2010, s 455* tax is deferred until nine months after the *end of the CTAP in which the loan is repaid or reduced,* with repayment interest arising on any delayed repayment. Given this lead time for repayment of the *CTA 2010, s 455* tax, owner-managers should always try to avoid triggering a *CTA 2010, s 455* liability by repaying their loans within nine months of the balance sheet date.

Director's overdrawn loan accounts

20.57 HMRC insist that the company's record keeping should ensure that balances of directors' loan accounts are accurate and kept up to date. HMRC are concerned that poorly kept records "may result in non-business expenditure incurred by the directors being incorrectly recorded or mis-posted in the business records and claimed in error as an allowable expense". Particular risk areas include the payment of personal bills, such as credit cards, personal expenses paid by company, and personal entertaining.

20.58   In practice, there is usually a potential *CTA 2010, s 455* exposure on overdrawn director-shareholder's current or loan accounts.

Focus

In many cases, an overdrawn loan account may not be established until sometime after the balance sheet date, eg when the accounts are completed or following certain audit adjustments. It is therefore important to establish the proper balance before the 'nine-month' due date for the *CTA 2010, s 455* tax. This will enable the owner-manager to decide whether to clear the balance by voting an additional bonus or declaring an appropriate dividend.

Dividends must be properly declared and documented to demonstrate that the debt due to the company has been repaid. Repayment via cheque to the company is the most robust way of demonstrating repayment.

20.59   If an overdrawn balance remains after the 'nine month' due date, the *CTA 2010, s 455* tax falls due and interest will begin to accrue. Where regular advances/loans are made to a company's shareholder director, HMRC will often contend that these have the character of 'earnings' and seek to apply PAYE and NIC on the relevant amounts. Proper loan documentation will help to rebut such challenges. To avoid HMRC seeking (unexpected) PAYE and NIC liabilities on regular withdrawals, where the owner-manager wishes to extract regular amounts from the company, it may be better for them to pay regular 'quarterly' dividends instead (see also **20.25**).

In cases where frequent advances have been accepted as loans under an HMRC enquiry, there may be insufficient evidence as to the amounts that have been cleared by subsequent repayment(s). Inspectors normally seek to apply the rule in *Clayton's* case (1816 MR Ch Vol 1, 572), which provides that repayments are set against the oldest debts first. Given that loans or advances may have been subject to different *CTA 2010, s 455* tax rates, it may be preferable to allocate the repayments against the loans/advances liable to the 32.5% rate in priority to those subject to the 25% charge.

Inspectors will not accept that separate 'director's' accounts can be aggregated or netted off each other since the *CTA 2010, s 455* charge arises where a close company 'makes any loan or advances any money' to a shareholder. HMRC seems to accept that genuine book entries (with supporting documentation) can be made where a credit balance is used to repay a debit balance. However, the *ICAEW Tax Faculty Guidance Note TAX 11/93* recommends that a company should draw a cheque to pay off the whole or part of the credit balance with another cheque being paid into the company to clear the debit balance. This will therefore provide firm evidence of the date the loan is repaid.

Interaction of FRS 102 and directors' loan accounts

20.60 The vast majority of owner-managed companies adopt FRS102, although some micro-entities exercise their option to apply FRS 105 rules.

FRS 102 lays down specific valuation rules for loans (which are likely to be treated as financial instruments), which may apply to directors loan accounts. (This potential complication does not arise if FRS 105 is adopted.)

There is an argument that the build-up of entries in the directors loan account over an accounting period is not a financing transaction, provided the loans are intended to be settled within a year. In practice, transactions between the directors and 'their' companies are often entered into on an informal basis. In any event, a strict application of the FRS 102 valuation rules is unlikely to give rise to any material 'intial difference'.

Therefore, to avoid the potential complexities of FRS 102 accounting treatment, owner-managers should specifically record that their loan accounts are repayable on demand. The loan accounts can then be recorded at 'cost' under FRS 102 (as was historically the case).

On the other hand, if the transactions on a directors' loan account are considered to be 'financing transactions', FRS 102 requires the balances to be accounted for under the amortised cost basis using the effective interest method. However, this can normally be avoided if a commercial rate of interest is charged. In such cases, there should be no (material) difference between the initial recognition amount and the amount received/settled on maturity. Furthermore, if the rate of interest charged is at least equal to HMRC's official rate, no tax charge arises under the 'beneficial loan' legislation (see **20.55**).

20.61 If no interest is charged (or is charged at less than a commercial rate) the loan account balance must be recorded at present value. This is likely to give rise to a 'shortfall' between the face value of the loan and its present value. In this case, the resultant debit would be treated in the company's books as a 'distribution' (para 11.13 of FRS 102). This reflects the benefit of the interest-free/cheap interest being provided to the shareholder.

For loans made after 31 December 2015, it is clear that the distribution (being an amount 'charged' to equity) would not be allowable for tax purposes. (The tax treatment of the 'distribution' for pre-1 January 2016 loans remains unclear.) However, future interest 'credits' over the life of the loan (as the 'discount unwinds) would still appear to be taxable, resulting in an asymetic tax treatment.

Example 20.10 – Treatment of 'long-term' interest-free loan to a director-shareholder

Andre is a 100% shareholder of Ayew Ltd, which draws up accounts to 31 March each year. On 1 April 2018, the company provides a £20,000 interest-free loan to him repayable on 31 March 2021. A comparable market interest rate is 6%.

The accounting entries would be:

	Dr	Cr
Director's loan account	16,792*	
Discount (= distribution)	3,207	
Cash		20,000
	20,000	20,000

* This is the present value of £20,000 received in three years time at a discount rate of 6%

Since the loan is made after 31 December 2015, the 'discount' would *not* be deductible for corporation tax purposes.

20.62   The 'individual' directors/shareholders tax treatment is *not* based on the FRS 102 accounting treatment. Consequently, any taxable benefit is calculated using the beneficial loan rules (see **20.55**). Also the *CTA 2010, s 455* charge is still based on the actual amount of the loan or advance (see **20.53**).

'Bed and breakfasting' of loan accounts

20.63   HMRC introduced specific legislation to counter the use of 'bed and breakfasting' arrangements in *FA 2013*.

Focus

Under the *FA 2013* changes, which apply for loans repaid after 19 March 2013, *CTA 2010, s 458* repayment relief can be denied in two different situations:

The 30-day repayment restriction

20.64   The new *CTA 2010, s 464C(1)* will apply where within a 30-day period:

- a shareholder has made repayments of 'their' *CTA 2010, s 455* loan (exceeding £5,000) ('relevant repayments'); and

- In a *subsequent accounting period*, new loans/advances (exceeding £5,000) are made to the same person or their associate (relevant chargeable payments).

This therefore catches the clearest form of bed and breakfasting arrangement. In such cases, *CTA 2010, s 458* repayment relief is only given *if and to the extent* that the *relevant repayments exceed the relevant chargeable payments*. In effect, the legislation only recognises the 'real' repayment (since repayments are matched with the amounts that have been re-lent shortly after the end of the relevant accounting period are).

An illustrative diagram showing the operation of the '30-day' rule is given below:

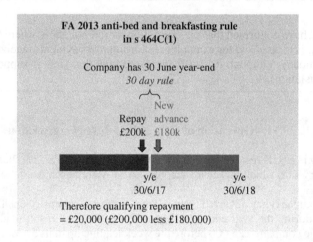

FA 2013 anti-bed and breakfasting rule in s 464C(1)

Company has 30 June year-end
30 day rule

New
Repay advance
£200k £180k

y/e   y/e
30/6/17   30/6/18

Therefore qualifying repayment
= £20,000 (£200,000 less £180,000)

However, importantly, this restriction does *not* apply if the amount repaid gives rise to an income tax liability in the individual shareholder's hands (*CTA 2010, s 464C(6)*). This would typically arise where a bonus is voted for or dividend is paid to 'clear' the shareholder-director's loan account, as is often the case in practice.

In practice, HMRC accept that the crediting of an interim dividend to a loan account represents 'payment' at the time the relevant book entry is made, since the amount is then 'placed unreservedly at the disposal of the directors/shareholders as part of their current accounts with the company'. Some company law purists would argue with that approach, contending that a payment requires a transfer of cash.

On a strict analysis of *CTA 2010, s 464C(6)*, the 'repayment' itself *must* give rise to the income tax charge. The Chartered Institute of Taxation (CIOT) (see *TAX Adviser, May 2014*) pointed out to HMRC that it is the entitlement to the bonus or dividend itself that gives rise to the income tax charge. Worryingly, recent correspondence between the CIOT and HMRC suggests that HMRC are taking a strict interpretation of this 'exemption'. It appears that HMRC considers that the exemption would only apply if the loan account were cleared by a book entry 'crediting' the relevant bonus or dividend from the (lending) company.

Many would argue that an appellate tribunal would adopt a purposive approach so that the 'income tax payment' requirement would be met where, for example, a company actually pays a *cash* dividend to a director, who then uses these monies to repay a loan account.

Focus

HMRC have confirmed that the exemption would not apply where the loan account is cleared by, for example, rent or interest payments received from the company (although it is difficult to see how this view is supported by the legislation).

Example 20.11 – Operation of *CTA 2010, s 464C(1)* restriction

Thierry is a (UK resident) executive director of, and also a 75% shareholder in Henry Ltd, which makes up accounts to 31 March each year.

The company has incurred some large personal expenses on Thierry's behalf during the year ended 31 March 2018, with the result that Thierry owes the company £25,000 before the week leading up to its 31 March 2018 year-end.

Thierry arranges to repay the £25,000 from his personal funds, with his cheque clearing the company's bank account on 28 March 2018. However, on 2 April 2018, he arranges for the company to advance a new loan of £20,000 to him.

Since the £25,000 repayment on 28 March 2018 was made within 30 days of a new loan of £20,000 (falling in the subsequent accounting period), it is matched with the new £20,000 loan first, so that only the excess amount is eligible for *CTA 2010, s 458* repayment relief, as follows:

	£
Repayment	25,000
Matched with new loan	(20,000)
Qualifying repayment	5,000
Therefore repayment of *s 455* tax = £5,000 × 32.5%	£1,625

There is no restriction in the repayment claim if the amount repaid gives rise to an income tax charge on the relevant shareholder or their associate. Thus, if Thierry had credited a dividend of £25,000 from Henry Ltd to his loan account, it would be treated as a full repayment of the loan, and the company would obtain the full *CTA 2010, s 455* tax repayment of £6,250. This is logical since HMRC will collect income tax from Thierry on the dividend payment.

The arrangements rule

20.65 The 'complementary' provision in *CTA 2010, s 464C(3)* potentially applies where the total amount of a shareholder's *CTA 2010, s 455* loan exceeds £15,000 before any repayment. If it does, the provisions in *CTA 2010, s 464C(4)* are triggered when a repayment is made, provided:

● arrangements had been made for one or more chargeable payments to be made to replace some, or all, of the amount repaid ...' and

● the amount of those chargeable payments exceeds £5,000.

In other words, this provision broadly requires that arrangements (which is a wide-ranging term) be in place (typically by the company and/or the relevant shareholder) to 'replace' some or all of the repayment. In such cases, the amount qualifying for repayment relief under *CTA 2010, s 458* is computed as:

Loan repayment(s)	X
Less: New loans/advances for which arrangements are in place	(X)
Qualifying repayment	X

It should be a little easier to prove whether there are arrangements actually in place for the company to grant fresh loans/advances. However, (as the CIOT Technical Team put it) 'any arrangement for a re-borrowing is likely to have involved a negotiation between the participator and the company that took place inside the head of the shareholder-director'. It is to be hoped that HMRC will adopt a sensible approach when applying this provision.

As with the '30 day' rule (see above), *CTA 2010, s 464C(3)* does *not* apply if the 'repayment' transaction gives rise to a taxable bonus or dividend (or waiver). Thus, if the loan is credited with a bonus (which is subjected to PAYE/NIC), this 'credit' will give rise to a valid repayment claim under *CTA 2010, s 458*.

Example 20.12 – Operation of *CTA 2010, s 464C(3), (4)* restriction

Winston holds 100% of the issued share capital of Reid Ltd, which makes up accounts to 30 September each year.

The management accounts show that Winston owed the company some £50,000 at 31 August 2018, which had been built up over the last 11 months.

Winston wishes to clear the loan account to avoid the *CTA 2010, s 455* liability. However, he cannot personally afford to repay it at present. Winston therefore asks his friend's company, Vaz Tê Ltd, for a short-term loan on the understanding that he would repay it within two months by taking a new loan from his company.

There is a significant risk that HMRC would contend that the 'arrangement' with Vaz Tê Ltd would be caught by *CTA 2010, s 464C(3)* and thus deny any claim for repayment relief.

On the other hand, Winston could clear his loan account with a dividend payment of (say) £70,000 on (say) 27 November 2018. Since his loan account was cleared by a taxable dividend, the repayment will qualify for *CTA 2010, s 458* relief (*CTA 2010, s 464C(6)*). As the loan would be 'cleared' by a taxable amount within nine months of the 30 September 2018 year-end, the *CTA 2010, s 455* tax would be discharged under *CTA 2010, s 458*.

Winston would not be liable to pay the income tax on his dividend (in 2018/19) until 31 January 2020.

CTA 2010, s 464A anti-avoidance charge on 'benefits' provided to shareholders

20.66 The *FA 2013* introduced a completely new weapon for dealing with 'indirect benefits' (as opposed to loans) enjoyed by close company shareholders. *CTA 2010, s 464A* imposes a 32.5% deemed 'corporation tax' charge on the relevant close company where:

- it is a party to tax avoidance arrangements (which are widely defined); and

- as a result of those arrangements, a 'benefit' is directly or indirectly conferred on a shareholder of the company (or their associate).

Where the shareholder receives the benefit before 6 April 2016, it is charged at the 25% tax rate.

The *CTA 2010, s 464A* charge will *not* apply where the benefit conferred on the participator would be subject to the 'normal' *CTA 2010, s 455* tax charge or an income tax charge.

HMRC considers that the *CTA 2010, s 464A* charge would be invoked in certain 'hybrid' partnerships where:

- an individual partner's capital account becomes overdrawn (after 19 March 2013); and

- that overdrawn account has effectively been financed by the undrawn profits (or capital introduced) of a corporate partner.

HMRC's explanatory notes indicate that the main target of this provision is to levy a tax charge where *individual* partners benefit as a result of the retention of profits in the partnership/LLP by a corporate partner. This 'benefit', which would otherwise be tax-free, would typically arise where individual partners reduce their own capital account or take sufficient drawings to overdraw their current/capital accounts.

In such cases, the (close) corporate partner could be liable to an *CTA 2010, s 464A* charge on the individual partner's overdrawn capital/current account (or, if lower, the amount funded by the corporate member).

Given that *CTA 2010, s 464A* can only be triggered where there are tax avoidance arrangements, we would expect the 32.5%/25% tax charge to be restricted to those cases where there is *deliberate* 'transfer of value' to 'related' individual partners via the partnership/LLP arrangements.

CTA 2010, s 464B contains a mechanism for repayment of the *CTA 2010, s 464A* tax charge if payments are returned to the company. However, such cases are likely to be rare since (in contrast to a loan), the 'benefit' conferred on the shareholder does not give rise to any repayment obligation.

It is hoped that HMRC would not use these widely drawn provisions as a carte blanche to attack normal commercial arrangements where individual partners/members simply draw profits earned in accordance with their profit share entitlements – it should be possible to show there is no tax avoidance motive here. Similarly, *CTA 2010, s 464A* should not apply where an individual partner's/member's drawings are 'financed' entirely from their own capital account (ie without relying on the capital account of a fellow corporate partner/ member).

Example 20.13 – Scope of *CTA 2010, s 464A* charge

Gareth is a 75% shareholder in Bale Ltd (a close trading company).

Both Gareth and Bale Ltd became equal partners in 'The Bale Partnership' on 1 April 2011, which draws up accounts to 30 September each year.

Under the terms of the partnership agreement, Bale Ltd and Gareth share profits in the ratio of 75%:25% respectively.

During the year ended 30 September 2018, the partnership generated profits of £1,500,000, which were shared as follows:

	£
Bale Ltd (75%)	1,125,000
Gareth (25%)	375,000
Total	1,500,000

Bale Ltd's profits are credited to its capital account and are left retained in the partnership business. On the other hand, Gareth has drawn over £800,000 from the business and, by the end of September 2018, his partnership capital account is overdrawn by some £400,000.

HMRC are likely to contend that *CTA 2010, s 464A* should apply to Gareth's overdrawn capital account.

The assertion would be that:

- the 'overdrawn' element represents a benefit conferred on Gareth; and
- this has been funded by Bale Ltd's undrawn profits.

The *CTA 2010, s 459* charge – deemed close company loans for certain arrangements

20.67 The normal *CTA 2010, s 455* charging rules are supplemented by a special *CTA 2010, s 459* charge, which may apply where a *s 455* charge does not normally bite.

In broad terms, a 32.5% (25% pre-6 April 2016) tax charge may be triggered under *CTA 2010, s 459*, where:

- under arrangements made by someone,

- a close company makes a loan that is *not* within the normal *CTA 2010, s 455* charge; and

- a person (other than the close company) makes a payment to a participator (or their associate), which is *not* subject to an income tax charge (*CTA 2010, s 459(3)*).

In such cases, the loan is treated as having been made to the 'participator' under *CTA 2010, s 455.*

CTA 2010, s 459 primarily aims to catch certain 'back-to-back arrangements' – such as where a close company deposits cash with (say) a bank on the understanding that the bank will make an advance or loan to a participator of that close company. These arrangements would firmly fall within this legislation.

However, the wording of *CTA 2010, s 459* is sufficiently wide to catch ('financial assistance' type) loans made in connection with certain type of company takeover (especially management buy-out deals), as illustrated below:

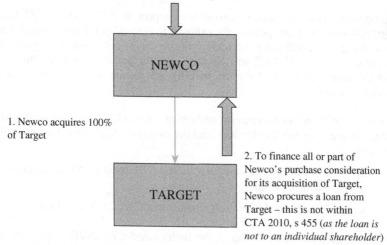

3. Newco makes a payment to the sellers of Target which is not subject to income tax in their hands (they are participators of Target since they would be on the share register of Target when the deal is completed).

NEWCO

1. Newco acquires 100% of Target

TARGET

2. To finance all or part of Newco's purchase consideration for its acquisition of Target, Newco procures a loan from Target – this is not within CTA 2010, s 455 (*as the loan is not to an individual shareholder*)

In practice, it is often possible to 'plan out' of the potential *CTA 2010, s 459* charge by arranging for Target to make an appropriate dividend to Newco (rather than a loan). The 'tax-free' dividend monies received by Newco are then used to discharge the purchase consideration payable to the sellers of Target. Since there is *no* loan to Newco, *CTA 2010, s 459* cannot apply.

HMRC continues to confirm that where the relevant conditions (as summarised above) are satisfied, it will seek to apply the *CTA 2010, s 459* provisions.

CTSA reporting obligations for *CTA 2010, ss 455* and *464A* tax

20.68   Under corporation tax self-assessment, the *CTA 2010 s 455* tax must be reported on the corporation tax return form CT600 and various details of loans made to participators, etc must be given on the supplementary page CT600A (even if the *CTA 2010, s 455* liability has been discharged by repayment or waiver). Companies that are liable to pay their corporation tax in instalments must include any anticipated or actual *CTA 2010, s 455* tax in their instalment liabilities. The same obligations also apply to any *CTA 2010, s 464A* tax (see **20.66**).

The CT600 return form must normally be submitted within 12 months from the end of the company's accounting period. Late returns attract a flat rate penalty of £100 increasing to £200 if the return is more than three months late. (These penalties become £500 and £1,000 respectively, if the company was subject to a flat penalty charge in each of its two preceding accounting periods.)

Companies must take care to ensure they report all *CTA 2010, s 455* loans correctly since they are potentially exposed to HMRC penalties. Penalties are now charged according to the underlying taxpayer behaviour that gave rise to the error. Thus, HMRC will charge a greater penalty where it can show that the understatement of the tax liability was deliberate (as opposed to an innocent error).

Penalties are based on the relevant amount of tax that has been understated, the nature of the taxpayer's behaviour and the extent of disclosure. For example, a penalty of:

- *up to 30%* will arise on any understated *CTA 2010, s 455* tax due to lack of reasonable care: or

- *up to 70%* on any deliberately understated *CTA 2010, s 455* tax.

For these purposes, in arriving at the understated *CTA 2010, s 455* tax, no reduction is made for any offset under *CTA 2010, s 458(2)* (where the loan has been subsequently repaid (see **20.56**)).

The relevant penalty would be substantially reduced where the taxpayer makes full disclosure or takes active steps to correct the mistake. No penalty should arise where the taxpayer makes a genuine mistake.

Example 20.14 – *CTA 2010, s 455* tax and interest on overdrawn director's loan

Mr Noble, a shareholder in Claret & Blue Captain Ltd (a close company), overdrew his director's loan account by £20,000 in November 2018. This amount was still outstanding at the end of the company's accounting period on 31 December 2018, although it was entirely cleared by the payment of a bonus on 30 June 2019.

The company's accounts, corporation tax computations and return form CT600 for the year ended 31 December 2018 were submitted to HMRC in September 2019.

The company must complete the supplementary page CT600A and submit it with the return. In Part 1, the company must show the loan of £20,000 made to Mr Noble during the period, but would also claim relief from the *CTA 2010, s 455* liability (in Part 2) as the loan was repaid by 30 September 2019 – ie within nine months of the end of the accounting period.

Mr Noble would also be subject to an employment income charge on the benefit of the interest-free loan. The company would also be subject to a Class 1A NIC charge on the same amount.

WAIVER OF LOANS TO SHAREHOLDERS

Income tax charge on shareholder

20.69 An income tax charge arises if the company releases or simply writes off a loan to a shareholder (or an associate of a shareholder) (*ITTOIA 2005, s 415*). The loan must be formally waived (which must be documented by a formal legal deed), as opposed to merely not being collected by the company.

Focus

Since 6 April 2016, loans formally waived or released no longer get the benefit of the 10% tax credit. Instead, the amount of the loan waived/released is taxed at the post-5 April 2016 'distribution' tax rates. The amount waived is treated as dividend income under *ITA 2007, s 19(1)(d)*. Thus, loan waivers can also benefit from the £2,000 'dividend' nil-rate band for 2018/19.

Thus, depending on the level of the shareholder's other income, the deemed 'dividend income' is taxed as the top slice of their total income in 2018/19 as shown below (ignoring the £2,000 dividend nil rate band):

Amount of loan waived/released	Tax rate applied
Up to £34,500	7.5%
£33,501 to £150,000	32.5%
More than £150,000	38.1%

Where the shareholder is a director (or an employee), the *ITTOIA 2005, s 415* charge also takes priority over any employment income tax charge on the waiver under *ITEPA 2003, s 188* (due to the statutory priority rule in *ITEPA 2003, s 188*). However, HMRC has been recently trying to assert that the waived amount should be regarded as earnings under general principles (see **20.70**)

It is fairly clear that if a waiver or release was in contemplation at the time the original 'loan' was made, then it is unlikely to be treated as a loan in the first place – there would be strong arguments for treating the payment as 'income' which would be characterised according to the underlying facts!

Provided any HMRC challenge to treat the loan waiver as 'earnings' can be successfully rebutted (see **20.70**), the loan waiver, release, or write-off should be taxed as dividend income under *ITA 2007, s 19*.

HMRC contention that amount waived is earnings

20.70   In recent times, HMRC has been trying to challenge loan waivers on the grounds that the amount waived was earnings based on basic principles within *ITEPA 2003, s 62* (as opposed to the deemed *ITEPA 2003, s 188* employment charge (see **20.69** above).

Many advisers remain unconvinced by HMRC's view on this. However, in the case of *Stewart Fraser Ltd v HMRC* [2011] UKFTT 46 (TC), the company had written off a loan to a shareholder-director. The taxpayer contended that the write-off was made in his capacity as a shareholder rather than a director, and therefore not considered to be earnings. Nevertheless HMRC successfully contended that the write-off was 'earnings' which gave rise to an NIC liability.

In giving their evidence, HMRC said that it considered that:

> 'Had they (the loans) been waived for him in his capacity as a shareholder then HMRC would have expected to see this discussed and approved at a shareholders' meeting involving all the shareholders.'

Following this useful statement, it would therefore be advisable for waivers/ write-offs of loans to participators to be approved at a general meeting of the shareholders or by an elected written resolution under *Companies Act 2006, ss 292* and *293*.

NIC treatment of loan waivers

20.71   Although the *ITTOIA 2005, s 415* charge takes precedence over the *ITEPA 2003, s 188* 'employment income' charge for income tax purposes, any such release is likely to be treated as 'earnings' for NIC purposes. 'Earnings' is widely defined for NIC purposes to include 'any remuneration or profit derived from the employment' (*SSCBA 1992, s 39(1)(a)*). HMRC's view is that given this wide coverage, the release of a director's loan would be seen as rewarding the director for services rendered and would thus be liable to Class 1 NICs.

However, following the ruling in the *Stewart Fraser* case (see **20.70** above), it may be possible to side step an NIC charge by following appropriate corporate procedures. In the *Stewart Fraser* case, the company lost its appeal that the loan write-off was made in Mr Fraser's capacity as a shareholder. The Tribunal could find no evidence for this since the *directors* had approved the write-off, not the shareholders. To demonstrate that Mr Fraser's loan had been waived in his capacity as a shareholder, HMRC would have expected to see this discussed and approved at a meeting of all the shareholders. Thus, applying this reasoning, provided a loan waiver is approved at a general meeting of the shareholders (or by a written shareholders resolution (see **20.70**)), it should be possible to avoid an NIC charge.

Clearly, if the shareholder is neither a director nor an employee, there can be no question of an NIC charge being levied on the release.

Novation of loans

20.72   The case of *Collins v Addies* [1992] STC 746 held that the novation of a shareholder loan gives rise to a release. The company had advanced loans to its two director shareholders and the company was subsequently sold. As part of the sale, the purchaser of the company agreed to take over these debts from the shareholders. Thus, their loans were novated so that the target company released the shareholders from their borrowings and the purchaser agreed to take the debts over. The purchaser eventually repaid these loans to the company. However, the court held that novation of the £68,000 debt constituted a taxable release under what is now *ITTOIA 2005, s 415*. The shareholders had argued that since the purchaser had agreed to take over their liability to the company, full consideration had been given and this was not therefore a 'release'. However, the court rejected this argument.

As illustrated by this case, the debtor (borrower) cannot assign the debt. A novation takes place under which the existing debtor is released from the debt and a new 'lender' (assignee) takes on a new debt (with the debtor). *ITTOIA 2005, s 415* will therefore catch situations where the 'creditor' company assigns (novates) the loans to someone else.

Recovery of *CTA 2010, s 455* tax

20.73   Where a loan is released or waived, the company can recover from HMRC any tax paid under *CTA 2010, s 455*. The amount is due for repayment nine months after the accounting period in which the loan is waived (see **20.66**).

Note that a loan waiver (upon which an *ITTOIA 2003, s 415* liability would arise) would enable the *CTA 2010, s 455* tax to be repaid in a 'bed and breakfasting' arrangement and the special rules in **20.63** would not apply.

Corporation tax treatment of loan waiver

20.74   A properly executed release of a loan (provided it is properly accounted for under GAAP) would reduce the amount of loan that is due to be paid which would be written-off against the company's profits.

However, the *FA 2010* introduced legislation preventing almost all owner-managed companies from claiming a loan relationship (non-trading) tax deduction for the release or write-off of a loan made to a shareholder (or associate thereof) (*CTA 2009, s 321A*). This rule (which applies to close companies) affects amounts that are written-off after 23 March 2010. Nevertheless, despite these changes, it remains possible for companies to deduct amounts written-off in respect of other loans (where the borrower is not a shareholder or one of their 'associates').

Before 24 March 2010, the loan relationship legislation (*CTA 2009, s 324(1)*) contained an apparent loophole, since it permitted relief to be claimed on the write-off of shareholder loans as well as other 'third party' loans. However, in practice, HMRC have been known to resist such claims for 'non-trading' debit relief under the loan relationship rules, contending that they are (already) blocked by various anti-avoidance provisions, such as *CTA 2009, s 444* (transactions not conducted on an arms' length basis).

Example 20.15 – *ITTOIA 2003, s 415* **tax liability on release of shareholder loan**

In June 2017, Hotspur Ltd (which is a close company) advanced an interest-free loan of £90,000 to Mr Alli, who is a 30% shareholder of the company. He does *not* work for Hotspur Ltd.

The loan remained outstanding nine months after the 31 December 2017 year end and therefore *CTA 2010, s 455* tax of £29,250 (32.5% × £90,000) was paid to HMRC on 1 October 2018.

In November 2018, the company decided to waive the £90,000 loan due from Mr Alli. Mr Alli and Hotspur Ltd entered into a formal deed to release the debt.

Hotspur Ltd

Since the company is 'close' and Mr Alli is a shareholder ('participator'), the *CTA 2009, s 321A* restriction applies to the amount written-off. Thus, the consequent loan relationship debit of £90,000 is not deductible for corporation tax purposes.

The *CTA 2010, s 455* tax of £29,250 also becomes repayable (which must be claimed), being due for repayment on 1 October 2019, ie nine months after the end of the accounting period in which the loan is waived – the year ended 31 December 2018.

Mr Alli

Assuming Mr Alli's total income (including the waiver) exceeds £150,000, his *ITTOIA 2005, s 415* charge in 2018/19 will be as follows:

	£
Amount waived *less* dividend 'nil-rate' band (£90,000 – £2,000)	88,000
Tax at 38.1%	33,528

It is important to note that if Mr Alli were a *director or employee* of Hotspur Ltd, the *ITTOIA 2005, s 415* charge would still prevail, but HMRC would also seek to impose a Class 1 NIC charge. Recently HMRC has contended that amounts of loans waived should be treated as earnings under *ITEPA 2003, s 62* – see **20.70** above.

BENEFITS IN KIND TO NON-WORKING SHAREHOLDERS

20.75

> **Focus**
>
> Certain expenses or benefits provided to a close company shareholder (or an associate of a shareholder) are treated as a distribution under *CTA 2010, s 1064*. Without these special provisions it would be possible to provide benefits to a non-working shareholder on a tax-free basis.

This 'deemed distribution' treatment does not apply where the expense or benefit is already taxed under the employment income rules in *ITEPA 2003*. Consequently, in practice, these rules would effectively apply to non-working shareholders being provided with living accommodation and other benefits or services (to the extent that they are not made good by the shareholder or their associate). These rules do not include pensions or lump sums payable on death or retirement.

The value of the distribution is taken to be the same amount that would have applied if the amount had been treated as an employment-related benefit. The recipient shareholder would be taxed on this amount in accordance with the relevant 'dividend taxation' rules.

The amount of the 'distribution' cannot be deducted against profits for corporation tax purposes

If a non-working shareholder was provided with a car, the distribution would be based on the scale benefit charge. This would not be the same figure as the depreciation and running costs that would have to be disallowed in calculating the company's taxable profits (since being incurred for a non-working shareholder, they would not generally be for the purposes of the trade).

APPENDIX – PLANNING CHECKLIST

20.76

> **PLANNING CHECKLIST – STRATEGIES FOR EXTRACTING FUNDS FROM THE COMPANY**
>
> **Company**
>
> - The extraction of funds is often influenced by the company's cash flow and working capital position.

- Where appropriate, shareholders can loan funds back to the company to restore liquidity and provide working capital.

- Dividend payments can easily be timed for optimum income tax efficiency in the hands of the shareholder(s).

- Corporate tax relief for bonuses can be effectively back-dated by making provision in the statutory accounts under the nine-month rule. However, care must be taken to ensure such provisions also comply with FRS 102/FRS 105.

Working shareholders

- Generally require a sensible mix of remuneration/bonuses and dividends. Adopting a profit extraction model of 'low salary/high dividends will often be tax-efficient.

- Some owner-managers wish to extract surplus cash funds from the company to remove them from any further business risk.

- To avoid high income tax rates on substantial salaries and bonuses, owner-managers could consider providing 'cheap' loans from the company. Such loans would only suffer employment tax at 1%/1.12% (ie official rate 2.5% × 40%/45%) for a complete tax year. The loans can be repaid when appropriate, although a *CTA 2010, s 455* charge will also arise if the loans are not repaid within nine months of the company year-end in which they were made.

- A *CTA 2010, s 455* liability is now likely to be triggered where an owner managed company makes a loan to a 'related' partnership or LLP (even where it is being made for genuine trading purposes). Similarly, a *CTA 2010, s 455* charge may also arise on loans to the trustees of a 'connected' trust.

- To avoid having to discount the value of directors' loan accounts under FRS 102, it is recommended to make the loans repayable on demand.

- The 'bed and breakfasting' of *CTA 2010, s 455* loans is not effective as a means of avoiding the *CTA 2010, s 455* tax or securing its repayment. However, these rules can enable the *CTA 2010, s 455* tax to be avoided/repaid where the loan account is cleared by means of a taxable bonus, dividend (or waiver of the loan).

- Owner-managers should consider bringing their loan accounts into credit by paying a dividend or 'large' bonus early in the tax year, thus enabling amounts to be drawn at a later date with no tax repercussions or RTI issues.

- It may be possible to avoid incurring Class 1 NICs on the waiver of directors overdrawn loan accounts by ensuring that this is approved at a general meeting of all the shareholders (or by a shareholders' written resolution).

- Dividends still remain attractive for shareholders who are only liable to lower or basic rate income tax. A small salary is usually worthwhile to provide a 'credit' for state pension purposes.

- Owner-managers can mitigate income tax on their earnings to the extent that they are paid out as pension contributions. Income tax relief for pension contributions is subject to the annual £40,000 'annual allowance' restriction. Also take into account any potential unused relief from the previous three years.

- Where the company's trading premises are personally owned by the controlling shareholder, it may be desirable to sell them to the company to obtain a tax-efficient extraction of cash.

Other employees

- Employees generally look for good remuneration packages with tax-efficient benefits (although there is now an increasing preference for cash).

- In appropriate cases, an incentive-based bonus scheme should be considered.

Non-working shareholders

- Dividends are much more tax-efficient as the company cannot claim tax relief for 'remuneration', particularly for non-working spouses. However, some care must be exercised to avoid the dividend being taxed on the owner-manager(s) under the settlement legislation.

- Consider paying pension contributions of up to £2,808 net (tax relief of up to £792 is added at source by HMRC) for non-working shareholders.

Chapter 21

Capital allowances on property transactions

Martin Wilson MA FCA
Adam Garrad BSc ATT MRICS
The Capital Allowances Partnership Ltd

SIGNPOSTS

- **Overview of capital allowances** – On a sale and purchase of property, the default position is that any capital allowances available will transfer across from seller to buyer. However, the amount transferred can be difficult to ascertain, and must comply with strict statutory rules which will in most cases require specialist advice (see **21.1–21.2**).

- **Calculation of expenditure on fixtures** – Statute prescribes that the amount allocated to fixtures, to be used by both seller and buyer in their tax returns, must be ascertained either by a just and reasonable apportionment under the *Capital Allowances Act 2001* (*CAA 2001*), *s 562* or by a joint election under *s 198* or *199* (see **21.3–21.10**).

- **Fixed value requirement** – Where a seller has claimed allowances on fixtures, the amount allocated to those fixtures on a sale must be supported by satisfying the fixed value requirement, which requires either a *s 198/s 199* election or a determination by the tax tribunal (see **21.11–21.15**).

- **Section 198 elections** – These elections can be useful, but they are not the panacea sometimes suggested. Very often they are misunderstood by both taxpayers and their advisers, and there are dangers inherent in relying on them, particularly for purchasers (see **21.16–21.22**).

- **Tribunal applications** – Taxpayers may be wary of applying to a tribunal, fearful of costs and the complexity of the system. However, a tribunal determination can be more easily and cheaply obtained than is often thought, and for purchasers in particular might give a better result than a *s 198/s 199* election (see **21.23–21.26**).

- **Mandatory pooling** – If the seller could have claimed allowances on fixtures, but has not done so, the buyer will only be able to claim allowances if the seller first pools the relevant expenditure. The allowances would then be passed on to the buyer, usually at the same amount (see **21.27–21.31**).

- **Consequences of failure to comply** – Failure to comply with the fixed value requirement or the mandatory pooling requirement will have dire consequences. The seller will likely face a clawback of any allowances he has ever claimed on the relevant fixtures, and the buyer will be unable to claim allowances going forward (see **21.32–21.36**).

- **Best practice for seller** – A seller may be able to effectively retain any capital allowances despite selling the property, or could face a major tax charge. Using this checklist will help to optimise the seller's tax position (see **21.37–21.38**).

- **Best practice for buyer** – A buyer should in most cases be entitled to claim capital allowances, but does need to comply with relevant legislation. Using this checklist will help to optimise the buyer's tax position (see **21.39–21.40**).

- **Contract clauses** – It is best practice to ensure that capital allowances are discussed in pre-contract enquiries and for appropriate clauses to be included in the sale and purchase contract. (see **21.41–21.47**).

OVERVIEW OF CAPITAL ALLOWANCES

21.1   Capital allowances are now generally only available on plant and machinery, which includes fixtures.

This work assumes a basic understanding of capital allowances on the part of the reader. For a detailed and comprehensive study, see the latest edition of *Capital Allowances: Transactions and Planning* by Martin Wilson and Steven Bone (Bloomsbury Professional).

The term 'plant and machinery' covers a wide variety of fixtures. Some are defined by statute, including (*CAA 2001, s 33A*)

- electrical systems (including lighting systems);

- cold water systems;

- space or water heating systems (ie heating and hot water), powered systems of ventilation, air cooling or air purification (ie mechanical ventilation and air conditioning);

- lifts, escalators and moving walkways; and

- external solar shading (ie *brise soleil*).

Others have been treated as plant by case law and long-standing practice. These include

- alarms;

- telephone and data systems;

- carpeting;

- door furniture;

- fixed furniture;

- fire protection systems;

- sanitary ware; and

- signage.

However, many other items will qualify, and it is sometimes easier to define plant and machinery by what it is not, ie land and buildings (ie 'bricks and mortar').

Currently, the first £200,000 of expenditure on plant in a year may be written off immediately through capital allowances, with any excess qualifying at either 8% (the first bulleted list above) or 18% (all other plant) per annum on a pooled, reducing balance basis.

21.2 On a sale and purchase of property, the default position is that any capital allowances available will transfer across from seller to buyer. However, the amount transferred can be difficult to ascertain, and must comply with strict statutory rules which will in most cases require specialist advice.

The default is a just and reasonable apportionment under *CAA 2001, s 562*, essentially a fair value apportionment of the total purchase price (see **21.5–21.7**). However, this can be bypassed if both seller and buyer agree an election under *CAA 2001, s 198* (see **21.16–21.22**).

Additional rules (described by HMRC as 'administrative requirements') apply where the seller has claimed, or was entitled to claim, allowances on fixtures. These are the fixed value requirement (see **21.11–21.15**) and the pooling requirement (see **21.27–21.31**).

The rules are complicated, and both sellers and buyers may be advised to take specialist advice and insert appropriate clauses into the sale and purchase agreement (see **21.41–21.47**).

CALCULATION OF EXPENDITURE ON FIXTURES

General principles

21.3 When a building is purchased second-hand, the buyer will be acquiring not only a shell building, but also any plant elements contained therein. This will include not just things that are obviously machinery, but also 'integral features' such as air conditioning or heating, and other plant and machinery fixtures.

It is possible for the purchaser to claim capital allowances on such plant. To the extent that such items are fixtures, they are treated as belonging to the purchaser of the building (*CAA 2001, s 181*).

Focus

The default position is that such a claim will be based on a 'just and reasonable' apportionment of the total purchase consideration, in accordance with *s 562* (which operates by default in the absence of a *s 198* joint election – see **21.16–21.23**). The intention is to apportion the purchase price to reflect the value that each constituent part makes to the value of the whole property (*Salts v Battersby* [1910] 2 KB 155). An apportionment is usually prepared using the VOA's formula approach (see **21.16**), which was endorsed by the First-tier Tribunal in *Bowerswood House Retirement Home Ltd v HMRC Comrs* [2015] UKFTT 0094 (TC).

In some circumstances, the amount will be restricted to whatever amount is properly brought into account as disposal proceeds by the vendor (*CAA 2001, s 185*). That said, it must nonetheless be emphasised that the matter is not entirely in the hands of the vendor because it is not the vendor's prerogative to unilaterally choose a disposal value (for example, tax written-down value), and the purchaser is not bound to accept the vendor's apportionment, however unfair that may be.

Furthermore, in the absence of an election under *s 198* (see **21.16–21.22**), the Inspector is not bound by any apportionment agreed between the parties and reflected in the purchase contract (*Fitton v Gilders and Heaton (Inspector of Taxes)* (1955) 36 TC 233; *Tapsell (Mr and Mrs) and Lester (Mr) (trading as Partnership 'The Granleys') v HMRC Comrs* [2011] UKFTT 376 (TC)).

Fixed value requirement

21.4 With effect from April 2012, where the vendor (or an earlier owner since April 2012) has pooled qualifying expenditure on plant or machinery fixtures, *CAA 2001, s 187A* makes the availability of capital allowances to a purchaser of fixtures conditional on the value of fixtures being established formally within two years of a transfer (the 'fixed value requirement'). This is generally satisfied either by making an election under *s 198* (see **21.16–21.22**) or by making a just apportionment then applying to the Tribunal for ratification (see **21.23–21.26**).

Apportionment methodology

21.5   The method of apportioning costs to determine qualifying expenditure is not prescribed by statute. It is, therefore, a matter for negotiation between the taxpayer, his advisers and HMRC. In accordance with the decision in *Salts v Battersby* [1910] 2 KB 155, the underlying aim of any method of apportionment should be to apportion the purchase price in proportion to the values of the constituent parts that go to make up the property.

Simply deducting a value for the land is not sufficient (*Bostock v Totham* (*Inspector of Taxes*) [1997] STC 764).

Similarly, in *Bowerswood House Retirement Home Ltd v HMRC Comrs* [2015] UKFTT 94 (TC), the taxpayer calculated an open market value for the land, and a new-build replacement cost for the qualifying assets (both at the actual purchase date) and simply deducted these from the total purchase price for the property to leave a balancing figure for the non-qualifying building expenditure. The tribunal considered this approach was flawed because it did not identify the value of all assets purchased on the same basis, and so was not a 'just and reasonable apportionment' as required by *CAA 2001, s 562*. The tribunal accepted that the VOA's preferred apportionment formula had been used extensively over many years in the context, and the tribunal was satisfied that it gave a just and reasonable result.

21.6   The VOA has expressed a preference for the following formula, which is almost always used in practice (VOA Manual, para 3.31):

$$Q = P \times (A/(B + C))$$

Where

Q = qualifying expenditure

A = the replacement cost of the qualifying assets

B = the replacement cost of the building (including plant content)

C = the land value (ie bare site value)

P = purchase consideration

The apportionment formula can have a significant impact on the value of a claim.

21.7

Example 21.1 – Just and reasonable apportionment

E Ltd acquired an office building for £40m in such circumstances that any expenditure qualifying for allowances was to be established by a just apportionment under *s 562*. Specialist capital allowances consultants determined the market/replacement values of the various components as follows:

Land	£5 million (C)
Building	£50 million (B)
Plant therein	£20 million (A)

The VOA formula gives the following qualifying expenditure.

Qualifying expenditure = £40 million × 20/(50 + 5) = 14.5 million

---

21.8   The VOA Manuals include a number of helpful instructions affecting the method of apportionment. They confirm (para 3.31) that plant ('A' in the formula) does not need to be written down due to its age, as age and obsolescence will be reflected in the purchase price. An exception is that if the purchase price is based 'largely or wholly' on the value of the land then the obsolete nature of the building will not be reflected in that price and it may be necessary to adjust the replacement costs for obsolescence (para 3.35).

21.9   The bare site ('C') should be taken as the open market value of the actual site at the date of purchase valued on the assumption that:

(i)   any reclamation works which have been carried out on the site which permanently enhance the value of the land should be included (eg removing underground obstructions or treating contamination);

(ii)   the valuation reflects the circumstances existing at the valuation date; and

(iii)   the interest valued will be the interest actually acquired (eg if a long leasehold, taking account of ground rent).

Presumably, where appropriate the assumptions will also still include the following factors listed in a previous version of the manual:

(iv)   the site is cleared of all building and external works;

(v)   access and services are available up to the boundary; and

(vi)   planning permission is available for the existing type of development (para 3.33).

21.10   The replacement costs used in the formula ('A' and 'B') should be taken as the estimated cost of replacing the building if work had commenced at the appropriate time as to have the building available for occupation at the date of purchase. It should include: (i) site works, but not any reclamation works which permanently enhance the value of the bare land; (ii) the cost of external works; (iii) professional fees; and (iv) finance charges (para 3.66).

FIXED VALUE REQUIREMENT

Additional rule from 2012

Focus

A new rule was introduced with effect from April 2012, where either the vendor or a previous earlier owner since April 2012 has pooled qualifying expenditure on plant or machinery fixtures.

In such circumstances, *CAA 2001, s 187A* makes the availability of capital allowances to a purchaser conditional on the value of fixtures being established formally within two years of a transfer (the 'fixed value requirement').

21.11   There is an alternative method of fixing the value that applies only in cases where an intermediate owner, who was not entitled to claim an allowance (such as a charity or pension fund), had failed to determine a fixtures apportionment with the past owner. It should be appreciated that until April 2014, when the pooling requirement took effect (see **21.27–21.31**), the new rules only applied where a relevant prior owner had pooled qualifying expenditure on the fixtures. If expenditure had not been pooled, the rules were initially unaffected.

When this rule applies

21.12   *Section 187A(1)* sets out the circumstances in which the new rules apply. They apply if:

● a buyer incurs capital expenditure on acquiring a property containing fixtures from another person (the seller), for the purposes of the buyer's business;

- the seller, or a previous owner, owned the fixtures at a relevant earlier time (see *s 187B(4)*) as a result of incurring expenditure on them for business purposes; and

- the seller, or a previous owner, pooled qualifying expenditure on plant or machinery in respect of the historic expenditure.

However, the new section does *not* apply if the previous owner was only entitled to relief by virtue of the contributions legislation in *CAA 2001, s 538*. The provisions also do not apply if the past owner was not entitled to claim plant and machinery allowances because they had already claimed industrial buildings allowances instead.

The key point here is that *s 187A* only applies if the seller, or a previous owner in the *relevant period* (effectively the period since the commencement of these rules in April 2012), had claimed plant and machinery allowances on the fixtures. It is therefore crucial to establish, for example through pre-contract enquiries, whether this is in fact the case. From April 2014, the rules are extended to situations where the seller could have claimed, whether they did so or not (see **21.27–21.31**).

Failure to comply

21.13   *Section 187A(3)* provides that the new owner's expenditure on fixtures qualifying for allowances is to be treated as nil if the 'fixed value requirement' applies but is not satisfied, or the 'disposal value statement requirement' (see below) applies but is not satisfied.

So, in all cases to which this section applies, one or other of the 'value' requirements will apply and must be satisfied if the purchaser is to claim allowances.

In practice, the 'fixed value requirement' will apply in the vast majority of cases and the 'disposal value statement requirement' is likely only to apply very infrequently. The disposal value statement requirement applies in circumstances where an election is not permitted and statute imposes disposal proceeds calculated as an apportionment of market value. For example, the transfer of property by means of a dividend in specie which is not a sale and the interest continues or is merged into another and, therefore, dealt with by *CAA 2001, s 196(1), table item 3*.

If either requirement is not met, neither the purchaser nor any future owner of those fixtures will be able to claim allowances. In the first instance, the purchaser's qualifying expenditure is deemed to be nil. On a subsequent sale, the new owner's claim will be restricted to the seller's disposal value under

CAA 2001, s 185 – because the seller's claim cannot exceed nil, his disposal value will also be limited to nil.

Satisfying the requirement

21.14 The 'fixed value' requirement applies where the past owner (that is, the current seller) is or has been required to bring the disposal value of the plant or machinery into account, and is met when one of two outcomes occurs. That is, either:

- 'a relevant apportionment of the apportionable sum has been made'; or

- the current owner has obtained certain statements where the property is acquired from someone other than 'the past owner' (the rare exception).

Section 187A(7) explains that a relevant apportionment is made if:

- a tribunal has determined the part of the sale price that constitutes the disposal value of the fixtures, on an application made by one of the affected parties within two years of the purchaser's acquisition (see **21.24–21.27**); or

- there has been a joint election, under either *CAA 2001, s 198* or *199*, as appropriate, between the past owner and the purchaser within two years of the acquisition (see **21.16–21.22**).

Focus

The overwhelming majority of commercial property transactions involving second-hand fixtures should involve a relevant apportionment, so that there will be the requirement for a reference to the tribunal, or for a joint election to be made, within two years of a sale. It must be emphasised that if this requirement is not met, the purchaser will obtain no allowances.

However, the seller must still account for disposal proceeds under the underlying legislation, possibly giving rise to a tax charge (*s 187B(6)*).

21.15

Example 21.2 – Failure to meet fixed value requirement

In 2009, Mr A bought fixtures in a property and claims an annual investment allowance in the amount of £100,000 (so the tax written-down value of

---

those fixtures is nil). After April 2012 he sells the property to B Limited and the fixtures are valued at £150,000.

The default position is that Mr A should account for disposal proceeds of £100,000 (actual proceeds, limited to original cost) and B Limited should be entitled to claim allowances on £100,000 (it paid more, but its claim is limited to the disposal value brought into account by the seller). This could be varied using a *s 198* election so that the seller retains more, or even all, of the allowances.

Because the sale takes place after April 2012, *s 187A* requires the fixtures value to be set in writing, either by a *s 198* election or by an application to the Tribunal for ratification.

If this is not done, then B Limited will be unable to claim allowances (its expenditure is deemed to be nil) but Mr A must still account for disposal proceeds of £100,000. As the tax written-down value of those fixtures is nil, A Limited potentially faces a balancing charge of £100,000 which could give rise to an immediate tax charge at up to 45%.

SECTION 198 ELECTIONS

Apportionment of consideration

Focus

As an alternative to a full just apportionment under *CAA 2001, s 562*, the parties to a property sale may jointly elect to fix the amount to be allocated to fixtures (*s 198*). Where a new lease is granted, the election may be made between lessor and lessee. In this case the election is under *s 199* but is otherwise identical to a *s 198* election.

21.16 The amount agreed under the election is limited to the original cost of those fixtures pooled by the seller. Obviously, if the total sale price (ie the price of the entire property, not just the fixtures) is less than the original cost of the fixtures, then the amount apportioned cannot exceed that.

There is no specified lower limit. In the Court of Appeal in *Revenue and Customs Comrs v Apollo Fuels Ltd and others* [2016] EWCA Civ 157, it was held (at [82]) that:

'Nil is not a number or an amount. It is a cipher of no value. There may, of course, be circumstances where the context in which the word "amount" is used indicates that it is to include nil.'

Within *CAA 2001* the context suggests that nil can be an amount for capital allowances disposal purposes. For example, *s 187A* stipulates that if the pooling, fixed value or disposal value statement requirements apply but are not satisfied, then the taxpayer's qualifying expenditure is nil. Therefore, it would seem permissible for a joint election to be made in the amount of nil, although £1 or £2 would be more normal in practice and would avoid the danger of the taxpayer inadvertently omitting to account for that nil disposal value in its tax return (by failing to visibly subtract the amount of nil from the relevant pool, or pools).

Form of election

21.17   The irrevocable election must be made jointly within two years after the date of the relevant transaction, and must include:

(a)   the names and Unique Taxpayer References (UTR) of both parties (from April 2012 where a party does not have a UTR the election should say so (*FA 2012, Sch 10, para 4; CAA 2001, s 201(3)(f)*));

(b)   sufficient information to identify both the relevant land (to which the fixtures are attached) and the machinery or plant;

(c)   details of the interest acquired; and

(d)   the amount fixed by the election (which must be quantified at the time the election is made (*s 201(2)*).

If an application has been made to the Tax Chamber of the First-tier Tribunal in time (see **21.23–21.26**), but has not been determined or has been withdrawn, and the parties to sale reach agreement, an election may be accepted even though the normal time limit has passed (*s 201(1A)*).

21.18   A formal election is the only way to guarantee an agreed apportionment at the outset (subject to it not being rejected by HMRC for technical reasons, such as not being submitted in time or deficient drafting: see **21.20–21.23**) – it is not sufficient that an apportionment is included in the purchase contract, as such an apportionment is not binding on HMRC (*Fitton v Gilders and Heaton (Inspector of Taxes)* (1955) 36 TC 233; *Tapsell (Mr and Mrs) and Lester (Mr) (trading as Partnership 'The Granleys') v HMRC Comrs* [2011] UKFTT 376 (TC)).

In most practical situations, it will *not* be to the purchaser's advantage to enter into an election, rather than rely on the default 'just apportionment' provisions of *CAA 2001, s 562*. Professional advice should be sought whenever a *s 198* election is proposed by the vendor.

Multiple properties

21.19 HMRC will accept a single election covering all the fixtures in a single property (but not multiple properties) – CA, para 26850. In practice, where an amount has been agreed between vendor and purchaser covering several properties, HMRC will accept an apportionment between the properties on a reasonable basis, such as book value or floor area.

In the context of an election covering all the fixtures in a property, the HMRC Capital Allowances Manual CA, para 26850 states:

> 'The fixtures rules work on an asset-by-asset basis. In practice, you may accept a degree of amalgamation of assets where this will not distort the tax computation. Provided that there are no specific factors which could give rise to distortion, you may accept an election covering all the fixtures in a particular property but not for a portfolio of properties.'

It is unclear what is meant by the term 'distortion'. It is arguable that distortion of 'the tax computation' does take place where the amount allocated to fixtures by an election under *s 198* is clearly insufficient, in that it bears no relation to the amount which has actually been paid for those fixtures, for example where an election for £1 covers assets clearly worth millions.

Distortion may also be relevant where the plant acquired consists of both integral features and other plant, and the election fails to allocate separate amounts to each.

Common errors in *s 198* elections

Focus

In practice, many elections appear to be technically invalid, for a variety of reasons.

Error (1) – including assets on which the seller has not claimed allowances

21.20 It is explicitly stated that the *CAA 2001, s 198* legislation applies 'if the disposal value of a fixture is required to be brought into account', which can only be the case if the vendor has claimed allowances on the fixtures concerned (*CAA 2001, s 64*). Some *s 198* elections purport to be made in cases where the vendor has not claimed allowances (for example, where the seller is a developer holding the property as trading stock, and therefore clearly not eligible for capital allowances, or where the seller was eligible to claim, but has confirmed in replies to pre-contract enquiries that he has not done so).

It is of the greatest importance to realise that an election under *s 198* can only cover plant on which the vendor has claimed allowances. The purchaser may still be able to claim allowances on an 'unrestricted' basis on other items of plant which were not identified as such by the vendor, and are in consequence not covered by the election.

Error (2) – failure to include the required information

21.21   *Section CAA 2001, s 201* sets out certain information which a *s 198* election *must* contain, including:

(a)   the amount fixed by the election (which must be quantified at the time the election is made: *s 201(2)*);

(b)   the name of each party to the election;

(c)   information sufficient to identify the plant or machinery;

(d)   information sufficient to identify the relevant land;

(e)   particulars of the interest being acquired (and the date of the transaction); and

(f)   the UTR of each party to the election (from April 2012, where a party does not have a UTR the election should say so (*FA 2012, Sch 10, para 4*; *CAA 2001, s 201(3)(f)*)).

Nothing in the legislation requires the election to be signed. It simply must be a joint election, so any evidence of agreement should suffice, such as being a contractual obligation within a sale and purchase agreement for a property, or the fact that both parties have submitted a copy of the election to HMRC.

Some of the required information is often omitted, with the result that the election may arguably be invalid. For example, an inspector would seem to be within his rights if he rejected an election which failed to give the tax reference numbers of each party.

With the introduction of the 'fixed value requirement' (see **21.11–21.15**) and the 'pooling requirement (see **21.27–21.31**) it is increasingly likely that HMRC will reject invalid elections, as to do so may mean that allowances are entirely clawed back from sellers, but denied to purchasers. Taxpayers would be unwise to rely on poorly worded elections, just because they have been accepted in the past. The drafting of elections presents a major risk to professional advisers, and capital allowances specialists should be involved.

Error (3) – failure to adequately identify the fixtures

21.22   The requirement presenting the greatest practical difficulty appears to be the obligation for 'information sufficient to identify the plant or machinery'. In a great many cases, the lack of detail could arguably invalidate the whole election. The following are the problems most commonly seen.

(1)   Many elections refer simply to 'all the fixtures at the property', 'all fixed plant and machinery', or equivalent wording. This either purports that a perfect capital allowances claim has been made, covering every conceivable qualifying item (which is improbable), or there must be serious doubt (apparently shared by HMRC) whether this is sufficient to identify the plant or machinery which is purportedly subject to the election.

(2)   Some elections merely refer to a standard list of fixtures which may be typically found in a building (normally with no values against any of the descriptions), but which may or may not be present in the actual property which is the subject of the election. Again, this is insufficient to identify the plant or machinery which is purportedly subject to the election. For example, some elections have listed a lift among the items of plant, when no lift actually existed.

(3)   Some elections in effect combine the two points above by referring to 'all the fixtures at the property, including but not limited to' the assets shown on an attached standard list. It is difficult to see how such terminology can be consistent with the legislation.

(4)   Some elections refer to an inventory of fixtures and fittings, which typically includes both fixtures and chattels. *Section 198* can only relate to fixtures. Therefore, if an election purports to relate to fixtures and chattels (with no separate amounts allocated), the entire election would appear to be invalid. This is because the legislation states that the amount fixed by an election must be quantified at the time the election is made. Where the amount allocated to the fixtures (rather than the chattels) is not clear, the amount cannot be said to be fixed.

(5)   When elections refer to 'all fixtures at a property', they often do so without considering whether or not the fixtures concerned have been subject to a claim. Frequently, allowances will only have been claimed on some of the fixtures, in which case, the election is invalid, as to the extent that it relates to assets which have not been subject to a claim, no disposal value is required to be brought into account.

(6)   The election sometimes claims to cover assets that appear to be ineligible (broadly, assets which are not accepted as plant), in which case it is clearly invalid. It should also be remembered that an election under *s 198* relates only to fixtures, and not to movable plant (that is, chattels).

If an election purports to relate to both eligible assets and ineligible assets (with no separate amounts allocated), the entire election would again appear to be invalid, as the amount fixed by the election (for qualifying assets) has not been quantified at the time the election is made.

TRIBUNAL APPLICATIONS

A means of satisfying *section 187A*

21.23 Since April 2012, *s 187A* has required both buyers and sellers of property to fix the value attributed to fixtures by determining a 'relevant apportionment of the apportionable sum' (*CAA 2001, s 187A(7)*).

Focus

This means that:

- either party must prepare an apportionment under *CAA 2001, s 562* then apply to the Tax Chamber of the First-tier Tribunal in order to ratify the amount (*CAA 2001, s 187A(7)(a)*); or

- the parties must enter into a *s 198* election to agree disposal value of the fixtures subject to capital allowances (*CAA 2001, s 187A(7)(b)*).

The time limit for both the above alternatives is two years from the date of completion of the property transfer.

The Tribunal process – overview

21.24 Most taxpayers are reluctant to go before any court or tribunal. However, the application for a determination under *CAA 2001, s 187* is meant to be a relatively informal process. It is generally paper-based (ie no hearing); if there is a formal hearing, it will, in most cases, be straightforward. The Tribunal is used to hearing accountants and self-represented litigants – there will rarely be any need to employ a barrister or even a solicitor. The time and costs should therefore be modest.

The Tribunal determines the facts (and can only find on basis of evidence presented). Documentation is therefore key.

Applications under *s 187* are dealt with by the Tax Chamber of First-tier Tribunal (which is not strictly a court). It is, of course, independent of government or HMRC, and is made up of a Tribunal panel, including a Tribunal judge and in some cases a tax expert, plus a Tribunal clerk.

The process is governed by the *Tribunal Procedure (First-tier Tribunal) (Tax Chamber) Rules 2009, SI 2009/273* (see: www.gov.uk/tax-tribunal).

Relevant Practice Directions and Practice Statements are available at www. judiciary.gov.uk/publications/.

Application

21.25   Either the buyer or seller must start proceedings by written application. There is no official form to complete, so the application will take the form of a letter, or more probably a formal report and covering letter. This should show:

- name and address of party (and representative – if any);

- address where documents can be sent;

- name and address of other party;

- the reason for making the application, referring to *CAA 2001, s 187*;

- relevant facts;

- the desired result.

The application must be made within two years of completion, and it is recommended to use a postal method which provides proof of delivery.

The Tribunal will invite the other party to join the proceedings (if they wish to do so), so it is not possible for one party to obtain a Tribunal determination without the other party knowing! The Tribunal may invite HMRC to be joined as party (or HMRC can ask to be joined, or simply to submit evidence). The Tribunal will supply both the other party and HMRC with a copy of the application – provided this properly applies the law, experience shows that HMRC rarely wishes to become involved.

The fixed value requirement is satisfied when the Tribunal determines the seller's disposal value.

It is determined on the 'balance of probabilities' (ie is it more than 50% likely), not on the 'beyond reasonable doubt' burden of absolute proof.

Documentation is key, the Tribunal determines the facts and can only find on the basis of the evidence presented.

Appeals against decisions are limited to questions of law (not questions of fact).

Determination

21.26   The two-year deadline relates only to the application to the Tribunal; there is no formal deadline for the Tribunal to determine the issue.

If an application to the Tribunal has been made, the normal two-year deadline for making a *s 198* election is extended until Tribunal application is determined or withdrawn. Consequently, it may be possible to use the Tribunal as a way of eliciting information from an uncooperative seller and encouraging the seller to enter into a *s 198* election.

Alternatively, because an election may be rejected, some taxpayers may wish to consider having 'two strings to their bow'. They may wish to submit a 'protective' Tribunal application (running in tandem with election). Then, if HMRC reject the election, they are still (provided the Tribunal application has not been determined) within the extended deadline for correcting it.

MANDATORY POOLING

Additional rule from 2014 – the 'pooling requirement'

Focus

With effect from April 2014, *CAA 2001, s 187A* makes the availability of capital allowances to a purchaser of fixtures further conditional on previous business expenditure on qualifying fixtures being pooled before a subsequent transfer on to that new purchaser (the 'pooling requirement'). This is in addition to the 'fixed value requirement' in **21.11–21.15** above.

21.27   *Section 187A(1)* sets out the circumstances in which the new rules apply. They apply if:

- a buyer incurs capital expenditure on acquiring a property containing fixtures from another person (the seller) for the purposes of his business;

- the seller, or a previous owner, owned the fixtures at a relevant earlier time (see *s 187B(4)*) as a result of incurring expenditure on them for business purposes; and

- the seller, or a previous owner, was entitled to claim plant and machinery allowances (PMAs) in respect of the historic expenditure.

Could the seller have claimed?

21.28   The key point here is that *s 187A* now applies if the seller, or a previous owner in the relevant period (effectively the period since the commencement of these rules in April 2012), was *entitled* to claim allowances on the fixtures (eg the seller is an owner-occupier or investor subject to UK tax). It is therefore crucial to establish, for example through pre-contract enquiries, whether this is in fact the case. It is worth emphasising that, from April 2014, these rules apply where the seller *could have* claimed; before then, they applied only where the seller had, in fact, pooled qualifying expenditure.

The pooling requirement does not apply in circumstances where the seller was not entitled to claim. Generally, it will not apply for the following reasons:

- the asset is a chattel (the pooling requirement only applies to fixtures);

- the seller's expenditure was not capital (eg a builder or property dealer);

- the seller was not carrying on a qualifying activity (eg a house owner selling a home to a business);

- the seller is not within the scope of UK income or corporation tax and capital allowances (eg councils, charities, pension funds);

- the seller's expenditure was not accepted as being in respect of plant and machinery.

An example of the last-mentioned will be expenditure on cold water systems, general electrical and lighting systems, and external solar shading, where the seller incurred expenditure prior to April 2008. Before that date, such items were not regarded as plant and machinery, but would now qualify as integral features. Such assets are not caught by the fixed value and pooling requirements.

Failure to comply

21.29   *Section 187A(3)* provides that the new owner's expenditure on fixtures qualifying for allowances is to be treated as nil if (from April 2014) the 'pooling requirement' is not satisfied.

So, in all cases to which this new section applies, the pooling requirement must be satisfied. Of course, once the expenditure has been pooled, the sale will be one to which one or other of the 'value' requirements will also apply (see **21.13**).

Timing

21.30 The 'pooling requirement' is that the historic expenditure must have been allocated to a pool in a chargeable period beginning on or before the day on which the past owner ceased to own the fixture, or the past owner claimed a first-year allowance on the expenditure (or any part of it).

Consequently, where this rule applies, a property purchaser will only be able to claim allowances on fixtures if the seller has claimed (or at least pooled the expenditure, whether or not allowances were actually claimed). In practice, pooling requires the expenditure to have been included in a tax return. Where it is essential to demonstrate that this has been done, it would be prudent to refer to the relevant expenditure in the 'white space' for other information on the return.

HMRC guidance on *CAA 2001, ss 187A* and *187B* is not in its capital allowances manual but can be found in 'Plant and Machinery: Allowances on Fixtures When There's a Change of Ownership' at www.gov.uk/guidance/plant-and-machinery-allowances-on-fixtures-when-theres-a-change-of-ownership.

21.31

Example 21.3 – The pooling requirement

A Limited sells a property to B Limited. Their advisers complete form CPSE.1 (pre-contract enquiries) and disclose that they have never claimed capital allowances on fixtures.

B Limited now needs to consider whether A Limited could have claimed allowances (ie did it meet the criteria to do so) even though no claim was actually made. If the answer is yes (ie A Limited carries on a qualifying activity and incurred capital expenditure on fixtures), then B Limited can claim capital allowances, but only by getting A Limited to satisfy the pooling requirement.

Normally, B Limited would commission specialist capital allowances advisers to prepare a claim based on A Limited's original expenditure. The amount of that claim would then be pooled by A Limited (referred to in a tax return) and would then in most cases be reflected in a *s 198* election.

If these steps are not followed, B Limited will not be able to claim capital allowances on those fixtures. A Limited is in the same position whether these steps are followed or not (ie it has not and will not claim allowances).

CONSEQUENCES OF FAILING TO COMPLY

Buyers

21.32 *CAA 2001, s 187A(3)* provides that the new owner's expenditure on fixtures qualifying for allowances is to be treated as nil if (from April 2014) the 'pooling requirement' (see **21.27–21.31**) is not satisfied.

So, in all cases to which this new section applies, the pooling requirement must be satisfied.

The pooling requirement does not apply if it would have been impossible for the seller to pool the relevant expenditure. Common reasons for this are:

- the expenditure was on revenue rather than capital account (for example, the seller is a builder or property trader);

- the seller does not have a qualifying activity (for example, the property being sold was his own residence);

- the fixtures (or some of them) were not regarded as plant and machinery when the seller bought them (for example, if the seller bought the property before April 2008, and the property contains electrical, lighting and cold water systems which qualify for allowances now, but not at the time the seller acquired them).

21.33 Of course, once the expenditure has been pooled, the sale will be one to which one or other of the 'value' requirements will also apply (see **21.13**), if that was not already the case by virtue of the seller having already made a claim.

So although it is true to say that the buyer will not be entitled to allowances if the pooling requirement is not met, the reverse is not immediately true – even if the pooling requirement is met, the fixed value requirement still remains to be satisfied.

Buyers could be 'caught out' by the relatively relaxed deadline attached to the pooling requirement. The rule is that the historic expenditure must have been allocated to a pool in a chargeable period beginning on or before the day on which the past owner ceased to own the fixture, or the past owner claimed a first-year allowance on the expenditure (or any part of it). But the deadline for satisfying the fixed value requirement may be earlier.

Example 21.4 – Pooling and fixed value deadlines

C Limited makes up its accounts to 31 December each year. On 5 January 2018, C sells freehold premises to D Limited. C has never claimed

---

allowances, but D wants to be able to do so. They agree, therefore, that C will pool the relevant expenditure then pass on the allowances to D by means of a *s 198* election.

C must pool the expenditure in its return for the period to 31 December 2018. That chargeable period began on 1 January 2018 and is therefore 'a chargeable period beginning on or before the day on which the past owner (C) ceased to own the fixture'.

The return for that period must be submitted by 31 December 2019 and can be amended by 31 December 2020 (usual self-assessment filing deadlines apply). So, in effect, the pooling deadline is 31 December 2020 (nearly three years after the date of sale).

The seller, however, defers dealing with the pooling requirement until the deadline is approaching, and only pools the expenditure in June 2020. This is six months before the time limit.

D Limited, having been notified, then turns its attention to the fixed value requirement, and is shocked to realise that that time limit expired on 4 January 2020 (two years after completion) and that, consequently, that deadline has been missed, and no capital allowances are available.

21.34

Focus

Section 187A(3) provides that the new owner's expenditure on fixtures qualifying for allowances is to be treated as nil if the 'fixed value requirement' applies but is not satisfied, or the 'disposal value statement requirement' applies but is not satisfied (see **21.11–21.15**).

If either requirement is not met, neither the purchaser nor any future owner of those fixtures will be able to claim allowances. In the first instance, the purchaser's qualifying expenditure is deemed to be nil. On a subsequent sale, the new owner's claim will be restricted to the seller's disposal value under *s 185* – because the seller's claim cannot exceed nil, his disposal value will also be limited to nil.

Sellers

21.35 If a seller fails to comply with the pooling requirement, he will not suffer any direct tax consequence – he had never claimed allowances, and now he never can. As he had not claimed, he is not required to bring any disposal proceeds into the pool, and he cannot suffer any balancing charge or clawback of allowances.

However, if the seller has agreed in the contract to pool the relevant expenditure and fails to do so, he will be in breach of contract and can expect the buyer to seek redress for the additional tax payable by the buyer as a result of the foregone allowances.

If a seller fails to comply with the fixed value requirement (for example by failing to submit a *s 198* election), it is not only a problem for the buyer. The seller must account for disposal proceeds of fixtures in the normal way, which effectively means a just apportionment of the total sale price. Where a property is sold at a profit (ie for more than original cost) this will generally mean a reversal of all the allowances the seller has ever claimed. At best, where the seller owns other properties, there will be reduced allowances in future; at worst, there will be an immediate tax charge.

21.36

Example 21.5 – Failure to comply – effect on seller

C Limited sells freehold premises to D Limited. The fixtures in the property are valued at £150,000. Their original cost was £125,000 but because Annual Investment Allowances were available, they have a tax written-down value of nil. The parties agree to enter into a *s 198* election in the amount of £1, so that C Limited does not suffer a balancing charge.

However, the parties fail to submit the election in time (within two years of completion). As the fixed value requirement has not been satisfied, whilst D Limited cannot claim any allowances, C Limited is required to account for disposal proceeds equal to the original cost of £125,000.

If this is C Limited's only property (such that the disposal proceeds are not 'lost' in a much larger pool value relating to assets in other properties), it will face a balancing charge of £125,000 which at 19% gives rise to an immediate tax charge of £23,750.

BEST PRACTICE FOR SELLERS

Checklist

21.37 Every transaction is different, and will have its own particular features. Specialist advice should always be taken. The seller should be looking to minimise any clawback of allowances previously claimed. The easiest way to achieve this is by entering into a *s 198* election for an amount no greater than the tax written-down value of any fixtures on which allowances have been claimed.

Sellers' and buyers' interests are generally diametrically opposed, so parties should not assume that the optimal result for them will be cost-free for the other party.

21.38 The following checklist identifies the most common issues.

- Have fixtures allowances been claimed in the past on assets now being sold?

- What was the cost of the relevant fixtures, and what is their estimated or approximate tax written-down value (the difference between these two figures will in most cases be the amount potentially clawed back on sale)?

- Is the property being sold for more than original cost (if not, the size of any clawback may be reduced)?

- Do you want to retain allowances, or are you prepared to pass them on to the buyer (the default position)?

- Is a *s 198* election proposed and what amount is to be allocated to fixtures?

- If no allowances have been claimed, are you prepared to do so now, before passing them on to the buyer?

- Does the contract make it clear what has been agreed on capital allowances, and what timescales or deadlines apply?

BEST PRACTICE FOR BUYERS

Checklist

21.39 Every transaction is different, and will have its own particular features. Specialist advice should always be taken. The buyer should be looking to maximise allowances, which will involve establishing the tax history of any fixtures (including any necessary restrictions of the amount claimable) and taking appropriate steps to ensure allowances are transferred as part of the transaction.

1091

21.40 *Capital allowances on property transactions*

Sellers' and buyers' interests are generally diametrically opposed, so parties should not assume that the optimal result for them will be cost-free for the other party.

Buyers should be wary of entering into *s 198* elections without proper thought. Such an election can never increase the amount of a claim beyond the default position (ratifies, where necessary, by the Tribunal) and in many cases will give a worse result.

21.40 The following checklist identifies the most common issues.

- When did the seller acquire the property (if it was before April 2008, a claim for pre-commencement integral features may be possible)?

- What was the original cost of the property to the seller (fixtures claims may be restricted to an apportionment of the seller's cost, rather than the current purchase price)?

- Are fixtures included in the sale?

- Are chattels included in the sale?

- Is any of the plant a long-life asset?

- Is any of the plant an 'integral feature'?

- Has a joint election been made (or is one proposed) regarding the value of fixtures?

- Is the cost of fixtures restricted by claims made by the seller or a previous owner?

- Has a different type of allowances (eg research and development allowances) previously been claimed in respect of fixtures?

- Is the transaction subject to the provisions of *CAA 2001, s 187A*, requiring mandatory pooling by the seller (ie where the seller was entitled to claim capital allowances but did not do so), or a formal fixed value statement (ie where the seller has claimed and it is necessary for the buyer to formally establish a value for qualifying expenditure incurred) or both?

- Have relevant warranties been sought from the seller?

- Does the contract make it clear what has been agreed on capital allowances, and what timescales or deadlines apply?

CONTRACT CLAUSES

Due diligence – pre-contract enquiries

Focus

In almost all cases, it will be appropriate for a sale and purchase agreement to include specific clauses relating to capital allowances. However, the precise nature of those clauses will depend on the circumstances of the case – for example, whether the seller has claimed allowances, or could claim if required, and whether there is proposed to be a *s 198* election.

21.41 On any property acquisition, one would expect the purchaser, through his solicitor, to ask a number of standard questions of the vendor, some of which will relate to capital allowances. These questions need to be answered by the vendor to the purchaser's satisfaction – they are important and can have a significant impact on the purchaser's claim for allowances. Answers such as 'not applicable' are generally unacceptable. The vendor should be pressed to explain *why* it thinks such an answer is appropriate. Readers' attention is drawn to *Clarke v Iliffes Booth Bennett (a firm)* [2004] EWHC 1731 (Ch), [2004] All ER (D) 369 (Jul), where it was held that a solicitor has a duty to understand a contract (for example, tax matters) to the extent necessary to give proper advice to the client.

21.42 The most widely used version of these questions is form Commercial Property Standard Enquiries 1 (CPSE.1), 'General pre-contract enquiries for all commercial property transactions', prepared by members of the London Property Support Lawyers Group and endorsed by the British Property Federation (since 28 February 2014, capital allowances being dealt with in enquiry 32). The latest version (v 3.6 at the time of writing) is available online from Practical Law and is free to use, subject to certain conditions.

In Scotland, CPSE.1 is not generally used, but the underlying issues are the same as in the rest of the UK, and advisers should ensure that identical or similar enquiries are made.

Contract clauses and warranties

21.43 There can be no definitive list of contract clauses and warranties because what is appropriate depends upon many factors, not least the circumstances of the particular transaction.

At best, illustrative clauses and warranties can act as a catalyst in the agreement of contract terms. The following are listed for that purpose only – it is essential that specific professional advice should be obtained.

The required clauses and warranties will depend to a great extent on the history of the property and the proposed division of capital allowances between seller and purchaser.

Where the seller has claimed allowances and the parties will enter into a s 198/s 199 election on completion

21.44   On completion, the seller and the buyer shall make an election in respect of the fixtures under *CAA 2001, s 198*.

Both the buyer and the seller shall:

- provide all necessary information to each other and take all reasonable steps required to make the election;

- submit a copy of the election to HMRC with their tax return for the first period affected by the election;

- take all reasonable steps to ensure that the amounts fixed by the election are accepted by HMRC; and

- reflect the amounts fixed by the election in their respective tax computations and returns.

The seller warrants that no person has a 'prior right' as defined by *CAA 2001, s 181* in relation to any of the fixtures.

Where the seller has claimed allowances and the parties will apply to the Tax Chamber of the First-tier Tribunal for a just and reasonable allocation of allowances

21.45   The seller and the buyer agree that within [six months] of completion the [seller/buyer] shall make an application to the Tribunal for a just and reasonable apportionment of the purchase price to the fixtures.

Both the buyer and the seller shall reflect the amounts fixed by the Tribunal in their respective tax computations and returns.

The seller shall:

- use its best endeavours to supply such documents and information relating to the capital allowances history of the fixtures (including information relating to the entitlement of previous owners to capital allowances) as the buyer may request; and

- take such action as is reasonably necessary to assist the buyer in making the application and any claim it may make for capital allowances.

The seller warrants that no person has a 'prior right' as defined by *CAA 2001, s 181* in relation to any of the fixtures.

Where the seller was entitled to claim allowances, but has not done so

21.46   The seller will provide all such information and assistance as is necessary for the buyer to claim capital allowances on any fixtures in respect of which the seller was entitled to claim capital allowances, but has not done so.

For all such fixtures, the seller will, in its tax return for the period in which completion takes place, allocate its expenditure on those fixtures to a pool in accordance with *CAA 2001, ss 53* and *54*.

The seller agrees to submit all returns and take all reasonable steps to ensure acceptance by HMRC of the pooling of expenditure.

The seller warrants that no person has a 'prior right' as defined by *CAA 2001, s 181* in relation to any of the fixtures.

The seller agrees that it will enter into an election under *CAA 2001, s 198* for an amount equal to the seller's qualifying expenditure on those fixtures.

Where the seller has not claimed allowances, and was not entitled to do so

21.47   The seller warrants that:

- it has not claimed, and has at no time been entitled to claim, allowances for capital expenditure on the provision of the fixtures;

- no person who is treated as having owned the fixtures during a period ending on or after [1/6] April 2014 has claimed, or was entitled to claim, allowances for capital expenditure on the provision of the fixtures; and

- no person has a 'prior right' as defined by *CAA 2001, s 181* in respect of any of the fixtures.

21.47 *Capital allowances on property transactions*

The seller acknowledges that after completion the buyer may seek to agree a just and reasonable apportionment of the purchase price to fixtures with HMRC. The seller shall:

- use its best endeavours to supply such documents and information relating to the capital allowances history of the fixtures (including information relating to the entitlement of previous owners to capital allowances) as the buyer may request; and

- take such action as is reasonably necessary to assist the buyer in any claim it may make for capital allowances in respect of the fixtures.

Index